PAÍSES DE HABLA HISPANA

CUBA
- Gentilicio: cubano/a
- Tamaño: 44.218 millas cuadradas
- Número de habitantes: 11.061.886
- Etnia(s): blancos 37%, mulatos 51%, negros 11%
- Lenguas habladas: el español
- Moneda: el peso cubano, el peso convertible
- Economía: azúcar, tabaco, turismo
- Alfabetización: 99.8%

REPÚBLICA DOMINICANA
- Gentilicio: dominicano/a
- Tamaño: 18.816 millas cuadradas
- Número de habitantes: 10.219.630
- Etnia(s): mulatos 73%, blancos 16%, negros 11%
- Lenguas habladas: el español
- Moneda: el peso dominicano
- Economía: azúcar, café, cacao, tabaco, cemento
- Alfabetización: 90.2%

Madrid
ESPAÑA
Ceuta
ISLAS BALEARES

ESPAÑA
- Gentilicio: español/a
- Tamaño: 194.896 millas cuadradas
- Número de habitantes: 47.370.542
- Etnia(s): blancos
- Lenguas habladas: el castellano (español), el catalán, el gallego, el euskera
- Moneda: el euro
- Economía: maquinaria, textiles, metales, farmacéutica, aceituna, vino, turismo, textiles, metales
- Alfabetización: 97.7%

ISLAS CANARIAS

PUERTO RICO
- Gentilicio: puertorriqueño/a
- Tamaño: 3.435 millas cuadradas
- Número de habitantes: 3.674.209
- Etnia(s): blancos 76%, negros 7%, otros 17%
- Lenguas habladas: el español y el inglés
- Moneda: el dólar americano
- Economía: manufactura (farmacéuticos), turismo
- Alfabetización: 90.3%

HONDURAS
- Gentilicio: hondureño/a
- Tamaño: 43.277 millas cuadradas
- Número de habitantes: 8.448.465
- Etnia(s): mestizos 90%, indígenas 7%, negros 2%, blancos 1%
- Lenguas habladas: el español y lenguas indígenas amerindias
- Moneda: el lempira
- Economía: bananas, café, azúcar, madera, textiles
- Alfabetización: 85.1%

NICARAGUA
- Gentilicio: nicaragüense
- Tamaño: 50.193 millas cuadradas
- Número de habitantes: 5.788.531
- Etnia(s): mestizos 69%, blancos 17%, negros 9%, indígenas 5%
- Lenguas habladas: el español y lengua indígena (miskito)
- Moneda: el córdoba
- Economía: procesamiento de alimentos, químicos, metales, petróleo, calzado, tabaco
- Alfabetización: 78%

VENEZUELA
- Gentilicio: venezolano/a
- Tamaño: 362.143 millas cuadradas
- Número de habitantes: 28.459.085
- Etnia(s): mestizos 69%, blancos 20%, negros 9%, indígenas 2%
- Lenguas habladas: el español y lenguas indígenas
- Moneda: el bolívar fuerte
- Economía: petróleo, metales, materiales de construcción
- Alfabetización: 95.5%

Malabo

GUINEA ECUATORIAL

COLOMBIA
- Gentilicio: colombiano/a
- Tamaño: 439.735 millas cuadradas
- Número de habitantes: 47.745.783
- Etnia(s): mestizos 58%, blancos 20%, mulatos 14%, negros 4%, indígenas 4%
- Lenguas habladas: el español
- Moneda: el peso colombiano
- Economía: procesamiento de alimentos, petróleo, calzado, oro, esmeraldas, café, cacao, flores, textiles
- Alfabetización: 93.6%

BOLIVIA
- Gentilicio: boliviano/a
- Tamaño: 424.165 millas cuadradas
- Número de habitantes: 10.461.053
- Etnia(s): mestizos 30%, indígenas 55%, blancos 15%
- Lenguas habladas: el español y lenguas indígenas (quechua, aymara)
- Moneda: el boliviano
- Economía: gas, petróleo, minerales, tabaco, textiles
- Alfabetización: 91.2%

GUINEA ECUATORIAL
- Gentilicio: guineano/a, ecuatoguineano/a
- Tamaño: 10.830 millas cuadradas
- Número de habitantes: 701.001
- Etnia(s): fang 86%, otras etnias africanas 14%
- Lenguas habladas: el español, el francés y lenguas indígenas (fang, bubi)
- Moneda: el franco CFA
- Economía: petróleo, madera, cacao, café
- Alfabetización: 94.2%

PARAGUAY
- Gentilicio: paraguayo/a
- Tamaño: 157.047 millas cuadradas
- Número de habitantes: 6.623.252
- Etnia(s): mestizos 95%
- Lenguas habladas: el español y lengua indígena (guaraní)
- Moneda: el guaraní
- Economía: azúcar, carne, textiles, cemento, madera, minerales
- Alfabetización: 93.9%

CHILE
- Gentilicio: chileno/a
- Tamaño: 292.257 millas cuadradas
- Número de habitantes: 17.216.945
- Etnia(s): mestizos 65%, blancos 25%, indígenas 5%
- Lenguas habladas: el español y lengua indígena (mapudungun)
- Moneda: el peso chileno
- Economía: minerales (cobre), agricultura, pesca, vino
- Alfabetización: 98.6%

URUGUAY
- Gentilicio: uruguayo/a
- Tamaño: 68.037 millas cuadradas
- Número de habitantes: 3.324.460
- Etnia(s): blancos 88%, mestizos 8%, negros 4%
- Lenguas habladas: el español
- Moneda: el peso uruguayo
- Economía: carne, metales, textiles, productos agrícolas
- Alfabetización: 98.7%

ARGENTINA
- Gentilicio: argentino/a
- Tamaño: 1.065.000 millas cuadradas
- Número de habitantes: 42.610.981
- Etnia(s): blanco 97%
- Lenguas habladas: el español y lenguas indígenas (mapudungun, quechua)
- Moneda oficial: el peso argentino
- Economía: carne, trigo, lana, petróleo
- Alfabetización: 97.9%

- Gentilicio: Nationality
- Tamaño: Size
- Número de habitantes: Population
- Etnia(s): Ethnic group(s)
- Lenguas habladas: Spoken Languages
- Moneda oficial: Currency
- Economía: Economy
- Alfabetización: Literacy

FRASES ÚTILES EN LA CLASE DE ESPAÑOL

Tengo una pregunta.	*I have a question.*	
Repita, por favor.	*Could you repeat, please?*	
Más despacio, por favor.	*Slower, please.*	
No entiendo.	*I don't understand.*	
No sé.	*I don't know.*	**Tú**
¿Cómo se dice...?	*How do you say . . .?*	
¿Cómo se escribe...?	*How do you spell . . .?*	
¿Cómo?	*What did you say?*	
¿Puedo ir al baño?	*May I go to the bathroom?*	

Atención, clase.	*Pay attention, class.*	
Silencio, por favor.	*Quiet, please.*	
Escuchen.	*Listen.*	
Abran el libro en la página...	*Open your book to page . . .*	
Cierren los libros.	*Close your books.*	
Escriban este dictado.	*Write down this dictation.*	
Pasen la tarea hacia el frente.	*Pass your homework to the front.*	**Tu profesor/a**
Saquen una hoja de papel.	*Take out a piece of paper.*	
Formen grupos de tres.	*Form groups of three.*	
Ve a la pizarra.	*Go to the chalkboard.*	
Levántense.	*Stand up.*	
Siéntense.	*Sit down.*	
Hablen con su compañero/a.	*Talk to your classmate.*	

WileyPLUS

Now with: **ORION**, An Adaptive Experience

WileyPLUS is a research-based, online environment for effective teaching and learning.

WileyPLUS builds students' confidence because it takes the guesswork out of studying by providing students with a clear roadmap:

- what to do
- how to do it
- if they did it right

It offers interactive resources along with a complete digital textbook that help students learn more. With *WileyPLUS*, students take more initiative so you'll have greater impact on their achievement in the classroom and beyond.

WileyPLUS

ALL THE HELP, RESOURCES, AND PERSONAL SUPPORT YOU AND YOUR STUDENTS NEED!

www.wileyplus.com/resources

1st DAY OF CLASS ...AND BEYOND!

2-Minute Tutorials and all of the resources you and your students need to get started

WileyPLUS
Student Partner Program

Student support from an experienced student user

Wiley Faculty Network

Collaborate with your colleagues, find a mentor, attend virtual and live events, and view resources
www.WhereFacultyConnect.com

WileyPLUS
Quick Start

Pre-loaded, ready-to-use assignments and presentations created by subject matter experts

Technical Support 24/7 FAQs, online chat, and phone support
www.wileyplus.com/support

© Courtney Keating/iStockphoto

Your Digital Solutions Specialist, providing personal training and support

Pura vida

Beginning Spanish

Norma López-Burton

University of California, Davis

Laura Marqués Pascual

University of California, Santa Barbara

Cristina Pardo Ballester

Iowa State University

WILEY

VICE PRESIDENT AND PUBLISHER	Laurie Rosatone
SPONSORING EDITOR	Elena Herrero
ASSOCIATE EDITOR	Maruja Malavé
PROJECT EDITOR	Jennifer Brady
EDITORIAL PROGRAM ASSISTANT	Alejandra Barciela
FREELANCE DEVELOPMENTAL EDITOR	Mercedes Roffé
EDITORIAL OPERATIONS MANAGER	Melissa Edwards
DIRECTOR, MARKETING COMMUNICATIONS	Jeffrey Rucker
MARKET SPECIALIST	Glenn A. Wilson
MARKETING MANAGER	Kimberly Kanakes
SENIOR PRODUCT DESIGNER	Thomas Kulesa
SENIOR PRODUCTION EDITOR	William A. Murray
MEDIA SPECIALIST	Anita Castro
PHOTO RESEARCH	Felicia Ruocco
SENIOR DESIGNER	Thomas Nery
COVER DESIGNER	Thomas Nery
COVER PHOTO CREDITS	Smartphone: © edel/Shutterstock
	Smartphone inset photo: Kimberly Morris
	Tablet: © A-R-T/Shutterstock
	Tablet inset photo: Christina Samson
	Camera: © Aeolos/iStockphoto
	Camera inset photo: Norma López-Burton

This book was set in 10/12 Sabon LT Std Roman by PreMediaGlobal and printed and bound by RR Donnelley.

Founded in 1807, John Wiley & Sons, Inc. has been a valued source of knowledge and understanding for more than 200 years, helping people around the world meet their needs and fulfill their aspirations. Our company is built on a foundation of principles that include responsibility to the communities we serve and where we live and work. In 2008, we launched a Corporate Citizenship Initiative, a global effort to address the environmental, social, economic, and ethical challenges we face in our business. Among the issues we are addressing are carbon impact, paper specifications and procurement, ethical conduct within our business and among our vendors, and community and charitable support. For more information, please visit our website: www.wiley.com/go/citizenship.

Evaluation copies are provided to qualified academics and professionals for review purposes only, for use in their courses during the next academic year. These copies are licensed and may not be sold or transferred to a third party. Upon completion of the review period, please return the evaluation copy to Wiley. Return instructions and a free of charge return shipping label are available at: www.wiley.com/go/returnlabel. If you have chosen to adopt this textbook for use in your course, please accept this book as your complimentary desk copy. Outside of the United States, please contact your local representative.

ISBN: 978-1-118-08710-7
BRV ISBN: 978-1-118-51476-4

Printed in the United States of America

10 9 8 7 6 5 4 3 2 1

Norma
López-Burton

A basic human need is to be understood, and for the last thirty years this has guided me, no more than here in *Pura vida*.

My crusade of breaking stereotypes began in 1981 shortly after I started teaching Spanish at UC Davis. It was then that this Puerto Rican was surprised to learn that many assumed I liked spicy foods and celebrated *El día de los muertos*. That made me wonder: What other generalizations does this culture hold dear? Imagine further my shock when I saw *all* the textbooks of the day—and most still do—lump all sorts of people into one homogenous group: "Our Hispanic Friends!"

And so for twenty years as program coordinator I have purposefully built a curriculum in which all activities would be truly communicative, and all instructors would present culture in a sensitive and consistent manner. It turns out this has been my calling.

This passion extends to my writing. I was lead author for the graduate methodology text, *On Being a Language Teacher*. "My goal in all three texts is to elicit meaningful communication and teach skills of cultural competency."

I have shared the dream of *Pura vida* with two former graduate students, now colleagues: Laura Marqués Pascual and Cristina Pardo Ballester. I am indebted to these two extraordinarily hard-working authors who never wavered from giving their best. Thank you.

And finally, if anyone has met *my* need of being understood, it is my husband, Tom. I dedicate this book to him and look forward to sharing the fruits of *our* labor.

I studied Hispanic literature and linguistics at the Universidad de Alcalá, Madrid, Spain. During my time as a college student I spent a year in Durham, England, where I studied literature and linguistics with British students. It was during my year abroad that I got interested in how people learn languages. I later moved to the United States to complete my graduate studies. I earned a MA in teaching English as a second language from Bowling Green State University, and a PhD in Hispanic Linguistics from the University of California, Davis. I am now the language program director at the University of California, Santa Barbara, where I also teach Spanish and linguistics courses at various levels.

Dedico este libro a mis padres, Juan José y Teresa, por su inmensa paciencia y apoyo.

Laura Marqués
Pascual

Cristina Pardo
Ballester

I am from Granada, Spain where I received a bachelor's degree in translation and interpretation with a major in French interpretation and a minor in English translation. My passion for languages started in elementary school where I learned about French culture from my French teacher. This passion or languages led to spending an extensive amount of time in Belgium and to traveling around the world. Eventually, I settled in Reno, Nevada, where I received my M.A. in foreign languages and literatures at the University of Nevada, Reno, while teaching Spanish language courses. I moved to New York City to teach Spanish and French at various high schools. My teaching experiences led me to complete my PhD in Hispanic linguistics with an emphasis in second language acquisition from the University of California, Davis. I am currently an assistant professor of Spanish and the lower-division language program coordinator in the Department of World Languages and Cultures at Iowa State University. This textbook, *Pura vida*, represents my commitment to beginning language learners, and my passion for teaching the culture and the language of the Spanish-speaking world.

Dedico este libro a Albert y a nuestra hija Olympia y a mi querida hermana María Belén, por toda la paciencia y comprensión que tuvieron conmigo durante varios años de dedicación y esfuerzo escribiendo *Pura vida*.

Capítulo 2: Día a día, p. 57

México y Guatemala	Learning objectives	Palabra por palabra

Sección 1 — **La rutina diaria, p. 58**

	Learning objectives	Palabra por palabra
	• Discover different realities in Mexico • Tell time • Discuss daily activities and actions • Recognize the use of **vos** • Understand a different concept of punctuality	• Las actividades diarias, p. 60 • ¿Qué hora es?, p. 60 • Los números del 1 al 59, p. 62 ♻

Sección 2 — **De compras, p. 78**

	• Negotiate in an open market • Describe clothing • Identify colors • Use numbers from 60 and on • Talk about what I and other people like • Tell what you are planning to do • Understand the different concept of physical contact	• El mercado al aire libre, p. 80 • Los colores, p. 80 • La ropa, p. 81 • Los números del 60 al 10.000, p. 81

Capítulo 3: La vida doméstica, p. 97

Costa Rica y Panamá	**Sección 1** — **En familia, p. 98**	
	• Understand the origin of the two last names in Hispanic names • Recognize and describe family relationships • Describe people's physical appearances and emotional states • Describe what you and other people do daily • Express age and possession • Recognize some differences between Spanish and U.S. families	• El árbol genealógico, p. 100 • Las partes del cuerpo: La apariencia física, p. 101

Sección 2 — **En casa, p. 118**

	• Compare diverse dwellings • Describe a house and its neighborhood • Use numbers from 10,000 • Make comparisons • Express location and existence • Understand the life in a neighborhood	• La casa, los muebles y el vecindario, p. 120 • Los números del 10.000 en adelante, p. 122

Capítulo 10: La salud y el bienestar, p. 377

Capítulo 11: Un mundo global, p. 415

Capítulo 12: Los hispanos en Estados Unidos, p. 453

Estados Unidos	Learning objectives	Palabra por palabra

Sección 1   La inmigración, p. 454

- Discuss issues related to immigration
- Understand the problems immigrants face
- Express hopes, wishes, uncertainty, doubt and advice
- Express subjective opinions about events in the past
- Consider possibilities

- Más nacionalidades, p. 456 ♻
- La inmigración, p. 457

Sección 2   La comunidad hispana, p. 473

- Discuss issues related to Hispanics in the U.S.
- Talk about changes in someone's life
- Talk about changes in emotional states
- Describe people or objects in detail

- La herencia cultural, p. 475
- Los asuntos sociales y políticos, p. 476

Preface

¡Pura vida! In *Pura vida* (*Life is good*), Spanish is more than vocabulary and grammar, just as Spanish-speaking cultures are more than products and practices. In this learner-centered introductory program, the authors' commitment to a methodology based on true-to-life experiences brings Spanish to life *Pura vida* is the discovery of a Spanish-speaking world through the experiences of *real* people who share anecdotes and reflections on those experiences. Students relate to these people and make deeper, more meaningful connections between language and culture than in other programs, and acquire Spanish with an unparalleled sense of personal engagement.

In this 12-chapter introductory program, students don't learn Spanish only *for* real life, but also *from* real life. They discover that there is not just one homogeneous Hispanic culture, but rather, that each Spanish-speaking country has its own rich, unique culture and that the people who live in these countries speak one common language with different accents, characteristics, and idiosyncrasies. This first-edition program offers *truly* seamless integration of cultural notions and language instruction, and features 100 percent contextualized and personalized activities.

HALLMARKS OF THE PROGRAM

Cross-cultural approach.   Culture is not just an add-on in *Pura vida*. The national standards call for the integration of a particular content with language aims. With *Pura vida,* students learn a new language and use it to learn about the different Hispanic cultures. Students discover cultural differences, rather than being told about them in disjointed, stand-alone "Did you know?" sidebars.

Pura vida takes a cross-cultural approach. In every *Una perspectiva/Otra perspectiva* section, cultural notions are introduced through the eyes of real people living in or visiting the target country. From the point of view of a visitor from the United States, students begin to observe cultural similarities and differences, which invite them to reflect on their own culture as they learn about the other. From the point of view of a citizen from the target country, students start to understand the other perspective and how people of that culture perceive them. This cross-cultural approach promotes cultural understanding and intercultural competence.

All vocabulary and grammatical structures are introduced in context through meaningful, comprehensible input stories *(La pura verdad)* based on real-life events as experienced by U.S. citizens living in Spanish-speaking countries. These input stories lend a reality lacking in most Spanish textbooks. PowerPoint® images and lecture scripts are provided for the instructor to aid in the narration. These input stories are written with the limited comprehension skills of first-year Spanish students in mind.

Contextualized, personalized, and task-based practice.   Informed by research in second language acquisition, *Pura vida* places structures that have been shown to be acquired first by second language learners earlier in the grammar sequence. For example, **estar** + *location* is usually acquired before **estar** + *adjective*.

In keeping with widely accepted beliefs, we assume that the learner does not need to know every word s/he hears in order to understand the message directed at him or her. However, the learner must be able to understand most of the language for acquisition to happen (i.e., input has to be comprehensible and meaningful). In *Pura vida*, grammar and vocabulary are introduced for the first time in context through the meaningful and comprehensible stories in *La pura verdad*. These stories, in turn, provide a context for the *Hablando de gramática* section, where all examples draw on the cultural notions and country explored in the chapter. Following the principle of comprehensible and meaningful input, starting very early in the program, all direction lines are in Spanish.

Research shows that for an activity to be communicative a real-life outcome is needed. In *Pura vida,* activities are rooted in the context of the real-life stories of Americans visiting Spanish-speaking countries, tap into students' own lives and perspectives, or are written to have students *do something* with the language from their own personal perspective. Practice for the sake of practice is not part of the *Pura vida* experience.

Modes of communication (interpretive, interpersonal, and presentational). Focused on developing interpretive skills, readings in *Entérate* are based on a variety of sources to cover a wide range of genres and incorporate the vocabulary, grammar structures, and cultural focus of each chapter. It also provides *Estrategias para leer* with strategic directions to guide the reading process. The accompanying activities help students build reading skills such as predicting content, understanding the main idea, or identifying supporting details. In addition, all readings are accompanied by pre- and post-reading activities that go beyond merely checking comprehension—language-focus tasks guide students through the actual process of interpreting written texts.

Writing tasks develop written presentational skills with a strategy and focused topic. *En tus propias palabras* includes *Estrategias para escribir,* a step-by-step guide through those aspects that are most problematic for our students. *Estrategias para escribir* emphasizes process to develop writing skills.

Oral expression, both interpersonal and presentational, is emphasized throughout the program, with the inclusion of guided collaborative tasks that require interaction and negotiation of meaning and that encourage students to report their findings to the class. *Estrategias para conversar* that accompany *Ponte en mi lugar* sections also provide students with key words, expressions, and phrases that will help them build oral fluency.

Recycling and reinforcement of content. Because language is inherently cumulative, *Pura vida* reinforces high-frequency vocabulary and key structures throughout the book. Starting in Chapter 2, there is at least one grammar or vocabulary topic recycled in every chapter.

Visual Walkthrough

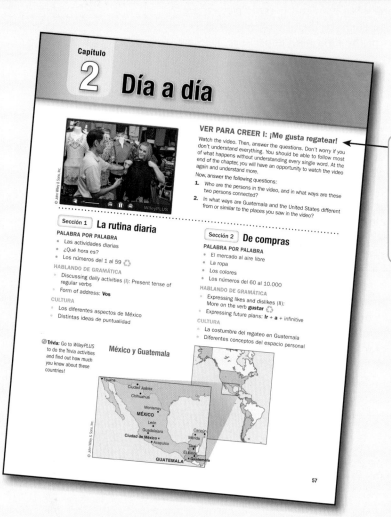

Chapters open with the **Pura vida** video and questions that activate background knowledge and introduce the chapter theme in the context of the experiences of real people. This video highlights cross-cultural comparisons following the approach of the book. See p. 94.

Photos and questions further establish the chapter theme and extend the opportunity to tap into background knowledge as students continue their discovery of language and culture.

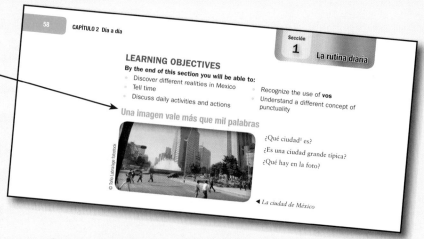

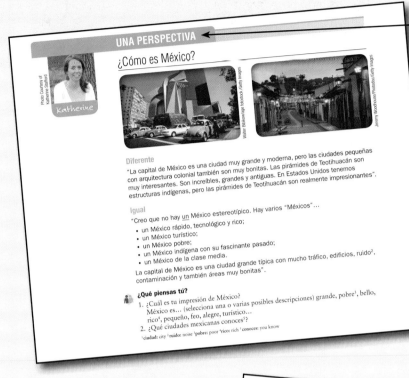

UNA PERSPECTIVA

¿Cómo es México?

Katherine

Photo: Courtesy of Katherine Stafford

Walter Bibikow/age fotostock /Getty Images

Jeremy Woodhouse/Photodisc/Getty Images

Diferente

"La capital de México es una ciudad muy grande y moderna, pero las ciudades pequeñas con arquitectura colonial también son muy bonitas. Las pirámides de Teotihuacán son muy interesantes. Son increíbles, grandes y antiguas. En Estados Unidos tenemos estructuras indígenas, pero las pirámides de Teotihuacán son realmente impresionantes".

Igual

"Creo que no hay un México estereotípico. Hay varios "Méxicos"…
- un México rápido, tecnológico y rico;
- un México turístico;
- un México pobre;
- un México indígena con su fascinante pasado;
- un México de la clase media.

La capital de México es una ciudad grande típica con mucho tráfico, edificios, ruido², contaminación y también áreas muy bonitas".

¿Qué piensas tú?
1. ¿Cuál es tu impresión de México?
   México es… (selecciona una o varias posibles descripciones) grande, pobre³, bello, rico⁴, pequeño, feo, alegre, turístico…
2. ¿Qué ciudades mexicanas conoces⁵?

¹ciudad: city ²ruido: noise ³pobre: poor ⁴rico: rich ⁵conoces: you know

---

Through the eyes of someone from the U.S. living in the featured country, students observe cultural differences first-hand, and reflect on their own culture in **¿Qué piensas tú?**.

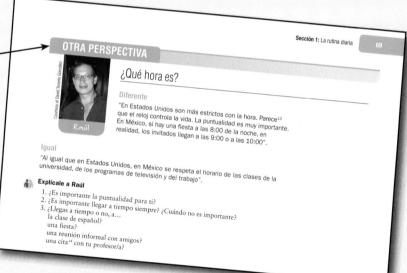

OTRA PERSPECTIVA

¿Qué hora es?

Raúl

Courtesy of David Tenorio González

Diferente

"En Estados Unidos son más estrictos con la hora. Parece¹³ que el reloj controla la vida. La puntualidad es muy importante. En México, si hay una fiesta a las 8:00 de la noche, en realidad, los invitados llegan a las 9:00 o a las 10:00".

Igual

"Al igual que en Estados Unidos, en México se respeta el horario de las clases de la universidad, de los programas de televisión y del trabajo".

Explícale a Raúl
1. ¿Es importante la puntualidad para ti?
2. ¿Es importante llegar a tiempo siempre?
3. ¿Llegas a tiempo o no, a… ¿Cuándo no es importante?
   la clase de español?
   una fiesta?
   una reunión informal con amigos?
   una cita¹⁴ con tu profesor/a?

Through the eyes of a visitor to the U.S., students find out how people from other countries perceive this country's practices and beliefs. **Explícale a…** compels students to reflect on their own culture.

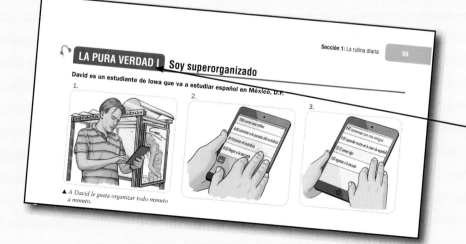

LA PURA VERDAD I Soy superorganizado

David es un estudiante de Iowa que va a estudiar español en México, D.F.

1.

2.

3.

▲ A David le gusta organizar todo minuto a minuto.

Graphic presentations introduce new vocabulary, linguistic structures, and culture in the context of *real-life* stories.

New vocabulary is reinforced in an illustrated context.

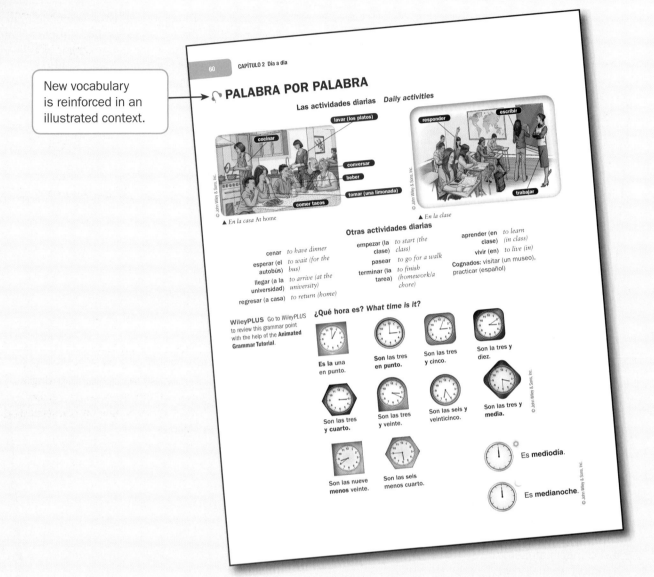

60 CAPÍTULO 2 Día a día

PALABRA POR PALABRA

Las actividades diarias *Daily activities*

▲ *En la casa At home*

▲ *En la clase*

Otras actividades diarias

cenar	*to have dinner*
esperar (el autobús)	*to wait (for the bus)*
llegar (a la universidad)	*to arrive (at the university)*
regresar (a casa)	*to return (home)*

empezar (la clase)	*to start (the class)*
pasear	*to go for a walk*
terminar (la tarea)	*to finish (homework/a chore)*

| aprender (en clase) | *to learn (in class)* |
| vivir (en) | *to live (in)* |

Cognados: visitar (un museo), practicar (español)

WileyPLUS Go to *WileyPLUS* to review this grammar point with the help of the **Animated Grammar Tutorial**.

¿Qué hora es? *What time is it?*

Es la una en punto.

Son las tres en punto.

Son las tres y cinco.

Son la tres y diez.

Son las tres y cuarto.

Son las tres y veinte.

Son las seis y veinticinco.

Son las tres y media.

Son las nueve menos veinte.

Son las seis menos cuarto.

Es **mediodía**.

Es **medianoche**.

¿Qué dicen los mexicanos?

- Hablamos mañana.	*We'll talk tomorrow.*
- <u>Ándale pues</u>.	*OK.*
<u>¡Híjole!</u> ¡Está caro!	*Wow! That's expensive!*
<u>Platica</u> mucho.	*He/she <u>talks</u> a lot.*
- No puedo ir a la plaza <u>contigo</u>.	*I can't go to the plaza <u>with you</u>.*
- <u>Pues, ni modo</u>.	*Oh, too bad!*
¿Me esperas <u>tantito</u>?	*Could you wait for me for just <u>a little bit</u>?*

¿Qué dicen los…? introduces colloquialism, idiomatic expressions, or vocabulary used in the countries explored.

Role-play activities prompt the student to use Spanish in a realistic situation, complete with cultural nuance. **Estrategias para conversar** offers strategies for effective interaction, such as how to ask for details or clarification.

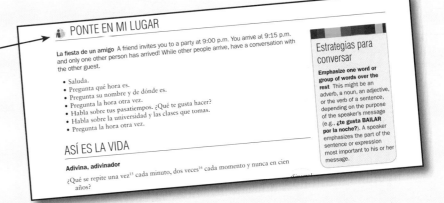

PONTE EN MI LUGAR

La fiesta de un amigo A friend invites you to a party at 9:00 p.m. You arrive at 9:15 p.m. and only one other person has arrived! While other people arrive, have a conversation with the other guest.

- Saluda.
- Pregunta qué hora es.
- Pregunta su nombre y de dónde es.
- Pregunta la hora otra vez.
- Habla sobre tus pasatiempos. ¿Qué te gusta hacer?
- Habla sobre la universidad y las clases que tomas.
- Pregunta la hora otra vez.

ASÍ ES LA VIDA

Adivina, adivinador

¿Qué se repite una vez[15] cada minuto, dos veces[16] cada momento y nunca en cien años?

Estrategias para conversar

Emphasize one word or group of words over the rest This might be an adverb, a noun, an adjective, or the verb of a sentence, depending on the purpose of the speaker's message (e.g., **¿te gusta BAILAR por la noche?**). A speaker emphasizes the part of the sentence or expression most important to his or her message.

ENTÉRATE

Antes de leer

1. **¿Qué tipo de texto es?** Whether you realize it or not, you quickly categorize texts by their format, layout, the images that accompany them, and also by their titles and subtitles. What is your first impression of the following text? By just looking at the design of the reading and its format, can you identify what the content might be?
   a. horoscope
   b. finding pen pals or email friends
   c. letters to the editor

Estrategias para leer

Cognates These words are similar in both languages. For example, **pasatiempos** and *pastimes*, or **música** and *music*, are cognates. Even at this level you may understand a lot of Spanish words because there are so many that are similar in English.

These readings focus on the vocabulary, grammar, and cultural notions of the chapter. **Estrategias para leer** develops reading skills through pre-reading and post-reading activities.

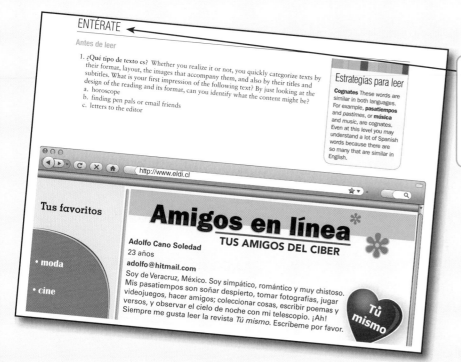

http://www.eldi.cl

Tus favoritos
- moda
- cine

Amigos en línea*
TUS AMIGOS DEL CIBER

Adolfo Cano Soledad
23 años
adolfo@hitmail.com
Soy de Veracruz, México. Soy simpático, romántico y muy chistoso. Mis pasatiempos son soñar despierto, tomar fotografías, jugar videojuegos, hacer amigos; coleccionar cosas, escribir poemas y versos, y observar el cielo de noche con mi telescopio. ¡Ah! Siempre me gusta leer la revista *Tú mismo*. Escríbeme por favor.

Tú mismo

Writing tasks are accompanied by **Estrategias para escribir,** which offers strategies and stresses process to develop writing skills.

EN TUS PROPIAS PALABRAS

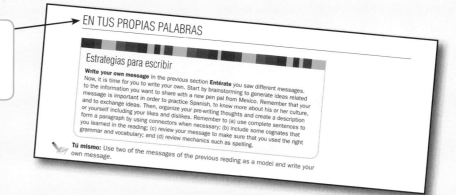

Estrategias para escribir

Write your own message In the previous section **Entérate** you saw different messages. Now, it is time for you to write your own. Start by brainstorming to generate ideas related to the information you want to share with a new pen pal from Mexico. Remember that your message is important in order to practice Spanish, to know more about his or her culture, and to exchange ideas. Then, organize your pre-writing thoughts and create a description of yourself including your likes and dislikes. Remember to (a) use complete sentences to form a paragraph by using connectors when necessary; (b) include some cognates that you learned in the reading; (c) review your message to make sure that you used the right grammar and vocabulary; and (d) review mechanics such as spelling.

Tú mismo: Use two of the messages of the previous reading as a model and write your own message.

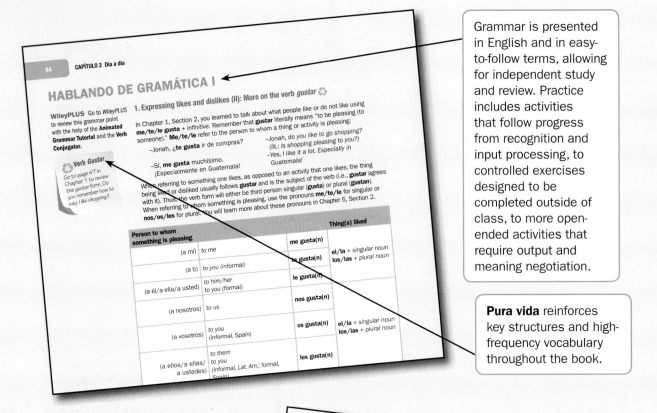

Grammar is presented in English and in easy-to-follow terms, allowing for independent study and review. Practice includes activities that follow progress from recognition and input processing, to controlled exercises designed to be completed outside of class, to more open-ended activities that require output and meaning negotiation.

Pura vida reinforces key structures and high-frequency vocabulary throughout the book.

All activities, from those focused on input processing to those involving interpersonal communication, are entirely rooted in the context of the real people appearing throughout *Pura vida* or in the context of the students' own realities and experiences.

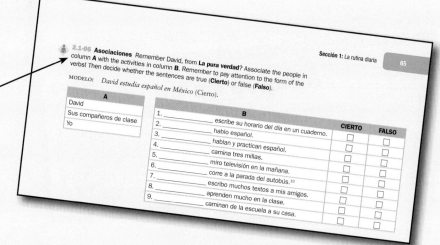

Communicative activities, tasks, and games offer a fun way for students to practice their Spanish working in pairs, small groups, or as a whole class. A culminating task-based activity that synthesizes content from the whole chapter anchors this section, which also includes **Presta atención** (listening) and **Por escrito** (writing) that tie together the new grammar structures, vocabulary, and cultural content of the chapter.

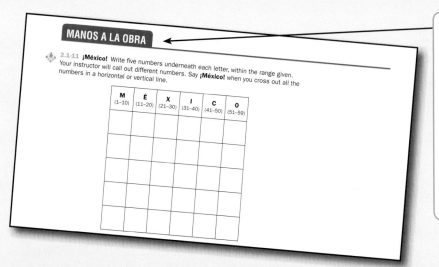

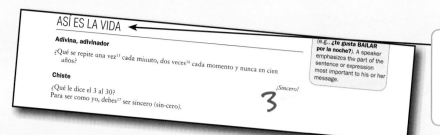

ASÍ ES LA VIDA

Adivina, adivinador

¿Qué se repite una vez[15] cada minuto, dos veces[16] cada momento y nunca en cien años?

Chiste

¿Qué le dice el 3 al 30?
Para ser como yo, debes[17] ser sincero (sin-cero).

¡Sincero!

3

(e.g., **¿te gusta BAILAR por la noche?**). A speaker emphasizes the part of the sentence or expression most important to his or her message.

> Sayings, simple jokes, and tongue twisters that are connected thematically or grammatically with the rest of the chapter reflect cultural beliefs and behaviors.

> Internet activities immerse students in the real online world in Spanish. Specific instructions are highlighted as a way to navigate the web to find the desired sites.

@Arroba@

WileyPLUS Go to *WileyPLUS* to find more **Arroba** activities.

Las revistas Explore in your favorite browser information about "Revistas de México para adolescentes." Look for magazines you can find online. Then, check the website from the selected magazine. Answer the following questions:

1. ¿Qué temas presenta esa revista? Escribe cuatro temas.
2. Escribe cinco cognados de la página web. Modelo: foro – *forum*
3. ¿Qué temas son importantes para ti?
4. ¿Qué diferencias hay entre la página web de la revista en español y la página web de una revista en inglés?

> This ***Pura vida*** video program highlights cross-cultural comparisons in the same way as the *Perspectivas* sections. Pre-viewing, viewing, and post-viewing activities support comprehension, linguistic analysis, and cultural comparisons.

94   CAPÍTULO 2 Día a día

VER PARA CREER II: ¡Me gusta regatear!

WileyPLUS Go to *WileyPlus* to see this video and to find more video activities.

Antes de ver

Answer these questions and compare your answers with a classmate:

1. ¿Vas a mercados al aire libre con frecuencia?
2. ¿A qué mercados al aire libre vas?
3. ¿Qué productos compras en los mercados al aire libre?
4. En los mercados al aire libre, ¿son fijos los precios de los productos?
5. ¿Qué es importante hacer para comprar el producto a mejor precio?
6. En los mercados al aire libre que conoces, ¿hay muchos productos para los turistas?

Después de ver

1. ¿Entendiste? What did you understand? Select an answer to see what you know about the information presented in the video.

1. ¿De dónde es Melanie?
   a. Melanie es de Guatemala.
   b. Melanie es de Antigua.
   c. Melanie es de Washington.
2. ¿Dónde vive Melanie ahora?
   a. Vive en Antigua.
   b. Vive en Washington.
   c. Vive en Estados Unidos.
3. ¿Por qué le gusta el mercado a Melanie?
   a. Porque le gusta caminar y regatear.
   b. Porque hay de todo y es barato.
   c. Porque le gustan las flores y ropa.
4. ¿Qué colores de blusas le muestra el vendedor?
   a. Morada, verde y negra
   b. Morada, negra y blanca
   c. Morada, azul y negra
5. ¿Qué tipo de diseño tiene la blusa que le muestra el vendedor?
   a. Tiene un diseño muy artesanal.
   b. Tiene un diseño muy moderno.
   c. Tiene un diseño muy joven.
6. ¿Cuántos quetzales quiere el vendedor por la blusa?
   a. El vendedor quiere 150 quetzales.
   b. El vendedor quiere 80 quetzales.
   c. El vendedor quiere 90 quetzales.

2. Comprar en los mercados Would you like to visit an open-air market in an Spanish-speaking country? Which one?

3. Enfoque cultural Do you bargain in the United States? When and where? What is the difference between bargaining in your country and in a Spanish-speaking country?

AUTOPRUEBA

VOCABULARIO

I. ¿Cómo se dice...

1. ...cuando algo no cuesta mucho dinero?
2. ...cuando negocias con un vendedor para no pagar el precio original?
3. ...cuando el precio no es negociable?
4. ...cuando algo cuesta mucho dinero?
5. ...cuando algo pasa de un precio alto a un precio más bajo?

II. ¿Qué hay en el mercado? What kind of clothes would you sell at a market in Guatemala? Use colors and prices to describe your items.

1. _____
2. _____
3. _____
4. _____
5. _____

III. How much is it in Quetzales? ($1 = 8 quezales)

1. Tres blusas a $15 cada una son _____ quetzales.
2. Cuatro vestidos a $32 cada uno son _____ quetzales.
3. Cinco aretes a $8 cada par son _____ quetzales.
4. Seis DVD a $9 cada uno son _____ quetzales.

GRAMÁTICA

I. ¿Qué te gusta? What do you think the following people like? Select among the following list.

visitar México
ir de compras
llevar reloj
regatear

la ropa cara
caminar por la ciudad
mirar a la gente
los mercados de artesanías

1. yo
2. mi profesor/a de español
3. mis padres
4. mi compañero/a de clase
5. mi amigo/a

II. De viaje por Guatemala You are in Guatemala with your family and some friends. What are all of you going to do there?

1. Mis amigos _____ comprar muchos regalos.
2. Mi hermana _____ estudiar la cultura.
3. Yo _____ visitar los museos.
4. Mi madre _____ caminar por toda la ciudad.
5. Todos nosotros _____ practicar español.

CULTURA

1. Which activity is customary at open-air markets in Guatemala?
2. What's the Guatemalan currency?
3. Mention some interesting places to visit in Guatemala.
4. What do some Guatemalans do for *Semana Santa*?

REDACCIÓN

At the market! Write a paragraph about a day out in the market. You need to buy a few things for a wedding you are attending.

MODELO: El sábado voy a ir al mercado al aire libre. Me voy a comprar... Me gusta...

EN RESUMIDAS CUENTAS, AHORA PUEDO...

☐ negotiate in an open market.
☐ describe clothing.
☐ identify colors.
☐ use numbers fr...
☐ talk about what...
☐ tell what you ar...
☐ understand the...

> This section includes a self-test and **En resumidas cuentas,** a checklist of what the learner is capable of doing, saying, and understanding at the end of the section.

🎧 VOCABULARIO ESENCIAL

Sustantivos

el anillo	*ring*
el arete/pendiente	*earring*
la artesanía	*arts and crafts*
la camisa	*shirt*
el cinturón	*belt*
la comida	*food*
la falda	*skirt*
la flor	*flower*
el mercado (al aire libre)	*outdoors market*
el oro	*gold*
los pantalones	*pants*
la plata	*silver*
el precio (fijo)	*(fixed) price*
la pulsera	*bracelet*
el regalo	*gift*
el reloj	*watch*
la ropa	*clothing*
el sombrero	*hat*
el traje	*suit*
el vestido	*dress*
las zapatillas de deporte/los tenis	*tennis shoes*
los zapatos	*shoes*

Cognados: la blusa, la bota, el color

Verbos

comprar	*to buy*
gustar	*to like*
ir	*to go*
ir de compras	*to go shopping*
rebajar	*to reduce*
regalar	*to buy a present*
regatear	*to negotiate price*
vender	*to sell*

Cognados: costar (o-ue), insistir

Expresiones

¿Cuánto cuesta/cuestan...?	*How much is/are . . . ?*
el mes/año que viene, el próximo mes/año	*next month/year*
esta noche	*tonight*
la semana que viene, la próxima semana	*next week*
Para Ud., Q25. Buen precio...	*For you, Q25. It's a good price...*

Pase, pase, adelante... (pasado) mañana	*Come in, come in, . . . (the day after) tomorrow*
por la mañana/tarde/noche	*in the morning/afternoon/evening*
¿Qué llevas?	*What are you wearing?*
¿Qué busca/desea?	*What are you looking for?*
¿Qué te gusta llevar?	*What do you like to wear?*

Adjetivos

amarillo/a	*yellow*
anaranjado/a/naranja	*orange*
azul	*blue*
barato/a	*cheap, inexpensive*
blanco/a	*white*
caro/a	*expensive*
gris	*gray*
marrón/café	*brown*
negro/a	*black*
rojo/a	*red*
rosado/a	*pink*
verde	*green*
violeta/morado/a	*purple*

Los números

sesenta	*sixty*
setenta	*seventy*
ochenta	*eighty*
noventa	*ninety*
cien	*one hundred*
ciento uno	*one hundred and one*
ciento diez	*one hundred and ten*
doscientos	*two hundred*
trescientos	*three hundred*
cuatrocientos	*four hundred*
quinientos	*five hundred*
seiscientos	*six hundred*
setecientos	*seven hundred*
ochocientos	*eight hundred*
novecientos	*nine hundred*
mil	*one thousand*
mil uno	*one thousand and one*
mil cien	*one thousand one hundred*
mil ciento uno	*one thousand one hundred and one*
dos mil	*two thousand*
diez mil	*ten thousand*

> All the new vocabulary is collected with the English translations and cognates for quick reference.

THE COMPLETE PROGRAM

For a desk copy or electronic access to any of these program components, please contact your local Wiley sales representative, call our Sales Office at 1-800-CALL-WILEY (1-800-225-5945), or contact us online at www.wiley.com/college/lopezburton.

Student Textbook
978-1-118-08710-7
The textbook is organized into 12 chapters plus a Preliminary chapter, each of which is divided into two sections.

Annotated Instructor's Edition
978-1-118-38170-0
The Annotated Instructor's Edition includes a variety of marginal annotations with teaching tips, scripts for the listening activities, expansion activities, and answers to discrete point exercises.

Activities Manual
978-1-118-51474-0
The Activities Manual, both printed upon request and online through *WileyPlus*, will provide much-needed, outside-the-classroom practice tools for listening, reading, writing, speaking, and learning cultural knowledge. The Activities Manual supports the structures, vocabulary, and cultural information presented in the textbook. The Answer Key appears at the end of the book. Electronic files for the Answer Key as well as for the audio scripts are available on the *Pura vida* Instructor Companion Site at www.wiley.com/college/lopezburton and in *WileyPLUS* as an Instructor Resource.

Video
To be used in the classroom or assigned as online work, *Pura vida* has one video per chapter featuring an American living in the target country and accompanied by locals, as s/he shows us something pertinent to the theme and grammar of the chapter. The student in the classroom will hear natural speech patterns in various Spanish accents. This video will highlight cross-cultural comparisons following the approach of the book. The textbook includes instructor and student support activities that present strategies for previewing, viewing, and post-viewing. Video segments are available digitally in *WileyPLUS* and on the Instructor and Student Companion Sites.

Explore Your Ordering Options
The textbook is available in various formats. Consider an eBook, loose-leaf binder version, or a custom publication. The textbook is also available through *All Access Pack,* which includes WileyPLUS access code, Wiley e-textbook for mobile devices, and the interactive activities included in the *Manos a la obra* section of the textbook. Learn more about our flexible pricing, flexible formats, and flexible content at www.wiley.com/college/sc/puravida/options.html.

WileyPLUS
www.wileyplus.com
WileyPLUS is an innovative, online teaching and learning environment, built on a foundation of cognitive research that integrates relevant resources, including the entire digital textbook, in an easy-to-navigate framework that helps students study effectively. Online *Activities Manual,* available in *WileyPLUS,* builds students' confidence because it takes the guesswork out of studying by providing a clear roadmap to academic success. With *WileyPLUS,* instructors and students receive 24/7 access to resources that promote positive learning outcomes. Throughout each study session, students can assess their progress

and gain immediate feedback on their strengths and weaknesses so they can be confident they are spending their time effectively.

What Do Students Receive with WileyPLUS?

An easy-to-navigate, interactive online version of the textbook is organized by sections.

- Related supplemental material reinforces learning objectives.
- Innovative features such as self-evaluation tools improve time management and strengthen areas of weakness.

One-on-one engagement. With *WileyPLUS* for *Pura vida,* students receive 24/7 access to resources that promote positive learning outcomes. Students engage with related activities in various media, including:

- **Blackboard IM functionality:** Student collaboration tool with IM, whiteboard, and desktop sharing capabilities.
- **Audio Program:** The Audio Program includes recordings for the listening activities in the textbook, vocabulary in *Palabra por palabra* and in the list at the end of the chapters, and the listening activities in the *Activities Manual.* The Audio Program is available in *WileyPLUS* and on the Book Companion Site at www.wiley.com/college/lopezburton.
- **Wimba Voice Response Questions and Wimba VoiceBoards:** Recording functionality that allows instructors to test students' speaking skills.
- **Electronic Activities Manual:** Allows instructors to assign Workbook and Lab Manual activities which are then sent straight to the gradebook for automatic and manual grading options. Available in the assignment section in *WileyPLUS*.
- **In-text activities:** Assignable electronic versions of select textbook activities that test students' understanding of grammar and vocabulary.
- **Animated grammar tutorials:** Animation series that reinforces key grammatical lessons.
- **Map quizzes:** Interactive study tool that tests students' geographical knowledge of Spanish speaking countries and cities.
- **Audio flashcards:** Offers pronunciation, English/Spanish translations, and chapter quizzes.
- **Verb conjugator:** Supplemental guides and practice for conjugating verbs.
- **English grammar checkpoints:** Alphabetical listing of the major grammar points from the textbook that allows students to review their use in the English language.
- *La pronunciación:* Guide that offers basic rules and practice for pronouncing the alphabet, diphthongs, accent marks, and more.

Measurable Outcomes: Throughout each study session, students can assess their progress and gain immediate feedback. *WileyPLUS* provides precise reporting of strengths and weaknesses, as well as individualized quizzes, so that students are confident they are spending their time on the right things. With *WileyPLUS*, students always know the exact outcome of their efforts.

What Do Instructors Receive with *WileyPLUS*?

WileyPLUS provides reliable, customizable resources that reinforce course goals inside and outside of the classroom as well as tracking of individual student progress. Pre-created materials and activities help instructors optimize their time:

- **Instructor Resource Manual (IRM)** contains complete syllabi, teaching tips, and expansion on the cultural information, with helpful suggestions to implement a cross-cultural approach effectively, as well as keys for teaching grammatical structures that students find problematic. Crossword puzzles, Jeopardy-style games, and info-gap or task-based activities are also included for each chapter.
- **Sample Syllabi** are included for quarters and semesters.

- **PowerPoint Presentations:** The PowerPoint presentations complement some sections of the textbook such as *Ver para creer, La pura verdad, Palabra por palabra, Así es la vida,* and selected activities to do in class.
- **Image Gallery:** Collection of the photographs, illustrations, and artwork from each chapter of the textbook.
- **Prebuilt Question Assignments:** Available in a variety of options, these prebuilt electronic quizzes allow instructors to test students' understanding of vocabulary, grammar, and culture, as well as their reading, writing, listening, and speaking skills.
- **Test bank:** Collection of assignable questions that allow instructors to build custom exams; select Test bank questions are also available in Word documents.
- **Printable exams with answer keys, audio files, and scripts:** All of the components that instructors need to distribute printed exams in class. There are three different exam versions per chapter.
- **Lab Manual audio script:** Script for each of the listening activities in the chapter.
- **Gradebook:** *WileyPLUS* provides access to reports on trends in class performance, student use of course materials, and progress toward learning objectives, helping inform decisions and drive classroom discussions.

WileyPLUS with ORION—Adaptive Learning Tool

WileyPLUS is now equipped with an adaptive learning module called ORION. Based on cognitive science, *WileyPLUS* with ORION provides students with a personal, adaptive learning experience so they can build their language skills and use their study time most effectively. *WileyPLUS* with ORION helps students learn by learning about them. Powering our *Grammar Checkpoint,* ORION also gives students a personalized and adaptive way to brush up on the basic language concepts they need (What's a pronoun? What do adverbs do?) in order to learn how grammar works in the language they're studying.

The *En* vivo option

With the *En vivo* option, regularly scheduled, live, online coaching sessions reinforce language skills and further explore cultural notions. A special set of activities per each chapter provides a framework for conversation, and a native-speaking language coach encourages students to practice the Spanish they're learning in weekly coaching sessions. For more information, contact your Wiley representative or visit www.wiley.com/college/sc/envivo.

Spanish Reader

You can create your own cultural Spanish Reader to accompany *Pura vida,* choosing from a wide variety of authentic articles written by journalists and writers from the 21 Spanish-speaking countries. Visit mywiley.info/puntoycoma for more information.

Student Companion Site

www.wiley.com/college/lopezburton
The Student Companion Site contains complimentary self-tests, audio flashcards, the Verb Conjugator or System with practice handouts, accompanying audio for the textbook, and Lab Manual, map quizzes, and videos.

Instructor Companion Site

www.wiley.com/college/ lopezburton
The Instructor Companion Site includes the student resources mentioned above, plus handouts, answer keys, scripts, and audio files to accompany chapter level, mid-term, and final exams. It also includes a Word version of the Test Bank, an image gallery, answer keys for the Lab Manual, and audio and video scripts.

Acknowledgments

We, the authors of *Pura vida,* wish to express our heartfelt thanks to our amazing editor, Elena Herrero, for her expert guidance, dedication, patience, and friendship. Her contribution to *Pura vida* has been invaluable. It has been a privilege to work with her.

We would also like to express our gratitude to Glenn Wilson, a visionary who came in contact with *Pura vida* a few years ago and understood *Pura vida*'s vision and potential. This book would not have been possible without him.

Furthermore, we want to thank Magali Iglesias for believing in us and Mercedes Roffé and Alejandra Barciela for their attention to detail.

Our deep appreciation goes to the rest of the team at John Wiley & Sons for their effort, professionalism, and expertise delivering the first edition of *Pura vida*: the marketing team: Jeff Rucker, Kimberly Kanakes, Glenn Wilson; the production team: Bill Murray, Micheline Frederick; the media team: Tom Kulesa, Jennifer Brady, and Beth Pearson.

Our book would not be complete without our colleagues in charge of the *Instructors Resources Manual*: Jesús David Jerez Gómez, Ben Schmeiser, Debra Herrick, and Amy Bodrozic. The *En vivo* author: Helga Winkle. And the *Student Activities Manual* authors: Tasha Lewis, Marcus Welch, and Adolfo Carrillo Cabello. We appreciate their hard work and patience.

A special thanks to all listed below for sharing with us your wonderful stories and great photos for the *Perspectivas* sections: Shelley Cheney Ackermann, Catalina Adams, Mark Adams, Mark Ackermann, Elena Atanasiu, Fernando Aveiga, Isabel Baboun Garib, Noemia Melissa Binney, Héctor Bombiella Medina, Jonah Brown, Miranda Buseman, Leslie A. Burton, Thomas A. Burton, Thomas P. Burton, Aina Cabra Riart, Rebecca Conley, Consuelo Cervantes, Daniel Chui, Carolyne Crolotte Mesquita, Katie Clarkson, Melissa Corbett, Claudia Darrigrandi, Emily Davidson, Alfida Deaza, Sergio Díaz Luna, Annabelle Dolidon, Nicole Ellis, Chad M Gasta, Myriam Gonzales-Smith, Andronike Halbrook, Rachel Haywood Ferreira, Elias Hernández, Iris Hernández, Alexandra Hernández-Pardo, Natalia Hernández-Pardo, Juan Hernando Vázquez, Byron Hoy, Michael Harris, Claire Ihlendorf Burke, Cindy Irusta, Elizabeth Jara, Timothy Johnson, Emily Kuffner, Brad Langer, Olga Lazchuk y familia, Tania Lizarazo, Jesse Long, Megan Mayzelle, Juan Miranda, Julia Medina, Lola Miralles, Miguel Montesinos, Kimberly Morris, Kenny Ogorzalek, María Belén Pardo Ballester, María Pilar Pardo Ballester, Teresa Pascual García, Yolanda Jacqueline Peláez, Angélica Sofía Reina Páez, Wilma Isabel Pillot, Orlando Ríos Cabral, Flor Romero de Slowing, Brittany Schon, Ryan Sokol, David Tenorio González, Tracy Quan, Christina Sansom, Katherine Stafford, Albert Van Geelen, Ana Varela Tafur, Marta Vessoni de Lence, Eva Michelle Wheeler, Julie Wilhelm, Karina Zelaya.

We also wish to thank the following reviewers and contributors from across the nation for their observations, their important scrutiny, and their creative ideas.

Christina Agostinelli, *University at Buffalo, The State University of New York*

Felipe Hugueño Machuca Alfaya, *University at Buffalo*

Frances Alpren, *Vanderbilt University*

Laura Arribas, *University at Buffalo, The State University of New York*

Corinne Arrieta, *American River College*

Bárbara Avila-Shah, *University at Buffalo, The State University of New York*

Rene Baca, *New Mexico Highlands University*

Damián Bacich, *California State San Jose, San Jose*

Youngmin Bae, *Los Angeles City College*

Carmen Bárcenas, *Lone Star College–North Harris*

Maria Bauluz, *Santa Clara University*

Mónica Beviá, *Cornell University*

Adrián Pérez Boluda, *California State University, Northridge*

Sara Bostwick, *Lansing Community College*

Sara Blossom Bostwock, *Lansing Community College*

Joanna Bradley, *East Carolina University*

Tatiana Calixto, *University of Michigan*

Manuel Camacho, *San Joaquin Delta College*
Araceli Canalini, *Chicago State University*
Monica Cantero, *Drew University*
Juan Carlos, *Truman State University*
Lissette Castro, *Mount San Jacinto College*
Robert Chierico, *Chicago State University*
Beatriz Cobeta, *George Washington University*
Sandra Correa, *Arizona State University*
William Denver, *Armstrong Atlantic State University*
Oscar Diaz, *Middle Tennesse State University*
Isabel Domínguez, *University at Buffalo, The State University of New York*
Lucía Dzikowski, *Seminole State College*
Kimberley Eherenman, *University of San Diego*
María Encisco, *Saddleback College*
Luz Escobar, *Tarrant County College District South*
Addison Everett, *Dixie State College*
Ronna Felt, *Nassau Community College, SUNY*
Diane Forbes, *Rochester Institute of Technology*
Diana Frantzen, *University of Wisconsin–Madison*
Ellen Friedrich, *Valdosta State University*
Inés Vaño García, *University at Buffalo, The State University of New York*
Chad Gasta, *Iowa State University*
Amy Ginck, *Messiah College*
David Jerez Gómez, *California State University, San Bernardino*
Jesus-David Jerez-Gomez, *California State San Bernadino*
Jesús David Jerez Gómez, *California State University, San Bernardino*
Tania Gomez, *College of State Benedict*
María A. Gómez, *Florida International University*
Pedro Gómez, *University of Nevada, Reno*
Kate Grovergrys, *Madison Area Technical College*
Angela Erickson Grussing, *Saint John's University*
James Gustafson, *Southern Utah University*
Greg Harris, *Indiana Univ South Bend*
Mary Hartson, *Oakland University*
Heather Hennes, *Saint Josephs University*
Miriam Hernández Rodríguez, *University of California, Berkeley*
Todd Hernandez, *Marquette University*
Jerry Hoeg, *Pennsylvania State University, Fayette*
Carmen Jany, *California State University, San Bernardino*
Amarilis Hidalgo de Jesús, *Bloomsburg University*
Liliana Jurewiez, *Indiana University of Pennsylvania*
Liliana Elizabeth Jurewiez, *Indiana University of Pennsylvania*
Nieves Knapp, *Brigham Young University–Provo*
Lina Lee, *University of New Hampshire*
Marta Lence, *Iowa State University*
Sonia Llacer, *Tacoma Community College*
Sonia Zuniga Lomeli, *Santa Barbara City College*
Rosa López Cañete, *East Carolina University*
Tania Muiño Loureiro, *Northeastern University*
Jessica Lynam, *Christopher Newport University*
Bernard Manker, *Grand Rapids Community College*
Marcelino Marcos, *Lakeland Community College*
Rob Martinson, *Brigham Young University–Provo*
Lydia Masanet, *Mercer University*
Nancy Mason, *Dalton State College*

Fernando Mayoral, *Edison State College*
Fernando Mayoral, *Edison State College*
Marco Mena, *Massbay Community College*
Denise Minor, *California State University, Chicago*
Denise Minor, *California State University, Chicago*
Deborah Mistron, *Middle Tennessee State University*
Patricia Moore-Martinez, *Temple University*
Maria Yazmina Moreno-Florido, *Chicago State University*
María Gabriela Muñiz, *Butler University*
Janet Navarro, *Purdue University Calumet*
Robert Norton, *Missouri State University*
William Otañez, *Coastal Carolina University*
Charles Paus, *University Park Campus*
Tammy Pérez, *San Antonio College*
Corinne Pubill, *Salisbury University*
Judith García Quismondo, *Seton Hill University*
Judith García Quismondo, *Seton Hill University*
Rajiv Rao, *University of Wisconsin, Madison*
Scott Rex, *Southern Oregon University*
Duane Rhoades, *University of Wyoming*
María del Mar Rosa Rodríguez, *Carnegie Mellon University*
Angelo Rodríguez, *Kutztown University of Pennsylvania*
Linda Roy, *Tarrant County College District South*
karen Rubio, *University of Tulsa*
Christine Sabin, *Sierra College*
Laura Sanchez, *Bethel University*
José Sandoval, *Coastal Cardina Community College*
Alex Sandoval, *Coastal Carolina CC*
Kayrn Schell, *University of San Francisco*
Michael Schinasi, *East Carolina Univeristy*
Benjamin Schmeiser, *Illinois State University*
David Schuettler, *The College of Saint Scholastica*
Laura Ruiz Scott, *Scottsdale CC*
Laura Ruiz-Scott, *Scottsdale Community College*
Jason Smith, *Southern Utah University*
Alexander Steffanell, *Lee University*
Michael Tallon, *University of the Incarnate Word*
Carrie Tamburo, *Seattle Central Community College*
Daniel Trego, *Michigan State University*
Jan Underwood, *Portland Community College*
Victoria Uricoechea, *Winthrop University*
Phyllis VanBuren, *Saint Cloud State University*
Leonor Vázquez, *University of Montevallo*
Gloria Vélez-Rendón, *Purdue University Calumet*
Celines Villalba, *Rutgers, The State University of New Jersey*
Grazyna Walczak, *Valdosta State University*
Erin Weber, *Cedarville University*
Alice Weldon, *University of North Carolina at Asheville*
Marcus Welsh, *Pacific University*
Julie Wilhelm, *Iowa State University*
Elizabeth Willingham, *Calhoun Community College*
Mercedes Windver, *Lansing Community College*
Andrew Wiseman, *Cedarville University*
Catherine Wiskes, *University of South Carolina, Columbia*
Gabriela Zapata, *University of Southern California*
Teresa Zmurkewycz, *Saint Josephs University*
Eduardo Acuna Zumbado, *Missouri State University*
Eve Zyzik, *University of California, Santa Cruz*

Preliminar ¡A conocerse!

VER PARA CREER I *(Seeing is believing)*: ¡Bienvenido al mundo hispano!

In this video you will learn how to greet people in the Hispanic world. For now, pay attention to their gestures. Don't worry if you cannot understand everything. After watching the video, answer the following questions:

1. How do people in the video greet each other?
2. Are the people in the video from the same country?

PALABRA POR PALABRA *(Word by word)*

- Saludos y despedidas
- Presentaciones (informales y formales)
- Los números del 0 al 59

HABLANDO DE GRAMÁTICA *(Talking about grammar)*

- Formal and informal forms of address: Use of **tú** and **usted** (Ud.)
- The Spanish alphabet and pronunciation
- Identifying gender and number: Nouns and articles

CULTURA

- La diferencia entre *tú* y *usted*
- Distintos tipos de saludos

Mark Scott / Photographer's Choice / Getty Images

LEARNING OBJECTIVES
By the end of this section you will be able to:
- Greet and introduce others
- Understand the difference between **tú** and **usted**
- Spell words in Spanish
- Identify gender and number
- Count to 59

Una imagen vale más que mil palabras *(An image is worth a thousand words)*

In these photos, there are people from the United States, Latin America, and Spain. Can you guess where each of them is from?

Visage / Stockbyte / Getty Images

© Cardinal / Corbis

© Somos Images / Alamy

 CP-01 ¿Por qué estudiar español?[1] In groups of three or four, take this quiz and together discover the historical and present-day facts that tie the Spanish language to the United States.

1. Spanish is a Romance language. Why is it called so?
   a. Because it is a romantic language.
   b. Because Spanish was spoken throughout the Roman Empire.
   c. Because Spanish is derived from Latin, a language spoken by the Romans.
2. Spanish is . . .
   a. the most spoken language in the world.
   b. the second most spoken language in the world.
   c. the third most spoken language in the world.
3. The number of Spanish speakers in the United States is approximately . . .
   a. 20 million.
   b. 50 million.
   c. 15 million.
4. How is the Spanish language present in your community?
5. Name five states that have Spanish names.
6. Name major cities in the United States with Spanish names.

© PNC / Brand X Pictures / Getty Images

[1]¿Por qué estudiar español?: Why study Spanish?

🎧 PALABRA POR PALABRA

Saludos y despedidas *Greetings and expressions of farewell*

> Hola, ¿cómo estás?

> Más o menos.

> Buenos días, ¿qué tal?

> Bastante bien.

> Hola, ¿cómo está usted?

> Muy bien, gracias.

Saludos	*Greetings*
Hola, ¿cómo estás?	*Hi, how are you? (informal)*
Hola, ¿cómo está usted?	*Hi, how are you? (formal)*
Buenos días, ¿qué tal?	*Good morning, how's it going?*
¡Fenomenal!	*Great!*
Bastante bien.	*Pretty good.*
Más o menos.	*So-so.*
Muy bien, gracias.	*Very well, thank you.*

Coloquialismos

¡Pura vida!	*Great! (Literally, "Pure life" or "nothing but life")*
¿Qué hubo?	*What's up?*
¿Cómo estamos?	*How are we doing?*
¿Qué me cuentas?	*What's going on?*
Pues, ahí nomás.	*Well, hanging in there.*

> Buenos días. ¿Cómo estás, Roberto?

> Buenos días. Bien, gracias, ¿y usted, doña Carmen?

Buenos días.	*Good morning.*
Buenas tardes.	*Good afternoon.*
Buenas noches.	*Good evening./Good night.*

Hola, me llamo...	*Hi, my name is . . .*
¿Cómo te llamas?	*What's your name?*
Mucho gusto.	*Nice to meet you.*
Encantado/a.	*Nice to meet you.*

Hasta la vista.	*See you soon. (Lit. Until I see you again.)*
Que tengas un buen fin de semana.	*Have a nice weekend. (informal)*

Despedidas	*Expressions of farewell*
Adiós.	*Goodbye.*
Hasta pronto.	*See you soon.*
Hasta mañana.	*See you tomorrow.*
Hasta luego.	*See you later.*

Coloquialismos	
(Ahí) nos vemos.	*See ya.*
Nos vemos mañana.	*See you tomorrow.*
Que la pases bien.	*Have a good time. (infor.)*
Que te diviertas.	*Have fun. (infor.)*

Presentaciones informales

Mi nombre es...	*My name is . . .*
Mi apellido es...	*My last name is . . .*
Te presento a...	*Let me introduce you to . . . (informal)*
Quiero presentarte a...	*Let me introduce you to . . . (informal)*
Gusto en conocerte.	*Nice to meet you.*
Encantado/a.	*Nice to meet you.*

Presentaciones formales

Titles of respect

Sr.	Señor	*Mister*
Srta.	Señorita	*Miss*
Sra.	Señora	*Mrs.*
D.ª	Doña	*Title of respect used with first names (f)*
	Don	*Title of respect used with first names (m)*

Quiero presentarle a...	*I would like to introduce you to . . . (formal)*
Le presento a...	*I would like to introduce you to . . . (formal)*
Igualmente.	*Likewise.*

CP-02 Asociaciones Match the greetings with the answers.

_C_ 1. ¿Qué me cuentas?   a. Igualmente.

_F_ 2. Hola, ¿cómo está?   b. Más o menos, ¿y tú?

____ 3. Hola, me llamo Clara. ¿Cómo te llamas?   c. No mucho, ¿y tú?

____ 4. Mucho gusto.   d. Adiós.

____ 5. Hola, ¿qué tal?   e. Eduardo, gusto en conocerte.

____ 6. Nos vemos mañana.   f. Bastante bien, gracias, ¿y usted?

CP-03 Diálogos Complete this dialogue and practice it with a classmate.

Estudiante 1: Hola, me llamo ___Chris___. ¿Cómo ___estás___?

Estudiante 2: ___Bien___, gracias. Yo me llamo _____.

Estudiante 1: Mucho gusto.

Estudiante 2: ___mucho gusto___. igualmente

Estudiante 1: _____ a mi nuevo amigo de la clase de español,

___amigo___.

Estudiante 3: Gusto en conocerte.

Estudiante 2: _____.

CP-04 ¡Mucho gusto!

Paso 1: Introduce yourself to five classmates.

MODELO: Estudiante 1:   *Hola, me llamo Ana. ¿Cómo te llamas?*
           Estudiante 2:   *Me llamo Rubén.*
           Estudiante 1:   *Mucho gusto.*
           Estudiante 2:   *Encantado.*

Paso 2: Now, introduce the people you have met to the rest of the class.

MODELO: *Él/Ella se llama* _____.

CP-05 Papa caliente When you receive the hot potato, introduce yourself:

MODELO: *Me llamo Victoria.*

After introducing yourself, repeat the names of the three classmates before you. Can you remember all names? If not, ask them.

MODELO: *Él se llama Lucas, ella se llama Amanda, él se llama… ¿cómo te llamas?*

CP-06 Hola, buenas tardes You meet the following people in the street. Greet them, ask them how they are, and say goodbye. Decide who will be **Estudiante 1** and who will be **Estudiante 2**. Each student will play the roles below.

MODELO: Estudiante 1 (as himself):   *Buenas tardes, señor Mireles, ¿cómo está usted?*
           Estudiante 2 (as Señor Mireles):   *Muy bien, gracias, ¿y tú?*

Estudiante 1:
el/la profesor/a de español
el médico
Doña Teresa

Estudiante 2:
el señor Mireles
el/la mejor amigo/a
el presidente de Estados Unidos

LA PURA VERDAD *(Nothing but the truth)* ¿Tú o usted?

La mamá de la Srta. Silva visita la clase de español.

1.

2.
¡Hola!

3.
Clase, les presento a mi mamá, la Sra. Silva. Mamá, esta es mi clase de español.

4.
Hola, ¿cómo están?

5.
Muy bien, gracias, ¿y tú?

6.
¿Cómo está usted?

7.
¡Usted, usted!

8.

9.
Bien, muy bien, gracias.

© John Wiley & Sons, Inc.

CP-07 ¿Tú o usted? Listen to the questions and select a logical answer.

1. a. Porque el saludo es muy informal.
   b. Porque el saludo es muy formal.
2. a. ¿Cómo estás, mamá? ¿Estás bien?
   b. ¿Cómo está, mamá? ¿Está bien?
3. a. Muy bien, gracias, Srta. Silva.
   b. Bueno, hasta mañana, Srta. Silva.

HABLANDO DE GRAMÁTICA

WileyPLUS Go to *WileyPLUS* to review this grammar point with the help of the **Animated Grammar Tutorial**.

1. Formal and informal forms of address: Use of *tú* and *usted* (*Ud.*)

Spanish uses different forms of address, depending on the relationship between the people who are speaking. Factors such as age and social position play important roles. In English, we use *you* for both a formal or an informal relationship. This never changes, so we never really have to think about the type of relationship that the people who are talking have. In Spanish, **tú** is the usual form of address when the relationship is informal; **usted** is generally used when the relationship is more distant or formal. The following are only guidelines and vary from one Spanish-speaking country to another. In general:

- Children, parents, students, and friends usually address each other as **tú**:

¿Cómo estás, papá?   How are you, Dad?
¿Qué tal, mamá?   How are you, Mom?

- Outside the family, young people address older people as **usted.** The older person will probably address the younger as **tú**:

Young person: ¿Cómo se llama usted?   *What is your name (sir)?*
Older person: Me llamo Manuel   *My name is Manuel Rivera, and you?*
   Rivera, ¿y tú?

- Doctors, lawyers, professors, and other professionals are usually treated as **usted**, even if they are approximately the same age (or even older) and have the same social standing:

Dr. Lagos, ¿cómo está usted hoy?   *Dr. Lagos, how are you today?*
Profesor Cedeño, le presento a   *Professor Cedeño, I'd like to introduce you*
   mi hijo Carlos.   *to my son, Carlos.*

- Students often address professors as **usted.** The professor may treat the student as **tú** or **usted.** This formal treatment is something that is changing in some countries, particularly in Spain where greater familiarity between professors and students has become more common. However, in many Spanish-speaking countries, the relationship between professors and students generally remains formal.

Buenos días, profesora Bonilla.   *Good morning, Professor Bonilla.*
   ¿Cómo está?   *How are you?*
Buenas tardes, profesor Rojas.   *Good afternoon, Professor Rojas.*
   ¿A qué hora es la clase?   *At what time is the class?*

- The general rule of thumb is, if in doubt, use **usted.** On the one hand, some people might be amused if you "incorrectly" treat them as **usted,** but they won't be offended. On the other hand, if you use **tú** and they expected to be treated as **usted,** they might feel that you are being disrespectful. Sometimes if you treat someone as **usted** who would like to be treated as **tú,** the person will say: **¿Por qué no nos tuteamos?** It means, "Why don't we treat each other as **tú?**" and it's like saying: "Call me by my first name."

Vosotros and ustedes

In Spain the plural of **tú** is **vosotros** but in the rest of the Spanish-speaking world the plural of **tú** is **ustedes** both in formal and informal situations:

¿**Vosotros** sois estudiantes? (in Spain)   *Are you all students?*
¿**Ustedes** son estudiantes? (in Lat. Am.)   *Are you all students?*

Vosotros sois muy pacientes. (in Spain)   *You are all very patient.*
Ustedes son muy pacientes. (in Lat. Am.)   *You are all very patient.*

In some countries people use **vos** instead of **tú.** In Argentina, Uruguay, Paraguay, and most of Central America (Costa Rica, El Salvador, Nicaragua, Guatemala, and Honduras) and in some parts of Colombia and Venezuela, people use **vos** instead of **tú,** but not **vosotros.**

CP-08 **¿Tú o usted?** Decide whether you should use **tú** or **usted** to address the following people:

1. The man at the corner kiosk who sells you the newspaper every day
2. An elderly lady to whom you have offered your seat in the bus
3. Your younger sister's best friend
4. Your dentist
5. A student you stop on campus to ask the time

CP-09 **Mucho respeto** Look at the drawings below and fill out their empty speech bubbles with their formal or informal greetings.

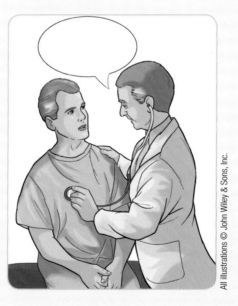

All illustrations © John Wiley & Sons, Inc.

CP-10 **¿Formal o informal?** Stand up, walk around the classroom, meet, and introduce your new acquaintances. Decide whether to use the formal or informal form of address.

MODELO: Estudiante 1:   *Te presento a Eva.* o *Le presento a la profesora González.*
               Estudiante 2:   *Gusto en conocerte.* o *Mucho gusto.*
               Estudiante 3:   *Igualmente.* o *Encantado/a.*

2. The Spanish alphabet and pronunciation

Below is the Spanish alphabet with its 27 letters. **Ñ *(eñe)*** is not in the English alphabet. The letter "h" is always silent in Spanish.

From country to country: The pronunciation of some letters like the *c, g, j, ll, r, x, y,* and *z* could vary from country to country. The letters *b* and *v* can also be called **be larga, be grande,** and **ve chica,** respectively. The letter *w* can also be called **doble ve.**

WileyPLUS Go to **La pronunciación** section in *WileyPLUS* to review the pronunciation through different audio activities.

Letra	Se dice	Ejemplo
a	a	**A**lberto; Mar**í**a
b	be	**B**ernab**é**
c	ce	**C**armen; Mer**c**edes
d	de	**D**iego; ma**d**re
e	e	**E**milia; T**e**resa; Jos**é**
f	efe	**F**elipe; Al**f**redo
g	ge	**G**abriel; Vir**g**ilio
h	hache	**H**oracio; a**h**í
i	i (i latina)	**I**rene; Jac**i**nto; com**í**
j	jota	**J**ulia; Ale**j**andro
k	ka	**k**ilogramo
l	ele	**L**o**l**a; Migue**l**
m	eme	**M**arta; Car**m**en
n	ene	**N**orma; Her**n**án
ñ	eñe	ni**ñ**a; Mu**ñ**oz
o	o	**O**livia; R**o**bert**o**
p	pe	**P**edro; Ló**p**ez
q	cu	**Q**uique; Ro**q**ue
r	erre	**R**omán; Fe**r**nando
s	ese	**S**usana; Marco**s**
t	te	**T**eodoro; Vic**t**oria
u	u	**Ú**rsula; H**u**go; t**ú**
v	uve	**V**alverde; u**v**a
w	uve doble	**W**álter; **w**hisky
x	equis	se**x**o; e**x**amen
y	ye o i griega	**Y**olanda; le**y**
z	zeta	**Z**oilo; Gon**z**alo, Pére**z**

¡OJO! *(Watch out!)*

The letter r

Although the letter **r** may be found at the beginning, middle, or end of a word, the pronunciation varies. If an **r** is found at the beginning of a word, it is trilled, while if a single **r** is found in the middle of a word, is softer.

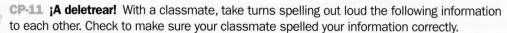

CP-11 ¡A deletrear! With a classmate, take turns spelling out loud the following information to each other. Check to make sure your classmate spelled your information correctly.

1. Your last name
2. Your mother's maiden name
3. The name of your street
4. Your e-mail (@ is **arroba** in Spanish)
5. A cool website that you like

CP-12 Mensajes de texto Spell out loud the word in Spanish and the "texting" version to a classmate. Check each other's spelling to make sure you spelled it correctly.

MODELO: texto → *txt*
"texto" *se deletrea te-e-equis-te-o y en* texting *es te-equis-te*

Estudiante 1

1. fiesta → fsta
2. por favor → xfa
3. personas → pers

Estudiante 2

4. problema → prblm
5. excelente → exclnt
6. besos → bss

Ns vms mñn en la fsta*

*Nos vemos mañana en la fiesta.
See you tomorrow at the party.

3. Identifying gender and number: Nouns and articles

WileyPLUS Go to *WileyPLUS* to review this grammar point with the help of the **Animated Grammar Tutorial**.

A. Nouns

In both English and Spanish, nouns denote people, animals, or objects. Nouns are those words that can be preceded by an article such as "the" or "a" in English. In English, sometimes nouns have a gender. For example, a sailor will usually refer to a ship as *she*. And sometimes a noun helps to differentiate between male and female: *doe* and *buck*, *king* and *queen*.

Spanish is different—*all* nouns have gender, either masculine or feminine. **La mesa** (table) is a word with feminine gender. It does not mean that a table necessarily has feminine characteristics. **El libro** (book) is masculine—it does not mean the book itself is masculine. In Spanish, most nouns that end in **a** are feminine. Most nouns that end in **o** are masculine. When nouns do not end in **o** or **a**, and the noun has an adjective, we can often guess the noun's gender by looking at whether the adjective ends in **o** or **a**.

Here are some common masculine and feminine nouns:

Feminine Nouns		Masculine Nouns	
la cas**a**	the house	el niñ**o**	the child
la sierr**a**	the sierra	el univers**o**	the universe
la vid**a**	the life	el bañ**o**	the bathroom
la pizarr**a**	the blackboard	el aut**o**	the car
la fiest**a**	the party	el text**o**	the text

Gender benders

Language evolution creates exceptions to the rules, in this case, gender. It is important to become familiar with these special cases since the gender of a word impacts other words that refer to it. You will simply have to memorize these exceptions. The good news is that words with the same ending are usually of the same gender. For example, all words ending in **-dad** are feminine.

Some words that come from Greek and end in **–ma**, **–pa**, or **–ta** are masculine:

la activi**dad**	the activity
la liber**tad**	the freedom
la creativi**dad**	the creativity

el ma**pa**	the map
el plane**ta**	the planet
el siste**ma**	the system

The reverse is possible, too. A common feminine word that ends in **o** is **la mano** (the hand). There are also some common words that end in **o** but are feminine because they are abbreviations of words that end in **a**:

la fotografí**a**	la fot**o**	the photo
la motocicle**ta**	la mot**o**	the motorcycle

And finally, here are some common words that don't end in either **o** or **a**.

Masculine		Femenine	
el cin**e**	the cinema	la universi**dad**	the university
el gara**je**	the garage	la estupid**ez**	the stupidity
el pape**l**	the paper	la lec**ción**	the lesson
el banqu**ete**	the banquet	la direc**ción**	the direction
el so**l**	the sun	la actit**ud**	the attitude
el avi**ón**	the airplane	la cost**umbre**	the custom

Plural of nouns

To form the plural of nouns, follow these two rules:

1. Add **-s** to a noun ending in a vowel:

    mapa → mapas, estudiante → estudiantes

2. Add **-es** to a noun ending in a consonant:

    actividad → actividades, lección → lecciones

B. Definite and indefinite articles

The definite article in English has only one form, *the*: *the* man, *the* woman, *the* children. In Spanish, the definite article varies, depending on the gender of the noun and whether it is singular or plural:

	Masculine	**Feminine**
Singular	**el** libr**o** (*the book*)	**la** profesor**a** (*the teacher*)
	el niñ**o** (*the child*)	**la** secretari**a** (*the secretary*)
Plural	**los** libr**os** (*the books*)	**las** profesor**as** (*the teachers*)
	los niñ**os** (*the children*)	**las** secretari**as** (*the secretaries*)

When you learn a new noun, your life will be easier if you learn it with its definite article.

The indefinite article in English has two singular forms: *a* and *an*. The plural is *some*. In Spanish, gender and number determine the indefinite article, just as for the definite article.

	Masculine	**Feminine**
Singular	**un** libr**o** (*a book*)	**una** mes**a** (*a table*)
	un profesor (*a teacher*)	**una** ventan**a** (*a window*)
Plural	**unos** libr**os** (*some books*)	**unas** mes**as** (*some tables*)
	unos profesor**es** (*some teachers*)	**unas** ventan**as** (*some windows*)

Note that the indefinite article **un** is used when it is followed by a masculine noun: for example, **un libro**, not **uno libro** (a common mistake).

 CP-13 Objetos de la clase Here is a list of objects and people that you can see in the drawing on p.13, but the article is missing. Place each noun with its corresponding item and add the masculine or feminine definite article as needed:

bolígrafo	*pen*	mochila	*backpack*
calculadora	*calculator*	papel	*paper*
lápiz	*pencil*	pizarra	*board*
libro	*book*	profesora	*professor*
mapa	*map*	pupitre	*desk*

© John Wiley & Sons, Inc.

CP-14 Lista de compras[2] Classes will be starting soon and you have to go out and do some shopping. Write a list of all the things you will need for class. You will need more than one of some items, so use the plural and place **unos** or **unas** in front of each noun, depending on the gender. You may only need one of other items, in which case use **un** or **una.**

Lista de compras

CP-15 Clase de español With a classmate, look at the list below and decide what words are related to your Spanish class. Don't forget to add the feminine or masculine article. Then, report to the class. Can the class agree on which item or items do not belong to the Spanish class?

MODELO: *diccionario*   <u>*el diccionario* (✔)</u>

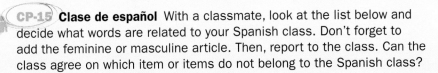

universidad	_____	calculadora	_____
mapas	_____	actividad	_____
fotografía	_____	lápices	_____
problema	_____	poema	_____
lecciones	_____	temas	_____
libros	_____	garaje	_____
bolígrafo	_____	banquete	_____

[2]**Lista de compras:** Shopping list

PALABRA POR PALABRA

Los números del 0 al 59 *(Numbers from 0 to 59)*

1	*uno*	11	*once*	21	*veintiuno*
2	*dos*	12	*doce*	22	*veintidós*
3	*tres*	13	*trece*	23	*veintitrés*
4	*cuatro*	14	*catorce*	24	*veinticuatro*
5	*cinco*	15	*quince*	25	*veinticinco*
6	*seis*	16	*dieciséis*	26	*veintiséis*
7	*siete*	17	*diecisiete*	27	*veintisiete*
8	*ocho*	18	*dieciocho*	28	*veintiocho*
9	*nueve*	19	*diecinueve*	29	*veintinueve*
10	*diez*	20	*veinte*	30	*treinta*
				40	*cuarenta*
				50	*cincuenta*

CP-16 En el restaurante You are at a restaurant with a group of friends. Calculate the tip you'll leave.

$\times \rightarrow$ multiplicado por
$= \rightarrow$ son

WileyPLUS Go to WileyPLUS to review this grammar point with the help of the **Animated Grammar Tutorial**.

MODELO: *$11,02 (20%) → $11,02 × 0,2 = $2,20*
Once dólares y dos centavos multiplicado por cero coma dos, son dos dólares y veinte centavos de propina[3].

1. $8,12 (18%)
2. $22,10 (10%)
3. $29,25 (11%)
4. $15,12 (15%)
5. $16,02 (13%)

CP-17 ¡El precio justo![4] Your instructor will show you several articles. In groups, decide how much each article costs. Then, decide which group is closer to the actual price.

MODELO: Grupo 1: *¿Cinco dólares?*
Grupo 2: *¿Diez dólares y 20 centavos?*

CP-18 ¿Qué es? Your instructor is going to say the number of certain objects that may be found in the classroom. As a whole class, try to guess what the object is.

CP-19 Por escrito: Un diálogo Write a dialogue between you and a good friend. Include a greeting, your name, a question, and a farewell.

¡OJO! *(Watch out!)*

Introduce yourself

My name is Sonia.
Me llamo Sonia.
Me llamo ~~a~~ Sonia.

Tú: *¡Hola!*...

Tu amigo: _____

Tú: _____

Tu amigo: _____

Tú: _____

[3] la propina: the tip   [4] ¡El precio justo!: The price is right!

PONTE EN MI LUGAR *(Put yourself in my shoes)*

Una persona famosa Assume the personality of a famous person (e.g., Antonio Banderas or Sonia Sotomayor). Introduce yourself to others.

MODELO: Estudiante 1: *Hola, me llamo Antonio Banderas. ¿Cómo te llamas tú?*
Estudiante 2: *Me llamo Jennifer López.*
Estudiante 1: *Mucho gusto.*
Estudiante 2: *Encantada.*
Estudiante 1: (to another student) *Jennifer, te presento a Sofía Vergara.*
Estudiante 3: *Gusto en conocerte.*

> ## Estrategias para conversar
>
> **Focus on familiar vocabulary** Use the words you have already learned and do not translate from English.

ASÍ ES LA VIDA *(Such is life)*

Expresión: ¡No entiendo ni jota!

¡No entiendo ni jota!

▲ *¿Cuál es el equivalente en inglés?*

Rima *(Rhyme)*

–¡Hola, hola, Coca-Cola!
–¿Qué te pasa, calabaza?[5]
–Nada, nada limonada[6].

¿Hay una rima similar en inglés?

Trabalenguas

Repeat this tongue twister as fast as possible.

"R" con "r" cigarro[7].
"R" con "r" carril[8].
Rápido corren los carros
por la carretera del ferrocarril[9].

Adivina, adivinador *(Riddle)*

1. ¿Qué hay siempre en el medio del mar?[10]
2. Un minuto tiene una, un momento tiene dos, un segundo ninguna[11].

 **@Arroba@**

WileyPLUS Go to *WileyPLUS* to find more **Arroba** activities.

Dímelo cantando Go online to your favorite video browser and look for songs in Spanish about greetings. Try for example "hola + songs" or other Spanish greetings to search for songs. Share your results with your classmates and instructor. Do you understand what they say? Do you dare to sing the song with your Spanish classmates?

---

[5] What is happening, pumpkin? [6] Nothing, nothing, lemonade. [7] An r with an r makes the word "cigar." [8] Two r's together make the word "track." [9] Cars go fast on the railroad tracks. [10] What is always in the middle of the sea? [11] A minute has one, a moment has two, a second has none.

ENTÉRATE *(Find out)*

Estrategias para leer

Cognados At this stage, you cannot expect to understand every word in every reading. Nevertheless, you can still comprehend a lot because you understand cognates that help you grasp the main idea.

Cognates are words that are similar in both languages. For example, **música** and *music* are cognates. Even at this level you can understand a lot of Spanish because there are many cognates that resemble words in English. As a matter of fact, 40 percent of the English vocabulary is Latin-based. Pay attention to the following differences in the cognates:

1. In Spanish, except for **rr** and **ll**, double consonants do not exist as in English. For example: **difícil** (*difficult*).
2. The combination *ph* in English is replaced in Spanish by **f** as in the word **filosofía,** and the combination *ch* is replaced by **c** or **qu**. For example: the words **rico** (*rich*) and **máquina** (*machine*).
3. Those words that in English end in *-ity, -ed, -tion,* or *-ly,* in Spanish end in **-dad, -ado, -ido, -ción,** or **-mente**. For example: city/**ciudad,** educated/**educado,** situation/**situación,** commonly/**comúnmente.**

Antes de leer

En la universidad Decide if the following senteces are true (Cierto) or false (Falso).

C	F	
☐	____	1. Para estudiar en la universidad, lleno[12] una solicitud.
____	☐	2. Una solicitud no tiene información personal.
☐	____	3. Para estudiar en la universidad necesito prepararme bien.

application

SOLICITUD DE ADMISIÓN PARA PROGRAMAS DE POSGRADO

1. PROGRAMA DE POSGRADO

Apellidos _____

               (Apellido paterno)   (Apellido materno)

Nombre(s) _____

Programa de posgrado solicitado: ❏ Maestría   ❏ Doctorado

Nombre del programa: _____

2. FINANCIAMIENTO

¿Cómo va a financiar sus estudios? _____

3. DATOS PERSONALES

Fecha de nacimiento (DD/MM/AA)		Lugar de nacimiento (Provincia y país)	
Sexo (H/M)		Nacionalidad	
Estado civil		Nº de pasaporte	

[12]**lleno:** I fill out

Contacto de emergencia:

Nombre	Teléfono

4. DOCUMENTOS QUE SE DEBEN ADJUNTAR

–Dos fotografías tamaño pasaporte. Escribir su nombre en el reverso.

–Dos fotocopias del documento de identificación.

–Una fotocopia de los diplomas universitarios obtenidos.

–En el caso de estudiantes extranjeros de países no hispanohablantes: Copia de certificación para acreditar dominio funcional del español.

–Currículum vítae.

–Dos cartas de referencia.

–Cumplir con los requisitos específicos según el programa.

5. DECLARACIÓN JURADA

Declaro que toda la información en esta solicitud es cierta.

_____   _____

FIRMA   FECHA

Nota: Esta solicitud con la información requerida debe ser entregada directamente o enviada a:
ESTUDIOS DE POSGRADO   UNIVERSIDAD DE LA FUENTE   Av. Paseo Colón 850, 4º Piso, Ala N

Después de leer

1. En el texto Identify five cognates in the reading.

2. ¿Entendiste? Select the answers according to the reading. Sometimes there is more than one correct answer.

1. Muchos estudiantes hispanos tienen...
   a. el apellido del padre.
   b. el apellido de la madre.
   c. el apellido del padre y de la madre.
2. En la solicitud se requiere...
   a. el certificado de nacimiento.
   b. la fecha de nacimiento.
   c. el lugar de nacimiento.
3. La solicitud necesita...
   a. la firma del candidato.
   b. la firma del padre.
   c. la firma de la madre.
4. La solicitud...
   a. se envía por correo electrónico.
   b. se entrega directamente.
   c. se envía por correo tradicional.

EN TUS PROPIAS PALABRAS *(In your own words)*

Estrategias para escribir

Meaning Use a dictionary and identify the meanings of the words you consider important to understand the **Entérate** reading. For example: **Nacionalidad** (feminine noun) is *Nationality*.

WileyPLUS Go to *WileyPLUS* to see this video and to find more video activities.

Fill out the form in pages 16–17 with your personal information.

VER PARA CREER II: ¡Bienvenido al mundo hispano!

Antes de ver

With a classmate answer the questions to be prepared before watching the video.

1. How do you greet your friends and family?
2. How do you greet your boss or your teacher?
3. In which countries is Spanish spoken?

Después de ver

1. ¿Entendiste? After watching the video select the correct answers.

1. Sofía and Daniel from Peru greet each other with…
   a. a handshake.
   b. a kiss.
   c. two kisses.
2. Two friends from Spain greet each other with…
   a. a handshake.
   b. a kiss.
   c. two kisses.
3. Two old friends greet each other with…
   a. a hug.
   b. a kiss.
   c. a handshake.
4. Physical contact is very important…
   a. at work, with family and with friends.
   b. only with family.
   c. only with old friends.

2. Los saludos When does a Hispanic greet with the following?
   -un abrazo
   -un beso/dos besos
   -dando la mano

3. Enfoque cultural
   a. If you were in Spain and your Spanish teacher introduces you to a Spanish girl of your own age . . .
      -How would you address her?
      -What do you do to greet her?
   b. Now, you are in the United States and your Spanish teacher introduces you to another Spanish girl of your own age . . .
      - Do you greet her in the same way that you did in Spain?
      - Why?

AUTOPRUEBA *(Self-Test)*

VOCABULARIO

I. El banco de Argentina Write some checks to pay out your share of some bills while you were in Argentina. Write out the numbers in Spanish.

1. To El Ateneo bookstore: $29,18 _____
2. To the store Chango mas: $14,21 _____
3. To your Argentinian roommate: $15,13 _____

II. Minidiálogos Write a mini dialogue for each situation.

a. Saluda a tu profesor a las 2:00 de la tarde.

Tú: _____

El/La profesor/a: _____

Tú: _____

b. Saluda, pregunta cómo está y despídete[13] de tu profesor a las 9:00 de la mañana.

Tú (saludo): _____

Prof. (respuesta): _____

Tú (pregunta): _____

Prof. (respuesta): _____

Tú (despedida): _____

Prof. (respuesta): _____

c. Presenta un amigo a otro amigo.

Tú: _____

Amigo 1: _____

Amigo 2: _____

GRAMÁTICA

I. Saludos y presentaciones Imagine that your friends are very important people. How would someone address them? Change the sentences below from informal to formal.

MODELO: *Elena, te presento a Irene.*

→ Doña Elena, le presento a la profesora Irene García.

1. Hola, Javier, ¿cómo estás?
2. Buenos días, ¿cómo te llamas?
3. Ángela, te presento a Liliana Hierro.

II. En el salón de clase Identify which objects are masculine and which are feminine. Write the indefinite article (*un, unos, una, unas*).

_____ tiza   _____ pizarra   _____ mapa

_____ mochila   _____ papeles   _____ ventanas

_____ libros   _____ números   _____ mesa

_____ preguntas   _____ profesor   _____ pupitres

III. ¿Cómo se escribe? You receive some text messages from abroad and you translate them to a friend.

MODELO: "K psa" es "Qué pasa?" → "Ka-pe-ese-a" *es "qu-u-e pe-a-ese-a"*

1. "fsta exclnt" es "la fiesta es excelente"

_____

2. "mi prblm tq" es "mi problema es que te quiero"

_____

3. "salu2 a t2" es "saludos a todos"

_____

CULTURA

¿Tú o usted? Decide whether to address the following people in the formal or informal way.

MODELO: *el doctor* → *usted*

1. mi profesora de español
2. mi mamá
3. mi dentista
4. mi compañero de clase
5. el Sr. Rodríguez
6. mi profesora de historia
7. doña Elena
8. un niño

REDACCIÓN

Write a dialogue between you, your Spanish teacher, and a friend. Include a greeting, one question, one introduction, and a farewell.

EN RESUMIDAS CUENTAS, AHORA PUEDO...
(To sum up, now I can...)

☐ greet and introduce others.

☐ understand the difference between **tú** and **usted**.

☐ spell words in Spanish.

☐ identify gender and number.

☐ count to 59.

---

[13]**despídete:** say goodbye

🎧 VOCABULARIO ESENCIAL

Sustantivos

el/la amigo/a	*friend*
el apellido	*last name*
el bolígrafo	*pen*
la despedida	*farewell*
el lápiz	*pencil*
el libro	*book*
la mochila	*backpack*
el nombre	*name*
la pizarra	*board*
el pupitre	*student desk*
el saludo	*greeting*
el/la señor/a	*Mr./Mrs.*
la señorita	*miss*
la ventana	*window*

Cognados: la actividad, la calculadora, el diccionario, el/la estudiante, la fotografía, la lección, el mapa, el papel, el problema, el/la profesor/a, el tema, la universidad

Números

uno	*one*
dos	*two*
tres	*three*
cuatro	*four*
cinco	*five*
seis	*six*
siete	*seven*
ocho	*eight*
nueve	*nine*
diez	*ten*
once	*eleven*
doce	*twelve*
trece	*thirteen*

catorce	*fourteen*
quince	*fifteen*
dieciséis	*sixteen*
diecisiete	*seventeen*
dieciocho	*eighteen*
diecinueve	*nineteen*
veinte	*twenty*
veintiuno	*twenty-one*
treinta	*thirty*
cuarenta	*forty*
cincuenta	*fifty*
Hay...	*There is . . .* *There are . . .*

Expresiones

Adiós.	*Goodbye.*
Bastante bien.	*Pretty well.*
Buenos días.	*Good morning.*
Buenas noches.	*Good evening./ Good night.*
Buenas tardes.	*Good afternoon.*
¿Cómo está usted?	*How are you? (formal)*
¿Cómo estás?	*How are you? (informal)*
¿Cómo te llamas?	*What's your name? (i)*
Encantado/a.	*Nice to meet you.*
¡Fenomenal!	*Great!*
Gracias.	*Thank you.*
Gusto en conocerte.	*Nice to meet you.*
Hasta la vista.	*See you soon. (Lit. Until I see you again.)*
Hasta luego.	*See you later.*
Hasta mañana.	*See you tomorrow.*
Hasta pronto.	*See you soon.*

Hola.	*Hi.*
Le presento a...	*would like to introduce you to*
Igualmente.	*Likewise.*
Más o menos.	*So-so.*
Me llamo...	*My name is . . .*
Mucho gusto.	*Nice to meet you.*
Muy bien, gracias.	*Very well, thank you.*
Nos vemos mañana.	*See you tomorrow.*
Por favor.	*Please.*
Que la pases bien.	*Have a good time.*
¿Qué tal?	*How's it going?*
Que te diviertas.	*Have fun (i).*
Que tengas un buen fin de semana.	*Have a good weekend (i).*
Quiero presentarte a...	*I'd like you to meet . . . (informal)*
Quiero presentarle a...	*I would like to introduce you to . . . (f)*
Te presento a...	*I'd like to introduce you to . . . (informal)*

Coloquialismos

(Ahí) nos vemos.	*See ya.*
¿Cómo estamos?	*How are we doing?*
¡Pura vida!	*Great! (Lit. Nothing but life!)*
Pues, ahí nomás.	*Well, hanging in there.*
¿Qué hubo?	*What's up?*
¿Qué me cuentas?	*What's going on?*

La sala de clases

© John Wiley & Sons, Inc.

VER PARA CREER I: Una visita a la UNAM

Watch the video. Then, answer the following questions. Don't worry if there are things you don't understand. You should be able to follow most of what happens without understanding every single word. At the end of the chapter, you will watch the video again and you will understand more.

Think about what you saw in the video and answer the following questions:

1. Where are the people in the video? What are they doing there?
2. From what you can see in the video, in which ways is this university in Mexico similar to a US university?
3. Which Spanish words did you understand?

Sección 1	¿De dónde eres?

PALABRA POR PALABRA
- La descripción física y de personalidad
- Los países hispanohablantes y las nacionalidades

HABLANDO DE GRAMÁTICA
- Describing and identifying people, places, and things: The verb **ser** and subject pronouns
- Describing people, places, and things: Adjective agreement and position

CULTURA
- Diferencias en las formas de expresarse
- La diversidad racial de los países hispanohablantes

Sección 2	En clase

PALABRA POR PALABRA
- Los días de la semana y los meses del año
- Las clases y las carreras
- Los pasatiempos y las actividades en el tiempo libre

HABLANDO DE GRAMÁTICA
- Expressing likes and dislikes (I): **Gustar** + infinitive
- Requesting information: Interrogative words

CULTURA
- El sistema de evaluación académica en algunos países hispanohablantes
- Los calendarios académicos en escuelas y universidades en EE. UU. y países hispanohablantes

Los países hispanohablantes

© John Wiley & Sons, Inc.

LEARNING OBJECTIVES

By the end of this section you will be able to:

- Describe and identify people, places, and things
- Tell and ask where you and others are from
- Name all of the Spanish-speaking countries
- Understand that there is a diverse variety of peoples in Spanish-speaking countries

Una imagen vale más que mil palabras

1.

Photo Courtesy of Ana Varela

2.

© Kreder Katja / Prisma / Age Fotostock America, Inc.

3.

© 2010 Ramiro Olaciregui / Flickr / Getty Images

4.

© Travel Ink / Gallo Images / Getty Images

Guess where these photos were taken!

UNA PERSPECTIVA

Photo Courtesy of Melissa Corbett

Melissa

Formas de expresarse

Diferente

"Mi impresión de los latinoamericanos es que son simpáticos[1] y amistosos. Mi amigo Carlos, que es ecuatoriano, se expresa con mucha emoción. Él habla con las manos[2]. Es muy expresivo".

Igual

"Un país no tiene el monopolio de una característica en particular. En todos los países hay personas buenas y malas, inteligentes y tontas, simpáticas y antipáticas".

 ¿Qué piensas tú? Read each of the following statements and place a check mark in the boxes that you think apply to each statement.

	Es una generalización.	Es un estereotipo cierto.	Es un estereotipo falso.
1. Los políticos estadounidenses hablan con las manos.	☐	☐	☐
2. Los estadounidenses son distantes y antisociales.	☐	☐	☐
3. Otros grupos, como los italianos, se expresan con mucha emoción.	☐	☐	☐
4. Los latinoamericanos son muy simpáticos.	☐	☐	☐
5. Los estadounidenses son rápidos y eficientes.	☐	☐	☐

[1]**simpáticos:** nice [2]**manos:** hands

LA PURA VERDAD I   ¿De dónde son?

En la clase de español de la Sra. Aponte, los estudiantes hablan sobre los latinoamericanos.

1.

triste   vanidosa   alegre   simpática   entusiasta   chistosa   atlético   estudioso

serio   desorganizado   creativo   enamorada   organizada   perezoso   religiosa

2.

Necesito ideas para un proyecto sobre Latinoamérica para mi clase de sociología.

3.

Cinco personas trabajan en el laboratorio. Los dos técnicos son de Latinoamérica.

4.

Hay dos técnicos en el laboratorio ahora, pero no son latinoamericanos.

5.

Sí, sí son latinoamericanos. Juan es de Argentina y Ana es de Cuba.

1.1-01 ¿Cómo son? Listen to the narration and decide which adjectives cannot be attributed to the same person.

1. _____
2. _____
3. _____

🎧 PALABRA POR PALABRA

La descripción física y de personalidad   *Physical and personality description*

buena   malo   alegre   aburrida   chistoso   listo

alto/a	*tall*	**divertido/a**	*fun*	**simpático/a**	*nice, likeable*
amistoso/a	*friendly*	**flaco/a**	*thin*	**tacaño/a**	*stingy*
antipático/a	*unpleasant*	**fuerte**	*strong*	**testarudo/a**	*stubborn*
atrevido/a	*daring*	**gordo/a**	*fat*	**tonto/a**	*silly/not smart*
bajo/a	*short*	**gracioso/a**	*funny*	**vanidoso/a**	*vain*
cuidadoso/a	*careful*	**guapo/a**	*pretty*		

Cognados: atlético/a, atractivo/a, conservador/a, creativo/a, curioso/a, (des)organizado/a, entusiasta, estudioso/a, expresivo/a, extrovertido/a, flexible, generoso/a, hipócrita, idealista, (im)paciente, (in)dependiente, inteligente, interesante, introvertido/a, (ir)responsable, liberal, modesto/a, optimista, pesimista, popular, religioso/a, romántico/a, sentimental, serio/a, sincero/a, sociable, talentoso/a, tímido/a

Tiene el pelo/Es de pelo...
He/She has (type) hair.

negro   rubio   castaño   rojo

Es pelirroja.

Tiene el pelo/Es de pelo...
He/She has (type) hair.

largo y lacio   corto y rizado

Tiene la piel/Es de piel...
His/Her skin is...

negra o morena   trigueña   blanca

Los países hispanohablantes y las nacionalidades *Spanish-speaking countries and nationalities*

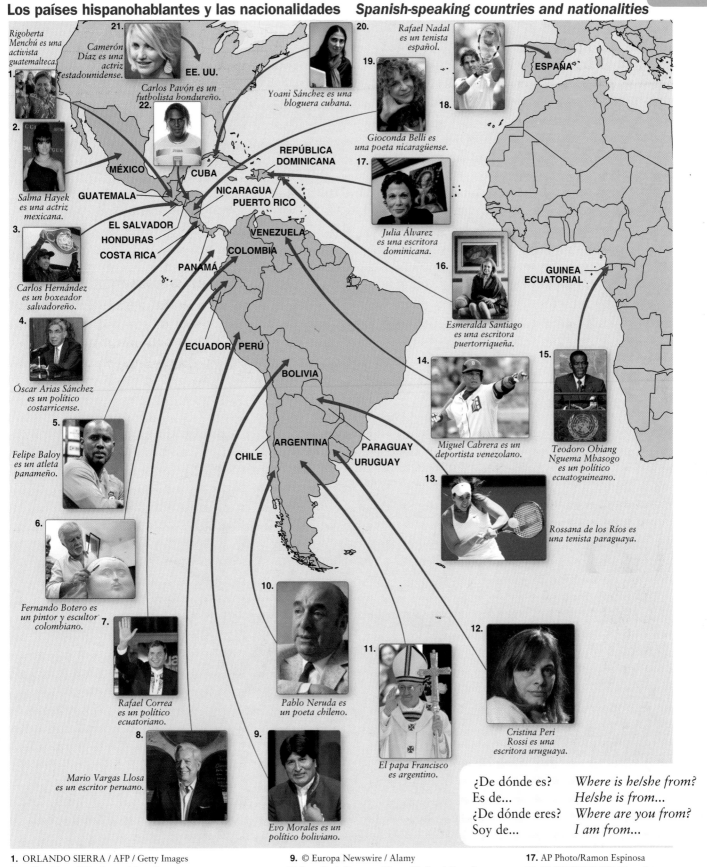

Rigoberta Menchú es una activista guatemalteca.

Camerón Díaz es una actriz estadounidense.

Carlos Pavón es un futbolista hondureño.

Yoani Sánchez es una bloguera cubana.

Rafael Nadal es un tenista español.

EE. UU.

ESPAÑA

Gioconda Belli es una poeta nicaragüense.

MÉXICO **CUBA**

REPÚBLICA DOMINICANA

Salma Hayek es una actriz mexicana.

GUATEMALA

NICARAGUA

PUERTO RICO

EL SALVADOR

HONDURAS

COSTA RICA

VENEZUELA

COLOMBIA

PANAMÁ

Julia Álvarez es una escritora dominicana.

Carlos Hernández es un boxeador salvadoreño.

GUINEA ECUATORIAL

Óscar Arias Sánchez es un político costarricense.

ECUADOR **PERÚ**

BOLIVIA

Esmeralda Santiago es una escritora puertorriqueña.

Miguel Cabrera es un deportista venezolano.

Teodoro Obiang Nguema Mbasogo es un político ecuatoguineano.

Felipe Baloy es un atleta panameño.

ARGENTINA **PARAGUAY**

CHILE **URUGUAY**

Rossana de los Ríos es una tenista paraguaya.

Fernando Botero es un pintor y escultor colombiano.

Rafael Correa es un político ecuatoriano.

Pablo Neruda es un poeta chileno.

Cristina Peri Rossi es una escritora uruguaya.

Mario Vargas Llosa es un escritor peruano.

El papa Francisco es argentino.

Evo Morales es un político boliviano.

¿De dónde es?	*Where is he/she from?*
Es de...	*He/she is from...*
¿De dónde eres?	*Where are you from?*
Soy de...	*I am from...*

1.1-02 Famosos In pairs, select the description that best fits each public figure.

1. Gloria Estefan	a. argentino, simpático, atlético
2. Carlos Santana	b. estadounidense, liberal, moreno
3. Lionel Messi	c. cubana, talentosa, de piel blanca
4. Sonia Sotomayor	d. colombiana, chistosa, de pelo largo
5. Sofía Vergara	e. mexicano, creativo, de pelo rizado
6. Barack Obama	f. puertorriqueña, lista, de pelo negro
7. Javier Bardem	g. español, atractivo, expresivo

 1.1-03 Cita a ciegas[3] You have found a perfect match for a classmate. Answer your classmate's questions by describing the person in a positive light.

MODELO: serio/a

             a. bonito/a   b. sentimental   c. chistoso/a

Estudiante 1:   *¿Es seria?*
Estudiante 2:   *No, ella es <u>chistosa</u>.*

1. ¿Es tacaño/a? No, él/ella es _____.
   a. alto/a   b. generoso/a   c. alegre
2. ¿Es aburrido/a? No, él/ella es _____.
   a. divertido/a   b. guapo/a   c. bonito/a
3. ¿Es tonto/a? No, él/ella es _____.
   a. trabajador/a   b. bueno/a   c. listo/a
4. ¿Es antipático/a? No, él/ella es_____.
   a. malo/a   b. cuidadoso/a   c. simpático/a
5. ¿Es vanidoso/a? No, él/ella es_____.
   a. pelirrojo/a   b. modesto/a   c. curioso/a
6. ¿Es hipócrita? No, él/ella es_____.
   a. sincero/a   b. amistoso/a   c. atlético/a
7. ¿Es testarudo/a? No, él/ella es _____.
   a. responsable   b. generoso/a   c. flexible
8. ¿Es pesimista? No, él/ella es_____.
   a. independiente   b. optimista   c. organizado/a

1.1-04 La persona ideal

 Paso 1: Complete the following statements with your opinion.

MODELO: El estudiante ideal es... *estudioso, organizado y cuidadoso.*

1. El amigo ideal es...
2. La profesora ideal es...
3. El compañero de cuarto ideal es...
4. El hombre o la mujer ideal es...
5. Los padres ideales son...

 Paso 2: Now share your opinions with a classmate.

MODELO: Estudiante 1:   *En tu opinión, ¿cómo es el estudiante ideal?*
              Estudiante 2:   *Es estudioso, organizado y cuidadoso.*
              Estudiante 1:   *¡Sí, para mí también!* o *No, para mí el estudiante ideal es...*

[3] **cita a ciegas:** blind date

1.1-05 ¿Cómo soy?

Paso 1: Using three adjectives, write a personal description of yourself on a piece of paper and turn it in to your instructor. It is important to be honest!

MODELO:　*Tengo el pelo largo, soy inteligente y soy desorganizada.*

Paso 2: Your instructor will distribute the pieces of paper. Look for the person that matches the description in the piece of paper that you received. Ask your classmates to help you find the person that best matches the description.

MODELO:　*¿Eres inteligente? ¿Eres desorganizada?*

1.1-06 Dilo con mímica[4] Your instructor will tell you a personality trait. Act it out so that the rest of the class can try to guess what it is.

1.1-07 El horóscopo

Paso 1: Read to a classmate his or her horoscope. Your classmate will listen and write it down. You do the same.

Piscis ♓
Usted es muy independiente y trabajador/a. No es muy romántico/a y sus relaciones no son estables.

Aries ♈
Usted es un/a líder, es entusiasta, agresivo/a y muy listo/a, pero impulsivo/a.

Tauro ♉
Usted es muy paciente. No es cruel. Es muy sentimental y romántico/a. Usted es muy expresivo/a.

Géminis ♊
Usted es muy sociable y artístico/a. Los amigos y la conversación son muy importantes en su vida.

Cáncer ♋
Usted es una persona amable y simpática. Es una persona intensamente honesta y romántica.

Leo ♌
Usted es persistente y agresivo/a. El dinero ($) es muy importante. Es trabajador/a y fuerte.

Virgo ♍
Usted es una persona práctica y organizada. Es una persona seria y trabaja mucho. La puntualidad es importante para usted. No es muy sociable.

Libra ♎
Usted es artístico/a, versátil y sociable. La conexión social por Internet es su adicción. No es impulsivo/a, pero es un poco triste.

Escorpio ♏
Usted es romántico/a y persistente, pero es un poco tímido/a. Es una persona trabajadora y selectiva en sus relaciones.

Sagitario ♐
Usted es optimista y alegre. Los amigos, la fiesta y la aventura son importantes para usted. Es una persona honesta y simpática.

Capricornio ♑
Usted es una persona profunda, determinada y organizada. Su personalidad es muy atractiva. Es tímido/a y serio/a.

Acuario ♒
Usted es una persona elegante, sofisticada y artística. No es una persona conservadora. Es amistoso/a y generoso/a pero un poco testarudo/a.

Paso 2: Ask whether the description fits or not.

MODELO:　Estudiante 1:　*¿Eres como la descripción del horóscopo?*
　　　　　　Estudiante 2:　*¡No! No soy sociable, soy muy tímida.*

Paso 3: Report to class how the horoscope described your partner correctly or incorrectly.

[4]dilo con mímica: act it out

HABLANDO DE GRAMÁTICA I

WileyPLUS Go to *WileyPLUS* to review this grammar point with the help of the **Animated Grammar Tutorial** and the **Verb Conjugator**.

1. Describing and identifying people, places, and things: The verb *ser* and subject pronouns

A. The forms of the present tense of the verb **ser** *(to be)* are as follows:

Singular		
Yo	**soy**	*I am*
Tú	**eres**	*You are (informal)*
Él/Ella	**es**	*He/she is*
Ud.	**es**	*You are (formal)*

Plural		
Nosotros/Nosotras	**somos**	*We are*
Vosotros/Vosotras	**sois**	*You are (informal)*
Ellos/Ellas	**son**	*They are*
Uds.	**son**	*You are*

Notice that there is only one verb form for **él, ella,** and **usted** and only one verb form for **ellos, ellas,** and **ustedes**.

B. In English, subject pronouns always precede the verb because most of the times it would be impossible to know to whom the verb refers. Consider the following:

The verb *to take*	
I take	*We take*
You take	*You take*
He/she takes	*They take*

The conjugation is always the same except in the case of the *he/she* form. But if you look at the conjugations of the verb **ser** again, it is obvious that there are many differences. If subject pronouns are omitted, the only confusion could be with the third-person singular (**él, ella,** and **usted**) and plural (**ellos, ellas,** and **ustedes**). Context usually allows you to identify the person. Consequently, subject pronouns are only used for special emphasis. For example: **Yo soy el doctor, no él.** Using subject pronouns frequently sounds unnatural in Spanish.

C. You also use the verb **ser** to express:

a. Permanent physical or mental characteristics

Mi hermano Rafa **es** gordo, pero mi hermano Daniel **es** muy flaco.	*My brother Rafa is fat, but my brother Daniel is very thin.*
Pepe **es** inteligente.	*Pepe is intelligent.*
Gloria **es** generosa.	*Gloria is generous.*

b. Origin

Yo **soy de** Bolivia, pero mi amigo **es de** Paraguay.	*I am from Bolivia, but my friend is from Paraguay.*

c. To identify people and things

Gloria, mira, ella **es** mi amiga Ana.	*Gloria, look, this is my friend Ana.*
¿Qué **es** esto? **Es** mi libro de español.	*What is this? This is my Spanish book.*

1.1-08 Lola y Elena Lola is talking to her friend Elena. Which pronouns does she use to talk about the following people?

MODELO: Lola → _yo_

1. Lola y Elena	_____	5. el profesor de Lola	_____
2. Lola y su amigo Raúl	_____	6. una amiga de Elena	_____
3. unos amigos de Elena	_____	7. unas amigas de Elena	_____
4. Elena	_____	8. Elena y su amigo	_____

1.1-09 Diálogo Complete this dialogue with the correct forms of the verb **ser**.

John: Hola, _____ John. ¿Cómo estás?

Clara: Bien, gracias. Yo _____ Clara, gusto en conocerte. Ella _____ mi amiga Gloria. John, tú _____ estudiante de español, ¿verdad?

John: ¡Sí, claro! Mi clase_____ muy divertida. Y ustedes, ¿_____ estudiantes de español? ¡Hablan español muy bien!

Clara: No, no. ¡Nosotras _____ de Argentina!

1.1-10 ¿De dónde eres?

Paso 1: Ask around the classroom to find out where your classmates are from. Write down the information.

MODELO: Estudiante 1: ¿De dónde eres?
Estudiante 2: Yo soy de...
Estudiante 3: ¿Tú eres de _____? ¡Yo también! o Yo soy de...

Paso 2: Now, report to the class.

MODELO: Ellos son de...
Nosotros somos de...
Él/Ella es de...

1.1-11 Los famosos de la clase Think about a famous person and assume their identity.

Paso 1: Prepare answers to the following questions. Think about one more question and answer it too.

Preguntas posibles:
1. ¿Cómo se llama?
2. ¿De dónde es?
3. ¿Cómo es su personalidad en público?
4. ¿Cómo es con su familia?
5. ¿Cuál es su característica física o de personalidad favorita?
6. ¿?

Paso 2: Then walk around the classroom and interview at least three famous people. Your classmates will interview you too. Remember to keep the interview in the **usted** form since these are famous people that you just have met.

Paso 3: Now, choose the most interesting person you have interviewed and introduce him/her to the class.

MODELO: Ella se llama Sonia Sotomayor y es puertorriqueña. En público es muy seria y trabajadora, pero en casa es alegre y expresiva...

LA PURA VERDAD II   ¿Amigo o amiga?

Gabriela es una estudiante de EE. UU. que habla con dos amigos de España. Gabriela describe a su amiga, pero sus amigos están confundidos.

1.

¿Quieres ir al cine con nosotros?

Sí. ¿Y mi amiga?

2.

¡Claro! ¡Por supuesto[5]! ¿Es simpática?

Sí, es muy simpático e inteligente.

3.

¿Cómo se llama?

Se llama Terri. Ella es bonita, flaca y atlética. Tiene el pelo largo y negro.

4.

¡Es una amiga fantástico, muy graciosos!

5.

¿   ?

6.

¿Invitamos a José María también?

¿José María?

1.1-12 ¿Cómo son? Listen to the description and draw the person.

[5]**por supuesto:** of course

HABLANDO DE GRAMÁTICA II

2. Describing people, places, and things: Adjective agreement and position

A. Placement: In Spanish and English, adjectives describe nouns. In English, adjectives precede the noun: a *big* house, an *intelligent* girl, *serious* students.

In Spanish, adjectives usually follow the noun they describe: **una casa *grande,* una muchacha *inteligente,* estudiantes *serios.***

B. Gender and number agreement: In addition, adjectives must agree in number and gender with the noun they modify. Most adjectives have either a masculine form (ending in **-o**) or a feminine form (ending in **-a**):

	Masculine	**Feminine**
Singular	un bolígrafo negr**o** *(a black pen)*	una profesora argentin**a**
Plural	dos estudiantes cuban**os**	tres mujeres español**as**

Adjectives ending in **-e, -ista**, and most consonants have the same form for masculine or feminine: **un niño feliz / una niña feliz; un profesor paciente / una profesora paciente, un hombre pesim*ista* / una mujer pesim*ista.***

To form the plural, add **-es** to adjectives that end in a consonant: **idea*l* → idea*les*; popula*r* → popula*res.*** Add an **-s** to adjectives that end in a vowel: **alto → altos; seria → serias; estadounidense → estadounidenses.**

C. Accents: If the masculine form of the adjective has a written accent in the last syllable, the feminine form does not need an accent:

un estudiante franc**és**　　　　una estudiante franc**esa**

D. Adjectives of nationality: Notice that adjectives denoting nationality are written with a lowercase letter. The name of the country, however, is written with a capital letter:

Rubén es de **C**uba. Es **c**ubano.　　*Rubén is from Cuba. He's Cuban.*
Inés es de **C**olombia. Es **c**olombiana.　　*Inés is from Colombia. She's Colombian.*

E. *Muy*: You can intensify an adjective by placing the adverb **muy** in front of it:

Andrés es **muy** trabajador.　　*Andrés is very hardworking.*
Amalia es **muy** generosa.　　*Amalia is very generous.*

1.1-13 Asociaciones For each sentence, decide what the most appropriate ending is and complete the word with the right gender and number agreement.

MODELO:　Antonio Banderas es un actor... *muy atractivo.*

_____ 1. La clase de español...
_____ 2. Rafael y Lydia no son de Cuba...
_____ 3. Usualmente, una persona sociable...
_____ 4. El/La profesor/a...
_____ 5. Los estudiantes de español...
_____ 6. Salma Hayek y Penélope Cruz...

a. es muy pacient___ con los estudiantes.
b. no es aburrid___, es muy interesant___.
c. son muy chistos___.
d. son puertorriqueñ___.
e. son actrices muy famos___.
f. es extrovertid___.

WileyPLUS Go to *WileyPLUS* to review this grammar point with the help of the **Animated Grammar Tutorial**.

1.1-14 Gente diferente Replace the prepositional phrases with nouns in the following sentences with adjectives to describe people. Replace **mucho/gran** with **muy** when necessary.

MODELO: Pedro habla con seriedad.   →   *Pedro es serio.*

1. María es una chica de gran inteligencia.
2. Juan es un estudiante con mucha curiosidad.
3. Pepe es un muchacho con mucha paciencia.
4. Javier es una persona de ideas conservadoras.
5. Bárbara es una niña con mucha alegría.

1.1-15 Las nacionalidades

 Paso 1: With a partner, ask about the personality of the following people. Then try to think about someone else with the same nationality. Make sure to use the right gender and number agreement.

MODELO: Óscar Arias Sánchez es un nobel de la paz costarricense.
            Estudiante 1:   *¿Cuál es la nacionalidad de Óscar Arias Sánchez?*
            Estudiante 2:   *Es costarricense.*
            Estudiante 1:   *¿Hay más personas costarricenses famosas?*
            Estudiante 2:   *Sí, por ejemplo...*

1. Evo Morales es el presidente de Bolivia.
2. El beisbolista Robinson Canó es de la República Dominicana.
3. El músico Ricardo Arjona es de Guatemala.
4. Violeta Chamorro, primera presidenta mujer en Latinoamérica, es de Nicaragua.
5. Los padres de Marc Anthony son de Puerto Rico.
6. El baloncestista Pau Gasol es de España.
7. Lionel Messi es de Argentina.

 Paso 2: Now, share your answers with your class. Which pair of students could add more names to each nationality?

1.1-16 Una descripción

 Paso 1: Using the verb **ser**, write down the following information about yourself.

- The city you are from
- Your country of origin
- Your nationality
- Description of your personality (at least three characteristics)
- The color and length of your hair (*Mi pelo _____*).

 Paso 2: Now read your description to a classmate. Listen for similarities or differences. Then, write a short paragraph together and report it to the class.

MODELO: *_____ y yo somos románticos/as.*
            _____ es un poco tímido/a, pero yo soy muy sociable...

1.1-17 El adivinador As one volunteer faces the class, the instructor will write the names of two students on the board and quickly erase them. The volunteer will solicit descriptions from the class so he can guess who they are.

MODELO: Estudiante: *¿Son altos?*
            Clase: *Un estudiante es alto y la otra estudiante es baja.*

OTRA PERSPECTIVA

Courtesy of Consuelo Cervantes

Consuelo

El continente americano

Diferente

"Las personas de Estados Unidos se llaman a sí mismas[6] 'americanas' y el término no incluye a los canadienses, mexicanos, panameños, chilenos, brasileños, etc. Pero todas las personas nacidas en América del Norte, América Central y América del Sur son americanas. Yo soy de México y soy americana también".

Igual

"El nombre oficial de México es Estados Unidos Mexicanos. Es muy similar al nombre de Estados Unidos de América".

Explícale a Consuelo

1. En el resto del mundo, ¿cómo llaman a las personas de Estados Unidos?
2. ¿Qué países forman parte de América del Norte?
3. ¿Sabes[7] cuál es el origen del nombre "América"?

MANOS A LA OBRA

1.1-18 Una fiesta en la Casa Internacional There is a party at the International House. Ask a classmate about the silhouettes in order to find out who they are.

MODELO: Estudiante 1: ¿Cómo es Suyapa?
Estudiante 2: Ella es _____.
Estudiante 1: ¿De dónde es ella?
Estudiante 2: Es hondureña.

© John Wiley & Sons, Inc.

[6]**sí mismas:** themselves [7]**sabes:** do you know?

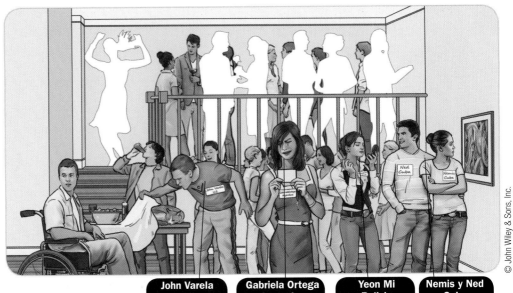

John Varela
Estados Unidos   Gabriela Ortega
Argentina   Yeon Mi
Bolivia   Nemis y Ned
Cuba

1.1-19 ¿Cómo son tus compañeros? Ask your classmates about their personalities.

MODELO: Estudiante 1:   *¿Eres tímido?*
Estudiante 2: *No, no soy tímido.*   o   *Sí, soy tímido.*

	Nombre		Nombre
optimista	_____	extrovertido/a	_____
idealista	_____	inteligente	_____
romántico/a	_____	cuidadoso/a	_____
atlético/a	_____	atrevido/a	_____
conservador/a	_____	curioso/a	_____

1.1-20 ¿Quién es? Select a classmate and write his/her description on a separate piece of paper. Then read it out loud; the rest of the class has to guess who the person is.

MODELO: *Este estudiante es de piel trigueña, de pelo largo y negro. Es sincero, romántico e inteligente. Es estadounidense. ¿Quién es?*

1.1-21 ¡Grafología!

Paso 1: Write down the following passage and then pass it on to a classmate. He/she will analyze your handwriting.

De tin marín de dos pingüé, cúcara, mácara títere fue...

Paso 2: Now examine your classmate's handwriting in order to analyze his or her personality. Look at the graphology analysis in the Appendix.

¿Cómo es la 't'? ¿Cómo es la 'm'? ¿Cómo es la 'i'? ¿Cómo es la inclinación?

¿Cómo es el tamaño[8]? ¿Cómo es la personalidad de tu compañero/a?

Paso 3: Now discuss with your classmate your assessment of his/her personality based on your analysis.

MODELO: Estudiante 1:   *Tú eres ambicioso/a, ¿no?*
Estudiante 2: *¿Ambicioso? No, no soy ambicioso...*

[8]**tamaño:** size

1.1-22 Presta atención: Marisa Listen to the audio twice and decide whether the information is true (**Cierto**) or false (**Falso**). If it is false, provide the correct information.

WileyPLUS Go to *WileyPLUS* and listen to **Presta atención.**

1. Marisa es colombiana.   Cierto   Falso
_____

2. Los padres de Marisa son españoles.   Cierto   Falso
_____

3. Los padres de Marisa son simpáticos.   Cierto   Falso
_____

4. Marisa y su padre son graciosos.   Cierto   Falso
_____

5. La madre de Marisa es graciosa.   Cierto   Falso
_____

6. Marisa y su madre tienen el pelo rubio.   Cierto   Falso
_____

¡OJO!

Gender agreement
You already know some Spanish vocabulary. In this activity you are going to use a lot of descriptive adjectives. You have already learned that many adjectives change their ending in order to agree in gender with the object or person they refer to. Put this knowledge in practice when you write the **acróstico** in this activity and double check correct gender agreement when you're done.

1.1-23 Por escrito: Un acróstico Using the vocabulary from **Palabra por palabra**, write an acrostic in Spanish. First, use your name or last name and match an adjective or noun with each letter of your name or last name. Then, write one sentence per word using the verb **ser**. Read your text to a classmate. He/she has to know how to spell your name or last name.

MODELO: *Cristina: C = cuidadosa, r = rizado, i = introvertida, s = seria, t = testaruda,*
i = irresponsable, n = negro, a = azul

Cuidadosa	*Soy cuidadosa.*
Rizado	*Mi pelo es rizado.*
Introvertida	*Soy introvertida.*
Seria	*Soy seria.*
Testaruda	*No soy testaruda.*
Irresponsable	*No soy irresponsable.*
Negro	*Mi pelo es negro.*
Azul	*Mi color favorito es el azul.*

WileyPLUS Go to *WileyPLUS* to find more **Arroba** activities.

¿Cómo son los famosos? Explore using your favorite browser for information about one of the famous people below. Look for his/her picture and describe him/her using the vocabulary and grammar presented in the chapter. Don't forget to add their nationalities. Then share your description with your classmates.

Carlos Baute, Thalía, Paulina Rubio, Ricky Martin, Alejandro Sanz

👥 PONTE EN MI LUGAR

Estrategias para conversar

Using physical resources and nonverbal clues Use *physical resources* to boost the conversation. Objects, images, graphics, and diagrams can be used to "inspire" a conversation. These external elements help to break the ice and at the same time prevent you from getting stuck in a dialogue by bringing up new ideas or vocabulary words that otherwise would not come up.

Physical gestures can also help you to communicate. When learning a language, it is natural to not be able to understand at first a lot of what is said. There are many ways of communicating nonverbally using gestures. Let's try some:

To say you don't understand: Raise your shoulders and show the palms of your hands.

To say you agree: Smile and nod. Give the thumbs-up.   **To say you disagree**: Shake your head. Give the thumbs-down.

¡Qué guapo/a! Imagine that you are in a party with one of your classmates. You both see an attractive person and go to meet him/her. Strike up a conversation. Introduce yourself and your classmate, ask where the person is from, tell where you and your classmate are from, and say something unflattering about your classmate because he/she is competing with you. Remember that you can use nonverbal gestures to help you communicate.

ASÍ ES LA VIDA

© John Wiley & Sons, Inc.

Adivina, adivinador

Si una persona dice "¡Eres un sol!", ¿qué quiere decir?

Chiste

¿Qué tienen en común un elevador y una mariposa[9]?
Respuesta: ¡Los dos van[10] de "flor en flor"!

© John Wiley & Sons, Inc.

ENTÉRATE

Estrategias para leer

Predicting content When reading a text, understanding the title can help you better understand the content of the reading. The title usually informs about the main idea of the text. Visual aids such as photos, charts, graphics, or even the layout of the text are also a good source of information about the general topic of the reading.

Antes de leer

1. ¿Qué tipo de texto es? Look at the text and answer the following questions.

   a. By the looks of the text, decide what the text is going to be: an essay, a blog, a letter, or an email.
   b. By the title, guess what the text will be about: something funny, something serious, something important.

2. ¿Cómo es tu grupo musical favorito? Now with a partner, talk about your favorite musical group using the following questions.

¿Cómo es? ¿De dónde es el grupo? ¿Cómo son sus fanes? ¿Cómo es su tipo de música?

3. Noticias In groups of three or four, imagine that you are groupies and are really obsessed with your favorite musical group. Then, come up with a list of ideas of news headlines that you could read in a magazine or the Internet.

MODELO: 1. *Un accidente en un concierto*   3. _____

2. _____   4. _____

[9]**mariposa** butterfly [10]**van** they go

Los Chistosos

FORO

| Elige tu Foro ▾ | | Buscar |

Foro » Música » Punk » **grupo de fans de Los Chistosos**

Lista 1-15 de 160 [1] 2 3 4 5 » de 11   « Anterior | Siguiente »

Cris
(Valencia, España)

⇨ **Responder**

Es mi grupo musical favorito. **Tengo recuerdos** de Los Chistosos de un concierto en la universidad. El grupo es interesante y gracioso. Soy feliz con mis recuerdos de la universidad y el grupo de Los Chistosos, pero hay un problema con el grupo.

I have memories

Ana
(Madrid, España)

⇨ **Responder**

Yo también tengo recuerdos. ¿Cuál es el problema?

Javi
(Georgia, EE. UU.)

⇨ **Responder**

Sí, ¿cuál es el problema? Los Chistosos son optimistas. No tienen problemas porque por ejemplo Andrea es muy sociable y sincera. También es dulce. Me gusta mucho. Me gusta su pelo rojo, me gusta su alegría y su paciencia. Es una mujer excelente. **La quiero**, pero también quiero a Violeta. Me gusta la música pop de Los Chistosos.

I love her, I care for her

Cristal
(Sevilla, España)

⇨ **Responder**

¿Cómo? ¿Qué me cuentas, Cris? No entiendo.

Javi
(Georgia, EE. UU.)

⇨ **Responder**

Sí, no entiendo ni jota.

Cris
(Valencia, España)

⇨ **Responder**

En febrero hay un concierto en Madrid.

Cristal
(Sevilla, España)

⇨ **Responder**

¿Y eso es un problema?

Javi
(Georgia, EE. UU.)

⇨ **Responder**

Quiero fotos, quiero su música alegre en el concierto de Madrid. **Me gusta** mucho el grupo musical Los Chistosos.

I like

Cris
(Valencia, España)

⇨ **Responder**

El problema es que Violeta y Jorge tienen un romance.

Cristal
(Sevilla, España)

⇨ **Responder**

¿Cómo? Pero Andrea es la amiga íntima de Jorge, ¿no?   ☺

Después de leer

1. En el texto In the preliminary chapter you learned about cognates. Identify ten cognates in the reading.

2. ¿Entendiste? Select the correct answer.

1. ¿Cómo es Andrea según la lectura?
   a. Es una mujer idealista.
   b. Es rebelde y tiene pocos fanes.
   c. Es sociable y habla con sinceridad.
2. ¿Quiénes no comprenden?
   a. Cris y Ana
   b. Ana y Javi
   c. Cristal y Javi
3. ¿Cuándo hay un concierto?
   a. en diciembre
   b. en febrero
   c. en agosto
4. ¿Cuál es el problema?
   a. El grupo musical Los Chistosos no tiene conciertos.
   b. La amiga íntima de Jorge se llama Ana.
   c. Andrea y Violeta no son amigas ahora.

EN TUS PROPIAS PALABRAS

Estrategias para escribir

Connectors Transition words allow us to connect ideas. It is important to use basic sentence connectors when writing a paragraph to give cohesion to those paragraphs and, in the end, to your text. Here are some frequently used connectors and their objective.

- To provide information that offers an alternative: **pero** (*but*)
- To joint related information: **y** (*and*)
- To add information: **también** (*also, too*)
- To clarify information: **por ejemplo** (*for example*), **es decir** (*that is*), **en otras palabras** (*in other words*)
- To give a reason: **porque** (*because*)

¿Cómo es Natalia? Use the connectors that you have learned in **Estrategias para escribir** to help you describe the person in the picture. Use your imagination when answering these questions:

- ¿Cómo es Natalia físicamente?
- ¿Qué otras características personales tiene?
- ¿De dónde es? ¿Cuál es su nacionalidad?

◀ *Natalia es...*

AUTOPRUEBA

VOCABULARIO

I. La persona ideal In your opinion, what are the characteristics of the ideal person?

MODELO:　¿Tiene el pelo largo?　→　*No, tiene el pelo corto.*
　　　　　¿Es tacaño/a?　　　　→　*No, es generoso/a.*
　　　　　¿Es inteligente?　　　→　*¡Sí, claro!*

1. ¿Es antipático/a?
2. ¿Es aburrido/a?
3. ¿Es introvertido/a?
4. ¿Tiene el pelo rizado?
5. ¿Es serio/a?
6. ¿Es pesimista?
7. ¿Es conservador/a?
8. ¿Es responsable?
9. ¿Es hipócrita?
10. ¿Es pelirrojo/a?

II. ¿De dónde son? What is the nationality of the following people?

MODELO:　El rey Juan Carlos es de España.
　　　　　→　*Él es español.*

1. Los padres de Jennifer López son de Puerto Rico.
2. Andy García es de Cuba.
3. Emilio Estévez es de Estados Unidos.
4. Jorge Ramos es de México.
5. La mamá de Benjamin Bratt es de Perú.
6. La mamá de Raquel Welch es de Bolivia.
7. Yo soy de...
8. Mi mamá y mi papá son de... Ellos...

GRAMÁTICA

I. ¿Cómo son los amigos? Change the adjectives and verbs to write new sentences.

MODELO:　Pepita es simpática y trabajadora. (Marco)
　　　　　→　*Marco es simpático y trabajador.*

1. Dolores es lista y sociable. (Pedro)
2. Carlos es gordo y divertido. (Esteban y Paco)
3. Pedro es una buena persona y también es alegre. (Maite y Zulma)
4. Carmen y Ana son testarudas y tontas. (Rafael y Jorge)
5. Yo soy estudioso y bajo. (Mi mejor amigo y yo)
6. Tú eres muy atrevido. (Mis compañeros de clase)

II. ¿De dónde son? Write sentences to talk about these people's origin.

MODELO:　Javier / Uruguay
　　　　　→　*Javier es de Uruguay. Es uruguayo.*

1. Mercedes y Guillermo / Chile
2. Amanda y Pilar / Panamá
3. Mi profesor/a de español /¿?
4. Tú / Puerto Rico
5. Yo / ¿?

CULTURA

¿Dónde se habla español? Name the Spanish-speaking countries that you have studied in this section.

1. Nombra dos países del Caribe.
2. Nombra tres países de América Central.
3. Nombra seis países de América del Sur.
4. Nombra un país de Europa y uno de África.

REDACCIÓN

Write a description of two people you admire or dislike. Include: name, origin, personality and some physical characteristics.

EN RESUMIDAS CUENTAS, AHORA PUEDO...

☐ describe myself.

☐ describe others.

☐ tell where I am from.

☐ ask where others are from.

☐ name all Spanish-speaking countries.

☐ understand that there is variety of peoples in Spanish-speaking countries.

🎧 VOCABULARIO ESENCIAL

Adjetivos

aburrido/a	*boring*
alegre	*happy*
alto/a	*tall*
amistoso/a	*friendly*
antipático/a	*unpleasant*
atrevido/a	*daring*
bajo/a	*short*
blanco/a	*white (skin)*
bueno/a	*good*
castaño/a	*chestnut*
chistoso/a	*funny*
corto/a	*short (hair)*
cuidadoso/a	*careful*
divertido/a	*fun*
flaco/a	*thin*
fuerte	*strong*
gordo/a	*fat*
gracioso/a	*funny*
guapo/a	*pretty*
lacio/a	*straight*
largo/a	*long*
listo/a	*smart*
malo/a	*bad*
moreno/a	*black (skin or hair)*
negro/a	*black (skin or hair)*
pelirrojo/a	*redhead*
rizado/a	*curly*
rubio/a	*blonde*
simpático/a	*nice, likable*
tacaño/a	*stingy*
testarudo/a	*stubborn*
trigueño/a	*dark-skinned*
tonto/a	*silly/not smart*
vanidoso/a	*vain*

Cognados: atlético/a, atractivo/a, conservador/a, creativo/a, curioso/a, (des)organizado/a, entusiasta, estudioso/a, expresivo/a, extrovertido/a, flexible, generoso/a, hipócrita, idealista, (im)paciente, (in)dependiente, inteligente, interesante, introvertido/a, (ir)responsable, liberal, modesto/a, optimista, pesimista, popular, religioso/a, romántico/a, sentimental, serio/a, sincero/a, sociable, talentoso/a, tímido/a

Nacionalidades de los países hispanos

argentino/a	*Argentine*
boliviano/a	*Bolivian*
chileno/a	*Chilean*
colombiano/a	*Colombian*
costarricense	*Costarican*
cubano/a	*Cuban*
dominicano/a	*Dominican*
ecuatoriano/a	*Ecuadorian*
español/a	*Spanish*
estadounidense	*American*
guatemalteco/a	*Guatemalan*
ecuatoguineano/a	*Equatoguinean*
hondureño/a	*Honduran*
mexicano/a	*Mexican*
nicaragüense	*Nicaraguan*
panameño/a	*Panamanian*
paraguayo/a	*Paraguayan*
peruano/a	*Peruvian*
puertorriqueño/a	*Puerto Rican*
salvadoreño/a	*Salvadoran*
uruguayo/a	*Uruguayan*
venezolano/a	*Venezuelan*

Verbos y expresiones

¿De dónde eres?	*Where are you from?*
Es de...	*He/She is from . . .*
ser	*to be*
Él/ella es de piel/de pelo...	*His/her skin/hair is . . .*
Él/Ella tiene (el pelo/la piel)	*He/She has ([type] hair/ skin)*

LEARNING OBJECTIVES

By the end of this section you will be able to:

- Name the months and the days of the week
- Talk about classes, majors, careers, and hobbies
- Discuss preferences by expressing likes and dislikes
- Request information using interrogative words
- Be familiar with the academic calendars and grading system of some Hispanic countries

Una imagen vale más que mil palabras

Courtesy of Jesús Pardo Ballester

Look at the picture and answer the following questions.

¿Cuántos niños hay?
¿Hay profesoras?
¿Llevan[1] los niños uniforme?
¿Cómo es la sala de clases?

UNA PERSPECTIVA

¿Un 7 en español?

Diferente

"En el sistema educativo de Chile no califican con A, B, C, D y F. Califican con números del 1 al 7. Siete es A, seis es B, cinco es C, cuatro es D, tres, dos y uno son F. Su calificación puede ser[2] 6,2 o 5,8 o 4,3. Con los números, la coma en español funciona como el punto en inglés".

Casi igual

"La escuela primaria de Chile va de los grados uno al ocho; y la escuela secundaria, de los grados nueve al doce".

Tim

Courtesy of Tim Johnson

¿Qué piensas tú? ¿Qué es normal para ti?

	muy común	común	raro	muy raro
1. Usar números y no letras como A, B y C.	☐	☐	☐	☐
2. Usar la coma y no los puntos para decimales.	☐	☐	☐	☐
3. Considerar el grado siete como escuela primaria.	☐	☐	☐	☐

[1] **llevan:** they are wearing [2] **puede ser:** could be

LA PURA VERDAD I   Una estudiante estadounidense en Argentina

Regina es una estudiante de EE. UU. Ella va a estudiar en la Universidad de Buenos Aires, Argentina, por nueve meses.

1.

2.

3.

4.

5.

6.

© John Wiley & Sons, Inc.

1.2-01 La Universidad de Buenos Aires Listen to the narration and decide if the conclusion is true (**Cierto**) or false (**Falso**). If it is **Falso**, say what the correct answer is.

	C	F	
1.	☐	☐	_____
2.	☐	☐	_____
3.	☐	☐	_____

🔊 PALABRA POR PALABRA

Los días de la semana y los meses del año   *Days of the week and months of the year*

mes →

semana →

día →

ENERO

Lun	Mar	Mié	Jue	Vie	Sáb	Dom
	1	2	3	4	5	6
7	8	9	10	11	12	13
14	15	16	17	18	19	20
21	22	23	24	25	26	27
28	29	30	31			

FEBRERO

Lun	Mar	Mié	Jue	Vie	Sáb	Dom
				1	2	3
4	5	6	7	8	9	10
11	12	13	14	15	16	17
18	19	20	21	22	23	24
25	26	27	28			

MARZO

Lun	Mar	Mié	Jue	Vie	Sáb	Dom
				1	2	3
4	5	6	7	8	9	10
11	12	13	14	15	16	17
18	19	20	21	22	23	24
25	26	27	28	29	30	31

ABRIL

Lun	Mar	Mié	Jue	Vie	Sáb	Dom
1	2	3	4	5	6	7
8	9	10	11	12	13	14
15	16	17	18	19	20	21
22	23	24	25	26	27	28
29	30					

MAYO

Lun	Mar	Mié	Jue	Vie	Sáb	Dom
		1	2	3	4	5
6	7	8	9	10	11	12
13	14	15	16	17	18	19
20	21	22	23	24	25	26
27	28	29	30	31		

JUNIO

Lun	Mar	Mié	Jue	Vie	Sáb	Dom
					1	2
3	4	5	6	7	8	9
10	11	12	13	14	15	16
17	18	19	20	21	22	23
24	25	26	27	28	29	30

JULIO

Lun	Mar	Mié	Jue	Vie	Sáb	Dom
1	2	3	4	5	6	7
8	9	10	11	12	13	14
15	16	17	18	19	20	21
22	23	24	25	26	27	28
29	30	31				

AGOSTO

Lun	Mar	Mié	Jue	Vie	Sáb	Dom
			1	2	3	4
5	6	7	8	9	10	11
12	13	14	15	16	17	18
19	20	21	22	23	24	25
26	27	28	29	30	31	

SEPTIEMBRE

Lun	Mar	Mié	Jue	Vie	Sáb	Dom
						1
2	3	4	5	6	7	8
9	10	11	12	13	14	15
16	17	18	19	20	21	22
23	24	25	26	27	28	29
30						

OCTUBRE

Lun	Mar	Mié	Jue	Vie	Sáb	Dom
	1	2	3	4	5	6
7	8	9	10	11	12	13
14	15	16	17	18	19	20
21	22	23	24	25	26	27
28	29	30	31			

NOVIEMBRE

Lun	Mar	Mié	Jue	Vie	Sáb	Dom
				1	2	3
4	5	6	7	8	9	10
11	12	13	14	15	16	17
18	19	20	21	22	23	24
25	26	27	28	29	30	

DICIEMBRE

Lun	Mar	Mié	Jue	Vie	Sáb	Dom
						1
2	3	4	5	6	7	8
9	10	11	12	13	14	15
16	17	18	19	20	21	22
23	24	25	26	27	28	29
30	31					

Estación del año: ▢ invierno ▢ primavera ▢ verano ▢ otoño   ↑ fin de semana

© John Wiley & Sons, Inc.

Los días de la semana	*The days of the week*
lunes	*Monday*
martes	*Tuesday*
miércoles	*Wednesday*
jueves	*Thursday*
viernes	*Friday*
sábado	*Saturday*
domingo	*Sunday*

¿Qué día es hoy?	*What day is today?*
Hoy es miércoles.	*Today is Wednesday.*
¿Cuál es la fecha de hoy?	*What is today's date?*
Hoy es miércoles, 24 de agosto de 2014.	*Today is Wednesday, August 24th, 2014.*
¿Cuándo es tu cumpleaños?	*When is your birthday?*
Es el viernes, 23 de agosto.	*It's Friday, August 23rd.*
¿Cuándo es tu clase de español?	*When is your Spanish class?*
Los lunes, miércoles y jueves.	*Mondays, Wednesdays, and Thursdays.*

Las clases y las carreras *Courses and careers*

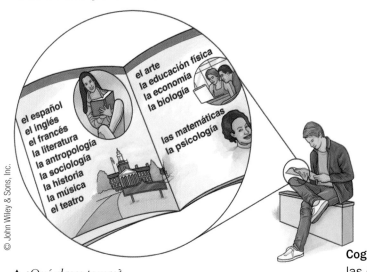

| el español | la literatura | la antropología | la sociología | la historia | la música | el teatro |
| el inglés |
| el francés |

el arte
la educación física
la economía
la biología

las matemáticas
la psicología

© John Wiley & Sons, Inc.

▲ *¿Qué clases tomas?*

la asignatura	*subject, class*
el derecho	*law*
el diseño	*design*
la enfermería	*nursing*
la especialización	*major, specialization*
la informática	*computer science*
los negocios	*business*
la química	*chemistry*
el trabajo social	*social work*
la escuela (primaria/ secundaria)	*(elementary/high) school*
el/la profesor/a	*teacher, instructor*

Cognados: las ciencias políticas, el comercio, las comunicaciones, la educación, la estadística, las finanzas, la medicina, las relaciones internacionales, la ingeniería

Otras actividades *Other activities*

caminar	*to walk*
hacer ejercicio	*to exercise*
ir al cine	*to go to the movies*
pintar	*to paint*
salir con amigos	*to go out with friends*

Los pasatiempos y las actividades en el tiempo libre *Pastimes and leisure activities*

esquiar
jugar al tenis
cantar
escuchar música
patinar
nadar
dormir
mirar/ver la televisión
estudiar
hacer yoga
bailar
leer
correr
hablar por teléfono celular/móvi
viajar
ir de compras
tocar un instrumento

© John Wiley & Sons, Inc.

Preferencias *Preferences*

¿Qué te gusta hacer?	*What do you like to do?*
Me gusta...	*I like . . .*
No me gusta...	*I (don't) like . . .*
Le gusta...	*He or she likes . . .*
No le gusta...	*He or she doesn't like...*

1.2-02 ¿Cuándo es tu cumpleaños?

Paso 1: Look at this year's calendar and see on which day of the week you will have (or had) your birthday. Write it on the first row of the table (and practice how to say it if necessary!) Then walk around the classroom asking as many students as possible the day of their birthdays.

MODELO: Estudiante 1: *¿Cuándo es tu cumpleaños?*
Estudiante 2: *Mi cumpleaños es el lunes, 15 de abril.*

NOMBRE	FECHA	DÍA DE LA SEMANA

Try to find at least one of the following:

1. Seven students with their birthdays on a different day of the week.
2. At least five students with their birthdays on a different month.
3. At least three students with their birthdays on the same month as yours.

Paso 2: Who is the first person in the class to gather information for each of those three tasks?

1.2-03 Energía With a partner, decide which of the following activities require more energy. Rank the activities from 1 to 11, 1 being the activity that requires the least energy.

_____ hablar por teléfono   _____ mirar la televisión

_____ ir de compras   _____ nadar

_____ esquiar   _____ salir con amigos

_____ patinar   _____ leer

_____ viajar   _____ hacer yoga

1.2-04 El calendario escolar argentino With a partner, compare the Argentinian school calendar with the school calendar in the United States according to the months that Regina attends classes on page 42.

1. ¿En qué meses es verano y no hay clases en Estados Unidos? ¿Y en Argentina?
2. ¿Qué meses constituyen el primer[3] semestre en EE. UU.? ¿Y en Argentina?
3. ¿Qué meses constituyen el segundo[4] semestre en EE. UU.? ¿Y en Argentina?
4. Trivia: ¿Qué día es de mala suerte[5] en EE. UU.? ¿Y en Argentina?

En Chile el primer semestre es en los meses de marzo, abril, mayo, junio y parte de julio. El segundo semestre es en los meses de agosto, septiembre, octubre, noviembre y parte de diciembre. Las vacaciones son en los meses de enero y febrero.

---

[3] **primer:** first [4] **segundo:** second [5] **suerte:** luck

¡Qué coincidencia!
¡Qué interesante!
¡Genial!
¡Qué aburrido!
¡Qué horrible!

1.2-05 La vida en la universidad

Paso 1: Complete the following sentences with your information.

1. Mi carrera es...
2. Mi clase favorita es...
3. Una clase que no me gusta es...
4. Mi profesor/a favorito/a es...
   (características de personalidad)
5. En mi tiempo libre me gusta...

Paso 2: Now interview a classmate and write down his/her answers.
Use the expressions on the left to make it more interesting.

1. ¿Cuál es tu carrera?
2. ¿Cuál es tu clase favorita?
3. ¿Qué clase no te gusta?
4. ¿Cómo es tu profesor/a favorito/a?
5. ¿Qué te gusta hacer en tu tiempo libre?

MODELO: Estudiante 1:   *¿Cuál es tu carrera?*
              Estudiante 2:   *Mi carrera es psicología.*
              Estudiante 1:   *¿Sí? ¡Qué coincidencia! ¡Mi carrera también es psicología!*

Paso 3: Write a short paragraph about you and your classmate and read it to the class.

MODELO: *La carrera de _____ es
psicología y mi carrera también
es psicología...*

1.2-06 ¿Fáciles o difíciles? Ask your
classmate if these classes are easy or difficult.

MODELO: *¿Es fácil o difícil la clase
de español?*

	muy fácil	fácil	difícil	imposible
1. diseño	☐	☐	☐	☐
2. matemáticas	☐	☐	☐	☐
3. educación física	☐	☐	☐	☐
4. biología	☐	☐	☐	☐
5. informática	☐	☐	☐	☐
6. sociología	☐	☐	☐	☐
7. teatro	☐	☐	☐	☐
8. estadística	☐	☐	☐	☐
9. ciencias políticas	☐	☐	☐	☐
10. ¿?	☐	☐	☐	☐

1.2-07 ¿Qué te gusta? Listen to your instructor and indicate what you like and dislike
by standing under the appropriate response, forming a human graph. Which is the most
popular pastime among the students in the class?

	Me gusta mucho	Me gusta	Me gusta muy poco	No me gusta
dormir				
cantar				
tocar un instrumento				
correr				
bailar				
esquiar				
escuchar música				
ir de compras				
viajar				

HABLANDO DE GRAMÁTICA I

1. Expressing likes and dislikes (I): *Gustar* + infinitive

WileyPLUS Go to *WileyPLUS* to review this grammar point with the help of this **Animated Grammar Tutorial** and the **Verb Conjugator**.

The verb **gustar** in Spanish means that something is "pleasing to you," it gives you pleasure or you like it. In English, we usually would say, "I like this car," but we could also say, "This car is pleasing to me" or even, "To me, this car is pleasing." Keep in mind this form and it will be easier to use **gustar** correctly.

Gustar is often used with an infinitive to express the idea that you enjoy an activity gives. For example:

Me gusta **estudiar** español.   *I like studying Spanish.*
Te gusta **ir** a clase.   *You like going to class.*

(a mí)	**me** gusta	*I like*
(a ti)	**te** gusta	*you like*
(a él/a ella/a Ud.)	**le** gusta	*he/she/you (formal) like*

Notice that the pronoun **le** may refer to **a él, a ella** or **a usted.** If the context does not make it clear who is being referred to, the preposition **a** + *the person's name* is used to clarify:

A mi madre le gusta hacer ejercicio.   *My mother likes working out.*
A Enrique le gusta cantar.   *Enrique likes singing.*

Even if the context is clear, you may want to add the prepositional phrase **a** + *pronoun* (e.g. **a mí, a ti, a él/a ella/a usted**) for extra emphasis:

A Celia le gusta nadar por la mañana,   *Celia likes swimming in the morning,*
    pero **a mí** me gusta pintar.   *but what I like is painting.*

You can express different degrees of liking something using **mucho** or **nada:**

¿**No** te gusta ir de compras?   *You don't like going shopping?*
Sí, ¡me gusta **mucho**! Pero a mi   *Yes, I like it a lot! But my mom*
    madre **no** le gusta **nada.**   *doesn't like it at all.*

(a mí)		**me** gusta	
(a ti)	(no)	**te** gusta	(mucho) + *infinitive*
(a él/a ella/a Ud.)		**le** gusta	

 1.2-08 ¡Muchas actividades! For each one, write a sentence expressing who among your friends likes to do it.

MODELO: *A James le gusta salir con los amigos.*

jugar al tenis	hablar por teléfono	escuchar música
viajar	leer en su tableta	ir al cine

1.2-09 ¿Te gusta hacer ejercicio? Complete the dialogue with me, te, le, mí, ti, or usted.

Prof. Herrera: Laura, _te_ gusta mucho hacer ejercicio, ¿no?

Laura: Sí, _____ gusta mucho. Y a _____, ¿_____ gusta hacer ejercicio?

Prof. Herrera: Bueno, a _____ _____ gusta hacer yoga, ¿y a _____?

Laura: Sí, también _____ gusta mucho.

LA PURA VERDAD II ¿Cómo soy en realidad?

Xavier es un estudiante de EE. UU. que chatea por Internet con una muchacha del Uruguay.

1.

> Xavier: ¡Hola! Paula, ¿no?
> Paula: Sí. ¿Cómo te llamas?
> Xavier: ¡Soy Xavier!

2.

> Paula: ¿De dónde eres?
> Xavier: Soy de... de...

Sacramento no es famosa...

> Xavier: Soy de San Francisco. ¿Y tú?

3.

> Paula: ¡Qué interesante! ¿Qué estudias?

Tomo una clase de bádminton... No...

> Xavier: Me gusta mucho estudiar química.

4.

> Paula: ¿Qué te gusta hacer?

Me gusta comer, mirar la tele, dormir, beber cerveza... no...

> Xavier: Me gusta escuchar música clásica.

5.

> Paula: ¡Genial! ¿Cómo eres?

Ella está en Uruguay, por qué no...

> Xavier: ¿Yo? Soy alto, de pelo negro, corto, ojos verdes, fuerte...

6.

> Paula: ¡Qué guapo! ¿Tienes una foto?

¡Oh, no!

 1.2-10 A conocerse por Internet Listen to the narration and choose the best option.

1. A Paula le gusta una persona...
   a. como el Xavier de verdad. b. como el Xavier inventado. c. estudiosa.
2. Paula es...
   a. introvertida. b. atlética. c. trabajadora.
3. A Paula le gusta...
   a. la ciencia. b. la política. c. la medicina.

HABLANDO DE GRAMÁTICA II

2. Requesting information: Interrogative words

To ask for information in Spanish, ask questions with interrogative words. All interrogative words carry a written accent and are preceded by the inverted question mark:

WileyPLUS Go to *WileyPLUS* to review this grammar point with the help of the **Animated Grammar Tutorial**.

Interrogative words

¿Cómo?	*How? or What?*	¿Cómo se dice...?
¿Cuál? ¿Cuáles?	*Which (one)? or What?*	¿Cuál es tu clase favorita? ¿Cuáles son tus amigos?
¿Cuándo?	*When?*	¿Cuándo es tu cumpleaños?
¿Cuánto/a?	*How much?*	¿Cuánto es?
¿Cuántos/as?	*How many?*	¿Cuántos estudiantes son?
¿Dónde?	*Where?*	¿Dónde es la clase?
¿De dónde?	*Where from?*	¿De dónde es la profesora?
¿Quién? ¿Quiénes?	*Who?*	¿Quién es esa estudiante? ¿Quiénes son los chicos?
¿De quién(es)?	*Whose?*	¿De quién es?
¿Qué?	*What? Which?*	¿Qué te gusta hacer?
¿Por qué?	*Why?*	¿Por qué son amigos?

To express *which*, as in *which one?*, use **cuál/cuáles** + *verb* or **qué** + *noun* + *verb*:

¿**Cuál** te gusta más?	*Which one do you like better?*
¿**Cuál** es tu favorita?	*Which one is your favorite?*
¿**Qué** libro te gusta más?	*Which book do you like better?*
¿**Qué** clase prefieres?	*Which class do you prefer?*

To express *what*, use **cuál/cuáles** + *verb* and **qué** + *noun* + *verb*, except when asking for a definition or an explanation, in which case **qué** is used.

¿**Cuál** es tu número de teléfono?	*What is your telephone number?*
¿**Cuál** es tu nacionalidad?	*What is your nationality?*
¿**Qué** día es hoy?	*What day is today?*
¿**Qué** es esto? Es mi libro de español.	*What is this? This is my Spanish book.*

1.2-11 Preguntas en la clase de español Match the question in the column on the left with the answers in the column on the right.

1. ¿De dónde es usted?
2. ¿Cómo se dice "to study"?
3. ¿Cuál es la capital de Perú?
4. ¿Cómo se escribe tu nombre?
5. ¿Cuándo es el examen?
6. ¿Quién es Enrique Peña Nieto?

a. El presidente de México.
b. Se escribe R-I-C-A-R-D-O.
c. Lima
d. ¡El examen es el lunes!
e. Soy de la República Dominicana.
f. "Estudiar"

1.2-12 En el teléfono Two friends are on the phone and you only hear one side of the conversation. Based on the answers, what is the question?

GABRIELA

1. _____
2. _____
3. _____
4. _____
5. _____
6. _____
7. ¡Fantástico! Buena suerte y hasta mañana.

AMELIA

1. Estoy muy bien, ¿y tú?
2. ¿Mi nuevo amigo? Es un compañero de trabajo social.
3. Es inteligente y muy guapo.
4. Se llama Carlos Mújica.
5. M-ú-j-i-c-a
6. Es de Caracas, Venezuela.
7. Gracias. ¡Hasta luego!

 1.2-13 Cuestionario

Paso 1: You are the secretary of the Spanish Club in your school and have to fill out this questionnaire for all the new members. Interview a classmate to find out his/her information.

BIENVENIDO AL CLUB DE ESPAÑOL
Cuestionario de inscripción

Pregunta 1 | ¿Cómo se llama?
Respuesta |

Pregunta 2 | ¿Cuál es su nacionalidad?
Respuesta |

Pregunta 3 | ¿Cuál es su carrera?
Respuesta |

Pregunta 4 | ¿Qué asignaturas le gusta estudiar?
Respuesta |

Pregunta 5 | ¿Qué actividades le gusta hacer en su tiempo libre?
Respuesta |

Pregunta 6 | ¿Quién es su profesor/a de español?
Respuesta |

Pregunta 7 | ¿De dónde es él o ella?
Respuesta |

Continuar   Cancelar

© John Wiley & Sons, Inc.

Paso 2: Now, write a short paragraph to introduce the new member of the club at the next meeting.

MODELO: *El/La nuevo/a miembro se llama...*

OTRA PERSPECTIVA

Courtesy of Claudia Darrigrandi

Claudia

En Chile es diferente

Diferente

"En Chile, en los grados 11 y 12 de la escuela secundaria tienes que[6] especializarte[7] en humanidades o en ciencias. En las universidades generalmente no estudias por cuatro años para obtener un título universitario como en Estados Unidos. Se estudia una carrera específica (economía, enfermería, historia, etc.) y las carreras toman usualmente cinco años".

Igual

"Las carreras muy especializadas (arquitectura, medicina, ingeniería, etc.) toman más tiempo, hasta ocho años más o menos. Al final, el número de años en la universidad es más o menos igual".

Explícale a Claudia

1. ¿Se especializan los estudiantes en la escuela secundaria en Estados Unidos?
2. ¿Cuántos años toma la carrera de medicina en Estados Unidos? ¿Y la carrera de derecho?

MANOS A LA OBRA

1.2-14 Tu cumpleaños Stand up and ask each other, **¿Cuándo es tu cumpleaños?** Form a circle with your classmates starting with the people who were born in the month of January.

1.2-15 ¡Encuesta!

Paso 1: Complete the following sentences with the most appropriate interrogative word. Then, interview two or three classmates.

MODELO: *¿Qué* te gusta hacer?

1. ¿_____ estás?
2. ¿_____ te llamas?
3. ¿_____ es tu personalidad? ¿Eres extrovertido/a, tímido/a...?
4. ¿_____ estudias en la universidad?
5. ¿Tomas muchas clases? ¿_____ clases tomas?
6. ¿_____ es tu clase favorita?
7. ¿_____ eres? ¿Eres de Estados Unidos?
8. ¿_____ es tu número de teléfono?

Paso 2: Which one of your classmates is more like you? Introduce him or her to the class.

MODELO: _____ *es muy similar a mí. A él/ella le gusta...*

[6] **tienes que:** you have to [7] **especializarte:** choose your career

1.2-16 Los pasatiempos de los compañeros Move around the classroom and ask each of your classmates a different question until you complete the list with the names of your classmates answering accordingly.

MODELO: Estudiante 1: *¿Te gusta hablar por teléfono con tus amigos?*
Estudiante 2: *Sí, me gusta hablar por teléfono con mis amigos.*

¿A quién de la clase le gusta...   Nombre

correr solo/a?   _____

estudiar español los fines de semana?   _____

leer *National Geographic*?   _____

¿A quién de la clase no le gusta...

esquiar?   _____

estudiar en el verano?   _____

mirar la televisión?   _____

bailar en las fiestas?   _____

chatear?   _____

ir al cine?   _____

 1.2-17 ¿Cierto o falso? On a piece of paper, write down an activity that you like to do (or do not like to do). Read it out loud. The class will guess whether the sentence is true or false.

MODELO: Estudiante 1: *Me gusta dormir en el sofá.* (falso)
Estudiante 2: *Es falso. No te gusta dormir en el sofá.*
Estudiante 1: *Correcto. Es falso. Me gusta dormir en la cama.*

WileyPLUS Go to *WileyPLUS* and listen to **Presta atención.**

 1.2-18 Presta atención: La semana de Pedro Listen to the audio twice and select an answer.

1. Los padres de Pedro son...
   a. de Estados Unidos.
   b. de Francia.
   c. de Perú.
   d. de Ecuador.
2. Pedro es estudiante de...
   a. ingeniería y comercio.
   b. música y comercio.
   c. comercio y francés.
   d. negocios y francés.
3. Pedro tiene clases con Ana...
   a. los lunes y martes.
   b. los miércoles y jueves.

   c. los martes.
   d. los lunes, miércoles y viernes.
4. Pedro...
   a. corre con sus amigos los lunes.
   b. habla con sus amigos los sábados.
   c. estudia mucho los domingos.
   d. habla por teléfono los domingos.
5. A Pedro le gusta...
   a. escuchar música.
   b. estudiar mucho en el fin de semana.
   c. salir con sus amigos y bailar.
   d. ir a clase de ingeniería.

 1.2-19 Por escrito: ¿Cómo eres?

Paso 1: Your classmates do not know you very well, so you decide to write a description about yourself. Include the following in your description:

- Tu nombre
- Descripciones físicas y de carácter
- Tus intereses y las actividades que te gustan
- Las asignaturas que no te gustan
- Tu nacionalidad
- Tu día favorito, ¿por qué?

(MODELO: *Me llamo María*).
(MODELO: *Soy delgada, rubia, simpática...*)
(MODELO: *Me gusta correr y bailar*).
(MODELO: *No me gusta estudiar química*).
(MODELO: *Soy estadounidense*).
(MODELO: *Mi día favorito es el domingo porque...*)

Paso 2: Now, use the list to write your description. Use transition words (see **Estrategias para escribir**, page 38) to connect your ideas.

MODELO: *Me llamo María y soy simpática, de pelo rubio, paciente y muy alta. Me gusta hacer muchas cosas. Por ejemplo, me gusta correr y bailar. También me gusta escuchar música pop y música clásica, pero no me gusta estudiar química porque es difícil. Soy estadounidense y me gusta jugar al fútbol americano los sábados. Mi día favorito es el domingo porque me gusta ver tres o cuatro películas, pero no me gusta el lunes porque soy estudiante y mi primera clase es a las ocho.*

 PONTE EN MI LUGAR

Estrategias para conversar

Negotiating meaning When conversing with your partner, if you do not understand something, or you do not know how to say something, ask questions to your partner. You already know some expressions (**no entiendo, más despacio por favor...**) and questions (**¿cómo se dice...?, ¿cómo?,** etc.). Use these expressions that you learned as "chunks" of language to keep the conversation going. If your partner cannot help you, use gestures, nonverbal clues or try to explain the concept with different words. By collaborating with your partner you will negotiate meaning, and this will help you to have a successful conversation.

La primera semana de clases During the first week of classes you are talking to a classmate about the classes he/she is taking. Have a dialogue following the steps below. Use the expressions above in **Estrategias para conversar** when necessary.

- Saluda.
- Pregunta el nombre y la nacionalidad.
- Pregunta sobre: sus clases, su clase favorita, el nombre del/de la profesor/a de su clase favorita, una descripción del/de la profesor/a, el país de origen del/de la profesor/a, la clase que no le gusta.
- ¿Qué te gusta hacer en el fin de semana?
- Despídete[8] porque tienes clase ahora.

ASÍ ES LA VIDA

Adivina, adivinador

¿Cuál es el día más largo[9] de la semana?

Rima

Treinta días trae[10] noviembre
con abril, junio y septiembre;
los demás[11], treinta y uno
excepto febrero mocho[12]
que solo trae veintiocho.

 ¡OJO!

Correct your writing
Think of writing as a process, not just as a product. In this exercise, **Paso 1** informs you about the purpose of the writing (a personal description), and your audience (your classmates). In **Paso 2** you have to use connectors (see page 38) to link those previous ideas. Then, revise your grammar (including: subject–verb agreement, noun–adjective agreement, and pronouns) and your vocabulary, and look for errors in spelling, punctuation, and accents.

FEBRERO						
Lun	Mar	Mié	Jue	Vie	Sáb	Dom
				1	2	3
4	5	6	7	8	9	10
11	12	13	14	15	16	17
18	19	20	21	22	23	24
25	26	27	28			

ABRIL						
Lun	Mar	Mié	Jue	Vie	Sáb	Dom
1	2	3	4	5	6	7
8	9	10	11	12	13	14
15	16	17	18	19	20	21
22	23	24	25	26	27	28
29	30					

JULIO						
Lun	Mar	Mié	Jue	Vie	Sáb	Dom
1	2	3	4	5	6	7
8	9	10	11	12	13	14
15	16	17	18	19	20	21
22	23	24	25	26	27	28
29	30	31				

[8]**despídete:** say goodbye [9]**más largo:** longest [10]**trae:** brings [11]**los demás:** the rest [12]**mocho:** cut short

 **WileyPLUS** Go to *WileyPLUS* to find more **Arroba** activities.

Universidades hispanas Explore in your favorite browser information about a university from a Hispanic country such as **Universidad Nacional de Colombia**, **Universidad Nacional Autónoma de México**, or **Universidad de Buenos Aires**. Look for information about **carreras**, **tours de la universidad**, **curso académico**, and **fotos de la universidad**. Then, answer these questions:

¿Qué cursos son familiares para ti? ¿Qué cursos son nuevos?
¿Es esta universidad similar a tu universidad?
¿Cómo es el calendario académico?

VER PARA CREER II: Una visita a la UNAM

WileyPLUS Go to *WileyPLUS* to see this video and to find more video activities.

Antes de ver

Before watching the video, answer the following questions:

1. ¿Qué asignaturas te gustan?
2. Además de español, ¿qué lenguas[13] ofrece tu universidad?
3. ¿De dónde son los estudiantes internacionales de tu universidad?

Después de ver

1. ¿Entendiste? Once you've seen the video, choose the right answer for each question.

1. ¿En qué país está la UNAM?
   a. en México
   b. en Costa Rica
   c. en Venezuela
2. ¿Cuántos estudiantes hay en la UNAM?
   a. Hay pocos estudiantes.
   b. Hay millones de estudiantes.
   c. Hay más de 200.000 estudiantes.
3. ¿De dónde son los estudiantes de la UNAM?
   a. Son de Estados Unidos y de Brasil.
   b. Son de todo el mundo.
   c. Son de México.
4. ¿Qué estudian las personas del video?
   a. Estudian español.
   b. Estudian inglés.
   c. Estudian lingüística.
5. ¿Cómo es la UNAM?
   a. Es pequeña.
   b. Es privada.
   c. Es ordenada.

2. Estudiar en el extranjero ¿Te gusta estudiar en el extranjero? ¿Dónde? ¿Cuándo? ¿Por qué?

3. Enfoque cultural ¿Son diferentes los estudiantes extranjeros de la UNAM a los de tu universidad? ¿De qué países son? ¿Qué estudian los estudiantes extranjeros en tu universidad?

[13] **lenguas:** languages

AUTOPRUEBA

VOCABULARIO

I. ¿Qué clases necesita? Write three subject classes that a student could take for each of these specializations:

Medicina
1. _____
2. _____
3. _____

Negocios
1. _____
2. _____
3. _____

Relaciones internacionales
1. _____
2. _____
3. _____

II. Las clases y el calendario

1. ¿Cuál es la fecha de hoy?
2. ¿Cuándo es tu cumpleaños?
3. ¿Qué días tienes la clase de español?
4. ¿En qué meses no vas[14] a la universidad?
5. ¿En qué estaciones no te gusta estudiar?

GRAMÁTICA

I. ¿Cómo somos? Indicate what each of the persons below likes doing.

> bailar   viajar   hacer yoga
> comprar   estudiar

MODELO: un compañero de clase   →   *A Juan le gusta cantar.*

1. un compañero de clase
2. mi profesor/a
3. yo
4. una compañera de clase
5. mi amigo

II. En una fiesta You meet someone you are very interested in. Ask the person questions using the cues provided.

MODELO: Estar bien, estar mal   →   *¿Cómo estás?*

1. Nombre: _____
2. Nacionalidad: _____
3. Clases, gustar: _____
4. Nombre, profesor/a: _____
5. Hacer, gustar: _____
6. (tu) Asignatura, favorita: _____

CULTURA

1. ¿En qué meses y estaciones hay clase en las universidades de América del Sur?
2. ¿En qué meses y estaciones no hay clase?
3. ¿Tienen el mismo sistema de calificación que en Estados Unidos (A, B, C, D y F)? Explica tu respuesta.

REDACCIÓN

Un amigo en internet. A new e-friend from Spain wants to get to know you better. Write an e-mail telling him/her a little about yourself. Include the following information:

- A greeting
- Your name
- Your nationality
- A physical description of yourself
- Your personality
- Where you live
- Where you study
- What you study
- What you like to do in your free time
- A farewell

EN RESUMIDAS CUENTAS, AHORA PUEDO...

☐ talk about what I like and what I don't like to do.

☐ talk about my major and my classes.

☐ ask questions using interrogative words.

☐ name the days of the week and the months.

☐ understand the differences among academic calendars in Spanish-speaking countries.

☐ understand the grading system in Spanish-speaking countries.

---

[14] **vas:** you go

⌒ VOCABULARIO ESENCIAL

Sustantivos

la escuela (primaria/ secundaria)	*(elementary/high) school*
el/la profesor/a	*teacher, instructor*

Las clases y las carreras *Courses and careers*

la asignatura	*subject, class*
el derecho	*law*
el diseño	*design*
la enfermería	*nursing*
el español	*Spanish*
la especialización	*major, specialization*
la informática	*computer science*
los negocios	*business*
la química	*chemistry*
el trabajo social	*social work*

Cognados: la antropología, el arte, la biología, las ciencias políticas, el comercio, las comunicaciones, la economía, la educación (física), la estadística, las finanzas, el francés, la historia, la ingeniería, el inglés, la literatura, las matemáticas, la medicina, la música, la psicología, las relaciones internacionales, la sociología, el teatro

Expresiones

¿Cuál es la fecha de hoy?	*What is today's date?*
¿Cuándo es tu cumpleaños?	*When is your birthday?*
el fin de semana	*the weekend*
el tiempo libre	*free time*
Hoy es...	*Today is . . .*
(No) Le gusta...	*He/She (doesn't) like(s)...*
(No) Me gusta...	*I (don't) like . . .*
¿Qué clases tomas?	*What classes do you take?*
¿Qué día es hoy?	*What day is today?*
¿Qué te gusta hacer?	*What do you like to do?*

Los meses *Months*

enero	*January*
febrero	*February*
marzo	*March*
abril	*April*
mayo	*May*
junio	*June*
julio	*July*
agosto	*August*
septiembre	*September*
octubre	*October*
noviembre	*November*
diciembre	*December*

Los días de la semana *Days of the week*

el lunes	*Monday*
el martes	*Tuesday*
el miércoles	*Wednesday*
el jueves	*Thursday*
el viernes	*Friday*
el sábado	*Saturday*
el domingo	*Sunday*

Las estaciones *Seasons*

invierno	*winter*
primavera	*spring*
verano	*summer*
otoño	*fall*

Verbos

bailar	*to dance*
caminar	*to walk*
cantar	*to sing*
correr	*to run*
dormir	*to sleep*
escuchar (música)	*to listen (to music)*
esquiar	*to ski*
estudiar	*to study*
hablar por teléfono (celular/ móvil)	*to talk on the (cell) phone*
hacer ejercicio	*to exercise*
hacer yoga	*to do yoga*
ir al cine	*to go to the movies*
ir de compras	*to go shopping*
jugar (al tenis)	*to play (tennis)*
leer	*to read*
mirar/ver la televisión	*to watch TV*
nadar	*to swim*
patinar	*to skate*
pintar	*to paint*
salir con amigos	*to go out with friends*
tocar un instrumento	*to play an instrument*
viajar	*to travel*

VER PARA CREER I: ¡Me gusta regatear!

Watch the video. Then, answer the questions. Don't worry if you don't understand everything. You should be able to follow most of what happens without understanding every single word. At the end of the chapter, you will have an opportunity to watch the video again and understand more.

Now, answer the following questions:

1. Who are the persons in the video, and in what ways are these two persons connected?
2. In what ways are Guatemala and the United States different from or similar to the places you saw in the video?

| Sección 1 | **La rutina diaria** |

PALABRA POR PALABRA

- Las actividades diarias
- ¿Qué hora es?
- Los números del 1 al 59 ♻

HABLANDO DE GRAMÁTICA

- Discussing daily activities (I): Present tense of regular verbs
- Form of address: **Vos**

CULTURA

- Los diferentes aspectos de México
- Distintas ideas de puntualidad

| Sección 2 | **De compras** |

PALABRA POR PALABRA

- El mercado al aire libre
- La ropa
- Los colores
- Los números del 60 al 10.000

HABLANDO DE GRAMÁTICA

- Expressing likes and dislikes (II): More on the verb **gustar** ♻
- Expressing future plans: **Ir** + **a** + infinitive

CULTURA

- La costumbre del regateo en Guatemala
- Diferentes conceptos del espacio personal

Trivia: Go to *WileyPLUS* to do the Trivia activities and find out how much you know about these countries!

México y Guatemala

LEARNING OBJECTIVES

By the end of this section you will be able to:

- Discover different realities in Mexico
- Tell time
- Discuss daily activities and actions
- Recognize the use of **vos**
- Understand a different concept of punctuality

Una imagen vale más que mil palabras

¿Qué ciudad¹ es?

¿Es una ciudad grande típica?

¿Qué hay en la foto?

◀ *La ciudad de México*

UNA PERSPECTIVA

Katherine

Photo Courtesy of Katherine Stafford

¿Cómo es México?

Walter Bibikow/age fotostock/Getty Images

Jeremy Woodhouse/Photodisc/Getty Images

Diferente

"La capital de México es una ciudad muy grande y moderna, pero las ciudades pequeñas con arquitectura colonial también son muy bonitas. Las pirámides de Teotihuacán son muy interesantes. Son increíbles, grandes y antiguas. En Estados Unidos tenemos estructuras indígenas, pero las pirámides de Teotihuacán son realmente impresionantes".

Igual

"Creo que no hay <u>un</u> México estereotípico. Hay varios "Méxicos"…

- un México rápido, tecnológico y rico;
- un México turístico;
- un México pobre;
- un México indígena con su fascinante pasado;
- un México de la clase media.

La capital de México es una ciudad grande típica con mucho tráfico, edificios, ruido², contaminación y también áreas muy bonitas".

 ¿Qué piensas tú?

1. ¿Cuál es tu impresión de México?
   México es… (selecciona una o varias posibles descripciones) grande, pobre³, bello, rico⁴, pequeño, feo, alegre, turístico…
2. ¿Qué ciudades mexicanas conoces⁵?

¹**ciudad:** city ²**ruido:** noise ³**pobre:** poor ⁴**rico:** rich ⁵**conoces:** you know

LA PURA VERDAD I | Soy superorganizado

David es un estudiante de Iowa que va a estudiar español en México, D.F.

1.

2.

7:00 correr tres millas
8:00 caminar a la parada del autobús
8:10 tomar el autobús
8:30 llegar a la escuela

3.

8:45 conversar con mis amigos
9:00 ¡aprender mucho en la clase de español!
12:15 comer algo
1:00 regresar a la escuela

▲ *A David le gusta organizar todo minuto a minuto.*

4.

3:00 caminar a casa
3:25 llegar a casa
3:30 conversar con mis amigos
4:45 estudiar español

5.

6:00 comer con la familia
6:50 pasear con amigos
9:00 mirar un programa de televisión
10:00 leer en la cama

6.

▲ *Los compañeros de David llegan a clase a las nueve menos diez.*

 2.1-01 Agenda Listen to David's instructor's agenda and arrange her activities in chronological order.

La hora	Actividad
9:00	
9:45	
10:30	
11:10	
12:15	
1:05	
1:30	
3:00	

🎧 PALABRA POR PALABRA

Las actividades diarias *Daily activities*

▲ *En la casa* At home

▲ *En la clase*

Otras actividades diarias

cenar	to have dinner	empezar (la clase)	to start (the class)	aprender (en clase)	to learn (in class)
esperar (el autobús)	to wait (for the bus)	pasear	to go for a walk	vivir (en)	to live (in)
llegar (a la universidad)	to arrive (at the university)	terminar (la tarea)	to finish (homework/a chore)	Cognados: visitar (un museo), practicar (español)	
regresar (a casa)	to return (home)				

WileyPLUS Go to *WileyPLUS* to review this grammar point with the help of the **Animated Grammar Tutorial**.

¿Qué hora es? *What time is it?*

Es la una en punto.

Son las tres **en punto.**

Son las tres y cinco.

Son la tres y diez.

Son las tres **y cuarto.**

Son las tres y veinte.

Son las seis y veinticinco.

Son las tres y **media.**

Son las nueve **menos** veinte.

Son las seis menos cuarto.

Es **mediodía.**

Es **medianoche.**

¿A qué hora...?   *At what time...?*

¿A qué hora la profesora llega a la universidad?	*At what time does the teacher arrive at the university?*
Llega a las ocho en punto **de la mañana. Llega a tiempo.**	*She arrives at eight o'clock in the morning. She arrives on time.*
Regresa a casa a las seis **de la tarde.**	*She gets back home at six in the evening.*
Cena a las ocho **de la noche.**	*She has dinner at eight in the evening.*

▲ *Las ocho en punto de la mañana*

© John Wiley & Sons, Inc.

Reloj de 24 horas   *24-hour clock*

Courtesy of Norma López-Burton

TULUM	$63	2358	TULUM	$63 1415		TULUM	$66
CARRILLO PTO	$100	2358	CHETUMAL	$191 1415 1545 2030			
KM 50	$138	2358	ESCARCEGA	$359 2030			
PETO	$160	2358	PALENQUE	$443 1415 1545 20 30		XCARET	$50
TZUCACAB	$159	2358	OCOSINGO	$495 1415 1545 20 0			
TEKAX	$178	2358	SANCRISTOBAL	$539 1415 1545			
OXKUTZCAB	$188	2358	TUXTLA GTEZ	$581 1415 1545		XELHA	$50
TICUL	$195	2358	COMITAN	$615 2030			
			CD CUAHUTEMOC	$650 2030		09:15	10
MERIDA	$162	2355	MOTOZINTLA	$730 2030			
CAMPECHE	$277	2355	HUIXTLA	$761 2030			
			TAPACHULA	$786 2030			

★ SR·PASAJERO
★ AQUI PUEDE ADQUIRIR SU VIAJE DE REGRESO, AHORRE TIEMPO
★ Y EVITE LARGAS FILAS EN OTRAS TERMINALES.

© John Wiley & Sons, Inc.

¿A qué hora sale el autobús para Mérida?	*At what time does the bus leave for Merida?*
Sale a las **23:55.** Sale a las veintitrés cincuenta y cinco.	*It leaves at 23:55.*
¿A qué hora sale el autobús para Tapachula?	*At what time does the bus leave for Tapachula?*
Sale a las **20:30.** Sale a las veinte treinta.	*It leaves at 20:30.*

¿Qué dicen los mexicanos?

- Hablamos mañana.	*We'll talk tomorrow.*
- Ándale pues.	*OK.*
¡Híjole! ¡Está caro!	*Wow! That's expensive!*
Platica mucho.	*He/she talks a lot.*
- No puedo ir a la plaza contigo.	*I can't go to the plaza with you.*
- Pues, ni modo.	*Oh, too bad!*
¿Me esperas tantito?	*Could you wait for me for just a little bit?*

2.1-02 ¿Qué hacen estas personas famosas? With a classmate, select the activity that best corresponds to each of these artists and celebrities.

MODELO: Laura Esquivel → *Laura Esquivel escribe muy bien.*

1. George López
2. Carlos Santana
3. Frida Kahlo
4. Gael García Bernal
5. Salma Hayek

a. trabaja en películas de Hollywood.
b. pinta "Diego y yo" en 1944.
c. habla con el público.
d. toca la guitarra y canta.
e. actúa en *Diarios de motocicleta*.

2.1-03 ¿Qué hora es...? With a classmate, complete and act out each of the following dialogues. Don't look at each other's vignettes.

Estudiante 1:

1.  2.  3.  4.

© John Wiley & Sons, Inc.

Estudiante 2:

1. 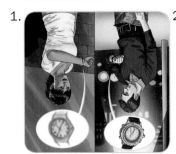 2.  3.  4.

© John Wiley & Sons, Inc.

1. Estudiante 1: ¿Qué hora es? ¿Son _____?

   Estudiante 2: No, son _____.

2. Estudiante 1: ¿Qué hora es? ¿Son _____?

   Estudiante 2: No, _____.

3. Estudiante 1: ¿Son _____?

   Estudiante 2: No, _____.

4. Estudiante 1: Mi reloj no funciona, ¿son _____?

   Estudiante 2: No, _____.

2.1-04 ¿A qué hora es...? You are at home with a friend deciding what to watch on TV.

Paso 1: Select four programs that you think your friend would like and then recommend them to your friend.

MODELO:

Estudiante 1:	*Te recomiendo el programa* Cristina. *Es un programa de variedades.*
Estudiante 2:	*¿A qué hora es?*
Estudiante 1:	*Es a las 2 de la mañana.*
Estudiante 2:	*Mmmhhh, no me gusta ver la televisión por la noche...*

Paso 2: Now decide what you are going to watch among the programs you and your friend recommended and tell the rest of the class. What is the most popular program and time to watch TV among your classmates?

Paso 3: In pairs, talk about your favorite TV shows.

¿Cuál es tu programa favorito? ¿A qué hora es? ¿Qué tipo de programa es?

 2.1-05 Los gustos

Paso 1: Looking at the drawings, ask your partner what these people like to do. Hint: Remember the words learned in Chapter 1.

MODELO: *¿Qué le gusta hacer a David?*
            A David le gusta jugar videojuegos.

 CANAL 4 TV – PROGRAMACIÓN
Jueves 11 de febrero

06:00	*Avance informativo* (noticias)[6]
06:45	*Guasanga* (infantil)
08:00	*Hoy* (variedades)
10:30	*Arriesga TV* (entretenimiento)
12:00	*Se vale* (variedades)
14:00	*A la mesa* (cocina)[7]
15:00	*A las 3* (noticias)
16:00	*Ellas con las estrellas* (variedades)
17:00	*La barranca de la muerte* (cine)
19:00	*Mar de amor* (telenovela)
21:00	*A las 9* (noticias)
22:00	*Nada es para siempre* (serie)
23:30	*Solo de fútbol* (deportes)
01:30	*¿Qué me pasa, doctor?* (salud)[8]
02:00	*Cristina* (variedades)[9]
04:00	*Clásicos de control* (variedades)
05:00	*Tercer grado* (interés general)

© John Wiley & Sons, Inc.

1. A David le gusta...

2. A la profesora le gusta...

© John Wiley & Sons, Inc.

3. A Nidia le gusta...

Paso 2: Now talk about yourself with your partner. Are you more like David, like **la profesora** or like Nidia? What do you like to do?

Yo soy más como _____ porque en casa me gusta _____, pero fuera de casa me gusta _____.

[6]**noticias:** news [7]**cocina:** cooking [8]**salud:** health [9]**variedades:** variety

HABLANDO DE GRAMÁTICA I

WileyPLUS Go to *WileyPLUS* to review this grammar point with the help of the **Animated Grammar Tutorial** and the **Verb Conjugator**.

1. Discussing daily activities (I): Present tense of regular verbs

Spanish verbs are classified in three groups, depending on their endings: **-ar**, **-er**, and **-ir** verbs. These are the infinitive endings, and **mirar, comer,** or **escribir** are the infinitive form of the verbs. In English, the infinitive form of a verb consists of two words: *to look, to eat, to write.* The infinitive is the form we find in dictionaries. As in English, some Spanish verbs are regular and some are irregular. In this chapter you will learn the present tense of regular verbs.

In order to form different tenses (present, past, future), you have to conjugate the verb by dropping the infinitive ending (**-ar, -er, -ir**) and adding the appropriate endings according to the tense and subject of the verb. To form the present tense of regular verbs, substitute the infinitive ending with the present tense endings.

Regular *-ar* verbs

Singular		Plural	
(yo)	-o	(nosotros/as)	-amos
(tú)	-as	(vosotros/as)	-áis
(él, ella, Ud.)	-a	(ellos/ellas/Uds.)	-an

Regular *-er/-ir* verbs

Singular		Plural	
(yo)	-o	(nosotros/as)	-emos/-imos
(tú)	-es	(vosotros/as)	-éis/-ís
(él, ella, Ud.)	-e	(ellos/ellas/Uds.)	-en

	mirar	comer	escribir
	(to look at, to watch)	*(to eat)*	*(to write)*
(yo)	mir**o**	com**o**	escrib**o**
(tú)	mir**as**	com**es**	escrib**es**
(él, ella, Ud.)	mir**a**	com**e**	escrib**e**

	mirar	comer	escribir
(nosotros/as)	mir**amos**	com**emos**	escrib**imos**
(vosotros/as)	mir**áis**	com**éis**	escrib**ís**
(ellos/as, Uds.)	mir**an**	com**en**	escrib**en**

In Spanish, the present tense is used to express different meanings. *I speak* (simple present, habitual action), *I am speaking* (action in progress), or *I will speak* (near future) can all be translated as the single form (**yo**) **hablo.**

The present tense can also be used to discuss past events, and it is widely used to narrate history. This is the historical present:

Frida Kahlo y Diego Rivera **se casan** en 1929.

Frida Kahlo and Diego Rivera get married in 1929.

In Chapter 1, Section 1 you learned that personal pronouns (*I, you, he,* etc.) are used much less frequently in Spanish than in English because the verb endings usually tell us to whom the verb refers. Compare with English: *I/you/we/they look, He/she look***s***. In Spanish there is no need to use personal pronouns unless you have to avoid ambiguity or to add emphasis:

Él habla español, pero **yo** solo hablo inglés.

He speaks Spanish, but I only speak English.

Ellos llegan a casa a las dos, **nosotros** llegamos a las tres.

They get home at two, we get home at three.

2.1-06 Asociaciones Remember David, from **La pura verdad**? Associate the people in column **A** with the activities in column **B**. Remember to pay attention to the form of the verbs! Then decide whether the sentences are true (**Cierto**) or false (**Falso**).

MODELO: *David estudia español en México* (Cierto).

A
David
Sus compañeros de clase
Yo

B	CIERTO	FALSO
1. _____ escribe su horario del día en un cuaderno.	☐	☐
2. _____ hablo español.	☐	☐
3. _____ hablan y practican español.	☐	☐
4. _____ camina tres millas.	☐	☐
5. _____ miro televisión en la mañana.	☐	☐
6. _____ corre a la parada del autobús.[10]	☐	☐
7. _____ escribo muchos textos a mis amigos.	☐	☐
8. _____ aprenden mucho en la clase.	☐	☐
9. _____ caminan de la escuela a su casa.	☐	☐

2.1-07 Cuestionario I

Paso 1: Complete the following questionnaire with information about yourself.

Yo

MODELO: *¿Qué toman con la cena?*   _Tomo agua._

1. ¿Qué cereal comes por la mañana?   _____
2. ¿Qué programa de televisión miras los jueves?   _____
3. ¿Qué bebes cuando tienes sed[11]?   _____
4. ¿A qué hora regresas los sábados por la noche?   _____
5. ¿Dónde vives?   _____
6. ¿Cuándo paseas por la ciudad?   _____

Paso 2: Now use the **tú** form of the verbs to interview a classmate. Write down his or her answers.

MODELO: Estudiante 1: *¿Qué tomas con la cena?*   _Mi compañero toma agua con limón._

Estudiante 2: *Tomo agua con limón.*

Paso 3: Now write a short paragraph to describe similarities and differences. What do you both do? How do you differ?

MODELO: *Los dos tomamos agua con la cena, pero él... y yo...*

[10]**parada del autobús:** bus stop [11]**tienes sed:** you are thirsty

2.1-08 Actividades de los estudiantes

Paso 1: Write down how frequently you do the activities on the following list. Use the **¿Con qué frecuencia?** expressions.

MODELO: comer en la cafetería de la universidad
→ *A veces como en la cafetería de la universidad.*

ACTIVIDADES	FRECUENCIA
1. llegar a tiempo a clase	
2. conversar en español con amigos fuera de clase	
3. hablar de política en clase	
4. visitar un museo	
5. aprender sobre otros países	
6. estudiar vocabulario nuevo	
7. preguntar en clase a el/la profesor/a	
8. practicar deportes	

¿Con qué frecuencia? *How frequently?*

a menudo	*often*
a veces	*sometimes*
casi nunca	*hardly ever*
(casi) siempre	*(almost) always*
con frecuencia	*frequently*
dos/tres/cuatro… veces por semana	*twice/three/four… times a week*
dos/tres/cuatro… veces por mes	*twice/three/four… times a month*
los fines de semana	*on the weekends*
muchas veces	*many times*
nunca	*never*
todas las mañanas	*every morning*
todas las noches	*every night*
todas las tardes	*every afternoon*
todos los días	*everyday*
una vez por semana	*once a week*

 Paso 2: Now ask a classmate and complete a similar table.

MODELO: Estudiante 1: *¿Con qué frecuencia comes en la cafetería?*
Estudiante 2: *Nunca como en la cafetería de la universidad porque es muy cara.*

ACTIVIDADES	FRECUENCIA
1. comer en la cafetería	Nunca come en la cafetería.
…	…

 Paso 3: Write a short paragraph to report to the class.

MODELO: *Paula siempre llega a tiempo a clase, y también siempre _____ pero nunca…*

LA PURA VERDAD II   No es una vida loca

Tres meses después[12], David está acostumbrado a la vida en México.

1.

▲ *Camina a la universidad.*

2.

▲ *David espera el autobús.*

3.

Buenos días.

▲ *David llega a las 9:00 en punto.*

4.

▲ *La clase termina a las 2:00.*

5.

¿A qué hora almorzamos?

Pues, ahorita.

▲ *Los niños corren. David habla con la señora.*

6.

▲ *Todos almuerzan.*

7.

▲ *La señora mira una telenovela.*

8.

9.

10.

All illustrations © John Wiley & Sons, Inc.

2.1-09 **La vida en México** Listen to the narration and decide which activity does not belong in the series.

   1. a   b   c
   2. a   b   c
   3. a   b   c

[12] después: later

HABLANDO DE GRAMÁTICA II

2. Form of address: *Vos*

The subject pronoun **vos** is used as an equivalent or instead of **tú** in several Spanish-speaking countries. The use of **vos** as a form of address is known as **voseo**. In general, the use of **vos** usually entails more intimacy than **tú** in those places where both forms are used (Guatemala and most of Central America). However, in some areas only **vos** is used, never **tú** (Argentina, Paraguay, and Uruguay).

In most countries **vos** has its own corresponding conjugated form in the present tense, which is similar to the **vosotros** form but without the final **-i-** for those verbs ending in **-ar** and **-er**. For those verbs ending in **-ir**, the **vosotros** and the **vos** form is the same:

(vosotros) miráis	→	(vos) mirás
(vosotros) coméis	→	(vos) comés
(vosotros) escribís	→	(vos) escribís

Tú form	**Vos** equivalent
¿Comes tamales con frecuencia?	*¿Comés tamales con frecuencia?*
¿Caminas mucho?	*¿Caminás mucho?*
¿Miras la televisión por la noche?	*¿Mirás la televisión por la noche?*

2.1-10 Cuestionario 2 You are traveling to Guatemala for your next vacation and you will be hearing the **vos** form of address.

 Paso 1: Use the questions from activity **2.1-07** and adapt them to use the **vos** form. Interview a different classmate and note their answers.

MODELO: Estudiante 1: ¿Qué tomás con la cena?
           Estudiante 2: Tomo agua.

                                    Mi compañero toma agua con la cena.

1. ¿Qué comés por la mañana?   _____
2. ¿Qué programa de televisión mirás los jueves? _____
3. ¿Qué tomás cuando tenés sed?   _____
4. ¿A qué hora regresás los sábados por la noche? _____
5. ¿Dónde vivís?   _____
6. ¿Cuándo paseás por la ciudad?   _____

 Paso 2: Now write a short paragraph in which you describe similarities and differences between the two classmates that you have interviewed in both questionnaire activities.

MODELO: *Las dos toman agua con la cena, pero Jennifer toma jugo y Cindy siempre toma agua.*

OTRA PERSPECTIVA

Courtesy of David Tenorio González

Raúl

¿Qué hora es?

Diferente

"En Estados Unidos son más estrictos con la hora. Parece[13] que el reloj controla la vida. La puntualidad es muy importante. En México, si hay una fiesta a las 8:00 de la noche, en realidad, los invitados llegan a las 9:00 o a las 10:00".

Igual

"Al igual que en Estados Unidos, en México se respeta el horario de las clases de la universidad, de los programas de televisión y del trabajo".

Explícale a Raúl

1. ¿Es importante la puntualidad para ti?
2. ¿Es importante llegar a tiempo siempre? ¿Cuándo no es importante?
3. ¿Llegas a tiempo o no, a...
   la clase de español?
   una fiesta?
   una reunión informal con amigos?
   una cita[14] con tu profesor/a?

MANOS A LA OBRA

2.1-11 ¡México! Write five numbers underneath each letter, within the range given. Your instructor will call out different numbers. Say **¡México!** when you cross out all the numbers in a horizontal or vertical line.

M (1–10)	É (11–20)	X (21–30)	I (31–40)	C (41–50)	O (51–59)

[13] **Parece:** It seems [14] **cita:** appointment

2.1-12 Un domingo en el Parque de Chapultepec, en Ciudad de México

 Paso 1: What are these people doing on a Sunday? Work with a classmate to find six differences between the two drawings.

A

B

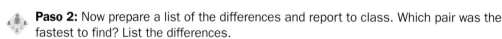

Estudiante 1: Describe el dibujo A: *En mi dibujo, un hombre corre.*
Estudiante 2: Describe el dibujo B: *En mi dibujo, tres muchachas corren.*

 Paso 2: Now prepare a list of the differences and report to class. Which pair was the fastest to find? List the differences.

2.1-13 ¿Cómo es la persona ideal?

Paso 1: In groups of three or four, decide which are the typical activities or actions that describe the following people.

MODELO: El profesor ideal *explica bien, inspira y motiva a los estudiantes.*

1. El padre/La madre ideal...
2. La pareja ideal...
3. El/La estudiante ideal...
4. El/La amigo/a ideal...
5. El/La hijo/a ideal...

 Paso 2: Now, report to the class. What are the opinions of the class as a whole?

© John Wiley & Sons, Inc.

2.1-14 ¿Qué haces durante el día? What do you do on a daily basis? Ask your classmates and write the name of those who respond affirmatively.

MODELO: Estudiante 1:   *¿Hablas por teléfono?*
            Estudiante 2:   *Sí, hablo por teléfono con otros amigos. /*
                             No, no hablo por teléfono.

¿Quién de la clase...   Nombre

  1. habla mucho por teléfono con sus padres?   _____

  2. estudia todo el vocabulario?   _____

  3. llama a sus amigos por la noche?   _____

  4. escribe mensajes de texto?   _____

  5. mira videos de YouTube?   _____

  6. come mucho?   _____

  7. mira a la gente pasar?   _____

  8. habla de política?   _____

  9. escucha música?   _____

2.1-15 ¡Una foto en familia!

 Paso 1: Bring a personal picture to class. Show the picture to a classmate and talk about it.

–Describe what you are doing in the picture and say how frequently you do this with your family.
–Describe the place.
–Describe the time.
–Explain why you like the picture.

MODELO: *En esta foto como con mi familia. Todos los días ceno con mis padres y mi hermana. En esta foto estamos de vacaciones. Estamos en un restaurante francés. Son las ocho de la noche y en el restaurante hay turistas estadounidenses, italianos y españoles. Me gusta la foto porque paso tiempo con mi familia y me gusta hablar, comer y beber con ellos. En la foto celebramos el 25 aniversario de mis padres.*

Paso 2: Describe your friend's picture to the class; share the information and explain why the picture is important to him or her.

▲ *Una cena con la familia Hernández*

MODELO: *En esta foto Natalia come con su familia. A Natalia le gusta la foto porque le gusta comer, beber y hablar con su familia.*

WileyPLUS Go to *WileyPLUS* and listen to **Presta atención.**

2.1-16 Presta atención: El paseo de David You will now learn more about David's life in Mexico. Listen carefully and select the appropriate answers.

1. David pasea con sus amigos el…
   a. lunes.
   b. miércoles.
   c. viernes.
   d. sábado.

2. En la plaza David ve a…
   a. amigos de la universidad.
   b. amigos de su familia mexicana.
   c. amigos del autobús.
   d. sus amigos mexicanos.

3. David decide…
   a. regresar a casa después del paseo.
   b. aceptar la invitación de sus amigos mexicanos.
   c. beber un café con sus amigos.
   d. visitar la plaza a menudo.

4. David regresa a casa…
   a. después de pasear por la plaza.
   b. después de bailar en la discoteca.
   c. después de hablar con su familia.
   d. después de caminar solo por la plaza.

5. David regresa a casa…
   a. a las once de la noche.
   b. a las dos de la mañana.
   c. a las tres de la mañana.
   d. a las cinco de la mañana.

2.1-17 Por escrito: Una carta personal Write a personal letter to a friend answering these questions:

- ¿Qué estudias este semestre (trimestre/año)?
- ¿A qué hora son tus clases?
- ¿Dónde comes?
- ¿A qué hora comes?
- ¿Adónde vas por la noche?
- ¿Te gusta bailar por la noche?
- ¿Dónde haces la tarea?
- ¿Trabajas mañana?
- ¿Cuándo?
- ¿…?

Then, review the grammar, vocabulary, and the spelling. Use the format in the illustration as a model.

¡OJO!

Proofreading
Before turning in your letter, proofread your writing to make sure that subjects and verbs, and nouns, articles, and adjectives agree in time, gender, and number, and make sure all words are spelled correctly, including accent marks.

Monterrey,
29 de agosto de 2014

Querida Elisa:

Hoy es 29 de agosto y estoy aquí en casa …

Un beso

PONTE EN MI LUGAR

La fiesta de un amigo A friend invites you to a party at 9:00 p.m. You arrive at 9:15 p.m. and only one other person has arrived! While other people arrive, have a conversation with the other guest.

- Saluda.
- Pregunta qué hora es.
- Pregunta su nombre y de dónde es.
- Pregunta la hora otra vez.
- Habla sobre tus pasatiempos. ¿Qué te gusta hacer?
- Habla sobre la universidad y las clases que tomas.
- Pregunta la hora otra vez.

ASÍ ES LA VIDA

Adivina, adivinador

¿Qué se repite una vez[15] cada minuto, dos veces[16] cada momento y nunca en cien años?

Chiste

¿Qué le dice el 3 al 30?
Para ser como yo, debes[17] ser sincero (sin-cero).

> *¡Sincero!*

 **WileyPLUS** Go to *WileyPLUS* to find more **Arroba** activities.

Las revistas Explore in your favorite browser information about "Revistas de México para adolescentes." Look for magazines you can find online. Then, check the website from the selected magazine. Answer the following questions:

1. ¿Qué temas presenta esa revista? Escribe cuatro temas.
2. Escribe cinco cognados de la página web. Modelo: foro – *forum*
3. ¿Qué temas son importantes para ti?
4. ¿Qué diferencias hay entre la página web de la revista en español y la página web de una revista en inglés?

ENTÉRATE

Antes de leer

1. **¿Qué tipo de texto es?** Whether you realize it or not, you quickly categorize texts by their format, layout, the images that accompany them, and also by their titles and subtitles. What is your first impression of the following text? By just looking at the design of the reading and its format, can you identify what the content might be?
   a. horoscope
   b. finding pen pals or email friends
   c. letters to the editor

---

[15] **una vez:** once [16] **dos veces:** twice [17] **debes:** you should

2. **¿De qué trata?** See if you can identify the content of each message. Obviously, the first part is the person's name, age, and email address. After skimming through the information in Adolfo's and Andrés' messages, can you guess what **pasatiempos** means?
  a. pastimes   b. courses studied   c. time in the past
3. **Cognados** Before you read the messages for meaning, look through the two of the messages and make a list of at least six cognates.

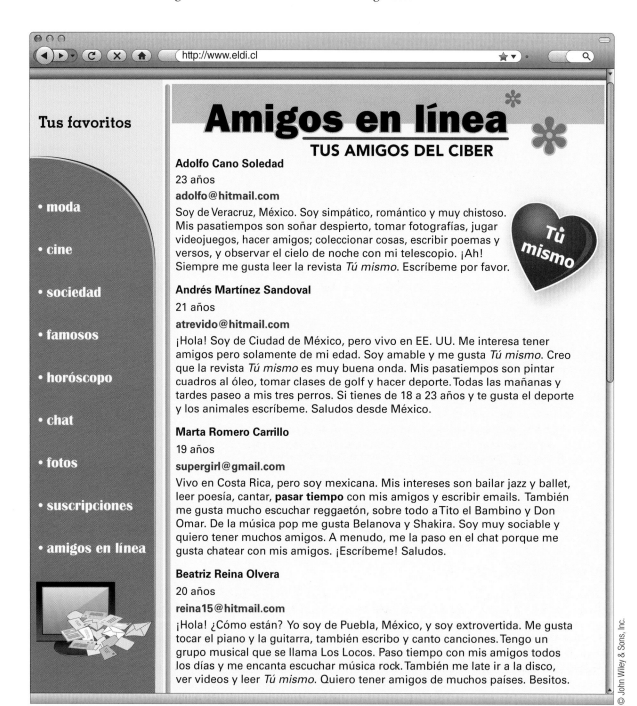

http://www.eldi.cl

Tus favoritos

- **moda**
- **cine**
- **sociedad**
- **famosos**
- **horóscopo**
- **chat**
- **fotos**

to spend time

- **suscripciones**
- **amigos en línea**

Amigos en línea
TUS AMIGOS DEL CIBER

Adolfo Cano Soledad

23 años

adolfo@hitmail.com

Soy de Veracruz, México. Soy simpático, romántico y muy chistoso. Mis pasatiempos son soñar despierto, tomar fotografías, jugar videojuegos, hacer amigos; coleccionar cosas, escribir poemas y versos, y observar el cielo de noche con mi telescopio. ¡Ah! Siempre me gusta leer la revista *Tú mismo*. Escríbeme por favor.

Tú mismo

Andrés Martínez Sandoval

21 años

atrevido@hitmail.com

¡Hola! Soy de Ciudad de México, pero vivo en EE. UU. Me interesa tener amigos pero solamente de mi edad. Soy amable y me gusta *Tú mismo*. Creo que la revista *Tú mismo* es muy buena onda. Mis pasatiempos son pintar cuadros al óleo, tomar clases de golf y hacer deporte. Todas las mañanas y tardes paseo a mis tres perros. Si tienes de 18 a 23 años y te gusta el deporte y los animales escríbeme. Saludos desde México.

Marta Romero Carrillo

19 años

supergirl@gmail.com

Vivo en Costa Rica, pero soy mexicana. Mis intereses son bailar jazz y ballet, leer poesía, cantar, **pasar tiempo** con mis amigos y escribir emails. También me gusta mucho escuchar reggaetón, sobre todo a Tito el Bambino y Don Omar. De la música pop me gusta Belanova y Shakira. Soy muy sociable y quiero tener muchos amigos. A menudo, me la paso en el chat porque me gusta chatear con mis amigos. ¡Escríbeme! Saludos.

Beatriz Reina Olvera

20 años

reina15@hitmail.com

¡Hola! ¿Cómo están? Yo soy de Puebla, México, y soy extrovertida. Me gusta tocar el piano y la guitarra, también escribo y canto canciones. Tengo un grupo musical que se llama Los Locos. Paso tiempo con mis amigos todos los días y me encanta escuchar música rock. También me late ir a la disco, ver videos y leer *Tú mismo*. Quiero tener amigos de muchos países. Besitos.

Después de leer

1. En el texto Identify in the messages in the previous page examples of the vocabulary and grammar topics you studied in this section: (1) verbs in the present tense, (2) infinitives, and (3) expressions to indicate the frequency of doing activities.

2. ¿Entendiste? Read the four messages and select or answer with the appropriate information according to the reading.

1. ¿Quién toca un instrumento?
   a. Adolfo
   b. Andrés
   c. Marta
   d. Beatriz
2. ¿Quién baila y por qué?
   a. Adolfo, porque es chistoso.
   b. Andrés, porque le gusta el deporte.
   c. Marta, porque bailar es uno de sus intereses.
   d. Beatriz, porque le gusta la discoteca.
3. ¿Quiénes son lectores?
   a. Adolfo y Andrés leen con frecuencia.
   b. Andrés lee libros en inglés.
   c. Marta y Beatriz leen poco.
   d. Todos leen.
4. ¿Qué significa "La revista *Tú mismo* es buena onda"?
   a. Es una revista aburrida.
   b. Es una revista buena.
   c. Es una revista negativa.
   d. Es una revista con ondas.
5. ¿Qué significa "me late ir a la disco"?
   a. Quiero un café en la disco.
   b. Me gusta ir a la disco.
   c. Ahoritita mismo quiero bailar.
   d. Detesto la música de la disco.
6. ¿Cómo se llama la persona que tiene los intereses más similares a los tuyos[18]? ¿Qué intereses tienen en común?

EN TUS PROPIAS PALABRAS

Estrategias para escribir

Write your own message In the previous section **Entérate** you saw different messages. Now, it is time for you to write your own. Start by brainstorming to generate ideas related to the information you want to share with a new pen pal from Mexico. Remember that your message is important in order to practice Spanish, to know more about his or her culture, and to exchange ideas. Then, organize your pre-writing thoughts and create a description or yourself including your likes and dislikes. Remember to (a) use complete sentences to form a paragraph by using connectors when necessary; (b) include some cognates that you learned in the reading; (c) review your message to make sure that you used the right grammar and vocabulary; and (d) review mechanics such as spelling.

 Tú mismo: Use two of the messages of the previous reading as a model and write your own message.

---

[18] **tuyos:** yours

AUTOPRUEBA

VOCABULARIO

I. ¿Qué hora es? All your friends have a different time! Look at these clocks and say what time it is.

1.  2.  3.

4.  5.

II. ¿A qué hora…? Write down at what time these student's classes and activities take place.

MODELO: *Toma matemáticas de las ocho a las nueve menos diez.*

Clase de español 10:30–12:00
Comer en la cafetería de la universidad 12:05–1:10
Clase de biología 1:30–2:50
Clase de tenis en el gimnasio 3:45–5:00
Hablar con amigos en el café 5:15–7:45
Cenar con la familia 7:16–8:00

1. _____
2. _____
3. _____
4. _____
5. _____
6. _____

GRAMÁTICA

I. Las actividades de mis amigos Use the verbs in the list to write complete sentences with information about your friends and your best friend specifically. Connect the sentences with **pero**.

MODELO: *Mis amigos bailan en las fiestas, pero a mi amiga Cristina no le gusta bailar.*

leer   mirar   ver   correr   cenar   practicar   escribir

II. De visita en México o Guatemala What do you and your friends do when you visit a country like Mexico or Guatemala? Select one of the following verbs for each sentence and write the appropriate form of the present tense.

caminar   escribir   comer   hablar   beber
mirar   visitar

1. Mis amigos y yo _____las ciudades más importantes.
2. No me gusta ir en taxi, a mí me gusta _____.
3. Nosotros todos _____ la comida local.
4. Mi amigo Gerardo es un casanova. Él _____ poemas a las muchachas y _____ con ellas en español.
5. Mis padres _____ artesanía en los mercados.
6. ¿Y los mexicanos? Ellos _____ limonada, ¡qué rica!

CULTURA

1. When is it important to be on time in Mexico?
2. At what time (approximately) do they have lunch and dinner in Mexico?
3. In countries like Mexico or Guatemala, is it common to see children still up at 10 p.m.?

REDACCIÓN

Write about the activities that you do during a typical day and at what time. Answer the following questions:

- ¿Qué haces por la mañana, por la tarde y por la noche y a qué hora en un día típico?
- ¿Qué te gusta hacer todos los días? ¿Qué te gusta hacer a veces?

EN RESUMIDAS CUENTAS, AHORA PUEDO…

☐ discover the different realities in Mexico.

☐ tell time.

☐ discuss daily activities and actions.

☐ recognize the use of **vos.**

☐ understand a different concept of punctuality.

⌒ VOCABULARIO ESENCIAL

Sustantivos

el autobús	*bus*
la casa	*house, home*

Cognados: la actividad, la familia

Expresiones

¿A qué hora es...?	*What time is . . . ?*
Es medianoche.	*It's midnight.*
Es mediodía.	*It's noon.*
¿Qué hora es?	*What time is it?*
Es la / Son las...	*It is…*
en punto	*o'clock*
y cuarto	*quarter past*
y media	*thirty past*
menos cuarto	*a quarter to*
de la mañana	*in the morning*
de la tarde	*in the afternoon*
de la noche	*in the evening/at night*

Verbos

aprender	*to learn*
beber	*to drink*
cenar	*to have dinner*
cocinar	*to cook*
comer	*to eat*
empezar	*to start*
escribir	*to write*
esperar	*to wait*
lavar (los platos)	*to wash (the dishes)/ to do the dishes*
llegar (a)	*to arrive (to)*
llegar a tiempo	*to arrive/be on time*
pasear	*to go for a walk*
regresar	*to return*
terminar	*to finish*
tomar	*to take / drink*
trabajar	*to work*
vivir	*to live*

Cognados: conversar, practicar, responder, visitar

LEARNING OBJECTIVES

By the end of this section you will be able to:

- Negotiate in an open market
- Describe clothing
- Identify colors
- Use numbers from 60 and on

- Talk about what I and other people like
- Tell what you are planning to do
- Understand the different concept of physical contact

Una imagen vale más que mil palabras

Wendy Connett/Robert Harding World Imagery/Getty Images

¿Qué hacen las personas de la foto?

¿Hay algo similar en tu comunidad?

¿Crees que las cosas son más caras[1] o más baratas[2] que en un gran almacén?

◀ *Un mercado al aire libre*

UNA PERSPECTIVA

Photo Courtesy of Ryan Sokol

Robert

La ropa y el mercado

Diferente

"En Guatemala, en general, observo que las personas llevan ropa un poco más formal en el trabajo y a la universidad. Las secretarias, las recepcionistas y los empleados[3] de la tiendas de ropa se visten[4] más formalmente que en EE. UU. También veo que en muchos mercados se puede negociar el precio. Esto se llama *regatear*".

©Marta NASCIMENTO/REA/Redux

Igual

"Las personas que trabajan en las oficinas se visten muy bien, pero los jóvenes, al igual que en Estados Unidos, llevan camisetas y *jeans*. En Estados Unidos también podemos regatear cuando compramos casas o automóviles".

 ¿Qué piensas tú? Con un/a compañero/a, habla sobre la ropa que usamos en Estados Unidos y marca con una X la situación correspondiente.

1. ¿Dónde llevamos ropa formal en EE. UU.?
   - _____ en el trabajo
   - _____ en fiestas
   - _____ en reuniones familiares
   - _____ en la universidad
2. ¿Cuándo llevamos ropa informal en EE. UU.?
   - _____ en un avión
   - _____ en casa
   - _____ cuando salimos con amigos
   - _____ en la universidad

3. ¿Cuándo regateamos en Estados Unidos?
   - _____ en los supermercados
   - _____ cuando compramos automóviles
   - _____ en las ventas de garaje[5]
   - _____ cuando compramos casas

---

[1]**caras:** expensive [2]**baratas:** cheap [3]**empleados:** employees [4]**se visten:** they dress [5]**ventas de garaje:** garage sales

LA PURA VERDAD I   ¡Barato, barato!

Jonah es un estudiante de Estados Unidos que vive en Guatemala. Una mañana, decide visitar un mercado al aire libre.

1.

▲ *Mercado Central en la ciudad de Guatemala*

2.

3.

4.

5.

6.

7.

8.

All illustrations © John Wiley & Sons, Inc.

2.2-01 **Más compras en el mercado** Listen to the narration and decide which article is the cheapest or the most expensive.

1. ¿Qué es más barato?
   a. los sombreros   b. las blusas   c. los pantalones
2. ¿Qué es más caro?
   a. las camisas   b. los zapatos   c. los relojes
3. ¿Qué es más caro?
   a. los anillos   b. los trajes   c. las pulseras

PALABRA POR PALABRA

El mercado al aire libre *Outdoor market*

¿Qué dicen en el mercado?	*What is said in the market?*
Es muy barato/a.	*It is very cheap.*
Es muy caro/a.	*It is very expensive.*
¿Cuánto cuesta/cuestan...?	*How much is it/are they?*
Para Ud., Q25. Buen precio...	*For you, Q25. It's a good price...*
Pase, pase, adelante...	*Come in, come in...*
¿Qué busca/desea?	*What are you looking for?*
el precio (fijo)	*(fixed) price*

¿Qué hacen?	*What do they do?*
comprar	*to buy*
ir de compras	*to go shopping*
rebajar	*to reduce*
regalar	*to buy a present*
regatear	*to negotiate a price*
vender	*to sell*

Cognados: costar, insistir

Los colores

Photo Courtesy of Elena Herrero

La ropa y los complementos	*Clothing and accessories*
la artesanía	*arts and crafts*
la comida	*food*
la flor	*flower*
las zapatillas de deporte/los tenis	*tennis shoes*
la plata	*silver*
el oro	*gold*
el regalo	*present*
el reloj	*watch*
el traje	*suit*
los zapatos	*shoes*

Cognados: la blusa, la bota

© John Wiley & Sons, Inc.

Para hablar de la ropa

¿Qué llevas?	*What are you wearing?*
¿Qué te gusta llevar?	*What do you like to wear?*

Los números del 60 al 10.000

60	*sesenta*
70	*setenta*
80	*ochenta*
90	*noventa*
100	*cien*
101	*ciento uno*
110	*ciento diez*
200	*doscientos*
300	*trescientos*
400	*cuatrocientos*
500	*quinientos*

600	*seiscientos*
700	*setecientos*
800	*ochocientos*
900	*novecientos*
1.000	*mil*
1.001	*mil uno*
1.100	*mil cien*
1.101	*mil ciento uno*
2.000	*dos mil*
10.000	*diez mil*

¿Qué dicen los guatemaltecos?

¡Perfecto! ¡Está a todo dar!	*Perfect! It's super cool!*
Ya te agarro la onda.	*I understand you now.*
Son mis cuates.	*They are my friends.*
¡Está padre/padrísimo!	*That's very cool!*

All of these expressions are also used in other Spanish-speaking countries.

2.2-02 ¿Qué venden? You are visiting a market in Antigua, Guatemala, with a friend. Look at the objects on the table. Which ones are appropriate for you, for your friend, and for both of you?

© John Wiley & Sons, Inc.

Para ti	Para él/ella	Para los dos
_____	_____	_____
_____	_____	_____
_____	_____	_____
_____	_____	_____

 2.2-03 ¿Qué te gusta?

 Paso 1: Complete the sentences with information that is true about you.

1. Mi color favorito es el…
2. No me gusta nada el color…
3. Me gusta ir de compras en…
4. Frecuentemente compro…
5. En un mercado al aire libre me gusta comprar…
6. En mi opinión, un buen regalo para un hombre en su cumpleaños es… y para una mujer…
7. En mi opinión, nunca debes regalar…

Paso 2: Now, transform the sentences into questions. Interview a classmate and write down his or her answers.

MODELO: Estudiante 1: Mi color favorito es el azul.   →   *¿Cuál es tu color favorito?*
Estudiante 2: Mi color favorito es el azul.

Paso 3: Now write a short paragraph to describe similarities and differences between the two of you. Do you have similar opinions?

MODELO: *El color favorito de los dos es el azul y a los dos nos gusta ir
de compras en…*

2.2-04 ¿Cuánto cuesta? In pairs, take turns interviewing each other. Make a list of what the other person is wearing and the approximate price of each article.

MODELO: Estudiante 1:   *¿Cuánto cuestan los tenis que llevas?*
                 Estudiante 2:   *Pues, cuestan $40 más o menos.*

2.2-05 ¡A comprar! In activity **2.2-02** you choose the articles that you wanted to buy. Now it is time to talk to the seller.

Paso 1: Get together with another classmate who is the seller. Use your list from activity **2.2-02** to ask the price of each article; write down the price.

MODELO: Cliente 1:   *¿Cuánto cuestan los aretes de oro?*
                 Vendedor: *Cuestan Q1.200 (mil doscientos quetzales).*
                 Cliente 2:   *Ay no, son muy caros. ¿Y cuánto cuesta/n…?*

▲ *El quetzal es la moneda de Guatemala.*

Paso 2: Choose the articles that you want to buy and calculate the total.

MODELO: Cliente 1:   *Bien, vamos a comprar…*
                 Cliente 2:   *En total, todo cuesta…*

Para ti   Para él/ella   Para los dos

_____   _____   _____

_____   _____   _____

Total: _____   Total: _____   Total: _____

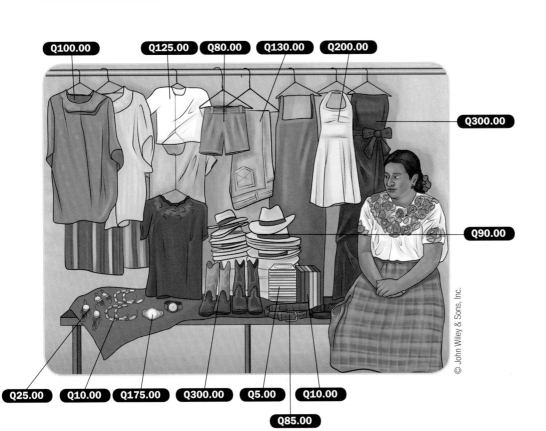

HABLANDO DE GRAMÁTICA I

WileyPLUS Go to *WileyPLUS* to review this grammar point with the help of the **Animated Grammar Tutorial** and the **Verb Conjugator.**

♺ Verb *Gustar*

Go to page 47 in Chapter 1 to review the gustar form. Do you remember how to say: I like shopping.?

1. Expressing likes and dislikes (II): More on the verb *gustar* ♺

In Chapter 1, Section 2, you learned to talk about what people like or do not like using **me/te/le gusta** + *infinitive*. Remember that **gustar** literally means "to be pleasing (to someone)." **Me/te/le** refer to the person to whom a thing or activity is pleasing:

–Jonah, ¿**te gusta** ir de compras?

–Sí, **me gusta** muchísimo. ¡Especialmente en Guatemala!

–Jonah, do you like to go shopping? (lit.: Is shopping pleasing to you?)

–Yes, I like it a lot. Especially in Guatemala!

When referring to something one likes, as opposed to an activity that one likes, the thing being liked or disliked usually follows **gustar** and is the subject of the verb (i.e., **gustar** agrees with it). Thus, the verb form will either be third person singular (**gusta**) or plural (**gustan**). When referring to whom something is pleasing, use the pronouns **me/te/le** for singular or **nos/os/les** for plural. You will learn more about these pronouns in Chapter 5, Section 2.

Person to whom something is pleasing			Thing(s) liked
(a mí)	*to me*	**me gusta(n)**	**el/la** + *singular noun* **los/las** + *plural noun*
(a ti)	*to you (informal)*	**te gusta(n)**	
(a él/a ella/a usted)	*to him/her to you (formal)*	**le gusta(n)**	
(a nosotros)	*to us*	**nos gusta(n)**	
(a vosotros)	*to you (informal, Spain)*	**os gusta(n)**	**el/la** + *singular noun* **los/las** + *plural noun*
(a ellos/a ellas/ a ustedes)	*to them to you (informal, Lat. Am.; formal, Spain)*	**les gusta(n)**	

–¿**Les gusta** la ropa que hay en los mercados al aire libre?

–Sí, y también **nos gustan** las artesanías.

–Do you like the clothes that they have at open-air markets?

–Yes, and we also like arts and crafts.

• **Le/les** may refer to different people. If the context does not make it clear to whom something is pleasing, the preposition **a** + *the person's name* is used to clarify:

A los padres de Jonah **les gustan** los regalos de Guatemala.

Jonah's parents like the presents from Guatemala.

• To express dislike for something, insert **no** before the pronoun **me, te, le, nos, os, les**. You can express different degrees of liking something using **mucho** or **nada**:

–¿**No** les gusta regatear?

–No, ¡**no** nos gusta **nada**! Pero a Jonah le gusta **mucho**.

–You don't like bargaining?

–No, we don't like it at all! But Jonah likes it a lot.

2.2-06 ¿Qué tal una blusa? Today, Jonah is in the market. Complete the dialogues with **me, te, le, nos, les** and **gusta** or **gustan**.

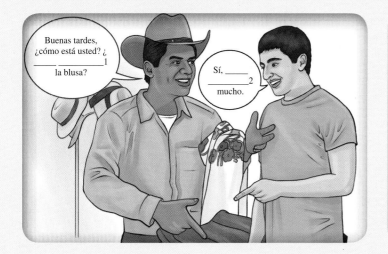

2.2-07 ¿Te gusta o no?

Paso 1: Complete the following sentences with vocabulary words from **Palabra por palabra**. Pay attention to the verb form!

	Estudiante 1	Estudiante 2
1. Me gusta…	_____	_____
2. No me gusta…	_____	_____
3. Me gusta mucho…	_____	_____
4. No me gustan nada…	_____	_____
5. Me gustan muchísimo…	_____	_____

Paso 2: Now change the statements into questions and interview two classmates to find out what they like.

MODELO: 　Estudiante 1: 　*A mí me gusta muchísimo regatear, y a ti,*
　　　　　　　　　　　　 ¿te gusta regatear?
　　　　　 Estudiante 2: 　*No, a mí no me gusta mucho.*

Paso 3: With the information on **Pasos 1 y 2**, write down two sentences with **nos** and two sentences with **les** to report your results to the class.

MODELO: 　*A nosotros tres nos gusta(n)…*
　　　　　　A Pablo y a Miranda (no) les gusta(n) (mucho)…

LA PURA VERDAD II Planes para las vacaciones

Un grupo de amigos que estudian español en México hablan sobre sus planes para las vacaciones de Semana Santa.

2.2-08 **Después de la procesión** Listen to the narration and decide if the sentences are true (**Cierto**) or false (**Falso**).

	CIERTO	FALSO
1. A Sonia no le gusta caminar y pasear.	☐	☐
2. A Ana y a Sonia les gusta la cultura maya.	☐	☐
3. Las dos van a comprar ropa en Santa Cruz.	☐	☐

HABLANDO DE GRAMÁTICA II

2. Expressing future plans: *Ir + a +* infinitive

It is possible to talk about the near future in Spanish by using the verb **ir** + **a** + verb in the infinitive. In Chapter 2, Section 1 you learned that the infinitive is the non-conjugated form of the verb, which in English it consists of two words, like *to buy* (**comprar**), *to eat* (**comer**), and *to live* (**vivir**).

–¿**Vas a comprar** ese vestido verde?	–*Are you going to buy that green dress?*
–No, **voy a comprar** la camiseta marrón.	–*No, I am going to buy the brown t-shirt.*
–Bien, porque después **vamos a ver** más tiendas con otras cosas bonitas.	–*OK, because we are going to see more stores with other beautiful things.*

WileyPLUS Go to *WileyPLUS* to review this grammar point with the help of the **Animated Grammar Tutorial** and the **Verb Conjugator**.

ir (*to go*)			
(yo)	voy	(nosotros/as)	vamos
(tú)	vas	(vosotros/as)	vais
(él, ella, Ud.)	va	(ellos, ellas, Uds.)	van

This construction is used frequently to talk about what we are going to do later today, tomorrow, next week, next month, etc.

Time expressions to talk about future plans	
esta noche	*tonight*
(pasado) mañana	*(the day after) tomorrow*
la semana que viene, la próxima semana	*next week*
el mes/año que viene, el próximo mes/año	*next month/year*
por la mañana/tarde/noche	*in the morning/afternoon/evening*

You can also use **ir** + **a** + *noun* in order to express destination. To ask where someone is going, use the interrogative word **adónde.**

–Sonia ¿**adónde** vas de vacaciones?	–*Where are you going on vacation?*
–**Voy a** Antigua.	–*I'm going to Antigua.*

¡OJO!

a + el = al

2.2-09 ¿Adónde van estas personas y qué van a hacer? Write sentences that describe each of the following drawings.

◀ *Jonah va al mercado. Va a comprar regalos para la familia.*

▲ *1. Jonah…*

▲ *2. Ana y Sonia…*

▲ *3. Mis amigos y yo…*

▲ *4. Los estudiantes de español…*

▲ *5. Esta noche, yo…*

2.2-10 Los planes

 Paso 1: Complete the sentences with information about you.

MODELO: *Esta noche <u>voy a estudiar para la clase de español</u>.*

1. Esta noche…
2. Mañana por la mañana…
3. El próximo sábado…
4. El verano que viene…
5. Las próximas vacaciones…

 Paso 2: Now, change the statements into questions and interview a classmate.

MODELO: Estudiante 1:   *¿Vas a estudiar español esta noche?*
           Estudiante 2:   *No, voy a mirar mi programa favorito.*

 Paso 3: With the information you have gathered, write a short paragraph to report to the class.

MODELO: *Esta noche Nora va a… pero yo voy a…*
           Mañana por la mañana nosotros/as dos vamos a…

 ### 2.2-11 Planes para el fin de semana

 Paso 1: Working with a partner, ask each other questions to find out what these friends did. Each of you has half of the information. Then, ask each other what you are going to do this weekend.

MODELO: Estudiante A: *¿Ana y Sonia <u>van a mirar</u> una película?*
           Estudiante B: *No, no <u>van a mirar</u> una película.*
           Estudiante A: *Y tú, ¿<u>vas a mirar</u> una película?*
           Estudiante B: *Sí, <u>voy a mirar</u>… o No, no <u>voy a mirar</u> una película.*

Estudiante A	Jonah	Ana y Sonia	compañero/a
Mirar una película	sí		
Dormir hasta muy tarde		sí	
Comer en un restaurante	no	no	
Jugar al tenis		sí	
Estudiar en la biblioteca	no		
Mirar la televisión			
Ir de compras			

Estudiante B	Jonah	Ana y Sonia	compañero/a
Mirar una película	no		
Dormir hasta muy tarde	sí		
Comer en un restaurante			
Jugar al tenis	sí		
Estudiar en la biblioteca		sí	
Mirar la televisión	no	no	
Ir de compras	no		

Paso 2: At the end, decide if you have similar plans for the weekend and report to the class.

MODELO: *Mi compañero/a y yo no vamos a hacer las mismas cosas porque él/ella va a… y yo…*

OTRA PERSPECTIVA

Flor

Espacio personal

Diferente

"Pienso que hay más contacto físico en Guatemala. Es posible ver a dos hombres, si son familia o muy amigos, caminar con una mano en el hombro[6] del otro. Es común ver a dos mujeres, si son amigas, caminar del brazo.[7] Los besos[8] y los abrazos son parte de mi vida. En Estados Unidos, ¿los hombres se abrazan? ¿Las mujeres caminan del brazo?"

Igual

"Cuando recién conocemos a alguien,[9] los guatemaltecos le damos la mano, como en EE. UU. En situaciones de trabajo o en el mundo de los negocios es muy común darse la mano. En Guatemala, también nos damos la mano en ocasiones formales, igual que en Estados Unidos".

 Explícale a Flor ¿Qué es más común ver en Estados Unidos?

	muy común	común	poco común
1. Dos mujeres que caminan del brazo por la calle.	☐	☐	☐
2. Dos amigos que se saludan con un abrazo.	☐	☐	☐
3. Dos hombres que se dan la mano.	☐	☐	☐
4. Dos mujeres que se saludan con un beso… dos besos…	☐	☐	☐
5. Dos hombres que caminan con una mano en el hombro.	☐	☐	☐

[6] **hombro:** shoulder [7] **del brazo:** arm in arm [8] **besos:** kisses [9] **cuando recién conocemos a alguien:** when we are meeting someone

MANOS A LA OBRA

 2.2-12 Sitios turísticos You are visiting Guatemala with a friend and you are trying to decide what to do.

Paso 1: Talk to your partner about places of interest to you. You can use these questions:

1. ¿Qué te gusta visitar?
2. ¿Cuándo vas a ir?
3. ¿Qué te gusta?

Paso 2: Decide which places you are visiting. Use transition words such as **pero, porque, y, por ejemplo, también**…

MODELO: *Vamos a visitar Antigua, porque nos gusta la arquitectura colonial y también…*

BIENVENIDOS A GUATEMALA

El Museo Popol Vuh

akg-images/Bildarchiv Steffens

Abierto de lunes a sábado: 9:00 a 12:00 y 14:00 a 17:30

Una de las colecciones de arte de la civilización maya más importante: cerámica, máscaras, esculturas, altares

Antigua, Guatemala

© Ocean/Corbis

- *Ciudad Patrimonio de la Humanidad por la UNESCO*
- *Arquitectura colonial*
- *Patios españoles*
- *Catedral de San José*
- *Museo Colonial*
- *Convento de Santa Catalina*

Las ruinas de Kaminal Juyú

© Radius Images/Alamy

 Abierto de lunes a domingo: 8:00 a 16:00 horas

- *Sitio arqueológico prehispánico*
- *Grandes templos*
- *Campo de fútbol antiguo*
- *Objetos de cerámica*
- *Museo*

Parque Nacional de las Naciones Unidas

© Stefano Paterna/Alamy

- *Espacio verde protegido en el área metropolitana de Ciudad de Guatemala*
- *Lago de Amatitlán*
- *Volcán de Pacaya*
- *Exposición natural de reptiles y serpientes*
- *Actividades de canopy, bicicleta, campamentos*
- *Vistas impresionantes*

2.2-13 ¿Cuánto cuesta? Your instructor will show you articles such as pencils, coins, books, etc. In groups, guess the price of each article. The group that comes the closest to guessing the price, without going over, wins.

2.2-14 Adivinos

Paso 1: In groups, select a classmate and guess what your classmate's future will be like in 20 years.

MODELO: *Esta persona va a ser un profesor muy famoso en una universidad. Va a hablar español muy bien. Va a tener una casa en México y va a tener cinco hijos…*

Paso 2: Taking turns, the leader of each group informs the class about the future of a student. The class will guess the name of the student.

2.2-15 ¿A quién de la clase…? Find out more about the likes and dislikes of your classmates. Move around the classroom and ask a different question to each classmate. Write down the names of those classmates.

MODELO: Estudiante 1: *¿Te gusta el color morado?*
  Estudiante 2: *Sí, me gusta el color morado.*

¿A quién le gusta(n) …   Nombre

  regatear?   _____

  los precios fijos?   _____

  llevar reloj?   _____

  los anillos de oro?   _____

  las faldas?   _____

  las artesanías?   _____

2.2-16 Vacaciones con la clase Pretend you are going on vacation to Mexico or Guatemala with a classmate.

Paso 1: Prepare two lists: List 1 should include four things you would like to buy and the country (Mexico or Guatemala) in which you want to buy them. List 2 should include three places of interest and activities you would like to do in those places.

Paso 2: With your classmate decide which country you will visit, then share your shopping list and places to shop. Select two articles you would like to buy and two places you would like to visit together. One place must be a craft store or an open-air market to buy a present for a classmate, a friend, or a family member. Discuss prices and colors.

MODELO: Estudiante 1: *Vamos a ir a México porque hay...*
  Estudiante 2: *¿Por qué no vamos a Guatemala en la Semana Santa?*
  En Guatemala hay…
  Estudiante 1: *Me gustan las artesanías.*
  Estudiante 2: *A mí también me gustan las artesanías.*
  Estudiante 1: *¿Vamos a comprar al Mercado Central?*
  Estudiante 2: *Sí, vamos al mercado central y al centro de Antigua.*
  Estudiante 1: *¿Vamos a comprar un poncho para John?*
  Estudiante 2: *Sí, pero los ponchos de artesanía son muy caros.*
  Cuestan 200 quetzales…
  Estudiante 1: *Sí, pero vamos a regatear…*

Paso 3: Share the selected present for your classmate, friend, or family member with the whole class.

MODELO: *En Guatemala compramos un poncho gris para John porque a él*
  le gustan mucho los ponchos.

WileyPLUS Go to *WileyPLUS* and listen to **Presta atención**.

2.2-17 Presta atención: De paseo por Guatemala Sonia spends several days in Guatemala. Listen to the audio twice in order to learn more about her vacations. Then, decide whether each statement is true (**Cierto**) or false (**Falso**).

	CIERTO	FALSO
1. Flor es de Iowa.	☐	☐
2. Sonia es amiga de Flor.	☐	☐
3. Flor llama por teléfono a Sonia.	☐	☐
4. Sonia va al mercado central con su amiga.	☐	☐
5. Sonia compra un regalo para Flor.	☐	☐
6. Sonia compra dos pulseras de plata baratas.	☐	☐
7. Flor compra unos pendientes por 100 quetzales.	☐	☐
8. Los pendientes rojos son para la mamá de Sonia.	☐	☐
9. Sonia invita a Flor a comer.	☐	☐
10. Las dos amigas comen comida típica de México.	☐	☐

2.2-18 Por escrito: Planes para ir de compras Think about your favorite store to buy clothes. Then write a paragraph answering the questions below. Make sure that **gustar** and **ir** are conjugated correctly. Do not forget to check for agreement between (a) subjects and verbs; (b) nouns and adjectives; and (c) articles and nouns.

1. ¿Qué tipo de ropa vas a comprar?
2. ¿Qué colores te gustan para la ropa?
3. ¿Qué actividades vas a hacer antes comprar?
4. ¿Cuánto dinero vas a usar para cada compra?
5. ¿Con quién vas a ir a tu tienda favorita?
6. ¿Qué día y cuándo te gusta ir de compras?

¡OJO!

Using connectors
When writing a paragraph use simple connectors such as **primero** (first), **segundo** (second), **tercero** (third), and **finalmente** (finally) or **por último** (lastly). Remember other connectors you have learned in **Estrategias para escribir** Chapter 1, Section 1, such as **y, pero, porque,** and **también**.

PONTE EN MI LUGAR

Estrategias para conversar

Practice using pauses to formulate ideas Novice Spanish speakers tend to make many "sound pauses" (thinking sounds such as *mmm, eeeeeh*) while they are trying to remember the word they need to convey a message. Use the silent pause to formulate your ideas and to find the vocabulary and expression that you need to communicate.

En el mercado You are at an open-air market and want to do some shopping. Decide with a classmate who will be the client and who will be the sales clerk.

Sales clerk: Your goal is to sell all your merchandise and make the most money possible.

Client: Your goal is to buy five presents for your family and spend the least money possible.

MODELO:
Cliente:	*¿Cuánto cuestan estos aretes anaranjados?*
Vendedor:	*Muy baratos. Cuestan 90 pesos solamente.*
Cliente:	*¡90 pesos es mucho! ¿50 pesos?*
Vendedor:	*¡No, no! 75 pesos para ti. Insisto. Es una buena rebaja.*
Cliente:	*No, no me gustan mucho. 50 pesos o nada.*
Vendedor:	*Mira, para ti 60 pesos. Es mi precio final.*
Cliente:	*Bien, voy a comprar los aretes.*

ASÍ ES LA VIDA

Rima

Roja mi chaqueta.	*Red is my jacket.*
Rojo mi pantalón.	*Red are my pants.*
La vergüenza es roja	*Embarrassment is red*
como el corazón.	*as the heart.*

Jaguar you?

Chiste

¿Qué le dice un jaguar a otro jaguar?
Hint: pronounce "jaguar" with a Spanish "J".
Jaguar you?

WileyPLUS Go to *WileyPLUS* to find more **Arroba** activities.

La ropa de Guatemala

Paso 1: Explore in your favorite browser information about the typical Guatemalan clothes. Can you find an image of a **huipil?** Now, answer the following questions:

¿Qué es un huilpil?
¿Qué usos tiene?
¿Qué colores tiene?

Paso 2: Now that you know better the typical **huipil,** do we have in the United States any clothing that could be comparable? Why is it comparable? Bring photos to the class with both clothing items.

VER PARA CREER II: ¡Me gusta regatear!

WileyPLUS Go to *WileyPlus* to see this video and to find more video activities.

Antes de ver

Answer these questions and compare your answers with a classmate:

1. ¿Vas a mercados al aire libre con frecuencia?
2. ¿A qué mercados al aire libre vas?
3. ¿Qué productos compras en los mercados al aire libre?
4. En los mercados al aire libre, ¿son fijos los precios de los productos?
5. ¿Qué es importante hacer para comprar el producto a mejor precio?
6. En los mercados al aire libre que conoces, ¿hay muchos productos para los turistas?

Después de ver

1. ¿Entendiste? What did you understand? Select an answer to see what you know about the information presented in the video.

1. ¿De dónde es Melanie?
   a. Melanie es de Guatemala.
   b. Melanie es de Antigua.
   c. Melanie es de Washington.
2. ¿Dónde vive Melanie ahora?
   a. Vive en Antigua.
   b. Vive en Washington.
   c. Vive en Estados Unidos.
3. ¿Por qué le gusta el mercado a Melanie?
   a. Porque le gusta caminar y regatear.
   b. Porque hay de todo y es barato.
   c. Porque le gustan las flores y ropa.
4. ¿Qué colores de blusas le muestra el vendedor?
   a. Morada, verde y negra
   b. Morada, negra y blanca
   c. Morada, azul y negra
5. ¿Qué tipo de diseño tiene la blusa que le muestra el vendedor?
   a. Tiene un diseño muy artesanal.
   b. Tiene un diseño muy moderno.
   c. Tiene un diseño muy joven.
6. ¿Cuántos quetzales quiere el vendedor por la blusa?
   a. El vendedor quiere 150 quetzales.
   b. El vendedor quiere 80 quetzales.
   c. El vendedor quiere 90 quetzales.

2. Comprar en los mercados Would you like to visit an open-air market in an Spanish-speaking country? Which one?

3. Enfoque cultural Do you bargain in the United States? When and where? What is the difference between bargaining in your country and in a Spanish-speaking country?

AUTOPRUEBA

VOCABULARIO

I. ¿Cómo se dice...

1. ...cuando algo no cuesta mucho dinero?
2. ...cuando negocias con un vendedor para no pagar el precio original?
3. ...cuando el precio no es negociable?
4. ...cuando algo cuesta mucho dinero?
5. ...cuando algo pasa de un precio alto a un precio más bajo?

II. ¿Qué hay en el mercado? What kind of clothes would you sell at a market in Guatemala? Use colors and prices to describe your items.

1. _____
2. _____
3. _____
4. _____
5. _____

III. How much is it in Quetzales? ($1 = 8 quezales)

1. Tres blusas a $15 cada una son _____ quetzales.
2. Cuatro vestidos a $32 cada uno son _____ quetzales.
3. Cinco aretes a $8 cada par son _____ quetzales.
4. Seis DVD a $9 cada uno son _____ quetzales.

GRAMÁTICA

I. ¿Qué te gusta? What do you think the following people like? Select among the following list.

visitar México	la ropa cara
ir de compras	caminar por la ciudad
llevar reloj	mirar a la gente
regatear	los mercados de artesanías

1. yo
2. mi profesor/a de español
3. mis padres
4. mi compañero/a de clase
5. mi amigo/a

II. De viaje por Guatemala You are in Guatemala with your family and some friends. What are all of you going to do there?

1. Mis amigos _____ comprar muchos regalos.
2. Mi hermana _____ estudiar la cultura.
3. Yo _____ visitar los museos.
4. Mi madre _____ caminar por toda la ciudad.
5. Todos nosotros _____ practicar español.

CULTURA

1. Which activity is customary at open-air markets in Guatemala?
2. What's the Guatemalan currency?
3. Mention some interesting places to visit in Guatemala.
4. What do some Guatemalans do for *Semana Santa*?

REDACCIÓN

At the market! Write a paragraph about a day out in the market. You need to buy a few things for a wedding you are attending.

MODELO: El sábado voy a ir al mercado al aire libre. Me voy a comprar... Me gusta...

EN RESUMIDAS CUENTAS, AHORA PUEDO...

☐ negotiate in an open market.

☐ describe clothing.

☐ identify colors.

☐ use numbers from 60 and on.

☐ talk about what I and other people like.

☐ tell what you are planning to do.

☐ understand the different concept of physical contact.

VOCABULARIO ESENCIAL

Sustantivos

el anillo	ring
el arete/pendiente	earring
la artesanía	arts and crafts
la camisa	shirt
el cinturón	belt
la comida	food
la falda	skirt
la flor	flower
el mercado (al aire libre)	outdoors market
el oro	gold
los pantalones	pants
la plata	silver
el precio (fijo)	(fixed) price
la pulsera	bracelet
el regalo	gift
el reloj	watch
la ropa	clothing
el sombrero	hat
el traje	suit
el vestido	dress
las zapatillas de deporte/los tenis	tennis shoes
los zapatos	shoes

Cognados: la blusa, la bota, el color

Verbos

comprar	to buy
gustar	to like
ir	to go
ir de compras	to go shopping
rebajar	to reduce
regalar	to buy a present
regatear	to negotiate price
vender	to sell

Cognados: costar (o-ue), insistir

Expresiones

¿Cuánto cuesta/cuestan...?	How much is/are . . . ?
el mes/año que viene, el próximo mes/año	next month/year
esta noche	tonight
la semana que viene, la próxima semana	next week
Para Ud., Q25. Buen precio...	For you, Q25. It's a good price...
Pase, pase, adelante...	Come in, come in, . . .
(pasado) mañana	(the day after) tomorrow
por la mañana/tarde/noche	in the morning/afternoon/evening
¿Qué llevas?	What are you wearing?
¿Qué busca/desea?	What are you looking for?
¿Qué te gusta llevar?	What do you like to wear?

Adjetivos

amarillo/a	yellow
anaranjado/a/naranja	orange
azul	blue
barato/a	cheap, inexpensive
blanco/a	white
caro/a	expensive
gris	gray
marrón/café	brown
negro/a	black
rojo/a	red
rosado/a	pink
verde	green
violeta/morado/a	purple

Los números

sesenta	sixty
setenta	seventy
ochenta	eighty
noventa	ninety
cien	one hundred
ciento uno	one hundred and one
ciento diez	one hundred and ten
doscientos	two hundred
trescientos	three hundred
cuatrocientos	four hundred
quinientos	five hundred
seiscientos	six hundred
setecientos	seven hundred
ochocientos	eight hundred
novecientos	nine hundred
mil	one thousand
mil uno	one thousand and one
mil cien	one thousand hundred
mil ciento uno	one thousand one hundred and one
dos mil	two thousand
diez mil	ten thousand

La vida doméstica

© John Wiley & Sons, Inc.

VER PARA CREER I: ¡Qué casa tan ecológica!

Watch the video without audio and try to understand the general gist of the video in order to answer the following questions. While watching, try to remember the vocabulary that you have already studied in previous chapters.

Think about what you saw in the video and answer the following questions:

1. Where are the people from the video?

2. In what ways are Costa Rica and the U.S. different or similar from the places you saw in the videos?

Sección 1	**En familia**

PALABRA POR PALABRA

- El árbol genealógico
- Las partes del cuerpo: La apariencia física

HABLANDO DE GRAMÁTICA

- Discussing daily activities (II): Present tense of stem-changing and irregular verbs ♻
- Expressing possession: Possessive adjectives
- Describing physical and emotional states: Expressions with **tener**

CULTURA

- Los dos apellidos
- Diferencias y similitudes con las familias hispanas

Sección 2	**En casa**

PALABRA POR PALABRA

- La casa, los muebles y el vecindario
- Los números del 10.000 en adelante

HABLANDO DE GRAMÁTICA

- Making comparisons: Comparisons of equality and inequality; the superlative
- Expressing location and existence: **Estar** + location and **hay**

CULTURA

- Distintos tipos de viviendas
- La vida en el vecindario: "el qué dirán"

⚙ **Trivia:** Go to *WileyPLUS* to do the **Trivia** activities and find out how much you know about these countries!

Costa Rica y Panamá

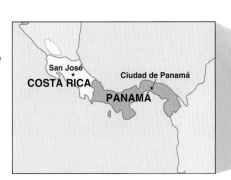

San José
COSTA RICA

Ciudad de Panamá
PANAMÁ

© John Wiley & Sons, Inc.

LEARNING OBJECTIVES

By the end of this section you will be able to:

- Understand the origin of the two last names in Hispanic names
- Recognize and describe family relationships
- Describe people's physical appearances and emotional states
- Describe what you and other people do daily.
- Express age and possession
- Recognize some differences between Spanish and U.S. families

Una imagen vale más que mil palabras

REPUBLICA DE COSTA RICA REGISTRO CIVIL

CERTIFICA

****

```
QUE EN EL REGISTRO DE  M A T R I M O N I O S  DE: LA PROVINCIA DE SAN JOSE
DICE QUE    : MARC DAVID ADAMS ADAMS
C/COMO      : ****************************
DE          : VEINTIDOS AÑOS
NACIONALIDAD: ESTADOUNIDENSE

HIJO DE     : DENIS ADAMS
NACIONALIDAD: ESTADOUNIDENSE
Y DE        : VIRGINIA ADAMS
NACIONALIDAD: ESTADOUNIDENSE

CONTRAJO MATRIMONIO CON:
            : ANA CATALINA SOTO SOLANO
C/COMO      : ****************************
DE          : VEINTITRES AÑOS
NACIONALIDAD: COSTARRICENSE
```

Courtesy of Catalina Adams

◀ *Certificado de matrimonio costarricense*

Examine the document and decide whether the following statements are true (**Cierto**) or false (**Falso**). If they are false, explain why.

	C	F
Este documento certifica dónde vive una persona.	☐	☐
La oficina de registros está en San José, Costa Rica.	☐	☐
Marc es costarricense.	☐	☐
El nombre completo de Marc en Costa Rica es Marc David Adams Adams.	☐	☐

UNA PERSPECTIVA

Courtesy of Elena Atanasiu

Helen

¿Cómo te llamas?

Diferente

"En Costa Rica las personas tienen uno o dos nombres y dos apellidos. Es un poco confuso para mí. Primero va el apellido del padre y después el de la madre. Mi nombre en Estados Unidos es Helen Atanasiu y en Costa Rica es Helen Atanasiu Downie. Downie es el apellido de mi madre".

Igual

"Algunas veces, si el niño tiene el mismo nombre que el papá, 'hijo' se añade[1] al final del nombre. Por ejemplo: Ángel Luis López, hijo. Esto es equivalente a 'Jr.'"

© blickwinkel / Alamy

▲ *Carmen Figueroa, Carlos Álvarez y su hijo Francisco José Álvarez Figueroa.*

 ¿Qué piensas tú?

1. ¿Cómo nombran a los niños en tu país? ¿De dónde viene[2] el primer nombre? ¿Y el segundo nombre? ¿Y el apellido?
2. ¿Cuál es el nombre completo de tu papá? ¿Y el de tu mamá?
3. ¿Cómo sería[3] tu nombre en Costa Rica?

[1] **se añade:** is added [2] **viene:** comes [3] **sería:** would be

LA PURA VERDAD I　Una nueva familia

Marc es estadounidense. Ahora está estudiando en Costa Rica en casa de una familia costarricense.

1.

2.

3.

4.

5.

6.
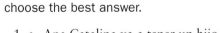

3.1-01　La nueva familia Listen to what Marc's parents say after the phone call and choose the best answer.

1. a. Ana Catalina va a tener un hijo.
   b. Ana Catalina va a casarse con un costarricense.
   c. Marc va a casarse.
2. a. Los padres piensan que Ana Catalina es guapa.
   b. Los padres piensan que Ana Catalina no es muy guapa.
   c. Los padres piensan que va a ser guapa.
3. a. Ellos quieren ir a Costa Rica.
   b. Ellos no planean ir a Costa Rica.
   c. Ellos piensan que cuesta mucho dinero ir a Costa Rica.

🎧 PALABRA POR PALABRA

El árbol genealógico   *Family tree*

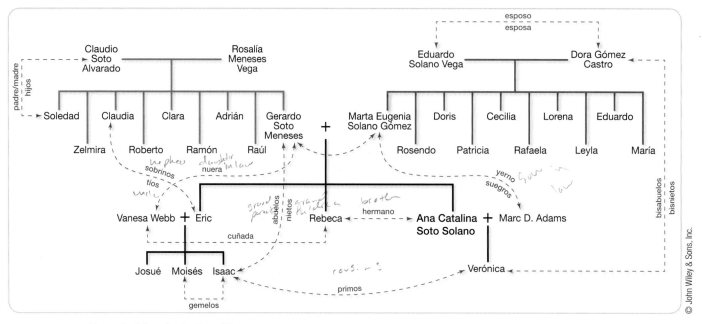

Para hablar de la familia

el apodo	*nickname*
casado/a	*married*
el familiar/pariente	*relative*
el/la hermanastro/a	*stepbrother/stepsister*
la madrastra	*stepmother*
materno/a	*mother's side*
el/la medio/a hermano/a	*half brother/half sister*
el/la novio/a	*boyfriend/girlfriend*
el padrastro	*stepfather*
los padres	*parents, fathers*
paterno/a	*father's side*
soltero/a	*single*

viudo/a	*widow/widower*
casarse	*to get married*

Cognados: divorciado/a, la familia, la mamá, el papá, la relación, separado/a

*Soltero, casado, separado, divorciado, viudo, are accompanied by the verb estar/ser.

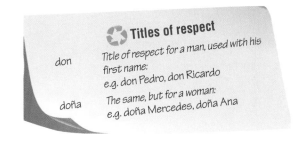

♻ Titles of respect

don — *Title of respect for a man, used with his first name:* e.g. don Pedro, don Ricardo

doña — *The same, but for a woman:* e.g. doña Mercedes, doña Ana

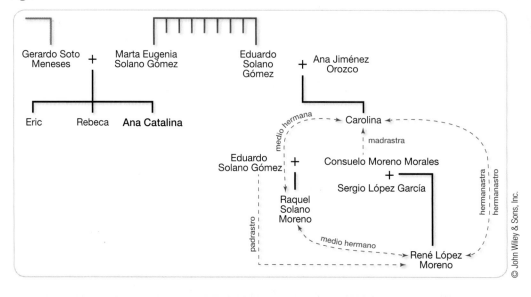

Las partes del cuerpo: La apariencia física

Parts of the body: Physical appearance

Rebecca Emery / Photodisc / Getty Images

- la cabeza
- la nariz
- el pelo
- el ojo
- la oreja
- la boca
- la cara
- los labios
- el diente

¿Qué dicen los ticos (costarricenses)?

¿Cómo estás?	*How are you?*
¡Pura vida!	*Great!*
Es <u>un chunche</u> que me encontré.	*It is a <u>thingy</u> I found.*
*Es muy arrogante. <u>¡No tiene abuela!</u>	*He is a braggart. <u>He toots his own horn!</u> (Lit. He doesn't have a grandmother.)*
Marc va a <u>ahorcarse</u> mañana.	*Marc is going <u>to get married</u> tomorrow.*
*Estoy cansado. <u>Voy a planchar la oreja</u>.	*I am tired. <u>I am going to sleep</u>. (Lit. I am going to iron my ear.)*

*These expressions are also used in other Spanish-speaking countries.

Parecerse	*To look like*
¿A quién te pareces?	*Who do you look like?*
Yo me parezco a mi papá.	*I look like my dad.*
Tú te pareces a tu mamá.	*You look like your mom.*
Él se parece a mí.	*He looks like me.*
Nosotros nos parecemos.	*We look alike.*
Ellos se parecen a...	*They look like. . .*

Courtesy of Laura Marqués-Pascual

3.1-02 ¿Cierto o falso? Look at Ana Catalina's family tree in page 100 and decide whether each statement is true (**Cierto**) or false (**Falso**). Correct the false statements.

C   F

- ☐ ☐ 1. Los dos abuelos de Ana Catalina se llaman Claudio y Eduardo.
- ☐ ☐ 2. La madre de Ana Catalina se llama Verónica.
- ☐ ☐ 3. Ana Catalina tiene once tías.
- ☐ ☐ 4. Verónica tiene tres primos en total.
- ☐ ☐ 5. La nuera de Marta Eugenia se llama Zelmira.
- ☐ ☐ 6. Gerardo tiene tres nietas.

3.1-03 Las personas de la familia Read the following definitions and look for the corresponding word in the **Palabra por palabra** section.

MODELO: Esta persona es la esposa de tu padre, pero no es tu madre.   →   *madrastra*

1. Estas personas son los hijos de tus tíos. _____
2. Esta persona es el esposo de tu hermana. _____
3. Esta persona es el abuelo de tu madre. _____
4. Son un esposo y una esposa legalmente separados. _____
5. Es una persona que no tiene esposo/a. _____
6. Son dos personas que solo tienen el mismo padre o la misma madre. _____

 3.1-04 Un árbol genealógico Build a classmate's family tree using the questions below. Ask more questions if necessary.

1. ¿Cómo se llaman tus padres? ¿Están casados, separados o divorciados?
2. ¿Cómo se llaman tus abuelos paternos? ¿Y tus abuelos maternos?
3. ¿Tu papá tiene hermanos? ¿Y tu mamá? ¿Cuántos?, etc.
4. ¿Tienes hermanos? ¿Cuántos? ¿Cómo se llaman? ¿Tienes hermanastros/as o medios hermanos/as?
5. ¿Tus hermanos están casados? ¿Tienen hijos? ¿Cuántos sobrinos tienes?
6. ¿Tú estás casado/a? ¿Tienes hijos?

 3.1-05 **¿Quién se parece a quién?**

Paso 1: Write five sentences to describe your family. You can write true or false statements.

MODELO: *Yo me parezco a mi mamá. Tenemos los ojos iguales, pero también me parezco a mi abuelo paterno en las orejas.*
            o
            Yo no me parezco a nadie, pero mi hermano se parece a mi papá porque...

Paso 2: Now, with a picture, talk to a classmate and describe your family. Use the sentences from **Paso 1**. Your classmate has to look at the picture and decide if the sentences are true or false.

MODELO: Estudiante 1:   *Ella es mi mamá. Yo me parezco a ella.*
            Estudiante 2:   *Falso, tú no te pareces a tu mamá. En mi opinión, te pareces más a tu papá.*

HABLANDO DE GRAMÁTICA I

1. Discussing daily activities (II): Present tense of stem-changing and irregular verbs ♻

WileyPLUS Go to *WileyPLUS* to review this grammar point with the help of the **Animated Grammar Tutorial** and the **Verb Conjugator**.

A. Stem-changing verbs

Some verbs in Spanish undergo a change in their stem vowel (i.e., the last vowel before the infinitive endings **-ar, -er, -ir**) except for the **nosotros** and **vosotros** forms. The three possible stem changes are o → ue, e → ie, e → i.

Stem-changing verbs

	o → ue	e → ie	e → i
Infinitive:	**contar** *(count)*	**entender** *(understand)*	**repetir** *(repeat)*
(yo)	cuento	entiendo	repito
(tú)	cuentas	entiendes	repites
(él/ella/Ud.)	cuenta	entiende	repite
(nosotros/as)	contamos	entendemos	repetimos
(vosotros/as)	contáis	entendéis	repetís
(ellos/ellas/Uds.)	cuentan	entienden	repiten

Verbs that you will find in this section whose stems change:

o → ue	e → ie	e → i
almorzar *(to have lunch)* **contar** *(to count, to tell)* **costar** *(to cost)* **dormir** *(to sleep)* **encontrar** *(to find)* **jugar** *(to play) (u>ue)* **poder** *(to be able to)* **volver** *(to return)*	**empezar** *(to begin)* **entender** *(to understand)* **perder** *(to lose)* **pensar** *(to think)* **preferir** *(to prefer)* **querer** *(to want)*	**repetir** *(to repeat)* **pedir** *(to ask for, to order)* **servir** *(to serve)*
—**Cuesta** muchísimo volar a Costa Rica; no **encuentro** nada a buen precio. Por eso no **puedo** ir a la boda de Marc y Ana Catalina. —*It costs a lot to fly to Costa Rica; I can't find anything at a good price. For this reason I can't go to Marc and Ana Catalina's wedding.*	—No **entiendo** por qué Marc y Ana Catalina **quieren** casarse en Costa Rica. —*I don't understand why Marc and Ana Catalina want to get married in Costa Rica.*	—Me **piden** el número de Marc. ¿Me **repites** su número, por favor? —*They are asking me for Marc's number. Could you repeat his number to me, please?*

 3.1-06 La sorpresa de Marc Read the following paragraph about the day Marc gave some surprising news to his family.

Marc puede *comunicarse con su familia de Estados Unidos por videoconferencia; es muy barato. La familia de Marc no entiende muy bien cómo es la vida en Costa Rica, por eso, Marc siempre cuenta con todo detalle su vida en San José. Él cuenta qué come, con quién habla y hasta qué mira en la televisión. Hoy piensa darles una sorpresa a sus padres. Está nervioso y no encuentra las palabras adecuadas. Finalmente, empieza con la pregunta: "Mamá, ¿te cuento una gran noticia[4]? ¡Ana Catalina va a ser mi esposa!". Su madre dice: "Hijo, ¡no entiendo nada!", pero su padre dice: "¡Mi hijo no pierde el tiempo!".*

[4]**noticia:** piece of news

Paso 1: Write down all the stem-changing verbs (there are 9 in total). Attention! No all verbs in the paragraph are stem-changing verbs.

MODELO: 1. _____*puede*_____

2. _____   4. _____   6. _____   8. _____

3. _____   5. _____   7. _____   9. _____

Paso 2: ¿Cierto o falso? Read the paragraph again and decide if the following statements are true (**Cierto**) or false (**Falso**). If they are false, write the correct information.

	C	F
1. Llamar a Estados Unidos por videoconferencia <u>cuesta</u> mucho dinero.	☐	☐
2. Hoy sus padres <u>encuentran</u> a Marc muy tranquilo.	☐	☐
3. Marc <u>empieza</u> su confesión con una pregunta.	☐	☐
4. La madre de Marc dice: "Hijo, ¿cuándo <u>vuelves</u>?".	☐	☐
5. El padre <u>piensa</u> que Marc no <u>pierde</u> el tiempo en Costa Rica.	☐	☐

> ♻ Please see **Hablando de gramática** in Chapter 2, Section 1 for present tense of regular verbs.

♻ **3.1-07 El Canal de Panamá**

Paso 1: In order to know more about the Panama Canal complete the paragraph with the correct form of verbs from the list.

> repetir   costar   pensar   empezar   poder   tener

Cuando los barcos llegan al Canal, _____₁ el viaje por el océano Atlántico. Si no pasan por el Canal, los barcos _____₂ que dar toda la vuelta⁵ por América del Sur. Muchos barcos _____₃ este viaje muchas veces al año, pero hay restricciones para pasar. Por ejemplo, los barcos no _____₄ medir⁶ más de 110 pies de ancho⁷. El precio es bastante caro y depende del tamaño⁸; _____₅ de $1.500 a más de $140.000 por barco. ¿Tú _____₆ que es caro?

Paso 2: Now, write a short paragraph (4-5 sentences) in order to answer the following questions. In your paragraph use these verbs:

> querer   preferir   pensar   tener

1. ¿Quieres visitar el Canal de Panamá? ¿Por qué?
2. ¿Hay algún canal similar en Estados Unidos?
3. ¿Qué otros lugares de interés hay en Panamá?

MODELO: *El Canal de Panamá es famoso porque... Pienso que...*

▲ *Los barcos pasan por el Canal de Panamá todos los días.*

© Frans Lanting/Corbis

B. Irregular verbs

There are some verbs in Spanish with an irregular first-person (**yo**) form. You can think of these as "**-go**" verbs:

Verbs with an irregular yo form

Infinitive:	hacer *(to do, to make)*	poner *(to put, to place)*	salir *(to leave, to go out)*	traer *(to bring)*
(yo)	**hago**	**pongo**	**salgo**	**traigo**
(tú)	haces	pones	sales	traes
(él/ella/Ud.)	hace	pone	sale	trae
(nosotros/as)	hacemos	ponemos	salimos	traemos
(vosotros/as)	hacéis	ponéis	salís	traéis
(ellos/ellas/Uds.)	hacen	ponen	salen	traen

⁵ **dar toda la vuelta:** to go around ⁶**medir:** to measure ⁷**ancho:** width ⁸**tamaño:** size

Salir is used with different prepositions depending on what you want to express. Use **salir de** to talk about leaving a certain place. Use **salir con** to talk about going out with someone:

Salgo de casa a las 5 de la tarde.   I leave the house at 5 in the afternoon.
Vamos a **salir con** nuestros amigos   We are going out with our friends from
    de Costa Rica.   Costa Rica.

Some other verbs are irregular in the **yo** form and all other forms except for **nosotros** and **vosotros**. Notice that **venir** is a stem-changing verb (**e → ie**) with an irregular **yo** form.

Infinitive:	**venir** (to come)	**oír** (to hear)
(yo)	**vengo**	**oigo**
(tú)	**vie**nes	**oy**es
(él/ella/Ud.)	**vie**ne	**oy**e
(nosotros/as)	venimos	oímos
(vosotros/as)	venís	oís
(ellos/ellas/Uds.)	**vie**nen	**oy**en

 3.1-08 El e-mail de Marc Marc is in Costa Rica and he writes an e-mail to his friend Steve, who studies Spanish in the United States.

Paso 1: Help him complete this e-mail with the correct form of the following verbs:

> hacer (x2)   pensar   practicar   volver   venir   contar   poder   salir (x2)   traer   querer

---

Asunto: ¡Pura vida!

Hola Steve:

¿Qué tal va todo? **¿Cómo va tu vida universitaria?** La vida en San José es genial y mi familia costarricense es muy simpática. Todas las mañanas _____, de casa a las 9 para ir al curso intensivo de español. Hablo español cada día mejor. ¡Ahora _____₂ chistes en español! Tú también estudias español, ¿no? **¿Tú** _____₃ **que es difícil? ¿Por qué** _____₄ **aprender esta lengua?**
   Por las tardes (5) _____₅ ejercicio en el gimnasio. **¿Tú qué deportes** _____₆**?** Cuando _____₇ a casa, paso por el mercado. ¡Siempre _____₈ fruta a casa porque mi madre costarricense _____₉ unos licuados⁹ deliciosos! **¿Cuándo** _____₁₀ **a visitarme?** ¡Así tú _____₁₁ practicar español! **¿Cuáles son tus planes?** Bueno, _____₁₂ con unos amigos en cinco minutos, otro día escribo más. ¡Espero tu respuesta!

¡Pura vida!
Marc

Paso 2: Imagine that you are Steve. Write an e-mail to Marc. Answer the questions in bold.

 3.1-09 Preguntas personales First, answer the following questions about your daily routine. Pay attention to the conjugation of the verbs! Then, use the questions to interview a classmate. Write down his/her answers and present this information to the class.

1. ¿Entiendes todo en clase?
2. Cuándo haces la tarea de español, ¿antes o después de clase?
3. ¿Oyes música mientras estudias español?
4. ¿Dónde pones tu libro y tu cuaderno cuando vas a clase?
5. ¿A qué hora sales de tu casa para venir a clase?
6. ¿Siempre traes todos los materiales necesarios para la clase?

⁹ licuados: smoothies

LA PURA VERDAD II Ahora es "nuestro"

Marc y Ana Catalina miran el álbum de boda con la familia de Marc.

1.

2.

3.

4.

5.

6.

© John Wiley & Sons, Inc.

3.1-10 Ahora es "nuestro" Listen to the narration. Then, change what you hear from "mine" to "ours." Hint: Pay attention to the endings (number and gender).

1. _____
2. _____
3. _____
4. _____
5. _____

HABLANDO DE GRAMÁTICA II

2. Expressing possession: Possessive adjectives

Possessive adjectives in English show ownership: *his* book, *their* house. Just like in English, Spanish possessive adjectives are always placed in front of the noun, but they need to agree in number and, if applicable, also in gender, with the noun that follows.

WileyPLUS Go to *WileyPLUS* to review this grammar point with the help of the **Animated Grammar Tutorial**.

yo	**mi(s)**	*my*
tú	**tu(s)**	*your (informal)*
él/ella/Ud.	**su(s)**	*his, her, your (formal)*

nosotros/as	**nuestro(s), nuestra(s)**	*our*
vosotros/as	**vuestro(s), vuestra(s)**	*your (informal, Spain)*
ellos/ellas/Uds.	**su(s)**	*their, your (formal)*

Here are some examples of the use of Spanish possessive adjectives that show agreement in number and gender with the noun that follows:

¡OJO!

mi yerno — *my son-in-law*
su tío — *his/her uncle/their uncle*
nuestra abuel**a** — *our grandmother*

mis yerno**s** — *my sons-in-law*
sus tío**s** — *their uncles, your* (formal) *uncles*
nuestras abuel**as** — *our grandmothers*

Accents
Accents are important to differentiate words such as **tú**, which means *you*, and **tu**, which means *your*.

In English, sometimes there is a distinction of gender in the possessive adjective depending on the possessor: *his* mother, *her* mother. On the contrary, Spanish adjectives agree in number and gender with the noun that follows, not with the possessor:

nuestr**os** herman**os** — *our brothers*
nuestr**as** herman**as** — *our sisters*

Note that the possessive adjective **su(s)** can have various meanings. For example, in the sentence **Su hermano está en Panamá** we are not sure whose brother he is. When the context can't clarify the owner, use **de**: **¿El hermano *de quién*? El hermano *de Felipe.***

 3.1-11 ¿Quién es quién en esta familia? Match the people with their relatives.

Pablo dice:
1. Jorge
2. Rosario y Rafael
3. Dolores

a. es **mi** madre.
b. son **mis** abuelos.
c. es **mi** hermano.

Rosario y Rafael dicen:
4. Jorge y Anita
5. Dolores
6. Paco

d. es **nuestro** yerno.
e. es **nuestra** hija.
f. son **nuestros** nietos.

3.1-12 ¿De quién es? Complete the sentences with the possessive adjectives and the corresponding nouns to know what these people say.

Modelo

Es <u>mi casa</u> y es <u>mi bicicleta</u>.

▲ ¿Qué dice Antoñito?

David, aquí tienes... y, Yeon Mi, aquí tienes...

▲ 1. ¿Qué dice la profesora?

Señora, aquí tiene... y...

▲ 2. ¿Qué dice Sara?

Él es...

Y ellas son...

▲ 3. ¿Qué dicen los abuelos?

Niños, aquí tienen...

▲ 4. ¿Qué dice la abuela?

Ella es... y ellos...

▲ 5. ¿Qué dice Antonio?

3. Describing physical and emotional states: Expressions with *tener*

An important stem-changing verb with an irregular **yo** form is **tener** (*to have*). **Tener** is used to express ownership:

Tengo tres hermanos, pero **no tengo** hermanas.	*I have three brothers, but I don't have any sisters.*
En casa **tenemos** dos animales, un perro y un gato.	*At home we have two pets, a dog and a cat.*

WileyPLUS Go to *WileyPLUS* to review this grammar point with the help of the **Animated Grammar Tutorial** and the **Verb Conjugator.**

Tener (to have)	
(e → ie)	
(yo)	**tengo**
(tú)	**tie**nes
(él/ella/Ud.)	**tie**ne
(nosotros/as)	tenemos
(vosotros/as)	tenéis
(ellos/ellas/Uds.)	**tie**nen

Tener is also used in some "fixed" expressions (**tener** + *noun*) that can't be translated literally. Most of these expressions are translated as *to be* + *adjective* in English.

tener... años	to be. . . years old	**tener sed**	to be thirsty
tener razón	to be right	**tener frío**	to be cold
tener sueño	to be sleepy	**tener calor**	to be hot
tener miedo	to be afraid	**tener (buena/mala) suerte**	to have (good/bad) luck
tener hambre	to be hungry	**tener ganas de...** *(+ infinitive)*	to feel like (doing something)

¿Cuántos años **tienes**? **Tengo** 20 años, ¿y tú?	*How old are you? I am 20 years old, and you?*
Tengo sed. **Tengo** ganas de tomar un refresco.	*I am thirsty. I feel like having a soda.*
Creo que **tienes** razón.	*I think you are right.*
Tienen hambre y quieren comer ya.	*They are hungry and they want to eat already.*
¿**Tienes** calor? ¿Abro la puerta?	*Are you hot? Should I open the door?*

To indicate *very*, use **mucho/a** before the noun:

Tienes mucho sueño, ¿verdad?	*You are very sleepy, aren't you?*

3.1-13 La fiesta del abuelo Match these situations with the **tener** expressions in the second column to describe this birthday party.

_____ 1. Esta noche vamos a celebrar el cumpleaños de mi abuelo.

_____ 2. Vamos a comer ahora porque mi hermano Juan...

_____ 3. A mi cuñada Cristina no le gusta el aire acondicionado porque siempre...

_____ 4. Mi novio y yo bebemos mucha limonada.

_____ 5. Mis primos Isabel y Jorge quieren dormir en el sofá porque...

_____ 6. Mi padrastro abre la ventana porque...

_____ 7. Al final todos mis familiares y yo jugamos al bingo, ¡y mi tío gana mucho dinero! Él siempre...

a. tiene mucha hambre.

b. tiene mucha suerte.

c. tiene mucho calor.

d. ¡Tenemos mucha sed!

e. tiene frío.

f. tienen mucho sueño.

g. ¡Ya tiene 72 años!

3.1-14 ¡No sé nada de Costa Rica!

Paso 1: Carolina, Marc's friend from Mexico, asks questions about Costa Rica. Complete the dialogue using an expression with **tener** in the correct form.

Carolina: ¿Qué comida es buena en Costa Rica?

Marc: Si[10] _____₁, puedes comer un "casado". Es un plato combinado de varias cosas. Es riquísimo. Si _____₂, una limonada es perfecta.

Carolina: ¿Debo llevar un suéter?

Marc: En Costa Rica no vas a _____₃. Es un clima tropical.

Carolina: _____₄ de ir a una playa[11]. ¿Cuál me recomiendas?

Marc: Si te interesa el ecoturismo, te recomiendo la playa Bejuco.

Carolina: ¿Hay tiburones[12]? Yo les _____₅ a los tiburones.

Marc: Eso, ¡no sé!

Paso 2: Now, write a paragraph (4–5 sentences) in order to answer the following questions. Use expressions with **tener** in your paragraph.

1. ¿Quieres visitar Costa Rica? ¿Por qué?
2. ¿Tienes ganas de comer comida costarricense?
3. ¿Qué otros lugares de interés hay en Costa Rica que tienes ganas de visitar?

MODELO: *Quiero visitar Costa Rica porque... Tengo ganas de...*

▲ *Carolina va a comer el tradicional "casado" costarricense.*

▲ *Playa Bejuco*

¹⁰**si:** if ¹¹**playa:** beach ¹²**tiburones:** sharks

3.1-15 ¿Quién aquí...? Ask and respond to questions following the model. Write down your classmate's name when his or her answer is affirmative. The first one to complete a vertical or horizontal line with affirmative answers wins!

MODELO: Estudiante 1:   *¿Tienes miedo a la oscuridad?*
                 Estudiante 2:   *Sí, tengo miedo a la oscuridad.*

PURA VIDA			
Tiene ganas de ir a Costa Rica.	Tiene hambre ahora.	Tiene sueño.	Tiene frío.
Tiene ganas de tomar una siesta.	Tiene un abuelo que no tiene dientes.	Tiene calor.	Prefiere caminar a correr.
Tiene miedo a los tiburones.	Viene de otro país.	No tiene hermanos.	Entiende todo lo que dice la profesora.
Duerme menos de 6 horas.	Tiene una familia grande (6+).	Juega al fútbol con sus parientes.	No se parece a sus padres.
Tiene la nariz igual que su padre/ madre.	Hace ejercicio por la mañana.	Pone sus libros en una mochila.	Tiene menos de 20 años.

 3.1-16 ¿Tenemos familias similares?

Paso 1: Write down five statements about your family using **mi/mis** with words from **Palabra por palabra**.

MODELO: *Mis primas son gemelas y tienen veinte años.*

Paso 2: Using your previous sentences write at least five questions for your classmates. Use **tu/tus** or **su/sus** if necessary. Then interview two of your classmates to find out.

Estudiante 1:   *¿Tienes primas o primos? ¿Tus primas son gemelas? ¿Tu prima tiene veinte años?*
Estudiante 2:   *Sí, tengo dos primos. Mis primos no son gemelos, pero uno de mis primos tiene veinte años...*

Paso 3: Find out which classmate has a family similar to yours and then explain why your families are similar.

MODELO: *Nuestras familias son muy similares. Nuestros primos...*

Courtesy of Alejandra Barciela

◀ *Los hermanos Barciela en una celebración con sus respectivos hijos y esposos.*

OTRA PERSPECTIVA

Courtesy of Tania Lizarazo

Tania

¿Con quién vives?

Diferente

"Somos la familia Durán. Mi papá se llama Fabio Durán y mi mamá, Antonieta Mora. Mi hermano mayor, Fernando, está casado y tiene gemelos. Mis otros hermanos, Carmelo y Marianela, viven en casa con nuestros padres. Carmelo tiene 25 años y Marianela tiene 31 años. No es raro que los hijos adultos vivan en la casa de sus padres. ¿Por qué los hijos en Estados Unidos deben irse a los 18 años?"

Igual

"Las familias ahora son más pequeñas que en el pasado, igual que en Estados Unidos".

Explícale a Tania ¿Qué es más común en Estados Unidos? Comenta con tu compañero/a.

	Muy común	Común	Neutral	Poco frecuente	Nada frecuente
1. Un abuelo que vive con sus hijos y nietos	☐	☐	☐	☐	☐
2 Una familia con más de cinco hijos	☐	☐	☐	☐	☐
3. Padres divorciados	☐	☐	☐	☐	☐
4. Un(a) hijo(a) de 26 años que vive con sus padres	☐	☐	☐	☐	☐
5. Un(a) muchacho(a) soltero(a) de 22 años que no vive con sus padres	☐	☐	☐	☐	☐
6. Tener medios hermanos y hermanas	☐	☐	☐	☐	☐

MANOS A LA OBRA

3.1-17 Una familia ideal In groups of three or four, decide which two students in the class make an ideal couple. Build a family tree using your classmate's names and decide who are the couple's children, grandchildren, and relatives. Make sure you use the correct possessive adjectives. Then present the family tree to the rest of the class.

MODELO: *Karen es la esposa de Tom. Ellos son un matrimonio perfecto.*
            Tienen tres hijos. Sus hijos son...

3.1-18 ¡Hablemos de la familia!

Paso 1: Do you want to know more about your classmates' family? Walk around the class asking questions to three students. Write down their answers.

1. ¿A quién te pareces de tu familia? ¿En qué te pareces (boca, pelo, orejas...)?

	Estudiante 1	Estudiante 2	Estudiante 3
A quién:	a. _____	b. _____	c. _____
En qué:	a. _____	b. _____	c. _____

2. ¿A quiénes ves más, a tu familia materna o a tu familia paterna? ¿Prefieres a tu familia materna o paterna? ¿Por qué?

	Estudiante 1	Estudiante 2	Estudiante 3
A quién veo:	a. _____	b. _____	c. _____
A quién prefiero:	a. _____	b. _____	c. _____
Por qué:	a. _____	b. _____	c. _____

3. ¿Qué parientes tienes (bisabuelos, primos, sobrinos, nietos, suegros)? ¿Cómo se llaman? ¿Cuántos años tienen?

	Estudiante 1	Estudiante 2	Estudiante 3
Parientes:	a. _____	b. _____	c. _____
Nombres:	a. _____	b. _____	c. _____
Años:	a. _____	b. _____	c. _____

4. ¿Qué tienes ganas de hacer con tu familia? ¿Piensas hacer algo especial o diferente?

	Estudiante 1	Estudiante 2	Estudiante 3
Tengo ganas de:	a. _____	b. _____	c. _____
Pienso hacer:	a. _____	b. _____	c. _____

5. ¿A qué juegan cuando están en una fiesta familiar? En las fiestas familiares, ¿qué almuerzan o cenan?

	Estudiante 1	Estudiante 2	Estudiante 3
Jugamos:	a. _____	b. _____	c. _____
Almorzamos/ Cenamos:	a. _____	b. _____	c. _____

6. ¿Tienes más tíos por el lado materno o por el lado paterno? ¿Qué tíos y primos van a las fiestas familiares?

	Estudiante 1	Estudiante 2	Estudiante 3
Tengo:	a. _____	b. _____	c. _____
Van:	a. _____	b. _____	c. _____

Paso 2: In groups of six, compare your answers to each question and mark the answers you have in common with other students. Then, the leader of the group informs the whole class:

MODELO: *En nuestro grupo, muchos estudiantes se parecen a sus madres en el pelo.*

3.1-19 La pareja ideal

Paso 1: Fill out the column "Para mí" with the characteristics of what would be your "ideal partner." Then, ask two classmates about their ideal partner.

MODELO: Estudiante 1: *¿Cómo es tu pareja ideal? ¿Cuántos años tiene?*
Estudiante 2: *Para mí, la pareja ideal tiene aproximadamente…*

	Para mí	Para mi compañero/a 1	Para mi compañero/a 2
Edad			
Estatura			
Pelo			
Se parece a…			
Boca			
Ojos			
Su carácter debe ser…			
Su carácter no debe ser…			

Paso 2: Share your ideas with your classmates: *¿Piensas que hay algún estudiante que se parece a la "pareja ideal" de tu compañero/a? ¿A quién recomiendas como su posible "pareja ideal"? ¿Una persona de la clase? ¿Una persona famosa?*

MODELO: *Pienso que la pareja ideal de mi compañero/a puede ser Paula, porque…*

3.1-20 **Presta atención: ¿Es lógico?** Indicate whether each statement you hear is logical (**Lógico**) or illogical (**Ilógico**) based on a series of statements that you will hear. If it is illogical, explain why.

WileyPLUS Go to *WileyPLUS* and listen to **Presta atención.**

	Lógico	Ilógico
1.	☐	☐
2.	☐	☐
3.	☐	☐
4.	☐	☐
5.	☐	☐

¡OJO!

Writing an e-mail
When writing the e-mail in Paso 2, use your knowledge of writing and receiving e-mails in English. Complete as follows: 1) **De:** (write your name and address); 2) **Para:** (write the name of the person you send the message); 3) **Asunto:** (indicate what the e-mail is about, i.e., **Mi familia**). Use connectors to present your ideas in a logical order. When editing your message, make sure the content is well organized.

3.1-21 **Por escrito: Tu primo panameño** You have a second cousin in Panama who you didn't know. He has found you on Facebook. He wants to write a report about your mother's side of the family and needs a short paragraph about your family.

Paso 1: Begin by writing down a list with the following information: members of your family, physical descriptions for each member, age (mother, father. . .), nationalities, personalities, and occupation.

Paso 2: Use the previous list to write an e-mail (short paragraph) to your cousin about your family. Do not forget to include a greeting (*Querido primo...*) and good-bye (*Responde pronto, un beso...*).

Paso 3: Then, in class: (a) Exchange your email with a classmate. (b) Review the conjugations for all verbs and do the necessary corrections. (c) Respond to your classmate's email. (d) Rewrite your email using your classmate's comments. (e) Pass the message and answer to your instructor.

PONTE EN MI LUGAR

Estrategias para conversar

Keeping the conversation going During the conversation, feel free to express your own opinion by showing agreement or disagreement with others. The following are expressions you should try to learn as "chunks of language" in order to keep your conversation going.

Agreement:		**Disagreement:**	
Por supuesto.	*Of course.*	No tiene(s) razón.	*You are wrong.*
Tiene(s) razón.	*You are right.*	De ninguna manera.	*No way.*
Estoy de acuerdo.	*I agree.*	No estoy de acuerdo.	*I disagree.*

Tu familia costarricense

Paso 1: In the summer you are going to study and live in Costa Rica. You need to call your Costa Rican family to ask them a few questions. Write down the questions.

Paso 2: With a partner take turns playing the Costa Rican father or mother to respond questions from **Paso 1**. In your answers use the expressions from **Estrategias para conversar** to express agreement or disagreement when possible.

WileyPLUS Go to *WileyPLUS* to find more **Arroba** activities.

El viaje You would like to travel this summer to San Jose, Costa Rica. Search in your favorite browser for information in Spanish to look for a round-trip flight. In which days and times are the tickets cheaper? How many connections do you have? In which month are you flying? When do you return to the U.S.? Write a paragraph with that information and compare your results with your classmates. With the whole class decide who found the cheapest ticket and share this information with your instructor in Spanish.

ASÍ ES LA VIDA

Adivina, adivinador

1. Dos padres y dos hijos caminan por la calle. ¿Cuántas personas hay en el grupo?
2. Cada uno de los tres hermanos tiene una hermana. ¿Cuántos son en total?

© John Wiley & Sons, Inc.

Chiste

Unos padres que esperan su segundo hijo piensan qué nombre le van a poner. Deciden llamarlo Roberto. Su otro hijo de 3 años escucha atentamente y, muy contento, dice: "¡Ah, qué bueno! ¡Ahora vamos a pensar en los apellidos!".

ENTÉRATE

Estrategias para leer

Identifying the main idea When reading for comprehension, the first sentence usually states the topic or the main idea of a text. The following sentences provide additional information, comparisons, and examples to support the main idea. The last sentence summarizes the main idea of the reading. These sentences will give you the *who* and the *what* in order to identify the main idea of the reading passage.

Antes de leer

1. Tu familia Think about your family and select three expressions or words to describe the concept of family according to your culture.

☐ Núcleo de la familia   ☐ Apoyo moral

☐ Parientes de la familia   ☐ Encuentros frecuentes

☐ Amigos   ☐ Fiestas familiares

2. La familia de Jorge Jorge is from Monteverde, Costa Rica, but now he is an exchange student and lives in Michigan with an American family. Jorge writes on his blog about the concept of the Hispanic family. Scan the reading **"La vida en familia"** to identify the main idea. What cognates did you find while you were scanning?

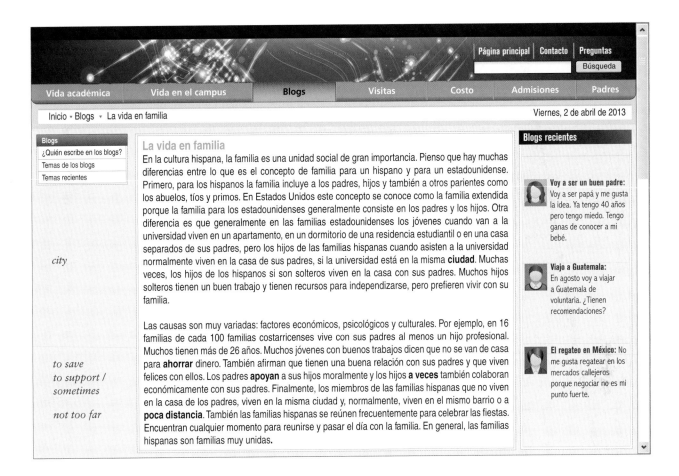

Página principal | Contacto | Preguntas

Búsqueda

| Vida académica | Vida en el campus | Blogs | Visitas | Costo | Admisiones | Padres |

Inicio ▾ Blogs ▾ La vida en familia   Viernes, 2 de abril de 2013

Blogs
- ¿Quién escribe en los blogs?
- Temas de los blogs
- Temas recientes

city

to save
to support /
sometimes

not too far

La vida en familia

En la cultura hispana, la familia es una unidad social de gran importancia. Pienso que hay muchas diferencias entre lo que es el concepto de familia para un hispano y para un estadounidense. Primero, para los hispanos la familia incluye a los padres, hijos y también a otros parientes como los abuelos, tíos y primos. En Estados Unidos este concepto se conoce como la familia extendida porque la familia para los estadounidenses generalmente consiste en los padres y los hijos. Otra diferencia es que generalmente en las familias estadounidenses los jóvenes cuando van a la universidad viven en un apartamento, en un dormitorio de una residencia estudiantil o en una casa separados de sus padres, pero los hijos de las familias hispanas cuando asisten a la universidad normalmente viven en la casa de sus padres, si la universidad está en la misma **ciudad**. Muchas veces, los hijos de los hispanos si son solteros viven en la casa con sus padres. Muchos hijos solteros tienen un buen trabajo y tienen recursos para independizarse, pero prefieren vivir con su familia.

Las causas son muy variadas: factores económicos, psicológicos y culturales. Por ejemplo, en 16 familias de cada 100 familias costarricenses vive con sus padres al menos un hijo profesional. Muchos tienen más de 26 años. Muchos jóvenes con buenos trabajos dicen que no se van de casa para **ahorrar** dinero. También afirman que tienen una buena relación con sus padres y que viven felices con ellos. Los padres **apoyan** a sus hijos moralmente y los hijos **a veces** también colaboran económicamente con sus padres. Finalmente, los miembros de las familias hispanas que no viven en la casa de los padres, viven en la misma ciudad y, normalmente, viven en el mismo barrio o a **poca distancia**. También las familias hispanas se reúnen frecuentemente para celebrar las fiestas. Encuentran cualquier momento para reunirse y pasar el día con la familia. En general, las familias hispanas son familias muy unidas.

Blogs recientes

Voy a ser un buen padre: Voy a ser papá y me gusta la idea. Ya tengo 40 años pero tengo miedo. Tengo ganas de conocer a mi bebé.

Viajo a Guatemala: En agosto voy a viajar a Guatemala de voluntaria. ¿Tienen recomendaciones?

El regateo en México: No me gusta regatear en los mercados callejeros porque negociar no es mi punto fuerte.

Después de leer

1. En el texto Identify two possessive adjectives in the reading and at least one sentence with information to support the main idea of the text.

2. ¿Entendiste? Indicate whether the following sentences are true (**Cierto**) or false (**Falso**). If the sentence is false, correct the statement.

	C	F
1. No hay diferencias entre las familias hispanas y las estadounidenses.	☐	☐
2. La familia hispana incluye a los padres, hijos y parientes.	☐	☐
3. Los hispanos cuando van a la universidad en su ciudad viven con sus padres.	☐	☐
4. Los jóvenes solteros viven con sus padres porque no tienen trabajo.	☐	☐
5. Los miembros de una familia hispana viven en la misma ciudad.	☐	☐

EN TUS PROPIAS PALABRAS

Now write a short composition about your family and traditions in your family. When writing your composition, answer the following questions:

- ¿En qué consiste la familia para ti?
- ¿Vives cerca o lejos de tu familia? ¿Por qué?
- ¿Cómo es tu relación con tu familia?
- ¿Dónde viven tus abuelos?
- ¿Con qué frecuencia se reúne tu familia para celebrar fiestas?
- ¿Tus padres te apoyan económicamente?

Estrategias para escribir

Generating ideas Before writing your first draft, brainstorm your ideas related to the family topic. In order to generate ideas and add content to your writing think about what your readers want to know and give information about *who* (**¿quién?**), *what* (**¿qué?, ¿cuál?**), *where* (**¿dónde?**), *when* (**¿cuándo?**), *why* (**¿por qué?**) and *how* (**¿cómo?**). You can also use these words to ask questions about similar or different topics that you would like your reader to answer.

AUTOPRUEBA

VOCABULARIO

I. ¿Quién es quién? You want to get to know the family of your Costa Rican friend. Your friend explains who each person is.

MODELO: Estudiante 1:   *¿Quién es ella?*
Estudiante 2:   *Es la hermana de mi padre, o sea, es mi tía.*

1. ... ella? Es la esposa de mi hermano, o sea, es mi _____.
2. ... él? Es el esposo de mi tía, o sea, es mi _____.
3. ... ella? Es la madre de mi sobrino, o sea, es mi _____.
4. ... ella? Es la hija de mi tía, o sea, es mi _____.
5. ... él? Es el padre de mi esposo, o sea, es mi _____.

II. ¿Cómo se dice? Tell a friend the word in Spanish for the following:

1. No estar casado/a
2. Separación legal
3. Un título de respeto antes de un nombre
4. Otra palabra para "familiares"
5. Un nombre que dan los amigos o familiares

GRAMÁTICA

I. Mi primo Fill in the blanks to learn more about an interesting relative. Use the appropriate forms of the verbs below.

pensar   empezar (x2)   almorzar   volver
poder   contar   querer   dormir   preferir

Mi primo Roberto es diferente. Yo _____₁ que no es muy normal. Todos nosotros _____₂ el día con un "buenos días", pero él _____₃ con el periódico porque _____₄ hablar de política. Él _____₅ ser el presidente de Costa Rica algún día y no _____₆ hablar de otra cosa. Él desayuna, _____₇ y cena política. Siempre _____₈ historias y cosas interesantes de los gobernantes. Algunas veces se _____₉ con el periódico en la mano y al día siguiente, ¡_____₁₀ al mismo tema!

II. Reuniones familiares In a family reunion we see interesting things. Choose the most logical explanation to the questions below.

1. ¿Por qué Quique mira el reloj constantemente?
   a. Porque tiene hambre.
   b. Porque tiene prisa.
   c. Porque tiene sed.
2. ¿Por qué Félix come mucho?
   a. Porque tiene razón.
   b. Porque tiene miedo.
   c. Porque tiene hambre.
3. ¿Por qué es tan pequeño mi sobrino?
   a. Porque tiene tres años.
   b. Porque tiene sueño.
   c. Porque tiene frío.
4. ¿Por qué llora el bebé?
   a. Porque tiene hambre.
   b. Porque tiene prisa.
   c. Porque tiene razón.
5. ¿Por qué beben agua fría?
   a. Porque tienen frío.
   b. Porque tienen calor.
   c. Porque tienen miedo.

III. ¿Cómo es mi familia? Fill in the blanks with the right possessive adjective in order to find out about a family tradition.

Cuando yo visito a _____₁ familia, a veces _____₂ padres organizan una fiesta familiar. Siempre viene _____₃ tío Alberto. Es el único hermano de _____₄ padre. _____₅ esposa se llama Juliana. Ella viene de una familia muy grande. _____₆ hermanos (los hermanos de ella) se llaman Andrés, Marta, Luis, Gregorio, Ana y Francisco. _____₇ hermano Roberto y _____₈ esposa Irene tienen cuatro hijos. Ellos dicen: "_____₉ hijos son todos muy inteligentes. _____₁₀ dos hijos mayores son médicos y _____₁₁ dos hijas son profesoras". _____₁₂ fiestas familiares siempre son muy divertidas.

CULTURA

1. ¿Qué quiere decir "pura vida"?
2. ¿Qué se considera "familia" en Costa Rica?
3. Si el papá se llama Ángel Luis López Román y la mamá se llama Lina Rosa Santos Rodríguez, ¿cuáles son los apellidos de su hijo, Rafael?

REDACCIÓN

Describe your favorite relative. Include his/her name, nickname, relationship, marital status, age, personality, what activities (s)he likes, and why this person is your favorite relative. Do you look like this relative?

EN RESUMIDAS CUENTAS, AHORA PUEDO...

- ☐ understand why many Hispanics have two last names.
- ☐ name family relationships.
- ☐ describe someone's marital status.
- ☐ describe physical resemblance of family members.
- ☐ talk about what families do.
- ☐ say to whom something belongs.
- ☐ describe physical and emotional states with the verb **tener**.
- ☐ say how old a person is.
- ☐ recognize some differences between Spanish and U.S. families.

🎧 VOCABULARIO ESENCIAL

Sustantivos

la boca	*mouth*
la cabeza	*head*
la cara	*face*
el diente	*tooth*
la nariz	*nose*
el pelo	*hair*
los labios	*lips*
el ojo	*eye*
la oreja	*ear*
el/la abuelo/a	*grandfather/ grandmother*
el apodo	*nickname*
el/la bisabuelo/a	*great grandfather/ grandmother*
el/la bisnieto/a	*great grandchild*
el/la cuñado/a	*brother/sister-in-law*
el/la esposo/a	*spouse*
el familiar/ pariente	*relative*
el/la gemelo/a	*identical twin*
el/la hermanastro/a	*stepbrother/ stepsister*
el/la hermano/a	*brother/sister*
el/la hijo/a	*son/daughter*
la madrastra	*stepmother*
la madre	*mother*
el/la medio/a hermano/a	*half brother/ sister*
el/la nieto/a	*grandson/ granddaughter*

el/la novio/a	*boyfriend/ girlfriend*
la nuera	*daughter-in-law*
el padrastro	*stepfather*
el padre	*father*
los padres	*parents, fathers*
el/la primo/a	*cousin*
el/la sobrino/a	*nephew/niece*
el/la suegro/a	*father/ mother-in-law*
el/la tío/a	*uncle/aunt*
el yerno	*son-in-law*

Cognados: la familia, la mamá, el papá, la relación

Adjetivos

casado/a	*married*
materno/a	*mother's side*
paterno/a	*father's side*
soltero/a	*single*
viudo/a	*widow/widower*

Cognados: divorciado/a, separado/a

Verbos

almorzar (ue)	*to have lunch*
casarse	*to get married*
contar (ue)	*to count*
costar (ue)	*to cost*
dormir (ue)	*to sleep*
encontrar (ue)	*to find*
entender (ie)	*to understand*
hacer	*to do, to make*

jugar (ue)	*to play*
oír	*to hear*
parecerse	*to look like*
pedir (i)	*to ask for*
pensar (ie)	*to think*
perder (ie)	*to lose*
poder (ue)	*to be able*
poner	*to put*
preferir (ie)	*to prefer*
querer (ie)	*to want*
repetir (i)	*to repeat*
salir	*to leave, to go out with*
servir (i)	*to serve*
tener (ie)	*to have*
traer	*to bring*
venir	*to come*
volver (ue)	*to return*

Expresiones

tener... años	*to be. . . years old*
tener buena/ mala suerte	*to be lucky/ unlucky*
tener calor	*to be hot*
tener frío	*to be cold*
tener ganas de...	*to feel like . . .*
tener hambre	*to be hungry*
tener miedo	*to be afraid*
tener razón	*to be right*
tener sed	*to be thirsty*
tener sueño	*to be sleepy*

LEARNING OBJECTIVES

By the end of this section you will be able to:

- Compare diverse dwellings
- Describe a house and its neighborhood
- Use numbers from 10,000
- Make comparisons
- Express location and existence
- Understand the life in a neighborhood

$1 = 1 Balboa (2013)

Una imagen vale más que mil palabras

¿Cuánto cuestan las casas?

¿Cuál es la moneda de Panamá? ¿A cuánto está el cambio[1]?

¿Cómo son las casas de Panamá comparadas con las de la ciudad donde vives ahora? ¿Más caras o más baratas? ¿Más grandes o más pequeñas? ¿Más modernas o más antiguas?

Bienes Raíces

1.Condominios de lujo Calle Boca Ríos 155 Privado, campo de golf, balcón extendido. **395.840 Balboas**

2.Apartamento de 3 habitaciones, Casco antiguo, Panamá, recientemente renovado, cocina grande. **570.350 Balboas**

3.Villa de 2 habitaciones Chiriqui, Panamá. Para un tour virtual visitar nuestra página web. **479.290 Balboas**

© John Wiley & Sons, Inc.

UNA PERSPECTIVA

Casas diferentes

Courtesy Thomas A. Burton

Tab

Diferente

"Fui[2] a Panamá a visitar a unos amigos. Muchas casas son diferentes a las casas de mi vecindario[3] en Estados Unidos. La casa de mis amigos Osvaldo y Roberto, y muchas otras casas, tienen rejas[4] ornamentales. Las casas son de cemento. Muchas no tienen garajes cerrados, sino[5] abiertos".

Courtesy of Norma Lopez-Burton

Courtesy of Norma Lopez-Burton

Courtesy of Norma Lopez-Burton

▲ *Casas con rejas*

Igual

"Hay casas muy grandes y ricas, con alarmas, pero también hay casas pequeñas y pobres, igual que en Estados Unidos".

 ¿Qué piensas tú? ¿Qué es más común ver en tu vecindario de Estados Unidos? ¿Es similar a Panamá? Utiliza las siguientes frases:

	Muy común	Común	Poco frecuente	Muy poco frecuente
1. Rejas en las casas o los edificios	☐	☐	☐	☐
2. Casas o edificios con alarmas	☐	☐	☐	☐
3. Casas de cemento	☐	☐	☐	☐
4. Casas de madera[6]	☐	☐	☐	☐
5. Casas con garajes cerrados	☐	☐	☐	☐

[1]**cambio:** exchange [2]**fui:** I went [3]**vecindario:** neighborhood [4]**rejas:** iron works [5]**sino:** but [6]**madera:** wood

LA PURA VERDAD I ¿Qué dirá la gente?

Lisa es una estadounidense de Nuevo México. Sus abuelos son de Honduras. Planea estudiar en Panamá por un año. Ahora está en la casa de una familia panameña.

1.

2.

3.

4.

¿Quieres venir a estudiar conmigo?

5.

6.

7.

¡Pero él no es mi novio!

¡No importa! ¿Qué dirá la gente?

8.

© All illustrations John Wiley & Sons, Inc.

▲ *No está bien estudiar en el dormitorio.*

3.2-01 ¿Qué dirá la gente? Listen to the narration and decide if the following statements are true (**Cierto**) or false (**Falso**). If they are false, explain why.

	C	F	
1.	☐	☐	_____
2.	☐	☐	_____
3.	☐	☐	_____
4.	☐	☐	_____
5.	☐	☐	_____

PALABRA POR PALABRA

La casa, los muebles y el vecindario *House, furniture, and neighborhood*

El exterior de la casa *The exterior of the house*

Para hablar de la vivienda			grande	*big*
amueblado/a	*furnished*		la habitación/el cuarto	*room*
bonito/a	*pretty*		la seguridad	*safety*
el centro	*downtown*		las flores	*flowers*
el edificio	*building*		la ubicación	*location*
el piso	*floor*		la vivienda	*housing*
el precio	*price*		luminoso/a	*bright*
el vecindario	*neighborhood*		pequeño/a	*small*
el/la vecino/a	*neighbor*		un piso/dos pisos	*one story/two stories*

Cognados: el apartamento, el garaje, la zona

La cocina y el comedor *The kitchen and the dining room*

Verbos

alquilar *to rent*
comprar *to buy*

Cognado: el refrigerador

La sala   *The living room*

Cognados: el aire acondicionado, la cortina, la lámpara, el sofá, la televisión/el televisor

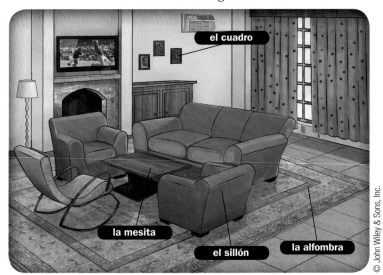

- el cuadro
- la mesita
- el sillón
- la alfombra

© John Wiley & Sons, Inc.

El dormitorio   *The bedroom*

- el armario/el ropero
- el escritorio
- la cama
- la computadora
- la mesita de noche
- el espejo
- la cómoda

© John Wiley & Sons, Inc.

El baño   *The bathroom*

- la ducha
- el mosaico/el azulejo
- el papel higiénico
- el bidé
- el inodoro
- el lavabo/el lavamanos
- la tina/la bañera

© John Wiley & Sons, Inc.

Los números del 10.000 en adelante *Numbers from 10,000 and on*

25.000 (veinticinco mil) balboas

126.000 (ciento veintiséis mil) balboas

499.500 (cuatrocientos noventa y nueve mil quinientos) balboas

1.600.000 (un millón seiscientos mil) balboas

© John Wiley & Sons, Inc.

¿Qué dicen los panameños?

¿Te gusta **mi chantín**?	*Do you like my house?*
¿Qué te parece **mi nave**?	*What do you think about my car?*
*Este patio **está chévere**.	*This yard is cool!*
*Le importa mucho "**el qué dirán**".	*He/She is very concerned about appearances.*

*This expression is also used in other Spanish-speaking countries.

¡OJO!

Hay muchas advertencias para casas en el periódico.

¿Advertencias? ¿De qué?

Oh, anuncios. Hay muchos anuncios.

Sí, mira, para vender casas.

© John Wiley & Sons, Inc.

▲ **Advertencia** *means "warning,"* **anuncio** *means "advertisement" or "ad."*

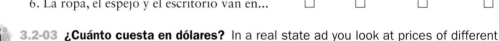
3.2-02 ¡Mudanza![7] You are helping a friend to move into a new place.

¿Dónde van las cosas? ¿En la cocina, la sala, el dormitorio o el baño?

	la cocina	la sala	el dormitorio	el baño
1. Las toallas, el papel higiénico y el espejo van en...	☐	☐	☐	☐
2. La lámpara, el sillón y la televisión van en...	☐	☐	☐	☐
3. La cama, la mesita de noche y la cómoda van en...	☐	☐	☐	☐
4. Los cuadros, los estantes y el sofá van en...	☐	☐	☐	☐
5. El microondas, la estufa y el refrigerador van en...	☐	☐	☐	☐
6. La ropa, el espejo y el escritorio van en...	☐	☐	☐	☐

3.2-03 ¿Cuánto cuesta en dólares? In a real state ad you look at prices of different houses in Costa Rica. Help each other calculate the prices in dollars. Decide which house you prefer and why, and then report to the class.

1 dólar = 500 colones aproximadamente (en 2013)

MODELO: Estudiante 1: *Esta casa cuesta 40.500.000 colones. ¿Cuánto cuesta en dólares?*
Estudiante 2: *Cuesta $81.000*

[7]**mudanza:** move

GUANACASTE, TAMARINDO

Casa nueva, espaciosa, tres cuartos, dos baños, jardín, magnífica vista.

PUNTARENAS, SANTA TERESA DE CÓBANO

Casa moderna y bonita, dos cuartos, 2 baños, pisos de mosaicos.

© John Wiley & Sons, Inc.

1. ¿Cuánto cuesta la casa de Guanacaste?		
Precio:	C 64.880.000,00	$_____
Pago inicial:	C 6.976.000,00	$_____
Pago mensual:	C 270.000,00	$_____

2. ¿Cuánto cuesta la casa de Puntarenas?		
Precio:	C 50.800.000,00	$_____
Pago inicial:	C 5.540.000,00	$_____
Pago mensual:	C 210.300,00	$_____

 3.2-04 Veo, veo In groups of four, take turns to guess one of the objects from the section **Palabra por palabra.**

MODELO: Estudiante 1: *Veo, veo.*
             Grupo: *¿Qué ves?*
           Estudiante 1: *Una cosita.*
             Grupo: *¿Con qué letrecita?*
           Estudiante 1: *Con la letrecita "l".*
             Grupo: *¿Lavabo? ¿Lámpara?*

 3.2-05 ¡Tu casa!

Paso 1: With a classmate, take turns interviewing each other about the place where you live. Describe your house or apartment.

1. ¿Dónde vives? ¿Vives en una casa o en un apartamento? ¿Cuál es tu dirección? ¿Cuántos pisos tiene?
2. ¿Cómo es tu cuarto? ¿Qué muebles tienes? ¿Te gustan?
3. Y la cocina, ¿cómo es? ¿Es grande o pequeña? ¿Qué aparatos[8] tiene?
4. ¿Cuál es tu cuarto favorito? ¿Por qué?
5. ¿Qué parte de tu casa detestas limpiar?
6. En tu casa, ¿usan el garaje para el carro o para almacenar[9] cosas?

Paso 2: Now compare both places. Be prepared to report to the rest of the class what is similar and what is different.

MODELO: *Los dos vivimos en una casa con patio, pero su casa tiene tres cuartos y mi casa tiene cinco cuartos...*

[8] **aparatos:** appliances [9] **almacenar:** to store

HABLANDO DE GRAMÁTICA I

WileyPLUS Go to *WileyPLUS* to review this grammar point with the help of the **Animated Grammar Tutorial**.

1. Making comparisons

A. Comparisons of equality

A. When comparing characteristics that are roughly equal or similar, use the phrase "**tan** + *adjective/adverb* + **como**" (*as. . . as*). Notice that although the adjective must agree in number and gender with the noun, "**tan + ... + como**" do not change:

La cocina de la casa de Panamá es **tan** grande **como** la cocina de la casa de Lisa en Estados Unidos.	The kitchen in the house in Panama is as big as the kitchen in Lisa's house in the United States.
Ella no limpia la cocina **tan** bien **como** él.	She doesn't clean the kitchen as well as he does.

When comparing characteristics that are not equal, use **no** in front of the main verb:

La casa de Panamá **no** es **tan** cara **como** la casa de Lisa en Nuevo México.	The house in Panama is not as expensive as Lisa's house in New Mexico.

B. When comparing nouns, use the phrase "**tanto/a/os/as** + *noun* + **como**" (*as many/as much . . . as*). Note that **tanto/a/os/as** is an adjective and has to agree with the noun that follows:

Esta casa tiene **tantas** ventan**as como** tu casa.	This house has as many windows as your house.
La casa de Lisa en Estados Unidos tiene **tantos** cuart**os como** la casa de Panamá.	Lisa's house in the United States has as many rooms as the house in Panamá.

C. When comparing activities, use *verb* + **tanto como**:

En Panamá, Lisa estudia **tanto como** en Estados Unidos.	In Panama, Lisa studies as much as she does in the United States.

 3.2-06 ¿Son similares? Look at the drawings and decide if the following statements are true (**Cierto**) or false (**Falso**). If they are false, write the correct information.

© John Wiley & Sons, Inc.

MODELO: El dormitorio es tan espacioso como la sala.
→ *Falso. El dormitorio <u>no</u> es tan espacioso como la sala.*

▲ 1. *Las rejas de la ventana de la casa gris no son tan decorativas como las rejas de la ventana de la casa marrón.*

C   F

☐   ☐

▲ 2. *La lámpara blanca es tan grande como la lámpara verde.*

C   F

☐   ☐

© John Wiley & Sons, Inc.

▲ 3. *El televisor pequeño no es tan moderno como el televisor grande.*

C   F

☐   ☐

© John Wiley & Sons, Inc.

▲ 4. *La casa gris no es tan bonita como la casa blanca.*

▲ 5. *La silla es tan cómoda como el sillón.*

▲ 6. *El microondas es tan caro como la estufa.*

C	F	C	F	C	F
☐	☐	☐	☐	☐	☐

3.2-07 ¿Son similares? Compare these houses and rooms.

MODELO: Mi casa / tu casa: cuartos →
            Mi casa no <u>tiene tantos cuartos</u> como tu casa.

1. Mi casa / la casa de mi mejor amigo/a: espacio
2. Mi garaje / el garaje de mi mejor amigo/a: cosas
3. Mi dormitorio / el dormitorio de mis padres: muebles
4. Mi jardín / el jardín de la casa de mis vecinos: flores
5. Mi refrigerador / el refrigerador de mis padres: comida
6. La sala / mi dormitorio: ventanas

3.2-08 Mi casa y la casa de mis padres Complete the following paragraph with the appropriate comparative words **tanto/a/os/as, tan** or **como**.

La casa donde yo vivo con mis compañeros de la universidad es similar, pero también es diferente a la casa de mis padres. Primero, mi casa tiene ＿＿＿＿＿＿＿＿＿ dormitorios ＿＿＿＿＿＿＿＿＿ la casa de mis padres. Sin embargo, la casa donde yo vivo no es ＿＿＿＿＿＿＿＿＿ nueva ＿＿＿＿＿＿＿＿＿ la casa de mis padres. En mi casa no hay ＿＿＿＿＿＿＿＿＿ espacio ＿＿＿＿＿＿＿＿＿ en la casa de mis padres. Cuando estoy en la universidad no estudio ＿＿＿＿＿＿＿＿＿ ＿＿＿＿＿＿＿＿＿ cuando estoy de visita en casa de mis padres. Es fácil estudiar en casa de mis padres porque no es ＿＿＿＿＿＿＿＿＿ divertida ＿＿＿＿＿＿＿＿＿ nuestra casa. ¡Nosotros hacemos muchas fiestas!

B. Comparisons of inequality

A. When comparing things that are not equal, use **más/menos +** *adjective/adverb/ noun* **+ que** (*more/less. . . than*):

Las casas cercanas a la playa son **más** caras **que** las casas que están en el campo.

The houses near the beach are more expensive than the houses in the countryside.

Hay **menos** roperos y **menos** estantes en la casa de Lisa en Estados Unidos **que** en la casa de Panamá.

There are fewer closets and fewer shelves in Lisa's house in the United States than in the house in Panama.

When comparing activities, use *verb* **+ más/menos + que**:

En Panamá, Lisa gasta **menos que** en Estados Unidos.

In Panama, Lisa spends less than in the United States.

Lisa trabaja con la computadora **más que** su familia panameña.

Lisa works on the computer more than her Panamanian family does.

B. Some adjectives and adverbs have special comparative forms:

bueno/a, bien → **mejor(es)**

malo/a, mal → **peor(es)**

Mi vencidario es **peor** que el de Lisa, pero mis vecinos son **mejores**.

My neighborhood is worse than Lisa's, but my neighbors are better.

C. When comparing age, use **mayor que** (*older than*) and **menor que** (*younger than*):

Fernando es **mayor que** Alberto.   *Fernando is older than Alberto.*
Alberto es **menor que** su hermano   *Alberto is younger than his brother*
Fernando.   *Fernando.*

D. With numbers, use **de** instead of **que**:

Esta casa cuesta **más de** 1.000.000   *This house costs more than*
de dólares.   *$1,000,000.*

 3.2-09 Dos casas de Panamá Compare these two houses and describe five differences. Use **tanto/a/os/as... como**. Keep in mind: *número de ventanas, número de balcones, número de puertas, flores, palmeras en el jardín, personas que viven en la casa.*

A.    B.

© John Wiley & Sons, Inc.

MODELO: número de ventanas →
    La casa 1 tiene <u>más ventanas</u> que la casa 2.

3.2-10 Compara Panamá y Estados Unidos In pairs compare both countries' statistics. Student 1 will look at Panama's stats in the inside cover of this book. Student 2's information is in box.

MODELO: Estudiante 1:   *¿Cuántos años es el término del presidente en Estados Unidos?*
    Estudiante 2:   *Cuatro años.*
    Estudiante 1:   *¿Cuántos años es el término del presidente en Panamá?*
    Estudiante 2:   *Cinco años.*
    El término del presidente de Panamá es más largo que el de Estados Unidos.

Estadísticas de Estados Unidos: tamaño 9.826.675 km²; habitantes 316.668.567; amerindios 0.97%; alfabetización 99%

1. ¿Cuántos habitantes hay en...?
2. ¿Cuál es el tamaño de...?
3. ¿Qué porcentaje de indígenas hay en...?
4. ¿Cuál es el nivel de alfabetización en...?

C. The superlative

A. When expressing that something has the highest or lowest degree of a quality, use the superlative form **el/la/los/las** (*noun*) + **más/menos** + *adjective/adverb* + (**de**) (*the most/least. . .*):

Esta casa es **la más** cara **de** todas.   *This house is the most expensive of all.*
Este vecindario es **el mejor de** la ciudad.   *This neighborhood is the best in the city.*

B. When expressing that something shows a very high degree of a quality without comparing it to others, use the superlative ending **–ísimo**.

Panamá es un país increíble. ¡Me gusta   *Panama is an amazing country. I like it*
    muchísimo!   *a lot!*

When the superlative ending is added to an adjective, it should agree in gender and number with the noun it modifies (**–ísimo/a/os/as**):

El programa de estudios en Panamá
es **baratísimo** y los estudiantes
estadounidenses están
contentísimos con sus familias.

*The study program in Panamá is very
cheap and the American students
are really happy with their host
families.*

Summary of comparative forms		
Comparisons of equality	(no) **tan** + *adjective/adverb* + **como** (no) *verb* + **tanto como**	(no) **tanto/a/os/as** + *noun* + **como**
Comparisons of inequality	**más/menos** + *adjetive/adverb* + **que** **más/menos** + **de** + *number*	*verb* + **más/menos** + **que**
Superlative	**el/la/los/las** + **más/menos** *adjective/adverb* + **de**	*adverb* + **–ísimo**, *adjective* + **–ísimo/a/os/as**
Special forms	**mejor, peor, mayor, menor**	

 3.2-11 ¡A comparar! Write five sentences using the superlative form (**el/la/los/las...
de**) and the superlative ending (**–ísimo/a**). Pay attention to irregular forms!

MODELO: las casas de San José / las casas de la ciudad de Panamá / las casas de
Beverly Hills (caras)
*Las casas de Beverly Hills son <u>las más caras de</u> todas. ¡Son unas casas
<u>carísimas</u>!*

1. San José / la ciudad de Panamá / la ciudad de Nueva York (moderna)
2. Costa Rica / Panamá / Estados Unidos (grande)
3. las playas de Costa Rica / de Panamá / de California (buenas)
4. el clima de Costa Rica / el clima de Panamá / el clima de la ciudad de Nueva York (frío)
5. la presidenta de Costa Rica / el presidente de Panamá / el presidente de Estados Unidos (famoso)

 3.2-12 ¡Busco habitación! You and your friend are going to study in Panama and you need to rent a room. Compare similarities and differences among these three rooms (price, location, comfort, look, services, furniture, size, etc). Decide which one is the best and report your conclusions to the class.

1. Linda habitación para alquilar, 350 balboas
Linda habitación principal en apartamento en Camino Real, excelente ubicación en zona centro, fácil acceso a supermercados y universidad, ideal para estudiantes, acceso a cocina y lavandería[10], baño privado, garaje incluido. Para más información, llamar al 67-123454.

2. Habitación en apartamento nuevo, 300 balboas
Habitación amueblada en apartamento de nueva construcción, aire acondicionado, baño privado, servicio de wifi y TV por cable incluido, acceso a piscina, lavandería y garaje. Llamar al 67-789 889.

3. Habitación para estudiantes, 280 balboas
Habitación para una o dos personas muy luminosa, baño compartido, zona tranquila y con mucha seguridad, cerca de la universidad y centros comerciales. Para más información:
habitaciónalquiler@puravida.com.

© John Wiley & Sons, Inc.

MODELO: Estudiante 1:   *La habitación 2 <u>no es tan bonita como</u> la habitación 3.*
Estudiante 2:   *Sí, pero la habitación 2 es <u>menos bonita que</u> la habitación 1.
La habitación 1 es <u>la más bonita de</u> las tres...*

[10]**lavandería:** laundry room

LA PURA VERDAD II ¿Cómo son las casas?

Los padres de Lisa están en Nuevo México. Piensan comprar una casa y tienen curiosidad sobre las casas en Panamá.

1. ¿Cómo estás, Lisa? ¿Te gusta Panamá? ¿Te gusta la comida? ¿Es muy picante allí? ¿Tienes muchos amigos? ¿Estudias mucho?

2. ¡Dios mío, cuántas preguntas! A ver, no, la comida no es picante. La comida de Nuevo México es muchísimo más picante.

3. Pues, depende, si están cerca de la playa, son más caras. Si están en el campo son más baratas. Hay casas en el campo que cuestan unos 60.000 balboas, en la Playa Venao cuestan unos 90.000 balboas y en la Costa Pedasi hay casas que cuestan más de 100.000 balboas.

¿Las casas son caras allá?

4. Y tu casa, ¿cómo es?

5. Esta es la sala. Es más pequeña que la sala de nuestra casa, pero es muy bonita.

6. Aquí tenemos muchas más flores y árboles que en nuestra casa.

7. La cocina es más o menos igual. Es tan grande como la nuestra.

8. Pero tengo un problema. En el baño hay un bidé, ¡y no sé cómo se usa!

© John Wiley & Sons, Inc.

3.2-13 ¿Qué hay en las habitaciones? Listen and decide whether each statement is logical or illogical.

	Ilógico	Lógico	
1.	☐	☐	_____
2.	☐	☐	_____
3.	☐	☐	_____

HABLANDO DE GRAMÁTICA II

2. Expressing location and existence: *Estar* + location and *hay*

A. *Estar* + location. There are two different verbs to express *to be* in Spanish: **ser** and **estar**. You have already been exposed to these two verbs and have been using them in conversation. **Ser** was presented in Chapter 1, Section 1. Now you are going to learn how to use **estar** to talk about location of people, places, and things.

Estar (*to be*) + en + lugar (*place*)		
(yo)	**estoy**	*I am*
(tú)	**estás**	*you are* (informal, singular)
(él/ella/Ud.)	**está**	*he/she/it is* or *you are* (formal, singular)
(nosotros/as)	**estamos**	*we are*
(vosotros/as)	**estáis**	*you are* (informal, plural, Spain)
(ellos/ellas/Uds.)	**están**	*they are* or *you are* (formal, plural)

Lisa y Mario **están en el cuarto** de Lisa.   *Lisa and Mario are in Lisa's room.*
La casa de la familia panameña **está**   *The Panamanian family's home is in a*
  en un barrio muy bueno.   *very good neighborhood.*

3.2-14 ¿Dónde están? Lisa is talking to her brother, who is in the U.S., through video conference. Use the appropriate form of the verb **estar** to combine the phrases in column A with those in column B.

MODELO: Tu hermana... / en el baño. → *Tu hermana está en el baño.*

A
1. La casa...
2. Ahora yo...
3. No puedes ver a mis padres panameños; ellos...
4. Mi hermano panameño y yo...
5. ¿Y tú...

B
a. en mi dormitorio.
b. en la casa de una amiga.
c. en tu casa?
d. en casa los dos.
e. en el centro de la ciudad.

B. The use of *hay*
When expressing something's existence, Spanish uses the verb **haber** in its irregular form **hay**, which does not change for either singular (*there is*) or plural (*there are*):

–¿**Hay** horno en la cocina?   –*Is there an oven in the kitchen?*
–No, no hay horno.   –*No, there isn't an oven.*

Hay muchos azulejos en el baño.   *There are many tiles in the bathroom.*

To express *there isn't* or *there aren't* you should say **no hay**. The definite article is usually omitted:

No hay bidé en el cuarto de baño.   *There isn't a bidet in the bathroom.*

WileyPLUS Go to *WileyPLUS* to review this grammar point with the help of the **Animated Grammar Tutorial** and the **Verb Conjugator**.

Summary of *estar* + location and *hay*

Use the verb **estar** to talk about *location*. Don't forget, **hay** emphasizes *existence*, not *location*. Compare the following:

–¿**Hay** baño en este restaurante?   –*Is there a bathroom in this restaurant?*
–Sí, hay baño.   –*Yes, there is a bathroom.*
–¿Dónde **está (el baño)**?   –*Where is it?*
–Está al lado[11] de la cocina.   –*It's next to the kitchen.*

3.2-15 ¿Cómo es su casa? Carmen lives in Panama City. Complete the paragraph with **hay** or the appropriate form of **estar**.

La sala de Carmen está llena de cosas. Al lado del sofá _____ unas fotos de
toda la familia. En el salón también _____ un piano. El piano _____
en el centro del salón. Al lado del piano _____ una lámpara. Carmen lee mucho.
Sus libros favoritos _____ en el estante. En la sala también _____
dos alfombras muy caras y muy bonitas.

3.2-16 Una habitación de hotel en la península de Papagayo Look at the room and tell how many of the following items are there.

MODELO: *Hay dos cortinas.*
   1. espejo(s)
   2. mesita(s)
   3. cuadro(s)
   4. escritorio(s)
   5. silla(s)
   6. sofá(s)
   7. ¿?

¿Qué no hay en la habitación que es importante en tu opinión?

[11] **al lado:** next to

OTRA PERSPECTIVA

María Teijeiro / Photodisc / Getty Images

Emilia

Nuestros vecinos

Diferente

"Veo que en Estados Unidos la gente no acostumbra a salir a caminar por las tardes o a hablar con sus vecinos. En Panamá caminamos con nuestros amigos, vamos a la plaza, hablamos en un café... También algunos son expertos en la vida de sus vecinos... lo que hacen, a qué hora, por qué..."

Igual

"En las ciudades grandes, donde hay más apartamentos, los vecinos están menos unidos".

Explícale a Emilia

1. ¿Por qué no caminamos mucho en Estados Unidos?
2. ¿Crees que en este país somos más reservados?
3. ¿Hablas con frecuencia con tus vecinos? ¿Con tus amigos?
4. ¿A cuántos vecinos saludas cada día? ¿Cómo se llaman?

MANOS A LA OBRA

 3.2-17 ¿Cuánto cuesta mi casa? A volunteer has to guess the price of another student's house. The volunteer's group can help by saying **más** or **menos.**

 3.2-18 ¿En mi clase, quién...? Ask your classmates to find out to whom the following statements apply. The goal is to get a horizontal line.

REJAS				
Tiene una computadora Macintosh.	No tiene televisión.	Tiene una cama enorme.	Tiene buenos vecinos.	Tiene un refrigerador muy pequeño.
Tiene tres baños en su casa.	Estudia en el comedor.	No tiene microondas.	Tiene dos ventanas en su cuarto.	Come frente a la televisión.
Tiene un dormitorio muy feo.	Pasa mucho tiempo en su jardín.	Tiene vecinos horribles.	Tiene un patio.	No tiene baño privado.

 3.2-19 ¡La casa más surrealista! With a group of classmates, draw the floorplan of an imaginary house. Describe to the class what's in each room, where the rooms are, etc. Which group can design the most surrealistic house?

 3.2-20 La casa de nuestras vacaciones You want to rent a house during the summer in Costa Rica or Panama with some friends, but you don't have a lot of money.

Paso 1: Write a list of features that you would like the house to have, plus furniture and other amenities that you consider important (e.g., *barata, grande, amueblada... número de cuartos/muebles que necesitan*).

Paso 2: Now look at these ads and decide which property you prefer. Compare them (*características, ubicación, precio, número de dormitorios...*) and reach a consensus regarding which one you will rent.

1. Palo Seco, Costa Rica, 860.000.00 colones / US$1.700 por mes

Linda casa frente a la playa, a 7 km. de Palo Seco, aire acondicionado, 4 dormitorios, 2 baños completos, cocina renovada con nuevos estantes, lavaplatos, horno y refrigerador, muy luminosa, piso de mosaicos, todo exterior

2. Apartamento en Jacó, Costa Rica, 1.000.000 colones / US$ 2.000 por mes

2 habitaciones, 2 baños, vistas espectaculares a la playa, salita, comedor, cocina amueblada, seguridad 24 horas, terraza cubierta

3. Casa en la Urbanización *Corona Garden,* Betania, Panamá, B/US$1.700 por mes

Zona centro, 2 pisos, 3 habitaciones, 3 baños, sala comedor y sala familiar, terraza, patio, garaje cubierto, lavandería separada. Urbanización privada con área social, piscina, guardia de seguridad y salón de fiestas

4. Casa en Ciudad de David, Chiriquí, Panamá, B/US$900 por mes

4 habitaciones, 2 baños, piso de azulejos, zona suburbana con fácil acceso al centro, gran terreno, muy luminosa, zona tranquila. Totalmente amueblada, refrigerador, lavadora, microondas

MODELO: Estudiante 1: *Me gusta la casa de Betania porque tiene <u>más baños que</u> la casa de Chiriquí.*

Estudiante 2: *Sí, pero no tenemos mucho dinero y la casa de Chiriquí es <u>la más barata</u> de todas...*

Estudiante 3: *Sí, la casa de Chiriquí tiene más habitaciones que la casa de Betania.*

Paso 3: Report to the class which house you have selected. Which is the most popular house in the class?

WileyPLUS Go to *WileyPLUS* and listen to **Presta atención.**

3.2-21 Presta atención: ¿Qué es? Your instructor will read some descriptions. Read carefully and select the most appropriate word for each one.

1. a. el lavaplatos   b. el fregadero   c. la refrigerador
2. a. la piscina   b. el ropero   c. la ducha
3. a. el horno   b. la estufa   c. el microondas
4. a. la alfombra   b. las cortinas   c. los estantes
5. a. el lavabo   b. el bidé   c. el inodoro
6. a. el dormitorio   b. el espejo   c. el armario
7. a. el tejado   b. la vivienda   c. la vecina
8. a. la cama   b. el cuarto   c. el comedor

3.2-22 Por escrito: Se busca vivienda

Paso 1: A   Imagine that you are studying next year in Costa Rica. You place an ad in the newspaper to rent an apartment. Write your ad using the information below. (e.g., *Busco un apartamento baratísimo*).

- Comienza con la expresión "Se busca apartamento".
- El lugar donde quieres alquilar (ciudad, avenida...)
- El tipo de vivienda y número de habitaciones (1 dormitorio, 2 baños y 1 cocina)
- Tipo de muebles (cama, sofá...)
- Precio del alquiler por mes (800.000 colones...)
- Características del edificio (gimnasio, piscina) y del vecindario (ubicación, seguridad...)
- Tu información de contacto (número de teléfono, correo electrónico...)

B. Imagine that you have a property in Costa Rica that you want to rent it out. Prepare a flyer with the information in the list. **1.** Use comparisons (*es el más bonito del vecindario*). **2.** Use **estar** (*está cerca del mercado*). **3.** Use **hay** (*hay piscina en el patio*). Start your paragraph with the expression **"Se alquila..."** and continue with the list above.

Paso 2: Look for the classmate who has the apartment you are looking for.

A. The tenant needs to ask questions to the owner using comparisons and the superlative. Remember to use the information you wrote for your ad.

MODELO: *¿Hay...? ¿Está en...? ¿Es el apartamento más barato?*

B. The owner needs to convince the potential tenant that his/her apartment is the best one in the city. Use comparisons, the superlative, **estar** + location, and **hay**:

MODELO: *Hay un supermercado cerca del parque. El apartamento está en...*

 PONTE EN MI LUGAR

¡OJO!

For rent
Think of a real flyer to help you find and rent an apartment or think about your real world experience when you have looked for a place to live. Make sure that the content of the flyer you are planning on placing on a website is well organized and informative.

Estrategias para conversar

On the phone Remember to express your own opinion by using the "chunks of language" you already know, like phrases to express agreement **por supuesto** or to express disagreement **de ninguna manera** (from **Estrategias para conversar** in Chapter 3, Section 1). Now you will learn how to request to talk to someone on the phone and how to find out who is answering the phone:

To request to talk to someone:

¿Está (nombre de la persona)?	Is (name of the person) there?
¿Podría hablar con (nombre de la persona)?	Could I talk to (name of the person)?

To find out who is answering your call:

¿Con quién hablo?	Who am I talking to?
¿Quién es?/¿Quién habla?	Who is this?

To request something:

Llamo por... (el anuncio)	I am calling because of. . . (e.g., the ad)
Busco...	I am looking for. . .

To offer something:

Ahora mismo podría (+infinitivo)	Right now I could (+infinitive)

Un apartamento You are looking for an apartment in Panama City. You want to rent the apartment for six months for you and two friends. With your classmate, decide who is the owner of the apartment. The person looking for a place to stay calls the owner to inquire about an apartment advertised in a newspaper. Use the expressions in **Estrategias para conversar** in Chapter 3, Sections 1 and 2.

Owner: Pick up the phone and answer the questions by the person interested in your property.

Person looking for apartment: Ask about the price, the number of rooms, bathrooms; request information about the kitchen, the type of house, and the neighborhood.

 **WileyPLUS** Go to *WileyPLUS* to find more **Arroba** activities.

La ruta panamericana Explore in your favorite browser information about the **Carretera Panamericana** that goes through Costa Rica and Panama. Then answer the questions:

1. ¿Qué es la Carretera Panamericana?
2. ¿De dónde a dónde se extiende?
3. ¿Está terminada la carretera? ¿Por qué?
4. ¿Cómo se llama el lugar donde la carretera está cortada?

ASÍ ES LA VIDA

Expresión: De tal palo tal astilla

Maestra: Manolito es excelente en matemáticas.
Mamá: Su papá es profesor de matemáticas.
Maestra: Claro, ¡de tal palo, tal astilla!

¿Hay una expresión similar en inglés?
¿En qué aspecto eres como tu papá o tu mamá?

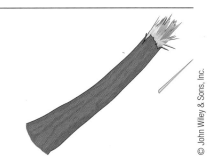

VER PARA CREER II: ¡Qué casa tan ecológica!

WileyPLUS Go to *WileyPLUS* to see this video and to find more video activities.

Antes de ver

With your partner, answer the following questions:

Para ti, ¿cuál es el mejor lugar de tu casa? ¿Por qué? ¿Tienes un jardín con piscina en tu casa? ¿Tienes patio en tu casa?

Después de ver

1. ¿Entendiste? Answer the following questions after watching the video.

1. ¿Dónde está José Luis?
2. ¿Cuál es el lugar favorito de José Luis? ¿Por qué?
3. ¿Es esta vivienda más grande que tu casa?
4. ¿Qué hay en la cocina?
5. ¿Dónde almuerza José Luis a veces?
6. ¿Para qué sirven los paneles solares?

2. La vida verde Ask questions to your classmate about the house you just saw in the video.

MODELO: ¿Hay...? ¿Está en...?

3. Enfoque cultural ¿Qué es importante para ti en una vivienda (precio, ubicación, seguridad, luminosidad...)? Para ti, ¿es importante la vivienda? ¿Por qué? ¿Qué tienen en común las casas de Costa Rica y las de tu país?

AUTOPRUEBA

VOCABULARIO

I. La vivienda Which one of the following words does not belong in the group?

1. vecinos, refrigerador, fregadero, cocina
2. piscina, patio, rejas, estante
3. inodoro, tejado, espejo, bañera
4. ducha, lavabo, cómoda, tina
5. dormitorio, comedor, sala, mosaico

II. La casa de Rubén Blades A famous Panamanian singer, Rubén Blades, invites you to his house. Write down five **muebles** or objects that you could find in his living room and in his bedroom.

Sala: Dormitorio:

1. mesita   1. _____
2. sillon   2. _____
3. alfombra   3. _____
4. cuadro   4. _____
5. _____   5. _____

III. ¿Cuánto cuesta? Say out loud or write down how much the following cost.

1. Instalar una piscina. ($45.560)

_____

2. Comprar una casa grande con vista al mar. ($1.460.935)

_____

3. Tener vacaciones de lujo (*luxurious*) en Costa Rica. ($52.780)

_____

GRAMÁTICA

I. ¡Un baño de lujo! What can you find in the bathroom of a luxurious mansion? Complete the paragraph with **hay** or the appropriate form of **estar**.

En el baño _____₁ una ducha, un inodoro, pero no _____₂ tina, sino un *jacuzzi* que _____₃ cerca de una ventana. También _____₄ una televisión y dos espejos muy grandes que _____₅ cerca de los lavabos. ¡_____₆ tres lavabos!

II. Ciudades Compare the cities of Panama, Washington, D.C., and San Jose.

Ciudad de Panamá, Panamá

708.738 habitantes
106 millas cuadradas
3 colores en la bandera
Es una ciudad muy bonita.

San José, Costa Rica

342.977 habitantes
17,23 millas cuadradas
3 colores en la bandera
Es una ciudad muy bonita.

Washington, D.C., EE. UU.

599.657 habitantes
17,7 millas cuadradas
3 colores en la bandera

CULTURA

1. ¿Qué partes de las casas de Panamá son diferentes a las de una casa típica de Estados Unidos?
2. ¿Qué frase en español expresa desacuerdo por la opinión de otras personas?
3. ¿Cuál es la moneda de Costa Rica? ¿Y la de Panamá?

REDACCIÓN

Describe your ideal house if money were not an issue. Include:
- Ubicación *location*
- Vecindario *neighborhood*
- Habitaciones *bedrooms*
- El por qué de cada elección *why*

EN RESUMIDAS CUENTAS, AHORA PUEDO...

☐ compare different types of houses.

☐ describe a house, its rooms, and its neighborhood.

☐ use numbers from 10,000.

☐ make comparisons.

☐ express location and existence with the verbs **estar** and **hay**.

☐ understand the concept of **el qué dirán**.

VOCABULARIO ESENCIAL

Sustantivos

la alfombra	*rug*
el apartamento	*apartment*
el árbol	*tree*
el armario/el ropero	*closet*
el azulejo/el mosaico	*tile*
el baño	*bathroom*
la cama	*bed*
la casa	*house*
la cocina	*kitchen*
el comedor	*dining room*
la cómoda	*dresser*
el cuadro	*painting*
el dormitorio	*bedroom*
la ducha	*shower*
el edificio	*building*
el escritorio	*desk*
el espejo	*mirror*
el estante	*shelf*
la estufa	*stove*
el fregadero	*kitchen sink*
la flor	*flower*
la habitación/el cuarto	*room*
el horno	*oven*
el inodoro	*toilet*
el jardín	*garden*
el lavabo/el lavamanos	*bathroom sink*

el lavaplatos	*dishwasher*
la mesa	*table*
la mesita	*coffee table*
la mesita de noche	*nightstand*
el microondas	*microwave*
el mueble	*furniture*
el papel higiénico	*toilet paper*
el patio	*backyard*
la piscina	*swimming pool*
el piso	*floor, story*
el precio	*price*
la puerta	*door*
la reja	*(ornamental) wrought iron*
la sala	*the living room*
la seguridad	*safety*
la silla	*chair*
el sillón	*armchair*
el tejado	*tiled roof*
la tina/la bañera	*bathtub*
la ubicación	*location*
el vecindario	*neighborhood*
el/la vecino/a	*neighbor*
la ventana	*window*
la vivienda	*housing*

Cognados: el aire acondicionado, el balcón, el bidé, el centro, la computadora, la cortina, el garaje, la lámpara, el refrigerador, el sofá, el televisor/la televisión, la terraza, la zona

Adjetivos

amueblado/a	*furnished*
bonito/a	*pretty*
grande	*big*
luminoso/a	*bright*
mayor	*older*
mejor	*better*
menor	*younger*
peor	*worse*
pequeño/a	*small*

Verbos

alquilar	*to rent*
comprar	*to buy*
estar	*to be*
hay	*there is/there are*

Expresiones

cien mil	*one hundred thousand*
diez mil	*ten thousand*
quinientos mil	*five hundred thousand*
un millón	*one million*
dos millones	*two millions*

4 El trabajo y la ciudad

VER PARA CREER I: ¡Me encanta mi trabajo!

Antes de ver el video, piensa en los temas que vas a estudiar en este capítulo. Cuando veas el video, presta atención a las imágenes y al tema general para poder contestar estas preguntas.

1. ¿Qué lugares hay en el video?
2. ¿Qué actividades hacen las chicas?
3. ¿Cómo son las chicas?

Sección 1 ¡A trabajar!

PALABRA POR PALABRA
- Oficios y profesiones
- El mundo profesional

HABLANDO DE GRAMÁTICA
- Expressing obligation: **Tener que**, **deber**, and **hay que**
- Discussing daily activities and changes of state: Pronominal verbs and reflexive pronouns
- Interrogative words ♻

CULTURA
- Las entrevistas de trabajo en los países hispanos y Estados Unidos
- Las prioridades al buscar un trabajo

Sección 2 La ciudad

PALABRA POR PALABRA
- La ciudad
- La ubicación
- El tiempo

HABLANDO DE GRAMÁTICA
- Expressing intention, motive and movement: The prepositions **por, para, en, a, de**
- Talking about actions in progress: The present progressive
- Identifying, describing, and talking about location: More on **ser** and **estar** ♻

CULTURA
- La forma de expresar las direcciones y medir las distancias en Nicaragua
- El clima en América Central

El Salvador, Honduras y Nicaragua

🌐 **Trivia:** Go to *WileyPLUS* to do the Trivia activities and find out how much you know about these countries!

LEARNING OBJECTIVES

By the end of this section you will be able to:

- Identify differences of a job interview in the U.S. and in Hispanic countries
- Describe yours and other's professions
- Talk about your obligations
- Describe your daily routine
- Describe your emotions
- Request information
- Identify your priorities when applying for a job

Una imagen vale más que mil palabras

Courtesy of Luz de piedra.

luz DE piedra S.A.
ARQUITECTOS
www.luzdepiedra.com
info@luzdepiedra.com
T(506) 22 33 90 84

Courtesy of Choco Museo.

CHOCO
café museo
Granada, Nicaragua
(505) 2552-4678
ChocoMuseo@gmail.com
www.ChocoMuseo.com
Calle Atravesada, frente a Bancentro

Mira las tarjetas de presentación.

¿Con qué profesiones se relacionan?

¿Cómo se llaman las compañías?

¿Cómo nos podemos comunicar con ellos?

¿Qué tarjeta crees que es la más atractiva?

UNA PERSPECTIVA

Courtesy of Michael Harris

Mike

Entrevista de trabajo[1]

Diferente

"Un amigo salvadoreño tiene que ir a una entrevista de trabajo. Le pregunto cómo son las entrevistas en su país. Mi amigo responde: 'Me piden una foto, me preguntan sobre mi experiencia y mi educación, pero también me preguntan cuántos años tengo, si estoy casado o soltero, si tengo hijos, de dónde soy... Si es posible, yo también menciono el nombre de alguna persona que ellos conozcan[2]'. Una conexión personal es importante".

Igual

"El nivel de educación y la experiencia son importantes. También hay muchas oficinas muy modernas con computadoras, fax, correo electrónico, fotocopiadoras, conexiones de alta velocidad de Internet... igual que en EE. UU".

 ¿Qué piensas tú? ¿Qué es frecuente en una entrevista de trabajo?

	Muy frecuente	Poco frecuente
1. Preguntas personales	☐	☐
2. Preguntas sobre tu experiencia	☐	☐
3. Preguntas sobre tu educación	☐	☐
4. Ir adecuadamente vestido/a	☐	☐
5. Mencionar a alguna persona conectada a la empresa	☐	☐
6. Hablar sobre tu familia	☐	☐

¿Es legal en Estados Unidos hacer preguntas sobre el estatus de residencia? ¿Y sobre el estado civil[3]? ¿Por qué?

¿Es apropiado mencionar a una persona conocida[4] en EE. UU.?

[1]**entrevista de trabajo:** job interview [2]**que ellos conozcan:** that they may know [3]**estado civil:** marital status [4]**mencionar a una persona conocida:** name someone you know

LA PURA VERDAD I | Necesito un trabajo

Gabriel quiere extender su visita a El Salvador, pero necesita un trabajo porque no tiene dinero[5]. ¿Qué trabajo puede conseguir?

1. periodista · abogado · médico · gerente · programador de computadoras · enfermero · ingeniero · dentista · escritor

A ver si hay puestos[6] para mí. No, estos trabajos son para personas con una carrera[7].

2. secretario · vendedor · conserje · maestro de inglés · cocinero · niñero · mesero · peluquero · recepcionista · dependiente

---

3.

Posibilidades

Cocinero/a

Pro: Me gusta cocinar.
Contra: No sé cocinar comida salvadoreña.

Peluquero/a

Pro: Puedo cortar[8] el pelo de mis primos.
Contra: No tengo diploma de cosmetología.

Mesero/a

Pro: Tengo experiencia en Estados Unidos.
Contra: El trabajo es durante el día y yo estoy ocupado con mis clases.

4.

Posibilidades

Conserje

Pro: No necesito experiencia.
Contra: No se gana mucho dinero.

Vendedor/a

Pro: Las horas son flexibles.
Contra: No soy muy persuasivo en español.

Secretario/a o recepcionista

Pro: Es fácil.
Contra: Son ocho horas diarias y yo tengo que asistir a clase.

5.

Posibilidades

Niñera

Pro: Puedo jugar todo el día.
Contra: Prefieren a una mujer, no a un hombre.

Dependiente

Pro: Es fácil.
Contra: La tienda está lejos.

Maestro/a

Hay mucha demanda, y me gusta este trabajo. ¡Sí, este puesto es una posibilidad!

4.1-01 ¿Qué trabajo es? Gabriel considera todos los anuncios y lee en voz alta la descripción de cada puesto. Indica a qué puesto se refiere.

1. a. niñera
   b. vendedor
   c. enfermero

2. a. mesero
   b. secretario
   c. cocinero

3. a. maestro
   b. conserje
   c. dependiente

[5]**dinero:** money [6]**puesto:** position [7]**carrera:** career [8]**cortar:** to cut

PALABRA POR PALABRA

Oficios   *Trades*

la cocinera   el electricista   la secretaria   la aeromoza   el bombero   el cartero   la artista   la peluquera   el mecánico   el conserje   la camarera/mesera   el dependiente   la niñera

¡OJO!

Articles

In Spanish there is no need to use an article in front of a profession unless you are adding more information. For example: **Soy policía. Soy un policía muy paciente.**

Soy un estudiante.

Soy estudiante.

Profesiones

la médica   la enfermera   la maestra   la ingeniera   la dentista   la abogada   la escritora   la periodista   la gerente

El mundo profesional   *The professional world*

la carta de presentación	*cover letter*
la carta de recomendación	*letter of recommendation*
el currículum vítae	*résumé*
el empleo	*employment*
la empresa	*company (business)*
la entrevista (de trabajo)	*(job) interview*
el/la gerente	*manager*
el/la jefe/a	*boss*
la práctica en empresa	*internship*
el policía	*police officer (m)*
la mujer policía[9]	*police officer (f)*
el puesto	*job/position*
el trabajo	*job/work*
el sueldo	*salary/wage*
la solicitud	*application*
el/la vendedor/a	*salesperson*

Cognados: el/la arquitecto/a, el/la candidato/a, el chofer, el/la profesor/a, el/la programador/a, de computadoras, el/la atleta, el/la piloto, el/la recepcionista

[9]*The word **mujer** has to be included for a female police officer because "**la policía**" means the police force.*

© John Wiley & Sons, Inc.

Para hablar del trabajo

conseguir (un trabajo)	*to get (a job)*
cortar	*to cut*
ganar (dinero)	*to earn, make money*
limpiar	*to clean*
solicitar (un trabajo)	*to apply (for a job)*

¿Qué dicen los salvadoreños?

Ese profesor es <u>un barco</u>.	*That professor is <u>easy</u>, not strict. (Lit., That professor is a boat.)*
Estoy <u>deschambado</u>.	*I am <u>unemployed</u>.*
Hay que <u>ganarse el pan</u>.*	*One must <u>make a living</u>. (Lit., One has to earn the bread.)*
Trabaja <u>de sol a sol</u>.*	*He/She works <u>long hours</u>. (Lit., He/She works from sun to sun.)*

*Estas expresiones también se usan en otros países hispanohablantes. ¿Hay expresiones similares en inglés?

 4.1-02 ¿Cuál es la profesión más apropiada? Con un/a compañero/a, decide cuál es la profesión más apropiada para estas personas.

1. **Miguel:** Le gusta mucho ayudar a personas en situaciones de emergencias. También le gusta mucho hacer ejercicio y estar en forma. No tiene miedo a las situaciones peligrosas[10].
2. **Clara:** Quiere ir a la universidad y le gusta estudiar durante muchos años. Le gusta mucho hacer experimentos mecánicos e inventar nuevos aparatos.
3. **Patricia:** Es muy paciente y le gusta cuidar[11] a la gente. Le interesa ayudar a personas enfermas, pero no quiere estudiar durante muchos años en la universidad.
4. **Javier:** Le gusta mucho trabajar y jugar con computadoras. Le interesan los códigos y lenguajes artificiales. No es muy activo y también quiere un trabajo con horario flexible.
5. **Maribel:** No le gusta estudiar y no quiere ir a la universidad. Le interesan los tratamientos estéticos y siempre se peina con estilos diferentes.

 ¡OJO!

A job or a profession? **Puestos** are jobs or positions. An **oficio** is a job for which you need special training and a skill that it is not acquired at a university, and a **profesión** is the same as an occupation or profession and generally requires a college education.

 4.1-03 Cuestionario Comenta con un/a compañero/a estas profesiones o trabajos e intenten llegar a un consenso en sus opiniones.

MODELO: Estudiante 1:   *¿Qué piensas de ser abogado?*
Estudiante 2:   *Pienso que es aburrido.*
Estudiante 1:   *Sí, pero un abogado gana mucho dinero, ¿no?*

abogado	aburrido / interesante
enfermero	bueno / malo
peluquero	(no) hay que estudiar mucho
médico	peligroso
camarero	fácil / difícil
bombero	(no) gana mucho dinero
vendedor	(no) tiene un horario flexible
gerente	ayuda a muchas personas
programador	
¿?	

[10]**peligrosas:** dangerous [11]**cuidar:** take care

4.1-04 ¿Trabajas?

Paso 1: Entrevista a dos compañeros, para completar las dos versiones de esta entrevista.

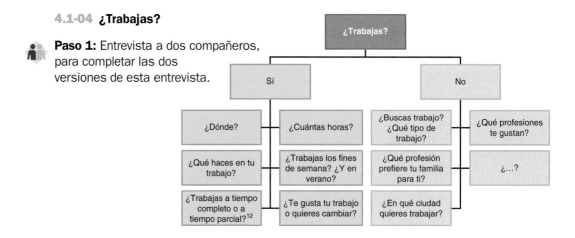

Paso 2: ¿Con quién te identificas más? Comenta tus impresiones con la clase.

MODELO: *Me identifico más con Lindsay porque ella no tiene trabajo y le gustan las mismas profesiones que a mí...*

4.1-05 Planes profesionales

Paso 1: Pregunta a varios compañeros de clase qué quieren ser y qué planes profesionales tienen después de terminar los estudios universitarios.

MODELO: Estudiante 1:   *¿Qué profesión quieres tener?*
Estudiante 2:   *Yo quiero ser médico. Después de terminar mis estudios universitarios voy a ir a la escuela de medicina.*
Estudiante 1:   *Yo no quiero estudiar más. Voy a buscar un trabajo como contable, pero primero voy a hacer prácticas en una empresa.*

Paso 2: Comenta los resultados con la clase. ¿Hay dos o más compañeros que quieren tener la misma profesión? Si la respuesta es sí, ¿tienen esos compañeros los mismos planes?

HABLANDO DE GRAMÁTICA I

WileyPLUS Go to *WileyPLUS* to review this grammar point with the help of the **Animated Grammar Tutorial** and the **Verb Conjugator.**

1. Expressing obligation: *Tener que*, *deber*, and *hay que*

In Spanish, four common verb phrases are used to talk about obligation, duty or need. With a few nuances, they are all used similarly in English.

tener que + *infinitive* (*to have to*)

Tenemos que ir a clase mañana.   *We have to go to class tomorrow.*

deber + *infinitive* (*should, ought to*)

Debo limpiar todo antes de salir   *I ought to clean up everything before*
de casa.   *leaving home.*

Even though both **tener que** and **deber** express obligation and may be interchangeable, generally speaking **tener que** expresses a slightly stronger sense of obligation than **deber**, which expresses a more moral or ethical obligation.

---

[12]a tiempo completo o a tiempo parcial: full or part-time

Hay que (*one must*) + *infinitive* is an invariable impersonal expression and cannot be conjugated like **tener que** and **deber**.

> **Hay que** saber usar muy bien un procesador de textos para ser secretaria.
>
> *One must know how to use a word processor really well in order to be a secretary.*

 ¡OJO!

¿*Tener que* or *necesitar*?

In English, we use *to have* and *to need* to express obligation interchangeably. In Spanish, you may be understood if you use **tener que** and **necesitar** interchangeably, but to a native speaker of Spanish it sounds strange. Using a form of **necesitar** means that you are actually in *need* of something, or lacking something, like needing a job. The word **necesitar** does not precede an action, only a noun:

> **Tengo que buscar** trabajo, pero antes **tengo que escribir** mi currículum vítae.
>
> *I need to look for a job, but before that I need to write my résumé.*
>
> Esta empresa **necesita empleados** cualificados.
>
> *This company needs qualified employees.*

4.1-06 ¿Qué hacen estos profesionales? Combina los números con las letras para formar oraciones.

Los abogados...
1. tienen que   a. ser honestos.
2. deben   b. defender a los clientes.
3. necesitan   c. una clientela.

Un/a maestro/a...
1. tiene que   a. una pizarra.
2. debe   b. ser entusiasta.
3. necesita   c. leer muchos exámenes.

Los cocineros...
1. tienen que   a. muchos ingredientes.
2. deben   b. cocinar para otros.
3. necesitan   c. lavarse las manos.

Los estudiantes de español...
1. tenemos que   a. practicar fuera de clase.
2. debemos   b. el libro de texto para estudiar.
3. necesitamos   c. estudiar para los exámenes.

4.1-07 Obligaciones. ¿Cuáles son las obligaciones de estas personas? Combina una frase de cada columna para formar oraciones sobre sus obligaciones.

MODELO: Un médico... / examinar a los pacientes.
→ *Un médico <u>tiene que</u> examinar a los pacientes.*
Para ser arquitecto / estudiar muchos años.
→ *Para ser arquitecto <u>hay que</u> estudiar muchos años.*

1. Para ser electricista...		muchos libros
2. Una estudiante...	hay que	ser valiente
3. Una mujer policía...	debe	saber dibujar
4. Un arquitecto...	tiene que	tener mucho cuidado
5. Una niñera...	necesita	tener talento
6. Para ser artista...		paciencia

4.1-08 Para ser un buen médico... El hermano de Gabriel, Rafael, habla de su carrera como médico y sus obligaciones profesionales. Completa su descripción con la forma apropiada de **tener que**, **deber** o **hay que**.

En general, para ser médico _____ estudiar la carrera de medicina, y después _____ hacer la residencia en un hospital. Las personas que quieren ser médicos _____ ser muy pacientes y _____ tratar a personas con problemas de todo tipo. Ser médico es un trabajo difícil, con muchas obligaciones. Por ejemplo, yo trabajo con dos enfermeras y todos los días nosotros _____ ver muchos pacientes. Yo _____ examinar a todos los pacientes, y las enfermeras _____ preparar la medicación necesaria. Frecuentemente, nosotros _____ trabajar también los fines de semana. ¡Esto es lo peor de la profesión! Si tú quieres estudiar medicina, ¡antes _____ preguntarte si realmente te gusta este tipo de vida!

LA PURA VERDAD II | La rutina de Gabriel

Gabriel consigue dos trabajos temporales porque necesita dinero. ¿Cómo es su rutina?

1.

2.

3.

4.

5.

6.

© John Wiley & Sons, Inc.

4.1-09 La rutina después del trabajo Escucha la narración y escoge la mejor opción.

1. a. Tiene que quitarse la ropa.
   b. Tiene que ponerse una camisa limpia.
   c. Tiene que peinarse.
2. a. Debe limpiar las ventanas.
   b. Debe cocinar algo delicioso.
   c. Debe vestirse bien.
3. a. Tiene que levantarse temprano.
   b. Tiene que afeitarse.
   c. No tiene que hacer nada.

HABLANDO DE GRAMÁTICA II

2. Discussing daily activities and changes of state: Pronominal verbs and reflexive pronouns

WileyPLUS Go to *WileyPLUS* to review this grammar point with the help of the **Animated Grammar Tutorial** and the **Verb Conjugator**.

A. Reflexive events
Reflexive events are those in which someone does something to or for himself/herself. Reflexive events are signaled in Spanish by the use of reflexive pronouns. Compare these examples:

Non reflexive

Por la mañana, Gabriel **mira** el reloj.
In the morning Gabriel looks at the clock.

Por las noches, Gabriel **lava** los pisos de la escuela.
At night, Gabriel mops the school floors.

Reflexive

Antes de salir, **se mira** en el espejo.
Before going out, he looks at himself in the mirror.

Cuando llega a su casa, **se lava** los dientes y **se pone** el pijama.
When he gets home, he brushes his teeth and puts on his pajamas.

In the left column, the subject of the verb (i.e., *Gabriel*) is looking at or washing something (e.g., *el reloj, los pisos*), so a reflexive pronoun is not needed. In the right column, only the subject (*Gabriel*) is involved in the action (i.e., performs the action to himself), thus the reflexive pronoun **se** is used.

B. Reflexive pronouns and pronominal verbs
In Spanish, many verbs are used with reflexive pronouns more often than not, even if the event is not truly reflexive (i.e., the subject is not acting upon him/herself). These verbs are known as pronominal verbs. You have already been using one of these verbs: **llamar(se)**.

¿Cómo **te llamas**?   **Me llamo** Patricia y ella **se llama** Sara.

Note that the subject pronoun (**yo**) and the reflexive pronoun (**me**) refer to the same person.

		llamarse		despertarse (e → ie) *(to wake up)*
(yo)	me	llamo	me	desp**ie**rto
(tú)	te	llamas	te	desp**ie**rtas
(él, ella, Ud.)	se	llama	se	desp**ie**rta
(nosotros/as)	nos	llamamos	nos	despertamos
(vosotros/as)	os	llamáis	os	despertáis
(ellos, ellas, Uds.)	se	llaman	se	desp**ie**rtan

Below are some verbs that usually take a reflexive pronoun (please note that most of these verbs can also be used without the reflexive pronoun to express a non reflexive event).

To talk about the daily routine:			
acostar(se)	to lie down	duchar(se)	to take a shower
afeitar(se)	to shave (oneself)	lavar(se)	to wash (oneself)
bañar(se)	to bathe (oneself)	levantar(se)	to get up
cepillar(se)	to brush (teeth or hair, usually)	maquillar(se)	to put on makeup
despertar(se) (e → ie)	to wake up	peinar(se)	to comb (one's hair)
dormir(se) (o → ue)	to fall asleep	sentar(se) (e → ie)	to sit down

No reflexive pronoun used: Reflexive pronoun used:
    La mamá **acuesta** a los niños a las ocho.   Ella **se acuesta** unas horas más tarde.
    The mom puts the children to bed at eight.   *She goes to bed a few hours later.*

To talk about cloth:	
vestir(se) (e → i)	*to get dressed*
poner(se)	*to put (something) on (oneself)*
quitar(se)	*to take clothes off*

No reflexive pronoun used: Reflexive pronoun used:
    Gabriel **pone** sus papeles en el portafolio.   Después **se pone** la chaqueta y sale de casa.
    Gabriel puts his papers in his briefcase.   *Then he puts his jacket on and leaves the house.*

To talk about changes of state or mood:			
sentir(se) (e → ie)	*to feel*	divertir(se)	*to enjoy oneself*
enojar(se)	*to become angry, to get upset*	aburrir(se)	*to get bored*

No reflexive pronoun used: Reflexive pronoun used:
    Gabriel **siente** mucha presión por hacer   Al final del día, Gabriel **se siente** muy
      un buen trabajo.   cansado.
    Gabriel feels a lot of pressure to do a   *At the end of the day Gabriel feels really*
      good job.   *tired.*

C. Placement of the reflexive pronouns

The reflexive pronouns (**me, te, se, nos, os, se**) are placed immediately before the conjugated verb or attached at the end if the verb is in the infinitive:

Before the conjugated verb:	After the infinitive:
Siempre <u>me</u> visto bien. *I always dress up.*	Me gusta vestir<u>me</u> bien. *I like to dress up.*
Mi padre <u>se</u> acuesta temprano. *My father goes to bed early.*	Mi padre prefiere acostar<u>se</u> temprano. *My father prefers to go to bed early.*

<u>Nos</u> vamos a maquillar antes de salir.
We are going to put on make-up before
   going out.
	Vamos a maquillar<u>nos</u> antes de salir.
	We are going to put on make-up before
	   going out.

D. The possessive or the article?

Note that in English we say "I wash <u>my</u> face" or "I brush <u>my</u> teeth." In Spanish, use an article, not a possessive, to refer to parts of the body or articles of clothing.

    Me cepillo **los** dientes tres veces al día.   *I brush my teeth three times a day.*
    Me pongo **la** chaqueta para ir a trabajar.   *I put on my jacket to go to work.*

By saying **me cepillo**, you are already indicating that you are brushing something that is part of you; using the possessive in this case would make the sentence redundant.

The following verbs have a slightly different meaning or add a different emphasis when used with the reflexive pronoun.			
subir	*to raise, to go up*	subirse	*to get up (on a horse or bus)*
dormir	*to sleep*	dormirse	*to fall asleep*
ir	*to go*	irse	*to leave*
caer	*to fall (like snow)*	caerse	*to fall down*
marchar	*to march*	marcharse	*to leave*
beber	*to drink*	beberse	*to drink up (the whole drink)*
comer	*to eat*	comerse	*to eat it all up*

4.1-10 ¿Eventos reflexivos o no? Mira las historias de **La pura verdad**, decide si estas situaciones son eventos reflexivos y completa estas oraciones de la manera más lógica.

El dilema de Gabriel

1. Gabriel no sabe qué puesto solicitar. Solo habla con sus amigos de posibles opciones, pero ellos están cansados[13] de escuchar a Gabriel. Gabriel...
   a. se aburre.   b. aburre a sus amigos.
2. Gabriel compara muchas opciones de trabajo. Pero no puede decidirse. Gabriel...
   a. siente que sus amigos están frustrados.
   b. se siente frustrado.
3. Al final Gabriel decide ser maestro de inglés. Gabriel decide...
   a. hacerse maestro de inglés.
   b. hacer muchas cosas.

Las mañanas de Gabriel

4. Por las mañanas Gabriel está muy cansado porque duerme poco. Gabriel...
   a. mira el reloj a las 7 de la mañana.
   b. se mira en el espejo a las 7 de la mañana.
5. A las 7:50, Gabriel...
   a. se levanta.   b. levanta pesas[14].
6. Después de levantarse, Gabriel...
   a. lava el auto.
   b. se lava la cara.
7. Antes de salir, Gabriel decide...
   a. ponerse una corbata[15].
   b. poner la corbata en el armario.

4.1-11 ¿Qué hace una enfermera del Hospital Rosales en El Salvador? Indica el orden cronológico con números.

En casa, antes de ir a trabajar...

3 se ducha en cinco minutos para no llegar tarde al hospital.
2 se levanta 15 minutos después.
1 se despierta muy temprano.
4 se maquilla muy poco.
5 se viste muy rápido.

En el Hospital Rosales...

6 se siente cansada.
3 baña a los pacientes.
1 se pone el uniforme blanco.
7 regresa a casa.
5 trabaja más horas por la tarde.
2 despierta a los pacientes.
4 almuerza y se acuesta unos minutos.

4.1-12 La rutina de Pedro Completa el párrafo con la forma apropiada de los verbos. Decide si debes usar el pronombre reflexivo o no.

En mi casa, mi padre _despierta_ (despertar/se) a todos mis hermanos muy temprano. A mí eso no me gusta. Yo _enojo_ (enojar/se), porque no me gusta _levanto_ (levantar/se) temprano, y él _enoja_ (enojar/se) porque yo no _levanto_ (levantar/se) inmediatamente. Además, mi padre _pone_ (poner/se) furioso cuando mis hermanas pasan mucho tiempo en el baño. ¡Ellas _maquilla_ (maquillar/se) y _peinan_ (peinar/se) durante horas! Por fin salen del baño y yo en cinco minutos _cepillo_ (cepillar/se) los dientes, _afeito_ (afeitar/se) y _ducho_ (duchar/se). ¡Es una injusticia!

4.1-13 Nuestra rutina

Paso 1: Entrevista a un/a compañero/a para saber más sobre su rutina.

1. ¿A qué hora te levantas los días que tienes clase de español?
2. ¿A qué hora te despiertas los fines de semana?
3. ¿Desayunas antes o después de ducharte?
4. ¿Prefieres ducharte o bañarte?
5. ¿Te maquillas todos los días?
6. ¿Cómo te sientes en la clase de español?

Paso 2: Ahora, escribe un pequeño párrafo para comparar la rutina de tu compañero/a con tu rutina. ¿Son similares? ¿En qué se diferencian?

MODELO: *La rutina de Diana y mi rutina son muy diferentes. Los días que tenemos clase de español, ella se levanta a las... pero yo me levanto a las...*

[13]**cansado:** tired [14]**pesas:** weighs [15]**corbata:** tie

OTRA PERSPECTIVA

Courtesy of Karina Zelaya

Karina

¿Trabajar cerca o lejos?

Diferente

"En general, parece que en Estados Unidos la gente cambia de trabajo, de ciudad, de casa y de esposo con más frecuencia que en El Salvador. Cuando obtiene un trabajo mejor, el estadounidense se muda con su familia y empieza un nuevo trabajo. ¿Por qué?"

Igual

"Muchos trabajos son de 9:00 de la mañana a 5:00 de la tarde con una hora de almuerzo, como en Estados Unidos".

 Explícale a Karina

1. Si tienes la oportunidad de tener un empleo lejos de tus padres, ¿te mudas? ¿Por qué?
2. ¿Estás de acuerdo? En Estados Unidos....
   a. la familia nuclear es más importante que los abuelos y tíos.
   b. el teléfono y el transporte aéreo hacen las distancias más cortas.
   c. un buen trabajo es importante para progresar en la vida.
   d. es importante estar cerca de tu familia.

MANOS A LA OBRA

 4.1-14 **¿En qué profesión...?**

Paso 1: Con un/a compañero/a, hablen sobre las obligaciones de cada profesión.

MODELO: abogados
  Estudiante 1:   *Los abogados siempre tienen que ponerse corbata para mostrar que*
                  son profesionales.
  Estudiante 2:   *Sí, y también deben afeitarse siempre.*

escritores	levantarse temprano
gerentes	maquillarse/afeitarse siempre
maestros	vestirse muy bien siempre
aeromozos	lavarse las manos con frecuencia
choferes	ponerse un uniforme
ingenieros	sentirse inspirados
conserjes	tener buenas relaciones con sus empleados

Paso 2: Ahora, lleguen a un consenso. ¿Qué profesión tiene las obligaciones más estrictas? ¿Y las menos estrictas? ¿Están de acuerdo con el resto de la clase?

4.1-15 Adivina, adivinador... ¿Cuál es mi profesión? Piensa en una profesión. Después, en grupos, túrnense para adivinar cuál es la profesión de sus compañeros. Unos estudiantes hacen preguntas y los otros estudiantes solo pueden responder "sí" o "no".

MODELO: Estudiante 1: *¿Tienes que ponerte uniforme?*
Estudiante 2: *Sí.*
Estudiante 1: *¿Trabajas en una escuela?*
Estudiante 2: *Sí.*
Estudiante 1: *¿Eres conserje?*
Estudiante 2: *¡Sí, muy bien! Ahora tú.*

4.1-16 ¡Quiero saber más! Después de hablar con un/a compañero/a sobre su rutina diaria en la actividad **4.1-13**, quieres saber más sobre él/ella.

Paso 1: Escribe una serie de preguntas, con las palabras interrogativas y los verbos de la lista.

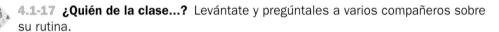
acostarse   dormirse   ponerse   sentirse   enojarse   aburrirse   divertirse

1. ¿Cómo...?
2. ¿Quién/es...?
3. ¿Cuándo...?

4. ¿Dónde...?
5. ¿Qué...?
6. ¿Cuál/es...?

> **Interrogative words**
>
> Hay muchas palabras interrogativas en español. ¿Las recuerdas? Puedes repasar estas palabras en **Hablando de gramática** del Capítulo 1, Sección 2. ¿Recuerdas cuándo usamos **qué** y cuándo usamos **cuál**?

Paso 2: Ahora, entrevista a tu compañero/a. Después, coméntale a la clase lo más interesante de sus respuestas.

4.1-17 ¿Quién de la clase...? Levántate y pregúntales a varios compañeros sobre su rutina.

MODELO: Estudiante 1: *¿Te <u>levantas</u> después de las 12?*
Estudiante 2: *No, no me <u>levanto</u> después de las 12.*

MÉDICA					
Se levanta después de las doce los sábados.	Se ducha más de una vez al día.	Se afeita las piernas.	Se despierta antes de las 6:00 de la mañana.	Se acuesta a las 3:00 de la mañana algunas veces.	Se siente frustrado/a con el trabajo.
Se ducha por cinco minutos.	Se pone perfume todos los días.	Se maquilla todos los días.	Se peina por más de 10 minutos.	Se duerme en la clase de español.	Se quita los zapatos en la clase.
Se peina varias veces al día.	Se afeita todos los días.	Se cepilla los dientes.	Se lava las manos antes de comer.	Se divierte en la clase de español.	Se pone perfume para ir a bailar.

4.1-18 Dilo con mímica Tu profesor/a te va a dar una frase que vas a representar haciendo mímicas. Tu grupo debe adivinar qué frase es en menos de 20 segundos.

4.1-19 ¡Es solo un juego! ¿A quién selecciono? Imaginen que hay un desastre ecológico y hay que fundar una nueva ciudad. Ustedes son responsables de seleccionar a seis personas para empezar una nueva comunidad. Hay diez candidatos. ¿A quiénes de la lista van a aceptar?

1. un policía
2. una médica de 36 años sin experiencia
3. un arquitecto de 75 años
4. una abogada de 26 años
5. un profesor de español de 30 años
6. una estudiante de filosofía muy inteligente
7. un mecánico de aviones
8. un dentista de 60 años
9. una actriz famosa, rica y perezosa de 28 años
10. una secretaria de 45 años que escribe 70 palabras por minuto

WileyPLUS Go to *WileyPLUS* and listen to **Presta atención.**

4.1-20 Presta atención: ¿Qué profesión es? Escucha el audio y selecciona el nombre de la profesión que coincide con la descripción.

1. a. el piloto	b. el programador	c. el policía	d. el peluquero
2. a. el cocinero	b. el chofer	c. el mesero	d. el aeromozo
3. a. el atleta	b. el gerente	c. el ingeniero	d. el cartero
4. a. el mecánico	b. el profesor	c. el conserje	d. el escritor

4.1-21 Por escrito: Una carta de recomendación Una persona que conoces busca trabajo. Escribe una carta de recomendación para él/ella. Incluye su trabajo actual, características personales y su educación. Explica por qué esa persona es la apropiada para el puesto.

MODELO:

¡OJO!

Formal Letter
Use the format of this letter, beginning with the location, date and a greeting. Use the model as an example, giving information such as the applicant's personal traits, academic preparation, and applicant's current job. This is a formal letter, so use a formal register using **usted** instead of the **tú** form.

Hospital Santo Tomás

San Salvador, 7 de noviembre de 2013

A quien corresponda:

Julieta Fernández es enfermera y trabaja en la clínica Santo Tomás. Julieta es una persona muy sociable, amistosa y cuidadosa. Trabaja muy bien con los médicos, pacientes y otras enfermeras. Julieta estudió enfermería en la Universidad de El Salvador. Recomiendo a Julieta para el trabajo de enfermera por ser la mejor enfermera de esta clínica.

Atentamente,

Marco Prado
Director del Hospital Santo Tomás

PONTE EN MI LUGAR

Estrategias para conversar

Asking for clarification
When asking for clarification, these are some strategies you can use:

- Repeat the word or phrase as a question (e.g., *¿Camarero?*)
- Ask your partner to explain (e.g., *¿Qué significa "camarero"?*)
- Let your partner see that you don't understand (e.g., *¿Qué? ¿Cómo dices?*)
- Propose another word with a similar meaning (e.g., *Lo mismo que mesero.*)

¿Cómo es tu trabajo? Vas a pasar un año en Honduras para estudiar y mejorar el español. Estás interesado/a en trabajar en ese país. Los padres de un/a amigo/a viven en Estados Unidos, pero son hondureños y vivieron 20 años en Tegucigalpa.

Paso 1: Con un/a compañero/a selecciona un papel: el padre o la madre de tu amigo/a o el/la estudiante estadounidense. Si no comprendes a tu compañero/a, debes hacer preguntas para verificar tu comprensión. Recuerda usar las estrategias para conversar.

Paso 2: El/La estudiante estadounidense comienza la conversación:

Estudiante estadounidense:

a. Saluda formalmente al padre/la madre del/de la amigo/a (usa "usted").
b. Pregunta si puedes hacerle unas preguntas sobre los trabajos en su país de origen.
c. Pide información sobre las horas de trabajo en su país de origen y la posibilidad de encontrar trabajo en Honduras.
d. Pregunta si tiene contactos en Honduras para conseguir un trabajo durante el verano.

Padre o madre hondureños:

a. Saluda al/a la amigo/a de tu hijo/a (usa "tú").
b. Pide que te explique por qué quiere información sobre los trabajos en Honduras.
c. Explica que el horario depende del trabajo.
d. Pregunta sobre sus intereses, qué le gusta, qué no le gusta y la experiencia profesional que tiene.
e. Pregunta dónde trabaja, qué hace en el trabajo, qué le gusta y qué no le gusta.
f. Pregunta si puede trabajar en Honduras.
g. Menciona la idea de hacer prácticas en alguna compañía sin ganar dinero.

WileyPLUS Go to *WileyPLUS* to find more **Arroba** activities.

El currículum vítae
Explora en tu buscador favorito información sobre qué debes incluir en tu currículum vítae en español. ¿Qué diferencias hay entre un currículum vítae en español y otro en inglés?

ASÍ ES LA VIDA

Chiste

Un periodista corre con su cámara hasta un pequeño avión que espera en una pista[16] del aeropuerto.

Periodista:	*¡Vámonos! ¡Rápido!*
Piloto:	*¿Rápido? ¿Por qué?*
Periodista:	*Quiero ver el incendio[17]. Vuela más bajo[18].*
Piloto:	*Es difícil controlar el avión. Tengo miedo. ¿Por qué tenemos que ir hacia el incendio?*
Periodista:	*¡Porque soy periodista y tengo que fotografiar el incendio!*
Piloto:	*¡¿Un periodista?! ¿Usted no es mi instructor?*

[16]**pista:** runway [17]**incendio:** fire [18]**Vuela...** fly lower

Adivina, adivinador

La bolsa, compañera,
me acompaña con frecuencia.
Voy de casa en casa
llevando correspondencia.
¿Quién soy?

ENTÉRATE

Estrategias para leer

Skimming is a reading strategy in which you read quickly in order to identify the main idea of the text, rather than reading for comprehension. Skimming works well to look for places, names, and dates. There are many strategies that can be used when skimming. You already learned some of them in previous chapters:

- In the Preliminary Chapter, Chapter 1 and Chapter 2 you learned that visual aids (layout of the text, title, illustrations) as well as recognizing cognates are useful tools to learn about the content.
- In Chapter 3, Section 1 you learned to read the first and last sentences of the text in order to get an idea about the content.

Antes de leer

1. Un nuevo trabajo Imagina que tienes un trabajo con un buen sueldo pero no eres feliz, así que quieres buscar otro trabajo. Reflexiona un poco a partir de las siguientes preguntas para saber qué tipo de trabajo te interesa.

1. ¿Cuáles son tus habilidades?
   a. Hablo otro idioma
   b. Trabajo bien con la gente
   c. Soy organizado/a
   d. Otras habilidades
2. ¿Qué nivel de educación tienes?
   a. Escuela secundaria
   b. Un año en la universidad
   c. Una maestría
   d. Otro nivel
3. ¿Qué tipo de carrera te interesa?
   a. Psicología
   b. Educación
   c. Negocios
   d. Otras carreras
4. ¿Qué oración te describe mejor?
   a. Me gusta ser el centro de atención.
   b. Me gusta aprender solo, sin ayuda.
   c. Me gusta analizar información.
   d. Me gusta viajar. No me gustan las oficinas.

2. Carreras.com Lee rápidamente el texto de la lectura. Recuerda todas las estrategias que ya sabes (título, cognados, fotos…). ¿Qué tipo de texto es? ¿Cuál es el tema?

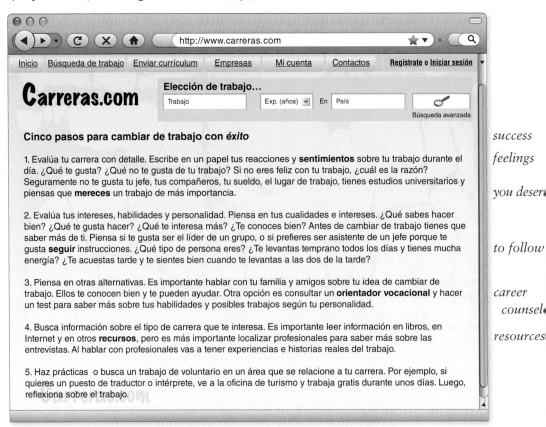

http://www.carreras.com

Inicio   Búsqueda de trabajo   Enviar currículum   Empresas   Mi cuenta   Contactos   **Regístrate** o **Iniciar sesión**

Carreras.com

Elección de trabajo…

Trabajo   Exp. (años)   En   País

Búsqueda avanzada

Cinco pasos para cambiar de trabajo con *éxito*

1. Evalúa tu carrera con detalle. Escribe en un papel tus reacciones y **sentimientos** sobre tu trabajo durante el día. ¿Qué te gusta? ¿Qué no te gusta de tu trabajo? Si no eres feliz con tu trabajo, ¿cuál es la razón? Seguramente no te gusta tu jefe, tus compañeros, tu sueldo, el lugar de trabajo, tienes estudios universitarios y piensas que **mereces** un trabajo de más importancia.

2. Evalúa tus intereses, habilidades y personalidad. Piensa en tus cualidades e intereses. ¿Qué sabes hacer bien? ¿Qué te gusta hacer? ¿Qué te interesa más? ¿Te conoces bien? Antes de cambiar de trabajo tienes que saber más de ti. Piensa si te gusta ser el líder de un grupo, o si prefieres ser asistente de un jefe porque te gusta **seguir** instrucciones. ¿Qué tipo de persona eres? ¿Te levantas temprano todos los días y tienes mucha energía? ¿Te acuestas tarde y te sientes bien cuando te levantas a las dos de la tarde?

3. Piensa en otras alternativas. Es importante hablar con tu familia y amigos sobre tu idea de cambiar de trabajo. Ellos te conocen bien y te pueden ayudar. Otra opción es consultar un **orientador vocacional** y hacer un test para saber más sobre tus habilidades y posibles trabajos según tu personalidad.

4. Busca información sobre el tipo de carrera que te interesa. Es importante leer información en libros, en Internet y en otros **recursos**, pero es más importante localizar profesionales para saber más sobre las entrevistas. Al hablar con profesionales vas a tener experiencias e historias reales del trabajo.

5. Haz prácticas o busca un trabajo de voluntario en un área que se relacione a tu carrera. Por ejemplo, si quieres un puesto de traductor o intérprete, ve a la oficina de turismo y trabaja gratis durante unos días. Luego, reflexiona sobre el trabajo.

success

feelings

you deser

to follow

career
counsel

resources

Después de leer

1. En el texto. Sin consultar el diccionario, contesta: ¿Qué significa la palabra *recursos*? ¿Cómo lo sabes? ¿Es una palabra en singular o en plural? ¿Es un sustantivo, un verbo o un adjetivo?

Ahora busca la palabra *recurso* en el diccionario. ¿Cuántos significados aparecen en el diccionario? ¿Qué otra palabra sinónima en español se usa para decir *recursos*?

2. ¿Entendiste? Lee los cinco pasos para cambiar de trabajo con éxito y selecciona la/s respuesta/s correcta/s.

1. Cuando una persona tiene que evaluar su trabajo quiere...
   a. saber si es feliz en su trabajo.
   b. hablar con su jefe rápidamente.
   c. ir a trabajar todos los fines de semana.
2. Si buscas trabajo...
   a. debes conocer tus habilidades.
   b. debes saber qué personalidad tienes.
   c. debes saber tus intereses.

3. Para tener más opciones tienes que...
   a. consultar con tu jefe.
   b. consultar con tu familia y amigos.
   c. consultar con un orientador.
4. Se recomienda...
   a. trabajar gratis de voluntario.
   b. cambiar de trabajo cada mes.
   c. hablar con profesionales.

EN TUS PROPIAS PALABRAS

Estrategias para escribir

Fast writing You already know some Spanish vocabulary and now it is time for you to engage with content and review in order to reflect on what you know. A strategy to start writing and, in the end, to produce more writing is by engaging in rapid writing. The purpose of rapid writing is to allow you to record what you know about a topic without worrying about any errors. Put this strategy in practice by following these steps:

- Think about a topic to write, such as "the perfect job."
- Write as fast as you can in Spanish.
- Do not worry about corrections or erasing your mistakes.
- Write for one minute. Do not stop before.
- Don't lift your pen from the paper.
- If you get stuck, jumpstart your brain by rewriting previous words.
- After a minute, count and record the number of words you have written.
- Check spelling.

El trabajo de mis sueños. Piensa en tu experiencia de trabajo y en tus estudios, después escribe un párrafo sobre tu trabajo ideal. Ese pequeño diario puede ayudarte a aclarar tus ideas sobre tu futuro. Lee estas preguntas y después escribe el párrafo usando la estrategia de escribir rápido.

- ¿Qué estudias?
- ¿Tienes experiencia de trabajo relacionada con tus estudios?
- ¿Cómo eres personalmente? ¿Tímido, sociable...?
- ¿Buscas un trabajo para ayudar a la gente?
- ¿En qué lugar quieres trabajar?

AUTOPRUEBA

VOCABULARIO

I. Profesiones ¿Qué profesiones asocias con...

1. clases, libros, estudiantes?
2. medicina, uniforme, pacientes?
3. computadoras, teléfonos, público?
4. ejercicio, televisión, dinero?
5. criminales, justicia, público?

II. Un día en la vida de una peluquera Ordena las actividades en el día de una peluquera en orden cronológico.

_____ a. Se acuesta y se duerme.

_____ b. Se pone el uniforme y se peina.

_____ c. Se despierta y se ducha.

_____ d. Después de trabajar, se siente cansada.

_____ e. Peina y maquilla a muchas clientas.

_____ f. Se sienta a almorzar.

_____ g. Se quita el uniforme cuando regresa a casa.

GRAMÁTICA

I. ¿Qué hacen estos profesionales? Con los verbos de la lista, escribe oraciones completas para describir las actividades de estas personas.

MODELO: Un bombero (despertarse)
→ *Un bombero se despierta con una alarma de incendios.*

| afeitarse | lavarse | dormirse | peinar | ducharse |

1. Los médicos...
2. Los atletas a veces...
3. Mi peluquero/a...
4. Yo...
5. Nosotros, los estudiantes, a veces...

II. ¿Qué deben o tienen que hacer estas personas?

MODELO: Un cocinero... **tiene que** *lavarse las manos antes de cocinar.*

1. Un conserje...
2. Un mesero...
3. Un bombero...
4. Un programador de computadoras...
5. Yo, estudiante de español,...

CULTURA

1. ¿Qué tipo de preguntas son aceptables en una entrevista de trabajo en un país como El Salvador?
2. ¿Qué consideración impide cambiar de trabajo con frecuencia en muchos países hispanos?

REDACCIÓN

Escribe una pequeña redacción para describir qué haces durante la semana. Incluye información sobre:

- **Tu rutina por la mañana:** ¿A qué hora te levantas, te bañas, sales a trabajar, sales a estudiar?
- **En el trabajo:** ¿Dónde trabajas? ¿Cuántas horas? ¿Qué haces en el trabajo? ¿Cómo es tu jefe?
- **La universidad:** ¿Qué clases tomas? ¿A qué hora? ¿Cuántas horas estudias?
- **Tu rutina al final del día:** ¿A qué hora te acuestas los días laborales? ¿A qué hora te acuestas los fines de semana?
- **Una conclusión:** ¿Cómo es tu vida en general? ¿Muy ocupada? ¿Muy divertida? ¿Interesante? ¿Aburrida?, etc.

EN RESUMIDAS CUENTAS, AHORA PUEDO...

☐ hablar sobre oficios, puestos y profesiones.

☐ hablar sobre las obligaciones de un trabajo.

☐ hablar sobre los cambios de estado emocional.

☐ hablar sobre mi rutina diaria y la de otros.

☐ hacer preguntas

☐ entender mejor una entrevista de trabajo en un país hispano.

☐ comparar el mercado de trabajo entre Estados Unidos y los países hispanos.

VOCABULARIO ESENCIAL

Sustantivos		Verbos	
el/la abogado/a	*lawyer*	aburrir(se)	*to get bored*
el/la aeromozo/a	*flight attendant*	acostar(se)	*to lie down*
el/la bombero/a	*firefighter*	afeitar(se)	*to shave (oneself)*
el/la camarero/a, mesero/a	*waiter/waitress*	bañar(se)	*to bathe (oneself)*
la carta de presentación	*cover letter*	cepillar(se)	*to brush (teeth or hair, usually)*
la carta de recomendación	*letter of recommendation*	conseguir (un trabajo)	*to get (a job)*
el/la cartero/a	*mail carrier*	cortar	*to cut*
el/la cocinero/a	*cook*	deber	*must, ought, should*
el/la conserje	*janitor*	despertar(se) (ie)	*to wake up*
el currículum vítae	*résumé*	divertir(se)	*to enjoy oneself*
el/la dependiente	*sales clerk*	dormir(se) (ue)	*to fall asleep*
el empleo	*employment*	duchar(se)	*to take a shower*
la empresa	*company (business)*	enojar(se)	*to become angry, to get upset*
el/la enfermero/a	*nurse*	ganar (dinero)	*to earn, make (money)*
la entrevista (de trabajo)	*(job) interview*	hay que	*one must*
el/la escritor/a	*writer*	lavar(se)	*to wash (oneself)*
el/la gerente	*manager*	levantar(se)	*to get (oneself) up*
el/la ingeniero/a	*engineer*	limpiar	*to clean*
el/la jefe/a	*boss*	maquillar(se)	*to put on makeup*
el/la maestro/a	*teacher*	peinar(se)	*to comb (one's hair)*
el/la médico/a	*doctor, physician*	poner(se)	*to put (something) on (oneself)*
la mujer policía	*police officer (f)*	quitar(se)	*to take clothes off*
el/la niñero/a	*baby sitter*	sentar(se) (ie)	*to sit down*
el oficio	*job/trade*	sentir(se) (ie)	*to feel*
el/la peluquero/a	*hairdresser*	solicitar (un trabajo)	*to apply (for a job)*
el/la periodista	*journalist*	tener (que)	*to have (to)*
el policía	*police officer (m)*	vestir(se) (i)	*to get dressed*
la práctica en empresa	*internship*		
el puesto	*job/position*		
la solicitud	*application*		
el sueldo	*salary/wage*		
el trabajo	*job/work*		
el/la vendedor/a	*salesperson*		

Cognados: el/la atleta, el/la arquitecto/a, el/la artista, el/la candidato/a, el/la chofer, el/la dentista, el/la electricista, el/la mecánico/a, el/la piloto, la profesión, el/la profesor/a, el/la programador/a de computadoras, el/la recepcionista, el/la secretario/a

LEARNING OBJECTIVES

By the end of this section you will be able to:

- Compare addresses and directions in the U.S. and Central America
- Identify places in a city and talk about location
- Talk about the weather
- Express intention, motive and movement
- Talk about actions in progress

▲ *El lago Nicaragua (el mar Dulce)*

Una imagen vale más que mil palabras

¿Por qué crees que el lago[1] Nicaragua se llama mar Dulce?

¿Conoces otros lagos en Latinoamérica?

¿Vives cerca de un lago?

UNA PERSPECTIVA

Eva

¿Dónde vives?

Diferente

"En Nicaragua las calles y carreteras principales tienen números o nombres, pero las otras calles no. No tienen números ni nombres. Las direcciones orales o postales dan un punto de referencia y una distancia. Por ejemplo: 'De la farmacia Altamira, 10 cuadras[2] al lago, allí está mi casa' o 'Del bar, dos cuadras a la costa, allí vive mi mamá'. Para los que viven en el área no hay problema, pero si estás de visita, como yo, y no estás familiarizado con el punto de referencia, "estás fregado"[3], como dicen los nicaragüenses. Otra cosa curiosa es que señalan[4] un sitio o a una persona con los labios".

Igual

"Muchas carreteras[5] principales y calles tienen nombres y números como en Estados Unidos. El sistema de correos funciona bien".

¿Qué piensas tú?

1. ¿Las direcciones se dan con puntos de referencia, o siempre hay calles y números para identificarlas en EE. UU.?
2. ¿Es fácil o difícil encontrar tu casa? ¿Es fácil explicar cómo llegar a tu casa?
3. ¿Qué gesto[6] haces cuando quieres señalar algo?

---

[1]**lago:** lake [2]**cuadras:** blocks [3]**estar fregado/a:** to be out of luck [4]**señalar:** to point [5]**carreteras:** highways [6]**gesto:** gesture

LA PURA VERDAD I   ¿Cómo llego?

Alexis es un joven de Estados Unidos que llega a Nicaragua y quiere visitar a su amigo nicaragüense, Moisés Medina.

1.

"Moisés vive en la Colonia Miguel Bonilla, detrás de la UNAN, de la Farmacia Soler, dos cuadras al sur y tres cuadras arriba."

2.

Bueno, hay que tomar la Carretera Norte y continuar para abajo. Camina por la Avenida Bolívar al sur y sigue preguntando.

Disculpe, señor, ¿cómo llego al barrio Miguel Bonilla?

3.

Disculpe, señorita, ¿cómo llego al barrio Miguel Bonilla?

Está lejos, creo que está detrás de la UNAN. Hay que seguir hacia el sur, por la UNAN y seguir preguntando.

4.

Aquí está la UNAN, pero, ¿dónde está la Farmacia Soler?

Está cerquitita, ahí nomás, sigue por esa calle y está a mano izquierda.

Disculpe, señor, ¿cómo llego a la Farmacia Soler?

5.

¿Arriba?

"De la Farmacia Soler, cuatro cuadras al sur y tres cuadras arriba."

6.

Disculpa, ¿cómo llego a la casa de Moisés Medina?

Es la casa que está al lado de la palma real.

¡Gracias!

No hay de qué.

© John Wiley & Sons, Inc.

4.2-01 El vecindario de Moisés Alexis y Moisés van a visitar a un amigo del vecindario. Escucha la narración.

1. Traza la trayectoria en el mapa.
2. ¿Cuándo pueden ir al lago?
   a. Pueden ir al lago mañana por la mañana.
   b. Pueden ir al lago mañana por la tarde.
   c. Pueden ir al lago hoy.
3. ¿Dónde está la parada de autobús?
   a. En frente de la casa de Moisés.
   b. Lejos de la casa de Moisés.
   c. Al este de la casa de Moisés.

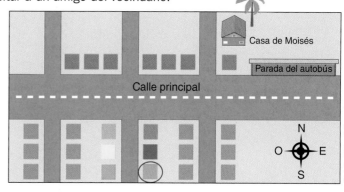

Casa de Moisés

Parada del autobús

Calle principal

N
O   E
S

© John Wiley & Sons, Inc.

PALABRA POR PALABRA

La ciudad *The city*

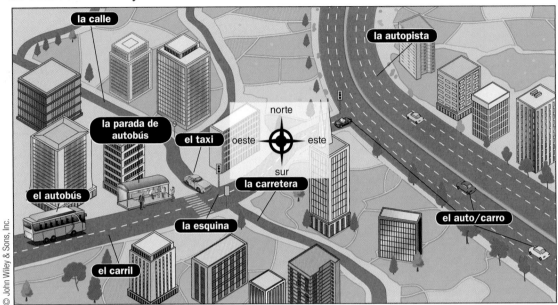

Lugares en la ciudad	Places in the city
el barrio	neighborhood
(la oficina de) correos	post office
la cuadra	city block
el cine	movie theatre
la dirección	address/direction

la discoteca	night club
el estacionamiento	parking lot
el pueblo	town
la plaza	square

Cognados: el aeropuerto, la avenida, el banco, el bar, la estación, la farmacia, el hospital, el hotel, el kilómetro, la milla, el museo, el punto de referencia, el restaurante, el supermercado, el teatro

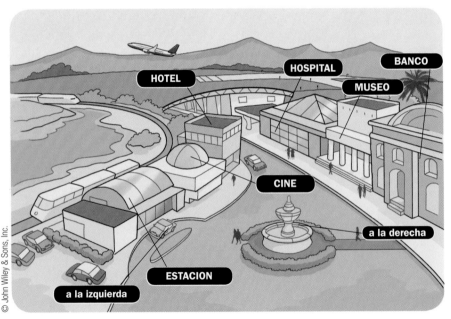

La ubicación *Location*

abajo	*down*
arriba	*up*
seguir	*to continue, follow*

1. El museo está **entre** el hospital y el banco.
2. La estación está **cerca de** la fuente.
3. El aeropuerto está **lejos de** la fuente.
4. El cine está **al lado de** la estación.
5. El hotel está **delante del** hospital.
6. El tren está **detrás de** la estación.
7. El auto está **en frente del** hotel.
8. El hospital está **al final de** la calle.

Expresiones

Disculpe, ¿cómo llego a...?	*Excuse me, how do I get to . . . ?*
Siga por la derecha.	*Continue on the right hand side.*

El tiempo *The weather*

▲ *En la playa* hace mucho sol *y* calor. Hace buen tiempo *para nadar.*

llover

la lluvia

el viento

▲ Hace mal tiempo. Está lloviendo *y* hace mucho viento. *¡Parece un* huracán*!*

la nieve

nevar

▲ *Aquí en Nicaragua no* hace frío *ni* nieva. Hace fresco.

¿Qué tiempo hace? *What's the weather like?*

Hace sol.	*It is sunny.*
Hace (mucho) calor.	*It is (very) hot.*
Hace (mucho) viento.	*It is (very) windy.*
Hace fresco.	*It is cool (neither hot nor cold).*
Hace buen/mal tiempo.	*The weather is good/bad.*
(No) Hace frío.	*It is (not) cold.*
Llueve (mucho).	*It rains (a lot).*
No nieva.	*It doesn't snow.*
Está nublado.	*It is cloudy.*
Hay tormenta.	*It is stormy.*
Hay niebla.	*It is foggy.*
Hay humedad.	*It is humid.*
Hay un huracán.	*There is a hurricane.*
¿Qué temperatura hace?	*What's the temperature?*
Hace 40 grados C.	*It is 40 degrees C.*

Conversiones

Grados centígrados a Fahrenheit: $°C \times 1.8 + 32 = °F$
Grados Fahrenheit a centígrados: $(°F - 32) \times 0.56 = °C$
1 milla = 1.6 kilómetros
km/h = kilómetros por hora
mi/h o mph = millas por hora

¿Qué dicen los centroamericanos?

Dobla a la derecha y está <u>ahí nomás</u>.*	*Turn right and it's <u>right there</u>.*
Yo soy <u>catracho/a</u>.	*I am <u>Honduran</u>.*
Si no conoces el área, <u>estás fregado</u>.	*If you don't know the area <u>you are out of luck</u>.*
Él/Ella no es de aquí. Es <u>nica</u>.	*He/She is not from here. He/She is <u>Nicaraguan</u>.*
Nunca gano. Estoy <u>salado</u>.	*I never win. I have <u>bad luck</u> (Lit., salty).*

*Esta expresión también se usa en otros países hispanohablantes.

4.2-02 Callejeando por San Salvador Mira el mapa del centro de San Salvador. Tu profesor/a va a decir dónde están algunos lugares y edificios de interés. Escucha con atención y escribe el número que corresponde a cada lugar en el mapa.

Lugares:

_8_ Plaza Gerardo Barrios

____ Palacio Nacional

____ Teatro Nacional

____ Plaza Comercial España

____ Supermercado La Despensa

____ Biblioteca Nacional

____ Centro comercial El Rosario

____ Centro escolar República de Argentina

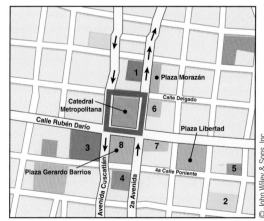

4.2-03 ¿Con qué frecuencia? Con un/a compañero/a, túrnense para decir con qué frecuencia hacen las siguientes actividades y por qué.

MODELO: ir al supermercado en carro
    Estudiante 1:   *¿Con qué frecuencia vas al supermercado en carro?*
    Estudiante 2:   *Nunca voy al supermercado en carro porque está muy cerca de mi casa.*
    Estudiante 1:   *Yo voy siempre en carro. ¡Mi casa está muy lejos del supermercado!*

1. tomar un taxi
2. manejar[7] por la autopista   siempre
3. visitar el museo de la ciudad   muchas veces
4. ir a la oficina de correos   a veces
5. correr por el parque   casi nunca
6. ir de compras al centro   nunca

4.2-04 ¿Cuándo haces estas actividades?

Paso 1: Con un/a compañero/a, túrnense para hacerse preguntas para saber cuándo hacen las siguientes actividades.

MODELO: ponerse una chaqueta
    Estudiante 1:   *¿Cuándo te pones una chaqueta?*
    Estudiante 2:   *Me pongo una chaqueta cuando hace fresco.*

                                                            hace fresco
1. patinar   hace frío
2. caminar en las montañas   hace calor
3. jugar con la nieve   hace viento
4. tomar el sol   llueve
5. llevar un paraguas   nieva
6. ...

Paso 2: Por lo general, ¿ustedes coinciden en sus respuestas o hacen algo diferente?

4.2-05 ¿Qué te gusta hacer cuando...?

Paso 1: Con un/a compañero/a, túrnense para ver si tienen los mismos gustos. ¡No olviden reaccionar a las respuestas de su compañero/a!

MODELO: hace mucho calor
    Estudiante 1:   *¿Qué te gusta hacer cuando hace mucho calor?*
    Estudiante 2:   *Me gusta beber té helado en una terraza.*
    Estudiante 1:   *Sí, a mí también* o *Yo prefiero estar en casa con el aire acondicionado.*

1. hace sol   5. hay niebla
2. hace mucho frío   6. hay lluvia
3. hace fresco   7. hace buen tiempo
4. hace viento   8. hace mal tiempo

¿Recuerdas como usar el verbo gustar? Es un poco diferente a los otros verbos, ¿verdad? Mira la sección **Hablando de gramática** del Capítulo 1, Sección 2, para recordar cómo usar este verbo.

Paso 2: Ahora, comenta los resultados con la clase. ¿Qué les gusta hacer a los dos?

MODELO: *Cuando hace mucho calor, a nosotros nos gusta beber té helado.*
                o
           No nos gusta hacer las mismas cosas, parece que somos muy diferentes.

4.2-06 ¿Conoces bien tu ciudad?

Paso 1: Con un/a compañero/a, habla sobre tu ciudad. Pregúntale dónde queda algún lugar.

MODELO: *¿Dónde está la oficina de correos?*
           Está en el centro, en frente del Hospital General.

Paso 2: Comenta con la clase: ¿Conoce tu compañero/a bien tu ciudad? ¿Por qué?

[7]manejar: to drive

HABLANDO DE GRAMÁTICA I

1. Expressing intention, motive, and movement: The prepositions *por, para, a, de* and *en*

WileyPLUS Go to *WileyPLUS* to review this grammar point with the help of the **Animated Grammar Tutorial**.

Prepositions are connectors between words. You already know some prepositions, such as **en** to express location, or the preposition **por** in many fixed expressions such as **por favor, por ejemplo** or **por fin**.

Por and **para** are two prepositions that are generally translated as *for* in English. However, they have different meanings in Spanish.

A. Use **por** to...
- express duration of an activity (although you can omit **por** in this case, or use **durante** instead); for this reason **por** is always used in fixed expressions such as **por la mañana, por la tarde, por la noche**:

Camina (**por/durante**) diez minutos más o menos.	*Walk for ten minutes more or less.*
Todos los días Alexis corre (**por/durante**) una hora.	*Everyday Alexis runs for an hour.*
Por la noche duermen en el Hotel Colón.	*At night you sleep in Hotel Colón.*

- indicate the reason or motive for an action (as in *because of* or *in behalf of*):

Alexis decidió visitar Nicaragua **por** su interesante historia arqueológica.	*Alexis decided to visit Nicaragua because of its interesting archeological history.*
Ahora que Alexis está en Nicaragua, le gusta muchísimo **por** su gente.	*Now that Alexis is in Nicaragua, he likes it a lot because of its people.*

B. Use **para** to...
- express what something is intended for:

Alexis compró una mochila **para** su viaje.	*Alexis bought a backpack for his trip.*
También compró muchos regalos **para** sus padres.	*He also bought a lot of presents for his parents.*

- express purpose or goal (as in *in order to*), in which case it is followed by an infinitive:

Alexis va a Nicaragua **para** estudiar antropología.	*Alexis goes to Nicaragua to study anthropology.*
Para entender las direcciones a la casa de Moisés, tiene que preguntar a varias personas.	*In order to understand the directions to Moises' house, he has to ask several people.*

C. To talk about movement through space, use **por, para, en, a, de** in the following way:
- Use **por** to express movement through, on or along a place:

Camina **por** esa calle tres cuadras más.	*Walk on that street for three more blocks.*
Tienes que pasear **por** el centro; es precioso.	*You have to walk around the city center; it is beautiful.*

- Use **para** to indicate movement towards a destination:

Toma la carretera norte y continúa **para** Managua.	*Take the north road and continue towards Managua.*
El autobús **para** la UNAN sale a las 9 de la mañana.	*The bus leaves to the UNAN at 9 am.*

- When discussing means of transportation, use **en**:

  Alexis va a hacer el tour arqueológico **en** tren.

  Alexis is going to do the archeological tour by train.

  Los padres de Alexis van a llegar **en** avión.

  Alexis's parents will arrive by plane.

- With the verb **ir**, use **a** to indicate direction towards a place. If **a** is followed by **el**, use the contracted form **al (al = a + el)**:

  Alexis quiere **ir al** centro de la ciudad y después **a** las ruinas de León Viejo.

  Alexis wants to go to the city center, and then to the ruins of Leon Viejo.

- To express that you are coming from a place, use **de**:

  ¿**De** dónde vienes?

  Where are you coming from?

  Vengo **de** Managua.

  I am coming from Managua.

4.2-07   **De viaje**   Liliana va a viajar a Honduras y les escribe un mensaje electrónico a sus padres para contarles los detalles. Completa el mensaje con la preposición adecuada (**por, para, en, de, a**) e indica por qué usas esa preposición.

Queridos mamá y papá:

_____ fin mañana salgo _____ Honduras. Mi itinerario es
el siguiente: voy a viajar _____ avión el día 17 de febrero. Voy a pasar
una semana visitando las ruinas cerca de Tegucigalpa. También me gustaría pasear
_____ el centro de la ciudad. Después pienso ir _____ las
famosas ruinas de Copán, _____ admirar algunos de los monumentos más
importantes de la civilización maya. Allí pienso quedarme _____ dos días.
Regreso _____ mi viaje el día 26. Quisiera pasar más tiempo en Honduras,
pero el día 27 tengo que empezar a trabajar otra vez.

Un abrazo,
Liliana

4.2-08   **El viaje de Alexis**   Antes de ir a Nicaragua, Alexis habla de su viaje con unos amigos. Completa las oraciones combinando las frases de las dos columnas con las preposiciones **por, para, en, de** and **a**.

MODELO: Tengo que comprar muchas cosas / mi viaje
        → *Tengo que comprar muchas cosas **para** mi viaje.*

1. Quiero ir...
2. Quiero visitar Nicaragua...
3. Voy a hacer un tour...
4. Voy a viajar...
5. Voy a comprar muchos regalos...
6. Voy a estar en Managua...
7. Me gusta Nicaragua...
8. Vuelvo...

a. una semana.
b. todo el país.
c. conocer bien su historia.
d. Nicaragua.
e. todos mis amigos.
f. tren.
g. su belleza[8] natural.
h. Nicaragua el 27 de este mes.

4.2-09   **¡Tu visita a América Central!**   Ahora eres tú quien hace planes para viajar a América Central. Completa las siguientes oraciones de manera lógica.

1. En este viaje voy a ir a...
2. Me gusta América Central por...
3. En América Central voy a viajar mucho en...
4. Voy a visitar mercados al aire libre para...
5. Voy caminar mucho por...
6. Voy a estar allí por...
7. Voy a comprar _____ para...
8. Voy a regresar de _____ el día...

[8]belleza: *beauty*

LA PURA VERDAD II   **Una visita de sus padres**

Los padres de Alexis vienen a visitarlo. Llegan al aeropuerto de Managua.

1.

Bienvenidos a Managua. La hora local es la 1:15 de la tarde. Hoy hace 31 °C en Managua.

2.

3.

¿Dónde hay wifi?

Pues, arriba, cerca de la cafetería, por las tiendas. Por allí hay wifi.

4.

5.

Yo voy a llegar primero.

Vamos al hotel en bus.

6.

4.2-10 ¿Qué hacer? Escucha lo que pasa con Alexis y sus padres y selecciona la mejor opción.

1. a. Esperar en el aeropuerto por tres horas más.
   b. Ir en autobús.
   c. Ir en taxi.
2. a. ...estudiar español.
   b. ...buscar un buen restaurante en Internet.
   c. ...llamar a la policía.
3. a. Está pidiéndoles un celular a otras personas.
   b. Está buscando un lugar con mejor conexión.
   c. Está mirando el accidente.

HABLANDO DE GRAMÁTICA II

WileyPLUS Go to *WileyPLUS* to review this grammar point with the help of the **Animated Grammar Tutorial** and the **Verb Conjugator**.

2. Talking about actions in progress: Present progressive

When you want to emphasize that an action is being carried out at the moment of speaking, you use the present progressive:

Ahora mismo Alexis **está haciendo** la maleta.	*Right now Alexis is packing his suitcase.*
Sus padres **están esperando** en el aeropuerto mientras él **está manejando**.	*His parents are waiting at the airport while he is driving.*

Form the present progressive with the present tense of **estar** + *the present participle*. In English, the present participle is the *-ing* form of a verb. In Spanish, the present participle (**gerundio** in Spanish) is formed by dropping the infinitive ending and adding **-ando** (**-ar** verbs), or **-iendo** (**-er** and **-ir** verbs).

	estar	+	*present participle*
(yo)	estoy		
(tú)	estás		
(él, ella, Ud.)	está		habl**ando**
(nosotros/as)	estamos		com**iendo**
(vosotros/as)	estáis		escrib**iendo**
(ellos, ellas, Uds.)	están		

Stem-changing verbs change **o → u** and **e → i** in the present participle. Verb stems of an **-er** or **-ir** that end in a vowel, form the present participle with **-yendo**.

decir → d**i**ciendo	servir → s**i**rviendo	dormir → d**u**rmiendo	leer → le**y**endo
pedir → p**i**diendo	sentir → s**i**ntiendo	oír → o**y**endo	traer → tra**y**endo

The use of present progressive in Spanish is much more restricted than in English; in Spanish it is only used to talk about an *activity or action in progress* at the moment:

Alexis es el chico que **está leyendo** la guía.	*Alexis is the guy who is reading the guide. (reading is what he is doing right now)*

Never use the present progressive to talk about a future event (as in English). In Spanish, the simple present is used instead:

¿A qué hora **sales** mañana?	*At what time are you leaving tomorrow?*
El sábado **hacemos** la visita turística por Managua.	*On Saturday we are going on a tour around Nicaragua.*

4.2-11 Preparativos para el viaje Alexis sale de viaje mañana y toda su familia está participando en los preparativos. Escribe lo que está haciendo cada persona.

1. Alexis...
2. Su padre...
3. Su madre...
4. Los gatos...
5. Sus hermanos...

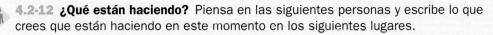 **4.2-12 ¿Qué están haciendo?** Piensa en las siguientes personas y escribe lo que crees que están haciendo en este momento en los siguientes lugares.

MODELO: Mi hermano / restaurante
→ *Mi hermano* <u>*está cenando*</u> *con un amigo.*

1. Mi profesor(a) de español / su oficina
2. Mi mejor amigo/a / su cuarto
3. Mi padres / en casa
4. Mi compañero/a de clase / biblioteca
5. Yo / ¿?

3. Identifying, describing, and talking about location: More on *ser* and *estar*

 Puedes repasar el verbo **ser** *en* **Hablando de gramática** *del Capítulo 1, Sección 1, y el verbo* **estar** *en* **Hablando de gramática** *del Capítulo 3, Sección 2.*

As you already know, there are two different verbs to express *to be* in Spanish: **ser** and **estar**. As you learned in Chapter 1, Section 1, **ser** is used to define, classify or identify an object or person:

¿Qué **es** esto? **Son** las <u>ruinas</u> de Copán.   *What's this? They are the ruins of Copan.*
Alexis **es** <u>amigo</u> mío.   *Alexis is my friend.*
El Salvador **es** el <u>país</u> más pequeño de   *El Salvador is the smallest country in*
  América Central.   *Central America.*

As such, it is only natural that we use **ser** to talk about origin:

Alexis **es** (un chico) <u>de Estados Unidos</u>.   *Alexis is (a guy) from the U.S.*

A. Ser/estar with adjectives
- Use **ser** + *adjective* when naming a characteristic that distinguishes the person or thing from other persons or things:

El Museo de Arqueología Maya **es** impresionante.   *The Museum of Mayan Archeology is impressive* (i.e., you are describing the museum as opposed to other museums).

La artesanía maya **es** muy apreciada por los turistas.   *Mayan crafts are very appreciated by tourists* (i.e., you are describing the crafts as opposed to other things tourists might like).

- Use **estar** + *adjective* to describe a condition that distinguishes a person's or thing's current state from other possible states of *itself*.

El museo **está** cerrado hoy.   *The museum is closed today* (i.e., the museum is open sometimes).

Estos artículos de artesanía **están** rebajados.   *These crafts are on sale* (i.e., they were not on sale before).

B. Ser/estar + *location*
- As you learned in Chapter 3, Section 2, we use **estar** for the location of people, places, and things:

Las ruinas de Copán **están** en el oeste de Honduras.   *The ruins of Copan are in western Honduras.*
La casa de Moisés **está** cerca de la Farmacia Soler.   *Moise's house is close to Farmacia Soler.*

- Use **ser** for the location and time of events (not physical objects):

La celebración del Solsticio de Primavera **es** en el Templo Mayor a las 6 de la mañana.   *The Spring Solstice celebration takes place at the main temple at 6 in the morning.*
La fiesta de cumpleaños de Alexis **es** en la casa de Moisés.   *Alexis's birthday party is at Moise's house.*

¡OJO!

Ser and ***estar***
As a verb of identification, we always use **ser** (never **estar**) followed by a noun, a noun phrase, or a pronoun.

~~Estoy~~ estudiante. → **Soy** estudiante.

Ella ~~está~~ la organizadora del tour → Ella **es** la organizadora del tour.

La organizadora ~~está~~ ella → La organizadora **es** ella.

USES OF *SER* AND *ESTAR*	
Use ser...	**Use estar...**
1. With **adjectives** to describe a characteristic Las ruinas son impresionantes. *The ruins are impressive.*	1. With **adjectives** to describe a condition Las ruinas están abandonadas. *The ruins are abandoned.*
2. For **location** and time of events La celebración es en el Templo Mayor. *The celebration takes place at the main temple.*	2. For **location** of people, places and things Las ruinas están lejos de Tegucigalpa. *The ruins are far from Tegucigalpa.*
3. With **nouns** to define, identify or classify a person/object Las ruinas son el mejor reflejo de la cultura maya. *The ruins are the best example of the Mayan culture.*	3. With **present participle** to describe an action in progress Hoy Alexis está visitando las ruinas. *Today Alexis is visiting the ruins.*

 4.2-13 Alexis prepara su viaje Alexis quiere tener toda la información posible. Completa sus oraciones combinando las frases con la forma apropiada de **ser** o **estar**.

MODELO: Nicaragua / un país centroamericano
→ *Nicaragua es un país centroamericano.*

1. Nicaragua...   en agosto.
2. La capital de Nicaragua...   al suroeste del lago de Managua.
3. Managua...   cálida todo el año.
4. La temperatura en Managua...   Managua.
5. Las fiestas de Santo Domingo...   entre Honduras y Costa Rica.
6. En Managua los museos...   cerrados los lunes.

 4.2-14 Una foto Después de su viaje, Alexis le enseña fotos a su mejor amiga. Completa la descripción de la foto más especial con la forma adecuada de **ser** o **estar**.

Mira, estos _____e_____ mis amigos nicaragüenses. Aquí _____ todos en un restaurante. Mi amigo Iván __*esta*__ en el centro. Él __*estan*__₂ muy contento porque _____₃ su fiesta de graduación. Las chicas que _____₅ detrás de Iván __*son*__ sus hermanas. Ellas _____₈ muy simpáticas, pero aquí _____₉ un poco cansadas, ¿las ves?

 4.2-15 Una visita a las ruinas Con un/a compañero/a, describe a las personas de la foto contestando a las preguntas. ¡Usen la imaginación!

MODELO: Estudiante 1:   *¿Dónde están estas personas?*
Estudiante 2:   *Creo que están en...*
Estudiante 1:   *Pues yo creo que están en... porque...*

1. ¿Quiénes son estas personas?   4. ¿De dónde son?
2. ¿Cómo son?   5. ¿Dónde están?
3. ¿Cómo están?   6. ¿Qué están haciendo?

Ahora, describan la foto a la clase. ¿Están de acuerdo los otros estudiantes con su descripción?

Bill Bachmann / Photo Researchers / Getty Images

OTRA PERSPECTIVA

Courtesy of Miguel Montesinos

Miguel

¿A qué distancia?

Diferente

"En El Salvador calculamos distancias en kilómetros, no en millas. Si me explican algo en millas, no puedo visualizar la distancia. Tengo que convertir el número en kilómetros, entonces puedo 'ver' la distancia. También es interesante que en EE. UU. calculan las distancias por tiempo. 'Está a diez minutos o está a tres horas[9]'. Nosotros no decimos eso".

Casi igual

"Al escribir la dirección postal usamos la calle y el número como en Estados Unidos, pero con una pequeña diferencia: nuestra dirección se escribe con la calle primero y el número después. Por ejemplo: Calle Colón #245, San Salvador".

Explícale a Miguel

1. ¿Qué es más largo, un kilómetro o una milla?
2. ¿Puedes visualizar distancias en kilómetros inmediatamente?
   a. ¿Qué es más rápido, una velocidad de 60 kilómetros por hora o 50 millas por hora?
   b. ¿Qué está a tres kilómetros de distancia desde donde tú estás ahora?

MANOS A LA OBRA

4.2-16 ¿Qué están haciendo? En Honduras, tu clase de español espera en una parada de autobús para hacer una excursión al Parque de la Leona en Tegucigalpa. Tu amigo/a conoce a algunos estudiantes y tú a otros. Mira el dibujo y explica qué está haciendo cada estudiante para poder identificarlo/a. ¡No mires el dibujo de tu compañero/a!

MODELO: Estudiante 1:   *Un chico está durmiendo.*
                Estudiante 2:   *Bien, ya lo veo.*
                Estudiante 1:   *Se llama Armando.*
                Estudiante 2:   (escribe el nombre)

© John Wiley & Sons, Inc.

[9]**Está a... minutos/horas:** It is . . . minutes/hours away.

4.2-17 ¿Dónde está? Con un/a compañero/a, mira el mapa de Managua y localiza algunos lugares. Tu compañero/a tiene 15 segundos para encontrarlos y decir dónde está ¡en español!

MODELO: Estudiante 1: *¿Dónde está la Yo no pude encontrar en el mapa la Plaza de la República. ?*

Estudiante 2: *¡Aquí está! Está en la 6a Calle Noreste, en frente del Parque Central.*

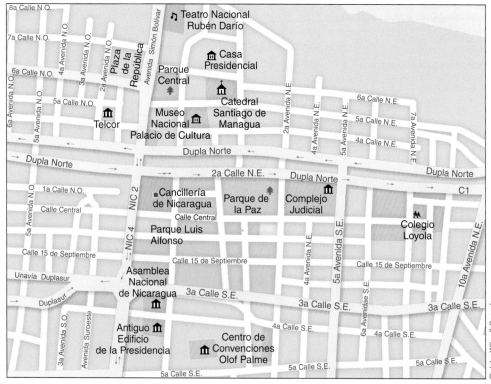

4.2-18 Tu ciudad

Paso 1: Con un/a compañero/a, habla sobre lo siguiente:

1. ¿Dónde está tu casa? ¿Cómo se llama tu barrio?
2. ¿Vives cerca o lejos del centro? ¿A cuántas millas o kilómetros está tu casa del centro?
3. ¿Vives cerca de un museo, una estación, una iglesia u otro punto de referencia? ¿Cuáles? ¿Cómo se llaman?
4. ¿Hay un buen supermercado, un estacionamiento o una oficina de correos en tu barrio? ¿Qué lugares frecuentas en tu barrio?
5. ¿Cuál es tu lugar favorito de tu ciudad? ¿Vas allí con frecuencia? ¿Por qué?
6. ¿Qué tiempo hace en tu ciudad? ¿Cómo es el clima en cada estación?
7. ¿Te gusta tu barrio y tu ciudad? ¿Por qué? ¿Qué no tiene tu ciudad que crees que es importante tener?

Paso 2: Después, escriban un pequeño párrafo. ¿En qué aspectos coinciden los dos? ¿En qué no coinciden?

MODELO: Mi compañero/a y yo vivimos en el área metropolitana de Los Ángeles. Él/Ella vive en Culver City y yo vivo en el centro. A los dos nos gusta que casi casi siempre hace buen tiempo, pero no nos gusta que es muy seco y casi nunca llueve...

Paso 3: Por último, informen a la clase. ¿Viven en el mismo lugar? Si la respuesta es sí, ¿coinciden en todo o en nada? Si no viven en la misma ciudad, ¿qué diferencias hay?

4.2-19 Película muda[10] En grupos, preparen una breve escena muda. Actúen en frente de la clase. La clase tiene que adivinar qué está pasando y narrar la escena. ¡Recuerden usar el gerundio!

4.2-20 Poder de observación Observa el dibujo por un minuto y trata de recordar lo más posible. Dile a un/a compañero/a todo lo que recuerdas[11]. Tu compañero/a va a confirmar o a modificar tu respuesta.

MODELO: Estudiante 1:   *El niño está montando en bicicleta.*
Estudiante 2:   *No, está llorando, al lado de su bicicleta.*

[10] **película muda:** silent film [11] **todo lo que recuerdas:** everything that you remember [12] **billetes de lotería:** lottery tickets

WileyPLUS Go to *WileyPLUS* and listen to **Presta atención.**

4.2-21 Presta atención: En la carretera Carolina sale de trabajar. Cuando está en el carro recibe una llamada de su hija. Escucha con atención y decide qué respuesta es más apropiada según la conversación.

1. ¿Qué problema tiene la mamá?
   a. La mamá tiene mucho trabajo y tiene que estudiar.
   b. La mamá está en la esquina pero hace mal tiempo.
   c. Hace mal tiempo y va muy lenta con el carro.
2. ¿Qué le dice la hija a su mamá?
   a. Ven rápido a casa.
   b. Ve tranquila que no pasa nada.
   c. Te veo en dos horas.
3. ¿A qué velocidad va su mamá?
   a. A 15 kilómetros por hora.
   b. A 25 millas por hora.
   c. A 25 kilómetros por hora.
4. ¿Por qué la hija dice que está cansada?
   a. Porque tiene que ir al trabajo.
   b. Porque tiene mucha tarea y exámenes.
   c. Porque su mamá tiene problemas.
5. ¿Cuándo va a llegar la mamá a casa?
   a. En una hora.
   b. En breves momentos.
   c. En tres horas.

4.2-22 Por escrito: El mapa de un estado Imagina que tienes un/a amigo/a en Honduras que quiere visitar Estados Unidos. No conoce nada de Estados Unidos y quiere información sobre un estado de tu país. Tu amigo/a te escribió un mensaje con información de su ciudad. Ahora tú escríbele un correo electrónico describiendo el mapa del estado donde vives incluyendo un itinerario con posibles lugares para visitar. En tu mensaje incluye:

a. Referencias espaciales (*al norte, al sur, a... kilómetros de..., de... a, en...,* etc.)
b. Vocabulario de este capítulo para indicar los lugares que hay (*¿Qué hay? Hay una oficina de correos, un estacionamiento...*)
c. Información sobre el lugar (*¿Dónde está?*)
d. Información sobre el tiempo que hace en esos lugares (*Hace 25 grados Celsius en verano...*)
e. Otra información relevante
f. Recuerda incluir un saludo (*Hola...*) y una despedida (*hasta luego, hasta pronto, nos vemos, hasta la próxima...*)

MODELO:
¡Hola, David! Aquí te mando algo de información sobre Tegucigalpa, la ciudad donde vivo. Yo vivo en la avenida de... Exactamente estoy al lado de la calle 10 sureste. Al sur está... Al este se encuentra... y al norte se encuentra... En el verano hace buen tiempo... En Tegucigalpa me gusta ir al cine y a bailar a un... También me gusta ir... Bueno, David, te cuento más en mi próximo mensaje.

Hasta la próxima,
Esther

¡OJO!

Revise your writing
When writing the composition about your state in the **Por escrito** activity, do not forget to revise your writing for vocabulary and grammar use:

1. Try to include new vocabulary and expressions.
2. Avoid repeating words by using synonyms.
3. Avoid using false cognates.
4. Simplify your sentences if you do not know complex grammar.

PONTE EN MI LUGAR

¡Una fiesta! Estás en San Salvador y llamas a tu amigo Roque. Roque te invita a una fiesta en su casa. El Estudiante 1 comienza la conversación.

Estudiante 1:

a. llama por teléfono y pregunta por Roque
b. pregúntale a Roque qué está haciendo en este momento
c. cómo va la fiesta
d. pregunta qué están haciendo los invitados
e. la dirección de la casa de Roque

Estudiante 2 (Roque):

a. responde al teléfono
b. explica que estás en una fiesta de graduación de tu hermano
c. da detalles sobre la fiesta
d. invita a tu amigo/a
e. explica cómo llegar a tu casa

ASÍ ES LA VIDA

Expresión: Al mal tiempo, buena cara

Ramón: *No sé qué hacer porque no tengo trabajo.*
 Mario: *Bueno, ¡al mal tiempo, buena cara!*

¿Qué significa esta expresión? ¿Sabes otras expresiones en inglés con un significado similar?

Adivina, adivinador

¿Qué es, qué es,
que te da en la cara
y no lo ves?

Estrategias para conversar

Giving clarification When trying to get your message across to other people in Spanish or other foreign language, there are several strategies you can use if you do not know or cannot remember a word (e.g., **carril**).

• Define the words (e.g., **En una carretera, es por donde van los autos**).

• Use another word (e.g., **una calle**).

• Give examples (e.g., **Como en la carretera I-80 donde hay líneas para los autos**).

WileyPLUS Go to *WileyPLUS* to find more **Arroba** activities.

@Arroba@

El tiempo ¿Cómo es el tiempo donde vives? ¿Cómo es el tiempo en Honduras, Nicaragua o El Salvador? Busca en tu buscador favorito información para comparar y contrastar el tiempo de la ciudad donde vives con el tiempo de una ciudad hispana de los tres países mencionados. Busca "pronóstico del tiempo en _____"; por ejemplo "pronóstico del tiempo en Tegucigalpa" o "pronóstico del tiempo en San Salvador". Escribe una redacción y comparte tus respuestas con la clase. En tu redacción incluye lo siguiente:

1. El tiempo para mañana en tu ciudad y en la ciudad hispana
2. Los grados centígrados para el fin de semana en esas ciudades
3. Otro tipo de pronóstico[13] en las dos ciudades

---

[13] **pronóstico:** forecast

VER PARA CREER II: ¡Me encanta mi trabajo!

WileyPLUS Go to *WileyPLUS* to see this video and to find more video activities.

Antes de ver

Con la ayuda de un/a compañero/a contesta estas preguntas para reflexionar sobre el tema del video que vas a ver.

1. ¿Qué lugares visitas en una ciudad cuando haces turismo?
2. ¿Te gusta ir a los museos? ¿Por qué?
3. ¿Tienes buena orientación en un lugar nuevo?
4. ¿Cuál es el trabajo de un guía turístico?
5. ¿Qué tiempo hace en tu ciudad ahora?

Después de ver

1. ¿Entendiste? Gabriela es una estadounidense que ahora vive en Granada, Nicaragua. Su vida es muy diferente a su vida en Estados Unidos. Presta atención al video para saber más sobre lo que hace Gabriela en Granada.

1. ¿Qué trabajo tiene Gabriela?
   a. Tiene un empleo de traductora.
   b. Tiene un empleo de vendedora.
   c. Tiene un empleo de guía turística.
2. ¿Por qué está nerviosa Gabriela?
   a. Está nerviosa porque no conoce bien los lugares del tour.
   b. Está nerviosa porque no sabe comunicarse en inglés.
   c. Está nerviosa porque le gusta la ciudad, pero no los museos.
3. Según Gabriela…
   a. en EE. UU. las direcciones son iguales que las direcciones en Nicaragua.
   b. en su país y en Nicaragua las direcciones son la distancia y un número.
   c. en Nicaragua dan direcciones con un punto de referencia y una distancia.
4. ¿Qué tiempo hace en Granada?
   a. Hace muy buen tiempo.
   b. Nunca hace sol.
   c. En el invierno nieva.
5. ¿De dónde es Gabriela?
   a. Gabriela es de Granada.
   b. Gabriela es de Minnesota.
   c. Gabriela es de Chicago.

2. Un tour en tu ciudad Uno de ustedes es el guía turística y el otro es un/a turista. Decidan quién es el guía y quién el turista. Después, escriban una conversación para representarla en la clase.

3. Enfoque cultural ¿Cómo se diferencia la geografía donde tú vives de la geografía de Nicaragua? ¿Cómo das direcciones para ubicar un lugar en tu país? ¿Cómo se diferencian esas direcciones de las de Nicaragua?

AUTOPRUEBA

VOCABULARIO

I. ¿Qué es? Lee la definición y di qué es.

autobús   kilómetro   carretera   este   taxi

1. Es un espacio por donde circulan los carros.
2. Es un medio de transporte público que puede transportar a muchas personas.
3. Es la dirección por donde sale el sol.
4. Es un medio de transporte público para una, dos o tres personas solamente.
5. Es el equivalente a 1.6 millas.

¿Dónde está? Mira el mapa y determina dónde está la embajada.

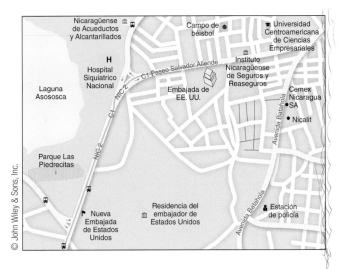

1. Está _____ de la laguna Asososca.
2. Está _____ del campo de béisbol.
3. Está _____ del Instituto Nicaragüense de Seguros.
4. Está _____ la carretera C1 y la Avenida Batahola.
5. La residencia del embajador está _____ la embajada.

III. ¿Qué tiempo hace hoy en América Central? Mira el mapa y describe qué tiempo hace en los siguientes lugares. ¡Atención! ¡Las temperaturas están en grados centígrados!

1. San Salvador
2. Tegucigalpa
3. Managua
4. Puerto Cabezas
5. Ciudad de Guatemala

Ciudad de Guatemala 24°
Tegucigalpa 16°
Puerto Cabezas 28°
San Salvador 18°
Managua 20°

GRAMÁTICA

I. El aeropuerto Para saber cómo se llega al aeropuerto, completa los espacios en blanco con la preposición correcta (**por, para en, de, al**).

_____₁ llegar al aeropuerto es mejor ir _____₂ autobús. Ir _____₃ la embajada _____₄ aeropuerto va a tomar como una hora. _____₅ la mañana hay muchos autobuses que pasan _____₆ la embajada cada 30 o 45 minutos.

II. Probablemente Piensa en las actividades que probablemente estas personas están haciendo ahora.

1. Mi profesor/a está _____ en el Departamento de Español.
2. Mis padres están _____ en casa.
3. Mi mejor amigo está _____ en su cuarto.
4. Mi compañero/a de la clase de español está _____ en la biblioteca.
5. Yo _____ en _____.

III. Preguntas personales Completa las preguntas con la forma adecuada de **ser** o **estar** y después contesta con información personal.

1. ¿Cómo _____estás_____ hoy?
2. ¿Cómo _____es_____ tu personalidad?
3. ¿De dónde _____eres_____?
4. ¿Dónde _____está_____ ahora?
5. ¿Qué _____está_____ haciendo ahora?

CULTURA

1. ¿Cómo son las direcciones en Nicaragua? (Hay más de una respuesta posible).
   a. Se dice el número primero y luego la calle.
   b. Se basa en puntos de referencia.
   c. Se dice la calle primero y después el número.
   d. Son difíciles para los extranjeros.
2. ¿En Honduras o Nicaragua? ¿En qué país...
   a. hay un lago muy grande?
   b. hay una ciudad que se llama Tegucigalpa?

EN RESUMIDAS CUENTAS, AHORA PUEDO...

☐ reconocer lugares característicos de las ciudades.

☐ describir el tiempo.

☐ identificar, describir y hablar sobre ubicaciones.

☐ hablar sobre acciones que están pasando ahora.

☐ expresar intención, motivo y dirección de movimiento.

☐ comparar las direcciones entre Estados Unidos y América Central.

VOCABULARIO ESENCIAL

Sustantivos

la autopista	*highway*
el auto/carro	*car*
la avenida	*avenue*
el barrio	*neighborhood*
la calle	*street*
la carretera	*road*
el carril	*lane*
el cine	*movie theatre*
la ciudad	*city*
la cuadra	*city block*
la dirección	*address, direction*
la discoteca	*night club*
la esquina	*corner*
el estacionamiento	*parking lot*
el este	*east*
la lluvia	*rain*
el lugar	*place*
la nieve	*snow*
el norte	*north*
el oeste	*west*
(la oficina de) correos	*post office*
la parada de autobús	*bus stop*
la plaza	*square*
el pueblo	*town*
el sur	*south*
el tiempo	*weather*
el viento	*wind*

Cognados: el aeropuerto, el autobús, el banco, el bar, la estación, la farmacia, el hospital, el hotel, el kilómetro, la milla, el museo, el punto de referencia, el restaurante, el supermercado, el taxi, el teatro

Verbos

llover	*to rain*
nevar	*to snow*
seguir	*to continue, follow*

Adverbios y preposiciones de lugar

abajo	*down*
arriba	*up*
cerca	*near*
delante (de)	*in front (of)*
detrás (de)	*behind*
en frente (de)	*in front (of)*
entre	*in between*
lejos	*far*
a la derecha	*to the right*
a la izquierda	*to the left*
al lado (de)	*next (to)*
al final (de)	*to the end (of)*

Expresiones

Disculpe, ¿cómo llego a...?	*Excuse me, how do I get to. . . ?*
Siga por la derecha.	*Continue on the right hand side.*
¿Qué tiempo hace?	*What's the weather like?*
Está nublado.	*It is cloudy.*
Hace buen/mal tiempo.	*The weather is good/bad.*
Hace (mucho) calor.	*It is (very) hot.*
Hace fresco.	*It is cool.*
LLueve (mucho).	*It rains (a lot).*
No nieva.	*It doesn't snow.*
(No) Hace frío.	*It is (not) cold.*
¿Qué temperatura hace?	*What's the temperature?*
Hace ___ grados F/C.	*It is ___ degrees F/C.*
Hace sol.	*It is sunny.*
Hace (mucho) viento.	*It is (very) windy.*
Hay tormenta.	*It is stormy.*
Hay niebla.	*It is foggy.*
Hay humedad.	*It is humid.*
Hay un huracán.	*There is a hurricane.*

5 La vida social

VER PARA CREER I ¡A bailar!

Mira el video sin sonido y contesta las preguntas. Presta atención a las imágenes para descifrar el contenido del video.

1. ¿Adónde crees que va el chico?
2. ¿Qué hace el chico en ese lugar? Menciona dos actividades.
3. ¿Qué hacen el chico y la chica al final del video?

Sección 1 — Música y ¡a bailar!

PALABRA POR PALABRA
- Los instrumentos
- Bailes del Caribe

HABLANDO DE GRAMÁTICA
- Talking about actions in progress: The present progressive ♻
- Avoiding repetition: Direct object pronouns
- Saying what you know: The verbs **saber** and **conocer**
- Interrogative words ♻

CULTURA
- Los cumpleaños y las quinceañeras
- La cultura del baile

Sección 2 — Celebraciones

PALABRA POR PALABRA
- Las celebraciones: La boda y el bautizo
- Otras celebraciones

HABLANDO DE GRAMÁTICA
- Talking about future plans: **Ir** + **a** + verb ♻
- Saying for whom something is done: Indirect object pronouns
- Discussing exchanges and reporting: The verbs **dar** and **decir**
- Expressing likes and dislikes (III): Verbs like **gustar** ♻

CULTURA
- Diferentes costumbres a la hora de celebrar
- La festividad de los Reyes Magos

Puerto Rico, República Dominicana y Cuba

Trivia: Go to *WileyPLUS* to do the **Trivia** activities and find out how much you know about these countries!

LEARNING OBJECTIVES

By the end of this section you will be able to:

- Understand the importance of dancing in the Caribbean countries and the **quinceañera** celebration
- Talk about different Caribbean rhythms and instruments
- Describe celebrations
- Use direct object pronouns to avoid repetition
- Say what you know
- Request information by asking direct questions

Una imagen vale más que mil palabras

Tim Dolan Photography/ UpperCut Images / Getty Images

¿Cuántos años cumple la niña?

¿Cuántos años tienen los invitados aproximadamente?

¿Qué están haciendo los invitados?

◄ *Una familia dominicana celebra los cinco años de la niña.*

UNA PERSPECTIVA

Courtesy Norma Lopez-Burton

Leslie

Los quince años

Diferente

"Fui a una gran fiesta de cumpleaños[1] en Puerto Rico. Allí, la celebración se llama 'quinceañero[2]', pero en México se llama 'quinceañera o 'fiesta quinceañera'. La celebración de los quince años es muy importante en el Caribe y muchos países hispanos porque, en teoría, este cumpleaños marca el paso de ser una niña a ser una mujer adulta. El evento varía mucho de país en país y de familia en familia. A veces consiste en una ceremonia religiosa seguida de una recepción; otras veces es solo una gran fiesta. La celebración de los quince años es similar a una boda; hay invitaciones, música, comida, flores, decoraciones, invitados[3], regalos y baile. Hay de todo, ¡excepto el novio!"

Igual

"El cumpleaños número dieciséis o el *Sweet Sixteen* también es especial en EE. UU. Dependiendo de la situación económica de cada familia, la celebración puede hacerse en la casa, un club social o un hotel".

 ¿Qué piensas tú? Decide si es **Cierto** o **Falso** y di por qué piensas así.

	Cierto	Falso
1. El quinceañero y el *Sweet Sixteen* son similares.	☐	☐
2. Hay un cumpleaños muy importante en Estados Unidos: el número 18.	☐	☐
3. Hay un evento social en Estados Unidos que marca el paso de un/a niño/a a un adulto: el *Senior Prom*.	☐	☐

[1]**cumpleaños:** birthday [2]**quinceañero:** 15th birthday celebration [3]**invitados:** guests

LA PURA VERDAD I   ¡Feliz Año Nuevo!

Tom y Tatiana son unos jóvenes estadounidenses que están visitando Puerto Rico. Hoy es Día de Año Viejo y van a bailar a una fiesta.

1.

¡Vamos a esperar el año nuevo bailando y escuchando música! ¡Hay que divertirse!

2.

Es un conjunto de salsa. Mira los instrumentos. ¿Te gusta este ritmo?

3.

¿Quieres bailar?

No, gracias; ahora no.

4.

Ahora están tocando un merengue. ¡Qué chévere! ¿Quieres bailar ahora?

No, gracias.

5.

Tom, no quiero bailar. Estoy cansada, no me gusta el reguetón y quiero irme a casa. Puedo tomar un taxi, no te preocupes. Adiós.

¡Lo siento!

6.

¿Lo siento?

© John Wiley & Sons, Inc.

5.1-01 El Año Nuevo Escucha la narración y contesta **Cierto** o **Falso**. Si es falso, explica por qué.

1. _____   2. _____   3. _____   4. _____

PALABRA POR PALABRA

Los instrumentos

las maracas · el bajo · el saxofón · el cantante · el trombón · la trompeta · el micrófono · la guitarra · los timbales · las congas · los bongós · el piano · la banda / el grupo / el conjunto (musical)

© John Wiley & Sons, Inc.

Para hablar de la música

la canción	*song*	animar	*to enliven*
el/la músico/a	*musician*	bailar	*to dance*
la pareja	*couple, partner*	cantar	*to sing*
los pasos de baile	*dance steps*	gritar	*to shout*

Cognados: el concierto, la música, la percusión, el ritmo

Cognados: celebrar, invitar

Bailes del Caribe   *Dances from the Caribbean*

el bolero
el chachachá
el mambo

la salsa
el reguetón

el merengue
la bachata

la cumbia

© John Wiley & Sons, Inc.

Expresiones

dar la vuelta	*to spin around*
hacer/dar una fiesta (sorpresa)	*to have/give a (surprise) party*
pasarlo/pasarla bien	*to have a good time*
¿Quieres bailar?	*Do you want to dance?*

¿Qué dicen los caribeños?

Hay una fiesta esta noche. <u>¡Qué chévere!</u>	*There is a party tonight. <u>Cool!</u>*
En Puerto Rico todos somos <u>boricuas</u>.	*In Puerto Rico we are all <u>boricuas</u>. (Taino word for Puerto Rican.)*
Les gusta bailar merengue porque son de <u>Quisqueya</u>.	*They like to dance merengue because they are from the <u>Dominican Republic</u>. (Taino word for the island.)*
Los <u>guajiros</u> son del corazón de Cuba.	*<u>Guajiros</u> are from the heart of Cuba. (Cubanism for people who live and work on the countryside.)*
Qué buena música. Vamos a <u>echar un pie</u>.	*What great music. Let's dance.*

5.1-02 ¿Qué sabes de música?

Paso 1: ¿Qué instrumentos asocias con...?

Rodrigo Varela/WireImage/Getty Images

AP Photo/Mike Albans

©Jeff Morgan 08/Alamy

▲ *José Feliciano*   ▲ *Tito Puente*   ▲ *Manuel Mirabal*

1. José Feliciano
2. Tito Puente
3. Manuel Mirabal
4. la música clásica
5. la percusión
6. el jazz
7. la salsa
8. el reguetón

Paso 2: Ahora, escribe una lista similar con el nombre de cinco músicos o grupos que conozcas. Pregúntale a un/a compañero/a qué instrumentos asocia con los nombres de tu lista. Después coméntale a la clase qué sabe de música tu compañero/a.

MODELO: *Mi compañero/a sabe mucho/poco de música porque...*

5.1-03 ¿Te gusta bailar?

Paso 1: Lee las siguientes preguntas y añade dos más. Después, conversa con un/a compañero/a sobre sus preferencias y gustos relacionados con la música.

1. ¿Sabes bailar? ¿Bailas algún ritmo caribeño, latinoamericano o español? ¿Cuál?
2. ¿Dónde bailas? ¿Vas a conciertos frecuentemente? ¿Vas a las discotecas?
3. ¿Cuándo te diviertes más, cuando vas a un concierto o cuando vas a una discoteca con tus amigos?
4. Cuando vas a un concierto, ¿gritas o animas al cantante o grupo?
5. ¿Qué hace tu familia para celebrar las ocasiones especiales? ¿Bailan, cantan, juegan, conversan? ¿Lo pasas bien en las fiestas familiares?

Paso 2: ¿Hay algunos aspectos en los que coinciden? ¿En cuáles coinciden y en cuáles no? Escriban un pequeño párrafo. Después, presenten su párrafo a la clase.

MODELO: *Los/Las dos bailamos y vamos a las discotecas frecuentemente, pero no a los conciertos...*

5.1-04 ¿Quién soy? Piensa en un cantante o grupo musical famoso. Después, en parejas, túrnense para adivinar quién es. Sigan el modelo.

MODELO: Estudiante 1:   *¿Estás en un grupo musical?*
Estudiante 2:   *No, soy una cantante solista.*
Estudiante 1:   *¿Eres estadounidense?*
Estudiante 2:   *No, soy cubana.*
Estudiante 1:   *¿Eres cantante de salsa?*
Estudiante 2:   *Sí.*
Estudiante 1:   *¡Eres Celia Cruz!*
Estudiante 2:   *¡Sí, muy bien!*

 5.1-05 ¡Música! Tu amigo/a está en la fiesta de **La pura verdad** con Tom y Tatiana.

Paso 1: Tú lo/la llamas a su celular para que te cuente qué está pasando.

MODELO: preparar
Estudiante 1:   *¿Qué pasa en el escenario?*
Estudiante 2:   *Los músicos <u>están preparando</u> los instrumentos.*

seguir los pasos	pasarlo bien/mal	animar
divertirse	aprender la letra[4]	tocar
gritar	cantar una canción	bailar
		mirar

1. ¿Qué instrumentos tocan los músicos?
2. ¿Qué hacen las personas que escuchan la banda?
3. ¿Qué pasa con Tatiana?
4. ¿Qué hace Tom?
5. ¿Qué hace el músico con el micrófono?
6. ¿Qué haces con una canción?

Paso 2: Ahora, piensen en dos preguntas más. Tu amigo/a también quiere saber qué estás haciendo tú.

7. _____
8. _____

 Paso 3: Después, informen a la clase sobre las diferentes actividades que están haciendo.

MODELO: *Pues él está bailando con una chica en esa fiesta, pero yo estoy… Los dos nos estamos divirtiendo.*

> **⟳ Talking about actions in progress: The present progressive**
>
> In **La pura verdad**, Tom says to Tatiana:
>
> *Ahora **están tocando** un merengue.*
>
> Tom is using the present progressive to talk about an action that is happening at that moment.
>
> Do you remember...
>
> 1) how to conjugate the present progressive?
> 2) which verbs are irregular?
>
> Go to **Hablando de gramática**, Chapter 4, Section 2, to check your answers.

[4]**la letra:** lyrics

HABLANDO DE GRAMÁTICA I

I. Avoiding repetition: Direct object pronouns

A. If someone asked you, "Do you play the trumpet often?" you could reply: "Yes, I play it every day." In this example, *the trumpet* is the direct object and *it* is the direct object pronoun. Direct objects receive the action of the verb and answer the questions *who/ whom?* or *what?*: "*What* do you play?" "The trumpet." The direct object can be a single word or a complete phrase. Direct object *pronouns* replace the names of specific direct object *nouns* (such as *the trumpet*) and agree with them in number and gender.

WileyPLUS Go to *WileyPLUS* to review this grammar point with the help of the **Animated Grammar Tutorial**.

Direct object pronouns

Singular		Plural	
me	me	**nos**	us
te	you *(familiar)*	**os**	you *(familiar, Spain)*
lo	you *(formal)*, him, it *(m)*	**los**	you *(formal)*, them *(m, m+f)*
la	you *(formal)*, her, it *(f)*	**las**	you *(formal)*, them *(f)*

Direct object	
Tito Puente toca **los timbales**.	*Tito Puente plays the timbales.*
¿Ves a **Gloria Estefan** bailando?	*Do you see Gloria Estefan dancing?*
Direct object pronouns	
Tito Puente **los** toca.	*Tito Puente plays them.*
¿**La** ves bailando?	*Do you see her dancing?*

Note that in Spanish, when the direct object refers to one or more specific *persons*, the word **a** is placed before the direct object, such as in the example above, "¿**Ves** *a* **Gloria Estefan bailando**?". This Spanish **a** is called the personal **a**. It is required and has no equivalent in English.

B. Direct object pronouns generally precede conjugated verbs. When a negative word is present, the pronoun is placed between the negative word and the conjugated verb.

¿Tocas **la guitarra** en las fiestas?	*Do you play the guitar at parties?*
No, no toco **la guitarra**.	*I don't play the guitar.*
¿**La** tocas en las fiestas?	*Do you play it at parties?*
No, no **la** toco.	*I don't play it.*

When the conjugated verb is followed by an infinitive or present participle (**gerundio**), the direct object pronoun may be attached to the end of either of these forms *or* it may be placed before the conjugated verb.

¿Vamos a bailar **la cumbia panameña** hoy?	*Are we going to dance the Panamanian cumbia today?*
¿**La** vamos a bailar hoy?	*Are we going to dance it today?*
O: ¿Vamos a bailar**la** hoy?	
¿Están practicando **los pasos nuevos**?	*Are you practicing the new steps?*
¿**Los** están practicando?	*Are you practicing them?*
O: ¿Están practicándo**los**?	

Note the addition of a written accent on the present participle when the pronoun is attached.

C. The neuter direct object pronoun **lo** usually refers to an idea, a statement, an action, or a situation. The neuter direct object pronoun corresponds to the English words *it* or *that*.

Me dicen que esta canción es de Daddy Yankee, pero no **lo** creo.	*They tell me that this song is sung by Daddy Yankee, but I don't believe it.*
Lo siento, pero no quiero bailar.	*I'm sorry (about it), but I don't want to dance.*
Lo veo y no **lo** creo.	*I see it, but I don't believe it.*

5.1-06 Músicos ¿Con qué asocias las siguientes cosas? Contesta con pronombres.

MODELO: las guitarras eléctricas
Las asocio con un grupo de rock.

1. la música clásica
2. el rock duro
3. los ritmos latinos

4. las canciones de amor
5. los megaconciertos

5.1-07 Un dúo especial Romeo Santos y Usher se preparan para cantar en vivo en la ceremonia de los *Latin Grammys*. Completa su conversación con el pronombre de objeto directo apropiado según el contexto.

Romeo: No tengo la letra de la canción que vamos a cantar. ¿_____ tienes tú?

Usher: Sí, _____ tengo. Y tú, ¿vas a tocar las congas?

Romeo: No, no _____ voy a tocar. Todavía tenemos que practicar los pasos nuevos. No _____ sé muy bien. ¿Me puedes ayudar a practicar la coreografía que vamos a hacer?

Usher: Sí, _____ puedo ayudar, pero… ¿qué hace aquí este cable? ¿Puedes mover _____ por favor?

Romeo: Sí, claro, ya está. Muy bien, ¿practicamos entonces?

▲ *Romeo Santos y Usher cantan "Promise" a ritmo de bachata.*

5.1-08 El concierto del año

Paso 1: Tu amigo/a y tú se están preparando para ir a un concierto de Jennifer López. Uno/a de ustedes está muy ansioso/a y hace muchas preguntas. El/La otro/a contesta las preguntas reemplazando las palabras subrayadas con el pronombre de objeto directo apropiado y da más información.

MODELO: Estudiante 1:   *¿Tenemos el coche para ir al concierto?*
            Estudiante 2:   *Sí, lo tenemos. No te preocupes.*

1. ¿Tienes las entradas?
2. ¿Vienes a buscarme a casa para ir juntos?
3. ¿Tienes la dirección del estadio?
4. ¿Sabes qué grupo toca antes que Jennifer?
5. ¿Tienes el plano del estadio para pasarnos a la zona VIP?
6. …
7. …

Paso 2: Hagan un plan para ir al concierto: Dónde se van a encontrar, a qué hora, cómo van a ir, etc. Escriban una pequeña nota para invitar a otro/a amigo/a.

▲ *Don Omar es un famoso cantante de reguetón puertorriqueño.*

▲ *Luis Fonsi es un cantante de baladas románticas y pop latino.*

 5.1-09 ¿Cuál es tu opinión?

Paso 1: Usando las siguientes palabras, comparte tu opinión con tus compañeros.

adorar   preferir   tolerar   respetar   detestar   conocer   odiar[5]

MODELO: La clase de español
            Estudiante 1:   *¿Qué piensas de la clase de español?*
            Estudiante 2:   *¡La adoro! Siempre la recomiendo.*
            Estudiante 1:   *¡Yo también! / Yo no, yo prefiero la clase de ciencias políticas.*

Don Omar	la música clásica
las fiestas de las fraternidades	los boleros
los bailes formales	Luis Fonsi
la ópera	el reguetón
el rap	la música *country*

Paso 2: Ahora, informen a la clase qué opiniones comparten todos los miembros del grupo. ¿Hay alguna opinión común a toda la clase?

MODELO: *Todos creemos que Luis Fonsi es un buen cantante. Nosotros lo admiramos porque...*

[5] **odiar:** to hate

LA PURA VERDAD II   ¿Quieres bailar?

1.

2. —¿Quieres bailar?
—¡NO, GRACIAS!

3. Hola, me llamo Tom. ¿Quieres bailar?

Sí. Me llamo Nina.

4. ¡Pero esto es merengue! El ritmo del merengue es más fácil.

No sé bailar salsa.

5. Diez, nueve, ocho, siete, seis, cinco, cuatro, tres, dos, uno. ¡Feliz Año Nuevo!

6. ¿Lo siento?

¡Lo siento!

 5.1-10 ¿Quieres bailar? Escucha la narración y selecciona la mejor opción.

1. ...
   a. Ella lo mira.
   b. El papá lo mira.
   c. Él la mira.

2. ...
   a. Los puede seguir.
   b. Tom baila muy bien.
   c. No los puede seguir.

3. ...
   a. Él la ayuda.
   b. Ella lo ayuda.
   c. Ella lo besa.

HABLANDO DE GRAMÁTICA II

2. Saying what we know: The verbs *saber* and *conocer*

WileyPLUS Go to *WileyPLUS* to review this grammar point with the help of the **Animated Grammar Tutorial** and the **Verb Conjugator**.

Saber and **conocer** are two verbs that mean "to know." Both verbs have an irregular **yo** form.

saber *(to know facts, information)*			
(yo)	**sé**	(nosotros/as)	sabemos
(tú)	sabes	(vosotros/as)	sabéis
(él, ella, Ud.)	sabe	(ellos/ellas/Uds.)	saben

conocer *(to know people, places)*			
(yo)	**conozco**	(nosotros/as)	conocemos
(tú)	conoces	(vosotros/as)	conocéis
(él, ella, Ud.)	conoce	(ellos/ellas/Uds.)	conocen

A. Saber means to know facts or information.

¿**Sabes** quién canta "Oye cómo va"?	*Do you know who sings "Oye cómo va"?*
¿**Sabes** cómo se llama esta banda?	*Do you know the name of this band?*

When followed by an infinitive, **saber** means *to know how to do something*.

Mi primo **sabe** bailar el chachachá.	*My cousin knows how to dance the cha-cha.*
Nina **sabe** bailar salsa y ayuda a Tom.	*Nina knows how to dance salsa and helps Tom.*

B. Conocer means *to know a person, to meet a person for the first time,* or *to be familiar with a place or thing*. Note that when **conocer** means *to meet or know a person*, it is followed by the personal **a**. Remember that the personal **a** refers to one or more specific persons (animals or characters) and is needed in Spanish before a direct object.

En la fiesta Tom conoce **a** Nina; después de conocerla, bailan juntos.	*At the party Tom meets Nina; after meeting her, they dance together.*
Conozco **al** cantante de esa banda de rock.	*I know the singer of that rock band.*
¿Conoces **a** esta banda?	*Are you familiar with this band?*

Conocer has several degrees of familiarity. For clarification, you may add an explanation to your sentence.

Conozco a Don Omar, no en persona, pero conozco su música.	*I know Don Omar—not in person, but I know his music.*
Conozco a Don Omar, mi amigo me lo presentó.	*I know Don Omar, a friend introduced him to me.*
Conozco a Don Omar; es mi amigo.	*I know Don Omar; he is my friend.*

Or you may say:

Lo conozco de nombre.	*I know who he is.*
Lo conozco en persona.	*I know him personally.*
Lo conozco; es mi amigo.	*I know him; he is my friend.*

These are other verbs that end in **-cer** or **-cir** that follow the same pattern as **conocer** in the **yo** form (**-zco**):

agradecer	*to thank*
(des)aparecer	*to (dis)appear*
ofrecer	*to offer*
parecer, parecerse	*to seem, to resemble*
producir	*to produce*
reconocer	*to recognize*
traducir	*to translate*

5.1-11 Nina y Tom ¿Recuerdas a Nina y Tom, los personajes de **La pura verdad**? Combina las oraciones de la columna A con las oraciones de la columna B para completar el relato de Tom sobre esa noche.

A

_____ 1. Nina me dice que mi cara le parece familiar y me pregunta: "¿Te conozco?".

_____ 2. Entonces me pregunta si quiero bailar con ella.

_____ 3. Sin embargo, Nina y yo bailamos y ella dice que bailo muy bien.

_____ 4. Después de bailar mucho, tenemos sed.

_____ 5. Esa noche Nina quiere practicar inglés conmigo.

_____ 6. Nina me parece una chica increíble.

B

a. Agradezco la invitación pero reconozco que no sé bailar bien.

b. Yo traduzco unas frases del inglés al español para ella.

c. A ella le parezco un buen bailarín⁶.

d. Me ofrezco para ir al bar y comprar una bebida.

e. ¡Reconozco que ella me gusta mucho!

f. Yo digo: "La verdad es que me parezco mucho a un cantante famoso".

5.1-12 ¿Qué sabes de música latina? Entrevista a un/a compañero/a sobre la música latina.

Paso 1: Primero, completa las siguientes preguntas con la forma apropiada de *saber* o *conocer*.

1. ¿(Tú) _____ qué pareja cubana es muy poderosa en el mundo de la música y ahora vive en EE. UU.?

2. ¿(Tú) _____ a otros cantantes o músicos cubanos?

3. Aparte del chachachá, ¿(tú) _____ qué otros ritmos tropicales tienen su origen en Cuba?

4. ¿(Tú) _____ alguna emisora de radio⁷ dominicana?

5. ¿(Tú) _____ cuál es una celebración ideal para vivir la música, los bailes y la forma de pasarlo bien de los dominicanos?

6. ¿(Tú) _____ a Juan Luis Guerra? ¿(Tú) _____ de dónde es, o qué tipo de música canta?

Paso 2: Después de investigar las respuestas a las preguntas, entrevista a dos compañeros de la clase y anota sus respuestas.

MODELO: Estudiante 1: ¿*Sabes* quién es la cantante cubana de salsa más famosa en todo el mundo?

Estudiante 2: *Sí sé. Se llama Celia Cruz.*

Paso 3: Entre los tres, escriban un pequeño párrafo para informar al resto de la clase.

MODELO: *Nosotros tres sabemos que Celia Cruz es la cantante cubana más famosa, pero no sabemos... También conocemos a... pero no conocemos a... etc.*

Con la ayuda de su profesor/a, decidan qué grupo de la clase está mejor informado.

5.1-13 ¿A quién conoces y qué sabe hacer?

Paso 1: Completa las siguientes listas.

Tres actividades que sé hacer.

1. _____
2. _____
3. _____

Tres personas que conozco bien.

1. _____
2. _____
3. _____

Paso 2: Ahora, levántate y busca entre tus compañeros quién tiene la lista más parecida a la tuya. Después, con tu compañero/a, informa a la clase.

MODELO: Estudiante 1: ¿Tú *sabes* tocar la guitarra eléctrica?

Estudiante 2: *Sí, sí sé. También sé...*

Mi compañero/a _____ y yo sabemos tocar la guitarra eléctrica...

YN / Splash News/Newscom

▲ *Juan Luis Guerra y Enrique Iglesias cantan juntos "Cuando me enamoro".*

⁶**bailarín:** dancer ⁷**emisora de radio:** radio station

OTRA PERSPECTIVA

Huntstock / Getty Images

Diego

Todos bailan

Diferente

"En Puerto Rico en la mayoría de las fiestas la gente baila, incluso los niños aprenden a bailar desde pequeños. Es importante saber bailar para divertirse. Recuerdo que mi hermano y yo practicábamos[8] pasos nuevos frente al espejo. Pero veo que a los jóvenes de EE. UU. no les gusta bailar. ¿Es verdad?"

Igual

"En nuestras fiestas también hay comida, bebida y mucha conversación. A los jóvenes les gusta divertirse juntos".

Explícale a Diego

1. ¿A qué edad aprende una persona a bailar en EE. UU.?
2. ¿Sabes bailar? ¿A qué edad aprendiste[9]?
3. ¿Es común ir a una fiesta y no bailar?
4. ¿Qué hacen las personas en una fiesta en EE. UU.?
5. ¿Por qué a los adolescentes de EE. UU., en general, no les interesa bailar?

@Arroba@

WileyPLUS Go to *WileyPLUS* to find more **Arroba** activities.

¡A bailar! Explora en tu buscador favorito y busca videos para aprender a bailar salsa, merengue, bachata u otro baile que te interese. Apunta la dirección del video que te gusta para compartir con tu profesor/a y compañeros. Comparte con la clase el tipo de baile que te gusta, por qué te gusta y los pasos que incluye. ¿Qué baile es más fácil o más complicado?

MODELO: *Quiero aprender a bailar salsa porque es popular en muchos países. Se baila con una pareja y en línea.*

MANOS A LA OBRA

5.1-14 ¿Conocemos a los estudiantes de la clase?

Paso 1: Lee la siguiente lista de preguntas y piensa en dos preguntas más con los verbos **saber** o **conocer**. Después, entrevista a un/a compañero/a.

1. ¿Sabes el nombre de todos tus compañeros de clase? Menciona diez.
2. ¿A quién conoces bien? ¿Qué sabes de esa persona?
3. ¿Sabes quién es un fiestero[10]?
4. ¿Sabes quién toca un instrumento musical? ¿Quién? ¿Qué toca?
5. ¿Qué sabes del/de la profesor/a?

Paso 2: Después de conversar, ¿cuál es su conclusión? ¿Conocen bien a sus compañeros? Informen a la clase. Después, con toda la clase, decidan quién es la persona que más sabe sobre los otros compañeros.

MODELO: *Nosotros conocemos mucho/poco a nuestros compañeros...*
              Por ejemplo (no) sabemos...

[8]**practicábamos:** we used to practice [9]**aprendiste:** did you learn [10]**fiestero:** party animal

5.1-15 ¿Eres curioso/a?

Paso 1: Ahora, para conocer mejor a tus compañeros, levántate y pregúntales lo siguiente a diferentes compañeros de tu clase, usando **saber** o **conocer**. Usa los pronombres de objeto directo. Luego, escribe los resultados.

MODELO: Estudiante 1 (tú):   *¿Sabes bailar el mambo?*
Estudiante 2:   *Sí, sé bailarlo. / No, no sé bailarlo.*
Estudiante 1 (escribes):   *John sabe bailar el mambo.*

1. ¿_____ tocar las congas?
2. ¿_____ la ciudad de La Habana?
3. ¿_____ la letra de la canción "Cuando me enamoro"?
4. ¿_____ el nombre de los indígenas nativos de Cuba?
5. ¿_____ algún restaurante dominicano o puertorriqueño?
6. ¿_____ dónde está San Juan?

Paso 2: Después, comparte tus resultados con la clase. ¿Fue difícil o fácil completar la actividad?

MODELO: *Parece que nadie de la clase sabe/conoce…*

5.1-16 Vamos a hacer una fiesta

servir
limpiar
ofrecer
preparar
traer
su casa
la música y el equipo de
    sonido
los bocadillos[11]
la comida
la casa después de la
    fiesta

Paso 1: En grupos de cinco, decidan cuál es el motivo o la ocasión y cúando y dónde se puede celebrar la fiesta. Después, organicen los preparativos. Usen el vocabulario de la izquierda.

MODELO: Estudiante 1:   *¿Quién va a mandar **las invitaciones**?*
Estudiante 2:   *El profesor **las** va a mandar.*

Paso 2: Después, entre los cinco, escriban una nota para describir el plan de la fiesta e invitar a su profesor/a. ¡Él/Ella va a decidir cuál es la mejor fiesta y a cuál va a asistir!

MODELO: *Profesor/a, vamos a celebrar una fiesta en casa de…*

5.1-17 ¿Sabe o no sabe? Esta es una versión del juego *Verdad o consecuencia*.

Paso 1: Piensa en una persona famosa, por ejemplo, Raúl Castro, o en un dato[12], por ejemplo, el número de países de habla hispana.

Paso 2: Después, la clase se divide en grupos. El líder de un grupo les pregunta a las personas de otro grupo:

Grupo A: *¿Saben quién es Raúl Castro?*
Grupo B: *Sí, sabemos que es un político cubano. / No, no sabemos quién es.*

Su profesor/a va a proponer un reto[13] si no saben la respuesta.

5.1-18 ¡Hablemos de música y bailes!

Paso 1: ¿Qué sabes sobre la música hispana? Camina por la clase y haz cada pregunta a tres estudiantes diferentes. Escribe las respuestas.

1. ¿Conoces la música de JLo? ¿Comprendes las canciones de JLo en español? ¿Traduces las canciones al inglés? Usa los pronombres de objeto directo en tus respuestas.

Conocer: a. _____   b. _____   c. _____
Comprender: a. _____   b. _____   c. _____
Traducir: a. _____   b. _____   c. _____

[11]**bocadillos:** sandwiches/snacks [12]**dato:** fact [13]**reto:** challenge

2. ¿Qué cantantes/grupos cantan en inglés y español? ¿Qué cantantes/grupos cantan reguetón/boleros/cumbias?

Dos idiomas: a. _____   b. _____   c. _____

Género: a. _____   b. _____   c. _____

3. ¿Qué bailes son populares en Puerto Rico? ¿Qué instrumentos se usan en el reguetón?

Bailes: a. _____   b. _____   c. _____

Instrumentos: a. _____   b. _____   c. _____

4. ¿Reconoces la música de salsa, cumbia o merengue cuando la oyes? ¿Cuándo escuchas música en español? ¿Conoces personalmente a algún/a artista? ¿A quién? Usa los pronombres de objeto directo en tus respuestas.

Reconocer: a. _____   b. _____   c. _____

Cuándo: a. _____   b. _____   c. _____

Conocer: a. _____   b. _____   c. _____

Paso 2: En grupos de cuatro, compara las respuestas de cada pregunta y marca las respuestas que tienes en común con otros estudiantes. Luego, el portavoz de cada grupo informa al resto de la clase.

MODELO: *En nuestro grupo, la mayoría de los estudiantes conocen la música de JLo, pero John no **la** conoce. Además, a veces comprendemos sus canciones, pero cuando Kate no **las** comprende **las** traduce al inglés.*

5.1-19 Presta atención: Un mensaje telefónico Tom llama por teléfono a Nina, pero no hay nadie en casa y deja un mensaje en el contestador automático. Escucha el mensaje una vez y selecciona las mejores respuestas según el audio.

WileyPLUS Go to *WileyPLUS* and listen to **Presta atención.**

1. Tom quiere...
   a. salir a bailar con Nina.   b. invitarla a una fiesta.   c. llamarla por teléfono.
2. Tom dice que...
   a. se conocen del fin de año.   b. en el fin de año hay una fiesta.   c. la conoce por un amigo.
3. Tom dice que...
   a. él cumple años.   b. su amigo cumple años.   c. Nina cumple años.
4. El amigo de Tom...
   a. sabe bailar salsa.   b. la llama por teléfono.   c. organiza una fiesta.
5. Tom quiere...
   a. aprender a bailar.   b. tener una cita.   c. a y b

5.1-20 Por escrito: ¡Un día festivo! Imagina que estás en un concierto de varios grupos musicales en el estadio de tu universidad. Es un día festivo para la universidad.

Paso 1: Haz una lista de lo que ves en el concierto:

- el tipo de gente que hay
- la variedad de grupos musicales y tipos de música
- los tipos de instrumentos musicales
- qué hacen las personas para divertirse

Paso 2: Ahora, usando los detalles de la lista, escribe un párrafo para describir ese día festivo. Incluye una introducción y una conclusión.

Paso 3: En grupos de cuatro estudiantes, lean los párrafos. Ofrezcan ideas a sus compañeros para mejorar la composición. Después, escriban la versión final para entregársela[14] a su profesor/a.

¡OJO!

Direct object pronouns
Use direct object pronouns to make your writing less redundant. When proofreading your composition, remember to double check that those pronouns agree with the person or object they refer to in gender and number.

[14] **entregársela:** turn it in

PONTE EN MI LUGAR

Estrategias para conversar ♻

Asking direct questions Direct questions take place normally during conversation. In Spanish they can be introduced by a verb, as in **¿Vienes al baile?**, or by interrogative words, as in **¿Cuándo viajas?** Look back at **Hablando de gramática,** Chapter 1, Section 2. for a review of these words. Do you remember when to use **qué** and when you need to use **cuál**? Here are some different ways to ask direct questions:

¿Dónde/cómo/cuándo/cuánto + *verb*?	¿Dónde es la fiesta? ¿Cómo te llamas?
¿Cuánto/a/os/as + *noun*?	¿Cuántas chicas van a la fiesta?
¿Cuál/es + *verb*?	¿Cuál quieres: el de arriba o el de abajo?
¿Qué + *verb*?	¿Qué bebes?
¿Qué + *noun*?	¿Qué música te gusta?
¿Quién/es + *verb*?	¿Quién va a venir a la fiesta?

With a preposition:

¿En dónde? ¿De dónde?	¿De dónde vienes?
¿Desde cuándo?	¿Desde cuándo sabes bailar salsa?
¿A cuál? ¿Con cuál?	¿Con cuál combina mejor?
¿A qué? ¿De qué?	¿A qué fiesta vas?
¿A quién? ¿Con quién?	¿Con quién vas a la discoteca?

Tu cumpleaños Quieres planear una fiesta para tu cumpleaños y quieres tener muchos invitados. Llama por teléfono a tres amigos para invitarlos a tu fiesta. Un/a compañero/a es tu mejor amigo/a y te hace preguntas sobre la hora, el día, el lugar de la fiesta, la música, el baile. Habla con tres de tus compañeros y ellos van a llamar e invitar a más amigos. Usa las **Estrategias para conversar** para hacer preguntas.

ASÍ ES LA VIDA

© John Wiley & Sons, Inc.

Expresión: Estoy en la cuerda floja[15]

Ramón: *Oye, Julio, conozco a una chica increíble que quiere salir contigo. ¿Quieres conocerla?*

Julio: *Nooooo, no gracias. Yo tengo novia. Además, **estoy en la cuerda floja** con ella. Está furiosa conmigo y creo que va a dejarme[16]. No, gracias, no quiero más problemas.*

¿Qué significa esta expresión? ¿Hay un equivalente en inglés? ¿Sabes cuál es?

ENTÉRATE

Estrategias para leer

Scanning Scanning is a reading strategy in which you look over a text quickly and superficially in order to find specific information, like when you are looking for a particular word or name. For example, you may be looking for a particular movie in the new releases listing of a movie theater, the title of a song or the name of a singer on the cover of a specific CD or DVD, or the time and channel of a TV show in a newspaper. Remember, *skimming* is when you read fast to get the gist of the passage; *scanning* is when you search for specific information because you already know what you are looking for.

---

[15] **cuerda floja:** tightrope [16] **dejarme:** leave me

Antes de leer

1. Revistas de entretenimiento El artículo que vas a leer es sobre una persona famosa. ¿Qué revistas conoces en inglés que publiquen artículos de este tipo? ¿Qué temas lees en ese tipo de revistas? ¿Qué tipo de artículo crees que vas a leer? ¿Algo literario? ¿Algo sobre historia?

2. Nombres Mira el texto por encima[17] y busca nombres de personas, películas o programas y lugares o ciudades.

3. Carlos Ponce Busca en el Internet quién es Carlos Ponce. ¿De dónde es? ¿Qué tipo de música canta? ¿Tienes alguna de sus canciones? ¿Te gustan?

CANALES Y SERVICIOS ▼

Entretenimiento

| PORTADA | CINE & DVD | MÚSICA | TELEVISIÓN | GENTE FAMOSA | FOTOS | VIDEOS | NOTICIAS | DIVIÉRTETE | EXCLUSIVOS | AWARDS CENTRAL | ENGLISH |

BUSCA [_____] En Terra ▼ Buscar

La vida amorosa de Carlos Ponce

Alexander Tamargo/ Getty Images Entertainment / Getty Images

Sabemos mucho sobre la vida profesional de Carlos Ponce. No sólo es un famoso actor y cantante boricua. También es un buen presentador, compositor y productor. Como cantante, **publica** su primer álbum en 1998, de título Carlos *Ponce*. Recientemente, en 2012, **grabó** el éxito musical *Me llevas*. En televisión, algunas de sus telenovelas más exitosas son *Sentimientos ajenos, Perro amor o Dos hogares*. En 2013 **actuó** como protagonista en la telenovela *Santa Diabla*. Una de sus famosas series de televisión de Estados Unidos del año 2012 es *Hollywood Heights*. Este actor es un profesional de la televisión, pero también del cine. Algunas de sus películas más populares son *Just my luck, Complete Guide to Guy, Meet Me in Miami y Couples Retreat*.

releases

recorded

acted

Pero, ¿qué sabemos de la vida personal de Carlos Ponce? ¿Y de sus romances? El famoso puertorriqueño, hijo de padres cubanos, nace en San Juan el 4 de septiembre de 1972. Carlos tiene cuatro hermanos. La familia es muy importante para él. En 1986 conoce a Verónica Rubio. Más tarde, la pareja se casa y tiene cuatro hijos: dos hijos biológicos y dos hijas gemelas adoptadas en Rusia. Para él la familia es lo primero. El trabajo viene después. Sólo es un medio para vivir. En 2010 Carlos Ponce y Verónica se divorcian. **Sin embargo**, hoy en día, Carlos tiene una buena relación con la madre de sus hijos y son buenos amigos.

However

Después de leer

1. En el texto
  1. Identifica tres cognados en la lectura.

2. ¿Entendiste?
  1. ¿Cuál es el trabajo de Carlos Ponce?
  2. ¿De qué país es Carlos Ponce?
  3. ¿Qué nacionalidad tienen sus padres?
  4. ¿Tiene hijos Carlos Ponce?
  5. ¿Cómo es la relación actual de Carlos y Verónica?
  6. ¿Cuál el nombre de la telenovela más reciente de Carlos Ponce?

---

[17] **Mirar (un texto) por encima:** to scan (a text)

EN TUS PROPIAS PALABRAS

Estrategias para escribir

Writing a dialogue In this chapter we will write dialogues **(diálogos)**. A dialogue is a conversation between two or more people who are exchanging ideas, feelings, and opinions directly, and not through a third person. Dialogues are a dynamic way to express ideas. One can use idiomatic expressions in dialogues to make them fun and interesting for the reader. The style of a dialogue can be ironic, elegant, or colloquial, for example. A dialogue can include figurative language, and can be used as a writing tool to express elements too complicated to convey in a narrative form.

In Spanish, each statement in a dialogue is introduced by a dash **(guión)**. **Guiones** replace quotation marks in English. Most dialogues are introduced by a descriptive narrative that sets the scene, as you can see in the example below.

En una fiesta de cumpleaños Héctor y Angélica están en una fiesta de cumpleaños. Héctor está enamorado de ella, pero ella no lo sabe.

–Hola Héctor, ¿cómo estás?

–¿Yo?

–¡Claro que tú! ¿Cómo estás?

–Pues, bien, escuchando la música. ¿Te gusta?

–Está chévere. ¿Conoces a Roberto?

–¿Es tu novio?

–No, es mi primo.

–¡Ah, qué bien! Digo[18]... qué bien que conoces a alguien en la fiesta.

–Aquí hay mojitos, ¿quieres uno?

–Sí, te quiero, digo... sí, la quiero, digo... sí, quiero uno, gracias.

–¿Estás bien?

–¿Yo? Claro que sí. No estoy nervioso para nada. ¿Por qué?

–Por nada. ¿Te gusta bailar?

–No, ¿y a ti?

–Sí.

–Pues, a mí también, en realidad. ¿Quieres bailar?

–Sí, ¡cómo no!

Courtesy Angélica S. Reina Paez

Escribe un diálogo serio o chistoso sobre la siguiente situación: Una conversación entre dos amigos/as. Uno/a de ellos/as es muy tímido/a y le pide consejos[19] al/a la otro/a para conocer a un/a muchacho/a que le gusta.

---

[18]**digo:** I mean [19]**consejos:** advice

AUTOPRUEBA

VOCABULARIO

I. Dile a un/a amigo/a ¿Qué instrumentos hay en un conjunto de salsa?

_____

_____

II. Un/a amigo/a te pregunta Di cómo se llama…

1. un espacio enfrente de la banda donde la gente baila.
2. un baile de la República Dominicana.
3. instrumentos de percusión pequeños que se tocan cada una en una mano.
4. una forma de celebrar un cumpleaños.
5. el baile que es el resultado de una combinación de ritmos caribeños.

GRAMÁTICA

I. Fiesta en la clase ¿Qué vas a hacer? Sustituye la frase en negrita con un pronombre para no repetir el objeto directo.

MODELO: Están tocando un merengue. Quiero bailar el merengue.
→ _Quiero bailarlo._

1. Me gustan **las congas.** Quiero tocar **las congas.**
2. Necesitamos música buena. Yo traigo **la música.**
3. ¿Quién va a limpiar **la casa?** Yo voy a limpiar **la casa.**
4. ¿Quién va a invitar **al profesor?** Kim va a invitar **al profesor.**
5. Antonio y Ramón no están aquí. María va a llamar **a Antonio y a Ramón.**

II. ¡Se las sabe todas! Tu amigo/a piensa que lo sabe todo y siempre contesta afirmativamente a todas tus preguntas o comentarios. Completa las preguntas con **saber** o **conocer** y escribe sus respuestas.

MODELO: ¿Conoces a la quinceañera? → _La conozco._

1. Esta banda es nueva, ¿la _____?
2. ¿ _____ cuántos años tiene la quinceañera?
3. ¿ _____ si la quinceañera toca el piano?
4. ¿ _____ a mis amigas?
5. ¿ _____ esta discoteca?

CULTURA

1. ¿De dónde son los siguientes bailes?
   a. merengue
   b. mambo
   c. salsa
2. Explica dos características diferentes de una fiesta de cumpleaños en Estados Unidos y de una fiesta en el Caribe.

REDACCIÓN

Escribe un diálogo entre tú y un/a amigo/a que quiere visitar un país del Caribe. Contesta sus preguntas sobre los bailes, la música, las fiestas, qué decir, qué expresiones coloquiales puede usar, etc.

EN RESUMIDAS CUENTAS, AHORA PUEDO…

☐ entender la cultura del baile y la celebración de la quinceañera.

☐ hablar de diferentes ritmos e instrumentos caribeños.

☐ describir las celebraciones y hablar de acciones en progreso.

☐ evitar la repetición de ciertas palabras al comunicarse.

☐ distinguir entre **saber** y **conocer.**

☐ hacer preguntas para obtener más información.

🎧 VOCABULARIO ESENCIAL

Sustantivos

el bajo	*bass*
el baile	*dance*
la canción	*song*
el/la cantante	*singer*
el conjunto (musical)	*(music) band*
el/la músico/a	*musician*
la pareja	*couple, partner*
el paso de baile	*dance step*

Cognados: la bachata, la banda, el bolero, los bongós, el chachachá, el concierto, las congas, la cumbia, el grupo, la guitarra, el instrumento, el mambo, las maracas, el merengue, el micrófono, la música, la percusión, el piano, el reguetón, el ritmo, la salsa, el saxofón, los timbales, el trombón, la trompeta

Verbos

agradecer	*to thank*
animar	*to enliven*
bailar	*to dance*
cantar	*to sing*
conocer	*to know or be familiar with*
gritar	*to shout*
ofrecer	*to offer*
parecer, parecerse	*to seem, to resemble*
reconocer	*to recognize*
saber	*to know (a fact)*
traducir	*to translate*

Cognados: celebrar, (des)aparecer, invitar, producir

Expresiones

dar la vuelta	*spin around*
hacer/dar una fiesta (sorpresa)	*to have/give a (surprise) party*
pasarlo/pasarla bien	*to have a good time*
¿Quieres bailar?	*Do you want to dance?*

LEARNING OBJECTIVES

By the end of this section you will be able to:

- Understand the celebration of **Los Reyes Magos**
- Describe and compare celebrations in the Caribbean and the United States
- Use indirect object pronouns to say for whom something is done
- Discuss exchanges and report
- Express likes and dislikes with verbs other than **gustar**
- Talk about future plans

Una imagen vale más que mil palabras

▲ *Los tres Reyes Magos son Melchor, Gaspar y Baltasar.*

¿Qué está haciendo este niño?

¿Qué quiere de los Reyes Magos[1]?

¿En qué mes ocurre esto?

¿Cuándo llegan los Reyes Magos?

¿Conoces a alguien que celebre el Día de los Reyes Magos?

UNA PERSPECTIVA

Un funeral

Daniel

Diferente

"En un funeral en la República Dominicana noté[2] que era menos organizado. Vi a niños corriendo, muchas personas hablando y otras rezando[3]. Algunas personas estaban llorando mucho y otras bebiendo café. No sirven comida como en Estados Unidos".

Igual

"Un funeral también es una ocasión para reunirse con la familia y los amigos para recordar a la persona fallecida[4]. Vestirse de negro es algo que se hace en muchos países".

¿Qué piensas tú?

¿Hay niños en los funerales en Estados Unidos?
¿Fuiste[5] a un funeral en Estados Unidos? ¿Por qué sirven comida?
¿Por qué está el féretro[6] cerrado generalmente?

[1] **Reyes Magos:** Three Wise Men/Three Kings [2] **noté:** I noticed [3] **rezar:** to pray [4] **fallecida:** deceased [5] **fuiste:** did you go [6] **féretro:** casket

LA PURA VERDAD I   ¡No me gustan las bodas!

Lucas es un estudiante de medicina que hace una pasantía[7] en La Habana, Cuba. Su amiga Nemis lo invita a una boda.

1.

2.

3.

4.

▲ Ahora a la recepción.

5.

6.

5.2-01 **Otra boda** Escucha la narración y decide si las oraciones son **Lógicas** o **Ilógicas**. Si son ilógicas, explica por qué.

    L   I

1. ☐   ☐ _____
2. ☐   ☐ _____
3. ☐   ☐ _____

[7]**pasantía:** internship [8]**juzgado:** court house

PALABRA POR PALABRA

Las celebraciones

La boda *Wedding*

las damas | la madrina | la novia | los novios | el novio | los caballeros

el anillo

el ramo

el cura

el padrino

el brindis

▲ *En la boda se casan los novios.*

Para hablar de celebraciones

la despedida de soltero/a	*bachelor/bachelorette party*
el juez de paz	*justice of the peace*
el juzgado	*the courthouse*
el/la invitado/a	*guest*
la luna de miel	*honeymoon*
el regalo	*gift*
el/la testigo	*witness*

Verbos

tirar (el ramo)	*to throw (the bouquet)*

Cognados: el banquete, la ceremonia, el funeral, la recepción

El bautizo *Baptism*

el/la ahijado/a	*godson/goddaughter*
la iglesia	*church*
la madrina	*godmother*
el padrino	*godfather*

Expresiones

¡Felicidades!	*Congratulations!*
¡Que vivan los novios!	*Cheers for the newlyweds! Hooray for the happy couple!*
¡Salud!	*Cheers! (Lit., Health!)*

© John Wiley & Sons, Inc.

Otras celebraciones

el Día de Año Viejo/ la Nochevieja	*New Year's Eve*
el Día de Año Nuevo	*New Year's Day*
el Día de los Reyes Magos	*Three Wise Men/ Three Kings Day*
el cumpleaños	*birthday*
el/la quinceañero/a	*15th birthday celebration*
la Nochebuena	*Christmas Eve*
la Navidad	*Christmas*

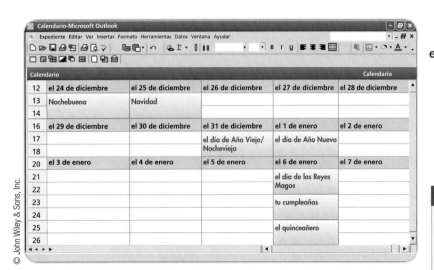

Varias de estas celebraciones son cristianas, pero también hay otras religiones en Cuba, la República Dominicana y Puerto Rico. Oficialmente, Cuba es un estado secular. La mayoría de la población es cristiana, pero también hay muchas personas que practican la santería, y otras personas que no practican ninguna religión. También hay pequeñas comunidades de judíos y musulmanes. En la República Dominicana, la mayoría de la población es cristiana (católica y protestante), con pequeñas comunidades de otras religiones. En Puerto Rico la mayoría de la población también es cristiana.

¿Qué dicen los caribeños?

Está cerca de la barra porque le gusta <u>darse el palo</u>.	*He is next to the bar because he <u>likes to drink</u>.*
*La fiesta fue <u>un relajo</u>.	*The party was <u>a lot of fun</u>.*
No quiere ayudar. <u>No da ni un tajo</u>.	*She doesn't want to help. She <u>doesn't lift a finger</u>.*
*Creo que voy a <u>ir en guagua</u>.	*I think I am going to <u>take the bus</u>.*
*Para la fiesta del Año Viejo voy a <u>tirar la casa por la ventana</u>.	*For New Year's Eve I am <u>not going to spare any expense</u>.*

*These expression are also used in other Spanish-speaking countries.

5.2-02 ¿Qué va primero y qué va después?

 Paso 1: Con un/a compañero/a, piensen en lo que pasa en las bodas y organicen esta lista en orden cronológico. Después, añadan dos situaciones más.

_____ a. Los novios se besan.
_____ b. Se da el brindis.
_____ c. La gente baila.
_____ d. Se celebra la despedida de soltero.
_____ e. Los novios intercambian los anillos.
_____ f. Se van de luna de miel.
_____ g. La novia tira el ramo de flores.
_____ …
_____ …

Paso 2: Ahora, comenten con la clase sus respuestas incluyendo sus adiciones a la lista. ¿Cómo es de larga la lista generada entre toda la clase?

5.2-03 ¿Dónde ocurre?

Paso 1: Completen la siguiente tabla. Decidan dónde ocurre cada cosa.

1. La novia tira el ramo de flores a un grupo de amigas o a sus damas.
2. El cura le echa agua al bebé.
3. Los novios se van de viaje.
4. Los novios dicen: "Sí, quiero".
5. El novio y la novia tienen fiestas separadas.
6. Las damas y los caballeros hablan con los invitados.
7. Los padrinos prometen ser parte de la vida del ahijado.

MODELO: El padrino da el brindis. → *Ocurre en la recepción de la boda.*

el bautizo	la despedida de soltero/a	la boda	la recepción/ el banquete de bodas	la luna de miel

Paso 2: Ahora, piensen qué más ocurre en estos eventos y después comenten sus ideas con la clase. ¿Qué grupo tiene una tabla más completa?

5.2-04 Bodas y bautizos

Paso 1: Hablen sobre estas ceremonias en parejas.

1. ¿Cómo son las bodas en tu opinión? ¿Son emocionantes, aburridas, tristes, románticas, alegres…? ¿Por qué?
2. ¿Qué parte de una boda es más divertida, más larga, más sentimental o más feliz? ¿Por qué?
3. ¿Quieres casarte algún día? ¿Por qué?
4. ¿Qué tipo de boda prefieres: grande y elaborada, pequeña y sencilla, formal o informal? ¿Por qué?
5. ¿Estás bautizado/a? ¿Tienes padrinos? ¿Quiénes son? ¿De dónde son y cómo se llaman?
6. ¿Sabes cómo son las bodas en otros países o en otras culturas? ¿Qué es diferente? ¿Qué es similar?

Paso 2: Ahora, escriban un pequeño párrafo. ¿En qué aspectos coinciden los dos? ¿En qué no coinciden?

MODELO: *Mi compañero/a y yo pensamos que las bodas son… porque… La parte de una boda que nos parece más aburrida es…*

Paso 3: Compartan con la clase sus párrafos y las cosas en las que coinciden. ¿En qué aspecto no coincide nadie?

5.2-05 ¡La boda del año! En grupos de tres o cuatro, planeen la boda de una persona famosa. Ustedes están invitados.

Talking about future plans: **Ir + a** + verb

Do you remember which structure we use to talk about future plans? Go to **Hablando de gramatica**, in chapter 2, section 2, to review this grammar point.

Paso 1: Decidan quién es la novia o el novio afortunado (puede ser una persona de la clase). Después preparen cada aspecto de la boda. ¿Dónde va a ser? ¿Quiénes son los invitados? ¿Cómo va a ser? ¿Va a haber música, va a hablar el padrino, van a bailar los novios, van a tirar el ramo de flores?

MODELO: *En la despedida de soltero, vamos a tener mucha música. También vamos a beber cerveza…*

1. despedida de soltero
2. despedida de soltera
3. la boda
4. la recepción
5. la luna de miel

Paso 2: Después, entre todos, escriban una invitación para describir el plan de la boda e invitar a su profesor/a y sus compañeros de clase. ¡Cada persona debe decidir a qué boda va a asistir!

MODELO: *¡Carlos Ponce y _____ se casan! Los invitamos a la boda el día…*

Entre toda la clase hagan una votación. ¿Qué boda va a tener el mayor número de invitados?

Boda de
Damián y Raquel

Julián Romero Jiménez y
Mª Rosario García González

Francisco Fuentes Escudero y
Mª Carmen Vadillo Muñoz

Nos complace comunicarles el enlace de nuestros hijos

Damián
y
Raquel

Que se celebrará el próximo 26 de julio,
a las 6:30 de la tarde en la Santa Iglesia Catedral.

Deseamos que nos acompañen en este día.
Cena y recepción: Villa El Rincón

HABLANDO DE GRAMÁTICA I

1. Saying for whom something is done: Indirect object pronouns

WileyPLUS Go to *WileyPLUS* to review this grammar point with the help of the **Animated Grammar Tutorial**.

In Chapter 5, Section 1 you learned about direct objects and direct object pronouns. Direct objects receive the action of the verb and answer the questions *who/whom?* or *what?*

What?	¿Compras tú **las entradas** para el concierto?	Sí, yo **las** compro.
	Are you going to buy the tickets for the concert?	*Yes, I'll buy them.*
Who?	¿Vas a ver **a Carlos** después?	Sí, **lo** voy a ver.
	Are you going to see Carlos later?	*Yes, I'll see him.*

The indirect object is the indirect recipient of the action of the verb and answers the questions *to/for whom?* or *to/for what?*: "To whom do you write those letters? To my sister." In this example, *you* is the subject of the verb, *letters* is the direct object, and *to whom/ to my sister*, the indirect object. You have already been using these pronouns when talking about likes and dislikes. Remember:

A Lucas no **le gusta** bailar en las bodas.	*Lucas doesn't like dancing at weddings. (Lit., Dancing at weddings is not pleasing to Lucas.)*

A. If someone asked you, "Do you send birthday cards *to your sister?*" you might answer: "Yes, I send a card *to her* every year." In this example *to your sister* is an indirect object noun phrase and *to her* is the indirect object pronoun. The indirect object usually, but not always, refers to people. Indirect object pronouns replace specific indirect object nouns (*to my sister* becomes *to her*) and agree with them in number and gender.

Indirect object pronouns

Singular		Plural	
me	*to/for me*	**nos**	*to/for us*
te	*to/for you (familiar)*	**os**	*to/for you (familiar, Spain)*
le	*to/for you (formal), him, her*	**les**	*to/for you (formal), them*
To whom?	¿Escribes **a tu novia** todos los días? Sí, **le** escribo todos los días. *Do you write to your girlfriend everyday? Yes, I write to her everyday.*		
For whom?	¿**Me** compras las entradas, por favor? *Would you buy the tickets for me, please?*		

B. You may have noticed that in Spanish the indirect object pronoun often appears in the sentence at the same time as the noun itself. This *never* occurs in English.

A Lucas no **le** gustan mucho las bodas.	*Lucas doesn't like weddings too much. (Lit., Weddings are not very pleasing to Lucas.)*
¿**Nos** prestas el carro **a Nemis y a mí** para ir a la boda?	*Would you lend the car to Nemis and me to go to the wedding?*

C. Indirect object pronouns follow the same rules of placement as direct object pronouns.

1. They usually go before the conjugated verb. If the sentence is negative, the indirect object pronoun is placed between the negative word and the verb:

–¿**Les** cuentas tus problemas **a tus padres?**	–*Do you tell your parents about your problems?*
–Sí, siempre **les** cuento todo.	–*Yes, I always tell them everything.*
–No, no siempre **les** cuento todo.	–*No, I don't always tell them everything.*

2. When a conjugated verb is followed by an infinitive or a present participle (ending in **-ndo**), the indirect object pronoun may be attached to the end of these forms or it may be placed before the conjugated verb. There is no difference in meaning. (Note that when attaching pronouns to present participles you will need to add a written accent mark over the vowel that normally carries the stress.)

¿Vamos a comprar**les** un regalo?	*Are we going to buy the present for them?*
¿**Les** vamos a comprar un regalo?	
Estoy escribiéndo**te** ahora.	*I am writing to you now.*
Te estoy escribiendo ahora.	

5.2-06 La boda de Carla Carla nos cuenta los detalles de su boda. Indica quién es el sujeto (la persona que hace la acción) en cada oración.

MODELO: Me promete amor eterno. → *mi nuevo esposo*

los invitados   mi esposo   el fotógrafo   el padrino   mis padres

1. Me pagan el banquete.
2. Nos saca muchas fotos a mi nuevo esposo y a mí.
3. Me pone el anillo de bodas.
4. Nos hace un brindis especial.
5. Me dicen "¡Felicidades!".
6. Nos ofrecen muchos regalos.

5.2-07 El cumpleaños de Carla Carla hace una fiesta para celebrar su cumpleaños. Combina las oraciones de la primera columna con las más apropiadas de la segunda.

_____ 1. Carla quiere invitar a muchos amigos.

_____ 2. Por fin hoy es el cumpleaños de Carla.

_____ 3. Nuestro amigo Rafa no sabe dónde está la casa de Carla.

_____ 4. En la fiesta, mi amigo Juan está deprimido y solo quiere darse el palo.

_____ 5. Rafa y yo queremos bailar.

_____ 6. Juan y yo tenemos sed.

_____ 7. Carla está muy contenta con su regalo.

a. Carla nos ofrece una bebida.

b. Voy a regalarle un suéter.

c. Le gusta muchísimo el suéter.

d. Les escribe a todos un *e-mail* para invitarlos.

e. Le explico cómo llegar.

f. Me explica qué le pasa.

g. Le preguntamos a Carla si tiene CD de salsa.

5.2-08 ¿Qué pasa en un bautizo? Carla quiere bautizar a su hijo y le explica a una amiga cómo es un bautizo católico.

Paso 1: Completa su narración con los pronombres de objeto indirecto. Mira las palabras subrayadas como referencia.

Para empezar, los padres _____*le*_____₁ preguntan <u>al cura</u> en qué fecha es posible bautizar al bebé. Entonces, unas semanas antes, los padres _____₂ envían invitaciones <u>a los familiares y amigos</u> para asegurarse de que vienen todos. Antes del bautizo, el cura _____₃ explica <u>a los padrinos</u> qué deben hacer. En la ceremonia, el cura _____₄ echa⁹ agua <u>al bebé</u>. Como en una boda o un cumpleaños, los invitados _____₅ llevan regalos <u>al bebé</u>. Por ejemplo, <u>a mí</u> mis padres _____₆ ofrecen pagar un almuerzo después de la ceremonia. Seguramente mis padres _____₇ van a llevar <u>a todos nosotros</u> a un restaurante delicioso.

⁹echa: pours

Paso 2: Ahora, Carla quiere saber sobre una celebración importante en tu cultura. Escribe un pequeño párrafo (de cuatro o cinco oraciones) para describir esta celebración. En tu párrafo, contesta sus preguntas. Usa los pronombres de objeto indirecto en tus respuestas.

1. ¿Hay que enviar invitaciones antes de la celebración? ¿A quién le envías las invitaciones?
2. ¿Hay que darles instrucciones especiales a los invitados o a otras personas? ¿A quién hay que darle instrucciones? ¿Quién da las instrucciones?
3. ¿Hay que llevar regalos? ¿Quién da los regalos? ¿A quién le da los regalos?
4. ¿Hay comida? ¿Quién les sirve la comida a los invitados?

MODELO: *Una celebración muy importante en mi familia es… Primero…*

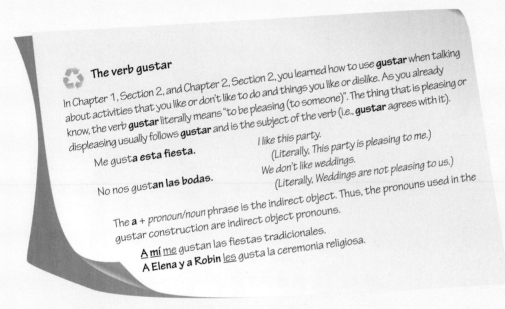

The verb gustar

In Chapter 1, Section 2, and Chapter 2, Section 2, you learned how to use **gustar** when talking about activities that you like or don't like to do and things you like or dislike. As you already know, the verb **gustar** literally means "to be pleasing (to someone)". The thing that is pleasing or displeasing usually follows **gustar** and is the subject of the verb (i.e., **gustar** agrees with it).

Me gust**a esta fiesta.**
    I like this party.
    (Literally, This party is pleasing to me.)
No nos gust**an las bodas.**
    We don't like weddings.
    (Literally, Weddings are not pleasing to us.)

The **a** + pronoun/noun phrase is the indirect object. Thus, the pronouns used in the gustar construction are indirect object pronouns.

A mí <u>me</u> gustan las fiestas tradicionales.
A Elena y a Robin <u>les</u> gusta la ceremonia religiosa.

5.2-09 ¡Qué gustos tan diferentes! Vas a planificar una fiesta con dos compañeros de clase y vas a invitar al resto de la clase. Pero primero, hay que saber qué les gusta o qué no les gusta a ustedes tres.

Paso 1: Escribe en los espacios en blanco cosas diferentes que te gustan o que no te gustan de las celebraciones o fiestas.

MODELO: *En una fiesta no me gusta <u>usar platos de plástico.</u>*

Ideas: la comida vegetariana, las bebidas alcohólicas, llevar regalos, bailar, los dulces, cantar…

En una fiesta (no) me gusta/n…

1. _____   5. _____
2. _____   6. _____
3. _____   7. _____
4. _____

Paso 2: Entrevista a dos compañeros de clase para ver si a ellos les gustan las mismas cosas.

MODELO: Estudiante 1:   *¿<u>Te gusta</u> usar platos de plástico en las fiestas?*
            Estudiante 2:   *Sí, <u>sí me gusta</u>, es más cómodo. o. No, <u>no me gusta</u>, producen mucha basura.*

Paso 3: Ahora, escriban un pequeño informe para presentarlo en clase.

MODELO: *Los tres preferimos usar platos de cerámica porque no <u>nos</u> gusta usar platos de plástico. A _____ y a _____ no <u>les</u> gusta llevar regalos, pero a mí…*

LA PURA VERDAD II Los Reyes Magos

Los Reyes Magos van a estar en la plaza y Tato tiene que llevar a su sobrina Anita a verlos. Tato invita a Ismael.

1.

Tengo que llevar a mi sobrina a ver a los Reyes Magos. ¿Quieres venir con nosotros?

¡Sí, cómo no!

2.

¿Qué les vas a pedir a los Reyes?

Yo quiero un videojuego, un celular, un iPod y una hermanita.

3.

4.

¿Eres obediente? ¿Te gusta la escuela?

Yo quiero un videojuego, un celular, un iPod y una hermanita.

5.

6.

No, él me parece muy viejo. ¡Está perdiendo el pelo! Creo que no sabe qué es un iPod.

¿Crees que vas a recibir tus regalos?

5.2-10 Los Reyes Magos: ¿Qué pasa después? Escucha la narración y selecciona la mejor opción:

1. a. Les dicen a los niños que no tienen más dulces.
   b. Les dicen que Melchor está cansado.
   c. Les dicen que van a estar en otro lugar por la tarde.
2. a. A Ismael le encantan los Reyes Magos.
   b. Ismael quiere hablar con Baltasar.
   c. A Ismael le molesta el calor.
3. a. A Anita le molesta el calor y quiere irse a su casa.
   b. Anita quiere hablarle a Ismael.
   c. Anita quiere hablarle a otro Rey Mago.

HABLANDO DE GRAMÁTICA II

2. Discussing exchanges and reporting: The verbs *dar* and *decir*

Two common verbs usually used together with indirect object pronouns are **dar** and **decir**.

WileyPLUS Go to *WileyPLUS* to review this grammar point with the help of the **Animated Grammar Tutorial** and the **Verb Conjugator**.

dar *(to give)*			
(yo)	doy	(nosotros/as)	damos
(tú)	das	(vosotros/as)	dáis
(él, ella, Ud.)	da	(ellos/ellas/Uds.)	dan

decir *(to say, to tell)*			
(yo)	digo	(nosotros/as)	decimos
(tú)	dices	(vosotros/as)	decís
(él, ella, Ud.)	dice	(ellos/ellas/Uds.)	dicen

A. Dar means "to give." Note the irregular first person form ending in **-y** (like **estoy**.)

Anita **le da** su carta **a Melchor**.	*Anita gives her letter to Melchor.*
Los Reyes **les dan** caramelos **a los niños**.	*The Three Kings give candy to the children.*

B. Decir means "to say" or "to tell" (not "to speak" or "to talk", which is **hablar**!). Note that the irregular first person form is spelled with a **g**, and that four of the conjugation forms have an **i** in the stem.

Anita **le dice a Melchor** que quiere un iPod.	*Anita tells Melchor that she wants an iPod.*
Melchor **le dice:** "Primero tengo que saber si eres obediente".	*Melchor tells her: "First I have to know if you are obedient."*

Other verbs of transfer (such as *dar*) and communication (such as *decir*) commonly used with indirect object pronouns are:	
aconsejar	*to advise*
contar (o → ue)	*to tell, to narrate (e.g., a story)*
contestar	*to answer*
devolver (o → ue)	*to return (something)*
enviar	*to send*
escribir	*to write*
explicar	*to explain*
mandar	*to send*
mostrar (o → ue)	*to show*
ofrecer (c → zc)	*to offer*
pedir (e → i)	*to ask for, to request*
preguntar	*to ask*
prestar	*to lend*
regalar	*to give (as a gift)*
responder	*to respond*

5.2-11 La visita a los Reyes Anita está entusiasmada después de ver a los Reyes Magos y relata su visita. Combina las oraciones de la primera columna con la segunda.

_____ 1. Hay muchos niños en la calle y Tato no quiere perderme.

_____ 2. Todos los niños quieren tocar a los Reyes.

_____ 3. Los Reyes son muy simpáticos y tienen muchos dulces para nosotros.

_____ 4. Melchor habla mucho conmigo.

_____ 5. Yo espero mi turno para hablar con Melchor.

_____ 6. Los Reyes saben que soy muy obediente.

a. Todos esperamos nuestro turno y les damos la mano y un beso.

b. Le doy mi carta a Melchor con la lista de regalos que quiero recibir.

c. Por esta razón siempre me dan muchos regalos.

d. Me dice: "Te doy un caramelo si me das la carta".

e. Me da la mano para tenerme cerca.

f. Nos dan muchos caramelos a todos los niños.

5.2-12 El video de felicitación Para la boda de Carla y Marcos, los invitados les hacen un video de felicitación a los novios. La abuela de Carla no oye bien y Carla le repite todo a su abuela. Completa el informe de Carla con la forma correcta del verbo *decir*.

Todos los invitados están muy contentos. La exnovia de Marcos nos _____$_1$ "Buena suerte". Mis tíos nos aconsejan y nos _____$_2$ el secreto para mantener un matrimonio feliz. Mis padres gritan juntos: "Nosotros les _____$_3$: ¡Felicidades!", y mi mamá agrega: "Yo les _____$_4$, ¡queremos nietos pronto, por favor!". La última que aparece es la madre de Marcos. Ella me _____$_5$: "Bienvenida a la familia, hija".

5.2-13 ¿Con quién interactúas frecuentemente?

Paso 1: Completa las siguientes oraciones con información sobre ti.

MODELO: *A veces le regalo flores a mi madre porque le gustan mucho.*

1. Le(s) doy los mejores regalos de cumpleaños a _____ porque _____.

2. _____ me aconseja devolver siempre las llamadas porque _____.

3. Siempre le(s) digo "¡Felicidades!" por su cumpleaños a _____.

4. Le(s) escribo mensajes de correo electrónico todos los días a _____ porque _____.

5. _____ me manda(n) mensajes de texto todos los días porque _____.

6. Siempre le(s) ofrezco mi ayuda a _____ porque/cuando _____.

7. A veces les pido _____ a mis padres porque/cuando _____.

Paso 2: Ahora, usa las oraciones del **Paso 1** para crear preguntas y entrevistar a alguien de la clase.

MODELO: *¿A quién le regalas flores por su cumpleaños? ¿Por qué?*

¿Cuál es la conclusión? ¿Interactúan con la misma gente? ¿En qué coinciden? ¿En qué no?

3. Expressing likes and dislikes (III): Other verbs like *gustar*

WileyPLUS Go to *WileyPLUS* to review this grammar point with the help of the **Animated Grammar Tutorial** and the **Verb Conjugator**.

You have already been discussing likes and dislikes with the verb **gustar**. In Spanish, there are many other verbs that function like **gustar**. In this section you will learn some of them.

encantar	*to like a lot, to love something*	Nos encanta la tradición de los Reyes Magos. *We love the tradition of the Three Wise Men.*
fascinar	*to love, to be fascinated by something*	Me fascinan las fiestas sorpresa. *I love surprise parties.*
importar	*to care about something, to matter*	No me importa no ser invitado a las bodas. *I don't mind not being invited to weddings. (Lit., It doesn't matter to me.)*
molestar	*to bother*	¿Les molesta la música alta? *Does the loud music bother you?*
parecer	*to seem*	¿Te parece buena idea comprar este regalo? *Do you think it is a good idea to buy this present? (Lit., Does it seem like a good idea to you?)*
(des)agradar	*to (dis)please*	Me agradan las celebraciones familiares. *I like family celebrations. (Lit., Family celebrations are pleasing to me.)*
caer bien/mal	*to like/dislike someone*	No me caen bien los invitados. *I don't like the guests.*
aburrir	*to bore*	A Lucas le aburren las bodas. *Weddings bore Lucas.*

As with **gustar**, the prepositional phrase **a + mí, ti, él/ella, nosotros/as, vosotros/as, ustedes, ellos/as** should be used to clarify to whom something is pleasing, important, bothering, etc.

Just like with **gustar**, in order to agree when someone makes a statement using one of these verbs, use the following expressions with **también/tampoco**. Don't forget to always use the personal **a**!

Negative statement:

–No me caen bien estos invitados.   –*I don't like these guests.*
–A mí tampoco.   –*Me, neither.*

Positive statement:

–¡Me encanta la comida que nos sirven!   –*I love the food they are serving us!*
–¡A mí también!   –*Me, too!*

In order to disagree with a statement, use **sí/no**.

–No me caen bien estos invitados.   –*I don't like these guests.*
–A mí sí.   –*I do.*
–¡Me encanta la comida que nos sirven!   –*I love the food they serve us.*
–A mí no.   –*I don't.*

5.2-14 ¿Recuerdas qué le pasa a Lucas? Mira la historia de Lucas en **La pura verdad I** y decide si las siguientes oraciones son **ciertas** o **falsas**. Si son falsas, escribe la información correcta.

C   F

☐   ☐   1. En Cuba no tienen mucho dinero, pero les fascina celebrar las bodas de forma especial.

☐   ☐   2. A Nemis le desagradan las bodas.

☐   ☐   3. A Nemis le cae bien Lucas y lo invita a la boda de su hermana.

☐   ☐   4. A Lucas las bodas le aburren.

☐   ☐   5. A Lucas le parece muy divertido asistir a dos bodas en un día.

5.2-15 ¡Te invito! Nemis invita a Lucas a la boda de su hermana Carla. Completa el diálogo con el pronombre de objeto indirecto y la forma apropiada de los verbos de la lista.

> fascinar   aburrir   encantar   importar   parecer   caer (bien/mal)

Nemis: Lucas, mi hermana Carla se casa. ¡Estoy emocionada! ¡ _____ las bodas!

Lucas: Pues a mí no. A mí las bodas _____.

Nemis: ¡Pero esta boda es importante para mí! Mi familia no puede tirar la casa por la ventana pero a nosotros _____ celebrar la boda de mi hermana de forma especial. Además, a mi hermana _____ muy bien. ¡Estás invitado!

Lucas: Está bien. _____ la cultura cubana y tu hermana _____ muy simpática. ¿Cuándo es la boda?

Nemis: El sábado a las dos de la tarde. Entonces, ¿vas a venir?

Lucas: Sí, sí, allí voy a estar.

5.2-16 ¿Y tú qué piensas de las bodas?

Paso 1: Después de leer sobre las opiniones de Nemis y Lucas, escribe cinco oraciones con tus opiniones usando los verbos de la lista.

> gustar   encantar   fascinar   molestar   aburrir   (des)agradar

Ideas posibles:

el banquete, la comida, el baile, la recepción, la ceremonia…
ver a la familia, bailar, ponerme ropa elegante, gastar dinero en un regalo…

MODELO: Me _agrada_ conocer gente nueva en las bodas.

Paso 2: Con un/a compañero/a, comparen sus opiniones. ¿Piensan igual?

MODELO: Estudiante 1: ¿Te _gusta_ conocer gente nueva en las bodas?
Estudiante 2: ¡Sí, me _encanta_! ¿Y a ti?
Estudiante 3: A mí también. Es una buena ocasión para conocer gente nueva.

Paso 3: Entre ambos, escriban un pequeño párrafo para informar a la clase sobre las opiniones en las que coinciden.

MODELO: A nosotros dos nos _agrada_ conocer gente nueva en las bodas y también nos _encanta_…

OTRA PERSPECTIVA

Courtesy Wilma Isabel Pillot

Wilma Isabel

¿Cuántos años tienes?

Diferente

"En Estados Unidos tengo que recordar llevar identificación porque si no la tengo, no puedo comprar alcohol. En Puerto Rico, al igual que en muchos otros países, no es legal beber ni comprar alcohol si eres menor de edad, pero esto no se cumple[10] estrictamente. El alcohol se compra en los supermercados. En un supermercado no siempre piden identificación para verificar la edad, especialmente si parece que tienes más de 18 años".

Casi igual

"La edad legal para beber alcohol en Puerto Rico es 18 años. Al igual que en Estados Unidos, te piden una identificación, como la licencia de conducir, para verificar tu edad. La ley existe en ambos países, pero la práctica de pedir identificación para verificar la edad es menos común que en Estados Unidos".

Explícale a Wilma

1. ¿Tenemos una edad mínima para beber alcohol? ¿Cuántos años debes tener? ¿Estás de acuerdo?

2. ¿Cómo crees que afecta a la juventud tener una ley estricta sobre el comsumo de alcohol?

MANOS A LA OBRA

5.2-17 ¿Quién le sirve a quién? ¿Qué pasa después de la boda? ¿Qué exigen[11] los dos?

Paso 1: Con un/a compañero/a asuman el papel de una pareja recién casada. Responde a las demandas de tu pareja.

MODELO: Estudiante 1: *Vas a servirme el desayuno todas las mañanas.*
Estudiante 2: *No/Sí voy a servirte el desayuno todas las mañanas.*
Me molesta/agrada cocinar.

Estudiante 1 dice:
1. Vas a escribirles *e-mails* a mis padres.
2. Vas a darme masajes en los pies.
3. Vas a prepararnos la cena todas las noches.

Estudiante 2 dice:
1. Vas a escribirme poemas de amor todas las semanas.
2. Vas a regalarme cosas caras en mi cumpleaños.
3. Vas a darnos (a mí y a mis amigos) dinero para divertirnos durante el fin de semana.

Paso 2: Presenten a la clase los resultados. ¿Cuáles son las reacciones de su pareja? ¿Creen que van a tener una buena relación? ¿Por qué si o por qué no?

MODELO: *Él/Ella dice que debo servirle el desayuno todas las mañanas, pero a mí no me agrada cocinar...*

[10] **se cumple:** enforced [11] **exigir:** to demand

5.2-18 ¿Qué escribimos? Traten de formar una oración en la pizarra. Escriban una palabra a la vez[12], hasta completar una oración. ¿Qué grupo lo hace más rápido?

MODELO: Estudiante 1 escribe: *Le*
Estudiante 2 escribe: *regalo*
Estudiante 3 escribe: *un*
Estudiante 4 *escribe: ramo de flores.*

 5.2-19 ¿Quién aquí...? Levántate y hazles las siguientes preguntas a tus compañeros. Escribe el nombre del/de la compañero/a que conteste afirmativamente.

MODELO: Estudiante 1:   *¿Vas a casarte este año?*
Estudiante 2:   *Sí, voy a casarme este año. / No, no voy a casarme este año.*

1. ¿Les ofreces ayuda a tus amigos cuando hacen una fiesta? _____
2. ¿Vas a la iglesia casi todos los domingos? _____
3. ¿No quieres casarte nunca? _____
4. ¿Le regalas flores a tu novio/a? _____
5. ¿Lloras en las bodas o en las películas? _____
6. ¿Les haces regalos a tus amigos en sus cumpleaños? _____

Después, comenta tus resultados con la clase. ¿Fue fácil o difícil completar la actividad?

MODELO: *Parece que nadie de la clase le regala...*

 5.2-20 ¡Escrúpulos! ¿Tienes escrúpulos? En grupos de dos o tres, lean las siguientes situaciones y digan qué van a hacer o qué van a decir en cada situación.

1. Una amiga se va a casar pronto. Tú sabes que el novio tiene una relación con otra mujer. ¿Le dices la verdad a tu amiga?
2. Te dan un regalo muy grande y muy caro pero muy feo. Con mucho entusiasmo te preguntan: "¿Te gusta, te gusta?". ¿Les dices la verdad o les dices una mentira como: "Ay, sí, me encanta, gracias"?
3. Estás en una boda que, en tu opinión, es un desastre. El novio te pregunta: "¿Qué te parece mi boda? Magnífica, ¿no?". ¿Qué le dices?
4. Una buena amiga te da un regalo caro pero a ti no te agrada. Le das las gracias y le dices que te gusta. Una semana después tienes que ir a una boda y no tienes dinero para comprar un regalo. ¿Usas el regalo de tu amiga?

WileyPLUS Go to *WileyPLUS* and listen to **Presta atención.**

 5.2-21 Presta atención: Una conversación entre Anita y su tío Tato Después de ver a los Reyes Magos, Anita habla con su tío. Escucha la conversación y selecciona las respuestas más apropiadas, según el audio.

1. El tío Tato le dice a Anita que...
    a. su amigo Ismael va con ellos a ver a los Reyes.
    b. su amigo Ismael tiene que ir a ver a unos amigos.
    c. su amigo Ismael tiene que ir al supermercado.
2. Tato dice que...
    a. su amigo Ismael no tiene tiempo para ver a los Reyes.
    b. su amigo Ismael va a ver a los Reyes más tarde.
    c. su amigo Ismael es mayor para ver a los Reyes.
3. Tato le dice a Anita que...
    a. Ismael no sabe con qué rey quiere hablar.
    b. Ismael quiere pedirles regalos a los tres Reyes.
    c. él no sabe a qué rey Ismael le va a pedir regalos.

[12] **a la vez:** at a time

4. Tato...
   a. sabe qué regalos quiere Ismael.
   b. no sabe si Ismael va a ver a los Reyes.
   c. no sabe qué regalos quiere Ismael.

5. Anita...
   a. quiere saber si Tato es realmente amigo de Ismael.
   b. piensa que Tato conoce bien a su amigo.
   c. le pregunta a Tato dónde está su amigo Ismael.

 5.2-22 Por escrito: Una boda Imagina que vas a ir con un/a amigo/a a la boda de una persona que no conocen. Van el próximo sábado.

Escribe un diálogo entre tu amigo/a y tú. Incluye los verbos nuevos de esta sección como: *encantar, fascinar, (des)agradar, aburrir, molestar, parecer, ir a* + infinitivo, *ser, estar, dar, decir* y los pronombres de objeto indirecto y directo.

En el diálogo, habla sobre lo siguiente:
- cuándo es la boda;
- qué ropa van a ponerse;
- qué van a hacer en la boda;
- cómo es la recepción, qué gente asiste, qué opinas sobre las bodas, etc.

Tu amigo/a puede preguntar sobre el tipo de boda, el lugar de la boda, la comida, etc.

 ¡OJO!

Grammar Review
Since you already know some grammar structures, make sure that you are accurately expressing the meaning you intended by reviewing your grammar after writing the dialogue.

PONTE EN MI LUGAR

Una celebración En grupos de tres o cuatro seleccionen a una persona y piensen en un tipo de celebración (cumpleaños, boda, quinceañero, benei mitzvá, etc.). Después, planeen la celebración: ¿Dónde tiene lugar? ¿Qué se celebra? ¿Quién dirige la celebración? ¿Cuándo es la celebración? ¿Quién asiste? ¿Qué costumbres se practican? ¿Cuánto dura? ¿En qué países o culturas se celebra? Después, el grupo prepara un diálogo y lo actúa. Por ejemplo, una boda: ¿Se celebra en una iglesia o en un juzgado? ¿A qué religión pertenece la celebración? ¿Hay un cura o un juez de paz? Un narrador describe la acción y nombra a todos los participantes. En el diálogo hablen sobre el baile, las conversaciones, el brindis, la comida, las bebidas, el fotógrafo y lo que dice el festejado[13]. Recuerda usar **Estrategias para conversar** para hacer preguntas directas.

---

[13]**festejado:** guest of honor

ASÍ ES LA VIDA

Adivina, adivinador

Solo una vez al año
tú celebras ese día,
y conmemoras la fecha
en que llegaste a la vida.
¿Qué fiesta es?

Redondo, redondo,
pequeño y sin fondo[14].
¿Qué es?

WileyPLUS Go to *WileyPLUS* to find more **Arroba** activities.

@Arroba@

Los regalos Explora en tu buscador favorito las palabras *almacenes* y *hogar*. Piensa en una persona que va a casarse pronto, como un hermano, un amigo, un primo, un padre, etc. Haz una lista de artículos de regalos y quién los va a regalar. ¿Qué le vas a regalar tú? ¿Qué le van a regalar otros invitados de la boda? Después, comparte tus oraciones con dos de tus compañeros y comenta sobre el regalo. Sigue el modelo.

MODELO: Estudiante 1: *Mi primo se casa el 21 de abril. Mis padres le van a regalar un televisor.*

Estudiante 2: *¡Qué bien! Mi hermana se casa en un mes. Yo le voy a regalar un florero.*

VER PARA CREER II: ¡A bailar!

WileyPLUS Go to *WileyPlus* to see this video and to find more video activities.

Antes de ver

En este video vamos a visitar Puerto Rico. Con un/a compañero/a, contesta o comenta lo siguiente:

1. ¿Conoces Puerto Rico? ¿Qué ciudades conoces?
2. ¿Qué expresión en inglés conoces para la palabra *chévere*?
3. ¿Qué bailes se bailan en Puerto Rico?
4. ¿Qué significa *boricua*?

Después de ver

1. ¿Entendiste? Después de ver el video, decide si las oraciones son **ciertas** o **falsas**. Si es falso, explica por qué.

1. Justin es un puertorriqueño que vive en Puerto Rico.
2. Kate es la prima de Justin y es puertorriqueña.
3. Justin y Kate son novios y se van a casar.
4. Hoy es el cumpleaños de la novia de Justin.
5. Kate invita a Justin a ir a la discoteca.
6. Nuyorican es una discoteca en el Viejo San Juan.

2. En la discoteca En parejas, escriban un diálogo usando palabras de esta lista. Represéntenlo delante de la clase.

caer bien/mal   molestar   importar   regalar   animar   agradecer   saber   conocer
paso de baile   cumbia   pareja   canción

Tema: Kate y Justin se encuentran en la discoteca. Justin está muy contento porque es su cumpleaños. Justin quiere bailar con Kate toda la noche pero Kate no siempre quiere bailar con él. ¿Por qué? ¿Qué pasa?

3. Enfoque cultural ¿Qué bailes e instrumentos son típicos en tu cultura?

[14]**fondo**: bottom

AUTOPRUEBA

VOCABULARIO

I. ¿Qué es? Contesta las preguntas de vocabulario.

1. ¿Cómo se llaman las mujeres que son amigas de la novia y participan en su boda?
2. ¿Cómo se llaman los hombres que son amigos del novio y participan en su boda?
3. ¿Cómo se llama la cosa que la novia tira a las mujeres solteras de la boda?
4. ¿En qué lugar te puedes casar si no quieres casarte en una iglesia?
5. ¿Qué celebran los padres que llevan a su bebé a la iglesia para ponerle agua?

II. ¿Qué o quién es? Lee las oraciones y decide quiénes son las siguientes personas o qué son las cosas. Usa la lista de palabras. ¡Ojo! Hay más palabras que oraciones.

el anillo   los padrinos   la iglesia   el padre
el novio   el cura   los invitados

1. Es una persona que puede casar a dos personas.
2. Es un hombre que tiene una relación con otra persona y quiere casarse con esa persona.
3. Son las personas que asisten a una celebración.
4. En un bautizo, son dos personas encargadas de un bebé. Son como los padres.
5. Es un lugar sagrado donde hay bautizos y bodas.

GRAMÁTICA

I. Buenos modales ¿Qué debemos hacer en una boda? Completa los espacios en blanco con el pronombre de objeto indirecto apropiado.

1. Tres semanas antes, los padres _____ mandan las invitaciones a los familiares.
2. Nosotros los invitados _____ tiramos arroz a los novios.
3. Todos _____ decimos "felicidades" al novio.
4. Nosotros _____ damos un regalo a los novios.
5. Unas semanas después, la novia _____ manda una nota de agradecimiento a nosotros los invitados.

II. ¿A quién le dices eso? Di quién dice las siguientes frases.

MODELO: ¿Me quieres? (la novia a su pareja)
→ *La novia le dice a su pareja: "¿Me quieres?".*

1. Felicidades (nosotros al padre de la novia)
2. Te bautizo en el nombre del Padre… (el cura al bebé)
3. Siempre lloro en las bodas. (yo a todos)
4. ¡No lo hagas! (los amigos al novio)
5. ¡Sí, quiero! (el novio a su pareja)

III. ¡Vamos de boda! Tu hermana se va a casar y todos están preparando la boda. Habla de las cosas que les gustan y que no les gustan a cada persona de la familia. Completa los espacios con el verbo equivalente a "gustar" adecuado de la lista.

interesar   encantar   molestar   parecer   aburrir

1. Mi hermana está muy contenta organizando su boda. A mi hermana _____ organizar su boda.
2. Yo detesto las bodas. Hay mucha gente y me siento claustrofóbico. A mí _____ las bodas con mucha gente.
3. Mi madre y yo opinamos que el banquete es demasiado caro. A mi madre y a mí _____ excesivo el banquete.
4. Mis hermanos están muy aburridos durante la ceremonia. A ellos _____ las bodas.
5. ¿Y tú? ¿Tienes interés por las bodas? ¿Y a ti? ¿_____ bodas?

CULTURA

1. ¿Son diferentes las bodas en Cuba a las bodas en Estados Unidos? ¿En qué son similares? ¿En qué son diferentes?
2. ¿Hay una edad mínima para beber alcohol en países como Puerto Rico?
3. Explica qué pasa el 6 de enero en Puerto Rico y la República Dominicana.

REDACCIÓN

Escríbele una carta a un amigo en la República Dominicana describiendo una boda típica de Estados Unidos. Dile qué diferencias hay con las bodas de la República Dominicana. Di qué cosas se hacen en una despedida de soltero/a, en la ceremonia, en la recepción, etc.

EN RESUMIDAS CUENTAS, AHORA PUEDO…

☐ hablar sobre bodas y otras celebraciones.

☐ reconocer las diferencias culturales en funerales, bodas, bautizos y otras celebraciones

☐ decir para quién hacemos algo.

☐ decir quién *dice* o *da* algo a alguien.

☐ hablar de gustos y preferencias.

☐ hablar de planes de futuro.

VOCABULARIO ESENCIAL

Sustantivos

el/la ahijado/a	godson/goddaughter
el anillo	ring
el bautizo	baptism
la boda	wedding
el brindis	the toast
el caballero	groomsman
el cumpleaños	birthday
el cura	priest
la dama	bridesmaid
la despedida de soltero/a	bachelor/bachelorette party
el Día de Año Nuevo	New Year's Day
el Día de los Reyes Magos	Three Kings Day
el/la quinceañero/a	15th birthday celebration
el Día de Año Viejo/la Nochevieja	New Year's Eve
la iglesia	church
el/la invitado/a	guest
el juez de paz	justice of the peace
el juzgado	courthouse
la luna de miel	honeymoon
la madrina	maid of honor, godmother
la Navidad	Christmas
la Nochebuena	Christmas Eve
la novia	bride/girlfriend
el novio	groom boyfriend
los novios	newlyweds/boyfriend and girlfriend
el padrino	best man, godfather
el ramo (de flores)	bouquet
el regalo	gift
el/la testigo	witness

Cognados: la ceremonia, el funeral, la recepción, el banquete, la celebración

Verbos

aconsejar	to advise
caer bien/mal	to like/dislike someone/or not
contar (ue)	to tell, to narrate (e.g., a story)
contestar	to answer
dar	to give
decir	to say
(des)agradar	to (dis)please
devolver (ue)	to return (something)
encantar	to like a lot, to love something
enviar	to send
explicar	to explain
fascinar	to love, to be fascinated by something
importar	to care about something, to matter
mandar	to send
molestar	to bother
mostrar	to show
ofrecer (zc)	to offer
preguntar	to ask
prestar	to lend
regalar	to give (as a gift)
tirar (el ramo)	to throw (the bouquet)

Expresiones

¡Felicidades!	Congratulations!
¡Salud!	Cheers! (Lit., Health!)
¡Que vivan los novios!	Cheers for the newlyweds!/ Hooray for the happy couple!

6 Un viaje al pasado

© John Wiley & Sons, Inc.

VER PARA CREER I: ¡Qué antiguo!

Antes de ver el video, con un(a) compañero/a, repasa el contenido de este capítulo ¿Cuál es el título? ¿Qué país vas a estudiar? ¿Conoces algunas ciudades de este país? ¿Qué tema piensas que puede tratar? Al ver el video, presta atención al contenido para poder contestar las preguntas.

1. ¿En qué lugar están las dos amigas?

2. ¿Qué hacen?

3. ¿Qué lugares visitan?

Sección 1	Lecciones de historia

PALABRA POR PALABRA

- La historia
- Los números ordinales

HABLANDO DE GRAMÁTICA

- Talking about events in the past (I): The preterit tense of regular verbs
- Talking about events in the past (II): The preterit of the verbs **ir** and **ser**
- Saying how long ago something happened: **Hace** + time + **que**
- Avoiding repetition: Direct object pronouns ♻

CULTURA

- España: Historia, lenguas y comunidades autónomas
- El centro histórico de la ciudad

Sección 2	Arte de ayer y de hoy

PALABRA POR PALABRA

- El arte
- Los procesos creativos
- Más colores ♻

HABLANDO DE GRAMÁTICA

- Talking about events in the past (III): The preterit tense of irregular and stem-changing verbs ♻
- Possessive adjectives ♻
- Pointing out people and objects: Demonstrative adjectives and pronouns
- Recognizing the *vosotros* form of address

CULTURA

- Algunos artistas españoles y sus obras
- La arquitectura y el espacio urbano

España

Trivia: Go to *WileyPLUS* to do the **Trivia** activities and find out how much you know about these countries!

© John Wiley & Sons, Inc.

LEARNING OBJECTIVES

By the end of this section you will be able to:

- Understand the history and art of Spain
- Use ordinal numbers
- Talk about events in the past using the preterit tense of regular verbs, **ir**, and **ser**
- List important events in your life

- Use **hace** + time + **que** to specify when something happened
- Practice using direct object pronouns
- Understand the importance of the historic downtown

Una imagen vale más que mil palabras

¿Quiénes, en el mundo antiguo[1], construyeron este tipo de estructura?

¿En qué años más o menos dominaron el mundo los romanos?

¿Hay este tipo de arquitectura en Estados Unidos?

▲ *Anfiteatro de Mérida, España*

UNA PERSPECTIVA

Jesse

Diferente

"En Madrid tomé una clase de historia de España con otros estudiantes internacionales. Los españoles sí que tienen que estudiar muchos siglos de historia. Desde el 3000 a. C. al 711 d. C., muchos grupos diferentes habitaron la Península Ibérica: los íberos, los fenicios, los celtas, los griegos, los romanos, los visigodos y los musulmanes[2]. Varios de esos grupos, como los romanos o los visigodos, fueron invasores. Todas esas invasiones forman lo que son los españoles de hoy".

Igual

"Los primeros pobladores del continente norteamericano, o sea, los distintos grupos de nativos, sufrieron una gran invasión europea".

¿Qué piensas tú?

1. ¿Qué grupos se establecen en el continente norteamericano?
2. ¿Qué grupos nativos en el territorio estadounidense tratan de resistir la constante inmigración europea?
3. ¿Sabes cuántos años tiene más o menos Estados Unidos? ¿Cuántos años tiene más o menos España?

---

[1] **antiguo:** ancient [2] **musulmán:** muslim

LA PURA VERDAD I   ¡Qué familia!

Gabriel estudia español en Madrid. Su profesora le cuenta a su clase la historia de los Reyes Católicos.

1.

2.

▲ *Una fascinante historia de intriga y amor.*

3.
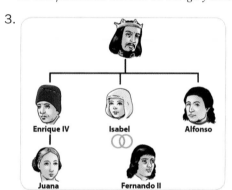

4.

▲ *Isabel y Fernando se casan el 19 de octubre de 1469.*

5.

6.
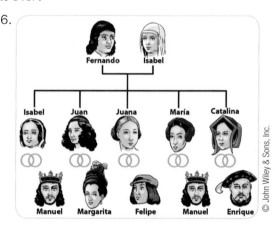

© John Wiley & Sons, Inc.

6.1-01 La intriga continúa... Escucha la narración y selecciona la oración que mejor explica lo que dice.

1. a. Los Reyes Católicos derrotan al rey Boabdil.
   b. Los Reyes Católicos invaden Arabia Saudita.
   c. Los Reyes Católicos destruyen la Alhambra.
2. a. Catalina es la tercera hija.
   b. María es la primera hija.
   c. Catalina es la quinta hija de los reyes.
3. a. El rey Fernando y su hija son enemigos.
   b. Isabel y su hija son enemigos.
   c. Juana gana la lucha.

🔊 PALABRA POR PALABRA

La historia

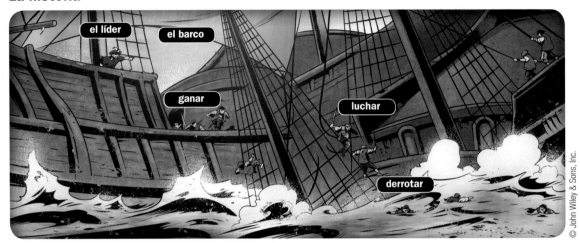

el líder · el barco · ganar · luchar · derrotar

a. C. (antes de Cristo)	*B.C. (Before Christ)*	el aliado	*ally*
d. C. (después de Cristo)	*A.D. (in the year of our Lord)*	la dictadura	*dictatorship*
		la Edad Media/Moderna	*middle/modern ages*
derrotar	*defeat*	la época	*age/era*
elegir	*to elect*	la guerra (civil)	*(civil) war*
fundar	*to establish*	el poder	*power*
ganar	*to win*	la reina	*queen*
gobernar	*to rule*	el rey	*king*
habitar	*to inhabit*	el siglo	*century*
luchar	*to fight*	el tratado	*treaty*
nacer	*to be born*	el viaje	*voyage*

Cognados: atacar, conquistar, establecer, explorar, invadir, terminar

Cognados: la conquista, la constitución, el/la enemigo/a, la democracia, el/la dictador/a, el imperio, la independencia, la invasión, el líder, la monarquía

Alfonso I · Alfonso II · Alfonso III · Alfonso IV · Alfonso V

Alfonso VI · Alfonso VII · Alfonso VIII · Alfonso IX · Alfonso X

Los números ordinales

primer(o)/a*	*first*
segundo/a	*second*
tercer(o)/a*	*third*
cuarto/a	*fourth*
quinto/a	*fifth*
sexto/a	*sixth*
séptimo/a	*seventh*
octavo/a	*eighth*
noveno/a	*ninth*
décimo/a	*tenth*

* When followed by a masculine noun, **primero** and **tercero** drop the -o ending: **El primer presidente de Estados Unidos fue George Washington.**

6.1-02 ¡Prueba de historia! Con un/a compañero/a, pon en orden la siguiente lista. ¿Qué ocurre primero y qué ocurre después?

_____ a. Los españoles establecen la primera misión de San Agustín en Florida en el siglo XVI.

_____ b. Estados Unidos derrota a España en la Guerra hispano-estadounidense en 1898.

_____ c. Cristóbal Colón descubre las Américas en busca de las Indias.

_____ d. Los romanos conquistan la Península Ibérica.

_____ e. Empieza la transición democrática después de la muerte de Franco.

_____ f. Los españoles exploran y establecen misiones en California.

_____ g. Francisco Franco es dictador de España entre 1936 y 1975.

_____ h. Los musulmanes invaden la Península Ibérica en el siglo VIII.

¿Qué dicen los españoles?

- Tenemos que estar allí en 10 minutos.	- *We have to be there in 10 minutes.*
- Pues <u>venga</u>, vámonos ya.	- *OK, let's go, let's leave already.*
- ¿Vamos al cine a ver una peli?	- *Why don't we go to the theater to watch a movie?*
- <u>Vale</u>.	- *OK.*
- Tuvo que pagar una multa de 1.000 euros.	- *He had to pay a fine of 1,000 euros.*
- ¡Qué <u>pasada</u>!	- *Unbelievable!*
¡Madre mía! ¿Qué ha pasado aquí?*	*Oh my goodness! What happened here?*
¡<u>Venga</u> ya! ¿Piensas que voy a creer eso?	*Oh, come off it! Do you think I'm going to believe that?*

*Esta expresión se usa en otros países hispanohablantes también.

6.1-03 Líderes

Paso 1: ¿Conocen a estas personas? Con un/a compañero/a, traten de recordar por qué son personajes históricos.

1. Hernán Cortés	a. Es reina de España entre 1479 y 1504.
2. Francisco Pizarro	b. Llega a las Américas pensando que es la India.
3. Los reyes Fernando e Isabel	c. Derrota al último emperador inca.
4. Cristóbal Colón	d. Demuestra que las Américas no son parte de Asia.
5. Américo Vespucio	e. Conquista a los aztecas.
6. Isabel la Católica	f. Conquistan Granada, el último reino árabe en España.

Paso 2: Ahora, piensa en un líder histórico y pregúntale a tu compañero/a por qué es un personaje histórico. ¿Qué piensan? ¿Saben de historia, o no?

6.1-04 ¿Qué palabra es?

Paso 1: ¿Con qué palabras de la sección **Palabra por palabra** asocian los siguientes eventos, personas o situaciones?

1. Es el resultado de la separación política de otro país.
2. Es la persona que está casada con el rey.
3. Es un sistema político en el que los ciudadanos deciden quiénes son sus representantes.
4. Es un sistema político en el que los ciudadanos no deciden quién es su líder.
5. Es el resultado de la invasión y conquista de muchos territorios.
6. Es un documento que se escribe normalmente al final de una guerra.

Paso 2: Ahora, elijan tres palabras de la sección **Palabra por palabra** y escriban tres definiciones para leerlas a la clase. El resto de la clase tiene que adivinar cuál es la palabra. ¡Atención! Recuerden que para definir siempre usamos el verbo *ser*.

MODELO: *Es un/a... que...*
            Es el/la... que...

6.1-05 La línea del tiempo

Paso 1: Con un/a compañero/a, habla sobre la historia de la Península Ibérica. Túrnense y sigan el orden de las preguntas. Anoten sus respuestas.

MODELO: Estudiante 1: *¿Qué rey de España es también rey de Alemania?*
Estudiante 2: *Carlos V (quinto)*

Estudiante 1

Los romanos conquistan la península. **S. III a. C.**

Alfonso X y la Escuela de Traductores de Toledo **S. XIII**

Carlos V de Alemania es también rey de España. **1516**

Juan Carlos I, rey de España **1975**

S. VIII a. C. Fundación de las colonias griegas de Ampurias y Roses en la costa mediterránea

S. V Primeras invasiones germánicas

1492 Salida de La Pinta, la Niña y la Santa María hacia las Indias

1561 Felipe II establece Madrid como la capital de España.

© John Wiley & Sons, Inc.

Estudiante 2

Estudiante 1

1. ¿En qué siglo fundan los griegos las primeras colonias en la Península Ibérica?
3. ¿En qué siglo empiezan las invasiones germánicas?
5. ¿Cuándo salió la expedición de Colón hacia las Indias?
7. ¿Qué rey establece Madrid como la capital de España en 1561?

Estudiante 2

2. ¿En qué siglo conquistan la Península Ibérica los romanos?
4. ¿Qué rey patrocina[3] la Escuela de Traductores de Toledo?
6. ¿Cuándo fue rey de España Carlos V?
8. ¿Quién pasó a ser rey de España en 1975?

Paso 2: Ahora, piensa en tres eventos históricos importantes de tu país y prepara tres preguntas para tu compañero/a. Después, decidan: ¿saben mucho de historia?

 6.1-06 Hablemos de historia

Paso 1: Hablen sobre lo siguiente:

1. ¿Debemos estudiar historia? ¿Sí? ¿No? ¿Por qué?
2. ¿Qué período o época de la historia es más interesante para ti? ¿Qué años? ¿Por qué?
3. ¿Qué período piensas que es el menos interesante? ¿Por qué?
4. ¿Qué personaje histórico admiras más? ¿Cuál detestas? ¿Por qué?
5. Imagina que puedes viajar en el tiempo. ¿Qué personaje histórico quieres observar?
6. ¿Conoces algunos tratados importantes? ¿Cuáles?

Paso 2: Después, escriban un pequeño informe. ¿En qué aspectos coinciden los dos? ¿En qué no coinciden?

MODELO: *Mi compañero/a (nombre del compañero/a) y yo pensamos que estudiar historia es importante porque... Yo admiro mucho a... pero mi compañero/a admira a.... Los tratados que conocemos son...*

Paso 3: Por último, informen a la clase. ¿Coinciden en todo, o en nada? ¿En qué aspecto no coinciden con nadie de la clase?

[3]**patrocinar:** to sponsor

HABLANDO DE GRAMÁTICA I

1. Talking about events in the past (I): The preterit tense of regular verbs

To talk about completed actions in the past, in Spanish we use the preterit (or simple past) tense.

WileyPLUS Go to *WileyPLUS* to review this grammar point with the help of the **Animated Grammar Tutorial** and the **Verb Conjugator.**

Los musulmanes **llegaron** a la Península Ibérica en el año 711.	*The Moors arrived in the Iberian Peninsula in the year 711.*
Cristóbal Colón **descubrió** un continente en ruta hacia las Indias.	*Christopher Columbus discovered a continent in route to the Indies.*

To form the preterit of regular verbs, substitute the infinitive ending by the preterit endings:

-ar			
(yo)	-é	(nosotros/as)	-amos
(tú)	-aste	(vosotros/as)	-asteis
(él, ella, Ud.)	-ó	(ellos/ellas/Uds.)	-aron

-er/-ir			
(yo)	-í	(nosotros/as)	-imos
(tú)	-iste	(vosotros/as)	-isteis
(él, ella, Ud.)	-ió (-yó)*	(ellos/ellas/Uds.)	-ieron (-yeron)*

	ganar *(to win)*	**nacer** *(to be born)*	**invadir** *(to invade)*
(yo)	gan**é**	nac**í**	invad**í**
(tú)	gan**aste**	nac**iste**	invad**iste**
(él, ella, Ud.)	gan**ó**	nac**ió**	invad**ió**
(nosotros/as)	gan**amos**	nac**imos**	invad**imos**
(vosotros/as)	gan**asteis**	nac**isteis**	invad**isteis**
(ellos/ellas/Uds.)	gan**aron**	nac**ieron**	invad**ieron**

El rey Fernando de Aragón **nació** en 1452. Se **casó** con Isabel de Castilla en 1469. Juntos **invadieron** el reino de Granada y **ganaron** la guerra contra los árabes. Así, **conquistaron** y **unificaron** casi toda la Península Ibérica bajo el reino de España.	*The king Fernando of Aragon **was born** in 1452. He **married** Isabel of Castille in 1469. Together they **invaded** the kingdom of Granada and **won** the war against the Moors. This way they **conquered** and **unified** almost all of the Iberian Peninsula as the kingdom of Spain.*

*When the verb stem ends in a vowel (e.g., **le-er, o-ír, ca-er, constru-ir, cre-er**), the **-i-** in the third person ending becomes **-y-**.

caer → cayó, cayeron
construir → construyó, construyeron

Los incas **construyeron** un imperio en los actuales territorios de Perú, Bolivia, Ecuador y parte de Chile y Argentina.	*The Incas built an empire in the territories of Perú, Bolivia, Ecuador, and part of Chile and Argentina.*
El inca Atahualpa **cayó** prisionero en la batalla de Cajamarca.	*The Inca Atahualpa was taken prisoner in the battle of Cajamarca.*

In regular preterit forms, the stress is always on the last syllable of the **yo** and **él/ella/Ud**. conjugations, and it is indicated by a written accent mark. The written accent marks in some of the preterit endings differentiate the word from another of the verb's tense. For example:

hablo → *I speak*   habl**ó** → *he/she spoke*

The verbs **dar** and **ver** do not take written accents in the preterit except in the **vosotros** form (**disteis, visteis**).

Regular verbs that end in **-car**, **-gar**, and **-zar** (**tocar**, **jugar**, **empezar**, etc.) change in the **yo** form to keep the sound of the infinitive form:

buscar	→	bus**qu**é	[~~buscé~~]
llegar	→	lle**gu**é	[~~llegé~~]
almorzar	→	almor**c**é	[~~almorzé~~]

Busqué el libro de historia por toda la casa, pero no lo encontré.

I looked for the history book all over the house but I didn't find it.

Llegué tarde a la clase y me perdí la presentación sobre Juana la Loca.

I arrived late to class and I missed the presentation on Juana la Loca.

6.1-07 ¿Presente o pasado? Lee las siguientes oraciones y decide si son afirmaciones en el presente o en el pasado. ¡Pon atención a la forma del verbo!

1. Alfonso X el Sabio fundó la Escuela de Traductores de Toledo.
2. Los Reyes Católicos gobernaron en el territorio que hoy conocemos como España.
3. En España hay una monarquía, pero los reyes no gobiernan.
4. En España los ciudadanos eligen a sus gobernantes.
5. Los ciudadanos españoles eligieron a Mariano Rajoy como presidente en un proceso democrático.

6.1-08 La primera expedición de Cristóbal Colón Pon en orden cronológico estos eventos históricos.

_____ a. Tres carabelas⁴ (la Pinta, la Niña y la Santa María) salieron del Puerto de Palos el 3 de agosto de 1492.

_____ b. Después de explorar la isla⁵ de Guanahani (San Salvador), Cristóbal Colón continuó su viaje y llegó a Cuba.

_____ c. Cristóbal Colón recibió fondos de Fernando e Isabel para financiar la primera expedición a las Indias.

_____ d. El 12 de octubre, Rodrigo de Triana gritó: "¡Tierra!".

_____ e. Los taínos de la isla de Guanahani en el Caribe recibieron a los españoles e intercambiaron regalos con ellos.

_____ f. Después de llegar a tierra, llamaron a la isla San Salvador.

6.1-09 Trafalgar ¿Qué sabes de la batalla de Trafalgar? Completa el párrafo con los verbos de la lista en el pretérito para saber más sobre este evento histórico.

atacar   terminar   luchar   significar   derrotar   ocurrir   empezar   informar

La batalla de Trafalgar _____₁ en 1805. En esta batalla, los aliados Francia y España _____₂ contra la armada británica. La batalla _____₃ al mediodía. La flota inglesa _____₄ primero y _____₅ completamente a la flota franco-española. El almirante Nelson murió⁶ en el combate, pero justo antes, unos marineros le _____₆ de la victoria inglesa. La batalla _____₇ a las 6:30 de la tarde. Esta derrota _____₈ el fin de España como potencia⁷ colonial en el mundo.

---

⁴**carabela:** caravel, a kind of sailing ship developed in the 15th century by the Portuguese
⁵**isla:** island ⁶**murió:** died ⁷**potencia:** power

6.1-10 La llegada a las Américas Escribe oraciones combinando los elementos de cada columna con la forma apropiada de los verbos en el pretérito.

Los marineros[8]   llamar   "indios" a los habitantes.
                   llegar   a la isla de de San Salvador.
                   ver   algo luminoso durante la noche.
Cristóbal Colón   tomar   "Vamos a morir, queremos regresar".
                   gritar   posesión de las tierras en nombre de los Reyes Católicos.

2. Talking about events in the past (II): The preterit of the verbs *ir* and *ser*

The verbs **ir** and **ser** have identical forms in the preterit. The context in which the verbs appear will clarify which one is being used.

ser / ir *(to be / to go)*		
(yo)	fui	*I was/went*
(tú)	fuiste	*you were/went*
(él, ella, Ud.)	fue	*he/she was/went; you (sing., formal) were/went*
(nosotros/as)	fuimos	*we were/went*
(vosotros/as)	fuisteis	*you (plural, infomal, Spain) were/went*
(ellos/ellas/Uds.)	fueron	*they were/went; you (plural, formal) were/went*

Ampurias y Rosas **fueron** las primeras colonias griegas en la Península Ibérica.
Cristobal Colón **fue** a las islas Canarias antes de continuar su viaje a las Indias.

Ampurias and Rosas were the first Greek colonies in the Iberian Peninsula.
Cristobal Colón went to the Canary Islands before continuing his journey to the Indies.

6.1-11 Bernal Díaz del Castillo Completa el siguiente párrafo con los verbos de la lista en la forma apropiada del pretérito para saber más sobre la vida de este personaje histórico.

ir (x2)   ser   escribir   encontrar   nacer   recibir

Bernal Díaz del Castillo _____₁ aproximadamente en 1496 en un pueblo pequeño de España y _____₂ una educación simple. _____₃ a las Américas en 1517 para hacer fortuna, pero _____₄ pocas oportunidades. Más tarde, en 1519, _____₅ a la península de Yucatán en una expedición con Hernán Cortés. Durante la campaña con Cortés, _____₆ sus crónicas sobre la conquista de Nueva España. Al final de su vida, _____₇ gobernador de Guatemala.

6.1-12 Entrevista histórica Bernal Díaz del Castillo fue conquistador y escribió sobre la historia de la conquista de las Américas. ¿Puedes pensar en las preguntas que Carlos V, rey de España, hizo a Bernal cuando lo conoció? Con un/a compañero/a, repasen la información y los verbos de la actividad **6.1-11** para completar esta entrevista histórica.

MODELO: ¿Cuándo <u>conociste</u> a Hernán Cortés?
           <u>Conocí</u> a Hernán Cortés antes de viajar con él.

Carlos V: ¿En qué año _____₁?
Bernal: _____₂ en 1496.
Carlos V: ¿Qué _____₃?
Bernal: _____₄ una educación muy simple.
Carlos V: ¿Cuándo _____₅?
Bernal: _____₆ al Nuevo Mundo con Hernán Cortés en 1514.
Carlos V: ¿Qué _____₇?
Bernal: _____₈ sobre la crónica de la conquista de Nueva España.

---
[8]**marineros:** sailors

LA PURA VERDAD II   Moros⁹ y cristianos

Julia es una turista de Estados Unidos que visita a unos amigos de Alicante y observa El Desembarco, un festival muy divertido que se celebra en Villajoyosa.

1.

▲ *Las Fiestas de Moros y Cristianos* **se celebran** *en Villajoyosa en honor a Santa Marta del 24 al 31 de julio.*

2.

3.

4.

Mira, llegaron los barcos. Empezó la invasión.

5.

© John Wiley & Sons, Inc.

6.1-13 La celebración continúa Escucha la narración de las festividades de Villajoyosa en Alicante, España. Selecciona la oración que mejor explica lo que dice.

1. a. Julia no regresó al festival al día siguiente.
   b. Julia miró otra lucha entre los moros y los cristianos.
   c. Los moros ganaron otra vez.
2. a. El día siguiente fue todo más tranquilo.
   b. Todos descansaron el día siguiente.
   c. El día siguiente se celebró la victoria de los cristianos.
3. Los últimos dos días...
   a. hicieron un desfile por la calle donde no había música.
   b. Julia comió paella.
   c. no fue muy divertido.

⁹**moros:** people from North Africa, mainly from Morocco, most of which were Muslims, that conquered Spain in the eighth century and were finally driven out in the fifteenth century.

HABLANDO DE GRAMÁTICA II

3. Saying how long ago something happened: *Hace* + time + *que*

WileyPLUS Go to *WileyPLUS* to review this grammar point with the help of the **Animated Grammar Tutorial**.

In order to express *how long ago* or *since when*, the expression **hace** + *amount of time* is used in Spanish:

El desfile acabó **hace 5 minutos**.   *The parade ended 5 minutes ago.*

Use **hace** + *time* + **que** if followed by a verb in the preterit:

Hace muchos años que comenzó la democracia.   *Democracy started many years ago.*

To ask how long ago something took place use **¿Cuánto (tiempo) hace que** + *verb*?

–**¿Cuánto tiempo hace que** fuiste a Barcelona?   –*How long ago did you go to Barcelona?*
–Hace dos años.   –*Two years ago.*

6.1-14 Historia deportiva ¿Cuánto tiempo hace que ocurrieron estos importantes eventos deportivos?

▲ *Iker Casillas recibió el premio Guante Dorado en 2010.*

PIERRE-PHILIPPE MARCOU/AFP/ Getty Images

MODELO: ¿Cuánto tiempo hace que los Lakers contrataron a Pau Gasol? (2008)
→ *Hace _____ años que lo contrataron.*

1. ¿Cuánto tiempo hace que fueron los Juegos Olímpicos de Barcelona? (1992)
2. ¿Cuánto tiempo hace que la selección española de fútbol ganó la Copa Mundial? (2010)
3. ¿Cuánto tiempo hace que Rafael Nadal ganó de la medalla de oro[10] de tenis en los Juegos Olímpicos de Pekín? (2008)
4. ¿Cuánto tiempo hace que el ciclista Miguel Indurain ganó el Tour de Francia por quinta vez? (1995)
5. ¿Cuánto tiempo hace que el futbolista Iker Casillas recibió el premio **Guante Dorado**[11] al mejor portero[12]? (2010)

6.1-15 Preguntas de historia Con un/a compañero/a, contesta las siguientes preguntas con los pronombres de objeto directo apropiados y ofrece más información. Puedes buscar la información en Internet o en algún libro de referencia. ¿Coincide tu información con la de tu compañero/a?

Avoiding repetition: Direct object pronouns

In Chapter 5, Section 1, you learned how to use direct object pronouns to avoid repetition of a noun phrase already introduced in the discourse.

Direct object pronouns			
Singular		**Plural**	
me	me	**nos**	us
te	you (familiar)	**os**	you (familiar)
lo	you (formal), him, it (m)	**los**	you (formal), them (m, m+f)
la	you (formal), her, it (f)	**las**	you (formal), them (f)

MODELO: Estudiante 1:   ¿Quiénes conquistaron *el oeste* de Estados Unidos? *(los europeos)*
Estudiante 2:   *Lo* conquistaron los europeos.
Estudiante 1:   *¿Cuánto tiempo hace que* los europeos *lo* conquistaron?
Estudiante 2:   *Hace aproximadamente 200 años que*...

1. ¿Cómo llamaron los romanos a la Península Ibérica? (Hispania)
2. ¿Quiénes invadieron la Península Ibérica en el año 711? (los moros)
3. ¿Qué marinero fue el primero que vio el continente? (Rodrigo de Triana)
4. ¿Quiénes recibieron a los españoles cuando llegaron al Caribe? (los taínos)
5. ¿Quién gobernó España durante la dictadura de los años 1939-1975? (Francisco Franco)

---

[10]**oro:** gold [11]**Guante Dorado:** Golden Glove [12]**portero/a:** goalkeeper

OTRA PERSPECTIVA

Courtesy of Cristina Pardo-Ballester

Cristina

Diferente

"Un verano visité a mi amiga Christie, que vive en Sacramento, California. Ella me llevó a un lugar muy bonito y turístico que se llama 'el Viejo Sacramento'. ¡Es como las películas, con caballos[13] y tiendas antiguas! Me dijo que a mediados del siglo XIX muchas personas fueron al oeste de Estados Unidos por la 'fiebre del oro'. Fue todo muy interesante y le pregunté a Christie: 'Es muy bonito, ¿pero dónde vive la gente?'. Ella me dijo: 'El viejo Sacramento es una atracción turística, no es un lugar donde vive gente'. En España mucha gente vive en el centro histórico. ¿Por qué en muchas ciudades de Estados Unidos la gente no vive en el centro histórico?"

Igual

"En España también preservamos la parte más antigua de una ciudad y el centro histórico también es el centro turístico".

 Explícale a Cristina

1. ¿Sabes que las partes antiguas de algunas ciudades en Estados Unidos son atracciones turísticas? ¿Por qué crees que es así?
2. ¿Sabes en qué fecha se fundó la ciudad donde vives ahora?

MANOS A LA OBRA

 6.1-16 Entrevista En grupos de tres, un estudiante asume la personalidad de un personaje famoso de la historia. Los otros dos estudiantes le hacen preguntas personales. Si la persona famosa no sabe la respuesta, ¡tiene que usar la imaginación!

MODELO: *Cristóbal Colón, ¿con quién habló esta mañana? ¿Qué comió anoche? ¿Dónde nació? ¿Cuándo nació?*

 6.1-17 ¡Peligro! En grupos, prueben con este juego sus conocimientos de la historia de España y Estados Unidos.

Guerras	Líderes	Edad Media (siglos V–XV)	Edad Moderna (siglos XV-XVIII)	Estados Unidos
❑ 100 euros	❑ 100 euros	❑ 100 euros	❑ 100 euros	❑ 100 euros
❑ 200 euros	❑ 200 euros	❑ 200 euros	❑ 200 euros	❑ 200 euros
❑ 300 euros	❑ 300 euros	❑ 300 euros	❑ 300 euros	❑ 300 euros
❑ 400 euros	❑ 400 euros	❑ 400 euros	❑ 400 euros	❑ 400 euros
❑ 500 euros	❑ 500 euros	❑ 500 euros	❑ 500 euros	❑ 500 euros

 6.1-18 Escenas de historia En grupos de cuatro personas, representen una escena de un evento histórico importante.

Paso 1: En grupo, escriban una pequeña narración del evento. Usen al menos dos personajes importantes. Usen verbos de la sección **Palabra por palabra** en el pretérito.

[13] **caballos:** horses

Paso 2: Decidan quiénes del grupo van a representar a los personajes. Preparen una actuación corta sin palabras. Representen la escena frente al resto de la clase. El resto de los estudiantes de la clase tienen que narrar las acciones de la escena.

MODELO: *Hernán Cortés llegó a Tenochtitlán y habló con Moctezuma...*

Al final, la clase debe decidir: ¿Cuál fue la mejor representación? ¿Quiénes fueron los mejores actores? ¿Cuál es la historia o el evento más interesante?

6.1-19 Los judíos[14] en la España medieval ¿Qué sabes de la relación entre los judíos, los musulmanes y los cristianos en la época medieval? Lee el siguiente párrafo y luego sigue los pasos para completar la actividad.

Entre los siglos XI y XIII, la relación entre los judíos y los cristianos es tranquila. La Edad Media es el período en que tres religiones distintas (los judíos, los musulmanes y los cristianos) viven en la península en armonía. Por eso, mucha gente la llama "la España de las tres culturas". Muchos años después, esta relación cambia. En el siglo XIV, las dificultades económicas del país empeoran la situación para los judíos, ya que mucha gente los culpa de la crisis económica y los considera enemigos. En esos siglos, los cristianos tienen el poder. Los sentimientos antisemitas crecen en las ciudades, y estos sentimientos culminan en un ataque contra los judíos en Sevilla en 1391. Pasa el tiempo y las persecuciones contra los judíos continúan. En 1492, Fernando e Isabel controlan los últimos dominios árabes en la península y declaran una reconquista de España a favor de los cristianos. En ese año, los Reyes Católicos conquistan Granada y ordenan la expulsión de los judíos y los musulmanes de los reinos de Castilla, Aragón y Granada. La solución para los dos grupos: la conversión al cristianismo. Les dan cuatro meses para convertirse al cristianismo o abandonar España. Muchos judíos se convierten; otros deciden salir del país. Antes de salir, deben vender sus casas a precios muy bajos. La mayoría emigra al norte de África. Los Reyes Católicos expulsan del país a más de 50,000 judíos.

Paso 1: Un/a compañero/a lee el primer párrafo y tú el segundo párrafo.

Cambia los verbos que están en presente al pretérito. Después comparen sus respuestas con las del compañero/a e identifiquen juntos los infinitivos y los sujetos de esos verbos.

MODELO: Los musulmanes son fieles.   →   *Los musulmanes fueron fieles.*
           Infinitivo: *ser*
           Sujeto: *los musulmanes*

Paso 2: Con ayuda de tu compañero/a, busca en el primer párrafo tres pronombres de objeto directo y subráyalos. Después digan cuáles, a qué o a quiénes se refiere el pronombre de objeto directo.

MODELO: *Los musulmanes viajan y finalmente ellos <u>los</u> aceptan.*
           Pronombre de objeto directo: *los*
           Referente: *los musulmanes*

Paso 3: Con ayuda de un/a compañero/a, contesta las siguientes preguntas usando el vocabulario del capítulo:

1. ¿En qué época conviven en la península tres religiones?
2. ¿En qué siglos las relaciones entre los judíos y los cristianos es tranquila?
3. ¿Por qué se considera enemigos a los judíos en el siglo XIV?
4. ¿Por qué deciden salir del país los judíos?

6.1-20 Presta atención: ¿Cuál es o quiénes son? En este capítulo aprendiste mucha historia. Ahora vas a escuchar más información sobre historia mundial. Presta atención para saber cuánta historia sabes. Después de escuchar dos veces la información sobre cada número, selecciona la respuesta más adecuada según tus conocimientos.

1. a. Cristóbal Colón   b. Juana la Loca   c. El rey Boabdil
2. a. Francisco Pizarro   b. Fernando de Magallanes   c. Hernán Cortés
3. a. los taínos   b. los incas   c. los aztecas
4. a. Abraham Lincoln   b. John F. Kennedy   c. Barack Obama
5. a. los griegos   b. los celtas   c. los romanos

[14]judíos: jews

WileyPLUS Go to *WileyPLUS* and listen to **Presta atención.**

¡OJO!

Marking time
When writing a biography use time expressions (**en 1492, hace cien años...**) and time markers (**antes, después, durante, luego...**) to ensure that you understand the chronological order of the events. For example: **Isabel de Castilla nació en Ávila en 1451 y diez años después se fue a Segovia.**

6.1- 21 Por escrito: Una biografía Busca un personaje importante de las artes en España y escribe su biografía usando Internet (por ejemplo, Diego Velázquez, Francisco de Goya, Miguel de Cervantes, Federico García Lorca...). Usa el pretérito. Contesta en tu texto las siguientes preguntas:

- ¿Dónde y cuándo nació?
- ¿Dónde vivió?

- ¿Por qué es importante? ¿Qué hizo?
- ¿Dónde, cuándo y cómo murió?

PONTE EN MI LUGAR

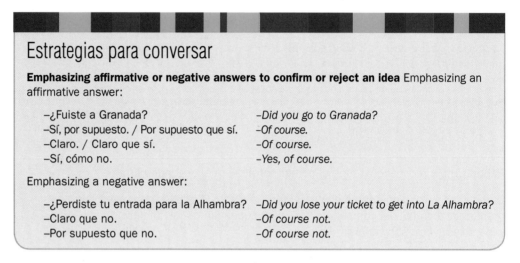

Estrategias para conversar

Emphasizing affirmative or negative answers to confirm or reject an idea Emphasizing an affirmative answer:

–¿Fuiste a Granada?   –Did you go to Granada?
–Sí, por supuesto. / Por supuesto que sí.   –Of course.
–Claro. / Claro que sí.   –Of course.
–Sí, cómo no.   –Yes, of course.

Emphasizing a negative answer:

–¿Perdiste tu entrada para la Alhambra? –Did you lose your ticket to get into La Alhambra?
–Claro que no.   –Of course not.
–Por supuesto que no.   –Of course not.

¿Qué hacer en Granada? Estás en Granada y el cuarto día decides ir a la Oficina de Turismo para informarte sobre los lugares que puedes visitar porque después de tres días en la ciudad no viste mucho.

Paso 1: Decide con un/a compañero/a quién va a ser el/la turista y quién va a ser el/la empleado/a de la Oficina de Turismo. Miren juntos el plano de la ciudad.

El/La turista…

- entra a la oficina y saluda.
- explica que no conoce la ciudad y dice que quiere información.
- hace preguntas (p. ej., dónde, cómo…). Repasa los interrogativos en el Capítulo 1, Sección 2, y el Capítulo 4, Sección 1, para hacer las preguntas.

El/La empleado/a…

- contesta las preguntas del turista haciendo nuevas preguntas en el pretérito.
- usa las estructuras *tener que* o *deber* (repasa el Capítulo 4, Sección 1).
- usa *poder* u otros verbos irregulares (repasa el Capítulo 3, Sección 1) y *estar* (repasa el Capítulo 3, Sección 2).

Usen las expresiones de **Estrategias para conversar** para enfatizar respuestas afirmativas o negativas (*¡Sí, cómo no!…*) cuando sea posible. También intenten usar los pronombres de objeto directo cuando puedan.

Paso 2: Sigan el modelo e incluyan más lugares de interés, como el Albaicín, el Sacromonte y la catedral. El/La turista tiene que recordar que si el/la empleado/a hace una pregunta en pretérito, él/ella tiene que contestar en pretérito también.

MODELO:

Turista: *¡Hola! Mire usted, llevo ya cuatro días en Granada y no conozco la ciudad. ¿Podría/Puede darme información sobre Granada?*

Empleado/a: *Sí, cómo no. Aquí la tiene, en el plano.*

Turista: *Ummm. ¿Qué lugares de interés puedo visitar en Granada?*

Empleado/a: *¿Fue ya a visitar la Alhambra?*

Turista: *No, no la visité. Yo solo fui al centro. ¿Dónde está la Alhambra? ¿Cómo llego allí?*

Empleado/a: *Usted puede ir en autobús, en taxi o a pie. Mire en este plano. Usted está aquí, en la Plaza de Santa Ana. Para llegar a la Alhambra tiene que subir por la Cuesta de Gomérez.*

Turista: *¿Qué otros lugares me aconseja visitar?*

Empleado/a: *¿Paseó por el Generalife?*

Paso 3: Compartan el diálogo con el resto de la clase. Al final del diálogo, vuelve a recordar tres lugares que puedes visitar en Granada.

ASÍ ES LA VIDA

▲ *No hay moros en la costa.*

Adivina, adivinador

Fruta es, ciudad también;
gran reino fue y ahora bonita ciudad es.

Expresión: No hay moros en la costa.

1. ¿Cuál es el equivalente en inglés?
2. ¿A qué momento histórico hace referencia esta expresión?

WileyPLUS Go to *WileyPLUS* to find more **Arroba** activities.

@Arroba@

Los museos de Andalucía Busca una página web de los museos de Andalucía para hacer un paseo virtual de esta comunidad autónoma de España. Abre la página web http://www.museosdeandalucia.es. Explora una página para aprender sobre los distintos tipos de museos que hay en Andalucía y en qué ciudades están. Selecciona y explora dos o tres museos de diferentes ciudades. Toma nota sobre los museos que seleccionaste y compártelos con tus compañeros.

ENTÉRATE

Estrategias para leer

Review of reading strategies You already learned a few strategies in previous chapters:

Recognizing cognates, using a dictionary, predicting the content by using visual elements, anticipating the content by considering the title, guessing the meaning from the context, skimming (read quickly in order to identify the main idea of the text), and scanning (look through a text fast in order to find specific information, such as looking for answers to specific questions or searching for a particular word). Now, try to use these strategies together.

Antes de leer

1. El mapa Mira el mapa de la lectura que es tu elemento visual para predecir el contenido. Después, responde estas preguntas.

1. ¿Qué océano está al oeste de la Península Ibérica?
2. ¿Qué mares rodean la Península Ibérica?
3. ¿Qué islas hay en España?
4. ¿Dónde están Ceuta y Melilla?
5. ¿En qué parte de España se encuentra Andalucía?

2. Predicción Lee el título de la lectura: ¿De qué crees que puede tratar la lectura?

Las lenguas y comunidades autónomas de España

Colloquial Latin, or Proto-Romance

El español, también llamado castellano, es una lengua romance porque viene del **latín vulgar**. El latín vulgar también se conoce como latín hablado y fue la lengua que se habló en la Península Ibérica durante los 200 años antes de Cristo. Del latín vulgar nacieron varios dialectos, es decir, variedades del latín. Estos dialectos o variedades del latín terminaron siendo idiomas romances. En España hoy día se hablan tres idiomas o lenguas romances: el castellano o español, el gallego y el catalán. Otra lengua que se habla en el País Vasco, otra comunidad autónoma española, es el euskera o vasco, pero

to come from

esta lengua no **procede** del latín. En 1975 murió el dictador

Francisco Franco y tres años más tarde se firmó la Constitución de 1978. Con esta Constitución, España se organizó como una democracia y reconoció su diversidad lingüística. En la constitución también se indica que todos los españoles tienen el deber y el derecho de hablar castellano. El español o castellano pasó a ser la lengua oficial del estado español, pero los estatutos de las comunidades autónomas o las regiones de España reconocieron las otras tres lenguas españolas.

La Constitución reconoció que España está formada por 17 comunidades autónomas (Andalucía, Aragón, Asturias, Cantabria, Castilla-La Mancha, Castilla y León, Cataluña, Extremadura, Galicia, las islas Baleares, las islas Canarias, La Rioja, Madrid, Murcia, Navarra, País Vasco y Valencia) y las ciudades Ceuta y Melilla. Desde que los españoles **aprobaron** la Constitución en 1978, cada comunidad autónoma tiene una organización lingüística, política, económica y cultural. Por ejemplo, en Galicia se habla gallego. Santiago de Compostela es una de las ciudades más conocidas de la comunidad porque allí se encuentra la catedral, que atrae a peregrinos cristianos desde los tiempos medievales, y la Real Universidad de Santiago de Compostela, una de las universidades más antiguas del mundo y una de las más prestigiosas de España. En Cataluña se habla catalán y es la región de famosos artistas, como Pablo Picasso, Salvador Dalí y Antonio Gaudí. También en Cataluña se hacen los famosos castillos humanos conocidos como los *castells*. Otro ejemplo es Andalucía, con **herencia** árabe porque en el año 711 los árabes conquistaron España. La herencia árabe **se conserva** especialmente en algunos ejemplos de la arquitectura, como la Alhambra de Granada y la Mezquita de Córdoba. Resumiendo, cada comunidad autónoma tiene su belleza y su historia.

to approve

heritage
to survive

Después de leer

1. En el texto Identifica un mínimo de veinte cognados en la lectura.

2. ¿Entendiste? Contesta las preguntas según la información de la lectura:
1. ¿Cuál es el origen del español?
2. ¿Cuántas lenguas se hablan en España?
3. ¿Cuál es la lengua oficial de España?
4. ¿Desde cuándo tiene España un gobierno[15] democrático?
5. ¿Cuántas comunidades autónomas hay en España? Menciona algunas.
6. ¿En qué parte de España se habla vasco?

EN TU PROPIAS PALABRAS

Estrategias para escribir

Writing a topic sentence will help you write a well-structured paragraph. A good topic sentence…

–appears at the beginning of a paragraph.
–states the main idea of the paragraph.
–is neither too specific nor too general.
–gives information on only one topic of interest.
–attracts the attention of the reader.
–makes a personal statement.

Now compare the following sentences focusing on the characteristics listed above. Decide which one is a good topic sentence to write a report about the south of Spain.

1. Hay ocho ciudades y muchos pueblos en Andalucía.
2. Jaén no tiene muchos habitantes, pero es tan bella como otras ciudades de Andalucía.
3. Andalucía, una comunidad autónoma situada en el sur de España, es el lugar ideal para disfrutar de unas vacaciones con la familia.
4. Las vistas de la ciudad de Granada desde la Torre de la Vela son increíbles.

If you haven't made a decision, do sentences 2 and 4 give you specific information? Is sentence 1 too general? If your answer is yes, you probably noticed that number 3 encompasses all the six characteristics above.

[15] **gobierno:** government

Informe sobre España

Paso 1: Para tu clase de español tienes que escribir un informe sobre España. Antes de empezar, contesta las siguientes preguntas para recordar lo que sabes sobre España. Si no sabes responder alguna de estas preguntas, busca la respuesta en Internet o en alguna otra fuente:

- ¿Cuál es la capital de España?
- ¿Cuántas lenguas se hablan en España?
- ¿En dónde está Andalucía y qué es?
- ¿Qué evidencia hay de la presencia histórica de los árabes en España?
- ¿Qué forma de gobierno hay en España?
- ¿Cómo está organizado políticamente el territorio de España?

Paso 2:

Imagina que cuando estabas en la escuela secundaria fuiste a España de viaje de estudios. Con la información de las preguntas anteriores, escribe un informe para presentar en tu clase de español. Indica lo que sabes de España y lo que hiciste allí. Intenta usar el presente, el pretérito y la estructura hace + *tiempo* + que. Incluye el vocabulario de: la historia de España, la geografía (Capítulo 4, Sección 2) y el vecindario (Capítulo 3, Sección 2) cuando sea posible. No olvides incluir una oración que indique el tema del informe siguiendo las estrategias para escribir.

Paso 3: En clase, pásale tu redacción a un/a compañero/a. Él/ella repasa:
1. El contenido:
   - ¿Es interesante?
   - ¿Hay una oración para indicar el tema de la redacción?
   - ¿Están conectadas las ideas?
2. La gramática:
   - ¿Concuerdan los verbos con los sujetos?
   - ¿Concuerdan los adjetivos con los sustantivos?
   - ¿Son correctas las raíces y las terminaciones de los verbos en presente y en pretérito?
3. El vocabulario:
   - ¿Están las palabras escritas correctamente?
   - ¿Hay palabras que se refieran a la historia, la geografía y el vecindario?

Con las sugerencias de tu compañero/a, vuelve a escribir tu redacción para entregársela a tu profesor/a.

▲ *Traje típico de Valencia, España.*

AUTOPRUEBA

VOCABULARIO

I. Historia Contesta las siguientes preguntas con palabras del vocabulario.

MODELO: ¿Qué organizó Cristóbal Colón en 1492?
→ *Un viaje.*

1. ¿Qué ocurrió en Estados Unidos entre 1861 y 1865?
2. ¿Qué tipo de gobierno impuso Francisco Franco en España?
3. ¿Quién fue Fernando II?
4. ¿Qué declararon las trece colonias inglesas de América del Norte en 1776?
5. ¿Qué establecieron los romanos durante cinco siglos?

II. Un amigo te pregunta Di cómo se llama:

1. una forma de gobierno con un rey o una reina.
2. un período de cien años.
3. el resultado de invadir un territorio.
4. un documento que firman los representantes de dos o más países.
5. el enfrentamiento armado entre dos países.

GRAMÁTICA

I. Personajes históricos Combina los elementos de la columna A con elementos de la columna B para escribir oraciones completas con la forma apropiada del pretérito.

1. Los españoles / ser
2. Los romanos / controlar
3. Isabel la Católica / financiar
4. Cristóbal Colón / ir
5. Los ingleses / conquistar
6. Los estadounidenses / elegir

a. el viaje de Cristóbal Colón a las Indias.
b. el oeste de América del Norte.
c. los primeros en fundar una colonia en Florida.
d. la Península Ibérica.
e. a buscar una ruta más corta.
f. a Obama como presidente en 2012.

II. Carta de Hernán Cortés al emperador Carlos V
Completa el siguiente fragmento de la carta de Hernán Cortés sobre la reunión con Moctezuma. Usa la forma apropiada del pretérito de los verbos de la lista.

> llevar   recibir   ir   sentarse   visitar   salir
> esperar   volver   empezar   tomar

Mis hombres y yo _____ de la ciudad de Iztapalapa a Tenochtitlán. Allí nosotros _____ al emperador de los mexicas[16]. Moctezuma nos _____ en la gran plaza. Después, él me _____ de la mano y me _____ a una gran sala. Los dos _____ en unas sillas muy decoradas, y después Moctezuma _____ de la sala. Yo _____ unos momentos, y después Moctezuma _____ con muchas joyas de oro y muchas finas piezas de ropa y _____ a hablar de la historia de su pueblo.

III. Historia de Estados Unidos ¿Cuánto tiempo hace que ocurrieron estos eventos? Escribe oraciones completas con los siguientes elementos.

MODELO: La Guerra hispano-estadounidense / ocurrir (1898)
→ *La Guerra hispano-estadounidense ocurrió hace más de un siglo.* o *Hace más de un siglo que ocurrió la Guerra hispano-estadounidense.*

Ponce de León / descubrir Florida (1513)
El *Mayflower* / llegar a la costa este de América del Norte (1620)
Las trece colonias / declarar la independencia de Estados Unidos (1776)
La Guerra Civil de Estados Unidos / ser (1861-1865)
México / perder todos sus territorios al norte del río Bravo (1848)

CULTURA

1. ¿Qué reina le dio dinero a Cristóbal Colón para hacer su viaje?
2. ¿Quiénes invadieron la Península Ibérica y vivieron allí durante ocho siglos?
3. ¿Qué festividad se celebra en Alicante en julio?
4. ¿Qué conmemoran estas festividades divertidas?
5. ¿Qué es la Alhambra? ¿Dónde está?

REDACCIÓN

Escribe un pequeño informe sobre tu estado o país de origen, o sobre los orígenes de tu familia. Incluye por lo menos cinco eventos importantes. Usa conectores como *primero, segundo, después, al final*, etc.

EN RESUMIDAS CUENTAS, AHORA PUEDO...

☐ hablar sobre la historia de España y reconocer su diversidad cultural y lingüística.
☐ usar números ordinales
☐ relatar eventos históricos.
☐ usar el pretérito de los verbos regulares y de *ser* e *ir* para hablar del pasado.
☐ usar la expresión **hace** + tiempo + **que** para especificar cuándo ocurrió algo.
☐ evitar repetir ciertas palabras al hablar.
☐ entender la importancia del centro histórico de una ciudad.

[16]**mexicas:** indigenous people of the Valley of Mexico, known today as the rulers of the Aztec empire.

🎧 VOCABULARIO ESENCIAL

Sustantivos

el aliado	*ally*
el barco	*ship*
la dictadura	*dictatorship*
la Edad Media/Moderna	*middle/modern ages*
la época	*age or era*
la guerra (civil)	*(civil) war*
el poder	*power*
la reina	*queen*
el rey	*king*
el siglo	*century*
el tratado	*treaty*
el viaje	*voyage*

Cognados: la conquista, la constitución, la democracia, el/la dictador/a, el/la enemigo/a, la historia, el imperio, la independencia, la invasión, el/la líder, la monarquía

Verbos

derrotar	*to defeat*
elegir	*to elect*
fundar	*to establish*
ganar	*to win*
gobernar	*to rule*
habitar	*to inhabit*
luchar	*to fight*
nacer	*to be born*

Cognados: atacar, conquistar, establecer, explorar, invadir, terminar,

Adjetivos

primer(o)/a	*first*
segundo/a	*second*
tercer(o)/a	*third*
cuarto/a	*fourth*
quinto/a	*fifth*
sexto/a	*sixth*
séptimo/a	*seventh*
octavo/a	*eighth*
noveno/a	*ninth*
décimo/a	*tenth*

Expresiones

a. C. (antes de Cristo)	*B.C. (Before Christ)*
d. C. (después de Cristo)	*A.D. (in the year of our Lord)*

LEARNING OBJECTIVES

By the end of this section you will be able to:

- Compare different urban spaces
- Describe works of art
- Talk about events in the past using the preterit tense of irregular and stem-changing verbs
- Express possession
- Point out people and objects
- Use other forms of address
- Understand Spanish art and talk about artists

▲ *Un castell en Vilafranca del Penedès, Barcelona.*

Courtesy of Aina Cabra-Riart

Una imagen vale más que mil palabras

¿En qué consiste esta torre? ¿Cuántos niveles tiene?

¿Crees que esta construcción tiene algún propósito?

¿A qué se compara lo que ves en la foto con una práctica que es común en las escuelas y universidades de Estados Unidos?

UNA PERSPECTIVA

Lo antiguo y lo moderno

Courtesy of Christina Samson

Tina

Diferente

"En España hay muchos edificios que son antiguos y tienen mucha historia. Hay monumentos maravillosos, palacios y catedrales mucho más antiguos que los edificios más antiguos de Estados Unidos. Para una persona de España, los monumentos históricos de Estados Unidos no son tan antiguos".

Igual

"En España también hay muchos edificios modernos con diseños futuristas como la Ciudad de las Artes y las Ciencias, en Valencia; la Torre Agbar y la Torre Marenostrum (Sede de Gas Natural), en Barcelona; los rascacielos de Cuatro Torres Business Area, en Madrid; y el Museo Guggenheim, en Bilbao."

¿Qué piensas tú?

1. ¿Cuáles son los monumentos de Estados Unidos más antiguos que conoces? ¿Cuándo se construyeron[1], más o menos?
2. ¿Qué edificios son impresionantes o importantes en tu estado o ciudad?
3. ¿Qué monumentos de tu país te gustan más? ¿Dónde están?

[1] se construyeron: were built

LA PURA VERDAD I | Un fin de semana en Barcelona

Amanda, una estudiante de Estados Unidos que estudia en Granada, viaja con unas amigas a Barcelona para pasar el fin de semana.

1.

¡Mira ese monumento!

2.

3.

¿Qué pasó en las noticias?

4.
¡Venga ya! No entiendo. Creo que tengo que estudiar más.

¡Ahh, creo que es catalán!

5.

Casi todo es en catalán, pero hay una película[2] en español: "La piel que habito". El director es Pedro Almodóvar, así es que debe de ser una buena película.

6.

La construcción de la Basílica de la Sagrada Familia empezó en 1882. Gaudí comenzó a trabajar en la basílica en 1883.

All Illustrations © John Wiley & Sons, Inc.

7.

© David Ryznar / Shutterstock.com

8.
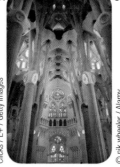
Clicks / E+ / Getty Images

9.

© nik wheeler / Alamy

6.2-01 **El tour de la basílica** Escucha en la narración lo que pasó en el tour de la basílica. Selecciona la oración que mejor explica la narración.

1. a. Amanda y sus amigas subieron a una torre de la basílica.
   b. Subir a una torre de la basílica les tomó una hora.
   c. Las autoridades no les permitieron subir a una torre.
2. a. Terminaron de construir la primera fachada en 1987.
   b. La primera fachada es la más decorada.
   c. La segunda fachada no tiene esculturas.
3. a. Terminaron la tercera fachada en el año 2002.
   b. La tercera fachada es la más pequeña de las tres, pero es la más bonita.
   c. Amanda vio un dibujo de la tercera fachada.

[2] **película:** film, movie

PALABRA POR PALABRA

Imagno / Hulton Archive / Getty Images

▲ Las Meninas *de Diego Velázquez*

El arte

antiguo/a	*old, ancient*
el autorretrato	*self portrait*
el castillo	*castle*
el cuadro	*painting*
el lienzo	*canvas*
la luz	*light*
la mezquita	*mosque*
la obra de arte	*work of art*
la obra maestra	*masterpiece*
el paisaje	*landscape*
la pintura (al óleo)	*(oil) painting*
el retrato	*portrait*
la torre	*tower*

Cognados: el arco, la arquitectura, la basílica, la catedral, el cine, el estilo, la escultura, la estatua, la fachada, la fotografía, la literatura, el monumento

Adjetivos para hablar de arte: abstracto/a, barroco/a, colonial, contemporáneo/a, gótico/a, medieval, moderno/a, romano/a

Los procesos creativos

construir	*to build*	diseñar	*to design*
crear	*to create*	esculpir	*to sculpt*
dibujar	*to draw*	pintar	*to paint*

El/La artista: el actor, la (actriz), el/la arquitecto/a, el/la director/a, el/la escultor/a, el/la pintor/a

♻Más colores   *More colors*

azul (oscuro, claro, marino)	*(dark, light, navy) blue*
color vivo	*bright color*
color vino	*burgundy*
dorado	*golden*
plateado	*silver*
turquesa	*turquoise*
verde (oliva, claro, oscuro)	*green (olive, light, dark)*

¿Qué dicen los españoles?

Alfonso me cae superbien. Es muy <u>majo</u>.	*I really like Alfonso. He's a <u>very nice</u> guy.*
-¿Te gustan mis nuevos zapatos?	*-Do you like my new shoes?*
-Sí, ¡qué <u>chulos</u>! Son muy <u>guays</u>.	*-Yes, <u>how cool</u>! They are really <u>cool</u>.*
-¿Has visto esto?	*-Have you seen this?*
-Sí, ¡<u>cómo mola</u>!	*-Yes, <u>very cool</u>!*
-No puedo creerlo. ¡<u>Me quedo a cuadros</u>!	*-I can't believe it. <u>I'm astonished</u>!*
-¡Qué niño más <u>mono</u>!*	*-What a <u>cute</u> little boy!*

*Esta expresión se usa en otros países hispanos también.

♻ **Colors**
Remember that you already studied colors in Chapter 2, Section 2? Review that vocabulary before learning these new words.

6.2-02 ¿Qué sabes de arte?

Paso 1: ¿Qué tipo de arte asocias con...?

1. Pedro Almodóvar

2. Joan Miró

3. Antoni Gaudí

4. Cervantes	8. el metal
5. el autorretrato	9. la luz
6. el lienzo	10. la fachada
7. la estatua	11. el paisaje

Paso 2: Ahora, escribe una lista similar con el nombre de cinco artistas que conozcas. Pregúntale a un/a compañero/a qué tipo de arte asocia con los nombres de la lista y qué sabe de ellos. Después, comenten con la clase cuánto saben de arte. ¿Conocen a todos los artistas mencionados en clase?

6.2-03 Obras de arte

¿Qué son estas obras de arte? ¿Con qué tipo de estilo las asocias? ¿Sabes dónde están? Consulta con un(a) compañero/a y busquen juntos la respuesta.

MODELO: la Sagrada Familia
Estudiante 1:   *¿Cuál es esta obra de arte?*
Estudiante 2:   *Es la Sagrada Familia.*
Estudiante 1:   *¿Qué tipo de obra es?*
Estudiante 2:   *Es una <u>basílica</u> de <u>arquitectura modernista.</u>*
Estudiante 1:   *¿Sabes dónde está?*
Estudiante 2:   *En Barcelona.*

1. Los relojes blandos *o* La persistencia de la memoria, *de Dalí*

2. Monumento a Colón

3. *La mezquita de Córdoba*

4. El Laberinto del Fauno

5. Don Quijote de la Mancha

6. *El acueducto de Segovia*

6.2-04 ¿Te gusta el arte? Lee las siguientes preguntas y piensa en otras dos preguntas. Después, con un/a compañero/a, conversen sobre sus gustos artísticos.

Paso 1:

1. ¿Te gusta el arte? ¿Qué tipo te gusta más? ¿Qué estilo es tu favorito? ¿Por qué?
2. ¿Vas a museos frecuentemente? ¿Qué tipo de obras te gusta ver en los museos? ¿Qué museo es tu favorito?
3. ¿Tienes talento artístico? ¿Te gusta crear, diseñar, pintar, dibujar o construir cosas?
4. ¿Cuál es tu artista favorito? ¿Qué hace? ¿Cómo son sus obras?
5. ¿Qué sabes del arte de España? ¿Conoces la obra de artistas españoles? ¿Qué obra maestra de España quieres ver o visitar?
6. ...
7. ...

Paso 2: ¿Hay algunos aspectos en los que coinciden? ¿En cuáles coinciden y en cuáles no? Escriban un pequeño párrafo sobre aquellos aspectos en los que sí coinciden.

MODELO: *A los dos nos gustan varios tipos de arte. Nos gusta mucho la arquitectura de estilo gótico. Los dos hemos visto la catedral...*

6.2-05 Adivina, adivinador... ¿quién soy? Piensa en un/a artista famoso/a. Después, en parejas, túrnense para adivinar en qué artista pensó el/la compañero/a.

MODELO: Estudiante 1:   *¿Qué tipo de arte haces?*
Estudiante 2:   *Hago pintura.*
Estudiante 1:   *¿Eres norteamericano/a?*
Estudiante 2:   *No, soy español.*
Estudiante 1:   *¿En qué época viviste?*
Estudiante 2:   *Viví en el siglo XX.*
Estudiante 1:   *¿Cómo son tus cuadros?*
Estudiante 2:   *Modernos, de vivos colores y abstractos.*
Estudiante 1:   *¡Eres Joan Miró!*
Estudiante 2:   *¡Sí, muy bien!*

HABLANDO DE GRAMÁTICA I

WileyPLUS Go to *WileyPLUS* to review this grammar point with the help of the **Animated Grammar Tutorial** and the **Verb Conjugator**.

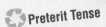 **Preterit Tense**

Do you remember how to use regular verbs in the past? You may want to go back to Section 1, before you start learning this new grammar point.

1. Talking about events in the past (III): The preterit tense of irregular and stem-changing verbs

A. Irregular verbs

In Chapter 6, Section 1, you learned the preterit forms of regular verbs ending in **-ar, -er,** and **-ir** and of the irregular verbs **ser** and **ir.** The following verbs are also irregular. All these verbs have irregular stems that differ from the present tense. All endings are the same except for **dar,** which takes the endings from regular verbs ending in **-er** and **-ir.**

	Irregular stem	Stem + irregular endings *(yo, tú, él/ella/Ud. nosotros/as, vosotros/as, ellos/ellas/Uds.)*
dar	**d-**	di, diste, dio, dimos, disteis, dieron
decir	**dij-**	dije, dijiste, dijo, dijimos, dijisteis, dijeron
estar	**estuv-**	estuve, estuviste, estuvo, estuvimos, estuvisteis, estuvieron
hacer*	**hic-**	hice, hiciste, hizo, hicimos, hicisteis, hicieron
poder	**pud-**	pude, pudiste, pudo, pudimos, pudisteis, pudieron
poner	**pus-**	puse, pusiste, puso, pusimos, pusisteis, pusieron
querer	**quis-**	quise, quisiste, quiso, quisimos, quisisteis, quisieron
saber	**sup-**	supe, supiste, supo, supimos, supisteis, supieron
tener	**tuv-**	tuve, tuviste, tuvo, tuvimos, tuvisteis, tuvieron
traducir	**traduj-**	traduje, tradujiste, tradujo, tradujimos, tradujisteis, tradujeron
traer	**traj-**	traje, trajiste, trajo, trajimos, trajisteis, trajeron
venir	**vin-**	vine, viniste, vino, vinimos, vinisteis, vinieron

- There is no stress shift in the first person singular (**yo**) and the third person singular (**Ud./él/ella**) forms in irregular verbs.

  Amanda **estuvo** aquí ayer y **hablé** con ella. Le **dije** que el autobús a Barcelona es más barato que el tren.

  Amanda was here yesterday and I talked to her. I told her that the bus to Barcelona is cheaper than the train.

- There are no accent marks on the **yo** and **Ud./él/ella** forms of **dar** because they consist of only one syllable.

  –¿Ya me **diste** las entradas para la Sagrada Familia?
  –Sí, te las **di** esta mañana.

  Did you give me the entrance tickets for the Sagrada Familia already?
  Yes, I gave them to you this morning.

- Verbs whose stem ends in **j** add **-eron** instead of **-ieron** for the **Uds./él/ella** form.

  Las chicas **trajeron** muchos recuerdos de Barcelona.

  The girls brought a lot of souvenirs from Barcelona.

- *The third person singular (**Ud./él/ella**) of **hacer** changes the **-c-** to an **-z-** in order to preserve the sound.

  Ese fin de semana **hizo** muy buen tiempo en Barcelona.

  That weekend the weather was very nice in Barcelona.

- The preterit form of **haber** is **hubo** (*there was/were*).

  En un fin de semana no **hubo** tiempo de verlo todo.

  In just one weekend there was no time to see it all.

6.2-06 **El fin de semana en Barcelona** Lee el siguiente párrafo sobre el viaje de Amanda y sus amigas a Barcelona, e identifica los verbos irregulares en el pretérito.

Amanda y sus amigas <u>fueron</u> a Barcelona de vacaciones y estuvieron allí varios días. Viajaron en autobús y desde la ventana vieron el paisaje y varias ciudades. Cuando llegaron al hotel, pusieron las mochilas sobre la cama y Amanda empezó a ver la tele, ¡pero no entendió nada de lo que dijeron en las noticias! Al principio, se sorprendió mucho, pero luego se dio cuenta[3] de que en Cataluña también hablan otra lengua, el catalán. Al día siguiente, las chicas hicieron una visita guiada por la ciudad. Las chicas no entendieron el folleto[4] en catalán, pero el guía les tradujo todo al español. Por la tarde quisieron visitar el Palau[5] de la Música, pero llegaron tarde y no pudieron entrar. Entonces decidieron ir a un bar en la Plaza Real a comer unas tapas.

Paso 1: Escribe abajo todos los verbos irregulares en el pretérito que hay en el párrafo. ¡Atención! No todos los verbos son irregulares.

MODELO: 1. _____ *fueron* _____

2. _____   4. _____   6. _____   8. _____

3. _____   5. _____   7. _____   9. _____

Paso 2: ¿Cierto o falso? Lee el párrafo otra vez y decide si las siguientes oraciones son ciertas o falsas. Si son falsas, escribe la información correcta.

C	F	
☐	☐	1. Cuando llegó al hotel, Amanda puso su mochila sobre la cama.
☐	☐	2. Amanda tradujo las noticias de la televisión para sus amigas.
☐	☐	3. Amanda pudo leer el folleto en catalán.
☐	☐	4. Las chicas no tuvieron muchos problemas para entender al guía.
☐	☐	5. Las chicas no supieron adónde ir a comer unas tapas.

6.2-07 **El e-*mail* de Amanda** Amanda sigue con su visita por España y le escribe un e-*mail* a su amiga Loli, que está en Madrid.

Paso 1: Amanda tiene problemas con los verbos irregulares en el pretérito. Ayúdala a completar este e-*mail* con la forma correcta de los verbos de la lista.

estar   decir   poder   visitar   querer   llegar   ir   ser   hacer (x2)   tener

Asunto:	Viaje a Barcelona

¡Hola, Loli!
¿Qué tal va todo? Mi viaje a Barcelona _____₁ genial. Mis amigas y yo _____₂ allí tres noches. Nosotras _____₃ una visita guiada de la ciudad, y en tres días _____₄ la oportunidad de visitar muchos museos. Tú me _____₅ que Barcelona es una ciudad increíble, ¡y tienes razón! Me enamoré del azul turquesa del mar y del verde paisaje. El último día _____₆ visitar el Palau de la Música, pero no _____₇ porque _____₈ tarde. Ahora estamos en Valencia, y mañana salimos para Sevilla. ¡Estoy entusiasmada! Y tú, ¿adónde _____₉ durante las últimas vacaciones? ¿Qué lugares o a quién _____₁₀? ¿Qué _____₁₁ de especial?

Te mando un abrazo, y ¡espero tu respuesta!

Amanda

Paso 2: Imagina que eres Loli. Escribe un breve e-*mail* para Amanda. ¡Contesta todas las preguntas del e-*mail* de Amanda!

[3]**darse cuenta:** to realize, [4]**folleto:** brochure [5]**Palau:** Catalan for "palacio" or palace in English

B. Stem-changing verbs

Verbs ending in **-ir** that undergo a stem change in the present (see Chapter 3, Sección 1) also change in the preterite, but only in the third person singular and plural.

	dormir (o →u)	**pedir (e → i)**
(yo)	dormí	pedí
(tú)	dormiste	pediste
(él/ella/Ud.)	durmió	pidió
(nosotros/as)	dormimos	pedisteis
(vosotros/as)	dormisteis	pedimos
(ellos/ellas/Uds.)	durmieron	pidieron

Amanda y sus amigas **durmieron** un par de horas durante el viaje en autobús a Barcelona.
En la oficina de turismo **pidieron** folletos en español, no en inglés ni en catalán.

Amanda and her friends slept for a couple of hours during the bus trip to Barcelona.
At the tourism office, they asked for brochures in Spanish, not in English or Catalan.

These are other verbs whose stems change in the preterite in the third person singular and plural:

conseguir *(to get)*	consiguió, consiguieron
competir *(to compete)*	compitió, compitieron
elegir *(to choose)*	eligió, eligieron
preferir	prefirió, prefirieron
repetir *(to repeat)*	repitió, repitieron
seguir	siguió, siguieron

sentir(se)	(se) sintió, (se) sintieron
servir	sirvió, sirvieron
sugerir *(to suggest)*	sugirió, sugirieron
vestir(se)	(se) vistió, (se) vistieron
morir *(to die)*	murió, murieron

Amanda y sus amigas **eligieron** ir a Barcelona en autobús porque es muy barato. También **consiguieron** un hotel en el centro a un buen precio.
En la Sagrada Familia, **prefirieron** escuchar al guía en español y no en inglés.

Amanda and her friends chose to go to Barcelona by bus because it is very cheap. They also got a hotel downtown for a good price.
At the Sagrada Familia, they preferred to listen to the tour guide in Spanish instead of English.

6.2-08 La interesante vida de Pablo Picasso Escoge la mejor palabra entre paréntesis para saber más sobre este famoso pintor español.

◀ *El famoso cuadro* Guernica *(1937) se encuentra en el Museo Reina Sofía en Madrid.*

Pablo Picasso (**nací/nació**)[1] en Málaga, España, en 1881. Picasso (**fui/fue**)[2] el artista que desarrolló el cubismo. (**Su/Sus**)[3] obra como artista (**fue/fueron**)[4] muy prolífica, con más de 13.000 cuadros, 100.000 impresiones y grabados, 34.000 ilustraciones y 300 esculturas. Muchas veces las mujeres de (**su/sus**)[5] vida le (**servimos/sirvieron**)[6] de inspiración para sus obras. Con (**tu/su**)[7] primera esposa, Olga, (**tuve/tuvo**)[8] un hijo llamado Pablo, como (**vuestro/su**)[9] padre. Aún casado con Olga, (**viví/vivió**)[10] una relación sentimental con Marie-Thérèse, madre de (**sus/su**)[11] hija. Una tercera relación (**seguimos/siguió**)[12] unos años después con Dora Maar. En 1943 (**conocieron/conoció**)[13] a Françoise Gilot y juntos (**tuvimos/tuvieron**)[14] dos hijos, Claude y Paloma. En 1961 le (**pedí/pidió**)[15] la mano a Jacqueline Roque y (**se casó/se casaron**)[16] con ella. Pablo Picasso (**murieron/murió**)[17] en 1973. A pesar de[6] su ocupada vida personal, Picasso (**consiguió/ conseguí**)[18] ser uno de los artistas más famosos del siglo XX.

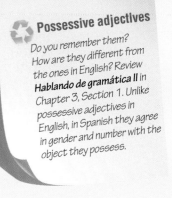

Possessive adjectives

Do you remember them? How are they different from the ones in English? Review **Hablando de gramática II** in Chapter 3, Section 1. Unlike possessive adjectives in English, in Spanish they agree in gender and number with the object they possess.

Paul Popper / Popperfoto/Getty Images

◀ *Picasso*

6.2-09 Preguntas personales Tu profesor/a de español quiere conocer mejor a los estudiantes de su clase. Contesta las siguientes preguntas en detalle. ¡Atención a la conjugación de los verbos!

1. ¿Por qué **elegiste** estudiar español? ¿Quién te **sugirió** la idea de estudiar español? ¿Por qué **preferiste** estudiar español a estudiar otra lengua?
2. Antes de estudiar español, ¿**estudiaste** otra lengua? ¿**Seguiste** estudiando esa lengua después de empezar a estudiar español? ¿A qué nivel[7] **llegaste** en tus estudios de la otra lengua?
3. ¿Cómo te **sentiste** cuando **tuviste** que hablar en español por primera vez?
4. ¿**Fuiste** alguna vez a un país hispanohablante? ¿A cuál? ¿Cómo **fue** tu experiencia?
5. ¿Qué lugares **visitaste** en ese país? ¿Qué obras de arte o arquitectura **viste**?
6. ¿Te **sirvió** la visita a ese país para practicar español?

Paso 2: Ahora, usa las preguntas para entrevistar a un/a compañero/a. Escribe sus respuestas y después presenta la información a la clase.

MODELO: *Mi compañero/a ... eligió estudiar español porque... Además, sus padres le sugirieron la idea de estudiar español porque...*

[6]**a pesar de:** despite of [7]**nivel:** level

LA PURA VERDAD II | Una visita a Granada

Los padres de Amanda vienen de Estados Unidos a visitar a su hija, que estudia en Granada. Los dos hablan muy bien el español.

1.

Quiero ir de compras.

Muchas tiendas están cerradas porque es Semana Santa.

2.

Yo quiero ir a ver la ciudad.

Podéis ir a ver la Alhambra y el Albaicín. También podéis ir a ver las procesiones, si queréis.

3.

¿Veis aquel palacio árabe muy grande? Es la Alhambra.

4.

¿Veis aquellas montañas muy altas? Es Sierra Nevada. El mes pasado fuimos a esquiar y nos divertimos muchísimo.

5.

¿Veis aquella colina que está allí? Es el Albaicín.

6.

¡Mira estos niños qué monos!

Mira aquellas capuchas[8].

© John Wiley & Sons, Inc.

6.2-10 Una visita a la Alhambra Escucha la narración y selecciona la oración que mejor explique lo que narra.

1. a. La Alhambra fue el palacio donde vivió el último rey moro en España.
   b. La Alhambra va a ser un lugar muy popular.
   c. Los padres de Amanda pudieron comprar los billetes el mismo día.
2. a. Fueron a la Alhambra por la mañana y a otro castillo rojo por la tarde.
   b. El guía les dijo que *Alhambra* quiere decir "castillo blanco".
   c. Pasaron todo el día en la Alhambra.
3. a. El rey murió en aquella montaña.
   b. La madre del sultán lloró en aquella montaña.
   c. El rey lloró porque no pudo defender la Alhambra.

[8] **capuchas:** hoods

HABLANDO DE GRAMÁTICA II

2. Pointing out people and objects: Demonstrative adjectives and pronouns

Demonstrative adjectives point at specific objects or people; they identify the noun they refer to in relation to the person speaking. Demonstrative adjectives always precede the noun they refer to, and like all adjectives, they agree in gender and number with the noun.

WileyPLUS Go to *WileyPLUS* to review this grammar point with the help of the **Animated Grammar Tutorial**.

Demonstrative adjectives

		Aquí *(here)* close to the speaker		Ahí *(there)* at a short distance from the speaker		Allí o allá *(over there)* far from the speaker	
(masc.) (fem.)	*this*	**este** cuadro **esta** escultura	*that*	**ese** cuadro **esa** escultura	*that*	**aquel** cuadro **aquella** escultura
(masc.) (fem.)	*these*	**estos** cuadros **estas** esculturas	*those*	**esos** cuadros **esas** esculturas	*those*	**aquellos** cuadros **aquellas** esculturas

–**Este** cuadro de Velázquez es mi obra preferida de todo el museo.

–*This painting by Velázquez is my favorite piece in the museum.*

–Pues a mí me gusta más **esa** escultura naranja que está ahí.

–*I like that orange sculpture there more.*

–¿En serio? ¿No te gusta más **aquella** escultura gris en la entrada?

–*Really? Don't you prefer that gray sculpture by the entrance?*

Demonstrative adjectives become pronouns when used without the noun they refer to, when it is clear from the context what we are talking about. They are pronouns because they replace the noun they refer to. Demonstrative pronouns are used to avoid repetition. They are identical to demonstrative adjectives, and they still have to agree in gender and number with the object or person they refer to.

Demonstrative pronouns

Aquí *(here)* close to the speaker		Ahí *(there)* at a short distance from speaker		Allí *(over there)* far from speaker	
this one	**este** **esta**	*that one*	**ese** **esa**	*that one*	**aquel** **aquella**
these ones	**estos** **estas**	*those ones*	**esos** **esas**	*those ones*	**aquellos** **aquellas**

–Me gusta **este** cuadro de Velázquez y **este** de Goya.

–*I like this painting by Velázquez and this one by Goya.*

–Sí, **estos** son bonitos, pero a mí me gusta más **ese**.

–*Yes, these ones are beautiful, but I like that one better.*

–Sí, **ese** es bonito también. Es muy parecido a **aquel** que nos gustó en la otra sala.

–*Yes, that one over there is beautiful too. It is very similar to that one that we liked in the other room.*

When we want to point at something and we don't know what it is, or we don't know its name, or we are not referring to a concrete object (e.g., a situation, or something someone has said), we use the neuter demonstrative pronouns **esto**, **eso**, **aquello**.

The speaker doesn't know the name:

¿Cómo se dice **eso** en inglés?

*How do you say **that** in English?*

The speaker doesn't know what it is:

¿Qué es **esto**? ¿Para qué sirve?

*What is **this**? What is it for?*

The speaker is referring to an entire situation:

Aquello no me gustó nada...

*I didn't like **that** at all. . .*

6.2-11 La visita a la Alhambra Amanda y sus padres visitan la Alhambra. Amanda quiere explicarles todo. Elige qué adjetivo demostrativo usarías.

1. Amanda y sus padres están en un mirador[9] en una torre de la Alhambra. Amanda señala[10] un barrio de casas blancas en la distancia y dice:

   Este/Ese/Aquel barrio de casas blancas es el Albaicín.

2. Desde la torre, Amanda y sus padres ven un palacio al lado de la Alhambra. Amanda dice:

   Este/Ese/Aquel edificio marrón claro de ahí es el Palacio de Carlos V.

3. La guía les muestra una montaña en la distancia y les dice:

   ¿Ven **esta/esa/aquella** montaña de allí? Se llama el Suspiro del Moro.

4. Amanda y sus padres están en un patio de la Alhambra, enfrente de una fuente. Amanda señala las esculturas de animales y dice:

   Estas/Esas/Aquellas estatuas son leones.

5. Amanda y sus padres están en un patio. Al fondo[11] hay una pared con arcos. Amanda dice:

   Vamos ahí, a ver **estos/esos/aquellos** arcos árabes.

6. Amanda y sus padres están dentro de una sala. Amanda dice:

   Esta/Esa/Aquella sala se usó para celebrar las audiencias del rey.

▲ *Sala de Comares, la Alhambra*

All illustrations © John Wiley & Sons, Inc.

age fotostock / SuperStock

[9] **mirador:** lookout point [10] **señalar:** to point [11] **al fondo:** in the background

6.2-12 **En la Plaza Real** Amanda y sus amigas llegan a la Plaza Real después de pasar el día explorando Barcelona. Completa el diálogo de las chicas con los adjetivos o pronombres demostrativos apropiados. Pon atención a las palabras clave *aquí, ahí* o *allí*.

¹²**ambiente:** atmosphere

3. Recognizing the *vosotros* form of address

As you already know, in Spanish there are different subject pronouns and forms of address depending on the relationship that the people who are speaking have. In the **Capítulo Preliminar** you learned how factors such as age and social position play important roles. In English we use *you* for both the singular and plural. In Spanish, when addressing one person only **tú** (*informal*); **usted** (formal); and more than one person **ustedes** (for both formal and informal).

In most of the Spanish-speaking world except for Spain, there is only one plural form of address, **ustedes**, which is both the formal and informal form of address. However, in Spain the plural of **tú** is **vosotros**, and it is used as the informal counterpart of **ustedes**. In Spain, **ustedes** is used only to address two or more people formally. **Vosotros** is used in more colloquial registers or when addressing people you are familiar with. As you may have noticed, the verb form for **vosotros** has been included with all other verb conjugation forms throughout the book.

	Singular	Plural (Latin America)	Plural (Spain)
Informal	Hola, **tú eres** el amigo de Amanda, ¿verdad?	¡Hola muchachos! **Ustedes son** los amigos de Amanda, ¿verdad?	¡Hola chicos! **Vosotros sois** los amigos de Amanda, ¿verdad?
	Hi, you are Amanda's friend, right?	*Hi guys! You are Amanda's friends, right?*	
Formal	Buenas tardes, señor. ¿**Usted** es el invitado de la Srta. Burton?	Buenas tardes, señores. ¿**Ustedes son** los invitados de la Srta. Burton?	Buenas tardes, señores. ¿**Ustedes son** los invitados de la Srta. Burton?
	Good afternoon, sir. Are you Ms. Burton's guest?	*Good afternoon, gentlemen. Are you Ms. Burton's guests?*	

6.2-13 Las próximas vacaciones Vas a viajar a España durante tus próximas vacaciones y tienes que acostumbrarte[13] a usar *vosotros*.

 Paso 1: Entrevista a dos compañeros usando la forma de *vosotros* y apunta las respuestas de los dos. Después, cambia de grupo; otro/a compañero/a te entrevistará a ti.

	Mi compañero/a	Mi compañero/a
1. ¿Dónde **estuvisteis**?	_____	_____
2. ¿**Pudisteis** visitar museos?	_____	_____
3. ¿**Visitasteis** monumentos u obras de arte?	_____	_____
4. ¿**Contemplasteis** vistas desde un mirador?	_____	_____
5. ¿**Paseasteis** por ciudades antiguas?	_____	_____
6. ¿**Admirasteis** arquitectura regional o pintoresca[14]?	_____	_____
7. ¿**Disfrutasteis** de paisajes hermosos?	_____	_____
8. ¿**Salisteis** por la noche?	_____	_____

Paso 2: Finalmente, escribe un pequeño párrafo para describir similitudes[15] y diferencias entre tus dos compañeros.

MODELO: *Los dos fueron de vacaciones, y los dos fueron a países hispanohablantes, pero (John) fue a… y (Sarah) fue a…*

[13] acostumbrarse: to get used to [14] pintoresco: picturesque, quaint [15] similitudes: similarities

OTRA PERSPECTIVA

Courtesy of Laura Marqués Pascual

Laura

El espacio urbano

Diferente

"En Estados Unidos veo que muchas cosas son grandes: los edificios, las calles, los centros comerciales, las mesas en los restaurantes, las porciones de comida, los vasos de refrescos, los automóviles, etc. También hay mucho espacio urbano y mucho espacio público, pero no ves mucha gente caminando por las calles. Normalmente, el centro de la ciudad es cuadriculado[16]. ¡Es difícil perderse[17]!"

Igual

"En España hay iglesias, catedrales, museos, grandes centros comerciales y palacios enormes también. Algunos barrios nuevos también son cuadriculados".

Explícale a Laura

1. ¿Por qué tenemos la impresión de que muchas cosas son grandes en los Estados Unidos?
2. ¿Por qué muchos centros de ciudades están diseñados como una cuadrícula?
3. ¿Por qué no es común caminar?

MANOS A LA OBRA

6.2-14 La vida de Salvador Dalí Con un/a compañero/a, pon las oraciones en orden cronológico para saber más sobre su vida.

Paso 1: Elijan cada uno una columna. Cambien individualmente los verbos al pretérito.

Estudiante 1

_____ A. <u>Pinta</u> el famoso cuadro *La persistencia de la memoria*.

_____ B. <u>Conoce</u> a Gala; <u>dice</u>: "Amo a Gala más que a mi madre, más que a mi padre, más que a Picasso y más que al dinero".

_____ C. <u>Nace</u> en España en 1904.

Estudiante 2

_____ D. Se <u>hace</u> cubista, como Picasso.

_____ E. <u>Muere</u> en 1989.

_____ F. <u>Cambia</u> su imagen. <u>Empieza</u> a llevar el pelo largo, una corbata grandísima y una capa hasta los pies.

Paso 2: Tomen turnos para leer cada uno sus oraciones en voz alta. Juntos decidan qué oración corresponde a cada ilustración, para ponerlas en orden.

1.   2.   3.   4.   5.   6.

Topham / The Image Works © Salvador Dalí, Fundació Gala-Salvador Dalí, Artists Rights Society (ARS), New York 2013

© Gonzalo Azumendi / age fotostock

All illustrations © John Wiley & Sons, Inc.

[16] **cuadriculado/a:** squared, gridded [17] **perderse:** to get lost

6.2-15 ¿Por qué son famosos? La clase se va a dividir en grupos. El/La profesor/a va a decir el nombre de una persona famosa. Cada grupo tiene que pensar y escribir quiénes fueron esas personas y por qué fueron famosas. Cada grupo que consiga dar una respuesta correcta gana un punto.

MODELO: *Fue un pintor cubista muy famoso. Pintó La persistencia de la memoria y contribuyó a la creación del movimiento cubista.* → *Salvador Dalí*

6.2-16 ¿Cuándo hiciste estas actividades? Levántate y hazles a tus compañeros las siguientes preguntas. Escribe el nombre del/de la compañero/a que conteste afirmativamente.

MODELO: visitar alguna ciudad antigua
Estudiante 1: *¿Visitaste alguna ciudad antigua?*
Estudiante 2: *Sí, visité Córdoba. Estudié dos meses allí.*

	Nombre	visitó
visitar alguna ciudad antigua	_____	_____
ver una exposición de escultura	_____	_____
entrar en una catedral gótica	_____	_____
conducir por calles muy estrechas	_____	_____
repetir un curso	_____	_____
sugerir un curso de español a un amigo	_____	_____
estar de vacaciones en un país hispanohablante	_____	_____
ir a un museo de pintura	_____	_____
diseñar un proyecto gráfico o artístico	_____	_____

WileyPLUS Go to *WileyPLUS* and listen to **Presta atención.**

¡OJO!

Replacing information
Now that you know how to use subject pronouns (**yo, tú, él...**), object pronouns (**lo, la, le, les...**), and demonstrative adjectives (**este, esto, esta, estos...**), you can use them to replace information that has been previously identified or mentioned in a text. This way you can eliminate excessive repetition and have a more cohesive writing. Now, read this paragraph and look for cohesion:

En Granada, la gente come tapas en los bares y son gratis. Comen las tapas con alguna bebida alcohólica o con refrescos. Los bares son lugares para la familia y para los amigos. Nosotros vemos a nuestros amigos en los bares y tenemos buenas conversaciones. Las conversaciones pueden ser largas o muy largas.

How could you make this paragraph less repetitive and more cohesive?

 6.2-17 Presta atención: Un paseo por Barcelona Dos amigas están paseando por el centro histórico de Barcelona. Escucha la conversación para tener más información sobre las actividades que hicieron por la mañana.

1. ¿De qué se sorprenden las chicas?
   a. de la cantidad de gente que hay en las Ramblas
   b. de un cuadro de Picasso que se vende en las Ramblas
   c. de la cantidad de estatuas que hay en las Ramblas
2. ¿Qué tipo de estatuas mencionan las chicas?
   a. estatuas en forma de torre, fachada, cuadros
   b. diferentes estatuas con balcones
   c. todas las estatuas son de colores vivos
3. ¿Por qué Carmen quiere ir al teatro del Liceo?
   a. porque le interesa la historia del arte
   b. porque es un teatro de ópera
   c. porque un señor famoso lo compró
4. ¿Qué pasó con el teatro del Liceo?
   a. Hubo un accidente y no se volvió a abrir.
   b. Hubo dos accidentes en años diferentes.
   c. Unos señores lo vendieron a un colegio.
5. ¿Qué quiere ver también Carmen?
   a. el barrio del Raval
   b. el escultor Botero
   c. el gato del Raval

6.2-18 Por escrito: Madrid, día y noche Imagina que tus padres te pagaron el viaje y un hotel para pasar una semana en Madrid durante las vacaciones de primavera. A tu vuelta, ellos te piden que escribas en tu blog un tipo de guía de entretenimiento. Fíjate en la caja de **¡Ojo!** para mejorar tu escritura. Escribe sobre...

- las actividades que hiciste para entretenerte;
- los lugares de interés (plazas, parques, calles...) a los que fuiste;
- los espectáculos a los que asististe (teatro, cine);
- el arte (museos, monumentos...) y la vida nocturna (bares, discotecas, restaurantes, pubs).

PONTE EN MI LUGAR

Entrevista a un español famoso

Paso 1: Vas a preparar una entrevista con un/a compañero/a para dramatizarla en frente de la clase. Un/a estudiante es periodista y el otro/la otra es un/a famoso/a actor o actriz español/a (p. ej., Antonio Banderas, Javier Bardem, Penélope Cruz, etc.) que vive en Estados Unidos.

El periodista quiere saber lo siguiente: (a) el número de películas en las que ha actuado desde que comenzó a ser actor/actriz, (b) las fechas en que salieron las películas, (c) cuánto tiempo hace que vive en Estados Unidos y por qué decidió ir a vivir allí, (d) los premios que ganó, (e) cuál es su película favorita, y (f) cuál es su actor favorito y por qué.

La persona famosa contesta todas las preguntas con creatividad, usando la imaginación, de manera que las respuestas sean divertidas. No olvides usar expresiones como *claro que sí, por supuesto que no*... para enfatizar tus respuestas afirmativas y negativas.

Paso 2: Después de escuchar varias entrevistas, la clase escoge la mejor. **¡Ojo!** No puedes votar por tu propia entrevista.

> ### Estrategias para conversar ♻
>
> **Emphasize your answers by going beyond *Sí* and *No*.** As you learned in Chapter 6, Section 1, you can use expressions such as **claro que sí**, **desde luego** or **por supuesto** when you want to say *of course*. Use **claro que no** or **por supuesto que no** when you express *of course not*.

ASÍ ES LA VIDA

Adivina, adivinador

Sobre lienzo, o en papel,
qué bien aplica el color,
con lápices o pincel.

Rima: ¿Quién es?

Azul o
rosa o
cubista
siempre artista

@Arroba@   **WileyPLUS** Go to *WileyPLUS* to find more **Arroba** activities.

Los museos de Madrid Imagina que vas a estar un solo día en Madrid con un/a amigo/a. A los dos les gustan mucho los museos. Convence a tu compañero/a de que el museo que a ti te interesa es el mejor de la ciudad. Usa el vocabulario del capítulo y estructuras como *tener que, deber* (Capítulo 4, Sección 1), *saber, conocer* (Capítulo 5, Sección 1), *decir, dar* (Capítulo 5, Sección 2), *ser y estar* (Capítulo 4, Sección 2) y *gustar* (Capítulo 1, Sección 2 y Capítulo 2, Sección 2): Es una pintura (románica/gótica/barroca); Son pinturas del siglo (XV/XVI/...); Estoy interesado en el (cubismo/surrealismo/impresionismo/...).

Instrucciones para el chat:

Estudiante 1: Encuentra en tu buscador favorito una página web del Museo del Prado. Busca información sobre las obras de arte de el Greco, Francisco de Goya o Diego Velázquez. Selecciona un pintor y busca información sobre el estilo de sus pinturas. Después, convence a tu compañero/a de que este es el museo más interesante.

Estudiante 2: Encuentra en tu buscador favorito una página web del Museo Reina Sofía. Busca información sobre las obras de arte de Pablo Picasso, Salvador Dalí o, Joan Miró. Sigue los pasos del Estudiante 1. Convence a tu compañero/a de que este es el museo más interesante de Madrid.

Decidan el museo que van a visitar e informen a la clase.

VER PARA CREER II: ¡Qué antiguo!

WileyPLUS Go to *WileyPLUS* to see this video and to find more video activities.

Antes de ver

Con un/a compañero/a, contesta las preguntas para comprender mejor el contenido del video y las diferencias culturales.

1. ¿Son antiguas las plazas estadounidenses? ¿Cuántos siglos tienen?
2. ¿Vives en el centro de la ciudad? ¿Por qué?
3. ¿Piensas que necesario usar el coche a diario? ¿Por qué?
4. ¿Qué expresiones dicen los españoles?

Después de ver

1. ¿Entendiste? Tina enseña inglés en Madrid y el fin de semana su amiga Marta la visita. Después de ver el video, responde estas preguntas.

1. ¿De qué ciudad es Marta?
   a. de Madrid   b. de Sevilla   c. de Alicante
2. ¿Cuándo llegó Marta a Madrid?
   a. ayer   b. esa mañana   c. hace una semana
3. ¿Qué expresión usa Marta cuando ve la Plaza Mayor?
   a. ¡Qué guay!   b. ¡Madre mía!   c. ¡Venga, vamos!
4. ¿En qué siglos construyeron la Plaza Mayor?
   a. en los siglos XIX y XX   b. en los siglos XV y XVI   c. en los siglos XVI y XVII
5. ¿Adónde van las amigas después de visitar la Plaza Mayor?
   a. a otra plaza más   b. a un restaurante.   c. a visitar el barrio
      antigua   antiguo   Malasaña
6. ¿Qué se hace en Nochevieja en España?
   a. Se celebra con la familia sin salir a la calle.
   b. Se comen doce uvas y se sale a bailar.
   c. Se celebra con amigos y a las doce se vuelve a casa.
7. ¿Qué echa de menos Marta de España?
   a. Echa de menos la espontaneidad para quedar con los amigos.
   b. Echa de menos comer en restaurantes elegantes.
   c. Echa de menos la familia.

2. De tapas En el video, Tina y Marta van al restaurante Botín para comer. ¿Crees que "ir de tapas" es particular de la cultura española? Describe el ambiente y la decoración del restaurante. ¿Qué hace la gente? ¿Es parecido a los restaurantes de tu ciudad? ¿En qué se diferencia? ¿Qué tiene en común?

3. Enfoque cultural ¿Vive algún/alguna amigo/a tuyo/a en otro país/estado/ciudad? ¿Crees que tu amigo/a puede ser tu guía turístico de ese lugar? ¿Por qué?

AUTOPRUEBA

VOCABULARIO

I. ¿Qué aprendiste?

MODELO: ¿Qué puedes ver en las Ramblas de Barcelona?
estatuas, artistas, arte

1. ¿Qué colores nuevos conoces?
2. ¿Cómo se llama el cuadro que un pintor pinta de sí mismo?
3. ¿Desde qué edificio alto puedes ver muy bien un paisaje?
4. ¿Qué edificios antiguos se ven en España?

II. ¿Qué recuerdas? Lee las oraciones y después identifica los objetos, lugares, actividades, personas con una o varias palabras.

1. ¿Qué actividades hace un artista?
2. ¿A qué edificio va un musulmán para rezar?
3. ¿En qué edificio puede haber una princesa?
4. ¿Qué le gusta pintar a un pintor?

GRAMÁTICA

I. En el cine Laura y Cristina están en la puerta del cine decidiendo qué película ver. Completa su diálogo con la forma correcta de los adjetivos demostrativos para saber más sobre sus gustos.

Laura: Cristina, mira _____ película que acaba de salir.

Cristina: Sí, ayer vi _____ película con mi hermana.

Laura: Vaya, pues entonces, ¿qué te parecen _____ películas de allí lejos. No veo los nombres porque no tengo las gafas.

Cristina: ¡Ah! _____ póster que está allá lejos es de una película de Antonio Banderas y _____ otro cartel que está ahí es de una película con Penélope Cruz. Me gustaría ver la película de Antonio Banderas.

Laura: Pues venga, vamos a comprar las entradas.

II. Los colores ¿Qué hicieron estas personas en la ciudad? Completa las oraciones formando oraciones para saber lo que hicieron. Usa el pretérito y cambia el género de los adjetivos cuando sea necesario.

1. Los pintores / crear / fachadas / azul marino
2. El arquitecto / diseñar / torres / plateado
3. Los escultores / esculpir / estatuas / dorado
4. Los trabajadores / poner / los carteles / de color verde oscuro / en el cine
5. La directora / pintar / monumentos / gótico / de color vino

III. El fin de semana en Granada Imagina que pasaste el fin de semana en Granada. Contesta las preguntas en pretérito según lo que hiciste.

1. ¿Fuiste a la Alhambra?
_____

2. ¿Anduviste o condujiste a la Alhambra?
_____

3. ¿Anduviste por los jardines del Generalife?
_____

4. ¿Estuviste en el Albaicín? ¿Qué hiciste allí?
_____

5. ¿Viste el Sacromonte? ¿Por qué sí o por qué no?
_____

CULTURA

1. ¿Qué diferencia hay entre los edificios antiguos de Estados Unidos y los de España?
2. ¿Cuáles son algunos pintores, arquitectos o directores españoles importantes?
3. ¿Qué ciudades españolas conoces ahora?
4. ¿Cómo se diferencia el espacio urbano de Estados Unidos del de España?

REDACCIÓN

Imagina que es el año 2025. Escribe una miniautobiografía. Menciona los eventos principales de tu vida incluyendo los últimos diez años. Incluye:

- cuándo y dónde naciste;
- cuántos hermanos tenías;
- a qué escuelas fuiste;
- cuándo te graduaste de la universidad;
- ¿te casaste?;
- ¿tuviste hijos?;
- ¿conseguiste un buen trabajo?;
- ¿qué haces ahora en el 2025?

EN RESUMIDAS CUENTAS, AHORA PUEDO...

☐ comparar diferentes espacios urbanos.

☐ describir obras de arte.

☐ hablar en el pasado.

☐ expresar posesión.

☐ identificar personas y objetos en el espacio físico.

☐ identificar y reconocer el uso del pronombre y la forma verbal de **vosotros**.

☐ entender el arte español y hablar de los artistas.

⌔ VOCABULARIO ESENCIAL

Sustantivos

la actriz	*actress*
el autorretrato	*selfportrait*
el castillo	*castle*
el cuadro	*painting*
el lienzo	*canvas*
la luz	*light*
la mezquita	*mosque*
la obra de arte	*work of art*
la obra maestra	*masterpiece*
el paisaje	*landscape*
la pintura (al óleo)	*(oil) painting*
el retrato	*portrait*
la torre	*tower*

Cognados: el actor, el arco, el/la arquitecto/a, la arquitectura, el arte, el/la artista, la basílica, la catedral, el cine, el/la director/a, el/la escultor/a, la escultura, la estatua, el estilo, la fachada, la fotografía, la literatura, el monumento, el/la pintor/a

Verbos

competir	*to compete*
conseguir	*to get*
construir	*to build*
crear	*to create*
dibujar	*to draw*
diseñar	*to design*
elegir	*to choose*
esculpir	*to sculpt*
pintar	*to paint*
repetir	*to repeat*
sugerir	*to suggest*
morir	*to die*

Adjetivos

antiguo/a	*old, ancient*
azul (oscuro, claro, marino)	*(dark, light, navy) blue*
color vino	*burgundy*
color vivo	*bright color*
dorado/a	*golden*
plateado/a	*silver*
turquesa	*turquoise*
verde (oliva, claro, oscuro)	*green (olive, light, dark)*

Cognados: abstracto/a, barroco/a, colonial, contemporáneo/a, gótico/a, medieval, moderno/a, romano/a

Expresiones

ahí	*there*
allí/allá	*over there*
aquí	*here*

Los restaurantes y las comidas

© John Wiley & Sons, Inc.

VER PARA CREER I: ¡Buen provecho!

Lauren es una estadounidense que está de visita en Argentina. Después de ver el video vas a poder contestar las preguntas y aprender sobre la comida y bebidas en Argentina.

1. ¿Dónde está Lauren? ¿A qué lugares va?
2. ¿Qué muestra Francisco con tanto entusiasmo en el Café Tortoni?
3. ¿Qué bebidas escuchaste o viste en el video?

Sección 1 ## ¿Qué comemos?

PALABRA POR PALABRA

- Los alimentos y las comidas

HABLANDO DE GRAMÁTICA

- Present tense of stem-changing verbs ♻
- Saying how life used to be: Imperfect tense (regular and irregular verbs)
- Expressing affection and size: Diminutive suffixes

CULTURA

- El mate y otros productos típicos
- Los hábitos alimenticios

Sección 2 ## A la mesa

PALABRA POR PALABRA

- En el restaurante
- A cocinar

HABLANDO DE GRAMÁTICA

- Expressions with **tener** ♻
- Giving instructions: Formal commands
- Making impersonal statements and deemphasizing authorship: Impersonal and passive **se**
- The **vos** form of address ♻

CULTURA

- Los restaurantes chilenos
- Las comidas regionales

Go to *WileyPLUS* to do the **Trivia** activities and find out how much you know about these countries!

Argentina, Chile y Uruguay

Antofagasta
Salta
La Serena
La Rioja
URUGUAY
Mendoza
Buenos Aires
Santiago ★
ARGENTINA
Talca
Montevideo
CHILE
Santa Rosa · Viedma
Chiloé
Rawson
Ushuaia

© John Wiley & Sons, Inc.

LEARNING OBJECTIVES

By the end of this section you will be able to:

- Talk about your eating habits now and in the past
- Talk about how things used to be
- Express size and endearment with the diminutive form
- Discuss regional differences in eating habits and traditional foods

Una imagen vale más que mil palabras

© Rudy Girón

¿Se encuentran platos similares en Estados Unidos?

¿Se venden en Estados Unidos partes como el corazón, los intestinos u otros órganos de algún animal?

¿Cómo se muestra la carne en los supermercados donde vives?

◄ *Mondongo: plato a base de trocitos del estómago de la vaca*

UNA PERSPECTIVA

Courtesy of Brad Langer

Brad

La yerba mate

Diferente

"Fui a Buenos Aires, Argentina, a estudiar por tres meses. Allí muy pronto traté de hacer amigos. No tuve problemas porque los argentinos son siempre muy simpáticos, pero no me sentí realmente parte de un grupo hasta que me invitaron a tomar mate.

La yerba mate es un tipo de té que se puede beber individualmente o en grupo. Una persona pone la yerba en el mate, introduce la bombilla[1], añade agua caliente y lo pasa a otro del grupo. Esta persona bebe, añade más agua y así sucesivamente. Todos beben usando el mismo mate y la misma bombilla. Es un acto social popular y para mí fue un honor ser invitado".

Casi igual

"¿Conoces alguna costumbre similar en Estados Unidos? ¿Compartimos algo para comer del mismo plato o beber de la misma copa? Creo que sí. Algunas veces mis amigos y yo comemos nachos y salsa de la misma bolsa y algunas veces pedimos un plato de comida para compartir entre todos, pero no es un ritual social".

 ¿Qué piensas tú? Contesta **Cierto** o **Falso** según tu opinión y justifica por qué piensas así.

	Cierto	Falso
1. Tenemos un ritual similar entre amigos.	☐	☐
2. Me siento bien bebiendo café o té de la taza[2] de un amigo.	☐	☐
3. Está bien compartir aperitivos, como por ejemplo, nachos de una misma bolsa.	☐	☐

[1] **bombilla:** metal straw used for drinking mate [2] **taza:** cup

LA PURA VERDAD I   Un supermercado

Julia es una estudiante de Texas que fue a estudiar a Mendoza, Argentina. Es su primera visita a un supermercado en este país.

1.

2.

3.

4.

5.

6.

7.

8.

© John Wiley & Sons, Inc.

7.1-01 En el supermercado Escucha la conversación entre Julia y el dependiente del supermercado. Haz un círculo alrededor de los ingredientes que ellos mencionan y que aparecen en la ilustración.

1.

2.

© John Wiley & Sons, Inc.

PALABRA POR PALABRA

Los alimentos y las comidas *Food and meals*

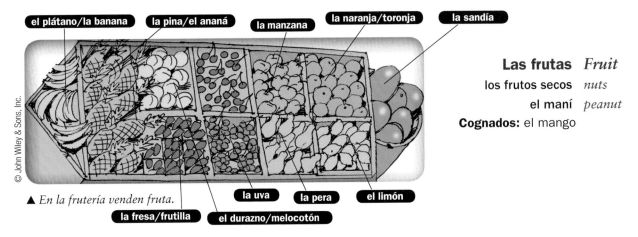

el plátano/la banana · la piña/el ananá · la manzana · la naranja/toronja · la sandía

Las frutas *Fruit*
los frutos secos *nuts*
el maní *peanut*
Cognados: el mango

la uva · la pera · el limón
la fresa/frutilla · el durazno/melocotón

▲ *En la frutería venden fruta.*

© John Wiley & Sons, Inc.

Las verduras y legumbres *Vegetables and legumes*
Cognados: la coliflor, la espinaca

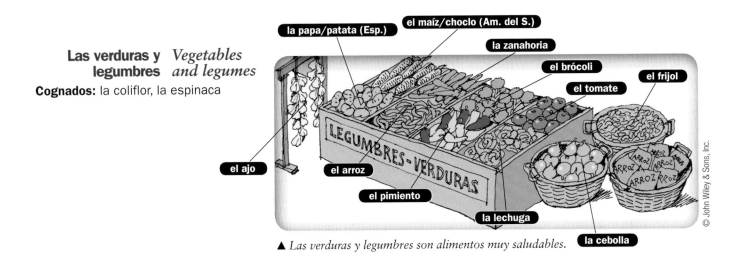

la papa/patata (Esp.) · el maíz/choclo (Am. del S.) · la zanahoria · el brócoli · el tomate · el frijol

LEGUMBRES - VERDURAS

el ajo · el arroz · el pimiento · la lechuga · la cebolla

▲ *Las verduras y legumbres son alimentos muy saludables.*

© John Wiley & Sons, Inc.

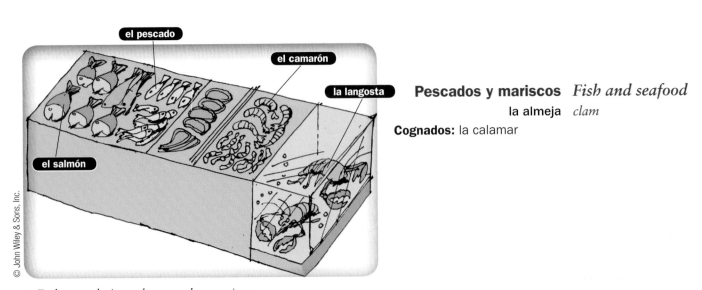

el pescado · el camarón · la langosta

Pescados y mariscos *Fish and seafood*
la almeja *clam*
Cognados: la calamar

el salmón

© John Wiley & Sons, Inc.

▲ *En la pescadería venden pescado y mariscos.*

Carnes *Meat*

el pavo   *turkey*
el tocino   *bacon*

▲ *En la carnicería venden carne.*

El desayuno *Breakfast*

la leche (de soja)   *(soy) milk*
la mantequilla   *butter*
la miel   *honey*

Cognados: el café, el cereal, el yogur

▲ *El desayuno*

Para hablar de la comida

el almuerzo   *lunch*
el asado/la parrillada   *BBQ*
la cena   *dinner*
la grasa   *fat*
la merienda   *a snack (between lunch and dinner)*
la receta   *a recipe*

Cognados: la dieta, la pasta

desayunar   *to have breakfast*
merendar (e→ie)   *to snack (between lunch and dinner)*
picar   *to snack (at any time)*
preparar   *to make, prepare, cook*
¿Quieres algo de tomar/picar?   *Would you like something to drink/a snack?*

Adjetivos

dulce   *sweet*
graso/a   *fatty*
picante   *hot*
saludable   *healthy*

¿Qué dicen los argentinos y los uruguayos?

<u>Che</u>, Ricardo, ¿necesitás algo?   *Hey Ricardo, do you need something?*

¿Adónde vas, <u>flaco</u>?   *Where are you going, buddy? (general term used for a young person)*

Unos <u>pibes</u> me ayudaron.   *Some <u>young guys</u> helped me.*

*No lo puedo comprar porque no tengo <u>plata</u>.   *I can't buy it because I don't have <u>money</u>.*

Hoy es el cumpleaños de mi <u>viejo/a</u>.   *Today is my <u>father's/mother's</u> birthday.*

¡Los <u>chiquilines</u> me vuelven loco!   *The <u>kids</u> are driving me crazy.*

*Esta expresión también se usa en otros países hispanos.

7.1-02 ¿Qué alimento es?

Paso 1: Lean las definiciones y busquen la palabra correspondiente de la sección **Palabra por palabra**.

_____ 1. Es una fruta muy grande, verde por fuera y roja por dentro, que contiene mucha agua.

_____ 2. Es una fruta de verano, que tiene la piel muy suave y que usamos para hacer mermelada.

_____ 3. Es una verdura de color naranja que tiene mucha vitamina A.

_____ 4. Es una fruta roja por dentro y por fuera, pequeña, con hojas verdes, con un aroma dulce.

_____ 5. Es una verdura de hojas verdes grandes, que no tiene mucho sabor, y que es la base de muchos otros platos con verduras frescas.

_____ 6. Es una fruta muy pequeña y redonda, de color verde o morado, con la que se hace vino.

Paso 2: Ahora, elijan tres palabras de la sección **Palabra por palabra** y escriban tres definiciones para leerlas a la clase. ¡Atención! Recuerden que para definir siempre usamos el verbo _ser_.

7.1-03 ¿Cuál es más saludable?

 Paso 1: Con un/a compañero/a, considera los siguientes alimentos. Decidan cuál es el más saludable y ordenen la lista del 1 (más saludable) al 10 (menos saludable).

_____ a. las manzanas   _____ f. las chuletas de puerco

_____ b. la leche de vaca   _____ g. el queso crema

_____ c. la leche de soja   _____ h. los huevos

_____ d. las galletas   _____ i. el jugo de naranja

_____ e. el pavo   _____ j. las papas fritas

 Paso 2: Ahora, comparen sus respuestas con las de los otros grupos de la clase. ¿Todos tienen la misma opinión? ¿Qué alimento está en el puesto número 1 para la mayoría de los grupos? ¿Y en el número 10?

7.1-04 El menú del estudiante En grupos de tres, decidan cuál es el menú ideal para el estudiante universitario que no tiene mucho dinero, pero que quiere llevar una dieta equilibrada[3]. En cada comida principal deben incluir carbohidratos, proteínas, frutas y verduras. Deben crear un menú barato y saludable.

	Desayuno	Almuerzo	Merienda	Cena
Carbohidratos				
Proteínas o derivados de la leche				
Frutas y verduras				

Presenten su menú a la clase. ¿Están todos de acuerdo?

[3] **equilibrada:** balanced

La nueva pirámide alimenticia

Ocasional: carne roja, carne procesada y mantequilla
Cereales: arroz blanco, pan y pasta
Papas
Bebidas con azúcar y dulces
Grasas
Sal

Opcional:
alcohol con moderación
(adultos)

Lácteos bajos en grasas[4]
(1–2 porciones diarias)

Frutos secos, legumbres,
tofu (3–7 porciones semanales)

Pescado, carnes magras[5]
y huevos (1–2 porciones diarias)

Frutos secos, legumbres

Pescado, carnes
magras y huevos

Frutas y verduras
(> 5 porciones diarias)
Aceites y grasas vegetales
saludables (3–4 porciones diarias)

Diario para la mayoría
de las personas:
complejo
multivitamínico
con suplemento
de vitamina D

VITAMINA C

Frutas y verduras

Aceites y grasas
vegetales
saludables

Cereales, pasta

Cereales integrales:[6]
arroz integral,
pasta integral, avena[7], etc.
(1–2 porciones diarias)

Agua (4–8 vasos diarios)

Ejercicio + dieta equilibrada = vida sana

© John Wiley & Sons, Inc.

7.1-05 ¿Cómo es tu dieta?

Paso 1: Lee las siguientes preguntas y añade dos preguntas más a la lista. Después, entrevista a un/a compañero/a para saber más sobre su dieta. Contesta también sus preguntas.

1. ¿Crees que llevas una dieta equilibrada? ¿Por qué?
2. ¿Sigues las recomendaciones de la pirámide alimenticia? ¿Cómo?
3. ¿Comes carne? ¿Qué tipo de carne comes? ¿Eres vegetariano/a? Si eres vegetariano/a, ¿qué alimentos comes para incluir proteínas en tu dieta?
4. ¿Pierdes peso[8] con facilidad? ¿Haces alguna dieta especial? ¿<u>Prefieres</u> no comer muchos carbohidratos?
5. ¿Puedes ir a casa para almorzar, o <u>almuerzas</u> fuera de casa? ¿Qué <u>almuerzas</u> normalmente?
6. ¿Eres alérgico/a a algún alimento? ¿A cuál?

Paso 2: Después, escriban un pequeño informe. ¿En qué aspectos coinciden los dos? ¿En qué no coinciden?

MODELO: *Mi compañero/a y yo pensamos que llevamos una dieta bastante equilibrada porque... Sin embargo, él/ella almuerza siempre... y yo...*

Paso 3: Por último, informen a la clase. ¿Coinciden en todo, o en nada? ¿En qué aspecto no coincide nadie?

> ♻ **Present tense of stem-changing verbs**
>
> In Chapter 3, Section 1, you learned the present tense of irregular verbs. Some of these verbs undergo a change in the stem vowel. The three possible stem changes are o → ue, e → ie, e → i. Do you remember what are some of these stem-changing verbs? Take a minute to generate a list and see how many you remember. Then go to p. 103 to review the conjugation of these verbs.

---

[4]**lácteos bajos en grasas:** low fat dairy products [5]**magro/a:** lean [6]**cereales integrales:** whole grains [7]**avena:** oatmeal [8]**peso:** weight

HABLANDO DE GRAMÁTICA I

WileyPLUS Go to *WileyPLUS* to review this grammar point with the help of the **Animated Grammar Tutorial** and the **Verb Conjugator**.

1. Saying how life used to be: Imperfect tense (regular and irregular verbs)

In Spanish there are two main verb tenses to talk about the past: the *preterit* (which you learned in Chapter 6) and the *imperfect*. The *preterit* is used to view actions as completed and with a definite ending. The *imperfect* is used to talk about actions that do not have a stated end point.

The *imperfect* is formed by dropping the infinitive endings and adding the *imperfect* tense endings shown below. Verbs ending in **-er/-ir** share the same imperfect tense endings.

Regular verbs in the imperfect

Infinitive	desayunar	comer	servir*
(yo)	desayun**aba**	com**ía**	serv**ía**
(tú)	desayun**abas**	com**ías**	serv**ías**
(él, ella, Ud.)	desayun**aba**	com**ía**	serv**ía**
(nosotros/as)	desayun**ábamos**	com**íamos**	serv**íamos**
(vosotros/as)	desayun**abais**	com**íais**	serv**íais**
(ellos, ellas, Uds.)	desayun**aban**	com**ían**	serv**ían**

*Stem-changing verbs in the present are regular in the imperfect.

Irregular verbs in the imperfect

Infinitive	ser	ir	ver
(yo)	era	iba	veía
(tú)	eras	ibas	veías
(él, ella, Ud.)	era	iba	veían
(nosotros/as)	éramos	íbamos	veíamos
(vosotros/as)	erais	ibais	veíais
(ellos, ellas, Uds.)	eran	iban	veían

In English, there isn't a verb tense that is exactly equivalent to the imperfect. Thus, depending on the use or the context, the imperfect may be translated in different ways. There are three main uses of the imperfect:

A. To talk about *habitual actions* in the past (what *used to* or *would* happen):

Julia **iba** al supermercado todas las semanas pero a veces no **encontraba** nada de su lista.	*Julia used to go to the supermarket but sometimes she would not find anything on her list.*
Julia y sus amigos **probaban** alimentos nuevos casi todos los días.	*Julia and her friends would try new food items almost every day.*

B. To talk about *actions in progress* at a given time in the past (what *was* happening):

Julia **buscaba** un producto específico cuando llegó el vendedor.	*Julia was looking for a specific product when the seller came.*
A las 11 de la noche la familia argentina todavía **charlaba** animadamente en la sala.	*At 11 pm the Argentinean family were still chatting enthusiastically in the living room.*

C. *To describe* a situation or characteristics (people, places, things):

Julia **era** curiosa y no **tenía** miedo de probar cosas nuevas.	*Julia was curious and was not afraid of trying new things.*
Las calles de Mendoza **olían** a asado los domingos por la tarde.	*The streets of Mendoza smelled of BBQ on Sunday afternoons.*

Haber - Había

The irregular form **hay**, from the verb **haber**, means *there is/are*. **Había**, the imperfect form of **haber** means *there was/were*, and should be used when describing the past:

Había un asado en todas las casas.   ***There was*** a BBQ in every home.

 7.1-06 Diego Maradona, de niño Lee el siguiente párrafo sobre el futbolista argentino Diego Armando Maradona.

Diego Armando Maradona <u>vivía</u> en Villa Fiorito, un barrio pobre de Buenos Aires. Su mejor amigo se llamaba Goyo Carrizo, y juntos jugaban mucho con la pelota en las calles de su barrio. Querían ser jugadores de fútbol profesional para ayudar a sus familias económicamente. Sobre su infancia, Maradona dice lo siguiente: "Mi vieja me mentía[9] siempre, a la hora de comer decía que le dolía[10] el estómago, pero no era verdad… Lo decía porque no tenía suficiente comida para todos y ella prefería dejar la comida para nosotros. Mis papás trabajaban mucho para nosotros, pero éramos muchos y no había suficiente para todos". En el presente, Maradona es considerado como uno de los mejores jugadores de la historia del fútbol y el mejor jugador de la historia de los mundiales. Ya desde pequeño era un fenómeno.

Paso 1: Escribe todos los verbos en el imperfecto que encuentres en el párrafo (hay trece en total). ¡Atención! No todos los verbos están en el imperfecto. Después, indica por qué se usa el imperfecto en cada caso: *acción habitual, acción en progreso* o *descripción* en el pasado. Es posible que no encuentres en el párrafo ejemplos de los tres casos.

MODELO: 1. *vivía* (acción habitual)

2. _____
3. _____
4. _____
5. _____
6. _____
7. _____
8. _____
9. _____
10. _____
11. _____
12. _____
13. _____

▲ *Maradona jugaba en las calles de Villa Fiorito.*

▲ *Maradona en el Mundial de Fútbol de México en 1986*

Paso 2: ¿Cierto o falso? Lee el párrafo otra vez y decide si las siguientes oraciones son **Ciertas** o **Falsas**. Si son falsas, escribe la información correcta.

C   F

☐   ☐   1. El barrio de Maradona se llamaba Buenos Aires.

☐   ☐   2. Sus padres no tenían suficiente dinero para dar a sus hijos todo lo necesario.

☐   ☐   3. El padre de Maradona estaba desempleado.

☐   ☐   4. La mamá de Maradona se preocupaba mucho por sus hijos.

☐   ☐   5. De niño, Maradona quería tener la profesión de sus papás.

[9]**mentir:** to lie [10]**doler:** to hurt

7.1-07 Mafalda Las tiras cómicas de Mafalda, una niña argentina, son famosísimas en todos los países hispanohablantes. Completa el siguiente texto con el verbo correspondiente en la forma apropiada del imperfecto para saber más sobre Mafalda.

salir encantar preocupar tener entender ir ser (x2) haber hacer odiar estar

Mafalda _____₁ una niña muy inteligente y crítica que vivía en la Argentina de los años 60 y 70. Mafalda _____₂ 6 años en 1964, cuando sus historias aparecieron por primera vez. Con sus papás y su hermano Guille, los cuatro _____₃ una familia típica de Buenos Aires de clase media. Todos los días _____₄ a la escuela y, en verano, cuando _____₅ suficiente dinero, _____₆ de vacaciones con su familia. A Mafalda le _____₇ el mundo y sus problemas y no _____₈ por qué los adultos no _____₉ nada por resolverlos. _____₁₀ preocupada por la humanidad, la paz y los derechos humanos. Le _____₁₁ los Beatles y _____₁₂ la sopa.

7.1-08 ¿La dieta de nuestros padres era más saludable? La generación de nuestros padres y la nuestra no tienen la misma dieta.

Paso 1: Mira la siguiente lista y decide si cada frase representa o no los hábitos de la generación de tus padres. Indica **Cierto** o **Falso**, según corresponda. Después, cambia los verbos al imperfecto para escribir oraciones que describan los hábitos de esa generación.

MODELO: comer comida procesada
→ Falso: *Antes la gente no <u>comía</u> tanta comida procesada.*

C F
☐ ☐ 1. preocuparse por los ácidos transgrasos
☐ ☐ 2. tomar leche de soja
☐ ☐ 3. beber leche descremada
☐ ☐ 4. comer alimentos orgánicos
☐ ☐ 5. hacer dietas sin carbohidratos
☐ ☐ 6. complementar la dieta con vitaminas
☐ ☐ 7. ir al gimnasio
☐ ☐ 8. llevar una vida sedentaria
☐ ☐ 9. cocinar en casa la mayoría de las veces
☐ ☐ 10. haber índices altos de obesidad[11]

Paso 2: Ahora, comenta con un/a compañero/a los hábitos de la generación de tus padres. ¿Qué piensan? ¿Era la dieta de sus padres más saludable?

MODELO: Estudiante 1:   *Antes la gente no comía tanta comida procesada. La gente cocinaba más y comía productos más naturales.*
Estudiante 2:   *Sí, pero comían otras cosas como...*

[11]índices altos de obesidad: high obesity rates

LA PURA VERDAD II Cuando estaba en Argentina

Laura, una estudiante de doctorado, recuerda sus experiencias cuando estuvo tres meses en Argentina.

1.

2.

3.

4.

"¿Querés un bife?"
"No, gracias, soy vegetariana."
"Ahh, entonces, ¿querés pescado?"
"No, soy vegetariana."
"Ah, ya sé. ¿Qué tal unas empanadas de choclo?"

5.

"¡Hay olor a carne a la parrilla por toda la calle!]"

6.

"Mmm riquísimo" "Bárbaro" "Regio"

3 PM

7.

¿Qué tipo de carne es? Es lengua.

© John Wiley & Sons, Inc.

7.1-09 Cuando estaba en Argentina Escucha lo que pensaba Laura después de una semana en Argentina y decide si es **Cierto** o **Falso**. Si es falso, da la información correcta.

C   F

☐   ☐   1. Cuando Laura fue a Argentina, era vegetariana.

☐   ☐   2. Cuando probó la carne, le pareció deliciosa.

☐   ☐   3. La carne favorita de Laura era la lengua de vaca.

☐   ☐   4. Laura comía carne en la cafetería.

☐   ☐   5. Laura no quería comer pastas ni legumbres.

HABLANDO DE GRAMÁTICA II

WileyPLUS Go to *WileyPLUS* to review this grammar point with the help of the **Animated Grammar Tutorial.**

2. Expressing affection and size: Diminutive suffixes

Diminutives are suffixes that add new information to a word. They are used to express a smaller size, affection, endearment, or cuteness, and they are widely used in colloquial or familiar contexts. The most common diminutive suffix that you are probably familiar with is **-ito/a**. Another common suffix is **-illo/a.** These suffixes can be added to nouns and adjectives. The formation of these suffixes varies from region to region, but these are the most common rules:

Words ending in **-o** or **-a**	Drop the last vowel and add the suffix **-ito(s), -ita(s)**	galle**ta** → galle**tita** asad**o** → asad**ito**
Words ending in a consonant, except **n, r**	Add the suffix **-ito(s), -ita(s)**	arroz → arro**cito*** vegetal → vegetal**ito**
Words with more than two syllables ending in **-e**	Add the suffix **-ito(s), -ita(s)**	calient**e** → calent**ito** vinag**re** → vinag**rito**
One-syllable words that ends in a consonant	Add the suffix **-cito(s), -cita(s)** or **-ecito(s), -ecita(s)**	pan → pan**cito**, pan**ecito** flor → flor**cita**, flor**ecita**
One- or two-syllable words ending in **e, n, r**	Add the suffix **-cito(s), -cita(s)**	café → cafe**cito** limón → limon**cito**

Amanda, ¿quieres algo de tomar, un **juguito** o un **vasito** de agua?	*Amanda, would you like something to drink, a juice or a cup of water?*
No, gracias, pero sí una de esas **galletitas**. ¡Parecen muy ricas!	*No, thanks, but I would try one of those cookies. They look very good!*

*Some words undergo minor spelling changes when adding the diminutive suffix in order to preserve the original pronunciation:

Words ending in **-co/-ca** and **-go/-ga** change to **qu** and **gu,** respectively:
po**co** → po**quito**, ju**go** → ju**guito**.
Words ending in **-z** change to **-c-:** arroz → arro**cito**, luz → lu**cecita**

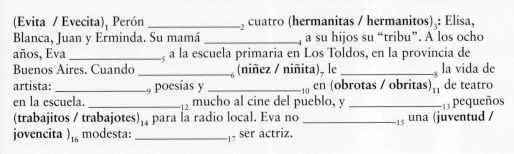

7.1-10 Eva Perón: ¿Una joven como las demás? Lee el siguiente texto sobre Eva Perón, esposa del expresidente de Argentina Juan Perón, y primera dama[12] de Argentina desde 1946 hasta su muerte, en 1952. Completa el texto con los verbos de la lista en imperfecto para saber más sobre sus orígenes, y decide qué forma del diminutivo es la más apropiada.

asistir   gustar   llamar   recitar   participar   querer   ser (x2)   tener   ir   hacer

(**Evita / Evecita**)₁ Perón _____₂ cuatro (**hermanitas / hermanitos**)₃: Elisa, Blanca, Juan y Erminda. Su mamá _____₄ a su hijos su "tribu". A los ocho años, Eva _____₅ a la escuela primaria en Los Toldos, en la provincia de Buenos Aires. Cuando _____₆ (**niñez / niñita**)₇ le _____₈ la vida de artista: _____₉ poesías y _____₁₀ en (**obrotas / obritas**)₁₁ de teatro en la escuela. _____₁₂ mucho al cine del pueblo, y _____₁₃ pequeños (**trabajitos / trabajotes**)₁₄ para la radio local. Eva no _____₁₅ una (**juventud / jovencita**)₁₆ modesta: _____₁₇ ser actriz.

[12]**primera dama:** first lady

▲ *Eva Perón en 1947*

OTRA PERSPECTIVA

Courtesy of Jessie
Jose DeLeon

Juan

¿Qué comer y cuándo?

Diferente

"En Mendoza, cuando yo era chico, siempre cenábamos entre las 9 y las 11 de la noche. Yo estaba muy acostumbrado a comer a esas horas. La primera vez que visité Estados Unidos, recuerdo que fuimos a un restaurante a las 10 de la noche y ¡ya estaba cerrado! No lo podía creer. También la carne asada se prepara de forma diferente en Argentina. En Mendoza, teníamos asadores[13] permanentes en el patio, no como las parrillas móviles de aquí. La carne se cocinaba muy lentamente condimentada con sal y algunas veces un poquito de pimienta, pero eso era todo. Mi papá le ponía chimichurri por encima. Aquí en Estados Unidos se cocina más rápido y pienso que la carne es un poco más seca[14]. En Estados Unidos veo que le ponen mucha, mucha salsa de barbacoa o está muy sazonada[15]. En Argentina la carne es tan buena que no es necesario ponerle muchos condimentos".

Igual

"El almuerzo es más o menos a la misma hora que en Estados Unidos, entre las 12 y la 1. Además, ¡los vinos de California son tan buenos como los de Mendoza!".

Explícale a Juan

1. ¿Por qué cenamos más temprano en Estados Unidos? ¿A qué hora cena tu familia?
2. ¿Por qué generalmente no tenemos asadores permanentes en nuestros patios? ¿Cómo es en tu casa? ¿Cuándo se usa la barbacoa?
3. ¿Te gusta asar[16] la carne? ¿Qué ingredientes y condimentos usas? ¿Le pones salsa a la carne?

MANOS A LA OBRA

7.1-11 ¿Qué comías cuando eras niño/a?

Paso 1: Mira la lista de la sección **Palabra por palabra** y completa la tabla. ¿Qué comías con frecuencia, a veces, raras veces o nunca?

	Con frecuencia	A veces	Raras veces	Nunca
Para desayunar				
Para almorzar				
Para merendar				
Para cenar				

Paso 2: Ahora entrevista a un/a compañero/a de clase para saber qué comía de niño/a.

MODELO: Estudiante 1: *¿Con qué frecuencia comías coliflor?*
  Estudiante 2: *Nunca comía coliflor, ¡no me **gustaba** nada! Pero comía muchas peras.*

[13] **asador/parrilla:** BBQ grill [14] **seco/a:** dry [15] **sazonar:** to season (meats, food) [16] **asar:** to roast, to grill

Paso 3: Escriban un pequeño párrafo para comparar sus dietas de niño/a.

MODELO: *Cuando era niño, con frecuencia* <u>*merendaba*</u> *pan con mantequilla de maní, pero a (nombre del compañero/a) no le* **gustaba.** *Él/Ella* **merendaba** *pan con mantequilla y mermelada... Los dos siempre* <u>*bebíamos*</u>*...*

Ahora, presenten a la clase los párrafos. ¿Qué comían y bebían con frecuencia los dos? ¿Qué no comían nunca? Con toda la clase, decidan: ¿Cuáles son los tres alimentos o bebidas que más les gustan a los niños estadounidenses? ¿Y los que menos les gustan?

7.1-12 Las preferencias en tu dieta

Paso 1: Pregúntale a tus compañeros de clase sobre sus preferencias a la hora de comer. Escribe el nombre del/de la compañero/a que conteste afirmativamente.

MODELO: Estudiante 1: <u>*¿Comes*</u> *yogur todos los días?*
Estudiante 2: *Sí,* <u>*¡me encanta*</u> *el yogur!*

Nombre del/de la compañero/a

¿Quién de la clase...

1. ... quiere llevar una dieta más saludable?   _____
2. ... pierde peso fácilmente?   _____
3. ... desayuna huevos con tocino una vez a la semana?   _____
4. ... prefiere el té al café?   _____
5. ... come frijoles con arroz?   _____
6. ... se sirve dos veces con frecuencia?   _____
7. ... almuerza en la cafetería de la universidad?   _____
8. ... le añade miel al café?   _____
9. ... puede ir a casa para almorzar?   _____
10. ... merienda fruta o frutos secos?   _____

Paso 2: Después, comenta tus resultados con la clase. ¿Fue fácil o difícil completar la actividad?

MODELO: *Parece que nadie de la clase...*

7.1-13 Vamos a hacer una fiesta En grupos de cinco, organicen una fiesta para celebrar... ¡Piensen en un buen motivo! Su profesor/a les va a decir cuánto dinero tienen para la fiesta.

Paso 1: Decidan cuál es el motivo o la ocasión para celebrar la fiesta. Después, organicen el menú y decidan quién va a traer o preparar cada cosa. Incluyan el precio de cada cosa. Tienen que ponerse de acuerdo y no pasarse del presupuesto.

Paso 2: Después, entre todos, escriban su menú para presentar a la clase.

MODELO: *Vamos a hacer una fiesta para celebrar...(nombre del evento). (nombre del/de la compañero/a)* va a traer...

¡La clase va a votar por el mejor menú!

Paso 3: Ahora, entre todos, decidan cuándo y dónde van a celebrar la fiesta.

7.1-14 Un concurso de comidas

Paso 1: Definan qué tipo de concurso de comida quieren hacer. Informen a su profesor/a sobre el tema de su concurso y trabajen en grupos con las personas interesadas en ese tema. Algunos ejemplos pueden ser: (1) ¿Qué chef prepara la mejor comida?
(2) ¿Quién prepara la comida más rápidamente sin la ayuda de un microondas?

Paso 2: Escriban un párrafo para hacerle publicidad a su concurso. Primero piensen en lo siguiente: ¿Qué concursos de comida conocen? ¿Participaron alguna vez en alguno? Ahora decidan:

1. por qué su concurso puede ser interesante y diferente a otros concursos;
2. qué ofrece su concurso comparándolo con otros concursos de comida;
3. las reglas del concurso en detalle: personas que pueden participar, ingredientes permitidos y no permitidos, horarios, privado o público, etc.

No olviden usar el vocabulario y la gramática estudiada en este capítulo (imperfecto y diminutivos).

Paso 3: Tu profesor/a va a escoger a cuatro estudiantes para que formen el jurado[17] con él/ella. Los grupos leen la publicidad del concurso y las reglas para participar. Los miembros del jurado anotan en un papel los puntos que le dan a cada grupo (4: muy bueno, 3: bueno, 2: regular, 1: muy regular). El jurado tiene que tener en cuenta:

1. la originalidad del concurso
2. el uso de vocabulario
3. el uso del pasado y los diminutivos en el contenido del concurso.

El jurado no puede votar por su propio grupo. Cuando todos los grupos presenten la información de sus concursos, una persona del jurado va a contar los puntos para cada grupo. El grupo con más puntos gana.

7.1-15 Presta atención: En la tienda uruguaya de Francisco Escucha el diálogo entre un vendedor y una clienta para averiguar el propósito de la conversación. Después, escucha el diálogo una vez más para indicar si los siguientes enunciados son **Ciertos** o **Falsos**. Si alguno es falso, explica por qué.

C   F

☐   ☐   1. Francisco tiene tomates de la semana pasada.

☐   ☐   2. Doña Marina compra seis kilos de tomates.

☐   ☐   3. Doña Marina tiene que comprar poco.

☐   ☐   4. Francisco no tiene huevos marrones.

☐   ☐   5. Doña Marina compra dieciocho huevos marrones.

☐   ☐   6. El vendedor se sorprende de que la señora compre 30 panes.

☐   ☐   7. Un amigo del hijo de doña Marina cumple años.

☐   ☐   8. El chivito es un plato típico uruguayo.

☐   ☐   9. La compra cuesta cien pesos.

WileyPLUS Go to *WileyPLUS* and listen to **Presta atención.**

7.1-16 Por escrito: Hace cinco años Escribe una breve narración sobre ti y sobre cómo era un día normal hace cinco años. ¿Dónde vivías? ¿Cómo eras físicamente? ¿Cómo era tu personalidad? ¿Dónde comías por la mañana, tarde y noche? ¿Qué comías casi siempre? ¿Qué comida no te gustaba? ¿Qué hacías cada día?

¡OJO!

Connectors

As you have learned in this chapter, in Spanish we use the imperfect tense to talk about habitual actions in the past and describe how life used to be. To make your writing more coherent, use discourse markers to enhance your description of the past: **en aquellos años** (*in those years*), **antes** (*before*), **entonces** (*back then*)...

[17]**jurado:** panel of judges

PONTE EN MI LUGAR

Estrategias para conversar

Keeping the conversation flowing Learn expressions that native speakers use in everyday speech to change the topic, start a sentence, or "buy time" when speaking. Sound as much like a native speaker as possible.

To change topic:
- Hablando de…   *Speaking of…*
- ¡Ah! Antes de que se me olvide…   *Oh! Before I forget…*
- Eso me recuerda a…   *That reminds me…*
- A propósito…   *By the way…*

To start a sentence:
- En este caso…   *In this case…*
- Después de todo…   *After all…*
- Por ahora…   *For now…*
- Por ejemplo…   *For instance…*

To buy time:
- ¡Ah! Quiere/s decir que…   *Oh! You mean…*
- Vamos a ver/A ver/Veamos   *Let's see*

Una invitación Imagina que estás en Uruguay y un amigo uruguayo te invita a su casa para cenar con su familia. Llegas temprano y tu amigo todavía no está en casa. Mientras esperas a tu amigo, conversas con su mamá o su papá. En la conversación, la mamá o el papá quiere saber más sobre ti. Con un/a compañero/a, decidan quién es el padre o la madre y quién es el/la invitado/a[18]. Usen las expresiones de **Estrategias para conversar** para que suene más coloquial e idiomático.

El padre quiere saber más sobre su invitado/a. Comienza la conversación y pregunta por…
- qué le encantaba comer de niño/a.
- qué no le gustaba.
- las comidas que la mamá del/de la invitado/a preparaba.
- las comidas típicas del país.
- las dietas en el país en comparación con Uruguay.

El/La invitado/a…
- contesta las preguntas.
- habla de sus comidas favoritas y típicas de su país.

Prepárense para interpretar la conversación en frente de la clase.

WileyPLUS Go to *WileyPLUS* to find more **Arroba** activities.

Una nueva receta   Escoge de las listas siguientes dos comidas de países diferentes. Después explora en tu buscador favorito recetas auténticas para esas comidas. Toma nota de los ingredientes y de los pasos para prepararla. ¿Qué comida elegiste? ¿Qué ingredientes no tienes en tu cocina? Después, dile a un/a compañero/a el nombre del plato, los ingredientes y decide si quieres preparar ese plato y probarlo.

- Comidas de Argentina: el locro, los chipá, la fainá o la milanesa "a caballo".
- Comidas de Uruguay: el chajá, las tortas fritas o la isla flotante.

[18]invitado/a: guest

ASÍ ES LA VIDA

Chiste

Ya sé por qué engordo[19]... es el champú.
Hoy vi que en la botella dice: "Para dar cuerpo y volumen".
Desde mañana, empiezo a ducharme con el detergente para los platos, que dice:
"Disuelve la grasa. Hasta la más difícil".

Adivina, adivinador

Un señor gordito
muy coloradito
no toma café
siempre toma té.
¿Qué verdura soy?

Fui a la plaza
y las compré bellas,
llegué a mi casa
y lloré con ellas.
¿Qué verdura soy?

© John Wiley & Sons, Inc.

ENTÉRATE

Estrategias para leer

The description A description aims at explaining, in a detailed and organized manner, certain aspects, characteristics, or features of something experienced or known. There are different types of descriptions such as describing a person, an object, or a process. Describing a process requires presenting the phases in order to indicate what happens in each phase and how it happens. In descriptions you can find different grammatical structures: the verbs **ser** and **tener** (to introduce a topic, give a definition, or explain different characteristics of something), or the verbs **ser** or **estar** followed by descriptive adjetives (such as **El pan es redondo; La carne está fría**). Connectors are also used especially when organizing different steps in a process (such as **primero, después, luego, finalmente**). Describing is mostly done in the imperfect tense to express habitual actions or to describe a situation (such as *Comía* **empanadas todos los domingos porque** *eran* **muy ricas**).

Antes de leer

1. ¡A comer! En la siguiente lista, señala con una cruz (x) los alimentos que te gustan. Si alguien de la clase no conoce algún alimento, tu profesor/a va a describirlo en español. Después, descubran cuáles son los tres alimentos favoritos de la clase.

- ☐ la cebolla
- ☐ la carne molida
- ☐ las papas
- ☐ el pimentón
- ☐ el pimiento
- ☐ las olivas
- ☐ los huevos duros
- ☐ el ajo

[19]**engordar:** to get fat

2. ¿Qué ves? Mira el texto, las fotos, el título y las primeras frases de cada párrafo. ¿De qué crees que trata cada párrafo? En tu respuesta, indica qué párrafo describe una situación en el pasado o presenta acciones habituales en el pasado. ¿El primero o el segundo? ¿Qué párrafo indica la descripción de un objeto, el segundo o el tercero? ¿Qué párrafo indica la descripción de un proceso, el segundo o el tercero?

Párrafo 1: _____

Párrafo 2: _____

El último párrafo: _____

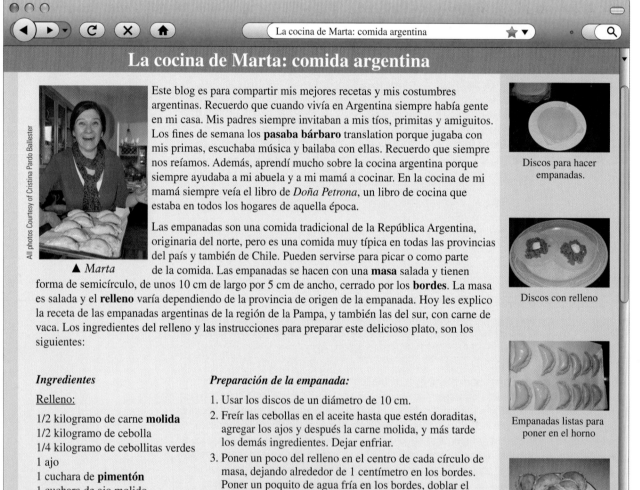

La cocina de Marta: comida argentina

La cocina de Marta: comida argentina

Este blog es para compartir mis mejores recetas y mis costumbres argentinas. Recuerdo que cuando vivía en Argentina siempre había gente en mi casa. Mis padres siempre invitaban a mis tíos, primitas y amiguitos. Los fines de semana los **pasaba bárbaro** translation porque jugaba con mis primas, escuchaba música y bailaba con ellas. Recuerdo que siempre nos reíamos. Además, aprendí mucho sobre la cocina argentina porque siempre ayudaba a mi abuela y a mi mamá a cocinar. En la cocina de mi mamá siempre veía el libro de *Doña Petrona*, un libro de cocina que estaba en todos los hogares de aquella época.

Discos para hacer empanadas.

to have a great time

▲ *Marta*

Las empanadas son una comida tradicional de la República Argentina, originaria del norte, pero es una comida muy típica en todas las provincias del país y también de Chile. Pueden servirse para picar o como parte de la comida. Las empanadas se hacen con una **masa** salada y tienen forma de semicírculo, de unos 10 cm de largo por 5 cm de ancho, cerrado por los **bordes**. La masa es salada y el **relleno** varía dependiendo de la provincia de origen de la empanada. Hoy les explico la receta de las empanadas argentinas de la región de la Pampa, y también las del sur, con carne de vaca. Los ingredientes del relleno y las instrucciones para preparar este delicioso plato, son los siguientes:

Discos con relleno

dough edges filling

Ingredientes

Relleno:

1/2 kilogramo de carne **molida**
1/2 kilogramo de cebolla
1/4 kilogramo de cebollitas verdes
1 ajo
1 cuchara de **pimentón**
1 cuchara de ajo molido
1 cuchara de orégano
3 huevos duros
100 gramos de olivas verdes, **picadas**

Preparación de la empanada:

1. Usar los discos de un diámetro de 10 cm.
2. Freír las cebollas en el aceite hasta que estén doraditas, agregar los ajos y después la carne molida, y más tarde los demás ingredientes. Dejar enfriar.
3. Poner un poco del relleno en el centro de cada círculo de masa, dejando alrededor de 1 centímetro en los bordes. Poner un poquito de agua fría en los bordes, doblar el disco por la mitad y cerrar.
4. Pintar las empanadas con huevo batido. Colocar las empanadas sobre una bandeja con un papel especial para cocinar. Cocinar al horno a 375 °F durante 20 minutos.

¡Buen provecho!

Empanadas listas para poner en el horno

ground

paprika

Empanadas listas para comer.
¡Buen provecho!

diced

All photos Courtesy of Cristina Pardo Ballester

© John Wiley & Sons, Inc.

Después de leer

1. En el texto. Identifica en el texto algunos ejemplos de: (1) verbos en imperfecto, (2) infinitivos, (3) diminutivos, (4) conectores y (5) preposiciones.

2. ¿Entendiste? Después de leer el texto, contesta estas preguntas:

1. ¿Cómo aprendió Marta a cocinar?
2. ¿Qué es el libro de *Doña Petrona*?
3. ¿Qué son las empanadas?
4. ¿De qué zona es la receta que se presenta en el blog?

 # EN TU PROPIAS PALABRAS

Estrategias para escribir

Incorporating location expressions When writing descriptions, it is a good idea to incorporate location expressions in the text. You use these expressions on a daily basis, when you describe where you went, describe a place, give directions to locate something in a specific place, or when you are listing a few things, etc. Some Spanish location expressions are: **al lado de** (*next to*); **dentro de** (*inside of*); **debajo de** (*under*); **en** (*in*); **encima de** (*on top of*); **delante de** (*in front of*); **hasta** (*up to, as far as*). These expressions will help you organize your writing and ensure that the reader understands the location or position of things included in your description.

Which of these sentences is easier to understand?

1. En una provincia del norte, como Salta, tenemos las empanadas salteñas; en el centro, las cordobesas; en el oeste las riojanas; y en la costa sur, las patagónicas.
2. En una provincia del norte como Salta tenemos las empanadas salteñas, las cordobesas en el centro, en el oeste las riojanas y las patagónicas en la costa.

Number 1 is easier because the writer organizes his/her ideas in a logical manner by including location expressions and by being consistent with the use of location expressions (**del norte, en el centro, en el oeste y en la costa sur**).

Tu cocina Acabas de inventar una receta nueva. Escribe una carta a un programa de televisión para compartir tu receta con todo el mundo. Comienza explicando cómo se te ocurrió esa receta y por qué decidiste pensar en una receta nueva. Luego, prepara una lista con los ingredientes de esa comida y los pasos para preparar esa receta en casa. No olvides usar las expresiones de lugar cuando expliques los pasos de la receta para tener una receta organizada (p. ej., *En la carne pongo…*).

▲ *María Pilar cocinando*

Courtesy of María Belén Pardo Ballester

AUTOPRUEBA

VOCABULARIO

I. Programa para perder peso El hotel Termas de Río Hondo, en la provincia de Santiago del Estero, Argentina, ofrece varios tratamientos de salud. Consulta la pirámide alimenticia de la actividad 7.1-05 y elabora un menú para este programa con los alimentos de la sección de **Palabra por palabra**. Incluye tres alimentos en cada comida, excepto en la merienda.

	Desayuno	Almuerzo	Merienda	Cena
Viernes				
Sábado				
Domingo				

II. Fuera de lugar Encierra en un círculo la palabra que no pertenece al grupo.

1. chorizo / pera / chuleta / bistec
2. fresas / duraznos / plátanos / miel
3. pavo / espinaca / coliflor / pimiento
4. frijoles / tomates / almejas / zanahorias
5. té / café / maní / jugo
6. lechuga / langosta / ajo / cebolla
7. camarones / pescado / tocino / calamares

GRAMÁTICA

I. Cuando estaba en la escuela secundaria... Usa los verbos de la lista para hablar de las dietas de estas personas cuando tú estabas en la escuela secundaria.

> merendar almorzar beber comer desayunar
> cocinar preparar

1. En la escuela, yo...
2. En casa, yo...
3. Mis padres...
4. Mi mejor amigo/a y yo...
5. En casa, mi familia...
6. Yo...

II. Recuerdos de mi familia chilena Jesse pasó un verano con una familia chilena. Ahora recuerda las comidas que su mamá chilena le preparaba. Completa el párrafo con los verbos en el imperfecto.

> cenar ser (2x) gustar estar cocinar decir

Carla me _____₁ humitas, que es un plato del sur de Chile. Mi mamá chilena me _____₂ que las humitas se comen en el verano y que se parecen al tamal mexicano. ¡_____₃ deliciosas! El relleno _____₄ de choclo y cebolla. El charquicán _____₅ otro plato que me _____₆ mucho. El charquicán es un plato de los indígenas mapuches[20], que tiene verduras. Normalmente nosotros _____₇ a las nueve y media de la noche.

III. El menú del chef Adolfo Marta quiere celebrar el cumpleaños de su hija pequeña y le pide ayuda a su amigo Adolfo. Lee la conversación entre Adolfo y Marta y usa los diminutivos para completar el diálogo.

Marta: Adolfo, necesito tu ayuda para preparar el menú para la fiesta de cumpleaños de mi hija (Luisa) _____₁. Quiero invitar a almorzar a todas sus (amigas) _____₂ y a todos sus (primos) _____₃.

Adolfo: Puedes empezar con unas (empanadas) _____₄, y después servirles unos (platos) _____₅ de pollo con verduras. Para los adultos, si te parece bien, podrías preparar un pavo al horno con (papas) _____₆ a la crema. Y de postre, para los niños, unos (chocolates) _____₇ y para los mayores, unas (galletas) _____₈ de limón.

Marta: Me parece espléndido, Adolfo. Mil gracias. ¿Por qué no te vienes tú también, con Margarita y los chicos?

CULTURA

1. ¿Qué comidas son típicas de Argentina?
2. ¿Qué bebidas toma la gente por lo general en Argentina y Uruguay?
3. ¿A qué hora se acostumbra cenar en Argentina?

REDACCIÓN

Escribe dos párrafos describiendo algunos aspectos de tu infancia. ¿Cómo eras de niño/a? ¿Dónde vivías? ¿Qué te gustaba comer? ¿Qué te gustaba beber? ¿Te gustaba la escuela? ¿Qué almorzabas en la escuela? ¿Qué hacías después de la escuela? ¿Tenías hermanos y hermanas? ¿Lo pasaban bien?

EN RESUMIDAS CUENTAS, AHORA PUEDO...

☐ hablar sobre comida.
☐ hablar sobre alimentos en el pasado y en el presente.
☐ hablar de cómo eran las cosas antes.
☐ expresar tamaño y afecto con el diminutivo.
☐ comentar diferencias regionales en las comidas.

---

[20]**indígenas mapuches:** group of indigenous people who live in south-central Chile and southwestern Argentina

VOCABULARIO ESENCIAL

Sustantivos

el ajo	*garlic*
el alimento	*food*
la almeja	*clam*
el almuerzo	*lunch*
el arroz	*rice*
el asado/la parrillada	*BBQ*
el bistec/bife	*beef steak*
el camarón	*shrimp*
la carne (de res/vaca)	*(beef) meat*
la cebolla	*onion*
la cena	*dinner*
el chorizo	*sausage*
la chuleta (de cerdo/puerco)	*(pork) chop*
el desayuno	*breakfast*
el durazno/melocotón (Esp.)	*peach*
la fresa/la frutilla (Arg.)	*strawberry*
el frijol	*bean*
el fruto seco	*nut*
la galleta/galletita	*cookie or cracker*
la grasa	*fat*
el huevo	*egg*
el jugo (de naranja)	*(orange) juice*
la langosta	*lobster*
la leche (de soja)	*(soy) milk*
la lechuga	*lettuce*
la legumbre	*legume*
el maíz/choclo (Am. del S.)	*corn*
el maní	*peanut*
la mantequilla	*butter*
la manzana	*apple*
el marisco	*seafood*
la merienda	*afternoon snack*
la miel	*honey*
la naranja/toronja	*orange*

el pan	*bread*
la papa/patata (Esp.)	*potato*
el pavo	*turkey*
la pera	*pear*
el pescado	*fish*
el pimiento	*bell pepper*
la piña/el ananá (Am. del S.)	*pineapple*
el plátano/la banana	*banana*
el pollo	*chicken*
el queso	*cheese*
la receta	*recipe*
la sandía	*watermelon*
el té	*tea*
el tocino	*bacon*
la uva	*grape*
la verdura	*vegetables*
la zanahoria	*carrot*

Cognados: el brócoli, el café, el calamar, el cereal, la coliflor, la dieta, la espinaca, la fruta, el limón, el mango, la pasta, el salmón, el tomate, el yogur

Verbos

desayunar	*to have breakfast*
merendar (ie)	*to have an afternoon snack*
picar	*to snack*

Cognados: preparar

Expresiones

¿Quieres algo de tomar/picar?	*Would you like something to drink/a snack?*

Adjetivos

dulce	*sweet*
graso/a	*fat/fatty*
picante	*hot*
saludable	*healthy*

LEARNING OBJECTIVES

By the end of this section you will be able to:

- Follow and write recipes
- How to interact in a restaurant
- Give instructions in formal situations
- Make impersonal statements
- Use **vos** to talk to other people
- Use **tener** in different expressions
- Be familiar with the traditional Chilean cuisine

Una imagen vale más que mil palabras

¿Qué ingredientes puedes ver en el churrasco italiano?

¿Qué piensas de la cantidad?

Si estás en Chile, ¿pides este plato?

Courtesy of Norma Lopez-Burton

▲ *El churrasco italiano es muy popular en Chile.*

UNA PERSPECTIVA

Courtesy of Norma Lopez-Burton

Philip

Tipos de comida

Diferente

"Andaba un día por la Plaza de Armas, en Santiago, cuando vi que había muchas tiendas, puestos y restaurantes pequeños. Unos puestos vendían *mote con huesito*, que es una bebida típica dulce y rica. En varios restaurantes vendían pizza. ¡Qué pizzas tan curiosas! La pizza en Chile es diferente porque se ponen muchos ingredientes que son grandes y casi no se ve el queso. Además, el pan es muy grueso[1]. Había pizzas con carne de vaca, mariscos, verduras, etc. Eran muy diferentes a las pizzas que se conocen en Estados Unidos".

Igual

"Debido a la gran influencia de la inmigración europea en Chile, hay mucha comida italiana y alemana. Se come mucha pasta con pan, carne y mariscos. Como en muchos países hoy en día, hay una gran variedad de comidas para los distintos gustos de los chilenos, pero la comida italiana es una de las más populares, igual que en Estados Unidos".

 ¿Qué piensas tú?

1. ¿Hay restaurantes de otras culturas en tu vecindario o en tu ciudad? ¿Te gustan? ¿Cuál es tu favorito?
2. ¿Cómo varía la popularidad de los tipos de comida según la geografía de Estados Unidos? Menciona algunas diferencias en los hábitos alimenticios dentro de Estados Unidos.
3. ¿Crees que eres aventurero/a con la comida? ¿Te gusta probar comida nueva?

[1]**grueso:** thick

LA PURA VERDAD I   Un restaurante chileno

Antonia Morales es de Puerto Rico y su amigo, Ariel, es de Estados Unidos. Los dos son turistas en Chile. Ariel está aprendiendo español.

1.

¿Tienen una reservación? ¿Dónde prefieren sentarse?

¿Qué es la ensalada de palta?²

No sé.

¿Qué es "a lo pobre"?

No sé.

¿Qué es el chupe?

No sé.

¿Qué es la paila marina?

No sé.

2.

Pero, hablas español, ¿no?

¡Pues, eso pensaba, pero ahora no sé!

3.

¿Qué es el chupe?

Es un plato de mariscos.

¿Qué es la paila marina?

Es una sopa de mariscos.

¿Qué es "a lo pobre"?

Una comida con dos huevos fritos encima.

4.

Yo voy a probar la paila marina.

Quisiera la ensalada de palta y el bistec a lo pobre.

5.

Gracias. ¿Me puede traer más agua mineral?

¡Buen provecho!

6.

Una amiga chilena me dijo que la propina en Chile no es un porcentaje fijo como en Estados Unidos.

No sé cuánto debemos dejar de propina. ¿Qué tal 15% o 20%?

© John Wiley & Sons, Inc.

7.2-01 ¿Qué pasa en un restaurante? Escucha la narración y decide qué artículos no corresponden.

1. _____   _____
2. _____   _____
3. _____   _____

²**palta:** (Arg., Chile, Perú y Ur.) avocado

PALABRA POR PALABRA

En el restaurante

el/la mesero/a, camarero/a, mozo/a
la servilleta
la taza
los cubiertos
el vaso
la copa
la cuchara
el tenedor
la sal
el plato
la pimienta
el cuchillo
el mantel
la cuenta   el menú/la carta   la propina   el plato hondo

© John Wiley & Sons, Inc.

Para hablar de la comida

¡Buen provecho!	*Enjoy your meal!*
¿Desea/n algo de comer/tomar?	*Would you like something to eat/to drink?*
¿Me podría traer...?	*Could you bring me. . .?*
¿Qué quiere/s comer/beber?	*What do you want to eat/drink?*
¡Qué rico!	*How delicious!*
¿Qué trae...?	*What comes with. . .?*
frito/a	*fried*
el aceite	*oil*
el aderezo	*dressing*
la comida chatarra/basura	*junk food*
la especia	*spice*
la mayonesa	*mayonnaise*
la mostaza	*mustard*
el vinagre	*vinegar*
hacer una reservación/reserva	*to book a table*
ordenar/pedir (e>i)	*to order*
pagar la cuenta	*pay the bill*
para llevar	*to go*
poner la mesa	*to set the table*

Palermo Viejo

Primer plato
(First course/Appetizer)

Ensalada
(salad)
Empanadas de carne
(turnover filled with meat)
Empanadas de queso
(turnover filled with cheese)
Empanadas de mariscos
(turnover filled with seafood)

Segundo plato
(Main course/Entrée)

Churrasco italiano
(steak, avocado, mayonaise and tomato sandwich)
Pescado frito
(fried fish)
Pollo asado
(roasted chicken)

Acompañamientos
(Side dishes)

Papas fritas
(French fries)
Sopa del día
(soup of the day)

Postres
(Desserts)

Flan
(sweet custard)
Helado
(ice cream)
Torta
(cake)
Pastel
(pie)
Ensalada de fruta
(fruit salad)

Bebidas
(Beverages)

Agua mineral
(spring water)
Agua con gas
(sparkling water)
Refrescos
(soft drinks)
Vinos
(wines)
Cerveza
(beer)

© John Wiley & Sons, Inc.

A cocinar *Cooking*

la fuente
la olla
el caldero
la sartén
la cacerola

© John Wiley & Sons, Inc.

agregar	*to add*
añadir	*to add*
asar	*to roast, to grill*
calentar (>ie)	*to heat up*
cortar	*to cut*
cubrir/tapar	*to cover*
freír (>i)	*to fry*
hervir (>ie)	*to boil*
hornear	*to bake*
mezclar	*to mix*
pelar	*to peel*
picar	*to dice*
probar (>ue)	*to taste, to try (food)*
seguir una receta	*to follow a recipe*

¿Qué dicen los chilenos?

Voy <u>al tiro.</u>	*I am going <u>right away.</u>*
Él es <u>un cabro</u> de 10 años.	*He is a 10-year-old <u>kid</u>.*
Me duele la <u>guata</u>.	*I have a <u>stomach</u> ache.*
Yo como <u>harta</u> carne.	*I eat <u>a lot</u> of meat.*
¡<u>Caen</u> <u>patos asados</u>!	*<u>It's so hot!</u> (Lit., <u>Roasted ducks are falling</u> from the sky.)*

7.2-02 Fuera de lugar Estudia las siguientes listas y decide cuál es el elemento que no corresponde.

1. taza, vaso, plato hondo, copa, mantel
2. aceite, aderezo, especia, cuchara, mostaza
3. servilleta, mantel, copa, tenedor, cacerola
4. olla, cubiertos, caldero, sartén, fuente
5. jugo, té, pimienta, refresco, vino
6. cuchillo, helado, flan, pastel, torta

7.2-03 ¿Qué es? Lean las definiciones y busquen la palabra correspondiente en la sección **Palabra por palabra**.

_____ 1. Es un recipiente grande que usamos para poner la comida o servir la ensalada.

_____ 2. Es un recipiente grande de metal donde se calienta la sopa u otras comidas.

_____ 3. Es una bebida con gas que tiene diferentes sabores, como fresa, limón, etc.

_____ 4. Es un recipiente de metal que usamos para freír comida.

_____ 5. Es un cubierto que usamos para cortar la carne.

_____ 6. Es una pieza de tela³ que se pone sobre la mesa cuando vamos a comer.

_____ 7. Es un líquido graso con el que preparamos aderezos para ensaladas.

_____ 8. Es una cantidad de dinero que dejamos para el mesero cuando pagamos la cuenta.

³**tela:** fabric

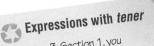

Expressions with _tener_

In Chapter 3, Section 1, you learned the present tense of the irregular verb **tener**. You also learned some fixed expressions with **tener** that can't be translated literally and usually translate as _to be_ + adjective. Do you remember some of these expressions? Take a minute to generate a list and see how many you remember. Then go to p. 108 to check if you remembered them all.

Paso 2: Ahora, elijan tres palabras de la sección **Palabra por palabra** y escriban tres definiciones para leerlas a la clase. ¡Atención! Recuerden que para definir siempre usamos el verbo _ser_.

MODELO: _Es un/a… que…_

7.2-04 ¿Qué comemos?

Paso 1: ¿Qué comes o bebes en estas situaciones? Piensa en dos o tres productos para cada situación.

a. Al mediodía tienes prisa porque solo tienes 10 minutos para llegar a tu clase.
b. Te despiertas muy temprano para ir al trabajo y tienes sueño. No quieres preparar nada complicado.
c. Estás en otro país y tienes miedo de probar platos o comidas nuevas.
d. Tienes sed y tienes mucho calor, pero te duele un poco el estómago.
e. Tienes ganas de comer torta, pero estás a dieta.
f. Tienes frío y te duele la garganta.
g. Tienes mucha hambre, pero tu refrigerador está vacío y no tienes mucho dinero.

Paso 2: En grupos, comenten sus respuestas. ¿Coincides con tus compañeros? Después, decidan qué es mejor comer o beber en estas situaciones.

MODELO: Estudiante 1:   _Cuando tengo prisa, yo siempre compro una barra de granola y un café para llevar._
Estudiante 2:   _Sí, eso es buena idea. Yo a veces compro una ensalada para llevar…_

Paso 3: Presenten sus ideas a la clase. ¿Están todos de acuerdo?

7.2-05 ¿Qué prefieres?

Paso 1: Lee las siguientes preguntas y añade una pregunta más a la lista. Después, entrevista a un/a compañero/a para saber más sobre sus preferencias en materia de comidas.

1. ¿Sabes cocinar? ¿Cocinas con frecuencia o prefieres comer fuera?
2. ¿Qué plato preparas muy bien? ¿Cómo o dónde aprendiste la receta de este plato?
3. ¿Qué te gusta más comer y beber en una fiesta? ¿Qué comidas y bebidas les sirves a tus invitados en una fiesta? ¿Compras comida preparada?
4. ¿Cuáles son tus restaurantes favoritos? ¿Qué tipos de restaurantes son? ¿Cuántas veces a la semana comes en un restaurante?
5. ¿Pones la mesa cuando vas a comer? ¿Qué artículos o cubiertos pones siempre? ¿Cuáles no pones nunca?
6. ¿Qué desayunas, almuerzas o cenas normalmente? ¿Cuál es tu postre favorito?
7. ¿Comes comida rápida, comida chatarra o comida preparada? ¿Cuándo y con qué frecuencia? ¿Qué pides de acompañamineto?
8. Cuando vas a un restaurante, ¿pides siempre un primer y un segundo plato? ¿O un solo plato? ¿Compartes algún plato?
9. …

Paso 2: Después, escriban un pequeño informe. ¿En qué aspectos coinciden los dos? ¿En qué no coinciden?

MODELO: _Mi compañero/a y yo tenemos preferencias muy diferentes. A mí me encanta cocinar y… sin embargo, él/ella…_

Paso 3: Por último, presenten a la clase el informe. ¿Coinciden en todo o en nada? ¿En qué aspecto no coincide nadie?

HABLANDO DE GRAMÁTICA I

1. Giving instructions: Formal commands

You have already seen command forms (also know as the *imperative* mood) in the instructions for activities. In Spanish there are two sets of commands. Formal commands (**los mandatos formales**) are used when you want to give instructions or directions to people with whom you have a formal relationship—those you would normally address as **usted**. Informal commands, which you will learn in Chapter 10, are used with people you would address as **tú**.

Formal commands are formed by dropping the ending of the first person singular form in the present tense indicative (e.g., **-o** or **-oy** in the **yo** form) and adding the opposite theme vowel. That is, verbs ending in **-ar** add **-e/n**, verbs ending in **-er** and **-ir** add **-a/n**.

> Si van a Montevideo, **cenen** en el restaurante Francis y **pidan** el salmón. ¡Es lo mejor del menú! Para terminar, **prueben** el tiramisú.
>
> *If you go to Montevideo, have dinner at Restaurant Francis and order the salmon. It is the best thing on the menu! At the end of the meal, try the tiramisu.*

WileyPLUS Go to *WileyPLUS* to review this grammar point with the help of the **Animated Grammar Tutorial** and the **Verb Conjugator**.

infinitive	yo form	usted (singular formal command)	ustedes (plural formal command)
prepar**ar**	prepar**o**	prepar**e**	prepar**en**
calent**ar** (e>ie) *to heat up*	calient**o**	calient**e**	calient**en**
com**er**	com**o**	com**a**	com**an**
remov**er** (o>ue) *to stir up*	remuev**o**	remuev**a**	remuev**an**
añad**ir**	añad**o**	añad**a**	añad**an**
ped**ir** (e>i) *to order*	pid**o**	pid**a**	pid**an**
-ar verbs → add **-e** (**usted**) or **-en** (**ustedes**) **-er**, **-ir** verbs → add **-a** (**usted**) or **-an** (**ustedes**)			

Verbs ending in **-car**, **-gar**, and **-zar** undergo a spelling change to **-qu**, **-gu**, **-c**, in order to maintain the original pronunciation.

infinitive	yo form	usted (singular formal command)	ustedes (plural formal command)
agregar	agreg**o**	agre**gu**e	agre**gu**en
picar	pic**o**	pi**qu**e	pi**qu**en
almorzar	almuerz**o**	almuer**c**e	almuer**c**en

Estar, ir, and **ser** have irregular command forms.

estar	→	esté/n	**Esté** tranquilo. Ya viene su comida. *Don't worry. Your meal is coming.*
ir	→	vaya/n	No **vayan** al restaurante La fogata. El servicio es muy malo. *Don't go to the restaurant La fogata. Service is very bad.*
ser	→	sea/n	¡No **sea** tímido y pruebe platos nuevos! *Don't be shy! Try new dishes.*

The formal command of **dar** is **dé** and it takes a written accent to distinguish it from the preposition **de.**

> En Chile, Argentina y Uruguay, **dé** la propina que usted piense que merece el servicio.
>
> *In Chile, Argentina, and Uruguay, leave the tip that you think the service deserves.*

Formal commands with pronouns

Direct, indirect, and reflexive pronouns are attached at the end of the affirmative command forms.

Mézclelo varias veces.   *Stir <u>it</u> several times.*

Después, **agréguele*** una pizca de sal.   *Then add a pinch of salt <u>to it</u>.*

*There is a written accent when the stress falls on the third-to-last syllable.

In negative command forms, the pronoun precedes the verb.

No **se sienten** aquí, por favor, aquella   *Don't sit here, please, that table*
mesa es mejor.   *is better.*

No **le pidan** la cuenta aún; vamos a pedir   *Do not ask him for the bill yet; we're*
postre primero.   *going to order dessert first.*

 7.2-06 Nuestra comunidad recomienda... Lee este foro de recomendaciones de restaurantes de Santiago de Chile.

¿Quiere publicar anuncios de su restaurante? Contáctenos.	Ver todos los anuncios

Comer en Santiago ★ ★ ★ ★ ★

<u>Explore</u> los mejores restaurantes de Santiago. El restaurante Portada de Sol ofrece los mejores platos de la comida peruana. No sea tímido y pruebe una de las especialidades de la casa, o déjese llevar por las recomendaciones de la dueña. Dé una buena propina porque la atención y el servicio también son buenísimos. En el barrio Brasil, vaya al restaurante Las Vacas Gordas; sirven las mejores carnes. Llame antes de ir y haga una reserva, porque siempre está lleno. Si va con su pareja, reserven la mesa frente al balcón, es muy romántico. Admire la bellísima decoración: es verdaderamente original. Para beber, pida el pisco sour, que es excelente. De postre, el flan es muy recomendable. ¡Buen provecho!

Paso 1: Escribe todos los mandatos formales que hay en el texto (son once en total). ¡Atención! No todos los verbos del texto son mandatos. Después indica cuál es el infinitivo de cada mandato.

MODELO: 1. *Explore* (explorar)

2. _____   7. _____
3. _____   8. _____
4. _____   9. _____
5. _____   10. _____
6. _____   11. _____

Paso 2: ¿A cuál de estos dos restaurantes prefieres ir y por qué?

Paso 3: Escribe una pequeña entrada para un foro de recomendaciones de restaurantes de tu ciudad. Recomienda qué deben beber, comer o hacer los clientes. En tus recomendaciones, utiliza por lo menos seis de los siguientes verbos en la forma de mandato.

pedir   ordenar   tomar   beber   dar   hacer
hacer una reservación   sentarse   atreverse   ir

7.2-07 Los buenos modales[4] en la mesa ¿Conoces las reglas básicas de los buenos modales en la mesa? Completa las siguientes reglas con mandatos formales. Sustituye las palabras subrayadas con el pronombre de objeto directo o indirecto que corresponda.

> dejar   lavarse   hablar   hacer   terminar   limpiarse   tocar   usar (x2)   poner

1. _____1 las manos antes de comer. Las manos siempre deben estar limpias para tomar los cubiertos y los vasos.

2. _____2 la servilleta desdoblada sobre sus piernas. _____3 exclusivamente para limpiarse los labios y los dedos.

3. No _____4 con la boca llena y no _____5 ruido al comer.

4. Antes de beber, _____6 de comer la comida que tiene en la boca y _____7 los labios con la servilleta.

5. No _____8 los alimentos que no va a comer. Si toca un alimento, no _____9 en la fuente para otras personas.

6. No _____10 sus cubiertos para servirse alimentos de las fuentes que son para todos.

Paso 2: ¿Son estas reglas básicas las mismas que en Estados Unidos? ¿Hay alguna regla que sea diferente? Añade tres reglas más a esta lista de buenos modales en la mesa en Estados Unidos.

7.2-08 ¿Quién lo dice? Antonia y Ariel, los personajes de **La pura verdad,** están en el Restaurante Pomaire.

Paso 1: Indica si las siguientes oraciones las dice el mesero (M), o Antonia o Ariel, los clientes (C).

M   C

☐   ☐   1. Tráiganos la cuenta, por favor.

☐   ☐   2. ¿Quiere mi opinión? Pídalo "a lo pobre".

☐   ☐   3. Pasen por aquí, señores.

☐   ☐   4. Siéntense en esta mesa; es la mejor.

☐   ☐   5. Déjenos el menú unos minutitos más, gracias.

☐   ☐   6. Prueben la paila marina, está exquisita.

☐   ☐   7. Qué rico. Sírvanos un poco más de vino, por favor.

Paso 2: Imaginen que están en su restaurante favorito. Decidan cuál es el restaurante y escriban cinco oraciones para el camarero usando mandatos formales.

---

[4]**modales:** manners

LA PURA VERDAD II   Pescado en escabeche

Victoria quiere aprender a cocinar un plato chileno sin carne. La señora de la casa le enseña a cocinar pescado en escabeche[5].

1.

2.

Ingredientes

Una taza de vinagre blanco,   Harina
½ taza de agua   ½ tazade aceite de oliva
Una cucharadita de pimienta   Una cebolla grande
4 hojas de laurel   Una zanahoria
½ cucharadita[6] de sal   ½ pepino verde
4 filetes de pescado blanco

3.

1. Se pone el agua, el vinagre, la pimienta, las hojas de laurel en una olla.
2. Se hierve por dos minutos.
3. Se quita del fuego y se deja enfriar.

4.

4. Se añaden sal y pimienta a los filetes.
5. Se cubren con harina.

5.

6. Se calienta el aceite en una sartén grande.
7. Se frien los filetes de pescado por 4 minutos por cada lado.

6.

8. Se pelan la cebolla y la zanahoria.
9. Se pican la cebolla, el pepino y la zanahoria.

7.

¡Qué rico!

10. Se agrega el líquido al pescado.
11. Se pone en el refrigerador de 8 a 24 horas.

8.

7.2-09 Pescado en escabeche Victoria quiere hacer la receta del pescado en escabeche para sus amigos. Escucha el procedimiento y corrige las tres instrucciones que no están bien.

1. _____
2. _____
3. _____

[5]**pescado en escabeche:** marinated fish [6]**cucharadita:** teaspoon

HABLANDO DE GRAMÁTICA II

2. Making impersonal statements and deemphasizing authorship: Impersonal and passive se

WileyPLUS Go to *WileyPLUS* to review this grammar point with the help of the **Animated Grammar Tutorial.**

You already know the pronoun **se** as a reflexive pronoun for third person singular (**él, ella, usted**) or plural (**ellos, ellas, ustedes**) in sentences such as **Ella se mira en el espejo.** In this section you will learn about the use of **se** to deemphasize authorship. When talking about activities for which the subject is unknown, general, nonspecific, or just not the focus of the event, Spanish uses impersonal or passive **se.**

There is not an exact equivalent to the impersonal **se** in English. Instead, there are different ways of expressing impersonality in English, such as with the nonspecific subjects *people, they, you,* or *one.* Consider the following statements:

> *People in Argentina eat late.*
> *They eat late in Argentina.*
> *One eats late in Argentina.*

Spanish speakers use the impersonal **se** to express the same concept.

> *En Argentina **se** cena tarde.*

The impersonal **se** is always used with the verb in the third person singular in the present tense:

En Chile **se come** mucho en restaurantes.	*People eat in restaurants a lot in Chile.*
En Uruguay **se come** de maravilla, y además es barato.	*They eat very well in Uruguay, and it is also cheap!*

Passive se (se pasivo)

Passive sentences in English[7] are usually translated using passive **se.** The verb following passive **se** can be either singular or plural if it refers to a plural noun. In passive **se** constructions the verb can appear in any tense.

En Chile **se cultivan** más de veinte especies diferentes de manzanas.	*More than twenty different types of apples are grown in Chile.*
En el siglo XIX **se plantaron** viñedos franceses en las regiones cercanas a Santiago.	*In the nineteenth century, French vineyards were planted in the regions near Santiago.*

7.2-10 Cocina chilena Lee la descripción de estos platos chilenos.

▲ *El ajiaco*

El ajiaco no es un plato original chileno, también <u>se cocina</u> en otros países de América Latina, pero se come por todo el país. Generalmente se prepara con las sobras[8] de carne de un gran asado. En el caldo[9] de la carne asada se agregan papas, cebollas picadas, ají[10], perejil, sal, pimienta, comino y orégano. Esta deliciosa sopa ayuda a componer el cuerpo y da energía para ir al trabajo o para seguir disfrutando el evento que se celebra.

---

[7] *Passive sentences in English are formed using the verb* **to be** *+ past participle, such as* Fresh produce is sold here, *or* Several languages are spoken in México. [8] **sobras:** left overs [9] **caldo:** broth [10] **ají:** chili

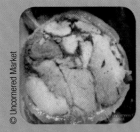

© Uncomered Market

Para el arrollado se utilizan la pulpa y el tocino del cerdo, ajo, pimienta y comino a gusto, se enrolla todo en piel de cerdo. Se forma un cilindro, se pincela con salsa de ají y se cocina luego en un caldo. Cuando los invitados comienzan a llegar, ya se huele el sabroso aroma de esta preparación. Es un plato que se prepara para celebrar las Fiestas Patrias[11] del 18 de septiembre.

▲ *Arrollado huaso*

Pablo Neruda le dedicó una oda y lo hizo famoso, especialmente en Isla Negra, donde el poeta tenía una de sus casas. Sin embargo, el caldillo se sirve en toda la costa central de Chile. Se toma como primer plato porque no es nada pesado[12]. Se hace de diferentes maneras, pero siempre se presenta muy caliente. Se combina con almejas, además de un buen vino blanco.

James Strange / Flickr / Getty Images

▲ *Caldillo de congrio*

Paso 1: Anota todas las formas del *se pasivo* que encuentres en el texto (son diecisiete en total). ¡Atención! Después indica cuál es el sustantivo al que se refiere el verbo.

MODELO: 1. *se cocina* (el ajiaco)

2. _____
3. _____
4. _____
5. _____
6. _____
7. _____
8. _____
9. _____

10. _____
11. _____
12. _____
13. _____
14. _____
15. _____
16. _____
17. _____

Paso 2: ¿Cuál de estos tres platos te gusta más y por qué?

Paso 3: Escribe una pequeña descripción de un plato que siempre comes con tu familia. Indica cuándo se come, cómo se sirve, con qué se sirve, etc. En grupos de cuatro, cada estudiante lee su descripción al grupo. El resto del grupo tiene que adivinar qué plato es.

7.2-11 ¿Dónde se hace...?

Paso 1: Indica si las siguientes actividades se hacen en el supermercado (S), el restaurante (R) o la cocina (C).

_____ 1. Se cortan las verduras.

_____ 2. Se deja propina.

_____ 3. Se lavan los platos.

_____ 4. Se paga en la caja.

_____ 5. Se pide la carta al camarero.

_____ 6. Se usan diferentes tenedores para cada plato.

_____ 7. Se pide la cuenta.

_____ 8. Se va con la lista de la compra.

Paso 2: Ahora piensa en un lugar y escribe cinco oraciones de actividades que se hacen en ese lugar.

Paso 3: Lee la descripción a tus compañeros de grupo. Ellos tienen que adivinar qué lugar es.

---

[11] Las **Fiestas Patrias** se celebran para conmemorar la formación de Chile como un estado o nación independiente de España
[12] pesado: heavy

Courtesy of Elizabeth Jara

Isabel

El arte de cocinar

Diferente

"Viví en Estados Unidos tres años y una cosa que observé fue que mis amigos estadounidenses no cocinaban mucho. Mientras yo preparaba sopas y guisos[13], ellos comían comida ya preparada, como pizza congelada[14], taquitos congelados o verduras congeladas. También compraban comida semi-preparada, como fideos[15] ramen, o macarrones con queso. Para 'preparar' estos platos solo tienes que añadir leche, mantequilla o agua. Las salsas para los espaguetis y la salsa de 'barbacoa', como la llaman en Estados Unidos, estaban ya preparadas también. ¿Por qué prefieren comer comidas preparadas a cocinar?".

Igual

"A la gente joven le gusta comer afuera y a veces también les gusta comer comida rápida o preparada. No toda la comida rápida es buena para la salud, pero a los jóvenes eso no les importa mucho. Lo importante es disfrutar y pasar el rato con los amigos".

Explícale a Isabel

1. ¿Con qué frecuencia cocinas? ¿Con qué frecuencia compras o comes comidas preparadas? ¿todos los días, casi todos los días, a veces, casi nunca, nunca…?
2. ¿Por qué no se cocina mucho en Estados Unidos? Selecciona una o varias razones y explica por qué.
   a. Porque cocinar toma mucho tiempo.
   b. Porque somos muy eficientes.
   c. Porque no somos buenos cocineros.
   d. Porque preferimos las comidas preparadas.
   e. Porque no nos gusta cocinar.
   f. Porque es más fácil comprar algo hecho.
   g. ¿Otra razón?
3. ¿Te gusta cocinar? ¿Qué te gusta cocinar?

MANOS A LA OBRA

7.2-12 ¿Qué preferís? Vas a viajar a Uruguay durante tus próximas vacaciones. Te vas a quedar en casa de una amiga y su familia, y quieres practicar el *voseo* porque lo vas a usar todo el tiempo.

Paso 1: Modifica las preguntas de la actividad 7.2-05 cambiando las formas del verbo a la forma de *vos*. Recuerda que la forma de *vos* está basada en la forma de *vosotros*.

MODELO: ¿Cocinas con frecuencia?
         → ¿*Cocinás con frecuencia?*

1. ¿ _____ (Saber)₁ cocinar? ¿Preferís comer fuera?
2. ¿Qué plato _____ (preparar)₂ muy bien? ¿Cómo o dónde aprendiste la receta de este plato?

[13]**guiso:** stew [14]**congelado/a:** frozen [15]**fideos:** noodles

The *vos* form of address

In Chapter 2, Section 1, you learned about the vos form of address. The use of **vos** as a form of address is known as **voseo**. In Argentina, Paraguay, and Uruguay (among other countries), vos is used instead of tú, and it has its own corresponding conjugated form in the present tense. If you travel to these countries you will have to be able to use this form. Do you remember how to conjugate the vos form of a verb? Consider the following examples:

—¿**Querés** algo de comer?

—No, pero si me **ofrecés** un cafecito, te lo acepto.

Go to p. 68 to check if you were correct on how to conjugate the **vos** form.

3. ¿Qué comidas y bebidas les _____ (servir)$_3$ a tus invitados en una fiesta? ¿ _____ (Comprar)$_4$ comida preparada?

4. ¿Cuáles son tus restaurantes favoritos? ¿Qué tipos de restaurante son? ¿Cuántas veces a la semana _____ (comer)$_5$ en un restaurante?

5. ¿_____ (Poner)$_6$ la mesa cuando vas a comer? ¿Qué artículos o cubiertos siempre _____ (poner)$_7$?

6. ¿Qué _____ (desayunar)$_8$, _____ (almorzar)$_9$ o _____ (cenar)$_{10}$ normalmente? ¿Qué _____ (pedir)$_{11}$ siempre de acompañamiento? ¿Cuál es tu postre favorito?

Paso 2: Ahora, practica la forma de vos. Entrevista a otro/a compañero/a y anota sus respuestas. Luego, escribe un pequeño párrafo para describir similitudes y diferencias entre los dos compañeros que entrevistaste en las dos actividades.

MODELO: *Los dos saben cocinar, pero _____ (nombre) prefiere… y _____ (nombre) prefiere…*

Paso 3: Por último, informen a la clase. ¿Coinciden en todo o en nada? ¿En qué aspecto no coincide nadie?

7.2-13 ¿Quién aquí…?

Paso 1: Levántate y hazles a tus compañeros las siguientes preguntas. Escribe el nombre del/de la compañero/a que conteste afirmativamente. Luego, comparte tu lista con la clase.

MODELO: Estudiante 1:   ¿**Comes** helado cuando estás triste o estresado/a?
            Estudiante 2:   *No, no como helado cuando estoy triste.* o *Sí, siempre como helado cuando estoy estresado/a.*

¿Quién de la clase…	Nombre del/de la estudiante
1. … come helado cuando está triste o estresado?	_____
2. … siempre pide papas fritas como acompañamiento?	_____
3. … usa cubiertos de plástico en casa para no lavarlos?	_____
4. … nunca come comida chatarra?	_____
5. … siempre usa mantel cuando come en casa?	_____
6. … pide el café en taza de cerámica en la cafetería?	_____
7. … sabe hornear muy bien?	_____
8. … prefiere el agua con gas en lugar de agua mineral?	_____
9. … siempre adoba la carne antes de asarla?	_____
10. … siempre pide el café para llevar?	_____

Paso 2: Después, comenta tus resultados con la clase. ¿Fue fácil o difícil completar la actividad?

MODELO: *Parece que nadie de la clase…*

7.2-14 ¿Qué recomiendan? Tu profesor/a va a presentar varias situaciones en las que hay personas visitando Argentina y Chile. En grupos, tienen un tiempo limitado para escribir recomendaciones usando mandatos formales. El grupo con más recomendaciones para cada situación, gana.

MODELO:
    Profesor/a: Estoy en un restaurante de Valparaíso y no sé qué pedir.

    Grupo: *Pida el bistec "a lo pobre".*
              Pruebe el pisco sour.

7.2-15 La inauguración de un restaurante

Paso 1: Escribe un anuncio para hacer publicidad a un restaurante uruguayo. Es un restaurante nuevo que vas a abrir con tu socio/a: tu compañero/a. Primero, discute con tu compañero/a la información que quieren poner en el anuncio contestando estas preguntas:

- ¿Cómo se llama el restaurante?
- ¿Dónde está el restaurante?
- ¿Qué comida típica se sirve?
- ¿Cuáles son las características más importantes del restaurante?
- ¿Qué actividades se ofrecen? ¿Organizan eventos?
- ¿Se come barato/bien/tranquilo?
- ¿Se aceptan reservas?

 Paso 2: Ahora, piensen en un lema o eslogan atractivo. El lema tiene que incluir una expresión con el verbo *tener* y por lo menos una palabra del vocabulario.

MODELO: El restaurante se llama La Fogata.   →   *La Fogata tiene prisa.*

Paso 3: Hoy es el día de la inauguración del restaurante. Hay mucho trabajo. Tu socio/a y tú están muy nerviosos. Imaginen que tienen cinco empleados. Les dan órdenes a los empleados. Túrnense para dar un total de seis órdenes.

MODELO:
    Problema: Hay mesas y sillas en todos los rincones del restaurante.
    Tú: *¡Pongan las mesas y las sillas en su lugar!*

Paso 4: Ahora, lee la información sobre tu restaurante al resto de tus compañeros. Incluye el nombre, eventos y comidas típicas que se ofrecen en el restaurante. Incluye también el lema de tu negocio y si hubo problemas con los empleados o los clientes. La clase tiene que votar por el mejor. Tu profesor/a va a escoger a cuatro estudiantes para que formen el jurado con él/ella. Los miembros del jurado anotan en un papel los puntos que le dan a cada grupo (4: muy bueno, 3: bueno, 2: regular, 1: muy regular). El grupo con más puntos gana.

 7.2-16 Presta atención: El curanto Jorge es chileno y hoy nos habla de una comida típica de Chile que se llama "curanto". Escucha dos veces el audio y decide cuál es la respuesta más apropiada.

▲ *El curanto es un plato muy popular en Chile.*

WileyPLUS Go to *WileyPLUS* and listen to **Presta atención.**

1. El curanto es un plato típico…
    a. de la costa central de Chile y Patagonia.
    b. de las islas del norte y sur de Chile.
    c. de las islas del sur de Chile y Patagonia.
2. El curanto es una…
    a. gran comida social, comunitaria y para la familia.
    b. gran comida social que preparan los indígenas.
    c. gran comida para la familia.
3. El curanto se prepara…
    a. en casa de algún miembro de la familia.
    b. en un centro comunitario indígena.
    c. al aire libre, como por ejemplo, en la playa.

4. El curanto se prepara…
    a. para dar las gracias a los que ayudaron en reparar una casa.
    b. para celebrar que todos los vecinos compraron papas.
    c. cada mes para agradecer a los indígenas por esa tradición.
5. Se ponen hojas[16] de plantas encima de los mariscos y…
    a. encima se ponen más hojas y piedras.
    b. encima se ponen carnes y luego se ponen vegetales.
    c. después se pone una olla para cocinar carnes.
6. El curanto está listo en…
    a. una hora.   b. dos horas.   c. tres horas.

---

[16] **hojas:** leaves

© Egmont Strigl/ Imagebroker RF/ age fotostock

7.2-17 Por escrito: Libro de cocina Tu profesor/a quiere crear un libro de cocina con las mejores recetas de sus estudiantes. Escribe tu receta favorita usando los conectores que se presentan en la sección **¡Ojo!** Usa las preguntas de apoyo: ¿Cómo se llama la receta? ¿Cuándo se come esa comida? ¿Dónde se come? ¿De qué ingredientes se compone la receta? ¿Cuánto tiempo toma preparar ese plato? ¿Es fácil o difícil de preparar?

 ¡OJO!

Connectors
In **7.2-17** you are going to write a recipe and you need to give instructions in a specific order. Use the following discourse markers to organize your recipe:

1. Primero… (*first*), lo primero es… (*the first thing is*)
2. Después/luego/a continuación... (*next*)
3. Por último/finalmente/al final… (*finally, lastly*)

PONTE EN MI LUGAR

Estrategias para conversar

Being polite You have already learned how to use formal commands in Spanish. For example, you can use them to give orders (Tráigame la cuenta) or instructions (Ponga sal y pimienta). However, when interacting with other people and using formal commands (**usted** or **ustedes**), you can politely get someone's attention by accompanying the command with expressions such as **por favor, perdone, disculpe** (*excuse me*) and **si no le importa/molesta** (*if you don't mind*).

Compare these sentences and determine which ones are more polite:

1. —Tráiganos un plato hondo.
   —Por favor, tráiganos un plato hondo.

2. —La sopa está fría. Caliéntela un poco más.
   —Perdone, la sopa está fría. Si no le molesta, caliéntela un poco más.

El Fogón Imagina que estás en Montevideo, Uruguay, y vas con un/a amigo/a al restaurante El Fogón. En grupos de tres, decidan quién es el/a mesero/a, y quiénes son los clientes. Después, con ayuda del/de la mesero/a, mantengan una conversación: pidan el menú, pregunten por el plato especial de la casa, digan qué platos y postres quieren comer y pidan un buen vino para acompañar la comida. Finalmente, su profesor/a seleccionará varios grupos para que interpreten la conversación en frente de la clase. No olviden usar las **Estrategias para conversar.**

MODELO:

Mesero:	*Buenas tardes, ¿Qué desean ustedes?*
Cliente 1:	*¿Podría traernos el menú?*
Mesero:	*¡Sí, cómo no! Aquí lo tienen.*
Cliente 2:	*¿Qué lleva…?*
Mesero:	*Lleva…*
Cliente 1:	*¡Ah! Quiere decir… Quisiera de primer plato… y de segundo plato…*
Cliente 2:	*¿Cómo se prepara…?*
Mesero:	*Se hornea…*
Cliente 2:	*Vamos a ver, para mí…*

Mesero:	*¿Desean ustedes algo más?*
Cliente 1:	*Sí…*
Mesero:	*¿Y para tomar?*
Cliente 1:	*Para tomar…*
Mesero:	*En un momento les traigo…*
Cliente 3:	*Disculpe, si no le molesta, tráigame…*

ASÍ ES LA VIDA

Expresión: Disfruta, come y bebe, que la vida es breve.

Alexandra: *¿Postre? Mejor no, que voy a engordar.*

Natalia: *No te preocupes tanto por la dieta.* **Disfruta, come y bebe, que la vida es breve.**

¿Qué significa esta expresión?

¿Conoces una expresión en inglés similar a esta?

Adivina, adivinador

Soy blanco, soy tinto.
De color todo lo pinto.
Estoy en la buena mesa
y me subo a la cabeza.

© John Wiley & Sons, Inc.

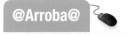 **@Arroba@**

WileyPLUS Go to *WileyPLUS* to find more **Arroba** activities.

Un menú en español

Paso 1: Explora en tu buscador favorito un menú en español de un restaurante en una de estas regiones: (1) Córdoba o Misiones (Argentina); (2) Colonia, Maldonado o Punta del Este (Uruguay); (3) Viña del Mar o Chiloé (Chile).

Paso 2: Después contesta estas preguntas y comenta tus respuestas con un/a compañero/a: ¿Qué plato especial ofrece el restaurante? ¿Qué te gustaría pedir de primer plato y de postre? ¿Qué ingredientes tienen esas comidas? ¿Ofrece el restaurante alguna bebida típica de la región? ¿Cómo se llama?

Paso 3: Con un/a compañero/a, decide qué comidas y bebidas te gustaría probar de esas regiones y explica por qué te gustaría probarlas.

WileyPLUS Go to *WileyPLUS* to see this video and to find more video activities.

VER PARA CREER II: ¡Buen provecho!

Antes de ver

Con ayuda de un/a compañero/a, responde estas preguntas.

1. En el pasado, ¿qué tipo de comidas te gustaba comer?
2. ¿Hay una comida o dulces típicos de tu estado o ciudad?
3. Cuando tú eras pequeño/a, ¿bebían tus padres u otros adultos vino en las comidas?
4. ¿Compraste alguna vez cerveza o vino cuando eras pequeño/a?

Después de ver

1. ¿Entendiste? Francisco conversa con su amiga Lauren sobre las costumbres de Argentina. Después de escuchar el video, responde las siguientes preguntas.

1. ¿Qué dice Lauren cuando saluda a Francisco?
   a. Que tiene hambre y quiere comer.
   b. Que está contenta de que hace calor.
   c. Que quiere volver a Nueva York.
2. ¿Qué son las facturas?
   a. unas cuentas para pagar
   b. los recibos del teléfono
   c. pasteles y otros dulces
3. ¿En qué tipo de cafetería están los amigos?
   a. en un café muy moderno
   b. en un café histórico
   c. en un café universitario
4. ¿Quién iba a ese café?
   a. todos los argentinos
   b. muchos turistas
   c. escritores famosos
5. ¿Qué comida tienen en el restaurante que van a almorzar?
   a. tienen comida americana
   b. tienen comida vegetariana
   c. tienen todo tipo de asado
6. ¿Quién mandaba a Francisco a comprar vino?
   a. su padre
   b. su madre
   c. su abuelo
7. ¿Qué es la Feria de Mataderos?
   a. Es un lugar de cultura gauchesca.
   b. Es un lugar de cultura francesa.
   c. Es un lugar de cultura italiana.
8. ¿Qué se vende en la Feria de Mataderos?
   a. Se vende todo tipo de ropa y joyas.
   b. Se venden libros argentinos.
   c. Se vende comida típica y artesanías.

2. La producción del vino ¿Qué diferencias hay entre el clima de Argentina y el clima de California?

3. Enfoque cultural Como buen argentino, Francisco sabe mucho de vinos y seguramente tiene una experiencia muy diferente a la tuya. ¿Qué diferencias culturales menciona Francisco entre la venta de vino en Estados Unidos y en Argentina? (Menciona dos).

AUTOPRUEBA

VOCABULARIO

I. ¿Cómo se dice? Contesta las siguientes preguntas con palabras o expresiones del vocabulario.

1. ¿Qué se utiliza para tomar un té?
2. ¿Qué expresión se dice al empezar a comer?
3. ¿Cómo se llama la persona que sirve la mesa en un restaurante?
4. ¿Qué puede ser con gas o mineral?
5. ¿Qué se usa para freír pescado?

II. ¿Qué hay en el restaurante?

1. ¿Quién sirve la comida y las bebidas en un restaurante?
2. ¿Qué usas para limpiarte la boca o las manos?
3. ¿En qué se sirve el vino?
4. ¿En qué se sirve una sopa?
5. ¿Con qué comes la sopa?

GRAMÁTICA

I. ¿Qué puedo comer? ¿Cuáles son los consejos de un médico a un paciente que quiere perder peso[17]? Escribe las respuestas del médico a las preguntas de su paciente.

MODELO: ¿Puedo comer las papas fritas?
          No, no las coma.

1. ¿Debo comer verduras?
2. ¿Cómo preparo las verduras?
3. ¿Puedo acompañar la comida con pan?
4. ¿Puedo comer dulces?
5. ¿Puedo beber la leche descremada?

II. Receta fácil: Empanadas de carne ¿Quieres preparar unas deliciosas empanadas de carne al estilo chileno? Completa la receta con el *se* pasivo y los verbos de la lista.

> hornear   dejar   añadir   deber   cortar
> mezclar   agregar   poner   picar

Ingredientes

500 g de carne picada (sin mucha grasa)
masa para empanadas
1/4 kg de tomates
1/4 kg de cebollas
1/2 pimiento pequeño
6 limones
sal
1/4 de taza de aceite
orégano, pimienta, comino, ajo

1. _____ la carne en una fuente con el jugo de 4 limones y _____ durante una hora.
2. _____ las cebollas, el tomate y el pimiento.
3. _____ las verduras, las especias, la sal y el aceite a la carne. Debe reposar durante 1 hora más.
4. _____ exprimir todo el líquido de la mezcla.
5. _____ la masa en forma de círculos.
6. _____ la mezcla de carne en los círculos.
7. _____ durante 25 minutos.

CULTURA

Lee la lista y selecciona las comidas típicas chilenas.

1. el churrasco italiano
2. la paella
3. las empanadas de carne
4. los burritos
5. el ajiaco

REDACCIÓN

Escribe un diálogo de dos personas que están en un restaurante. Incluye una descripción de la mesa, qué dice el mozo, qué piden las dos personas para beber, para comer y de postre. ¿Qué opinión tienen sobre la comida?

EN RESUMIDAS CUENTAS, AHORA PUEDO...

☐ seguir y escribir recetas de comida.

☐ hacer una reserva en un restaurante y ordenar la comida.

☐ utilizar el vos para dirigirme a otros.

☐ usar *tener* en distintas expresiones.

☐ dar instrucciones en situaciones formales.

☐ hablar de forma impersonal.

☐ reconocer algunas comidas típicas chilenas.

---

[17]**perder peso:** to lose weight

VOCABULARIO ESENCIAL

Sustantivos

el aceite	*oil*
el acompañamiento	*side dish*
el aderezo	*dressing*
el agua (mineral/con gas)	*(spring/sparkling) water*
la bebida	*drink*
la cacerola	*pan*
el caldero	*cast iron pot*
la carta/el menú	*menu*
la cerveza	*beer*
el churrasco	*steak*
la comida chatarra/basura	*junk food*
la copa	*wine glass*
el cubierto	*cutlery*
la cuchara	*spoon*
el cuchillo	*knife*
la cuenta	*bill/check*
la empanada (de carne, de queso, de marisco)	*(meat, cheese, seafood) turnover*
la ensalada	*salad*
la especia	*spice*
el flan	*sweet custard*
frito/a	*fried*
la fuente	*bowl*
el helado	*ice cream*
el mantel	*tablecloth*
el/la mesero/a, camarero/a, mozo/a	*waiter, waitress*
la mostaza	*mustard*
la olla	*soup pot*
el pastel	*pie*
la pimienta	*pepper*
el plato	*dish, plate*
el plato hondo	*soup dish*
el primer plato	*first course/appetizer*
el segundo plato	*main course/entrée*
el postre	*dessert*
la propina	*tip*
el refresco	*soft drink, soda*
la sal	*salt*
la sartén	*frying pan*
la servilleta	*napkin*

la sopa (del día)	*soup (of the day)*
la taza	*coffee cup*
el tenedor	*fork*
la torta	*cake*
el vaso	*glass*
el vinagre	*vinegar*
el vino	*wine*

Cognados: la mayonesa, el restaurante

Verbos

agregar	*to add*
añadir	*to add*
asar	*to roast, to grill*
calentar (>ie)	*to heat up*
cortar	*to cut*
cubrir/tapar	*to cover*
freír (>i)	*to fry*
hervir (>ie)	*to boil*
hornear	*to bake*
mezclar	*to mix*
ordenar/pedir	*to order*
pelar	*to peel*
picar	*to dice*
probar (>ue)	*to taste, to try (food)*
remover (<ue)	*to stir up*

Adjetivos

frito/a	*fried*

Expresiones

¡Buen provecho!	*Enjoy your meal!*
¿Desea/Desean algo de comer/tomar?	*Would you like something to eat/drink?*
hacer una reservación/reserva	*to book a table*
¿Me podría traer...?	*Could you bring me . . . ?*
pagar la cuenta	*pay the bill/check*
para llevar	*to go*
poner la mesa	*to set the table*
el primer/segundo plato	*first/main course*
¿Qué quiere/s comer/beber?	*What do you want to eat/drink?*
¡Qué rico!	*How delicious!*
¿Qué trae...?	*What comes with . . . ?*
seguir una receta	*to follow a recipe*

El mundo del entretenimiento

© John Wiley & Sons, Inc.

VER PARA CREER I: La belleza de Cartagena de Indias

Adam visita a su amiga colombiana Jahira en Cartagena de Indias. Repasa el contenido de las Secciones 1 y 2, y piensa en los temas que este video puede incluir. Después de ver el video, contesta las preguntas.

1. ¿Qué viste de Colombia? ¿Hay diferencias con los Estados Unidos?
2. ¿Qué te impresionó de Cartagena?
3. ¿Qué hacen los amigos al final del video?

Sección 1	**Los juegos y los deportes**

PALABRA POR PALABRA

- Los deportes
- El fútbol
- Los juegos

HABLANDO DE GRAMÁTICA

- Giving instructions: Formal commands ♻
- The present participle ♻
- Narrating in the past: The preterit vs. the imperfect tense ♻

CULTURA

- Juegos y deportes populares en Colombia
- La importancia de los deportes en las universidades

Sección 2	**El cine y la televisión**

PALABRA POR PALABRA

- La televisión
- El cine
- Los medios de comunicación

HABLANDO DE GRAMÁTICA

- Verbs like **gustar**: **Parecer** + *adjective* ♻
- Expressing negation: Negative and indefinite words
- Avoiding repetition (II): Double object pronouns ♻

CULTURA

- La cultura del doblaje
- La popularidad de las telenovelas en Venezuela y Colombia

Colombia y Venezuela

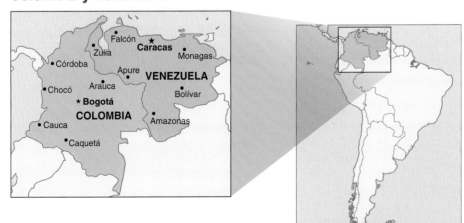

© John Wiley & Sons, Inc.

Trivia: Go to *WileyPLUS* to do the Trivia activities and find out how much you know about these countries!

LEARNING OBJECTIVES

By the end of this section you will be able to:

- Talk about sports and games
- Narrate events in the past
- Talk about actions in progress
- Give instructions in a formal way
- Understand the importance of sports in universities
- Discover games and sports popular in Colombia

Una imagen vale más que mil palabras

© imagebroker/Alamy

¿A qué están jugando estos niños?

¿Hay niñas jugando?

¿Qué tipo de juego les gusta jugar a los niños en Estados Unidos durante el recreo[1]?

UNA PERSPECTIVA

Courtesy Rebecca Conley

Rebecca

Deportes populares

© Tampa Bay Times /Zumapress

J. Raley-Al Wire "Al Wire Photo Service"/ Newscom

Diferente

"El deporte más popular en Colombia es el fútbol[2]. Se puede decir que aproximadamente un 70% de la sección de deportes de todos los periódicos es sobre fútbol. Mientras en Estados Unidos idolatramos[3] a los jugadores de béisbol, de baloncesto o de fútbol americano como Michael Jordan, LeBron James o Peyton Manning, el ídolo de los colombianos es Carlos 'el Pibe' Valderrama, un famosísimo exfutbolista colombiano. Muchos aficionados al fútbol a veces se ponen pelucas como el pelo de Valderrama cuando asisten a los partidos".

Igual

"A muchos colombianos —especialmente los de la costa norte del país, que es parte del Caribe— también les gusta el béisbol. Se juega al béisbol de octubre a enero y por eso se llama la Liga de Invierno. Hay algunos jugadores colombianos que juegan en las grandes ligas de Estados Unidos, entre ellos, Julio Teherán y José Quintana".

¿Qué piensas tú?

1. ¿Qué deportes son los más populares en Estados Unidos? ¿Y en el mundo?
2. ¿Crees que el fútbol es popular en Estados Unidos? Del uno al diez, ¿qué calificación le das?
3. ¿Por qué crees que no es tan popular el fútbol?

[1] **recreo:** break, recess [2] **fútbol** is the term for soccer. Football is known as **fútbol americano.** [3] **idolatrar:** idolize

LA PURA VERDAD I   ¿Qué más podemos hacer?

Daniel es un turista estadounidense que visita a su amigo Sergio, que vive en Bogotá. Daniel conoció a Sergio en Estados Unidos. Ahora Sergio le muestra algunos lugares de su ciudad.

1.

Yo estudié allí, en la Pontificia Universidad Javeriana.

¿Qué deportes practican en tu universidad?

2.

Yo era arquero.

3.

¿Qué deporte practicabas tú en la universidad?

4.

5.

Sí, pero algunas cartas son diferentes.

¿Puedo jugar con ellos?

6.

¡Oh, son diferentes!

© John Wiley & Sons, Inc.

 8.1-01 **¿Qué juego es?** Escucha la narración y decide cuál es el juego que describe.

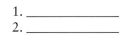

1. _____
2. _____
3. _____

♫ PALABRA POR PALABRA

Los deportes

- hacer esquí acuático
- el ciclismo/montar en bicicleta
- el bate
- el béisbol
- el baloncesto
- el voleibol (de playa)
- hacer senderismo
- el atletismo
- andar en patineta/monopatín
- montar a caballo
- la pesca
- pescar
- levantar pesas
- patinar en línea
- la natación

© John Wiley & Sons, Inc.

El fútbol

- el entrenador
- el estadio
- el jugador
- el balón
- el arquero
- el campo de fútbol

© John Wiley & Sons, Inc.

Para hablar de deportes

el/la aficionado/a	*fan*
el atletismo	*track and field*
la cancha	*court*
el deporte (extremo/de riesgo)	*(extreme) sport*
la pelota	*ball*
el campeonato	*championship*
el/la deportista	*athlete*
el equipo	*tean*
el juego	*game*
la liga	*league*
el partido (de fútbol, de tenis, de baloncesto)	*(soccer, basketball) match, game*
el tenis de mesa	*ping-pong*
animar (a un equipo)	*to cheer (a team)*
hacer/jugar a un deporte	*to play/practice a sport*
hacer snowboarding	*to snowboard*
ser aficionado/a (de)	*to be a fan (of)*
silbar	*to whistle*
¿De qué equipo eres?	*What team do you support?*
Soy de...	*My team is . . .*

Cognados: el hockey, el golf, el rugby, el tenis

Los juegos *Games*

el videojuego

las damas

Está perdiendo.

Está ganando.

las cartas

el juego de mesa

la ficha

el tablero

el ajedrez

los dados

© John Wiley & Sons, Inc.

¿Qué dicen los colombianos?

Ese muchacho es un <u>buñuelo</u>.	*That guy is <u>new</u>.*
Él es un <u>cachaco</u>.	*He is <u>from Bogotá</u>.*
*¡Qué <u>chévere</u>!	*Great!*
*Metió el gol <u>de chiripa</u>.	*He scored a goal by <u>sheer luck</u>.*
¡<u>Yuca</u>! Perdimos el partido.	*What <u>bad luck</u>! We lost the match.*

*Esta expresión se usa en otros países hispanos también.

 8.1-02 ¿Qué asocias con...?

Paso 1: En grupos, piensen en qué deportes o juegos asocian con las siguientes palabras.

1. arquero
2. bicicleta
3. raqueta
4. piscina

5. cancha
6. tablero
7. fichas
8. balón

Paso 2: Ahora, escribe una lista con el nombre de cinco deportistas o atletas que conozcas. Pregúntale a tus compañeros qué deporte asocian con los nombres de tu lista. Después, coméntale a la clase cuánto saben tus compañeros de grupo de deportes.

8.1-03 ¿Somos activos o sedentarios?

Paso 1: En grupos, clasifiquen los deportes y juegos de la sección de **Palabra por palabra** en las siguientes categorías.

Se juega en equipo	Se practica de forma individual	Es una actividad tranquila/sedentaria	Es un deporte peligroso/de riesgo	Es una actividad física muy intensa

Paso 2: Después, hablen de las actividades que practican o que les gusta seguir en los medios. ¿A qué categoría pertenecen? ¿Son activos o son sedentarios? ¿Les gustan los deportes tranquilos o los de riesgo? ¿Los deportes de equipo o los individuales? Pueden llegar a más de una conclusión.

8.1-04 ¿Eres aficionado/a a los deportes?

Paso 1: Lee las siguientes preguntas y piensa en otra pregunta que te gustaría hacer. Después, conversa con un/a compañero/a sobre los deportes y los juegos.

1. ¿Haces ejercicio con frecuencia? ¿Cuántas veces a la semana? ¿Qué ejercicio haces?
2. ¿Practicas algún deporte? ¿Cuándo lo practicas? ¿Te gustan los deportes extremos o de riesgo?
3. ¿Cuál es tu deporte favorito? ¿Sigues alguna liga? ¿De qué equipo eres?
4. ¿Asistes a partidos de algún deporte? ¿Ves deportes por televisión?
5. ¿Eres aficionado/a de algún atleta en particular? ¿De quién y por qué?
6. ¿Montas en bicicleta para moverte por tu ciudad? ¿Andas en patineta o monopatín? ¿Crees que es seguro? ¿Por qué?
7. ...

Paso 2: Con la información de tu compañero/a, escribe un párrafo para contestar a la siguiente pregunta: ¿Quién es más aficionado/a a los deportes?

> MODELO: *A los/las dos nos gusta hacer ejercicio, pero creo que (nombre de tu compañero/a) es más aficionado/a de los deportes porque...*

8.1-05 Las reglas del juego

Paso 1: ¿Conoces las reglas del Monopolio? Completa las siguientes reglas con los verbos de la lista en la forma singular del mandato formal.

Giving instructions: Formal commands

In Chapter 7, Section 2, you learned how to use formal commands (**los mandatos formales**) when giving instructions to people with whom you have a formal relationship— those you would normally address as **usted**. Do you remember how to form the formal commands? Study the following examples:

Juegue con nosotros. **Tire** los dados para ver cuál es su turno.

Play with us. **Throw** the dice to see what your turn is.

Jugar and **tirar** are two verbs that end in **-ar**. What is the rule for verbs ending in **-er** and **-ir**? And what are the three verbs that have irregular formal command forms?

mover   comprar   tomar   construir   evitar   declarar
seguir   olvidar   pagar   tirar

1. _____ los dados y _____ las fichas alrededor del tablero.
2. _____ el mayor número de propiedades posible. _____ la cantidad de dinero escrita en el "Título de propiedad".
3. No _____ cobrar[4] el alquiler a los jugadores que paran en sus propiedades.
4. Si cae en las casillas[5] de *Suerte* o *Caja de Comunidad*, _____ una carta y _____ las instrucciones.
5. _____ casas y hoteles en sus propiedades.
6. Si no tiene dinero, _____ la bancarrota[6].
7. _____ ir la cárcel. Es mejor moverse y poder comprar propiedades.

Paso 2: Piensen en un juego conocido (tradicional, de video, para computadoras o teléfonos) y escriban las reglas básicas del juego, siguiendo el modelo del Monopolio. Presenten sus reglas a la clase. El resto de la clase debe adivinar qué juego es.

8.1-06 Adivina, adivinador... ¿quién soy? Piensa en un/a deportista o atleta famoso/a. Después, en parejas, túrnense para adivinar en qué persona famosa pensó tu compañero/a.

MODELO:

Estudiante 1:	*¿Formas parte de un equipo?*
Estudiante 2:	Sí, formo parte de un equipo de fútbol.
Estudiante 1:	¿Con qué equipo juegas?
Estudiante 2:	Juego con el Atlético de Madrid.
Estudiante 1:	¿Eres español?
Estudiante 2:	No, soy colombiano.
Estudiante 1:	¡Eres Radamel Falcao García!
Estudiante 2:	¡Sí, muy bien!

▲ *Radamel Falcao cuando ganó la Liga Europea en 2012 con el Atlético de Madrid*

Denis Doyle/Getty Images Sport / Getty Images

HABLANDO DE GRAMÁTICA I

1. Narrating in the past (I): The preterit vs. the imperfect tense

So far you have learned that there are two different simple past tenses in Spanish, the *preterit* (**pretérito**) and the *imperfect* (**imperfecto**).

A. The preterit

The preterit usually translates into simple past in English. In Chapter 6 you learned that we use the preterit to talk about . . .

a. **completed actions** in the past: the preterit is used to talk about a certain event that the speaker views as finished and completed by a certain time point—even if the event or action lasted for some time.

> **Estudié** en esa universidad del 2010 al 2014.
>
> *I studied in that university from 2010 to 2014.*
>
> Ayer **fuimos** a la universidad y después **jugamos** un partido de fútbol.
>
> *Yesterday we went to the university and then we played a soccer game.*

b. **single, punctual actions** or events that happened at a particular point in time.

> Daniel **visitó** a su amigo Sergio en agosto. **Llegó** el día 2 y **se fue** el día 12.
>
> *Daniel visited his friend Sergio in August. He arrived on the 2nd and left on the 12th.*

The following phrases usually appear with the preterit to indicate a point in time for completed or single events:	
ayer	*yesterday*
anoche	*last night*
anteayer	*the day before yesterday*
la semana pasada	*last week*
el lunes/martes... pasado	*last Monday/Tuesday . . .*
el fin de semana/mes/año pasado	*last weekend/month/year*
un día, una vez	*one day, once*
de repente	*suddenly*
ya	*already*
hace... (que)	*. . . ago*

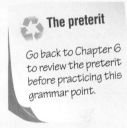

The preterit

Go back to Chapter 6 to review the preterit before practicing this grammar point.

8.1-07 El viaje de Daniel

Paso 1: Lee las siguientes oraciones sobre el viaje de Daniel a Colombia en **La pura verdad** y decide si son **ciertas** (C) o **falsas** (F). Corrige las oraciones falsas con la información verdadera.

C   F

☐   ☐   _____ a. Durante el paseo, Sergio y Daniel **hablaron** de política.

☐   ☐   _____ b. Sergio le **mostró** a Daniel el campo de fútbol.

☐   ☐   _____ c. Daniel se **sentó** a jugar a las cartas con dos señores.

☐   ☐   _____ d. Más tarde, **pasaron** por un centro comercial lleno de gente jugando a las cartas, al ajedrez y al dominó.

☐   ☐   _____ e. Durante el paseo **vieron** la universidad a la que **asistió** Sergio.

☐   ☐   _____ f. Un día, Sergio **llevó** a Daniel a montar en bicicleta.

Paso 2: Ahora, ¿puedes poner en orden cronológico las oraciones para contar el día de Sergio y Daniel en **La pura verdad**?

WileyPLUS Go to *WileyPLUS* to review this grammar point with the help of the **Animated Grammar Tutorial** and the **Verb Conjugator**.

8.1-08 ¿Cuándo fue la última vez que...?

Paso 1: Escribe cuándo fue la última vez que hiciste cada actividad: **ayer, anoche, la semana pasada, hace dos días, hace un mes,** etc.

MODELO: levantar pesas   →   *Levanté pesas ayer.*

1. jugar a un deporte de equipo (¿cuál?)
2. hacer ejercicio
3. jugar a un juego de mesa (¿cuál?)
4. hacer un deporte al aire libre (¿cuál?)
5. ver un partido por televisión (¿de qué?)
6. montar en bicicleta

Paso 2: Convierte las oraciones del **Paso 1** en preguntas.

MODELO: levantar pesas   →   *¿Cuándo fue la última vez que levantaste pesas?*

Paso 3: Ahora, haz las preguntas a tus compañeros. ¿Puedes encontrar a dos personas que dieron respuestas iguales a las tuyas en por lo menos tres actividades? Presenta los resultados a la clase.

MODELO: *Victoria y Diana también levantaron pesas ayer.*

The imperfect

You may want to review the imperfect tense in Chapter 7 before you start practicing the preterit and the imperfect together.

B. The imperfect

In Chapter 7 you learned that the **imperfect** translates into different tenses in English, and it is used to talk about. . .

a. ongoing, repeated or **habitual actions** in the past (what would happen or used to happen).

Sergio **jugaba** mucho al fútbol.   *Sergio used to play soccer a lot.*

b. to describe a situation, people, places or things in the past (how things were or used to be).

A Sergio le **encantaba** el fútbol. **Era** el   *Sergio loved soccer. He was the team's*
arquero del equipo.   *goalkeeper.*

8.1-09 Sergio y Daniel Lee el siguiente párrafo sobre Sergio y Daniel. Escribe en una hoja de papel todos los verbos en el imperfecto (hay 15 en total). Después, indica por qué se usa el imperfecto en cada caso: (1) **acción habitual** o (2) **descripción** de la situación, lugar, personas o cosas.

Cuando Sergio era niño jugaba al Monopolio y a las damas con sus amigos. También hacía deportes, pero sobre todo, jugaba mucho al fútbol. Todos le decían que era muy bueno. Sergio y Daniel eran amigos. Daniel era estadounidense y Sergio colombiano, pero tenían mucho en común. Los dos practicaban varios deportes, aunque Daniel era más atlético que Sergio. Se llevaban muy bien porque aunque venían de países diferentes, compartían la pasión por los deportes de equipo y además tenían personalidades similares.

MODELO: 1. *era (descripción)*

8.1-10 ¿Qué hacías y cómo eras?

Paso 1: Escribe seis oraciones sobre tus experiencias en la escuela secundaria: cómo eras, qué hacías y con qué frecuencia lo hacías, qué deportes practicabas, etc.

MODELO: *Nunca asistía a competiciones deportivas.*

Paso 2: Convierte las oraciones del **Paso 1** en preguntas. Luego, entrevista a dos compañeros. ¿Quién de los dos se parece más a ti? Informa a la clase.

MODELO: *¿Asistías a competiciones deportivas?*

C. Simultaneous and interrupting events

So far you have learned the different uses for the preterit and the imperfect. However, often both tenses are used within the same sentence. Because the imperfect is used to signal that an action was not finished, it is often used to describe a scene in which two events were simultaneously in progress. The word **mientras** (*while*) is often used in these cases:

Mientras Sergio **manejaba,** Daniel le **hacía** muchas preguntas.	*While Sergio was driving, Daniel was asking many questions.*
En la plaza, los niños **corrían** y los mayores **jugaban** a las cartas.	*At the square, the kids were running and the older people were playing cards.*

On the other hand, we use the preterit to indicate an action that interrupts an ongoing scene, event, or action in progress. Actions in progress in the past are usually expressed in the imperfect (for states) or the imperfect progressive (**estaba, estabas, estaba, estábamos, estaban** + gerund) for activities:

Sergio **estaba manejando** por el centro cuando **pasaron** por una plaza.	*Sergio was driving around downtown when they passed by a square.*
Ellos **estaban jugando** a las cartas cuando Daniel **se sentó** con ellos.	*They were playing cards when Daniel sat down with them.*

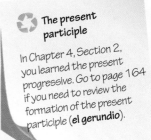

The present participle

In Chapter 4, Section 2, you learned the present progressive. Go to page 164 if you need to review the formation of the present participle (**el gerundio**).

 8.1-11 ¿Qué pasó cuando...? Mira otra vez las viñetas de **La pura verdad** en la página 297.

Paso 1: Completa cada oración con la mejor opción.

1. Sergio manejaba el coche mientras...
   a. él y Daniel hablaban de deportes.
   b. él y Daniel hacían planes para las siguientes dos semanas.
2. Sergio estaba manejando cuando...
   a. le mostró a Daniel la universidad.
   b. decidieron ir a ver un partido.
3. Sergio le mostraba a Daniel el campo de fútbol mientras...
   a. le contaba cómo era ser estudiante universitario en Colombia.
   b. le hablaba de sus días como arquero del equipo.
4. Sergio le estaba mostrando a Daniel el campo de fútbol cuando...
   a. le preguntó: "¿A qué jugabas tú en la universidad?".
   b. Daniel dijo: "¿Qué más podemos hacer estas dos semanas?".
5. Mientras unos niños patinaban, otros...
   a. miraban a Sergio y Daniel.
   b. jugaban al Monopolio.

Paso 2: ¿Qué más pasó? Completa las dos oraciones de forma apropiada.

6. Los dos amigos estaban caminando hacia la plaza cuando...
7. Daniel jugaba a las cartas mientras...

 8.1-12 La última vez que alguien me llamó... Piensa en la última vez que alguien te llamó por teléfono y escribe un pequeño párrafo contestando a las siguientes preguntas.

1. ¿Cuándo fue la última vez que alguien te llamó por teléfono?
2. Cuando sonó el teléfono, ¿qué estabas haciendo? ¿Dónde estabas?
3. ¿Cuánto tiempo hablaste con la persona que te llamó?
4. Cuando acabó la conversación, ¿cómo te sentías? ¿Contento/a, triste, preocupado/a? ¿Por qué?

LA PURA VERDAD II | Partido de fútbol

Alberto, un amigo de Sergio, invita a Daniel a ver un partido de fútbol entre los Millonarios de Bogotá y el Deportivo de Cali.

1.

2.

3.

4.

5.

6.

© John Wiley & Sons, Inc.

8.1-13 ¿Qué pasó después? Escucha la narración de lo que les pasó después a Daniel y a Alberto en el estadio y selecciona la respuesta correcta.

1. ¿Qué hizo Daniel?
   a. Siguió silbando.
   b. Se sentó.
   c. Salió del estadio.
2. ¿Qué hizo mal?
   a. Animó al equipo contrario.
   b. Silbó, y eso era negativo para su equipo.
   c. Silbó, y eso se considera vulgar en Colombia.
3. ¿Qué pasó al final?
   a. Se sintió mal y salió del estadio.
   b. Ganó Cali.
   c. Ganaron los Millonarios.

HABLANDO DE GRAMÁTICA II

WileyPLUS Go to *WileyPLUS* to review this grammar point with the help of the **Animated Grammar Tutorial** and the **Verb Conjugator.**

2. Narrating in the past (II): The preterit vs. the imperfect tense

A. Using the preterit and imperfect together

When narrating in the past, the preterit and the imperfect may be used together; it is often difficult to tell a story without using both. Because the imperfect is used to describe a situation in the past, it is only natural that we use this tense to describe the background, often "setting the stage" for other actions or events to take place. That is, we use the imperfect to provide background information (**el trasfondo**) for a story (such as the season, the weather, date or time, or to describe the people, places and objects involved in the situation). On the other hand, because we use the preterit to talk about completed, single, or punctual actions, we use it in order to allow the main events in the story, to advance and move forward.

Imperfect: Sets the scene Describes the surroundings Adds background description/information	Preterit: Tells what happened
Sergio **quería** aprender a hablar bien inglés... *Sergio wanted to learn how to speak English well. . .*	... y **decidió** estudiar un año en una universidad de EE. UU. *. . . so he decided to study at a university in the U.S. for a year.*
Le **gustaba** mucho el fútbol... *He liked soccer a lot. . .*	... y por eso **entró** en un equipo para jugar en una pequeña liga. *. . . and that's why he got onto a team to play in a small league.*
Daniel **jugaba** en el mismo equipo... *Daniel played on the same team. . .*	... y así es como se **conocieron.** *. . . and that's how they met each other.*
Les **gustaban** las mismas cosas... *They liked the same things. . .*	... y por eso se **hicieron** muy buenos amigos. *. . . that's why they became very good friends.*
	Después de un año, Sergio **volvió** a Colombia. *After a year, Sergio went back to Colombia.*
Los dos amigos siempre **mantenían** mucho contacto. *The two friends were in contact all the time.*	
	Por fin, un día Daniel **decidió** ir a Colombia a visitar a su amigo. *Finally one day, Daniel decided to go to Colombia to visit his friend.*

- - - Imperfect
——— Preterit

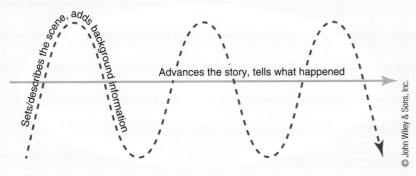

Sets/describes the scene, adds background information

Advances the story, tells what happened

© John Wiley & Sons, Inc.

▲ *Narrating in the past using preterit and imperfect*

8.1-14 La historia incompleta del viaje de Daniel En **8.1-07** pusiste en orden la historia de **El viaje de Daniel.** Ahora, tienes que completarla con más detalles e información. Mira las viñetas de **La Pura Verdad** y completa la historia poniendo las oraciones **a-d** en el lugar adecuado.

*Durante la visita de Daniel, un día los dos amigos **fueron** en coche a ver la universidad a la que **asistió** Sergio. _____*
*₁ Durante el paseo, Sergio y Daniel **hablaron** mucho de deportes y su vida de estudiantes universitarios. _____₂ Por eso Sergio le **llevó** a Daniel a ver el campo de fútbol. Más tarde **pasaron** por muchos lugares interesantes _____₃. A Daniel le **llamó** mucho la atención un grupo de señores que **jugaban** a las cartas y **quiso** sentarse con ellos. _____₄ Se **sorprendió** mucho, porque **vio** que las cartas eran diferentes.*

a. Cuando **paseaban,** vieron a muchos niños que **jugaban** al Monopolio, al fútbol y a las damas.

b. Sergio **manejaba** mientras le **mostraba** la ciudad a Daniel.

c. Cuando Daniel **estaba** listo para jugar con los hombres que jugaban en la plaza, **vio** que las cartas **eran** cartas españolas.

d. Sergio **era** el arquero cuando **jugaba** con el equipo de fútbol, y Daniel **quería** ver el campo.

 8.1-15 El partido de fútbol Mira las viñetas de **La pura verdad** en la página 304 que describen la anécdota de Daniel en el partido de fútbol. Escoge la forma correcta del verbo para completar lo que Alberto les contó a sus amigos al día siguiente.

Hace unos días (**invité/invitaba**)₁ a Daniel, el amigo de Sergio, a ver un partido de fútbol. Daniel (**estuvo/estaba**)₂ muy emocionado, y me (**preguntó/preguntaba**)₃: "¿Lo dices en serio?". Él es estadounidense y (**tuvo/tenía**)₄ muchas ganas de ver un partido de fútbol en Colombia. El día del partido, todos los aficionados que estaban en el estadio (**llevaron/llevaban**)₅ camisetas del color de su equipo. (**Fue/Era**)₆ un día muy bonito. Todos (**animaron/animaban**)₇ a los jugadores y les (**gritaron/gritaban**)₈ "¡Arriba Deportivo!". En la mitad del partido, Vladimir Marín (**salía/salió**)₉ a jugar. ¡Entonces, para animar al jugador, Daniel se (**levantó/levantaba**)₁₀ y (**silbó/silbaba**)₁₁ muy fuerte! Todas las personas que (**estuvieron/estaban**)₁₂ alrededor se (**sorprendieron/sorprendían**)₁₃ muchísimo. Entonces lo (**agarré/agarraba**)₁₄ de la camiseta y él se (**sentó/sentaba**)₁₅. Al final le (**expliqué/explicaba**)₁₆ que en Colombia no puedes silbar para animar a alguien!

B. Summary of the preterit and the imperfect

Imperfect	Preterit
A. Indicates an **ongoing, habitual, or repeated action** with no emphasis on the beginning or end. Daniel **hacía** mucho ejercicio cuando **estudiaba** en la universidad. *Daniel did a lot of exercise when he was studying at the university.*	A. Indicates a **completed event, action, or condition** with a clear beginning, end, or timeframe. Daniel **hizo** mucho ejercicio ayer. *Daniel exercised a lot yesterday.*
B. Describes an **action in progress.** Por la tarde, los niños **jugaban** en la plaza. *In the afternoon the kids would play in the plaza.*	B. Indicates a **one-time, single, punctual, sudden action,** or change of condition, or an action **that interrupts** an action in progress expressed in the imperfect. Los hombres **estaban jugando** a las cartas cuando Daniel y Sergio **llegaron.** *The men were playing cards when Daniel and Sergio arrived.*
C. **Describes characteristics or conditions** of people, places, things or a situation; provides **background information** or supporting details. Sergio y Daniel **eran** amigos de la infancia. *Sergio and Daniel were friends since childhood.*	C. Indicates a **series of completed and consecutive events;** moves the story forward. Un día, Daniel **decidió** ir a visitar a Sergio. Lo **llamó** y **compró** un billete de avión a Bogotá. *One day, Daniel decided to go visit Sergio. Daniel called him and bought a plane ticket to Bogota.*

8.1-16 ¿Qué pasó al final? Contesten las siguientes preguntas sobre Daniel y sus aventuras en Colombia. Después de responder, miren el cuadro de arriba e indiquen en el espacio en blanco qué uso del pretérito o del imperfecto escogieron para sus respuestas (A, B o C).

_____ 1. ¿Quiénes eran Sergio y Daniel?

_____ 2. ¿Cómo eran?

_____ 3. ¿Adónde llevó Sergio a Daniel durante su paseo por la ciudad?

_____ 4. ¿Qué había en la plaza?

_____ 5. ¿Por qué se sorprendió Daniel?

_____ 6. ¿Quién invitó a Daniel a un partido de fútbol?

_____ 7. ¿Llovió mucho el día del partido?

_____ 8. ¿Qué pasó cuando salió Mayer Candelo al campo?

_____ 9. ¿Qué pasó al final?

OTRA PERSPECTIVA

Courtesy of Sergio Díaz-Luna

Sergio

Diferente

"Creo que en Estados Unidos el béisbol es tan popular como el fútbol en Colombia. Hay muchos equipos, unos con más dinero que otros, y todos participan en una liga para al final decidir cuál es el mejor equipo del país. Nuestra competencia nacional se llama la Copa Colombia (o la Copa del patrocinador[7]). También participamos en la Copa América, en la que participan muchos países de todo el continente, y también en la Copa Mundial cada cuatro años. Pero algo curioso para mí es que en Estados Unidos el campeonato de béisbol se llama 'la Serie Mundial'. ¿Por qué la llaman 'la Serie Mundial' si no hay equipos de otros países?"

Igual

"El fútbol femenino tiene mucha popularidad y prestigio tanto en Estados Unidos como en Colombia. En los dos países el equipo femenino sale mejor en los torneos[8] internacionales que el equipo masculino. El equipo de fútbol femenino de Colombia obtuvo el segundo lugar en la Copa Sudamericana, un puesto mejor que el que obtuvo el equipo masculino. De igual manera, el equipo femenino de fútbol de Estados Unidos ganó la Copa Mundial dos veces y el equipo masculino todavía ninguna".

Explícale a Sergio

1. ¿Por qué le llaman "la Serie Mundial" al campeonato de béisbol si no hay equipos de otros países?
2. ¿Hay competiciones internacionales de béisbol? ¿Cómo sale Estados Unidos en esas competencias?
3. ¿Participa el béisbol en los Juegos Olímpicos?

MANOS A LA OBRA

8.1-17 Colombianos famosos

Paso 1: En grupos pequeños, escriban tres oraciones originales sobre colombianos famosos. Indiquen qué imaginan que hacían cuando eran niños para divertirse, qué piensan que ellos hicieron ayer y qué creen están haciendo ahora mismo.

MODELO: Shakira
Cuando era niña jugaba a ser bailarina.
Ayer por la tarde dio un concierto en Bogotá.
Ahora mismo está trabajando en su último álbum.

Paso 2: Comenten sus oraciones con la clase. ¿Cuál de las actividades para cada persona piensan que es más probable?

8.1-18 Dilo con mímica Tu profesor/a te va a dar una frase que vas a representar haciendo mímica. En veinte segundos, tu grupo debe adivinar qué frase es. ¿Qué grupo tiene los mejores actores?

MODELO: *Samuel estaba tomando un refresco cuando el equipo metió un gol.*

---

[7]**patrocinador:** sponsor [8]**torneo:** tournament

8.1-19 Dilemas y soluciones

Paso 1: Piensa en tres dilemas o problemas que tuviste en alguna ocasión. Prepara cuatro o cinco oraciones para describir la situación. Puedes usar las siguientes preguntas para organizar tus ideas.

1. ¿Cuál era el problema?
2. ¿Cuándo fue? ¿Cuántos años tenías?
3. ¿Qué hacías? ¿Dónde estabas? ¿Con quién estabas?
4. ¿Cómo te sentías al ver qué estaba sucediendo eso?
5. ¿Qué pasó al final? ¿Cómo lo solucionaste?

 Paso 2: Comenta con un/a compañero/a las situaciones que describieron. Descríbele a tu compañero/a: (1) cuál era el problema (da la mayor cantidad posible de detalles e información) y (2) explica (en el pretérito) qué hiciste para solucionarlo. Tu compañero/a tiene que pensar en por lo menos dos preguntas más sobre la situación que le cuentas.

MODELO: Estudiante 1: *¿Qué dilema tenías?*
Estudiante 2: *Estaba en la escuela secundaria, me iba a graduar y no sabía a qué universidad asistir.*
Estudiante 1: *¿Qué opciones tenías?*
Estudiante 2: …

 Paso 3: Después de hablar con dos o tres compañeros, comenta con la clase quién tuvo el dilema más difícil, interesante, extraordinario, etc.

 8.1-20 ¿Qué pasó después?

Paso 1: Su profesor/a le va asignar a cada grupo una de las siguientes situaciones. Ustedes tienen que terminar el relato de manera creativa en por lo menos cuatro oraciones.

WileyPLUS Go to *WileyPLUS* and listen to **Presta atención.**

1. Era un día muy bonito y caluroso, y estabas en casa. Estabas estudiando para un examen que tenías al día siguiente cuando sonó el teléfono…
2. Era un día soleado de invierno y estabas haciendo senderismo con tus amigos. Se hizo de noche y no tenían luz para ver el camino. El teléfono no funcionaba…
3. Estabas levantando pesas en el gimnasio cuando de repente se fue la luz y nadie podía ver nada. Una persona se cayó por las escaleras y…
4. Estabas jugando un partido de baloncesto con tus amigos. Tu equipo estaba perdiendo cuando un jugador del equipo contrario cometió una falta[9] que el árbitro[10] no vio. Entonces…

Paso 2: Cada grupo representa su historia frente a la clase, con una persona como narrador/a. Al final, la clase tiene que votar qué historia fue la más original.

 8.1-21 Presta atención: Los Juegos Sudamericanos del 2010 Vas a escuchar una conversación entre un colombiano y su amigo estadounidense. El colombiano le comenta los Juegos Sudamericanos del 2010. Después de escucharlo, selecciona la respuesta más adecuada.

1. Héctor es colombiano. Él es de…
   a. la ciudad de Medellín.   b. la ciudad de Bogotá.   c. la ciudad de Barranquilla.
2. Los Juegos Sudamericanos…
   a. se celebraron en Medellín.   b. se celebraron en Bogotá.   c. se celebraron en Barranquilla.
3. ¿Cuántos países participaron en los Juegos Sudamericanos?
   a. Participaron veinticinco.   b. Participaron quince.   c. Participaron cincuenta.

[9]**cometer una falta:** to commit a foul [10]**árbitro:** referee

4. ¿Qué tipo de medallas ganó Colombia?
   a. Ganó solamente   b. Ganó medallas en   c. Ganó medallas en
      medallas en atletismo.   patinaje y motociclismo.   ciclismo y patinaje.
5. ¿Cuántos turistas viajaron a Colombia para ver los Juegos?
   a. alrededor de dos   b. alrededor de quince   c. alrededor de doce
      mil turistas.   mil turistas.   mil turistas.
6. ¿Por qué gastaron mucho dinero en la ciudad donde se celebraron los Juegos?
   a. para mostrar que hay muchos buenos atletas colombianos
   b. para decorarla y asegurarse que había seguridad en la ciudad
   c. para asegurarse que iban muchos turistas a los Juegos

 8.1-22 Por escrito: Un acontecimiento inolvidable Escribe una breve narración de tres párrafos sobre un evento que viviste tú o una persona cercana a ti: una aventura peligrosa, una fiesta sorpresa, la primera vez que hiciste algo, un viaje al extranjero. En cada párrafo incluye la idea principal del párrafo con detalles y ejemplos. Sigue los pasos de la sección **¡Ojo!** y usa el pretérito y el imperfecto.

PONTE EN MI LUGAR

Estrategias para conversar ♻

Showing interest in a conversation In Chapter 5, Section 2, you learned some expressions to help you maintain the natural flow of a conversation. You can go back to that section to review some of those expressions. These are some new expressions you can try this time:

Eché de menos no ir a…	I missed not going to. . . !
Lo que te perdiste, ¡no te puedes imaginar!	You cannot imagine what you missed!
¡Ni te imaginas lo que pasó!	You cannot even imagine what happened!
¡Qué mal!	That's too bad!
¿Qué pasó?	What happened?

When using these expressions, don't forget to use intonation and emotion in your reactions.

Un partido. Un/a amigo/a y tú hablan sobre un partido importante de tu universidad. Usen las **Estrategias para conversar.**

Estudiante 1: Esta semana estás muy ocupado/a con tus clases porque tienes un examen cada día y no tuviste tiempo para ir a ver el último partido de fútbol americano de tu universidad. En un breve descanso llamas a tu mejor amigo/a: (a) explícale por qué no fuiste al partido; (b) pregúntale cómo fue el partido y qué ocurrió con los jugadores y el entrenador; (c) pregúntale cómo era el ambiente del estadio (la gente que había, el clima, la duración del partido…); (d) despídete.

Estudiante 2: Responde la llamada telefónica de tu amigo/a y responde a sus preguntas; (a) cuéntale que el entrenador estaba enfadado y los aficionados estaban silbando porque el mejor jugador tuvo que retirarse del campo (cuenta por qué); (b) cuéntale que, durante el partido, conociste a una persona especial (describe a la persona con detalle y cuéntale todos los detalles de cómo se conocieron); (c) despídete.

 ¡OJO!

Using preterit and imperfect when narrating in the past

If you are telling a story in the past, in *the first paragraph* you should set the scene, usually in the imperfect tense (**Cuando tenía** 15 años). In a *second paragraph*, use the preterit to introduce a new idea, and use the imperfect to provide supporting details or to talk about the state of mind of the persons participating in the action (**Un día decidí… pero estaba** un poco nervioso porque...). In the *third paragraph* conclude the story by telling the result (**Al final...**).

ASÍ ES LA VIDA

Chiste

Dos amigos van por primera vez a un partido de fútbol. No saben nada de fútbol y después de un rato se dan cuenta de que todos están insultando al árbitro:

—¡Idiota!

—Oye, ¿a quién le están diciendo eso?

—A la persona de la camiseta negra.

—¡Ah! No me sorprende, lleva media hora en el campo y todavía no tocó el balón.

Adivina, adivinador

Juegan en la cancha
más altos que bajos,
meten la pelota
dentro de los aros.
¿Qué deporte es?

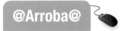

WileyPLUS Go to *WileyPLUS*
to find more **Arroba** activities.

CNN en español: vive la noticia

Paso 1: Explora en tu buscador favorito la página de CNN en español. Después selecciona una noticia interesante y léela.

Paso 2: Escribe un breve resumen de la noticia que leíste.

Paso 3: Comparte la información con un/a compañero/a y conversen sobre ese tema. ¿Conocía tu compañero/a esa noticia?

Paso 4: Informen al/a la profesor/a sobre las noticias más actuales que encontraron.

ENTÉRATE

Estrategias para leer

A narrative Narrating is telling a story in order to inform about something or to tell about an experience. This story may be real or imaginary. It could be a biography, in which a series of personal events are presented in a chronological order. A story can also narrate historical events in the order that they occurred. However, it could also be a short story or a novel without a chronological order. Readers understand a story by looking at discourse markers (e.g., **antes, en esa época, luego…**). The use of *preterit* and *imperfect* tenses are related to the narrative text. The *preterit* tense is used to talk about past actions and events in order to inform about what happened and when. The *imperfect* tense is used to describe the background, to describe the conditions or circumstances that caused the action, and to talk about an ongoing action interrupted by a new one or habitual actions.

Antes de leer

1. Deportistas famosos Di a qué deportistas hispanohablantes famosos conoces y qué deporte hacen.

2. La vida de alguien ¿Conoces bien la vida de algún famoso?

3. El pibe ¿Sabes qué significa *pibe*?

La vida de Carlos "el Pibe" Valderrama

Brian Bahr /Getty Images Sports / Getty Images

Cuando se habla del fútbol colombiano, muchos colombianos nombran al Pibe, una figura que hoy día se recuerda tanto por su talento en el fútbol como por su particular cabello rubio estilo afro, y su bigotito. Su figura se parecía más a la de un cantante de música moderna que a la de un futbolista como él, que ponía orden en la cancha, guiaba a sus compañeros y encantaba al público con sus pases. Carlos Alberto Valderrama, conocido por todos como el Pibe, es el mejor jugador de fútbol colombiano de la historia.

Carlos "el Pibe" Valderrama nació el 2 de septiembre de 1961 en Santa Marta, Colombia. Su madre se llamaba Justa Palacio y su padre llevaba el mismo nombre que su hijo, Carlos Valderrama, aunque todos sus compañeros de fútbol lo conocían como Jaricho. Desde que el Pibe era un bebé, su padre lo llevaba a todos lados y lo mostraba **con orgullo.** El contraste de piel entre padre e hijo llamaba mucho la atención, ya que su padre era de piel muy oscura y su hijo de piel más blanca. Pero ¿por qué lo llamaban el Pibe?

proudly

La historia del **apodo** el Pibe comenzó porque su padre también jugaba al fútbol y desde muy pequeño llevaba a su hijo a los entrenamientos. Cuando Jaricho no llevaba a su hijo, Rubén Deibe, el **entrenador** de Jaricho, preguntaba por él y decía: "¿y el pibe cómo está?". Así que después, su padre, madre, hermanos y el resto de la familia también comenzaron a llamarlo el Pibe.

nickname
coach

© William Bello / age fotostock

Carlos Valderrama pasó su infancia como cualquier niño. Estudió la primaria en el colegio John F. Kennedy y después de las clases del colegio jugaba al fútbol en la calle o en la cancha La Castellana del barrio Pescaíto. Tanto el Pibe como sus dos hermanos, Roland y Alan, exfutbolistas profesionales, aprendieron a jugar al fútbol también en el barrio Pescaíto. Después, en la secundaria, jugó para el equipo del Liceo Celedón, que era donde él estudiaba. En 1979 se graduó de bachiller del Liceo Celedón. A pesar de que él quería ser **odontólogo**, estaba claro que el fútbol le atraía más y era parte de su vida. Así que en 1981 pasó a formar parte de su equipo profesional más querido, el Unión Magdalena. Jugó al fútbol durante 23 años en varios equipos de su país (por ejemplo, los Millonarios; Deportivo Cali; Independiente Medellín; y Joven) y también en equipos de Francia, España y Estados Unidos. Se lo considera el mejor jugador sudamericano de los años 1987-1993.

dental surgeon

En el 2002, en Santa Marta y al lado del Estadio Eduardo Santos, levantaron una enorme estatua de la figura del jugador, un monumento de bronce de seis metros de altura y siete toneladas para **homenajear** al reconocido Pibe Valderrama. En el 2004, Valderrama se retiró formalmente del fútbol, aunque todavía juega con sus compañeros y de vez en cuando aparece en programas de televisión. El Pibe es sin duda una gran figura del fútbol y sigue en la memoria del pueblo colombiano.

to honor

Después de leer

1. En el texto

1. Identifica todos los verbos en pretérito. Después, fíjate en el cuadro de la página 306 y decide por qué se usa el pretérito en cada caso: (a) acción, evento o condición completa; (b) acción puntual, única, que ocurre una vez, que ocurre de repente, cambio de condición o una acción que interrumpe a otra acción; o (c) una serie que indica eventos completos y consecutivos.
2. Identifica todos los verbos en imperfecto. Después, fíjate en el cuadro de la página 306 y decide por qué se usa el imperfecto en cada caso: (a) acción en desarrollo, habitual o repetida en el pasado; (b) acción en progreso; o (c) descripción/trasfondo.
3. Ahora, compara esta biografía de el Pibe Valderrama con la descripción de la infancia de Maradona en el Capítulo 7, Sección 1. ¿Qué diferencias notas? ¿Cuál de los dos textos te parece más descriptivo? ¿En cuál hay más acción? ¿Puedes explicar el uso del pretérito y el imperfecto en cada una de las narraciones?

2. ¿Entendiste? Organiza estos acontecimientos en orden cronológico usando números del 1 al 7.

_____ a. Hoy día sigue jugando al fútbol con sus amigos.

_____ b. Jugaba en el barrio Pescaíto de Santa Marta.

_____ c. Nació el 2 de septiembre de 1961.

_____ d. Quería ser odontólogo, pero al final decidió ser futbolista.

_____ e. Se graduó de bachiller en el Liceo Celedón.

_____ f. Jugó al fútbol profesionalmente durante 23 años.

_____ g. En Santa Marta pusieron una gran estatua de bronce en su honor.

EN TUS PROPIAS PALABRAS

Estrategias para escribir

Writing a narration When writing a narrative in Spanish, get used to follow this structure: (1) an introduction, (2) a sequence of events, and (3) a conclusion. With the introduction, you will orient your readers by setting the scene and giving enough details to describe the event and the characters clearly. Try to keep a chronological order in your narrative and include discourse markers (check the **¡Ojo!** of Chapter 6, Section 1, and Chapter 7, Section 1 and Section 2) to ensure your story is easy to follow. After including enough details you will lead the reader to the climax of the story by solving the tensions and revealing the mysteries and actions of the characters, or the events around them. Finally, present the outcome of those actions. Conclude your story by presenting an ending or letting the reader imagine it.

Now, read the short story, pay attention to the use of imperfect and preterit tenses, and answer the questions:

En aquellos años **vivía** en el campo con mis abuelos. La vida de la naturaleza me **gustaba** porque me **sentía** tranquilo y feliz. Todo a mi alrededor **era** bello: el verde de los árboles, el agua cristalina del río, el rojo atardecer.[11] **Escuchaba** a todos los animales del campo. Mi abuelita me **preparaba** buenas comidas. **Jugaba** al fútbol con mi abuelo. Pero cuando **cumplí** quince años, mi vida **cambió** porque me **mudé** a la ciudad con mi papá. **Empecé** a trabajar en una fábrica de metales y por la noche **asistía** a clases. **¡Era** una vida muy dura! Pero mi papá me **ayudaba** con la tarea, y después de unos años **terminé** los estudios secundarios y **me anoté** en la universidad.

1. ¿Cuándo se usa el imperfecto?
2. ¿Cuándo se usa el pretérito?
3. Identifica tres partes en el párrafo anterior: introducción, desarrollo y conclusión.

As you have noticed the imperfect tense is used to provide background information, to describe the surroundings, the people and the situation (**vivía, me gustaba, me sentía, era, escuchaba, preparaba, jugaba...**) and the preterit tense is used to indicate a sudden change (**cumplí, cambió, me mudé...**), and to tell what happened in a series of consecutive events that advance the story along the timeline (e.g., **empecé, terminé** and **anoté**).

▲ *Rafael Nadal, tenista español ganador de varios campeonatos y torneos*

GLYN KIRK / AFP / Getty Images

La vida de un deportista famoso

Paso 1: Escribe un artículo sobre la vida de un deportista famoso de cualquier nacionalidad para la sección de deportes del periódico de tu universidad. En tu narración, incluye el pretérito y el imperfecto. Primero, di en el artículo por qué vas a hablar de ese deportista en particular. ¿Es famoso? En los siguientes párrafos, incluye: su lugar y su fecha de nacimiento, los eventos más importantes de su vida (p. ej., medallas o campeonatos ganados). Desarrolla tu narración de forma organizada y con una secuencia apropiada. Divide tu escrito en tres partes (introducción, eventos o acciones importantes, conclusión de los eventos). No olvides usar expresiones de tiempo (p. ej., En esa época, antes, luego, etc.). Repasa **¡Ojo!** y **Por escrito** del Capítulo 6, Sección 1, y el Capítulo 7, Sección 1.

Paso 2: Después de escribir Intercambia tu artículo con un/a compañero/a. Ayuda a tu compañero/a a corregir su narración. Al corregir, usa la siguiente lista:

- ¿Tiene un título original? ¿Se corresponde con la historia del texto?
- ¿Tiene un mínimo de tres párrafos?
- ¿Qué información presenta en la introducción?
- ¿Hay una acción o conflicto después de la introducción?
- ¿Es interesante la conclusión?

- ¿Usó correctamente las formas del pretérito y del imperfecto?
- ¿Tienen acento escrito todos los verbos en pretérito o imperfecto que lo necesitan?
- ¿Te interesa esta biografía? ¿Por qué?
- ¿Crees que hay algo más que el autor debe decir?

Paso 3: Últimas decisiones Ahora, lee los comentarios de tu compañero/a y piensa en las siguientes preguntas:

- ¿Qué piensa tu compañero/a del título de tu redacción? ¿Vas a hacerle cambios?
- ¿Vas a seguir las sugerencias de tu compañero/a? ¿Por qué?
- ¿Crees que tu compañero/a te ha ayudado? ¿Cómo?

[11] atardecer: sunset

AUTOPRUEBA

VOCABULARIO

I. Los deportes y otras actividades Encierra en un círculo la palabra que no pertenece al grupo.

1. deportista / jugador / entrenador / atletismo
2. pelota / béisbol / balón / ajedrez
3. entrenador / competir / ganar/ perder
4. tenis / voleibol / rugby / dados
5. esquiar / silbar / nadar / pescar

II. ¿Qué deporte es? Identifica de qué deporte se trata y escribe el nombre.

1. Se usa un balón blanco que se pasa por encima de una red con las manos o los brazos; a veces la gente lo juega en la playa.
2. Si no tienes una bicicleta no puedes practicar este deporte.
3. Hay nueve jugadores en cada equipo y usan un bate y una pelota.
4. Hay once jugadores en cada equipo y juegan con un balón que solo pueden tocar con los pies.
5. Si no tienes esquís y no estás en el agua no puedes practicar este deporte.

GRAMÁTICA

I. Interrupciones Ayer tenías la intención de hacer muchas cosas, pero no pudiste terminar nada. Completa cada oración con uno de los pares de verbos de la lista. Pon uno de los verbos en el pretérito y el otro en el imperfecto progresivo.

manejar / parar   ver / llamar   hacer / empezar
estudiar / venir   jugar / ir(se)

1. _____ un partido de béisbol muy interesante cuando mis padres me _____ por teléfono.
2. _____ español para un examen cuando un amigo _____ a casa a visitarme.
3. _____ muy rápido cuando un policía me _____.
4. _____ a las cartas con mis amigos cuando _____ la luz.
5. _____ senderismo cuando _____ a llover.

II. Breve historia de la conquista y la colonia Elige la forma correcta del pretérito o del imperfecto para completar esta breve historia de Colombia.

Tres grandes culturas (**poblaban/poblaron**)$_1$ el territorio colombiano durante la época precolombina: la chibcha, la caribe y la arwac. Cada una de estas culturas (**vivía/vivió**)$_2$ en un área diferente de Colombia. La estructura sociopolítica de los chibchas (**era/fue**)$_3$ matriarcal. Los

arwacs, por otro lado, (**tenían/tuvieron**)$_4$ una organización mixta de matriarcado y patriarcado. Los caribes (**eran/fueran**)$_5$ un pueblo guerrero y comerciante. La economía de estos pueblos (**consistía/consistió**)$_6$ en la agricultura, la caza, la pesca y la recolección.

Cuando (**llegaban/llegaron**)$_7$ los europeos, (**encontraban/encontraron**)$_8$ un pueblo disperso. La diversidad de lenguas, costumbres, religiones y zonas geográficas se (**convertían/convirtieron**)$_9$ en una desventaja para los nativos. El proceso de colonización (**comenzaba/comenzó**)$_{10}$ en 1509, cuando los conquistadores (**fundaban/fundaron**)$_{11}$ las primeras ciudades. En la época de la colonización los nativos (**ofrecían/ofrecieron**)$_{12}$ el oro como intercambio mientras los colonizadores les (**vendían/vendieron**)$_{13}$ espejos, telas[12] y otros artículos de mínimo valor. Durante este período, la Iglesia (**impuso/imponía**)$_{14}$ la religión católica en todos los territorios y (**facilitaba/facilitó**)$_{15}$ su administración por los colonizadores españoles.

La gente estaba descontenta cuando (**empezaba/empezó**)$_{16}$ el movimiento independentista de España, a principios del siglo XIX.

CULTURA

Decide si la oración es **cierta** (C) o **falsa** (F). Corrige las que sean falsas.

	C	F
1. El deporte más popular en Colombia es el fútbol.	☐	☐
2. El equipo de fútbol femenino colombiano gana más campeonatos que el masculino en las competiciones internacionales.	☐	☐
3. Otros deportes populares en Colombia son el esquí y el hockey.	☐	☐
4. Carlos Valderrama fue un jugador de béisbol muy famoso en Colombia.	☐	☐

REDACCIÓN

Piensa en un/a atleta que admiras y escribe unas líneas sobre su vida.

¿Quién es? ¿Cuál es su deporte? ¿Por qué lo/la admiras? ¿Qué hizo? ¿Qué ocasión especial recuerdas de su carrera?

EN RESUMIDAS CUENTAS, AHORA PUEDO...

☐ hablar sobre juegos y deportes.

☐ dar instrucciones en situaciones formales.

☐ narrar eventos en el pasado.

☐ expresar acciones que están en progreso.

☐ hablar sobre el fútbol y su popularidad en Colombia.

☐ entender diferencias culturales relacionadas a los deportes.

---

[12] **tela:** material, fabric

🎧 VOCABULARIO ESENCIAL

Sustantivos

el/la aficionado/a	*fan*
el ajedrez	*chess*
el/la arquero/a	*goalkeeper*
el atletismo	*track and field*
el baloncesto	*basketball*
el balón	*(soccer, basket) ball*
el campeonato	*championship*
el campo de fútbol	*soccer field*
la cancha	*court*
las cartas	*cards*
los dados	*dice*
las damas	*checkers*
el deporte (extremo/de riesgo)	*(extreme) sport*
el/la deportista	*athlete*
el/la entrenador/a	*coach / trainer*
el equipo	*team*
la ficha	*piece*
el fútbol	*soccer*
el juego	*game*
el juego de mesa	*board game*
el/la jugador/a	*player*
la liga	*league*
la natación	*swimming*
el partido (de fútbol, de tenis, de baloncesto)	*(soccer, tennis, basketball) match, game*
la pelota	*ball*
la pesca	*fishing*
el tablero	*board*
el tenis de mesa	*ping-pong*
el videojuego	*videogame*
el voleibol (de playa)	*(beach) volleyball*

Cognados: el bate, el béisbol, el ciclismo, el estadio, el golf, el hockey, el rugby, el tenis

Verbos y expresiones verbales

animar (a un equipo)	*to cheer (a team)*
andar en patineta/ monopatín	*to skateboard*
ganar	*to win*
hacer/jugar (ue) a un deporte	*to play/practice a sport*
hacer esquí acuático	*to water ski*
hacer senderismo	*to hike*
hacer snowboarding	*to snowboard*
levantar pesas	*weight-lifting*
montar a caballo	*horseback riding*
montar en bicicleta	*to ride a bike*
patinar en línea	*line skating*
perder (ie)	*to lose*
pescar	*to go fishing*
ser aficionado/a (de)	*to be a fan (of)*
silbar	*to whistle*

Expresiones

anoche	*last night*
anteayer	*the day before yesterday*
ayer	*yesterday*
¿De qué equipo eres?	*What team do you support?*
Soy de…	*My team is . . .*
de repente	*suddenly*
un día, una vez	*one day, one time*
el fin de semana/mes/ año pasado	*last weekend/month/year*
el lunes/martes… pasado	*last Monday/Tuesday . . .*
mientras	*while*
la semana pasada	*last week*
ya	*already*

Sección 2 — El cine y la televisión

LEARNING OBJECTIVES

By the end of this section you will be able to:

- Talk about TV shows, movies, and media
- Express likes and dislikes when talking about entertainment
- Express negation
- Use double object pronouns to avoid repetition
- Understand the popularity of soap operas in Venezuela and Colombia

Una imagen vale más que mil palabras

¿Reconoces el título de la película?

¿Crees que es necesario traducir los títulos?

¿Traducimos los títulos de las películas extranjeras en Estados Unidos?

© Summit Entertainment/Photofest

UNA PERSPECTIVA

Courtesy Rachel Haywood Ferreira

Rachel

Las películas

Diferente

"En Venezuela, las películas extranjeras, o sea, películas de Estados Unidos, Rusia, Francia, Dinamarca, etc., no se doblan[1], sino que tienen subtítulos en español. Cada vez que voy al cine para ver una película en inglés con subtítulos en español, me siento un poco rara porque yo soy siempre la primera que se ríe y un momento después (después de leer los subtítulos) el resto del público se ríe. Las películas para niños sí se doblan y, aunque[2] yo entiendo bastante bien el español, los labios y las palabras no coinciden y esto me confunde un poco".

Igual

"En Estados Unidos también tenemos películas con subtítulos, pero no muchas porque en Estados Unidos el público prefiere las películas en inglés. Muy pocas películas extranjeras tienen éxito. Los dibujos animados[3] que vienen del Japón, como Bola de Dragón y Pokemon, también se doblan".

¿Qué piensas tú?

1. ¿Te molesta ver películas con subtítulos? ¿Por qué?
2. ¿Qué películas extranjeras viste recientemente?
3. ¿Sabes por qué las películas extranjeras no tienen mucho éxito en Estados Unidos?

---

[1]**doblar:** to dub [2]**aunque:** although [3]**dibujos animados:** cartoons

LA PURA VERDAD I | Televisión

Samuel es un turista que está visitando Venezuela por un mes. Tiene muchos amigos en Caracas y Maracaibo. Su amigo venezolano, Marcelo, lo invita una tarde a ver juntos la televisión.

1.

2.

3.

4.

5.

6.

 8.2-01 ¿Qué tipo de programa es? Escucha la narración y decide a qué tipo de programa o película se refiere.

1. a. las comedias románticas   b. los comerciales   c. los programas de concurso
2. a. las películas de ciencia ficción   b. las novelas   c. las películas animadas
3. a. las películas con subtítulos   b. los documentales   c. los noticieros

◐ PALABRA POR PALABRA

La televisión

PURA VISION.com
24 horas de información

Inicio Mercadeo Blogs RSS Señal en vivo Titulares de prensa Contáctenos

S E Ñ A L
EN VIVO
Abril 21, 2012 11:45 am

Inicio » Programación

Empresa	Cobertura	¿Por qué invertir?	Programación	Tarifas TV	Tarifas web	Tarifas móvil

LUNES	MARTES	MIÉRCOLES	JUEVES	VIERNES	SÁBADO	DOMINGO	HORA/DÍA	
			PROGRAMACIÓN					
		HIMNO NACIONAL					12:00 AM	
PROGRAMA DE INVESTIGACIÓN		NOTICIAS					12:04 AM	● el noticiero
							12:30 AM	
NOTICIAS		NOTICIAS ECONÓMICAS				35 MM	1:00 AM	
		GRADO 33				RECORRIENDO REALIDADES	1:30 AM	
EL MUNDO ECONÓMICO		BRÚJULA INTERNACIONAL				SÁBADO EN LA NOCHE	2:00 AM	● el programa de variedades
CON TEODORO							2:30 AM	
TOCANDO FONDO		TNN					3:00 AM	
		RCN				TNN	3:30 AM	
TNN	SIN FLASH	RECORRIENDO REALIDADES	35 MM	ALTA POSTURA	ALTA DENSIDAD	NOTICIAS	4:00 AM	
		NOTICIAS					4:30 AM	
						RECORRIENDO REALIDADES	5:00 AM	
		DEL DICHO AL HECHO			RADAR DE LOS BARRIOS	SIN FLASH	5:30 AM	
		HIMNO NACIONAL					6:00 AM	
					SIN FLASH	LO MEJOR DE 35 MM	6:04 AM	
		PROGRAMA DE VARIEDADES			TNN		6:30 AM	
							7:00 AM	
					EL CAPITÁN CENTELLA		7:30 AM	● los dibujos animados
							8:00 AM	
		SOLUCIONES					8:30 AM	
		TELE NOVELA			A QUE TE RÍES		9:00 AM	● la comedia
					TNN WORLD REPORT	EL MUNDO ECONÓMICO	9:30 AM	
		LA VIUDA JOVEN			DEPORTES	CON TEODORO	10:00 AM	● la telenovela
					TELE REALIDAD	TOCANDO FONDO	10:30 AM	
					SIN FLASH		11:00 AM	
					ASÍ COCINA SOUCY	REPORTEROS	11:30 AM	
		A QUE TE RÍES			NOTICIAS		12:00 m. A 1:00 PM	
					SIN FLASH	PLAY BALL	1:00 PM	
		FLASH y PLANETA GENTE			ANTESALA 35 MM	BIOGRAFÍA	1:30 PM	
		TRAMPOLÍN A LA FAMA			DEPORTES	TNN	2:00 PM	● el concurso
					ALTA DENSIDAD	PROGRAMA DEPORTE	2:30 PM	
		NOTICIAS ECONÓMICAS			NOTICIAS		3:00 PM	
SIN FLASH	RECORRIENDO REALIDADES	35 MM	ALTA POSTURA	ALTA DENSIDAD	TNN	OTRA VISIÓN	3:30 PM	
		NOTICIAS					4:00 PM	
		PROGRAMA DE ENTREVISTAS			CALA		4:30 PM	
					TNN destinos		5:00 PM	
					RECORRIENDO REALIDADES	ALO VENEZUELA	5:30 PM	
		CORAZÓN APASIONADO			NOTICIAS		6:00 PM	
					ALTA POSTURA		6:30 PM	
					OTRA VISIÓN	PROGRAMA DE INVESTIGACIÓN	7:00 PM	
					35 MM		7:30 PM	
		GRADO 33			BIOGRAFÍA	REPORTEROS	8:00 PM	
	TNN	PROGRAMA DE INVESTIGACIÓN		TNN			8:30 PM	
		NOTICIAS					9:00 PM	
							9:30 PM	
		BUENAS NOCHES			SÁBADO EN LA	YO PROMETO	10:00 PM	

© John Wiley & Sons, Inc.

el canal (de televisión)	*TV channel*	**el/la presentador/a (de televisión)**	*newsreader, TV host(ess)*
el anuncio/comercial	*TV commercial*	**el programa (de variedades)**	*(variety) show*
el concurso	*competition, contest*	**la programación**	*programming, schedule*
los dibujos animados	*cartoons*	**la telenovela**	*soap opera*
el noticiero	*news program*		

Cognados: la comedia, el episodio, la serie

© John Wiley & Sons, Inc.

la película de animación   **la película dramática**   **la comedia**   **la película romántica**   **la película de acción/suspenso**

El cine

la entrada	*movie ticket*
la película (de terror)	*(horror) movie*
el personaje	*character*
el premio	*award*
el/la protagonista	*main character*
la trama	*plot*

Cognados: la ciencia ficción, los efectos especiales, el/la crítico/a (de cine/teatro), el documental, el/la espectador/a, los subtítulos

Los medios de comunicación *Media*

la actualidad	*current affairs*
la emisora de radio	*radio station*
la noticia	*piece of news*
las noticias (internacionales, nacionales, locales)	*(international, national, local) news*
el periódico	*newspaper*
el/la periodista	*journalist*
la prensa	*press*
la revista	*magazine*

Cognados: la radio, el/la reportero/a

¿Qué dicen los venezolanos?

*Los casetes <u>son del año de la pera.</u>	*Cassettes <u>are very old.</u>*
*¡<u>Chévere</u>!	*Good, cool*
*¡Esos <u>culebrones</u> son adictivos!	*Those <u>soap operas</u> (lit., big snakes) are addictive!*
*Un <u>pana</u> mío me lo dijo.	*A <u>good friend</u> of mine told me about it.*
*¡<u>Qué vaina</u>! No encuentro mis lentes.	*<u>What a drag!</u> I can't find my glasses.*

*Estas expresiones se usan en otros países hispanos también.

Para hablar del entretenimiento

¿De qué (se) trata?	*What is it about?*
¿Qué hay en la tele?	*What's on TV?*
la obra de teatro	*theater play*
actual	*current*
aburrido/a	*boring, tedious*
animado/a	*lively*
controvertido/a	*controversial*
doblado/a	*dubbed*
emocionante	*exciting, thrilling*
entretenido/a	*entertaining*
gracioso/a	*funny*
doblar	*to dub*
grabar	*to record*
representar/interpretar (un personaje)	*to play (the part of . . .)*
tener éxito	*to be successful*
tratar(se) de	*to be about*

Cognados: actuar, informar; el control remoto

8.2-02 ¿Qué hacen?

Paso 1: Expliquen lo que hacen o quiénes son estas personas.

MODELO: el actor   →   *El actor actúa en películas u obras de teatro.*

1. el/la presentador/a
2. el personaje
3. el/la reportero/a
4. el periodista
5. el crítico
6. el/la director/a
7. el/la protagonista
8. el/la espectador/a

Paso 2: Ahora, escriban la definición de otras dos palabras de **Palabra por palabra**. Van a leerle las definiciones a la clase, y sus compañeros las van a adivinar.

8.2-03 El nombre de...

Paso 1: En grupos de tres, piensen en un ejemplo para cada una de las siguientes categorías.

1. el concurso de televisión con los mejores premios
2. una película con una trama muy complicada
3. la emisora de radio más popular entre los estudiantes de tu universidad
4. una película que recibió varios premios Óscar
5. una serie de televisión con muchísima audiencia
6. un personaje difícil de interpretar
7. un documental muy controvertido
8. una película con efectos especiales impresionantes

Paso 2: Ahora, comenten sus respuestas con otros dos grupos y escriban un informe para presentar a la clase.

MODELO: *Todos están de acuerdo en que _____ es una película con efectos especiales impresionantes. Sin embargo, hay variedad de opiniones respecto a una película con trama complicada. Según la clase, _____, _____ y _____ tienen una trama complicada.*

8.2-04 El programa es...

Paso 1: Piensa en un tipo de programa o noticia y después comenta qué te parece.

1. aburrido/a
2. animado/a
3. gracioso/a
4. controvertido/a
5. emocionante
6. entretenido/a

Paso 2: Comenta tus respuestas con un/a compañero/a. ¿Puedes encontrar tres compañeros que coincidan contigo en —por lo menos— dos respuestas?

MODELO: Estudiante 1:   *Los programas deportivos me parecen súper aburridos.*
Estudiante 2:   *A mí también.* o *A mí no. A mí me encantan. Son los más interesantes de la programación.*

8.2-05 ¿Estás informado?

Paso 1: Hablen sobre cómo se informan ustedes de las noticias.

1. ¿Lees el periódico? ¿Con qué frecuencia? ¿Qué periódico lees?
2. ¿Estás informado de las noticias internacionales? ¿Qué está pasando ahora?
3. ¿Lees revistas? ¿Qué revistas lees? ¿Con qué frecuencia?
4. ¿Cómo prefieres informarte de las noticias? ¿Por qué?
5. ¿Cuál es tu noticiero favorito? ¿Por qué? ¿En qué canal es?
6. ¿Escuchas la radio con frecuencia? ¿Qué emisora(s) escuchas?

Paso 2: Escriban un pequeño informe. ¿En qué aspectos coinciden los dos? ¿En qué no coinciden? Por último, informen a la clase. ¿Crees que tu compañero/a está bien informado/a?

MODELO: *Mi compañero/a y yo leemos todos los días el periódico _____. A mí no me interesan las noticias locales pero a él/ella sí le interesan...*

Verbs like **gustar**: **Parecer** + *adjective*

In Chapter 5, Section 2, you learned the verb **parecer** (+ *adjective*) to express opinions/impressions about something/someone. This verb works like the verb "to seem" in English. Just like with the verb **gustar**, the thing/person that is being discussed is the subject of the verb (i.e., **parecer** agrees with it).

<u>Ese artículo</u> me parece muy interesante.

I think this program is very interesting (literally, This program seems very interesting to me).

<u>Esas series</u> nos parecen entretenidas.

We think those shows are entertaining (literally, Those shows seem entertaining to us).

The **a** + pronoun/noun phrase is the indirect object. Thus, the pronouns used with **parecer** are indirect object pronouns.

<u>A mí</u> los programas de concurso **me** parecen emocionantes.

Pues <u>a Marcelo y a Samuel</u> **les** parecen una pérdida de tiempo.

HABLANDO DE GRAMÁTICA I

WileyPLUS Go to *WileyPLUS* to review the grammar point with the help of the **Animated Grammar Tutorial**.

1. Expressing negation: Negative and indefinite words

You have already been using some indefinite words like **algo** and some negative words like **nada, nunca,** or **nadie**. Here are some other indefinite and negative words:

Negative and indefinite pronouns

algo	*something, anything*	Sé **algo** sobre el cine venezolano.
todo	*everything*	**Todo** el cine venezolano es muy interesante.
nada	*nothing, not anything*	**No** sé **nada** sobre el cine venezolano.
alguien	*someone, anyone*	**Alguien** de la clase sabe algo sobre el cine venezolano.
nadie	*no one, nobody*	**Nadie** de la clase sabe nada sobre el cine venezolano.

Negative and indefinite adjectives

todo/a/os/as	*all*	**Todos** los programas eran interesantes.
algún, alguna/os/as	*some, any*	**Algunos** programas eran interesantes.
ningún, ninguna/os/as	*none, any*	**Ningún** programa era interesante.

Negative and indefinite adverbs

siempre	*always*	La mamá de Marcelo **siempre** ve esa telenovela. La mamá de Marcelo ve esa telenovela **siempre**.
nunca, jamás	*never*	Marcelo **nunca** ve telenovelas. Marcelo **no** ve telenovelas **nunca**.
también	*also*	La hermana de Marcelo **también** ve esa telenovela. La hermana de Marcelo ve esa telenovela **también**.
tampoco	*neither, not either*	Samuel **tampoco** ve telenovelas. Samuel **no** ve telenovelas **tampoco**.

Negative and indefinite conjunctions

o... o	*either... or*	Podemos ver **o** esta película **o** esta serie.
ni... ni	*either... nor*	No quiero ver **ni** esta película **ni** esta serie.

A. Double negation

In Spanish, the negative adverb should always precede the verb:

Samuel todavía **no** habla bien español y por eso **no** entiende las noticias.	*Samuel still doesn't speak Spanish well so he doesn't understand the news.*
Marcelo **nunca** ve películas románticas.	*Marcelo never watches romantic movies.*

The negative forms **nadie, nada** o **ningún, ninguno/a** can follow or precede the verb. If they follow the verb, we must use a negative word before the verb. Notice that this may result in double negatives, which is very common in Spanish.

Samuel **no** entiende **nada** cuando el presentador habla muy rápido.	*Samuel does not understand anything when the newsreader speaks very fast.*
Samuel **tampoco** ve películas románticas **nunca**.	*Samuel never watches romantic movies, either.*

B. The adjectives *algún* and *ningún*

Alguno/a/os/as and **ningún/ninguno/a** are adjectives that agree in gender and number with the noun they modify. **Alguno** and **ninguno** are shortened to **algún** and **ningún** when followed by a singular, masculine noun. We can use these forms as pronouns to replace a noun already referred to. In this case they match the gender and number of that noun.

¿Quieres ver **algún** programa de televisión?	Do you want to watch **any** program on TV?
No, no me gusta ninguno.	No, I don't like any (of them).
¿Prefieres ver **alguna** de las películas que dan en el cine?	Do you prefer to watch **any** of the movies they are now playing at the theater?
Tampoco me gusta **ninguna** de las que están dando ahora.	I don't like **any** of the ones playing now.

8.2-06 ¿Qué hay en la tele? Lee el siguiente párrafo sobre Marcelo y Samuel.

Marcelo y Samuel están en casa viendo la televisión, pero hoy <u>no</u> hay <u>nada</u> interesante. A Marcelo no le gusta ningún programa. Además, a Samuel no le gustan ni las noticias ni las series de comedia en español. A veces hay comerciales muy graciosos en la televisión venezolana pero a Samuel no le parecen graciosos tampoco. Entiende algunas palabras, pero el problema es que no entiende ninguno de los chistes. Por fin encuentran la serie "Amigos". A Marcelo le encanta, y a Samuel también, porque conoce algunos episodios, recuerda los chistes y eso le ayuda a entender algo más.

Paso 1: Escribe todas las palabras indefinidas y negativas que hay en el párrafo. Si hay negación doble en la misma oración, escribe las dos palabras en la misma línea.

MODELO: 1. ___*no/nada*___

2. _____   6. _____

3. _____   7. _____

4. _____   8. _____

5. _____   9. _____

Paso 2: ¿Cierto o falso? Lee el párrafo otra vez y decide si las siguientes oraciones son **ciertas** o **falsas**. Si son falsas, escribe la información correcta usando palabras indefinidas o negativas.

MODELO: A Marcelo le gustan **todas** las películas románticas.
          → *Falso; No le gusta **ninguna** película romántica.*

C   F

☐   ☐   1. Hoy en la tele **no** hay **muchos** programas interesantes.

☐   ☐   2. A Samuel **no** le gusta **ninguno** de los programas que ven.

☐   ☐   3. Samuel entiende **todos** los chistes de los comerciales.

☐   ☐   4. A veces encuentran **algún** programa que les gusta a los dos.

☐   ☐   5. Al final[4] **no** encuentran **nada** para ver en la televisión.

---

[4] **al final:** at the end

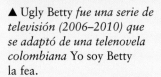

▲ Ugly Betty *fue una serie de televisión (2006–2010) que se adaptó de una telenovela colombiana* Yo soy Betty la fea.

8.2-07 Yo soy Betty, la fea Completa el siguiente párrafo sobre la telenovela colombiana con la forma adecuada de las palabras negativas o indefinidas. ¡Presta atención a la concordancia de los adjetivos!

ningún	ninguno/a	nada	todo/a/os/as
algún	alguno/a	también	

Beatriz Aurora Pinzón, también conocida como Betty, es muy inteligente y tiene una maestría en finanzas, pero no es linda y no se preocupa _____1 por su apariencia física. Betty no puede conseguir _____2 entrevista de trabajo porque sus fotos son tan feas que arruinan su impresionante currículum vitae. Finalmente consigue un puesto de secretaria en una empresa de modas, donde _____3 sus compañeros de trabajo guapos y perezosos la tratan muy mal porque no hay _____4 otro empleado tan inteligente como ella. _____5 críticos afirman que *Betty la fea* tuvo tanto éxito porque antes _____6 telenovela tenía por protagonista a una muchacha "fea". Además, la telenovela retrata⁵ de manera realista las luchas⁶ de clase y raza en algunas zonas de América Latina. Sin embargo, al final, la telenovela termina como _____7 las otras. Betty se transforma en una guapa ejecutiva y se casa con el jefe de la empresa, **a pesar de que**⁷ ella sabe que no es un príncipe azul.

Después de su éxito en Colombia, la telenovela tuvo mucho éxito en _____8 países, como Estados Unidos, Alemania o Italia. _____9 existen _____10 adaptaciones de la telenovela, como la versión estadounidense *Ugly Betty*.

8.2-08 ¿Vemos los mismos programas?

Paso 1: Contesta las siguientes preguntas con información verdadera sobre ti y añade alguna explicación.

MODELO: ¿**Alguien** de tu familia ve los mismos programas que tú?
→ *No, **nadie** ve los mismos programas que yo.* o *Sí, mi hermana y yo vemos los mismos programas y a veces los vemos juntos/as.*

1. ¿Ves alguna telenovela? ¿Sabes el nombre de alguna telenovela popular ahora en Estados Unidos?
2. ¿Prefieres ver algún noticiero en particular?
3. Cuando ves el noticiero, ¿ves todas las noticias, o algunas no te interesan?
4. ¿Alguna vez vas al cine a ver películas extranjeras?
5. ¿Alguien que conoces trabaja en el cine o la televisión?
6. ¿Hay algo en especial de la programación que siempre ves?

Paso 2: Ahora, entrevista a un/a compañero/a de clase. Él/Ella también te va a hacer preguntas a ti. En general, ¿quién de los dos está mejor informado/a sobre la programación del cine y la televisión? ¿Tienen los mismos gustos?

---

⁵**retratar:** to portray ⁶**lucha:** struggle ⁷**a pesar de que:** despite the fact that

LA PURA VERDAD II Viendo la telenovela

Samuel está de visita en la casa de Marcelo. Mientras Marcelo está ocupado, Samuel se sienta junto a la madre de Marcelo, que está mirando una telenovela.

1.

¿Qué pasa?

Estoy viendo la telenovela 'La viuda joven'. La viuda se llama Abril Armas. Nadie sabe cómo sufre. ¡Nadie!

2.

¿De qué trata la telenovela?

La baronesa Inma mató a sus cuatro esposos pero el detective Alejandro no puede hacer nada. ¡No puede probar nada!

3.

¿Cómo sabe que mató a sus cuatro esposos?

Mi vecina me lo dijo ayer. La baronesa se lo confesó al cura.

4.

Esa mujer es muy mala. No quiere a nadie. Nunca piensa en los demás[8]. Ahora está seduciendo a Alejandro. ¡Qué mala! Ella va a pagar algún día."

5.

¡Ajá! ¡El cura va a confesar!

¿A quién? ¿Se lo va a decir al detective?

6.

¿No te lo dije? ¡Sí te lo dije! ¡Ella va a pagar!

© John Wiley & Sons, Inc.

8.2-09 ¿Qué va a pasar en el próximo episodio? Doña Juanita y su vecina hablan por teléfono sobre qué va a pasar en el próximo episodio. Escucha qué dicen y selecciona la oración que mejor lo describe.

1. Sobre el secreto, la vecina piensa que...
   a. los esposos se lo van a decir al cura.
   b. el detective se lo va a decir a la policía.
   c. el cura se lo va a decir al detective.
2. Sobre qué va a pasar en el episodio de mañana, doña Juanita piensa que...
   a. el detective no está enamorado de nadie.
   b. el cura no va a decir nada.
   c. el detective no va a hablar nunca con el cura.
3. Sobre el detective, piensa que...
   a. no va a decidir nada.
   b. no quiere a ninguna de las dos mujeres.
   c. va a estar solo al final.

[8] **los demás:** the others

HABLANDO DE GRAMÁTICA II

WileyPLUS Go to *WileyPLUS* to review the grammar point with the help of the **Animated Grammar Tutorial**.

♻ 2. Avoiding repetition (II): Double object pronouns

In Chapter 5 you learned how to use direct and indirect object pronouns to avoid redundancy. Remember that you use direct object pronouns to replace the direct object of a sentence. The direct object receives the action of the verb and answers the questions *What?* or *Whom?*

¿Doña Juanita ve **esa telenovela**?	*Doña Juanita watches that soap opera?*
Sí, **la** ve todos los días.	*Yes, she watches it everyday.*

We use indirect object pronouns to replace the indirect object of a sentence. The indirect object answers the question *To whom?* or *For whom?*

¿**Me** pasas el control remoto, por favor?	*Can you pass the remote control to me, please?*

It is very common to use two pronouns together.

¿**Me** pasas **el control remoto**, por favor?	*Can you pass the remote to me, please?*
Sí, ahora **te lo** paso.	*Yes, I'll pass it to you right now.*

A. Order of pronouns

When the two object pronouns appear in the same sentence, they always appear together. The indirect object pronoun always preceeds the direct object pronoun. This is the opposite order in which these pronouns are placed in English.

♻ **Direct and Indirect pronouns**

Do you remember how to use direct and indirect object pronouns? Go back to Chapter 5 to review that content before learning this grammar point.

	Indirect object pronoun	Direct object pronoun
(le) →	me te **se**	lo/la/los/las
(le) →	nos os **se**	

¿**Me** compras **la entrada**?	*Can you buy the ticket for me?*
Está bien, **te la** compro, pero la próxima vez **me la** compras tú a mí.	*Ok, I'll buy it for you, but next time you buy it for me.*

B. Placement of pronouns

As with single object pronouns, double pronouns are placed before a conjugated verb. If the sentence is negative, the pronouns are placed between the negative word and the verb:

¿**Me** pasas el **control remoto**?	*Can you pass me the remote control?*
No, no **te lo** paso porque no **lo** tengo.	*No, I won't pass it to you because I don't have it.*

When a verb phrase has an infinitive or a present participle (ending in **-ndo**), the pronouns may be attached to the end of these forms or they may be placed before the conjugated verb. If attached to the infinitive or to the participle, there is a written accent mark over the vowel that carries the stress.

¿Vas a compra**rme las entradas**?	→	¿Vas a comprár**melas**?
¿**Me** vas a comprar **las entradas**?	→	¿**Me las** vas a comprar?
Are you going to buy the tickets for me?	→	*Are you going to buy them for me?*

Estoy comprándo**telas** ahora. / **Te las** estoy comprando ahora.
I am buying them for you right now.

C. le → se

The indirect object pronouns **le** and **les** change to **se** when followed by **lo, la, los, las.** This is *not* a reflexive **se.**

Por fin Samuel **le** pasó **los pañuelos.** →	Por fin Samuel **se los** pasó.
Finally Samuel passed the tissues to her.	*Finally Samuel passed them to her.*
Doña Juanita les prometió que va → a dejar **de ver la novela.**	Doña Juanita **se lo** prometió.
Doña Juanita promised to them that she would stop watching the soap opera.	*Doña Juanita promised it to them.*

D. Object pronouns with *decir*

Unlike in English, it is very common to use the pronoun **lo** with the verb **decir** when the direct object is implied (i.e., it is something already said or known):

¿No **te lo** dije? ¡Sí **te lo** dije!	*Didn't I tell (it to) you? Yes I told (it to)*
¡Ella lo va a pagar!	*you! She is going to pay for it!*

E. Pronoun doubling

You may have noticed that in Spanish the indirect object pronoun often appears in the sentence at the same time as the indirect object itself. Given that **se/le/nos** can refer to both singular and plural indirect objects, it is often followed by a prepositional phrase with **a** to clarify who the indirect object is (if it is not clear from the context) or to add emphasis.

¿**Nos** prestas el carro **a Gloria y a mí** para ir al cine? ¿Cuándo **nos lo** puedes prestar?	*Would you lend me and Gloria the car to go to the movies? When can you lend it to us?*
Ya **se lo** dije **a doña Juanita.**	*I already told doña Juanita.*

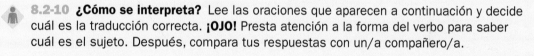

8.2-10 ¿Cómo se interpreta? Lee las oraciones que aparecen a continuación y decide cuál es la traducción correcta. **¡OJO!** Presta atención a la forma del verbo para saber cuál es el sujeto. Después, compara tus respuestas con un/a compañero/a.

	A	**B**
1. Me invitó al cine Marcelo.	☐ *Marcelo invited me to the movies.*	☐ *I invited Marcelo to the movies.*
2. ¿La entrada? Nos la compró él.	☐ *The ticket? He bought it for us.*	☐ *The ticket? We bought it for him.*
3. No le di el dinero para comprarlas.	☐ *He didn't give me the money to buy them.*	☐ *I didn't give him the money to buy them.*
4. Te lo expliqué ayer.	☐ *I explained to you yesterday.*	☐ *You explained it to me yesterday.*
5. Nos acompañó Gloria.	☐ *We accompanied Gloria.*	☐ *Gloria accompanied us.*

8.2-11 ¿Qué pasó? Samuel recuerda lo que pasó en casa de Marcelo.

Paso 1: En las siguientes oraciones, identifica quién hace la acción del verbo en negrita: Marcelo, Samuel o doña Juanita.

1. Marcelo tenía el control remoto y yo **se lo pedí.**
2. Cuando encontramos un programa que nos gustaba a los dos, **me lo pasó.**
3. Cuando fui a casa de Marcelo, su madre me dijo: "Marcelo llega más tarde. ¿No **te lo dijo?**".
4. Doña Juanita lloraba y me pidió los pañuelos;[9] **se los di** inmediatamente.
5. Doña Juanita me dijo que la trama de la telenovela era muy complicada. **Me la contó** con todo detalle.
6. Después tomamos café. **Me lo sirvió** con unas galletitas muy ricas.

[9] **pañuelos:** tissues

Paso 2: Ahora, elige la respuesta basándote en las oraciones del **Paso 1**.

1. ¿Quién le pasó el control remoto?
   a. Se lo pasó a Marcelo.
   b. Se lo pasó Samuel.
   c. Se lo pasó Marcelo.
2. ¿A quién le pasó el control remoto?
   a. Se lo pasó a Marcelo.
   b. Se lo pasó a Samuel.
   c. Se lo pasó Samuel.

3. ¿Quién pidió los pañuelos?
   a. Se los pidió a Samuel doña Juanita.
   b. Se la pidió doña Juanita a Samuel.
   c. Se los pidió Samuel a doña Juanita.
4. ¿Qué pasó con las galletitas?
   a. Se las sirvió a doña Juanita.
   b. Se las sirvió doña Juanita.
   c. Se las sirvió Marcelo.

 8.2-12 Una tarde en el cine Samuel nos cuenta cómo fue su tarde en el cine.

Paso 1: Combina las oraciones de la primera columna con la que corresponda de la segunda.

____ 1. Marcelo quería invitar a unos amigos al cine.

____ 2. Yo no sabía dónde estaba el cine y le pregunté a Marcelo.

____ 3. Marcelo dijo que no había que preocuparse por las entradas. Creo que va a comprarlas.

____ 4. Marcelo nos pidió nuestra opinión sobre las películas de la cartelera.

____ 5. Al final, decidimos ver una película en inglés con subtítulos en español.

____ 6. Durante la película, Gloria estaba un poco frustrada y hablé con ella.

____ 7. Yo era el único que entendía todos los chistes.

a. **Se la** dimos.
b. Gloria no quería ver esa, pero **la** convencimos.
c. **Nos las** compró él.
d. **Le** pregunté qué **le** pasaba.
e. **Se los** tuve que explicar a Marcelo y a Gloria porque los chistes son difíciles de entender.
f. **Nos lo** dijo a Gloria y a mí.
g. Marcelo **me lo** explicó.

Paso 2: Ahora, contesta estas preguntas. Decide si debes usar el pronombre de objeto directo, el de objeto indirecto, o los dos.

MODELO: ¿Quién invitó <u>a Samuel y a Marcelo</u> al cine?
           Marcelo los invitó o Los invitó Marcelo.

1. ¿Quién <u>les</u> compró <u>las entradas</u>?
2. ¿Quién le explicó <u>a Samuel</u> <u>cómo llegar al cine</u>?
3. ¿A quién <u>le</u> dieron Samuel y Gloria <u>su opinión sobre las películas</u>?
4. ¿Quiénes convencieron <u>a Gloria</u> de ver una película con subtítulos?
5. ¿Quién le preguntó <u>a Gloria</u> <u>por qué se sentía frustrada</u>?
6. ¿Quién entendió <u>todos los chistes</u> de la película?

OTRA PERSPECTIVA

Courtesy of Yolanda Jacqueline
Peláez

Yolanda

Las telenovelas

Diferente

"Las telenovelas son muy populares en Venezuela. Una amiga de mi madre miraba cuatro telenovelas al día; dos durante la tarde y dos por la noche. En Venezuela, las telenovelas de la noche son las mejores y las más populares, mientras que en Estados Unidos solo hay telenovelas durante el día.

Las telenovelas son historias que duran uno o dos años. Cuando termina una, empieza otra con otro nombre, otros actores y otra historia. En Estados Unidos solo tienen un nombre, los actores mueren y regresan a la vida y algunas telenovelas nunca terminan: *Hospital general* empezó en 1963 y todavía continúa. ¿Por qué? Además, ¿por qué las llaman 'óperas de jabón'?".

Igual

"Tanto las telenovelas venezolanas como las de Estados Unidos son un poco adictivas y todas tienen elementos de intriga, traición y amor. Todas terminan cada episodio con algo chocante para que quieras ver el próximo episodio. Son todas muy melodramáticas, ¿no?".

Explícale a Yolanda

1. ¿Son populares las telenovelas en Estados Unidos?
2. ¿Por qué no tienen fin las novelas en Estados Unidos?
3. ¿Por qué las llaman "óperas de jabón"?

MANOS A LA OBRA

8.2-13 ¿Y tú qué piensas?

Paso 1: Completa las siguientes oraciones con información sobre tus gustos.

1. Siempre veo...
2. Nunca veo...
3. Me gustan mucho...
4. No me gustan...
5. Los programas de... me parecen...
6. Las películas de... no me parecen...
7. Algunas series que me encantan son...
8. Una noticia de actualidad que me interesa es...

Paso 2: Comenta tus respuestas con un/a compañero/a. ¿Piensan igual?

MODELO: Estudiante 1:   **Algunos** periódicos que leo son... *Últimas Noticias* y *El Universal*.

Estudiante 2:   *¡Yo también! Siempre leo* Últimas Noticias *porque...*

o

Yo no, no leo **ni** *Últimas Noticias* **ni** *El Universal porque... Yo leo* El Nacional *porque sus artículos son...*

Paso 3: Entre los dos, escriban un pequeño párrafo para informar a la clase sobre aquellas opiniones en las que coinciden.

MODELO: *A nosotros dos nos encantan las series de... Tenemos la misma opinión sobre....*

8.2-14 El cine y la televisión

Paso 1: Escribe por lo menos cinco preguntas con los siguientes términos.

MODELO: las telenovelas → *¿Ves telenovelas? ¿Qué telenovelas ves?*

1. programas de concursos
2. películas extranjeras
3. películas con subtítulos o dobladas
4. presentador/a de televisión
5. emisora de radio

6. efectos especiales
7. noticiero
8. canal de televisión
9. ¿?

Paso 2: Ahora, usa las preguntas para entrevistar a un/a compañero/a y saber más sobre sus gustos y opiniones sobre el cine y la televisión. ¿Coinciden en sus respuestas?

8.2-15 ¿Qué película es? Clasifiquen las siguientes películas según su género. Después, relaten la trama y cuenten de qué trata con el mayor número de detalles posibles para que sus compañeros adivinen qué película es.

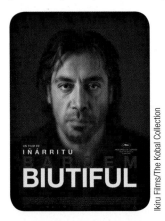

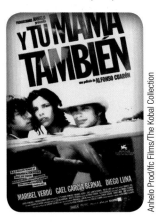

MODELO: *Es una película de suspenso que trata de... Ganó tres premios Óscar, uno al mejor actor, otro a la mejor actriz secundaria y otro a la mejor fotografía...*

8.2-16 ¡¿Debo hacer qué?! ¿Qué pasa en la oficina de un periódico? ¿Qué les pide el director a sus empleados?

Paso 1: En grupos de tres, escojan entre los personajes de **director, periodista** y **editor** y respondan a lo que dice cada uno.

MODELO: Director: *Vas a servirme el café todas las mañanas.*
              Periodista: *Esa no es la tarea de un periodista. No voy a servírselo.*

1. Vas a buscar <u>las mejores noticias</u>.
2. Vas a mejorar <u>la reputación del periódico</u>.
3. Vas a mandar**le** <u>los artículos</u> al editor a tiempo.
4. Vas a escribir**le** <u>los comunicados de prensa</u>[10] a la dirección del periódico.
5. Vas a organizar**nos** <u>las ruedas de prensa</u>[11].
6. Vas a sacar <u>las fotografías de las noticias</u>.
7. Vas a diseñar <u>las páginas</u> del periódico.
8. Vas a editar**me** <u>los *e-mails*</u> para mi familia.
9. ¿?

Paso 2: Ahora, informen a la clase. ¿Cuáles son las reacciones del editor y del periodista? ¿Creen que van a tener una buena relación? ¿Por qué?

MODELO: *El director me dice que tengo que editarle los mensajes para su familia, pero yo digo que no se los voy a editar porque no me parece...*

8.2-17 Un concurso televisivo Con un grupo, vas a crear un programa de televisión de concursos sobre un tema de tu interés. Sigue los pasos y no olvides ser original.

Paso 1: Definan qué tipo de concurso televisivo quieren hacer (p. ej., programa tipo *El gran hermano...*). Informen a su profesor/a sobre el tema del concurso y trabajen en grupos pequeños con las personas interesadas en cada tema.

Paso 2: Escriban un párrafo para describir el programa respondiendo las siguientes preguntas:

- ¿Quién va a presentar el programa? ¿Alguien especial?
- ¿A qué personas se les permite participar (abuelos, niños, gente joven, etc.)?
- ¿Qué actividades hacen los participantes en el programa (siempre se los pone en parejas para...)?
- ¿Qué tipo de cosas (dinero, viajes, coches, etc.) les ofrece el presentador del concurso a los participantes?
- ¿En qué canal (cable, público, etc.) se ofrece el programa?
- ¿A qué audiencia le va a gustar el programa?
- ¿Qué aspecto del programa prepara a los participantes para la vida real?
- ¿En qué se diferencia tu concurso de otros concursos y por qué podría resultar interesante?

Escriban cuatro o cinco preguntas para el/la presentador/a con el objetivo de obtener información sobre los participantes y presentarlos al principio[12] del programa. Las preguntas tienen que estar relacionadas con el tema del programa. Los participantes deben contestar las preguntas.

MODELO: Un concurso relacionado con la música
          Presentador/a: *¿<u>Siempre</u> vas a conciertos en tu tiempo libre?*
          Participante: *Sí, <u>siempre</u> que tengo tiempo voy.*
          Presentador/a: *¿Les pones canciones románticas a tus amigos/as?*
          Participante: *Sí, <u>se las</u> pongo.*

Al terminar las preguntas, el/la presentador/a dice unas palabras para dar comienzo al concurso. **¡OJO!** Todos deben usar el vocabulario y la gramática estudiada en este capítulo (palabras indefinidas y negativas, y pronombres dobles).

---

[10]**comunicado de prensa:** press release [11]**rueda de prensa:** press conference [12]**al principio:** at the beginning

Paso 3: Tu profesor/a va a escoger a cuatro estudiantes para que formen el jurado. Tu profesor/a también va a formar parte del jurado. Los grupos leen la descripción del concurso y las preguntas del presentador para conocer a los participantes. Los miembros del jurado anotan en un papel los puntos que le dan a cada grupo (4, muy bueno; 3, bueno; 2, regular; 1, muy regular). El jurado tiene que tener en cuenta los siguientes criterios:

1. la originalidad del concurso con la descripción y preguntas del presentador;
2. el uso del vocabulario del capítulo;
3. el uso de la gramática (los pronombres dobles y las palabras indefinidas y negativas) en el contenido del concurso.

El jurado no puede votar por su propio grupo. Cuando todos los grupos terminen de presentar la información sobre sus concursos, una persona del jurado va a contar los puntos para cada grupo. El grupo con más puntos gana.

8.2-18 **Presta atención:** *Ciudad Bendita* Samuel está en casa de Marcelo y va a empezar una telenovela. Escucha atentamente para saber más sobre la telenovela y la conversación entre Samuel y la familia de Marcelo. Después, decide si las siguientes afirmaciones son **ciertas** (C) o **falsas** (F). Corrige las respuestas falsas.

WileyPLUS Go to *WileyPLUS* and listen to **Presta atención**.

C F

☐ ☐ 1. Marcelo dice que son las cuatro de la tarde y la telenovela va a empezar.

☐ ☐ 2. Marcelo llama a su mamá y a su abuela.

☐ ☐ 3. Juan Lobo es el esposo de Bendita.

☐ ☐ 4. Juan Lobo es músico.

☐ ☐ 5. La mamá de Marcelo quiere ver la telenovela en silencio.

☐ ☐ 6. Samuel se disculpa.

☐ ☐ 7. Marcelo dice que le cuenta la trama al final del episodio.

8.2-19 **Por escrito: La trama de una telenovela** Tu abuelo no pudo ver el último episodio de su telenovela favorita. Como mañana es su cumpleaños, vas a escribir el resumen del episodio que no vio para dárselo de regalo sorpresa. Debes usar los pronombres de objeto directo e indirecto para no repetir los nombres de las personas y objetos mencionados.

MODELO: *En un capítulo de la telenovela* Ciudad Bendita *vemos a Juan Lobo que escribe una canción para Bendita. Se la escribe con mucho amor porque él está enamorada de ella...*

 ¡OJO!

More on replacing information
In a previous section of **¡OJO!** (Chapter 6, Section 2) you learned how to write a more cohesive writing by using direct object pronouns (**lo, la, etc.**) and demonstrative pronouns (**este, ese, etc.**) and by eliminating superfluous subject pronouns (**yo, tú, etc.**) whenever possible. Now, add to this list double object pronouns (**me lo, te la, se los**) to make your writing less redundant. When proofreading your composition, remember to double check that those pronouns agree in gender and number with the person or object they refer to.

PONTE EN MI LUGAR

Estrategias para conversar

Participating in a debate or conversation (I) When participating in a conversation, you can use different resources to ask for clarification.

✓ Due to lack of understanding:
   —Lo siento, pero no entiendo la pregunta. *(I'm sorry, but I don't understand the question.)*
✓ For clarification or reformulation:
   —¿Qué quiere/s decir? *(What do you mean?)*
   —¿Podría/s explicar(me) eso con más detalle? *(Could you be more specific?)*
   —¿Podría/s darme un ejemplo? *(Could you give me an example?)*
   —¿Podría/s aclararme eso, por favor? *(Could you clarify that for me, please?)*
✓ To ensure you understood the speaker:
   —Entonces, ¿para ti/usted...? *(So, in your opinion/for you...?)*
   —¿Lo que quiere/s decir es que...? *(You mean that...?)*

Entrevista Un canal venezolano emite[13] programas deportivos, de opinión, de cine, además de películas, telenovelas y series extranjeras. Imagina que caminas por una calle de Caracas con un/a amigo/a venezolano/a y un/a presentador/a de un canal los quiere entrevistar sobre un tema específico. Uno de ustedes es el/la presentador/a y los otros dos estudiantes son los entrevistados. No olviden usar las **Estrategias para conversar.**

Presentador/a: Escoge un tema específico de abajo y pide información a la gente de la calle. Primero, explícales que te gustaría grabarlos para tu canal. Hazles preguntas interesantes. Al final de la entrevista, dales las gracias a los entrevistados.

¿Cómo presenta la televisión (en películas, telenovelas, series, etc.) los siguientes temas?

• la violencia
• la felicidad
• la fantasía
• la telebasura

Entrevistado/a 1: Dile al/a la presentador/a que le puedes contestar sus preguntas sin problema. Contéstalas con detalles. Al responder, piensa en lo que muestra la televisión y cómo es la realidad que vive la mayoría de la gente (venezolanos, estadounidenses, colombianos, etc.).

Entrevistado/a 2: Comenta la opinión de tu compañero/a. ¿Estás de acuerdo o en desacuerdo? ¿Por qué?

WileyPLUS Go to *WileyPLUS* to find more **Arroba** activities.

Jorge Ramos Es un periodista y escritor mexicano y, según la revista *Time*, uno de los 25 hispanos más influyentes de Estados Unidos. Busca en Internet información sobre este periodista. Después, contesta estas preguntas para compartir la información con tus compañeros:

1. ¿En qué canal de televisión trabaja?
2. ¿A qué personajes entrevistó durante su carrera/recientemente?
3. ¿Qué libros ha escrito?
4. ¿Obtuvo algún premio por su trabajo? ¿Cuál/es?

[13]**emitir:** to broadcast

ASÍ ES LA VIDA

Adivina, adivinador

Es como una caja grande
metida en la habitación
por la que salen curiosos
los de la programación.

"¿Qué piensas del Canal de Panamá?"

Me parece que tiene una buena programación.

© John Wiley & Sons, Inc.

VER PARA CREER II: La belleza de Cartagena de Indias

WileyPLUS Go to *WileyPlus*
to see this video and to find
more video activities.

Antes de ver

Contesta estas preguntas con ayuda de un/a compañero/a.

1. ¿Sabes algo sobre Colombia?
2. ¿Conoces algunos colombianos famosos? ¿Quiénes?
3. ¿Ves telenovelas? ¿Cómo se llaman algunas telenovelas conocidas?
4. ¿Te gusta el café? ¿Con cuánta frecuencia tomas café?

Después de ver

1. ¿Entendiste? Adam visita Cartagena de Indias con su amiga Jahira. Escucha el video y después selecciona la respuesta más adecuada.

1. ¿En qué año construyeron el teatro Adolfo Mejía?
   a. en 1311   b. en 1611   c. en 1911
2. ¿En qué lugar vieron una escultura de Fernando Botero?
   a. en la Torre del Reloj
   b. en el barrio Getsemaní
   c. en la Plaza de Santo Domingo
3. ¿En dónde se conocieron los padres de Jahira?
   a. en el Bazurto Social Club
   b. en el barrio Getsemaní
   c. en la universidad de Cartagena
4. ¿Qué le explica Jahira a Adam sobre la telenovela colombiana *Betty La Fea*?
   a. que se ven mucho en el cine y en todos los países
   b. que le gusta la trama, se relaciona con la protagonista
   c. que son muy populares en Colombia y son chistosas

2. Una visita a la ciudad ¿Qué ventajas puede tener Adam visitando la ciudad con su amiga colombiana? Menciona por lo menos tres.

3. Enfoque cultural En Estados Unidos ¿se ven las telenovelas tanto como en Colombia? ¿Ven los hombres estadounidenses tantas telenovelas como los colombianos?

AUTOPRUEBA

VOCABULARIO

I. ¿A qué se dedican? Circula la palabra que menos se asocia con la profesión dada. Explica por qué seleccionaste esa palabra.

1. el/la crítico/a
   - a. la trama
   - b. el control remoto
   - c. la película
   - d. la actriz
2. el/la reportero/a
   - a. interpretar
   - b. las noticias
   - c. la emisora
   - d. informar
3. el/la periodista
   - a. grabar
   - b. doblar
   - c. escribir
   - d. informar
4. el actor
   - a. representar
   - b. interpretar
   - c. grabar
   - d. actuar
5. el/la presentador/a
   - a. la actualidad
   - b. el concurso
   - c. el noticiero
   - d. los dibujos animados

II. El cine y la televisión Empareja cada palabra con su definición o descripción.

_____ 1. la trama

_____ 2. la telenovela

_____ 3. el espectador

_____ 4. la revista

_____ 5. el premio

_____ 6. el protagonista

_____ 7. el documental

a. una publicación periódica con artículos y a veces con fotos

b. el actor o actriz principal de una película

c. la secuencia de eventos de una película, una obra de teatro o una novela

d. historia que se narra por episodios por televisión

e. un tipo de película o programa

f. la persona que ve una obra de teatro, una película o un programa

g. es un regalo o recompensa que se da por hacer algo bien

GRAMÁTICA

I. Doña Juanita está muy negativa hoy Doña Juanita está de muy mal humor esta tarde. Escribe las respuestas a las preguntas de Marcelo con las expresiones negativas apropiadas.

1. ¿Quieres ver **algún** programa en especial?
2. ¿**Siempre** ves las noticias internacionales?
3. ¿Hay **algo** que te gusta de los noticieros?
4. ¿Vas a ir al cine con **alguien**?
5. ¿Qué quieres: alquilar un película o ir al cine?

II. Tomando café con doña Juanita Samuel le cuenta a Gloria cómo fue su tarde con doña Juanita. Recuerda **La pura verdad** y completa las siguientes oraciones con los pronombres de objeto directo e indirecto juntos.

MODELO: Cuando Marcelo me invitó a su casa, le llevé pasteles a su madre. _Se los_ llevé porque ella es muy simpática.

1. Vi los pañuelos y _____ pasé a doña Juanita porque lloraba viendo la telenovela.
2. ¿El café? _____ ofreció doña Juanita pero yo _____ serví a ella.
3. ¿Las galletitas? _____ ofreció doña Juanita también. También me dio unas para ti y _____ traje.

CULTURA

1. ¿Qué tipo de programa de televisión es muy popular en Venezuela y Colombia?
2. ¿Qué diferencias hay entre esos programas y los de Estados Unidos?
3. ¿Ven muchas películas extranjeras en Venezuela y Colombia? ¿Cómo las entienden?

REDACCIÓN

Escribe la trama de una película que te gustó mucho.

- ¿Cómo se llamaba la película? ¿De dónde era?
- ¿Quiénes eran los actores principales?
- ¿De qué se trataba la película?
- ¿Cuál te pareció la mejor parte? ¿Y la peor? ¿Y la más interesante?
- ¿Te gustó cómo termina?

EN RESUMIDAS CUENTAS, AHORA PUEDO...

☐ hablar de cine, televisión y entretenimiento.

☐ expresar mi opinión.

☐ expresar negación.

☐ evitar la repetición de cosas y personas al expresarme.

☐ entender la popularidad de las telenovelas en Colombia y Venezuela.

VOCABULARIO ESENCIAL

Sustantivos

la actualidad	*current affairs*
el anuncio/el comercial	*TV commercial*
el canal (de televisión)	*TV channel*
el concurso	*competition, contest*
los dibujos animados	*cartoons*
la emisora de radio	*radio station*
la entrada	*movie ticket*
el medio de comunicación	*media*
la noticia	*piece of news*
las noticias (internacionales, nacionales, locales)	*(international, national, local) news*
el noticiero	*news program*
la obra de teatro	*theater play*
la película (de acción, de animación, de suspenso, de terror, dramática, romántica)	*(action, animation, suspense, horror, drama, romance) movie*
el periódico	*newspaper*
el/la periodista	*journalist*
el personaje	*character*
el premio	*award*
el/la presentador/a (de televisión)	*newsreader, TV host(ess)*
la prensa	*press*
la programación	*programming, schedule*
el programa (de variedades)	*(variety) show*
el/la protagonista	*main character*
la revista	*magazine*
la telenovela	*soap opera*
la trama	*plot*

Cognados: actuar, la ciencia ficción, la comedia, el control remoto, el/la crítico/a (de cine/ teatro), el documental, los efectos especiales, el entretenimiento, el episodio, el/la espectador/a, la radio, el/la reportero/a, la serie, los subtítulos

Adjetivos

aburrido/a	*boring, tedious*
actual	*current*
animado/a	*lively*
controvertido/a	*controversial*
emocionante	*exciting, thrilling*
entretenido/a	*entertaining*
gracioso/a	*funny*

Verbos

doblar	*to dub*
grabar	*to record*
representar/interpretar (un personaje)	*to play (the part of . . .)*
tratar(se) de	*to be about*

Cognados: actuar, informar

Palabras negativas e indefinidas

algo	*something, anything*
alguien	*someone, anyone*
algún, alguna/os/as	*some, any*
nada	*nothing, not anything*
nadie	*no one, nobody*
ni... ni	*neither. . . nor*
ningún, ninguna/os/as	*none, any*
nunca, jamás	*never*
o... o	*either. . . or*
siempre	*always*
también	*also*
tampoco	*neither, not either*
todo	*everything*
todo/a/os/as	*all*

Expresiones

¿De qué (se) trata?	*What is it about?*
¿Qué hay en la tele?	*What's on TV?*
tener éxito	*to be successful*

© John Wiley & Sons, Inc.

VER PARA CREER I:
Un paseo por Cotopaxi

Con ayuda de tu profesor/a, crea una lista de vocabulario que se relacione con los parques nacionales. Después, mira el video y contesta las preguntas.

1. ¿Dónde están las dos chicas?

2. ¿Cómo es la geografía en ese lugar?

3. ¿Hay algún lugar parecido en Estados Unidos?

Sección 1	**La geografía y el clima**

PALABRA POR PALABRA

- La geografía
- El tiempo ♲

HABLANDO DE GRAMÁTICA

- Introduction to the subjunctive mood and formation of the present subjunctive
- Expressing obligation and giving advice: Present subjunctive with impersonal expressions and verbs of influence
- **Deber, tener,** and **hay que** ♲
- Indirect object pronouns ♲

CULTURA

- La altitud en Ecuador
- Las regiones y el clima

Ecuador y Perú

© John Wiley & Sons, Inc.

Sección 2	**Los animales y el medio ambiente**

PALABRA POR PALABRA

- Los animales
- El medio ambiente

HABLANDO DE GRAMÁTICA

- Expressing likes and dislikes: Verbs like **gustar** ♲
- Expressing subjective reactions: Present subjunctive with verbs of emotion
- Expressing uncertainty: Present subjunctive with expressions of doubt
- Making comparisons: Superlatives and absolute superlatives ♲

CULTURA

- Las hojas de coca
- Distintas perspectivas sobre ecología

🌐 **Trivia:** Go to *WileyPLUS* to do the **Trivia** activities and find out how much you know about these countries!

335

LEARNING OBJECTIVES

By the end of this section you will be able to:

- Talk about geography and climate
- Express obligation and advise
- Try to influence others to do something
- Get familiar with diverse climates and environments
- Practice using indirect object pronouns to say for whom something is done

Una imagen vale más que mil palabras

Courtesy of Brittany Schon, Shannon Mitchell and Lisa Nelson

ECUADOR
LATITUD: 0°- 0'- 0"
LONG. OCC. 78°-27'-8"

▲ *Estas estudiantes caminan sobre la línea que divide el hemisferio norte y el hemisferio sur.*

¿Dónde están estas estudiantes: en el país de Ecuador o en la línea del ecuador?

¿Qué diferencias de geografía y clima esperas ver si estás en la latitud cero?

¿Sabes en qué latitud está el área donde vives?

UNA PERSPECTIVA

Courtesy of Emily Kuffner

Emily

La altura en Ecuador

Diferente

"Lógicamente, mientras más cerca una persona está de la línea del ecuador, más calor hace, pero no es así en Quito, la capital de Ecuador. ¡En Quito hace fresco todo el año! Claro, Quito está muy alto en las sierras y la temperatura no varía mucho. La temperatura máxima va de 19 a 20 grados centígrados (entre 66 y 68 grados Fahrenheit) y la mínima de 9 a 11 grados centígrados (entre 48 y 52 grados Fahrenheit).

Cuando fui a Quito constantemente tenía frío. También me afectó el 'soroche', que es un malestar[1] producido por la altitud. Quito está a 2.800 metros de altura (9.200 pies). Eso me pasó el primer día. El resto del tiempo la pasé muy bien".

Igual

"En Colorado hay varias ciudades que están a más de una milla de alto (una milla equivale a 5.280 pies). Los turistas y especialmente los atletas sienten inmediatamente los efectos de la altitud. Para evitar el soroche, hay que evitar hacer ejercicio y hay que beber mucha agua. En un día o dos, desaparecen los síntomas".

¿Qué piensas tú?

1. Ecuador tiene varias ciudades en la costa. ¿Qué tiempo crees que hace en la costa?
2. ¿Te sentiste mal alguna vez debido a la altitud? ¿Dónde? ¿Qué hiciste?
3. ¿Qué ciudades se conocen por su clima? Menciona algunas ciudades de EE.UU. y el tipo de clima que tienen.

[1] **malestar:** physical discomfort

LA PURA VERDAD I   Visita a Ecuador

Tito va a Ecuador a visitar a un amigo. Su amigo ecuatoriano prometió llevarlo a muchos sitios.

1. ¡Bienvenido a Quito, mi pana!

Gracias. ¡Ay, hace frío!

2. ¿Adónde quieres ir primero? Ecuador tiene 4 regiones: la sierra, la costa, el oriente y el archipiélago de Colón.

3. Esta es la región del oriente. Es muy tropical y hace mucho calor. Llueve casi todo el año.

4. El archipiélago está muy protegido por su importancia ecológica. El clima es tropical y hay muchos animales exóticos.

5. En la costa hace mucho calor. La temperatura es de 35 °C, o 95 °F. La gente de Guayaquil es muy fiestera. Nosotros somos más reservados y serios.

6. ¡La sierra es bacana! Ahora estamos en la estación seca, de mayo a noviembre. Allí hay 30 volcanes y seis están activos. Podemos subir al Cotopaxi y jugar en la nieve.

7. ¿Adónde quieres ir primero?

A Guayaquil, a la costa, donde hace sol, calor y hay mucha humedad.

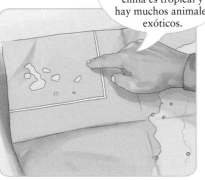

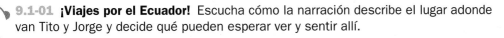

© John Wiley & Sons, Inc.

9.1-01 ¡Viajes por el Ecuador! Escucha cómo la narración describe el lugar adonde van Tito y Jorge y decide qué pueden esperar ver y sentir allí.

1. a. una selva tropical   b. una playa   c. el río Amazonas
2. a. soroche otra vez   b. mucho calor   c. humedad
3. a. muchos hoteles   b. nieve   c. animales exóticos

◠ PALABRA POR PALABRA

La geografía

el bosque	*forest*
la estación seca	*dry season*
la estación lluviosa	*rainy season*
el lago	*lake*
el nivel del mar	*sea level*
el paisaje	*landscape*
la selva tropical	*tropical forest*

Cognados: la altitud, la Amazonía, el cañón,
el desierto, la humedad, la jungla

♻ El tiempo

Está nublado por las tardes.

En la sierra hace frío.

En la costa hace calor y mucha humedad.

De junio a septiembre es la estación seca.

Siempre nieva en el Cotopaxi.

De octubre a mayo es la estación lluviosa.

En el bosque hay mucha humedad.

COLOMBIA

QUITO

OCÉANO PACÍFICO

E C U A D O R

PERÚ

© John Wiley & Sons, Inc.

¿Qué dicen los ecuatorianos?

Los ecuatorianos de la sierra (los serranos) usan mucho el diminutivo: **amiguito, hijito, casita, ropita, mamita,** etc.

*¡Bacán!	*Cool!*
—Me invitó a cenar.	*He invited me to have*
—¡Qué <u>bacano</u>!	*dinner.*
	What a <u>nice person</u>!
Sale con un <u>pelado</u>	*She's going out with a*
muy simpático.	*very nice <u>guy</u>.*
*<u>No seas malito</u>,	*<u>Don't be mean</u>, lend*
préstame tu carro.	*me your car.*

*Esta expresión también se usa en otros países hispanos.

9.1-02 ¿De qué hablamos?

Paso 1: Lean las definiciones y busquen la palabra correspondiente en la sección **Palabra por palabra.** Después, escriban una oración con esa palabra que incluya un ejemplo real.

MODELO: Es una extensión de tierra con muchos árboles. → *<u>Bosque</u>. Cerca de mi casa, en San Francisco, hay un bosque impresionante de secuoyas que se llama Muir Woods.*

1. Es una montaña con forma de cono de la que sale lava.
2. Es un accidente geográfico[2] provocado por un río que produce una depresión profunda.
3. Es una corriente de agua que corre hacia el mar.
4. Es el límite político y a veces también geográfico que separa un país de otro.
5. Es una zona geográfica muy árida, caracterizada por la falta de agua y vegetación.
6. Es una serie de montañas conectadas.
7. Es un lugar adonde llegan barcos grandes y donde pueden estacionarse.
8. Es un terreno plano entre dos montañas.

Paso 2: Ahora, elijan tres palabras de la sección **Palabra por palabra** y escriban tres definiciones que van a leerle a la clase. ¡Atención! Recuerden que para definir siempre usamos el verbo **ser.**

MODELO: *Es un/a… (que)…*

---

[2]**accidente geográfico:** geographical feature

9.1-03 ¿Con qué frecuencia? Hablen sobre con qué frecuencia hacen las siguientes actividades dentro de su país.

MODELO:　caminar por un cañón
　　　　　Estudiante 1:　*¿Con qué frecuencia caminas por un cañón?*
　　　　　Estudiante 2:　*Nunca camino por un cañón porque no vivo cerca de ninguno.*
　　　　　Estudiante 1:　*Yo tampoco.*

　muchas veces　a veces　casi nunca　nunca

1. ir a la costa
2. cruzar una frontera
3. hacer senderismo por la selva tropical
4. escalar montañas
5. nadar en el mar
6. hacer esquí acuático en un lago
7. subir a un volcán
8. pescar en un río
9. pasear por un puerto

El tiempo (el clima)

Do you remember how to talk about the weather?

What are some expressions used to describe the weather?

In the section **Palabra por palabra** from Chapter 4, Section 2, you learned some expressions to describe the weather in Spanish. Please review that section before completing activity **9.1-04**.

 9.1-04 ¿Qué tiempo hace en...?

 Paso 1: Mirando las fotos y usando lo que aprendiste en **La pura verdad**, habla con un/a compañero/a sobre el tiempo que hace en estos lugares.

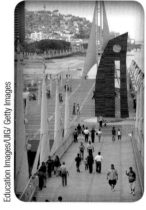

▲ *Quito*　　▲ *Volcán Cotopaxi, en la región de la sierra*　　▲ *Selva amazónica ecuatoriana*　　▲ *Guayaquil, en la costa*

Paso 2: Ahora, piensen en tres lugares o regiones geográficas del mundo. ¿Saben qué tiempo hace allí?

MODELO:　el desierto del Sahara
　　　　　→ *Hace muchísimo calor durante el día, pero hace frío durante la noche. Nunca llueve y el clima es muy seco.*

9.1-05 Adivina, adivinador... Piensa en una zona o accidente geográfico. Después, túrnense para adivinar en qué accidente geográfico pensó tu compañero/a. Las preguntas deben tener respuesta de Sí o No.

MODELO:　Estudiante 1:　*¿Está en el hemisferio norte?*
　　　　　Estudiante 2:　*No, está en el hemisferio sur.*
　　　　　Estudiante 1:　*¿Está en Ecuador?*
　　　　　Estudiante 2:　*No, está en la frontera de Perú y Bolivia.*
　　　　　Estudiante 1:　*¿Es una cordillera?*
　　　　　Estudiante 2:　*No, es un lago.*
　　　　　Estudiante 1:　*¡Es el lago Titicaca!*
　　　　　Estudiante 2:　*¡Sí, muy bien!*

HABLANDO DE GRAMÁTICA I

1. Introduction to the subjunctive mood and formation of the present subjunctive

WileyPLUS Go to *WileyPLUS* to review this grammar point with the help of the **Animated Grammar Tutorial** and the **Verb Conjugator**.

So far you have already studied a few verb tenses in Spanish such as the present, the preterit and the imperfect. These tenses correspond to what is called the *indicative mood*, and they are used to report events—to talk about facts and events as objective and part of reality.

Para evitar el soroche, **bebo** mucha agua.

To avoid altitude sickness, I drink a lot of water.

Jorge **toma** té de coca.

Jorge drinks coca tea.

The subjunctive mood, by contrast, is used to express emotional reactions, wishes, hopes, requests, doubts, and other subjective reactions to events and the actions of others.

Para evitar el soroche te recomiendo [que **bebas** mucha agua].

To avoid altitude sickness, I recommend [that you drink a lot of water].

Jorge sugiere [que **tomes** té de coca].

Jorge suggests [that you take coca tea].

The subjunctive also exists in English, though for the most part the forms of subjunctive and indicative forms coincide. Study the following examples:

Indicative	Subjunctive
I always **take** warm clothes when traveling.	He recommends that I **take** warm clothes when traveling.
She usually **arrives** on time.	It is urgent that she **arrive** on time (and not "that she arrives").

Subjunctive constructions are much more common in Spanish than in English, and the nuances expressed by the Spanish subjunctive may be translated with a variety of different constructions in English.

In Spanish, the subjunctive usually appears in a dependent clause introduced by **que**, which is used to connect two clauses, a main or independent clause and a subordinate or dependent clause. In the sentence *He recommends that I take warm clothes*, *He recommends* is the main clause (i.e., expresses a complete thought), and *that I take warm clothes* is the subordinate clause that cannot stand on its own.

In this and the following chapters, you will be introduced to different contexts and uses of the present subjunctive. For now, let's get familiar with the forms.

Forms of the present subjunctive

The forms of the present subjunctive are the same forms you already know for the formal commands. Drop the ending of the first person singular form in the present tense indicative (e.g., **-o** or **-oy** in the **yo** form) and add the opposite theme vowel. That is, verbs ending in **-ar** add **-e/n**, verbs ending in **-er**, **-ir**, add **-a/n**.

Formal command
Si viajan a Ecuador, **vayan** a la costa.   *If you travel to Ecuador, go to the coast.*

Present subjunctive
Si viajan a Ecuador, les sugiero que **vayan** a la costa.

If you travel to Ecuador, I suggest that you go to the coast.

Infinitive	yo form	Add opposite theme vowel	
visit**ar**	visit**o**	**-e**	visit**e**, visit**es**, visit**e**, visit**emos**, visit**éis**, visit**en**
beb**er**	beb**o**	**-a**	beb**a**, beb**as**, beb**a**, beb**amos**, beb**áis**, beb**an**
conoc**er***	conozc**o**	**-a**	conozc**a**, conozc**as**, conozc**a**, conozc**amos**, conozc**áis**, conozc**an**
consum**ir**	consum**o**	**-a**	consum**a**, consum**as**, consum**a**, consum**amos**, consum**áis**, consum**an**
sal**ir***	salg**o**	**-a**	salg**a**, salg**as**, salg**a**, salg**amos**, salg**áis**, salg**an**

*All verbs with irregular **yo** forms in the present indicative, follow the same pattern in the present subjunctive.

All verbs ending in **-car**, **-gar**, **-zar**, **-ger** and **-guir** undergo spelling changes in all forms.

Verbs ending in *-car, -gar, -zar, -ger, -guir*	
sacar (c > qu)	saque, saques, saque, saquemos, saquéis, saquen
llegar (g > gu)	llegue, llegues, llegue, lleguemos, lleguéis, lleguen
organizar (z > c)	organice, organices, organice, organicemos, organicéis, organicen
proteger (g > j)	proteja, protejas, proteja, protejamos, protejáis, protejan
seguir (gu > g)	siga, sigas, siga, sigamos, sigáis, sigan

There are six irregular verbs in the present subjunctive. You are already familiar with these conjugations, which are the same as for formal commands (see p. 283).

Irregular verbs in the present subjunctive	
dar	dé, des, dé, demos, deis, den
estar	esté, estés, esté, estemos, estéis, estén
haber	haya, hayas, haya, hayamos, hayáis, hayan
ir	vaya, vayas, vaya, vayamos, vayáis, vayan
saber	sepa, sepas, sepa, sepamos, sepáis, sepan
ser	sea, seas, sea, seamos, seáis, sean

Stem-changing verbs follow the same pattern as in the present indicative, but have an additional change in the **nosotros/as** and **vosotros/as** form.

Stem-changing verbs		
o > u, ue	dormir	duerma, duermas, duerma, durmamos, durmáis, duerman
e > i	servir	sirva, sirvas, sirva, sirvamos, sirváis, sirvan
e > ie, i	preferir	prefiera, prefieras, prefiera, prefiramos, prefiráis, prefieran

The present subjunctive of **haber** is **haya.**

No creo que **haya** problema en acampar allí.

I don't think it is a problem to camp there.

 9.1-06 Preparando el viaje Antes de viajar a Ecuador, Tito le escribe un mensaje a Jorge para pedirle consejos.

Lee el mensaje que Jorge le escribe a Tito con sus recomendaciones.

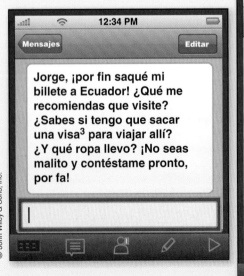

Jorge, ¡por fin saqué mi billete a Ecuador! ¿Qué me recomiendas que visite? ¿Sabes si tengo que sacar una visa[3] para viajar allí? ¿Y qué ropa llevo? ¡No seas malito y contéstame pronto, por fa!

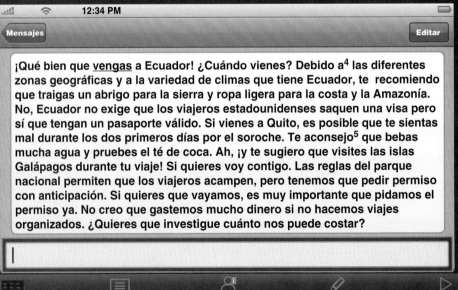

¡Qué bien que <u>vengas</u> a Ecuador! ¿Cuándo vienes? Debido a[4] las diferentes zonas geográficas y a la variedad de climas que tiene Ecuador, te recomiendo que traigas un abrigo para la sierra y ropa ligera para la costa y la Amazonía. No, Ecuador no exige que los viajeros estadounidenses saquen una visa pero sí que tengan un pasaporte válido. Si vienes a Quito, es posible que te sientas mal durante los dos primeros días por el soroche. Te aconsejo[5] que bebas mucha agua y pruebes el té de coca. Ah, ¡y te sugiero que visites las islas Galápagos durante tu viaje! Si quieres voy contigo. Las reglas del parque nacional permiten que los viajeros acampen, pero tenemos que pedir permiso con anticipación. Si quieres que vayamos, es muy importante que pidamos el permiso ya. No creo que gastemos mucho dinero si no hacemos viajes organizados. ¿Quieres que investigue cuánto nos puede costar?

[3]**sacar una visa:** to obtain a visa [4]**debido a:** due to [5]**aconsejar:** to advise

Paso 1: Escribe todos los verbos que encuentres en el párrafo anterior (son trece en total) en presente de subjuntivo. ¡Atención! No todos los verbos están en el subjuntivo. Después, indica cuál es el infinitivo de cada verbo.

MODELO: 1. *vengas (venir)*

2. _____   8. _____
3. _____   9. _____
4. _____   10. _____
5. _____   11. _____
6. _____   12. _____
7. _____   13. _____

Paso 2: ¿Cierto o falso? Ahora, lee el párrafo otra vez y decide si las siguientes oraciones son ciertas o falsas. Si son falsas, escribe la información correcta.

C   F

☐   ☐   1. No es seguro que Tito <u>viaje</u> a Ecuador.

☐   ☐   2. Solo es necesario llevar ropa de verano.

☐   ☐   3. Tito le dice a su amigo que no se <u>preocupe</u> por la visa.

☐   ☐   4. Jorge no cree que las islas Galápagos <u>sean</u> un buen lugar para visitar.

☐   ☐   5. Tito insiste en que <u>pidan</u> permiso para acampar.

9.1-07 ¿Quién lo dice?

Paso 1: Mira **La pura verdad I** y decide si las siguientes oraciones las dicen Tito **(T)** o Jorge **(J)**.

_____ 1. ¡No puedo creer que haga frío en Ecuador! Pensaba que siempre hacía calor.
_____ 2. Es posible que nieve en el Cocopaxi. Vamos a poder jugar con la nieve.
_____ 3. Te sugiero que bebas té de coca.
_____ 4. No es probable que te sientas mal durante más de dos días por el soroche.
_____ 5. Estoy muy contento de que visites Ecuador.
_____ 6. Es probable que veamos muchos animales exóticos en las islas Galápagos.
_____ 7. Quiero que vayamos a Guayaquil.

Paso 2: Ahora, en cada oración identifica cuál es el verbo que está en presente de subjuntivo (hay uno en cada oración). Después, analiza otra vez las oraciones. ¿Cuál es la palabra que precede al verbo en subjuntivo en todas las oraciones?

LA PURA VERDAD II　Escalar una montaña

Tito continúa visitando lugares nuevos con su amigo Jorge.

1.

Pues es importante que estés en buena forma. ¡Es la montaña más alta del mundo!

¿Sabes qué? ¡Quiero escalar el Chimborazo!

2.

Si se mide[6] desde el centro de la Tierra, el Chimborazo es la más alta. Si se miden desde el nivel del mar[7], es el Everest.

La montaña más alta del mundo es el Everest, ¿no?

3.

El Chimborazo es difícil de escalar. Es mejor que subas a la cima del volcán Cotopaxi. Cotopaxi es una palabra quechua que significa "dulce cuello de la luna".

4.

¡Es esencial que no nieve! Si nieva, no podemos subir.

5.

Es necesario que acampemos en Limpiopungo antes de subir mañana.

6.

¡Es preciso que haga buen tiempo mañana!

9.1-08　Escalar el Cotopaxi　Escucha cómo la narración describe la subida al volcán Cotopaxi y selecciona las oraciones que describen qué fue lo que pasó.

1. Sobre el clima...
   a. ellos saben que es esencial que haga buen tiempo.
   b. Jorge y Tito saben que es preciso que llueva.
   c. la radio pronostica buen tiempo.
2. ¿Qué pasa ahora?
   a. Parece que va a llover. No pueden subir.
   b. Está nevando, pero no mucho.
   c. Parece que va a hacer buen tiempo.
3. Al final...
   a. les tomó nueve horas subir al volcán.
   b. Jorge y Tito no subieron porque estaba nublado.
   c. Jorge y Tito no sacaron fotos porque en la cima estaba muy nublado.

[6]**Si se mide:** if one measures　[7]**nivel del mar:** sea level

HABLANDO DE GRAMÁTICA II

2. Expressing obligation and giving advice: Present subjunctive with impersonal expressions and verbs of influence

Complex sentences have more than one clause (and have a conjugated verb in each clause). A clause that depends on another to have meaning is a subordinate clause.

WileyPLUS Go to *WileyPLUS* to review this grammar point with the help of the **Animated Grammar Tutorial** and the **Verb Conjugator**.

Main clause	Subordinate clause
Sugiero *I suggest*	[que <u>estudies</u> mejor la geografía]. *[that you <u>study</u> geography better].*
Te aconsejo *I advise (to you)*	[que lo <u>busques</u> en Google™]. *[that you <u>look</u> it up on Google].*

The subjunctive mood is only used in <u>some</u> subordinate clauses, and <u>never</u> in main clauses. In this chapter you will learn how to recommend something and give advice, and how to express obligation with verbs of influence and impersonal generalizations that require the use of the subjunctive mood.

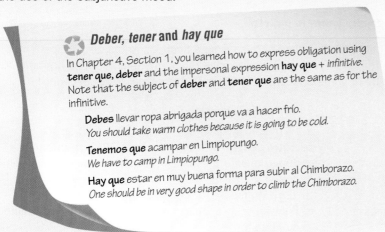

♻ *Deber, tener and hay que*

In Chapter 4, Section 1, you learned how to express obligation using **tener que, deber** and the impersonal expression **hay que** + *infinitive*. Note that the subject of **deber** and **tener que** are the same as for the infinitive.

Debes llevar ropa abrigada porque va a hacer frío.
You should take warm clothes because it is going to be cold.

Tenemos que acampar en Limpiopungo.
We have to camp in Limpiopungo.

Hay que estar en muy buena forma para subir al Chimborazo.
One should be in very good shape in order to climb the Chimborazo.

When someone requests or asks that someone else do something, use a *verb of influence* + **que** + *a verb in the subjuntive form*:

expression of influence (indicative)	+ **que** +	action requested (subjunctive)
Jorge **recomienda**	**que**	(nosotros) **subamos** al Cotopaxi.

This sentence involves two different subjects: the subject of the main clause (the one expressing the request) is different from the subject of the subordinate clause (the one being requested).

The following verbs of influence require the use of the subjunctive when the subject of the main clause and the subject of the subordinate are different:

aconsejar	*to advise*	prohibir	*to prohibit*
insistir (en)	*to insist (on)*	recomendar (e > ie)	*to recommend*
pedir (e > i)	*to ask for, to request*	sugerir (e > ie)	*to suggest*
permitir	*to permit*		

Ecuador no **requiere que saques** una visa.

Ecuador does not require that you get a visa.

Jorge **insiste en que no vayamos** al Chimborazo.

Jorge insists that we don't go to Chimborazo.

En vez de eso **recomienda que subamos** el Cotopaxi.

Instead, he recommends that we climb the Cotopaxi.

Impersonal generalizations may also be used to express recommendations or obligation. When the advice is a general comment and not directed to a specific person, we use the infinitive construction:

	Adjective	Infinitive
Es	esencial/preciso/necesario/importante/mejor	**estar** en buena forma. **acampar** en Limpiolungo.
It's	essential/necessary/important/better	*to be in good shape.* *to camp in Limpiolungo.*

However, if the advice or recommendation is directed to a specific person, we use **que + subjunctive**.

	Adjective	que + *subjunctive*
Es	esencial/preciso/necesario/importante/mejor	**que estés** en buena forma. **que acampemos** en Limpiolungo.
It's	essential/necessary/important/better	*that you are in good shape.* *that we camp in Limpiolungo.*

9.1-09 ¡Tengo que hacer la maleta[8]!

Paso 1: Tito está preparándose para su viaje a Ecuador. Antes de salir, está muy nervioso con todos los preparativos y le hace muchas preguntas a su hermano. Combina cada oración de la primera columna con la más apropiada de la segunda.

Tito dice:

_____ 1. ¡Debo comprar una maleta nueva!
_____ 2. Tengo que renovar el pasaporte.
_____ 3. ¿Crees que hay que sacar una visa también?
_____ 4. ¿Crees que debo llevar loción antimosquitos?
_____ 5. Jorge insiste en que me quede en su casa.
_____ 6. ¿Debo comprar una guía?
_____ 7. ¡Estoy muy emocionado con mi viaje! ¿Me ayudas a hacer la maleta?

Su hermano le contesta:

a. Es mejor que busques información en Internet.
b. Antes de renovarlo, es necesario que te tomes unas fotos.
c. Tengo mucho que hacer. ¡Te prohíbo que sigas pidiéndome cosas!
d. Te recomiendo que compres una mochila grande.
e. Pues no sé, te aconsejo que mires la página de la embajada de Ecuador.
f. Te sugiero que no cargues demasiadas cosas. Seguro que lo puedes comprar allí.
g. Entonces te aconsejo que le lleves un regalo, ¿no?

Paso 2: Imagina que un/a amigo/a ecuatoriano/a viene de visita y mientras está preparando su viaje te hace muchas preguntas. ¿Qué le contestas? Utiliza en tus respuestas algunas expresiones o verbos de la lista.

MODELO: ¿Debo sacar una visa para entrar en Estados Unidos?
→ *No sé, **te sugiero que** te informes en la página web de la embajada de Estados Unidos en Ecuador.*

es mejor que	aconsejar	tener que
(no) es necesario que	recomendar	deber
es preciso que	insistir	

1. ¿Es mejor que lleve una mochila grande o una maleta con rueditas[9]?
2. ¿Tengo que llevar alguna documentación específica?
3. ¿Debo llevar algo en particular?
4. ¿Me puedo quedar en tu casa?
5. ¿Debo comprar una guía?
6. ¿Qué más me recomiendas que haga antes de ir?

Paso 3: Ahora, con un/a compañero/a compara tus recomendaciones. ¿Cuáles de ellas son similares?

[8]**hacer la maleta:** to pack (a suitcase) [9]**rueditas:** little wheels

♻ Indirect object pronouns

In Chapter 5, Section 2, you learned that verbs whose meaning involve some kind of transfer (such as **dar**) or communication (like **decir**) are commonly used with indirect object pronouns. In the case of verbs that express communication, the indirect object indicates to whom something is being communicated.

Singular			Plural	
		nos	to/for us	
me	to/for me	**os**	to/for you (familiar, Spain)	
te	to/for you (familiar)	**les**	to/for you (formal), them	
le	to/for you (formal), him, her			

Verbs of influence such as **aconsejar, pedir, recomendar,** or **sugerir** are also often used with indirect object pronouns since one advises, asks, recommends, or suggests something to someone else.

Te sugiero que saques un permiso
   con antelación.

Nos aconsejan que estudiemos bien
   la zona antes de subir.

*I suggest that you get a permit
   ahead of time.*

*They advise (**us**) that we study
   the area well before climbing.*

9.1-10 El programa de voluntarios del Parque Nacional Jorge conversa con su amiga Fanny sobre el programa de voluntarios. Indica cuál es la palabra correcta de las dos opciones.

Jorge: Hola, Fanny, ¿ya te inscribiste[10] en el programa de voluntarios del parque que (**te / me**) recomendé?

Fanny: ¡Sí! (**Me / Te**) aconsejaste muy bien. Hice como (**te / me**) sugeriste. Ya fui a la primera reunión con el resto de los voluntarios. Hay una reunión una vez al mes. En esas reuniones la directora del programa (**le / nos**) da muchas recomendaciones.

Jorge: ¿Y qué (**les / le**) dice?

Fanny: Más que nada (**nos / le**) dice que (**prestamos / prestemos**) atención a los viajeros. No podemos permitir(**le / les**) que (**toquen / tocan**) o (**dan / den**) de comer a los animales. Tenemos que pedir(**les / le**) que no (**salen / salgan**) de las rutas establecidas. (**Nos / Les**) pedimos que (**respetan / respeten**) las reglas del parque.

Jorge: ¿Y por lo general los viajeros (**respeten / respetan**) las reglas?

Fanny: Sí, solo algunas veces (**les / nos**) decimos que no (**tomen / toman**) nada del parque, solo pueden tomar fotos.

Jorge: Bueno, pues qué bacán que estés haciendo ese trabajo.

Fanny: ¡Sí, estoy muy contenta!

[10]inscribirse: to sign up

Fernando

OTRA PERSPECTIVA

Las regiones y el clima

Diferente

"En Michigan hay cuatro estaciones en el año y en Ecuador dos: la estación lluviosa y la estación seca. En Michigan el clima cambia en un mismo lugar. En Ecuador el clima de un lugar es constante. Solo es diferente en otros lugares. En la sierra hace frío, en el valle central es primaveral y en la costa hace calor. ¡Qué interesante!, ¿no?".

"En la sierra, mucha gente tiene manchas rojizas[11] o color marrón en la cara. Es un efecto combinado del viento, el sol y el frío. A la gente que vive en Michigan no le pasa esto. ¿Por qué?"

Igual

"Estados Unidos es un país muy grande y, como Ecuador, tiene una geografía muy variada. Tiene montañas muy altas, desiertos, valles, playas, lagos, ríos y volcanes. Tiene clima frío, caluroso, húmedo y también tropical. Ecuador tiene la misma variedad geográfica y climática, pero todo esto en un país del tamaño del estado de Colorado. Increíble, ¿no?"

 Explícale a Fernando

1. ¿Es normal quemarse con el sol[12] en invierno?
2. ¿Hay cuatro estaciones donde vives?
3. ¿Adónde vas si quieres ver nieve en verano? ¿Adónde vas si quieres disfrutar de la playa en invierno?

MANOS A LA OBRA

 9.1-11 Una visita al Parque Nacional

Paso 1: Con un/a compañero/a, busquen en Internet información sobre el Parque Nacional de las islas Galápagos o lean la siguiente página informativa para los visitantes del parque. Después, hagan una lista de las recomendaciones que consideran más importantes.

Si usted está pensando en visitar las islas Galápagos, hagan algunas recomendaciones:

1. Es importante que...
2. Es preciso que...
3. Es necesario que...

SUDAMERICANA DE TURISMO   ANDES

Inicio ⊛ Islas Galápagos ⊛ **RECOMENDACIONES PARA VISITAR GALAPAGOS**

RECOMENDACIONES PARA VISITAR GALAPAGOS   🖨 ✉

Parque Nacional
GALÁPAGOS
Ecuador

Quienes visitan Galápagos tienen la oportunidad de proteger las islas... o hacerles daño. Para que su aporte sea positivo y ayude a conservar Galápagos, el Parque Nacional le pide que respete las siguientes reglas.

LAS REGLAS DEL PARQUE NACIONAL GALAPAGOS

1. Por su naturaleza única, las plantas, animales y rocas, deben permanecer en su sitio para no causar alteración alguna. No es permitido tomar nada de las islas, a excepción de fotos.

2. Cada isla del archipiélago es un lugar único por su flora, fauna y paisajes, cualquier introducción de organismos extraños como: animales, semillas, plantas e insectos causan serios problemas. Su colaboración es muy importante evitando que esto suceda.

3. Los animales de Galápagos no deben ser tocados ni acariciados para su seguridad y porque estos rápidamente pueden perder su docilidad y alterar su comportamiento.

4. La fauna endémica y nativa de Galápagos tiene su forma natural de alimentación, por lo tanto no se debe dar ningún tipo de alimento ya que les puede hacer daño.

5. Las aves marinas de Galápagos abandonan sus nidos si se las molesta o se las persigue, dejando caer sus huevos o polluelos al suelo, o dejándolos expuestos al sol; por lo cual, usted puede observar a las aves a una distancia de no menor a dos metros.

6. Para mantener a las islas en su mayor estado natural posible, está prohibido el ingreso de cualquier organismo vivo desde el continente e inclusive su traslado entre islas. Plantas semillas, insectos, plagas y enfermedades son peligrosos para el frágil ecosistema insular.

7. Los sitios de visita del Parque Nacional Galápagos, se encuentran marcados y señalados para garantizar su seguridad. Usted no debe salirse de los senderos.

8. La basura de cualquier tipo interfiere en los procesos naturales y le quita el encanto al paisaje único de las islas. No arroje basura en los sitios de visita, en el mar o en las cercanías de las islas, los lobos marinos sacan los tarros que se depositan en el fondo del mar y juegan con ellos hiriéndose sus narices; los plásticos pueden ser comidos por las tortugas marinas y morir por obstrucción del tubo digestivo.

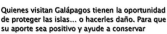

[11] **manchas rojizas:** reddish spots or burns
[12] **quemarse:** get sunburn

Las autoridades del parque...

    4. recomiendan a los viajeros que...

    5. prohíben que...

    6. permiten que...

Paso 2: Piensen en un parque natural o nacional que conozcan los dos y escriban tres recomendaciones para un/a viajero/a. Sean lo más específicos posible.

Si usted está pensando en visitar _____,

    1. es mejor que...

    2. es importante que...

    3. es esencial que...

Después, presenten sus recomendaciones a la clase. El resto de la clase tiene que adivinar de qué parque natural o nacional se trata. ¿Qué pareja da las mejores recomendaciones?

9.1-12 ¿Cómo es tu compañero/a de viaje ideal?

Paso 1: Piensa en un lugar de Perú o Ecuador que te gustaría visitar. Tuviste una mala experiencia en el último viaje y ahora quieres encontrar a un/a compañero/a de viaje ideal. Escribe una lista de seis características que te gustaría encontrar en el/la compañero/a ideal.

MODELO: interesar(le) ir a la playa

          → *(No) es necesario/esencial/preciso que le interese ir a la playa porque vamos a ir a la montaña.*

Lugares posibles:

▲ *Lago Titicaca (Perú)*

▲ *Machu Picchu (Perú)*

▲ *Parque Nacional Cotopaxi (Ecuador)*

▲ *Cuzco (Perú)*

importar(le) usar el transporte público
gustar(le) acampar
preferir alojarse en hoteles baratos o albergues
fumar
quejarse por todo

levantarse tarde
llevar mucho equipaje
ser muy exigente[13]
ser delicado/a[14] con la comida
gustar(le) salir de fiesta

Paso 2: En grupos pequeños, comenten sus listas. Digan qué lugar les gustaría visitar y qué es importante para ustedes en un/a compañero/a de viaje. Decidan si los miembros de su grupo pueden viajar juntos o no. Si crees que los miembros de tu grupo no son buenos compañeros, busca otro grupo mejor.

[13] **exigente:** demanding [14] **delicado/a:** picky

9.1-13 Excursiones en *jeeps* rosas Imaginen que trabajan para la empresa estadounidense *Pink Jeep Tours*, que ofrece servicios de excursiones guiadas en Arizona y Nevada, y que quieren ofrecer un servicio de excursiones guiadas para los turistas en *jeeps* de color rosa en Ecuador. Primero es importante que el dueño de la empresa comprenda la importancia de ofrecer sus servicios en Ecuador. Sigan los pasos para completar la actividad.

Paso 1: La clase se divide en grupos de cuatro. Todos los miembros del grupo tienen que aportar ideas y designar a un/a líder para escribir el informe. Para convencer a su jefe del negocio, tienen que escribir un informe con la siguiente información. Usen el vocabulario de **Palabra por palabra**.

1. Tipos de clima y geografía de Ecuador
2. Cuatro lugares (p. ej.: selva amazónica, Quito...) donde se van a ofrecer las excursiones
3. Descripción de la excursión (p. ej.: explorar la flora y la fauna de la selva amazónica)
4. Precios de cada excursión para adultos y niños
5. Beneficios para la empresa (p. ej.: ganancias, popularidad)

Paso 2: Ahora que tienen un informe sobre Ecuador y los tipos de excursiones que van a ofrecer a los turistas, tienen que mostrar al jefe (su profesor/a) que el negocio va a tener éxito. Su jefe está indeciso porque abrir el mismo negocio en Ecuador cuesta mucho dinero. Usen la lista de expresiones o verbos y no olviden incluir el pronombre de objeto indirecto cuando sea necesario.

MODELO: insistir
→ *Le insistimos que abra este negocio en Ecuador porque el clima caluroso y tropical en la selva amazónica atrae a turistas.*

es mejor que	aconsejar	tener que
(no) es necesario que	recomendar	deber
es preciso que	insistir	pedir

WileyPLUS Go to *WileyPLUS* and listen to **Presta atención.**

Paso 3: Cada grupo trata de convencer al/a la profesor/a de que las futuras excursiones organizadas son un buen negocio en Ecuador. El líder de cada grupo presenta la información al/a la profesor/a. Al final, su profesor/a va a decidir qué grupo lo/a convenció para abrir el negocio en Ecuador porque presentó mejor información.

9.1-14 Presta atención: Consejos para viajar María José es guía de turismo y aconseja a unos estudiantes estadounidenses sobre actividades que pueden hacer durante un viaje por Ecuador y Perú. Escucha y selecciona la opción más adecuada.

1. María José aconseja ver el lago Titicaca...
   a. para aprender sobre la cultura inca.
   b. para poder hacer senderismo.
   c. para ver las famosas tortugas galápagos.
2. El lago Titicaca...
   a. está en Ecuador y es navegable.
   b. está entre Ecuador y Perú.
   c. está entre Bolivia y Perú y es navegable.
3. Si te gusta el sol, el agua y...
   a. los turistas, visita las islas Galápagos.
   b. los animales, visita las islas Galápagos.
   c. los incas, visita las islas Galápagos.

4. Hay tortugas gigantes...
   a. por todo Ecuador y Perú.
   b. en las islas Galápagos del Ecuador.
   c. en las Galápagos y el lago Titicaca.
5. El Camino Inca...
   a. está en Perú.
   b. está en Ecuador.
   c. está en los dos países.
6. Machu Picchu es...
   a. una ciudad de ruinas aztecas.
   b. una ciudad de ruinas incas.
   c. una ciudad del Ecuador.

¡OJO!

Reviewing your essay
Review vocabulary by checking spelling and agreement (gender and number) between articles and nouns, between nouns and all adjectives, and between subjects and verbs. Make sure that you are not using false cognates. Avoid repeating words. Instead, use synonyms, or you could also check if some words can be replaced by a direct or indirect object pronoun.

Try to include, if possible, new grammatical structures, and don't forget to make sure that every sentence has a conjugated verb and the correct verb forms.

9.1-15 Por escrito: La selva amazónica Trabajas para la oficina del programa de estudios en el extranjero de tu universidad. Recientemente visitaste la selva amazónica y tu jefa te pide que escribas un informe descriptivo sobre la jungla. Repasa la caja de **¡OJO!** para mejorar tu descripción.

PONTE EN MI LUGAR

Estrategias para conversar

Ways for participating in a debate or conversation (II) In Chapter 3, Section 1 you learned some phrases to express agreement (**Por supuesto, tienes razón,** and **estoy de acuerdo**) or disagreement (**No tienes razón, ni mucho menos, de ninguna manera** and **no estoy de acuerdo**) when giving your opinion. Sometimes you agree or disagree with your interlocutor, but want to offer an alternative to your interlocutor's opinion. Here are some useful expressions for providing other possibilities:

• Quizás *(+ subjunctive)* tengas razón, pero…	*You may be right, but . . .*
• A lo mejor *(+ indicative)* tienes razón, pero…	*Maybe you are right, but . . .*
• Puede que *(+ subjunctive)* esté equivocado, pero…	*Perhaps I am mistaken, but . . .*
• Es posible que *(+ subjunctive)* cambie de idea, pero…	*It is possible that I will change my mind, but . . .*

Las vacaciones Un/a amigo/a está indeciso/a sobre el país que quiere visitar en sus próximas vacaciones. Uno/a de ustedes debe ser la persona que va de vacaciones a Perú y el/a otro/a es el/a amigo/a que lo/a quiere convencer de que viaje a Ecuador. No olviden usar las **Estrategias para conversar**.

Amigo/a: Explícale a tu amigo/a que estás pensando viajar en tus próximas vacaciones a Perú. Infórmale sobre el número de días que tienes para viajar, tus actividades favoritas, los lugares que quieres visitar y el tipo de clima que te gusta.

Turista a Perú: Convence al turista de que viaje a Ecuador. Para convencerlo, infórmale sobre actividades diferentes que puede hacer en Ecuador, lugares donde puede quedarse a un precio económico e información sobre la cultura y la vida de los ecuatorianos.

Proyecto global Imagina que tienes que hacer un proyecto global para tu clase de español. Escoge uno de los siguientes temas: música andina, las líneas de Nazca, Ingapirca, la cordillera de los Andes. Busca en Internet información sobre el tema que elegiste. Después de estudiar la información, escribe un resumen que incluya lo siguiente:

- tema escogido y dónde se encuentra;
- cómo es;
- por qué lo recomiendas;
- si quieres estudiar más sobre este tema y por qué.

ASÍ ES LA VIDA

© John Wiley & Sons, Inc.

Expresión: "Año de nieves, año de bienes"

Fermín: Tenemos mucho trabajo este verano.
Ramón: Sí, ya sabes, **año de nieves, año de bienes.**
Fermín: Sí, tuvimos suerte con el tiempo.

¿Sabes qué significa el refrán?
¿Hay refranes o expresiones similares en inglés?

Adivina adivinador

En verano barbudo[15]
y en invierno desnudo[16],
¡esto es muy duro!
¿Qué es?

ENTÉRATE

Estrategias para leer

Thesis and development of an essay When reading an essay, you need to identify a topic and a thesis. The thesis is the focus of the text and what the essay is going to be about. In the first paragraph of the essay, the writer provides readers with some background about the topic and introduces a thesis. The background should describe why this topic is interesting and why he or she decided to write about. The conclusion of thesis is usually located in the last sentence of the paragraph. A good thesis needs to be creative and precise. The content of the essay will be based on the thesis. Once you have identified the thesis of a reading, look for details and reasons in the text that support it. In each paragraph you should find a reason supported by details, examples, and facts. The last paragraph in the text is a summary of the thesis. When reading **La Avenida de los Volcanes, Ecuador,** think about the thesis and the reasons that support it.

Antes de leer

1. Actividades al aire libre Lee la siguiente lista y piensa en dos actividades para cada uno de los temas presentados.

MODELO: las montañas → *escalar montañas o hacer senderismo*

el bosque tropical	el volcán	la isla
la Amazonía	la playa	la sierra

[15]**barbudo:** with a beard [16]**desnudo:** naked

2. ¿Qué ves? Mira rápidamente el texto, el formato y el título. Contesta las siguientes preguntas:

- ¿De qué crees que va a tratar este texto?
- ¿Qué tipo de consejos crees que vas a leer aquí?
- ¿Quién crees que escribe el texto?

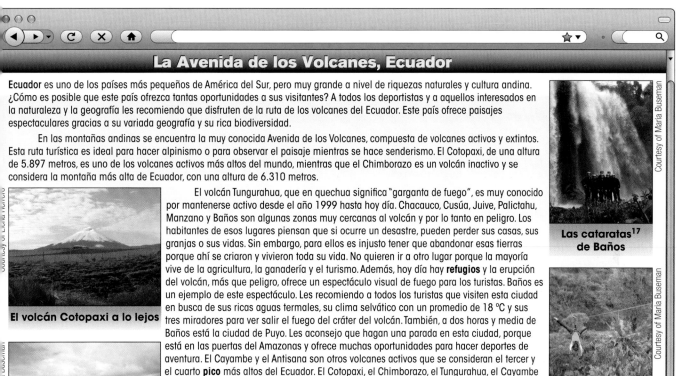

La Avenida de los Volcanes, Ecuador

Ecuador es uno de los países más pequeños de América del Sur, pero muy grande a nivel de riquezas naturales y cultura andina. ¿Cómo es posible que este país ofrezca tantas oportunidades a sus visitantes? A todos los deportistas y a aquellos interesados en la naturaleza y la geografía les recomiendo que disfruten de la ruta de los volcanes del Ecuador. Este país ofrece paisajes espectaculares gracias a su variada geografía y su rica biodiversidad.

En las montañas andinas se encuentra la muy conocida Avenida de los Volcanes, compuesta de volcanes activos y extintos. Esta ruta turística es ideal para hacer alpinismo o para observar el paisaje mientras se hace senderismo. El Cotopaxi, de una altura de 5.897 metros, es uno de los volcanes activos más altos del mundo, mientras que el Chimborazo es un volcán inactivo y se considera la montaña más alta de Ecuador, con una altura de 6.310 metros.

El volcán Tungurahua, que en quechua significa "garganta de fuego", es muy conocido por mantenerse activo desde el año 1999 hasta hoy día. Chacauco, Cusúa, Juive, Palictahu, Manzano y Baños son algunas zonas muy cercanas al volcán y por lo tanto en peligro. Los habitantes de esos lugares piensan que si ocurre un desastre, pueden perder sus casas, sus granjas o sus vidas. Sin embargo, para ellos es injusto tener que abandonar esas tierras porque ahí se criaron y vivieron toda su vida. No quieren ir a otro lugar porque la mayoría vive de la agricultura, la ganadería y el turismo. Además, hoy día hay **refugios** y la erupción del volcán, más que peligro, ofrece un espectáculo visual de fuego para los turistas. Baños es un ejemplo de este espectáculo. Les recomiendo a todos los turistas que visiten esta ciudad en busca de sus ricas aguas termales, su clima selvático con un promedio de 18 °C y sus tres miradores para ver salir el fuego del cráter del volcán. También, a dos horas y media de Baños está la ciudad de Puyo. Les aconsejo que hagan una parada en esta ciudad, porque está en las puertas del Amazonas y ofrece muchas oportunidades para hacer deportes de aventura. El Cayambe y el Antisana son otros volcanes activos que se consideran el tercer y el cuarto **pico** más altos del Ecuador. El Cotopaxi, el Chimborazo, el Tungurahua, el Cayambe y el Antisana son algunos de los volcanes que forman la Avenida de los Volcanes. Es importante que todos sepan que esta ruta ecológica se puede recorrer en vehículo, en bicicleta o caminando. A lo largo de la ruta hay lugares para dormir, descansar y admirar. ¿Qué más puede uno pedir?

Para terminar, solo decir que visiten este país mágico que está lleno de vida. Los volcanes, los pueblos pintorescos y la jungla amazónica son motivos suficientes para viajar hasta el corazón de los Andes. Ecuador tiene mucho que ofrecer a todos los turistas que buscan algo nuevo y original. Si no son personas interesadas en la montaña o la selva, tienen la opción de visitar las impresionantes islas Galápagos y la Costa del Sol de este país.

El volcán Cotopaxi a lo lejos

Isla Bartolomé en las islas Galápagos

Las cataratas[17] de Baños

shelters

Deportes de aventura en Mindo

peak

Courtesy of Maria Buseman

Después de leer

1. En el texto

1. Identifica la tesis. ¿Dónde está y cuál es?
2. Identifica en cada párrafo las ideas que apoyan[18] la tesis (una por párrafo sin incluir la introducción).
3. Identifica todos los adjetivos descriptivos que se usan en el texto anterior para describir el paisaje y la naturaleza de Ecuador de manera positiva.
4. Identifica las formas verbales que están en subjuntivo (seis en total). ¿A qué expresión o verbo le siguen?
5. Identifica seis conectores en el texto. ¿Conoces conectores similares o equivalentes? Consulta la caja de conectores de las **Estrategias para escribir en la siguiente página.**

[17]**cataratas:** waterfalls [18]**apoyan:** support

2. ¿Entendiste?

1. ¿Qué actividades deportivas se pueden hacer en la ruta de los volcanes?
2. ¿Qué volcanes están activos y cuál es peligroso?
3. ¿Por qué algunos ecuatorianos quieren seguir viviendo en zonas de peligro?
4. ¿Qué atractivos hay para los turistas en Baños?
5. Además de volcanes y selva, ¿qué otro tipo de geografía hay en Ecuador?

EXPANSIÓN:

Paso 1: Contesta las siguientes preguntas con ayuda de tu compañero/a.

1. ¿Lees blogs de viaje?	3. ¿Hay algún blog al que estás suscrito?
2. ¿Lees algún blog?	4. ¿Escribes algún blog? ¿De viajes o sobre qué?

Paso 2: Si escribes un blog, ¿Qué tipo de recomendaciones puedes hacer a las personas que escriben un blog?

MODELO: 1. Recomiendo que las entradas sean cortas.   3. Es importante que…
             2. Es mejor que…   4. Les recomiendo que…

Paso 3. Ahora, recomienda a tus compañeros algunos blogs que conozcas y explica por qué los recomiendas.

MODELO: 1. Te sugiero que leas el Blog de María José   3. Te sugiero que…
                porque da consejos para viajar a Ecuador.
             2. Recomiendo que…   4. Les pido que…

 ## EN TUS PROPIAS PALABRAS

Estrategias para escribir

Connectors Connector words are used to connect ideas, details, or clauses in order to show a logical relationship between them. Combining ideas by using connectors also helps with the clarity, cohesion, and organization of writing. Let's review those that we have learned and learn a few more:

Putting ideas together:	Adding information:	Contrasting ideas:
primero (*first*), segundo (*second*), tercero (*third*) lo primero es (*the first thing is*), después (*next*), luego (*then, next*), a continuación (*next*) por último, finalmente (*finally, last*), al final (*at the end*), para terminar (*finally*)	además (*also, moreover, furthermore*) también (*also*)	no obstante (*however*) sin embargo (*nevertheless*) pero (*but*) aunque (*although*) en cambio/por otro lado (*on the other hand*) mientras (*while*) por el contrario (*contrary to, in contrast*)

Giving examples/ideas		
por ejemplo (*for example*) es decir (*that is*) o sea (*that is*) tal/es como (*such as*) en otras palabras (*in other words*)		

Emphasizing an statement:	Expressing consequences:	Making general statements:
de cualquier forma, de todos modos (*in any event/case*)	así (*so*) por eso/por lo tanto (*therefore, that is why, for that reason*) como consecuencia (*as a consequence*) por esta razón (*for this reason*)	en general (*in general*) generalmente (*generally*) como regla general (*as a general rule*)

▲ *Tortugas galápagos*

▲ *Lobos marinos descansando bajo el sol*

▲ *Unos turistas buceando en las islas Galápagos*

Las islas Galápagos Imagínate que viajaste a Ecuador y quieres compartir tu experiencia. Vas a escribir un blog sobre las islas Galápagos. Investiga el tema en Internet. Después, convence a tus lectores de que es mejor visitar las islas Galápagos que cualquier otra parte de Ecuador. Sigue los siguientes pasos:

- Escribe una introducción explicando que vas a escribir sobre Ecuador y específicamente sobre las islas Galápagos. Explica por qué es mejor viajar a las islas Galápagos. No olvides incluir tu tesis al final del primer párrafo.
- Escribe uno o dos párrafos con información que apoye tu tesis con ejemplos y datos. Apóyate en estas u otras fotos de las islas Galápagos para describir el lugar.
- Introduce información para convencer a los lectores de que una visita a las islas Galápagos es una excelente opción. Añade adjetivos descriptivos de carácter positivo.
- Para terminar, escribe una conclusión explicando por qué ir a las Galápagos es una buena opción de viaje.
- No olvides usar conectores para organizar ideas y dar claridad y cohesión a cada párrafo del texto.

AUTOPRUEBA

VOCABULARIO

I. ¿De qué hablamos? Combina cada definición con la palabra que le corresponde.

_____ 1. Es una zona de muchos árboles.

_____ 2. Es un terreno plano entre las montañas.

_____ 3. Es la selva tropical más grande del mundo.

_____ 4. Es la orilla del mar.

_____ 5. Es una extensión de tierra rodeada de agua.

a. la Amazonía
b. el bosque
c. una isla
d. la playa
e. el valle

GRAMÁTICA

I. Consejos para la clase de español Tus amigos quieren aprender español rápidamente. Observa las ilustraciones y dales consejos.

© John Wiley & Sons, Inc.

MODELO:　Es necesario que _tomen clases de español._

1. Es importante que...
2. Es mejor que...
3. Les recomiendo que...
4. Les aconsejo que...
5. Les sugiero que...
6. Es preciso que...

II. Consejos de viaje Después de estudiar el Capítulo 9, ahora eres un/a experto/a sobre Ecuador. Tienes un/a amigo/a que está preparando su viaje a Ecuador y te pide consejos. ¿Qué le dices? Contesta sus preguntas utilizando los siguientes verbos y expresiones. No olvides usar los pronombres de objeto indirecto con los verbos de influencia.

| sugerir | recomendar | aconsejar | es mejor... |

MODELO:　¿Qué época del año es la ideal para visitar Ecuador?　→　_Te recomiendo que vayas durante la estación seca._

1. ¿A qué parte de Ecuador me recomiendas que vaya?
2. ¿Qué me aconsejas que tome para calmar los efectos del soroche?
3. Tengo una maleta grande y una mochila de expedición. ¿Qué me sugieres que lleve?
4. ¿Qué excursiones puedo hacer?
5. ¿Qué ropa es la más adecuada para el viaje?

CULTURA

1. Si vas a viajar a Ecuador, ¿debes llevar ropa de invierno o de verano? ¿Por qué?
2. ¿Qué es el archipiélago de Colón? ¿Por qué son famosas esas islas?
3. ¿Qué montañas importantes de Ecuador conoces?
4. ¿Qué es el soroche y cómo se puede aliviar?

REDACCIÓN

Piensa en un lugar que has visitado o quieres visitar algún día. Describe la geografía y el clima del lugar. Recomiéndale al lector qué actividades se pueden hacer allí, qué ropa llevar, cuándo es mejor ir y cuándo no.

EN RESUMIDAS CUENTAS, AHORA PUEDO...

☐ hablar sobre la geografía de Ecuador.

☐ hablar sobre todo tipo de climas.

☐ dar recomendaciones.

☐ expresar obligación.

☐ practicar el uso del pronombre para evitar repeticiones.

☐ hablar sobre Perú y Ecuador y sus diferentes regiones.

⌕ VOCABULARIO ESENCIAL

Sustantivos

el bosque	*forest*
la cordillera	*mountain range*
la estación lluviosa/seca	*(rainy/dry) season*
la frontera	*border*
la isla	*island*
el lago	*lake*
la montaña	*mountain*
el nivel del mar	*sea level*
el paisaje	*landscape*
la playa	*beach*
el puerto	*harbor*
el río	*river*
la selva tropical	*tropical forest*
la sierra	*highlands*

Cognados: la altitud, la Amazonía, el cañón, la costa, el desierto, la geografía, la jungla, la humedad, el valle, el volcán

Adjetivos

preciso/a	*necessary*

Cognados: esencial, importante, necesario/a

Verbos

acampar	*to go camping*
aconsejar	*to advise*
pedir (i)	*to request*
sugerir (ie)	*to suggest*

Cognados: insistir (en), permitir, prohibir, recomendar (ie)

LEARNING OBJECTIVES

By the end of this section you will be able to:

- Name different kinds of animals
- Discuss environmental problems
- Express subjective reactions and uncertainty
- Compare facts

- Express likes and dislikes
- Be acquainted with the consumption of coca leaves in Peru
- Express different perspectives on ecology

Una imagen vale más que mil palabras

Estas son líneas vistas[1] desde un avión. ¿Qué forma de animal tienen estas líneas?

¿Hay algo similar en Estados Unidos?

¿Quién hizo las líneas? ¿Cuál es la teoría del origen de estas líneas?

◄ *Las líneas de Nazca*

Jim Dyson/ Getty Images News / Getty Images

UNA PERSPECTIVA

Photo Courtesy of Tracy Quan

Tracy

La coca

Diferente

"Cuando fui a Perú, me sorprendió ver que se venden hojas de coca fresca en la calle, y que es legal. En mis paseos vi que había muchos productos de coca: refrescos de coca, té de coca, galletitas y hasta caramelos de coca. ¡Los niños pueden comprarlos! Me di cuenta[2] de que la coca es un estimulante muy suave, como la cafeína de los refrescos que tomamos en Estados Unidos. ¡No es una droga!".

Igual

"El consumo[3] de café en Estados Unidos es similar al consumo de coca en Perú. El café es un estimulante suave, ¡excepto cuando tomas mucho! Hay helado con sabor a café, y hay dulces y chocolates que contienen café y que los niños pueden comprar. Muchos de nuestros refrescos también tienen cafeína".

▲ *Dulce de coca*

© Bjorn Svensson / Alamy

¿Qué piensas tú?

1. ¿Crees que debe prohibirse la coca? ¿Por qué?
2. Si algún día se desarrolla una droga basada en el café, ¿debería prohibirse el café en Estados Unidos?
3. ¿Probarías[4] algún producto con coca si vas al Perú? ¿Por qué?

[1] **vistas:** seen [2] **darse cuenta:** to realize [3] **consumo:** consumption [4] **probarías:** would you taste

LA PURA VERDAD I | Animales de Perú

Bruno es un fotógrafo que nos dice lo que vio en persona y a través de la cámara.

1.

2.

3.

4.

5.

6.

© John Wiley & Sons, Inc.

 9.2-01 Animales que encuentra en Perú Bruno habla por Skype con sus hermanos sobre los animales exóticos que ve en Perú. Escucha y selecciona lo que describe.

1. Bruno describe...
   a. una alpaca.   b. una tortuga.   c. una rana.
2. Bruno describe...
   a. un cerdo.   b. un conejo.   c. un cuy.
3. Bruno comió...
   a. oveja.   b. alpaca.   c. llama.

⁵ **hueso:** bone

PALABRA POR PALABRA

Los animales

Los animales domésticos

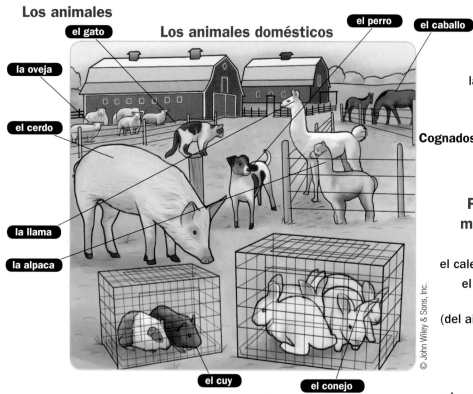

el gato · el perro · el caballo · la oveja · el cerdo · la llama · la alpaca · el cuy · el conejo

© John Wiley & Sons, Inc.

la araña	*spider*
la mariposa	*butterfly*
la rana	*frog*
la tortuga	*turtle*

Cognados: el delfín, el insecto, el mosquito

Para hablar del medio ambiente	*To talk about the environment*
la basura	*garbage*
el calentamiento global	*global warming*
el cambio climático	*climate change*
la contaminación (del aire, del agua, etc.)	*(air, water, etc.) pollution*
el derrame	*oil spill*
el desecho	*waste*
el/la ecologista	*environmentalist*
el envase (desechable)	*(disposable) container*
la escasez	*shortage*
el papel	*paper*
el petróleo	*oil*
el reciclaje	*recycling*
el recurso (natural)	*(natural) resource*
el vidrio	*glass*
ahorrar	*to save*
contaminar (el aire, el agua)	*to pollute (the air, the water)*
desarrollar	*to develop*
estar en peligro de extinción	*to be endangered*
tirar	*to throw away*

Cognados: conservar, consumir, la deforestación, la ecología, la energía (eléctrica, renovable...), el esmog, la especie, la fauna, el pesticida, el plástico, proteger, la reforestación, reciclar

Los animales salvajes *Wild animals*

el cóndor · el pájaro · el reptil · la serpiente · el pez

© John Wiley & Sons, Inc.

¿Qué dicen los peruanos?

¿Me das un <u>canceroso</u>, por favor?	*Would you give me a <u>cigarette</u>, please?*
Voy a la fiesta de Manu <u>de cajón</u>.	*I'm <u>absolutely</u> going to Manu's party.*
Tengo ganas de tomarme una <u>cholita</u>.	*I feel like drinking a <u>cholita</u> (beer mixed with coca-cola).*
No para de <u>lorear</u>.	*He/She does not stop <u>talking</u>.* (loro = parrot)
<u>Él es un zanahoria</u>.	*He doesn't drink or smoke.*

9.2-02 ¿De qué hablamos?

Paso 1: Lean las definiciones y busquen la palabra correspondiente en la sección **Palabra por palabra**.

MODELO: Es un tipo de energía procedente de una fuente que se regenera automáticamente.
→ *La energía renovable.*

1. Es la modificación del clima con respecto al historial climático debido a causas humanas o naturales.
2. Es un proceso de tratamiento[6] de un producto usado para obtener un nuevo producto.
3. Es la alteración negativa del estado natural de la tierra, el agua o la atmósfera mediante la introducción de un agente externo.
4. Es el aumento de la temperatura de la atmósfera y los océanos.
5. Es un recipiente de plástico, cartón u otro material que sirve para contener y guardar un producto.
6. Es un tipo de insecto volador[7] que puede tener alas grandes de bonitos colores.

Paso 2: Ahora, elijan tres palabras de la sección **Palabra por palabra** y escriban tres definiciones para leerlas a la clase. ¡Atención! Recuerden que para definir siempre usamos el verbo *ser*.

MODELO: *Es un/a… (que)…*
Es el/la… que…

9.2-03 Adivina, adivinador… Piensa en un animal. Después, túrnate con un/a compañero/a para adivinar en qué animal pensó cada uno. Las preguntas solo pueden tener respuestas del tipo Sí o No.

MODELO: Estudiante 1:   *¿Es un animal doméstico?*
Estudiante 2:   *No, es un animal salvaje.*
Estudiante 1:   *¿Vive en la selva?*
Estudiante 2:   *No, vive en el mar.*
Estudiante 1:   *¿Es inteligente y sociable?*
Estudiante 2:   *Sí.*
Estudiante 1:   *¡Ya sé, es el delfín!*
Estudiante 2:   *¡Sí, muy bien!*

---

[6]**tratamiento:** treatment [7]**volador:** flying

Expressing likes and dislikes: Verbs like gustar

In Chapter 5, Section 2 you learned different verbs like **gustar** to express likes and dislikes. These verbs work like the verb *to seem* in English.

Me preocupa [la escasez de agua].

I worry about the water shortage.
(Lit., The water shortage worries me.)
Mosquitoes bother us.

Nos molestan [los mosquitos].

As you already know, these verbs require the use of indirect object pronouns. The optional **a** + pronoun/noun is used to clarify or add emphasis.

A Bruno le fascina la vida salvaje.

Bruno is fascinated with wildlife.
(Lit., Wildlife fascinates Bruno.)
It doesn't fascinate me! Mosquitoes bother me and snakes scare me.

¡Pues **a mí** no! Los mosquitos me molestan y las serpientes me dan miedo.

With a partner, generate a list of as many verbs like **gustar** as you remember. Then, go back to the section **Hablando de gramática II** in Chapter 5, Section 2, and see if you remembered all of them. Are there any other verbs like **gustar** you are familiar with?

9.2-04 ¿Te gusta la vida salvaje? Levántate y hazles a tus compañeros las siguientes preguntas. Escribe el nombre del/de la compañero/a que conteste afirmativamente.

MODELO: Estudiante 1: *¿Te dan miedo las arañas?*
Estudiante 2: *Sí, ¡me dan mucho miedo! / No, no me dan miedo para nada.*

¿A quién de la clase...   Nombre del/la compañero/a

1. ...le encantan los perros? _____
2. ...le asustan las serpientes? _____
3. ...le fascinan los caballos? _____
4. ...le gusta reciclar y reutilizar materiales? _____
5. ...le encanta participar en reforestaciones? _____
6. ...le agrada tener peces en su casa? _____
7. ...le desagradan los delfines? _____
8. ...le interesa la ecología? _____
9. ...le molesta usar bolsas de plástico en el supermercado? _____
10. ...le aburre hablar de temas del medio ambiente? _____

9.2-05 ¿Qué problema es más serio para la supervivencia[8] del planeta?

Paso 1: Consideren los siguientes problemas ecológicos. Decidan cuál es el más serio, y ordenen la lista del 1 (más serio) al 10 (menos serio). Deben llegar a un consenso.

_____ a. la contaminación del aire
_____ b. la contaminación de los ríos y el mar
_____ c. la contaminación acústica
_____ d. la escasez de petróleo
_____ e. la escasez del agua
_____ f. la deforestación
_____ g. las especies en peligro de extinción
_____ h. la acumulación de desechos
_____ i. el cambio climático
_____ j. los residuos radioactivos

Paso 2: Ahora, comenta con tus compañeros qué haces tú para remediar cada uno de estos problemas. En general, ¿creen que su grupo está preocupado por el medio ambiente? ¿Piensan que hacen suficiente? ¿Qué más pueden hacer que no hacen? Informen a la clase.

MODELO: *En general, a nosotros nos preocupan los problemas del medio ambiente, pero no hacemos mucho para solucionarlos. Por ejemplo, ninguno de nosotros...*

[8]supervivencia: *survival*

HABLANDO DE GRAMÁTICA I

1. Expressing subjective reactions: Present subjunctive with verbs of emotion

WileyPLUS Go to *WileyPLUS* to review this grammar point with the help of the **Animated Grammar Tutorial** and the **Verb Conjugator**.

We use the indicative mood when we want to declare (i.e., state as a fact) the event expressed by that verb. That is, we state that someone knows or assumes that something is real.

Hay mucha contaminación del aire en Lima.	*There is a lot of air pollution in Lima.*
Nunca **usamos** el transporte público.	*We never use public transportation.*

In Section 1, you learned that the subjunctive mood, in contrast, is used to express wishes, hopes, requests, doubts and other subjective reactions to the events expressed by that verb.

Me preocupa [que **haya** tanta contaminación del aire en Lima].	*It is worrisome to me that there is so much pollution in Lima.*
Es una lástima [que no **usemos** el transporte público].	*It is a pity that we don't use the public transportation.*

Notice that in these two sentences we are not stating the information in the subordinate clause as a fact. Rather, we are expressing an opinion or subjective reaction about an event, which is already accepted as real. Thus, we use the subjunctive mood in a subordinate clause that follows main clauses that express a subjective reaction.

Main clause (subjective reaction)	Subordinate clause (verb in subjunctive)
Me preocupa Me molesta Es una lástima/pena No es extraño Es terrible Siento	[que **haya** tanta contaminación del aire en Lima]. [que no **usemos** el transporte público].

The following verbs and phrases, among others, express subjective reactions and require the use of the subjunctive when followed by a subordinate clause:

Es...	It is . . .
increíble	*incredible*
sorprendente	*surprising*
terrible	*terrible*
extraño	*strange*

raro	*odd*
genial	*great*
maravilloso	*marvelous*
ridículo	*ridiculous*
una lástima/pena	*a pity/shame*

Es una lástima que used no pueda ir a Machu Pichu.	*It is a pity that you cannot go to Machu Pichu.*
Es sorprendente que coman cuy en las regiones andinas.	*It is surprising that they eat Guinea pigs in the Andean regions.*

alegrarse (de)	*to be glad*
sentir (e>ie)	*to feel sorry*
temer	*to fear, to be afraid*

Siento que en el Amazonas **haya** tantos derrames de petróleo.	*I feel sorry/bad that in the Amazon River there are so many oil spills.*

A. Infinitive or subjunctive?

When expressing subjective reactions, the subordinate verb can be a subjunctive form (introduced by **que**) or an infinitive.

	Infinitive	Subjunctive
	If the subject of the subordinate verb and the person referred to in the main clause are the same:	If the subject of the subordinate verb and the person referred to in the main clause are different:
Me/te/le/nos/les... gusta, alegra, encanta, preocupa molesta, importa, etc.	<u>Me</u> gusta <u>reciclar</u>. (a mí) = (yo)	<u>Me</u> encanta que <u>recicles</u>. (a mí) ≠ (tú)
	To make generalizations:	**To specify about:**
Es... bueno/malo increíble sorprendente terrible extraño raro genial maravilloso ridículo una lástima/pena etc.	Es bueno <u>reciclar</u>. (en general)	Es bueno <u>que recicles</u>. (tú específicamente)

B. Verbs like *gustar*

In Chapter 5, Section 2, you learned different verbs like **gustar** to express opinions, impressions, and emotions about something. These verbs work like the verb "to seem" in English. These verbs can also be used with subordinate clauses to express an opinion about a specific event.

[La actitud del gobierno] **me parece** inaceptable. **Me parece** inaceptable [la actitud del gobierno].	*The attitude of the government seems unacceptable (to me).*
Me parece inaceptable [que el gobierno no **haga** nada]. [Que el gobierno no **haga** nada] **me parece** inaceptable.	*I find it unacceptable that the government is not doing anything. (Lit., It seems unacceptable to me that . . .)*
[La actitud del gobierno] **nos importa**. **Nos importa** [la actitud del gobierno].	*The attitude of the government matters to us.*
Nos importa [que el gobierno no **haga** nada].	*It matters to us that the government is not doing anything. (Lit., The fact that the government is not doing anything matters to us.)*

9.2-06 Informe del viaje Durante su viaje a Perú, Bruno le escribe un mensaje a su supervisora para comentarle sus impresiones.

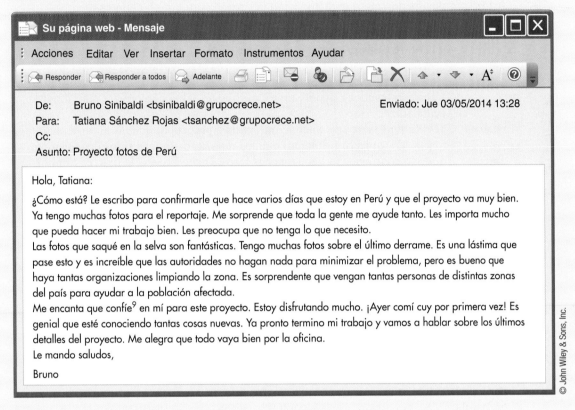

Su página web - Mensaje

Acciones   Editar   Ver   Insertar   Formato   Instrumentos   Ayudar

Responder   Responder a todos   Adelante

De: Bruno Sinibaldi <bsinibaldi@grupocrece.net>   Enviado: Jue 03/05/2014 13:28
Para: Tatiana Sánchez Rojas <tsanchez@grupocrece.net>
Cc:
Asunto: Proyecto fotos de Perú

Hola, Tatiana:

¿Cómo está? Le escribo para confirmarle que hace varios días que estoy en Perú y que el proyecto va muy bien. Ya tengo muchas fotos para el reportaje. Me sorprende que toda la gente me ayude tanto. Les importa mucho que pueda hacer mi trabajo bien. Les preocupa que no tenga lo que necesito.

Las fotos que saqué en la selva son fantásticas. Tengo muchas fotos sobre el último derrame. Es una lástima que pase esto y es increíble que las autoridades no hagan nada para minimizar el problema, pero es bueno que haya tantas organizaciones limpiando la zona. Es sorprendente que vengan tantas personas de distintas zonas del país para ayudar a la población afectada.

Me encanta que confíe[9] en mí para este proyecto. Estoy disfrutando mucho. ¡Ayer comí cuy por primera vez! Es genial que esté conociendo tantas cosas nuevas. Ya pronto termino mi trabajo y vamos a hablar sobre los últimos detalles del proyecto. Me alegra que todo vaya bien por la oficina.

Le mando saludos,

Bruno

Paso 1: Primero, busca todos los verbos en el presente de subjuntivo que encuentres en el párrafo (son diez en total). Después, completa la lista indicando cuál es la cláusula principal y cuál es la cláusula subordinada.

Cláusula principal:

1. *Me sorprende...*
2. _____
3. _____
4. _____
5. _____
6. _____
7. _____
8. _____
9. _____
10. _____

Cláusula subordinada:

que toda la gente me ayude tanto.
_____
_____
_____
_____
_____
_____
_____
_____
_____

Paso 2: ¿Cierto o falso? Ahora, lee el mensaje otra vez y decide si las siguientes oraciones son ciertas o falsas. Si son falsas, escribe la información correcta.

C   F

☐ ☐   1. A Bruno le aburre el trabajo que tiene que hacer en Perú.

☐ ☐   2. La gente con la que trabaja Bruno no lo ayuda mucho.

☐ ☐   3. A Bruno le preocupa el derrame.

☐ ☐   4. A Bruno le parece fantástica la respuesta de las autoridades.

☐ ☐   5. Bruno sabe que las cosas van bien en la oficina.

[9] confiar: to trust

9.2-07 ¿Qué sabes de Bruno? Beatriz, la jefa de la organización en la que trabaja Bruno, no sabe nada de él y le pregunta a Tatiana. Lee otra vez el mensaje de Bruno en 9.1-06 y después completa el diálogo con la opción correcta en cada caso.

Beatriz: ¡Hola, Tatiana! ¿Cómo estás? ¿Sabes algo de Bruno? Me (**encanta / preocupa**) que no (**tenemos / tengamos**) noticias de él.

Tatiana: ¡No te preocupes! Ayer recibí noticias de él. Hace varios días que está en Perú y todo va bien. Le (**molesta / sorprende**) que todas las personas con las que trabaja lo (**ayuden / ayude**) tanto, porque no sabía cómo iba a reaccionar la gente allí.

Beatriz: ¿De verdad? Si te soy sincera, me (**gusta / preocupa**) que las autoridades locales no (**quieren / quieran**) que los reporteros saquen fotos del derrame.

Tatiana: Todo lo contrario. Ya tiene muchas fotos. De hecho, a él le (**parece / importa**) increíble que tantas organizaciones ecológicas (**están / estén**) allí y les (**ofrezcan / ofrezca**) todos los permisos que necesitan.

Beatriz: ¡Me alegro! Ya sabes que me (**desagrada / importa**) mucho que este proyecto (**sale / salga**) bien.

Tatiana: Pues a Bruno le (**aburre / encanta**) que (**confiamos / confiemos**) en él para el proyecto y yo sé que va a hacer un trabajo excepcional.

Beatriz: ¡Genial! Ahora sí que estoy contenta por el resto del día.

9.2-08 Y tú, ¿qué opinas?

Paso 1: Usa las expresiones de la lista para expresar tus opiniones o reacciones sobre las siguientes noticias. Recuerda usar el verbo de la cláusula subordinada en la forma apropiada del subjuntivo.

(no) me preocupa que...   me alegra que...   es _____ que...

me parece _____ que...   es terrible/genial que...   siento que...

1. La contaminación atmosférica también afecta a Quito.

2. El gobierno de Ecuador trabaja para eliminar 1.400 fuentes de contaminación ambiental antes del 2016.

3. Perú prohíbe el uso de animales salvajes en los circos.

4. *Petroecuador* limpia la selva amazónica afectada por el derrame de petróleo.

5. La provincia de Huaraz pone en marcha[10] programas de reciclaje y reforestación.

6. El cóndor andino es una especie en peligro de extinción.

7. Perú se convierte en el mayor proveedor[11] de energía limpia y renovable de América del Sur.

▲ *Ciudad de Huaraz, Perú*

Paso 2: Ahora, compara tus opiniones con las de un/a compañero/a. Para cada noticia, ¿es su reacción positiva o negativa? ¿Coinciden en algunas reacciones, en ninguna o en todas?

[10]poner en marcha: to start up [11]proveedor: supplier

LA PURA VERDAD II | Un pueblo de los Andes

Kenny trabaja para *Ingenieros sin fronteras* y va a un pueblito de los Andes con su amigo Rob.

1.

2.

> Bienvenidos. Estamos muy contentos de que estén aquí.

3.

> Creo que no están hablando en quechua, ¿no?

4.

5.

> vidrio
> papel
> plástico

6.

> ¿Qué es esto?

© John Wiley & Sons, Inc.

9.2-09 ¿Qué creen que esté pasando? Escucha lo que les pasó a los ingenieros y decide cuál es la explicación más probable.

1. ¿Cuál es el problema?
   a. Es posible que la comida sea muy mala.
   b. Es probable que el plato tenga carne y él es vegetariano.
   c. Es posible que piense que es muy poca comida.
2. ¿Por qué entiende todo?
   a. Es posible que estén hablando en inglés.
   b. Es probable que estén hablando en quechua.
   c. Es posible que estén hablando en español.
3. ¿Qué le pasa?
   a. Es posible que Kenny quiera más comida.
   b. Es posible que Kenny esté triste porque le gustó mucho vivir allí y ahora tiene que irse.
   c. Es probable que piense que ellos fueron antipáticos.

HABLANDO DE GRAMÁTICA II

WileyPLUS Go to *WileyPLUS* to review this grammar point with the help of the **Animated Grammar Tutorial** and the **Verb Conjugator**.

2. Expressing uncertainty: Present subjunctive with expressions of doubt

As you already know, the indicative mood is used to report and to talk about facts and events as objective and a part of reality. Thus, we use the indicative mood when we want to declare (i.e., state as a fact) the event expressed by that verb: we make a statement about something that someone knows or assumes to be real.

Están hablando quechua.
They are speaking quechua.

Creo [que **están** hablando quechua].
I think [they are speaking quechua].

When we do not want to state or assume but want to express uncertainty or we are just considering a possibility about an event, the subjunctive is used in the subordinate clause:

Dudo/No creo/Es posible [que **estén** hablando quechua].
I doubt/I don't think/It's possible [that they are speaking quechua].

Thus, we use the indicative after main clauses that state or assume the veracity or reality of an event, and we use subjunctive after main clauses that express uncertainty and possibility, or to deny the occurrence an event.

Statements	Indicative
Está claro que... Es verdad/cierto que... No hay duda de que... Estoy seguro/a de que...	**están** muy contentos de estar allí.
Assumptions	**Indicative**
Creemos que... Pienso que... Me parece que... Es seguro que... Supongo que...	no **saben** dónde están.

Uncertainty/Negation	Subjunctive
No está claro que... No es verdad/cierto/seguro que... No creemos que... No pienso que... No me parece que... No estoy seguro/a de que...	**estén** muy contentos de estar allí.
Possibility	**Subjunctive**
(No) Es posible que... Quizás/Tal vez... *(maybe)* (No) Es probable que...	no **sepan** dónde están.

9.2-10 ¿Qué dicen? Mira otra vez la historia de Kenny y Rob en **La pura verdad II** y completa el diálogo.

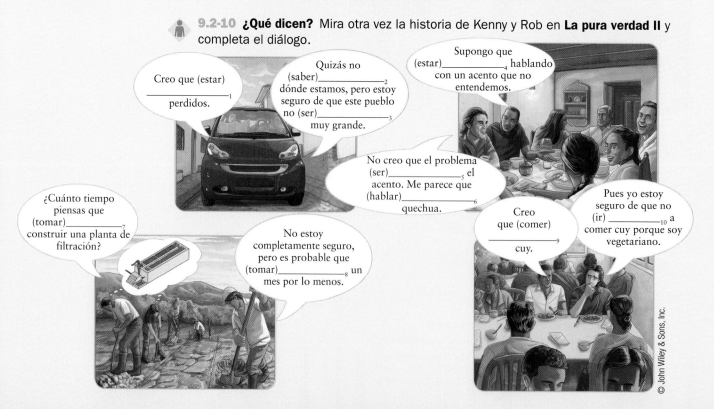

Creo que (estar) _____ perdidos.₁

Quizás no (saber) _____₂ dónde estamos, pero estoy seguro de que este pueblo no (ser) _____₃ muy grande.

Supongo que (estar) _____₄ hablando con un acento que no entendemos.

No creo que el problema (ser) _____₅ el acento. Me parece que (hablar) _____₆ quechua.

¿Cuánto tiempo piensas que (tomar) _____₇ construir una planta de filtración?

No estoy completamente seguro, pero es probable que (tomar) _____₈ un mes por lo menos.

Creo que (comer) _____₉ cuy.

Pues yo estoy seguro de que no (ir) _____₁₀ a comer cuy porque soy vegetariano.

9.2-11 **La presentación del proyecto** Kenny y Rob regresan a Estados Unidos y dan una presentación sobre la construcción del sistema de filtración de agua en la sierra de Miraflores.

Paso 1: Lee la presentación de Kenny y Rob.

Rob: *... el sistema de filtración lenta con arena es el sistema de tratamiento de agua más antiguo del mundo. Está considerado el mejor porque elimina la mayoría de las bacterias y residuos de pesticidas. Por ejemplo, tiene mayor eficacia que el sistema de filtración biológica. Además, purifica el agua sin contaminar el medio ambiente.*

Kenny: *Los habitantes del pueblo trabajan muy duro para conseguir agua potable. La construcción de esta planta los va a ayuda a solucionar la escasez de agua que....*

Paso 2: Ahora, completa los comentarios y preguntas de los asistentes a la presentación con la forma adecuada del subjuntivo o el indicativo de los verbos.

1. **Es verdad que** este sistema _____ el más antiguo del mundo. **Está claro que** _____ considerado el mejor y **no hay duda de que** _____ la mayoría de las bacterias y residuos.
2. Pues yo **dudo que** este sistema _____ el más antiguo del mundo, y para mí **no está tan claro que** _____ considerado el mejor. ¿**Están ustedes seguros de que** _____ la mayoría de bacterias y residuos?
3. Yo estudio sistemas de filtración y **es cierto que** _____ considerado el mejor sistema de todos. **Estoy completamente seguro de que** _____ el agua sin contaminar el medio ambiente.
4. **Es posible que** no _____ considerado el mejor sistema de todos, pero **no dudo que** _____ mayor eficacia que la filtración biológica.
5. Pues yo sé que **es verdad que** los habitantes del pueblo _____ duro para conseguir agua potable[12], y **me parece maravilloso que** nosotros los _____ a solucionar la escasez.

© John Wiley & Sons, Inc.

[12] **agua potable:** drinking water

OTRA PERSPECTIVA

Myriam

La basura y el reciclaje

Diferente

"La primera vez que fui de compras en Estados Unidos me llamó la atención que en las tiendas usaban muchas bolsas y envases. Me sorprendió mucho ver el exceso de bolsas plásticas en los supermercados y en los restaurantes de comida rápida. Muchas veces le ofrecen al cliente una doble bolsa plástica porque tienen miedo de que una sola se rompa. En Perú se usan menos bolsas y envoltorios[13]. Además, en Perú tienes que pagar extra por las botellas de soda o traer una botella vacía para reemplazar la nueva. ¡Las botellas son caras!"

Igual

"En Perú también hay mucha conciencia sobre la conservación del ambiente, la ecología, el reciclaje y la deforestación. Tenemos grupos que protestan contra la construcción de oleoductos[14], ya que los derrames accidentales pueden contaminar mucho la tierra".

 Explícale a Myriam

1. ¿Crees que se usan demasiado las bolsas plásticas en los supermercados y las tiendas de Estados Unidos? ¿Y en los restaurantes de comida rápida? ¿Por qué?
2. ¿Conoces grupos interesados por conservar el medio ambiente?
3. ¿Hay áreas en Estados Unidos donde la gente se interesa más sobre el medio ambiente y el reciclaje que en otras?

MANOS A LA OBRA

 9.2-12 ¿Respetas el medio ambiente?

Paso 1: Entrevista a un/a compañero/a sobre los siguientes temas medioambientales.

1. ¿Cuáles son los problemas medioambientales más serios en el área donde vives? ¿Crees que existe una solución para este problema? ¿Haces algo para reducir el impacto de este problema?
2. ¿Reciclas? ¿Hay buenos programas de reciclaje en tu comunidad? ¿Por qué?
3. ¿Haces algo para conservar los recursos naturales? ¿Andas en bicicleta o caminas para gastar menos gasolina? ¿Usas menos calefacción en invierno o menos aire acondicionado en verano? ¿Ahorras agua? ¿Cómo?
4. ¿Vas mucho a restaurantes y cafeterías donde usan envases desechables para la comida y las bebidas? ¿Usas estos envases desechables con frecuencia o prefieres evitarlos? ¿Llevas otros envases alternativos, como por ejemplo, una taza de metal?
5. ¿Conoces algún país hispanohablante? ¿Crees que en ese país son respetuosos con el medio ambiente? ¿Contaminan más o menos que en EE.UU.?
6. En general, ¿crees que eres respetuoso con el medio ambiente?

Paso 2: Después, escriban un pequeño informe. ¿En qué aspectos coinciden los dos? ¿En qué no coinciden?

MODELO: *Mi compañero/a _____ y yo nos preocupamos por el medio ambiente. Sin embargo, pienso que _____ es más activista que yo porque...*

Paso 3: Por último, compartan su informe con la clase. ¿Crees que tu compañero/a es respetuoso/a con el medio ambiente?

[13]**envoltorio:** wrapping, packaging [14]**oleoducto:** oil pipeline

9.2-13 El más... y el mejor

 Paso 1: Completa las oraciones con tus opiniones sobre los siguientes temas.

MODELO: El animal más desagradable de una ciudad *es la rata, porque siempre anda entre la basura.*

1. La comida más desagradable[15] o el animal más desagradable
2. El animal más hermoso de la selva
3. El animal doméstico más útil
4. El animal con mayor peligro de extinción
5. El recurso natural más amenazado
6. La peor manera de gastar agua
7. La mejor manera de reducir el consumo de envases desechables

 Paso 2: Compara tus respuestas con las de un/a compañero/a. ¿Están de acuerdo? Si no están de acuerdo, intenten convencer al otro de su opinión usando las expresiones de la lista u otras parecidas. ¡Enfatiza tu opinión usando superlativos!

(no) creer que...	(no) está claro que...	es posible que...
(no) pensar que...	(no) es evidente que...	es probable que...
(no) dudo que...	(no) es verdad/cierto que...	quizás, tal vez...

MODELO: *No creo que la rata sea el animal más desagradable. Yo pienso que la cucaracha es el animal más desagradable. ¡Es asquerosísima![16] Siempre vive en la basura también y además...*

9.2-14 El candidato "verde"

 Paso 1: Imagina que eres un/a candidato/a para alcalde[17] de tu ciudad. Escribe tres cosas que vas a hacer con respecto al medio ambiente si los ciudadanos te eligen.

MODELO: *Si me eligen, voy a prohibir las megafiestas universitarias en la playa porque producen muchísima basura y desechos. Contaminan la playa y cuesta mucho dinero limpiarla.*

Paso 2: En grupos de tres, interpreten los papeles del/de la candidato/a y dos periodistas. El/La candidato/a habla de lo que va a hacer. Los periodistas toman apuntes y cuando el/la candidato/a termina, hacen comentarios o preguntas. Usen las palabras de la lista:

Dudo que...	Me preocupa que...
No creo que usted...	Me parece que...
Es improbable que usted...	Es bueno que... pero...
(No) Estoy seguro de que usted...	Me alegro de que... pero...

MODELO: Periodista 1: *Señor/a _____, ¿qué propone usted para reducir el esmog urbano?*
             Periodista 2: *Ese es un asunto muy serio. Voy a aumentar los impuestos de...*
             Periodista 3: **Es genial que usted** tome *esas medidas, pero* **es probable que** encuentre *mucha oposición...*

 Paso 3: Para terminar, dos grupos presentan su conferencia de prensa a la clase. El resto de la clase escucha las dos conferencias y al final vota por el mejor candidato.

---

[15] **desagradable:** disgusting [16] **asqueroso/a:** disgusting [17] **alcalde:** mayor

---

Making comparisons: Superlatives and absolute superlatives

Do you remember how to express that something has the highest or lowest degree of a quality? And how do we express that something shows a very high degree of a quality without comparing it to others?

Ese es el problema más serio de todos. ¡Es un problema gravísimo!

Go back to section **Hablando de gramática I** in Chapter 3, Section 2, to review the formation of the superlative before doing activity **9.2-13**.

9.2-15 Problemas y soluciones sobre el mundo

Paso 1: Piensen en cinco de los problemas ambientales más problemáticos a nivel global. Pueden mirar la lista de la actividad 9.2-05.

Paso 2: Ahora, expliquen las causas de estos problemas. Propongan soluciones a estos problemas usando el subjuntivo y el vocabulario de **Palabra por palabra**. Sean realistas en sus opiniones.

MODELO: la escasez de energía
Causa: *Creo que la gente consume demasiada energía. Está claro que mucha gente prefiere usar su auto en vez de usar el transporte público.*
Solución: *Es necesario que usemos más el transporte público y que desarrollemos energías renovables.*

Paso 3: Ahora, usen la información de **Paso 2** para preparar un debate. Cada grupo presenta un problema ecológico y explica su(s) causa(s), y los miembros de otros grupos presentan posibles soluciones al problema. No olviden usar las palabras del vocabulario y el subjuntivo. Su profesor/a puede añadir otra pregunta sobre el mismo tema, con el objetivo de que presenten otro argumento a favor y otro en contra.

MODELO: Estudiante 1: *¿Qué puede hacer nuestra comunidad para terminar con* **la** *escasez de energía? Nuestra comunidad consume más energía eléctrica de la que necesita.*
Estudiante 2: *Es necesario que usemos más el transporte público.*
Estudiante 3: *No estamos de acuerdo. La energía es necesaria para la vida diaria. Es mejor que desarrollemos fuentes renovables de energía.*
Profesor/a: *¿Qué ventajas y desventajas tienen las energías renovables?*

WileyPLUS Go to *WileyPLUS* and listen to **Presta atención.**

9.2-16 Presta atención: Una charla del Ministro del Interior[18]
El Ministro del Interior de Estados Unidos presenta un plan para mejorar el medio ambiente. Escucha su presentación para saber más sobre estos problemas. Después, selecciona la respuesta correcta.

1. ¿Qué problemas menciona el Ministro del Interior?
   a. la deforestación y el uso de pesticidas
   b. un alto consumo de agua, energía eléctrica y pesticidas
   c. un alto consumo de agua, petróleo y electricidad
2. ¿Qué puede ocurrir si no resolvemos los problemas presentados por el ministro?
   a. Nuestro planeta va a mejorar día a día.
   b. La vida en el planeta va a desaparecer.
   c. Se van a reforestar los bosques.
3. ¿Por qué quiere el ministro que no se usen tanto los carros algunos días de la semana?
   a. Para evitar el tráfico cuando vayamos al trabajo.
   b. Para mejorar nuestra salud y usar menos petróleo.
   c. Para no usar tanto petróleo y tener un cielo sin contaminación.
4. ¿Por qué quiere crear leyes?
   a. porque es necesario proteger la naturaleza
   b. porque quiere conseguir más dinero
   c. porque no hay ninguna ley

9.2-17 Por escrito: La basura
Trabajas para el periódico de tu universidad y escribes un artículo sobre el tema de la basura. Antes de empezar a escribir: (a) especifica el problema (dónde, cuándo, quién, cómo, etc.); (b) piensa en algunos ejemplos que apoyen tus opiniones; (c) convence a los estudiantes de tus ideas. Usa las sugerencias de **¡OJO!**. Puedes usar estas preguntas para comenzar con tu artículo:

- ¿Qué se hace con toda la basura?
- ¿Es bueno quemar[19] la basura?
- ¿Es preferible que se tire al mar?
- ¿Qué debe hacer la comunidad para solucionar el problema?

[18] **Ministro del Interior:** Secretary of the Interior [19] **quemar:** to burn

¡OJO!

Structuring and revising your writing

When writing an essay you should include an introduction, a body to develop the reasons to support the thesis presented in the introduction, and a conclusion restating your thesis. Then revise the grammar and vocabulary. Check the sentences and clauses that need subjunctive or indicative mood. Did you use the right expressions to use the subjunctive? Or are those expressions used with the indicative?

PONTE EN MI LUGAR

Un ecologista desilusionado Tienes un/a amigo/a que está desilusionado/a con la organización ecológica a la que pertenece. Decidan quién quiere ser el/la ecologista desilusionado/a y quién es el/la amigo/a que le da consejos e ideas. Después, lean atentamente las siguientes descripciones para poder representar la situación. No olviden usar las **Estrategias para conversar**.

Estudiante 1: Eres un/a ecologista. Uno de los objetivos de tu organización es reducir la contaminación y promover el reciclaje de desechos de plástico, vidrio y papel. No estás contento/a con la organización. Explícale a un/a compañero/a: (a) las actividades de la organización que te preocupan, o te importan; (b) qué es necesario/importante/mejor/bueno que la organización haga; (c) los beneficios de la organización para la comunidad; (d) todo el trabajo que hizo la organización.

Estudiante 2: Tu compañero/a pertenece a una organización ecológica. Escucha la información sobre la organización y ofrécele ayuda. Pregúntale sobre: (a) el número de miembros de la organización; (b) las funciones de cada miembro; (c) la situación económica; (d) el trabajo del presidente; (e) días, horas y lugar de las reuniones; (f) sugiere ideas para ayudar a lograr sus objetivos.

Estrategias para conversar

Ways for participating in a debate or conversation (III) In Chapter 8, Section 2, you have learned to use some questions or statements to participate in a conversation when clarification of the topic is needed (e.g., **¿Qué quiere decir? ¿Podría clarificar eso?**, etc.). If you need to further clarify things, use these expressions:

Lo que quiero decir es que... + *indicative*
What I mean is . . .

Yo no digo que... + *subjunctive*
I'm not saying that . . .

   **WileyPLUS** Go to *WileyPLUS* to find more **Arroba** activities.

Organizaciones ecologistas Explora en tu buscador favorito información sobre una organización ecologista que trabaje para proteger el Parque Nacional de las islas Galápagos. Escribe un pequeño resumen sobre los objetivos de la organización, cómo se financia, el tipo de trabajo que hacen y quiénes participan. Comenta tu investigación con un/a compañero/a y decidan qué organización es más efectiva para proteger el medio ambiente de las Galápagos.

ASÍ ES LA VIDA

Expresión: "A caballo regalado no se le miran los dientes".

Ana: ¿Quieres unos tenis?
Ema: Sí, necesito unos tenis, pero ¿no los tienes en rojo?
Ana: No te quejes. **A caballo regalado no se le miran los dientes.**

¿Qué significa esta expresión?
¿Hay un equivalente en inglés? ¿Cuál es?

Adivina, adivinador

¿Cómo se llama,
se llama, se llama
el animal de carga
que viste de lana?

VER PARA CREER II: Un paseo por Cotopaxi

WileyPLUS Go to *WileyPLUS* to see this video and to find more video activities.

Antes de ver

Con ayuda de un/a compañero/a, responde estas preguntas.

1. ¿Conoces parques nacionales de tu país? ¿Quieres visitarlos?
2. ¿Qué volcanes activos o extintos conoces?
3. ¿Qué animales en peligro de extinción conoces?
4. ¿Cómo es la vegetación y la fauna de la Amazonía?

Después de ver

1. ¿Entendiste? Karen y su amiga María José visitan un lugar importante de Quito. Después de escuchar el video, responde las preguntas:

1. ¿Desde hace cuántos años vive Karen en Quito?
   a. Karen vive en Quito desde hace unos días.
   b. Karen vive en Quito desde hace una semana.
   c. Karen vive en Quito desde hace dos años.
2. ¿Qué significa "páramo" según María José?
   a. Es un refugio para los animales y la gente.
   b. Es un lugar donde hay un ecosistema.
   c. Es el interior de un volcán.
3. ¿Qué animal según María José está en peligro de extinción?
   a. Los cuyes están en peligro de extinción.
   b. Los loros están en peligro de extinción.
   c. Los cóndores están en peligro de extinción.
4. ¿Qué consejos le da María José a Karen para proteger a los animales en peligro de extinción?
   a. Le sugiere que alimente a los animales.
   b. Sugiere que se eduque a la gente.
   c. Le pide que los lleve a refugios nacionales.
5. ¿Qué actividad hace Karen al final del video?
   a. Ella monta en bicicleta.
   b. Ella monta a caballo.
   c. Ella hace *canopy*.

2. Actividades en la Hacienda El Porvenir Al final del recorrido por el Cotopaxi, Karen quiere saber más información sobre las actividades que se pueden practicar en la Hacienda El Porvenir. ¿Qué piensas del *canopy*? ¿Practicaste alguna vez esta actividad? ¿Dónde y cómo?

3. Enfoque cultural ¿Qué actividades de tu ciudad le recomiendas a un visitante? ¿Por qué?

AUTOPRUEBA

VOCABULARIO

I. ¿De qué hablamos? Lee las definiciones y busca la palabra correspondiente en la sección **Palabra por palabra.**

____ 1. Es un animal que puede volar.
____ 2. Es la posibilidad de desaparición de animales.
____ 3. Es la acción de defender a una persona, animal o cosa de un peligro.
____ 4. Es la acción de economizar o de no gastar algo.
____ 5. Es un líquido que se extrae de la tierra para producir gasolina.

a. peligro de extinción
b. el petróleo
c. ahorrar
d. un pájaro
e. proteger

II. ¿Hay soluciones? Empareja cada problema con la solución más apropiada.

____ 1. la deforestación
____ 2. la contaminación del agua
____ 3. tirar basura al suelo
____ 4. la escasez de energía
____ 5. la escasez de agua
____ 6. tirar envases de plástico y vidrio a la basura

a. plantar árboles
b. ahorrar agua
c. conservar electricidad
d. poner contenedores de reciclaje en las calles
e. poner la basura en los contenedores
f. no tirar basura a los ríos o el mar

GRAMÁTICA

I. Tus impresiones sobre Perú y Ecuador Aprendiste sobre estos países. ¿Cuáles son tus impresiones?

Es increíble/terrible/maravilloso/extraño/ sorprendente/raro/genial/una pena...

MODELO: La llama y la alpaca son animales autóctonos de América del Sur. → *Es sorprendente que la llama y la alpaca sean animales autóctonos de América del Sur.*

1. Las llamas no pueden vivir en zonas tropicales.
2. El cuy tiene un sabor similar al pollo.
3. Machu Picchu está situado a 2.430 metros (7.970 pies) sobre el nivel del mar.
4. La llama y la alpaca producen lana de gran calidad.

II. ¿Verdad o mentira? Decide si lo siguiente sobre Perú y Ecuador es cierto o falso.

(no) creo/pienso/dudo que...
(no) es cierto/verdad/probable que...

MODELO: Cuando están enojadas, las llamas escupen. → *Dudo que las llamas escupan. (Falso, sí escupen)*

1. Perú es del tamaño de Alaska.
2. Un escritor peruano, Mario Vargas Llosa, es mundialmente famoso.
3. En Perú, ni los militares ni los policías pueden votar en las elecciones.
4. La carne de llama no se come.
5. Otro nombre para el cuy es conejillo de Indias.

III. ¿Qué reacción te producen las siguientes situaciones? Usa las expresiones de la lista para expresar tus opiniones. Usa las frases entre paréntesis y presta atención a si hay cambio de sujeto o no.

(no) me preocupa (que)...   (no) me importa (que)...
me alegra (que)...   (no) me gusta (que)...
(no) me molesta (que)...

1. La escasez de lluvia afecta a nuestra ciudad.
2. La contaminación de los ríos provoca la muerte de millones de peces al año.
3. Intento reducir el consumo de gasolina.
4. El gato andino está en peligro de extinción.
5. Reciclo las bolsas de plástico.

CULTURA

Decide si la oración es **Cierta** o **Falsa**. Si es falsa, corrígela.

	Cierto	Falso
1. El español es la lengua materna de todos los peruanos.	☐	☐
2. La llama es natural de la costa.	☐	☐
3. El cuy no es una mascota, se cría para comer.	☐	☐
4. Las líneas de Nazca se pueden ver desde un avión.	☐	☐
5. Hay cocaína disponible para todos.	☐	☐

REDACCIÓN

Piensa en algo que te llama la atención sobre el medio ambiente, la contaminación, la belleza de la naturaleza, etc. Escribe qué te sorprende, te interesa o sientes acerca de estos temas.

EN RESUMIDAS CUENTAS, AHORA PUEDO...

☐ expresar gustos y preferencias.
☐ hacer comparaciones.
☐ nombrar animales en español.
☐ hablar sobre problemas medioambientales.
☐ expresar emociones y dudas.
☐ opinar sobre problemas ecológicos.
☐ entender el papel de la coca en la cultura andina.

VOCABULARIO ESENCIAL

Sustantivos

la araña	*spider*
el animal (doméstico/salvaje)	*(domestic/wild) animal*
la basura	*garbage*
el caballo	*horse*
el calentamiento global	*global warming*
el cambio climático	*climate change*
el/la cerdo/a	*pig*
el/la conejo/a	*rabbit*
la contaminación (del aire, del agua...)	*(air, water . . .) pollution*
el cuy	*guinea pig*
el derrame	*oil spill*
el desecho	*waste*
el/la ecologista	*environmentalist*
el envase (desechable)	*(disposable) container*
la escasez	*shortage*
el/la gato/a	*cat*
la mariposa	*butterfly*
el medio ambiente	*environment*
la oveja	*sheep*
el/la pájaro/a	*bird*
el papel	*paper*
el/la perro/a	*dog*
el petróleo	*oil*
el pez	*fish*
la rana	*frog*
el reciclaje	*recycling*
el recurso (natural)	*(natural) resource*
la serpiente	*snake*
la tortuga	*turtle*
el vidrio	*glass*

Cognados: la alpaca, el cóndor, la deforestación, el delfín, la ecología, la energía (eléctrica, renovable...), el esmog, la especie, la fauna, el insecto, la llama, el mosquito, el pesticida, el plástico, la reforestación, el reptil, la serpiente

Verbos

ahorrar	*to save*
contaminar (el aire, el agua)	*to pollute (the air, the water)*
desarrollar	*to develop*
tirar	*to throw away*

Cognados: conservar, consumir, proteger, reciclar

Expresiones

estar en peligro de extinción	*to be endangered*
quizás/tal vez	*maybe*

10 La salud y el bienestar

VER PARA CREER I: Mal de altura

Antes de ver el video, no te olvides de leer el título del capítulo para saber un poco sobre el posible tema del video. Conversa unos minutos con un/a compañero/a para compartir ideas sobre lo que esperas ver en este video. Después de ver y escuchar, contesta las preguntas.

1. ¿Dónde están los chicos del video?

2. ¿Qué le duele a un chico? Menciona una cosa.

3. ¿Qué viste en la segunda parte del video?

··

| Sección 1 | **La salud y la enfermedad** |

PALABRA POR PALABRA
- El cuerpo humano
- Los síntomas
- La salud: Los remedios y la enfermedad

HABLANDO DE GRAMÁTICA
- Giving instructions: Formal commands
- Expressing wants, desires, and hopes: Present subjunctive with verbs of volition
- Summary of the subjunctive mood

CULTURA
- La bebida preferida en Paraguay: el tereré
- La medicina alternativa

| Sección 2 | **Medicina y estilos de vida** |

PALABRA POR PALABRA
- Los estados de ánimo
- Los profesionales de la salud
- La salud: Hábitos saludables y prevención

HABLANDO DE GRAMÁTICA
- Describing people: **Ser** and **estar** + adjective
- Giving advice: Impersonal expressions with subjunctive
- Giving instructions and advice: Informal commands
- Expressing qualities: **Lo** + adjective

CULTURA
- La espiritualidad
- Diferentes estilos de vida

Trivia: Go to *WileyPLUS* to do the **Trivia** activities and find out how much you know about these countries!

Bolivia y Paraguay

LEARNING OBJECTIVES

By the end of this section you will be able to:

- Discuss health issues and treatments
- Identify the different parts of the body
- Give instructions
- Express hopes and wishes
- Talk about alternative medicine
- Understand bilingualism in Paraguay

Una imagen vale más que mil palabras

¿Reconoces los idiomas de este cartel?

¿Quiénes crees que hablan guaraní?

¿Se hablan idiomas indígenas en Estados Unidos? ¿Cuáles?

◀ *Los idiomas oficiales de Paraguay son el guaraní y el español.*

UNA PERSPECTIVA

Megan

Courtesy of Megan M. Mayzelle

La bebida preferida en Paraguay: el tereré

Diferente

"Cuando estuve en Paraguay vi que todos bebían una bebida con mucha cafeína llamada tereré. Es una hierba parecida al mate que se bebe en la Argentina, pero no se bebe con agua caliente, sino con agua muy fría. Se toma en una taza que se llama guampa que es como un termo decorado y se bebe con una bombilla¹. Es una bebida que se comparte con los amigos o familiares y todos beben del mismo envase. Yo pensé en los gérmenes². Si una persona está resfriada³, todos nos vamos a enfermar, pero mis amigos me aseguraron que el tereré mata los gérmenes. ¡Hay que relajarse!"

Casi igual

"En Paraguay se bebe mucho la Coca-Cola. También tienen una bebida que se llama 'vino con coca' (o sea, que mezclan la Coca-Cola y el vino tinto) que es similar a los *wine coolers* de Estados Unidos".

▲ *¿Quieres tereré?*

¿Qué piensas tú?

1. ¿Qué bebidas con cafeína se beben en Estados Unidos? ¿Qué bebes tú?
2. ¿Beben los niños de Estados Unidos refrescos con cafeína?
3. ¿Qué refresco es muy popular y típico de Estados Unidos?

¹**bombilla:** metal straw ²**gérmenes:** germs ³**estar resfriado/a:** to have a cold

LA PURA VERDAD I Un remedio alternativo

Megan fue voluntaria en la organización del Cuerpo de Paz[4] y pasó un año en Paraguay.

1.

2.

No me siento bien. Tengo dolor de estómago, náuseas y dolor de cabeza.

¿Qué te duele? ¿Te duele el oído? ¿Te duele la cabeza? ¿Tienes fiebre? ¿Tienes escalofríos?

3.

Este tereré te va a curar rápido. Le voy a poner un yuyo, que es una hierba que se llama cola de caballo.

¡Cola de caballo!

4.

Tómalo todo. Te va a curar el dolor de estómago.

5.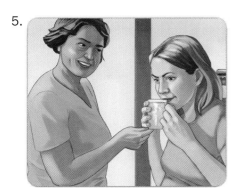

6.

¡Me siento bien y tengo hambre!

© John Wiley & Sons, Inc.

 10.1-01 Otro tipo de medicina Escucha lo que le pasa a Megan después de unas semanas de estar trabajando en Paraguay. Consulta la tabla de hierbas cuando sea necesario.

1. Megan quiere saber más sobre la medicina tradicional. ¿Cierto o falso?
2. Cuando la amiga de Megan no quería comer, Megan le preparó un tereré y le añadió...

Hierbas	Usos
anís	para el resfriado
menta	es un calmante[5]
eucalipto	para el resfriado, para la tos
cola de caballo	para el dolor de estómago

3. Cuando la madre le prepara un tereré a Aníbal, le añade...

[4]**Cuerpo de Paz:** Peace Corps [5]**calmante:** painkiller, tranquilizer

🎧 PALABRA POR PALABRA

♻ El cuerpo humano   *Human body*

Courtesy Megan M. Mayzelle

la cabeza · la oreja · la nariz · la boca · el ojo · el brazo · los dientes · la mano · el dedo · la cara · la espalda · el pie · la rodilla · la pierna · el tobillo · el dedo del pie

> ### ♻ Las partes del cuerpo
>
> In **Palabra por palabra** of Chapter 3, Section 1, you already learned some words to name parts of the head. Review that vocabulary before learning new words related to the human body.

Algunas partes internas

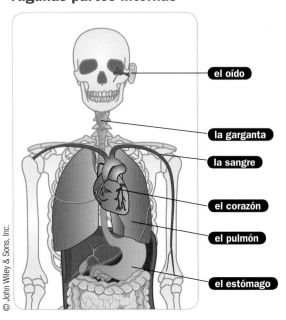

el oído · la garganta · la sangre · el corazón · el pulmón · el estómago

© John Wiley & Sons, Inc.

Los síntomas	Symptoms
estornudar	*to sneeze*
tener alergias	*to suffer from allergies*
tener comezón	*to have an itch*
tener dolor de (cabeza, estómago, oído)	*to have (a head, stomach, ear) ache*
tener escalofríos	*to have chills*
tener fiebre	*to have a fever*
tener mareos	*to feel dizzy*
tener migraña	*to have a migraine*
tener náuseas	*to feel nauseous*
tener tos/toser	*to have a cough*

La salud *Health*

curar	*to cure, to heal*
curarse	*to get well, to recover*
doler (ue)[6]	*to hurt*
enfermarse	*to get sick*
estar resfriado/a	*to have a cold*
mejorar	*to get better*
romperse un hueso	*to break a bone*
el seguro médico	*health insurance*
sentirse mal/bien	*to feel badly/well*
torcerse el tobillo	*to twist an ankle*
ponerle una inyección/vacuna a alguien	*to give somebody a shot/vaccine*

Adjetivos

congestionado/a	*congested*
débil	*weak*
enfermo/a	*sick*

Cognado: medicinal

Los remedios

la infusión/el té de hierbas	*herbal tea*
el jarabe para la tos	*cough syrup*

La enfermedad *Disease, illness*

el sida	*AIDS*
los gérmenes	*germs*
la gripe	*flu*
el malestar	*discomfort*
el resfriado	*cold*

Cognados: el antibiótico, la bronquitis, la cura, la diabetes, el diagnóstico, la infección, la medicina, la neumonía, el/la paciente, el tratamiento

El consultorio del médico

los medicamentos

El médico le pone una vacuna/inyección al niño.

Me duele la garganta

¿Qué te pasa? ¿Qué te duele?

la receta   las pastillas

© John Wiley & Sons, Inc.

¿Qué dicen los paraguayos?

¿Quieres un terieré?	*Would you like a terieré (tea-like cold drink)?*
Le voy a añadir un yuyo.	*I am going to add a medicinal herb.*
Hablo jopará.	*I speak Spanish with a lot of guaraní words.*
Nambrena, no quiero hacer esto.	*No, I don't want to do this.*

10.1-02 ¿Qué me pasa, doctor? Estas personas van al médico porque no se sienten bien. Le explican sus síntomas al médico. ¿Qué les dice él? ¿Cuál es su diagnóstico?

_____ 1. Doctor, estoy mareada, tengo náuseas y no tengo hambre.

_____ 2. Me duele la cabeza, estoy congestionada y estornudo mucho.

_____ 3. Estoy tosiendo mucho, me duele la garganta y también me es difícil respirar.

_____ 4. Tengo fiebre, escalofríos, dolor de garganta y me siento muy débil[7].

_____ 5. Tengo comezón en los ojos y estornudo mucho.

_____ 6. Tengo sed y hambre excesivas, y me siento débil todo el tiempo.

_____ 7. Me caí y me torcí el tobillo.

a. Tiene gripe.
b. Tiene el hueso roto.
c. Tiene diabetes.
d. Tiene alergia.
e. Está embarazada.
f. Tiene bronquitis.
g. Está resfriada.

---

[6]Doler is used as **gustar**, e.g., **Me/Te/Le/Nos/Les duele...** [7]**débil:** weak

10.1-03 ¿De qué hablamos?

Paso 1: Lean las definiciones y busquen la palabra correspondiente en la sección **Palabra por palabra.**

MODELO: Es una enfermedad contagiosa viral muy común que afecta a la nariz, la garganta y los pulmones.
→ *el resfriado*

1. Es una sustancia química que se usa para tratar infecciones.
2. Es la hoja de papel donde el médico prescribe medicamentos al paciente.
3. Es una enfermedad viral que provoca una infección en el sistema respiratorio y causa fiebre.
4. Es la articulación más grande del cuerpo humano que se encuentra en las piernas.
5. Es una medicina líquida que contiene azúcar y por lo menos un ingrediente activo y que se usa en el tratamiento de síntomas como la tos.
6. Es una enfermedad de los pulmones que viene acompañada de tos.
7. Son partes del cuerpo firmes, duras y resistentes, que forman el esqueleto.
8. Es un tipo de medicamento pequeño y de forma redonda que se traga[8] fácilmente.

Paso 2: Ahora, elijan tres palabras de la sección **Palabra por palabra** y escriban tres definiciones que van a leerle a la clase. ¡Atención! Recuerden que para definir siempre usamos el verbo *ser*.

MODELO: Es un/a... que...

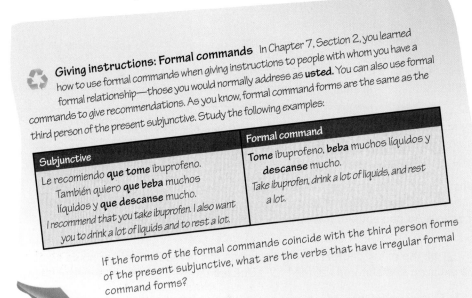

Giving instructions: Formal commands In Chapter 7, Section 2, you learned how to use formal commands when giving instructions to people with whom you have a formal relationship—those you would normally address as **usted**. You can also use formal commands to give recommendations. As you know, formal command forms are the same as the third person of the present subjunctive. Study the following examples:

Subjunctive	Formal command
Le recomiendo **que tome** ibuprofeno. También quiero **que beba** muchos líquidos y **que descanse** mucho. *I recommend that you take ibuprofen. I also want you to drink a lot of liquids and to rest a lot.*	**Tome** ibuprofeno, **beba** muchos líquidos y **descanse** mucho. *Take ibuprofen, drink a lot of liquids, and rest a lot.*

If the forms of the formal commands coincide with the third person forms of the present subjunctive, what are the verbs that have irregular formal command forms?

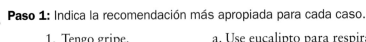 **10.1-04 ¿Qué recomienda el médico?** ¿Qué le dice el médico a sus pacientes si tienen los siguientes síntomas?

 Paso 1: Indica la recomendación más apropiada para cada caso.

_____ 1. Tengo gripe.
_____ 2. Estoy mareado/a.
_____ 3. Estoy deprimido/a.
_____ 4. Me duele la garganta.
_____ 5. Tengo dolor de estómago.
_____ 6. Estoy tosiendo mucho.
_____ 7. Tengo la nariz congestionada.

a. Use eucalipto para respirar mejor.
b. Vaya a la farmacia y compre un jarabe para la tos.
c. Prepare una infusión con anís, miel y limón y bébela despacio.
d. No coma grasas ni comidas picantes.
e. Tome ibuprofeno cada 6 horas hasta que le baje la fiebre.
f. Vea a un psicólogo o a un psiquiatra.
g. Siéntese y respire aire fresco.

[8] **tragar**: to swallow

Paso 2: Ahora, para cada malestar, piensa con un/a compañero/a en dos recomendaciones más por lo menos.

MODELO: Estudiante 1:   *Si tiene gripe, **descanse** mucho.*
               Estudiante 2:   *Sí, y también **beba** mucho líquido.*

10.1-05 ¿Qué haces si...?

Paso 1: ¿Qué haces en estas situaciones? ¿Qué tomas, con quién hablas, adónde vas? Piensa en dos o tres cosas que haces habitualmente si estás en una de estas situaciones.

a. Estás bailando con tus amigos en una discoteca y pisas[9] mal. Te tuerces el tobillo y te duele muchísimo.

b. Te duele la garganta y estás congestionado/a. Te vas a la cama por la noche pero no puedes dormir porque no puedes respirar.

c. Comiste algo en un restaurante y no te sientes bien. Te duele mucho el estómago y tienes muchas náuseas.

d. Comiste algo en un restaurante de comida rápida y tienes que ir al baño muchas veces.

e. Te duelen el cuerpo y la cabeza, tienes fiebre y ganas de vomitar. Te sientes muy débil y estás solo/a en casa.

f. Te caíste y te rompiste un diente. No te duele, pero se ve muy feo.

g. Comiste algo que te provocó una reacción alérgica muy fuerte. Tienes mucha comezón y la piel muy roja.

Paso 2: En grupos, comenten sus respuestas. ¿Coincides con tus compañeros? Después, decidan qué es mejor hacer en estas situaciones.

MODELO: Estudiante 1:   *Si estoy solo/a en casa y tengo fiebre y me siento muy mal, tomo unas pastillas de ibuprofeno y después llamo a mis padres.*
               Estudiante 2:   *Sí, eso es buena idea. Puedes tomar unas pastillas de ibuprofeno o aspirina. También llamo a mi madre cuando estoy enferma y ella me dice qué hacer.*

Paso 3: Ahora piensen en cada situación otra vez. ¿Conocen remedios naturales o tradicionales que puedan usar en cada situación? ¿Cuáles?

10.1-06 ¿Con qué frecuencia vas al médico? Hablen sobre con qué frecuencia les ocurren o hacen las siguientes cosas.

MODELO: ir al consultorio del médico
               Estudiante 1:   *¿Con qué frecuencia vas al médico?*
               Estudiante 2:   *Casi nunca voy al médico porque casi nunca estoy enfermo.*
               Estudiante 1:   *Yo sí voy bastante. Tengo alergia y voy una vez cada seis meses para que me pongan una inyección.*

         muchas veces   a veces   casi nunca   nunca

1. estar resfriado/a o tener gripe
2. tener dolor de cabeza
3. tener dolor de estómago
4. marearse
5. quedarse en casa por estar enfermo/a o sentirse mal
6. hacerse un examen médico general
7. tomar remedios naturales
8. tomar aspirinas u otro medicamento
9. ponerse una inyección o una vacuna
10. tomar antibióticos

[9] pisar: to step

HABLANDO DE GRAMÁTICA I

WileyPLUS Go to *WileyPLUS* to review this grammar point with the help of the **Animated Grammar Tutorial** and the **Verb Conjugator**.

1. Expressing wants, desires, and hopes: Present subjunctive with verbs of volition

As you already know, the indicative mood is used to talk about facts and events as objective and part of reality. We use the indicative mood when we declare (state as a fact) the content of the subordinate clause: We make a statement about something that someone knows or assumes it is real.

Carmen me dijo [que no **tengo** nada grave].	Carmen told me [that I don't have anything serious].
Carmen sabe [que este remedio **cura** el dolor de estómago].	Carmen knows that [this remedy cures stomach aches].

By contrast, when we talk about wishing that an event or situation were a certain way, we are not stating or assuming that situation or event is true. Rather, when we express a desire, want or wish, we are contemplating the possibility of an idea, since we are hoping that the event or situation (expressed in the subordinate clause) were true or becomes true.

Espero [que Carmen **tenga** razón y que no **sea** nada grave].	I hope [that Carmen is right and that it is nothing serious].
Ojalá [que este remedio me **cure** el dolor de estómago].	Let's hope [that this remedy cures stomach aches].

Thus, we use the subjunctive mood with the subordinate verb that follows main clauses that express a wish, want, or desire.

Main clause (expression of wish, want, or desire)	Subordinate clause (subjunctive verb)
Deseo Esperamos Ojalá Quieren	[que no **tengan** dolor de estómago]. [que Carmen **hable** primero con el médico].

The following verbs and phrases, among others, express wishes and require the use of the subjunctive when followed by a subordinate clause:

desear   Deseo [que se **cure** de su enfermedad].
I wish [that he would recover (gets cured) from his illness].

esperar   Esperamos [que te **mejores** pronto].
We hope [that you get well soon].

preferir   Prefiero [que **pruebes** un remedio natural antes de tomar pastillas].
I prefer [that you try a natural remedy before taking pills].

ojalá[10]   Ojalá [que me **vaya** bien con esta medicina].
Let's hope [that this medicine works well for me].

Infinitive or subjunctive?

When expressing wishes, the subordinate verb can be a subjunctive form (introduced by **que**) or an infinitive.

	Infinitive	Subjunctive
	If the subject of the subordinate verb and the person referred to in the main clause are the same:	If the subject of the subordinate verb and the person referred to in the main clause are different:
desear esperar querer preferir	Espero no tener dolor de estómago. (yo) = (yo)	Espero que no tengas dolor de estómago. (yo) ≠ (tú)

[10]Ojalá is an invariable expression derived from the Arabic *inchallah*, which literally means "God willing."

10.1-07 ¿Qué quieres que haga? Mira la historia de **La pura verdad I** y combina las oraciones de la primera columna con la más apropiada de la segunda.

_____ 1. Megan no se siente bien y quiere...
_____ 2. Carmen sabe que...
_____ 3. Carmen le dice a Megan que...
_____ 4. Carmen espera que...
_____ 5. Megan piensa: ¡Ojalá que...
_____ 6. Después de esa experiencia, Megan desea...
_____ 7. Megan quiere que...

a. aprender a usar las hierbas como remedios naturales.
b. Megan mejore después de tomar el tereré.
c. Carmen le enseñe todo lo que sabe sobre las hierbas medicinales.
d. dejar de tener escalofríos.
e. beba todo el tereré.
f. a Megan no le gusta mucho la bebida que le preparó.
g. el té de hierbas de Carmen me cure pronto el dolor de estómago!

10.1-08 El programa de voluntarios del centro de salud Megan conversa con su amiga Carmen sobre el programa de voluntarios. Indica cuál es la palabra correcta de las dos opciones.

Carmen: Megan, ¿ya empezaste a trabajar en el centro de salud?

Megan: ¡Sí! Me gusta mucho. Ojalá que me (**acostumbre / acostumbrar**) pronto al trabajo. Deseo que me (**consideren / considerar**) una buena voluntaria, porque quiero (**ayude / ayudar**) a la gente. Ya fui a la primera reunión con el resto de los voluntarios. Hay una reunión una vez al mes. En esas reuniones, la directora nos dice lo que esperan que (**hacemos / hagamos**).

Carmen: ¿Y qué les pide que (**hagan / hacer**)?

Megan: Pues algunos pacientes se sienten muy solos. Quieren que (**conversemos / conversamos**) con ellos, que (**ayudamos / ayudemos**) a las enfermeras y que (**atendemos / atendamos**[11]) a los familiares de los pacientes. Yo prefiero que los pacientes me (**diga / digan**) lo que necesitan, y entonces lo (**hago / haga**). Lo único que no (**podemos / podamos**) hacer es prestar atención médica porque todavía no somos doctores.

Carmen: Y los pacientes y el personal del centro, ¿están contentos con el trabajo de los voluntarios?

Megan: Pues espero que sí, porque quiero que (**continúe / continúen**) con ese programa.

10.1-09 Y tú, ¿qué esperas?

Paso 1: Usa las expresiones de la lista para expresar tus deseos o reacciones sobre las siguientes noticias. Recuerda usar el verbo de la cláusula subordinada en la forma apropiada del subjuntivo.

Espero que...
Deseo que...
Prefiero que...
Ojalá que...

1. El presidente de la república anunció una ley contra la desnutrición

2. En Paraguay analizan medidas para combatir el dengue[12]

3. Intervienen farmacias que venden medicamentos sin receta

4. Paraguay pide acceso universal a los medicamentos

5. Comienza hoy la campaña anual de vacunación contra la gripe

Paso 2: Ahora, compara tus opiniones con las de un/a compañero/a. Para cada noticia, ¿tienen el mismo deseo? ¿Coinciden en sus deseos, en ninguno o en todos?

MODELO: Alto riesgo de epidemia de dengue en tres zonas de Asunción
            Estudiante 1:   _**Espero que** termine la epidemia de dengue en Asunción._
            Estudiante 2:   _Yo también. Además, **espero que** descubran pronto una vacuna._

[11]**atender:** to assist, to help [12]Dengue fever, or breakbone fever, is a infectious tropical disease transmitted by a mosquito.

LA PURA VERDAD II   El Cuerpo de Paz

Paula fue voluntaria en el Cuerpo de Paz y también fue a Paraguay. Nos muestra sus fotos, nos habla de sus experiencias y les da consejos a futuros voluntarios.

1.

▲ *Trabajé en una escuela primaria.*

2.

▲ *Yo nunca aprendí guaraní. ¡Pero espero que ustedes aprendan un poco de guaraní!*

3.

▲ *Probé muchas comidas nuevas. Espero que prueben la comida local.*

4.

▲ *No compartí tereré con mis amigos. Espero que ustedes compartan esta bebida con sus amigos.*

5.

▲ *Probé la medicina tradicional. Si se enferman, prueben la medicina tradicional primero.*

6.

▲ *Aprendí a cocinar platos paraguayos. ¡Ojalá que aprendan a cocinar algo de Paraguay!*

10.1-10 Más consejos Escucha las experiencias de Paula y selecciona el consejo que les da a los nuevos voluntarios.

1. ¿Qué se puede hacer si se enferman?
   a. Les dice que vayan al médico con urgencia.
   b. Les dice que pidan medicina en la farmacia.
   c. Les dice que beban un tereré bien caliente.
2. ¿Qué aconseja sobre el guaraní?
   a. Quiere que aprendan guaraní porque es bueno para el corazón de los paraguayos.
   b. Quiere que aprendan guaraní porque es la lengua del corazón de los paraguayos.
   c. Quiere que aprendan guaraní para entender la televisión y los negocios.
3. ¿Qué dice sobre su experiencia en Paraguay?
   a. Espera que la experiencia de los nuevos voluntarios sea igual, buenísima.
   b. Dice que escriban todos los días porque van a olvidar mucho de Paraguay.
   c. Quiere que la experiencia de los nuevos voluntarios sea mejor que la suya.

HABLANDO DE GRAMÁTICA II

2. Summary of the subjunctive mood

In Chapter 9 you were introduced to the forms and uses of the subjunctive mood. Let's review what you have learned so far:

WileyPLUS Go to *WileyPLUS* to review this grammar point with the help of the **Animated Grammar Tutorial** and the **Verb Conjugator**.

- The subjunctive is used <u>only</u> in subordinate clauses, usually preceded by **que**.
- The subjunctive mood is used when we are <u>not</u> stating or assuming the veracity of the content in the subordinate clause.
- The subjunctive mood is used when the main clause expresses a request, an opinion, a subjective reaction, uncertainty, denial, possibility, a wish, or a hope.
- The subjunctive is used <u>only</u> when the subject of the main clause and the subject of the subordinate clause are <u>different</u>. If both clauses have the same subject, the infinitive form is used instead.

Indicative		Indicative
Main clause		Subordinate clause
1st subject = indicative Report State Assume	+ **que** +	2nd subject = indicative

Indicative		Subjunctive
Main clause		Subordinate clause
1st subject = indicative Influence Doubt Deny Consider possibility Express emotion, opinion Wish, want, desire	+ **que** +	2nd subject = subjunctive

Indicative	
Report/Statement/Assumption Dice que... Insiste en que... Pienso que... Creo que... Me parece que... Está claro que... Es evidente que... Es obvio que... No hay duda de que...	**tomas** demasiada azúcar.

Subjunctive	
Influence Dice que... Te aconsejo que... Te recomiendan que... Es mejor que... Es importante que...	no **tomes** tanta azúcar.
Doubt/Denial/Possibility No cree que... No pensamos que... No les parece que... Dudo que... Es posible que... Es probable que... Quizás...	**tomes** demasiada azúcar.
Emotion/Opinion Nos preocupa que... No me gusta que... No me importa que... Es increíble que... Es soprendente que... Es malo que... No es bueno que...	**tomes** tanta azúcar.
Wish/Want/Hope Quiero que... Desea que... Preferimos que... Esperan que... Ojalá que...	no **tomes** tanta azúcar.

Request or report?

With some verbs such as **decir** or **insistir** we can state or report information or we can ask someone to do something. As you already know, when we report or state information we use the indicative in the subordinate clause. If we are making a request, we use the subjunctive in the subordinate clause.

Report (indicative)	Request, command (subjunctive)
Me dijo [que **prepara** muchos remedios naturales]. *She told me [that she prepares many natural remedies.]*	Me dijo [que **prepare** este remedio natural]. *She told me [to prepare this natural remedy.]*
Insiste en [que nunca **tomamos** café con ella]. *She insists [that we never have coffee with her.]*	Insiste en [que **tomemos** café con ella]. *She insists [that we should have coffee with her.]*

10.1-11 ¿Cómo lo expresamos? De las siguientes oraciones, identifica cuáles requieren el uso del subjuntivo si las expresamos en español.

1. What does the doctor want?
2. The doctor says that he can't see me today.
3. The doctor wants me to go to his office tomorrow.
4. I prefer to take a medicinal herb before taking a pill.
5. It's strange that you ask the pharmacist for medical advice.
6. I doubt that the doctor will give me a shot.

 10.1-12 ¿Qué te dijo el médico? Después de ir al médico, les cuentas a tus amigos lo que te dijo. Primero tienes que pensar si las siguientes oraciones del médico son afirmaciones (A) o mandatos (M). Después, pon el verbo en la forma correcta del indicativo si son afirmaciones, o en subjuntivo si son mandatos o peticiones.

El médico dice:

__(A)__ 1. "Tu nivel de colesterol en la sangre **es** muy alto". → Me dice que mi nivel de colesterol en la sangre _es_ muy alto.

__(M)__ 2. "**Come** menos grasa". → Me dice que _coma_ menos grasa.

_____ 3. "**Tienes** una infección estomacal". → Me dice que _____ una infección estomacal.

_____ 4. "Cuando tengas comezón, **ponte** esta crema". → Me dice que _____ esta crema cuando tenga comezón.

_____ 5. "Muchas veces los escalofríos **vienen** asociados con la fiebre". → Insiste en que muchas veces los escalofríos _____ asociados con la fiebre.

_____ 6. "Los antibióticos no **funcionan** contra las infecciones de oído causadas por un virus..." → Él sabe que los antibióticos no _____ contra las infecciones de oído causadas por un virus.

_____ 7. "No **creas** que los antibióticos alivian todas las infecciones". → Me dice que no _____ que los antibióticos alivian todas las infecciones.

_____ 8. "Cuando tengas dolor de garganta, **prepara** una infusión de miel, anís y limón". → Me dice que _____ una infusión de miel, anís y limón para calmar el dolor de garganta.

10.1-13 ¡Exprésate!

 Paso 1: Completa las siguientes oraciones de manera correcta con una cláusula principal[13]. Complétalas de forma que se apliquen a ti. Puedes usar los verbos y las expresiones de la sección **Hablando de gramática II** o algunas de las expresiones que aprendiste en el Capítulo 9.

MODELO: ... no tener gripe este año. → _Espero_ no tener gripe este año.

1. ... que no me **enferme** nunca.
2. ... que mi familia siempre **disfrute** de buena salud.
3. ... que el seguro médico **sea** más barato.
4. ... que yo **tenga** el colesterol alto.
5. ... que yo **cuide** más mi alimentación.
6. ... que **descubran** una vacuna contra el sida.
7. ... **conocer** más remedios naturales.

 Paso 2: Ahora, compara tus opiniones con las de un/a compañero/a. ¿Tienen las mismas reacciones? ¿Coincidieron en algunas, en ninguna, en todas?

MODELO: Estudiante 1: _Espero no tener gripe este año._
Estudiante 2: _Yo también. ¡Es un problema tener gripe!_

[13]cláusula principal: main clause

OTRA PERSPECTIVA

Courtesy of Orlando Ríos Cabral

Orlando

La medicina alternativa

Diferente

"Muchos de mis amigos aquí en Estados Unidos tienen seguro médico, van al médico cuando se enferman y compran las medicinas en el supermercado o en las farmacias. En mi casa, en Paraguay, si tengo dolor de garganta, hago gárgaras[14] con agua caliente y sal. Mis amigos compran Cepacol. Si tengo gripe, yo tomo una infusión de anís, limón y miel. Mis amigos compran NyQuil. No veo que se usen medicinas naturales. ¿Por qué?"

Igual

"Nosotros también vamos al médico cuando la medicina alternativa no funciona. Tenemos un sistema de salud pública que es muy barato, pero también tenemos muchos hospitales privados, como en Estados Unidos".

Explícale a Orlando

1. ¿Por qué usamos muy pocos remedios naturales en Estados Unidos?
2. ¿Usas tú algún remedio natural cuando te enfermas?
3. ¿Por qué no tenemos un sistema de salud pública en Estados Unidos?

MANOS A LA OBRA

10.1-14 ¿Qué tal tu salud?

Paso 1: Entrevista a un/a compañero/a sobre los siguientes temas de salud.

1. ¿Cómo es tu salud en general? ¿Llevas una vida sana?
2. ¿Alguna vez te rompiste un hueso o te torciste un tobillo? ¿Qué te pasó? ¿Te dolió mucho?
3. ¿Cuándo fue la última vez que fuiste al médico? ¿Fue por algo grave[15] o fue un examen rutinario?
4. ¿Usas remedios naturales o siempre vas a la farmacia y compras medicinas sin receta para curar síntomas menos serios? ¿Qué remedios naturales conoces? ¿Qué medicinas compras sin receta?
5. ¿Alguna vez usaste alguna forma de medicina alternativa, como la acupuntura, la fitoterapia o la homeopatía? ¿Para qué? ¿Te sirvió?
6. ¿Crees que el gobierno de un país debe proveer seguro médico universal, o que es mejor que haya seguros médicos privados? ¿Por qué?

Paso 2: Después, escriban un pequeño informe. ¿En qué aspectos coinciden los dos? ¿En qué no coinciden?

MODELO: *Mi compañero/a y yo tenemos buena salud y llevamos una vida sana. Sin embargo, creo que a él le interesa más la medicina natural porque...*

[14]**hacer gárgaras:** to gargle [15]**grave:** serious

10.1-15 ¿Qué malestar tienes? Piensa en una enfermedad o malestar que conozcas. Describe los síntomas, lo que hay que hacer y lo que no hay que hacer. Túrnense para adivinar qué malestar es.

MODELO: Estudiante 1:   *Cuando tienes esta enfermedad, tienes la nariz congestionada, no puedes respirar y también tienes tos y dolor de cabeza. Hay que tomar mucho líquido, como té de hierbas o caldo de pollo, y puedes tomar jarabe para la tos o pastillas de ibuprofeno para el dolor.*
　　　　　Estudiante 2:   *¡Un resfriado!*

 10.1-16 En el consultorio del médico No te sientes bien y vas al médico. Con un/a compañero/a, representen los papeles de médico y paciente.

 Paso 1: El paciente piensa en un malestar o enfermedad y en los síntomas relacionados. El médico piensa en las preguntas que le puede hacer al paciente.

 Paso 2: El paciente le describe sus síntomas al médico y contesta sus preguntas. El médico hace todas las preguntas necesarias para poder diagnosticar la enfermedad y recomendar un tratamiento. El paciente le hace preguntas al médico para clarificar lo que debe o no debe hacer.

Diagnósticos	Recomendaciones
Gripe	Le recomiendo/aconsejo que...
Resfriado	Quiero que...
Infección de...	Debe/Tiene que...
Bronquitis	Es importante/necesario que...
Acidez de estómago[16]	
Diabetes	
Un hueso roto	
El tobillo torcido	
Neumonía	

MODELO:
　　Paciente: *Buenas tardes, doctor, no me siento muy bien. Estoy.../Me duele...*
　　Médico: *¿Qué le pasa?/¿Qué le duele?/¿Le duele...? Lo que usted tiene es... Primero... Después...*
　　Paciente: *¿Puedo...? ¿Debo...? ¿Es necesario que...? ¿Me recomienda que...?*

 Paso 3: El paciente quiere comparar diagnósticos y tratamientos, y busca a otro médico para ver si le da algún diagnóstico y tratamiento diferente. Después decide qué médico le parece mejor. El paciente comenta sus impresiones con el resto de la clase para ver si a otros pacientes les gustó el mismo médico.

10.1-17 Presta atención: En la tienda Michelle está débil y quiere ir a una tienda de medicinas y remedios naturales. Escucha la conversación dos veces para saber qué necesita.

WileyPLUS Go to *WileyPLUS* and listen to **Presta atención**.

1. ¿Qué hay en la tienda a la que entra Michelle?
   a. Hay mucha gente.
   b. Hay muchas hierbas.
   c. Hay bebidas naturales.
2. ¿Qué le dice Michelle a la señora de la tienda? Le dice...
   a. que le duele la espalda.
   b. que le duelen los pies.
   c. que le duelen los ojos.

[16]acidez de estómago: heartburn

3. ¿Qué dice Michelle de su dolor? Dice que...
   a. el problema es su cama.
   b. le duele por la noche.
   c. quiere curarse inmediatamente.
4. ¿Qué quiere la señora que atiende a Michelle?
   a. Quiere saber si tomó algo para el dolor.
   b. Quiere saber qué hizo ayer.
   c. Quiere saber si tuvo un accidente.
5. ¿Qué le da la señora de la tienda a Michelle?
   a. Le da un pequeño masaje.
   b. Le da un remedio natural.
   c. Le da un jarabe para la tos.

¡OJO!

Connectors
With a partner, generate a list of connector words like the ones provided on Chapter 1, Section 1, **Estrategias para escribir**. Can you add some more connector words to the list?

 10.1-18 Por escrito: En la universidad Un/a estudiante del primer año de universidad tiene problemas porque todo es muy diferente. No está comiendo bien, está subiendo de peso, no duerme bien, tiene problemas con las clases que está tomando y además no tiene amigos. En general, no lleva una vida tranquila y está desilusionado/a con su primer año en la universidad. Le contó sus problemas a un/a psicólogo/a de una revista para recibir consejo. Imagina que eres el/la psicólogo/a y contesta el mensaje del/de la estudiante. En tu mensaje, especifica los problemas del/de la estudiante y dale una solución explicándole lo que debe hacer. Usa expresiones para expresar tus deseos y opiniones y para influenciar al estudiante. No olvides usar la lista de conectores que preparaste.

PONTE EN MI LUGAR

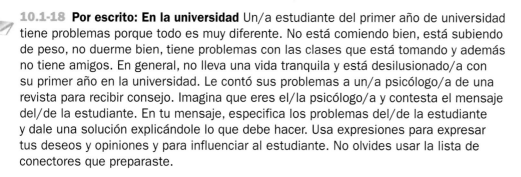

Estrategias para conversar

Giving and reacting to news In Chapter 5, Section 2 you learned some expressions to keep a conversation flowing. In Chapter 9, Section 2 you also learned impersonal expressions to express an opinion. Now, try to use the following Spanish expressions to react to good and bad news and keep the conversation going:

Para dar malas noticias:
¿Sabes lo que pasó?	*Do you know what happened?*
Tengo malas noticias...	*I have bad news . . .*

Para reaccionar ante malas noticias:
¡Qué mala suerte!	*What bad luck!*
¡Qué lástima!/¡Qué pena!	*What a pity!*

Para dar buenas noticias:
Es sorprendente que + *subjunctive*	*It is surprising that . . .*
¡Qué maravilla que + *subjunctive*	*How wonderful that . . .*

 @Arroba@

El salar de Uyuni
Explora en tu buscador favorito información sobre el salar de Uyuni para contestar estas preguntas: ¿Dónde está? ¿Qué metal produce el salar de Uyuni que se usa para tratar la bipolaridad? ¿Tiene otras funciones este metal? ¿Por qué es difícil extraer este metal del salar? Comparte la información que encuentres con tus compañeros.

WileyPLUS Go to *WileyPLUS* to find more **Arroba** activities.

En el hospital Un/a amigo/a sufrió un accidente y hay que ir a la sala de emergencia. Representen la situación. No olviden usar las **Estrategias para conversar**.

Estudiante 1: Llama a tu mejor amigo/a y dile que tienes que darle una mala noticia. Dile que su novio/a se rompió una pierna y se torció un tobillo en un accidente y que está en el hospital. Responde las preguntas de tu amigo/a.

Estudiante 2: Hazle preguntas a tu amigo/a sobre la salud de tu novio/a. Pídele información sobre el accidente y pregúntale en qué hospital está para ir a verlo/a lo antes posible.

ASÍ ES LA VIDA

Adivina, adivinador

¿Qué parte del cuerpo es?

Solo tres letras tengo
pero tu peso sostengo.
Si me tratas con cuidado,
te llevaré a cualquier lado.

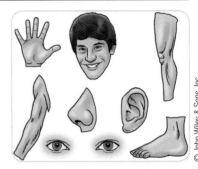

Expresión: Costar un ojo de la cara

Daniela: No me encuentro bien desde hace tres días
           y tengo que ir al médico.
Lola: ¿Y por qué no fuiste ayer?
Daniela: No tengo seguro médico y la consulta
           cuesta un ojo de la cara.

¿Sabes qué significa esta expresión?
¿Hay expresiones similares en inglés?

ENTÉRATE

Estrategias para leer

The journalistic report A news article in a newspaper is usually short. However, when the article is longer it may also incorporate a reporter's opinions about an issue or an event. In this type of text, the reporter may include anecdotes, descriptions, and quotations, among other things. The title provides the topic of the article and the first paragraph introduces the topic by catching the attention and interest of readers. In the first paragraph, the reporter usually tries to answer the key questions about the event or issue being covered—who, what, when, where, and why.

Now, read the title and the first paragraph from the reading. Then, scan the reading for the following information:

- Who has a problem?
- What kind of problem?
- When did this problem start?
- Where did this person go?
- Why did this person go to a specific place?

Antes de leer

1. La salud Con ayuda de un/a compañero/a, contesta las preguntas:

1. ¿Tienes fe en la medicina moderna?
2. ¿Usas alguna forma de medicina alternativa, como la acupuntura, la medicina naturista o la homeopatía? Explica.
3. ¿Compras hierbas medicinales? ¿Dónde? ¿Para qué?
4. Cuando tienes gripe, ¿qué síntomas tienes?
5. ¿Conoces remedios para aliviar algunos síntomas (por ejemplo, el dolor de estómago)?
6. ¿Te enfermas fácilmente?

Llegan las noticias desde Bolivia
Médicos kallawayas en Bolivia

Luis Martínez nació con problemas respiratorios y tuvo que pasar mucho tiempo en el hospital con cuidados intensivos. Ningún tratamiento de los médicos de El Alto lo ayudaba a mejorar. Es más, los médicos no parecían saber la razón de su problema. Su madre, Trinidad, que estaba desesperada, decidió visitar a un médico kallawaya.

"Estas son las hierbas que tiene que usar para preparar el remedio. Espero que lo prepare todos los días y le aconsejo que siga bien los pasos para hacerlo. Le recomiendo que, una vez preparado, lo consuma enseguida", dijo Walter, el médico kallawaya. Y continuó diciendo: "Los malestares de su hijo tienen cura, pero es un proceso lento y tiene que tener **fe**. Sin fe, las ceremonias rituales no curan al enfermo".

La cultura kallawaya llega de La Paz, Bolivia. La medicina kallawaya consiste en la cura de diferentes males y enfermedades. Sus técnicas medicinales se basan en **creencias** que datan del periodo preincaico mediante una clasificación antigua de plantas, animales, minerales, ceremonias rituales y espirituales. La visión holística de la medicina kallawaya consiste en unir la fuerza divina, la naturaleza y el cuerpo físico. Según sus creencias, cuando se pierde la fuerza divina desaparece la fuerza del cuerpo y por tanto la persona se enferma. El kallawaya se comunica con el paciente para aprender sobre sus males y ayudarlo a recuperar esa unión mediante el mundo de los espíritus y los recursos de la naturaleza.

La medicina kallawaya es de tradición oral y se transmite de generación en generación. Los padres y abuelos pasan sus **conocimientos** rituales y prácticas médicas a los niños varones. La cultura kallawaya no solo mantiene su lengua propia sagrada "kallawaya" sino que también mantiene una reputación nacional e internacional. Así pues, en el 2003, la UNESCO proclamó la cultura kallawaya Obra Maestra del Patrimonio Oral e Intangible de la Humanidad.

La medicina tradicional se practica en todos los estratos sociales del país. Se encuentra en las ciudades, el campo y todos los lugares de Bolivia, e incluso está siendo industrializada. Esto es común porque los remedios son asequibles, mientras que los servicios de la medicina moderna no lo son. Además, en muchos pueblos bolivianos no hay médicos, enfermeros o clínicas adonde ir, por eso acuden a la medicina alternativa de los kallawayas. En otros lugares rurales sí hay médicos y servicios modernos, pero muchos bolivianos no **se fían** de ellos porque los ven foráneos a su cultura.

Bolivia es un país rico en recursos, pero la mayoría de la población vive en la pobreza. Trinidad, la madre de Luis Martínez, vive en El Alto, la zona de los ricos. Trinidad, como mujer con dinero, llevó a su hijo Luis a clínicas privadas y a los mejores especialistas en medicina occidental. Sin embargo, la salud de su hijo no mejoraba con ningún tratamiento. Un día, una vecina le dijo: "Te recomiendo que lo lleves a un médico kallawaya. Creo que piensas que muchos de estos hombres no son sinceros, pero a mí me parece que lo son. Quizás piense así porque recibí un buen tratamiento con hierbas y rituales cuando perdí la **vista**. Luis necesita una buena salud y un buen tratamiento de un kallawaya. Realmente espero que no te demores en ir y que lo reciban pronto".

Hoy día, la medicina moderna ha controlado muchas enfermedades, pero no parece encontrar soluciones para enfermedades crónicas. Tanto los profesionales de la salud como los curanderos de Bolivia dicen que una combinación de ambas medicinas y tratamientos que sigan un enfoque holístico pueden ser la respuesta a diferentes tipos de males.

faith

belief

knowledge

to trust (someone)

eyesight

© John Wiley & Sons, Inc.

Después de leer

1. En el texto

1. Después de leer el texto con atención, escribe todas las oraciones que expresen recomendación, posibilidad, influencia, deseo y afirmación[17] (hay diez en total). Después, indica cuál es el verbo subordinado y si está en subjuntivo o indicativo.

MODELO: 1. *Espero que lo prepare todos los días...*
(esperanza; prepare)

2. _____ 5. _____ 8. _____
3. _____ 6. _____ 9. _____
4. _____ 7. _____ 10. _____

2. Finalmente, indica cuál es el sujeto del verbo principal y el sujeto del verbo subordinado.

MODELO: 1. *Espero que lo prepare todos los días...*
Sujeto del verbo principal (Walter), sujeto del verbo subordinado (usted)

2. _____ 5. _____ 8. _____
3. _____ 6. _____ 9. _____
4. _____ 7. _____ 10. _____

[17]**afirmación:** statement

2. ¿Entendiste?

1. ¿Por qué Trinidad está desesperada?
2. ¿En qué creencias se basa o se funda la medicina kallawaya?
3. ¿Por qué se enferma una persona, según las creencias kallawayas?
4. ¿Qué parte de la población tiene conocimientos kallawayas?
5. Menciona tres razones por las que los bolivianos acuden a la medicina alternativa.
6. ¿Cuál puede ser la solución para encontrar cura a algunos males?

3. Análisis Contesta las siguientes preguntas con ayuda de un/a compañero/a.

1. ¿Te gusta escribir en tu tiempo libre? ¿Qué escribes?
2. ¿Qué tipo de introducción presenta el autor en el artículo?
3. ¿Por qué crees que usa ese tipo de introducción?
4. El autor comenta más de una vez el tema presentado en la introducción. ¿Cuándo y por qué vuelve a escribir sobre ese tema?
5. ¿Qué te gusta leer más, artículos o entrevistas? ¿Por qué?

EN TUS PROPIAS PALABRAS

Estrategias para escribir

The use of punctuation and capitalization in Spanish

1. In Spanish, question and exclamation marks are used at the beginning and at the end of a sentence.

| ¿...? | ¿Entiendes? | Do you understand? |
| ¡...! | ¡Atención, por favor! | Attention, please! |

2. In Spanish, lowercase letters are used to write the names of languages, nationalities, days of the week, months, and seasons.

El quechua, el aimara y el español son lenguas que se hablan en la comunidad boliviana.

Quechua, Aymara, and Spanish are languages spoken in the Bolivian community.

3. When quotation marks are used to quote direct speech, notice that when you use them in Spanish, the punctuation (such as periods and commas) goes outside of the quotation mark.

Walter dijo: "Toma esta bebida".

Walter said "Take this drink."

Una entrevista Imagínate que eres periodista y tienes que escribir una historia para la página web de un periódico. Elige una de las enfermedades mencionadas abajo. Imagina que vas a hacerle una entrevista a una persona que tiene una de estas enfermedades. Escribe una redacción en forma de artículo como el presentado en la lectura de **Entérate**. Informa a tus lectores sobre cuáles son sus problemas de salud, cómo comenzaron los síntomas, cuáles son los tratamientos médicos, qué tipo de medicina (moderna o alternativa) ayuda, cuánto dura la enfermedad y cómo se siente actualmente. Puedes usar comillas (" ") para destacar frases usadas por la persona entrevistada en tu redacción como en el punto número 3 de las **Estrategias para escribir**.

Temas: diabetes, gripe, neumonía, bronquitis, sida

En el primer párrafo intenta informar sobre las cinco preguntas presentadas en las **Estrategias para leer** (¿quién? ¿qué? ¿dónde? ¿cómo? ¿por qué?). Usa conectores para tener párrafos coherentes y organizados. Presta atención a la puntuación y al uso de letras mayúsculas y minúsculas.

AUTOPRUEBA

VOCABULARIO

I. Las partes del cuerpo Mira las actividades de la lista y selecciona la parte del cuerpo que <u>no</u> se usa para hacer la actividad.

1. Correr: la nariz, los pies, las rodillas, los tobillos
2. Nadar: los brazos, las piernas, la cabeza, los oídos
3. Bailar: la cabeza, los brazos, la garganta, las piernas
4. Tocar el piano: los dedos, los pies, los ojos, la boca
5. Conducir un auto: las manos, la espalda, los pies, los ojos

II. Las enfermedades Contesta las preguntas usando palabras del vocabulario.

1. ¿Qué parte del cuerpo te duele si tienes neumonía?
2. ¿Qué te duele cuando tienes migraña?
3. ¿Qué enfermedad sufres si tienes mucha azúcar en la sangre?
4. ¿Qué enfermedad contagiosa puede transmitirse sexualmente?

GRAMÁTICA

I. La gripe Un amigo de la clase de español tiene gripe. ¿Qué le aconsejas? Usa los verbos o expresiones de la lista.

recomendar   aconsejar
es mejor/importante/bueno/necesario...

MODELO: quedarse en casa
→ *Te recomiendo que te quedes en casa.*

1. tomar una infusión de hierbas
2. descansar y tomar jarabe para la tos
3. hacer gárgaras si te duele la garganta
4. ir al consultorio del médico si tienes fiebre
5. beber mucho líquido

II. ¿Qué pasa? Una amiga está viajando por América Latina y no contesta tus *e-mails*. ¿Qué crees que pasa? Usa los verbos o expresiones de la lista.

ojalá   querer   esperar   preferir   desear

MODELO: Seguro que se está divirtiendo.
→ *Espero que se esté divirtiendo.*

1. Seguro que no está enferma.
2. Seguro que me escribe en unos días.
3. Seguro que regresa pronto.
4. Seguro que me trae regalos de Paraguay.
5. Seguro que está pasando tiempo con nuevos amigos.

CULTURA

Demuestra lo que aprendiste en este capítulo, seleccionando la mejor respuesta.

1. Una bebida muy típica de Paraguay es...
   a. la limonada
   b. el tereré
   c. el mate
2. La lengua indígena de Paraguay es...
   a. el quechua
   b. el aimara
   c. el guaraní
3. En Paraguay...
   a. la mayoría de la población es bilingüe.
   b. la minoría de la población es bilingüe.
   c. solo se habla español.
4. La medicina alternativa se usa...
   a. en Bolivia
   b. en Paraguay
   c. en Bolivia y Paraguay

REDACCIÓN

En este capítulo aprendiste sobre Bolivia y la medicina de los kallawayas. Escribe un párrafo sobre quién es este pueblo y qué tipo de medicina usan, qué hacen o qué tipo de tratamientos usan, dónde trabajan, y explica quiénes visitan a los médicos kallawayas y por qué.

EN RESUMIDAS CUENTAS, AHORA PUEDO...

☐ hablar sobre el cuerpo humano.

☐ describir síntomas y enfermedades.

☐ dar órdenes e indicaciones de manera formal.

☐ expresar deseos y esperanzas.

☐ entender la medicina alternativa.

☐ identificar las lenguas de Paraguay y Bolivia.

VOCABULARIO ESENCIAL

Sustantivos

el brazo	*arm*
el consultorio del médico	*doctor's office*
el corazón	*heart*
el cuerpo humano	*human body*
el dedo (de la mano/del pie)	*finger/toe*
la garganta	*throat*
el germen	*germ*
la gripe	*flu*
la enfermedad	*disease*
la espalda	*back*
el estómago	*stomach*
el jarabe para la tos	*cough syrup*
la infusión/el té de hierbas	*herbal tea*
el malestar	*discomfort*
la mano	*hand*
el medicamento	*medicine*
el oído	*(inner) ear*
la pastilla	*pills*
la pierna	*leg*
el pie	*foot*
el pulmón	*lung*
la receta	*prescription*
el resfriado	*cold*
la rodilla	*knee*
la salud	*health*
la sangre	*blood*
el seguro médico	*health insurance*
el sida	*AIDS*
el síntoma	*symptom*
el tobillo	*ankle*
la vacuna	*vaccine*

Cognados: el antibiótico, la bronquitis, la cura, la diabetes, el diagnóstico, la infección, la medicina, la neumonía, el/la paciente, el remedio, el tratamiento

Adjetivos

congestionado/a	*congested*
débil	*weak*
enfermo/a	*sick, ill*

Cognados: medicinal

Verbos

curar	*to cure, to heal*
curarse	*to get well, to recover*
enfermarse	*to get sick*
estornudar	*to sneeze*
doler (ue)	*to hurt*
mejorar	*to improve*

Expresiones

estar resfriado/a	*to have a cold*
ponerle una inyección/ vacuna a alguien	*to give somebody a shot/ vaccine*
romperse un hueso	*to break a bone*
sentirse mal/bien	*to feel badly/well*
tener alergias	*to suffer from allergies*
tener comezón	*to feel itchy*
tener dolor de (cabeza/ estómago/oído)	*to have (a head/stomach/ ear) ache*
tener escalofríos	*to have cold chills*
tener fiebre	*to have fever*
tener mareos	*to feel dizzy*
tener migraña	*to have a migraine*
tener náuseas	*to feel nauseous*
toser	*to cough*
torcerse el tobillo	*to twist an ankle*
¿Qué te duele?	*What hurts?*
¿Qué te pasa?	*What is the matter?*
Me duele...	*My . . . hurts*

LEARNING OBJECTIVES

By the end of this section you will be able to:

- Discuss emotional well-being
- Talk about healthy and unhealthy lifestyles
- Give and receive instructions and advice on health issues
- Describe people
- Express qualities
- Understand spirituality and lifestyles in Bolivia

Una imagen vale más que mil palabras

¿Cómo se puede saber si se tiene tuberculosis?

¿Tiene cura la tuberculosis? ¿Cuánto cuesta el tratamiento?

¿Por qué hablan de tuberculosis y discriminación al mismo tiempo?

Si tienes tos por más de 15 días, acude al centro de salud. La tuberculosis se puede curar. La discriminación también. Recuerda: El tratamiento de tuberculosis es gratis.

© John Wiley & Sons, Inc.

▲ *Letrero del gobierno municipal de El Alto, Bolivia*

UNA PERSPECTIVA

La espiritualidad en Bolivia

Courtesy of Kimberly Morris

Kim

Diferente

"Pasé una Semana Santa[1] en Bolivia y nunca vi el lado comercial de la Semana Santa que hay en Estados Unidos, como los huevos o los conejitos de Pascua[2], ni las rebajas[3] de Pascua. Fue una semana de contemplación espiritual y personal. Había una devoción y tranquilidad que me inspiró.

También observé que para los bolivianos es muy habitual mencionar a Dios en conversaciones ordinarias y coloquiales. Oí mucho, por ejemplo: 'Mañana voy a visitarte, si Dios quiere, o Dios mediante, o si Dios lo permite'. Cuando preguntan '¿Cómo estás?', es muy común oír 'Muy bien, gracias a Dios'. El nombre *Jesús* para un niño también es común".

Igual

"Estados Unidos, como Bolivia o la gran mayoría de los países hispanohablantes, es un país muy espiritual. Nosotros también nos referimos a Dios de forma directa (*God bless you, thank God, God willing* o *for God's sake*) o indirecta (*¡OMG!, ¡TGIF!, gosh, oh my goodness*).

Además, también usamos nombres religiosos para llamar a las personas, como *Joseph, Mary* o *Christopher, Christina, Christian,* que vienen de la palabra *Cristo,* y muchos otros nombres que vienen de textos religiosos, como la Biblia".

¿Qué piensas tú?

1. ¿Qué tienen que ver los huevos y los conejos con la Pascua en Estados Unidos?
2. ¿Qué otro día feriado religioso tiene un componente muy comercial en Estados Unidos?
3. ¿Conoces ciudades que tienen nombres religiosos en español?

[1] **Semana Santa:** Holy week [2] **conejitos de Pascua:** Easter bunnies [3] **rebajas:** sales

LA PURA VERDAD I   La vida de voluntaria

Aída fue voluntaria del Cuerpo de Paz. Pasó un año en Bolivia.

1.

¡Tengo que estudiar muchísimo!

▲ *¿Está estresada o está deprimida?*

2.

¡Sí, y puedo vivir en la comunidad por un año!

▲ *Está muy animada.*

3.
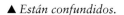

¡No me gusta volar!

¡Qué viaje tan largo!

▲ *Está nerviosa.*   ▲ *Está muy cansada.*

4.

No entiendo...

▲ *Están confundidos.*

5.

Esto cura la tos, un resfriado, alivia el estrés y te ayuda a calmarte.

▲ *Está enferma.*

6.
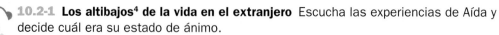

Me siento mejor.

▲ *Se siente relajada.*

10.2-1 Los altibajos⁴ de la vida en el extranjero Escucha las experiencias de Aída y decide cuál era su estado de ánimo.

1. ¿Cómo se sentía?
   a. Estaba nerviosa.   b. Estaba deprimida.   c. Estaba animada.
2. Al final del día,
   a. estaba cansada.   b. estaba aburrida.   c. estaba confundida.
3. ¿Qué le gustaba?
   a. Le gustaba estar débil.   b. Le gustaba relajarse.   c. Le gustaba estar animada.

⁴**altibajos:** ups and downs

PALABRA POR PALABRA

Los estados de ánimo *Moods*

emocionado/a, animado/a   cansado/a   deprimido/a   confundido/a   loco/a   contento/a   estresado/a

irritado/a   distraído/a   avergonzado/a   nervioso/a   débil   fuerte   tranquilo/a   triste

© John Wiley & Sons, Inc.

Los profesionales de la salud

el/la cirujano/a	*surgeon*
el/la enfermero/a	*nurse*
el/la oculista	*eye doctor*

Cognados: el/la cardiólogo/a, el/la dentista, el/la doctor/a, el/la farmacéutico/a, el/la psicólogo/a, el/la psiquiatra, el/la terapeuta

¿Qué dicen los bolivianos?

Susana es muy <u>chinchi</u>.	*Susana is very <u>immature</u>.*
Ten cuidado, hay un <u>paco</u> en cada esquina.	*Be careful, there is a <u>police officer</u> in every corner.*
Es un *<u>pelado</u> de 16 años.	*He is a 16-year-old <u>kid</u>.*
Me encantan las <u>pipocas</u>.	*I love <u>popcorn</u>.*

*Esta expresión también se usa en otros países hispanos.

Para hablar de la salud

el bienestar	*well-being*
el descanso	*rest*
engordar	*to gain on weight*
estar embarazada	*to be pregnant*
preocuparse (por)	*to worry (about)*
subir/bajar de peso	*to gain/lose weight*
tener estrés	*to suffer from stress*

Cognados: el análisis, el estrés

Hábitos saludables y prevención *Healthy habits and prevention*

adelgazar	*to lose weight*
calmarse	*calm down*
controlar (la ansiedad/el colesterol)	*control (your anxiety/ cholesterol)*
cuidar(se)	*to take care (of oneself)*
descansar	*to rest*
estar a dieta/hacer dieta	*to be on a diet/to diet*
relajarse	*to relax*
reducir el consumo (de alcohol/ grasa)	*to reduce (alcohol/fat) intake*
tener cuidado	*to be careful*

Cognados: meditar, prevenir

10.2-02 ¿Qué le duele?

Paso 1: Estas personas tienen problemas de salud y necesitan ayuda profesional. ¿A qué especialista deben ver?

MODELO: Miriam tiene demasiado trabajo y la semana pasada tuvo un ataque de ansiedad. → *Miriam tiene que ver al <u>psicólogo.</u>*

1. A Adela le duele la cabeza cuando lee y ve la televisión.
2. Elena va a hacerse una operación cosmética.
3. A Mercedes se le rompió un diente.
4. Javier está muy deprimido y tiene fobia social.
5. Jorge Luis tuvo un ataque al corazón y está en el hospital.
6. Carlos tiene que ir a la farmacia y comprar el antibiótico que le recetó el médico.
7. María tiene que hacer terapia de rehabilitación física.
8. Francisco va al hospital a dar una muestra de sangre.

Paso 2: Comenta con un/a compañero/a: ¿Alguna vez tuviste que ver a alguno de estos especialistas? ¿Por qué? ¿Qué te pasó?

10.2-03 ¿Cómo te sientes?

Paso 1: Utiliza los adjetivos de la sección **Palabra por palabra** (*nervioso/a, emocionado/a, deprimido/a, etc.*) o los adverbios *bien/mal* para decir cómo te sientes en las siguientes situaciones.

MODELO: Tienes que escribir un ensayo sobre un tema que te interesa mucho.
       → *Estoy emocionado.*

1. Regresas de un viaje de avión intercontinental.
2. No puedes tomar una decisión sobre algo importante (comprar un auto, elegir una especialidad en la universidad, etc.).
3. Tus vecinos hacen demasiado ruido y no puedes dormir.
4. Tienes un examen muy difícil al día siguiente.
5. Después de tener un accidente de auto no sabes si el seguro lo va a pagar.
6. Te dicen que un buen amigo tiene una enfermedad grave.
7. Tienes muchas cosas que hacer y no puedes hacerlas todas.
8. Tienes que ir al cardiólogo para una revisión del corazón.

Paso 2: Ahora, entrevista a un/a compañero/a para ver si se siente como tú en esas situaciones. ¿Se sienten igual o hay mucha diferencia entre sus reacciones a la misma situación?

MODELO: Estudiante 1:   *¿Cómo te sientes después de un viaje en avión intercontinental?*
                Estudiante 2:   *¡Me siento <u>contento</u> porque fue una gran experiencia!*
                Estudiante 1:   *¿Sí? ¡Qué suerte! Yo me siento <u>cansada.</u>*

♻ **Describing people: Ser and estar + adjective**

You already know that both **ser** and **estar** can be used with adjectives to describe people and things. Do you remember when to use one or the other? Go back to **Hablando de gramática II** in Chapter 4, Section 2, and try to explain the difference between these two sentences:

Aída **es** muy **distraída**. Siempre lo pierde todo.

Aída **está** muy **distraída** estos días. Creo que tiene problemas en casa.

We use **ser +** adjective when naming a characteristic that distinguishes that person from other persons. In the first sentence, Aída is pretty absent-minded if we compare her to other people. We use **estar +** adjective to describe a condition that distinguishes the person's current state from his or her usual state of being. Thus, in the second sentence, Aída is more distracted than usual, which means that she is not usually that way. Because English has only one equivalent to **ser/estar** (the verb *to be*), the subtleties of this difference are expressed with different adjectives or expressions in English.

Use **ser...** with adjectives to describe a characteristic.	Use **estar...** with adjectives to describe a condition or state.
Aída **es** muy aburrida. *Aída is very boring.* **Es** muy guapa. *She is very beautiful.*	Aída **está** muy aburrida. *Aída is very bored.* **Está** muy guapa. *She looks great.*

👥 **10.2-04 ¿Cómo eres? ¿Cómo estás?**

♻ **Paso 1:** Con los siguientes adjetivos, forma preguntas con *ser* y *estar* y entrevista a un/a compañero/a. ¡OJO! Algunos adjetivos son diferentes si los usas con *ser* o *estar*.

MODELO: serio/a
       Estudiante 1:   *En general, ¿eres una persona <u>seria</u>?*
       Estudiante 2:   *Pues sí, en general <u>soy bastante seria</u>. ¿Y tú?*
       Estudiante 1:   *Yo no, yo <u>soy muy animado</u>, aunque en la clase de español siempre <u>estoy bastante serio</u>.*

1. emocional
2. emocionado/a
3. irritable
4. irritado/a
5. alegre
6. distraído/a
7. tranquilo/a
8. nervioso/a

Paso 2: Compartan con la clase sus conclusiones sobre sus personalidades. ¿Cómo son ustedes? ¿Tienen características de personalidad similares o son muy diferentes? ¿Cómo se sienten estos días? ¿Tienen el mismo estado de ánimo?

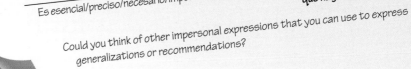

Giving advice: Impersonal expressions with subjunctive

You already know a few different ways of giving advice. In Chapter 4, Section 1, you learned how to express obligation and advice with **tener que, deber** and **hay que** + *infinitive*. In Chapter 9, Section 1, you also learned how to make impersonal generalizations to express recommendations. When the advice is generic and not directed to a specific person, we use the infinitive:

	Infinitive
Es esencial/preciso/necesario/importante/mejor	**estar** en buena forma.
	hacer más ejercicio.

However, if the advice or recommendation is directed to a specific person or persons, we use **que** + *subjunctive*:

	Subjunctive
Es esencial/preciso/necesario/importante/mejor	**que estés** en buena forma.
	que hagamos más ejercicio.

Could you think of other impersonal expressions that you can use to express generalizations or recommendations?

 10.2-05 **Recomendaciones para sentirse bien** Después de los altibajos de su viaje a Bolivia y la dura vida de voluntaria, Aída quiere sentirse mejor.

 Paso 1: Con un/a compañero/a, escriban todos los consejos que puedan para cada aspecto de su vida que Aída quiere mejorar.

Aída quiere...	Consejos:
adelgazar	Es importante...
estar más tranquila	Es mejor...
estar más fuerte	Es bueno...
estar menos distraída	Es necesario...
estar más animada	Es esencial...

 Paso 2: Comparen sus consejos con otras parejas de la clase. ¿Quién tiene la lista más larga?

HABLANDO DE GRAMÁTICA I

1. Giving instructions and advice: Informal commands

A. Afirmative informal commands

In Chapter 7, Section 2, you learned how to give instructions using formal commands. As you already know, in Spanish there are two sets of commands. Formal commands (**los mandatos formales**) are used when you want to give instructions or directions to people with whom you have a formal relationship—those you would normally address as **usted/ ustedes.** In this section you will learn how to use informal commands, which are used with people that you would address as **tú.** You are already familiar with these forms since they are used in many of the direction lines of the activities in this book:

Compara tus respuestas con las de un/a compañero/a. | *Compare your answers with a partner.*

You already know that the form of the **usted** command and the present subjunctive forms for the third person singular (**él, ella, usted**) and plural (**ustedes**) are the same. For the informal commands (**los mandatos informales**) use the third person form of the present indicative. These will be the command form you use with people who you would normally address as **tú.**

	Third person present indicative	Affirmative *tú* command
descansar	Aída no **descansa** lo suficiente. *Aida doesn't rest enough.*	**Descansa** un poco. *Rest a little.*
beber	También **bebe** mucho café. *She also drinks a lot of coffee.*	**Bebe** más infusiones y menos café. *Drink herbal teas and less coffee.*
subir	Nunca **sube** de peso. *She never puts on weight.*	**Sube** de peso un poquito, estás demasiado delgada. *Gain a little weight; you are too thin.*

The following verbs have irregular command forms.

decir	➜	di	**Di** lo que piensas. Te vas a sentir mejor. *Say what you think. You'll feel better.*
hacer	➜	haz	**Haz** más ejercicio. *Do more exercise.*
ir	➜	ve	**Ve** a una clase de meditación. *Go to a meditation class.*
poner	➜	pon	**Pon** esta hierba en la infusión. *Put this herb in the tea.*
salir	➜	sal	**Sal** un poco más y diviértete. *Go out more and have fun.*
ser	➜	sé	¡**Sé** más disciplinado y no dejes trabajo para mañana! *Be more disciplined and do not leave work for tomorrow!*
tener	➜	ten	**Ten** más paciencia; es muy pronto para ver resultados. *Have more patience; it is early to see results.*
venir	➜	ven	**Ven** conmigo a la clase de yoga. Te va a gustar. *Come with me to the yoga class. You'll like it.*

Direct, indirect, and reflexive pronouns are attached at the end of the affirmative command forms.

Si estás nerviosa, **siénta̱te*** y respira profundamente. | *If you are nervous, sit down and breathe deeply.*

Si estás deprimida y quieres hablar con alguien, **llámame***. | *If you are depressed and you want to talk to someone, call me.*

*A written accent is added when the stress falls on the third-to-last syllable.

WileyPLUS Go to *WileyPLUS* to review this grammar point with the help of the **Animated Grammar Tutorial** and the **Verb Conjugator.**

10.2-06 **Consejos para reducir el estrés** Lee este foro de recomendaciones para reducir el estrés.

Médicos en línea

INICIO | QUIÉNES SOMOS | CONTACTO | AVISO LEGAL | INICIAR SESIÓN

| **Salud y bienestar** | Vivir sano | Actualidad | Enfermedades | Pruebas diagnósticas |

Consejos para reducir el estrés

Aquí te ofrecemos unos consejos para prevenir o reducir el estrés.

DIETA Y EJERCICIO
- Lleva una dieta equilibrada, evitando las comidas pesadas que provocan digestiones lentas.
- Usa el tiempo para comer como momento de descanso.
- Controla el consumo de alcohol.
- Haz ejercicio todos los días.

DESCANSO
- Duerme lo suficiente, aproximadamente 7 u 8 horas diarias.
- Toma las vacaciones y los fines de semana como tiempo de ocio.
- Deja el trabajo en la oficina.

ORGANIZACIÓN
- Organiza tus tareas y establece horarios para no tener olvidos importantes.
- Planifica tus actividades con tiempo para no llegar tarde a tus citas[5] y obligaciones.
- Si no puedes hacerlo todo, selecciona las actividades más importantes.

TÉCNICAS DE CONTROL DE ANSIEDAD Y ESTRÉS
- Practica la relajación y la meditación, sobre todo si te sientes mal.
- Aprende a decir no.

VIDA SOCIAL
- Reconéctate con tus amigos.
- Todos los días dedica tiempo a hacer alguna actividad que te guste durante por lo menos una hora.
- Busca apoyo en tu familia o amigos.

© John Wiley & Sons, Inc.

Paso 1: Escribe todos los mandatos informales que hay en el texto (son dieciséis en total). ¡Atención! No todos los verbos del texto son mandatos. Después, indica cuál es el infinitivo de cada mandato.

MODELO: 1. ____lleva (llevar)____

2. _____	7. _____	12. _____
3. _____	8. _____	13. _____
4. _____	9. _____	14. _____
5. _____	10. _____	15. _____
6. _____	11. _____	16. _____

Paso 2: Comenta con un/a compañero/a. ¿Cuál de estos consejos sigues y cuáles no? ¿Crees que todos son consejos válidos, o crees que hay algunos más importantes que otros? Añadan dos consejos más a la lista.

MODELO: Estudiante 1: *¿Llevas una dieta equilibrada?*
Estudiante 2: *No mucho. Como mucha comida rápida porque es barata y no me gusta cocinar.*
Estudiante 3: *Puedes comer en restaurantes, pero busca opciones sanas. Come ensaladas o alimentos frescos y reduce el consumo de alimentos fritos.*

---

[5] **cita:** appointment

Paso 3: Ahora, escribe una pequeña entrada para un foro de recomendaciones de tu universidad. Recomienda qué deben hacer los nuevos estudiantes para combatir el estrés o la ansiedad del cambio de entorno. En tus recomendaciones, utiliza por lo menos seis de los siguientes verbos en la forma de mandato informal.

> hacer   ir   salir   ser   tener   sentirse   relajarse   descansar

B. Negative informal commands

Affirmative and negative informal commands are not the same. Negative informal commands are formed by dropping the ending of the first person singular form in the present tense indicative (e.g., **-o** or **-oy** in the **yo** form) and adding the opposite theme vowel + **s**. That is, verbs ending in **-ar** add **-es**, verbs ending in **-er**, **-ir**, add **-as**.

Infinitive	yo form	tú command	
descans**ar**	descans~~o~~	descans**es**	No **descanses** tanto. Luego te duele la cabeza si duermes mucho.
est**ar**	est~~oy~~	est**és**	No **estés*** triste. Todo tiene solución.
beb**er**	beb~~o~~	beb**as**	No **bebas** tanto café.
pon**er**(se)	pong~~o~~	pong**as**	No **pongas** tanta sal en la comida.
sub**ir**	sub~~o~~	sub**as**	No **subas** más de peso.
reduc**ir**	reduzc~~o~~	reduzc**as**	No **reduzcas** la cantidad de comida, solo la grasa.

Verbs ending in **-car, -gar, -zar** undergo a spelling change to **-qu, -gu, -c**, in order to maintain the original pronunciation.

Infinitive	yo form	tú command	ustedes
llegar	lleg~~o~~	lle**gu**e	No **llegues** tarde. Eso provoca mucho estrés.
buscar	busc~~o~~	bus**qu**es	No **busques** un psicólogo.
adelgazar	adelgaz~~o~~	adelga**c**es	No **adelgaces** más. Estás demasiado delgada.

Ir and **ser** have irregular forms.

ir	→	no vayas	**No vayas** al cardiólogo todavía.
ser	→	seas	**No seas** impaciente. Pronto vas a ver los resultados.

You may have noticed that all negative informal commands are identical to the second person singular (**tú**) form in the present subjunctive:

	Second person subjunctive	Negative tú command
descansar	No quiero [que **descanses** tanto]. *I don't want [you to rest so much.]*	**No descanses** tanto. *Do not rest so much.*
beber	Es posible [que **bebas** demasiado café]. *It is possible [that you drink too much coffee.]*	**No bebas** tanto café. *Do not drink so much coffee.*
subir	Es mejor [que no **subas** más de peso]. *It is better [that you don't put on more weight.]*	**No subas** más de peso. *Don't put on more weight.*

In negative command forms, the pronoun immediately precedes the verb.

No **te sientas** mal; es normal estar estresada al final del trimestre.   *Don't feel bad; it is normal to feel stressed at the end of the quarter.*

No **le pidas** consejo; él nunca se siente deprimido.   *Don't ask him for advice; he never feels depressed.*

*The command form of **estar** carries a written accent.

10.2-07 ¿Qué me recomiendas? Aída regresa a casa y su amiga, que también va a ir a Bolivia con el Cuerpo de Paz, le hace muchas preguntas. ¿Cuáles son los consejos de Aída? Escribe las respuestas en forma de mandato con los pronombres necesarios.

MODELO: ¿Debo <u>llevar</u> <u>mis medicinas para el asma</u>?
Sí, <u>llévalas</u>. Es posible que allí no las encuentres.

1. ¿Crees que es buena idea que yo <u>vaya</u> a Bolivia?

   ¡Por supuesto, _____! Va a ser una experiencia maravillosa.

2. ¿Debo <u>probar</u> <u>la comida local</u>?

   ¡Pues claro! _____. ¡Es deliciosa!

3. ¿Y cómo <u>me</u> <u>comunico</u> con los pacientes del hospital?

   Pues _____ con ellos en español.

4. ¿Tengo que <u>estudiar</u> <u>quechua</u>?

   No es obligatorio, pero _____, ¿por qué no?

5. ¿Es mejor <u>vivir</u> en una residencia o con una familia boliviana?

   No _____ en una residencia porque hay muchos estadounidenses. Con una familia vas a aprender mucho más.

10.2-08 Recomendaciones para Aída Vuelve a la historia de **La pura verdad I** y para cada estado de ánimo, dale un consejo de algo que Aída NO debe hacer y algo que SÍ debe hacer para sentirse mejor. Usa los verbos propuestos.

  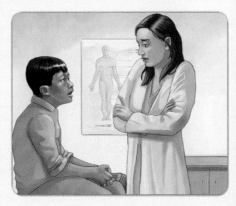

© John Wiley & Sons, Inc.

MODELO: Viñeta 1: preocuparse, priorizar, hacer
→ <u>No te preocupes</u>. <u>Prioriza</u> tus obligaciones y <u>haz</u> las tareas más importantes o difíciles primero.

Viñeta 2: ponerse más nerviosa, calmarse
Viñeta 3: perder la paciencia, aprender
Viñeta 4: preocuparse, tomar
Viñeta 5: quedarse en casa, salir

LA PURA VERDAD II   Una experiencia emocionante

Alex y Linda viven en Bolivia. Nos dan consejos y nos cuentan su experiencia en bicicleta en la famosa Carretera de la Muerte.

1.

Es mejor que vayas con ▶ un buen grupo, que tengan todo el equipo necesario y que lleven bicicletas extras.

◀ *Todos los años más de 200 personas mueren en esta carretera. ¡Es increíble que se use tanto!*

2.

3.

Mis amigos piensan que estoy loco. Es posible...

4.

¡Si Dios quiere!

¡Ten cuidado! Nos vemos abajo.

5.

▲ *Lo bueno es la vista y la emoción de la velocidad.*

6.

▲ *Lo emocionante es el peligro y la posibilidad de perder la vida.*

10.2-09 ¿Qué hacer y qué no hacer en la Carretera de la Muerte? Escucha la experiencia que tuvo Alex y decide qué consejos debes seguir.

1. ¿Qué aconseja Alex que hagas que él no pudo hacer?
   a. que saques fotos al bajar a toda velocidad.
   b. que no te concentres en la carretera.
   c. que pares en la carretera y saques fotos.
2. ¿Qué aconseja Alex que hagas?
   a. que escuches al guía.
   b. que bebas menos singani.
   c. que no sigas las reglas.
3. ¿Qué aconseja que hagas después de la aventura?
   a. que tomes algo para el dolor.
   b. que te relajes en un hotel.
   c. que nades en la piscina.

HABLANDO DE GRAMÁTICA II

2. Expressing qualities: *Lo* + adjective

To describe the general qualities or characteristics of something, use the neuter definite article **lo** + adjective (singular, masculine) + **es** when, followed by a noun or an infinitive.

> **Lo bueno** es la vista y la emoción de la velocidad.
>
> **Lo emocionante** es bajar la carretera tan rápido.

> *What's good is the view and the excitement of speed.*
>
> *The exciting part is going down the road so fast.*

Use **lo** + *adjective* + **son** when followed by a plural noun.

> **Lo interesante son** los cambios de temperatura y estación.

> *The temperature and season changes are the interesting part.*

Use **que** to introduce a subordinate clause.

> **Lo increíble es [que** yo siempre hago este tipo de locuras].

> *What is incredible is [that I am always up for this type of crazy stuff.]*

 10.2-10 ¡¿Y eso es lo bueno?! Completa el siguiente diálogo entre Alex y Linda mientras hacen planes para descender el camino de Yungas.

Alex: ¿Qué es _____ atractivo de esta carretera?

Linda: Lo _____ es que es la carretera más peligrosa del mundo.

Alex: ¡¿Y eso es bueno?!

Linda: Eh... pues no, lo bueno _____ las vistas y los contrastes de temperatura. Lo atractivo, lo bueno, lo emocionante _____ las curvas peligrosas, la emoción de la velocidad.

Alex: Puf... ¡ahora estoy nervioso! ¡Parece que lo mejor de esta aventura _____ llegar al destino con vida!

Linda: Sí, y lo peor es _____ si estás nervioso y tienes miedo, no lo vas a disfrutar. ¡Relájate! ¡Lo vamos a pasar bien!

10.2-11 ¿Qué es lo mejor de todo esto?

 Paso 1: Usa los siguientes adjetivos para describir una visita al médico o al dentista.

MODELO: bueno/malo   →   *Lo **bueno** de ir al médico es que puede curar tu enfermedad o malestar. Lo **malo** es que cuesta dinero.*

1. bueno/malo
2. peor/mejor
3. interesante/aburrido
4. normal/raro
5. fácil/difícil

 Paso 2: Ahora, compara tus opiniones con las de un/a compañero/a. Para cada aspecto, ¿pensaron en lo mismo? ¿Coinciden en sus opiniones sobre lo bueno y lo malo de ir al médico?

MODELO: Estudiante 1:   *Lo **bueno** de ir al médico es que te cura el dolor. ¡Lo **malo** es tener que pagar la consulta después!*

              Estudiante 2:   *Sí, es verdad. También lo **malo** es ¡que nunca sabes cuál va a ser el diagnóstico!*

OTRA PERSPECTIVA

Courtesy of Cindy Irusta

Cindy

Diferentes estilos de vida

Diferente

"El ritmo de la vida en las grandes ciudades de Estados Unidos es mucho más rápido que en mi país, Bolivia. Aquí en Estados Unidos la gente está conectada electrónicamente y están continuamente revisando sus mensajes de Facebook, *e-mail o,* Twitter, y parece que siempre están texteando hasta cuando manejan. Siento que hay urgencia en la comunicación. Nosotros en Bolivia también estamos conectados, pero también hay tiempo para verse en persona y compartir el mate. Siento que hay más tranquilidad y que hay un mayor sentido de familia y comunidad. Creo que nos tomamos más tiempo para hablar y escuchar con paciencia. El ir y venir[6] de Estados Unidos es estresante algunas veces".

Igual

"En las ciudades grandes como La Paz también hay un ritmo más rápido porque hay más actividad en general, más gente y más tráfico. Para ir de un lugar a otro, el esfuerzo es mayor. También estamos conectados electrónicamente, seguimos tuits[7] y texteamos también, pero con menos frecuencia o urgencia".

Explícale a Cindy

1. ¿Son estresantes o divertidas las conexiones electrónicas?
2. ¿Cuáles son las ventajas y desventajas de tanta conexión?
3. ¿Sientes que compartes tiempo con frecuencia con tu familia o tus amigos?

MANOS A LA OBRA

10.2-12 ¿Cómo te sientes?

Paso 1: Completa cada oración con información verdadera sobre ti.

1. Estoy irritado/a cuando...
2. Cuando estoy nervioso/a (no) tomo...
3. Cuando tengo estrés (no)...
4. Para relajarme...
5. La última vez que me sentí avergonzado/a fue cuando...
6. Cuando me siento triste...
7. Yo (no) sé controlar bien la ansiedad porque...
8. (No) Descanso lo suficiente porque...

Paso 2: Con las oraciones del **Paso 1**, forma preguntas y entrevista a un/a compañero/a.

MODELO: Cuando tengo estrés *no quiero hablar con nadie.*
    →   *¿Te molesta hablar con la gente cuando tienes estrés?*

Paso 3: Ahora, escriban un pequeño informe. ¿En qué aspectos coinciden los dos? ¿En qué no coinciden?

MODELO: *Mi compañero/a y yo tenemos personalidades muy diferentes. Por ejemplo, yo estoy irritado si las cosas no me salen bien y, sin embargo, ella...*

Por último, informen a la clase. ¿Coinciden en todo, en algunas cosas o en nada? ¿En qué aspectos no coincide nadie?

[6] **el ir y venir:** hustle and bustle [7] **tuit:** a tweet, a post made on Twitter

10.2-13 ¿Quién de la clase...? Levántate y hazles a tus compañeros las siguientes preguntas. Escribe el nombre de los compañeros que contesten afirmativamente.

MODELO: Estudiante 1: *¿Te pones rojo cuando estás avergonzado?*
Estudiante 2: *Sí, me pongo muy rojo/No, no me pongo rojo.*

¿Quién de la clase...   Nombre del/de la compañero/a

1. ... engorda cuando está estresado/a? _____

2. ... medita o hace yoga? _____

3. ... alguna vez se rompió un hueso? _____

4. ... se vuelve loco/a en la temporada de exámenes? _____

5. ... tiene problemas para relajarse antes de dormir? _____

6. ... se pone rojo/a cuando está avergonzado/a? _____

7. ... es muy distraído/a? _____

8. ... se levanta contento/a por las mañanas? _____

9. ... tiene una amiga que está embarazada? _____

 10.2-14 Anuncios de la salud y el bienestar Muchos anuncios usan mandatos informales para crear un mensaje más directo y más personal.

Paso 1: Inventen un anuncio sobre algún tema relacionado con la salud (cómo prevenir una enfermedad, la seguridad al manejar, un seguro médico, la Organización Mundial de Salud, etc.). Deben utilizar el vocabulario de este capítulo.

Paso 2: Presenten los anuncios a la clase. La clase va a votar por el anuncio más creativo, original y con el mejor eslogan.

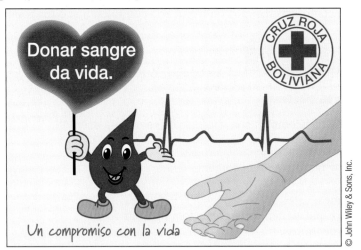

WileyPLUS Go to *WileyPLUS*
and listen to **Presta atención.**

 10.2-15 Presta atención: Hablando con una amiga Marta va para su trabajo y por la calle se encuentra a su amiga Angélica. Las dos hablan sobre la salud. Escucha el audio para saber qué le pasa a Angélica.

1. ¿Qué problemas tiene Angélica?
   a. Está a dieta porque quiere adelgazar.
   b. Está cansada y está subiendo de peso.
   c. Tiene el colesterol alto y está gorda.
2. Marta piensa que...
   a. Angélica está enferma.
   b. Angélica come mucho.
   c. Angélica se cuida poco.

3. ¿Por qué Angélica fue al hospital?
   a. Porque allí trabaja su amiga Marta.
   b. Porque le dolía la cabeza y el corazón.
   c. Porque tenía náuseas y estaba muy débil.
4. ¿Qué sospecha Angélica?
   a. Que está embarazada.
   b. Que tiene el colesterol muy alto.
   c. Que está enferma.
5. ¿Qué quiere Marta de Angélica?
   a. Quiere saber lo que piensa ella.
   b. Quiere que Angélica la llame mañana.
   c. Quiere que vaya al médico mañana.

10.2-16 Por escrito: Un informe de salud Escribe un informe sobre tu salud para enviarlo al director de un programa de estudios en el extranjero, o al entrenador de un equipo de un deporte (baloncesto, fútbol, vóleibol, etc.). Incluye: tu edad, las enfermedades que tuviste, tus hábitos actuales (buenos y malos) y cinco aspectos positivos y cinco negativos de tu condición física.

¡OJO!

Connectors
Let's review the box in **Estrategias para escribir** in Chapter 9, Section 1, with connector words.

🚶 PONTE EN MI LUGAR

Un accidente Después de sufrir un accidente de motocicleta, un/a paciente asiste a la consulta de un/a psicólogo/a. El/La paciente se siente bien físicamente, pero todavía necesita ayuda profesional. Decidan quién es el/la psicólogo/a y quién es el/la paciente. Usen las expresiones de las **Estrategias para conversar**.

Paciente: Da detalles del accidente de motocicleta y explícale a tu psicólogo/a que no tienes problemas físicos, pero que no te sientes bien emocionalmente. Explícale que necesitas ayuda porque desde el accidente no puedes usar ningún tipo de transporte y te dan mucho miedo las motocicletas.

Psicólogo/a: Escucha al paciente y pídele que te diga las actividades que normalmente hace (por ejemplo, deporte, hábitos de alimentación y bebida, actividades sociales, etc.). Después, explícale al paciente lo que debe hacer y hazle una serie de recomendaciones (por ejemplo, "*corre todos los días*"). Dile que esperas que haga todas las tareas de la lista. Haz una cita para la próxima semana.

Estrategias para conversar

Expressing satisfaction
In Chapter 10, Section 1, you learned a few expressions to react to good or bad news. Use these to express satisfaction or to praise someone:

¡Me alegro (de) que (+ *subjunctive*)!

¡Qué fabuloso que (+ *subjunctive*)!

¡Te felicito! Te alimentas muy bien.

ASÍ ES LA VIDA

Adivina, adivinador

El farmacéutico y su hija,
el médico y su mujer
se comieron nueve huevos
y todos tocaron a tres.

¿Cómo puede ser?

Chiste

Ya sé por qué engordo... Es el champú. En la botella dice "Para dar cuerpo y volumen". Desde mañana, empiezo a ducharme con el detergente para lavar platos, que dice "Elimina la grasa. Hasta la más difícil".

WileyPLUS Go to *WileyPLUS*
to find more **Arroba** activities.

Operación Sonrisa Operación Sonrisa es una fundación que trabaja con voluntarios en muchos países latinoamericanos (Paraguay, Bolivia, Brasil, Colombia, etc.). Busca en Internet información sobre esta fundación y contesta estas preguntas: ¿Cuáles son las profesiones de los voluntarios que trabajan en la fundación? ¿En qué lugares trabajan? Comenta con tus compañeros la información que encontraste. Después, contesta estas preguntas: ¿Conoces algún grupo de voluntarios? ¿Qué hace ese grupo? ¿Te gustaría trabajar como voluntario/a en algún grupo?

WileyPLUS Go to *WileyPLUS* to see this video and to find more video activities.

VER PARA CREER II: Mal de altura

Antes de ver

Con ayuda de un/a compañero/a, responde estas preguntas.

1. ¿Con qué frecuencia te enfermas?
2. ¿Te gusta ir al médico o prefieres tomar medicamentos naturales? ¿Por qué?
3. ¿Qué haces cuando estás deprimido/a?
4. ¿Qué hierbas medicinales conoces o usas?

Después de ver

1. ¿Entendiste? Brian acaba de llegar a Bolivia y no se siente bien. Después de ver el video, responde las siguientes preguntas para saber más sobre la situación de Brian.

1. ¿Qué le dice Jorge a Brian en la cafetería?
   a. Levántate y salúdame.
   b. Llega a la hora.
   c. Ven, siéntate.
2. ¿Qué síntomas tiene Brian?
   a. Tiene ansiedad.
   b. Tiene estrés.
   c. Tiene mareos.
3. ¿Qué piensa Jorge que tiene su amigo Brian?
   a. Piensa que tiene dolor de estómago.
   b. Piensa que tiene mal de altura.
   c. Piensa que tiene dolor de espalda.
4. ¿Qué bebe Brian?
   a. Bebe agua.
   b. Bebe una coca.
   c. Bebe té de coca.
5. ¿Por qué van al Mercado de las Brujas?
   a. Para buscar un remedio para el mal de amores.
   b. Para comprar medicinas tradicionales de farmacia.
   c. Para encontrarse con Sofía, la novia de Brian.

2. Enfermo en el extranjero Si estás en un país extranjero y te enfermas, ¿qué haces?

3. Enfoque cultural ¿Hay diferencias entre la visita de Brian y tus visitas al mercado? Explica.

AUTOPRUEBA

VOCABULARIO

I. En el consultorio de la Dra. Pascual Completa los consejos de la Dra. Pascual con una palabra o expresión del vocabulario de **Palabra por palabra**. Conjuga los verbos si es necesario.

MODELO: *Sr. López, es bueno <u>hacer ejercicio</u>, como por ejemplo, correr o practicar deportes.*

1. Sra. Cabello, usted está muy delgada. Tiene que _____ porque su peso es muy bajo.
2. Sra. Carrillo, usted tiene el colesterol muy alto y problemas del corazón. Debe visitar al _____.
3. Sra. Pardo, es importante que vaya al _____. Tiene un problema con los ojos.
4. Sr. Rodríguez, usted bebe demasiado. Debe reducir _____.
5. Sra. Reina, el examen indica que usted _____ de tres meses.

II. De voluntaria Nina está en Paraguay trabajando como voluntaria en una escuela. Llama a su padre por teléfono para contarle unos problemitas. Completa el diálogo con las palabras de la caja. ¡Ojo! Hay más palabras de las que necesitas. No olvides conjugar los verbos y cambiar el género y número de los adjetivos.

> nervioso/a   descansar   meditar
> estresado/a   calmarse   distraído/a
> engordar   relajarse   bienestar

Papá: ¿Cómo estás, hija?
Nina: No muy bien, papá. Estoy muy _____₁ Tengo que cuidar a estos niños pequeños cada día. ¡No prestan atención! Están muy _____₂.
Papá: Ya sabes que es bueno _____₃ para tener la mente tranquila.
Nina: Sí, papá, ya sé que el ejercicio es muy importante, pero no tengo tiempo. Además, como bebo mucho tereré para tener energía, también estoy _____₄.
Papá: Bueno, hija, tienes que _____₅ y aprender a _____₆. No te olvides de _____₇ al menos ocho horas al día. ¡Llámame pronto!
Nina: Sí, papá. ¡Hasta pronto!

GRAMÁTICA

I. ¿Qué le recomiendas? ¿Cuáles son los consejos que le das a un/a amigo/a que quiere llevar una vida más sana y tener menos estrés? Escribe tus respuestas con mandatos informales. Usa el pronombre de objeto directo cuando puedas.

MODELO: ¿Puedo <u>comer</u> <u>las papas fritas que me gustan</u>? → *No, no las comas.*

1. ¿Debo <u>reducir</u> <u>el consumo de alcohol</u>?
2. ¿<u>Visito al terapeuta</u> que me recomendaron?
3. ¿Tengo que <u>controlar</u> <u>el colesterol</u>?
4. ¿Puedo <u>comer</u> <u>mi postre favorito todos los días</u>?
5. ¿Puedo <u>hacer</u> <u>el trabajo de la oficina</u> en casa?
6. ¿Puedo <u>trabajar</u> los fines de semana?
7. ¿Cuántas horas debo <u>dormir</u>?

II. Lo mejor es... Usa los siguientes adjetivos para describir cómo es viajar al extranjero.

MODELO: bueno   →   *Lo bueno es que conoces lugares nuevos.*

1. malo
2. mejor
3. emocionante
4. peor
5. estresante

CULTURA

¿Qué has aprendido de Bolivia? Decide si las oraciones son ciertas o falsas. Si son falsas, corrígelas.

1. Singani es una medicina.
2. La Carretera de la Muerte es una atracción turística.
3. En Bolivia nadie se conecta electrónicamente.

REDACCIÓN

Javi está deprimido porque su novia no quiere seguir la relación con él. No sabe qué hacer para recuperar el amor de su vida. No quiere comer, ni salir con sus amigos. Solo quiere dormir y mirar el Internet esperando un correo electrónico de su exnovia. Imagina que eres psicólogo/a. Escríbele un mensaje ofreciéndole ayuda y dándole consejos. Usa la gramática estudiada en este capítulo.

EN RESUMIDAS CUENTAS, AHORA PUEDO...

☐ identificar a los profesionales de la salud.

☐ hablar sobre el estado de ánimo y el bienestar.

☐ dar o recibir consejos e instrucciones sobre salud y estado emocional.

☐ usar **lo** + adjetivo para describir características sobre una situación.

☐ entender el sentido de espiritualidad de Bolivia y otros países hispanos.

♪ VOCABULARIO ESENCIAL

Sustantivos

el bienestar	*well-being*
el/la cirujano/a	*surgeon*
el descanso	*rest*
el/la enfermero/a	*nurse*
el estado de ánimo	*mood*
el/la oculista	*eye doctor*

Cognados: el análisis, el/la cardiólogo/a, el/la dentista, el/la doctor/a, el estrés, el/la farmacéutico/a, el hábito, el/la psicólogo/a, el/la psiquiatra, el/la terapeuta

Verbos

adelgazar	*to lose weight*
calmarse	*to calm down*
cuidar (se)	*to take care (of oneself)*
descansar	*to rest*
engordar	*to gain weight*
preocuparse (por)	*to worry (about)*
relajarse	*to relax*

Cognados: meditar, prevenir (ie)[8]

Adjetivos

avergonzado/a	*embarrassed*
cansado/a	*tired*
confundido/a	*confused*
emocionado/a	*excited*
deprimido/a	*depressed*
distraído/a	*distracted, absent-minded*
fuerte	*strong*
loco/a	*crazy*
tranquilo/a	*calm*
triste	*sad*

Cognados: animado/a, contento/a, estresado/a, irritado/a, nervioso/a

Otras expresiones

controlar (la ansiedad/el colesterol)	*control (your anxiety/cholesterol)*
estar a dieta/hacer dieta	*to diet/be on a diet*
estar embarazada	*to be pregnant*
reducir (el consumo de alcohol/grasa)	*reduce (your alcohol/fat intake)*
subir/bajar de peso	*to gain/lose weight*
tener cuidado	*to be careful*
tener estrés	*to suffer from stress*

---

[8]**Prevenir** is conjugated like **venir.**

VER PARA CREER I: *Online* las 24 horas

Antes de mirar el video, conversa unos minutos con un/a compañero/a sobre la tecnología. Hablen sobre las razones para usar un teléfono inteligente o un celular parecido. Al ver el video, presta atención a lo que hacen los chicos con la tecnología. Después, contesta las preguntas.

1. ¿Dónde están los dos chicos?

2. ¿Qué tienen en las manos?

3. ¿Qué hacen los chicos con lo que tienen en las manos?

Sección 1	Redes

PALABRA POR PALABRA

- La tecnología

HABLANDO DE GRAMÁTICA

- Talking about the recent past: The present perfect tense
- Describing results: Participles used as adjectives
- Preterit vs. imperfect ♻

CULTURA

- La tecnología como parte de nuestras vidas
- La función de los teléfonos móviles y los cibercafés

Sección 2	De vacaciones

PALABRA POR PALABRA

- En el aeropuerto
- En el hotel
- Los medios de transporte ♻

HABLANDO DE GRAMÁTICA

- Double object pronouns ♻
- Talking about pending actions: Subjunctive with temporal conjunctions
- Talking about the future: The future tense

CULTURA

- Formas de viajar
- Viajeros con conciencia

Guinea Ecuatorial

Go to *WileyPLUS* to do the **Trivia** activities and find out how much you know about this country!

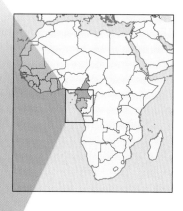

Roberto Soncin Gerometta / Lonely Planet Images / Getty Images

LEARNING OBJECTIVES

By the end of this section you will be able to:

- Discuss issues related to new technologies
- Talk about the use of new technologies in Spanish-speaking countries
- State what you and others have done and what has happened
- Describe the result of certain processes
- Convey different aspects of a narration

Una imagen vale más que mil palabras

¿Qué está haciendo esta chica?

En Chile hay 20 millones de usuarios de móvil, pero solo 3,5 millones que tienen teléfonos en su casa. ¿Por qué crees que ocurre esto?

¿Tienes un teléfono en casa o solo un móvil?

UNA PERSPECTIVA

Courtesy of Juan Hernando Vázquez

Hernando

Todos estamos conectados

Diferente

"Cuando viajo fuera de Estados Unidos, tengo que mantener la comunicación con mi familia y mi trabajo. Si no tengo mi computadora portátil, tengo que buscar cibercafés para usar el Internet y revisar mi *e-mail*. Ahora hay menos cibercafés porque hay *wifi* por todos lados, pero todavía se encuentran y son importantes en países como Guinea Ecuatorial. En cambio, no es fácil encontrar cibercafés en Estados Unidos".

AP Photo/Rebecca Blackwell

▲ *Un ciudadano de Guinea Ecuatorial hablando por teléfono móvil.*

Igual

"En mis viajes he visto[1] que todo el mundo está conectado. Muchas personas tienen computadoras, teléfonos inteligentes o móviles. Aun[2] en Guinea Ecuatorial, que es un país muy pobre, más del 60% de sus habitantes son usuarios de móvil. Muchos guineanos que viven en España se comunican por Internet con sus compatriotas. ¡Todo el mundo está conectado!".

 ¿Qué piensas tú?

1. ¿Por qué tenemos pocos cibercafés en Estados Unidos? ¿Por qué hay menos cibercafés en Europa y América Latina?
2. ¿Te sorprende que todo el mundo esté conectado? Explica por qué.

[1]**he visto:** I have seen   [2]**aun:** even

LA PURA VERDAD I   Viaje a Europa

Abel es un estudiante de historia que estudió español en Estados Unidos. Esta es su primera visita a Europa.

1.

> Tengo que cargar la batería.

2.

> ¿Me prestas tu computadora? La mía está en casa cargándose.

3.

> Los resultados de mi examen están en línea. Aquí tienen wifi gratis.

4.

> Nombre del usuario: arbravo33
> Contraseña: "¿Soy guapo?_Si³"¿¿Error??

5.

> Acuérdate de que el teclado de mi portátil es diferente al tuyo.

6.

© John Wiley & Sons, Inc.

11.1-01 ¡Más obstáculos! Escucha la siguiente la narración sobre los problemas de Abel. Decide si las siguientes oraciones son ciertas o falsas. Si son falsas, explica por qué.

	C	F
1. Abel no puede entrar al sitio web porque la computadora no funciona.	☐	☐
2. Abel no puede entrar al sitio web porque la batería no está cargada.	☐	☐
3. Abel puede entrar al sitio web pero olvidó su número de estudiante.	☐	☐

³Note that written accents are not used in e-mail or website addresses and passwords.

◔ PALABRA POR PALABRA

La tecnología

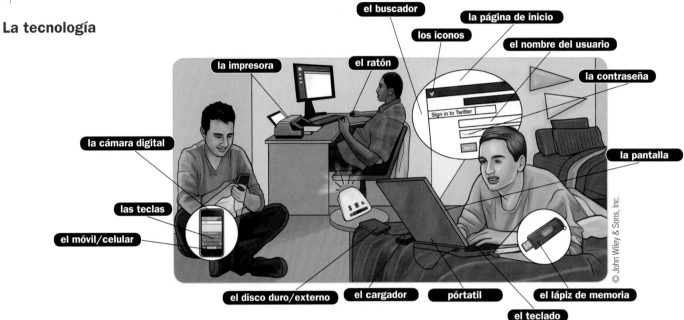

el buscador
la página de inicio
los iconos
el nombre del usuario
la impresora
el ratón
la contraseña
la cámara digital
la pantalla
las teclas
el móvil/celular
el disco duro/externo
el cargador
pórtatil
el lápiz de memoria
el teclado

© John Wiley & Sons, Inc.

Para hablar de tecnología

abrir una cuenta	*to set up an account*
adjuntar un archivo	*to attach a file*
apagar la computadora	*to turn off the computer*
descargar programas	*to download programs*
borrar lo que no quieres	*to delete what you don't want*
buscar una dirección de Internet	*to search for a URL*
cargar la batería	*to charge the battery*
chatear en línea	*to chat online*
colgar/poner videos en Internet	*to post videos on the Internet*
encender la computadora	*to turn on the computer*
enchufar la impresora	*to plug in the printer*
entrar a un sitio web	*to log in*
enviar mensajes electrónicos	*to send e-mails*
funcionar (la computadora, el aparato)	*to work (a computer, a device)*
grabar música	*to record music*
guardar los cambios	*to save changes*
imprimir documentos	*to print documents*
meter (el lápiz, el disco)	*to put in (the pen drive, the CD/DVD)*
navegar en la red	*to browse the net*
oprimir una tecla	*to press a key*
subir/cargar canciones	*to upload songs*
esperar que los aparatos funcionen	*to hope that devices work*

Cognados: chatear, conectar(se), (des)activar, textear

archivo (adjunto)	*(attached) document*	el reproductor (de audio/video/música/DVD)	*(audio/video/music/DVD) player*
el cable	*wire*	red social	*social*
carpetas	*folders*		

Cognados: el adaptador, la batería, el blog, el celular, la conexión
el documento, el *e-mail*, el monitor, el sitio web, la tableta, el virus, el wifi

¿Qué textean los hispanohablantes?

David, <u>tq</u> (te quiero)	*David, I love you.*
<u>A2</u> (adiós)	*Goodbye.*
<u>Pq</u> (porque) no tengo $	*Because I don't have any money.*
Chatea conmigo, <u>xfa</u> (por favor)	*Chat with me, please.*
<u>Q acs?</u> (¿Qué haces?)	*What are you doing?*

11.1-02 ¿De qué hablamos?

Paso 1: Lean las definiciones y busquen la palabra correspondiente en la sección **Palabra por palabra.**

MODELO: Es un dispositivo[4] que transmite corriente eléctrica a una batería o pila.
→ *el cargador*

1. Es un directorio para clasificar o guardar los documentos en una computadora.
2. Es un aparato que sirve para contestar llamadas telefónicas y grabar mensajes de voz cuando una persona no puede contestar el teléfono.
3. Es una combinación de letras, números o caracteres secretos que controlan el acceso a un recurso tecnológico.
4. Es una máquina que está conectada a la computadora y que sirve para imprimir documentos.
5. Es un dispositivo que guarda, organiza y reproduce archivos de audio.
6. Es el componente de la computadora que guarda todos los programas y los archivos.

Paso 2: Ahora, elijan tres palabras de la sección **Palabra por palabra** y escriban tres definiciones para leerlas a la clase. ¡Atención! Recuerden que para definir siempre usamos el verbo *ser.*

MODELO: *Es un/a... (que)...*

11.1-03 ¿Con qué frecuencia usas estas tecnologías? Comenten con qué frecuencia hacen lo siguiente:

MODELO: cargar la batería de la computadora
Estudiante 1: *¿Con qué frecuencia <u>cargas</u> la batería de la computadora?*
Estudiante 2: *Siempre tengo la batería cargándose porque siempre uso la computadora en casa y siempre está enchufada.*
Estudiante 1: *Yo también la cargo siempre que puedo.*

1. mandar archivos adjuntos
2. descargar música o archivos de audio de Internet
3. chatear con amigos
4. enviar mensajes electrónicos
5. comunicarse con la familia por videoconferencia
6. imprimir documentos en casa
7. colgar videos en internet
8. publicar entradas en blogs o foros de internet

siempre
(muy) frecuentemente
(casi) todos los días
a veces
de vez en cuando
casi nunca
nunca

[4]dispositivo: device

11.1-04 ¿Qué haces si...?

Paso 1: ¿Qué haces cuando la tecnología no funciona? ¿Qué otros recursos utilizas? Piensa qué haces cuando estás en una de estas situaciones.

a. Estabas escribiendo una redacción para tu clase de español, pero no guardaste los cambios y borraste todo por error.

b. Estás en tu casa y vas a imprimir una redacción para entregar en tu clase de español al día siguiente, pero se va la luz[5].

c. Estás solo en la calle y tienes que comunicarte con un amigo, pero tu teléfono no tiene batería.

d. Vas a dar una presentación de PowerPoint en clase y tu lápiz de memoria donde tienes el archivo no funciona.

e. Quieres mandarle un video a un amigo, pero el archivo es muy grande y no puedes mandarlo por *e-mail*.

f. Es la mitad del trimestre y tu computadora deja de funcionar. La llevas a la tienda y te dicen que es muy vieja y ya no pueden repararla.

Paso 2: En grupos, comenten sus respuestas. ¿Coincides con tus compañeros? ¿Alguna vez estuvieron en una situación problemática porque no funcionó la tecnología? ¿Dependen demasiado de la tecnología?

11.1-05 ¿Cuál es más necesario?

Paso 1: Con un/a compañero/a, considera los siguientes aparatos y avances informáticos. Decidan cuál es el más necesario y ordenen la lista con números del 1 (más necesario) al 10 (menos necesario).

_____ a. el contestador

_____ b. la impresora

_____ c. el adaptador

_____ d. el internet

_____ e. el *wifi*

_____ f. el reproductor de audio

_____ g. el teléfono inteligente

_____ h. el lápiz de memoria

_____ i. la computadora portátil

_____ j. las tabletas

Paso 2: Ahora, comparen sus respuestas con las de otros grupos de la clase. ¿Tienen todos la misma opinión? ¿Cuál está en el puesto número 1 para la mayoría de los grupos? ¿Y en el número 10?

[5] **se va la luz:** the power goes off

HABLANDO DE GRAMÁTICA I

1. Talking about the recent past: The present perfect tense

The Spanish present perfect[6] is roughly equivalent to the English present perfect. We use the present perfect to talk about a past event, which is still relevant, or has consequences, in the present situation.

WileyPLUS Go to *WileyPLUS* to review this grammar point with the help of the **Animated Grammar Tutorial** and the **Verb Conjugator.**

–¿Tienes tu computadora?
–Sí, pero no **he cargado** la batería.

–*Do you have your computer?*
–*Yes, but I haven't charged the battery.*

–¿Conoces este sistema operativo?
–Sí, lo **he usado** todo el tiempo desde que salió.

–*Are you familiar with this operating system?*
–*Yes, I have used it since it came out.*

–¿Está bien equipada tu universidad?
–Sí, en los últimos cinco años **han equipado** todos los salones de clase con la última tecnología.

–*Is your university well equipped?*
–*Yes, in the last five years it has equipped all classrooms with the latest technology.*

Form the present perfect with the present tense of **haber** + *the past participle*. In English, the past participle is the *-en* or *-ed* form of a verb (e.g., *I have eaten a lot*). In Spanish, the past participle is formed by dropping the infinitive ending and adding **-ado** (**-ar** verbs), or **-ido** (**-er** and **-ir** verbs).

	haber	past participle
(yo)	he	
(tú)	has	
(él, ella, usted)	ha	cargado
(nosotros/as)	hemos	encendido
(vosotros/as)	habéis	oprimido
(ellos, ellas, Uds.)	han	

The following verbs have irregular past participles:

abrir	**abierto**	morir	**muerto**
cubrir, descubrir	**cubierto, descubierto**	romper	**roto**
decir, contradecir	**dicho, contradicho**	poner	**puesto**
escribir	**escrito**	ver	**visto**
freír	**freído, frito**	volver, devolver	**vuelto, devuelto**
hacer, deshacer	**hecho, deshecho**	resolver	**resuelto**
imprimir	**imprimido, impreso**	satisfacer	**satisfecho**

Object and reflexive pronouns always precede the conjugated form of **haber**.

Le hemos comprado el último modelo de tableta.
Ya **te he enviado** el archivo.
No **la han instalado** correctamente.

We've bought <u>him</u> the last tablet model.
I have already sent <u>you</u> the file.
They haven't installed <u>it</u> correctly.

---

[6]In Spanish, the name for the present perfect tense is **pretérito perfecto.**

The following words usually accompany the present perfect since they make the action have a lasting effect until the present:

ya	*already*	**Ya** he comprado el teléfono que quería.
todavía, aún	*still*	**Todavía** no han podido reparar la computadora.
siempre	*always*	**Siempre** ha comprado los modelos de última generación.
nunca	*never*	**Nunca** he tenido interés por los aparatos electrónicos.

11.1-06 Las actividades de la clase

 Paso 1: ¿Qué ha pasado en la clase de español durante este trimestre/semestre? Indica cuál es el sujeto de cada oración.

MODELO: Has corregido nuestros exámenes.   →   *tú, profesor/a*

> yo
> usted (profesor/a)
> mi compañero/a
> nosotros los estudiantes
> mis compañeros y

1. Hemos aprendido a usar el teclado en español.
2. Ha asignado varios ejercicios de **Arroba** para hacer en casa.
3. Hemos entregado las tareas en línea por *WileyPLUS*.
4. Ha comparado sus respuestas conmigo.
5. He escrito varias redacciones.
6. Hemos tenido varios exámenes.
7. Han trabajado en grupo conmigo.

 Paso 2: Ahora, hagan una lista de por lo menos tres actividades más de la clase relacionadas con la tecnología.

MODELO: *Los estudiantes hemos impreso...*
           La profesora ha hecho varias presentaciones sobre...

Comenten su lista con el resto de la clase. Si juntan todas las listas, ¿cuántas actividades han mencionado en total?

11.1-07 ¿Qué hiciste y qué has hecho?

 Paso 1: Completa esta tabla con información sobre cosas que *hiciste* (o no) y que *has hecho* (o no) relacionadas con la tecnología.

MODELO: <u>*El año pasado imprimí* muchas tareas para mis clases, pero <u>*este año ya no he impreso*</u> tantas. La mayoría de las tareas las <u>*he entregado*</u> en línea.</u>

El año pasado...   Este año...
El mes pasado...   Este mes...
La semana pasada...   Esta semana...
Ayer por la mañana...   Esta mañana...

 Paso 2: Compara tus respuestas con las de un/a compañero/a. ¿Hay algo que *sí hicieron* los dos pero que después *no han hecho* más?

LA PURA VERDAD II **Presentación en español**

Leo es un estudiante de la Universidad Católica de Santiago de Chile. Va a dar una presentación en su clase de español.

1.

He terminado mi presentación y el archivo está en mi lápiz de memoria. ¡Fácil!

2.

La computadora está enchufada, está encendida… Ahora meto el lápiz… ¡Fácil!

3.

No puedo ver mi archivo. ¿Lo he metido bien? ¿Está roto? Voy a pedir ayuda…

4.

He esperado varios minutos y no veo el icono del lápiz de memoria. He revisado la compu. ¿He hecho algo mal?

5.

El problema es que es un poco complicado activar el lápiz de memoria. Va a tomar tiempo. ¿Has puesto el archivo en línea?

¡Sí!

6.

Pues ve a tu cuenta y así vas a poder abrir el archivo. Problema resuelto.

Lo sabía, fácil.

© John Wiley & Sons, Inc.

11.1-08 ¡Más problemas! Escucha los problemas de Leo. Decide cuál de las siguientes opciones describe mejor el problema.

1. ¿Cuál es el problema?
   a. No ha conectado la computadora al proyector.
   b. No ha dicho la palabra mágica *abracadabra*.
   c. No funciona el ratón.
2. ¿Qué ha pasado?
   a. Ha dicho *por favor*, pero no ha dicho *abracadabra*.
   b. Es posible que no haya electricidad.
   c. Ha cerrado su computadora.
3. ¿Cómo pudo continuar?
   a. Regresó la electricidad y continuó la presentación.
   b. Dio su presentación sin imágenes.
   c. La batería estaba cargada y mostró las imágenes en la pantalla de su computadora.

HABLANDO DE GRAMÁTICA II

2. Describing results: Participles used as adjectives

The past participle is a verbal adjective (i.e., it is an adjective derived from a verb) that expresses the result of a process:

–¿**Ha enchufado** la computadora?   –*Have you plugged in the computer?*
–Sí, ya está **enchufada** y **conectada**.   –*Yes, it is plugged in and connected.*

–¿**Has impreso** tu redacción?   –*Have you printed out your composition?*
–Sí, ya la tengo **impresa** y lista.   –*Yes, I have it printed and ready.*

When used as an adjective, the participle always agrees in gender and number with the noun it refers to. These are some common constructions with the participle as an adjective:

Noun + participle	Los archivos **protegidos** con contraseña son más seguros. Eso es un problema **resuelto**.
Estar + *participle*	Todos los archivos están **protegidos** con contraseña. El problema está ya **resuelto**.
Tener + *participle*	Tengo los archivos **protegidos** con una contraseña. Ya tenemos **resuelto** ese problema.

  11.1-09 ¿Qué problema ha tenido hoy Leo? Observa de nuevo la historia de **La pura verdad II** y combina las oraciones de la primera columna con la que corresponda de la segunda.

_____ 1. **He terminado** mi presentación.

_____ 2. **He enchufado** y **encendido** la computadora.

_____ 3. **He metido** el lápiz de memoria en el portal de conexión USB.

_____ 4. ¿**He hecho** algo mal?

_____ 5. Mientras tanto, algunos estudiantes ya **han llegado**.

_____ 6. No hay que preocuparse, porque he **puesto** mi archivo en línea.

a. Todo estaba **preparado** y ahora algo no funciona.

b. Están todos **sentados** en sus mesas.

c. Pero la luz del lápiz no está **encendida**.

d. **He entrado** en mi cuenta y ¡problema **resuelto**!

e. Está **guardada** en mi lápiz de memoria.

f. También está **conectada** al proyector.

  11.1-10 ¿Qué le pasó a Leo? Completa el siguiente párrafo con la forma correcta del participio de los verbos de la lista. Decide si debes usar el pretérito o el imperfecto.

encender	conectar	solucionar	preparar	guardar

Leo (tenía/tuvo)₁ que hacer una presentación para su clase y (quiso/quería)₂ tener todo _____₃ y _____₄ antes de la clase. El día de la presentación, cuando Leo (entraba/entró)₅ en el salón todavía no (había/hubo)₆ nadie. (Tenía/tuvo)₇ la presentación _____₈ en su lápiz de memoria. Primero (enchufaba/enchufó)₉ la computadora, después la (encendía/encendió)₁₀ y por último (metía/metió)₁₁ el lápiz en el puerto USB. Sin embargo, la luz del lápiz no (estaba/estuvo)₁₂ _____₁₃. Los estudiantes y la profesora (llegaban/llegaron)₁₄. Entonces Leo (llamaba/llamó)₁₅ al técnico y le (ayudaba/ayudó)₁₆. Leo (encontró/encontraba)₁₇ una copia del archivo en línea. Así que de un momento a otro tuvo todo _____₁₈.

♻ Preterit vs. Imperfect

You now know three different past tenses to talk about the past in Spanish: the present perfect, the preterit, and the imperfect. As you know, the preterit and the imperfect are usually used together to present actions and descriptions in a narration. Do you remember when each one is used? Go back to Chapter 8 to review the different ... these two verb ...s.

OTRA PERSPECTIVA

Courtesy Alfida Deaza

Alfi

¡Con o sin tecnología!

Diferente

"Soy estudiante de maestría en la República Dominicana. Tengo un poco de experiencia como maestra. He enseñado en una zona rural y sin tecnología, y en la ciudad, con tecnología. Ahora estoy en Estados Unidos continuando mis estudios. Veo que los profesores aquí son hábiles con todo tipo de tecnología, pero si algún equipo electrónico falla[7], es difícil para algunos continuar la clase. Para mí, no hay problema. Yo continúo felizmente con mi tiza".

Igual

"En la República Dominicana también estamos conectados al internet. Usamos las computadoras y el internet para mostrar videos, para llamar por Skype, para chatear, etc. También tenemos móviles y teléfonos inteligentes".

Explícale a Alfi

1. ¿Dependemos demasiado como sociedad de la tecnología? ¿Dependes tú mucho de la tecnología?
2. ¿Qué tipos de tecnología se usan en tus clases?
3. ¿Qué haces cuando no hay electricidad o internet? ¿Qué haces si se te pierde el móvil?

MANOS A LA OBRA

11.1-11 ¿Qué has hecho últimamente?

Paso 1: Completa la primera columna con información verdadera sobre ti.

MODELO: hacer un curso muy útil   →   <u>He hecho</u> *un curso de programación.*

	Yo	El/La compañero/a...
1. hacer un curso muy útil		
2. reparar un aparato electrónico		
3. colgar un video en internet sobre…		
4. romper algo muy valioso		
5. ver una película extranjera		
6. resolver una situación difícil o un problema		

Paso 2: Levántate y haz preguntas a tus compañeros para averiguar si alguien ha hecho algo similar. Escribe el nombre del/de la compañero/a que conteste afirmativamente.

MODELO: Estudiante 1:   *¿Has tomado un curso de programación?*
            Estudiante 2:   *No, no he tomado un curso de programación, pero he tomado un curso de _____ que me ha gustado mucho.*

Paso 3: ¿Qué estudiante tiene un mayor número de compañeros en la lista? ¿Quién ha tenido experiencias similares a las tuyas?

MODELO: *Samuel y yo hemos tomado un curso de...*

[7]**fallar:** to fail

11.1-12 Lo que he hecho en mi vida

Paso 1: Escribe en un papel tres oraciones describiendo cosas que has hecho (y no has hecho). Piensa en actividades poco comunes. Dos de las oraciones deben ser ciertas y una falsa.

MODELO: *He viajado a Tailandia.*
He saltado desde un avión con paracaídas[8].
He ganado una computadora portátil en una rifa[9].

Paso 2: En grupos de cuatro personas, túrnense para leer sus oraciones. Los otros miembros del grupo deben hacer preguntas sobre esa experiencia. La persona que contesta tiene que inventar detalles para la experiencia falsa.

MODELO: *¿Cuándo viajaste a Tailandia? ¿Con quién fuiste?*

Paso 3: El grupo vota para adivinar cuáles de las experiencias son falsas y cada persona revela cuál es falsa y cuáles no lo son.

11.1-13 Hablando sobre tecnología

Paso 1: Hablen sobre las ventajas y desventajas de usar estos aparatos. Después, contesta estas preguntas: ¿Puedes sobrevivir sin estos aparatos tecnológicos? ¿Sí? ¿No? ¿Por qué?

	Ventaja	Desventaja
MODELO: el GPS:	*indica el camino*	*distrae a la gente*
1. la tableta:	_____	_____
2. el teléfono inteligente:	_____	_____
3. la red *wifi*:	_____	_____
4. la computadora pórtatil:	_____	_____

Paso 2: Camina por la clase y habla con tus compañeros sobre el último aparato tecnológico que has usado recientemente o en el pasado. Usa la lista para hacer preguntas.

redes sociales	un teléfono inteligente	ser víctima de un virus informático
el lápiz de memoria	un libro electrónico	escribir un blog
una tableta	tener un virus	descargar música gratis

MODELO: Estudiante 1: *¿Qué has usado recientemente?*
Estudiante 2: *He usado una tableta.*
Estudiante 1: *¿Has usado cámaras digitales?*
Estudiante 2: *Sí, siempre las uso./No, saco fotos con el teléfono.*

Paso 3: ¿Conoces bien a tus compañeros? Escribe una oración de algo que has hecho recientemente (puede ser verdad o mentira) y que se relacione con la tecnología. Tu profesor/a va a pedirles a algunos que lean sus oraciones delante de la clase. La clase debe adivinar si es verdad o mentira.

MODELO: Voluntario: *He usado Skype esta mañana para hablar con mi familia (porque la última vez que hablé con ellos fue el año pasado).*
Clase: *¡Es verdad! Él ha hablado varias veces de usar Skype para hablar con su familia. / ¡No, no es verdad! No has hablado con tu familia.*
Voluntario: *Sí, he hablado con mi familia.*
No, no he hablado con mi familia.

---

[8]**paracaídas:** parachute [9]**rifa:** raffle

11.1-14 Presta atención: Un estudiante de intercambio Juan Tomás es guineano y ahora estudia en la Universidad de Valladolid, en España, como estudiante de intercambio. Escucha con atención para saber qué opina Juan Tomás de su nueva universidad.

WileyPLUS Go to *WileyPLUS* and listen to **Presta atención.**

1. ¿A qué tipo de clases está acostumbrado Juan Tomás?
   a. a clases que se enseñan en un salón de clase
   b. a clases a distancia
   c. a clases de formato híbrido
2. ¿A qué clase asiste Juan Tomás?
   a. a una clase de español sobre ingeniería/para ingenieros
   b. a una clase de inglés enfocado en ingeniería
   c. a una clase de ingeniería a distancia
3. ¿Por qué Juan Tomás dice que a veces asiste a clase en pijama?
   a. Porque el formato del curso le permite asistir a clase desde su casa.
   b. Porque es un estudiante que trabaja como tutor corrigiendo exámenes.
   c. Porque su clase es a las ocho y no tiene mucho tiempo para cambiarse de ropa.
4. ¿Por qué la mochila de Juan Tomás no pesa mucho ahora?
   a. Porque no asiste a muchas clases.
   b. Porque tiene libros electrónicos.
   c. Porque no lleva su computadora.
5. ¿Para qué usa Luis Miguel la tableta?
   a. para estudiar, porque toma clases en línea
   b. para comprar libros y otros productos
   c. para estudiar, divertirse y estar en contacto con sus amigos

11.1-15 Por escrito: Resumir información Hazle a un/a compañero/a estas preguntas y toma notas de sus respuestas. Después, escribe un resumen con la información que obtuviste y agrega una conclusión acerca de la posición de tu compañero/a con respecto a la tecnología: ¿está a favor o en contra?

- ¿Qué es una clase híbrida?
- ¿Cómo se diferencia una clase híbrida de una clase tradicional?
- ¿Has tenido oportunidad de tomar clases en línea o híbridas?
- ¿Cuánto tiempo has pasado hoy en el internet?
- ¿Qué has aprendido recientemente sobre la tecnología?
- ¿Consideras importante el internet para hacer tus tareas?

¡OJO!

Summarizing
In our daily lives, we share information we hear or see by summarizing. A good summary presents the main ideas in an organized and coherent manner by avoiding repetition or unimportant facts.

 # PONTE EN MI LUGAR

Estrategias para conversar

There are a few expressions that you can use *to complain about something*:

Quisiera hablar con usted/su supervisor sobre...	*I would like to talk with you/your supervisor about. . .*
Tengo una queja.	*I have a complaint.*

To acknowledge that you are doing your job:

Lo siento, pero hice lo que me pidió.	*I am sorry, but I did what you asked for.*
Solamente identifiqué el problema.	*I only identified the problem.*

To acknowledge that you understand the problem, but cannot help him:

Comprendo su frustración, pero no puedo ayudarlo.	*I understand your frustration, but I cannot help you.*
Lo siento, pero no puedo devolverle el dinero.	*Sorry, but I cannot give you back your money.*

Un negocio de reparaciones Formen parejas. Uno de ustedes usa la computadora todos los días para estudiar y para trabajar. Esta mañana la computadora no se ha encendido y hay que llevarla a una tienda de reparaciones. Decidan quién va a ser el empleado de la tienda y quién será el cliente con la computadora con problemas. Usen las expresiones de las **Estrategias para conversar**.

Cliente: Has descubierto un problema técnico en tu computadora. Has intentando reparar la computadora por tu cuenta, pero la pantalla sigue negra y no hay manera de repararla. La has llevado a una tienda de reparaciones, pero el resultado es que te han hecho pagar una cantidad de dinero para saber cuál es el problema de la computadora; además, te han hecho comprar una pieza nueva en otro negocio, pero tu computadora todavía no funciona. Habla con el empleado:

a. Cuando te salude el/la empleado/a, cuéntale que has pagado mucho dinero por la pieza que él o ella te recomendó.
b. El/La empleado/a te ha cobrado dinero por un diagnóstico que no tiene solución, así que exígele que te devuelva el dinero que has pagado por el diagnóstico.
c. Dile que tu computadora ahora funciona porque otra persona la ha arreglado sin necesidad de usar esa pieza tan cara que has comprado.
d. Insiste en que quieres que te devuelva tu dinero.

Empleado/a: Empieza la conversación saludando al cliente amablemente y diciéndole que te agrada verlo/a de nuevo. En la conversación…

a. Descríbele el diagnóstico que diste y la pieza que pediste.
b. Dile al cliente que primero tuviste que hacer un diagnóstico. Si el problema no tiene solución, no es tu culpa.
c. No puedes devolverle el dinero al cliente porque no compró la pieza en tu tienda y porque pasaste tres horas investigando el problema de la computadora.

Al final, lleguen a algún tipo de solución aceptable para los dos.

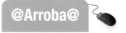

WileyPLUS Go to *WileyPLUS* to find more **Arroba** activities.

Personajes de Guinea Ecuatorial Busca en tu buscador favorito información sobre Donato Ndongo o Mefe para contestar estas preguntas: ¿Quién es? ¿Dónde vive? ¿En qué trabaja? ¿Por qué es importante en el mundo hispano? ¿Cómo se llaman algunas de sus obras? Comenta con tus compañeros la información que encuentres.

ASÍ ES LA VIDA

Adivina, adivinador

Llevo secretos a voces,
corriendo por esos mundos
y sin que nadie los oiga
los doy en unos segundos.
¿Quién soy?

Chiste

–¿Por qué se pone la computadora al lado de la ventana?
–Para tener Windows.

ENTÉRATE

Estrategias para leer

Spanish affixes: Learning new vocabulary Affixes are parts of words used to form new words. They can be added at the beginning of a word (as prefixes: **anti**natural) or at the end of the word (as suffixes: **libre**ría). The meaning or the category of words can change by adding an affix, for example:

- An adjective can become an adverb by adding **-mente** (*-ly*) at the end of the word: **suave > suavemente; veloz > velozmente**
- An adjective can become a noun by adding **-idad: sincero > sinceridad**
- An adverb can become a verb: **lejos> a-lej-ar**
- A noun can become a verb by adding **-ar, -er, -ir: formato > formatear**
- A verb can become a noun by adding **-ción: presentar > presentación**

These are some Spanish prefixes that will help you expand your vocabulary. Can you guess the meaning of these words?

a-, an- (*opposite/toward/addition*): analfabeto, adentro, agrupar

ante- (*before*): anteponer

anti- (*against*): antiaéreo, antivirus

contra- (*opposite*): contradecir

des- (*no*): desleal, desobedecer, desigual

extra- (*more than*): extraordinario

in-, im-, i- (*no*): ilegal, incierto, imposible

entre-, inter- (*between, reciprocity*): interurbano, internacional

pos-, post- (*later*): posponer

super-, sobre-, supra- (*superior*): sobrenatural, supranacional

sub- (*inferiority, low, under*): subsuelo, subterráneo

Antes de leer

1. La conexión virtual

1. ¿Qué opinas sobre el internet como medio social?
2. ¿Crees que todo el mundo usa el internet?
3. ¿Cuántas redes sociales conoces? ¿Las usas todas?
4. ¿Qué opinas sobre la amistad sin fronteras?

2. Predicciones sobre el texto

1. Lee el título y el subtítulo del texto. ¿Puedes predecir qué tema va a tratar? ¿Puedes adivinar la opinión de la autora?
2. ¿Qué te indica la foto? ¿Se relaciona la foto con el subtítulo de la lectura?
3. ¿Cómo se relaciona la foto con las dos primeras oraciones de la lectura?

Courtesy of María Belén Pardo Ballester

REDES SOCIALES: Ni son todos los que están, ni están todos los que son

Decía el filósofo griego Aristóteles que el ser humano no puede vivir solo y, si lo hace, acaba convirtiéndose en un dios o en una bestia. El deseo de vivir en sociedad es tan antiguo como la humanidad, aunque las formas han variado a través de la historia. Por eso, gracias al internet, el número de redes sociales ha crecido rápidamente en poco más de una década. Muchas personas se conectan con sus amigos y han hecho nuevas amistades, de manera virtual, creando así comunidades con intereses similares que comparten contenidos e interactúan.

Claro que, como ocurre con todos los cambios, mientras una importante parte del mundo felizmente se ha conectado, hay quien no quiere perder el contacto con el mundo tangible que lo rodea. ¿Y si todo ese universo de miradas que se cruzan y paseos que llevan a un encuentro casual y que han sido tradicionalmente el alimento del amor y la amistad, se pierden para siempre?

Internet user, web surfer
In fact

Afortunadamente, detrás de las pantallas hay personas, y aunque algunos mensajes de los **cibernautas** parecen las palabras de un robot, hay cosas que no cambian. Por ejemplo, lo que nos distingue como seres humanos es el instinto sociable; y eso no cambia en las comunidades virtuales. **De hecho**, la necesidad de asociarnos a grupos con intereses comunes es una de las razones del éxito de las redes sociales. Existen agrupaciones de educadores, médicos, madres de bebés, seguidores de un equipo de fútbol, estudiantes… El nombre de algunos sitios tales como *abuelos en la red.net*, *tuenti.com*… es suficiente para no entrar en ellos si "no estamos en la edad" o desconocemos sus "códigos lingüísticos".

A decir verdad, las relaciones que se crean en el ciberespacio reflejan el mundo real. Las personas que disfrutan de una vida social activa en la calle también es posible que sean muy sociables en el mundo virtual. Pero como me comenta un miembro de Twitter, "que tengas todo el mundo a tu disposición no significa que quieras o puedas conectarte con todo el mundo". De hecho, según datos de Facebook —la mayor de las redes sociales—, sus miembros establecen relaciones con un **promedio** de 120 contactos; sin embargo, realmente solo interactúan con unas siete o diez personas.

average

Lo que sí ha cambiado en la sociedad del siglo XXI es nuestro sistema de valores: el culto a los comportamientos permisivos, a la imagen, al consumismo, a la cultura como mercancía… son un hecho; pero también a la generosidad de compartir experiencias e ideas.

literacy

Conviene tener presente que para participar en la comunidad virtual se requiere un mínimo de **alfabetización** e infraestructura informática. Y eso solo incluye a una pequeña parte del planeta. Únicamente el 39% de la población mundial tiene acceso a internet. El resto no lo hace, bien porque no puede o porque no quiere.

El internet es un vehículo de comunicación muy útil, pero no el único. De modo que, lo mismo que los aviones no han erradicado a las bicicletas ni mucho menos a los pies, un correo electrónico siempre será una carta, aunque llegue antes.

Reproducido y adaptado de la revista Punto y Coma con permiso de Efe S.L.

Después de leer

1. En el texto

1. Cambiando los sufijos, ¿qué otras palabras se relacionarían con **sociedad, humanidad, amistad, comportamiento, permisivo, generosidad, mundial**?
2. En el texto hay por lo menos diez sufijos. ¿Cuántos puedes encontrar?

2. ¿Entendiste?

1. El texto nos indica que…
   a. ahora la gente prefiere relacionarse virtualmente.
   b. la autora está a favor de la tecnología porque las personas han hecho muchas amistades en redes sociales como Twitter y Facebook.
   c. la tecnología ha cambiado la vida social de algunas personas, pero las personas siempre han vivido en sociedad sin necesidad de la tecnología.
2. ¿Por qué la gente se asocia a diferentes grupos virtuales?
   a. Porque en esos grupos están sus amigos o nuevos amigos y pueden conseguir trabajo.
   b. Porque todo el mundo lo hace y la población mundial cambia a lo largo de la historia.
   c. Porque tienen intereses comunes y quieren aprender algo sobre un tema y conocer gente nueva.
3. Un usuario de una red social afirmó que…
   a. puedes conocer a mucha gente en el mundo virtual, pero no tienes contacto con todos.
   b. si conoces a mucha gente en Facebook o Twitter, más vas a hablar diariamente con ellos.
   c. con el internet conocemos gente nueva y por tanto siempre interactuamos con ellos.

4. Cuando la autora introduce el avión, la bicicleta, la carta y el correo electrónico…
   a. nos indica que los avances tecnológicos no eliminan otros medios de comunicación tradicionales.
   b. quiere convencer al público de que el internet es un avance tecnológico que la mayoría de la población mundial usa diariamente para comunicarse.
   c. nos aclara que la población mundial sigue avanzado y ya no se aprecia el pasado.

 # EN TU PROPIAS PALABRAS

Estrategias para escribir

Reviewing the language of your written work After writing your essay, reread what you have written and make sure you have included the following:

1. New learned vocabulary and synonyms have been used to avoid repeated words.
2. New words with affixes have been used.
3. There are no spelling and agreement (gender and number) mistakes between nouns and their accompanying words (adjectives, articles, etc.)
4. If you translated from English into Spanish complex sentences, rewrite them and simplify them using structures you already know.
5. Direct and indirect object pronouns have been used to avoid repetition.
6. All sentences have conjugated verbs and verb forms are correct (i.e., there is subject-verb agreement).
7. The essay is not a list of sentences but a few organized and coherent paragraphs.

Las redes sociales Imagínate que te ha pasado algo usando una red social y lo vas a comentar en tu blog. Tu redacción debe centrarse en cómo se usa el internet para participar en las redes sociales. ¿Qué piensas sobre este tema? ¿Cuáles son las ventajas y cuáles las desventajas? En tu redacción, incluye una introducción en la que presentes tu opinión, un desarrollo y una conclusión. Considera las siguientes preguntas como guía. Después, repasa las **Estrategias para escribir**.

I. Introducción
- ¿Qué son las redes sociales?
- ¿Cuál es la tendencia entre los jóvenes?
- ¿Cuál es tu opinión sobre el tema?

II. Cuerpo
- ¿Por qué es importante usar las redes sociales virtuales?
- Incluye un ejemplo específico de alguna de tus experiencias.
- ¿En qué se diferencia tu opinión de la opinión de tus padres?
- ¿Podrías sobrevivir sin usar las redes sociales?

III. Conclusión
- ¿Por qué te gustan o disgustan las redes sociales?
- ¿Qué conclusión podrías sacar de todo lo que has comentado?

AUTOPRUEBA

VOCABULARIO

I. ¿De qué se trata? Relaciona estas palabras con su significado.

1. guardar 3. pantalla 5. carpeta
2. chatear 4. teclado 6. red social

_____ a. Es una estructura social compuesta de personas conectadas por diferentes tipos de relaciones, como la amistad.

_____ b. Es la parte de la computadora que tiene teclas y se usa para escribir.

_____ c. Es la acción de comunicarse mediante mensajes electrónicos instantáneos.

_____ d. Es la parte plana de un monitor que retransmite visualmente la información.

_____ e. Es el acto de poner los documentos importantes en un lugar apropiado.

_____ f. Es un lugar donde ponemos y organizamos los archivos de una computadora.

II. ¡Mi teléfono no funciona! Ana llama a su hermano para felicitarlo por su cumpleaños, pero tiene un problema cuando está hablando con él. Completa el siguiente texto con las palabras de la lista para saber más sobre el problema de Ana. ¡Ojo! Hay dos palabras que no tienes que usar.

> carpeta enchufar móvil pantalla batería
> roto/a cubierto/a encender chatear descargar

Hace unos días estaba hablando con mi hermano por el
_____ cuando de repente la _____ dejó
de funcionar y la _____ se puso negra. Me enfadé
mucho, porque era su cumpleaños y hacía tiempo que no
hablaba con él. Así que entré a casa y quise _____
rápidamente el teléfono para volver a llamarlo, pero
estaba _____ porque no lo podía _____.
Así que llamé a mi hermano desde el teléfono de casa y le
expliqué lo que me pasó. Por suerte, él dijo que le gusta
_____ con sus amigos, y que también le gusta
_____ música, *podcasts* y videos en su nuevo
teléfono inteligente y que me regalaba su teléfono viejo.

GRAMÁTICA

I. ¡A llamar por Skype! Laura está en Estados Unidos y se quiere comunicar por Skype con sus padres, que están en España. Cambia lo que *hay que hacer* a lo que *ha hecho*.

MODELO: Hay que abrir una cuenta.
   → *Ya he abierto una cuenta.*

1. Ellos tienen que encender la computadora.
2. Laura tiene que decirles que se compren una cámara digital.
3. Laura y sus padres tienen que ponerse de acuerdo para llamar a una hora específica.
4. Laura tiene que calcular la diferencia de hora entre España y Estados Unidos.
5. Sus padres tienen que oprimir la tecla de "video" para que Laura pueda verlos.

II. Una lista Dos amigas se van de vacaciones a Puerto Rico. Una le pregunta a la otra lo que ya está hecho. Responde a sus preguntas con el participio del verbo.

MODELO: ¿Hiciste las maletas?
   → *Ya están hechas.*

1. ¿Hiciste la reserva para el tour a Vieques?
2. ¿Resolviste el problema de la tarjeta de crédito?
3. ¿Escribiste la dirección del lugar adonde vamos?
4. ¿Cancelaste el viaje a Ponce?
5. ¿Imprimiste las tarjetas de embarque[10] del avión?

CULTURA

¿Qué has aprendido en esta sección? Contesta **Cierto (C)** o **Falso (F)**. Si las oraciones son falsas, corrígelas.

	C	F
1. Hay conexiones de internet incluso en los países poco desarrollados.	☐	☐
2. No hay ningún país de habla hispana en Asia ni en África.	☐	☐
3. La capital de Guinea Ecuatorial es Nairobi.	☐	☐
4. Los teclados son iguales en todo el mundo.	☐	☐
5. Las redes sociales ayudan a las personas a mantenerse en contacto.	☐	☐

REDACCIÓN

Cuéntale a un/a amigo/a el último problema tecnológico que tuviste. Puede ser un problema con tu celular, con tu computadora o con una contraseña. ¿Qué pasó? ¿Qué problemas causó? ¿Cómo resolviste el problema al final?

EN RESUMIDAS CUENTAS, AHORA PUEDO...

☐ hablar de asuntos relacionados con las nuevas tecnologías.

☐ comparar el uso de las nuevas tecnologías en países hispanohablantes.

☐ hablar de qué ha ocurrido recientemente.

☐ describir el resultado de algunos procesos.

☐ expresar diferentes aspectos en una narración.

[10]tarjeta de embarque: boarding pass

🔊 VOCABULARIO ESENCIAL

Sustantivos

el archivo (adjunto)	*(attached) file*
el buscador	*browser*
el cable	*wire*
el cargador	*charger*
la carpeta	*folder*
la computadora (portátil)	*(laptop) computer*
el contestador	*answering machine*
la contraseña	*password*
el disco duro/externo	*hard drive*
la impresora	*printer*
el lápiz de memoria	*(USB) flash/pen drive*
el móvil/celular	*cell phone*
el nombre del usuario	*username*
la página de inicio	*home page*
la pantalla	*screen*
el ratón	*mouse*
las redes sociales	*social networks*
el reproductor (de audio/video/música/DVD)	*(audio/video/music/DVD) player*
la tecla	*key*
el teclado	*keyboard*

Cognados: el adaptador, la batería, el blog, la cámara digital, la conexión, el *e-mail*, el documento, el icono, el monitor, el sitio web, la tableta, la tecnología, el virus, el *wifi*

Adjectives and participles

abierto/a	*open, opened*
contradicho	*contradicted*
cubierto/a	*covered*
descubierto/a	*discovered*
deshecho/a	*undone*
devuelto/a	*returned (an object)*
dicho/a	*said, told*
encendido/a	*(turned) on*
escrito/a	*written*
freído/frito	*fried*
hecho/a	*done*
imprimido/a, impreso/a	*printed*
muerto	*died*
puesto/a	*put, placed*

resuelto/a	*solved*
roto/a	*broken*
satisfecho/a	*satisfied*
visto/a	*seen*
vuelto	*returned (a person)*

Verbos

abrir una cuenta	*to set up an account*
adjuntar un archivo	*to attach a file*
apagar la computadora	*to turn off the computer*
borrar lo que no quieren	*to delete what they don't want*
buscar una dirección de internet	*to search for a URL*
cargar la batería	*to charge the battery*
chatear en línea	*to chat online*
colgar/poner videos en Internet	*to post videos on the internet*
descargar programas	*to download programs*
funcionar (la computadora, el aparato)	*to work (a computer, a device)*
encender la computadora	*to turn on the computer*
enchufar la impresora	*to plug in the printer*
entrar a un sitio web	*to log in*
enviar mensajes electrónicos	*to send e-mails*
grabar música	*to record music*
guardar los cambios	*to save changes*
imprimir documentos	*to print documents*
meter (el lápiz, el disco)	*to put in (the pen drive, the CD/DVD)*
navegar	*to browse*
navegar en la red	*to browse the net*
oprimir una tecla	*to press a key*
subir/cargar canciones	*to upload songs*
esperar que los aparatos funcionen	*to hope that devices work*

Cognados: chatear, conectar(se), (des)activar, textear

Expresiones

aún	*still*
todavía	*still*
ya	*already*

LEARNING OBJECTIVES

By the end of this section you will be able to:

- Make arrangements for a trip
- Practice using double object pronouns to avoid repetition
- Talk about pending actions
- Talk about events in the future
- Get familiar with different situations when traveling

Una imagen vale más que mil palabras...

© Steve Lupton/Corbis

¿Qué diferencias hay entre el dólar y el euro?

¿Cuál es la ventaja de tener billetes[1] de diferentes tamaños?

¿Recuerdas a cuánto está el cambio entre el dólar estadounidense y el euro?

UNA PERSPECTIVA

Courtesy of Claire Ihlendorf

Claire

El viaje es un poco más caro

Diferente

"El año pasado, mi hermano y yo viajamos juntos a varios países. Cuando llegamos al aeropuerto de Buenos Aires, en Argentina, hicimos cola[2] en inmigración, como todos los pasajeros, pero cuando llegamos, nos dijeron que los estadounidenses teníamos que ir a otra ventanilla[3] primero. Los otros pasajeros pasaban sin problemas, pero nosotros no. Fuimos a la otra ventanilla y nos dijeron que teníamos que pagar $131 por persona para entrar al país. '¿Por qué nosotros tenemos que pagar y ellos no?', preguntamos. Nos contestaron con una palabra: 'Reciprocidad'. ¿Qué es reciprocidad?".

Igual

"Nosotros no sabíamos que el gobierno de Estados Unidos les cobra a los argentinos (y no solo a los argentinos) para obtener una visa para entrar a Estados Unidos. Así que el gobierno argentino, al igual que el de otros países, como Chile, instituyó la ley de reciprocidad".

¿Qué piensas tú?

1. ¿Crees que la reciprocidad es justa o no? Explica tu respuesta.
2. ¿Crees que pagar este dinero afecta el turismo en estos países?
3. ¿Afectaría tu decisión de ir a Argentina?

---

[1]**billetes:** bills [2]**hacer cola:** to stand in line [3]**ventanilla (de inmigración):** (immigration) office/window

LA PURA VERDAD I   De vacaciones a Chile

Rubén y Lucas han estudiado mucho todo el año y ahora están planificando unas vacaciones en Chile.

1.

Aquí hay buenos paquetes de vacaciones para Chile. Este incluye vuelo de ida y vuelta y un hotel de tres estrellas.

Nos podemos quedar con mi amigo Claudio, así no tenemos que pagar el alojamiento.

2.

Su atención, por favor. El vuelo #649 con destino a Santiago de Chile ha sido cancelado debido a problemas mecánicos. El próximo vuelo saldrá a las 10:00am, mañana jueves. Favor de acercarse al mostrador para recibir cupones para su alojamiento esta noche. Les agradecemos su paciencia. ¡Gracias!

3.

Aquí está LAN, Líneas Aéreas Nacionales.

4.

¡Mira este baño! Nos dieron cupones para comer en el restaurante del hotel. No está mal la demora.

Bienvenidos a bordo, señores pasajeros. La duración del vuelo será de 10 horas y treinta minutos.

5.

6.

¿Dónde estás estacionado?

No tengo carro. Vamos en metro, pero en media hora llegamos a casa.

© John Wiley & Sons, Inc.

11.2-01 En Santiago de Chile Escucha cómo la narración describe qué pasa después de llegar al aeropuerto. Selecciona la opción más posible.

1. a. El servicio de metro de Santiago es muy lento.
   b. Había mucha gente con maletas grandes.
   c. Pudieron sentarse y llegar en 30 minutos.
2. a. Claudio vive en un hotel de cuatro estrellas.
   b. Claudio les explicó qué líneas del metro tomar.
   c. Claudio vive en un apartamento de una habitación.
3. a. Se quedan en un hotel de tres estrellas.
   b. Se quedan en un hotel por una noche.
   c. Deciden quedarse cerca de la playa por cuatro noches.

PALABRA POR PALABRA

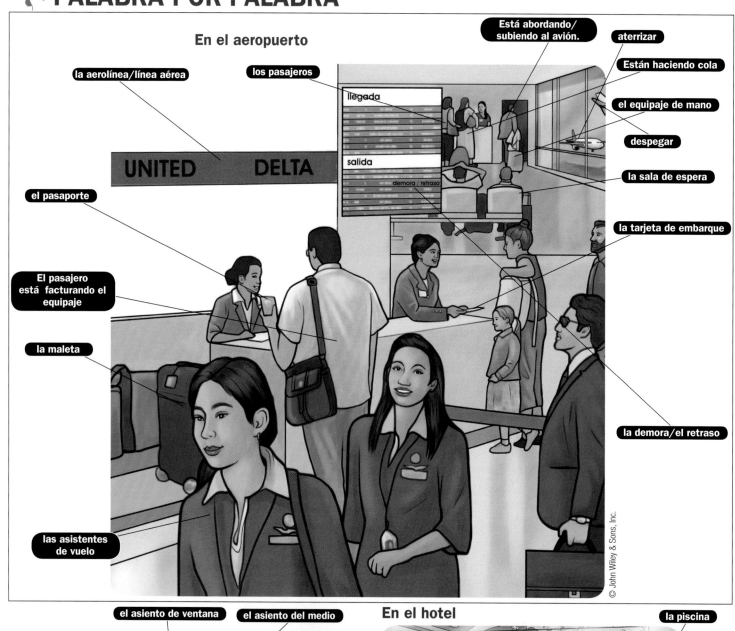

En el aeropuerto

- Está abordando/ subiendo al avión.
- aterrizar
- la aerolínea/línea aérea
- los pasajeros
- Están haciendo cola
- el equipaje de mano
- despegar
- llegada
- salida
- demora / retraso
- la sala de espera
- el pasaporte
- la tarjeta de embarque
- UNITED DELTA
- El pasajero está facturando el equipaje
- la maleta
- la demora/el retraso
- las asistentes de vuelo

© John Wiley & Sons, Inc.

- el asiento de ventana
- el asiento del medio
- En el hotel
- la piscina
- HOTEL EL CONQUISTADOR ★★★
- abrocharse el cinturón
- el asistente de vuelo
- el compartimento superior
- el asiento de pasillo
- el hotel de tres estrellas
- Se están registrando en el hotel.
- la recepción

© John Wiley & Sons, Inc.

© John Wiley & Sons, Inc.

Los medios de transporte   *Transportation means*

el barco	*the ship*
el crucero	*a sign announcing a cruise*
las líneas de metro	*subway lines*
el tren	*train*

Para hablar de los viajes

la aduana	*customs*
el alojamiento	*accommodations*
la clase turista	*coach (economy) class*
la estadía/estancia (en un hotel)	*(hotel) stay*
la habitación (sencilla, doble, triple)	*(single, double, triple) room*
el pasaje/billete (de ida/ de ida y vuelta)	*(one way/round trip) ticket*
pasar por seguridad	*to go through TSA area*
la primera clase	*first class/business class*
el vuelo (directo)	*(direct) flight*
hacer las maletas	*to pack*
ir al extranjero	*to go abroad*
pasar por la aduana	*to go through customs*
quedarse (en un hotel)	*to stay (in a hotel)*
retrasarse	*to be late*
volar	*to fly*

> **Transportation means**
>
> Do you remember the means of transportation that you studied in Chapter 4, Section 2?

¿Qué dicen los hispanohablantes?

Las pirámides me dejaron boquiabierto/a.	*The pyramids left me <u>dumbfounded</u>. (lit., with my mouth open)*
El largo viaje me ha dejado hecha polvo.	*The long trip left me <u>spent</u>. (lit., reduced to dust)*
Pagué el viaje con el sudor de mi frente.	*I paid for this trip with <u>hard work</u>. (lit., with the sweat of my brow)*
¡Que la/lo pases bien!	*Have fun!*
¡Que tengas un buen viaje!	*Have a good trip!*

11.2-02 ¿Qué va primero y qué va después?

Paso 1: Piensen en lo que pasa en un viaje, empezando con la planificación y los preparativos. Ordenen esta lista con números del 1 al 9, y después añadan tres más.

_____ a. llegar al aeropuerto

_____ b. abrocharse el cinturón de seguridad

_____ c. reservar y comprar los billetes de avión

_____ d. hacer cola

_____ e. registrarse en la recepción del hotel

_____ f. pasar por aduana

_____ g. facturar las maletas

_____ h. sacar el pasaporte

_____ i. hacer las maletas

_____ j. ...

_____ k. ...

_____ l. ...

Paso 2: Ahora, comenten con la clase sus respuestas incluyendo lo nuevo. ¿Cómo es de larga la lista generada entre toda la clase?

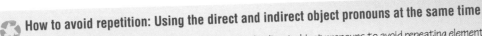

> ### How to avoid repetition: Using the direct and indirect object pronouns at the same time
>
> In Chapter 8, Section 2, you learned to use the direct and indirect object pronouns to avoid repeating elements of a sentence. Before reviewing the combined use of these pronouns, let's review how much you remember. Take a look at the following sentence:
>
> **El asistente de vuelo da la tarjeta de embarque a Lucas y a Rubén.**
>
> 1. Identify the direct and indirect objects.
> 2. Which pronouns do you use to replace each object?
> 3. Can you rewrite the sentence using both pronouns?
>
> Now go to Chapter 9, Section 1 to review the placement and order rules related to these pronouns before completing activity 11.2-03.

11.2-03 ¿Qué hacen con las maletas? Observa la historia de Lucas y Rubén y contesta las siguientes preguntas. Decide si debes usar el pronombre de objeto directo, el de objeto indirecto o los dos.

1. ¿A quién <u>le</u> dan <u>la tarjeta de embarque</u>?
2. ¿Dónde ponen <u>el equipaje de mano</u>?
3. ¿Qué hace Lucas con <u>el maní</u> que no le gusta?
4. ¿A quién <u>le</u> pagan <u>el impuesto de reciprocidad</u>?
5. ¿Quién <u>les</u> ofrece <u>alojamiento en Santiago</u>?

 11.2-04 Mis experiencias en los viajes

Paso 1: Entrevista a un/a compañero/a para saber un poco sobre sus experiencias de viajes.

1. ¿Te gusta viajar en avión o tienes miedo de volar? ¿Por qué si o por qué no?
2. ¿Alguna vez has sufrido una demora o retraso y perdiste un vuelo?
3. ¿Has tomado alguna vez un tren de alta velocidad? ¿Dónde?
4. ¿Has viajado en metro? ¿Qué metros conoces? ¿Cuál te ha gustado más?
5. ¿Alguna vez has viajado en barco o has hecho un crucero? ¿Adónde?

Paso 2: Después, escriban un pequeño informe. ¿En qué aspectos coinciden los dos? ¿En qué no coinciden?

MODELO: *Mi compañero/a tiene más experiencia que yo viajando en avión. El/Ella ha viajado a..., en cambio yo no he viajado nunca en avión. Sin embargo, los dos hemos ido a...*

Paso 3: Por último, informen a la clase. ¿Coinciden en todo, o en nada? ¿En qué aspecto no coincide nadie?

11.2-05 Buscando hotel Imagina que vas a ir de vacaciones a Dominical, en Costa Rica, y estás buscando alojamiento.

 Paso 1: Indica la importancia que las siguientes características y servicios tienen para ti.

	Totalmente necesario	Importante	Preferible	No me importa
1. baño privado				
2. internet gratis				
3. desayuno incluido				
4. vistas al mar				
5. aire acondicionado				
6. servicio diario de limpieza de habitaciones				
7. piscina				
8. registrarse en el hotel a cualquier hora				

Paso 2: Comparen sus respuestas con otros compañeros. Decide quién es un/a buen/a compañero/a de viaje y con quién piensas que es mejor no viajar porque no tienen las mismas preferencias.

HABLANDO DE GRAMÁTICA I

1. Talking about pending actions: Subjunctive with temporal conjunctions

The subjunctive is used after the following conjunctions of time only when the action is pending—that is, when it has not occurred yet. In contrast, if the action has been completed or is habitual, the indicative is used.

cuando	*when*	**hasta que**	*until*
después de que	*after*	**tan pronto como**	*as soon as*

The conjunction **antes de que** is always followed by the subjunctive, because it signals an action that has not yet occurred, even if the entire sequence of events takes place in the past.

	SUBJUNCTIVE **Pending action; yet to occur**	**INDICATIVE** **Completed or habitual action**
cuando	**Cuando lleguen** a la estación, tomen el metro. *When you arrive at the station, take the subway.*	**Cuando llegaron** a la estación, tomaron el metro. *When they arrived at the station, they took the subway.*
hasta que	Nos quedaremos con Mariana **hasta que pase** por seguridad. *We will stay with Mariana until she goes through security.*	Siempre nos quedamos con Mariana **hasta que pasa** por seguridad. *We always stay with Mariana until she goes through security.*
tan pronto como, en cuanto	Nos llamará **tan pronto como llegue** a la estación. *She will call us as soon as she arrives at the station.*	Siempre nos llama **tan pronto como llega** a la estación. *She calls us as soon as she arrives at the station.*
después de que	Nos iremos a casa **después de que ella facture** el equipaje. *We'll go home after she checks her luggage.*	Nos vamos a casa **después de que ella factura** el equipaje. *We go home after she checks the luggage.*
antes de que	Anunciarán la salida de tu vuelo **antes de que subas** al avión. *They will announce the departure of your flight before you board the plane.*	

As you already know, when the subject of the main clause and the subject of the subordinate clause are the same, the infinitive is used instead:

SUBJUNCTIVE **Change of subject**	**INFINITIVE** **No change of subject**
Nos quedaremos con él **hasta que pase** por seguridad.	Tiene que hacer cola **hasta pasar** por seguridad.
Nos iremos a casa **después de que él facture** el equipaje.	Pasaremos por seguridad **después de facturar** el equipaje.
Antes de que subas al avión te pedirán la tarjeta de embarque.	**Antes de subir** al avión tienes que mostrar la tarjeta de embarque.

WileyPLUS Go to *WileyPLUS* to review this grammar point with the help of the **Animated Grammar Tutorial**.

11.2-06 ¿Qué planes tienen para el viaje? Cuando ya están en el metro de camino a casa, Claudio les pregunta a Lucas y Rubén sobre su viaje.

▲ *Cambio de guardia frente a la Casa de la Moneda, Santiago de Chile*

▲ *Valparaíso*

▲ *Viña del Mar*

Claudio: ¿Tuvieron un buen viaje?

Rubén: Tan pronto como subimos al avión, nos dormimos. Hasta Dallas tuvimos muy buen viaje. Cuando llegamos a Dallas nos dijeron que el vuelo a Santiago estaba cancelado. Tuvimos que pasar la noche en Dallas, pero no nos importó, porque nos alojaron en un hotel de cuatro estrellas. Nos dieron un regalo en la recepción del hotel. En cuanto lleguemos a tu casa te muestro las fotos del hotel.

Claudio: Pues qué suerte tuvieron. Así pudieron descansar antes de hacer el vuelo más largo de Dallas a Santiago. ¿Y qué planes tienen?

Lucas: Después de pasar unos días en Santiago, vamos a ir a Valparaíso. Pero antes de ir a Valparaíso tienes que decirnos qué lugares debemos visitar allí.

Rubén: Cuando volvamos de Valparaíso tal vez vayamos a Viña del Mar hasta que tengamos que regresar a Santiago para tomar el vuelo de vuelta a Estados Unidos.

Claudio: Entonces, ¿van a pasar alguna noche en mi casa después de visitar Valparaíso?

Lucas: Tan pronto como hagamos planes definitivos te lo decimos.

Claudio: Bien, hacemos eso entonces.

Paso 1: Escribe todas las conjunciones temporales que encuentres en el párrafo e indica si se escriben con infinitivo, subjuntivo o indicativo. Después, indica si la acción es una acción pendiente[4] (que no ha ocurrido todavía) o pasada (que ya ocurrió).

MODELO: 1. *tan pronto como subimos (indicativo, acción pasada)*

2. _____   6. _____
3. _____   7. _____
4. _____   8. _____
5. _____   9. _____

[4]**pendiente:** pending

Paso 2: ¿Cierto o falso? Lee el párrafo otra vez y decide si las siguientes oraciones son ciertas o falsas. Si son falsas, escribe la información correcta.

C   F

☐   ☐   1. Cuando ven que había vuelos a Santiago a buen precio, deciden ir.

☐   ☐   2. Tan pronto como llegan al aeropuerto de Dallas, tienen que tomar el avión a Santiago.

☐   ☐   3. Después de que Claudio les da información sobre Valparaíso, Rubén y Lucas deciden ir.

☐   ☐   4. Antes de llegar a casa de Claudio, Rubén le muestra las fotos.

☐   ☐   5. Hasta que no regresen de Valparaíso no van a decidir qué día van a Viña.

11.2-07 El/La estudiante ideal

Paso 1: ¿Eres el/la estudiante ideal? ¿Normalmente haces todas estas cosas? Lee las siguientes oraciones y selecciona las que son verdaderas para ti.

☐   1. **En cuanto** termina la clase de español, estudio y hago la tarea para la clase siguiente.

☐   2. **Cuando** tengo un examen, estudio durante toda la semana previa.

☐   3. **Tan pronto como** el profesor devuelve un examen, lo reviso y corrijo mis errores.

☐   4. Nunca empiezo a recoger⁵ mis cosas **antes de que** termine la clase.

☐   5. Nunca llego **después de que** el profesor empieza la clase.

☐   6. Nunca salgo con mis amigos **hasta que** termino todas mis tareas.

Paso 2: Si alguna de esas afirmaciones no se aplica a ti, cámbiala proponiendo algún cambio para el futuro.

MODELO: 1. *Cuando termina la clase de español tengo una clase de matemáticas. Mañana, en cuanto termine la clase de matemáticas, voy a estudiar y hacer la tarea de español.*

Paso 3: Compara tus respuestas con las de un/a compañero/a. ¿Crees que tu compañero/a es el/la estudiante ideal? ¿Hacen las mismas cosas?

---

⁵recoger: to pick up

LA PURA VERDAD II | Vacaciones de primera

Tomás y Norma pasaron unas excelentes vacaciones en España y ahora una amiga les da instrucciones para ir de Barcelona al aeropuerto de Barajas, en Madrid.

1. Tenéis que llegar temprano a la Estació de Sants porque tendréis que pasar las maletas por seguridad para tomar el tren.

2. Si vais en primera clase estaréis muy cómodos, tendréis mucho espacio, os darán buena comida, mucha bebida, podréis mirar una película. Recibiréis mucha atención.

3. En la estación de Atocha en Madrid, tendréis que tomar el metro al aeropuerto de Barajas. Recordad que es un vuelo internacional. Llegad al aeropuerto tan pronto como sea posible. ¡Que tengáis un buen viaje!

4. Lo siento, pero estáis en la cola equivocada. Es allá.

Lo siento, pero no es aquí

5. Lo siento, pero no hay asientos en clase turista. Os pondré en primera clase.

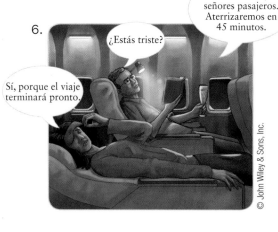

6. ¿Estás triste?

Sí, porque el viaje terminará pronto.

Su atención, señores pasajeros. Aterrizaremos en 45 minutos.

© John Wiley & Sons, Inc.

11.2-08 ¡Ventajas de viajar en primera clase! Escucha cómo describe la narración lo que pasa al final del viaje. Decide si las oraciones son ciertas (C) o falsas (F). Si son falsas, corrígelas.

	C	F
1. Norma y Tomás sacarán fotos de su viaje en primera clase.	☐	☐
2. Los pasajeros de primera clase esperan a que los de clase turista salgan primero.	☐	☐
3. La cola para pasar por inmigración es enorme. Norma y Tomás pasarán mucho tiempo en la cola.	☐	☐

HABLANDO DE GRAMÁTICA II

2. Talking about the future: The future tense

There are three different ways to talk about the future in Spanish.

The present tense:	**Salimos** mañana.	*We are leaving/We leave tomorrow.*
Ir a + *infinitive*:	**Vamos a ir** a Costa Rica.	*We are going to Costa Rica.*
The future tense:	**Viajaremos** en tren.	*We will travel by train.*

In Chapter 2, Section 2, you learned how to talk about future plans using **ir a** + *infinitive*. In this section you will learn the simple future tense.

WileyPLUS Go to *WileyPLUS* to review this grammar point with the help of the **Animated Grammar Tutorial** and the **Verb Conjugator.**

A. Forming the future tense

To form the future tense, add the following endings to the infinitive of the verb.

	volar	ver	subir
(yo)	volar**é**	ver**é**	subir**é**
(tú)	volar**ás**	ver**ás**	subir**ás**
(él, ella, Ud.)	volar**á**	ver**á**	subir**á**
(nosotros/as)	volar**emos**	ver**emos**	subir**emos**
(vosotros/as)	volar**éis**	ver**éis**	subir**éis**
(ellos, ellas, Uds.)	volar**án**	ver**án**	subir**án**

La duración del vuelo **será** de 10 horas y 30 minutos.	*The duration of the flight will be 10 hours and 30 minutes.*
Nos **quedaremos** en casa de mi amigo.	*We will stay at my friend's house.*

There are some irregular verbs in the future. These verbs have irregular future stems, but the endings are always regular.

Infinitivo	Raíz	
decir	**dir-**	
haber	**habr-**	
hacer	**har-**	-é
poder	**podr-**	-ás
poner	**pondr-**	-á
querer	**querr-**	-emos
saber	**sabr-**	-éis
salir	**saldr-**	-án
tener	**tendr-**	
venir	**vendr-**	

B. Uses of the future tense

We use the future tense to make predictions for a future time; that is, to express what will happen in the future or to ask someone to predict what may happen in the future:

–¿**Llegaremos** a tiempo?	*–Will we arrive on time?*
–Sí, **saldremos** temprano y ya **verás** cómo tenemos tiempo suficiente.	*–Yes, we'll leave early and you'll see that we'll have enough time.*

In addition to expressing what will happen, the future tense is also used to hypothesize about the present when we speculate or make assumptions of things that we are not totally certain about. Notice the English equivalents to this use of the future tense in Spanish.

–El vuelo se ha retrasado. ¿**Tendrá** problemas técnicos?	–*The flight has been delayed. I wonder if it has technical problems.*
–No te preocupes, probablemente **habrá** mucho tráfico.	–*Don't worry; I bet there is just a lot of traffic.*
–Me pregunto a qué hora **saldrá**.	–*I wonder what time the plane takes off.*

11.2-09 ¿Serán ricos? Leslie y Tab, los hijos de Norma y Tomás, hablan del regreso de sus padres.

Paso 1: Lee el diálogo e identifica todos los verbos en la forma del futuro.

Tab: ¿Qué sabes de papá y mamá?

Leslie: He hablado con ellos hace un par de horas. Estaban todavía en el aeropuerto de Barajas, en Madrid. Llegarán a San Francisco mañana por la mañana.

Tab: ¿Cómo vendrán a casa?

Leslie: Iré a buscarlos en el carro.

Tab: Cuando lleguen tendrán sueño y querrán dormir. Volar tantas horas será agotador[6].

Leslie: ¡No creas! Vuelan en primera clase. ¡Imagínate! Estarán ahora mismo en el avión.

Tab: ¡¿En primera clase?! Eso costará miles de dólares. ¿Serán ricos y nunca nos lo han dicho?

Leslie: Pues no sé... les preguntaremos cuando lleguen. Pero tendrán que mostrarme fotos o no les creeré.

Paso 2: Escribe todas las formas del futuro que encuentres en el párrafo (hay doce en total). Indica cuál es el sujeto y si se refiere a una *acción futura*, o a una *suposición*[7] o *conjetura* sobre el presente.

MODELO: 1. *llegarán (papá y mamá), acción futura*

2. _____	8. _____
3. _____	9. _____
4. _____	10. _____
5. _____	11. _____
6. _____	12. _____
7. _____	

---

[6] **agotador:** exhausting [7] **suposición:** assumption

Paso 3: Después de que Norma habla por teléfono con Leslie, habla con Tomás sobre las ventajas de viajar en primera clase. Completa el diálogo con la forma correcta del futuro de los verbos de la lista.

> preguntar salir volar creer poder dormir pensar ser tener hacer haber

Norma: Le he dicho a Leslie que _____₁ en primera clase. Se ha quedado muy sorprendida pero no le he querido dar detalles.

Tomás: ¡Ja, ja! Leslie _____₂ que somos ricos.

Norma: Cuando lleguemos a casa seguro que nuestros hijos nos _____₃ cómo es que hemos viajado en primera.

Tomás: ¡En primera clase! ¡_____₄ la primera vez en mi vida! _____₅ reclinar el asiento y _____₆ mucho espacio. _____₇ muy bien. ¡_____₈ los primeros y no _____₉ cola al llegar al aeropuerto!

Norma: Bueno, ¡pues _____₁₀ que sacar muchas fotos porque si no, nuestros hijos no nos _____₁₁!

11.2-10 ¿Qué harás?

Paso 1: Completa las siguientes oraciones con información que se aplica a ti.

MODELO: Cuando termine el trimestre *iré de vacaciones al extranjero.*

1. Tan pronto como termine todos mis exámenes finales…
2. Cuando termine el trimestre/semestre…
3. El verano que viene…
4. En cuanto me gradúe…
5. Cuando tenga suficiente dinero…

Paso 2: Ahora, transforma las oraciones en preguntas y entrevista a un/a compañero/a.

MODELO: Estudiante 1:   *¿Irás al extranjero cuando termine el trimestre?*
           Estudiante 2:   *No, creo que no tendré suficiente dinero para ir de vacaciones. Me quedaré unos días en casa de mis padres.*

Paso 3: Con la información que has recogido, escribe un pequeño párrafo sobre los dos.

MODELO: *Cuando termine el trimestre, Norma pasará unos días en casa de sus padres, pero yo… Tan pronto como terminemos con los exámenes finales, iremos a…*

OTRA PERSPECTIVA

Courtesy of Norma
Lopez-Burton

Iris

¿Aprender otra lengua o no?

Diferente

"Cuando mi familia y yo planificamos un viaje, parte de los planes es aprender a comunicarnos en la lengua del país adonde vamos. Yo he viajado a Francia, Alemania, Brasil y Estados Unidos, y antes de ir, memorizo el mayor número de frases posibles en inglés, francés, alemán o portugués. Especialmente, me aseguro de saber bien cómo decir 'hola', 'por favor' y 'gracias' en esos idiomas. En general, a los turistas estadounidenses no les interesa aprender otra lengua. Siempre esperan que los otros hablen inglés. Creen que no hay necesidad de aprender porque todo el mundo habla inglés. ¿Por qué no aprender otro idioma?".

Igual

"Antes no entendía por qué los turistas querían ver las pirámides y a los indígenas nativos de mi país con sus trajes típicos. ¿Por qué no visitar las ciudades modernas y las universidades que son más parte de mi realidad? Entonces me di cuenta de que nosotros hacemos lo mismo cuando venimos a Estados Unidos. Además de las ciudades importantes, también queremos ver a los vaqueros y el Viejo Oeste".

 Explícale a Iris

1. ¿Por qué la mayoría de los estados han aprobado una ley que determina el uso del inglés solamente (*English only*) en asuntos oficiales?
2. ¿Por qué en el resto del mundo se aprende inglés?
3. ¿Por qué es importante poder comunicarse en más de un idioma?

MANOS A LA OBRA

 11.2-11 Cuando me gradúe…

Paso 1: Levántate y hazles a tus compañeros las siguientes preguntas. Escribe el nombre del/de la compañero/a que conteste afirmativamente.

MODELO: Estudiante 1:   *¿**Buscarás** trabajo?*
            Estudiante 2:   *Sí, claro, **buscaré** trabajo/No, no **buscaré** trabajo porque ya
                             tengo uno, y bastante bueno.*

¿Quién de la clase cuando se gradúe…   Nombre del compañero/a

  1. … buscará trabajo?   _____

  2. … se mudará de ciudad?   _____

  3. … volverá a vivir con sus padres?   _____

  4. … dará una gran fiesta?   _____

  5. … hará un gran viaje?   _____

  6. … estudiará una maestría?   _____

  7. … hará una práctica de trabajo/empresa?   _____

  8. … seguirá estudiando español?   _____

Paso 2: Después, comenta tus resultados con la clase. ¿Quién piensas que tiene un plan mejor?

MODELO: *Pienso que el mejor plan es el de… porque…*

11.2-12 **Adivina, adivinador**

Paso 1: Formen grupos de cuatro. En su grupo, seleccionen a un/a compañero/a para que haga el papel de adivino/a y prediga el futuro de otro/a compañero/a del grupo. El/La adivino/a debe usar las siguientes frases:

cuando...   tan pronto como...   en cuanto...   después/antes de (que)...

MODELO: *Cuando te gradúes crearás una aplicación para teléfonos inteligentes y te harás rico/a. Después de ganar mucho dinero...*

Paso 2: Por turnos, el/la adivino/a de cada grupo informará a la clase sobre el futuro de un miembro del grupo. El resto de la clase tiene que adivinar de qué estudiante se trata.

11.2-13 **Nuestro viaje con los compañeros de clase**

Paso 1: Ahora que sabes tantas cosas de todos los países hispanohablantes, decide qué país quieres visitar. Prepara dos listas. En la lista 1, incluye tres lugares de interés y las actividades que quieres hacer allí. En la lista 2, incluye por lo menos tres cosas que tienes que hacer antes de salir de viaje.

Paso 2: Entre todos tus compañeros, busca a alguien que quiera viajar al mismo país que tú.

MODELO: Estudiante 1:   *Yo quiero viajar a Costa Rica, ¿y tú?*
           Estudiante 2:   *Yo también quiero viajar a Costa Rica, o sea que podemos viajar juntos.*

Paso 3: Después de encontrar a tu/s compañero/s de viaje, comparen sus listas. Deben ponerse de acuerdo en los lugares que visitarán, las actividades que harán y en cómo prepararán su viaje.

MODELO: Para decidir adónde ir y qué hacer:

▲ *Laguna azul en el Parque Nacional Manuel Antonio*

           Estudiante 1:   *Podemos ir a la península de Nicoya, a la costa central del Pacífico y al bosque lluvioso de Monteverde.*
           Estudiante 2:   *Sí, en la costa central visitaremos el Parque Nacional Manuel Antonio...*

           Para hacer los preparativos:
           Estudiante 1:   *Tenemos que buscar los billetes de avión.*
           Estudiante 2:   *Bien, tú buscarás los billetes. En cuanto decidamos en qué fechas ir, yo buscaré el alojamiento...*

Paso 4: Hagan una presentación en clase sobre su viaje. Incluyan la siguiente información:

- quiénes irán
- en qué fechas viajarán
- cuánto durará el viaje
- con qué aerolínea viajarán
- qué equipaje van a llevar

- qué harán antes de salir
- qué lugares visitarán
- dónde se alojarán
- etc.

MODELO: *Mis compañeros _____, _____ y yo iremos a Costa Rica.*
Saldremos de San Francisco el día... y volaremos a San José.

WileyPLUS Go to *WileyPLUS* and listen to **Presta atención.**

11.2-14 Presta atención: En una fiesta Unas amigas están en una fiesta y hablan sobre un viaje. Escucha su conversación y después contesta las preguntas:

1. ¿Por qué Elena no viajará más de tres veces en el año?
   a. Porque no tiene dinero y ya ha viajado mucho.
   b. Porque tiene mucho trabajo y no tiene tiempo.
   c. Porque es una persona realista y conoce su situación.
2. ¿Cuándo estuvo Elena en Taxco?
   a. Estuvo cuando era niña.
   b. Estuvo el verano pasado.
   c. Estuvo hace dos años.
3. ¿Por qué quiere volver a Taxco?
   a. Para visitar a sus amigos y a un artista.
   b. Porque le ofrecieron un trabajo de artista.
   c. Porque es un pueblo con mucho arte.
4. ¿Cómo llegará Elena de Cuernavaca a Taxco?
   a. Su amigo la busca en el aeropuerto.
   b. Irá en un avión pequeño.
   c. Irá en auto desde Cuernavaca.
5. ¿Con quién irá Elena a Guatemala?
   a. Irá con Roberto.
   b. Irá con Cristina.
   c. Irá sola.

11.2-15 Por escrito: Comprar en línea o en una agencia de viajes Actualmente, la mayoría de la gente compra sus pasajes en línea y cada vez hay menos agencias de viajes. Escribe un breve ensayo dando tu opinión al respecto. Puedes incluir algo sobre tus hábitos de viaje y ejemplos de experiencias propias o de tus amigos.

PONTE EN MI LUGAR

Estrategias para conversar

Sound like a native speaker Remember that in order to sound more like a native speaker there are some words or phrases you can use to fill awkward pauses or to buy time, such as **este...** (*uhmmm...*), **pues...** (*well...*), or **vamos a ver** (*let's see...*). Review the **Estrategias para conversar** in Chapter 7, Section 1 for more of these expressions.

Estudiar en el extranjero Ustedes van a estudiar en Valencia, España. Uno de los requisitos del programa es asistir a reuniones de orientación. Conversa con un/a compañero/a sobre las reuniones de orientación. Usen las **Estrategias para conversar** cuando puedan.

Estudiante 1: El jueves pasado no pudiste ir a la primera reunión de orientación del programa de verano en el extranjero. Durante la conversación:

a. Pregúntale sobre las cosas importantes que hicieron y que tú tendrás que hacer.
b. Pídele la información que presentaron en la reunión.
c. Pregúntale de qué hablarán en la próxima reunión.
d. Pregúntale si tomó notas sobre la información de la reunión.
e. Dale las gracias por su ayuda y dile que te ha sido muy útil.

Estudiante 2: Tu amigo/a no pudo ir a la primera reunión de orientación, así que tienes que pasarle la información. En la conversación:

a. Cuéntale lo que hiciste en la primera media hora y lo que él/ella tendrá que hacer en la próxima reunión: hacer una encuesta sobre la familia con la que quieren vivir; rellenar unos documentos sobre alimentación y enfermedades; y tomarse una foto para la tarjeta de estudiante.
b. Explícale que en la reunión se habló sobre las cosas que tienen que hacer los estudiantes: comprar el pasaje de avión; hacer o renovar el pasaporte; rellenar unos papeles para el visado; seleccionar los cursos que tomarán en el verano.
c. Dile que en la próxima reunión se hablará sobre el transporte y las costumbres en España (saludos, horario de comida, vida nocturna, etc.) y las familias de acogida.[8]
d. Dile que la información de la reunión está en la página web del programa. En la página hay unos documentos informativos y también un archivo de audio.
e. Pregúntale si necesita más información y después despídete.

¡OJO!

Improving your text
Review **Estrategias para escribir** in Chapter 11, Section 1 and Chapter 9, Section 1 to make sure you write a coherent and organized essay.

ASÍ ES LA VIDA

Chiste

Estaba un hombre haciendo cola para comprar un pasaje de avión. Como era la primera vez que compraba un pasaje y no estaba seguro de qué decir, se acercó a la muchacha que estaba delante de él para escuchar lo que pedía.

La chica dijo:
—Deme un pasaje para Florida, solo ida.

Entonces, al llegar el turno del hombre, este pidió:
—Deme un pasaje para Nueva York, solo York.

Adivina, adivinador

Soy pájaro sin nido
con las alas de metal,
las ruedas tengo de goma
y los ojitos de cristal.
¿Qué soy?

© John Wiley & Sons, Inc.

WileyPLUS Go to *WileyPLUS* to find more **Arroba** activities.

De viaje: Estadía gratis Hoy día, cada vez más jóvenes salen de sus ciudades o países en busca de viajes y aventuras. Explora en tu buscador preferido información sobre cómo viajar gratis o con poco dinero. Escribe un pequeño párrafo para comentar con tu clase la información que has encontrado. Estas preguntas te pueden ayudar: ¿Qué puedes hacer para conocer gente de otras culturas? ¿Qué alternativas hay para no gastar dinero en hoteles? ¿Quién te puede referir a personas de otras ciudades para visitar la ciudad sin necesidad de usar una guía turística?

[8] **familias de acogida**: host families

VER PARA CREER II: *Online* las 24 horas

WileyPLUS Go to *WileyPLUS* to see this video and to find more video activities.

Antes de ver

Con la ayuda de un/a compañero/a, responde estas preguntas para prepararte a ver el video.

1. ¿Qué aparatos electrónicos usas cuando vas de viaje?
2. ¿Qué redes sociales usas? ¿Por qué?
3. ¿Para qué tipo de actividades usas el internet con más frecuencia?
4. ¿Qué tipo de compras haces por internet?

Después de ver

1. ¿Entendiste? Daniel y Luis son amigos y están de vacaciones. Después de ver el video, contesta las preguntas para saber si comprendiste lo que van a hacer estos dos amigos durante sus vacaciones.

1. ¿Por qué está grabando Daniel?
   a. Porque quiere que sus amigos estadounidenses aprendan algo nuevo.
   b. Porque le encanta la tecnología y quiere tener un video con su amigo.
   c. Porque tiene que hacer un proyecto para una clase de civilización.
2. Según Luis…
   a. Xochimilco significa que hay muchos botes.
   b. Xochimilco significa lugar donde crecen las flores.
   c. Xochimilco significa lagos con islas pequeñas.
3. Según Luis, ¿quiénes construyeron islas sobre el lago?
   a. la civilización maya
   b. la civilización olmeca
   c. la civilización azteca
4. ¿Qué pasa cuando Luis y Daniel se están haciendo una foto?
   a. Una amiga llama a Luis por teléfono y está hablando con ella.
   b. Daniel se cae al agua.
   c. Luis canta con los mariachis.
5. ¿Dónde quiere quedarse Luis cuando esté en Costa Rica?
   a. en un hotel de dos estrellas que tiene piscina y habitaciones dobles
   b. en casa de Rocío porque se la ha recomendado un amigov
   c. en casa de su amigo porque está muy satisfecho con su gran casa
6. ¿Cómo quiere Daniel ir a Costa Rica?
   a. en un vuelo directo con una buena aerolínea
   b. en un vuelo directo que sea de ida y vuelta
   c. en un vuelo de ida y vuelta y que sea barato

2. Tus próximos viajes en el extranjero ¿Adónde viajarás en el futuro? ¿Qué lugares visitarás? ¿Por qué? ¿Buscarás alojamiento en un hotel, un hostal, con una familia de acogida o en un programa de intercambio?

3. Enfoque cultural ¿Qué viste en el video de México que hay o no hay en Estados Unidos? Explica.

AUTOPRUEBA

VOCABULARIO

I. De viaje Contesta las preguntas usando el vocabulario del capítulo para saber si puedes comunicarte en español durante tu viaje.

1. ¿Cómo se llama el lugar del aeropuerto donde uno espera antes de subir al avión?
2. ¿Qué documento se presenta al pasar por inmigración cuando llegas a un país?
3. ¿Cómo se llama el lugar que te asignan en un avión?
4. ¿Quiénes sirven la comida y las bebidas en un avión?
5. ¿Qué documento te dan en el aeropuerto después de facturar las maletas?

II. De vacaciones Antonio volará el próximo verano a Chile para visitar a su novia. Completa el diálogo entre ellos con el vocabulario de la lista y conjuga los verbos cuando sea necesario.

línea aérea	equipaje	avión	pasaje
equipaje de mano	metro	clase turista	
maletas	aeropuerto	aterrizar	

Antonio: ¡Hola, cariño! ¿Cómo estás?

Natalia: Bien, bien, pero te extraño[9].

Antonio: Sí, yo también. Por cierto, ¿sabes que he comprado el _____₁ para Chile?

Natalia: ¡Qué bien! Viajas en _____₂, ¿verdad?

Antonio: Pues la verdad es que voy a viajar en primera clase porque tenía muchas millas con mi _____₃ favorita.

Natalia: ¡Qué suerte! ¿Vas a traer mucho _____₄?

Antonio: Sí, tengo dos _____₅ y también voy a llevar un bolso pequeño como _____₆.

Natalia: ¿Qué día vuelas?

Antonio: Llego a Santiago el lunes. El _____₇ _____₈ a las ocho de la mañana.

Natalia: ¡Oh, no! No puedo estar en el _____₉ el lunes porque tengo que trabajar. Vas a tener que venir a mi casa en el _____₁₀.

Antonio: No te preocupes, mi amor. Nos vemos pronto.

Natalia: Hasta pronto.

GRAMÁTICA

I. ¿Qué harás con la maleta? Contesta las preguntas que Rubén le hace a Lucas usando el futuro y los pronombres de objeto directo e indirecto cuando sea posible.

1. ¿Qué harás con la maleta?
2. ¿Dónde pondrás el equipaje de mano?
3. ¿A quién le darás la tarjeta de embarque?
4. ¿Qué haremos con el cinturón de seguridad?
5. ¿Quién nos esperará en el aeropuerto?

II. ¿Cuándo lo harás? Completa las respuestas de Lucas con la frase entre paréntesis. Decide si debes usar indicativo o subjuntivo.

1. ¿Cuándo compraste los billetes de avión? (decidir el lugar)
   Después de que nosotros…
2. ¿Cuándo me enviarás la información del vuelo? (pagarme)
   Tan pronto como tú…
3. ¿Cuándo reservaste el hotel? (darme el número de teléfono)
   En cuanto tú…
4. ¿Con cuánto tiempo antes de un viaje haces la maleta? (terminar todos los exámenes finales)
   Yo siempre la hago cuando…

CULTURA

Lee las siguientes oraciones y corrige las oraciones falsas.

	C	F
1. "Reciprocidad" es hacer amigos en otros países.	☐	☐
2. El metro es un sistema de trenes.	☐	☐
3. El AVE es un sistema de trenes de alta velocidad en España.	☐	☐
4. El euro es la moneda de España y de América Latina.	☐	☐

REDACCIÓN

Piensa en un viaje memorable que hiciste. ¿Cuánto te costó? ¿Qué tipo de transporte usaste? ¿Con quién fuiste? ¿Tuviste problemas? ¿Hiciste amigos? ¿Cómo era el hotel? ¿Qué viste?

EN RESUMIDAS CUENTAS, AHORA PUEDO...

☐ hablar sobre viajes.

☐ entender ciertas situaciones a la hora de viajar.

☐ hablar sobre eventos futuros.

☐ hablar sobre hechos que aún no han sucedido.

☐ evitar la repetición.

[9] **te extraño:** I miss you

⌂ **VOCABULARIO ESENCIAL**

Sustantivos

la aduana	*customs*
la aerolínea/línea aérea	*airline*
el alojamiento	*accommodations*
el asiento (de pasillo/ ventana/del medio)	*(aisle/window/middle) seat*
el/la asistente de vuelo	*flight attendant*
el avión	*plane*
el barco	*ship*
el billete/pasaje (de ida/de ida y vuelta)	*(one-way/round-trip) ticket*
clase turista	*coach (economy class)*
el compartimento superior	*overhead compartment*
el crucero	*cruise*
la demora/el retraso	*delay*
el equipaje (de mano)	*(carry-on) luggage*
la estadía/estancia (en un hotel)	*(hotel) stay*
(dos, tres, cuatro) estrellas	*(two, three, four) stars*
la habitación (sencilla, doble, triple)	*(single, double, triple) room*
las líneas del metro	*subway lines*
la maleta	*suitcase*
los pasajeros	*passengers*

la piscina	*pool*
primera clase	*first class/business class*
la sala de espera	*waiting room*
la tarjeta de embarque	*boarding pass*
el tren	*train*
el vuelo (directo)	*(direct) flight*

Cognados: el aeropuerto, el hotel, el pasaporte, la recepción

Verbos y expresiones verbales

abordar/subir al avión	*to board (the plane)*
abrocharse el cinturón	*to fasten one's seatbelt*
aterrizar	*to land*
despegar	*to take off*
facturar el equipaje	*to check your luggage*
hacer cola	*to wait in line*
hacer las maletas	*to pack*
ir al extranjero	*to go abroad*
pasar por la aduana	*to go through customs*
pasar por seguridad	*to go through TSA area*
quedarse (en un hotel)	*to stay (in a hotel)*
registrarse	*to check in*
retrasarse	*to be late*
volar	*to fly*

Los hispanos en Estados Unidos

© John Wiley & Sons, Inc.

VER PARA CREER I: CLUES ayuda a inmigrantes

La inmigración no es un tema nuevo para ti. Con un/a compañero/a, intercambia opiniones sobre la inmigración. Después de ver el video, contesta las preguntas.

1. ¿Qué lugares has visto en el video?
2. ¿Qué palabras escuchaste o comprendiste?
3. ¿Qué tipo de gente has visto en el video?

Go to *WileyPLUS* to do the **Trivia** activities to find out how much you know about the United States.

Estados Unidos

© John Wiley & Sons, Inc.

Población hispana en EE. UU. (miles de personas/habitantes)

☐ 0–100 ☐ 501–1.000 ☐ 101–250 ☐ 251–500 ☐ >1.000

LEARNING OBJECTIVES

By the end of this section you will be able to:

- Discuss issues related to immigration
- Understand the problems immigrants face
- Express hopes, wishes, uncertainty, and doubt
- Express subjective opinions about events in the past
- Consider possibilities and offer advice

Una imagen vale más que mil palabras

¿Sabes cuál es el proceso para obtener la ciudadanía en Estados Unidos?

¿Crees que Estados Unidos es como una "ensalada", es decir, una mezcla de distintos ingredientes?

¿Cuál es el grupo más grande que ha emigrado a Estados Unidos?

UNA PERSPECTIVA

Julie

El miedo al cambio

Diferente

"He vivido en California por más de cuarenta años y he visto cómo la cultura hispana ha crecido y ha tenido una gran influencia en muchos aspectos de la vida en California. Como es natural, los humanos le tenemos miedo al cambio. Tenemos miedo de que esta nueva cultura vaya a dominar la nuestra. Pero no ha sido así. Muchos inmigrantes traen consigo su cultura y enriquecen[1] la nuestra, pero a la vez se asimilan y adquieren muchas de nuestras costumbres. Además, muchos de ellos contribuyen notablemente a mejorar nuestra sociedad. Los inmigrantes no significan un detrimento para nuestro pueblo, sino una inyección de vitalidad".

Igual

"Yo también soy un producto de la inmigración en Estados Unidos. Mis antepasados eran de Irlanda y Alemania. Seguramente, la sociedad en aquel tiempo también temió que los irlandeses y los alemanes fueran un detrimento para el país. Con el tiempo, todos nos asimilamos. Tenemos que aceptar que, a excepción de los indígenas americanos, todos los habitantes de Estados Unidos fuimos inmigrantes alguna vez".

¿Qué piensas tú?

1. ¿Cuál es la nacionalidad de tus antepasados?
2. ¿Qué aspectos de la cultura de tus antepasados conservas ahora o te habría gustado[2] conservar?
3. ¿Crees que la asimilación es importante para el país?

[1]**enriquecer:** enrich [2]**te habría gustado:** you would have liked

LA PURA VERDAD I   Historias de inmigrantes

Vivian, de Puerto Rico, nos cuenta cómo es su vida en EE. UU.

1.

Con tanto desempleo, tendré mejores oportunidades si continúo estudiando.

2.

▲ *Quiere estudiar en Texas porque tiene amigos allí.*

3.
Tengo que vivir aquí por un año para establecer la residencia legal en este estado y así pagar menos para estudiar.

4.
Aquí tengo que pagar más impuestos que en Puerto Rico.

5.
Echo de menos la comida, la música y el acento puertorriqueño.

Pues no te quejes: yo no sé si un día tendré que volverme a México. Es una lucha diaria encontrar trabajo.

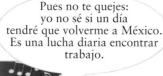

6.
¿Cómo estoy? Pues, mamá, estoy bien. Todo va bien.

© John Wiley & Sons, Inc.

12.1-01 ¡Problemas de inmigración! El amigo de Vivian le cuenta la historia de la inmigración en Texas y Vivian descubre que los mexicanos no siempre fueron los inmigrantes. Escucha la narración y selecciona la mejor respuesta.

1. En 1824, ¿quiénes eran los inmigrantes?
   a. los mexicanos   b. los estadounidenses   c. los texanos
2. En 1830…
   a. el gobierno mexicano logró detener la inmigración de Estados Unidos a México.
   b. el gobierno mexicano promovió la inmigración de Estados Unidos a México.
   c. el gobierno de México prohibió la inmigración de Estados Unidos.
3. ¿Qué pasó unos años después?
   a. La mayoría de origen estadounidense propuso la independencia de México.
   b. La mayoría de origen mexicano propuso deportar a los inmigrantes.
   c. La minoría de origen estadounidense propuso la independencia de México.

🎧 PALABRA POR PALABRA

♻ **Nationalities**
Remember: you can find the nationalities for the Spanish-speaking countries in Chapter 1, Section 1.

♻ **Más nacionalidades**

Estas son las nacionalidades de los países vecinos a los países hispanohablantes.

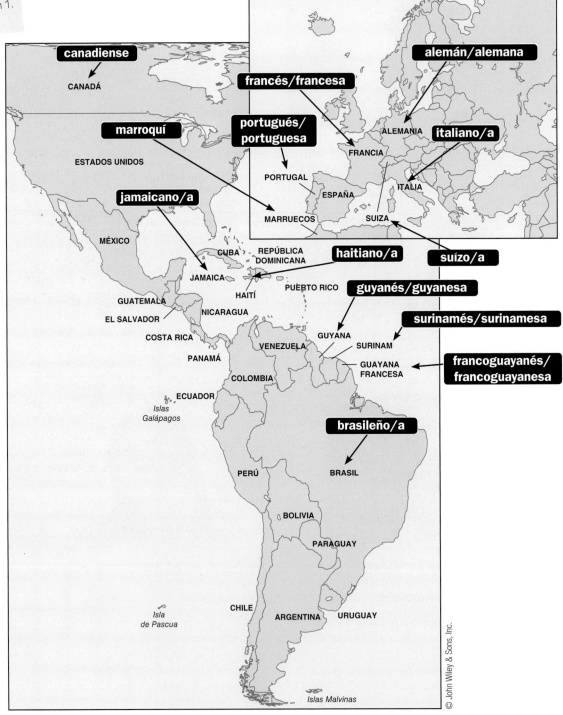

La inmigración

la (doble) ciudadanía	*(dual) citizenship*
el/la ciudadano/a	*citizen*
el (des)empleo	*(un)employment*
la (des)igualdad	*(in)equality*
la huelga	*strike*
los impuestos	*taxes*
el juramento a la bandera	*the pledge of allegiance*
la ley	*law*
la manifestación	*protest*
el permiso	*permit*

apoyar (una causa)	*to support (a cause)*
aprobar una ley	*to pass a law*
echar de menos	*to miss (something/someone)*
luchar por	*to fight for*

Cognados: la comunidad, la diversidad, el/la emigrante, emigrar, (i)legal, la (in)migración, el/la inmigrante, la marcha, la minoría, la nacionalidad, la oportunidad, el origen, el prejuicio, la protesta, el/la residente, la visa

12.1-02 ¿De qué hablamos?

Paso 1: Lee las definiciones y busca la palabra correspondiente en la sección **Palabra por palabra.**

MODELO: Es la línea divisoria entre dos países. → *la frontera*

1. Es un paro[3] voluntario de los trabajadores para mejorar su situación laboral.
2. Es el dinero que se paga al gobierno para financiar los gastos públicos.
3. Reunión de personas que protestan por algo en la calle.
4. Es una licencia o autorización para hacer algo.
5. Es una norma establecida por el gobierno que los ciudadanos deben cumplir.
6. Es una opinión, generalmente negativa, sin una base real o conocimiento[4] suficiente.
7. Es la desproporción económica y social entre diferentes personas.

Paso 2: Ahora, elijan tres palabras de la sección **Palabra por palabra** y escriban tres definiciones para leerlas a la clase. ¡Atención! Recuerden que para definir siempre usamos el verbo *ser.*

MODELO: *Es un/una/el/la... (que)...*

12.1-03 Palabras relacionadas
En grupos pequeños, piensen en todas las palabras que conocen relacionadas con los siguientes términos. Piensen en todo el vocabulario que ya conocen, no solo en el de esta sección. ¿Qué grupo sabe más palabras?

MODELO: documento → *documentar, documentación, documentado*

1. empleo
2. igual
3. permitir
4. ciudad
5. migrar
6. residencia

¿Qué dicen los hispanohablantes de Estados Unidos?

Quiero <u>aplicar</u> para ser ciudadano. (en vez de[5] *solicitar*)	*I want <u>to apply</u> to become a citizen.*
<u>La parada</u> del Día de los Muertos me gustó mucho. (en vez de *desfile*)	*I really liked the Day of the Dead <u>parade</u>.*
Trabaja de <u>paralegal</u> en esa oficina. (en vez de *asistente legal*)	*He/She works as a <u>paralegal</u> at that office.*
Este dinero es para pagar <u>la renta</u>. (en vez del *alquiler*)	*This money is to pay <u>the rent</u>.*
Compró una <u>van</u> para transportar la mercancía. (en vez de *camioneta*)	*He/She bought <u>a van</u> to transport the merchandise.*

---

[3]**paro:** interrupción de trabajo [4]**conocimiento:** knowledge [5]**en vez de:** instead of

12.1-04 Adivina, adivinador… ¿Cuál es mi nacionalidad? Imagina que eres un inmigrante o extranjero en EE. UU. Piensa en un país interesante (por ejemplo, un país hispanohablante), en tu país de origen o en el país de origen de tus antepasados[6]. Adopta esa nacionalidad. Después, en parejas, túrnense para adivinar cuál es la nacionalidad de su compañero/a.

MODELO: Estudiante 1:   *¿Vienes de las Américas?*
Estudiante 2:   *Sí, soy caribeño/a.*
Estudiante 1:   *¿En tu país la lengua oficial es el español o el francés?*
Estudiante 2:   *La lengua oficial es el español.*
Estudiante 1:   *¿La capital es La Habana?*
Estudiante 2:   *No, la capital es Santo Domingo.*
Estudiante 1:   *¡Eres dominicano/a!*
Estudiante 2:   *¡Sí, muy bien!*

The indicative vs. the subjunctive

In previous chapters, you have learned that the subjunctive appears in subordinate clauses (frequently introduced by **que**). However, the subjunctive is not always used in subordinate clauses. In many cases, the indicative is used instead. Therefore, every time you find a subordinate clause, you have to decide whether to use the indicative or the subjunctive.

With a classmate, write a list of situations or contexts where you would use the subjunctive in a subordinate clause. Do the same for the indicative. Afterward, still in pairs, try to determine whether the situations for each mood (subjunctive and indicative) have anything in common. Finally, review the chart in Chapter 10, Section 1 and compare your answers.

12.1-05 ¿Qué piensas sobre estos asuntos[7] sociales?

Paso 1: Completa las siguientes oraciones de manera correcta con una cláusula principal (prestando atención al uso del indicativo o subjuntivo en la cláusula subordinada). Complétalas con información verdadera sobre ti. Puedes usar los verbos y las expresiones de la sección **Hablando de gramática II** del Capítulo 10, Sección 1.

MODELO: … que nadie de mi familia **tenga** que emigrar por razones económicas.
→ *Espero* que nadie de mi familia **tenga** que emigrar por razones económicas.

1. … que no **aumente** el desempleo.
2. … que **haya** que continuar luchando con el propósito de…
3. … que el gobierno **use** el dinero de los impuestos para…
4. … que el español **es** el segundo idioma más hablado en EE. UU.
5. … que los hispanos no **son** una minoría en algunos estados, como California.
6. … **tener** doble ciudadanía algún día.
7. … que yo **tenga** que emigrar a otro país para tener una vida mejor.

Paso 2: Ahora, compara tus opiniones con las de un/a compañero/a. ¿Son iguales? ¿Coincidieron en algunas, en ninguna, en todas?

MODELO: Estudiante 1:   *Espero* que nadie de mi familia tenga que emigrar por razones económicas.
Estudiante 2:   *Yo también.* **Es una lástima que haya** personas en esa situación. *¡Debe ser muy difícil!*

---

[6]**antepasados:** ancestors [7]**asuntos:** issues

HABLANDO DE GRAMÁTICA I

1. Expressing subjectivity in the past: Introduction to the imperfect subjunctive

WileyPLUS Go to *WileyPLUS* to review this grammar point with the help of the **Animated Grammar Tutorial** and the **Verb Conjugator**.

So far you have studied a few verb tenses in Spanish and also different moods, such as the indicative, the subjunctive, and the imperative (i.e., formal and informal commands). In this chapter you will be introduced to a new verb tense of the subjunctive mood, the imperfect subjunctive.

Indicative	Subjunctive
Present	Present
Imperfect	Imperfect
Preterit	
Present Perfect	

As you already know, we use the indicative mood when we want to declare that the event expressed by the verb is a fact. That is, we state that someone knows or assumes that it is real.

Vivian no **es** una inmigrante. — *Vivian is not an immigrant.*

Sabemos que **es** ciudadana. — *We know that she is a citizen.*

In Chapters 9 and 10 you learned that the subjunctive mood, in contrast, is used to express wishes, hopes, requests, doubts, and other subjective reactions.

No creo que **sea** una inmigrante. — *I don't think she is an immigrant.*

Me alegra que **sea** ciudadana. — *I'm happy that she is a citizen.*

A. Form of the imperfect (past) subjunctive
The imperfect subjunctive of *all* verbs is formed by dropping the **-on** ending from the third person plural (**ellos, ellas, ustedes**) form of the preterit and adding the following endings:

	emigrar (emigraron)	deber (debieron)	permitir (permitieron)
(yo)	emigrar**a**	debier**a**	permitier**a**
(tú)	emigrar**as**	debier**as**	permitier**as**
(él, ella, Ud.)	emigrar**a**	debier**a**	permitier**a**
(nosotros/as)	emigrár**amos**	debiér**amos**	permitiér**amos**
(vosotros/as)	emigrar**ais**	debier**ais**	permitier**ais**
(ellos, ellas, Uds.)	emigrar**an**	debier**an**	permitier**an**

B. Use of the imperfect subjunctive
We use the imperfect subjunctive in cases in which we need to use the subjunctive, but when the subordinate verb refers to a past action.

	Indicative	Subjunctive
Sus padres **eran** puertorriqueños.	Supongo [que sus padres **eran** puertorriqueños]. *I assume [that her parents were Puerto Rican.]*	Dudo [que sus padres **fueran** puertorriqueños]. *I doubted [that her parents were Puerto Rican.]*
Sus padres no **dejaron** la isla.	Creo [que sus padres no **dejaron** la isla]. *I think [that her parents didn't leave the island.]*	No creo [que sus padres **dejaran** la isla]. *I don't think [that her parents left the island.]*

12.1-06 Cuando llegué a Texas

Paso 1: Vivian le cuenta a una amiga cómo fueron sus primeros meses en Texas. Lee el texto con atención.

Cuando terminé de estudiar en la UPR, decidí continuar estudiando. Es una lástima que no **pudiera** encontrar trabajo con el desempleo tan alto que había en Puerto Rico. Entonces unos amigos me aconsejaron que viniera a Texas. Me recomendaron que viviera aquí por un año antes de empezar a estudiar para obtener el permiso de residencia y me dijeron que trabajara con ellos en el restuarante. Cuando obtuviera la residencia, sería más barato ir a la universidad.

Al principio pensaba que iba a tener mejores oportunidades aquí. No pensaba que la vida fuera tan difícil para un ciudadano. Aunque tuviera la ciudadanía, a veces me sentía una ciudadana de segunda clase. También me sorprendió que hubiera tanta gente que no sabía que yo era ciudadana. En el restaurante me sorprendía que todos pensaran que yo era mexicana. ¡Para mí somos tan diferentes! La gente no creía que no me gustara la comida picante y muchas otras cosas que ellos asocian con la cultura hispana.

Paso 2: Ahora, escribe todas las expresiones que incluyen un verbo subordinado en *imperfecto de subjuntivo* (hay diez en total). Después, indica cuáles de los verbos se refieren a Vivian (V).

MODELO: 1. *Es una lástima que no* **pudiera**... (V)

2. _____
3. _____
4. _____
5. _____
6. _____
7. _____
8. _____
9. _____
10. _____

12.1-07 ¿Qué piensa Vivian? Ahora lee el párrafo otra vez y decide si Vivian opina o no lo siguiente. Si no opina de esa manera, escribe lo que sí opina.

Sí	No	
☐	☐	1. Me sorprendió que no supieran que yo soy puertorriqueña.
☐	☐	2. Fue una suerte poder venir a Texas.
☐	☐	3. Creía que la vida iba a ser más fácil como ciudadana de EE. UU.
☐	☐	4. Era lógico que muchas personas pensaran que yo no soy ciudadana.
☐	☐	5. Yo entendía que me confundieran con personas de otros países hispanos.

LA PURA VERDAD II | Ciudadana estadounidense

Elena es una periodista uruguaya que quiso quedarse en Estados Unidos. Este fue el proceso.

1.

> Tengo una visa de periodista que me dura tres años. Voy a cubrir las reuniones de las Naciones Unidas para el periódico donde trabajo.

2.

> Hace ya dos años que vivo aquí y cada día me gusta más este país.

3.

> Para quedarme necesitaría la tarjeta verde. Y para conseguir la tarjeta verde, tendría que conseguir antes un trabajo estable.

▲ *Echa de menos a su familia, pero igual quiere quedarse.*

4.

> Hace cinco años que conseguí la tarjeta verde. Ahora tengo que estudiar las respuestas a 200 preguntas para obtener la ciudadanía y hacer el juramento a la bandera. Ojalá que el examen no sea muy difícil.

5.

6.

> ¡Ahora puedo votar aquí!

© John Wiley & Sons, Inc.

12.1-08 ¡Cosas de inmigración! Escucha más datos interesantes sobre la inmigración y decide si las oraciones son **Ciertas** o **Falsas**. Si son falsas, ¿cuál es la información correcta?

C   F

☐ ☐ 1. En caso de la muerte del presidente y el vicepresidente, la tercera persona en línea para gobernar el país sería el secretario de estado.

☐ ☐ 2. Elena estaba nerviosa porque tendría que pagar aproximadamente $700 para tomar el examen por segunda vez.

☐ ☐ 3. Para ser ciudadano español o uruguayo tendría que aprender bien el idioma y vivir en el país diez años.

HABLANDO DE GRAMÁTICA II

WileyPLUS Go to *WileyPLUS* to review this grammar point with the help of the **Animated Grammar Tutorial** and the **Verb Conjugator**.

2. Discussing hypothetical situations: The conditional tense

When we talk about hypothetical circumstances, we use the conditional tense.

¿Por qué **emigrarías** a otro país?	*Why would you emigrate to another country?*

A. Form of the conditional tense

As with the future tense, the conditional of regular verbs is formed by adding the following endings[8] to the infinitive:

Infinitive	emigrar	deber	permitir
(yo)	emigrar**ía**	deber**ía**	permitir**ía**
(tú)	emigrar**ías**	deber**ías**	permitir**ías**
(él, ella, Ud.)	emigrar**ía**	deber**ía**	permitir**ía**
(nosotros/as)	emigrar**íamos**	deber**íamos**	permitir**íamos**
(vosotros/as)	emigrar**íais**	deber**íais**	permitir**íais**
(ellos, ellas, Uds.)	emigrar**ían**	deber**ían**	permitir**ían**

Yo **iría** a esa manifestación porque…	*I would go to that protest because…*

Verbs that have an irregular stem in the future tense also form the conditional with that same irregular stem and regular conditional endings.

¿**Sabrías** explicarme de qué trata esa ley?	*Would you explain to me what that law is about?*

The conditional of **hay** (*there is, there are*) is **habría** (*there would be*).

Si la economía del país fuera más fuerte, **habría** más inmigrantes.	*If the country's economy were stronger, there would be more immigrants.*

Infinitive	Stem	
decir	**dir-**	
haber	**habr-**	
hacer	**har-**	-ía
poder	**podr-**	-ías
poner	**pondr-**	-ía
querer	**querr-**	-íamos
saber	**sabr-**	-íais
salir	**saldr-**	-ían
tener	**tendr-**	
venir	**vendr-**	

B. Uses of the conditional

The conditional is used to express what would happen in a hypothetical situation. The hypothetical situations or circumstances are usually expressed in a subordinate clause introduced by **si** (*if*) followed by the imperfect subjunctive:

Subordinate clause	Main clause
Si + *imperfect subjunctive*	conditional
Si quisieras quedarte en EE. UU.,	¿qué **harías**?
If you wanted to stay in the U.S.,	*what would you do?*
Si me quedara en EE. UU.,	**trabajaría** como periodista en las Naciones Unidas.
If I stayed in the U.S.,	*I would work as a journalist for the United Nations.*

It is very often used to make polite or softened requests or suggestions. It is commonly used with verbs like **gustar, querer, preferir, poder**, etc.

¿**Podrías** ayudarme con este formulario?	*Could you help me with this form?*
¿Me **darías** el teléfono de tu abogada?	*Would you give me the phone number of your lawyer?*

---

[8]These endings are the same as the imperfect tense endings for **-er** and **-ir** verbs.

12.1-09 ¿Llamamos a Elena? Dos amigas de Elena hablan de ella.

Paso 1: Lee el diálogo y señala todas las formas del condicional.

Patricia: Oye, hace tiempo que no sé nada de Elena. <u>Podríamos</u> llamarla.

Cristina: ¡Sí! Pero deberíamos esperar porque en EE. UU. ahora es de noche.

Patricia: Si yo pudiera, también iría a Estados Unidos.

Cristina: ¿Has visitado Estados Unidos alguna vez? ¿De verdad irías allí a vivir?

Patricia: Bueno, si tuviera dinero suficiente por lo menos visitaría algunos lugares.

Cristina: Si yo fuera tú, le preguntaría a Elena si te puedes quedar en su casa unos días. Conocerías Nueva York y así sabrías si querrías vivir allí o no.

Patricia: ¡Tienes razón! ¿Podrías darme su dirección de *e-mail*?

Cristina: Yo le escribiría un mensaje por WhatsApp; así es más fácil.

Paso 2: Escribe todas las formas del condicional que encuentres en el párrafo (hay once en total). Después, indica quién es el sujeto del verbo, si Cristina, Patricia o las dos.

MODELO: 1. *Podríamos (las dos)*

Paso 3: Patricia está chateando con su amiga Elena para ver si puede pasar unos días con ella en su apartamento de Nueva York. Patricia quiere ser muy cortés[9]. Usa la forma apropiada del condicional del verbo más apropiado.

deber
importar
querer
preferir
poder
tener
quedarse
ir

Chateo

Patricia
Hola, Elena, me gustaría viajar a Estados Unidos y pasar unos días en la costa este. ¿_____₁ quedarme en tu casa?

Elena
Pues claro, Patricia, ¿cómo no?

Patricia
Y cuando esté allí, ¿te _____₂ mostrarme la ciudad?

Elena
Pues, durante el día tengo que trabajar, pero por las noches sí podemos hacer cosas juntas. _____₃ hacer una lista de lo que quieres ver, ¡porque hay mucho!

Patricia
¿Y tú no _____₄ a visitar Filadelfia y Boston conmigo?

Elena
Mira, la verdad, _____₅ quedarme en Nueva York mientras tú viajas, porque yo tengo mucho trabajo estos próximos meses y no _____₆ tiempo de hacer esos viajes contigo. ¿_____₇ venir con Cristina?

Patricia
¿Y _____₈ las dos en tu casa?

Elena
Claro, mujer, ¡no hay problema!

© John Wiley & Sons, Inc.

12.1-10 ¿Qué harías?

Paso 1: Completa las siguientes oraciones con información que se aplique a ti.

MODELO: Si tuviera que emigrar a otro país, *emigraría a un país hispanohablante porque ya hablo bastante bien español.*

1. Si mis condiciones laborales no fueran buenas…
2. Si en mi país no hubiera mucho desempleo…
3. Si fuera un inmigrante recién[10] llegado…
4. Si pudiera aprobar una nueva ley de inmigración…

Paso 2: Ahora, transforma las oraciones en preguntas y entrevista a un/a compañero/a.

MODELO: Estudiante 1:   *¿Emigrarías a un país hispanohablante?*
                Estudiante 2:   *Bueno, depende. Iría a Chile o a Argentina, porque…*

Paso 3: Con la información que has recogido, compara lo que tú harías con lo que haría tu compañero/a. ¿Harían lo mismo? Escribe un pequeño párrafo sobre ustedes dos.

[9]**cortés:** polite [10]**recién:** recently

OTRA PERSPECTIVA

Courtesy of Teresa Pascual Garcia

Teresa

¡No todo el mundo quiere ir a Estados Unidos!

Diferente

"A Estados Unidos va mucha gente de muchos países del mundo escapando de una mala situación política o buscando mejorar su vida porque no encuentran trabajo en su país. Es muy difícil y triste tener que dejar a la familia y empezar otra vez en un lugar extraño, con un idioma y una cultura diferente. Si todos tuvieran un buen trabajo, pocas personas dejarían su país y su familia. Sin embargo, parece que en Estados Unidos se piensa que todo el mundo quiere, sueña y lógicamente preferiría vivir en Estados Unidos. ¿Por qué?".

Igual

"En todo el mundo hay migración de un lado y del otro. A España han venido personas que emigraban especialmente de América Latina, África y Europa del Este buscando mejores oportunidades. También hay estadounidenses que prefieren vivir en España. Muchos de nosotros también pensamos que como España no hay otro país".

 Explícale a Teresa

1. ¿Por qué la gente emigra a Estados Unidos?
2. ¿Crees que un hispanohablante preferiría vivir en Estados Unidos más que vivir en su país?
3. ¿A qué países van a vivir algunos estadounidenses?

MANOS A LA OBRA

 12.1-11 Asuntos sociales

Paso 1: Entrevista a un/a compañero/a para saber un poco sobre su experiencia con estos asuntos sociales.

1. ¿Emigró alguien de tu familia a Estados Unidos? ¿Quién? ¿Qué sabes de su historia?
2. ¿Hay muchos inmigrantes en la ciudad en la que vives? ¿De dónde son?
3. ¿Tienes algún amigo que emigró de otro país a EE. UU.? ¿De dónde emigró? ¿Sabes si le gusta vivir en EE. UU. o si preferiría vivir en su país de origen?
4. ¿Conoces a alguna persona que haya emigrado a otro país? ¿Por qué razón? ¿Le gusta vivir en ese país o preferiría vivir en EE. UU.?
5. ¿Has participado en alguna manifestación alguna vez? ¿Por qué causa?
6. ¿Alguna vez has participado en una huelga? ¿Cuándo? ¿Por qué?
7. ¿Luchas por alguna causa? ¿Por cuál? ¿Qué haces para luchar por esa causa?

Paso 2: Después, escriban un pequeño informe. ¿En qué aspectos coinciden los dos? ¿En qué no coinciden?

MODELO: (Nombre del/de la compañero/a) *tiene más experiencia con personas de otros países que yo. Sus abuelos eran de Nicaragua y emigraron a Estados Unidos. Por eso conoce a muchos nicaragüenses. Sin embargo, los dos conocemos a personas que...*

Paso 3: Por último, presenten el informe a la clase. ¿En qué cosas coinciden? ¿En qué aspecto no coincide nadie?

12.1-12 **Si las cosas fueran diferentes...**

Paso 1: Levántate y hazles a tus compañeros las siguientes preguntas. Escribe el nombre del/de la compañero/a que conteste afirmativamente.

MODELO: Estudiante 1:   *¿Te casarías con un inmigrante?*
            Estudiante 2:   *Sí, no tendría ningún problema.*

¿Quién de la clase...   Compañero/a

1. ... cambiaría la ley de inmigración estadounidense?   _____

2. ... se iría a vivir a América Latina?   _____

3. ... preferiría vivir en Europa?   _____

4. ... emigraría a otro país por un sueldo más alto?   _____

5. ... participaría en una manifestación por los derechos
   de los inmigrantes?   _____

6. ... querría estudiar en otro país durante un año?   _____

Paso 2: Después, comparte tus resultados con la clase. ¿Fue fácil o difícil completar la actividad?

MODELO: *Parece que muchas personas preferirían... pero nadie...*

12.1-13 **La diversidad en la clase de español** Seguro que en tu clase de español hay estudiantes de orígenes muy diversos. Vamos a conocernos todos un poco mejor.

 Paso 1: Para conocer mejor a los compañeros de clase empieza por completar el siguiente formulario[11].

Nacionalidad: _____

País de residencia: _____

¿Tienes doble ciudadanía?   Sí ☐   No ☐

Nacionalidad de tus padres:_____

Nacionalidad de tus abuelos: _____

Idiomas que hablas en casa, con tu familia: _____

Otros idiomas que hablas: _____

Países donde has vivido: _____

Ciudad en la que resides: _____

Mayores problemas sociales en esa ciudad:_____

Causas que apoyas o por las que luchas: _____

Marchas o manifestaciones en las que has participado: _____

 Paso 2: Comparen su formulario con el de dos o tres compañeros. ¿Con quién tienes más en común? ¿Con quién tienes más diferencias? ¿Hay algún estudiante en la clase que tenga el mismo origen que tú? ¿Lo sabías o ha sido una sorpresa?

Paso 3: Comenten los resultados de su grupo con la clase. ¿Cuántos estudiantes hay con nacionalidades diferentes? ¿Cuántos estudiantes hay con orígenes diferentes? ¿Alguien tiene doble ciudadanía? ¿Cuántos luchan por la misma causa? ¿Qué piensan? ¿Es la clase de español una comunidad diversa, o es por el contrario una comunidad bastante homogénea?

[11]formulario: form

12.1-14 Un cambio de vida

Paso 1: Formen parejas. Pregúntense qué saben sobre sus familiares: ¿Hubo algún inmigrante en tu familia? ¿Quiénes eran, tus abuelos, padres, tíos? ¿Alguien de tu misma generación? ¿De dónde vinieron? ¿Qué hacían ellos allí? ¿Qué hacían antes de llegar a Estados Unidos? ¿Dónde se instalaron cuando llegaron? ¿En qué región? ¿Qué lengua hablaban en su lugar de origen? ¿Qué tradiciones o palabras aprendiste de ellos?

Paso 2: Ahora, imagínense que tienen que emigrar de su país por razones económicas, religiosas o políticas. ¿A qué país emigrarían? ¿Cómo emigrarían? ¿Por qué emigrarían a ese país? ¿Qué incentivos ofrece el país que seleccionaron? ¿Qué problemas tendrían que enfrentar allá? ¿Qué tipo de trabajo encontrarían en ese país?

Paso 3: Por último, comenta tus conclusiones con tu compañero/a: ¿Qué opinas? ¿Crees que es importante que haya diversidad en Estados Unidos? ¿Es importante que los inmigrantes que llegan a este país hablen inglés? ¿Qué esperas que el gobierno de tu país haga para que los inmigrantes se integren mejor en la sociedad?

12.1-15 Presta atención: Jorge Ramos Escucha la información sobre Jorge Ramos para saber por qué es tan famoso en Estados Unidos y selecciona la respuesta más adecuada.

WileyPLUS Go to *WileyPLUS* and listen to **Presta atención**.

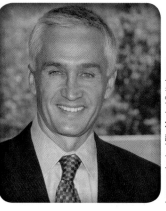

Lawrence Lucier / FilmMagic / Getty Images

1. ¿Quién es Jorge Ramos?
    a. Es periodista y escritor.
    b. Es político y periodista.
    c. Es un escritor de *People en Español*.
    d. Es político y escritor.
2. ¿Qué reconocimiento le dio la revista *Time* a Jorge Ramos?
    a. Es uno de los diez latinos con más influencia en Estados Unidos.
    b. Es uno de los diez latinos más admirados en Estados Unidos.
    c. Es uno de los veinticinco hispanos más influyentes de Estados Unidos.
    d. Es uno de los veinticinco mexicanos más famosos de Estados Unidos.
3. ¿En qué canal trabaja Jorge Ramos?
    a. Trabaja en CNN.
    b. Trabaja en Univisión.
    c. Trabaja en Telemiami.
    d. Trabaja en ABC-7.
4. ¿A qué político o escritor *no* ha entrevistado Jorge Ramos?
    a. a Barack Obama
    b. a Isabel Allende
    c. a Hugo Chávez
    d. a Raúl Castro
5. ¿Qué premio ganó en el 2011?
    a. Ganó un premio Emmy.
    b. Ganó el premio David Brinkley.
    c. Ganó el premio Ron Brown del Comité Nacional de Trabajo Infantil.
    d. Ganó un premio internacional de periodismo.

12.1-16 **Por escrito: Estudios en un país hispanoamericano**
Imagínate que estás llenando una solicitud para ingresar a
un programa de maestría o de doctorado en una universidad
hispanoamericana. Como eres extranjero/a, tienes que escribir
un párrafo explicando por qué te interesan las oportunidades
que ofrece estudiar en el país que seleccionaste y por qué no
podrías desarrollar esos intereses en Estados Unidos. Cuando
escribas, recuerda la sección **¡Ojo!**.

¡OJO!

Real-life goals
When writing a composition you *must have a
real-life goal in mind.* That's why when writing
you need to have a specific context, a purpose
for writing, a reader in mind, and the right use of
register, such as the use of **usted** or **tú** using a
formal and an informal register.

 ## PONTE EN MI LUGAR

Estrategias para conversar

Expressing courtesy As noted in **Hablando de gramática II**, the conditional is commonly used
to make requests and suggestions in a more courteous manner.
Here are some examples:

¿**Podría** indicarme cómo llenar este formulario?	*Would/Could you tell me how to fill out this form?*
¿**Sería** tan amable de…?	*Would you be so kind as to…?*
Me **gustaría** saber cómo puedo llegar a…	*I would like to know how can I get to…*
¿Le **importaría** decirme qué camino tomar para…?	*Would you mind telling me which way I could take to…?*

Perdido en Nueva York Un inmigrante recién llegado a la ciudad de Nueva York está
buscando la plaza Union Square. Está perdido y no habla inglés. Le pide ayuda a
un ciudadano que habla español. Decide si quieres ser el inmigrante perdido o la
persona que le ofrece ayuda. Usa el condicional y las expresiones de **Estrategias para
conversar** para tener una conversación cortés.

Inmigrante: Tienes muy mal sentido de orientación y no sabes llegar a Union Square.
Hablas con una persona que camina por la calle:

- Saluda y pide ayuda en español porque no sabes hablar inglés.
- Pregunta dónde está la plaza.
- Explícale que no tienes mucha información sobre la plaza (solo sabes que al lado[12]
  de la plaza hay una librería).
- Explícale que tienes miedo de tomar un trasporte público y que te gustaría saber
  cómo llegar a pie.
- Dale las gracias por su ayuda y despídete.

Ciudadano: Caminas por la calle y de repente alguien te llama la atención porque
necesita ayuda.

- Cuando empiece a hablar en español, dile que tiene suerte porque tú hablas español.
- Pregúntale el nombre de la plaza y cuando te lo diga, explícale que es grande y que
  necesitas saber si tiene que ir al lado sur, norte, este u oeste de la plaza.
- Después de aclarar el nombre y el lugar exacto, pregúntale si quiere ir caminando,
  en autobús o en metro.
- Después de darle instrucciones, saca un mapa de tu bolsa y dile que lo use si
  necesita ayuda.
- Despídete.

[12]**al lado:** next to

WileyPLUS   Go to *WileyPLUS* to find more **Arroba** activities.

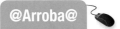

Espanglish ¿Sabes lo que significa *espanglish*? Busca información sobre este tema para responder las siguientes preguntas: ¿Qué es el *espanglish*? ¿Cuál es la causa del *espanglish*? ¿Has escuchado algunas expresiones o palabras en *espanglish*? ¿Cuáles? Comparte con un/a compañero/a la información que encuentres sobre el tema. Intercambien opiniones sobre el lugar que piensan que debería darse al *espanglish*: en la casa, en el trabajo, en la educación. Con un/a compañero/a, hagan una lista de palabras de *espanglish*. ¿Qué palabra es la más graciosa? ¿La más original? ¿La más extraña?

ASÍ ES LA VIDA

Adivina, adivinador

Cada país me reconoce,
pues yo lo represento,
suelo estar[13] en las alturas,
bajo el sol y frente al viento…
¿Quién soy?

Todos las piden,
nadie las respeta.
Si quieres saber qué es,
espera.
¿Qué es?

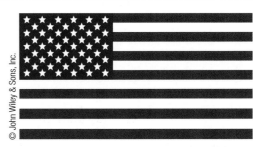

© John Wiley & Sons, Inc.

ENTÉRATE

Estrategias para leer

Expository texts An expository text is a written piece in which the author presents information about a situation without giving us his or her opinion. In an expository text, an objective thesis is presented and it comes from information collected about a specific topic. In Chapter 9, Section 1, you have learned that the thesis is the focus of a text. You also need to know that the title, the thesis or main idea, and the information presented in the body of the text help readers to reach a conclusion.

Antes de leer

1. Inmigrantes en Estados Unidos   Contesta las preguntas con un/a compañero/a.

- ¿Conoces inmigrantes que vivan en Estados Unidos? ¿De dónde vienen? ¿Trabajan? ¿Dónde?
- ¿Qué lenguas se hablan en Estados Unidos?
- ¿Cómo es la población de Estados Unidos?

---

[13]**suelo estar:** I'm usually

El nuevo **rostro** de Estados Unidos

face

NACIONALIDAD	CENSO 2000	CENSO 2010	PORCENTAJE 2010
Mexicanos	20.640.711	31.798.258	63%
Puertorriqueños	3.406.178	4.623.716	9,2%
Cubanos	1.241.685	1.785.547	3,5%
Dominicanos	764.945	1.414.703	2,8%
Costarricences	68.588	126.418	0,3%
Guatemaltecos	372.487	1.044.209	2,1%
Hondureños	1.044.209	633.401	1,3%
Nicaragüenses	177.684	348.202	0,7%
Panameños	91.723	165.456	0,3%
Salvadoreños	655.165	1.648.968	3,3%
Argentinos	100.864	224.952	0,4%
Bolivianos	42.068	99.210	0,2%
Chilenos	68.849	126.810	0,3%
Colombianos	470.684	908.734	1,8%
Ecuatorianos	908.734	564.631	1,1%
Paraguayos	8.769	20.023	-
Peruanos	233.926	531.358	1,1%
Uruguayos	18.804	56.884	0,1%
Venezolanos	91.507	215.023	0,4%
Españoles	100.135	635.253	1,3%
Latinos sin especificar nacionalidad	6.111.665	3.452.403	6,8%
Total de latinos en EE. UU.	35.305.818 (12,5%)	50.477.594	16,3%
Total de población en EE. UU.	281.421.906 (100%)	308.745.538	100%

"Ni ustedes ni yo vamos a estar aquí, pero en unos 100 años habrá más latinos, más hispanos, que blancos anglosajones en Estados Unidos. De alguna forma, Estados Unidos se está latinizando; o sea, es una verdadera revolución demográfica lo que estamos viendo en este país".

Estas palabras del periodista mexicano Jorge Ramos, en una entrevista con la Cadena Ser, vienen de los datos del último censo en Estados Unidos: ya son más de 50 millones los hispanos que viven en este país. Esta cifra representa más del 16% de la población, con un **crecimiento** del 43% en la última década, lo que significa que la comunidad hispana va en aumento. Además, según los estudios del gobierno estadounidense, para el año 2050 los hispanos muy probablemente lleguen a ser más de 132 millones. En este país existen ciudades donde el español es la lengua materna más hablada. En Miami, por ejemplo, el 70% de la población habla español. Otras ciudades, incluso, están en alrededor del 95%, como Hialeah, también en la Florida.

increase, growth

Cada año llegan miles de personas al país en busca de una vida mejor (sobre todo habitantes de América Central, como los salvadoreños, hondureños, nicaragüenses, etc.). Aproximadamente el 60% de los latinos ha nacido en Estados Unidos. Cada vez tienen mayor presencia en los medios de comunicación, en las universidades o en las esferas de poder. Por ejemplo, el número de latinos que **cursa estudios superiores** casi se ha triplicado en los últimos 30 años, pasando del 4% al 11%. Otro dato: el 12,1% de los nuevos admitidos en 2011 en la Universidad de Harvard es de origen latino, una cifra récord que supera al 10,3% del año anterior.

to study for a college degree

Además, esta comunidad ha adquirido un gran poder político: los analistas calculan que ningún político podría llegar a ser presidente de Estados Unidos sin contar con al menos el 40% del voto latino. Muchos **alcaldes** ya lo saben: es el ejemplo de Michael Bloomberg, quien además de estudiar español todos los días, realizó una fuerte campaña electoral en español en el 2009 para renovar su cargo de alcalde de la ciudad de Nueva York, donde aproximadamente el 30% de la población es latina.

mayors

No hay duda de que el rostro de Estados Unidos está cambiando y se está haciendo más hispano.

Después de leer

1. En el texto

1. ¿Cuál es la tesis o idea principal del texto?
   a. Ni ustedes ni yo vamos a estar aquí… en Estados Unidos.
   b. De alguna forma, Estados Unidos se esá latinizando...
   c. ... para el año 2050... lleguen a ser más de 132 millones.
2. ¿Qué tipo de evidencia se presenta en el cuerpo del texto para apoyar la idea principal?
   a. porcentajes, estadísticas y ejemplos
   b. citas, ejemplos y diagramas
   c. historias vividas y fotos
3. ¿Es la última oración de la lectura la conclusión? ¿Por qué sí o por qué no?

2. ¿Entendiste?

1. El texto nos indica que…
   a. la lengua oficial de Estados Unidos es el español.
   b. todos los inmigrantes son hispanos y cada vez hay menos.
   c. la comunidad hispana en Estados Unidos está aumentando.
2. El español…
   a. se habla más que el inglés en algunos lugares de Estados Unidos.
   b. es la lengua más hablada en todos los estados de Estados Unidos.
   c. se estudia cada vez más para poder relacionarse con los hispanos.
3. Muchos inmigrantes…
   a. que llegan a Estados Unidos saben cuál será su destino.
   b. vienen de América Central para tener una vida mejor.
   c. que vienen a Estados Unidos no hablan español.
4. Los políticos saben que…
   a. tendrán el voto de los hispanos si aumentan los impuestos.
   b. el inglés es la lengua oficial de las campañas electorales.
   c. necesitan el voto latino para poder ser elegidos.

 ## EN TU PROPIAS PALABRAS

Estrategias para escribir

In your own words When writing an expository text, you need to inform or describe the topic or facts that you are presenting without stating your opinion in a direct way (e.g., **Pienso que**…: *I believe that*). In order to write in a more objective manner without including your opinion, review Chapter 7, Section 2, **Hablando de Gramática II: se impersonal** and **se pasivo**. Remember that these are ways to express things in an impersonal way in Spanish.

In your first paragraph, include the main idea without superfluous information. In the body of your essay, you need to have evidence, such as anecdotes, quotes, or examples of the topic you are presenting. In the conclusion, restate your main idea, using different words, or present a question to open up the topic to the readers.

Espanglish En la actividad de **Arroba** buscaste información sobre lo que es el *espanglish*. Ahora, escribe un ensayo exponiendo la información que encontraste. No olvides que no estás dando tu opinión sobre si el *espanglish* es bueno o malo, solamente vas a exponer el tema. Sigue las **Estrategias para escribir** para poder presentar un buen informe.

© StockAB / Alamy

AUTOPRUEBA

VOCABULARIO

I. **¿Sabes lo que son?** Relaciona estas palabras con su significado.

1. la huelga
2. marroquí
3. los impuestos
4. el empleo
5. la inmigración
6. la igualdad

_____ a. Trato idéntico de todas las personas sin tener en cuenta, por ejemplo, la raza.

_____ b. Situación en la que la gente deja de trabajar para protestar por malas condiciones de trabajo.

_____ c. Es un trabajo, ocupación u oficio.

_____ d. Una persona que tiene la nacionalidad de Marruecos.

_____ e. Cantidad de dinero que se paga al estado para servicios públicos, como las carreteras.

_____ f. Movimiento de población que se refiere a la llegada de personas a un país.

II. **La vida de Miguel** Completa el diálogo con las palabras de la lista. ¡Ojo! Hay más palabras de las que necesitas. Conjuga los verbos y pon atención a la concordancia de los adjetivos.

> visa   luchar por   canadiense   residente   ciudadano/a
> echar de menos   portugués/portuguesa
> juramento a la bandera

Ana: ¿Eres de Portugal?

Tomás: Sí, soy _____1, pero ya llevo muchos años en EE. UU.

Ana: ¡Ah, sí! Entonces, ¿eres _____2 de EE. UU?

Tomás: Sí, hace como diez años que recité el _____3 de mi nuevo país, Estados Unidos.

Ana: ¿Y por qué viniste a Estados Unidos?

Tomás: Vine para no _____4 a mi novia. Tuve que dejar mi país y _____5 salvar el amor de mi vida. Y tú, ¿cuándo llegaste al país? ¿Eres _____6 de Estados Unidos?

Ana: No, no lo soy. Llegué hace un año y tengo una _____7 de estudiante.

GRAMÁTICA

I. **El recién llegado** Samuel es un canadiense que llegó a México hace solo dos meses. Ayúdalo a hacer estas peticiones de manera más cortés. Usa el verbo más apropiado.

> preferir   importar   traer   poder   decir

1. Al camarero de un bar: "Un café, por favor".
   ¿Me _____ un café, por favor?

2. A una persona que está caminando por la calle: "¿Qué hora es?".
   ¿Me _____ qué hora es, por favor?

3. En el banco: "Quiero cambiar dólares a pesos".
   ¿_____ cambiarme estos dólares a pesos?

4. En el supermercado, a una persona que está delante: "No puedo pasar".
   ¿Le _____ dejarme pasar, por favor?

5. En una tienda: "Esta camiseta me queda un poco pequeña. _____ una talla más grande".

II. **¿Qué pasaría?** Piensa qué pasaría o qué harías en estas situaciones. Completa las oraciones con un verbo diferente en cada una.

1. Si yo fuera el presidente de Estados Unidos...
2. Si mi mejor amigo quisiera emigrar a otro país...
3. Si mis padres vivieran en otro país...
4. Si yo no pudiera estudiar en la universidad...
5. Si hubiera mucho desempleo en mi ciudad...

CULTURA

Lee las siguientes oraciones y decide si son Ciertas o Falsas. Si son falsas, corrígelas.

C   F
☐   ☐ 1. Nunca ha habido emigración <u>de</u> Estados Unidos <u>a</u> México.

☐   ☐ 2. Los inmigrantes, en general, están tan contentos de estar en Estados Unidos que no echan de menos su cultura.

☐   ☐ 3. Para obtener la ciudadanía, muchos tienen que pasar un examen de 200 preguntas.

REDACCIÓN

Imagínate que por razones inevitables te ves obligado/a a emigrar a otro país.

- ¿A qué país irías? ¿Por qué?
- ¿Qué obstáculos crees que encontrarías?
- ¿Qué echarías de menos?

EN RESUMIDAS CUENTAS, AHORA PUEDO...

☐ hablar sobre temas de inmigración y nacionalidad.

☐ expresar subjetividad en el presente y el pasado.

☐ hablar de situaciones hipotéticas.

☐ hablar sobre los problemas que enfrentan los inmigrantes.

VOCABULARIO ESENCIAL

Sustantivos

el/la ciudadano/a	*citizen*
el (des)empleo	*(un)employment*
la (des)igualdad	*(in)equality*
la (doble) ciudadanía	*(dual) citizenship*
la huelga	*strike*
los impuestos	*taxes*
el juramento a la bandera	*the pledge of allegiance*
la ley	*law*
la manifestación	*protest*
el permiso	*permit*

Cognados: la comunidad, la diversidad, el/la emigrante, la (in)migración, el/la inmigrante, la marcha, la minoría, la nacionalidad, la oportunidad, el origen, el prejuicio, la protesta, el/la residente, la visa

Adjetivos

alemán/alemana	*German*
brasileño/a	*Brazilian*
canadiense	*Canadian*
francés/francesa	*French*
francoguayanés/ francoguayanesa	*French Guianese*
guyanés/guyanesa	*Guyanese*
haitiano/a	*Haitian*
italiano/a	*Italian*
jamaicano/a	*Jamaican*
marroquí	*Moroccan*
portugués/portuguesa	*Portuguese*
suizo/a	*Suisse*
surinamés/surinamesa	*Surinamese*

Cognados: (i)legal

Verbos

apoyar (una causa)	*to support (a cause)*
aprobar una ley	*to pass a law*
echar de menos	*to miss (something/ someone)*
luchar por	*to fight for*

Cognados: emigrar

LEARNING OBJECTIVES

By the end of this section you will be able to:

- Discuss issues related to Hispanics in the United States
- Talk about changes in someone's life
- Talk about changes in emotional states
- Describe people or objects in detail

Una imagen vale más que mil palabras

¿Crees que es un chiste? ¿Cuál es el propósito de este letrero?

¿En qué otras áreas de Estados Unidos se concentran comunidades que hablan otro idioma?

¿Has visitado comunidades donde se habla principalmente español? ¿Dónde? ¿Las puedes describir?

AP Photo/Lynne Sladky

▲ *Letrero en una escuela en Miami*

UNA PERSPECTIVA

Courtesy of Chad Gasta

Chad

Un día sin inmigrantes

Diferente

"La percepción general en Estados Unidos es que los inmigrantes son una carga negativa para la economía del país. ¿Pero cómo sería un día sin inmigrantes en algunos estados como Texas, Arizona, California o Nuevo México o en ciudades como Los Ángeles o Nueva York? Muchos inmigrantes ilegales trabajan en la agricultura, en restaurantes, en construcción, en hoteles, etc. ¿Y qué tal los inmigrantes legales? Sin ellos perderíamos médicos, enfermeras, escritores, doctores, músicos, pilotos, soldados, maestros, artistas y un gran número de profesores universitarios, entre otras cosas. ¿Cómo sería un día sin todos ellos?".

Igual

"Los inmigrantes también pagan impuestos. No pagan impuestos federales o estatales, pero los pagan como consumidores y se les descuenta de su salario. Cada vez que compran algo —zapatos, televisores, ropa o alimentos—, pagan impuestos de ventas. Y cada vez que pagan el alquiler, ayudan a pagar los impuestos a la propiedad. A los inmigrantes que tienen la tarjeta verde se les deducen del sueldo impuestos federales y contribuciones a la seguridad social, como a cualquier ciudadano. De una forma u otra, los inmigrantes contribuyen enormemente a la economía del país".

¿Qué piensas tú?

1. ¿Conoces a algún inmigrante?
2. ¿Cómo cambiaría/sería tu vida si no hubiera inmigrantes?
3. ¿En qué trabajarías si tuvieras que emigrar a otro país?

LA PURA VERDAD I   El activismo

Iliana Suárez, estudiante universitaria, nos dice a quién admira.

1.

¿Quién es Dolores Huerta? Pues, es una mujer estadounidense, nacida en California, de ascendencia mexicana. Dolores es una persona muy destacada.

2.

"Pensé que sería mejor organizar a los trabajadores agrícolas que ser la maestra de sus hijos hambrientos."

3.

► *Dolores Huerta fundó, junto con César Chávez, la Unión de Trabajadores Agrícolas (UFW).*

4.

◄ *Dolores organizó muchas marchas y manifestaciones de carácter político.*

5.

► *También recibió numerosos premios por su tarea como activista.*

6.

© John Wiley & Sons, Inc.

12.2-01 Más datos sobre Dolores Huerta Escucha más información sobre Dolores Huerta y completa las siguientes oraciones.

1. Los padres de Dolores Huerta...
   a. eran chicanos.
   b. eran mexicanos.
   c. eran de Stockton.
2. Cuatro de los hijos de Dolores Huerta...
   a. son sobrinos del activista César Chávez.
   b. son hijos del activista César Chávez.
   c. son líderes de la Unión de Trabajadores.
3. Dolores Huerta...
   a. recibió premios de escuelas en Texas, Colorado y California.
   b. recibió un premio del presidente de México.
   c. recibió honores de varias universidades de Estados Unidos.

🎧 PALABRA POR PALABRA

La herencia cultural *Cultural heritage*

▲ *Hay más de 50 millones de hispanos en Estados Unidos (según el censo de 2010). Estados Unidos es el tercer país con más hispanohablantes del mundo, después de México y España.*

Nuestra herencia

los antepasados/antecesores	*ancestors*
la ascendencia	*ancestry*
la demografía	*demographics*
el/la hispanohablante	*Spanish speaker*
la lengua materna	*mother language*
las raíces	*roots*
la raza	*race*

Cognados: bicultural, bilingüe, multicultural, multirracial

Los asuntos sociales y políticos

el/la activista destacado/a	*renown activist*
los derechos	*rights*
la jubilación	*retirement*
el nivel (de vida/socioeconómico)	*(living/socioeconomic) standard*
el perfil	*profile*
el rechazo	*rejection*
el sindicato	*labor union*
el tema (controvertido)	*(controversial) issue, topic*
la vivienda	*housing*

integrarse	*to be accepted, to join a group*
prosperar	*to prosper, to thrive*
rechazar (z>c)	*to reject*
reconocer	*to recognize*
triunfar, tener éxito	*to succeed, to be successful*

Cognados: el activismo, la asimilación, la comunidad, la discriminación, las elecciones, la identidad cultural, la influencia, la (in)justicia, la (in)tolerancia, la organización (política/laboral), la política, la sociedad

12.2-02 ¿De qué hablamos?

 Paso 1: Lee las definiciones y busca la palabra correspondiente en la sección **Palabra por palabra**.

MODELO: Es el grupo de la sociedad estadounidense que habla español como primera lengua o lengua materna.   →   *los hispanohablantes*

1. Es el idioma que aprendes de tus padres o en tu casa durante la infancia.
2. Es el conjunto de antecesores o antepasados de una persona.
3. Es el retiro del mundo laboral a causa de una edad avanzada establecida por la ley.
4. Es una casa, apartamento o habitación donde viven las personas.
5. Es una asociación de trabajadores creada para defender sus derechos laborales.
6. Es el conjunto de características particulares de una persona o un grupo.
7. Es el conjunto de características, ideas, costumbres, circunstancias sociales y/o culturales que se transmiten de padres a hijos.
8. Es el resultado de no aceptar, no admitir o resistirse a algo o a alguien.

 Paso 2: Ahora, elijan tres palabras de la sección **Palabra por palabra** y escriban sus definiciones para leérselas a la clase. ¡Atención! Recuerden que para definir siempre usamos el verbo ser.

MODELO: *Es un/una/el/la... (que)...*
           Es el proceso/la actividad de...

 12.2-03 Asociación de ideas ¿En cuántas palabras relacionadas con los siguientes conceptos pueden pensar? Hagan una lista. ¿Qué grupo sabe más palabras?

MODELO: la tolerancia   →   *la diversidad, la igualdad, la justicia social, el activismo, etc.*

1. el sindicato	5. el nivel de vida
2. la discriminación	6. la jubilación
3. la identidad cultural	7. la herencia cultural
4. la ascendencia	8. el bilingüismo

12.2-04 ¿Cómo es tu comunidad?

Paso 1: Entrevista a un/a compañero/a para saber un poco más sobre él/ella y su comunidad.

1. ¿Cuál es tu lengua materna? ¿Qué lengua hablas en tu casa?
2. ¿Conoces a alguien que tenga una lengua materna diferente del inglés?
3. ¿Tienes amigos hispanohablantes? ¿Son estadounidenses? ¿Cuál es su ascendencia?
4. ¿Formas parte de alguna organización política o laboral? ¿Admiras a algún activista destacado?
5. ¿Cómo es tu ciudad de origen? ¿Es multicultural o multirracial? ¿Cuáles son los grupos más numerosos?
6. ¿Crees que en tu ciudad/comunidad/grupo social se rechaza a ciertos grupos minoritarios?
7. ¿Qué entiendes por "asimilación"? ¿Crees que los hispanos de tu área están "asimilados"?
8. ¿Sabes lo que es la "hispanización"? ¿Crees que tu ciudad está "hispanizada"?

Paso 2: Después, escribe un breve informe sobre tu compañero/a. En la conclusión, resume si lleva un estilo de vida multicultural o si, por el contrario, su experiencia se concentra en una sola cultura.

MODELO: *Mi compañero/a tiene una experiencia de vida multicultural y diversa. Primero, él/ella habla inglés, pero su lengua materna es…*

Paso 3: Por último, informen a la clase. Después, como clase, decidan: ¿es su clase una clase diversa y multicultural, o forman ustedes una "comunidad" bastante homogénea?

12.2-05 ¿El país de las oportunidades?

Paso 1: Usando el vocabulario de **Palabra por palabra**, hagan una lista de lo mejor y lo peor que Estados Unidos ofrece a los extranjeros que vienen a vivir aquí. Elijan algunos de los siguientes temas sociales y díganle su opinión al resto del grupo.

MODELO: Estudiante 1: *Yo creo que en algunas zonas de Estados Unidos hay mucha diversidad racial y cultural, y para los inmigrantes es muy fácil comenzar una nueva vida.*

Estudiante 2: *Yo no estoy de acuerdo. Creo que en Estados Unidos todavía hay mucha intolerancia hacia otras culturas.*

1. la discriminación
2. la diversidad
3. la seguridad social
4. los impuestos
5. la (des)igualdad social
6. el nivel de vida
7. los derechos de los trabajadores
8. las oportunidades de prosperar o triunfar
9. el acceso a la educación
10. la (in)tolerancia hacia otras culturas

Paso 2: Elijan un tema sobre el que todos los miembros del grupo estén de acuerdo. Un/a secretario/a debe escribir los argumentos del grupo a favor o en contra.

Paso 3: Cada grupo presenta sus argumentos a la clase. Al final, entre todos decidan: ¿es fácil o difícil integrarse en Estados Unidos siendo extranjero o inmigrante?

HABLANDO DE GRAMÁTICA I

WileyPLUS Go to *WileyPLUS* to review this grammar point with the help of the **Animated Grammar Tutorial** and the **Verb Conjugator**.

1. Describing emotions and changes of state: The verbs **hacerse**, **volverse** and **ponerse**

A. True reflexives

In Chapter 4, Section 1, you learned about reflexive events and reflexive pronouns. Reflexive events are those in which someone is acting on himself/herself. Reflexive events are signaled in Spanish by the use of reflexive pronouns. Compare these examples.

Nonreflexive	Reflexive
Ella tuvo que cuidar **a sus padres**, que eran ancianos.	Ella tiene que cuidar**se**, porque trabaja demasiado.
She had to take care of her parents, who were elderly.	*She has to take care of herself, because she works too much.*
Cuando yo **la** vi, no me pareció una anciana.	Cuando **se** vio en el espejo dijo: "Parezco una anciana".
When I saw her, she didn't look elderly to me.	*When she saw herself in the mirror she said, "I look like an old woman."*

B. Pronominal and change-of-state verbs

You also learned that some verbs usually take a reflexive pronoun even if the action is not truly reflexive (i.e., the subject is not acting on him/herself). These are called pronominal verbs (**verbos pronominales**) and are very common in Spanish.

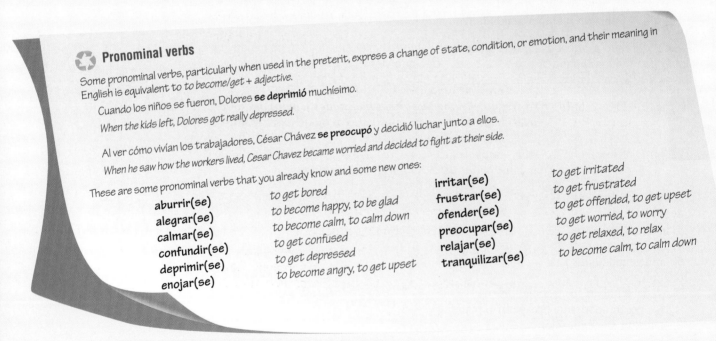

Pronominal verbs

Some pronominal verbs, particularly when used in the preterit, express a change of state, condition, or emotion, and their meaning in English is equivalent to *to become/get* + adjective.

Cuando los niños se fueron, Dolores **se deprimió** muchísimo.

When the kids left, Dolores got really depressed.

Al ver cómo vivían los trabajadores, César Chávez **se preocupó** y decidió luchar junto a ellos.

When he saw how the workers lived, Cesar Chavez became worried and decided to fight at their side.

These are some pronominal verbs that you already know and some new ones:

aburrir(se)	to get bored	irritar(se)	to get irritated
alegrar(se)	to become happy, to be glad	frustrar(se)	to get frustrated
calmar(se)	to become calm, to calm down	ofender(se)	to get offended, to get upset
confundir(se)	to get confused	preocupar(se)	to get worried, to worry
deprimir(se)	to get depressed	relajar(se)	to get relaxed, to relax
enojar(se)	to become angry, to get upset	tranquilizar(se)	to become calm, to calm down

12.2-06 El compañero de equipo más compatible Ya conoces bastante a tus compañeros de clase y has tenido oportunidad de trabajar con algunos de ellos. Ahora es el momento de saber quién sería tu compañero/a ideal para trabajar en un proyecto de la comunidad.

Paso 1: Indica si las siguientes afirmaciones se te aplican o no.

	Sí	No
1. Me aburro cuando tengo que trabajar solo/a.	☐	☐
2. Me divierto mucho cuando trabajo con niños.	☐	☐
3. Me irrito cuando no tengo suficiente tiempo para estudiar.	☐	☐
4. Me frustro si no entiendo qué tengo que hacer.	☐	☐
5. Me preocupo por mis notas.	☐	☐

Ahora, transforma estas oraciones en preguntas.

Paso 2: En grupos de cuatro, túrnense para hacer las preguntas. Todos deben responder cada pregunta. Al final, cada miembro del grupo tiene que decidir quién sería la persona más compatible con quien trabajar en un proyecto final.

MODELO: Estudiante 1:   *¿Se aburren cuando tienen que trabajar solos?*
          Estudiante 2:   *Yo no me aburro, a mí me gusta trabajar solo/a.*
          Estudiante 3:   *Yo sí me aburro; me divierte más trabajar en equipo.*

C. The verbs *ponerse*, *hacerse* and *volverse*

These verbs express a change of, emotion or condition in Spanish. **Ponerse** is used to express a spontaneous and nonpermanent change of mood.

ponerse... contento/a, feliz, de buen/mal humor, triste, nervioso/a, enfermo/a

Me puse muy **contenta** cuando supe que conocería a Dolores Huerta.	*I got very happy when I found out that I would meet Dolores Huerta.*
Se pone de mal humor cuando habla de temas controvertidos.	*He/she gets in a bad mood when he/she talks about controversial issues.*

Volverse is used to convey a more permanent change in character, personality, or behavior. It is more often used to talk about a negative change.

volverse... irritable, sensible, egoísta, autoritario/a, amigable, loco/a, radical, extremista, intolerante, (ir)responsable

Desde que es parte de esa organización, **se ha vuelto** muy **sensible**.	*Since he/she became part of that organization, he/she has become very sensitive.*
Te has vuelto muy **irritable** desde que trabajas en el sindicato.	*You've become very irritable since you began working for the union.*

Hacerse is used to express a personal, professional, or social development. It implies a gradual change, over a period of time, usually voluntary and effortful.

hacerse... mayor, viejo/a, rico/a, famoso/a, ciudadano/a, activista

Dolores Huerta **se hizo famosa** por luchar por los derechos de los trabajadores.	*Dolores Huerta became famous for fighting in favor of workers' rights.*
Después de 10 años, **me hice ciudadano**.	*After 10 years, I became a citizen.*

12.2-07 ¿Cómo te pones?

Paso 1: Usando *ponerse + adjetivo*, expresa cómo te sientes en estas situaciones.

1. cuando me va bien en un examen
2. cuando conozco a gente con quien puedo practicar español
3. cuando tengo mucho que estudiar
4. cuando no entiendo lo que dice el profesor
5. cuando intento decir algo y no sé cómo expresarlo

Paso 2: Entrevista a un/a compañero/a para ver si reacciona de la misma manera que tú. ¿Son parecidos o diferentes en su forma de reaccionar?

MODELO: *¿Te pones _____ cuando conoces a gente que habla español?*

LA PURA VERDAD II La vida de un poeta

Francisco X. Alarcón es un poeta y profesor chicano que enseña en la Universidad de California en Davis. En esta sección, el profesor Alarcón nos habla sobre su vida, su familia y su profesión.

1.

2.

3.
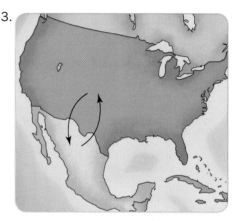

▲ *Francisco nació en Los Ángeles, pero creció en México. De niño iba y venía de México a Estados Unidos con frecuencia.*

4.

5.

▲ *Francisco es profesor y ha escrito varios libros de poesía. Se ha hecho famoso con sus libros de poemas bilingües para niños.*

12.2-08 Más datos sobre Francisco Alarcón Escucha más información sobre la vida de Francisco Alarcón. Luego, indica qué oración responde correctamente cada pregunta.

1. ¿A qué tipo de estudiantes está dirigido su programa?
   a. a aquellos estudiantes que han aprendido español como segunda lengua
   b. a aquellos estudiantes que no pueden escribir bien el español
   c. a aquellos estudiantes que han recibido instrucción formal en español
2. Francisco Alarcón...
   a. se alegra de que estén orgullosos de su cultura estadounidense.
   b. espera que aprendan a escribir ensayos y poemas.
   c. dice que es bueno aprender inglés primero.
3. Francisco Alarcón...
   a. escribe libros en inglés y español porque es bueno que los hispanos conserven la conexión con el español.
   b. escribe libros para enseñar español en la universidad.
   c. escribe libros que enseñan a sentirse orgullosos de hablar español.

HABLANDO DE GRAMÁTICA II

2. Describing objects or people: Subjunctive vs. indicative in adjective clauses

In Chapters 9, 10, and 11, you learned about the subjunctive mood and how it is required in some subordinate clauses. In this section you will learn about adjective clauses (clauses that have the same function as an adjective).

WileyPLUS Go to *WileyPLUS* to review this grammar point with the help of the **Animated Grammar Tutorial** and the **Verb Conjugator**.

Adjective	**Adjective clause**
Ese es un tema [muy controvertido].	*That is a [very controversial] issue.*
Ese es un tema [que causa mucha controversia].	*That is an issue [that causes a lot of controversy].*

When the adjective clause describes someone or something that we know for certain that exists and that we can identify, we use the indicative mood:

Es un poeta chicano [que **escribe** poemas bilingües].	*He's a Chicano poet [who writes bilingual poems].*
Estados Unidos es un país [que **tiene** mucha diversidad].	*The United States is a country [that has a lot of diversity].*

By contrast, when the adjective clause describes something or someone that is unknown, unspecified, or hypothetical, we use the subjunctive mood:

Queremos contratar a un poeta [que **escriba** poemas bilingües].	*We want to hire a poet [who writes bilingual poems].*
¿Conoces algún país [que **tenga** tanta diversidad como Estados Unidos]?	*Do you know of any country [that has as much diversity as the United States]?*

Following the same logic, when the adjective clause describes a nonexistent or negated antecedent, we use the subjunctive mood.

No queremos contratar a nadie [que **escriba** solo en inglés].	*We want to hire a poet [who writes bilingual poems].*
No conozco ningún país [que **tenga** tanta diversidad como Estados Unidos].	*I don't know of any country [that has as much diversity as the United States].*

12.2-09 El programa de español para hispanohablantes Francisco X. Alarcón, director del programa de español para hispanohablantes de la Universidad de California en Davis, enumera las características ideales de un programa de este tipo. Relaciona las dos columnas en la siguiente página para saber cuáles son esas características. Los elementos de las dos columnas completan la oración que comienza en el dibujo.

Para que un programa de español para hispanohablantes sea bueno, debe contar con...

© John Wiley & Sons, Inc.

_____ 1. profesores...

_____ 2. un libro de texto...

_____ 3. aulas y laboratorios de lengua...

_____ 4. una universidad...

_____ 5. un equipo de tutores...

_____ 6. una comunidad...

_____ 7. estudiantes...

a. que **apoye** nuestra labor.

b. donde **haya** un alto porcentaje de estudiantes hispanohablantes.

c. que **quieran** mejorar su español escrito y conectarse con sus raíces.

d. que **sepan** cuáles son las necesidades lingüísticas de los hispanohablantes en EE. UU.

e. que **estén** bien equipados.

f. que **sea** actual e interesante y que **tenga** buenos ejercicios.

g. que **estén** muy motivados.

 12.2-10 La familia de Francisco Alarcón

Paso 1: En una entrevista, Francisco Alarcón nos habla de cómo sus padres, que eran personas de origen humilde, prosperaron en Estados Unidos. Completa el texto de la entrevista con la forma apropiada del indicativo o del subjuntivo, según corresponda.

No conozco a nadie que *representa/represente*$_1$ el sueño americano como mis padres. Ellos son unas personas extraordinarias. Mis padres, que en México *eran/fueran*$_2$ campesinos[1], deciden emigrar a Estados Unidos. Aquí crían a sus siete hijos, que ahora *son/sean*$_3$ profesionales. Todos nosotros, que *somos/seamos*$_4$ la segunda generación, hemos prosperado. Mi hermano mayor, que ahora *trabaja/trabaje*$_5$ como director general de un hospital, es cirujano[2]. Tengo otro hermano que *es/sea*$_6$ arquitecto. Yo soy el que *escribe/escriba*$_7$ poemas. Mi hermano Carlos es cura en una iglesia que *tiene/tenga*$_8$ un área de influencia de unas 20.000 personas... No conozco ningún otro país donde *es/sea*$_9$ posible llegar tan lejos viniendo de un origen humilde. Mi madre siempre nos decía: "Hagan aquello que *quieren/quieran*$_{10}$ hacer, pero háganlo bien". Cuando escribo libros, no hay nada que me *inspira/inspire*$_{11}$ más que la historia de mi familia.

Paso 2: Imagina que vas a entrevistar a Francisco Alarcón y que tienes que preparar algunas preguntas.

1. ¿Conoce a alguien que...?
2. ¿Ha vivido en algún lugar donde...?
3. ¿Ha escrito algún libro que...?
4. ¿Nos puede recomendar otros autores chicanos que...?
5. ¿Puede hablarnos de algún premio que...?

[1]campesino/a: peasant [2]cirujano: surgeon

OTRA PERSPECTIVA

Courtesy of Norma
López-Burton

Norma

Los hispanos

Diferente

"Aquí en California muchas personas asumen que soy
mexicana, pero yo soy de Puerto Rico. Lo comprendo,
porque en California la mayoría de los hispanohablantes
vienen del sur de la frontera. Comprendo que la gente
crea que me gusta la comida picante (en Puerto Rico no comemos comida picante) o
que hago tortillas en casa (en Puerto Rico casi ni se venden). Tampoco me molesta
cuando la gente me pregunta: '¿Cómo obtuviste la ciudadanía?'. Los puertorriqueños
somos ciudadanos estadounidenses. Pero lo que sí encuentro raro es que aquí nos
clasifican a todos los que hablamos español como 'hispanos'. En nuestros respectivos
países no nos referimos a nosotros mismos como 'hispanos'. Decimos que somos
puertorriqueños, guatemaltecos, argentinos, bolivianos, etc. Cada país tiene una variedad
lingüística y una cultura diferente. ¿Por qué nos clasifican a todos como hispanos sin
distinguir entre los diferentes grupos?".

Igual

"Nosotros también clasificamos a las personas de China, Corea, Japón, Tailandia y
Vietnam como 'asiáticas u orientales'. Y sin embargo, las personas de esos países
también tienen idiomas y culturas diferentes. ¡Algunos hasta han sido enemigos! Pero
aun así los catalogamos a todos con la misma etiqueta[3]. Y lo más curioso es que no
llamamos 'asiáticas' a las personas de la India, ni de Pakistán, ni de Bangladés, ni de
Irán, aunque son de Asia. Interesante, ¿no? ¿Por qué será?".

Explícale a Norma

1. ¿Por qué en Estados Unidos se llama "hispanos" a todos los que hablan español
   como lengua materna?
2. ¿Qué significan para ti las palabras "hispano" y "latino"? ¿Hay alguna diferencia
   entre ellas? ¿Cuál de las dos usas más?
3. ¿Crees que hay una clasificación para todos los que hablan inglés en el mundo? ¿Por qué?

MANOS A LA OBRA

12.2-11 ¿Cómo te sientes cuando...?

Paso 1: Selecciona tres de las siguientes situaciones. Escribe en una hoja aparte cómo
te sientes en esas situaciones. Una de tus oraciones tiene que ser falsa.

MODELO: pensar en la jubilación   →   *Me aburro cuando pienso en la jubilación.*

1. pensar en la jubilación
2. usar estructuras nuevas en español
3. ver a personas ancianas con un mal nivel de vida
4. poder votar en las elecciones presidenciales
5. vivir en una sociedad...
6. leer libros sobre temas controvertidos

aburrirse
alegrarse
calmarse
confundirse
deprimirse
enojarse
irritarse
frustrarse
preocuparse
relajarse
tranquilizarse
ponerse (+ adjetivo)

[3]etiqueta: label

Paso 2: Léanles sus oraciones a los otros miembros del grupo. Ellos tienen que adivinar cuál es la reacción falsa y decir por qué.

MODELO: *Pienso que es falso que **te aburras** cuando **piensas** en la jubilación porque yo sé que tienes muchos planes para cuando dejes de trabajar.*

Paso 3: ¿Qué piensan? ¿Conocen bien a sus compañeros de grupo?

12.2-12 Busca a alguien que…

Paso 1: ¿Es tu clase de español una comunidad diversa? ¡Continúa investigando! Habla con el mayor número de compañeros posible y busca a alguien que…

1. tenga ascendencia de otro país (especifica qué país).
2. pertenezca a una organización política (¿cuál?).
3. trabaje para un sindicato (¿cuál?).
4. tenga amigos hispanohablantes (¿de dónde son? ¿cómo se llaman?).
5. sea bilingüe (especifica qué idiomas habla).
6. proceda de una familia multirracial (¿de qué etnicidad?).
7. se confunda siempre que habla español (¿con quién?).
8. admire a algún activista social (¿quién?).
9. se sienta orgulloso/a de sus raíces (¿cuáles?).

MODELO: Estudiante 1: *¿Eres bilingüe?*
Estudiante 2: *Sí, soy bilingüe. Hablo _____ y _____, ¿y tú?*

Paso 2: Después, informa a la clase. ¿Has encontrado a alguien para cada categoría?

MODELO: *No he encontrado a nadie que __sea__ bilingüe.*
Sí, he encontrado a dos personas que __son__ bilingües. Se llaman…

12.2-13 Los famosos en Estados Unidos Camina por la clase haciendo preguntas a tus compañeros y escribe el nombre de los estudiantes que contesten afirmativamente. Usa verbos pronominales en tus respuestas o *volverse/ponerse + adjetivo*.

Paso 1: ¿Cómo reaccionan tus compañeros cuando se habla sobre los siguientes temas?

MODELO: Estudiante 1: *¿Cómo reaccionas cuando alguien habla sobre los logros de los hispanos?*
Estudiante 2: *Me alegro muchísimo.*
Estudiante 1: (escribe) *Josh se alegra muchísimo cuando se habla sobre los logros de los hispanos.*

1. _____ los logros de los hispanos.
2. _____ la vida amorosa de los famosos.
3. _____ la educación bilingüe de los profesionales destacados.
4. _____ la vida bicultural que mencionan las letras de algunas canciones.
5. _____ los deportistas hispanos se destacan.
6. _____ no siempre algunos escritores dicen la verdad en sus artículos de opinión.
7. _____ las viviendas de los famosos valen millones de dólares.
8. _____ algunos comentaristas de la radio hacen comentarios negativos sobre los inmigrantes.

Paso 2: Ahora, comenta tus respuestas con el resto de la clase. En general, ¿reaccionan de manera similar ante estas situaciones? ¿Son ustedes una clase homogénea o diversa en cuanto a sus opiniones?

12.2-14 **Nuestra organización** Piensen en una organización estudiantil que quieran fundar. Debe ser una organización con una causa social o de ayuda a la comunidad.

Paso 1: Piensen en un nombre para su organización y una misión. Después, piensen en lo que puede hacer cada uno de ustedes en la organización.

MODELO: Estudiante 1:   *Yo trabajo con muchas empresas y puedo buscar patrocinadores*[4].
Estudiante 2:   *Yo soy muy buena con los números y puedo ser la tesorera.*
Estudiante 3:   *Yo tengo experiencia en... y puedo...*

Paso 2: Escriban una descripción. Deben incluir el nombre de su organización, la misión, lo que ya tienen y lo que necesitan.

MODELO: *La organización estudiantil "Hermanas Unidas" tiene como misión (ayudar/ favorecer/dar a conocer/luchar, etc)... y queremos llegar a personas que...*
Actualmente tenemos...
También contamos con varias personas que...
Necesitamos un traductor/representante/... que...
Buscamos un local donde reunirnos que...

Paso 3: Después de compartir sus descripciones y anuncios con la clase, el objetivo es encontrar lo que necesitan o están buscando entre las personas de la clase.

Paso 4: Cuando terminen de describir su organización y encuentren todo lo que necesitan y a las personas con el perfil que buscan, presenten su proyecto final a la clase.

WileyPLUS Go to *WileyPLUS* and listen to **Presta atención**.

 12.2-15 **Presta atención: El español en Estados Unidos** Unas compañeras de trabajo están hablando sobre un artículo que habla del español en Estados Unidos. Escucha para saber de qué trata el artículo. Selecciona la respuesta más adecuada para cada pregunta.

1. Según el artículo que Flor está leyendo en el año 2050...
    a. en Estados Unidos habrá más de 130 millones de latinos.
    b. el número de hispanohablantes será diez veces el de ahora.
    c. la Real Academia Española dejará de aceptar nuevas palabras.
2. El número de hispanos que vivirá en Estados Unidos en el futuro...
    a. no necesariamente hablará inglés.
    b. no tiene por qué ser hispanohablante.
    c. hablará español de manera fluida.
3. Según Flor, el término...
    a. "hispano" se refiere a un latino que habla español en Estados Unidos.
    b. "hispanounidense" se refiere a un hispano que vive en Estados Unidos pero no necesariamente habla español.
    c. "latino" se refiere a un hispano que habla un español diferente al de su país.
4. ¿Qué sabemos de las palabras "bagel" y "pretzel" según la conversación de Marta y Flor?
    a. que son palabras que tienen una buena traducción al español
    b. que los hispanos siempre las traducen cuando las usan
    c. que la Real Academia Española las aceptará
5. ¿Qué piensa Flor de la palabra "aplicar" en lugar de "solicitar"?
    a. que si mucha gente la usa, la RAE la aceptará
    b. que la RAE acepta la palabra "solicitar" y no va a agregar otra
    c. que los hispanohablantes usan solamente las palabras aceptadas por la RAE

---

[4]patrocinador: sponsor

¡OJO!

Structure your narration
In **Estrategias para escribir,**
Chapter 8, Section 1, you
learned that a narration has
(a) an introduction, (b) the
high point or climax of the
story and (c) a conclusion.
In your narration, remember
also to check for agreement,
verbal tenses, and the use of
subjunctive.

12.2-16 Por escrito: Un profesional extranjero Escribe una narracción sobre un profesional extranjero que trabaje y viva en Estados Unidos.

- ¿Cómo se llama?
- ¿Cuál es su profesión?
- ¿Por qué lo/la admiras?
- ¿De qué país es?
- ¿Cómo llegó a Estados Unidos?
- ¿Cómo se sintió al llegar a este país?
- ¿Hoy día es una persona destacada en su profesión?
- ¿Qué quieres que haga por ti o por el mundo?

PONTE EN MI LUGAR

Estrategias para conversar

To talk about disappointments In Chapter 10, Section 2, you learned a few expressions to express satisfaction or to praise someone. In this section, you will learn a few more expressions to express disappointment and to respond to those comments of disappointment.

To express disappointment

Me confunde que... (+ *subjuntivo*)	*It confuses me that . . .*
Me irrito/irrité cuando (+ *indicativo*)...	*I get/got irritated when . . .*
Me ofendió cuando me dijo (+ *indicativo*)....	*I got upset when you said . . .*

To respond to expressions of disappointment

Cálmese/Cálmate, no quería deprimirlo/a/ deprimirte.	*Calm down, I didn't want you to get depressed.*
Perdone/Perdona mi ignorancia, pero me frustra...	*I am sorry about my ignorance, but I get frustrated . . .*
Por favor no se/te enoje/s, realmente pensaba que...	*Please don't get angry, I really thought that . . .*

Mentiras Un/a amigo/a se molesta porque su mejor amigo/a le ha mentido. Decidan quién será el/la amigo/a que no dice la verdad y quién será el/la amigo/a ofendido/a. Sigan las instrucciones. Usen las expresiones que aparecen en **Estrategias para conversar** para expresar decepción.

El/La amigo/a mentiroso/a: Estás en la universidad y vives con tus padres porque no puedes ni quieres pagar el alquiler de un apartamento. Pasas mucho tiempo en casa de tu amigo/a preparando tareas, proyectos y divirtiéndote. Tu amigo/a quiere ir a tu casa porque cuando lo/a conociste le dijiste que vivías con dos chicos/as. Conversas con él/ella y de nuevo te menciona que quiere que, para el próximo proyecto en equipo, trabajen los dos en tu casa. Buscas excusas para poder trabajar en la biblioteca o en algún otro lado. Quieres decirle la verdad, pero no sabes cómo. Cuando tu amigo/a te exprese su decepción, pídele disculpas y explícale que no sabías cómo decirle la verdad por un comentario que él/ella hizo cuando lo/la conociste por primera vez.

El/La amigo/a ofendido/a: Estás cansado/a de que tu mejor amigo/a pase todo el tiempo en tu apartamento y nunca te invite a su casa. Te enteras que él/ella vive con sus padres y estás molesto/a porque te ha mentido. Quieres darle una oportunidad para que se disculpe y te dé explicaciones. Dile que quieres hacer el proyecto de física en su casa porque en tu casa no hay electricidad. Cuando te dé una excusa para no trabajar en su casa y te diga la verdad, demuéstrale tu decepción por tener un/a amigo/a mentiroso/a. Habla con él/ella y dile lo que opinas de esa situación y de sus mentiras.

ASÍ ES LA VIDA

Expresión: Nadie es profeta en su tierra.

Periodista: Entonces, ¿nació en Bolivia? ¿Cuándo llegó a Estados Unidos?
Rodrigo Montes: Sí, exactamente, nací en Sucre y llegué aquí a finales de los años 80.
Periodista: ¡Usted es un comentarista exitoso en la radio de Estados Unidos! ¿Tenía el mismo éxito cuando vivía en Bolivia?
Rodrigo Montes: No, allí nadie me conocía. Ya sabes: **nadie es profeta en su tierra.**

¿Qué significa esta expresión?
¿Hay un equivalente en inglés? ¿Cuál es?

Expresión: Quien tiene boca, se equivoca.

John: Soy americano.
Miguel: Yo también soy americano.
John: ¿Tú? ¿Pero no eres guatemalteco?
Miguel: ¿Y Guatemala no está en América? Soy americano porque Guatemala está en el hemisferio norte del continente americano.
John: Perdón, **quien tiene boca, se equivoca.**

¿Qué significa esta expresión?
¿Hay un equivalente en inglés? ¿Cuál es?

WileyPLUS Go to *WileyPLUS* to find more **Arroba** activities.

Hispanos en Estados Unidos Busca en tu buscador favorito información sobre tres personas hispanas que vivan en Estados Unidos y que sean muy conocidas aquí. Escribe una pequeña biografía contestando las preguntas: ¿Dónde nacieron? ¿Por qué son famosas? ¿En qué trabajan? ¿Qué aportan a la cultura hispana y a Estados Unidos? ¿Son conocidas internacionalmente? ¿Tienen doble ciudadanía o solamente una? ¿Dónde viven? Comenta con tus compañeros la información.

Aquí hay algunas personas: Janet Murguía / Alexis Bledel / Sandra Cisneros / Ellen Ochoa / Rolando Hinojosa / Carlos Santana / Gustavo Santaolalla / Alexa Vega / Ricky Martín / Andy García / Christina Aguilera / Dagne Zuniga / Sofía Vergara

WileyPLUS Go to *WileyPLUS* to see this video and to find more video activities.

VER PARA CREER II: CLUES ayuda a inmigrantes

Antes de ver

1. ¿Conoces a algún hispano? ¿De dónde es? ¿Cuál es su nacionalidad?
2. ¿Nació aquí en Estados Unidos o llegó con su familia de otro país?
3. ¿Qué hizo cuando llegó por primera vez a Estados Unidos? ¿Estudió? ¿Trabajó?
4. ¿Qué le recomendarías a una persona que llega por primera vez a Estados Unidos?

Después de ver

1. ¿Entendiste? Después de ver el video sobre CLUES, selecciona las respuestas más adecuadas según el contenido del video.

1. ¿Qué significa CLUES?
   a. Cultura Latina Unida en la Sociedad
   b. Servicios Comunitarios para los Hispanos
   c. Comunidades Latinas Unidas en Servicio
2. ¿Qué servicios ofrece CLUES?
   a. Ofrece programas para buscar empleo y también ofrece clases de inglés.
   b. Ofrece clases de diferentes profesiones como, por ejemplo, para ser profesora.
   c. Ofrece cualquier clase que un hispano necesite para tener mejor educación.
3. ¿Qué le aconseja la directora de empleo, que se llama Erika Nicholson, al inmigrante que llega a Minnesota?
   a. Le aconseja que sea paciente con los estadounidenses.
   b. Le aconseja que se registre a clases de inglés.
   c. Le aconseja que busque empleo sin entrenamiento.
4. ¿De qué son los talleres que se ofrecen en CLUES?
   a. Talleres para saber hacer la carta de presentación y para tener una entrevista exitosa.
   b. Talleres para conseguir muchas entrevistas y tener un empleo que le interese al inmigrante.
   c. Talleres de temas diversos relacionados con el nivel de vida estadounidense.
5. ¿Por qué se reúne la mujer del final del video con su consejero de empleo?
   a. Porque quiere darle las gracias ya que ha conseguido un trabajo que le interesa.
   b. Porque quiere tomar clases de inglés y no sabe cómo comenzar.
   c. Porque quiere que la ayude a conseguir un trabajo que le guste hacer.

2. La integración en un país ¿Qué le recomendarías a una persona que emigra a tu país? ¿Qué necesita el inmigrante para integrarse rápidamente al país? ¿Por qué?

3. Enfoque cultural ¿Cómo te sentirías si tuvieras que emigrar a otro país? ¿Qué razones te llevarían a irte a vivir a otro país?

AUTOPRUEBA

VOCABULARIO

I. ¿Sabes qué es? Lee las oraciones y escribe la palabra que define la oración.

1. Es una persona mayor con muchos años de edad.
2. Es una persona que habla español porque es su lengua materna.
3. Es cuando una persona deja de trabajar a cierta edad, como a los 60 o 65 años.
4. Es un ciudadano de Estados Unidos que tiene origen mexicano.
5. Es una persona que habla dos idiomas.

II. Conversación entre amigos Selecciona una palabra de la lista para completar el diálogo. ¡Ojo! Hay más palabras de las que necesitas.

> elecciones   sindicato   demografía   rechazar
> censo   población   triunfar

Víctor: ¿Sabes que según el _____ hay más de 50 millones de latinos que viven en Estados Unidos?

Marcos: No lo sabía. La _____ latina demuestra el aumento de la _____.

Víctor: Sí, tienes razón. Además, los hispanos juegan un rol importante en las _____ presidenciales por su activa participación.

Marcos: Sí, los demócratas y los republicanos saben que para _____, durante sus campañas deben comunicarse con los hispanos.

Víctor: Es verdad. El voto hispano ha sido decisivo en las últimas elecciones.

GRAMÁTICA

I. ¿Qué haces cuando...? Contesta las siguientes preguntas explicando qué haces en cada situación.

MODELO: ¿Qué haces cuando te sientes frustrado?
→ *Cuando me siento frustrado, hago algo para distraerme.*

¿Qué haces cuando...

1. te enojas?
2. te aburres?
3. te ofendes?
4. te sientes cansado/a?
5. te pones enfermo/a?
6. te alegras por algo bueno?
7. quieres relajarte?
8. necesitas tranquilizarte?

II. Buscando un compañero de conversación Escribe la forma correcta del verbo entre paréntesis usando el *indicativo* o el *subjuntivo*.

Pedro: Jaime, estoy buscando una persona que (hablar) _____ bien español y que (querer) _____ hacer un intercambio de conversación español/inglés con una amiga mía.

Jaime: Pues, tengo una amiga que (ser) _____ cubana y que (poder) _____ ayudarte.

Pedro: ¡Qué bueno! Tiene que ser alguien que (saber) _____ explicar bien la gramática y que (ser) _____ buena maestra. No quiero a alguien que no (tener) _____ experiencia como profesor de lengua.

Jaime: ¡Mi amiga Lía es la persona perfecta!

CULTURA

1. ¿Quién es Dolores Huerta? ¿Por qué es tan conocida?
2. ¿Quién es Francisco Alarcón? ¿A qué se dedica?
3. ¿Cómo contribuyen los inmigrantes a la economía de Estados Unidos?

REDACCIÓN

Entrevista a una persona bicultural que sea primera o segunda generación estadounidense. Escribe una biografía con esta información:

- Cuándo y dónde nació.
- De dónde son sus padres y sus antecesores.
- Qué trabajos tuvieron sus padres/sus antepasados.
- Qué idiomas habla en su casa.
- Qué costumbres conserva de sus padres o antepasados.
- Qué le gusta de su herencia cultural.

EN RESUMIDAS CUENTAS, AHORA PUEDO...

☐ hablar sobre temas relacionados con la política y la comunidad.

☐ describir emociones y cambios de estado usando verbos pronominales.

☐ describir objetos y personas usando cláusulas adjetivas.

☐ hablar de hispanos destacados.

☐ reconocer la contribución de los hispanos en EE. UU.

🔊 VOCABULARIO ESENCIAL

Sustantivos

el/la anciano/a	*elderly person*
los antepasados/ antecesores	*ancestors*
la ascendencia	*ancestry*
la demografía	*demographics*
los derechos	*rights*
la herencia	*inheritance*
el/la hispanohablante	*Spanish speaker*
la jubilación	*retirement*
la lengua materna	*mother language*
el nivel (de vida/ socioeconómico)	*(living/socioeconomic) standard*
las nuevas generaciones	*new generations*
el perfil	*profile*
las raíces	*roots*
la raza	*race*
el rechazo	*rejection*
el sindicato	*labor union*
el tema	*issue, topic*
la vivienda	*housing*

Cognados: el activismo, el/la activista, la asimilación, el bilingüismo, el censo, la comunidad, la discriminación, las elecciones, la identidad, la influencia, la (in)justicia, la (in)tolerancia, el/la líder, la organización, la política, la sociedad

Adjetivos

controvertido	*controversial*
destacado/a	*renown*

Cognados: bicultural, bilingüe, cubanoamericano/a, cultural, laboral, mexicoamericano/a, multicultural, multirracial, político/a, social

Verbos

integrarse	*to be accepted, to join a group*
prosperar	*to prosper, to thrive*
rechazar (z > c)	*to reject*
reconocer	*to recognize*
triunfar, tener éxito	*to succeed, to be successful*

¿Cómo es la m?

Orgulloso, vanidoso, arrogante, diplomático.

Agresivo.

Simple, calmado.

Tímido.

Materialista, indiferente.

¿Cómo es la i?

Artista.

Alegre.

Fuerte.

Curioso, ambicioso.

Energético

Cuidadoso, tímido.

Creativo, imaginativo.

¿Cómo es la t?

Cuidadoso, trabajador.

Perezoso, flojo.

Entusiasta, ambicioso.

Testarudo, determinado.

Imaginativo.

Sensible.

Perseverante.

¿Cómo es la inclinación?

 Sociable, extrovertido.

 Introvertido, callado.

 Paciente, consistente.

¿Cómo es el tamaño? (*size*)

El libro de español Amistoso, sociable.

El libro de español Detallista (*details are important*), reservado.

2 Verbos

Regular Verbs: Simple Tenses

Infinitive Present Participle Past Participle	Present	Imperfect	Indicative Preterit	Future	Conditional	Subjunctive Present	Imperfect	Imperative (commands)
hablar *to speak* hablando hablado	hablo hablas habla hablamos habláis hablan	hablaba hablabas hablaba hablábamos hablabais hablaban	hablé hablaste habló hablamos hablasteis hablaron	hablaré hablarás hablará hablaremos hablaréis hablarán	hablaría hablarías hablaría hablaríamos hablaríais hablarían	hable hables hable hablemos habléis hablen	hablara hablaras hablara habláramos hablarais hablaran	habla tú no hables hable Ud. hablen Uds. hablemos hablad no habléis
comer *to eat* comiendo comido	como comes come comemos coméis comen	comía comías comía comíamos comíais comían	comí comiste comió comimos comisteis comieron	comeré comerás comerá comeremos comeréis comerán	comería comerías comería comeríamos comeríais comerían	coma comas coma comamos comáis coman	comiera comieras comiera comiéramos comierais comieran	come tú no comas coma Ud. coman Uds. comamos comed no comáis
vivir *to live* viviendo vivido	vivo vives vive vivimos vivís viven	vivía vivías vivía vivíamos vivíais vivían	viví viviste vivió vivimos vivisteis vivieron	viviré vivirás vivirá viviremos viviréis vivirán	viviría vivirías viviría viviríamos viviríais vivirían	viva vivas viva vivamos viváis vivan	viviera vivieras viviera viviéramos vivierais vivieran	vive tú no vivas viva Ud. vivan Uds. vivamos vivid no viváis

Regular Verbs: Perfect Tenses

Indicative Present Perfect		Past Perfect		Future Perfect		Conditional Perfect		Subjunctive Present Perfect		Past Perfect	
he has ha hemos habéis han	hablado comido vivido	había habías había habíamos habíais habían	hablado comido vivido	habré habrás habrá habremos habréis habrán	hablado comido vivido	habría habrías habría habríamos habríais habrían	hablado comido vivido	haya hayas haya hayamos hayáis hayan	hablado comido vivido	hubiera hubieras hubiera hubiéramos hubierais hubieran	hablado comido vivido

Stem-changing -ar and -er Verbs: e → ie; o → ue

Present Participle Past Participle	Present	Imperfect	Indicative Preterit	Future	Conditional	Subjunctive Present	Imperfect	Imperative (commands)
pensar (ie) to think pensando pensado	**pienso** **piensas** **piensa** pensamos pensáis **piensan**	pensaba pensabas pensaba pensábamos pensabais pensaban	pensé pensaste pensó pensamos pensasteis pensaron	pensaré pensarás pensará pensaremos pensaréis pensarán	pensaría pensarías pensaría pensaríamos pensaríais pensarían	**piense** **pienses** **piense** pensemos penséis **piensen**	pensara pensaras pensara pensáramos pensarais pensaran	**piensa** tú no **pienses** **piense** Ud. **piensen** Uds. pensemos pensad no penséis
volver (ue) to return volviendo vuelto (irreg.)	**vuelvo** **vuelves** **vuelve** volvemos volvéis **vuelven**	volvía volvías volvía volvíamos volvíais volvían	volví volviste volvió volvimos volvisteis volvieron	volveré volverás volverá volveremos volveréis volverán	volvería volverías volvería volveríamos volveríais volverían	**vuelva** **vuelvas** **vuelva** volvamos volváis **vuelvan**	volviera volvieras volviera volviéramos volvierais volvieran	**vuelve** tú no **vuelvas** **vuelva** Ud. **vuelvan** Uds. volvamos volved no volváis

Other verbs of this type are:

e → ie: **atender, cerrar, despertarse, empezar, entender, nevar, pensar, perder, preferir, querer, recomendar, regar, sentarse**

o → ue: **acordarse de, acostarse, almorzar, colgar, costar, encontrar, jugar, mostrar, poder, probar, recordar, resolver, sonar, volar, volver**

Stem-changing -ir Verbs: e → ie, i; e → i, i; o → ue, u

Infinitive Present Participle Past Participle	Present	Imperfect	Indicative Preterit	Future	Conditional	Subjunctive Present	Imperfect	Imperative (commands)
sentir (ie, i) to feel, regret **sintiendo** sentido	**siento** **sientes** **siente** sentimos sentís **sienten**	sentía sentías sentía sentíamos sentíais sentían	sentí sentiste **sintió** sentimos sentisteis **sintieron**	sentiré sentirás sentirá sentiremos sentiréis sentirán	sentiría sentirías sentiría sentiríamos sentiríais sentirían	**sienta** **sientas** **sienta** **sintamos** **sintáis** **sientan**	**sintiera** **sintieras** **sintiera** **sintiéramos** **sintierais** **sintieran**	**siente** tú no **sientas** **sienta** Ud. **sientan** Uds. **sintamos** sentid no **sintáis**
pedir (i, i) to ask (for) **pidiendo** pedido	**pido** **pides** **pide** pedimos pedís **piden**	pedía pedías pedía pedíamos pedíais pedían	pedí pediste **pidió** pedimos pedisteis **pidieron**	pediré pedirás pedirá pediremos pediréis pedirán	pediría pedirías pediría pediríamos pediríais pedirían	**pida** **pidas** **pida** **pidamos** **pidáis** **pidan**	**pidiera** **pidieras** **pidiera** **pidiéramos** **pidierais** **pidieran**	**pide** tú no **pidas** **pida** Ud. **pidan** Uds. **pidamos** pedid no **pidáis**
dormir (ue, u) to sleep **durmiendo** dormido	**duermo** **duermes** **duerme** dormimos dormís **duermen**	dormía dormías dormía dormíamos dormíais dormían	dormí dormiste **durmió** dormimos dormisteis **durmieron**	dormiré dormirás dormirá dormiremos dormiréis dormirán	dormiría dormirías dormiría dormiríamos dormiríais dormirían	**duerma** **duermas** **duerma** **durmamos** **durmáis** **duerman**	**durmiera** **durmieras** **durmiera** **durmiéramos** **durmierais** **durmieran**	**duerme** tú no **duermas** **duerma** Ud. **duerman** Uds. **durmamos** dormid no **durmáis**

Other verbs of this type are:

e → ie, i: **divertirse, invertir, preferir, sentirse**

e → i, i: **conseguir, despedirse de, reírse, repetir, seguir, servir, teñirse, vestirse**

o → ue, u: **morir(se)**

Verbs with Spelling Changes

1. c → qu: tocar (model); also buscar, explicar, pescar, sacar

Infinitive / Present Participle / Past Participle	Indicative					Subjunctive		Imperative (commands)
	Present	Imperfect	Preterit	Future	Conditional	Present	Imperfect	
tocar *to play (musical instrument), touch*	toco	tocaba	**toqué**	tocaré	tocaría	**toque**	tocara	toca tú
tocando	tocas	tocabas	tocaste	tocarás	tocarías	**toques**	tocaras	no **toques**
tocado	toca	tocaba	tocó	tocará	tocaría	**toque**	tocara	**toque** Ud.
	tocamos	tocábamos	tocamos	tocaremos	tocaríamos	**toquemos**	tocáramos	**toquen** Uds.
	tocáis	tocabais	tocasteis	tocaréis	tocaríais	**toquéis**	tocarais	**toquemos**
	tocan	tocaban	tocaron	tocarán	tocarían	**toquen**	tocaran	tocad
								no **toquéis**

2. z → c: abrazar; also almorzar, cruzar, empezar (ie)

Infinitive / Present Participle / Past Participle	Present	Imperfect	Preterit	Future	Conditional	Present	Imperfect	Imperative (commands)
abrazar *to hug*	abrazo	abrazaba	**abracé**	abrazaré	abrazaría	**abrace**	abrazara	abraza tú
abrazando	abrazas	abrazabas	abrazaste	abrazarás	abrazarías	**abraces**	abrazaras	no **abraces**
abrazado	abraza	abrazaba	abrazó	abrazará	abrazaría	**abrace**	abrazara	**abrace** Ud.
	abrazamos	abrazábamos	abrazamos	abrazaremos	abrazaríamos	**abracemos**	abrazáramos	**abracen** Uds.
	abrazáis	abrazabais	abrazasteis	abrazaréis	abrazaríais	**abracéis**	abrazarais	**abracemos**
	abrazan	abrazaban	abrazaron	abrazarán	abrazarían	**abracen**	abrazaran	abrazad
								no **abracéis**

3. g → gu: pagar; also apagar, jugar (ue), llegar

Infinitive / Present Participle / Past Participle	Present	Imperfect	Preterit	Future	Conditional	Present	Imperfect	Imperative (commands)
pagar *to pay (for)*	pago	pagaba	**pagué**	pagaré	pagaría	**pague**	pagara	paga tú
pagando	pagas	pagabas	pagaste	pagarás	pagarías	**pagues**	pagaras	no **pagues**
pagado	paga	pagaba	pagó	pagará	pagaría	**pague**	pagara	**pague** Ud.
	pagamos	pagábamos	pagamos	pagaremos	pagaríamos	**paguemos**	pagáramos	**paguen** Uds.
	pagáis	pagabais	pagasteis	pagaréis	pagaríais	**paguéis**	pagarais	**paguemos**
	pagan	pagaban	pagaron	pagarán	pagarían	**paguen**	pagaran	pagad
								no **paguéis**

4. gu → g: seguir (i, i); also conseguir

Infinitive / Present Participle / Past Participle	Present	Imperfect	Preterit	Future	Conditional	Present	Imperfect	Imperative (commands)
seguir (i, i) *to follow*	**sigo**	seguía	seguí	seguiré	seguiría	**siga**	siguiera	sigue tú
siguiendo	sigues	seguías	seguiste	seguirás	seguirías	**sigas**	siguieras	no **sigas**
seguido	sigue	seguía	siguió	seguirá	seguiría	**siga**	siguiera	**siga** Ud.
	seguimos	seguíamos	seguimos	seguiremos	seguiríamos	**sigamos**	siguiéramos	**sigan** Uds.
	seguís	seguíais	seguisteis	seguiréis	seguiríais	**sigáis**	siguierais	**sigamos**
	siguen	seguían	siguieron	seguirán	seguirían	**sigan**	siguieran	seguid
								no **sigáis**

5. g → j: recoger; also escoger, proteger

Infinitive / Present Participle / Past Participle	Present	Imperfect	Preterit	Future	Conditional	Present Subj.	Imperfect Subj.	Imperative
recoger	**recojo**	recogía	recogí	recogeré	recogería	**recoja**	recogiera	
to pick up	recoges	recogías	recogiste	recogerás	recogerías	**recojas**	recogieras	recoge tú / no **recojas**
recogiendo	recoge	recogía	recogió	recogerá	recogería	**recoja**	recogiera	**recoja** Ud.
recogido	recogemos	recogíamos	recogimos	recogeremos	recogeríamos	**recojamos**	recogiéramos	**recojan** Uds. / **recojamos**
	recogéis	recogíais	recogisteis	recogeréis	recogeríais	**recojáis**	recogierais	recoged / no **recojáis**
	recogen	recogían	recogieron	recogerán	recogerían	**recojan**	recogieran	

6. i → y: leer; also caer, oír. Verbs with additional i → y changes: construir; also destruir, contribuir

Infinitive / Present Participle / Past Participle	Present	Imperfect	Preterit	Future	Conditional	Present Subj.	Imperfect Subj.	Imperative
leer	leo	leía	leí	leeré	leería	lea	**leyera**	lee tú / no leas
to read	lees	leías	leíste	leerás	leerías	leas	**leyeras**	lea Ud.
leyendo	lee	leía	**leyó**	leerá	leería	lea	**leyera**	lean Uds.
leído	leemos	leíamos	leímos	leeremos	leeríamos	leamos	**leyéramos**	leamos
	leéis	leíais	leísteis	leeréis	leeríais	leáis	**leyerais**	leed
	leen	leían	**leyeron**	leerán	leerían	lean	**leyeran**	no leáis
construir	**construyo**	construía	construí	construiré	construiría	**construya**	**construyera**	**construye** tú
to construct, build	**construyes**	construías	construiste	construirás	construirías	**construyas**	**construyeras**	no **construyas**
construyendo	**construye**	construía	**construyó**	construirá	construiría	**construya**	**construyera**	**construya** Ud.
construido	construimos	construíamos	construimos	construiremos	construiríamos	**construyamos**	**construyéramos**	**construyan** Uds.
	construís	construíais	construisteis	construiréis	construiríais	**construyáis**	**construyerais**	**construyamos**
	construyen	construían	**construyeron**	construirán	construirían	**construyan**	**construyeran**	construid / no **construyáis**

Irregular Verbs

Infinitive / Present Participle / Past Participle	Indicative					Subjunctive		Imperative
	Present	Imperfect	Preterit	Future	Conditional	Present	Imperfect	
caer	**caigo**	caía	caí	caeré	caería	caiga	cayera	cae tú
to fall	caes	caías	caíste	caerás	caerías	caigas	cayeras	no caigas
cayendo	cae	caía	**cayó**	caerá	caería	caiga	cayera	caiga Ud.
caído	caemos	caíamos	caímos	caeremos	caeríamos	caigamos	cayéramos	caigan Uds.
	caéis	caíais	caísteis	caeréis	caeríais	caigáis	cayerais	caigamos
	caen	caían	**cayeron**	caerán	caerían	caigan	cayeran	caed / no caigáis

Infinitive / Participles	Present	Imperfect	Preterite	Future	Conditional	Present Subjunctive	Imperfect Subjunctive	Commands
conocer *to know, to be acquainted with* conociendo conocido	conozco conoces conoce conocemos conocéis conocen	conocía conocías conocía conocíamos conocíais conocían	conocí conociste conoció conocimos conocisteis conocieron	conoceré conocerás conocerá conoceremos conoceréis conocerán	conocería conocerías conocería conoceríamos conoceríais conocerían	conozca conozcas conozca conozcamos conozcáis conozcan	conociera conocieras conociera conociéramos conocierais conocieran	conoce tú, no conozcas conozca Ud. conozcan Uds. conozcamos conoced no conozcáis
dar *to give* dando dado	doy das da damos dais dan	daba dabas daba dábamos dabais daban	di diste dio dimos disteis dieron	daré darás dará daremos daréis darán	daría darías daría daríamos daríais darían	dé des dé demos deis den	diera dieras diera diéramos dierais dieran	da tú, no des dé Ud. den Uds. demos dad no deis
decir *to say, tell* diciendo dicho	digo dices dice decimos decís dicen	decía decías decía decíamos decíais decían	dije dijiste dijo dijimos dijisteis dijeron	diré dirás dirá diremos diréis dirán	diría dirías diría diríamos diríais dirían	diga digas diga digamos digáis digan	dijera dijeras dijera dijéramos dijerais dijeran	di tú, no digas diga Ud. digan Uds. digamos decid no digáis
estar *to be* estando estado	estoy estás está estamos estáis están	estaba estabas estaba estábamos estabais estaban	estuve estuviste estuvo estuvimos estuvisteis estuvieron	estaré estarás estará estaremos estaréis estarán	estaría estarías estaría estaríamos estaríais estarían	esté estés esté estemos estéis estén	estuviera estuvieras estuviera estuviéramos estuvierais estuvieran	estés tú, no estés esté Ud. estén Uds. estemos estad no estéis
haber *to have* habiendo habido	he has ha hemos habéis han	había habías había habíamos habíais habían	hube hubiste hubo hubimos hubisteis hubieron	habré habrás habrá habremos habréis habrán	habría habrías habría habríamos habríais habrían	haya hayas haya hayamos hayáis hayan	hubiera hubieras hubiera hubiéramos hubierais hubieran	
hacer *to do, make* haciendo hecho	hago haces hace hacemos hacéis hacen	hacía hacías hacía hacíamos hacíais hacían	hice hiciste hizo hicimos hicisteis hicieron	haré harás hará haremos haréis harán	haría harías haría haríamos haríais harían	haga hagas haga hagamos hagáis hagan	hiciera hicieras hiciera hiciéramos hicierais hicieran	haz tú, no hagas haga Ud. hagan Uds. hagamos haced no hagáis

Infinitivo	Presente	Imperfecto	Pretérito	Futuro	Condicional	Presente (subjuntivo)	Imperfecto (subjuntivo)	Mandatos
ir *to go* **yendo** ido	voy vas va vamos vais van	iba ibas iba íbamos ibais iban	fui fuiste fue fuimos fuisteis fueron	iré irás irá iremos iréis irán	iría irías iría iríamos iríais irían	vaya vayas vaya vayamos vayáis vayan	fuera fueras fuera fuéramos fuerais fueran	ve tú no vayas vaya Ud. vayan Uds. vayamos id no vayáis
oír *to hear* **oyendo** **oído**	oigo oyes oye oímos oís oyen	oía oías oía oíamos oíais oían	oí oíste oyó oímos oísteis oyeron	oiré oirás oirá oiremos oiréis oirán	oiría oirías oiría oiríamos oiríais oirían	oiga oigas oiga oigamos oigáis oigan	oyera oyeras oyera oyéramos oyerais oyeran	oye tú no oigas oiga Ud. oigan Uds. oigamos oíd no oigáis
poder (ue) *to be able, can* pudiendo podido	puedo puedes puede podemos podéis pueden	podía podías podía podíamos podíais podían	pude pudiste pudo pudimos pudisteis pudieron	podré podrás podrá podremos podréis podrán	podría podrías podría podríamos podríais podrían	pueda puedas pueda podamos podáis puedan	pudiera pudieras pudiera pudiéramos pudierais pudieran	puede tú pueda Ud. puedan Uds.
poner *to put, place* poniendo **puesto**	pongo pones pone ponemos ponéis ponen	ponía ponías ponía poníamos poníais ponían	puse pusiste puso pusimos pusisteis pusieron	pondré pondrás pondrá pondremos pondréis pondrán	pondría pondrías pondría pondríamos pondríais pondrían	ponga pongas ponga pongamos pongáis pongan	pusiera pusieras pusiera pusiéramos pusierais pusieran	**pon tú** no pongas ponga Ud. pongan Uds. pongamos poned no pongáis
querer (ie) *to wish, want, love* queriendo querido	quiero quieres quiere queremos queréis quieren	quería querías quería queríamos queríais querían	quise quisiste quiso quisimos quisisteis quisieron	querré querrás querrá querremos querréis querrán	querría querrías querría querríamos querríais querrían	quiera quieras quiera queramos queráis quieran	quisiera quisieras quisiera quisiéramos quisierais quisieran	quiere tú no quieras quiera Ud. quieran Uds. queramos quered no queráis

Infinitive / Present Participle / Past Participle	Present	Imperfect	Preterite	Future	Conditional	Present Subjunctive	Imperfect Subjunctive	Commands
saber *to know* sabiendo sabido	sé sabes sabe sabemos sabéis saben	sabía sabías sabía sabíamos sabíais sabían	supe supiste supo supimos supisteis supieron	sabré sabrás sabrá sabremos sabréis sabrán	sabría sabrías sabría sabríamos sabríais sabrían	sepa sepas sepa sepamos sepáis sepan	supiera supieras supiera supiéramos supierais supieran	sabe tú, no sepas sepa Ud. sepan Uds. sepamos sabed, no sepáis
salir *to leave, go out* saliendo salido	salgo sales sale salimos salís salen	salía salías salía salíamos salíais salían	salí saliste salió salimos salisteis salieron	saldré saldrás saldrá saldremos saldréis saldrán	saldría saldrías saldría saldríamos saldríais saldrían	salga salgas salga salgamos salgáis salgan	saliera salieras saliera saliéramos salierais salieran	**sal tú**, no salgas salga Ud. salgan Uds. salgamos salid, no salgáis
ser *to be* siendo sido	soy eres es somos sois son	era eras era éramos erais eran	fui fuiste fue fuimos fuisteis fueron	seré serás será seremos seréis serán	sería serías sería seríamos seríais serían	sea seas sea seamos seáis sean	fuera fueras fuera fuéramos fuerais fueran	sé tú, no seas sea Ud. sean Uds. seamos sed, no seáis
tener *to have* teniendo tenido	**tengo** tienes tiene tenemos tenéis tienen	tenía tenías tenía teníamos teníais tenían	tuve tuviste tuvo tuvimos tuvisteis tuvieron	tendré tendrás tendrá tendremos tendréis tendrán	tendría tendrías tendría tendríamos tendríais tendrían	tenga tengas tenga tengamos tengáis tengan	tuviera tuvieras tuviera tuviéramos tuvierais tuvieran	**ten tú**, no tengas tenga Ud. tengan Uds. tengamos tened, no tengáis
traer *to bring* **trayendo** **traído**	**traigo** traes trae traemos traéis traen	traía traías traía traíamos traíais traían	traje trajiste trajo trajimos trajisteis trajeron	traeré traerás traerá traeremos traeréis traerán	traería traerías traería traeríamos traeríais traerían	traiga traigas traiga traigamos traigáis traigan	trajera trajeras trajera trajéramos trajerais trajeran	trae tú, no traigas traiga Ud. traigan Uds. traigamos traed, no traigáis

Infinitive / Present participle / Past participle	Present	Imperfect	Preterite	Future	Conditional	Present subjunctive	Imperfect subjunctive	Commands
venir to come **viniendo** venido (also **prevenir**)	**vengo** **vienes** **viene** venimos venís **vienen**	venía venías venía veníamos veníais venían	**vine** **viniste** **vino** **vinimos** **vinisteis** **vinieron**	**vendré** **vendrás** **vendrá** **vendremos** **vendréis** **vendrán**	**vendría** **vendrías** **vendría** **vendríamos** **vendríais** **vendrían**	venga vengas venga vengamos vengáis vengan	viniera vinieras viniera viniéramos vinierais vinieran	**ven** tú, no vengas venga Ud. vengan Uds. vengamos venid, no vengáis
ver to see **viendo** **visto**	**veo** ves ve vemos veis ven	**veía** **veías** **veía** **veíamos** **veíais** **veían**	**vi** viste **vio** vimos visteis vieron	veré verás verá veremos veréis verán	vería verías vería veríamos veríais verían	vea veas vea veamos veáis vean	viera vieras viera viéramos vierais vieran	ve tú, no veas vea Ud. vean Uds. veamos ved, no veáis

Spanish-English Glossary

A

a. C. (antes de Cristo) B.C. (Before Christ) 6.1
abajo down 4.2
el/la abogado/a lawyer 4.1
abril April 1.2
el/la abuelo/a grandfather/grandmother 3.1
aburrido/a boring, tedious 8.2, 1.1
aburrir(se) to get bored 4.1
acampar to go camping 9.1
el aceite oil 7.2, 9.2
el acompañamiento side dish 7.2
aconsejar to advise 5.2, 9.1
acostar(se) to lie down 4.1
la actriz actress 6.2
actual current 8.2
la actualidad current affairs 8.2
el aderezo dressing 7.2
la aerolínea/línea aérea airline 11.2
el/la aeromozo/a flight attendant 4.1, 11.2
afeitar(se) to shave (oneself) 4.1
el/la aficionado/a fan 8.1
agosto August 1.2
(des) agradar to (dis) please 5.2
agradecer to thank 5.1
agregar to add 7.2
el agua (mineral/con gas) (spring/sparkling) water 7.2
ahí there 6.2
el/la ahijado/a godson/goddaughter 5.2
el ajedrez chess 8.1
el ajo garlic 7.1
la alfombra rug 3.2
el aliado ally 6.1
algo something, anything 8.2
alguien someone, anyone 8.2
algún, alguna/os/as some, any 8.2
allí/allá over there 6.2
almorzar (ue) to have lunch 3.1
alquilar to rent 3.2
el alimento food 7.1, 2.2
la almeja clam 7.1
el almuerzo lunch 7.1
amarillo/a yellow 2.2
amueblado/a furnished 3.2
añadir to add 7.2
anaranjado/a/naranja orange 2.2, 7.1
andar en patineta /monopatín to skateboard 8.1
el anillo ring 2.2, 5.2
animado/a lively 8.2
el animal (doméstico/salvaje) (domestic/wild) animal 9.2
animar to enliven 5.1, 8.1
animar (a un equipo) to cheer (a team) 8.1, 5.1

anoche last night 8.1
anteayer the day before yesterday 8.1
antiguo/a old, ancient 6.2
el anuncio/el comercial TV commercial 8.2
el apartamento apartment 3.2
el apodo nickname 3.1
aprender to learn 2.1
aquí here 6.2
la araña spider 9.2
el árbol tree 3.2
el archivo (adjunto) (attached) file 11.1
el arete/pendiente earring 2.2
argentino/a Argentine 1.1
arriba up 4.2
el armario/el ropero closet 3.2
el arquero goalkeeper 8.1
el arroz rice 7.1
la artesanía arts and crafts 2.2
el asado/la parrillada BBQ 7.1
asar to roast, to grill 7.2
el atletismo track and field 8.1
el auto/carro car 4.2
el autobús bus 2.1, 4.2
la autopista highway 4.2
el autorretrato self portrait 6.2
la avenida avenue 4.2
ayer yesterday 8.1
azul blue 2.2
azul (oscuro, claro, marino) (dark, light, navy) blue 6.2
el azulejo/el mosaico tile 3.2

B

bailar to dance 1.2, 5.1
el baile dance 5.1
bajo/a short 1.1
el bajo bass 5.1
el balón (soccer, basket) ball 8.1
el baloncesto basketball 8.1
bañar(se) to bathe (oneself) 4.1
el baño bathroom 3.2
barato/a cheap, inexpensive 2.2
el barco ship 11.2, 6.1
el barrio neighborhood 4.2, 3.2
Bastante bien. Pretty well. P
la basura garbage 9.2
el bautizo baptism 5.2
beber to drink 2.1
la bebida drink 7.2
el bienestar well-being 10.2
el billete/pasaje (de ida/de ida y vuelta) (one way/round trip) ticket 11.2
el/la bisabuelo/a great grandfather/grandmother 3.1
el/la bisnieto/a great grandchild 3.1
el bistec/bife beef steak 7.1
blanco/a white, white (skin) 1.1, 2.2

la boca mouth 3.1
la boda wedding 5.2
el bolígrafo pen P
boliviano/a Bolivian 1.1
el/la bombero/a firefighter 4.1
bonito/a pretty 3.2, 1.1
borrar lo que no quieren to delete what they don't want 11.1
el bosque forest 9.1
brasileño/a Brazilian 12.1
el brazo arm 10.1
el brindis the toast 5.2
¡Buen provecho! Enjoy your meal! 7.2
Buenas noches. Good evening./Good night. P
Buenas tardes. Good afternoon. P
bueno/a good 1.1
Buenos días. Good morning. P
buscar una dirección de Internet to search for a URL 11.1
el buscador browser 11.1

C

caer bien/mal to like/dislike someone/or not 5.2
el caballero groomsman 5.2
el caballo horse 9.2
la cabeza head 3.1
el cable wire 11.1
el caldero cast iron pot 7.2
el calentamiento global global warming 9.2
calentar (>ie) to heat up 7.2
la calle street 4.2
la cama bed 3.2
calmarse to calm down 10.2
el/la camarero/a, mesero/a waiter/waitress 4.1
el camarón shrimp 7.1
el cambio climático climate change 9.2
la camisa shirt 2.2
caminar to walk 1.2
el campeonato championship 8.1
el campo de fútbol soccer field 8.1
el canal (de televisión) TV channel 8.2
la cancha court 8.1
la cacerola pan 7.2
la canción song 5.1
cansado/a tired 10.2
el/la cantante singer 5.1
cantar to sing 1.2, 5.1
la cara face 3.1
el cargador charger 11.1
cargar la batería to charge the battery 11.1
la carne (de vaca/res) (beef) meat 7.1
caro/a expensive 2.2
la carpeta folder 11.1

la carretera *road* 4.2
el carril *lane* 4.2
la carta de presentación *cover letter* 4.1
la carta de recomendación *letter of recommendation* 4.1
la carta/el menú *menu* 7.2
las cartas *cards* 8.1
el/la cartero/a *mail carrier* 4.1
la casa *house, home* 2.1, 3.2
casado/a *married* 3.1
casarse *to get married* 3.1
castaño/a *chestnut* 1.1
el castillo *castle* 6.2
catorce *fourteen* P
la cebolla *onion* 7.1
la cena *dinner* 7.1
cenar *to have dinner* 2.1
cepillar(se) *to brush (teeth or hair usually)* 4.1
cerca *near* 4.2
el/la cerdo/a *pig* 9.2
la cerveza *beer* 7.2
chatear en línea *to chat on line* 11.1
chileno/a *Chilean* 1.1
chistoso/a *funny* 1.1, 8.2
el chorizo *sausage* 7.1
la chuleta (de cerdo/puerco) *(pork) chop* 7.1
el churrasco *steak* 7.2
cien *one hundred* 2.2
cien mil *one hundred thousand* 3.2
ciento diez *one hundred and ten* 2.2
ciento uno *one hundred and one* 2.2
cinco *five* P
cincuenta *fifty* P
el cine *movie theatre* 4.2, 6.2
el cinturón *belt* 2.2
el/la cirujano/a *surgeon* 10.2
la ciudad *city* 4.2
la (doble) ciudadanía *(dual) citizenship* 12.1
la cocina *kitchen* 3.2
cocinar *to cook* 2.1
el/la cocinero/a *cook* 4.1
colgar/poner videos en Internet *to post videos on the Internet* 11.1
colombiano/a *Colombian* 1.1
color vino *burgundy* 6.2
color vivo *bright color* 6.2
el comedor *dining room* 3.2
comer *to eat* 2.1
la comida *food* 2.2, 7.1
la comida chatarra/basura *junk food* 7.2
¿Cómo está usted? *How are you? (formal)* P
¿Cómo estamos? *How are you doing?* P
¿Cómo estás? *How are you? (informal)* P
¿Cómo te llamas? *What´s your name? (informal)* P
la cómoda *dresser* 3.2
competir *to compete* 6.2
comprar *to buy* 2.2, 3.2
la computadora (portátil) *(laptop) computer* 11.1
el concurso *competition, contest* 8.2
el/la conejo/a *rabbit* 9.2
confundido/a *confused* 10.2
congestionado/a *congested* 10.1

el conjunto (musical) *(music) band* 5.1
conocer *to know or be familiar with* 5.1
conseguir *to get* 6.2
conseguir (un trabajo) *to get (a job)* 4.1
el/la conserje *janitor* 4.1
construir *to build* 6.2
el consultorio del médico *doctor's office* 10.1
contaminar (el aire, el agua) *to pollute (the air, the water)* 9.2
la contaminación (del aire, del agua...) *(air, water...) pollution* 9.2
contar (ue) *to count ; to tell, to narrate (e.g., a story)* 3.1, 5.2
el contestador *answering machine* 11.1
contestar *to answer* 5.2
contradicho/a *contradicted* 11.1
controlar (la ansiedad/ el colesterol) *control (your anxiety/cholesterol)* 10.2
la contraseña *password* 11.1
controvertido/a *controversial* 8.2, 12.2
la copa *wine glass* 7.2
el corazón *heart* 10.1
la cordillera *mountain range* 9.1
(la oficina de) correos *post office* 4.2
correr *to run* 1.2
cortar *to cut* 7.2, 4.1
corto/a *short (hair)* 1.1
costar (ue) *to cost* 3.1
costarricense *Costarican* 1.1
crear *to create* 6.2
¿Cuál es la fecha de hoy? *What is today's date?* 1.2
¿Cuándo es tu cumpleaños? *When is your birthday?* 1.2
¿Cuánto cuesta/cuestan...? *How much is/are . . .?* 2.2
la cuadra *city block* 4.2
el cuadro *painting* 3.2, 6.2
cuarenta *forty* 2.2
cuarto/a *fourth* 6.1
cuatro *four* P
cuatrocientos *four hundred* 2.2
cubano/a *Cuban* 1.1
el cubierto *cutlery* 7.2
cubierto/a *covered* 11.1
cubrir/tapar *to cover* 7.2
la cuchara *spoon* 7.2
el cuchillo *knife* 7.2
la cuenta *bill/check* 7.2
el cuerpo humano *human body* 10.1
cuidadoso/a *careful* 1.1
cuidar(se) *to take care (of oneself)* 10.2
el cumpleaños *birthday* 5.2
el/la cuñado/a *brother/sister-in-law* 3.1
el cura *priest* 5.2
curar *to cure, to heal* 10.1
curarse *to get well, to recover* 10.1
el currículum vítae *résumé* 4.1
el cuy *guinea pig* 9.2

D

d. C. (después de Cristo) *A.D.(in the year of our Lord)* 6.1
los dados *dice* 8.1
la dama *bridesmaid* 5.2
las damas *checkers* 8.1

dar *to give* 5.2
dar la vuelta *spin around* 5.1
de la mañana *in the morning* 2.1
de la noche *in the evening/at night* 2.1
de la tarde *in the afternoon* 2.1
de repente *suddenly* 8.1
deber *must, ought, should* 4.1
débil *weak* 10.1
décimo/a *tenth* 6.1
decir *to say* 5.2
el dedo (de la mano/del pie) *finger/ toe* 10.1
¿De dónde eres? *Where are you from?* 1.1
delante (de) *in front (of)* 4.2
la demografía *demographics* 12.2
el/la dependiente *sales clerk* 4.1
deprimido/a *depressed* 10.2
el deporte (extremo/de riesgo) *(extreme) sport* 8.1
el/la deportista *athlete* 8.1
¿De qué (se) trata? *What is it about?* 8.2
¿De qué equipo eres? *What team do you support?* 8.1
a la derecha *to the right* 4.2
el derecho *law* 1.2, 12.1
los derechos *rights* 12.2
el derrame *oil spill* 9.2
derrotar *to defeat* 6.1
desarrollar *to develop* 9.2
desayunar *to have breakfast* 7.1
el desayuno *breakfast* 7.1
descansar *to rest* 10.2
el descanso *rest* 10.2
descargar programas *to download programs* 11.1
descubierto/a *discovered* 11.1
¿Desea/Desean algo de comer/tomar? *Would you like something to eat/drink?* 7.2
el desecho *waste* 9.2
deshecho/a *undone* 11.1
la despedida *farewell* P
la despedida de soltero/a *bachelor/ bachelorette party* 5.2
despertar(se) (ie) *to wake up* 4.1
destacado/a *renown* 12.2
detrás (de) *behind* 4.2
devolver (ue) *to return (something)* 5.2
devuelto/a *returned (an object)* 11.1
el día de Año Nuevo *New Year´s Day* 5.2
el día de Año Viejo/la Nochevieja *New Year´s Eve* 5.2
el día de los Reyes Magos *Three Kings Day* 5.2
dibujar *to draw* 6.2
los dibujos animados *cartoons* 8.2
dicho/a *said, told* 11.1
diciembre *December* 1.2
la dictadura *dictatorship* 6.1
diecinueve *nineteen* P
dieciocho *eighteen* P
dieciséis *sixteen* P
diecisiete *seventeen* P
el diente *tooth* 3.1
diez *ten* P
diez mil *ten thousand* 2.2, 3.2
la dirección *address, direction* 4.2
el disco duro/externo *hard drive* 11.1
la discoteca *night club* 4.2

Disculpe, ¿cómo llego a...? *Excuse me, how do I get to...?* 4.2

diseñar *to design* 6.2

el diseño *design* 1.2

distraído/a *distracted, absent-minded* 10.2

divertido/a *fun* 1.1

divertir(se) *to enjoy oneself* 4.1

doblar *to dub* 8.2

doce *twelve* P

doler (ue) *to hurt* 10.1

el domingo *Sunday* 1.2

dominicano/a *Dominican* 1.1

dorado/a *golden* 6.2

dormir (ue) *to sleep* 3.1, 1.2

dormir(se) (ue) *to fall asleep* 4.1

el dormitorio *bedroom* 3.2

dos *two* P

dos mil *two thousand* 2.2

dos millones *two millions* 3.2

doscientos *two hundred* 2.2

la ducha *shower* 3.2

duchar(se) *to take a shower* 4.1

dulce *sweet* 7.1

el durazno/melocotón (Esp.) *peach* 7.1

E

echar de menos *to miss (something/someone)* 12.1

el/la ecologista *environmentalist* 9.2

ecuatoguineano/a *Equatoguinean* 1.1

ecuatoriano/a *Ecuadorian* 1.1

la Edad Media/ Moderna *middle/modern ages* 6.1

el edificio *building* 3.2

la emisora (de radio) *(radio) station* 8.2

el empleo *employment* 4.1

el/la enfermero/a *nurse* 4.1, 10.2

el envase (desechable) *(disposable) container* 9.2

el equipaje (de mano) *(carry-on) luggage* 11.2

el equipo *team* 8.1

Él/ella es de piel/de pelo... *His/her skin/hair is...* 1.1

el/la entrenador/a *coach / trainer* 8.1

el/la escritor/a *writer* 4.1

el escritorio *desk* 3.2

el español *Spanish* 1.1, 1.2

el espejo *mirror* 3.2

el/la esposo/a *spouse* 3.1

el estacionamiento *parking lot* 4.2

el estado de ánimo *mood* 10.2

el estante *shelf* 3.2

el este *east* 4.2

el estómago *stomach* 10.1

Él/Ella tiene (el pelo/la piel) *He/She has ([type] hair/skin)* 1.1

elegir *to elect* 6.1, 6.2

elegir *to choose* 6.2, 6.1

emocionado/a *excited* 10.2

emocionante *exciting, thrilling* 8.2

la empanada (de carne, de queso, de marisco) *(meat, cheese, seafood) turnover* 7.2

empezar *to start* 2.1

la empresa *company (business)* 4.1

en frente (de) *in front (of)* 4.2

en punto *o'clock* 2.1

Encantado/a. *Nice to meet you.* P

encantar *to like a lot, to love something* 5.2

encender la computadora *to turn on the computer* 11.1

encendido/a *(turned) on* 11.1

enchufar la impresora *to plug in the printer* 11.1

encontrar (ue) *to find* 3.1

enero *January* 1.2

enfermarse *to get sick* 10.1

la enfermedad *disease* 10.1

la enfermería *nursing* 1.2

enfermo/a *sick, ill* 10.1

engordar *to gain weight* 10.2

enojar(se) *to become angry, to get upset* 4.1

la ensalada *salad* 7.2

entender (ie) *to understand* 3.1

la entrada *movie ticket* 8.2

entrar a un sitio web *to log in* 11.1

entre *in between* 4.2

entretenido/a *entertaining* 8.2

la entrevista (de trabajo) *(job) interview* 4.1

enviar *to send* 5.2

enviar mensajes electrónicos *to send emails* 11.1

la época *age or era* 6.1

Es de... *He/She is from...* 1.1

Es la / Son las... *It is...* 2.1

Es medianoche. *It's midnight.* 2.1

Es mediodía. *It's noon.* 2.1

la escasez *shortage* 9.2

escribir *to write* 2.1

escrito/a *written* 11.1

escuchar (música) *to listen (to music)* 1.2

la escuela (primaria/secundaria) *(elementary/high) school* 1.2

esculpir *to sculpt* 6.2

la espalda *back* 10.1

español/a *Spanish* 1.1, 1.2

esperar *to wait* 2.1

esperar que los aparatos funcionen *to hope that devices work* 11.1

la especia *spice* 7.2

la especialización *major, specialization* 1.2

esquiar *to ski* 1.2

la esquina *corner* 4.2

esta noche *tonight* 2.2

Está nublado. *It is cloudy.* 4.2

la estación lluviosa/seca *(rainy/dry) season* 9.1

la estadía/estancia (en un hotel) *(hotel) stay* 11.2

estadounidense *American* 1.1

estar *to be* 3.2

estar a dieta/hacer dieta *to diet/be on a diet* 10.2

estar embarazada *to be pregnant* 10.2

estar en peligro de extinción *to be endangered* 9.2

estar resfriado/a *to have a cold* 10.1

estornudar *to sneeze* 10.1

(dos, tres, cuatro) estrellas *(two, three, four) stars* 11.2

estudiar *to study* 1.2

la estufa *stove* 3.2

explicar *to explain* 5.2

F

facturar el equipaje *to check in your luggage* 11.2

la falda *skirt* 2.2

el familiar/pariente *relative* 3.1

fascinar *to love, to be fascinated by something* 5.2

febrero *February* 1.2

¡Felicidades! *Congratulations!* 5.2

¡Fenomenal! *Great!* P

la ficha *piece* 8.1

el fin de semana *the weekend* 1.2

el fin de semana/mes/año pasado *last weekend/month/year* 8.1

al final (de) *to the end (of)* 4.2

flaco/a *thin* 1.1

el flan *sweet custard* 7.2

la flor *flower* 2.2, 3.2

francés/francesa *French* 12.1

francoguayanés/francoguayanesa *French Guianese* 12.1

el fregadero *kitchen sink* 3.2

freído/a *fried* 11.1, 7.2

freír (i) *to fry* 7.2

la fresa/ la frutilla (Arg.) *strawberry* 7.1

el frijol *bean* 7.1

frito/a *fried* 7.2, 11.1

la frontera *border* 9.1

el fruto seco *nut* 7.1

la fuente *bowl* 7.2

fuerte *strong* 1.1, 10.2

funcionar (la computadora, el aparato) *to work (a computer, a device)* 11.1

fundar *to establish* 6.1

el fútbol *soccer* 8.1

G

la galleta/ galletita *cookie or cracker* 7.1

ganar *to win* 6.1, 8.1

ganar (dinero) *to earn, make (money)* 4.1

la garganta *throat* 10.1

el/la gato/a *cat* 9.2

el/la gemelo/a *identical twin* 3.1

el/la gerente *manager* 4.1

el germen *germ* 10.1

gobernar *to rule* 6.1

gordo/a *fat* 1.1

grabar *to record* 8.2

grabar música *to record music* 11.1

Gracias. *Thank you.* P

gracioso/a *funny* 1.1, 8.2

grande *big* 3.2

la grasa *fat* 7.1

graso/a *fat/fatty* 7.1

la gripe *flu* 10.1

gris *gray* 2.2

gritar *to shout* 5.1

guapo/a *pretty* 1.1, 3.2

guardar los cambios *to save changes* 11.1

guatemalteco/a *Guatemalan* 1.1

la guerra (civil) *(civil) war* 6.1

(No) Le gusta... *He/She (doesn't) like(s)...* 1.2

gustar *to like* 2.2

Gusto en conocerte. *Nice to meet you.* P

guyanés/guyanesa *Guyanese* 12.1

H

la habitación (sencilla, doble, triple) *(single, double, triple) room* 11.2

la habitación/el cuarto *room* 3.2

habitar *to inhabit* 6.1

hablar por teléfono (celular/móvil) *to talk on the (cell) phone* 1.2

Hace (mucho) calor. *It is (very) hot.* 4.2

Hace (mucho) viento. *It is (very) windy.* 4.2

Hace ___ grados F/C. *It is ___ degrees F/C.* 4.2

Hace buen/mal tiempo. *The weather is good/bad.* 4.2

Hace fresco. *It is cool.* 4.2

(No) Hace frío. *It is (not) cold.* 4.2

Hace sol. *It is sunny.* 4.2

hacer *to do, to make* 3.1

hacer cola *to wait in line* 11.2

hacer ejercicio *to exercise* 1.2

hacer esquí acuático *to water ski* 8.1

hacer las maletas *to pack* 11.2

hacer senderismo *to hike* 8.1

hacer snowboarding *to snowboard* 8.1

hacer una reservación/reserva *to book a table* 7.2

hacer yoga *to do yoga* 1.2

hacer/dar una fiesta (sorpresa) *to have/give a (surprise) party* 5.1

hacer/jugar (ue) a un deporte *to play/practice a sport* 8.1

haitiano/a *Haitian* 12.1

Hasta la vista. *See you soon. (Lit. Until I see you again)* P

Hasta luego. *See you later.* P

Hasta mañana. *See you tomorrow.* P

Hasta pronto. *See you soon.* P

hay *there is/there are* 3.2

Hay humedad. *It is humid.* 4.2

Hay niebla. *It is foggy.* 4.2

hay que *one must* 4.1

Hay tormenta. *It is stormy.* 4.2

Hay un huracán. *There is a hurricane.* 4.2

Hay... *There is... There are...* P

hecho/a *done* 11.1

el helado *ice-cream* 7.2

la herencia *inheritance* 12.2

el/la hermanastro/a *stepbrother/stepsister* 3.1

el/la hermano/a *brother/sister* 3.1

hervir (ie) *to boil* 7.2

el/la hijo/a *son/daughter* 3.1

el/la hispanohablante *Spanish speaker* 12.2

Hola. *Hi.* P

hondureño/a *Honduran* 1.1

hornear *to bake* 7.2

el horno *oven* 3.2

Hoy es... *Today is . . .* 1.2

la huelga *strike* 12.1

el huevo *egg* 7.1

I

la (des) igualdad *(in)equality* 12.1

la iglesia *church* 5.2

Igualmente. *Likewise.* P

importar *to care about something, to matter* 5.2

la impresora *printer* 11.1

imprimido/a, impreso/a *printed* 11.1

imprimir documentos *to print documents* 11.1

los impuestos *taxes* 12.1

la informática *computer science* 1.2

la infusión/el té de hierbas *herbal tea* 10.1

el/la ingeniero/a *engineer* 4.1

el inodoro *toilet* 3.2

integrarse *to be accepted, to join ato be accepted, to join a group* 12.2

invierno *winter* 1.2

ir *to go* 2.2, 7.2

ir al cine *to go to the movies* 1.2

ir al extranjero *to go abroad* 11.2

ir de compras *to go shopping* 1.2, 2.2

el/la invitado/a *guest* 5.2

la isla *island* 9.1

italiano/a *Italian* 12.1

a la izquierda *to the left* 4.2

J

jamaicano/a *Jamaican* 12.1

el jarabe para la tos *cough syrup* 10.1

el jardín *garden* 3.2

el/la jefe/a *boss* 4.1

la jubilación *retirement* 12.2

el juego *game* 8.1

el juego de mesa *(board) game* 8.1

el jueves *Thursday* 1.2

el juez de paz *justice of the peace* 5.2

el/la jugador/a *player* 8.1

jugar (al tenis) *to play (tennis)* 1.2

jugar (ue) *to play* 3.1

el jugo (de naranja) *(orange) juice* 7.1

julio *July* 1.2

junio *June* 1.2

el juramento a la bandera *the pledge of allegiance* 12.1

el juzgado *court house* 5.2

L

los labios *lips* 3.1

lacio/a *straight* 1.1

al lado (de) *next (to)* 4.2

el lago *lake* 9.1

la langosta *lobster* 7.1

el lápiz *pencil* P

el lápiz de memoria *(USB) flash/pen drive* 11.1

largo/a *long* 1.1

el lavabo/el lavamanos *bathroom sink* 3.2

el lavaplatos *dishwasher* 3.2

lavar (los platos) *to wash (the dishes)/to do the dishes* 2.1

lavar(se) *to wash (oneself)* 4.1

Le presento a... *I would like to introduce you to...* P

leer *to read* 1.2

la leche (de soja) *(soy) milk* 7.1

la lechuga *lettuce* 7.1

la legumbre *legume* 7.1

lejos *far* 4.2

la lengua materna *mother language* 12.2

levantar pesas *weight-lifting* 8.1

levantar(se) *to get (oneself) up* 4.1

la ley *law* 12.1, 1.2

el libro *book* P

el lienzo *canvas* 6.2

la liga *league* 8.1

limpiar *to clean* 4.1

las líneas del metro *subway lines* 11.2

listo/a *smart* 1.1

llegar (a) *to arrive (to)* 2.1

llegar a tiempo *to arrive/be on time* 2.1

llover *to rain* 4.2

Llueve (mucho). *It rains (a lot).* 4.2

la lluvia *rain* 4.2

loco/a *crazy* 10.2

luchar *to fight* 6.1

luchar por *to fight for* 12.1

el lugar *place* 4.2

luminoso/a *bright* 3.2

la luna de miel *honeymoon* 5.2

el lunes *Monday* 1.2

el lunes/martes... pasado *last Monday/Tuesday . . .* 8.1

la luz *light* 6.2

M

la madrastra *stepmother* 3.1

la madre *mother* 3.1

la madrina *maid of honor, godmother* 5.2

el/la maestro/a *teacher* 4.1

el maíz/choclo (Am. del S.) *corn* 7.1

el malestar *discomfort* 10.1

la maleta *suitcase* 11.2

malo/a *bad* 1.1

(pasado) mañana *(the day after) tomorrow* 2.2

mandar *to send* 5.2

el maní *peanut* 7.1

la manifestación *protest* 12.1

la mano *hand* 10.1

el mantel *tablecloth* 7.2

la mantequilla *butter* 7.1

la manzana *apple* 7.1

maquillar(se) *to put on makeup* 4.1

la mariposa *butterfly* 9.2

marrón/café *brown* 2.2

marroquí *Moroccan* 12.1

el martes *Tuesday* 1.2

marzo *March* 1.2

Más o menos. *So-so.* P

materno/a *mother's side* 3.1

mayo *May* 1.2

mayor *older* 3.2

Me duele... *My . . . hurts* 10.1

(No) Me gusta... *I (don't) like . . .* 1.2

Me llamo... *My name is...* P

¿Me podría traer...? *Could you bring me...?* 7.2

el medicamento *medicine* 10.1

el/la médico/a *doctor, physician* 4.1

el/la medio/a hermano/a *half brother/sister* 3.1

el medio ambiente *environment* 9.2

el medio de comunicación *media* 8.2

mejor *better* 3.2

mejorar *to improve* 10.1

menor *younger* 3.2

menos cuarto *a quarter to* 2.1

el mercado (al aire libre) *outdoors market* 2.2

merendar (e→ie) *to have an afternoon snack* 7.1

la merienda *afternoon snack* 7.1

el mes/año que viene, el próximo mes/año *next month/year* 2.2

la mesa *table* 3.2

el/la mesero/a, camarero/a, mozo/a *waiter, waitress* 7.2

la mesita *coffee table* 3.2

la mesita de noche *nightstand* 3.2

meter (el lápiz, el disco) *to put in (the pen drive, the CD/DVD)* 11.1

mexicano/a *Mexican* 1.1

mezclar *to mix* 7.2

la mezquita *mosque* 6.2

el microondas *microwave* 3.2

la miel *honey* 7.1

mientras *while* 8.1

el miércoles *Wednesday* 1.2

mil *one thousand* 2.2

mil cien *one thousand hundred* 2.2

mil ciento uno *one thousand one hundred and one* 2.2

mil uno *one thousand and one* 2.2

mirar/ver la televisión *to watch TV* 1.2

la mochila *backpack* P

molestar *to bother* 5.2

la montaña *mountain* 9.1

montar a caballo *horseback riding* 8.1

montar en bicicleta *to ride a bike* 8.1

moreno/a *black (skin or hair)* 1.1, 2.2

morir *to die* 6.2

la mostaza *mustard* 7.2

mostrar *to show* 5.2

el móvil/ celular *cell phone* 11.1

Mucho gusto. *Nice to meet you.* P

el mueble *furniture* 3.2

muerto/a *died, dead* 11.1

la mujer policía *police officer (f)* 4.1

el/la músico/a *musician* 5.1

Muy bien, gracias. *Very well, thank you.* P

N

nacer *to be born* 6.1

nada *nothing, not anything* 8.2

nadar *to swim* 1.2

nadie *no one, nobody* 8.2

la naranja/ toronja *orange* 7.1, 2.2

la nariz *nose* 3.1

la natación *swimming* 8.1

navegar (la red) *to browse (the net)* 11.1

la Navidad *Christmas* 5.2

los negocios *business* 1.2

negro/a *black (skin or hair)* 1.1, 2.2

nevar *to snow* 4.2

ni...ni *neither...or* 8.2

nicaragüense *Nicaraguan* 1.1

el/la nieto/a *grandson/granddaughter* 3.1

la nieve *snow* 4.2

el/la niñero/a *baby sitter* 4.1

ningún, ninguna/os/as *none, any* 8.2

el nivel (de vida/socioeconómico) *(living/socioeconomic) standard* 12.2

el nivel del mar *sea level* 9.1

No nieva. *It doesn't snow.* 4.2

la Nochebuena *Christmas Eve* 5.2

el nombre *name* P

el nombre del usuario *username* 11.1

el norte *north* 4.2

Nos vemos mañana. *See you tomorrow.* P

las noticias (internacionales, nacionales, locales) *(international, national, local) news* 8.2

el noticiero *news program* 8.2

la noticia *piece of news* 8.2

novecientos *nine hundred* 2.2

noveno/a *ninth* 6.1

noventa *ninety* 2.2

la novia *bride/ girlfriend* 5.2

noviembre *November* 1.2

el novio *groom/ boyfriend* 5.2

el/la novio/a *boyfriend/girlfriend* 3.1

los novios *newly weds/ boyfriend and girlfriend* 5.2

la nuera *daughter-in-law* 3.1

las nuevas generaciones *new generations* 12.2

nueve *nine* P

nunca, jamás *never* 8.2

O

o...o *either...or* 8.2

la obra (de teatro) *(theatre) play* 8.2

la obra de arte *work of art* 6.2

la obra maestra *master piece* 6.2

ochenta *eighty* 2.2

ocho *eight* P

ochocientos *eight hundred* 2.2

octavo/a *eighth* 6.1

octubre *October* 1.2

el/la oculista *eye doctor* 10.2

el oeste *west* 4.2

el oficio *job/trade* 4.1

ofrecer (zc) *to offer* 5.1, 5.2

el oído *(inner) ear* 10.1

oír *to hear* 3.1

el ojo *eye* 3.1

la olla *soup pot* 7.2

once *eleven* P

oprimir una tecla *to press a key* 11.1

ordenar/pedir *to order* 7.2

la oreja *ear* 3.1

el oro *gold* 2.2

otoño *fall* 1.2

la oveja *sheep* 9.2

P

el padrastro *stepfather* 3.1

el padre *father* 3.1

los padres *parents, fathers* 3.1

el padrino *bestman, godfather* 5.2

pagar la cuenta *pay the bill/check* 7.2

la página de inicio *home page* 11.1

el paisaje *landscape* 6.2, 9.1

el/la pájaro/a *bird* 9.2

el pan *bread* 7.1

panameño/a *Panamanian* 1.1

la pantalla *screen* 11.1

los pantalones *pants* 2.2

la papa/patata (Esp.) *potato* 7.1

el papel *paper* 9.2

el papel higiénico *toilet paper* 3.2

para llevar *to go* 2.2, 7.2

Para Ud, Q25. Buen precio... *For you, Q25. It's a good price...* 2.2

la parada de autobús *bus stop* 4.2

paraguayo/a *Paraguayan* 1.1

parecer, parecerse *to seem, to resemble* 5.1

parecerse *to look like* 3.1

la pareja *couple, partner* 5.1

el partido (de fútbol, de tenis, de baloncesto) *(soccer, tennis, basketball) match, game* 8.1

los pasajeros *passengers* 11.2

pasar por la aduana *to go through customs* 11.2

pasar por seguridad *to go through TSA area* 11.2

pasarlo/pasarla bien *to have a good time* 5.1

Pase, pase, adelante... *Come in, come in . . .* 2.2

pasear *to go for a walk* 2.1

el paso (de baile) *(dance) step* 5.1

el pastel *pie* 7.2

la pastilla *pills* 10.1

paterno/a *father's side* 3.1

patinar *to skate* 1.2

patinar en línea *line skating* 8.1

el patio *backyard* 3.2

el pavo *turkey* 7.1

pedir (i) *to request* 3.1, 9.1

peinar(se) *to comb (one's hair)* 4.1

pelar *to peel* 7.2

la película (de acción, de animación, de suspenso, de terror, dramática, romántica) *(action, animation, suspense, horror, drama, romance) movie* 8.2

pelirrojo/a *redhead* 1.1

el pelo *hair* 3.1

la pelota *ball* 8.1

el/la peluquero/a *hairdresser* 4.1

pensar (ie) *to think* 3.1

peor *worse* 3.2

pequeño/a *small* 3.2

la pera *pear* 7.1

perder (ie) *to lose* 3.1, 8.1

el perfil *profile* 12.2

el periódico *newspaper* 8.2

el/la periodista *journalist* 4.1

el permiso *permit* 12.1

el/la perro/a *dog* 9.2

el personaje *character* 8.2

peruano/a *Peruvian* 1.1

la pesca *fishing* 8.1

el pescado *fish* 7.1, 9.2

pescar *to go fishing* 8.1

el petróleo *oil* 7.2, 9.2

el pez *fish* 9.2, 7.1

picante *hoy* 7.1

picar *to snack, to dice* 7.1, 7.2

el pie *foot* 10.1

la pierna *leg* 10.1

la pimienta *pepper* 7.2

el pimiento *bell pepper* 7.1

la piña/el ananá (Am. del S.) *pineapple* 7.1

pintar *to paint* 1.2, 6.2

la pintura (al óleo) *(oil) painting* 6.2

la piscina *swimming pool* 3.2, 11.2
el piso *floor, story* 3.2
la pizarra *board* P, 8.1
la plata *silver* 2.2, 6.2
el plátano/la banana *banana* 7.1
plateado/a *silver* 6.2, 2.2
el plato *dish, plate* 7.2
el plato hondo *soup dish* 7.2
la playa *beach* 9.1
la plaza *square* 4.2
poder (ue) *to be able* 3.1
el poder *power* 6.1
el policía *police officer (m)* 4.1
el pollo *chicken* 7.1
poner *to put* 3.1
poner la mesa *to set the table* 7.2
poner una inyección/vacuna a alguien *to give somebody a shot/vaccine* 10.1
poner(se) *to put (something) on (oneself)* 4.1
Por favor *Please* P
por la mañana/tarde/noche *in the morning/afternoon/evening* 2.2
portugués/portuguesa *Portuguese* 12.1
el postre *dessert* 7.2
la práctica en empresa *internship* 4.1
preciso/a *necessary* 9.1
preferir (ie) *to prefer* 3.1
preguntar *to ask* 5.2
la prensa *press* 8.2
preocuparse (por) *to worry (about)* 10.2
el/la presentador/a (de televisión) *newsreader, TV host(ess)* 8.2
prestar *to lend* 5.2
el precio *price* 3.2
el precio (fijo) *(fixed) price* 2.2
el premio *award* 8.2
primavera *spring* 1.2
el primer plato *first course/ appetizer* 7.2
el primer/segundo plato *first/main course* 7.2
primer(o)/a *first* 6.1
primera clase *first class/business class* 11.2
el/la primo/a *cousin* 3.1
probar (>ue) *to taste, to try (food)* 7.2
el/la profesor/a *teacher, instructor* 1.2, 4.1
el programa (de variedades) *(variety) show* 8.2
la programación *programming* 8.2
la propina *tip* 7.2
prosperar *to prosper, to thrive* 12.2
el/la protagonista *main character* 8.2
la puerta *door* 3.2
puertorriqueño/a *Puerto Rican* 1.1
Pues, ahí nomás *Well, hanging in there* P
el pueblo *town* 4.2
el puerto *harbor* 9.1
puesto/a *put, placed* 11.1
el puesto *job/position* 4.1
el pulmón *lung* 10.1
la pulsera *bracelet* 2.2
el pupitre *student desk* P
¡Pura vida! *Great! (Lit. Nothing but life.)* P

Q

¿Qué busca/desea? *What are you looking for?* 2.2

¿Qué clases tomas? *What classes do you take?* 1.2
quedarse (en un hotel) *to stay (in a hotel)* 11.2
¿Qué día es hoy? *What day is today?* 1.2
¿Qué hay en la tele? *What's on TV?* 8.2
¿A qué hora es...? *What time is . . . ?* 2.1
¿Qué hubo? *What's up?* P
¿Qué llevas? *What are you wearing?* 2.2
Que la pases bien *Have a good time* P
¿Qué me cuentas? *What's going on?* P
¿Qué quiere/s comer/beber? *What do you want to eat/drink?* 7.2
querer (ie) *to want* 3.1
¡Qué rico! *How delicious!* 7.2
el queso *cheese* 7.1
¿Qué tal? *How's it going?* P
Que te diviertas *Have fun (i)* P
¿Qué te duele? *What hurts?* 10.1
¿Qué te gusta hacer? *What do you like to do?* 1.2
¿Qué te gusta llevar? *What do you like to wear?* 2.2
¿Qué te pasa? *What is the matter?* 10.1
¿Qué temperatura hace? *What's the temperature?* 4.2
Que tengas un buen fin de semana. *Have a good weekend. (i)* P
¿Qué tiempo hace? *What's the weather like?* 4.2
¿Qué trae...? *What comes with...?* 7.2
¡Que vivan los novios! *Cheers for the newlyweds!/Hooray for the happy couple!* 5.2
¿Quieres algo de tomar/picar? *Would you like something to drink/ a snack?* 7.1
¿Quieres bailar? *Do you want to dance?* 5.1
Quiero presentarle a... *I would like to introduce you to...(formal)* P
Quiero presentarte a... *I'd like you to meet... (informal)* P
la química *chemistry* 1.2
quince *fifteen* P
el/la quinceañero/a *15th birthday celebration* 5.2
quinientos *five hundred* 2.2
quinientos mil *five hundred thousand* 3.2
quinto/a *fifth* 6.1
quitar(se) *to take clothes off* 4.1
quizás/ tal vez *maybe* 9.2

R

las raíces *roots* 12.2
el ramo (de flores) *bouquet* 5.2
la rana *frog* 9.2
el ratón *mouse* 11.1
la raza *race* 12.2
rebajar *to reduce* 2.2
rechazar *to reject* 12.2
la receta *recipe* 7.1, 10.1
el rechazo *rejection* 12.2
el reciclaje *recycling* 9.2
reconocer *recognize* 5.1, 12.2
el recurso (natural) *(natural) resource* 9.2
las redes sociales *social networks* 11.1
reducir (el consumo de alcohol/grasa) *reduce (your alcohol/fat intake)* 10.2

la reina *queen* 6.1
el refresco *soft drink, soda* 7.2
regalar *to buy a present* 2.2, 5.2
el regalo *gift* 2.2, 5.2
regatear *to negotiate price* 2.2
registrarse *to check in* 11.2
regresar *to return* 2.1, 3.1
la reja *(ornamental) wrought iron* 3.2
relajarse *to relax* 10.2
el reloj *watch* 2.2
remover *to stir up* 7.2
repetir (i) *to repeat* 3.1, 6.2
representar/interpretar (un personaje) *to play (the part of...)* 8.2
el reproductor (de audio/video/música/DVD) *(audio/video/music/DVD) player* 11.1
resuelto/a *solved* 11.1
retrasarse *to be late* 11.2
el retrato *portrait* 6.2
la revista *magazine* 8.2
el rey *king* 6.1
el río *river* 9.1
rizado/a *curly* 1.1
la rodilla *knee* 10.1
rojo/a *red* 2.2
romperse un hueso *to break a bone* 10.1
la ropa *clothing* 2.2
rosado/a *pink* 2.2
roto/a *broken* 11.1
rubio/a *blonde* 1.1

S

el sábado *Saturday* 1.2
saber *to know (a fact)* 5.1
la sal *salt* 7.2
la sala *the living room* 3.2
la sala de espera *waiting room* 11.2
salir *to leave, to go out with* 3.1
salir con amigos *to go out with friends* 1.2
¡Salud! *Cheers! (Lit. Health!)* 5.2
la salud *health* 10.1
saludable *healthy* 7.1
el saludo *greeting* P
salvadoreño/a *Salvadorian* 1.1
la sandía *watermelon* 7.1
la sangre *blood* 10.1
la sartén *frying pan* 7.2
satisfecho/a *satisfied* 11.1
seguir *to continue, follow* 4.2
seguir una receta *to follow a recipe* 7.2
segundo/a *second* 6.1
el segundo plato *main course/ entrée* 7.2
la seguridad *safety* 3.2
el seguro medico *health insurance* 10.1
seis *six* P
seiscientos *six hundred* 2.2
la selva *tropical tropical forest* 9.1
la semana pasada *last week* 8.1
la semana que viene, la próxima semana *next week* 2.2
el/la señor/a *Mr./Ms.* P
la señorita *miss* P
sentar(se) (ie) *to sit down* 4.1
sentir(se) (ie) *to feel* 4.1
sentirse mal/bien *to feel badly/well* 10.1
septiembre *September* 1.2

séptimo/a   *seventh*   6.1
ser   *to be*   1.1
ser aficionado/a (de...)   *to be a fan (of . . .)*   8.1
la serpiente   *snake*   9.2
la servilleta   *napkin*   7.2
servir (i)   *to serve*   3.1
sesenta   *sixty*   2.2
setecientos   *seven hundred*   2.2
setenta   *seventy*   2.2
sexto/a   *sixth*   6.1
el sida   *AIDS*   10.1
siempre   *always*   8.2
la sierra   *highlands*   9.1
siete   *seven*   P
Siga por la derecha.   *Continue on the right hand side.*   4.2
el siglo   *century*   6.1
silbar   *to whistle*   8.1
la silla   *chair*   3.2
el sillón   *armchair*   3.2
simpático/a   *nice, likable*   1.1
el sindicato   *labor union*   12.2
el síntoma   *symptom*   10.1
el/la sobrino/a   *nephew/niece*   3.1
solicitar (un trabajo)   *to apply (for a job)*   4.1
la solicitud   *application*   4.1
soltero/a   *single*   3.1
el sombrero   *hat*   2.2
la sopa (del día)   *soup (of the day)*   7.2
Soy de...   *My team is...*   8.1
subir/bajar de peso   *to gain/lose weight*   10.2
subir/cargar canciones   *to upload songs*   11.1
el/la suegro/a   *father/mother-in-law*   3.1
el sueldo   *salary/wage*   4.1
sugerir   *to suggest*   6.2, 9.1
suizo/a   *Suisse*   12.1
el sur   *south*   4.2
surinamés/surinamesa   *Surinamese*   12.1

T

el tablero   *board*   8.1, P
tacaño/a   *stingy*   1.1
también   *also*   8.2
tampoco   *neither, not either*   8.2
la tarjeta de embarque   *boarding pass*   11.2
la taza   *coffee cup*   7.2
el té   *tea*   7.1
Te presento a...   *I would like to introduce you to... (informal)*   P
la tecla   *key*   11.1
el teclado   *keyboard*   11.1
el tejado   *tiled roof*   3.2
la telenovela   *soap opera*   8.2
el tema   *issue, topic*   12.2
el tenedor   *fork*   7.2
tener (ie)   *to have*   3.1
tener (que)   *to have (to)*   4.1
tener alergias   *to suffer from allergies*   10.1
tener buena/mala suerte   *to be lucky/unlucky*   3.1
tener calor   *to be hot*   3.1

tener comezón   *to feel itchy*   10.1
tener cuidado   *to be careful*   10.2
tener dolor de (cabeza/estómago/oído)   *to have (a head/stomach/ear) ache*   10.1
tener escalofríos   *to have cold chills*   10.1
tener estrés   *to suffer from stress*   10.2
tener éxito   *to be successful*   8.2
tener fiebre   *to have fever*   10.1
tener frío   *to be cold*   3.1
tener ganas de...   *to feel like . . .*   3.1
tener hambre   *to be hungry*   3.1
tener mareos   *to feel dizzy*   10.1
tener miedo   *to be afraid*   3.1
tener migraña   *to have a migraine*   10.1
tener náuseas   *to feel nauseous*   10.1
tener razón   *to be right*   3.1
tener sed   *to be thirsty*   3.1
tener sueño   *to be sleepy*   3.1
tener... años   *to be... years old*   3.1
el tenis de mesa   *ping-pong*   8.1
tercer(o)/a   *third*   6.1
terminar   *to finish*   2.1
testarudo/a   *stubborn*   1.1
el/la testigo   *witness*   5.2
el tiempo   *weather*   4.2
el tiempo libre   *free time*   1.2
la tina/la bañera   *bathtub*   3.2
el/la tío/a   *uncle/aunt*   3.1
tirar   *to throw away*   9.2
tirar (el ramo)   *to throw (the bouquet)*   5.2
el tobillo   *ankle*   10.1
tocar un instrumento   *to play an instrument*   1.2
el tocino   *bacon*   7.1
todavía   *still*   11.1
todo   *everything*   8.2
todo/a/os/as   *all*   8.2
tomar   *to take / drink*   2.1
tonto/a   *silly/not smart*   1.1
torcerse el tobillo   *to twist an ankle*   10.1
la torre   *tower*   6.2
la torta   *cake*   7.2
la tortuga   *turtle*   9.2
toser   *to cough*   10.1
trabajar   *to work*   2.1
el trabajo   *job/work*   4.1
el trabajo social   *social work*   1.2
traducir   *to translate*   5.1
traer   *to bring*   3.1
el traje   *suit*   2.2
la trama   *plot*   8.2
tranquilo/a   *calm*   10.2
el tratado   *treaty*   6.1
tratar(se) de   *to be about*   8.2
trece   *thirteen*   P
treinta   *thirty*   P
el tren   *train*   11.2
tres   *three*   P
trescientos   *three hundred*   2.2
trigueño/a   *dark-skinned*   1.1
triste   *sad*   10.2
triunfar, tener éxito   *to succeed, to be successful*   12.2
turquesa   *turquoise*   6.2

U

la ubicación   *location*   3.2
un día, una vez   *one day, one time*   8.1
un millón   *one million*   3.2
uno   *one*   P
uruguayo/a   *Uruguayan*   1.1
la uva   *grape*   7.1

V

la vacuna   *vaccine*   10.1
vanidoso/a   *vain*   1.1
el vaso   *glass*   7.2, 9.2
el vecindario   *neighborhood*   3.2, 4.2
el/la vecino/a   *neighbor*   3.2
veinte   *twenty*   P
veintiuno   *twenty-one*   P
el/la vendedor/a   *salesperson*   4.1
vender   *to sell*   2.2
venezolano/a   *Venezuelan*   1.1
la ventana   *window*   P, 3.2
venir   *to come*   3.1
verano   *summer*   1.2
verde   *green*   2.2
verde (oliva, claro, oscuro)   *green (olive, light, dark)*   6.2
la verdura   *vegetables*   7.1
el vestido   *dress*   2.2
vestir(se) (i)   *to get dressed*   4.1
viajar   *to travel*   1.2
el viaje   *voyage*   6.1
el videojuego   *videogame*   8.1
el vidrio   *glass*   9.2, 7.2
el viento   *wind*   4.2
el viernes   *Friday*   1.2
el vinagre   *vinegar*   7.2
el vino   *wine*   7.2
el voleibol (de playa)   *(beach) volleyball*   8.1
violeta/morado/a   *purple*   2.2
visto/a   *seen*   11.1
viudo/a   *widow/widower*   3.1
la vivienda   *housing*   3.2, 12.2
vivir   *to live*   2.1
volar   *to fly*   11.2
volver (ue)   *to return*   3.1, 2.1
el vuelo (directo)   *(direct) flight*   11.2
vuelto   *returned (a person)*   11.1

Y

y cuarto   *quarter past*   2.1
y media   *thirty past*   2.1
ya   *already*   8.1, 11.1
el yerno   *son-in-law*   3.1

Z

la zanahoria   *carrot*   7.1
las zapatillas de deporte/los tenis   *tennis shoes*   2.2
los zapatos   *shoes*   2.2

English-Spanish Glossary

A

a quarter to   *menos cuarto*   2.1
A.D.(in the year of our Lord)   *d. C. (después de Cristo)*   6.1
(action, animation, suspense,   *la película (de acción,de horror, drama, romance) movie   animación, desuspenso, de terror,dramática, romántica)*   8.2
(disposable) container   *el envase (desechable)*   9.2
actress   *la actriz*   6.2
address, direction   *la dirección*   4.2
afternoon snack   *la merienda*   7.1
age or era   *la época*   6.1
AIDS   *el sida*   10.1
(air, water...) pollution   *la contaminación (del aire, del agua...)*   9.2
airline   *la aerolínea/línea aérea*   11.2
all   *todo/a/os/as*   8.2
ally   *el aliado*   6.1
already   *ya*   8.1, 11.1
also   *también*   8.2
always   *siempre*   8.2
American   *estadounidense*   1.1
ankle   *el tobillo*   10.1
answering machine   *el contestador*   11.1
apartment   *el apartamento*   3.2
apple   *la manzana*   7.1
application   *la solicitud*   4.1
April   *abril*   1.2
Argentine   *argentino/a*   1.1
arm   *el brazo*   10.1
armchair   *el sillón*   3.2
arts and crafts   *la artesanía*   2.2
(attached) file   *el archivo (adjunto)*   11.1
athlete   *el/la deportista*   8.1
(audio/video/music/DVD) player   *el reproductor (de audio/video/música/ DVD)*   11.1
August   *agosto*   1.2
avenue   *la avenida*   4.2
award   *el premio*   8.2

B

B.C. (Before Christ)   *a. C. (antes de Cristo)*   6.1
baby sitter   *el/la niñero/a*   4.1
bachelor/bachelorette party   *la despedida de soltero/a*   5.2
back   *la espalda*   10.1
backpack   *la mochila*   P
backyard   *el patio*   3.2
bacon   *el tocino*   7.1
bad   *malo/a*   1.1
ball   *la pelota*   8.1
banana   *el plátano/la banana*   7.1

baptism   *el bautizo*   5.2
basketball   *el baloncesto*   8.1
bass   *el bajo*   5.1
bathroom   *el baño*   3.2
bathroom sink   *el lavabo/el lavamanos*   3.2
bathtub   *la tina/la bañera*   3.2
BBQ   *el asado/la parrillada*   7.1
beach   *la playa*   9.1
(beach) volleyball   *el voleibol (de playa)*   8.1
bean   *el frijol*   7.1
bed   *la cama*   3.2
bedroom   *el dormitorio*   3.2
(beef) meat   *la carne (de vaca/res)*   7.1
beef steak   *el bistec/bife*   7.1
beer   *la cerveza*   7.2
behind   *detrás (de)*   4.2
bell pepper   *el pimiento*   7.1
bestman, godfather   *el padrino*   5.2
better   *mejor*   3.2
big   *grande*   3.2
bill/check   *la cuenta*   7.2
bird   *el/la pájaro/a*   9.2
birthday   *el cumpleaños*   5.2
black   *negro/a*   2.2, 1.1
black (skin or hair)   *moreno/a, negro/a*   1.1, 2.2
blonde   *rubio/a*   1.1
blood   *la sangre*   10.1
blue   *azul*   2.2
board   *la pizarra, el tablero*   P, 8.1
(board) game   *el juego de mesa*   8.1
boarding pass   *la tarjeta de embarque*   11.2
Bolivian   *boliviano/a*   1.1
book   *el libro*
border   *la frontera*   9.1
boring, tedious   *aburrido/a*   8.2, 1.1
boss   *el/la jefe/a*   4.1
bouquet   *el ramo (de flores)*   5.2
bowl   *la fuente*   7.2
boyfriend/girlfriend   *el/la novio/a*   3.1
bracelet   *la pulsera*   2.2
Brazilian   *brasileño/a*   12.1
bread   *el pan*   7.1
breakfast   *el desayuno*   7.1
bride/ girlfriend   *la novia*   5.2
bridesmaid   *la dama*   5.2
bright   *luminoso/a*   3.2
bright color   *color vivo*   6.2
broken   *roto/a*   11.1
brother/sister   *el/la hermano/a*   3.1
brother/sister-in-law   *el/la cuñado/a*   3.1
brown   *marrón/café*   2.2
browser   *el buscador*   11.1
building   *el edificio*   3.2
burgundy   *color vino*   6.2
bus   *el autobús*   2.1, 4.2
bus stop   *la parada de autobús*   4.2

business   *los negocios*   1.2
butter   *la mantequilla*   7.1
butterfly   *la mariposa*   9.2

C

cake   *la torta*   7.2
calm   *tranquilo/a*   10.2
canvas   *el lienzo*   6.2
car   *el auto/carro*   4.2
cards   *las cartas*   8.1
careful   *cuidadoso/a*   1.1
carrot   *la zanahoria*   7.1
(carry-on) luggage   *el equipaje (de mano)*   11.2
cartoons   *los dibujos animados*   8.2
cast iron pot   *el caldero*   7.2
castle   *el castillo*   6.2
cat   *el/la gato/a*   9.2
cell phone   *el móvil/ celular*   11.1
century   *el siglo*   6.1
chair   *la silla*   3.2
championship   *el campeonato*   8.1
character   *el personaje*   8.2
charger   *el cargador*   11.1
cheap, inexpensive   *barato/a*   2.2
checkers   *las damas*   8.1
Cheers! (Lit. Health!)   *¡Salud!*   5.2
Cheers for the newlyweds!/Hooray for the happy couple!   *¡Que vivan los novios!*   5.2
cheese   *el queso*   7.1
chemistry   *la química*   1.2
chess   *el ajedrez*   8.1
chestnut   *castaño/a*   1.1
chicken   *el pollo*   7.1
Chilean   *chileno/a*   1.1
Christmas   *la Navidad*   5.2
Christmas Eve   *la Nochebuena*   5.2
church   *la iglesia*   5.2
city   *la ciudad*   4.2
city block   *la cuadra*   4.2
(civil) war   *la guerra (civil)*   6.1
clam   *la almeja*   7.1
climate change   *el cambio climático*   9.2
closet   *el armario/el ropero*   3.2
clothing   *la ropa*   2.2
coach / trainer   *el/la entrenador/a*   8.1
coffee cup   *la taza*   7.2
coffee table   *la mesita*   3.2
Colombian   *colombiano/a*   1.1
Come in, come in, . . .   *Pase, pase, adelante...*   2.2
company (business)   *la empresa*   4.1
competition, contest   *el concurso*   8.2
computer science   *la informática*   1.2
confused   *confundido/a*   10.2
congested   *congestionado/a*   10.1
Congratulations!   *¡Felicidades!*   5.2

Continue on the right hand side. *Siga por la derecha.* 4.2
contradicted *contradicho/a* 11.1
control (your anxiety/cholesterol) *controlar (la ansiedad/el colesterol)* 10.2
controversial *controvertido/a* 8.2, 12.2
cook *el/la cocinero/a* 4.1
cookie or cracker *la galleta/ galletita* 7.1
corn *el maíz/choclo (Am. del S.)* 7.1
corner *la esquina* 4.2
Costarican *costarricense* 1.1
cough syrup *el jarabe para la tos* 10.1
Could you bring me...? *¿Me podría traer...?* 7.2
couple, partner *la pareja* 5.1
court *la cancha* 8.1
court house *el juzgado* 5.2
cousin *el/la primo/a* 3.1
cover letter *la carta de presentación* 4.1
covered *cubierto/a* 11.1
crazy *loco/a* 10.2
Cuban *cubano/a* 1.1
curly *rizado/a* 1.1
current *actual* 8.2
current affairs *la actualidad* 8.2
cutlery *el cubierto* 7.2
dance *el baile* 5.1
dark-skinned *trigueño/a* 1.1
daughter-in-law *la nuera* 3.1

D

(dance) step *el paso (de baile)* 5.1
(dark, light, navy) blue *azul (oscuro, claro, marino)* 6.2
December *diciembre* 1.2
demographics *la demografía* 12.2
depressed *deprimido/a* 10.2
design *el diseño* 1.2
desk *el escritorio* 3.2
dessert *el postre* 7.2
dice *los dados* 8.1
dictatorship *la dictadura* 6.1
died, dead *muerto/a* 11.1
dining room *el comedor* 3.2
dinner *la cena* 7.1
(direct) flight *el vuelo (directo)* 11.2
discomfort *el malestar* 10.1
discovered *descubierto/a* 11.1
disease *la enfermedad* 10.1
dish, plate *el plato* 7.2
dishwasher *el lavaplatos* 3.2
distracted, absent-minded *distraído/a* 10.2
Do you want to dance? *¿Quieres bailar?* 5.1
doctor, physician *el/la médico/a* 4.1
doctor's office *el consultorio del médico* 10.1
dog *el/la perro/a* 9.2
(domestic/wild) animal *el animal (doméstico/salvaje)* 9.2
Dominican *dominicano/a* 1.1
done *hecho/a* 11.1
door *la puerta* 3.2
down *abajo* 4.2
dress *el vestido* 2.2
dresser *la cómoda* 3.2

dressing *el aderezo* 7.2
drink *la bebida* 7.2
(dual) citizenship *la (doble) ciudadanía* 12.1

E

ear *la oreja* 3.1
earring *el arete/pendiente* 2.2
east *el este* 4.2
Ecuadorian *ecuatoriano/a* 1.1
egg *el huevo* 7.1
eight *ocho* P
eight hundred *ochocientos* 2.2
eighteen *dieciocho* P
eighth *octavo/a* 6.1
eighty *ochenta* 2.2
either...or *o...o* 8.2
(elementary/high) school *la escuela (primaria/secundaria)* 1.2
eleven *once* P
employment *el empleo* 4.1
engineer *el/la ingeniero/a* 4.1
Enjoy your meal! *¡Buen provecho!* 7.2
entertaining *entretenido/a* 8.2
environment *el medio ambiente* 9.2
environmentalist *el/la ecologista* 9.2
Equatoguinean *ecuatoguineano/a* 1.1
everything *todo* 8.2
excited *emocionado/a* 10.2
exciting, thrilling *emocionante* 8.2
Excuse me, how do I get to...? *Disculpe, ¿cómo llego a...?* 4.2
expensive *caro/a* 2.2
(extreme) sport *el deporte (extremo/de riesgo)* 8.1
eye *el ojo* 3.1
eye doctor *el/la oculista* 10.2

F

face *la cara* 3.1
fall *otoño* 1.2
fan *el/la aficionado/a* 8.1
far *lejos* 4.2
farewell *la despedida* P
fat *la grasa* 7.1
fat *gordo/a* 1.1
fat/fatty *graso/a* 7.1
father *el padre* 3.1
father/mother-in-law *el/la suegro/a* 3.1
father's side *paterno/a* 3.1
February *febrero* 1.2
fifteen *quince* P
15th birthday celebration *el/la quinceañero/a* 5.2
fifth *quinto/a* 6.1
fifty *cincuenta* P
finger/toe *el dedo (de la mano/del pie)* 10.1
firefighter *el/la bombero/a* 4.1
first *primer(o)/a* 6.1
first class/business class *primera clase* 11.2
first course/ appetizer *el primer plato* 7.2
first/main course *el primer/segundo plato* 7.2
fish *el pescado, el pez* 7.1, 9.2
fishing *la pesca* 8.1
five *cinco* P

five hundred *quinientos* 2.2
five hundred thousand *quinientos mil* 3.2
(fixed) price *el precio (fijo)* 2.2
flight attendant *el/la aeromozo/a* 4.1, 11.2
floor, story *el piso* 3.2
flower *la flor* 2.2, 3.2
flu *la gripe* 10.1
folder *la carpeta* 11.1
food *la comida, el alimento* 2.2, 7.1
foot *el pie* 10.1
For you, Q25. It's a good price... *Para Ud., Q25. Buen precio...* 2.2
forest *el bosque* 9.1
fork *el tenedor* 7.2
forty *cuarenta* P
four *cuatro* P
four hundred *cuatrocientos* 2.2
fourteen *catorce* P
fourth *cuarto/a* 6.1
free time *el tiempo libre* 1.2
French *francés/francesa* 12.1
French Guianese *francoguayanés/ francoguayanesa* 12.1
Friday *el viernes* 1.2
fried *frito/a, freído/a* 7.2, 11.1
frog *la rana* 9.2
frying pan *la sartén* 7.2
fun *divertido/a* 1.1
funny *chistoso/a, gracioso/a* 1.1, 8.2
furnished *amueblado/a* 3.2
furniture *el mueble* 3.2

G

game *el juego* 8.1
garbage *la basura* 9.2
garden *el jardín* 3.2
garlic *el ajo* 7.1
germ *el germen* 10.1
gift *el regalo* 2.2, 5.2
glass *el vaso, el vidrio* 7.2, 9.2
global warming *el calentamiento global* 9.2
goalkeeper *el arquero* 8.1
godson/goddaughter *el/la ahijado/a* 5.2
gold *el oro* 2.2
golden *dorado/a* 6.2
good *bueno/a* 1.1
Good afternoon. *Buenas tardes.* P
Good evening./Good night. *Buenas noches.* P
Good morning. *Buenos días.* P
grandfather/grandmother *el/la abuelo/a* 3.1
grandson/granddaughter *el/la nieto/a* 3.1
grape *la uva* 7.1
gray *gris* 2.2
great grandchild *el/la bisnieto/a* 3.1
great grandfather/grandmother *el/la bisabuelo/a* 3.1
Great! *¡Fenomenal!* P
Great! (Lit. Nothing but life.) *¡Pura vida!* P
green *verde* 2.2
green (olive, light, dark) *verde (oliva, claro, oscuro)* 6.2
greeting *el saludo* P

groom/ boyfriend *el novio* 5.2
groomsman *el caballero* 5.2
Guatemalan *guatemalteco/a* 1.1
guest *el/la invitado/a* 5.2
guinea pig *el cuy* 9.2
Guyanese *guyanés/guyanesa* 12.1

H

hair *el pelo* 3.1
hairdresser *el/la peluquero/a* 4.1
Haitian *haitiano/a* 12.1
half brother/sister *el/la medio/a hermano/a* 3.1
hand *la mano* 10.1
harbor *el puerto* 9.1
hard drive *el disco duro/externo* 11.1
hat *el sombrero* 2.2
Have a good time. *Que la pases bien.* P
Have a good weekend (i). *Que tengas un buen fin de semana.* P
Have fun (i). *Que te diviertas.* P
He/She (doesn't) like(s)… *(No) Le gusta…* 1.2
He/She has ([type] hair/skin) *Él/Ella tiene (el pelo/la piel)* 1.1
He/She is from … *Es de…* 1.1
head *la cabeza* 3.1
health *la salud* 10.1
health insurance *el seguro médico* 10.1
healthy *saludable* 7.1
heart *el corazón* 10.1
herbal tea *la infusión/el té de hierbas* 10.1
here *aquí* 6.2
Hi. *Hola.* P
highlands *la sierra* 9.1
highway *la autopista* 4.2
His/her skin/hair is … *Él/ella es de piel/de pelo…* 1.1
home page *la página de inicio* 11.1
Honduran *hondureño/a* 1.1
honey *la miel* 7.1
honeymoon *la luna de miel* 5.2
horse *el caballo* 9.2
horseback riding *montar a caballo* 8.1
(hotel) stay *la estadía/estancia (en un hotel)* 11.2
house, home *la casa* 2.1, 3.2
housing *la vivienda* 3.2, 12.2
How are you doing? *¿Cómo estamos?* P
How are you? (formal) *¿Cómo está usted?* P
How are you? (informal) *¿Cómo estás?* P
How delicious! *¡Qué rico!* 7.2
How much is/are …? *¿Cuánto cuesta/ cuestan…?* 2.2
How's it going? *¿Qué tal?* P
hoy *picante* 7.1
human body *el cuerpo humano* 10.1

I

I (don't) like … *(No) Me gusta…* 1.2
I would like to introduce you to… *Le presento a…* P
I would like to introduce you to…(informal) *Te presento a…* P

I would like to introduce you to…(formal) *Quiero presentarle a…* P
I´d like you to meet… (informal) *Quiero presentarte a…* P
ice -cream *el helado* 7.2
identical twin *el/la gemelo/a* 3.1
in between *entre* 4.2
(in)equality *la (des)igualdad* 12.1
in front (of) *delante (de), en frente (de)* 4.2
in the afternoon *de la tarde* 2.1
in the evening/at night *de la noche* 2.1
in the morning *de la mañana* 2.1
in the morning/afternoon/evening *por la mañana/tarde/noche* 2.2
inheritance *la herencia* 12.2
(inner) ear *el oído* 10.1
(international, national, local) news *las noticias (internacionales, nacionales, locales)* 8.2
internship *la práctica en empresa* 4.1
island *la isla* 9.1
issue, topic *el tema* 12.2
It doesn't snow. *No nieva.* 4.2
It is… *Es la / Son las…* 2.1
It is (not) cold. *(No) Hace frío.* 4.2
It is (very) hot. *Hace (mucho) calor.* 4.2
It is (very) windy. *Hace (mucho) viento.* 4.2
It is ___ degrees F/C. *Hace ___ grados F/C.* 4.2
It is cloudy. *Está nublado.* 4.2
It is cool. *Hace fresco.* 4.2
It is foggy. *Hay niebla.* 4.2
It is humid. *Hay humedad.* 4.2
It is stormy. *Hay tormenta.* 4.2
It is sunny. *Hace sol.* 4.2
It rains (a lot). *Llueve (mucho).* 4.2
It's midnight. *Es medianoche.* 2.1
It's noon. *Es mediodía.* 2.1
Italian *italiano/a* 12.1

J

Jamaican *jamaicano/a* 12.1
janitor *el/la conserje* 4.1
January *enero* 1.2
(job) interview *la entrevista (de trabajo)* 4.1
job/position *el puesto* 4.1
job/trade *el oficio* 4.1
job/work *el trabajo* 4.1
journalist *el/la periodista* 8.2, 4.1
July *julio* 1.2
June *junio* 1.2
junk food *la comida chatarra/basura* 7.2
justice of the peace *el juez de paz* 5.2

K

key *la tecla* 11.1
keyboard *el teclado* 11.1
king *el rey* 6.1
kitchen *la cocina* 3.2
kitchen sink *el fregadero* 3.2
knee *la rodilla* 10.1
knife *el cuchillo* 7.2

L

labor union *el sindicato* 12.2
lake *el lago* 9.1
landscape *el paisaje* 6.2, 9.1
lane *el carril* 4.2
(laptop) computer *la computadora (portátil)* 11.1
last Monday/Tuesday … *el lunes/martes… pasado* 8.1
last night *anoche* 8.1
last week *la semana pasada* 8.1
last weekend/month/year *el fin de semana/ mes/año pasado* 8.1
law *el derecho, la ley* 1.2, 12.1
lawyer *el/la abogado/a* 4.1
league *la liga* 8.1
leg *la pierna* 10.1
legume *la legumbre* 7.1
letter of recommendation *la carta de recomendación* 4.1
lettuce *la lechuga* 7.1
light *la luz* 6.2
Likewise. *Igualmente.* P
line skating *patinar en línea* 8.1
lips *los labios* 3.1
lively *animado/a* 8.2
(living/socioeconomic) standard *el nivel (de vida/socioeconómico)* 12.2
lobster *la langosta* 7.1
location *la ubicación* 3.2
long *largo/a* 1.1
lunch *el almuerzo* 7.1
lung *el pulmón* 10.1

M

magazine *la revista* 8.2
maid of honor, godmother *la madrina* 5.2
mail carrier *el/la cartero/a* 4.1
main character *el/la protagonista* 8.2
main course/ entrée *el segundo plato* 7.2
major, specialization *la especialización* 1.2
manager *el/la gerente* 4.1
March *marzo* 1.2
married *casado/a* 3.1
master piece *la obra maestra* 6.2
May *mayo* 1.2
maybe *quizás/ tal vez* 9.2
(meat, cheese, seafood) turnover *la empanada (de carne, de queso, de marisco)* 7.2
media *el medio de comunicación* 8.2
medicine *el medicamento* 10.1
menu *la carta/el menú* 7.2
Mexican *mexicano/a* 1.1
microwave *el microondas* 3.2
middle/modern ages *la Edad Media/ Moderna* 6.1
mirror *el espejo* 3.2
miss *la señorita* P
Monday *el lunes* 1.2
mood *el estado de ánimo* 10.2
Moroccan *marroquí* 12.1
mosque *la mezquita* 6.2
mother *la madre* 3.1
mother language *la lengua materna* 12.2
mother's side *materno/a* 3.1

mountain   *la montaña*   9.1
mountain range   *la cordillera*   9.1
mouse   *el ratón*   11.1
mouth   *la boca*   3.1
movie theatre   *el cine*   4.2, 6.2
movie ticket   *la entrada*   8.2
Mr./Ms.   *el/la señor/a*   P
(music) band   *el conjunto (musical)*   5.1
musician   *el/la músico/a*   5.1
must, ought, should   *deber*   4.1
mustard   *la mostaza*   7.2
My . . . hurts   *Me duele...*   10.1
My name is...   *Me llamo...*   P
My team is...   *Soy de...*   8.1

N

name   *el nombre*   P
napkin   *la servilleta*   7.2
(natural) resource   *el recurso (natural)*   9.2
near   *cerca*   4.2
necessary   *preciso/a*   9.1
neighbor   *el/la vecino/a*   3.2
neighborhood   *el vecindario, el barrio*
   3.2, 4.2
neither, not either   *tampoco*   8.2
neither...or   *ni...ni*   8.2
nephew/niece   *el/la sobrino/a*   3.1
never   *nunca, jamás*   8.2
new generations   *las nuevas*
   generaciones   12.2
New Year´s Day   *el día de Año*
   Nuevo   5.2
New Year´s Eve   *el día de Año Viejo/la*
   Nochevieja   5.2
newly weds/ boyfriend and girlfriend   *los*
   novios   5.2
news program   *el noticiero*   8.2
newspaper   *el periódico*   8.2
newsreader, TV host(ess)   *el/la presentador/a*
   (de televisión)   8.2
next (to)   *al lado (de)*   4.2
next month/year   *el mes/año que viene, el*
   próximo mes/año   2.2
next week   *la semana que viene, la próxima*
   semana   2.2
Nicaraguan   *nicaragüense*   1.1
Nice to meet you.   *Encantado/a. Gusto en*
   conocerte. Mucho gusto.   P
nice, likable   *simpático/a*   1.1
nickname   *el apodo*   3.1
night club   *la discoteca*   4.2
nightstand   *la mesita de noche*   3.2
nine   *nueve*   P
nine hundred   *novecientos*   2.2
nineteen   *diecinueve*   P
ninety   *noventa*   2.2
ninth   *noveno/a*   6.1
no one, nobody   *nadie*   8.2
none, any   *ningún, ninguna/os/as*   8.2
north   *el norte*   4.2
nose   *la nariz*   3.1
nothing, not anything   *nada*   8.2
November   *noviembre*   1.2
nurse   *el/la enfermero/a*   4.1, 10.2
nursing   *la enfermería*   1.2
nut   *el fruto seco*   7.1

O

o'clock   *en punto*   2.1
October   *octubre*   1.2
oil   *el aceite, el petróleo*   7.2, 9.2
(oil) painting   *la pintura (al óleo)*   6.2
oil spill   *el derrame*   9.2
old, ancient   *antiguo/a*   6.2
older   *mayor*   3.2
one   *uno*   P
one day, one time   *un día, una vez*   8.1
one hundred   *cien*   2.2
one hundred and one   *ciento uno*   2.2
one hundred and ten   *ciento diez*   2.2
one hundred thousand   *cien mil*   3.2
one million   *un millón*   3.2
one must   *hay que*   4.1
one thousand   *mil*   2.2
one thousand and one   *mil uno*   2.2
one thousand hundred   *mil cien*   2.2
one thousand one hundred and one
   mil ciento uno   2.2
(one way/round trip) ticket   *el billete/pasaje*
   (de ida/de ida y vuelta)   11.2
onion   *la cebolla*   7.1
orange   *anaranjado/a/naranja, la naranja/*
   toronja   2.2, 7.1
(orange) juice   *el jugo (de naranja)*   7.1
(ornamental) wrought iron   *la reja*   3.2
outdoors market   *el mercado (al aire*
   libre)   2.2
oven   *el horno*   3.2
over there   *allí/allá*   6.2

P

painting   *el cuadro*   3.2, 6.2
pan   *la cacerola*   7.2
Panamanian   *panameño/a*   1.1
pants   *los pantalones*   2.2
paper   *el papel*   9.2
Paraguayan   *paraguayo/a*   1.1
parents, fathers   *los padres*   3.1
parking lot   *el estacionamiento*   4.2
passengers   *los pasajeros*   11.2
password   *la contraseña*   11.1
pay the bill/check   *pagar la cuenta*   7.2
peach   *el durazno/melocotón (Esp.)*   7.1
peanut   *el maní*   7.1
pear   *la pera*   7.1
pen   *el bolígrafo*   P
pencil   *el lápiz*   P
pepper   *la pimienta*   7.2
permit   *el permiso*   12.1
Peruvian   *peruano/a*   1.1
pie   *el pastel*   7.2
piece   *la ficha*   8.1
piece of news   *la noticia*   8.2
pig   *el/la cerdo/a*   9.2
pills   *la pastilla*   10.1
pineapple   *la piña/el ananá (Am. del S.)*   7.1
ping-pong   *el tenis de mesa*   8.1
pink   *rosado/a*   2.2
place   *el lugar*   4.2
player   *el/la jugador/a*   8.1
Please.   *Por favor.*   P
plot   *la trama*   8.2
police officer (f)   *la mujer policía*   4.1

police officer (m)   *el policía*   4.1
pool   *la piscina*   11.2, 3.2
portrait   *el retrato*   6.2
Portuguese   *portugués/portuguesa*   12.1
post office   *(la oficina de) correos*   4.2
potato   *la papa/patata (Esp.)*   7.1
power   *el poder*   6.1
prescription   *la receta*   10.1, 7.1
press   *la prensa*   8.2
pretty   *guapo/a, bonito/a*   1.1, 3.2
Pretty well.   *Bastante bien.*   P
price   *el precio*   3.2
priest   *el cura*   5.2
printed   *imprimido/a, impreso/a*   11.1
printer   *la impresora*   11.1
profile   *el perfil*   12.2
programming   *la programación*   8.2
protest   *la manifestación*   12.1
Puerto Rican   *puertorriqueño/a*   1.1
purple   *violeta/morado/a*   2.2
put, placed   *puesto/a*   11.1

Q

quarter past   *y cuarto*   2.1
queen   *la reina*   6.1

R

rabbit   *el/la conejo/a*   9.2
race   *la raza*   12.2
(radio) station   *la emisora (de radio)*   8.2
rain   *la lluvia*   4.2
(rainy/dry) season   *la estación lluviosa/*
   seca   9.1
recipe   *la receta*   7.1, 10.1
recognize   *reconocer*   5.1
recycling   *el reciclaje*   9.2
red   *rojo/a*   2.2
redhead   *pelirrojo/a*   1.1
reduce (your alcohol/fat intake)   *reducir*
   (el consumo de alcohol/grasa)   10.2
rejection   *el rechazo*   12.2
relative   *el familiar/pariente*   3.1
renown   *destacado/a*   12.2
rest   *el descanso*   10.2
résumé   *el currículum vítae*   4.1
retirement   *la jubilación*   12.2
returned (a person)   *vuelto*   11.1
returned (an object)   *devuelto/a*   11.1
rice   *el arroz*   7.1
rights   *los derechos*   12.2
ring   *el anillo*   2.2, 5.2
river   *el río*   9.1
road   *la carretera*   4.2
room   *la habitación/el cuarto*   3.2
roots   *las raíces*   12.2
rug   *la alfombra*   3.2

S

sad   *triste*   10.2
safety   *la seguridad*   3.2
said, told   *dicho/a*   11.1
salad   *la ensalada*   7.2
salary, wage   *el sueldo*   4.1
sales clerk   *el/la dependiente*   4.1

salesperson *el/la vendedor/a* 4.1
salt *la sal* 7.2
Salvadorian *salvadoreño/a* 1.1
satisfied *satisfecho/a* 11.1
Saturday *el sábado* 1.2
sausage *el chorizo* 7.1
screen *la pantalla* 11.1
sea level *el nivel del mar* 9.1
second *segundo/a* 6.1
See you later. *Hasta luego.* P
See you soon. (Lit. Until I see you again) *Hasta la vista. Hasta pronto.* P
See you tomorrow. *Hasta mañana. Nos vemos mañana.* P
seen *visto/a* 11.1
self portrait *el autorretrato* 6.2
September *septiembre* 1.2
seven *siete* P
seven hundred *setecientos* 2.2
seventeen *diecisiete* P
seventh *séptimo/a* 6.1
seventy *setenta* 2.2
sheep *la oveja* 9.2
shelf *el estante* 3.2
ship *el barco* 11.2, 6.1
shirt *la camisa* 2.2
shoes *los zapatos* 2.2
short *bajo/a* 1.1
short (hair) *corto/a* 1.1
shortage *la escasez* 9.2
shower *la ducha* 3.2
shrimp *el camarón* 7.1
sick, ill *enfermo/a* 10.1
side dish *el acompañamiento* 7.2
silly/not smart *tonto/a* 1.1
silver *la plata, plateado/a* 2.2, 6.2
singer *el/la cantante* 5.1
single *soltero/a* 3.1
(single, double, triple) room *la habitación (sencilla, doble, triple)* 11.2
six *seis* P
six hundred *seiscientos* 2.2
sixteen *dieciséis* P
sixth *sexto/a* 6.1
sixty *sesenta* 2.2
skirt *la falda* 2.2
small *pequeño/a* 3.2
smart *listo/a* 1.1
snake *la serpiente* 9.2
snow *la nieve* 4.2
soap opera *la telenovela* 8.2
(soccer, basket) ball *el balón* 8.1
soccer *el fútbol* 8.1
soccer field *el campo de fútbol* 8.1
(soccer, tennis, basketball) match, game *el partido (de fútbol, de tenis, de baloncesto)* 8.1
social networks *las redes sociales* 11.1
social work *el trabajo social* 1.2
soft drink, soda *el refresco* 7.2
solved *resuelto/a* 11.1
some, any *algún, alguna/os/as* 8.2
someone, anyone *alguien* 8.2
something, anything *algo* 8.2
son/daughter *el/la hijo/a* 3.1
song *la canción* 5.1
son-in-law *el yerno* 3.1

So-so. *Más o menos.* P
soup (of the day) *la sopa (del día)* 7.2
soup dish *el plato hondo* 7.2
soup pot *la olla* 7.2
south *el sur* 4.2
(soy) milk *la leche (de soja)* 7.1
Spanish *español/a, el español* 1.1, 1.2
Spanish speaker *el/la hispanohablante* 12.2
spice *la especia* 7.2
spider *la araña* 9.2
spin around *dar la vuelta* 5.1
spoon *la cuchara* 7.2
spouse *el/la esposo/a* 3.1
spring *primavera* 1.2
(spring/sparkling) water *el agua (mineral/con gas)* 7.2
square *la plaza* 4.2
steak *el churrasco* 7.2
stepbrother/stepsister *el/la hermanastro/a* 3.1
stepfather *el padrastro* 3.1
stepmother *la madrastra* 3.1
still *todavía* 11.1
stingy *tacaño/a* 1.1
stomach *el estómago* 10.1
stove *la estufa* 3.2
straight *lacio/a* 1.1
strawberry *la fresa/ la frutilla (Arg.)* 7.1
street *la calle* 4.2
strike *la huelga* 12.1
strong *fuerte* 1.1, 10.2
stubborn *testarudo/a* 1.1
student desk *el pupitre* P
subway lines *las líneas del metro* 11.2
suddenly *de repente* 8.1
Suisse *suizo/a* 12.1
suit *el traje* 2.2
suitcase *la maleta* 11.2
summer *verano* 1.2
Sunday *el domingo* 1.2
surgeon *el/la cirujano/a* 10.2
Surinamese *surinamés/surinamesa* 12.1
sweet *dulce* 7.1
sweet custard *el flan* 7.2
swimming *la natación* 8.1
swimming pool *la piscina* 3.2, 11.2
symptom *el síntoma* 10.1

T

table *la mesa* 3.2
tablecloth *el mantel* 7.2
taxes *los impuestos* 12.1
tea *el té* 7.1
teacher *el/la maestro/a* 4.1
teacher, instructor *el/la profesor/a* 1.2, 4.1
team *el equipo* 8.1
ten *diez* P
ten thousand *diez mil* 2.2, 3.2
tennis shoes *las zapatillas de deporte/los tenis* 2.2
tenth *décimo/a* 6.1
Thank you. *Gracias.* P
(the day after) tomorrow *(pasado) mañana* 2.2
the day before yesterday *anteayer* 8.1
the living room *la sala* 3.2

the pledge of allegiance *el juramento a la bandera* 12.1
the toast *el brindis* 5.2
The weather is good/bad. *Hace buen/mal tiempo.* 4.2
the weekend *el fin de semana* 1.2
(theatre) play *la obra (de teatro)* 8.2
there *ahí* 6.2
There is a hurricane. *Hay un huracán.* 4.2
there is/there are *hay* 3.2
There is... There are... *Hay...* P
thin *flaco/a* 1.1
third *tercer(o)/a* 6.1
thirteen *trece* P
thirty *treinta* P
thirty past *y media* 2.1
three *tres* P
three hundred *trescientos* 2.2
Three Kings Day *el día de los Reyes Magos* 5.2
throat *la garganta* 10.1
Thursday *el jueves* 1.2
tile *el azulejo/el mosaico* 3.2
tiled roof *el tejado* 3.2
tip *la propina* 7.2
tired *cansado/a* 10.2
to (dis)please *(des)agradar* 5.2
to add *agregar, añadir* 7.2
to advise *aconsejar* 5.2, 9.1
to answer *contestar* 5.2
to apply (for a job) *solicitar (un trabajo)* 4.1
to arrive (to) *llegar (a)* 2.1
to arrive/be on time *llegar a tiempo* 2.1
to ask *preguntar* 5.2
to ask for *pedir (i)* 3.1
to bake *hornear* 7.2
to bathe (oneself) *bañar(se)* 4.1
to be *ser, estar* 1.1, 3.2
to be a fan (of . . .) *ser aficionado/a (de...)* 8.1
to be able *poder (ue)* 3.1
to be about *tratar(se) de* 8.2
to be accepted, to join ato be accepted, to join a group *integrarse* 12.2
to be afraid *tener miedo* 3.1
to be born *nacer* 6.1
to be careful *tener cuidado* 10.2
to be cold *tener frío* 3.1
to be endangered *estar en peligro de extinción* 9.2
to be hot *tener calor* 3.1
to be hungry *tener hambre* 3.1
to be late *retrasarse* 11.2
to be lucky/unlucky *tener buena/mala suerte* 3.1
to be pregnant *estar embarazada* 10.2
to be right *tener razón* 3.1
to be sleepy *tener sueño* 3.1
to be successful *tener éxito* 8.2
to be thirsty *tener sed* 3.1
to be. . . years old *tener... años* 3.1
to become angry, to get upset *enojar(se)* 4.1
to boil *hervir (>ie)* 7.2
to book a table *hacer una reservación/reserva* 7.2
to bother *molestar* 5.2

to break a bone *romperse un hueso* 10.1

to bring *traer* 3.1

to browse (the net) *navegar (la red)* 11.1

to brush (teeth or hair usually) *cepillar(se)* 4.1

to build *construir* 6.2

to buy *comprar* 2.2, 3.2

to buy *comprar* 3.2, 2.2

to buy a present *regalar* 2.2, 5.2

to calm down *calmarse* 10.2

to care about something, to matter *importar* 5.2

to charge the battery *cargar la batería* 11.1

to chat on line *chatear en línea* 11.1

to check in *registrarse* 11.2

to check in your luggage *facturar el equipaje* 11.2

to cheer (a team) *animar (a un equipo)* 8.1, 5.1

to choose *elegir* 6.2, 6.1

to clean *limpiar* 4.1

to comb (one's hair) *peinar(se)* 4.1

to come *venir* 3.1

to compete *competir* 6.2

to continue, follow *seguir* 4.2

to cook *cocinar* 2.1

to cost *costar (ue)* 3.1

to cough *toser* 10.1

to count *contar (ue)* 3.1, 5.2

to cover *cubrir/tapar* 7.2

to create *crear* 6.2

to cure, to heal *curar* 10.1

to cut *cortar* 7.2, 4.12

to dance *bailar* 1.2, 5.1

to defeat *derrotar* 6.1

to delete what they don´t want *borrar lo que no quieren* 11.1

to design *diseñar* 6.2

to develop *desarrollar* 9.2

to dice *picar* 7.2

to die *morir* 6.2

to diet/be on a diet *estar a dieta/hacer dieta* 10.2

to do yoga *hacer yoga* 1.2

to do, to make *hacer* 3.1

to download programs *descargar programas* 11.1

to draw *dibujar* 6.2

to drink *beber* 2.1

to dub *doblar* 8.2

to earn, make (money) *ganar (dinero)* 4.1

to eat *comer* 2.1

to elect *elegir* 6.1, 6.2

to enjoy oneself *divertir(se)* 4.1

to enliven *animar* 5.1, 8.1

to establish *fundar* 6.1

to exercise *hacer ejercicio* 1.2

to explain *explicar* 5.2

to fall asleep *dormir(se) (ue)* 4.1

to feel *sentir(se) (ie)* 4.1

to feel badly/well *sentirse mal/bien* 10.1

to feel dizzy *tener mareos* 10.1

to feel itchy *tener comezón* 10.1

to feel like . . . *tener ganas de...* 3.1

to feel nauseous *tener náuseas* 10.1

to fight *luchar* 6.1

to fight for *luchar por* 12.1

to find *encontrar (ue)* 3.1

to finish *terminar* 2.1

to fly *volar* 11.2

to follow a recipe *seguir una receta* 7.2

to fry *freír (>i)* 7.2

to gain weight *engordar* 10.2

to gain/lose weight *subir/bajar de peso* 10.2

to get *conseguir* 6.2

to get (a job) *conseguir (un trabajo)* 4.1

to get (oneself) up *levantar(se)* 4.1

to get bored *aburrir(se)* 4.1

to get dressed *vestir(se) (i)* 4.1

to get married *casarse* 3.1

to get sick *enfermarse* 10.1

to get well, to recover *curarse* 10.1

to give *dar* 5.2

to give (as a gift) *regalar* 5.2, 2.2

to give somebody a shot/vaccine *poner una inyección/vacuna a alguien* 10.1

to go *ir, para llevar* 2.2, 7.2

to go abroad *ir al extranjero* 11.2

to go camping *acampar* 9.1

to go fishing *pescar* 8.1

to go for a walk *pasear* 2.1

to go out with friends *salir con amigos* 1.2

to go shopping *ir de compras* 1.2, 2.2

to go through customs *pasar por la aduana* 11.2

to go through TSA area *pasar por seguridad* 11.2

to go to the movies *ir al cine* 1.2

to have *tener (ie)* 3.1

to have (a head/stomach/ear) ache *tener dolor de (cabeza/estómago/oído)* 10.1

to have (to) *tener (que)* 4.1

to have a cold *estar resfriado/a* 10.1

to have a good time *pasarlo/pasarla bien* 4.1

to have a migraine *tener migraña* 10.1

to have an afternoon snack *merendar (e→ie)* 7.1

to have breakfast *desayunar* 7.1

to have cold chills *tener escalofríos* 10.1

to have dinner *cenar* 2.1

to have fever *tener fiebre* 10.1

to have lunch *almorzar (ue)* 3.1

to have/give a (surprise) party *hacer/dar una fiesta (sorpresa)* 5.1

to hear *oír* 3.1

to heat up *calentar (>ie)* 7.2

to hike *hacer senderismo* 8.1

to hope that devices work *esperar que los aparatos funcionen* 11.1

to hurt *doler (ue)* 10.1

to improve *mejorar* 10.1

to inhabit *habitar* 6.1

to know (a fact) *saber* 5.1

to know or be familiar with *conocer* 5.1

to learn *aprender* 2.1

to leave, to go out with *salir* 3.1

to lend *prestar* 5.2

to lie down *acostar(se)* 4.1

to like *gustar* 2.2

to like a lot, to love something *encantar* 5.2

to like/dislike someone/or not *caer bien/mal* 5.2

to listen (to music) *escuchar (música)* 1.2

to live *vivir* 2.1

to log in *entrar a un sitio web* 11.1

to look like *parecerse* 3.1

to lose *perder (ie)* 3.1, 8.1

to love, to be fascinated by something *fascinar* 5.2

to miss (something/someone) *echar de menos* 12.1

to mix *mezclar* 7.2

to negotiate price *regatear* 2.2

to offer *ofrecer (zc)* 5.2

to order *ordenar/pedir* 7.2

to pack *hacer las maletas* 11.2

to paint *pintar* 1.2, 6.2

to peel *pelar* 7.2

to play *jugar (ue)* 3.1

to play (tennis) *jugar (al tenis)* 1.2

to play (the part of...) *representar/interpretar (un personaje)* 8.2

to play an instrument *tocar un instrumento* 1.2

to play/practice a sport *hacer/jugar (ue) a un deporte* 8.1

to plug in the printer *enchufar la impresora* 11.1

to pollute (the air, the water) *contaminar (el aire, el agua)* 9.2

to post videos on the Internet *colgar/poner videos en Internet* 11.1

to prefer *preferir (ie)* 3.1

to press a key *oprimir una tecla* 11.1

to print documents *imprimir documentos* 11.1

to prosper, to thrive *prosperar* 12.2

to put *poner* 3.1

to put (something) on (oneself) *poner(se)* 4.1

to put in (the pen drive, the CD/DVD) *meter (el lápiz, el disco)* 11.1

to put on makeup *maquillar(se)* 4.1

to rain *llover* 4.2

to read *leer* 1.2

to recognize *reconocer* 12.2

to record *grabar* 8.2

to record music *grabar música* 11.1

to reduce *rebajar* 2.2

to reject *rechazar (z > c)* 12.2

to relax *relajarse* 10.2

to rent *alquilar* 3.2

to repeat *repetir (i)* 3.1, 6.2

to request *pedir (i)* 9.1

to rest *descansar* 10.2

to return *regresar, volver (ue)* 2.1, 3.1

to return (something) *devolver (ue)* 5.2

to ride a bike *montar en bicicleta* 8.1

to roast, to grill *asar* 7.2

to rule *gobernar* 6.1

to run *correr* 1.2

to save changes *guardar los cambios* 11.1

to say *decir* 5.2

to sculpt *esculpir* 6.2

to search for a URL *buscar una dirección de Internet* 11.1

to seem, to resemble *parecer, parecerse* 5.1

to sell *vender* 2.2

to send *enviar, mandar* 5.2

to send emails   *enviar mensajes electrónicos*   11.1
to serve   *servir (i)*   3.1
to set the table   *poner la mesa*   7.2
to shave (oneself)   *afeitar(se)*   4.1
to shout   *gritar*   5.1
to show   *mostrar*   5.2
to sing   *cantar*   1.2, 5.1
to sit down   *sentar(se) (ie)*   4.1
to skate   *patinar*   1.2
to skateboard   *andar en patineta/ monopatín*   8.1
to ski   *esquiar*   1.2
to sleep   *dormir (ue)*   1.2, 3.1
to snack   *picar*   7.1
to sneeze   *estornudar*   10.1
to snow   *nevar*   4.2
to snowboard   *hacer snowboarding*   8.1
to start   *empezar*   2.1
to stay (in a hotel)   *quedarse (en un hotel)*   11.2
to stir up   *remover*   7.2
to study   *estudiar*   1.2
to succeed, to be successful   *triunfar, tener éxito*   12.2
to suffer from allergies   *tener alergias*   10.1
to suffer from stress   *tener estrés*   10.2
to suggest   *sugerir*   6.2, 9.1
to suggest   *sugerir (ie)*   9.1, 6.2
to swim   *nadar*   1.2
to take / drink   *tomar*   2.1
to take a shower   *duchar(se)*   4.1
to take care (of oneself)   *cuidar(se)*   10.2
to take clothes off   *quitar(se)*   4.1
to talk on the (cell) phone   *hablar por teléfono (celular/móvil)*   1.2
to taste, to try (food)   *probar (>ue)*   7.2
to tell, to narrate (e.g., a story)   *contar (ue)*   5.2, 3.1
to thank   *agradecer*   5.1
to the end (of)   *al final (de)*   4.2
to the left   *a la izquierda*   4.2
to the right   *a la derecha*   4.2
to think   *pensar (ie)*   3.1
to throw (the bouquet)   *tirar (el ramo)*   5.2
to throw away   *tirar*   9.2
to translate   *traducir*   5.1
to travel   *viajar*   1.2
to turn on the computer   *encender la computadora*   11.1
to twist an ankle   *torcerse el tobillo*   10.1
to understand   *entender (ie)*   3.1
to upload songs   *subir/cargar canciones*   11.1
to wait   *esperar*   2.1
to wait in line   *hacer cola*   11.2
to wake up   *despertar(se) (ie)*   4.1
to walk   *caminar*   1.2
to want   *querer (ie)*   3.1
to wash (oneself)   *lavar(se)*   4.1
to wash (the dishes)/to do the dishes   *lavar (los platos)*   2.1
to watch TV   *mirar/ver la televisión*   1.2
to water ski   *hacer esquí acuático*   8.1
to whistle   *silbar*   8.1
to win   *ganar*   6.1, 8.1

to work   *trabajar*   2.1
to work (a computer, a device)   *funcionar (la computadora, el aparato)*   11.1
to worry (about)   *preocuparse (por)*   10.2
to write   *escribir*   2.1
Today is . . .   *Hoy es...*   1.2
toilet   *el inodoro*   3.2
toilet paper   *el papel higiénico*   3.2
tonight   *esta noche*   2.2
tooth   *el diente*   3.1
tower   *la torre*   6.2
town   *el pueblo*   4.2
track and field   *el atletismo*   8.1
train   *el tren*   11.2
treaty   *el tratado*   6.1
tree   *el árbol*   3.2
tropical forest   *la selva tropical*   9.1
Tuesday   *el martes*   1.2
turkey   *el pavo*   7.1
(turned) on   *encendido/a*   11.1
turquoise   *turquesa*   6.2
turtle   *la tortuga*   9.2
TV channel   *el canal (de televisión)*   8.2
TV commercial   *el anuncio/el comercial*   8.2
twelve   *doce*   P
twenty   *veinte*   P
twenty-one   *veintiuno*   P
two   *dos*   P
two hundred   *doscientos*   2.2
two millions   *dos millones*   3.2
two thousand   *dos mil*   2.2
(two, three, four) stars   *(dos, tres, cuatro) estrellas*   11.2

U

uncle/aunt   *el/la tío/a*   3.1
undone   *deshecho/a*   11.1
up   *arriba*   4.2
Uruguayan   *uruguayo/a*   1.1
(USB) flash/pen drive   *el lápiz de memoria*   11.1
username   *el nombre del usuario*   11.1

V

(variety) show   *el programa (de variedades)*   8.2
vaccine   *la vacuna*   10.1
vain   *vanidoso/a*   1.1
vegetables   *la verdura*   7.1
Venezuelan   *venezolano/a*   1.1
Very well, thank you.   *Muy bien, gracias.*   P
videogame   *el videojuego*   8.1
vinegar   *el vinagre*   7.2
voyage   *el viaje*   6.1

W

waiter, waitress   *el/la mesero/a, camarero/a, mozo/a*   4.1, 7.2
waiting room   *la sala de espera*   11.2
waste   *el desecho*   9.2
watch   *el reloj*   2.2
watermelon   *la sandía*   7.1
weak   *débil*   10.1

weather   *el tiempo*   4.2
wedding   *la boda*   5.2
Wednesday   *el miércoles*   1.2
weight-lifting   *levantar pesas*   8.1
Well, hanging in there.   *Pues, ahí nomás.*   P
well-being   *el bienestar*   10.2
west   *el oeste*   4.2
What are you looking for?   *¿Qué busca/ desea?*   2.2
What are you wearing?   *¿Qué llevas?*   2.2
What comes with...?   *¿Qué trae...?*   7.2
What classes do you take?   *¿Qué clases tomas?*   1.2
What day is today?   *¿Qué día es hoy?*   1.2
What do you like to do?   *¿Qué te gusta hacer?*   1.2
What do you like to wear?   *¿Qué te gusta llevar?*   2.2
What do you want to eat/drink?   *¿Qué quiere/s comer/beber?*   7.2
What hurts?   *¿Qué te duele?*   10.1
What is it about?   *¿De qué (se) trata?*   8.2
What is the matter?   *¿Qué te pasa?*   10.1
What is today's date?   *¿Cuál es la fecha de hoy?*   1.2
What team do you support?   *¿De qué equipo eres?*   8.1
What time is . . . ?   *¿A qué hora es...?*   2.1
What time is it?   *¿Qué hora es?*   2.1
What´s going on?   *¿Qué me cuentas?*   P
What´s up?   *¿Qué hubo?*   P
What´s your name? (informal)   *¿Cómo te llamas?*   P
What's on TV?   *¿Qué hay en la tele?*   8.2
What's the temperature?   *¿Qué temperatura hace?*   4.2
What's the weather like?   *¿Qué tiempo hace?*   4.2
When is your birthday?   *¿Cuándo es tu cumpleaños?*   1.2
Where are you from?   *¿De dónde eres?*   1.1
while   *mientras*   8.1
white   *blanco/a*   2.2, 1.1
white (skin)   *blanco/a*   1.1, 2.2
widow/widower   *viudo/a*   3.1
wind   *el viento*   4.2
window   *la ventana*   P, 3.2
wine   *el vino*   7.2
wine glass   *la copa*   7.2
winter   *invierno*   1.2
wire   *el cable*   11.1
witness   *el/la testigo*   5.2
work of art   *la obra de arte*   6.2
worse   *peor*   3.2
Would you like something to drink/ a snack?   *¿Quieres algo de tomar/picar?*   7.1
Would you like something to eat/drink?   *¿Desea/Desean algo de comer/tomar?*   7.2
writer   *el/la escritor/a*   4.1
written   *escrito/a*   11.1

Y

yellow   *amarillo/a*   2.2
yesterday   *ayer*   8.1
younger   *menor*   3.2

Capítulo preliminar

la actividad
la calculadora
el diccionario
el/la estudiante
la fotografía
la lección
el mapa
el papel
el problema
el/la profesor/a
el tema
la universidad

Capítulo 1

la antropología
el arte
atlético/a
atractivo/a
la biología
las ciencias políticas
el comercio
las comunicaciones
conservador/a
creativo/a
curioso/a
(des)organizado/a
la economía
la educación (física)
entusiasta
la estadística
estudioso/a
expresivo/a
extrovertido/a
las finanzas
flexible
el francés
generoso/a
hipócrita
la historia
idealista
(im)paciente
(in)dependiente
la ingeniería
el inglés
inteligente
interesante
introvertido/a
(ir)responsable
liberal
la literatura
las matemáticas
la medicina
modesto/a
la música

optimista
pesimista
popular
la psicología
las relaciones
internacionales
religioso/a
romántico/a
sentimental
serio/a
sincero/a
sociable
la sociología
talentoso/a
el teatro
tímido/a

Capítulo 2

la actividad
la blusa
la bota
el color
conversar
costar (ue)
la familia
insistir
practicar
responder
visitar

Capítulo 3

el aire acondicionado
el balcón
el bidé
el centro
la computadora
la cortina
divorciado/a
la familia
el garaje
la lámpara
la mamá
el papá
el refrigerador
la relación
separado/a
el sofá
el televisor/la televisión
la terraza
la zona

Capítulo 4

el aeropuerto
el/la arquitecto/a
el/la artista

el/la atleta
el autobús
el banco
el bar
el/la candidato/a
el/la chofer
el/la dentista
el/la electricista
la estación
la farmacia
el hospital
el hotel
el kilómetro
la milla
el/la mecánico/a
el museo
el/la piloto
la profesión
el/la profesor/a
el/la programador/a de
computadoras
el/la recepcionista
el punto de referencia
el restaurante
el/la secretario/a
el supermercado
el taxi
el teatro

Capítulo 5

(des)aparecer
la bachata
la banda
el banquete
el bolero
los bongós
celebrar
la celebración
la ceremonia
el chachachá
el concierto
las congas
la cumbia
el funeral
el grupo
la guitarra
el instrumento
invitar
el mambo
las maracas
el merengue
el micrófono
la música
la percusión
el piano
producir
la recepción

el reguetón
el ritmo
la salsa
el saxofón
los timbales
el trombón
la trompeta

Capítulo 6

abstracto/a
el actor
el arco
el/la arquitecto/a
la arquitectura
el arte
el/la artista
atacar
barroco/a
la basílica
la catedral
el cine
colonial
la conquista
conquistar
la constitución
contemporáneo/a
la democracia
el/la dictador/a
el/la directora/a
el/la enemigo/a
el/la escultor/a
la escultura
establecer
la estatua
el estilo
explorar
la fachada
la fotografía
gótico/a
la historia
el imperio
la independencia
invadir
la invasión
el/la líder
la literatura
medieval
moderno/a
la monarquía
el monumento
el/la pintor/a
romano/a
terminar

Capítulo 7

el brócoli
el café

el calamar
el cereal
la coliflor
la dieta
la espinaca
la fruta
el limón
el mango
la mayonesa
la pasta
preparar
el restaurante
el salmón
el tomate
el yogur

Capítulo 8

actuar
el bate
el béisbol
el ciclismo
la ciencia ficción
la comedia
el control remoto
el/la crítico/a (de cine/
teatro)
el documental
los efectos especiales
el entretenimiento
el episodio
el/la espectador/a
el estadio
el golf
el hockey
informar
la radio
el/la reportero/a
el rugby
la serie
los subtítulos
el tenis

Capítulo 9

la alpaca
la altitud
la Amazonía
el cañón
el cóndor
conservar
consumir
la costa
la deforestación
el delfín
el desierto
la ecología
la energía (eléctrica,

renovable,...)
esencial
el esmog
la especie
la fauna
la geografía
la humedad
importante
el insecto
insistir (en)
la jungla
la llama
necesario/a
el mosquito
permitir
el pesticida
el plástico
prohibir
proteger
reciclar
recomendar (ie)
la reforestación
el reptil
la serpiente
el valle
el volcán

Capítulo 10

el análisis
animado/a
el antibiótico
la bronquitis
el/la cardiólogo/a
contento/a
la cura
el/la dentista
la diabetes
el diagnóstico
el/la doctor/a
el estrés
estresado/a
el/la farmacéutico/a
el hábito
la infección
irritado/a
la medicina
medicinal
meditar
nervioso/a
la neumonía
el/la paciente
prevenir (ie)
el/la psicólogo/a
el/la psiquiatra
el remedio
el/la terapeuta
el tratamiento

Capítulo 11

(des)activar
el adaptador
el aeropuerto
la batería
el blog
la cámara digital
chatear
conectar(se)
la conexión
el e-mail
el documento
el hotel
el icono
el monitor
el pasaporte
la recepción
el sitio web
la tableta
la tecnología
textear
el virus
el *wifi*

Capítulo 12

el activismo
el/la activista
la asimilación
bicultural
bilingüe
el bilingüismo
el censo
la comunidad
cubanoamericano/a
cultural
la discriminación
la diversidad
las elecciones
el/la emigrante
emigrar
la identidad
el/la inmigrante
la influencia
la (in) justicia
laboral
(i)legal
mexicanoamericano/a
la (in)migración
multicultural
multirracial
político/a
social
la (in)tolerancia
el/la líder
la marcha
la minoría
la nacionalidad
la oportunidad
la organización
el origen
la política
el prejuicio
la protesta
el/la residente
la sociedad
la visa

Índice

Dedication

This book is dedicated to educators everywhere. You create the future every single day. May this book help you foster a generation of upstanders who collectively become the solution to bullying.

Acknowledgments

No book is ever written alone. This book was created and brought to life with the help and input of so many talented, caring people. My deepest, most heartfelt thanks go to:

My wonderful publisher, Free Spirit. I'm deeply grateful for Free Spirit's flexibility and for all the work, time, and care that went into the book, including coordinating our national survey and enabling the many unheard voices of children to be included and heard. Very special thanks go to Judy Galbraith, whose vision makes Free Spirit Publishing an exceptional house of the highest integrity. Special thanks also go to the Free Spirit editorial and creative team whose work and talents contributed to this book in so many ways: Brianna DeVore, Darsi Dreyer, Douglas Fehlen, Steven Hauge, Heidi Hogg, Michelle Lee, Marjorie Lisovskis, and Charlie Mahoney.

The many teachers and counselors who participated in our survey. We couldn't have done it without you!

The 2,171 kids who filled out the survey and shared their real-life stories. Your words and experiences form the core of this book.

The many schools I've worked with over the past three years, talking to teachers and kids, conducting interviews, and being in classrooms. Special thanks to Cathy Brettman for going the extra mile in setting up student interviews.

The wonderful teachers at Berkeley Elementary School who sent in pictures and stories of peacemaking in action.

Librarians Laura Gruninger of the Lawrence Library and Pat Brown of Lawrence Intermediate School who provided excellent resource recommendations.

All of my family and friends who gave so much moral support in the years of hard work that went into the development, research, and writing of this book. Thanks for being there! Special thanks to my daughter in-law, Emy Drew, for the idea of "10-Minute Time Crunchers."

The folks at City Market in Lambertville, New Jersey, for the many hours I spent writing and drinking coffee at your sunny window.

Contents

Additional Material on the CD-ROM

Eight Enrichment Activities You Can Use at Any Time

    1. Prepare a Public Service Announcement (PSA)
    2. Write and Perform a Song
    3. Create a Book
    4. Perform a Puppet Show
    5. Connect with Another Classroom Online
    6. Meet with the School Administrator
    7. Contact the Press and Public Officials
    8. Create a Podcast

Schoolwide Bullying Response Protocols

Student Reporting of Bullying Form

Informational Handouts for Parents

    Four Steps to a More Peaceful Home
    Using Active and Reflective Listening
    10 Ways to Help Kids Stop Fighting
    Mediating Kids' Conflicts with the Win/Win Guidelines
    Helping Children Deal with Bullying
    Promoting Tolerance at Home

Poem

    You Belong

List of Reproducible Pages

Introduction

"He always teased me about my not being able to do something. Even though I knew what he said wasn't true, it killed me inside."
—4th-grade boy

"I didn't mean to hit him that hard. I just wanted him to stop saying stuff about me. He tried to hit me, but I ducked and kicked his shin. I was trying to tell him to stop, but he hit my arm. I didn't want to fight but I had no choice."
—6th-grade girl

"People call me names all the time. They call me fatty and fat boy and apple tree and cherry cheeks. I would like to know how to stop it."
—3rd-grade boy

"I try to ignore conflicts, but if I can't, I just hurt."
—5th-grade girl

"I've been through a lot. These kids don't like the way I look. They call me pimple face and the other day after school they kicked me in the ribs. I am so sick of being picked on."
—4th-grade boy

"Anger and bullying are among the major issues I see as a teacher."
—4th-grade teacher

"Things seem to start small and quickly grow bigger."
—5th-grade teacher

"How do you end the name-calling? This is a BIG problem. I have tried many things, and I have not found a way that really works. I am not seeing success this year."
—3rd-grade teacher

The quotes you just read are from students and teachers who were surveyed or interviewed for this book. Before I wrote the book, my publisher and I conducted a survey of 2,171 kids and 59 teachers in the United States and Canada to find out how bullying, peer cruelty, and conflicts impact their lives. Survey responses confirmed what media reports continue to tell us—that bullying is one of the greatest challenges our kids face today. Educators consistently reported that they were troubled by the bullying, name-calling, and meanness that take place among their students. Students expressed the same concerns: Seventy-three percent of the kids we surveyed said other kids are somewhat to very mean to each other. Forty-four percent said bullying happens often, every day, or all the time, and over 40 percent said they

1

see conflicts happening often or every day. Students also expressed, sometimes longingly and often poignantly, that they don't want to be hurt by bullying. Sixty-three percent of the children said that they wanted to learn how to stay out of physical fights. Eighty percent said that they wanted to learn ways to stop the bullying, avoid fighting, get along better with peers, and work out conflicts.

The problem of bullying persists despite the awareness and attention that many schools, teachers, and parents have put toward diminishing it. The purpose of *No Kidding About Bullying* is to help teachers and kids by getting to the root of the problem. While the book's goal is to prevent bullying, its approach to doing so is broad. Some of our most important work as educators is teaching kids how to navigate through an increasingly complex and violent world: helping them interact with all kinds of people and showing them how to work out differences, respect others, and be compassionate human beings who disavow cruelty in all its forms. Navigating the world successfully requires understanding that being respectful will get you a lot further in life than being mean-spirited. It requires remembering that inside every human being is a heart that beats and a mind that feels pain when unkind words are spoken. It requires choosing to be a person of conscience who does the right thing even when no one is looking. These are the concepts and behaviors kids need to absorb in order to eliminate bullying *and* to lead rewarding lives.

In my work as an educator focused on peacemaking, I have seen firsthand the transformation that can occur as kids begin to see the power of their own compassion and recognize the personal well-being that comes with following their own conscience. I have witnessed the empowerment students feel when they learn to stop and think before acting and to use deep breathing, self-calming, respectful listening, and peaceful conflict resolution to help them through challenging situations. By instilling these attitudes and practices in your students, you can establish a peaceful classroom environment while teaching kids skills that will enable them to have positive, peaceful relationships throughout their lives.

Facts About Bullying and Conflict in Children's Lives

Research on the Impact of Bullying

What's actually happening among our children? According to recent studies:

- The intensity of aggression involving children and teens has escalated dramatically.[1]
- Children are becoming involved in aggression at ever-younger ages.[2]
- In the United States, youth violence is the second leading cause of death for young people ages ten and up.[3]
- Kids who are bullied are five times more likely to be depressed and far more likely to be suicidal.[4]
- 50% of students in the United States are bullied.[5]

Not only do bullying and cruelty create an undercurrent of fear and mistrust among kids, they also affect learning and development, and can even impact a child's future mental health. According to the Center for Social and Emotional Education, "When children are bullied in an intermittent but ongoing manner it derails healthy development and a student's capacity to learn. In fact, more and more evidence suggests that this type of harassment leads to significant adolescent and adult psychiatric problems."[6]

Bullying expert Dr. Susan Limber, in proceedings before the American Medical Association, noted, "Children and youth who are bullied are more likely than other children to be depressed, lonely, anxious; have low self-esteem; feel unwell; and think about suicide."[7]

Data regarding school shootings is even more alarming. According to "The Final Report and Findings of the Safe School Initiative" conducted by the U.S. Secret Service and the U.S. Department of Education, even though the majority of attackers in thirty-seven school shootings came from two-parent families, had good grades, were involved in school activities, and had never been in trouble before, they shared the following characteristic:

"Almost three-quarters of the attackers felt persecuted, bullied, threatened, attacked, or injured by others prior to the incident. In several cases, individual attackers had

experienced bullying and harassment that was long-standing and severe. In some of these cases the experience of being bullied seemed to have a significant impact on the attacker and appeared to have been a factor in his decision to mount an attack at the school. In one case, most of the attacker's schoolmates described the attacker as 'the kid everyone teased.'"[8]

The negative impact of bullying goes beyond students who are bullied, affecting those who see it take place as well. According to the American Psychological Association, research suggests that "Students who watch as their peers endure the verbal or physical abuses of another student could become as psychologically distressed, if not more so, by the events than the victims themselves. . . . Bullies and bystanders may also be more likely to take drugs and drink alcohol."[9]

Kids who bully also are adversely affected. According to the American Academy of Pediatrics, "Children labeled by their peers as aggressors or bullies at age eight are more likely to end up incarcerated and are less likely to be steadily employed and in stable long-term romantic relationships by the time they reach age thirty. Consequently, bullying prevention programs have a long-term benefit for both bullies and victims."[10]

Research on What Impacts Kids Positively

Anyone who teaches knows how "contagious" emotions and behaviors are. If you've ever spent a year with a conflict-ridden class where bullying is prevalent, you probably know the feeling of throwing your hands up in frustration as bickering and meanness infected the entire atmosphere in your room.

But the good news is, positive emotions and behaviors also are contagious. Dr. Nicholas A. Christakis, a researcher at Harvard Medical School, explains, "Emotions have a collective existence—they are not just an individual phenomenon." He goes on to say that how you feel depends "not just on your choices and actions, but also on the choices and actions of people . . . who are one, two, and three degrees removed from you."[11]

People one, two, and three degrees removed . . . as in a class. And when positive emotions and behaviors are sparked in a class, they spread. Christakis and his research partner, James Fowler, hypothesize that "behaviors spread partly through the subconscious social signals that we pick up from those around us,

which serve as cues to what is considered normal behavior." Another likely cause of social contagions is mirror neurons in our brains, which cause us to mimic what we see in others.[12]

These findings reaffirm the importance of making concerted efforts to build empathy, social skills, and conscience in children. The results can be both immediate and long-lasting.

Harnessing positive contagious emotions can have a powerful effect in the classroom. Search Institute in Minneapolis did a comprehensive review of studies on the impact of a caring educational environment on kids. The research reveals that safe, supportive schools foster the following in students:

- higher grades
- higher engagement, attendance, expectations, and aspirations
- a sense of scholastic competence
- fewer school suspensions
- on-time progression through grades
- less anxiety, depression, and loneliness
- higher self-esteem and self-concept[13]

These findings reaffirm the importance of making concerted efforts to build empathy, social skills, and conscience in children. The results can be immediate and long-lasting:

- 57 percent of the time, bullying stops in less than ten seconds when peers intervene on behalf of the child who is being bullied.[14]
- When schools make a comprehensive commitment to changing their climate, and the entire school community is involved in preventing bullying, bullying can be reduced by 50 percent.[15]

The New York University Child Study Center offers an important reminder to educators: "Aggressive behavior is often first recognized as bullying behavior. Schools must be vigilant about spotting problems when they arise and direct in addressing them."[16]

By assiduously fostering empathy, conscience, and kindness along with teaching kids how to work out conflicts, deal with anger, and be "upstanders" for those who are bullied, I believe we can start reversing the trend of youth cruelty. At the same time, we can create a more peaceful atmosphere in our schools, ultimately setting the foundation for a healthier future for all of our children. Think of it as creating a contagion of kindness, compassion, and respect that spreads through your entire class and lasts all year—a contagion that dramatically reduces bullying and conflict.

About This Book

At the core of this book are 125 easy-to-use sessions that have been carefully designed to help you create a bully-free atmosphere where kids learn and thrive. These twenty-minute activities are easy to use and require very little preparation. The intent is to make bully prevention, conflict resolution, and social-emotional skill building realistic and realizable within the context of your already busy school day.

How the Book Is Organized

"Background for Conducting the Sessions and Working with Students" (pages 5–15) provides background information to help you use the book and instill its concepts and skills effectively. It includes information on how to help kids mediate conflicts, top keys for preventing bullying and conflict, and techniques for implementing the book's lessons into the daily routine.

Following that, the book is divided into two main parts:

Part One: Building Bully-Free Skills and Attitudes. The fifteen Core Sessions in Part 1 are the cornerstone of *No Kidding About Bullying*. They

Use as many or as few sessions as you like. Use them as a full curriculum from start to finish or as a shorter unit.

The activities can be easily integrated with the Olweus Bullying Prevention Program, Responsive Classroom, Second Step, or another social-emotional learning model. If you're not using any particular curriculum to build social skills, this book will be an important tool for introducing them.

introduce the concepts and skills that are the basis for all the other sessions in the book. See page 7 for more information about the Core Sessions.

Part Two: Getting Along and Staying Bully Free. Here you will find 110 sessions arranged in seven topic areas:

- Fostering Kindness and Compassion
- Managing Anger
- Preventing Conflict
- Responding to Conflict
- Addressing Name-Calling and Teasing
- Dealing with Bullying
- Accepting Differences

The structure for each session begins with a list of the key character traits and skills the session reinforces, a quick activity summary, and "Students will," which highlights specific things students will learn. Each session also includes:

Materials. The materials you will need to conduct the session, including reproducible handouts, are listed here. Other materials are easily obtained, such as chart paper or drawing materials.

Preparation. This is included as needed.

The session. Each session begins with an introduction followed by discussion, the main activity, and wrap-up. The activities vary and may include role plays, large- or small-group tasks, writing, drawing and other creative arts, and learning new information.

Follow-Up. Most sessions include a follow-up activity or suggestion to reinforce and, at times, help you monitor how students are doing incorporating the skills and concepts.

Extensions. Many sessions include optional extensions. These are often activities that require more time and allow students to do creative projects, practice skills, or share what they are learning with their families or other students.

Reproducible forms. Most activities include handouts. These are noted in the materials list and can be found at the end of each session; they are also included on the accompanying CD-ROM. Unless otherwise noted, you will need to print or copy a handout for each student prior to the session.

At the back of the book you will find several additional resources:

Pre- and Post-Test. This brief assessment, also on the CD-ROM, lets you measure students' attitudes and use of skills before and after taking part in *No Kidding About Bullying* sessions.

Survey About Conflicts form. A blank form is provided so you can conduct your own survey with students in your class or school; the survey also is included on the CD-ROM.

References and Resources. This is both a bibliography of resources used in developing the book and a selection of recommended books, websites, and other resources you may find helpful.

Index. With the index, you can look up a particular topic (such as calming strategies, gossiping, or physical bullying) or character trait (such as respect, collaboration, or self-control) and find sessions with that focus.

CD-ROM. The CD-ROM includes all of the reproducible forms from the book, additional resources for leading the sessions, and forms for sharing information with parents. The parent forms provide background about the concepts children are learning and suggestions for ways parents can support this at home.

Using the Book in Your Setting

Yours may be one of the many classrooms using the Olweus Bullying Prevention Program, Responsive Classroom, Second Step, or another social and emotional learning model. The activities in *No Kidding About Bullying* can be easily integrated with programs like these. If you're not using any particular curriculum to build social skills, this book will be an important tool for introducing them.

Depending on your needs, you may use as many or as few sessions as you like. Use them as a full curriculum from start to finish or as a shorter unit. In the latter case, conduct the Core Sessions first and follow up by focusing on a particular section (such as Managing Anger) or by conducting several activities from each section. You can also turn to specific sessions when you have an incident of bullying, unkindness, or conflict you want to address.

Using the sessions first thing in the morning is ideal. If you're already doing morning meetings, you can weave these sessions in after the greeting. If another time of the day works better for you, that's fine, too. The whole idea is to make them work for

you and your setting. Three times a week will give you maximum results. Even doing a session a week will make a big difference. The more you do, the better.

Although designed with a classroom in mind, this book can easily be used in other settings, including youth groups, faith-based programs, before- or after-school settings, counseling groups, scouting, camps, or any other environment where children are served. You will find the book useful if you are a classroom teacher, resource teacher, school counselor, youth group director, community program leader, camp counselor, religious educator, or parent.

Each session can be conducted in twenty minutes. You can spend more time if you wish, and reinforce concepts as time permits by using the follow-ups and extensions. Several sessions in each section address similar topics in different ways, allowing you to reinforce important skills and practices. There are also review sessions, including "10-Minute Time Crunchers."

Background for Conducting the Sessions and Working with Students

Before You Begin

Seven things will enhance the experience you and your students have with the *No Kidding About Bullying* sessions:

Circle. The sessions in this book will be most effective if done in a circle. This helps with listening, focus, and empathy. One of the most basic ways people connect is by simply looking at each other's faces when speaking. So many children spend hours each day behind a computer screen or video game; they're often more connected to a screen than to each other. As a result some kids may have become oblivious to each other's feelings and may find face-to-face interactions awkward. By seating your students in a circle, you can get them used to the practice of looking at the person who is speaking. Coach them to look around the circle when it's their turn to speak, and to wait until everyone is looking back at them.

Cueing kids to look at each other and tune in to what's being said can drastically improve communication skills and develop a greater sense of connectedness. The good listening and respectful attitudes fostered in the circle can also spill over into the rest of the day and make it easier to teach.

Globe. For many sessions, I strongly recommend having a globe handy. If you can, pick up the soft kind that's a cross between a ball and a pillow. You can order these through AAA, Amazon, or many other places on the Web. Here are three ways to use your globe as you conduct the sessions:

1. Let it serve as a visual reminder that we are part of the larger world. Hold up the globe periodically to remind kids that our actions make a difference and everything we do affects the people around us. They can make the world a better place starting right in their own classroom. Peace begins with each person.

2. Use it as a "talking object" to pass in the circle when you do the activities in this book. The person holding the globe is the only one to speak. When he or she is finished, the globe is passed to the next person.

> Working in pairs enables kids to immediately put into practice the many cooperative behaviors they are learning.

3. If you have a soft globe, you can use it as a ball to throw during review activities (for more on review activities, see the CD-ROM), allowing you to review concepts easily and quickly.

Working in pairs. Many sessions in this book have children working in dyads and, in some cases, small groups. These interactions enable kids to immediately put into practice many cooperative behaviors they are learning: listening, compassion, kindness, openness to another's ideas. Studies have shown that using dyads and cooperative learning in teaching situations makes a significant difference in students' ability to learn new concepts.[17]

My favorite way to get students into pairs is to prime them by saying, "In a moment we're going to partner up. Your most important job is to make sure no one is left out. Look around and make sure everyone is included." I always follow this up with immediate acknowledgment of kids who make sure no one is left out, especially if they forgo sitting with a friend

to be a partner to someone who doesn't have one. If I see students start rushing to be with friends instead of looking around to see if someone needs a partner, I stop the whole process and give a gentle reminder.

Assuming you have your kids in a circle, another way to get them to partner up is to randomly ask one child to raise his or her hand. After that, every second child raises a hand, alternating so half the students have hands raised. Kids with raised hands turn to the person on their right; this person becomes their partner. If there's an odd number, have one group triple up, or have the extra child be your partner.

Once students are in pairs, whether in chairs or seated on the floor, have them sit "knee to knee"—directly facing one another with their knees facing but not touching. This enables good eye contact and less distraction.

Charts. Many activities include creating a chart for or with students. Among these, there are seven that I recommend laminating and keeping up all year long as a visual reminder of the most important bullying prevention concepts in this book:

- **Our Agreements for a Get-Along Classroom:** Keep this chart somewhere in the front of the room for easy reference, high enough for everyone to see, but not so high you can't reach the agreements with a pointer. (This chart is introduced in Session 1.)

- **Respectful Listening:** This chart can be used all day long for every subject you teach. Display it where kids can't miss seeing it. (Introduced in Session 2.)

- **Peace Pledge:** You'll probably be using this every morning, so keep it in easy access for kids to view. You might want to have a different child lead the class in the pledge each day, so post it in a spot a student can stand next to. (Introduced in Session 6.)

- **Win/Win Guidelines for Working Out Conflicts** and **Rules for Using the Win/Win Guidelines:** Place these near your Peace Table or Peace Place (see page 8). Post them so they're readily accessible when two students sit down together to work out a conflict. (Introduced in Session 8.)

- **Stop, Breathe, Chill:** This is another good chart for your Peace Table area, although if space is limited, any place in the room will do. (Introduced in Session 9.)

- **No More Hurtful Words:** This is a pledge for students to live by and for you to refer to whenever they need a reminder to be kind. (Introduced in Session 22.)

- **Ways to Chill:** This chart can go in any spot where it's easily seen, even up high at the top of a wall. It will serve as a constant reminder of all the things students can do to calm down when angry. (Introduced in Session 40.)

Other charts recommended in sessions throughout the book can be left up as long as you need them, whether that's a day or two after you've completed the session or longer as a reinforcement. If possible, save any charts you take down. They can serve as helpful reminders of concepts you might want or need to review as the year goes on.

Student journals. Journals are used throughout the sessions in a variety of ways: for responding to a topic, airing personal experiences, brainstorming ideas, and more.

Provide students with notebooks to use as their journals. Have students decorate and personalize the cover. Keep a journal yourself and do the same exercises your students do. This will broaden your own understanding of the concepts in this book and expand your ability to empathize with what your kids are going through. If you choose to share any of your journal entries with your kids, it may help them open up even more.

Automatic writing. Some of the sessions employ automatic writing, a technique that can spark spontaneous thought and release ideas. In automatic writing, students should let their words flow out freely and land on the paper like coins spilling out of a bag. Neatness, grammar, and spelling don't count. After stating the given prompt, direct students to "write, write, write" for about three straight minutes without lifting pencil from paper until you say "Stop."

Automatic writing is about the unfolding of what's inside. Let students know that sometimes they may be surprised at what comes out. Whether they keep what they write confidential or share it with you and others is always up to them.

Students who have difficulty writing can draw their response, speak their words into a recorder, or dictate them to you, a classroom aide, or another student if this is comfortable for them.

Role plays. Role playing is a key learning strategy in *No Kidding About Bullying*. Role playing allows students to practice the bullying prevention and conflict resolution skills they are learning, making it easier to apply them in real-life situations.

Often the role plays provided are based on the Survey About Conflicts and interviews with students. Your students' own experiences will also make good sources for role plays, so invite these wherever you feel it is appropriate.

> Journals are used throughout the sessions in a variety of ways: for responding to a topic, airing personal experiences, brainstorming ideas, doing automatic writing, and more. Students who have difficulty writing can draw or dictate their responses.

Ask for volunteers to play the parts. If enough students don't volunteer, take a part yourself. If the actual situation being role-played resulted in a physical fight, allow only pantomimed movements.

Teach students these ground rules for role plays:

- Students who participate should never reveal personal information they're not comfortable sharing.
- No physical contact or swearing is allowed.
- Actors should not use real names.

If student actors get off track or start to act silly, stop the role play and remind them of its purpose and the ground rules.

Key Practices and Skills: The Core Sessions

The Core Sessions that comprise Part 1 introduce the most critical skills and attitudes for creating a bully-free environment. Some of the strategies in Part 1 will be reintroduced in Part 2 sessions, but are included early on so you can start the year with them. The Core Sessions were designed to help you do the following:

- create agreements for a peaceful, "get-along" classroom
- foster empathy, kindness, and acceptance
- teach respectful listening
- build trust and collaboration
- introduce the Win/Win Guidelines for Working Out Conflicts
- introduce the anger management strategy Stop, Breathe, Chill
- foster responsibility for one's actions

These initial sessions also include some important practices that will help you maintain an atmosphere of respect and kindness throughout the year: breathing for calmness, the process of visualization, a Peace Pledge to be recited each day, a ritual for setting aside upset feelings when entering the classroom, and the class Peace Table or Peace Place.

Deep Breathing

I recommend starting the activities in this book by leading students in a few rounds of deep breathing. Most kids like this practice. Taking a few deep breaths together is a ritual they learn to look forward to. Doing so helps them focus and sets a tone of calmness. Research shows that six deep abdominal breaths can literally lower the blood pressure.[18]

It's important that you get the feel of deep abdominal breathing before you teach it. See Session 4 (pages 28–29) for a thorough introduction to deep breathing. Practice so you're comfortable with the process.

Once you've taught it to your kids, you can use deep breathing throughout the day as a transition between lessons or as a way of lowering anxiety, tension, or nervous energy in your room. You can add visualization (see below) to the breathing, especially as a way of calming before tests.

The Process of Visualization

A number of the sessions incorporate visualization. This is a highly effective tool to help kids mentally rehearse situations where they need to calm themselves, manage anger, talk out a conflict, resist bullying, or use other strategies taught in this book. According to psychology professor and researcher Dr. Barbara Fredrickson, "Visualization has been shown to activate the same brain areas as actually carrying out those same visualized actions. That's why visualization has been such a powerful tool for winning athletes. Mental practice can perhaps be just as effective as physical practice."[19]

Students are introduced to visualization in Session 9. Session 37, pages 94–96, provides a more structured introduction along with a visualization script.

Leave It at the Door

We've all seen it happen. A child comes to school filled with anger, fear, or stress, then spends the day acting out. Leave It at the Door (Session 7) gives you a method you can use all year long to alleviate this. Many kids are under enormous stress. We don't always know which children might be sitting in our classroom with heavy burdens weighing on their hearts. The "Leave It at the Door" box is a place where kids can write down and discharge intense or difficult feelings the minute they walk into your classroom.

The purpose of this exercise is not to minimize feelings, but to help students transition to the school day so they can get along with classmates and learn. If students choose to let you read what they wrote (which is always optional), you then have an added window into their lives. If a child reveals something that requires follow-up or additional intervention, you can get the student the needed help. Should a student reveal serious family issues, any kind of abuse, feelings of depression, or thoughts of harming oneself, talk to your school counselor, nurse, or principal.

Having a tool for processing and communicating what's going on can be the lifeline that pulls a child out of hidden hurt or sadness. By letting out what's troubling them, kids are often more able to learn, and more apt to get along with peers rather than bully them.

Note: Make sure the box is sealed and has a narrow slit at the top so no one but you can take out what anyone else has written. Stress to students that everything they place in the "Leave It at the Door" box is confidential, and no one but the teacher is ever allowed to remove anything from it. Place the box on a shelf in your clear view. If you have concerns that anyone in the class might try to take out something another child has written, keep the box on your desk instead of by the door.

Peace Table

A Peace Table gives students a place in the room where they can retrieve their grounding when angry or upset. It's also a place to talk out conflicts. Set up a Peace Table in a corner of your room. On and near it have objects kids can use to calm themselves and restore composure: a Koosh ball, headsets with soothing music, books, stuffed animals, writing paper, markers, pencils, clay, and more. Near the Peace Table hang posters and drawings that nurture calmness. Post the Win/Win Guidelines for Working Out Conflicts and Rules for Using the Win/Win Guidelines (see page 36). Some teachers make flip cards with the Win/Win Guidelines for kids to hold when they're working out a conflict. Get students in the habit of going to the Peace Table to calm down and to talk things out when conflicts arise.

If space is an issue, create a Peace Place. Some teachers use a bean bag chair for this purpose. Put it in a corner and hang the Win/Win guidelines and rules nearby. Put together a Peace Box containing calming objects and place it next to the bean bag chair. A movable study carrel or screen is also a good idea if kids want privacy. "Quiet headphones" can block out noise for kids who tend to get overstimulated.

Moving away physically from the source can help kids "move" mentally and emotionally when they're angry or upset. Unhooking from the energy of anger, sadness, or frustration by squeezing a soft ball, listening to music, or writing in a journal helps kids learn that they have the ability to release and transform negative feelings in a healthy way. Giving kids the place and tools to do this helps make self-soothing and problem-solving intrinsic, rather than extrinsic. When we put the locus of control inside the child, we give the student a tool to use throughout life.

Using the Win/Win Guidelines for Working Out Conflicts

Kids who know how to work out conflicts are less likely to bully. That's one of the many reasons why teaching conflict resolution is so important. The ultimate goal is that kids will be able to use the Win/Win Guidelines independently when they have a conflict. However, it takes time to develop that comfort level. Many sessions in the Preventing Conflict and the Responding to Conflict sections of this book (pages 119–188) are devoted to role-playing conflicts real kids reported in the Survey About Conflicts and in interviews with students in schools. The more role plays they do, the more natural it will feel for your students to use the Win/Win Guidelines to resolve their own conflicts, rather than fighting, name-calling, or tattling.

You can help mediate students' conflicts using the Win/Win Guidelines. One caveat: be sure to teach the guidelines before using them as a mediation tool. The guidelines, described in the next column, are introduced individually in Sessions 8–14, and reviewed as a process in Session 15. See pages 36 and 47.

Note: The Win/Win Guidelines should not be used with bullying situations. Putting a child who is bullied face-to-face with the child who bullied him or her can be overwhelming and can cause a sense of intimidation and fear. See pages 10–12 and the Dealing with Bullying sessions (pages 217–260) for ways to address bullying.

Mediating Kids' Conflicts with the Win/Win Guidelines

It is best to mediate with no more than two students at a time. If a conflict involves more than two people, try to determine the two who are at the heart of the conflict. Then help them begin to resolve it, following the six guidelines:

1. **Cool off.** Separately, have each child take time out, get a drink of water, or do something physical to let off steam. Make sure both kids have cooled off completely before going to the next step. When it comes to conflicts, the number one mistake adults make is trying to get kids to talk out the problem while they're still mad. When tempers are calmer and tears are dried, sit down with them and go on to Guideline 2.

2. **Talk it over starting from "I," not "you."** Tell students they're both going to have a chance to say what's bothering them, but they're going to need to listen respectfully to each other without interrupting. Then ask each child to state what's on his or her mind, starting from "I," not "you." Example: "I'm mad 'cause you grabbed my pencil without asking" is a lot less inflammatory than "You're so mean. Give it back!"

3. **Listen and say back what you heard.** Guide kids to do this for each other: "Justin, can you repeat back the main idea of what Marcus just said?" Let them know that "saying back" doesn't indicate agreement, but shows respect, builds understanding, and makes it easier to work out the problem.

4. **Take responsibility for your role in the conflict.** In the majority of all conflicts both people have some degree of responsibility. Ask each student, "How were you even a little bit responsible for what happened?" Stay neutral here. This part needs to come from them. If a student is unwilling to take any responsibility at all, try gently coaxing by saying, "Is there something really small that you might have done, too?" If this step starts to stymie the whole process, move on to the next step.

5. **Come up with a solution that's fair to each of you.** Ask, "How can the two of you work out this conflict?" Or, "What can you do so this doesn't happen again?" Then wait. Don't give them solutions. It's important that they come up with their own.

If the conflict is a recurring or ongoing one, have them write down the solution and sign it.

6. **Affirm, forgive, thank, or apologize.** Ask, "Is there anything you'd like to say to each other?" Or, "Would you like to shake hands?"

If an apology is in order, ask, "Do you feel in your heart that you can give an apology?" If not, ask students to consider offering an apology at another time. Forcing apologies makes for inauthentic gestures and doesn't support the goal of getting along better.

At the beginning of conflict resolution and throughout the process as needed, remind students of the Rules for Using the Win/Win Guidelines:

1. Treat each other with respect. No blaming or put-downs.
2. Attack the problem, not the person.
3. No negative body language or facial expressions.
4. Be willing to compromise
5. Be honest.

Incorporating and Reviewing "Get-Along" Classroom Agreements

In Session 1, Introducing the Concept of a "Get-Along" Classroom, you and your students will create a chart called "Our Agreements for a Get-Along Classroom." These agreements are a contract that everyone signs and promises to follow. They form a scaffold for the entire year and are a working document that you and your class should revisit every few weeks. Here are five ways you can review the agreements and keep them alive:

"How are we doing?" check-in. Direct students' attention to items you think they need to work on. For example, you might ask them, "How do you think you're doing on listening when someone speaks?" Encourage students to be honest. When there are areas of challenges, lead a brief discussion on ways to deal with them. Then hold students accountable.

Check back in a few days to see if suggested improvements have been followed through on.

"Pat on the back" check-in. Ask students where they have shown improvement individually or as a group. Acknowledge them for improvements made and for positive steps along the way. Have kids acknowledge each other, too.

Goal setting. Have students choose items on the "get-along" classroom agreements they want to improve on. Have them write the items in their journals. Talk about action steps they can take to reach their goal. Goals can be for individuals or for the entire class. Encourage kids to be "support partners" for each other. For example, if Joey's attention drifts a lot and his goal is to be a better listener, Amy may agree to be his support partner, sitting next to him during lessons and giving him an agreed-upon silent signal when he loses focus. Support partners can also encourage and affirm when progress is made.

New student review. When a new child joins your class, have your students lead a complete review of your "get-along" classroom agreements, answering questions from the new student and talking about how the class is living the words of the agreements.

Share with family adults. As suggested in Session 1, copy the agreements from your wall chart and send them home with a cover letter. At your back-to-school open house, introduce your "Agreements for a Get-Along Classroom" and let parents know how you're using them.

Four Critical Ways for Teachers to Prevent Bullying

1. Model, teach, and reinforce kindness and compassion. By taking the time to teach kindness and compassion, you lay the foundation for a bully-free classroom. Three sections of this book will help you do this:

- The Core Sessions (pages 19–47)
- Fostering Kindness and Compassion (pages 51–81)
- Accepting Differences (pages 261–275)

What you model is key. As Albert Schweitzer once said, "Example is not the main thing in influencing others, it is the only thing." When he wrote these words, he had little idea that inside the human brain are millions of mirror neurons that cause us to mirror each other's behaviors, emotions, and facial expressions. Neuroscientists have recently discovered that this is why we tend to smile back when someone smiles at us, or frown when we see someone frowning. Mirror neurons are the reason kids' attitudes and behaviors are so contagious.[20]

It's also the reason teachers have even more influence than they realize. Mirror neurons are functioning all day long. Plus, kids watch us for clues as to how to behave, even when we think they're not. There have been times I've heard kids say things like, "I know my teacher doesn't like Mr. So-and-So. I see the look on her face every time he walks by." This attests to the need to be mindful of our body language and facial expressions as well as our words.

For some kids, we may be the most influential role models they have, so we need to hold ourselves to a high standard. When we tell kids to treat others with respect and they see us doing this ourselves, we make a powerful impact for the good. Their mirror neurons are sparked to follow our lead.

2. Make kids part of the solution, and hold them accountable. When kids have a role in coming up with their own rules and agreements, they are far more motivated to abide by them. That's why it's important to start by having your students define the kind of atmosphere they want to have in the classroom, then come up with agreements for creating it (Session 1).

It's also critical to hold your students accountable. Kids can be good at parroting back the right answer when it comes to respect, kindness, and acceptance. They often "talk the talk," but don't "walk the walk." Getting kids to "walk the walk" requires frequent check-ins on how they're applying what they're learning. For example, after you teach an anger management or assertiveness strategy, tell students you're going to want to hear how they apply it in real life. Mark a date in your plan book, and make sure you take five to ten minutes to check in with kids when that date arrives. Reinforce skills and concepts by conducting additional role plays for a given session or for other sessions that have the same focus.

Be sure to tell family adults about the *No Kidding About Bullying* program you are introducing in your classroom. Share information early in the year, and let parents know you'll be contacting them from time to time to see how their kids are applying what they've learned. Then keep in touch via email, your class website, or by sending information home with students.

3. Teach kids concrete strategies they can use when they're angry and in conflict. A study in the Canadian journal *Child Development* revealed that "Students who bully their classmates also tend to have lots of conflicts with parents, friends, and others."[21] Giving kids acceptable ways to deal with conflict and anger can cut back significantly on bullying.

Stop, Breathe, Chill (explained in Session 9) is the number one anger management strategy in this book. Many sessions that follow it show how to use this strategy when conflicts arise. Using Stop, Breathe, Chill yourself and sharing some personal examples with students can make the practice come alive for kids. The more they hear about your real-life applications the likelier they are to follow in your footsteps. Sharing how you handled challenges in angry situations can give your students the confidence to keep trying rather than give up when they meet challenges of their own. The road to managing anger and conflict is never easy. It requires us to be mindful of our old patterns and willing to change them. The role modeling you provide in this regard will be invaluable to your kids.

In terms of helping kids resolve conflicts, the key strategy is the Win/Win Guidelines, introduced in the Core Sessions. Following this, the Responding to Conflict section has twelve detailed sessions designed to help kids apply the Win/Win Guidelines in their lives. There are lots of actual conflicts described by students from our survey for your students to role-play, discuss, and brainstorm solutions to.

Be sure to tell parents about the *No Kidding About Bullying* program you are introducing in your classroom. Share information early in the year and keep in touch regularly.

4. Never look the other way when bullying takes place. Kids need to know that bullying and other acts of cruelty will not be tolerated. Sometimes adults pooh-pooh bullying, saying that it's always existed or that it's just part of life. But that doesn't make it acceptable. And, over time, bullying has changed. It is more insidious and pervasive, and is now part of what many experts see as an epidemic of cruelty among kids. In recent years the ubiquity of the Internet and cell phones has spurred widespread cyberbullying, which can start in elementary school.

Ignoring or minimizing the problem only allows it to grow. As educators, we must call kids on cruel behavior and hold them accountable. Not doing so actually reinforces it by sending a silent signal that cruelty and bullying are okay.

Most schools have some system of consequences for misbehavior as well as bullying response protocols. On the CD-ROM that accompanies this book you will find information regarding using these protocols. Also see the References and Resources on pages 282–284 for sources of schoolwide bullying prevention programs.

The Dealing with Bullying section (pages 217–260) contains nineteen sessions that give specific ways to help kids recognize different forms of bullying. It also teaches kids what to do if they or others are bullied and shows how to be an upstander, as opposed to a bystander, when bullying takes place. If bullying is going on in your classroom, don't rely solely on this section; the sessions on kindness, compassion, and acceptance are equally important, if not more so.

In fact, research reveals that kids who are bullied have certain social challenges in common. *The Journal of Clinical Child and Adolescent Psychology* reports that these students often have difficulty in at least one of the following three areas: reading nonverbal cues, understanding the meaning of social cues, and coming up with options for resolving conflicts.[22] Sessions throughout *No Kidding About Bullying* are designed to help kids improve in all of these areas through role play, empathy building, and activities that require them to observe and respond to the reactions of others. Students with poor social skills can improve in these areas when provided with good role models, effective strategies, and opportunities to practice social interactions.

Acknowledging and Affirming Students

John Milton once wrote, "Good, the more communicated, more abundant grows." One of the most powerful tools we have for making good things grow in our students is catching kids in the act of doing things right and affirming them for their positive acts. When you see students being kind, respectful, caring, or accepting, acknowledge it. Kindness is the antithesis of bullying. The more kind acts we can catch kids in the act of performing, the more we extinguish the roots of bullying.

Be like a detective on the lookout for kind words and actions. When you see kids cooling off when angry, talking out conflicts, or expressing compassion, acknowledge them. For students who feel embarrassed by compliments, make it private. Whisper your acknowledgement or jot it on a note. And make it specific: "I noticed how you helped Joe pick up his books when he dropped them. You didn't laugh, even though other kids did. That was a very kind thing to do. How did that feel for you?" By asking this question, you further reinforce the positive act.

Start and end sessions on a tone of affirmation by sincerely acknowledging individuals or the class as a whole for positives you've observed. Be sure to spread your acknowledgments out, so each child gets a chance to hear something positive at some point. It can be harder to find things to compliment with some kids than with others, so take note of progress made, moves in the right direction, sincere attempts to improve—the small, subtle things that often go unnoticed.

One of my favorite examples of positive change sparked by acknowledgment was with an intense fifth grader I'll call Miko. Miko was in a group I ran for at-risk kids who bullied and got into fights. He started the year angry, reactive, and quick with his fists. Although Miko constantly mumbled put-downs and gave nasty looks to other kids in the group, he had a lot of positive qualities. One day I took him aside and told him how much I enjoyed having him in the group—which I sincerely did—and shared all the positive things I saw in him: his intelligence, his strength, his vast potential. I asked him if he could try to let go of his reactions when kids in the group said or did things that got on his nerves. I told him he had the power to react less, and I said, "I have faith in you." His face completely changed when he heard those words. He admitted to me that he didn't know how to control his temper, so I showed him how to use Stop, Breathe, Chill.

Initially it was hard for Miko to contain his reactions when someone got on his nerves, but he started trying. When something was said that would ordinarily push his buttons, I would notice him consciously looking away (as opposed to giving a look) and breathing deeply. Each time he did this I'd acknowledge him privately. "You're gaining more control over your reactions," I would tell him, or, "You're really making an effort, and it's working." Often, he'd nod in agreement and give me a little smile. Over time, with consistent support and acknowledgment, Miko turned around. At the end of the year, he wrote these words:

> "I love our program because it helped me so much with handling my problems. It really helped me calm myself down when someone or something bothered me. It taught me respect. I'm sure it would help others like me, too."

Continuously catching Miko in the act of doing things right—even sincere attempts and small steps—helped Miko see his better self. He eventually learned that he had the ability to control himself, and when he did, he felt good. For kids who get in trouble all the time, this can be life-changing.

Also teach kids to acknowledge each other. For every kind word your kids speak, one fewer mean word is spoken. Moment to moment, words and actions add up to the atmosphere that's created in our classrooms. If we're consistently affirming positive words and actions, our students often follow suit, noticing the positives in each other and affirming them.

You can prompt student-to-student affirmations fairly easily. "Is there something anyone would like to acknowledge someone for?" is a good question to ask when you complete activities in this book. Things you can prime your kids to notice are:

- kindness in any form
- respect in any form
- helpfulness
- patience
- improvement in any area
- listening attentively
- hearing out someone you disagree with
- calming down when angry
- being an upstander

There are so many things worth acknowledging if our minds are primed toward the positive. In the classroom, when we get in the habit of paying each other sincere compliments, something magical can take root. I've seen it happen over and over.

Anticipating Challenges
Confidentiality

Make sure students understand that they should not bring other people's personal information into group discussions or role plays. Remind students not to use real names when describing bullying or conflict situations. Coach them to say, "Someone I know," "This kid," "A person in our school," "Someone in my home," or "A relative of mine." This applies for writing assignments as well. Journals, too, need to be confidential. The only time a journal entry should be shared is when the person who is writing in it chooses to share an entry with the teacher or the class during a session where optional sharing is designated.

> Be like a detective on the lookout for kind words and actions. Also teach kids to acknowledge each other.

What to Do If a "Red-Flag" Issue Comes Up

The sessions in this book may bring up some red-flag issues for kids. Bullying in and of itself can be one. Kids who are bullied can suffer from depression and even harbor suicidal thoughts. They may also have thoughts of harming someone else. If this or any other issue of major concern arises, talk to your school counselor, nurse, or principal. Discuss how to reach out supportively to the child's family adults and how to get further assistance for the child if need be. Sometimes just being there for the child yourself may be enough. I've known teachers who eat lunch with certain kids at least once a week, or invite them to help in the classroom and chat after school. Whatever avenue you take, consider the red flag a gift—this child is revealing that support is needed. Providing it can make all the difference in the world.

Finally, follow your school's policy guidelines on mandatory reporting of physical or sexual abuse.

Dealing with Disruptive Behavior

It's happened to all of us, and for some of us, it can happen every day: a student explodes, becomes defiant, or gets physical. What can we do? There's no silver bullet, but there are some things that can help.

Calm yourself first. Immediately take deep abdominal breaths and silently say a calming statement (*examples:* "I can handle this," "Cool and steady," "I'll stay calm"). Then lower your voice instead of raising it. These steps will help lower your own stress and provide a model of calmness for the child who's acting out as well as for the rest of the class.

Convey the attitude, "I am on your side." Once students think we no longer support them, we lose the chance to connect and help correct their negative behavior. At-risk kids, especially those who regularly get in trouble, need to believe we still care about them and believe in them even when they've lost control. Consequences can be given, but in the spirit of care and concern.

Let the student save face. Never back a disruptive child into a corner. If we threaten a child who's acting out, we can almost guarantee that he or she will choose a defensive or aggressive way out. ("You want me to go to the office. Try and make me!") Instead, phrase your response in a nonconfrontational way that doesn't further escalate the problem. Here's an example. Tina has just thrown an eraser at a student who made fun of her. You whisper to her: "Tina, I see you're upset right now. Why don't you take a break and get a drink of water?" If a consequence is in order, give it later, once Tina's volatility has subsided.

Make the child part of the solution. Ask, "What can *we* do to solve this problem?" Then come up with a plan together. Here's an example: Jessie always acts out during math lessons. After talking to him you discover that he doesn't get the math concepts you've been working on and his acting out is a mask for his feelings of frustration and inadequacy. Ask him what would help; then make some compromises and adaptations. Maybe Jessie can work with a partner, or maybe he can complete the few problems he understands and leave the rest till you can help him. Coming up with solutions together will put the locus of control back inside him, removing the sense of powerlessness that precipitated his acting out.

Use preventive maintenance. For some kids, calling out their name in front of the class is enough to set them off. Anticipate the anger triggers of kids who easily become disruptive, and do your best to avoid them. For example, if you know that embarrassment leads to outbursts, direct corrective comments to the child privately, or use a previously agreed upon signal. Here, too, involve the child in the solution. If Charlie is always interrupting lessons with inappropriate comments, speak to him privately, create a plan together, let him know you have faith in his ability to follow it, and affirm him when he does so.

Diffuse potentially explosive situations. Here are a few phrases you might use with a student who's on the verge of a meltdown:

- "What do you need to do to take care of yourself right now?"
- "I can see you're very upset. Is there someone you'd like to talk to?"
- "I'm depending on you to have a level head."
- "Did that action help you or hurt you?"
- "How about taking a break."

Put physical safety first. If a child gets physical and can't be readily calmed down, follow your school's policy for dealing with student violence and keeping all students safe.

"Gay" Name-Calling

It's not uncommon for elementary-age kids to put each other down using homophobic terms. Many students who filled out our survey wrote about the heartache of having a homophobic label attached to them. This example came from an 11-year-old boy:

> "It started at lunch when everybody decided I was gay. So that's what they started calling me, and I'm not. They also called me freak because I don't buy lunch, and a nerd because I get straight A's. It's not solved. About a month ago this kid calls me a nerd and other names. So I go tell my mom. The next day his best friend hits me in the face because I told on his friend. Then I got mad and I wanted to hit him back, but I didn't. Now it's the end of the school year. It's like every day without crying is an accomplishment. Even some of my friends have turned on me. It just makes me want to die."*

As this story painfully illustrates, students can be devastated by pejorative comments of this nature. Kids may use the term gay to label a child as homosexual. They may also use it as a kind of generic insult: "That's so gay!" But kids on the receiving end almost always take it as an embarrassing put-down. Here are some facts:[23]

- Anti-gay bullying is one of the most prevalent social problems in American schools.
- A study by the National Mental Health Association found that four out of five teens who are

---

* While the students' surveys were anonymous, the teachers' were not. When a student's story indicated a critical need for help, every effort was made to alert the child's teacher.

bullied for being perceived to be gay were actually heterosexual.

- Kids who are bullied are five times more likely to be depressed and far more likely to be suicidal.

Never look the other way when homophobic comments are made. Kids need to know that doing so is never okay. Session 110 will help you address this issue.

Integrating the Understandings in This Book Throughout the Day

The lessons in this book will live in their application. For systemic change to happen, it's critical to integrate the concepts and strategies presented in the sessions throughout the entire day. Here's how:

- Keep referring back to charts, signs, and quotes from each session, particularly your "Agreements for a Get-Along Classroom." Use them as living documents, tying them in to real-life situations in the classroom. For example, if one of your get-along agreements is "Treat others with respect," and something disrespectful happens, gesture toward the line in the chart about respect. Ask, "Was that respectful or not?" Remind students that every word and action counts. Before long, many kids will get in the habit of referring back to the charts themselves, keeping each other on track.

- Once again, affirm your kids for positive acts you witness. Continuously encourage students to affirm each other, too.

- Ask students to be aware of acts of respect, kindness, integrity, acceptance, and conscience performed by story characters or people they encounter in other content areas. Highlight acts of goodness, and ask students to comment on them.

- When students go to lunch, recess, classes in other rooms, or other special activities, remind them to keep abiding by their get-along classroom agreements. When they return, take a few minutes to hear how the activity went. Acknowledge positives, remediate negatives.

- At dismissal, remind your students to continue living what they're learning with their families, friends, and anyone else whose paths they cross. Follow up by checking in with them often about this.

- Invite guest speakers who reflect the values you are teaching. Teens who have overcome bullying or have been upstanders for others make good guests. So do people who've learned how to manage anger and deal with conflict. Kids enjoy and respond to real-life anecdotes and experiences.

- Refer to current events and ask students to speculate on how the values of respect, kindness, and compassion—or their opposites—might have made an impact on specific events of the day.

- Have students be on the lookout for examples of respect, kindness, compassion, acceptance, or conscience in the news, in movies, and on TV. Ask them to share examples they've come across. Have them go to MyHero.com for examples of everyday people doing extraordinary things.

- Look at conflicts in the news and have students talk about how those conflicts could be worked out using the strategies and concepts you are teaching.

Just about every session of *No Kidding About Bullying* zeros in on skills that not only help prevent bullying and conflict, but also help kids succeed in school. According to a survey of 8,000 teachers and parents by Dr. Stephen Elliott of Vanderbilt University, the following are among the top skills that help kids succeed in school:

- listening to others
- taking turns when talking
- getting along with others
- staying calm with others
- being responsible for one's own behavior [24]

In the pages ahead, you will find a wealth of activities that foster all of these skills. As you use them, be sure to share what's working for you in your classroom with your colleagues. Ask what's working for them. Find out what parents are doing at home to encourage their kids to show respect and kindness, manage anger, and resolve conflicts.

I also invite you to share your successes, challenges, and ideas with me. Please contact me in care of my publisher: help4kids@freespirit.com. I would love to hear from you.

In peace,
Naomi Drew

Notes

1. Goodman, Robin. "Aggression." New York University Child Study Center. Retrieved January 20, 2010, from www.education.com.

2. Ibid.

3. Centers for Disease Control and Prevention and the National Center for Injury Prevention and Control. "Understanding Youth Violence: Fact Sheet 2008." Retrieved January 18, 2010, from www.cdc.gov/ncipc/pub-res/YVFactSheet.pdf.

4. Fight Crime: Invest in Kids. Report released September 8, 2003. Retrieved January 28, 2010, from www.ncjfcj.org/content/blogcategory/240/236.

5. New York University Child Study Center. "May Is Mental Health Month: Fact-of-the-Day." Retrieved January 18, 2010, from www.aboutourkids.org/articles/may_mental_health_month_factoftheday.

6. Center for Social and Emotional Education. "Breaking the Bully-Victim-Witness Cycle." *School Climate Matters* 2, no. 2. (June 2008): 3.

7. Health Resources and Services Administration Maternal and Child Health Bureau. "What We Know About Bullying." U.S. Department of Health and Human Services.Retrieved January 18, 2010, from njbullying.org/documents/whatweknowaboutB.pdf.

8. U.S. Secret Service and U.S. Department of Education. "The Final Report of the Safe School Initiative: Implications for the Prevention of School Attacks in the United States." (May 2002): 30.

9. American Psychological Association. "The Mental Health Implications of Witness Status." *School Psychology Quarterly,* vol. 24, no. 4 (December 2009): 211–223. Retrieved February 4, 2010, from www.apa.org/news/press/releases/2009/12/witness-bullying.aspx.

10. American Academy of Pediatrics. "Bullying: It's Not OK." Retrieved January 18, 2010, from www.aap.org/ConnectedKids/samples/bullying.htm.

11. Belluck, Pam. "Strangers May Cheer You Up, Study Says." *The New York Times* (December 4, 2008).

12. Thompson, Clive. "Is Happiness Catching?" *The New York Times* Magazine. (September 13, 2009): 28.

13. University Outreach and Engagement at Michigan State University. "Best Practice Briefs," no. 31 (December 2004): 5.

14. Bullying.org. Retrieved January 20, 2010, from www.bullying.org/external/documents/Bullying.org_Bullying_Myths-Facts%20Pamphlet.pdf

15. Olweus, Dan, Susan Limber, and Sharon Mihalic. *Blueprints for Violence Prevention, Book Nine: Bullying Prevention Program.* Boulder, CO: Center for the Study and Prevention of Violence, 1999.

16. Goodman, Robin. "Aggression." New York University Child Study Center. Retrieved January 20, 2010, from www.education.com.

17. Slavin, Robert. *Cooperative Learning Theory, Research, and Practice.* Boston: Allyn and Bacon, 1995; cited in Nisbett, Richard E., *Intelligence and How to Get It* (New York: Norton, 2009), p. 72

18. Mori, Hisao, et al., "How Does Deep Breathing Affect Office Blood Pressure and Pulse Rate?" *Hypertension Research: Official Journal of the Japanese Society of Hypertension* 28, no. 6 (June 2005): 499–504.

19. Fredrickson, Barbara. *Positivity: Groundbreaking Research Reveals How to Embrace the Hidden Strength of Positive Emotions, Overcome Negativity, and Thrive.* New York: Crown Publishers, 2009.

20. Thompson, Clive. "Is Happiness Catching?" *The New York Times* Magazine (September 13, 2009): 28.

21. Pepler, Debra, et al. "Developmental Trajectories of Bullying and Associated Factors." *Child Development* 79, no. 2 (March/April 2008): 325–338.

22. Nixon, Robin. "Studies Reveal Why Kids Get Bullied and Rejected." Retrieved February 4, 2010, from news.yahoo.com/s/livescience/20100202/sc_livescience/studiesrevealwhykidsgetbulliedandrejected.

23. Kim, Bob, and Judy Logan. *Let's Get Real Curriculum Guide.* San Francisco: GroundSparks, 2004.

24. Gresham, F.M., and S.N. Elliot. *Social Skills Improvement System* (Bloomington, MN: Pearson Assessments, 2008). Reported by LiveScience in "10 Things Schools Don't Teach Well." Retrieved February 4, 2010, from www.livescience.com/health/070927-charm-school.html.

Part One

Building Bully-Free Skills and Attitudes

Congratulations on beginning! The activities you are about to start are the gateway to a bully-free classroom. These 15 sessions introduce the most fundamental concepts and strategies for creating an atmosphere of respect, compassion, and kindness. Once you have conducted them, your students will have the beginning information and skills they need to take part in any of the other activities in the book.

Specifically, the Core Sessions will help you:

- Work with students to create agreements for a peaceful, "get-along" classroom

- Foster students' empathy, kindness, and acceptance

- Teach respectful listening and the use of I-messages

- Build trust and collaboration in your classroom

- Introduce the Win/Win Guidelines for Working Out Conflicts

- Introduce the anger management strategy Stop, Breathe, Chill

- Foster in students a sense of personal responsibility for their actions

The Core Sessions

The Core Sessions that comprise Part 1 introduce the most critical skills and attitudes for creating a bully-free environment. Some of the strategies in Part 1 will be reintroduced and expanded upon in Part 2 sessions, but are included early on so students will have the basic understandings and tools they need to begin getting along better as a class and to get the most out of future sessions.

It is best, but not absolutely necessary, to do all of the Core Sessions in order. However, to be effective, sessions 8–15 should be conducted in sequence. They are key introductory sessions on conflict resolution, an essential skill for all students.

1. Introducing the Concept of a "Get-Along" Classroom
2. Respectful Listening
3. Great Listeners in Our Lives
4. Deep Breathing
5. Integrity
6. Peace Pledge
7. Leave It at the Door
8. Peace Table
9. Stop, Breathe, Chill
10. Introducing I-Messages
11. Practicing I-Messages
12. Reflective Listening
13. Taking Responsibility in Conflicts
14. Brainstorming Solutions to Conflicts
15. Win-Win Guidelines for Working Out Conflicts

Session 1: Introducing the Concept of a "Get-Along" Classroom

respect • collaboration

Session 1 lays the groundwork for a bully-free "get-along" classroom that will last all year long.

Students will

- identify qualities of a "get-along" classroom
- recognize their responsibility for helping create a safe and supportive learning climate
- create and sign an "Our Agreements for a Get-Along Classroom" chart

Materials

- globe (see page 6)
- chart paper and markers
- handouts: "Our Agreements for a Get-Along Classroom" (page 21, one copy); parent letter (page 22)
- *optional:* art materials for a classroom display

Introduction. Welcome your students and express how pleased you are about being their teacher. Let them know that this is an important meeting, one that will help them start to create a peaceful year where they get along with each other and treat each other with kindness and respect.

Discussion. Ask students their number one hope for the coming year, months, or weeks. Briefly discuss.

Hold up the globe and tell students that just as we are connected to each other as members of the same classroom, community, neighborhood, and country, we're also connected as members of the human family. By learning to get along and respect each other in the classroom, we're preparing ourselves to get along with all kinds of people in all kinds of settings.

Ask: **What kind of world would you like to grow up in?** Students will likely say things like safe, peaceful, fun, and healthy. Write the words on the board.

Activity. Now ask: **How about here in our own classroom? How would you like it to be in here?**

On chart paper, write the title *"Qualities of a Get-Along Classroom."* List what students say. As each child shares, pass the globe.

Next, ask: **What are things each of us can do to create a get-along classroom?** Have students pass the globe as they speak. On chart paper, write the title *"Our Agreements for a Get-Along Classroom."* List the agreements they suggest, stating them in the affirmative where possible; for example, instead of "No hitting" write "Keep your hands to yourself."

As you list the agreements, ask students to give specific examples for each. For example, if someone suggests, "Treat each other with respect," ask what that means in terms of actions (avoid using putdowns even when you're angry, refrain from rolling eyes or laughing when someone makes a mistake or says something you disagree with, etc.).

Keep the list short (seven or eight agreements) and be sure to leave enough room at the bottom for everyone's signature, including your own. When the chart is complete, ask several students to lead in reading it.

Explain what a contract is and let students know that this agreement is a special kind of contract. Ask students to sign their names to the bottom of the chart. You might say: **By signing a contract we give our word of honor. This means we promise to do everything in our power to live up to the agreements we are signing our name to.**

Wrap-Up. Affirm students for working together to come up with agreements they can use all year long. Hold up the globe and remind students that getting along with others and creating peaceful relationships starts with each of us. Say: **If we want our world to become a more peaceful place, it has to begin right here.**

Follow-Up. Laminate the "Our Agreements for a Get-Along Classroom" chart and hang it prominently in front of the room where you can refer to it every day. This is a living document to be continuously integrated into the daily life of your classroom.

Copy the agreements from the chart onto the "Our Agreements for a Get-Along Classroom" handout and make photocopies to send home with a parent letter. Use the letter on page 22 or write your own.

Extension. Have students create and decorate a classroom bulletin board display that includes the "Our Agreements for a Get-Along Classroom" chart. Use the display to incorporate other key classroom charts you make in future sessions.

Our Agreements for a Get-Along Classroom

1. _____
_____

2. _____
_____

3. _____
_____

4. _____
_____

5. _____
_____

6. _____
_____

7. _____
_____

8. _____
_____

Date: _____

Dear Parent/Guardian,

Our class is committed to creating a classroom filled with peace, respect, kindness, and compassion: a "get-along" classroom. Attached are agreements we came up with together to help us do this all year long. Please ask your child to tell you about these agreements and why they're so important.

Many parents are looking for ways to reinforce respect, kindness, compassion, and peace at home, so periodically I'll be sending you information to help with this. You are an important part of the peaceful community we're working to create this year, and I welcome your involvement.

Thank you for your support. If you have questions or suggestions, please feel free to contact me at any time.

Sincerely,

_____

Contact me at: _____

_____

_____

_____

_____

_____

Session 2: Respectful Listening

respect • personal responsibility

Session 2 helps students understand the value of listening respectfully to others.

Students will
- recognize the difference between disrespectful and respectful listening
- learn guidelines for respectful listening
- practice listening respectfully

Materials
- chart paper and marker
- handout: "Respectful Listening" (page 24)

Preparation. On a piece of chart paper, copy the "Respectful Listening" guidelines from the handout.

Introduction. Invite a student to come to the center of the circle to role-play a scenario with you. (In your role, you will be demonstrating disrespectful listening, so be sure to choose a student who won't become upset by this.) Ask: **What's your favorite thing about school?** As soon as the student responds, act distracted, fidget, avoid eye contact, interrupt, and then take over the conversation and make it about yourself. After the role play, ask the student you role-played with how she or he felt about the way you were listening.

Now, ask the class to verbally list all the things you did as a not-so-respectful listener.

Next, start the role play over again with the same question. This time play the part of a respectful, attentive listener. Ask the same question as before, and when the student answers, show interest by leaning in, nodding, making eye contact, and staying focused. Paraphrase something she or he says and follow up with a relevant question. At the end, ask the student you role-played with how she or he felt this time.

Discussion. Ask the class to identify everything they observed you doing as a respectful listener. List these things on board. Now show the chart you've prepared. Ask: **Is there anything we should add to this chart?**

Activity. Have students practice respectful listening in pairs, one partner as the Speaker and one as the Listener. Tell partners to sit directly across from one another looking at each other's faces. The Listener should ask the Speaker to describe his or her favorite things about school. The Listener then listens respectfully in the way that was modeled. Remind students to listen to each other as though no one else is in the room, giving their full attention to what's being said. After a few minutes, have students reverse roles.

Wrap-Up. Ask students to share what this experience was like for them. As each person shares, remind the student to look around the circle to see if everyone's listening before beginning to speak. Acknowledge respectful listening as it takes place. Pass out the "Respectful Listening" handout as a reminder of good listening habits.

Follow-Up. Laminate the "Respectful Listening" chart and hang it in a prominent place in the room. Refer back to it throughout the rest of the day, and use it daily.

Extension. Designate a day as "Respectful Listening Day." At the end of the day, do a brief check-in with the class to talk about how respectful listening affected their day.

Respectful Listening

Look at the person who is speaking.

Keep your body still, and focus your mind on what's being said.

Wait your turn to speak.

Listen with an open mind.

Take a deep breath if you have the urge to interrupt. Then focus your mind back on the speaker.

Session 3: Great Listeners in Our Lives

respect • personal responsibility

Session 3 helps students examine the impact great listeners have on others and honestly assess their own listening skills.

Students will

- share and discuss what makes a great listener
- recognize the role effective listening plays in helping people get along
- take inventory of their own listening strengths and weaknesses

Materials

- "Respectful Listening" chart from Session 2
- handouts: "A Great Listener in My Life" (page 26); "Check Your Listening" (page 27)
- student journals

Preparation. Prior to this session, pass out copies of the "A Great Listener in My Life" handout and have students complete it.

Introduction. Tell students that listening is the most fundamental way we show respect for others. Ask students how they feel when someone truly listens to them and cares about what they have to say. Share your own experience briefly.

Discussion. Ask students to take out their completed "A Great Listener in My Life" handouts. Have students pair up and share what they've written. Refer to the "Respectful Listening" chart, and remind students to use good listening as their partners share what they observed about great listeners in their lives.

Next, ask students to reconvene in the large circle and describe what the great listeners they observed do. Ask: **How does their respectful listening make other people feel?**

Activity. Pass out copies of the "Check Your Listening" handout and have students take a few minutes to assess their own listening habits. Encourage them to answer honestly. Then ask: **Which things on the list are you already good at? Which things do you need to work on?** Afterward, ask students to choose one or two listening goals to work on throughout the week. Have them write down their listening goals in their journals.

Ask: **How can being a good listener help people get along better?** Hold up or point to a globe and ask how our world would be different if people all over truly listened to what others had to say.

Wrap-Up. Close by reminding students that we each have the power to improve our listening, and when we do, our lives and relationships with others often get better.

Follow-Up. Be sure to revisit this activity at a later time so students can assess how they're doing with their listening goals.

A Great Listener in My Life

A person who is a great listener is: _____.

Here are some things I notice _____ doing
when he or she listens to me or someone else:

_____

_____

_____

_____

This is how I feel when I'm talking with this person:

_____

_____

_____

_____

Here's what I plan to do to become a better listener:

_____

_____

_____

_____

Check Your Listening

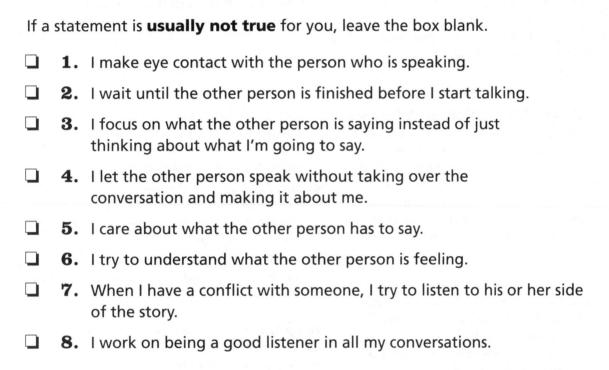

**Take this self-test about your listening skills.
For each statement:**

Check the box if it is **true most of the time.**

If a statement is **usually not true** for you, leave the box blank.

❏ **1.** I make eye contact with the person who is speaking.

❏ **2.** I wait until the other person is finished before I start talking.

❏ **3.** I focus on what the other person is saying instead of just thinking about what I'm going to say.

❏ **4.** I let the other person speak without taking over the conversation and making it about me.

❏ **5.** I care about what the other person has to say.

❏ **6.** I try to understand what the other person is feeling.

❏ **7.** When I have a conflict with someone, I try to listen to his or her side of the story.

❏ **8.** I work on being a good listener in all my conversations.

How did you do?

If you checked at least 4 of the statements, you already have some good listening skills.

If not, you are not alone. Many people have not yet learned how to listen. The good news is that everyone can learn to be a better listener. It just takes practice. Be part of the solution by really listening to what other people have to say!

Session 4: Deep Breathing

personal responsibility • compassion

Session 4 shows students how to become calm and focused through deep abdominal breathing.

Note: This is a basic and essential strategy for fostering calmness. Use it with your students at the start of each day and as often as needed throughout. It also works well as a transition between activities.

Students will
- understand that feeling peaceful and calm inside helps them be more peaceful with others
- learn and practice deep breathing as a way to feel calm and peaceful

Materials
- handout: "Deep Breathing Instructions" (page 29)

Introduction and Discussion. Ask: **What does it mean to be a peaceful person? If you want to be peaceful with others, where does it have to start?** Discuss briefly, emphasizing that being peaceful with others starts by being peaceful inside ourselves.

Ask students if they ever find it hard to feel peaceful inside. Discuss. Then ask: **What do you do to calm yourself when you feel upset, angry, scared, or stressed?**

Activity. Tell students you're going to teach them an important strategy that's easy to do, yet powerful in its impact. Say: **This is a strategy professional athletes and performers use to feel calm, focused, confident, and peaceful before a performance or game. It's called deep abdominal breathing.**

1. Have students sit up tall without tensing, hands on lower abdominal muscles just below the navel.
2. Have them imagine a balloon in the lower abdomen that fills with air as they inhale. (Make sure no one has anything in their mouths before beginning. Food, gum, or another object could cause them to choke.)

   Together, take a slow, deep breath all the way down into the imaginary balloon. Together, hold the breath in gently for a few seconds. (This should be a gentle, quiet breath, not the kind kids take when they're about to swim under water.)
3. Now have them slowly, quietly, and gently breathe out, "deflating" the imaginary balloon as they exhale.

   Repeat three times, extending the length of each exhalation. (If kids giggle, tell them that this sometimes happens at first. Encourage them to do

the breathing in a "mature" way, as an athlete or a performer would. Remind them that learning to do abdominal breathing will help whenever they feel tense about anything, including tests.)

4. After three deep breaths, have students remove their hands from the lower abdominal area and take two more slow, deep breaths with their hands resting in their laps.
5. Now have them take a few regular cleansing breaths, rolling shoulders and neck to release any areas of tension.

Wrap-Up. Ask students how they feel. Discuss. For those who might have felt dizzy, tell them not to inhale quite as deeply next time. Kids with asthma may be especially prone to dizziness.

Affirm students for any positive behavior you observed during this session. Pass out the "Deep Breathing Instructions" handout and ask students to practice deep breathing when they go to bed tonight and when they wake up in the morning.

Follow-Up. When students next arrive at school, start the day with deep breathing. Consider starting every day with this exercise and using it during transition times, too—it's a very effective way to help kids refocus.

Extension. In his book *Peace Is Every Step*, Nobel nominee Thich Naht Hanh suggests using the following words with deep breathing: "I breathe in and I calm my body. I breathe out and I smile." Share these words with your students. They're comforting to say before beginning deep breathing. The smile that comes afterward helps set a tone of warmth and connection.

Deep Breathing Instructions

1. Sit up tall with your hands resting on the lower abdominal muscles, just below the navel.

2. Imagine a balloon in your lower abdomen that will fill with air as you breathe in. Take in a slow, deep breath, breathing all the way down into the imaginary balloon. Hold the breath gently for a few seconds.

3. Slowly, quietly, and gently breathe out, "deflating" the imaginary balloon as you exhale.

   Repeat this process of deep breathing three times. Each time, exhale a little more slowly.

4. After three deep breaths, remove your hands from your lower abdomen and place them in your lap. Take two more deep breaths.

5. Finish with a few regular "cleansing" breaths. Roll your neck and shoulders to help release tension.

Session 5: Integrity

personal responsibility • integrity • decency

Session 5 helps students understand the meaning of integrity and reinforces the importance of doing what's right, even when no one is looking.

Students will
- identify specific actions that indicate a lack of integrity
- list actions that constitute integrity
- reflect on the importance of being a person of integrity

Materials
- chart paper and marker
- student journals

Preparation. On chart paper, write the following: *"Integrity—Doing the right thing even when no one is looking"*

Introduction. Write the word *integrity* on the board. Ask if anyone knows what it means.

Show the definition and ask a student to read it aloud. Ask the class: **What does this mean to you?** Discuss, asking for examples.

Discussion and Activity. Ask students if they think it's important to do the right thing, even if they know they won't get caught doing something wrong. Encourage them to say what they really feel, not just what they think you want to hear.

Tell students: **Here's something a real student said: "I was part of a gossip club. We made up rumors about people and spread them around the whole school."** *

Then ask: **Does this show integrity?** Ask what's wrong with doing what this person did and how the people affected by the student's actions probably felt about it.

If students say, "What if they never found out who did it?" ask: **How do you think the student feels about herself inside when she thinks about what she did?**

Bring out the notion that when we do something that's not right, a part of us knows it, and we often feel guilty. Say: **Whenever we do something that could intentionally hurt another person, we're not showing integrity.**

Ask students to name some other things that show a lack of integrity (lying, bullying, stealing, cheating, disrespecting adults and peers, etc.).

Ask what often happens to adults who engage in these kinds of activities. Guide students to understand that when someone develops a pattern of doing things that are hurtful and dishonest, the person usually does get caught eventually. Ask what other negative things can happen (people not trusting you, losing the respect of others, lack of self-respect, getting in trouble, etc.).

Say: **At one time or another, even really honest people might do something that lacks integrity. This doesn't mean they're bad people, it just means they've made a bad choice. How do you feel about yourself when you do things you know aren't right?**

Ask students to think of things that show integrity (telling the truth, treating others with kindness and respect, not taking things that don't belong to you, listening to adults, etc.). List these actions on chart paper under the title, "Integrity is . . ."

Wrap-Up. Ask students to do three minutes of automatic writing in their journals on the topic of integrity. (See page 7 for details on automatic writing.) Here's a prompt you can start them with: **Give examples of what it means to be a person of integrity.**

In closing, remind students that even if they've done something that lacks integrity, every day is an opportunity to do better.

Extension. Ask students to observe their own behaviors throughout the day, asking themselves the question, "Am I acting with integrity right now?" Then, before they go to bed, have them write in their journals about what they observed in themselves.

---

* Quotes attributed to real students come from interviews and from responses to the Survey About Conflicts conducted by the author and publisher. See pages 1 and 279–281 for further information.

Session 6: Peace Pledge

respect • collaboration • personal responsibility

In Session 6, your class will create a Peace Pledge that can be recited at the beginning of each day.

Students will
- identify actions that help make their classroom a peaceful place
- work together to brainstorm ideas and distill them into a pledge to be used all year long

Materials
- chart paper and marker
- *optional:* art materials for creating classroom display; "My Peace Pledge" handout (page 32)

Introduction. Gather your class in a circle. Hold up or point to the globe. Remind students: **We are all part of the same human family. Having a more peaceful world starts right here in our classroom. Getting along with each other is the first step.**

Discussion. Tell students that today they'll be creating a Peace Pledge to say together at the start of each day. Ask how a pledge might help your class set the tone for a peaceful day in which people get along and treat each other with respect. Discuss.

Ask students to suggest things that might be included in the pledge. List ideas on chart paper. As a group, decide which are the most important and meaningful suggestions for the pledge.

Activity. Work together as a class to integrate ideas and create a Peace Pledge that kids can live by. Compose the pledge on chart paper, keeping it short and concise.

When the pledge is complete, ask several students to lead in reading it together. For each line, ask students how they can live the words through real-life actions. Ask students to name things from the pledge they are going to work on personally.

Wrap-Up. Compliment students for coming up with the Peace Pledge collaboratively and for other positive behaviors you noticed (attentive listening, acceptance of each other's ideas, fairness, creativity, patience, kindness, etc.). Ask if anyone in the group would like to acknowledge a classmate.

Follow-Up. Laminate the Peace Pledge and hang it in a prominent place in your room.

Let your students know that you'll be checking in with them to see how they're living the words of the Peace Pledge.

Extension. Create a bulletin board or other classroom display with the Peace Pledge at the center. Give students "My Peace Pledge" handouts. Have them write down and illustrate one thing they plan to do as peacemakers. Display individual Peace Pledges around the class pledge.

Sample Peace Pledge

We pledge to be peacemakers
Throughout the day
And at all other times,
To be kind to others
And follow the Golden Rule.

My Peace Pledge

In order to be a peacemaker, I pledge to

_____

_____

_____

Session 7: Leave It at the Door

empathy for self and others

Session 7 introduces the idea of a "Leave It at the Door" box—a container where students can "leave" problems when they walk into your classroom.

Students will
- learn a strategy for letting go of problems and stressful feelings
- understand that they can use the "Leave It at the Door" box throughout the year
- use the technique of automatic writing to discharge any negative feelings they presently have

Materials
- a box (or another container) large enough to contain student notes
- paper and pens or pencils

Note: Be sure to read all of the "Leave It at the Door" information on page 8 before conducting this activity.

Note: The purpose of this activity is to teach students a technique for letting go of problems and upset feelings they've brought to school, and to help them transition to a school day in which they can effectively learn and get along with others. It is not intended to minimize or deny feelings or issues that need to be addressed. If you think a child needs further help, speak with the child's parent or your principal, guidance counselor, or school psychologist. See page 13 for more information on what you can do if students share serious issues.

Preparation. Create a "Leave It at the Door" box by decorating a box and making a slot in the top. Attach a sign to the front that says, *"Leave It at the Door."* Place paper and pens or pencils near the box, along with a sign stating: *"You don't have to keep bad feelings inside. Let go of them here."*

Introduction. Affirm students for any acts of respect or cooperation you've seen. Ask if anyone would like to acknowledge another student in the group.

Discussion. Ask students if they ever arrive at school in a bad mood, angry, sad, or stressed. Let them know it's normal to have these feelings, and that you have them, too. Discuss this as a group, sharing your own story (frustration from sitting in traffic, an argument you had with a family member, etc.).

Ask students what they do to let go of bad feelings. Discuss. Remind them that there are many positive ways we can help ourselves manage strong emotions. Say: **Writing is one good way to *unload* negative feelings—to let go of them.**

Hold up the "Leave It at the Door" box and tell students that this is a place where they can put any negative feelings they might come to school with.

Point out the paper and pencils, and explain that they can write about any negative emotions they're feeling as soon as they walk through the door of the classroom.

Unloading their feelings on paper and putting them in the box can help them feel better. Let them know that no one in the class gets to read what's inside the box except you, and even that is only if a student wants you to read what he or she has written.

Activity. Give each student a piece of paper. Say: **Think of something you'd like to leave at the door right now. It can be something from this morning or any other time.** Give students about three minutes to use automatic writing to unload the feelings they'd like to leave at the door.

Encourage students to completely "unload" what's on their minds. Make sure they know that neatness and spelling don't matter. Emphasize that whatever they write will be confidential. Say: **If you would like me to read what you've written sign your name, fold your paper and put my name on top. If you don't want me to read it, crumple the paper and put it in the box. At the end of day, I'll destroy all the crumpled papers, and I'll read the ones addressed to me.**

After three minutes, ask students to finish writing and put their papers in the box. Tell students they can add something to the "Leave It at the Door" box at anytime, but you are the only one who is ever allowed to take anything out. Stress that you are expecting every person in the class to honor the confidentiality of the "Leave It at the Door" box. Place the box on your desk or on a shelf in your clear view.

Wrap-Up. Ask students how they felt "unloading" their thoughts on paper. Be aware that this process can open up unsettling feelings for some children.

If that happens, take a few minutes to talk privately with the child. Tell students that the "Leave It at the Door" box will be there every day all day and can be used whenever needed.

Follow-Up. This process can reveal useful information and give you deeper insight into your students. Save the notes addressed to you and follow up with a brief written or privately spoken response. If a child wants to talk to you further, consider meeting with him or her after class or at lunch. Providing this kind of support can make a big difference in how students feel at school.

Session 8: Peace Table

calming • working out conflicts

Session 8 introduces the "Peace Table" as a place where students can calm themselves when feeling stressed, angry, or upset. It's also a place to go to work out conflicts. This session also introduces "Win/Win Guidelines for Working Out Conflicts" and reinforces Guideline 1: *Cool off.*

Students will

- share what they already do to calm themselves when angry or upset
- learn other things they can do to calm down when angry or upset
- gain awareness that they have the power to resolve conflicts in a peaceful way

Materials

- small table and chairs
- calming objects (Koosh ball, books, age-appropriate stuffed animals, paper, crayons, markers, music and headphones, etc.)
- chart paper and markers
- handouts: "Win/Win Guidelines for Working Out Conflicts" (page 36); parent letter (page 37)
- *optional:* "Time at the Peace Table," a song by Paulette Meiers on her *Come Join the Circle* CD (available at www.lessonsongs.com)

Note: You will find it helpful to read the "Peace Table" information on pages 8–9 before conducting this activity.

Preparation. On chart paper, write the "Win/Win Guidelines for Working Out Conflicts" and the "Rules for Using the Win/Win Guidelines" (see page 36). Laminate them.

Set up the Peace Table in a place in your room where students can go when they feel upset. Place the calming objects you have assembled on or near the table. Hang the Win/Win Guidelines and Rules next to the Peace Table.

Introduction. Ask students what they do to help themselves feel better when they're upset, stressed, sad, or angry. Discuss. Direct students' attention to the Peace Table you've set up. Tell them the Peace Table will be available to them all year long as a place to go if they need to feel calmer or work out a conflict.

Discussion. Ask: **What is a conflict?** See if students can accurately define the word. Here is a definition: **A conflict is a misunderstanding, disagreement, or fight between two or more people. It can also be something that goes on inside yourself.** (For example: *Should I punch this person or walk away?*)

Ask students if they see many conflicts going on in their school and neighborhood. Ask them to briefly describe some of the conflicts they see. (Caution them not to use real names.) Discuss.

Ask students: **Do you think it's normal to have conflicts?** Allow their attitudes to surface. Then let them know that conflict is normal and natural, but what makes some conflicts bad is the way we choose

to handle them. Emphasize that every person has the power to choose fair and respectful ways of handling conflict. Tell students you're going to show them a very important strategy for working out conflicts at the Peace Table, or anywhere else.

Activity. Direct attention to the "Win/Win Guidelines for Working Out Conflicts" chart. Ask for volunteers to read each guideline, along with the rules for using them. For Guideline 6, briefly explain the meaning of *affirm.* Say **When you affirm someone, you say something nice about the person. For example, "I'm glad we're still friends" or "I feel good about the way you listened to me."**

Tell students that Guideline 1, cooling off, is something they can always do at the Peace Table. Ask which objects on the table might help them calm down when they're angry or upset.

Ask what other objects they'd like to have on or near the Peace Table. Invite students to bring in objects they suggest.

Wrap-Up. Tell students you'll be going over every step of the Win/Win Guidelines very soon. Pass out individual copies of the "Win/Win Guidelines for Working Out Conflicts" and the parent letter. Ask students to display the guidelines at home and explain them to their families.

Extension. End with the song "Time at the Peace Table."

WiN/WiN Guidelines for Working Out Conflicts

1. Cool off.

2. Talk it over starting from "I," not "you."

3. Listen and say back what you heard.

4. Take responsibility for your role in the conflict.

5. Come up with a solution that's fair to each of you.

6. Affirm, forgive, thank, or apologize.

Rules for using the WiN/WiN Guidelines

1. Treat each other with respect.
   No blaming or put-downs.

2. Attack the problem, not the person.

3. No negative body language or facial expressions.

4. Be willing to compromise.

5. Be honest.

Date: _____

Dear Parent/Guardian,

Our class is committed to creating a "get-along" classroom filled with peace, respect, kindness, and compassion. Attached are "Win/Win Guidelines for Working Out Conflicts" that we are using in school. Please ask your child to tell you about these guidelines and what she or he is learning about them.

The guidelines can be used by people of all ages in many different settings. Reinforcing the guidelines at home will encourage your child to use them. I hope you will post them and use them whenever conflicts arise. The more you practice them, the more natural they will feel.

Thanks as always for your support. If you have questions or suggestions, please feel free to contact me.

Sincerely,

_____

Contact me at: _____

_____

_____

_____

_____

_____

Session 9: Stop, Breathe, Chill

personal responsibility • anger management • self-control

Session 9 introduces "Stop, Breathe, Chill," a powerful strategy for managing anger. It reinforces Win/Win Guideline 1: *Cool off.*

Note: This session builds on skills learned in Session 4. Complete Session 4 before introducing this one.

Students will

- identify body sensations, feelings, and thoughts they have when they get angry
- learn the terms *reptilian brain* and *neocortex* and how they relate to anger
- learn how to shift from the angry part of the brain (reptilian brain) and get to a calmer place
- understand that the front of the brain (neocortex) is their place of power, especially when conflicts occur

Materials

- "Win/Win Guidelines for Working Out Conflicts" chart from Session 8
- chart paper and markers
- handout: "Stop, Breathe, Chill" (page 39)

Preparation. On chart paper, write the words *"Stop," "Breathe,"* and *"Chill"* in a column.

Introduction. Point to Win/Win Guideline 1: *Cool off.* Tell students that today you're going to give them a very powerful strategy that will help them cool off, control their anger, and work out conflicts more peacefully.

Discussion. Tell students: **Here is something a real student said: "Sometimes I react without thinking and hurt the people who make me mad. I want to learn how to handle my anger better."**

Ask students if they can identify with this statement. Briefly discuss.

Now share another statement from a real student: **"I try to walk away when I'm in a conflict, but inside my body I feel really mad, so I can't."**

Ask: **How does your body feel when you get mad?**

Say: **Think about where the anger "lands" inside you. Does it land in your heart, causing it to pound? How about your stomach?** Have students point to the places in their bodies as they respond.

Say: **Sometimes anger can cause tightness in the neck or shoulders, pounding in the head, heat in the face, shakiness in the hands.** (Point to each place on yourself as you refer to it.) **Anger is fueled by two things: the feelings we feel in our bodies and the thoughts we think in our heads.**

Now ask students to recall angry thoughts they've had. Ask for one or two volunteers to share.

Activity. Tell students that these thoughts and body sensations come from the *reptilian brain.* Point to the base of your skull; have them do the same. Then say: **The *reptilian brain* is the part that takes over when**
we get angry. It causes us to react. When we react, we do things without thinking, sometimes things we regret. But there's another part of our brain that helps us think straight and *choose* a response. Touch the front of your forehead and have students do the same. **The front of the brain is called the *neocortex.* It is our place of true power.**

Refer to the "Stop, Breathe, Chill" chart. Say: **When anger strikes, if we stop, breathe, and chill, we can get *out* of our reptilian brain, and *into* our place of power. Let's try it now.**

Have students close their eyes and think of a time they got mad. Say: **Recall where the anger landed in your body. Remember your angry thoughts.** Give students a minute to do this.

Then say: **Now picture a big red stop sign, and silently tell yourself to STOP.** (Pause.) **Take some slow deep breaths.** (Breathe with them.) **Feel the oxygen calming your body and mind.**

Stopping and breathing takes you out of the reptilian brain into the front of the brain, your place of power. (Have students point to each place.)

Ask: **What can you do to chill out after you stop and breathe?** Write suggestions on the board.

Wrap-Up. Pass out copies of the "Stop, Breathe, Chill" handout. Ask students to take it home and think of other things they can do to chill out when they're angry—after they stop and breathe. Have them write their ideas in the space provided on the handout and bring it to the next session.

Follow-Up. Take a few minutes to discuss students' "Chill" ideas. You'll find additional ideas in several of the Managing Anger sessions (pages 83–118).

Stop, Breathe, Chill

1. Stop

Picture a big red stop sign, and silently tell yourself to **STOP**.

2. Breathe

Take some slow deep breaths. Feel the oxygen calming your body and mind.

3. Chill

Do an activity that helps you relax. You might:

drink some water	draw a picture	skateboard
look out the window	go for a walk	talk with a friend
play a game	play an instrument	write in a journal
exercise	shoot baskets	talk to a teacher
listen to music	color or paint	read a book
gaze at the sky	watch a movie	stretch
talk to a parent	spend time with a pet	_____
_____	_____	_____
_____	_____	_____

Session 10: Introducing I-Messages

respect • responsibility • collaboration • conflict resolution

Session 10 introduces I-messages as a neutral, nonaggressive way of expressing one's feelings or concerns when conflicts arise. It reinforces Win/Win Guideline 2: *Talk it over starting from "I," not "you."*

Students will

- understand the purpose, use, and value of I-messages
- understand that I-messages are always intended to be respectful, never sarcastic or hurtful
- practice using I-messages through role-play

Materials

- "Win/Win Guidelines for Working Out Conflicts" chart from Session 8
- student journals

Introduction. Point to Win/Win Guideline 2: *Talk it over starting from "I," not "you."* Tell students that today they're going to learn about I-messages—an important skill for working out conflicts. Say: **First, let's look at the way many people often react when they're in a conflict.**

Ask for two students to come to the center of the circle and role-play a conflict in which one takes a pencil from the other without asking. Have them argue, and make statements starting with "you." ("You better give it back or else," etc.)

Discussion. Now ask the class what made this conflict get worse. On the board, list some of the things that escalated the conflict. Emphasize that blaming, name-calling, and starting from "you" *escalate* conflicts—make them grow. Tell students that starting from "you" puts people on the defensive—makes them want to defend themselves and lash out at the other person.

Say: **Starting from "I" lets us state what's on our minds respectfully without blame or put-downs. When we start from "I," that's called an I-message. I-messages let people be *assertive* (speak up for themselves) without blame or put-downs.** Emphasize that the way an I-message is delivered is just as important as the words. Sarcasm is never okay.

Ask students to turn the following "you-message" into an I-message: **"You just cut in front of me. You're mean."** Possible I-message alternatives are:

- "I was here first. Please don't cut in front of me."
- "I don't like when people cut in front of me. Please get behind me."
- "I don't appreciate being cut in front of. Please move."

An easy way to teach I-messages is to have students start sentences with "I didn't like it when . . ." and then elaborate without blame. Example: "I didn't like it when you told my secret. I thought you understood that this was just supposed to be between us. Please don't do it again."

Notes About I-Messages: It's not necessary for kids to state how they feel when they use I-messages. While I-messages have traditionally included statements of feelings ("I feel hurt when . . ."), many experts now believe that a more neutral form of I-messages is preferable. Starting with "I feel" often leaves the person delivering the words vulnerable and open to more hurt. (For example, the respondent might reply, "You feel hurt. Good!") I-messages can also be followed by a request, as illustrated above.

The word *you* can be included in I-messages ("I didn't like when *you* grabbed the pencil out of my hand"). But you should not be used in an accusatory or blameful way.

Activity. Have students partner up and think of an I-message for the following scenario: **Your friend insists that you play soccer at recess today. You want to play softball.**

After a few minutes, ask students to share some of the I-messages they came up with. Here are a few possibilities:

- "I don't think it's fair that we always have to play soccer. How about playing softball for a change?"
- "I don't really want to play soccer today."
- "I don't like it when you try to force me to play something I don't want to play."

Have students share some of the I-messages they came up with. Help them assess whether the I-message respectfully got their point across.

Wrap-Up. Commend students on the effort they've put into coming up with I-messages. Remind them to use I-messages when real conflicts arise.

Follow-Up. Have students think about a conflict they recently had. Ask them to think of I-messages they might have used during the conflict. Have them list a few in their journals.

Extension. One of the most important I-messages is, "I have something on my mind." This opens the door to airing concerns or hurts that have been tucked away. Encourage students to think about something they'd like to discuss with a friend or family member, but haven't had the courage to broach. Tell them to rehearse—or even write down—what they'd like to say. Then suggest they approach the person by saying, "I have something on my mind."

Session 11: Practicing I-Messages

respect • personal responsibility • collaboration

Session 11 gives students more practice in formulating and delivering I-messages. The session reinforces Win/Win Guideline 2: *Talk it over starting from "I," not "you."*

Students will
- formulate I-messages for common conflicts
- understand that the way an I-message is delivered is just as important as the words that are spoken

Materials
- "Win/Win Guidelines for Working Out Conflicts" chart from Session 8

Introduction. Review what you taught in the last session, particularly that I-messages need to be delivered in a respectful way free of blame, put-downs, or sarcasm. Ask why I-messages are more effective for resolving conflicts than "you-messages." (You-messages put people on the defensive and make conflicts escalate; I-messages help us state what's on our mind respectfully so we can talk out conflicts.)

Activity. Say: **When you use an I-message, it's not just about the words you speak. It's also about how you say them.** Demonstrate an I-message with arms crossed and a hostile look on your face. Ask students what message your face and body are delivering.

Now have students form pairs and come up with I-messages for the following scenarios. (Students might also suggest scenarios for this activity.) Have them practice delivering the I-messages assertively and with *neutral* (not aggressive) body language. After each scenario, stop and ask a few partners to stand and deliver I-messages they came up with.

I-message scenarios:

- Someone in class makes fun of your shoes.
- You drop the ball during a game and someone calls you a name.
- You approach two classmates at recess and one of them says, "You can't hang out with us."

After each I-message is delivered, ask the class if it sounded both assertive and respectful. Were the person's body language and facial expression neutral and respectful?

Wrap-Up. Encourage students to use I-messages throughout the day, always being aware of *how* the words are being spoken. Remind them that body language, tone of voice, and facial expression are just as important as words.

Follow-Up. Ask students to create I-messages to deliver to someone in their lives. Have them practice saying the words in a mirror, observing their own body language and facial expression.

Session 12: Reflective Listening

compassion • conflict resolution

Session 12 introduces reflective listening and gives students the opportunity to practice it. The session reinforces Win/Win Guideline 3: *Listen and say back what you heard.*

Students will

- understand what reflective listening is and how it is used
- practice using reflective listening in a non-conflict situation

Materials

- "Win/Win Guidelines for Working Out Conflicts" chart from Session 8

Introduction. Ask students for examples of situations where they've used I-messages at home or in school. Ask: **How is it going?** Discuss briefly.

Tell students: **If we really want to resolve a conflict, the way we listen is as important as what we say. When someone gives us an I-message, we need to listen carefully and then** *paraphrase* **(say back) the main idea of what the person said. When we do this, we show that we care enough to listen, even if we disagree. Listening is the most powerful thing we can do to resolve conflicts.**

Discussion. Now point to Win/Win Guideline 3: *Listen and say back what you heard.* Ask: **Is this what people generally do when there's a conflict?** Ask students what they tend to do when the other person is speaking. (Many people think about what to say next, interrupt, or argue.) Speak honestly about what *you* tend to do. The more honest you are, the more it gives kids permission to be honest, too.

Activity. Explain that listening and saying back the main idea of what was said is called reflective listening; reflective listening can be used anytime, not just in conflicts. Say: **Now you're going to try using reflective listening in a neutral situation—one where there isn't a conflict. The more you practice reflective listening in regular conversations, the easier it will be to use when conflicts arise.**

Have a volunteer come to the center of the circle and help you demonstrate. Say to the volunteer: **Describe what you most like to do after school.**

Listen attentively, make eye contact, then paraphrase what the student says. You can start with the words "I'm hearing you say . . ." or "So. . . ." Afterward, ask the student if you got it right.

Now have students form pairs and face each other directly. Have each pair choose a Speaker and a Listener. Have the Listener ask, "Can you tell me about what you most like to do after school?" Caution Speakers not to let their response get too lengthy. Tell Listeners to listen with their full attention, as though no one else is in the room but the person they're listening to. When the Speaker is finished, the Listener needs to say back the main idea of what the Speaker said. If the Listener gets it wrong, the Speaker should repeat what he or she originally said, and the Listener should try again.

After a minute or two, have partners switch roles, so each one gets to be both Speaker and Listener.

Wrap-Up. Ask students how it felt to have someone truly listen to what they had to say. Discuss. Ask how reflective listening can help when it comes to working out conflicts.

Follow-Up. Tell students to practice reflective listening throughout the day; let them know you'll check in with them about how it went in the next session. Encourage them to try reflective listening at home and notice its impact on the people they listen to.

Session 13: Taking Responsibility in Conflicts

respect • personal responsibility • integrity • conflict resolution

Session 13 helps students understand that when conflicts arise, both people are usually responsible in some way, and that blaming only escalates conflicts. The session reinforces Win/Win Guideline 4: *Take responsibility for your role in the conflict.*

Students will
- examine a conflict they had and reflect on ways they may have been "even a little bit" responsible for some part of it
- role-play a conflict in which blaming prevents a peaceful outcome
- replay the conflict with people taking responsibility rather than blaming

Materials
- student journals
- "Win/Win Guidelines for Working Out Conflicts" chart from Session 8
- handout: "Responsibility Log" (page 45), several copies for each student

Introduction. Point to Win/Win Guideline 4: *Take responsibility for your role in the conflict.* Say: **One of the most important things we can do to work out conflicts is take responsibility for our part, even if we did something small.**

Discussion. On the board write the words *blaming* and *taking responsibility*. Ask: **What's the difference?** Discuss, guiding students to think about how often they blame rather than take responsibility in conflicts.

Discuss how common it is to blame rather than look at our own behavior and take responsibility for how we might have contributed to the conflict. Share this actual dialogue by a real sixth-grader (not her real name) that illustrates this, playing each of the roles yourself:

Allysa: My big sister is really mean to me.
Teacher: What does she do?
Allysa: She never lets me in her room, and I like to go in there.
Teacher: Do you ask permission first?
Allysa: No. I just go in.
Teacher: And then she gets angry with you?
Allysa: Yeah, and she calls me names.
Teacher: Why do you think she gets so mad?
Allysa: Because she's mean.
Teacher: Is there something you're doing that brings out her anger?
Allysa: Hey, this isn't my fault. My sister's supposed to be nice to me.

Teacher: Sounds like you're putting all the blame on her. How are you responsible for the problem, too?
Allysa: I shouldn't have to be responsible. I'm the youngest. She's the oldest and she should know better.

Ask students if they can see themselves in any part of Allysa's story. Discuss. Bring out the point that Allysa is avoiding taking responsibility for going into her sister's room without permission, and she's trying to pin the entire blame on her sister with the excuse of being younger. Ask: **Have you ever made excuses for something you shouldn't have done?** Invite examples. Nearly all of us do this at one time or another, so share a situation where you blamed rather than taking responsibility.

Ask students to think about a conflict in which the other person blamed them and refused to take responsibility for anything that went wrong. Discuss a few examples, reminding students not to use names or refer to anyone in the class. Ask students how it felt to be blamed. Ask: **Did blaming cause the conflict to get better, or worse?**

Say: **Now think of a time when *you* did the blaming.** Elicit one or two examples. Ask students if blaming the other person made the conflict get better or worse. Guide students to understand that blaming *escalates* conflicts—makes them grow bigger and worse—and prevents them from getting solved.

Now give students a moment to think about a conflict they've recently had. Say: **In almost all conflicts,** both people are responsible in some way. Can you think of a way you might have been *even a little bit responsible* for what happened? Share an example from your life to help kids open up about their own conflicts.

Tell students that taking responsibility is an act of courage, one that will help them better resolve any conflict that might come up. Say: **Taking responsibility for our part in a conflict can give the other person the courage to do the same.**

Activity. Ask for two volunteers to role-play the following conflict in a negative way. Ask them to use you-messages, blame each other, and refuse to take responsibility for their part:

Carl and Janie worked together on a class project. They just got it back, and discovered they only earned a C because an important part of the project had been left out.

When the role play is completed, ask the class to comment on what made the conflict escalate. Ask each role player how it felt to be blamed. Now have them reenact the conflict, this time taking responsibility for whatever they each did, even if it was something small.

Wrap-Up. Ask students: **Which role play turned out better? Why?** Ask how taking responsibility helps us resolve conflicts.

Follow-Up. Have students keep a "Responsibility Log" for the next week. Provide them with a few copies of the handout on page 45 so they can practice taking responsibility for their role in conflicts.

RESPONSibility Log

Taking responsibility helps people resolve conflicts. Use this sheet to help yourself take responsibility for your part in conflicts.

A conflict I had: (Briefly describe what happened in the conflict.)

_____

_____

_____

_____

Is there some way I was even a little bit responsible? Describe.

_____

_____

_____

_____

What could I have done differently?

_____

_____

_____

Session 14: Brainstorming Solutions to Conflicts

respect • personal responsibility • conflict resolution

Session 14 helps students understand that every conflict has many solutions, and if they're committed to working out conflicts, they can find fair solutions. The session reinforces Win/Win Guidelines 5 and 6: *Come up with a solution that's fair to each of you* and *Affirm, forgive, thank, or apologize.*

Students will

- work together with a partner to come up with fair solutions to conflicts
- recognize that conflicts can have a variety of possible solutions

Materials

- "Win/Win Guidelines for Working Out Conflicts" chart from Session 8
- student journals

Introduction. Tell students that every conflict has many solutions. Point to Win/Win Guideline 5: *Come up with a solution that's fair to each of you.* Say: **Today we're going to get some practice coming up with possible solutions to conflicts.**

Discussion. Ask: **How many of you get into conflicts with people over who's right and who's wrong?** Allow for a show of hands. Tell students you're going to share a story about two sixth graders whose friendship is about to fall apart over this issue. Read the following:

Tom and Jarrett always get into conflicts about who's right and who's wrong, and they're losing their patience with each other. Today it happens again. Tom says the book they've been reading in class is totally lame; Jarrett thinks it's really interesting. They start arguing over their opposing viewpoints, each trying to prove that the other is wrong. As usual they both end up walking away angry and frustrated.

Activity. Have students role-play Tom and Jarrett's conflict.

Now ask the class: **What are some possible solutions to this ongoing conflict?** List solutions kids come up with on the board under the title "Brainstorming Solutions." Some examples may include:

- Agree to drop the subject and do something else when disagreements come up.
- Refrain from discussing things they don't see eye to eye on—agree not to talk about them.
- Agree to hear each other out and try to understand the other person's point of view.
- When there's a point of disagreement, use one of the following phrases: "You have a right to your opinion," "I see it differently, but that's okay,"

"Even though I disagree, I respect your right to see things in a different way."

Have students partner up, discuss, and list in their journals at least five possible solutions to the following conflict.

Amy and Todd walk to school together each day. Todd is always on time, but Amy never is, so they often end up getting to school late. Amy is late again today.

Wrap-Up. Ask students to share the solutions they came up with. List their suggestions on the board. Refer again to Guideline 5 of the Win/Win Guidelines: *Come up with a solution that's fair to each of you.*

Now refer to Guideline 6 of the Win/Win Guidelines: *Affirm, forgive, thank, or apologize.* Have partners turn to each other, state which solution feels like a fair one, and imagine they have just worked out their conflict. Now have them either affirm (acknowledge), forgive, thank, or apologize to each other. Examples of affirming are, "I'm glad we're still friends." Or, "I appreciate the way you listened to me when I spoke." If apologies are given, they should be sincere.

Follow-Up. Have students write in their journals or talk to a trusted person about an ongoing conflict in their lives and consider possible solutions. Ask students to talk to the person they're in conflict with, brainstorm solutions together, and decide on a solution that's fair to both of them.

Extension. Keep a Question Box in your room. If students have conflicts they can't find solutions to, have them write about the conflict and put their paper in the box. Several times a week, have other students randomly select a conflict from the box, sit down with the person who wrote about it, and brainstorm solutions together.

Session 15: Win/Win Guidelines for Working Out Conflicts

respect • personal responsibility • conflict resolution

Session 15 reviews the Win/Win Guidelines and lets students practice using them through role play.

Note: This session builds on skills and attitudes learned in sessions 9, 10, 11, 12, 13, and 14. It's important to have completed these activities before conducting this one.

Students will

- role-play a conflict in the "old way"—negatively
- role-play a conflict using the Win/Win Guidelines
- understand that it's possible to resolve conflicts more peacefully when they use the Win/Win Guidelines

Materials

- "Win/Win Guidelines for Working Out Conflicts" and "Rules for Using the Win/Win Guidelines" charts from Session 8
- chart paper and marker

Preparation. Ask students to bring their copies of the "Win/Win Guidelines for Working Out Conflicts," distributed in Session 8 (page 36), to this session.

Introduction and Discussion. Ask students how they've been using the Win/Win Guidelines that they've learned in the last six sessions. Discuss. Be prepared for some students to complain about challenges they've encountered. Emphasize that challenges are normal. After more practice and role-playing, using the guidelines will start to feel more natural.

Activity. Ask for two volunteers to role-play a conflict. You can have students choose a conflict that's fairly common and role-play that one, or use this idea: **Person A shared a secret that Person B had wanted kept private.**

First, have students role-play the conflict in a negative way instead of using the Win/Win Guidelines. Before they begin, prime the rest of the class to note what the role players do that escalates the conflict. After the role play, ask: **What made this conflict get worse?**

Direct attention to the "Win/Win Guidelines for Working Out Conflicts" and "Rules for Using the Win/ Win Guidelines." Choose a few students to read each of the rules aloud. Explain any that need clarification.

Now have volunteers replay the conflict, this time using the guidelines and rules:

Guideline 1. Tell role players to start by cooling off (taking some deep breaths, getting a drink of water, walking away for a few moments, etc.).

After the role players have cooled off, direct them to go through the remaining guidelines:

Guidelines 2 and 3. Have the role players take turns telling each other what was bothering them, starting from "I," not "you." As one person gives an I-message, the other should listen and briefly paraphrase what was said: "I'm hearing you say that_____."

Guideline 4. Ask each student how he or she might be "even a little bit" responsible for the conflict.

Guideline 5. Ask the role players to brainstorm a number of solutions, then come up with one they can agree upon. Ask the class to suggest solutions, too.

Guideline 6. Ask role players to either affirm (acknowledge), forgive, thank, or apologize to each other. Resist making them apologize if they're not ready. Forced apologies are not effective.

Ask the class to evaluate why the conflict ended better when the role players used the Win/Win Guidelines. Discuss.

Wrap-Up. End the session by acknowledging your students for their openness to change and respectful, effective listening. Hold up or point to a globe and remind them that each time they try to work out conflicts respectfully, they're doing their part to make the world a little more peaceful.

Follow-Up. Check in with students occasionally on how they're doing as they use the Win/Win Guidelines. Provide refresher lessons on the guidelines, referring back to Sessions 9–14 as needed.

Extensions. Ask students to create a rap or cheer that tells how to use the Win/Win Guidelines or have students create a comic strip that shows people working out a conflict using the six guidelines.

Part Two

Getting Along and Staying Bully Free

All of the activities in Part Two of *No Kidding About Bullying* build on the fundamental bullying prevention skills and understandings introduced in the Core Sessions of Part One. In Part Two you will find 106 sessions designed to help you create a get-along classroom that can last all year. Sessions in this section are organized into seven topic areas:

- Fostering Kindness and Compassion
- Managing Anger
- Preventing Conflict
- Responding to Conflict
- Addressing Name-Calling and Teasing
- Dealing with Bullying
- Accepting Differences

Fostering Kindness and Compassion

Fostering kindness, compassion, and conscience is your most powerful tool for preventing and alleviating bullying. Current research tells us that the prime motivator for bullying is a need for power. Kids who bully tend to be impervious to the feelings of others. By teaching, modeling, and expecting kindness and compassion, we can create an environment where bullying becomes an "uncool" thing to do. This section also introduces the concept of being an upstander, one who stands up for those who are picked on.

Session 16: Creating Your Place in Other People's Memory Banks

respect • kindness • compassion • personal responsibility

Session 16 introduces the concept of a "memory bank"—the part of us that holds memories of the way we've been treated by others.

Students will

- understand that the way we treat people today creates memories of us that can last a long time, sometimes forever
- define two qualities they want to be remembered as having
- take greater responsibility for their words and actions

Materials

- small box (or other container) with a lid labeled "Memory Bank"
- notecards or slips of paper that students (and you) will put in the Memory Bank

Preparation. On chart paper, write: *"Our words and actions today create memories that will fill others' memory banks tomorrow."*

Introduction. Gather students in a circle. Affirm them as a class and individually for positive ways they've been treating one another. Ask students to think about acts of respect, kindness, or helpfulness that have taken place in the classroom recently. Ask if anyone would like to compliment a classmate. If no one does, give one more affirmation yourself.

Discussion. Hold up the Memory Bank you made. Explain that it represents the "memory bank" each of us has inside. Tell students that things we say and do now will go into people's memory banks, sometimes forever. Say: **Kind words and actions create positive memories. How about mean or hurtful words and actions—what kind of memories of us do they create?**

Share a positive memory of someone who showed kindness toward you. Next share the following negative memory from a real teacher:[*]

"Even though decades have passed, when I remember the person who bullied me, I still cringe. It gives me a stomachache. I can remember names he called me, his cruel laughter when I would walk by. The sight of his face in my mind brings me pain. If I were to see him today it would still bother me, even though we are both adults now."

Ask students to name some of the feelings this teacher holds in her memory bank about the person who bullied her. Write the feelings on a notecard or slip of paper and put it into the Memory Bank.

Now ask students to think of a positive memory that's stored in their memory banks of someone who was kind to them. Call on a student to share briefly.

Next ask students to think about their own place in other people's memory banks. Ask them how they would like to be remembered by others. Choose a few children to share aloud.

Display the statement you prepared. Say: **Our words and actions today create memories of us that will fill others' memory banks tomorrow.** Remind students that we have the power to create positive memories of ourselves through kind words and actions. Ask: **If we treat someone in a hurtful or unkind way, how will we be remembered?**

Activity. Pass out notecards or slips of paper and ask students to write two positive qualities for which they would like to be remembered (examples: caring, helpful, honest, fair). Get them started with this prompt: **"In future years, I want people to remember me as being _____ and _____."**

Have students read aloud the two qualities for which they would like to be remembered. Then have them put their papers in the Memory Bank. Ask what they can do now so people will remember them for the qualities they just named. List specific actions on the board.

Wrap-Up. Compliment students for any positive actions you observed during this session (honesty, kindness, good listening, sensitivity, etc.). Emphasize that these actions are creating good memories of them in people's memory banks.

---

[*] Quotes attributed to real teachers or students come from interviews and from responses to the Survey About Conflicts conducted by the author and publisher. See pages 1 and 279–281 for further information.

Session 17: How Do You Want to Be Remembered?

respect • kindness • compassion • personal responsibility

Session 17 asks students to define how they want to be remembered by peers over time and encourages them to be kind in word and action. This session is a follow-up to Session 16.

Students will
- envision how they want to be remembered by others ten years from now
- write about how they want to be remembered by others
- reflect on changes they need to make to be remembered in positive ways

Materials
- small box (or other container) with a lid labeled "Memory Bank"
- handout: "Creating My Place in Other People's Memory Banks" (page 54)

Introduction. Hold up the Memory Bank. Ask students what it represents (the place where we hold either positive or negative memories of others based on the way they treated us). Ask for a few students to share the qualities they would want to be remembered by. Tell students how you would like to be remembered by them, and describe what you're doing now to make that happen.

Activity. Ask students to close their eyes or look down. Say: **Imagine it is ten years from now. The people who know you now are remembering you back in (this year's) grade. What would you like them to be able to say about you? How would you like to be remembered by them?**

Give students a minute or two to envision this. Then have them open their eyes, get into pairs, and share what they envisioned.

Pass out the "Creating My Place in Other People's Memory Banks" handout and go over it briefly, making sure students understand each section. Allow five to ten minutes for students to complete the handout. If anyone needs more time, have them finish it later in the day.

Discussion. Ask for several volunteers to share what they wrote. Be sure to have them include actions they can take now to be remembered in a positive way by those who know them presently.

Wrap-Up. Ask students if they have any compliments for people who listened respectfully. End by reminding students that every moment is an opportunity to create positive memories of ourselves in other people's memory banks.

Follow-Up. When you see students acting in kind, compassionate ways, point out that they're creating positive memories of themselves in other people's memory banks. If you observe hurtfulness or meanness, ask, "What kind of memory might you be creating right now?"

Creating My Place in Other People's Memory Banks

Imagine it is ten years from today and people who know you are thinking about the person you were in the grade you're in now. Write a paragraph describing how you would like other people to remember you. Include the qualities you would like them to remember about you. Also include things you hope they will be able to say about you years from now.

_____

_____

_____

_____

What can you do now to be remembered in the ways you described above?

_____

_____

_____

_____

_____

What changes do you need to make so people will remember you in the way you hope they will?

_____

_____

_____

_____

Session 18: Choosing Kindness

kindness • respect • empathy • personal responsibility

Session 18 focuses on the need for kindness and empathy and guides students to choose kind actions over hurtful ones.

Students will
- describe how it feels to be treated unkindly
- understand that kindness is a gift they can give to each other every day

Materials
- handout: "What Real Kids Have to Say About Being Mean" (page 56)
- "Our Agreements for a Get-Along Classroom" chart from Session 1

Introduction. Gather students in a circle. Affirm several kids for acts of kindness and respect you've recently observed. Ask students if they think it's more common for kids to treat each other in kind ways or mean ways.

Discussion. Distribute handouts and read or have a student read the statistic at the top. Ask: **Does this sound right to you? How mean do you think kids are to each other?**

Read or have a student read the quoted story from the handout. Invite responses from students. Ask: **Has anything like this ever happened to you?**

Activity. Have students pair up. Ask them to think of a time they were treated in a mean way, sharing with their partner what happened and how it made them feel. Caution students not to use real names.

Next have students complete the bottom of the handout. After several minutes, have students share their experiences with the class, either reading what they wrote or talking about it. Ask them to describe how they felt when they were treated unkindly.

As students identify feelings, list them on chart paper under the heading "Being Treated Unkindly Makes People Feel . . ." After students share, ask for someone to lead in the reading of the chart.

Refer to your get-along classroom agreements and ask: **How can being kind help us create and keep the kind of get-along classroom we all want? Why is it important to constantly remember how our words and action affect others?**

Wrap-Up. On the board or on chart paper, write: "A gift we can all give each other is kindness." Say: **Giving kindness isn't just "acting nice." It's more about treating others the way we want to be treated.** Ask students to focus on kindness for the rest of the day

and to give the gift of kindness to each other as often as they can.

Follow-Up. Post the "Being Treated Unkindly Makes People Feel" chart and the statement "A gift we can all give each other is kindness." Keep referring back to each. As the day goes on, affirm kids for any kind acts you witness. Have students affirm each other, too. (You'll notice that after a while they'll do this automatically.) If you see an unkind act, ask, "Was that kind or unkind?" Sometimes just asking the question is enough to hold kids to account.

Relate the concept of kindness to characters in literature you read for the remainder of the day, or to people in articles and books used in other content areas.

Throughout this week and the next, when students go to lunch, remind them to keep giving the gift of kindness to everyone they come in contact with. When they return, take a few minutes to hear how it went. At dismissal, remind your students to continue giving the gift of kindness to their families and anyone else they cross paths with.

Note: It's possible when a student is nice to someone that the person may respond negatively. If a student reports this happening, help the student think about potential reasons behind the negative response. Could the person be angry about an unresolved problem between the two of them? If so, suggest the student talk to the person, find out what's going on, and see if they can work it out. Might the person be showing off and trying to impress friends by acting tough or be having a bad day? Or maybe the person has a completely unrelated problem. Encourage students to try not to take situations like these personally. Talk together with students about possible ways to handle specific situations, and encourage them to continue to give the gift of kindness to others.

What Real Kids Have to Say About
Being Mean

In a national survey of more than 2,100 students in grades 3–6:

73% (1,584 students) said they thought other kids are **somewhat** to **very mean.**

Here's what one student wrote:

"I'm a new kid at this school. At the beginning of the year everyone knew I was different. I am. Anyway, this is what happened: I tried to make friends with a few kids in my class, but they weren't interested. One kid really didn't like me. He whacked me on the back of the head and screamed at me. Later he did it again and yelled. The next day he did it again. I told him if he tried it again I would tell. He finally stopped. But then other kids were doing other things to me. It made starting in a new school really hard. Being the new kid is really hard. Being picked on makes it even worse."

What do YOU have to say about being mean?

How do you feel when someone is mean to you? What can we do to stamp out meanness?

_____

_____

_____

_____

_____

_____

_____

_____

Session 19: Take a Stand for Kindness

kindness • respect • empathy • personal responsibility

In Session 19, students reflect upon the importance of kindness and consider ways to be an "upstander"—someone who stands up for people who are mistreated.

Students will

- come up with words and actions they can use as upstanders who help kids who are being picked on or mistreated
- role-play a scenario in which upstanders intervene on behalf of a child who is being mistreated

Materials

- chart paper and marker
- handout: "The Courage to Be an Upstander" (page 59)

Introduction. Ask students to think of a time when someone they know was treated in a mean way. Ask for examples, cautioning kids not to use real names or other identifying factors. Suggest they start with, "Someone I know" or "Someone I saw out on the playground."

Ask students what they, personally, could have done to help. Say: **When you stand up for someone who's being mistreated, you're being an *upstander*. Sometimes it can be hard to be an upstander alone. Pairing up can give us the courage to speak up when we might otherwise be too afraid.**

Discussion. At the top of a piece of chart paper write: "Be an Upstander." Ask students what they can say or do to help someone who's being picked on. List their suggestions. Guide students to understand that upstanders are both respectful and direct, always making sure not to bully the person who's committing the hurtful act. Give the following example of an appropriate comment upstanders can use when they intervene: "Hey, it's not cool to treat someone that way." Ask for other suggestions and write them on the board.

Tell students that it's fine to address the person who's being mistreated, rather than the one who's doing the mistreating. Give the following example of a phrase they can use when they intervene: "Do you need some help? Why don't you come with us?" Ask for other suggestions and write them on the board.

Activity. Have students get into groups of four to role-play a scenario in which one child falls down on the playground and another person laughs, makes mean comments, and tries to get bystanders to join in. Have one child play the role of the person who

falls down, another play the role of the person who's being mean, and the other two act as upstanders who intervene together. Circulate as groups role-play, and give help where needed.

Afterward, have students reconvene in a circle. Ask how the role plays went. Ask: **What did the upstanders do? What did they say? Did their words and actions help? If the kid who was acting mean said nasty things to the upstanders, what did the upstanders do in response?** Emphasize that sometimes upstanders will need to say what they have to say and then walk away. Sticking around and arguing back and forth with the person who acted mean will only add fuel to the fire. It is best for upstanders to speak up assertively, then turn and walk away with the student they helped. They can say something like, "We're not going to listen to this." Discuss, and ask a few students to demonstrate. Emphasize that they should walk away tall and proud with heads held high.

(This is very important because some students think walking away shows weakness; it's critical to help them see walking away as a sign of strength. I often remind students of how Martin Luther King Jr. walked away, head held high when people hurled threats and racial epithets at him. Dr. King demonstrated the epitome of walking away tall and strong, walking away with dignity, not weakness.)

Ask students why it takes courage to be an upstander, especially when others are acting mean.

Then ask: **When you consider being an upstander for someone who's being mistreated, what might make it hard to actually do?** Briefly discuss, emphasizing that the more students practice being upstanders, the easier it becomes.

Note: Upstanders should never physically intervene. Make sure students know that if a fight is going on, or if kids are physically attacking another child, it's important to immediately seek the assistance of an adult. Stress that seeking help is not tattling or snitching. It's supporting the right every person has to be safe.

Wrap-Up. Point to the globe. Remind students that every time we are kind in word and deed, we send ripples of peace out into the world. Being an upstander is one of the highest forms of kindness we can give.

Follow-Up. Distribute the "Courage to Be an Upstander" handout and ask students to complete it on their own or with a classmate. Discuss students' handouts at the beginning of a future session.

Note: The handout asks students to learn about Miep Gies, a Dutchwoman born in 1919 who helped Anne Frank and her family stay in hiding from the Nazis during World War II.

The Courage to Be an Upstander

1. On the Internet, in an encyclopedia, or at the library, look up Miep Gies. Gies was a courageous upstander. What did Miep Gies do?

_____

_____

_____

_____

_____

_____

2. What might stand in your way of being an upstander for someone who's being mistreated? What can you do to overcome whatever might be in your way?

_____

_____

_____

_____

_____

_____

_____

_____

_____

Session 20: It's Cool to Be Kind

kindness • compassion • integrity • personal responsibility • decency

Session 20 helps students equate "coolness" with kindness, compassion, and integrity.

Students will
- learn a new way of looking at the word *cool*
- understand that being an upstander is a very high form of "coolness"
- role-play being an upstander

Materials
- *optional:* markers, colored pencils, or crayons

Preparation. On chart paper, write the following:

"**C**ompassionate
Outrageously kind
Often an upstander
Lives with integrity"

If you wish, have a student illustrate this chart ahead of time.

Introduction and Discussion. Ask: **What does being cool mean to you?** (Students may say things like being popular, having the right clothes, etc.) If someone does not suggest it, introduce the idea that there are other ways to be cool, especially when it comes to how we treat others. Ask: **Do you know someone who's cool because they're kind, fair, and treat people with respect?** Allow for responses. Say: **This form of coolness is the most powerful of all.** Give an example of someone you respect who's cool, kind, and caring.

Activity. Show students the "COOL" chart. Ask for a volunteer to read it aloud. Ask: **What does it mean to be compassionate?** Share the following definition: **Being compassionate means understanding the feelings of others and feeling what they feel in your own heart.** Clarify that feeling compassion doesn't mean feeling sorry for someone. It means feeling what the person is feeling: happiness, sadness, embarrassment, or any other emotion.

Ask students to think of a time a friend was sad and they felt their friend's sadness. (Example: A friend is grieving the loss of a beloved pet and you choke up when they tell you about it.) Ask students to think of a time when someone was extremely happy, and they felt happiness for that person.

Refer to the chart and ask: **How about outrageously kind—what does that mean?** Invite an example or share a story from your life.

Next, point to "Often an upstander." Ask students what an upstander does. Ask for an example.

Point to the final phrase, "Lives with integrity," and ask students the meaning of integrity. Share the following definition: **Showing integrity means doing the right thing, even when no one is looking.**

Wrap-Up. Direct students' attention to the chart again and ask how this definition of *cool* differs from one many people hold. Ask for a few volunteers to act out a situation where one or two people show outrageous kindness, integrity, and compassion by being upstanders for a classmate who's being picked on. Ask how standing up for others is a way of being cool.

Extension. Have students create posters using the COOL acrostic introduced in this session. Ask them to illustrate the posters with examples that reflect what the four letters stand for.

Session 21: Redefining Cool

kindness • compassion • integrity • respect

Session 21 helps kids further redefine coolness, equating it with kindness and other positive qualities. This session is a follow-up to Session 20.

Students will

- see the link between "coolness" and admirable qualities like compassion, kindness, and courage
- understand that it's never cool to be cruel, even though popular images often equate the two
- be encouraged to disavow cruelty

Materials

- "COOL" chart from Session 20 (page 60)
- photo of someone you admire and respect (a person you know, or someone of note, such as Martin Luther King Jr. or Eleanor Roosevelt)
- chart paper and marker
- drawing paper, markers, and crayons for each student
- *optional:* large mural paper

Introduction. Review the COOL chart, then show the picture you brought in of someone you admire and respect, linking the qualities this person has with words on the chart. Include other words like courage, creativity, and uniqueness if they apply. List these qualities on chart paper entitled, "The New Definition of Cool."

Discussion. Ask students to think of a cool person they respect and admire. Have them name some of the positive qualities this person possesses. Add them to the list.

Ask if it's ever cool to be cruel. Discuss, guiding students to understand that it is never cool to be cruel to another person. Write the following words on the board: "Being cruel is never cool."

Ask students to think about people in popular culture who are regarded as cool, but are actually cruel (such as certain video-game characters, violent movie heroes, etc.). Reiterate that cruelty cancels out coolness.

Encourage students to think of more qualities that can go on "The New Definition of Cool" list (intelligent, think for themselves, etc.).

Activity. Ask students to draw a picture of a cool person they admire and respect. Beneath it, have them write the following caption: "I respect _____. He/she is cool because _____."

Wrap-Up. Remind students that the qualities discussed today are what make people truly cool. End by reiterating that it's never cool to be cruel.

Follow-Up. Create a bulletin board or display with the heading "A New Definition of Cool" that incorporates the pictures students made.

Extension. Lay out mural paper, markers, and crayons. Ask a student to write "Cool Is:" in the center of the paper in large colorful letters. Then have the class colorfully write all of the qualities listed on the "New Definition of Cool" list plus others that might apply. Have them create corresponding illustrations. Somewhere on the mural should be the words, "Being cruel is never cool." When the mural is complete, hang it in the hallway. Let students know that this mural can help other kids in the school redefine what it means to be cool. Encourage them to be role models for the new definition of cool.

Session 22: Words That Hurt

compassion • kindness • conscience • respect • personal responsibility

Session 22 fosters compassion by guiding students to reflect upon the impact of hurtful words and actions

Students will
- reflect on the impact of name-calling, mean words, and hurtful gestures
- understand that hurtful words have no place in a get-along classroom

Materials
- handout: "What Real Kids Have to Say About Mean Words" (page 63)
- student journals
- *optional: The Misfits* by James Howe; poster paper and markers

Preparation. Write or type the quote from *The Misfits* (see Discussion, below) so you can display it for the class.

On chart paper, write the title *"No More Hurtful Words"* Beneath it, write: *"I pledge not to use words, jokes, or gestures that hurt others or put them down in any way."*

Introduction. Begin by asking volunteers to read aloud quotes about name-calling and put-downs from the handout. Ask students if any of the things kids said ring true for them. Discuss. Also talk about how they feel when they see other kids being put down or called names.

Discussion. Display the quoted passage, below, from *The Misfits* by James Howe, which gets right to the heart of why mean words and names hurt so much. In the book, these words are spoken by a boy who is overweight and unpopular, but still has the courage to run for president of the student council. He says these words in his speech to the whole student body:

> "Sticks and stones may break my bones, but names will never hurt me. Anybody who believes that has never been called a name. This is what I think about names. I think that names are a very small way of looking at a person. Another thing I think about names is that they do hurt. They hurt because we believe them. We think they are telling us something true about ourselves, something other people can see even if we don't."
>
> —Bobby Goodspeed, in *The Misfits* by James Howe

Ask students to respond to Bobby Goodspeed's words. Then ask: **Are there other actions or gestures that can hurt our feelings even if not a single word is spoken?** (Examples might include being laughed at or having people roll their eyes when you walk by.)

Ask: **In order to have a get-along classroom, why is it especially important that we not use hurtful words and gestures? What can we do as a class to put an end to different forms of hurtfulness?**

Activity. Allow three minutes for students to do automatic writing (see page 7) in their journals on how they've been affected by name-calling. Ask them to think about what they can do if they have the urge to say or do something hurtful to another person.

Wrap-Up. Direct students' attention to the pledge on the chart paper (and on their handouts). End by having everyone say the pledge together.

Follow-Up. Post the pledge in front of the room, referring to it daily.

Extension. Put students in pairs and pass out the poster paper and markers. Have students create posters entitled, "No More Hurtful Words or Actions." When posters are complete, have students hang them throughout the school.

What Real Kids Have to Say About
Mean words

In a national survey of more than 2,100 students in grades 3–6, kids reported the top three things that made them mad, caused conflicts, and led to fights: **being teased or made fun of, name-calling, rumors and gossip**

Here are some things kids said:

- "People call me names and make me, oh, so very mad."
- "I hate it when people call me loser, idiot, retard."
- "I cry when someone calls me names."
- "Someone called my friend stupid, slow, disgusting, and useless. No one stood up for her. It was horrible."
- "It stresses me out when people say mean things about my family."
- "Something that made me really mad was when this kid called me weird and gay. It led to a physical fight."

What do YOU have to say about mean words?

How do you feel when people make fun of you or call you names? Do you ever do this to people? If so, why?

_____

_____

_____

_____

Take the Pledge!

I pledge not to use words, jokes, or gestures that hurt others or put them down in any way.

_____
signature

Session 23: Standing Up for Those Who Are Mistreated

kindness • compassion • respect • personal responsibility • decency

Session 23 helps students think of ways they can support peers who are called names or teased in other ways and practice being upstanders.

Students will

- be guided to choose kind actions, particularly when others are being unkind
- role-play being upstanders in situations where someone is being treated with meanness or intolerance

Materials

- chart paper and marker
- handouts: "8 Ways to Be an Upstander" (page 65); "Kindness Worksheet" (page 67)

Preparation. On chart paper, write: *"I am only one; but still I am one. I cannot do everything, but still I can do something. I will not refuse to do the something I can do." —Helen Keller*

Introduction and Discussion. Ask students if they've ever chosen to be kind to someone everyone else was being mean to. Ask if they've ever been an upstander for someone who was being mistreated. Discuss, acknowledging how hard this can be.

Show the Helen Keller quote and invite a student to read it. Ask: **What is "something we can do" when someone's being called names or made fun of by others? Why does it take courage to choose to be kind when others aren't or to stick up for someone when no one else does?**

Activity. Present the following scenarios, or scenarios students suggest, and ask for volunteers to act them out. After each scenario, ask: **What kind choice could you make? What would an upstander do?**

- Brian gives the wrong answer to a question the teacher asks. Other kids start to snicker and make faces.
- Mindy comes to school wearing a shirt with a big stain on it. Her hair is all tangled and looks like it hasn't been washed in a while. A few kids hold their noses as she walks by.

- Jason has trouble reading. He stumbles over some simple words that most of the class can easily read. Someone makes a joke about Jason's reading. A few kids start to laugh.
- Jessie tends to be awkward around other kids. Sometimes she talks too loud. People find her annoying. She always ends up sitting alone at lunch.

Ask kids to list kind, caring choices that were demonstrated during the role plays. List responses on a piece of chart paper entitled, "Kind Choices We Can Make When People Are Unkind."

Distribute the "8 Ways to Be an Upstander" handout and review the ways to help people who are picked on. Encourage students to come up with other upstander actions to add to the handout.

Wrap-Up. Affirm students for acts of kindness, compassion, and good listening you observed during this session. Ask whether anyone would also like to acknowledge a classmate for any positive actions or attitudes.

Follow-Up. Have students complete the "Kindness Worksheet." Note that the worksheet will be used in Session 24.

8 ways to Be an upstander

1. Choose not to join in when people are picking on or laughing at someone.

2. Speak out against unkind words or actions.

3. Say something helpful to the person who's being picked on or laughed at.

4. Ask people who are teasing how it would feel if they were the ones being teased.

5. Ask the person who's being left out or picked on to join you in an activity.

6. Let an adult know what's going on.

7. _____

_____

_____

_____

_____

8. _____

_____

_____

_____

_____

Session 24: Thinking About Kindness

> **kindness • compassion • respect • personal responsibility • decency**
>
> Session 24 asks students to reflect on their willingness to be kind, even when others aren't.
>
> **Students will**
> - reflect on how kind they've been to others, and how others have been kind to them
> - reflect on the challenges of being kind when others aren't
> - role-play intervening when an act of unkindness takes place
>
> **Materials**
> - handout: "Kindness Worksheet" (page 67; see Preparation, below)

Preparation. Prior to this session, pass out copies of the "Kindness Worksheet" and ask students to complete it ahead of time and bring it to this session. Encourage students to answer the questions with complete honesty. Let them know you'll be completing the worksheet, too.

Introduction. Have students bring their "Kindness Worksheets" to the circle. Tell them you're going to be asking them to share their answers, and that you'll be sharing, too. Remind students not to use people's real names when they share, and to be as honest as possible.

Discussion. Discuss each question on the worksheet together:

- How kind have I been today?
- What acts of unkindness have I witnessed?
- What did I think when I saw the unkind acts taking place?
- What did I do when I saw the unkind acts taking place?
- What can I do if something like this happens again?
- What acts of kindness have I witnessed?
- What acts of kindness have I performed?

Talk together about realistic challenges kids face in trying to be kind when others aren't. For example, kids may say, "I wanted to say something when my friends were picking on somebody, but I didn't because I was afraid they might get mad at me." Or, "I'm afraid if I say something, I'll get picked on, too." Help students come up with viable solutions.

Activity. Ask for several volunteers to role-play the following scenario:

> **Jeffrey is in a wheelchair. When Nick and Kalil see him they call him names and make fun of him. They try to get their friends to join in. Nora and Chris are upset by this unkindness. They decide to be upstanders for Jeffrey.**

After the role play is complete, debrief with the class. How did the role play go? Ask Jeffrey: **How did you feel when Nora and Chris intervened?** Ask Nora and Chris: **How did you get the courage to be upstanders?** Ask Nick and Kalil: **How did it feel to have people step in when you were being mean?** Ask the class if they can picture themselves being upstanders for someone who's being mistreated.

Wrap-Up. Hold up or point to a globe. Ask students how our world might be different if people were kinder to each other. Challenge students to be kind in word and deed throughout the rest of the day.

Extension. Have students make a Kindness Commercial that they can deliver in person, in writing, over the school intercom, or on video. Arrange for them to take their commercial "on the road" to other classes and schools.

kindNess worksheet

Answer each question honestly. Use the back of this sheet or extra paper if you need more room.

How kind have I been today? _____

_____

_____

What acts of unkindness have I witnessed? (Don't use real names.)_____

_____

_____

What did I think when I saw the unkind acts taking place?_____

_____

_____

What did I do when I saw the unkind acts taking place? _____

_____

_____

What can I do if something like this happens again? _____

_____

_____

What acts of kindness have I witnessed? _____

_____

_____

What acts of kindness have I performed?_____

_____

_____

Session 25: Listening with Care and Openness

> **respect • personal responsibility**
>
> Session 25 gives students the opportunity to practice listening with an open, caring heart and mind when someone else speaks.
>
> **Students will**
> - review the elements of respectful listening
> - practice using respectful listening and paraphrasing what they hear
> - understand that listening respectfully shows care for others
>
> **Materials**
> - "Respectful Listening" chart from Session 2 (page 23)
> - handout: "How I Learned to Listen" (page 69)

Introduction. Review the "Respectful Listening" chart. Ask students how it feels when someone really cares about what they have to say, and listens with an open heart and mind. Briefly discuss. Tell your students how you feel when you are listened to in this way.

Tell students they will have the opportunity to practice listening with care and respect during this session.

Activity and Discussion. Ask for two volunteers to come to the center of the circle. Ask one student to describe to the other a birthday he or she celebrated that was especially happy. Tell the student who listens to do so with complete focus as though there's no one else in the room. When the first child finishes talking, have the child who listened paraphrase the main idea of what was said. The listener can start paraphrasing with the words "I'm hearing you say" or "It sounds like" and can also name the feeling the other person conveyed. Here's an example: "I'm hearing you say that your ninth birthday was the best ever. Your mom took you and five of your friends roller skating and then out for pizza. You sound really excited about it."

Ask the student who shared the birthday story how it felt to be listened to with such care and interest. Ask the listener: **What was it like to really care and pay attention while you listened?** Ask everyone:

What would it be like if people listened in this way more of the time?

Have a volunteer read aloud the story on the handout, from a student who realized she wasn't such a good listener and decided to become one.

Ask students to respond to the story.

Now have students pair up to practice respectful listening. Have pairs choose a Person A and Person B. Person A will ask Person B the question from the role play: "Can you tell me about a birthday you celebrated that was especially happy?" (Alternatively, Person A can ask another question you and students choose.) Person A needs to listen with total focus and then paraphrase the main idea (starting with "I'm hearing you say" or "It sounds like"). Person B can repeat anything important that might have been missed. If that happens, tell Person A to paraphrase it again. Then have partners switch roles so both get the chance to speak and listen.

Wrap-Up. Ask students how it felt to be listened to with care and respect. Ask how being good listeners might help them at school and in other parts of their lives. Discuss. Affirm students for good listening you observed.

Follow-Up. Tell students to continue practicing respectful listening throughout the day, including at home. Refer to the bottom of the handout and encourage them to notice the effect of their listening on others.

How I Learned to Listen

People used to always get annoyed with me, and I couldn't figure out why. One day it happened again—the kid who sat next to me seemed to get mad at me out of the blue. So I got up the courage to ask him why he was mad at me. He said it was because I was always interrupting. He said, "Every time I talk, you cut me off and start talking about what you want to talk about. You don't seem to care about what I have to say."

He was right. I always wanted to do the talking. I didn't have the patience to listen. The truth hurt, but I guess I needed to hear it. That night when I went home I started noticing how often I'd get the urge to interrupt. It was hard for me to stop. No wonder people kept getting mad at me!

I made up my mind I would change, but I didn't know how. So I decided to watch people who were really good listeners and see how they did it. I thought of this kid in my class named Saj and remembered how, whenever anyone talked to him, he always listened with complete interest. It felt so good to be around him.

I started paying more attention to what Saj did so I could learn from him. I noticed a couple of things right away: He was really patient and he never interrupted. He always looked right at you when you talked to him, like you were the only person in the room. His eyes never drifted over your head.

So I started trying to do what he did. I would think about how Saj listened whenever I was with anybody. I had to work hard to catch myself when I wanted to interrupt.

I'm doing a lot better now, and I have more friends. I like myself better now that I know how to truly listen.

Respectful Listening Challenge

Throughout the day try to listen as well as Saj did.
Tune in to the people you're listening to.
Show you care.

At the end of the day, think about the effect of your respectful listening on others and on yourself.

Session 26: Being Excluded

empathy • kindness • acceptance • personal responsibility • decency

Session 26 helps students see that excluding others is hurtful and encourages them to include kids who are left out.

Students will
- reflect on what it feels like to be excluded
- use reflective listening to hear and understand the feelings of another
- understand the importance of including others

Materials
- student journals
- *optional: Blubber* by Judy Blume

Introduction. Read aloud the following story a boy wrote in the Survey About Conflicts:

"Early in the school year no one I knew would play with me. I didn't know why. I asked if I could play with other people. They said no. I wandered around school looking for somebody to play with. No one would play with me. So I sat on the ground talking to myself. Fall and winter passed, still nobody."

Activity. Have students do several minutes of automatic writing in their journals about a time they were left out (or what it might have been like for the boy who wrote the story).

Ask students to pair up and read (or talk about) what they wrote. Ask them each to reflect back (paraphrase) the main idea of what the other person said. For example, "It sounds like you were really upset and lonely when your friends left you out."

Discussion. After students have shared with partners, have them reconvene in a circle. Ask them to share some of the thoughts and feelings that came up in this activity. Share your own feelings, too.

Ask: **What actions can each person take so no one in our class feels the way the boy who wrote the story felt?** Discuss. Then ask: **What can we do on the playground when someone isn't picked for a team or gets left out of games?**

Encourage students to talk about some of the real issues that come up for them when it comes to including someone they don't really want to include. As they speak, ask the class to think about viable solutions and practical actions they can take.

Wrap-Up. End by affirming students for acts of respect, kindness, compassion, and good listening you've observed. Ask if anyone in the group would like to acknowledge a classmate.

Extension. Have your students read *Blubber* by Judy Blume. In this book Linda gets picked on and excluded by Jill and other kids in the class. Things change when the tables are turned on Jill, forcing her to find out what it's like to be the one who's left out. Available in Spanish: *La ballena.*

Session 27: Put-Ups, Not Put-Downs

respect • kindness • compassion • decency

Session 27 helps students learn to use *put-ups*—sincere words of acknowledgment and encouragement.

Students will

- understand the meaning and purpose of put-ups
- contrast the impact of put-downs and put-ups
- generate ideas for put-ups they can give to each other

Materials

- chart paper and marker
- student journals
- *optional:* brown construction paper, other construction paper, scissors, crayons or markers

Preparation. On chart paper, write: *"Put-ups, not put-downs."*

Introduction and Discussion. Ask students how they feel when put-downs are used against them. Ask: **How do you feel when you see put-downs being used against others?** Discuss.

Ask students how they feel when someone says positive, complimentary, or encouraging words to them. Discuss.

Introduce the idea of *put-ups*—words and phrases that are positive, encouraging, and complimentary. Guide students to understand that a put-up should always be sincere and deserved: something the person giving it truly means and the person receiving it truly deserves, as opposed to a fake compliment. Demonstrate by giving a put-up to a student, such as: "Your listening has improved so much recently" or "I notice how you always offer a helping hand."

Ask for a few examples of put-ups from students. Encourage them to resist superficial statements like "Nice shirt," focusing instead on a person's positive actions, personal qualities, or character traits. Caution students that true put-ups are never used in a sarcastic way. Doing this turns put-ups into put-downs.

Refer to the words you wrote on the chart paper, "Put-ups, not put-downs." Ask a student to read them aloud. Ask: **Would this be a good policy for our class? Why?** Discuss.

Activity. Put students in pairs. On paper or in journals have them brainstorm as many put-ups as they can think of.

After about three minutes, have students share their put-ups with the class. List these on a chart entitled "Put-Ups." If no one comes up with "Nice try," suggest it yourself. Encourage kids to use this put-up when classmates make mistakes.

Wrap-Up. Tell your class the put-up chart will be posted as a reminder of things they can say each day. Acknowledge students for their teamwork and ideas and for any acts of kindness, compassion, and respectful listening you observed during this session.

Follow-Up. After the session, laminate the "Put-Ups" chart and post it prominently in the room. Keep using the put-ups listed on the chart, and remind students to do the same.

Extension. Have kids make a "Put-Up Tree" out of brown construction paper. Hang it on a wall in your room. Pass out leaves to every member of the class. Have them write a generic put-up (as opposed to a put-up directed at a specific person in the class) on each leaf. Hang the leaves on the tree. Refer to it often.

Session 28: Personal Put-Ups

respect • kindness • compassion • decency

In Session 28 you'll be affirming every student and giving students the opportunity to affirm each other.

Students will
- understand the importance of affirming each other with put-ups
- each receive a personal put-up from their teacher
- give personal put-ups to each other

Materials
- notecards
- student journals
- *optional:* chart paper and marker

Preparation. Prior to this session, on a notecard write a brief personal put-up for every child. It can be as simple as "You have a wonderful smile." Put the child's name at the top and sign your name at the bottom.

Introduction. Have students gather in a circle. If you haven't done Session 27, introduce the idea of put-ups now—words and phrases students can say to each other that are positive, encouraging, sincere, and complimentary. Put-ups might be about things someone's good at, talents or skills they possess, or positive qualities such as kindness, helpfulness, or a good sense of humor.

Activity. Tell students that you appreciate each and every one of them, and today you're going to give every person in the class an individual put-up. Go around the circle, affirming each student by name. Make direct eye contact with every child as you do this. Afterward, give all students their written put-ups.

Next, tell students they will now do a put-up activity with a partner. Explain that the activity is an opportunity for them to be kind and accepting toward their partner, whoever she or he might be. Have each student turn to the person he or she is sitting next to and face the person directly. Say: **Look at your partner. Think of something positive you've noticed about this person. Maybe he or she has shown kindness toward others or has a special talent. Maybe the person is helpful or caring or has a great sense of humor. Tell your partner the positive thing you've noticed about him or her. Look directly at your partner as you give your put-up.** Remind students: Even if you're not friends with each other, do your best to think of at least one positive thing you've sincerely noticed about this person. Be generous with kindness.

Discussion. After the activity, ask students how it felt to be affirmed with a put-up. Share how you felt as you watched your students giving each other put-ups. Ask students: **How does it feel when our classroom is filled with put-ups and we show care and kindness toward each other?**

Wrap-Up. Encourage students to keep affirming one another daily with personal put-ups. Tell them that put-ups contribute to the peace and kindness everyone wants to have in the classroom and in the world.

Follow-Up. Encourage students to give personal put-ups to other people in their lives, such as family members and friends. After they've given personal put-ups, suggest that they think or write in their journals about the impact of the put-ups upon the people who received them and upon their own lives.

Extension. Have each child randomly select the name of another classmate and write a letter of affirmation—a put-up letter—to the person whose name they chose. Prior to writing, take a few minutes to brainstorm with the class a general list of positive qualities people might possess. If time allows, you can also model on chart paper how to write a letter of affirmation to someone you don't know extremely well. Example:

Dear Kim,

I think you're a really caring person.

Last week when James forgot his markers you offered to share yours. And last week when Katie didn't have a snack you gave her part of yours. You are very kind, and I wish more people were like you. I'm glad you're in our class.

Sincerely, Mei Lee

Session 29: Rumors Are Unkind

respect • empathy • kindness • decency • personal responsibility

Session 29 fosters the understanding that rumors can poison the atmosphere around us. The session helps build a sense of personal responsibility when it comes to resisting spreading rumors.

Students will
- understand the negative impact of rumors
- understand the need to always avoid spreading rumors
- come up with words that can be used to deflect the spread of rumors

Materials
- colored construction paper
- chart paper and marker
- handout: "Rumors Are Unkind Reflection Sheet" (page 74)

Preparation. Prior to the session ask a pair of students to trace and cut out the outlines of one another's feet, each set on a different color construction paper.

Introduction. Compliment your students for any positive things you've observed in the area of respect, acceptance, empathy, or kindness.

Tell them that today you're going to be addressing the issue of rumors. Distribute the handout and ask a student to read the statistic it cites from the Survey About Conflicts: 64% of students listed rumors and gossip as the top cause of conflicts in their lives.

Ask students if they think rumors are a big problem. Discuss briefly.

Activity. Demonstrate the trajectory of a rumor by playing a short game of telephone. Whisper a rumor about a pretend person into the ear of the first student. Let the rumor spread through the circle.

Have the last person come to the center of the circle and stand on one set of footprints and share with the class whatever the rumor "morphed" into.

Have another student pretend to be the person the rumor was about. Have him or her come to the center of the circle and stand on the other set of footprints facing the first person.

Ask the second child to imagine what it would really be like to have had this rumor spread about him or her. How would it feel? Ask the child to look into the eyes of the other person and describe those feelings.

Ask the first child to paraphrase what was just said, reflecting back the main idea and feelings the other person conveyed. ("I'm hearing you say that . . .")

Discussion. Ask: **What do you think about the rumor we all took part in spreading?** Discuss briefly.

On the board, write, "Rumors hurt." Ask students to think about how rumors and gossip create conflicts. Discuss, reminding students not to use real names if they relate personal stories. Ask: **What do you think is the right thing to do if someone comes to you with a rumor? What can you say if someone gossips or tells you a rumor about someone else?**

Have students pair up and think of at least two responses that can be given to someone who approaches them with a rumor. Model one possible response before they begin: "I'm uncomfortable hearing this. Please don't tell me any more." Encourage students to start from "I," not "you."

After about five minutes have students share some of the responses they came up with for deflecting rumors. List them on chart paper under the title "Stamp Out Rumors."

Wrap-Up. Ask students to imagine what their classroom and school would be like if rumors were completely abolished. Call on a few students. Then ask: **Who does creating a rumor-free environment start with? Whose responsibility is it to make sure rumors don't get spread?**

Follow-Up. Have students complete the "Rumors Are Unkind Reflection Sheet," being as honest and thorough as they can. Note that the handout will be used in Session 30.

Rumors Are unkind
Reflection Sheet

In a national survey of more than 2,100 students in grades 3–6: **64% of students** surveyed listed rumors and gossip as the top cause of conflicts in their lives.

> **Here's what one student wrote:**
>
> "There were rumors being spread about what people were wearing and how they looked. This girl I know was making fun of my friend because her teeth were crooked. It kept getting worse. I don't think it's fair to make fun of people who don't look exactly like everybody else. Everyone is different."

What do YOU think about rumors?
Answer the following questions.

1. In the quoted story above, how do you think the people who were talked about felt? How would you feel if you were one of them?

_____

_____

2. Have you ever spread a rumor? What happened?

_____

_____

3. Have you ever had rumors spread about you? How did you feel?

_____

_____

4. When it comes to rumors, what can you do to be part of the solution?

_____

_____

Session 30: Stamp Out Rumors

respect • empathy • kindness • decency • personal responsibility

Session 30 empowers students to take responsibility toward stopping the rumor cycle. The session is a follow-up to Session 29.

Students will
- reflect on the impact of rumors in their lives
- role-play being an upstander for someone about whom rumors are being spread
- know how to be a part of the solution to rumors and gossip

Materials
- "Stamp Out Rumors" chart from Session 29 and markers
- completed handout: "Rumors Are Unkind Reflection Sheet" (page 74)
- *optional: Mr. Peabody's Apples* by Madonna

Preparation. Make sure students have completed the "Rumors Are Unkind Reflection Sheet" prior to this session. Have them bring their sheets to the circle at the start of the session.

Introduction. On the board write: "Rumors _____." Ask for a volunteer to come to the board and fill in the blank. (Acceptable answers can include: hurt, are unkind, make people mad, cause conflicts, etc.)

Discussion. Ask students to share the most important things they learned from the last session on rumors.

Have students take out their completed handouts. Go through each question and ask for volunteers to share their responses and reflections. Discuss.

Ask students if they've had the opportunity to apply what they learned about stopping the spread of rumors. Caution students not to use real names when sharing. Acknowledge that stopping the spread of a rumor can be harder when it's about someone you don't like. Help students recognize and understand that stopping *all* rumors is important.

Activity. Tell students they're going to have the chance to role-play a conflict that was sparked by a rumor spread about real kids. Read the following:

"**I was in a conflict when this girl emailed my friend and said all this mean stuff about us. Then she started telling the whole school all the things she'd written in the email, and these terrible rumors about us got started. It went so far that my friend and I finally went to the principal. The rumors stopped after the principal had us talk everything out.**"

Call on students to role-play the scene. Have a child play the role of one of the girls about whom the rumors were being spread. Have another child play the role of the girl who started the rumors. Have two more kids play the roles of upstanders who work to stop the rumor from going further when approached by the girl who is spreading it. Refer to the "Stamp Out Rumors" chart for examples of things the upstanders can say to stop rumors.

Wrap-Up. Refer back to the "Stamp Out Rumors" chart. Ask students if there are any other words or actions that can be added. Remind them that you'll be checking in from time to time to see how they're doing in regard to helping stop the rumor cycle.

Extensions. Have students work with a friend to make "Stamp Out Rumors" posters. Display the posters in the classroom and around the school.

Share the children's picture book *Mr. Peabody's Apples* by Madonna. Although the format of this book may seem more suited to younger students, its retelling of a three-hundred year old story depicting the impact of a single rumor has universal appeal.

Session 31: What Is Conscience?

respect • decency • integrity • compassion • personal responsibility

Session 31 helps students understand the meaning and purpose of conscience.

Students will

- understand the meaning of conscience
- reflect on why it's important to listen to the voice of one's conscience
- be better able to listen to the voice of their conscience, choosing right over wrong

Materials

- chart paper and marker
- handouts: "What Real Kids Have to Say About Struggling with Conscience" (page 77); "Doing What Is Right" (pages 80—81); "Conscience Interview" (page 78)

Preparation. On chart paper, write: *"Conscience—A feeling or knowledge of right and wrong that guides us to do what is right."*

Introduction. Write the word *conscience* on the board. Ask students what it means. Then share the definition you've prepared. Have a student read it aloud. Then paraphrase, saying: **Conscience is a kind of goodness inside each of us that can guide us to do the right thing.**

Discussion. Distribute copies of the "What Real Kids Have to Say About Struggling with Conscience" handouts and read or have a student read the real story from the Survey About Conflicts. Ask: **What did this boy's conscience first guide him to do? Why didn't he continue to follow his conscience? How did the boy feel at the end of the story?**

Ask students: **How does it feel to ignore what the goodness inside us guides us to do?** Discuss.

Ask students if there's a different way the boy who wrote the story could have handled this situation. Then ask: **Were the boy's friends in the story really true friends? Why or why not?** Guide students to understand that the boy who wrote the story ignored the voice of his conscience for the sake of kids whose actions were not those of true friends.

Activity. Ask students to pair up. Have them think of a time they struggled with conscience, describing to partners what happened and how they felt. Ask students to write about their experiences on the handouts or in their journals. After about five minutes, have students reconvene in a circle.

Ask students to share their experiences, either reading what they wrote or talking about it. Caution them not to use real names.

Wrap-Up. Ask students: **How does it feel to follow your conscience, even when it's a hard thing to do?** Emphasize that when people listen to the voice of their conscience, they usually end up feeling at peace with themselves, even if they had to make a hard choice. Encourage students to notice what their conscience is telling them in the days ahead.

Follow-Up. Have students complete the "Doing What Is Right" handout. Note that the worksheet will be used in Session 32.

Extension. Distribute the "Conscience Interview" handout and encourage students to interview someone and discuss the quote about conscience. At the beginning of the next session you conduct, invite students to share some of the things they learned from their interviews about conscience.

What Real Kids Have to Say About
Struggling with Conscience

In a national survey of more than 2,100 students in grades 3–6, here is what one student wrote:

"There is this one kid *everyone* picks on but me. Sometimes I would defend him, but when I did my friends called me weird. They stopped accepting me. This kid now thinks he's my best friend and bugs me all the time.

"My friends finally started to accept me again. Now I pretend to tease the other kid so I don't lose all my friends again. But I feel bad because I really feel sorry for him."

Write about a time you
struggled with your conscience:

_____

_____

_____

_____

_____

_____

_____

_____

_____

Conscience Interview

"Each person has inside a basic decency and goodness. If he listens to it and acts on it, he is giving a great deal of what it is the world needs most. It is not complicated but it takes courage. It takes courage for a person to listen to his own good." —Pablo Casals

1. **Interview someone you trust and respect.** Read the Pablo Casals quote to the person. Ask him or her these questions:

   • What does the quote mean to you?

   • Do you know someone who listened to his or her own goodness and acted on it, even though other people did not? What happened?

   • Do you think it takes courage to follow your conscience? Why?

2. **After your interview,** write about something you learned from the person you interviewed:

   _____

   _____

   _____

   _____

   _____

   _____

   _____

   _____

   _____

   _____

   _____

Session 32: Listening to the Voice of Your Conscience

respect • decency • integrity • personal responsibility

Session 32 gives students the opportunity to reflect on the importance of living by one's conscience.

Students will

- understand that the time is always right to do what's right
- be guided to take responsibility for choosing between right and wrong
- understand that they can make amends if they have done something wrong

Materials

- chart paper and marker
- handout: "Doing What Is Right" (pages 80–81; see Preparation, below)

Preparation. Prior to this session pass out copies of the "Doing What Is Right" handout and ask students to complete it ahead of time and bring it to this session.

Introduction. Write the word *conscience* on the board. Review the meaning of it—a feeling or knowledge of right and wrong that guides us to do what is right. Have students take out their completed "Doing What Is Right" handouts and ask a volunteer to read the Martin Luther King Jr. quote at the top: "The time is always right to do what is right."

Discussion and Activity. Ask students what the quote means to them. Discuss.

Go over the questions on the handout one by one, sharing and discussing students' ideas and responses.

Students may struggle with question 6. Some kids think telling an adult is "snitching"—and that this violates a code of ethics. Help them see that seeking the aid of an adult when someone is being harmed, especially when other measures have failed, can keep someone from being hurt and may prevent other bullying situations.

Note: You will want to continue to address the complex issues that students face regarding bullying. Many of the sessions that remain in Part 2 will be helpful to you, especially those in the Dealing with Bullying section, pages 217–260.

Ask: **How do you feel when you don't follow your conscience?** Discuss. Point out that everyone makes wrong decisions at times, and that we each can recognize our mistakes and work to do better next time.

Ask: **What can you do if you choose not to follow your conscience, and then feel guilty about it afterward?** Include in your discussion the importance of taking responsibility and apologizing if necessary. Ask students to think of a way they could make *amends*—do something to make things better—for something they did in the past.

Wrap-Up. Hold up or point to a globe. Say: **Having a more peaceful world depends on people of conscience doing the right thing. What do you think the world would be like if everyone listened to the voice of their conscience?**

Doing What IS Right

"The time is always right to do what is right." —Martin Luther King Jr.

1. Think of a book or movie where a person had to choose between doing what was right and what was wrong. What did the person do? Describe what happened.

_____

_____

_____

2. What did you think about the decision this person made?

_____

_____

_____

3. Think of a time you were faced with a decision between right and wrong. (For example: to tell the truth or not tell the truth, or to admit a mistake or pretend nothing happened.) What happened? What did you decide to do?

_____

_____

_____

Doing What Is Right (continued)

4. How did you feel about the decision you made?

_____

_____

_____

_____

5. Why do you think it's important to listen to your conscience and follow it?

_____

_____

_____

_____

6. If you see someone being bullied or picked on, what do you think is the right thing to do? How can your conscience help you do the right thing?

_____

_____

_____

_____

Managing Anger

Teaching kids how to control their anger is an important way to help prevent bullying. Sometimes incidences of bullying are triggered by angry interchanges and resentful feelings that follow. By providing kids with real-life tools to use when anger strikes, we set the stage for more positive relationships while diminishing seeds of resentment that might otherwise germinate into full-blown bullying.

This section provides step-by-step anger management strategies that are easy to use, highly effective, and become more and more natural for kids to apply each time they practice them. Breathing techniques, visualizations, and role plays are among the many activities you'll find in this section. You'll also find out how to help kids keep from getting physical when they're angry. Stop, Breathe, Chill (introduced in Session 9) is students' most powerful anger management strategy. Re-read that session for a step-by-step refresher before you begin the Managing Anger section.

Note: The sessions follow a sequence. Even if you don't use every session, conduct the ones you choose to do in the order they are presented.

33. Things That Make Us Mad
34. It's Okay to Be Angry, But Not to Be Cruel
35. Responding to Anger
36. Peaceful Place Visualization
37. Using Stop, Breathe, Chill in Real-Life Situations
38. Calming Statements
39. Picture the Cake, Blow Out the Candles (10-Minute Time Cruncher)
40. Other Ways to Chill Out
41. See Yourself Getting Calmer (10-Minute Time Cruncher)
42. Things We Do When We Get Angry
43. Breathe Out/Breathe In (10-Minute Time Cruncher)
44. How Are We Doing? (Review)
45. Getting Past Reacting
46. Don't Get Physical
47. Peace Shield
48. Using "Think-Alouds" (10-Minute Time Cruncher)
49. Anger Management Role Play
50. Getting Help with Anger (10-Minute Time Cruncher)

Session 33: Things That Make Us Mad

personal responsibility • anger management • self-control

Session 33 builds students' awareness of their anger triggers and guides them to use calming strategies that will help them "unhook" from negative reactions.

Students will

- understand that anger is a natural emotion that everyone feels at times
- explore common anger triggers in kids
- review Stop, Breathe, Chill as a way of constructively responding to anger

Materials

- handout: "What Real Kids Have to Say About Anger Triggers" (pages 85–86)
- *optional:* student journals

Introduction. Ask students to raise their hands if they ever get angry. Raise yours, too. Ask kids what makes them angry. Discuss briefly, making sure they understand that anger is a natural emotion we all feel from time to time.

Say: **Even though anger in itself isn't a bad thing, sometimes people make bad or harmful choices when they get mad. What are some negative choices people make when they get angry?** (hitting, yelling, name-calling, etc.)

Then continue: **The good news is that it's possible to react more calmly when we're angry and to be more in control of the choices we make. How might your life be better if you could avoid making negative, hurtful choices when you're angry?** Discuss.

Ask students to suggest a few positive choices they can make in the face of anger (deep breathing, walking away, telling themselves it's not worth it to lash out, etc.).

Discussion. Say: **Being aware of what makes us angry is the first step in gaining more control over how we react.** Share something that makes you really angry. Then ask: **What makes you really angry?** Allow for a couple responses.

Distribute the handouts and read or have a student read the top three anger triggers students reported in the Survey About Conflicts. Ask: **What does** *anger trigger* **mean? Can you relate to boys' and girls' top three anger triggers? What are some other anger triggers?**

Go around the circle having students, one at a time, read aloud the quotes about anger triggers. Then ask: **Which of these quotes do you identify with most?** Allow a few students to respond. Discuss.

Put students in pairs and give them a few minutes to share about things that make them really angry, describing how they feel when they get mad. Afterward, have students reconvene in the large circle. Ask them to look at the handout and find the part that can help them calm down when their anger is triggered (Stop, Breathe, Chill). Tell students they'll be getting lots of practice using this and other calming strategies in future sessions.

Wrap-Up. Reiterate that anger is a natural emotion, one we all have, and there are ways we can get in better control of our reactions when anger is triggered. Remind students to use Stop, Breathe, Chill the next time they feel angry. Say: **Remember, the minute you feel the anger in your body and mind, hold up a big red stop sign in your head and silently say "Stop." Then take a few slow, deep abdominal breaths. Let's take some now.** (Breathe together). **Then do something else to help yourself chill out. What might that be?**

Follow-Up. Let students know you'll be checking in with them about how they're using Stop, Breathe, Chill in real life. When you check in with your students, tell them how you're using it, too.

Extension. In journals, have students write the words "Anger Bin" at the top of a page. Tell them to write out or draw their anger in the "Anger Bin" next time they feel it, describing or showing what happened and how they reacted. Remind them that whatever they record is just for them and not to be shared with peers. Have them also write about or draw what they can do to calm down.

What Real Kids Have to Say About
Anger Triggers

In a national survey of more than 2,100 students in grades 3–6, kids answered a question about what makes them angry. Here are some things they said:

It makes me angry when people . . .

- talk behind my back
- say I did something that I didn't do
- hit me and pick on me because of my size
- call me weak and say no one likes me
- make fun of me because I don't have a mom
- hurt others for no reason
- pick on younger kids
- make me feel like I'm invisible
- talk to me but won't listen
- make threats
- judge me 'cause I'm different
- are racist when they talk about people's families
- tease me and say I'm poor and have moldy food
- throw stuff at me and flip my tray over
- lie, write notes, and tell people not to be my friend
- exclude me, steal stuff from me, and make fun of me
- say my name wrong on purpose
- say I'm ugly and then say, "Kidding!" and laugh
- make little jokes that are funny to them and not to me
- think they're way better than someone else

What Real Kids Have to Say About Anger Triggers (continued)

Here are the top 3 anger triggers from boys and girls who took the survey:

Top 3 Anger Triggers for Boys

1. name-calling
2. being made fun of
3. hitting, kicking, and pushing

Top 3 Anger Triggers for Girls

1. name-calling
2. being made fun of
3. gossiping

When you feel yourself getting angry, here's how to get in better control of your reactions:

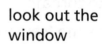

1. **Stop.** Picture a big red stop sign, and silently tell yourself to STOP.

2. **Breathe.** Take some slow deep breaths. Feel the oxygen calming your body and mind.

3. **Chill.** Do something that helps you calm down. You might:

go for a walk	play an instrument	look out the window
talk with a friend	drink some water	
play a game	exercise	draw

What else can you do to help yourself chill out?

Session 34: It's Okay to Be Angry, But Not to Be Cruel

compassion • decency • anger management • self-control

Session 34 helps students reflect on the impact of cruel words and actions and avoid using them when angry.

Students will

- gain greater sensitivity toward the feelings of others
- understand that using cruel words and gestures is never okay

Materials

- colored construction paper
- chart paper and marker
- handout: "What Real Kids Have to Say About Angry Reactions" (page 89)
- plain lined paper for brainstorming

Preparation. Prior to the session ask a pair of students to trace and cut out the outlines of one another's feet, each set on a different color construction paper. Also, on chart paper, write the following: *"I have the right to feel angry, but that doesn't give me the right to be cruel."*

Introduction. Gather students in a circle. Share the statement you've written and ask a student to read it aloud. Ask: **What does this statement mean to you?**

Say: **Anger is a natural emotion all people feel. However, using mean words or hurting others when we're angry is never okay.** Tell students how it makes you feel as a teacher when you see kids saying or doing mean things to each other. Ask students how they feel when they observe cruel acts.

Discussion. Distribute the handouts and read or have a student read the quotes from kids who responded to the Survey About Conflicts. Invite comments from students about how it feels to be treated meanly by someone who is angry.

Pass out the plain paper. Say: **We've been talking out how it feels to be hurt by the anger of others. Think about times *you* directed cruel words or actions toward someone you were mad at.**

Have students take their plain paper to a private spot. Give them about two minutes to individually brainstorm a list of hurtful words or gestures they or others have used in anger. Let students know that each list is confidential. No one will see it but them.

At the end of two minutes ask students to fold up their lists put them on or in their desks.

Have students return to the circle. Ask them how it felt to remember these hurtful words and actions. Discuss, cautioning students not to use real names.

Activity. Tell students they're now going to have an opportunity to look more closely at the impact of mean words. Place the sets of footprints in the middle of the circle so students standing on them will face one another. Ask for two volunteers, Student A and Student B. Have them stand on the footprints facing each other.

Then say: **Student A, I want you to "put yourself in the shoes" of someone who says hurtful things when she or he gets mad. While you're on the footprints, you will *be* that person.**

Student B, your role is to "put yourself in the shoes" of someone who takes things to heart and gets hurt easily.

Then say to Student A: **Imagine Student B accidentally bumped into you when you were lining up. You're mad! React to Student B with mean words.**

After hearing the words, ask Student B to describe for the class how these words made him or her feel.

If time allows, repeat the process with two more students, having each put themselves in the shoes of someone who reacts quickly with mean words and someone who feels hurt or offended as a result. Use scenarios similar to these, or invite students to suggest scenarios:

- Student B tries to pass a football to a friend, but the ball goes too far and hits Student A. Student A shouts at Student B, telling the student that he/she is terrible at football and every other sport.

- Student B is wearing a sweater that is out of style. Student A says mean things that embarrass Student B in front of other people.

With each role play, ask Student B how it felt to have mean words directed at him or her. If a child says "I don't care," ask the class how they would feel if they were the recipient of these words. Talk about how you would feel, too.

Talk about how sometimes what might seem like "no big deal" to one person can actually be very hurtful to another person.

Wrap-Up. Conclude the activity by having students do a "No More Mean Words and Actions" ritual.

Have them take the lists they wrote at the beginning of the session, tear them up into small pieces, and throw them away. As they throw away the pieces, ask everyone to make a silent promise not to use cruel words or actions, even when they're really mad. Remind them to use Stop, Breathe, Chill and other calming strategies when anger rises up.

Extension. Set a Daylong Challenge: Ask the class to have a day without mean words, including at home. Remind them to take a few slow deep breaths if they feel like they're going to react to someone in a hurtful way.

What Real Kids Have to Say About
Angry Reactions

In a national survey of more than 2,100 students in grades 3–6, kids wrote about negative ways they deal with anger. Here are some things they wrote:

> - "I have anger issues. Sometimes I'm able to walk away, but sometimes I yell back and say mean things even though I know I shouldn't."
> - "Sometimes I get so mad I smack people and call them jerks."
> - "I want to know how to get along better, cause sometimes I can be kind of mean. Sometimes I'll push or hit. I want to stop doing these things. Once I get into high school I could get into serious trouble."

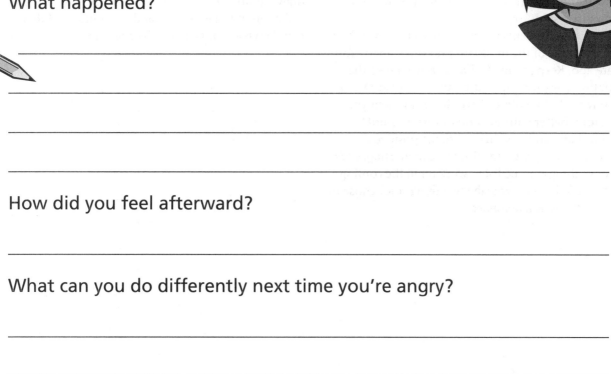

Write about a time you hurt someone (with words or actions) when you were angry.

What happened?

_____

_____

_____

_____

How did you feel afterward?

_____

What can you do differently next time you're angry?

_____

_____

Session 35: Responding to Anger

respect • anger management • self-control • personal responsibility

Session 35 encourages students to think about how they behave when they're angry and identify positive choices they can make in response to anger.

Students will
- complete a checklist of their positive and negative responses to anger
- evaluate whether responses they chose result in positive or negative outcomes
- identify healthy responses to anger they can work on developing

Materials
- handout: "When I Get Mad" (page 91)
- student journals

Introduction. Give each student a handout and go over it briefly. Then ask students to mark all of the responses to anger that they commonly have. If something they do isn't on the list, have them write it in at the bottom. Give students a few minutes to complete this.

Activity and Discussion. Have students get into pairs and talk about the items they checked off. After each item, have them ask themselves the question: **Did this choice make the situation get better or worse?** (Write the question on the board.) Have them discuss this together.

Next, have students reconvene in a circle. Ask them to share some of the things they do when angry. You share, too. Keep asking: **Did this choice make the situation (or problem) get better or worse? Did it help the relationship or harm it? Did it help you get along better with the other person or not?**

Now have students circle all of the positive responses to anger on the list. Have them choose two positive things on the list to work on in the coming weeks. Ask them to write the two things they chose in their journals as a reminder.

Wrap-Up. Go around the circle and have each student share one thing they plan to work on. Tell them what you plan to work on. Remind them that you'll be checking in with them about this during the week. Ask how doing this can help create a more peaceful classroom and world.

Extension. Ask students to remember a time they reacted to anger in a negative way. Tell them to think about what they did to make a situation between them and another person worse. Have them write or draw a journal entry about what happened, how they feel about it today, and what they would do if they could go back and change their reaction.

when I Get mad

When I get mad at someone, I usually . . .

- ❏ push, hit, punch, or kick the person
- ❏ walk away from the situation to cool off
- ❏ use put-downs or name-calling
- ❏ take slow, deep breaths
- ❏ yell
- ❏ curse
- ❏ roll my eyes or give a nasty look
- ❏ do something positive that helps me calm down
- ❏ gossip about the other person
- ❏ get even with the person
- ❏ refuse to talk to the other person
- ❏ discuss the problem with a trusted adult

- ❏ ask the person to stop doing whatever is making me angry
- ❏ use Stop, Breathe, Chill
- ❏ stuff my feelings down and try to ignore them
- ❏ take out my anger on someone else
- ❏ ignore the person
- ❏ tattle
- ❏ talk to the person respectfully about how I feel
- ❏ _____ _____
- ❏ _____ _____
- ❏ _____ _____

Think About It: Which of the checked items make the situation better?

Which work best? _____

_____

Two things I plan to work on:

1. _____

_____

2. _____

_____

Session 36: Peaceful Place Visualization

calming • personal responsibility

Session 36 introduces a visualization tool students can use to calm themselves when they feel angry, stressed, frightened, or upset. This calming technique can also help students relax and refocus before tests and during transition times.

Students will
- reflect on a place they've been where they felt calm and at peace
- learn a tool for calmness they can use daily, now and for the rest of their lives

Materials
- art and writing materials including paper, pencils, and markers
- handout: "Peaceful Place Visualization Script" (page 93)

Introduction. Tell students that today they'll be learning a very powerful way to feel calm inside, no matter what's happening on the outside.

Ask students to think of a place they've been where they felt happy, peaceful, relaxed, and safe. It can be a place close to home or far away. It might be a place from the past, like their grandmother's kitchen when they were little. (If students have difficulty coming up with a peaceful place, suggest they focus on a beach, park, or other natural setting.)

Call on students to share about their peaceful places. Share about yours. Make sure everyone in the class has come up with a peaceful place before going on with the activity.

Activity. Have students sit comfortably on the floor or in a chair; some kids may prefer to lie down on the floor. Tell students it's very important that they're completely silent during this activity. Ask them to close their eyes, cover them, or look down and take several slow, deep abdominal breaths.

Then read aloud the "Peaceful Place Visualization Script" (page 93), using a steady, calm voice.

When you finish reading the script, have students open their eyes. Ask how they feel. Allow a few students to share about the relaxing effect this visualization exercise had for them.

Assure any students who had difficulty envisioning their peaceful place that it often gets easier with practice. Let everyone know that doing this visualization on a regular basis can help them feel calmer and more relaxed, including before tests and other stressful events.

Ask students to take a few minutes to draw or write about their peaceful place. Encourage them to include as much vivid detail as possible. Drawing or writing in detail about their peaceful place will help them return to the vision of it whenever they need calmness.

Wrap-Up. Ask students to hang the drawing or story of their peaceful place in a spot where they'll see it every day. This can serve as a reminder of the peaceful place they hold inside. Their work can be displayed either in school or at home. Distribute the handout so students can use it at home.

Extensions. Suggest that students record their own voices reading the "Peaceful Place Visualization Script." Tell them they can listen to it before going to bed at night or at any time they feel stressed, upset, angry, or fearful.

Have students write a poem or haiku describing their Peaceful Place.

Peaceful Place Visualization Script

Close your eyes and breathe slowly and deeply. As you breathe, imagine your mind is a blank movie screen. Your screen is the color blue, a bright, soothing shade of blue, like the sky on a clear spring day. Allow this image to fill your mind completely.

Now project onto your screen an image of your peaceful place, a place you've been where you've felt happy, relaxed, peaceful, and safe. Let this peaceful place completely fill the screen of your mind. Allow it to grow so large that the blue screen melts away and all that's left is the vision of your peaceful place.

Now, step into your peaceful place. Imagine being there right now. Look around and notice the colors. Now listen to the sounds of your peaceful place. *(Pause.)*

Breathe deeply and inhale the scent of your peaceful place. Allow it to fill your body, brain, arms, and legs. *(Pause.)*

Allow the good feelings you had when you were last in this peaceful place to completely fill your heart and spread out into every cell, the way rays of the sun give warmth to everything they touch.

If any distracting thoughts come up, put them on a cloud, and let the cloud float them away. Then gently bring your focus back to your peaceful place and let the good feelings soak into every part of you.

Now feel yourself becoming fully at ease in own your skin. Let yourself be filled with a sense of well-being, confidence, peace, and happiness. Keep breathing slowly and deeply. *(Pause.)*

When you open your eyes, you will bring with you a complete sense of calmness, relaxation, and happiness. Now open your eyes and take these good feelings with you wherever you go throughout the rest of the day.

Session 37: Using Stop, Breathe, Chill in Real-Life Situations

> **respect • anger management • conflict resolution • self-control**
>
> Session 37 reinforces the core skill of Stop, Breathe, Chill and gives students an opportunity to mentally rehearse applying it to an actual situation.
>
> **Students will**
> - review how stopping and breathing helps them think more clearly and respond with better judgment when they are angry
> - review and practice the Stop, Breathe, Chill technique and visualize themselves using it in a real-life situation
>
> **Materials**
> - sign from Session 34: *"I have the right to feel angry, but that doesn't give me the right to be cruel"* (see page 87)
> - "Stop, Breathe, Chill" sign from Session 9 (see page 39)
> - handout: "How Stop, Breathe, Chill Can Help" (page 96)
> - student journals

Introduction. Recognize students for any kind acts or words you have observed in recent days; also affirm acts of self-control in the face of anger.

Refer to the sign, "I have the right to feel angry, but that doesn't give me the right to be cruel." Ask why it's important to resist using cruel words when we get angry (or at any other time).

Share with the class these words from real students:

"**My classmate made a face at me and I tried to control my anger, but I couldn't hold it in any longer. So I made a face back at her.**"

"**I was in a conflict with my brother. He kept coming into my room without asking. The last time he did it I felt the anger swell up inside me. I told him to get out but he shook his head no. My anger started flowing out all over.**"*

Ask students if they can identify with either of the statements. Briefly discuss.

Ask students how they've been using Stop, Breathe, Chill as a way to control their anger. Respond to comments and questions. Also tell students how you've used this strategy.

Note: Don't be surprised if someone says, "I used Stop, Breathe, Chill, but I still felt angry." Explain that Stop, Breathe, Chill doesn't completely erase angry feelings. What it does is help us gain greater control over our reactions, even when we still have some anger inside. The angry feelings might be there for a while, buy they'll have less control over us.

Say: **Using Stop, Breathe, Chill actually changes the way our brains work. Let's review.** Ask students what part of the brain angry reactions come from (the reptilian brain). Have them point to the base of the skull.

Ask what part of the brain Stop, Breathe, Chill takes them to (the front of the brain—the neocortex).

Ask why the front of the brain is the place of true power. (It's the part that allows us to think straight and choose a response instead of just reacting.)

Activity. Say: **The more we practice Stop, Breathe, Chill, the easier it is to use in real life.** Tell students they're going to be doing a visualization that will give them practice now. Tell them that visualization is the same technique many Olympic athletes use to help themselves accomplish their goals. Have students close their eyes, or cover them and look down, and picture a time they got mad. Say: **Recall where the anger landed in your body. Recall your angry thoughts. Recall what you actually did.** Give students a minute or so to do this.

Say: **Now let's replay the angry event. This time, you'll see yourself handle it with more control. Picture what happened that made you angry. Now imagine a big red stop sign, and silently tell yourself to STOP so you don't say or do something you'll regret.** (Pause.) **Take some slow, deep abdominal breaths.** (Breathe with students.) **Feel your body and mind calming down.** (Pause.)

---

* Quotes attributed to real students come from responses to the Survey About Conflicts conducted by the author and publisher. See pages 1 and 279–281 for further information.

Picture yourself doing something else that will help you chill out a little more, like walking away or getting a drink of water. (Pause.)

Now, imagine yourself feeling more in control. Decide what you're going to do next. Do you want to work things out with the person you're mad at? Or do you want to just let the problem go? Whatever you choose, picture yourself doing it. (Pause.) **See yourself feeling in control of yourself and proud of the choice you made.**

Have students open their eyes and share what they envisioned. If any students say they weren't able to visualize what you asked them to, let them know that visualization gets easier with practice.

Wrap-Up. Acknowledge the class for the important work they did today. Ask how the world could change if people all over learned how to control their anger better. Let them know they are part of helping this happen.

Follow-Up. Have students read and discuss with a family member the "How Stop, Breathe, Chill Can Help" handout. Ask them to write or draw in their journals an example of how they are applying Stop, Breathe, Chill in their lives.

How Stop, Breathe, Chill Can Help
Ideas from Real Kids

Here are some things students have to say about how using Stop, Breathe, Chill helps them:

"I was playing basketball and a player from the other team shoved me. I was going to shove her back, but I *thought about the consequences* and decided to stop, breathe, and chill instead. I told myself this wasn't worth fighting over. And it wasn't. *I was able to help my team win instead of getting a foul for fighting.*"

"Stop, Breathe, Chill helped me with my annoying sister. She started getting on my nerves the other day and *I almost called her a name. But then I stopped, took some breaths, and reminded myself that she's only four.*"

"I used Stop, Breathe, Chill with my mother. She was yelling at me to clean my room, and instead of talking back, I stopped and breathed. Then I told myself to just do it. I was going to have to do it anyway. *I avoided a fight with my mom and I didn't end up getting punished.*"

"I was in the cafeteria when someone rolled their eyes at me. Usually I would roll my eyes back at them. This time I reminded myself to stop and breathe. Then *I chilled out by saying the name of my dog. That always calms me down.* I was able to just walk away and forget about it then, instead of getting into a big thing."

"In touch football, this kid pushed me and yanked the ball out of my hand. I was ready to fight him for it, but I knew I'd get in trouble for that. So *I stopped and breathed and decided to play even harder and better. I ended up scoring three touchdowns.*"

"Knowing how to stop, breathe, and chill really helps me handle my anger. I can control myself better now. *Before, I would do things when I got mad that I'd feel guilty about.* Sometimes I would get punished. Now I can calm myself down and make a better choice. *I feel better about myself now.*"

Session 38: Calming Statements

In Session 38, students learn how calming statements can give them greater control over angry reactions.

Students will

- recognize that angry thoughts fuel angry feelings
- understand that calming thoughts can help diminish angry reactions
- come up with a personal calming statement to help them chill out whenever they feel angry

Materials

- "Stop, Breathe, Chill" sign from Session 9 (see page 39)
- handout: "Chill Out with Calming Statements" (pages 98–99)
- student journals

Introduction. Refer to the "Stop, Breathe, Chill" sign. Lead students in taking three slow, deep abdominal breaths.

Briefly review the way stopping and breathing helps people move to the place of power in the brain. Ask students: **Which part of the brain do angry reactions come from?** (The reptilian brain; point to the base of the skull.) **Which part of the brain helps us think straight and choose a response?** (The neocortex.) **Which part of the brain is our place of power?** (The neocortex; point to the front of the skull.) **How can we get out of our reptilian brain into the front of the brain?** (By stopping, breathing, and chilling.)

Tell students that they are now going to learn a very important skill for chilling out—a skill that will help them move out of the reptilian brain and into the front of the brain when they're angry.

Activity. Distribute the handout. Ask seven volunteers to stand and read aloud each of the seven paragraphs of the handout. Encourage them to read in the most expressive way possible, as though making a public service announcement on the radio or YouTube.

Afterward, invite questions and discuss what was just read. You might ask: **Have you noticed that when your anger is triggered, your mind is often filled with angry thoughts? How do these angry thoughts make you feel? Have you ever tried using a calming statement to help yourself calm down? How did that work for you?** Give an example of your own and ask for others.

Now have students work in pairs to come up with a personal calming statement that they write in their journals. After several minutes, go around the circle and have each student say aloud his or her calming statement.

Wrap-Up. Encourage students to use their calming statement every time they feel angry or annoyed, including at home. Tell them you'll be using yours and you'll be checking in with them to see how it went.

Follow-Up. The next time the class meets, check in with students to ask how it's going for them to use calming statements.

Extension. Have students create their own public service announcements (PSAs) or skits to teach other students about calming statements and how they can help people chill when they feel angry. Arrange for them to share the PSAs during the morning school announcements or to present their skits to another class.

Chill Out with Calming Statements

One of the main things that fuels anger is the thoughts we think: "I can't stand that kid!" "I'm ready to blow my top!" Thoughts like these make us even madder. Sure, angry thoughts are going to pop into your head when you feel mad. But if you keep focusing on them, you're going to end up feeling more and more angry and out of control.

When your mind is full of angry thoughts, there's a helpful way you can chill out: Use a calming statement. Calming statements are words you silently say in your brain that help you cool down. A calming statement helps put you back in control of *you.* Every time you think or say a calming statement to yourself, the place of power in your brain will start to take over and help you feel calmer. You'll be better able to deal with the other person when you're in control of yourself.

Here's an example of a calming statement: "I can handle this." It's simple. It's positive. And when you say it to yourself, it makes you feel like you really can handle whatever you're faced with. A calming statement can also be a line from a song or poem. It can be a simple phrase that reminds you of a peaceful place, like "Ocean waves."

Calming statements are so powerful because they reprogram your brain. It's like your brain is a computer and the calming statement is the command you're giving it. Even if you don't believe your calming statement right away, it will still work. Really! Say it like you mean it, and trust your brain to do its job. The more you use your calming statement, the more you'll start to actually feel calm.

Chill Out with Calming Statements (continued)

Here are some other calming statements you might want to use:

"I can keep my cool."

"I am in control."

"I have the power to stay calm."

"Peace now."

"Chill."

Now it's your turn. Come up with your own personal calming statement. You can choose one of the statements from this handout or make up your own. Remember, keep it short and positive. Choose something that makes you feel good when you say it.

Write your calming statement in your journal and on a separate piece of paper, too. That way you can hang it in a place where you can read it every day. Repeat it often. Picture it coming true. After a while, it will! Whenever you're faced with anger, your calming statement will help you stay in control.

Session 39: Picture the Cake, Blow Out the Candles (10-Minute Time Cruncher)

self-control • calming • anger management

Session 39 gives students a fun tool they can use to calm down when they feel angry or upset.

Students will
- learn a simple, effective visualization and breathing exercise

Materials
- *optional:* drawing paper and markers

Introduction. Tell students that you're going to give them a fun way to calm themselves called "Picture the cake, blow out the candles."

Activity. Say: Pretend that your birthday is today, and it's the most wonderful birthday ever. Everything is exactly how you want it to be, including the cake.

Ask for volunteers to briefly share about the cake they imagine.

Say: Now close your eyes and picture your cake. Picture the icing, the filling, and any special decorations you would like. (Pause.) Put your candles on the cake. Light them. Take a deep breath and blow out the candles.

Say: Okay, now let's do it again. Take a deep breath, blow out the candles.

Say: One last time . . . Take a deep breath, blow out the candles. Now open your eyes.

Wrap-Up. After the activity, ask students how they feel. Kids often really enjoy this activity and may be smiling. Encourage them to "Picture the cake, blow out the candles" anytime they feel angry, stressed, or upset.

Extension. Have students draw their ideal birthday cake. Encourage them to hang their pictures in their rooms at home to remind themselves to breathe deep and blow out the air as a way of calming themselves.

Session 40: Other Ways to Chill Out

calming • anger management • self-control

Session 40 reinforces the core skill of Stop, Breathe, Chill and introduces students to three modes of self-calming, so they will have an expanded range of ideas to call upon when they're angry, stressed, or upset.

Students will
- learn the three modes of chilling out: physical, quiet and calm, or distraction
- brainstorm ways to chill using all three approaches
- individually identify specific ways they can calm themselves when angry

Materials
- "Stop, Breathe, Chill" sign from Session 9 (see page 39)
- chart paper and marker
- student journals
- *optional:* drawing materials

Preparation. On the board or chart paper, write the following quote: *"The best remedy for a short temper is a long walk."* —Jacqueline Schiff

Introduction. Refer to the "Stop, Breathe, Chill" sign. Lead students in taking three slow, deep abdominal breaths. Then ask students how it's been going for them to use Stop, Breathe, Chill and calming statements in school, at home, or outside. Discuss. Share your own story, including challenges you've faced.

Discussion. At the top of the chart paper, write "Ways to Chill." Ask students: **What are some ways you chill out when you feel angry?** Discuss briefly, listing ideas on the chart paper. Then say: **There are lots of ways to chill out. Some people prefer to do something physical.** Show the Jacqueline Schiff quote and ask students if taking a walk works for them. Invite more examples of physical activity that can help people chill out; add these to the chart.

Say: **Another way to chill out is by finding something calm and quiet to do, like going to a quiet spot and reading. What are some other calm, quiet ways to chill out?** Elicit more suggestions, such as listening to music or writing in a journal. Add them to the "Ways to Chill" chart.

Continue: **A third way to chill out is to distract yourself by channeling your energy into something completely different. It's kind of like changing the channel on the TV.** Invite examples of distraction activities, such as cleaning one's room, making or building something, or helping someone. List more distraction ideas on the chart.

Activity. Have students pair up and brainstorm at least six new ways they can chill out when angry, upset, or stressed at school or home.

After about three minutes, ask students what they came up with. Add their ideas to the "Ways to Chill" chart.

Ask students: **Which of the ideas on our chart can you do here in our classroom?** Put a star ★ by each one.

Wrap-Up. In their journals, have students write down three chill-out strategies that can work for them. Say: **Your job is to put this into practice in real life. When you're angry, remember to stop, breathe, and then chill using your calming statement or another one of the ideas you've chosen. Also, in your journals write down the names of two trusted people you can talk to if you're still angry. I'll check in with you in a few days to see how it's going for you.**

Follow-Up. Laminate the "Ways to Chill" list and hang it in a prominent place. This will be one of your most important working documents throughout the year, one that students can refer to whenever they need a healthy channel for anger or stress.

The next time the class meets, check in with students to ask how their methods of chilling out are working for them.

Extension. Have students make pictures or posters showing ways they calm themselves when they are angry. Create a bulletin board or hallway display under the heading "Chill Out."

Ideas for a "Ways to Chill" Chart

put cold water on your face	read
go to a quiet spot	draw
do some physical exercise	model clay
★ write out what's bothering you	clean out a drawer
listen to music	ride your bike
talk to a friend	play with your pet
★ look at a poster or picture	do push-ups or sit-ups
★ use a calming statement	★ squeeze a Koosh ball
★ talk to an adult	★ remind yourself that you're bigger than the problem
★ look at the sky	take a bath or shower
★ think of something funny	★ put it in perspective—know this moment will pass
throw a ball	
go outside and run	

Session 41: See Yourself Getting Calmer
(10-Minute Time Cruncher)

self-control • anger management • personal responsibility

Session 41 gives students the opportunity to mentally rehearse chilling out.

Students will
- envision putting chill-out strategies into practice with a real-life conflict

Activity. Make sure students are seated comfortably. Say: Close your eyes or cover them. Breathe in slowly through your nose all the way down into the bottom of your stomach. Hold the breath in and slowly release it. Take another slow, deep breath all the way down, and let it calm your mind and body. Breathe out slowly.

Picture yourself having an angry conflict with someone. (Pause.)

In your mind, tell yourself to stop. Take a slow, deep calming breath. Now say your calming statement in your head. Picture yourself telling the other person that you're going to take a moment to chill out; then you'll come back to talk things over. (Pause.)

Picture yourself doing something from the "Ways to Chill" chart. (Pause.) Feel yourself getting calmer. You are more in control now. Picture yourself going back to talk about the problem. (Pause.)

Now picture yourself talking it out and coming to a fair solution. (Pause.)

Now open your eyes. Welcome back. How did it go?

Wrap-Up. Briefly discuss with students what they learned from doing this exercise.

Session 42: Things We Do When We Get Angry

anger management • self-control • personal responsibility

Session 42 reinforces the important understanding that we each have the ability to choose a response rather than simply react when we get angry.

Note: Review Sessions 10 and 11 (pages 40–41) prior to conducting this session.

Students will
- evaluate the outcomes of negative choices they might still make in response to anger
- identify things they can do to gain greater self-control when angry

Materials
- handout: "What Real Kids Do When They're Angry" (pages 104–105)
- chart paper; black and red marker

Introduction. Say: **You've been learning a lot of ways to better control anger. Change takes time, and sometimes it's hard to let go of old habits. Today we're going to evaluate how we're doing with managing anger now.**

Discussion. Distribute the handout and ask volunteers to read the comments from students about what they do when they're angry. Have students pair up and discuss what they do now when they get angry, noting positive changes and places where they may be stuck in negative patterns.

After a few minutes have students share in the large group about things they do when they get angry, noting positive changes or negative choices that still remain. List students' answers on chart paper.

When the list is complete, point to each action, one at a time, and ask: **Does doing this tend to make things get better or worse? How?** Put a red X by each action that makes things worse.

Ask: **What negative things happen when we do the things marked by an X?** (Punishment, guilt, retaliation, disappointing people we care about, disappointing oneself, etc.)

Then ask: **What can you do to help yourself avoid the choices that make things worse?** List these on a separate sheet of chart paper.

Activity. Ask for three volunteers to role-play the following scenario:

Three students have to come up with an idea for a science project. Student A keeps interrupting. Student B feels ready to lose his or her temper and say something mean. Student C notices and decides to say something that might help.

Have the role players act out the scenario, first using one or more of the negative actions on the list. Then have them replay it, this time using some of the positive strategies they've been learning. If they need prompting, here are some choices the players might make:

- Student C might suggest that they all take a break.
- Student B might excuse him/herself, get a drink of water, and think about an I-message to say. He or she can return to the group and deliver the I-message.
- Student B might use Stop, Breathe, Chill to calm down and then talk about the problem.

After the role play, debrief with the class. Ask what made things get worse the first time the scenario was acted out. What made things work out better the second time? What other choices could the players have made that might have helped?

Wrap-Up. Remind students to use the strategies you've been practicing together at home, after school, and throughout the day. Let them know you'll check in with them to hear how it's going.

Acknowledge acts of respect, listening, and compassion you observed during this session. Ask students if anyone wants to acknowledge somebody else.

Follow-Up. Have students answer the questions on their handout, either in writing or in discussion with a partner.

What Real Kids Do
When They're Angry

In a national survey of more than 2,100 students in grades 3–6, kids wrote about negative ways they deal with anger. Here are the top 5 things boys and girls reported doing when they're angry:

Top 5 Things Kids Do When They Get Mad

Boys

1. Walk away or ignore/avoid the person or situation.
2. Fight or do physical things such as hit, kick, push, or shove.
3. Try to stay calm.
4. Tell an adult.
5. Tell the person to stop.

Girls

1. Walk away or ignore/avoid the person or situation.
2. Tell an adult.
3. Talk/work it out.
4. Tell the person to stop.
5. Try to stay calm.

Here are some other things students said they did when they're angry:

"When I get mad sometimes I freak out."

"I count to ten, take a deep breath, and try to relax."

"When someone gets me mad I egg them on."

"I try to stay calm and not get worked up."

"I scream into my pillow when I get home."

"I usually stomp away."

"If someone makes me mad I call them names."

"I just try to sort it out in my head."

What Real Kids Do When They're Angry (continued)

What do YOU do when you're angry?

_____

_____

_____

What helps?

_____

_____

_____

Is there something you still do in response to anger that you need to change? Explain.

_____

_____

_____

_____

What can you do to make this change?

_____

_____

_____

_____

Session 43: Breathe Out/Breathe In
(10-Minute Time Cruncher)

calming • anger management • self-control

Session 43 introduces a way to breathe out anger and breathe in calmness.

Students will
- learn and practice a technique called Breathe Out/Breathe In

Introduction. Tell students you're going to show them a different way of breathing that can help them release anger and chill out. It's called Breathe Out/ Breathe In.

Activity. Ask students to remember a time they felt angry. Ask them to feel the anger in their bodies. Say: **Now, breathe out the anger you feel. Breathe it out as hard as you can.** Explain that they should not blow out, but rather exhale deeply with the mouth slightly open. Demonstrate this deep exhalation for students so they see the difference.

Next, have students take a slow, deep inhalation from all the way down in the lower abdomen. Demonstrate this deep inhalation.

Ask students to repeat this cycle of breathing. Say: **Breathe out the anger again. Breathe in the calmness.** (Pause.)

Repeat Breathe Out/Breathe In one more time.

Wrap-Up. Together with students, pretend to wipe the angry energy out of the air, the way you would "wipe" the air if it were filled with smoke. Tell students they can use Breathe Out/Breathe In as another way to Stop, Breathe, Chill.

Session 44: How Are We Doing? (Review)

anger management • self-control

Session 44 is a check-in with students on their application of the anger management strategies they are learning. It will enable you to provide support and encouragement where needed.

Students will

- review skills they have learned for calming down and choosing a response rather than reacting when angry
- Consider positive changes they have made and can make in the future to deal with anger in a healthy way

Materials

- handout: "What Real Kids Have to Say About Helpful Ways to Deal with Anger" (page 108)
- chart paper and marker
- "Stop, Breathe, Chill" sign from Session 9 (see page 39)
- "Ways to Chill" chart from Session 40 (see pages 100–101)
- student journals

Preparation. On the board or chart paper, write the following quote: *"For every minute you are angry, you lose sixty seconds of happiness." —Ralph Waldo Emerson*

Introduction. Lead students in taking three slow, deep abdominal breaths.

Invite a student to read the Ralph Waldo Emerson quote aloud. Ask students: **What do these words mean to you?** Discuss briefly. Then ask: **What is the most helpful thing about managing anger you've learned so far?** Discuss, referring to the "Stop, Breathe, Chill" sign and "Ways to Chill" chart.

Discussion. Distribute the handouts and ask for volunteers to read the statements from real students about managing anger in positive ways. Ask kids to respond to the ideas.

Remind students that managing anger can be challenging for all of us. The important thing is to keep working at it. Then ask: **What challenges are you having with managing anger? What successes are you having?** Discuss, offering suggestions and inviting them from other students. Let them know what works for you.

Activity. Ask students to think of a time in recent days when they felt angry and didn't let it get the best of them. What did they do to keep their cool?

Ask them to think of a time they got angry recently and didn't handle it well. Have them take out their journals and do some automatic writing, using this prompt: **Describe the situation that made you angry. Describe how you reacted, then come up with some things you could have done differently.**

Afterward, ask for volunteers to share what they wrote. Discuss.

Wrap-Up. Acknowledge students for showing compassion, self-control, and respect toward their classmates. Remind them to continue using anger management strategies at home.

Extension. Have students interview someone they admire and find out what the person does to manage anger, especially in moments when he or she feels really mad. Does the person have any special tips to share? Students can take notes in their journals and share any valuable ideas with the class.

What Real Kids Have to Say About
Helpful ways to Deal with Anger

In a national survey of more than 2,100 students in grades 3–6, kids wrote about positive ways they deal with anger. Here are some things they wrote:

- "I either talk to a friend who understands me, or I tell stuffed animals if there's no one to talk to."

- "I go outside and say to myself, 'Don't lose control.'"

- "With physical fights, I walk away and say, 'I don't fight.'"

- "I walk away so me and the other person can cool down. Sooner or later we forgive each other."

- "I find my calming point."

What are YOU going to do to help yourself better deal with anger the next time you're annoyed or in a conflict?

_____

_____

_____

_____

_____

_____

_____

Session 45: Getting Past Reacting

anger management • personal responsibility • self-control

Session 45 helps students gain additional insight into managing anger based on the example of a middle schooler who gained greater control over hers.

Students will

- examine more ways of gaining greater self-control in the face of anger
- come up with an action plan for responding to anger

Materials

- handout: "What Real Kids Have to Say About Making Changes" (pages 110–111; see Preparation, below)

Preparation. Prior to this session, pass out copies of the "What Real Kids Have to Say About Making Changes" handout and ask students to complete it ahead of time and bring it to this session.

Introduction. Have students bring their handouts to the circle. Explain that you will be asking people to share ideas they included on their "What Real Kids Have to Say About Making Changes" sheets; remind students not to use people's names when sharing.

Read or have a student read the quoted story from the handout.

Have students look back at the story and underline one line that's particularly meaningful to them. Ask for a few volunteers to read aloud the line they chose and to explain why they chose it.

Discussion. Discuss each question on the worksheet together:

- How does this student stop herself from reacting in ways that will get her in trouble?
- What did the girl do when the boys she passed were saying mean things about the way she looks and dresses?

- What is the most important thing you learned from this story?
- What words can you tell yourself to calm down when you're getting angry?
- What activity can you do to "take a break" from a situation that's making you mad?
- What can you do when it feels very hard to stay in control of anger?

Activity. Ask why it's important to have an action plan for staying in control when anger strikes. Tell students they're going to have a chance to share their action plans (at the bottom of the handout) with a partner now. Group students in pairs to briefly discuss the action plans they came up with. They can add more to their worksheets at this time.

Have students reconvene in a large circle and ask some students to share their action plans for gaining control over anger.

Wrap-Up. Affirm students for the work they are doing to manage anger, be more peaceful people, and get along together.

What Real Kids Have to Say About
Making Changes

In national survey of more than 2,100 students in grades 3–6:

64% said they want learn more about dealing with anger, conflict, and how to get along with others.

In the survey and in interviews, kids wrote about changes they're making to manage anger in better ways. Here is something a middle school girl shared:

"I used to yell and scream and curse if someone made remarks about me. Then I'd get in trouble and would get grounded and not be allowed to watch TV or go outside—all the things I like to do. It wasn't worth it.

"Now I'm trying to take everything step by step and think before I act. I'm starting to see a dramatic change in myself. Like today, these boys were talking mean about the way I dress and the way I look. I just kept walking. Once you get past that stage of reacting, you get to see who you really are. I know that inside I'm a kind, loving person. I don't need to do what everyone else does just to be cool."

What do YOU think about the girl's story?

How does this student stop herself from reacting in ways that will get her in trouble?

_____

_____

What did the girl do when the boys she passed were saying mean things about the way she looks and dresses?

_____

_____

_____

What Real Kids Have to Say About Making Changes (continued)

What is the most important thing you learned from this story?

_____

_____

What activity can you do to "take a break" from a situation that's making you mad?

_____

_____

What can you do when it feels very hard to stay in control of anger?

_____

_____

Action Plan

Make an action plan you can follow the next time anger strikes. List three things that can help you stay in control. Include words you can tell yourself that help you calm down.

_____

_____

_____

_____

_____

Session 46: Don't Get Physical

anger management • self-control • personal responsibility

Session 46 can help students learn how to manage anger when they feel on the verge of losing control and hurting or physically harming another person.

Students will

- understand why it is important not to get physical
- identify a variety of ways to keep from losing control when angry
- role-play ways to use temper tamers in anger-provoking situations

Materials

- handout: "What Real Kids Have to Say About Taming Their Tempers" (page 113)
- chart paper and marker
- student journals

Introduction and Discussion. Ask: **Why is it important not to get physical when we're angry?** Discuss. Ask what negative outcomes can result from physically hurting someone. (You can get in trouble, end up getting hurt, bring about retaliation, gain an enemy, etc.)

Note: Let students know that there are rare instances where people might have to defend themselves physically (for example, if someone attacks them and they have no other way out). But in most cases, physical responses should be avoided. Tell kids it takes more courage to stand tall and walk away from a fight than to let themselves be drawn into one.

Ask students what they do to avoid getting physical or saying things they'll later regret. Discuss briefly. Tell them what you did at their age.

Tell students that today you'll be discussing "temper tamers." Temper tamers can help them if they're really mad and feel like they're about to go out of control verbally or physically.

Pass out copies of the handout. Ask for volunteers to stand and read aloud the quotes from real kids. Tell students to follow along and underline the parts they find most useful.

After the quotes have been read, ask students to share what they found most helpful in the advice from other kids. Discuss.

At the top of a sheet of chart paper, write "Temper Tamers." Ask students to suggest temper tamers they can use to help themselves when their tempers are in danger of flaring and they're on the verge of lashing out physically. List their suggestions on the chart.

Activity. Have volunteers come to the center of the circle and role-play the following scenarios or scenarios they suggest. As time permits, have students enact the scenes more than once, using a different temper tamer each time.

- You are working hard on controlling your temper. The kid who sits next to you makes a joke about a bad grade you just got on a test. You feel like throwing your pencil at her. What do you do to tame your temper?

- You are working on controlling your temper. You're on the playground, and someone backs into you as he's trying to catch a ball. You feel like pushing him down, but you want to control your temper. What do you do?

Briefly discuss each role play, focusing on different temper tamers that were used and emphasizing the negative outcomes that were avoided as a result.

Wrap-Up. Have students choose three or four temper tamers and write them in their journals. Encourage them to use their temper tamers in real life when they are angry or losing control. Acknowledge students for the good work they are doing. See if anyone would like to acknowledge a classmate.

Extension. Tell students: **Think of a conflict in which you got so mad you completely lost it. Maybe you got physical, or maybe you said something cruel. Now think about what you could have done differently to tame your temper and maintain control of yourself. Create a comic strip showing the steps you would take.**

What Real Kids Have to Say About
Taming Their Tempers
Tips from Middle Schoolers

Here's what some middle school students said about ways they try to control their tempers:

"When someone gets me mad, I ask them why they said what they did. I try to understand. That usually helps us work it out. If I get really frustrated, I ball my fist up real tight and think what would happen if I react in a bad way. I know what might get me in trouble and I keep myself aware of the consequences."

"When someone gets me mad, I feel hyper and ready to hit. Things that help me calm down are going into the bathroom and taking a minute, sitting outside, or going in my room and playing my game when I'm home."

"If someone messes with me or calls me a name, I tell them to stop. I've learned how to manage my anger. I used to have a short fuse. I used to hit people real quick without thinking. Now I think things through first."

"I got a little squeeze ball. When I get mad, I squeeze it. Also I try to think of something else, something good from the past, like a place I went with my family when I was younger."

"If someone bothers you, walk away. If they're trying to hit you, you have the right to tell an adult. Don't worry about being called a snitch. Everyone has the right to protect themselves."

Session 47: Peace Shield

calming • self-respect • anger management

Session 47 introduces the concept of a Peace Shield*—a calming ritual students can use when faced with other people's anger.

Note: Be sure to complete Session 36, "Peaceful Place Visualization," prior to this session.

Students will

- learn a tool for calmness that can help them feel more safe and confident when someone is acting aggressively toward them
- visualize their own Peace Shields protecting them from other people's anger and hurtful behavior

Materials

- handout: "Peace Shield" (page 115)
- "Ways to Chill" chart from Session 40 (see pages 100–101)
- drawing paper and markers or colored pencils

Introduction and Discussion. Ask students how they feel when they are faced with an angry person. (Tell them not to use other people's names when describing situations of this nature.) Discuss.

Remind students of the reptilian brain, which is activated when people are angry. Tell students: **When someone else is mad, and you feel scared or angry in response, your fearful reaction starts in the reptilian brain, too. How do you feel when someone directs their anger at you? What happens inside your body?** (Fast pulse and heartbeat, hot face, etc.) **Which part of the brain helps you calm down and choose a response, instead of just reacting?** (The front of the brain or neocortex.)

Ask students what they're already doing to calm themselves and feel better when upset, hurt, or angry. If needed, remind them about Stop, Breathe, Chill; deep breathing; calming statements; and ideas from the "Ways to Chill" chart (Session 40). Tell students that all these things also help when they feel nervous, frightened, or threatened. Then say: **Today we'll learn about another technique you can use, called the Peace Shield.**

Activity. Read the "Peace Shield" handout aloud in a calming voice, pausing as needed for students to visualize. Afterward, ask students: **Were you able to picture your Peace Shield? How did it feel to imagine this invisible shield of protection?** Discuss.

Have students pair up and describe their Peace Shields to each other. Ask: **Can you think of ways your Peace Shield can help you at school and at home?** (For example, when someone makes them feel afraid by yelling, threatening, put-downs, etc.) Also describe how you are planning to use your Peace Shield. Without getting too personal, refer to situations they can relate to: being in the presence of a sharp-tongued neighbor or relative; having a conflict with someone who tries to put you down. Talk about locking in the power of your Peace Shield and focusing on the feeling of protection it gives you.

Wrap-Up. Remind students that they have the right and the power to protect themselves from people's anger, teasing, and other mistreatment. Say: **When you feel the need for protection from hurt, anger, or fear, remember to breathe deeply and put your Peace Shield in place. Feel it locking in your safety and locking out the harm that comes from bad feelings and mean words. The power of your Peace Shield will help you feel calmer and safer with people of any age who speak or act in aggressive ways.**

Encourage students to envision themselves surrounded by their Peace Shield whenever they feel the need.

Follow-Up. Give students their own copies of the handout. Have them draw a picture of themselves surrounded by their Peace Shield.

---

* Special thanks to student assistance counselor Virginia Abu Bakr for sharing with me the idea of the Peace Shield.

Peace Shield

Close your eyes. Take three slow, deep, calming breaths. Now go to your Peaceful Place. Let the good feelings you felt when you were there fill you up completely. Picture yourself standing tall and strong, feeling confident and happy. Now imagine yourself surrounded with an invisible shield of protection—a Peace Shield. Picture what the shield looks like to you. It is invisible to everyone else. Picture yourself surrounded by your Peace Shield. Picture it keeping you completely safe from harm. Your Peace Shield has the power to keep good feelings in and bad feelings out.

Take another slow deep breath.
On that breath you are "locking in" the power of your Peace Shield. Feel this happening now. The power of your Peace Shield is yours forever.

Start every day by closing your eyes and putting your Peace Shield in place. When you feel the need to protect yourself from anger or hurt, breathe deeply and feel your Peace Shield protecting you. See it locking in your safety and locking out anger and meanness. Use your Peace Shield anytime, day or night.

Session 48: Using "Think-Alouds"

(10-Minute Time Cruncher)

| anger management • personal responsibility • self-control • calming |

Session 48 helps you demonstrate to students the thought process that takes place when implementing core skills and anger management strategies.

Note: Conduct Session 47, "Peace Shield," prior to conducting this session.

Students will

- observe the process of thinking through and preparing to talk about a conflict
- review Stop, Breathe, Chill calming strategies and the Win/Win Guidelines for Working Out Conflicts
- understand that mental rehearsal and thinking things through are essential tools for dealing with conflicts

Materials

- "Win/Win Guidelines for Working Out Conflicts" chart from Session 8 (see page 36)
- "Stop, Breathe, Chill" chart from Session 9 (see page 39)
- "Ways to Chill" chart from Session 40 (see pages 100–101)

PART TWO
Managing Anger

Introduction and Activity. Tell your students that today you are going to model thinking aloud about how to deal with anger and conflict. You can use or adapt the following:

Imagine that someone has just done something to hurt my feelings. I need to say something, but I know if I do it now, I'm going to make it worse because I'm very upset. I'm going to show you how I would think this through, and what I would do. This is called a Think-Aloud.

First, I'm going to Stop, Breathe, Chill. (Point to the chart.) I'm going to stop and feel what I feel. I'm noticing that my heart is pounding very fast and my face feels hot. I'm going to breathe in deeply and then breathe out the bad feelings. I'll do this three times. Do it with me. (Breathe together.)

Now I'm going to calm myself down by saying my calming statement: "I can handle this." I'm also going to splash water on my face to calm myself some more. (Pretend you're doing that now.) And I'm also going to remind myself that this isn't the end of the world.

Maybe I'll take some more deep breaths to calm even more. Do this with me. (Breathe together.) I think I'll do something else from my "Ways to Chill" list. I know—I'll think about something funny. (Close your eyes and smile to yourself.)

(Open your eyes.) I'm starting to feel better now. I think I'll also talk confidentially—privately—with my aunt about what happened. She's a helpful listener. That way I can let go of some more anger before I talk with the person who hurt my feelings. (Pretend you're making a phone call to your aunt.)

Okay, now I'm ready to think about what I'm going to say. Let's see, start from "I," not "you." (Point to step 2 of the Win/Win Guidelines.) Hmm. Okay. Here's what I'm going to say: "I felt bad when you made that mean remark to me."

Let me practice that in the mirror so I can feel comfortable saying it. (Pretend to face a mirror and repeat your I-message a few times.)

(Face forward.) Good. Now I'll put on my Peace Shield so I feel safe and protected. (Pretend you're putting on your Peace Shield now.) Okay, now I'm ready to talk to the person who hurt my feelings.

Role-play talking to the person who hurt your feelings. Have a student play that part. Go through the steps of the Win/Win Guidelines.

Wrap-Up. Ask if students have any questions. Encourage them to suggest other ways you could have made yourself feel calmer, stronger, and more ready to face the person. Reassure students that it takes time and practice to put all the skills together. Emphasize that the more they practice, the easier it will become.

Extension. Have students get into pairs and do Think-Alouds of their own in response to an imagined conflict. Say: **This will be practice for a time in the future when you feel yourself getting angry. In your Think-Aloud, use Stop, Breathe, Chill. Try to remember the different ways you can calm yourself down. Then think about an I-message you can use. Put on your Peace Shield to help yourself feel ready to face the person you have a conflict with.**

Session 49: Anger Management Role Play

anger management • conflict resolution • self-control

Session 49 shows how to use anger management and conflict resolution skills in combination.

Note: Conduct Session 47, "Peace Shield," prior to conducting this session.

Students will

- review and practice anger management skills introduced so far
- brainstorm and role-play solutions to a common conflict
- evaluate the impact of calming strategies and mental preparation

Materials

- "Win/Win Guidelines for Working Out Conflicts" chart from Session 8 (see page 36)
- "Stop, Breathe, Chill" chart from Session 9 (see page 39)

Introduction. Say: **Today we're going to see how to put all the anger management skills we've been learning into practice when we're faced with an actual conflict. First let's put on our Peace Shields.**

Have students close their eyes or look down. Lead students in taking three slow, deep abdominal breaths. Then have them visualize themselves surrounded by their Peace Shields. Say: **The power of your Peace Shield is locked in; you are safe and protected behind it. Now picture someone standing in front of you calling you names. Picture the mean words bouncing off your Peace Shield. Feel yourself strong inside as you realize that no one's words can break through the power of your Peace Shield.** Pause and give students a few moments to envision in silence.

Now ask them to listen as you read aloud this story from a real student:

"These kids started teasing me about this girl they said I liked. Every day I would hear them say, 'Hey, how's your girlfriend treating you lately?' I told them to stop but they wouldn't. Then everybody started doing it. It kept getting worse and worse until finally I couldn't take it anymore."

Discussion and Activity. Ask: **What do you think this boy did next?** Discuss, being open to hearing negative or positive choices the boy might have made. Then ask: **What could he have done to make things better?**

Display or point to the "Stop, Breathe, Chill" and "Win/Win Guidelines for Working Out Conflicts" charts. Ask for two volunteers—one to play the child who started taunting the boy in the first place, and one to play the boy.

Before starting the actual role play, have the student playing the role of the boy who was taunted mentally prepare himself. Then have him demonstrate the following:

- using Stop, Breathe, Chill
- deciding what he's going to say before approaching the other boy
- rehearsing what he's going to say
- putting on his Peace Shield

See if the class has any other suggestions.

Now have him role-play approaching the other boy. Display or point to the Win/Win Guidelines. Guide the role players through the steps, with special emphasis on steps 1, 2, 3, and 5.

Win/Win Guidelines for Working Out Conflicts

1. Cool off.

2. Talk it over starting from "I," not "you."

3. Listen and say back what you heard.

4. Take responsibility for your role in the conflict.

5. Come up with a solution that's fair to each of you.

6. Affirm, forgive, thank, or apologize.

After the role play, discuss what happened. Ask: **How did it help to stop and breathe? What did the boy do to calm himself?** Ask the role player: **Did putting on your Peace Shield help? How?**

Wrap-Up. Remind students to use all the calming skills they've learned next time they are in a conflict in school or at home. Let them know that they will have more opportunities to practice using all of the Win/Win Guidelines for Working Out Conflicts.

Follow-Up. Put students into small groups and have them enact the same scenario or other scenarios you or the class come up with. Move from group to group, observing students, and providing coaching when necessary.

Session 50: Getting Help with Anger
(10-Minute Time Cruncher)

anger management • personal responsibility • calming

Session 50 helps students identify trusted adults they can talk to if they need support with anger or any other upset feelings.

Students will
- understand that talking to a trusted adult is a helpful thing to do when they're angry or upset about a problem
- determine at least two people they can go to for support

Materials
- chart paper and marker
- soft ball appropriate for throwing in class
- student journals

Activity. Say: **Talking out a problem helps people feel better and can also help them come up with solutions. It's important for each of you to have a trusted adult you can talk to when you're angry or upset.** Tell students who you used to talk to when you were their age. Also share about who you talk to now. On chart paper, list students' suggestions of trusted people they can talk to if they have a problem. Be sure to include parents or caregivers, other relatives, counselors, teachers, school social workers, youth group leaders, coaches, people affiliated with places of worship, neighbors, friends' parents.

Have students pair up and determine which trusted adults they can (or do) talk to when they're angry or upset about something.

After about three minutes, have them reconvene in a large circle. Throw the ball to a student and ask him or her to name a trusted person he or she can talk to. The student can say the person's role rather than actually naming the person. Have the student throw the ball to someone else who names a trusted person to go to. Continue until everyone has had a turn.

If a child doesn't have a trusted adult to go to, see the student after the session and help identify an appropriate person, perhaps someone at school.

Wrap-Up. At the front of their journals, have students write down the names of the two trusted adults they can go to for support. You may also want to share the toll-free phone number for Nineline (1-800-999-9999), a support hotline for young people.

Preventing Conflict

Teaching kids how to resolve conflicts respectfully and fairly helps cut back on bullying. Although it's not possible to eliminate conflict completely, it *is* possible to significantly reduce the amount and severity of conflicts in your classroom and school. This section will help you foster in your students a greater willingness and desire to work out differences rather than fight. The sessions were designed to help you nurture an attitude of conciliation in students, opening their minds to working out conflicts peacefully, and to provide important tools that help them do this. The activities in the Preventing Conflict sessions lay the groundwork for the Responding to Conflict activities on pages 165–188. You will want to conduct at least some of these sessions before conducting those.

Be sure to have these charts (introduced in Sessions 2, 8, and 9) displayed: "Respectful Listening," "The Win/Win Guidelines for Working Out Conflicts," and "Stop, Breathe, Chill."

51. Top 10 Conflict Starters

52. Conflict Habits, Part 1

53. Conflict Habits, Part 2

54. Positive and Negative Choices in Conflicts

55. Observing Conflict

56. Responsibility vs. Blame, Part 1

57. Responsibility vs. Blame, Part 2

58. Willingness to Work Out Conflicts

59. Willingness Blocks

60. Examining Our Willingness Blocks

61. Let's Compromise (10-Minute Time Cruncher)

62. Basement or Balcony? Part 1

63. Basement or Balcony? Part 2

64. Staying in the Balcony

65. Introducing Assertiveness

66. Conflict Solver Interviews

67. Staying Respectful with Someone You Don't Like

68. The Dignity Stance

69. Staying Out of Physical Fights

Session 51: Top 10 Conflict Starters

conflict resolution • cooperation • personal responsibility

Session 51 invites students to survey peers on common causes of conflict and compare their findings to results from the Survey About Conflicts.

Students will
- identify sources of their most common conflicts
- discover what other kids most often get into conflicts over
- reflect on how to be part of the solution to conflicts, especially those caused by teasing, gossip, name-calling, and exclusion

Materials
- chart paper and marker
- handouts: "What Are Your Conflict Starters?" (page 121); "Top 10 Conflict Starters" (page 122)
- student journals

Preparation. On chart paper, write the following: *"You can either be part of the problem or part of the solution."*

Introduction. Distribute copies of the "What Are Your Conflict Starters?" handout and read or have a student read the statistic at the top. Ask: **Does this sound right to you? How often do you see conflicts happening?** Discuss.

Activity and Discussion. Ask students to think about what they get into conflicts about. Pair up students and give them a minute or two to discuss this with their partner and write their ideas in the space provided on the handout. Ask a few students to share their answers with the class.

Now have students circulate around the room, asking three classmates, "What do you get into conflicts over most?" Have students write the answers in the last three blanks on their handouts.

After about five minutes, have students reconvene in a circle. Go around the circle and ask each student to read his or her list. Write the responses on chart paper. For repeat answers, make a tally mark next to the original answer each time it's given. When you have survey responses from all students, rank the top 10 answers in order. At the top of the chart paper, write: "Our Top 10 Conflict Starters."

Now pass out the "Top 10 Conflict Starters" handout. Ask students to compare the results from your classroom to findings from the Survey About Conflicts. Discuss. The survey responses will help your students see how much they have in common with other North American students regarding what

triggers conflicts. Regarding the top three conflict-starters—teasing, name-calling, and gossiping—ask students why all of these so often lead to conflict. Ask: **What do you think it would be like in our school if there wasn't as much teasing, name-calling, and gossip?** Refer to the sign you've created and guide students to understand that they each have the power to be part of the solution rather than part of the problem. Ask: **What does this mean to you?**

Wrap-Up. Ask: **If someone comes to you with gossip, what can you personally do to be part of the solution rather than the problem?** Discuss, then ask: **If someone teases you or calls you a name, is there something you can do to prevent it from turning into a conflict? What?**

Ask: **How about as a class? If we want to have a get-along classroom, what can we each do to be part of the solution?**

Follow-Up. Tell students what you do to be part of the solution. Have them ask a friend or family member this question: "Is there something you do when it comes to conflict so you can be part of the solution instead of being part of the problem?" Have them jot down notes in their journals so they can report back.

Extension. Have students interview older students about conflict starters and ask the older students what they think can be done about teasing, rumors, gossip, exclusion, and other conflict starters. Discuss what your students learned from their older counterparts.

what Are your Conflict Starters?

In a national survey of more than 2,100 students in grades 3–6:

48% (1,046 students) said they saw conflicts happening often, every day, or all the time.

What do YOU get into conflicts over most?

_____

_____

_____

_____

_____

Ask three classmates, "What do you get into conflicts over most?" Write the answers here.

1. _____

2. _____

3. _____

Think About It

Conflicts happen all the time! What can you do to be part of the solution instead of being part of the problem when it comes to conflicts?

_____

_____

_____

_____

Top 10 Conflict Starters

In a national survey of more than 2,100 students in grades 3–6, kids wrote about what situations most often lead to conflicts. Here are the Top 10 Conflict Starters reported in the survey:

1. Being teased or made fun of
2. Rumors and gossip
3. Name-calling
4. Being blamed for something
5. Someone being unfair
6. Being left out
7. Being picked on for being different
8. Cheating at games
9. Threats
10. Mean notes or text messages

Session 52: Conflict Habits, Part 1

conflict resolution • cooperation • respect • anger management • personal responsibility

Session 52 helps students understand that negative conflict habits can be changed.

Students will

- understand that everyone has conflict habits, some that are helpful and others that are harmful
- identify helpful and harmful conflict habits
- reflect on which harmful conflict habits they would like to change

Note: Review Sessions 10 and 11 (pages 40–41) prior to conducting this session.

Materials

- handouts: "Scripts About Conflict Habits" (pages 124–125, two copies); "Conflict Habits Self-Test" (page 126)
- student journals

Preparation. Make two copies of the "Scripts About Conflict Habits" handout. Keep one for yourself and cut out the three scripts from the other. Select three students to help lead this session. Their roles will be to read their scripts aloud to the class, share their own personal information as indicated, and ask discussion questions. Provide them with copies of their scripts prior to the session to help them feel comfortable reading aloud, sharing their stories, and inviting discussion from other students. Talk with them about the information they plan to share, and offer guidance as needed.

Introduction. Lead the class in taking three slow, deep abdominal breaths. Explain that you've asked three students to help lead today's session. Introduce the co-leaders and have them sit near you in the circle.

Discussion. Say: **Today we're going to talk about conflict habits and how they affect our lives. Our leaders will tell you some more about this.**

Allow about ten minutes for this student-led presentation and discussion. Begin by having Leader 1 read his or her script. At the discussion points, help student leaders guide brief conversations (one or two minutes) about helpful habits and other habits students would like to change.

Continue with Leader 2's explanation and brief discussion of harmful conflict habits. After Leader 3's reading and short discussion, have the class acknowledge the student leaders and see if anyone has any questions.

Activity. Have students pair up and discuss with a partner one harmful conflict habit they would like to change. Ask them to talk about things they can do to change the habit they've identified. Have them write the following heading on top of a page in their journals: "I have the power to change harmful conflict habits." Below this, tell them to write down the habit they plan to change, along with a few steps they will take to change it.

Wrap-Up. Pass out the "Conflict Habits Self-Test" and ask students to complete it before the next session. Have them check off the reactions they commonly have to conflicts and list others that are not included. Note that this handout will be used in Session 53.

Extension. Have students share with their parents or another trusted adult what they learned about conflict habits, talking together about conflict habits they each would like to change and thinking of ways to make that happen.

Scripts About Conflict Habits

Script for Leader 1

Habits are things we're used to doing. For example, we might brush our teeth at a set time, study in the same way each night, or even treat people in certain ways. Habits can be harmful or helpful. A helpful habit I have is _____

_____

_____.

What helpful habits do you have? *(Call on students to answer this question.)*

One habit I would like to change is _____.

What habits would you like to change? *(Call on students. Discuss.)*

Script for Leader 2

Helpful habits make life better. Eating healthy foods, getting to bed on time, and finishing homework are helpful habits that improve our lives. Harmful habits make life more difficult. Harmful habits like arguing and fighting, not studying for tests, and being disrespectful can cause problems and make our lives more difficult.

The way we react to conflict is a habit, too. Here's what one fifth-grader said about a habit he has when he's angry: "When someone gets me mad, I lose my temper. It's what I've always done. I don't know any other way." How many of you can identify with this? *(Discuss briefly.)*

This boy's habit of losing his temper is a harmful conflict habit. A harmful conflict habit I have is: _____.

What harmful conflict habits do you have? *(Discuss with other students.)*

$\longrightarrow$

Scripts About Conflict Habits (continued)

- -

Script for Leader 3

The good news is that habits can be changed! We can let go of harmful habits, and we can develop new healthy habits. Here's one student's story of success in turning a harmful conflict habit into a helpful one:

"I always used to yell and scream and curse if someone made me mad. I got in trouble a lot, and my friends didn't want to be with me. I decided to change. Now I try to take everything step-by-step. I try to find out the real story instead of flying off the handle. When I control my anger and talk out problems, I feel better inside. It's like I feel stronger."

This student succeeded in turning a harmful conflict habit to a helpful one. Now she feels better about herself. Her confidence is growing. She realizes that she has the power to change a negative conflict habit into a positive one.

Think about what you can do to change a harmful conflict habit into a helpful one. *(Discuss with other students.)*

- -

Conflict Habits Self-Test

Check the things you do **most often** when you have conflicts with people.

_____ 1. I say something mean to hurt the person's feelings.

_____ 2. I try to calm down before I speak.

_____ 3. I hurt the person physically.

_____ 4. I blame the other person.

_____ 5. I blame myself.

_____ 6. I look for ways to solve the conflict rather than just get what I want.

_____ 7. I don't say anything and wish I had.

_____ 8. I avoid using put-downs.

_____ 9. I spread rumors or lies about the person.

_____ 10. I try to understand the person's point of view.

_____ 11. I am willing to forgive the person for mistakes.

_____ 12. I threaten not to be friends with the person.

_____ 13. I send a mean text message about the person.

_____ 14. I do something to get even.

_____ 15. I am willing to compromise (give and take) rather than just have my way.

_____ 16. I talk things over with the person and try to work things out fairly.

_____ 17. I talk to an adult for advice (as opposed to tattling).

_____ 18. I apologize if I have done something wrong.

_____ 19. _____

_____ 20. _____

Here are my healthy conflict habits:

_____

_____

Here is a harmful conflict habit I plan to change:

_____

_____

Session 53: Conflict Habits, Part 2

conflict resolution • cooperation • respect • anger management

Session 53, a follow-up to Session 52, helps students further identify the helpful and harmful conflict habits they possess.

Students will

- identify and contrast helpful and harmful conflict habits that people can have
- gain deeper understanding of their own conflict habits and the impact they have
- reflect on why it's important to change harmful conflict habits into helpful ones

Materials

- completed handout: "Conflict Habits Self-Test" (page 126)

Preparation. Make sure students have completed the "Conflict Habits Self-Test" prior to this session. Have them bring their sheets to the circle at the start of the session.

Introduction. On the board make two large circles with the following headings: "Helpful Conflict Habits" and "Harmful Conflict Habits."

Ask for volunteers to come up, two at a time, and write in one circle or the other a helpful or harmful conflict habit that someone can have. Ask what happens when people are stuck in the pattern of harmful conflict habits.

Activity. Have students look at their completed "Conflict Habits Self-Test." Ask: **Which conflict habits would you personally like to change? Why?** Share one of your harmful conflict habits and its negative impact; then name a helpful conflict habit you would like to replace it with. Ask your students to name some harmful impacts of harmful conflict habits, followed by helpful conflict habits the harmful ones can be replaced by, and helpful impacts that could result. Remind your students that habits can be changed, and every day is an opportunity to change harmful habits into helpful ones.

Now ask: **What are some helpful conflict habits you already have?** Discuss. **How do your helpful conflict habits help you when you're in a conflict?**

Next put students in pairs and have them circle all of the healthy conflict habits on their sheets. Go over the sheets together afterward and make sure they have circled numbers 2, 6, 8, 10, 11, 15, 16, 17, and 18.

Answer questions and discuss. Have volunteers add any new helpful or harmful conflict habits to the circles on the board.

Wrap-Up. Tell students to underline at least one item on their handouts to work on over the next week. Ask them what they've learned so far that can help them turn their harmful conflict habits into helpful ones (deep breathing, calming statements).

Follow-Up. Check in with students over the next few days to see how they're doing in changing conflict habits. Mark your calendar for a brief check-in discussion in a week or so.

Extension. Conduct a follow-up session in which students share and role-play conflict habits they have changed for the better.

Session 54: Positive and Negative Choices in Conflicts

conflict resolution • decency • respect • personal responsibility

Session 54 helps students distinguish between positive and negative choices in conflicts, recognizing that they have the power to choose positive responses.

Students will

- understand that negative choices in conflicts generally lead to negative outcomes
- reflect on the positive outcomes that positive choices in conflicts lead to
- understand that their conscience can help them make positive choices in conflict situations

Materials

- chart paper and marker
- handouts: "What Real Kids Have to Say About Making Choices in Conflicts" (page 130); "Conflict Observation Reflection Sheet" (pages 131–132)
- sign from Session 31: "Conscience— A feeling or knowledge of right and wrong that guides us to do what is right" (see page 76)

Preparation. Divide a piece of chart paper into two columns. At the top of the left-hand column, write *"Positive Choices in Conflicts."* On the right, write *"Negative Choices in Conflicts."*

Introduction. Say: **Did you know that when we're faced with conflict, we always have choice as to how we're going to handle it? We can make a positive choice that will help resolve the conflict, or we can make a negative choice that ends up making the conflict get worse.**

Distribute the "What Real Kids Have to Say About Making Choices in Conflicts" handout. Ask for volunteers to read aloud the quotes from students on choices they make during conflicts. After each quote, ask: **"Positive choice or negative choice, what do you think?"** Discuss each response.

Referring to the sign, review the meaning of *conscience.* Ask: **Which quotes sounded like the kids were guided by their conscience?** Then say: **Sometimes we know we're making a negative choice, but we do it anyway. Does that ever happen to you? Why do you think people make negative choices?** Discuss.

Discussion and Activity. Ask students to think of a time they handled a conflict in a negative way (hitting, yelling, threatening). Ask how that conflict turned out. Say: **Conflicts often turn out badly when we react without thinking, or when we ignore our conscience. When we stop for even a few seconds,** think about the best thing to do, and choose how we're going to respond, things usually turn out better.

Ask students to think of a time they handled a conflict in a positive way (cooling off, hearing out the other person). Ask how the conflict turned out.

Have students brainstorm negative choices people make in conflicts. List them on the "Negative Choices in Conflicts" side of the chart. Be sure to include making negative faces and using negative body language and tone of voice. Then have students brainstorm positive choices people make in conflicts; list those on the other side of the chart.

Point to the right-hand column and ask: **What generally happens when we make negative choices like these?** (People get suspended, lose a friend, lose the trust of others.)

Ask: **What if someone gets in the habit of making negative choices in conflicts? What might happen as the person grows into adulthood?** (Perpetual trouble, loss of relationships, loss of a job, jail.)

Take a new sheet of chart paper and write at the top "Positive Outcomes of Positive Choices." Ask for examples of positive choices leading to positive results (keeping friends, staying out of trouble, greater self-respect, sense of personal pride). List the positive outcomes students name on the chart. Also discuss future positive outcomes that can result from making positive choices in conflict situations (happier relationships, more success in school and work, respect from others, peace of mind, admirable reputation).

Say: **How we handle conflicts can have a big impact on our lives. That's why learning how to work out conflicts respectfully is so important.** Ask: **If someone has trouble getting along with others right now, is it possible to change?** Discuss.

Wrap-Up. Remind students that they each have the power to respond to conflicts in positive ways. Each time they choose to make positive choices, they are creating a healthy pattern that will support them for the rest of their lives.

Follow-Up. Tell your students they're going to have the opportunity to observe conflicts that happen at school over the next few days. Pass out copies of the "Conflict Observation Reflection Sheet" and have students complete it. Note that this handout will be used in Session 55.

What Real Kids Have to Say About
Making Choices in Conflicts

In a national survey of more than 2,100 students in grades 3–6, kids wrote about choices they make during conflict. Here are some of the things they wrote:

	Positive	Negative
"Sometimes I yell back at people, even though I know I shouldn't."	❑	❑
"I yell and the other person yells and we keep yelling at each other."	❑	❑
"If I'm in a conflict and it's going in the wrong direction, I walk away and ask a fair friend to help."	❑	❑
"If someone starts to get physical with me, I punch them and hit them."	❑	❑
"I usually cry because I'm sensitive."	❑	❑
"I tell the truth about what happened, and I try to be fair."	❑	❑
"I kick the person who is bothering me in the shin."	❑	❑
"If they get mad at me I try to make them jealous."	❑	❑
"I try to talk things out before it can turn into a physical fight."	❑	❑
"I try to prove that I'm the one who's right."	❑	❑
"If I get into a conflict with someone, I usually gossip about them and start rumors."	❑	❑
"I try to compromise."	❑	❑
"I try to ignore the person. Then after a day or two, I go up to them and tell them how I feel."	❑	❑
"One time this girl in my class made up a story and said I punched her in the face on the bus. I didn't know what to do, but I decided to let it go. I thought, she's lying and I don't care. It's not my fault. So I ignored her. I was so happy I ignored her because I felt so good afterwards!"	❑	❑

Conflict Observation Reflection Sheet

Observe conflicts that take place in your school over the next few days. Notice what happens when conflicts arise in the classroom, hall, cafeteria, gym, and on the playground and bus. Then fill out this form. Be sure not to use people's names when filling out this sheet.

How often did you see conflicts taking place? Circle one.

Hardly ever   Once in a while   Often   All the time

In the following columns, write down some of the choices you saw people make when they got into conflicts. Use an extra sheet if necessary.

Negative choices: **Positive choices:**

_____   _____

_____   _____

_____   _____

_____   _____

What are the top 3 things you noticed kids having conflicts over?

1. _____

2. _____

3. _____

Conflict Observation Reflection Sheet (continued)

In the conflicts you observed, what were some things people did that made conflicts worse?

_____

_____

_____

_____

What positive choices did you observe—things that helped conflicts get worked out?

_____

_____

_____

_____

Were there better ways kids could have handled some of the conflicts you saw? Write about them here.

_____

_____

_____

_____

_____

_____

Session 55: Observing Conflict

conflict resolution • decency • fairness

Session 55 enables students to gain insights from having observed people in conflict. This session is a follow-up to Session 54.

Students will

- reflect on and evaluate choices made in conflicts they have observed
- determine which actions made conflicts better or worse
- role-play more positive ways conflicts they observed could have been handled

Materials

- completed handout: "Conflict Observation Reflection Sheet" (pages 131–132)
- student journals
- *optional:* "Our Top 10 Conflict Starters" chart from Session 51 (see page 120)

Preparation. Make sure students have completed the "Conflict Observation Reflection Sheet" prior to this session. Have them bring their sheets to the circle at the start of the session.

Introduction. Tell students they're going to have the opportunity to share things they've learned by observing conflicts. Remind them not to use people's names when sharing about the conflicts they observed, and not to discuss these conflicts after class. Ask: **What were some important things you discovered by observing conflicts?** Briefly discuss.

Discussion and Activity. Refer to the "Conflict Observation Reflection Sheet." Ask students the first question: **How often did you see conflicts taking place?** Ask what negative choices they observed. Discuss.

Put students in pairs and have them discuss negative choices people made that led to conflicts escalating and positive choices that helped conflicts get resolved. After a couple minutes, have students reconvene in the large circle. Discuss the negative and positive choices in the large group.

Cueing off of the last question from the sheet, ask for volunteers to role-play a conflict they observed, replacing negative conflict responses with positive ones. Role-play two or three different situations that were observed, with different volunteers acting in each. After each enactment, refer to the Win/Win Guidelines for Working Out Conflicts and ask: **Which of the guidelines did these people use? How did that help?**

Wrap-Up. Mention one or two of the top three conflict starters that several students noticed—something you consider to be an issue among your students or in your classroom. You may want to refer to your chart, "Our Top 10 Conflict Starters" as well. Say: **Imagine what our class would be like if every time this kind of conflict came up, each person made a positive choice and tried to resolve it in a fair, respectful way. How would that make things different here in our classroom (or school)?**

Follow-Up. Encourage students to write in their journals about a positive way a conflict they observed could have been handled, or a positive way a conflict of their own could have been handled.

Session 56: Responsibility vs. Blame, Part 1

> **personal responsibility • conflict resolution • cooperation**
>
> Session 56 helps students understand the importance of taking responsibility in conflicts rather than blaming.
>
> **Students will**
> - work in cooperative groups to learn important information about taking responsibility
> - understand that in most conflicts, both people are responsible in some way
> - understand that blaming causes conflicts to escalate
>
> **Materials**
> - handout: "Group Discussions About Taking Responsibility" (pages 135–137, two copies)
> - paper and pencil for Recorders (see Activity and Discussion, below)
> - chart paper and marker
>
> **Note:** Conduct this session and Session 57 in sequence.

Preparation. Make two copies of the "Group Discussions About Taking Responsibility" handout. Keep one for yourself; cut out the five sections of the other. For this session, you'll be giving one section to each of five small groups.

Introduction. Refer to Win/Win Guideline 4: *Take responsibility for your role in the conflict.* Tell students they're going to be working in groups, and each group will be receiving information to read and a question to discuss relating to taking responsibility in conflicts. Let them know that afterward the class will come together and a student from each group will report the key points his or her group discussed. Refer to the "Respectful Listening" chart and remind students to observe respectful listening guidelines as they interact in their groups.

Activity and Discussion. Divide the class into five groups and have each group choose a Leader, a Recorder, and a Reporter. Make sure Recorders have paper and pencils to write down important ideas from their group's discussion.

Pass a section of the handout to each group. Allow five minutes for Leaders to read aloud the information at the top, and for the group to discuss the question at the bottom. Remind Recorders to note the main ideas their group talks about so Reporters can present them to the class. Circulate and guide the groups' interactions as needed.

After five minutes, reconvene in a large circle. Beginning with Group 1, have each Reporter take about two minutes to tell the class what his or her group discussed regarding taking responsibility in conflicts. If the class has questions, anyone in the group may respond. On chart paper list key points from each Reporter as that student speaks. These will be reviewed in Part 2 (Session 57).

Wrap-Up. Compliment students for any positives you observed in terms of group interaction and respectful listening. Have Leaders and Reporters put their names on the top of the papers they have. Collect and save these to redistribute during the next session. Tell the class they'll be reviewing what they shared in their groups during the next session.

Follow-Up. Have students observe themselves in any conflicts they get into between now and the next session. Tell them to ask themselves the question, "Is there some way I may be even a little bit responsible for this conflict?" (Do this yourself so you can discuss your own experiences with your class during Part 2.)

Note: If the issue of bullying comes up during this session, here's some important information: In bullying situations, all involved do not share responsibility. Make sure students understand that kids who are bullied are not responsible for the bullying. The person who bullies is the responsible party and needs to be held accountable. For more information on bullying, see pages 10–12 and Dealing with Bullying (pages 217–260).

Group Discussions About Taking Responsibility

Group 1: Taking Responsibility

Read to the group:

Did you know that in nearly all conflicts, *both* people are at least a little responsible? Both people usually did something to make the conflict happen, get worse, or keep going. Blaming almost always makes conflicts get worse. But when even *one* person takes responsibility, the conflict will usually start to get better. When both people take responsibility, the conflict is likely to get solved. Taking responsibility rather than blaming is one of the most important things you can do.

Talk about it:

Think of a conflict you had. Was there a way you were *even a little bit* responsible? Discuss this in your group.

Group 2: The Problem with Blaming

Read to the group:

What do you think is the number one thing that keeps conflicts from getting worked out?

You're right if you said blaming.

When we blame the other person and don't take responsibility for our part, we make the conflict grow larger. Blaming usually makes the other person madder. Then the person will try to blame us back. Before long, instead of working out the conflict, we end up lost in the blame game. It's not hard to blame, but taking responsibility requires courage. The more you do it, the easier it gets. Next time you're in a conflict, try taking responsibility instead of blaming, and see what happens.

Talk about it:

Think of a conflict you had where you blamed the other person instead of taking responsibility. What ended up happening? Discuss this in your group.

Group Discussions About Taking Responsibility (continued)

- -

Group 3: Benefits of Taking Responsibility

Read to the group:

What positive things can happen when you take responsibility for something you did rather than blaming? What can happen when you really listen to what the other person has to say? Your power to make things better grows. Aside from getting the conflict resolved, many other good things may start to happen. Here are just a few:

- People will respect and admire you more.
- You will respect yourself more.
- You will have healthier relationships.
- You will get along better with your friends, classmates, teachers, and family members.
- People will trust you more.
- You will have fewer conflicts.

Talk about it:

What other benefits are there for taking responsibility? What other good things can happen? Discuss this in your group.

- -

Group 4: Why People Blame Instead of Taking Responsibility

Read to the group:

There is so much to gain from taking responsibility, and so little to gain from blaming! Why do so many people blame instead of taking responsibility? Here's what some kids say:

- "I always feel like I didn't do anything wrong."
- "It's usually the other person's fault."
- "I don't want to admit something and get in trouble."
- "What if the other person doesn't take responsibility, too? Then I look bad."
- "It scares me to admit what I've done."

Talk about it:

Do you ever blame instead of taking responsibility? Why? Discuss in your group. List more reasons people might not want to take responsibility for their role in a conflict.

- -

Group Discussions About Taking Responsibility (continued)

Group 5: Looking at Our Own Conflicts

Read to the group:

Even though taking responsibility for your part in conflicts can be a hard thing to do, people who've learned to do it feel happy they did. Taking responsibility is a sign of strength and maturity. Here's what one person said about taking responsibility rather than blaming:

"I used to blame. But I stopped doing it when I began to see that it just made things worse. When I started taking responsibility, I was able to get along better with people in my life."

What was your last conflict about? Did you take responsibility for your role in it or did you blame? Was there a way you were *even a little bit* responsible?

Talk about it:

Discuss with your group conflicts some of you have had. For each one, talk about what happened. How might each person have been at least a little bit responsible for the conflict happening or for its not getting solved?

Session 57: Responsibility vs. Blame, Part 2

personal responsibility • conflict resolution • cooperation

Session 57 reinforces the importance of taking responsibility in conflicts rather than blaming. This session is a follow-up to Session 56.

Students will

- work in cooperative groups to review important information about taking responsibility
- understand that in most conflicts, both people are responsible in some way
- review the concept that blaming causes conflicts to escalate

Materials

- soft globe or ball
- "Group Discussions About Taking Responsibility" sheets and Reporters' notes from Session 56 (see pages 135–137)
- chart with key points from Session 56 (see page 134)
- handout: "Responsibility vs. Blame" (pages 139–140)
- *optional:* student journals

Preparation. For the first half of this session, take down or cover up the chart you wrote in Session 56 with key points from the Reporters on taking responsibility. You'll be showing it after a short review.

Introduction. Gather students in a circle and tell them you want to do a quick review of what they learned in the previous session about taking responsibility versus blaming. Ask one or two students to state the most important thing they remember from the last session.

Discussion. To further review concepts on responsibility versus blame, throw the soft globe or ball to someone and ask the student to share something else she or he remembers from the preceding session. Have that student throw the ball to someone else. Continue with a few more students until most major concepts have been covered.

Have students get back into the same cooperative groups they were in during the last session. Pass out the sections of the "Group Discussions About Taking Responsibility" and the notes Reporters took. Give each group about three minutes to review what they discussed in the last session.

Activity. Have students reconvene in the large circle. Show the chart from the last session listing important ideas from each group. Ask students to

look over the list and see if there's anything else that should be added to it on taking responsibility versus blaming.

Now ask for a few volunteers to role-play a common conflict (ask the class to suggest one). Have role players blame each other for something that happened rather than take responsibility. Ask for two more volunteers to replay the conflict, this time with each person taking responsibility for something that happened. Afterward, debrief with the class, asking which role play worked better and why.

Wrap-Up. Direct attention to the "Respectful Listening" chart and ask the class how they think they did working in their groups and in the large circle. Have them acknowledge respectful listening they observed. Let students know that listening respectfully is a form of taking responsibility, too. The more we do it, the better everyone gets along.

Distribute the "Responsibility vs. Blame" handout and encourage students to read it and share it with parents and friends.

Extension. Have students keep a responsibility log in their journals. For one week ask them to note every conflict they have at home and in school, then answer this question for each: "Was there some way I was responsible, too, even if it was something small?"

Responsibility vs. Blame

Taking Responsibility

Did you know that in nearly all conflicts, *both* people are at least a little responsible? Both people usually did something to make the conflict happen, get worse, or keep going. Blaming almost always makes conflicts get worse. But when even *one* person takes responsibility, the conflict will usually start to get better. When both people take responsibility, the conflict is likely to get solved. Taking responsibility rather than blaming is one of the most important things you can do.

Think of a conflict you had. Was there a way you were *even a little bit* responsible?

The Problem with Blaming

What do you think is the number one thing that keeps conflicts from getting worked out?

You're right if you said blaming. When we blame the other person and don't take responsibility for our part, we make the conflict grow larger. Blaming usually makes the other person madder. Then the person will try to blame us back. Before long, instead of working out the conflict, we end up lost in the blame game. It's not hard to blame, but taking responsibility requires courage. The more you do it, the easier it gets. Next time you're in a conflict, try taking responsibility instead of blaming, and see what happens.

Think of a conflict you had where you blamed the other person instead of taking responsibility. What ended up happening?

Responsibility vs. Blame (continued)

Benefits of Taking Responsibility

What positive thing can happen when you're in a conflict and you take responsibility for something you did rather than blaming? What can happen when you really listen to what the other person has to say? Your power to make things better grows. Aside from getting the conflict resolved, many other good things may start to happen. Here are just a few:

- People will respect and admire you more.
- You will respect yourself more.
- You will have healthier relationships.
- You will get along better with your friends, classmates, teachers, and family members.
- People will trust you more.
- You will have fewer conflicts.

Why People Blame Instead of Taking Responsibility

There is so much to gain from taking responsibility, and so little to gain from blaming! Why do so many people blame instead of taking responsibility? Here's what some kids say:

- "I always feel like I didn't do anything wrong."
- "It's usually the other person's fault."
- "I don't want to admit anything and get in trouble."
- "What if the other person doesn't take responsibility, too? Then I look bad."
- "It scares me to admit what I've done."

Even though taking responsibility for your part in conflicts can be a hard thing to do, people who've learned to do it feel happy they did. Taking responsibility is a sign of strength and maturity. Here's what one person said about taking responsibility rather than blaming:

> "I used to blame. But I stopped doing it when I began to see that it just made things worse. When I started taking responsibility, I was able to get along better with people in my life."

> What was your last conflict about? Did you take responsibility for your role in it or did you blame? Was there a way you were *even a little bit* responsible?

Session 58: Willingness to Work Out Conflicts

conflict resolution • fairness • compromise

Session 58 focuses on the importance of being willing to resolve conflicts fairly, and impediments to doing so.

Students will

- learn that working out conflicts requires being willing to compromise, hear the other person out, and be patient
- understand that without willingness, conflicts can't get resolved.
- role-play using compromise, sincere listening, and patience to resolve a conflict

Materials

- chart paper and marker
- student journals

Preparation. Create a sign that says the following:

"Working out conflicts requires WILLINGNESS to:

1. *compromise*

2. *hear out the other person*

3. *be patient"*

Introduction. Compliment students on any progress you've observed in the ways they've been handling conflicts. Ask: **Do you ever find it hard to work out conflicts peacefully? What makes it hard for you?**

Discussion. Ask: **How do you feel when you're involved in a conflict that doesn't get resolved?** Discuss. Then say: **Having conflicts that aren't resolved makes most of us feel really bad. It can affect our mood, our energy, and our concentration. Has that ever happened to you?** Discuss.

Continue: **On the other hand, how do you feel when you've been successful at working out a conflict?** Discuss. Say: **Before any conflict can be worked out, one thing needs to be present: willingness to do so.**

Show the sign you made. Point to the word *willingness* and ask: **What does it mean to be willing to do something?** Ask students the meaning of *compromise*. Discuss, asking for examples. Also give an example of a time you compromised.

Ask: **Do you ever have trouble compromising? Hearing out the other person? Being patient?** Discuss. **Why do you think people sometimes aren't willing to work out conflicts peacefully?** (habit,

wanting power, needing to be right, fear of looking bad)

Referring to the sign, reiterate: **To be willing to work out conflicts, we need to be willing to compromise. We need to be willing to hear out the other person—really listen to what the other person has to say, even if we disagree. And we need to be patient. Working things out can take time. Sometimes, conflicts can get worked out even if only one person is willing. It's important to try to be that person.**

Ask students to think of conflicts they observed (or took part in) that didn't get resolved. Which of the three willingness skills might have been missing? Give a personal example.

Note: Sometimes kids get frustrated when they're willing to work out a conflict and the other person isn't. Let them know that it's still important to be willing to try. In time, the other person may follow suit. If not, at least you know you tried your best.

Activity. Ask for two volunteers to role-play a conflict that didn't get resolved. Use a scenario students suggest or the following conflict reported by a fifth-grade boy:*

Zach plays Ultimate Frisbee every day at school with a bunch of kids. Zach plays on one team and his friends Max and Steven play on the other. Zach is good at intercepting the Frisbee. When Zach's side is winning, Max and Steven get mad and say he's cheating. When the students go back inside after recess, Max and Steven call Zach names and

* Quotes and stories attributed to real students and teachers come from author interviews and from responses to the Survey About Conflicts conducted by the author and publisher. See pages 1 and 279–281 for further information.

No Kidding About Bullying   **141**

spread rumors that he cheats. Zach feels hurt and mad, especially because Max used to be his best friend. Today, he tells Max that he's not cheating and Max should quit saying he is. Max says, "Yeah—right!"

Have students take the parts of Zach and Max to role-play the conflict. Ask them to do something to chill out before facing each other. Guide the role players through the Win/Win Guidelines. Encourage them to compromise, really listen, and be patient so they can come to a fair solution. Let the class suggest solutions, too.

Afterward, ask students to assess how the conflict-solving went. Did Zach and Max show willingness to compromise? To hear each other out? Did they stay patient? Did they solve the conflict fairly?

Discuss any problems the two role players had in resolving the conflict. Emphasize that it takes practice to solve conflicts. Each time students practice willingness skills, this will get easier.

Wrap-Up. Acknowledge students for progress they're making in learning to get along and work out conflicts. Ask: **Why is it so important to be willing to work out conflicts? Which willingness skill is most challenging for you? Jot it down in your journal.**

Follow-Up. Ask students to write or draw in their journals about a time their most challenging willingness skill got in the way of working out a conflict. Have them reflect on what they plan to do differently next time.

Extension. Tell students to continue observing themselves when conflicts arise. Encourage them to ask themselves this question each time: "How willing am I to listen, compromise, and be patient?"

Session 59: Willingness Blocks

conflict resolution • fairness • compromise

Session 59 has students identify their personal willingness blocks—things that stand in their way of working out conflicts.

Materials

- chart paper and marker or "WILLINGNESS" skills sign from Session 58 (see page 141)
- handout: "What Are Your Willingness Blocks?" (page 144)
- two large wooden blocks

Preparation. If you have not already done so, create a sign that says the following:

"Working out conflicts requires WILLINGNESS to:

1. *compromise*

2. *hear out the other person*

3. *be patient"*

Introduction. Display the sign and introduce or review the three willingness skills needed to solve conflicts: willingness to listen, compromise, and be patient.

Say: **Today we're going to look at the opposite of willingness, something called *willingness blocks.* Willingness blocks are all the things we think, feel, and do that hold us back from working out conflicts.** Pass out the "What Are Your Willingness Blocks?" handout. Ask students to think of some recent conflicts they've had at school or at home, and fill out the quiz as honestly as possible. Let them know you'll be taking the quiz right along with them.

Discussion. After everyone has completed the quiz, ask students which willingness blocks they checked off. Share what yours are. Discuss.

Ask students: **When you hold onto your willingness blocks, are you able to work out conflicts peacefully? Why not?** Discuss.

Then ask: **What happens when people hold onto willingness blocks?** (They keep blaming others, conflicts escalate, they get into more conflicts.) **What other negative things happen when we go around having conflicts all the time?** Discuss outcomes like the following:

- We lose friends.
- We get punished.
- We're stressed out.
- People avoid us.

- We feel bad about ourselves.
- People start thinking we're troublemakers.
- Our health can be affected.
- We can set up a lifetime pattern of dealing with conflicts in negative ways.

Activity. Ask students to think of an unresolved conflict they've had at home or at school. Ask for two volunteers to role-play the conflict. Before they start, have each volunteer hold a block in front of themselves as if literally blocking the other person. Tell them to role-play the conflict with their willingness blocks in place, not listening, not compromising, and not being patient. Caution students not to use real names or physically touch each other.

Next, have the role players put down their blocks and replay the conflict, this time showing willingness to compromise, hear the other person out, and be patient. Guide them through Stop, Breathe, Chill and the Win/Win Guidelines.

Ask the class: **What was different this time? Which worked better—holding onto willingness blocks, or letting them go?** Discuss. **What's to be gained by letting go of our willingness blocks?**

Wrap-Up. Have students look at the handout they completed. Ask them to circle one or two willingness blocks they plan to work on giving up. Follow up with the class in about a week to see how they're doing with this.

Extensions. Have students continue observing themselves in conflicts, taking note of willingness blocks that come up. They can optionally write, draw, or record themselves talking about this, reflecting on what they can do to let go of their willingness blocks.

Start a Willingness Blog in your class where kids can comment on willingness blocks that come up and things they're doing to let go of them.

what Are your willingness Blocks?

When you're in a conflict, which willingness blocks apply to you? Check any that do. If you have a different willingness block than those listed, write it down.

- ☐ I want to show I'm "right" and make the other person "wrong."
- ☐ I don't want to look like a wimp.
- ☐ I think people will take advantage of me if I compromise.
- ☐ I like to be on top.
- ☐ I don't want to hear out someone I don't like or someone who did me wrong.
- ☐ Sometimes I'm afraid of looking stupid.
- ☐ Sometimes I feel too angry to work things out.
- ☐ It takes too long to talk things out.
- ☐ Sometimes I want to get even with the other person.
- ☐ I'd rather blame than take responsibility.
- ☐ I've always dealt with conflict one way and I don't know how to change.
- ☐ _____
- ☐ _____

When you hold onto willingness blocks, you can almost *guarantee* that your conflicts aren't going to get worked out. Ask yourself:

"Is it really worth holding onto my willingness block?"

Which willingness blocks are you willing to give up?

_____

_____

_____

Session 60: Examining Our Willingness Blocks

conflict resolution • fairness • compromise

Session 60 encourages students to reflect on the ramifications of holding onto their willingness blocks when they are faced with conflicts. This session is a follow-up to Session 59.

Students will

- review what willingness blocks are and the negative outcomes they lead to
- write about a time when a willingness block kept them from working out a conflict
- visualize themselves letting go of a willingness block and resolving a conflict successfully

Materials

- two large wooden blocks
- student journals
- *optional:* completed handout, "What Are Your Willingness Blocks?" (page 144)

Introduction and Discussion. Hold up the blocks and review by asking: **What are willingness blocks? What happens when people hold onto willingness blocks?** (We keep blaming others, conflicts escalate, we get into more conflicts.) **What other negative things happen when we go around having conflicts all the time?** Briefly review ideas discussed in Session 59 (loss of friends, punishment, stress, loneliness, negative lifetime pattern).

Ask: **What three things do we need to be willing to do to resolve conflicts?** (Compromise, hear the other person out, be patient.) **Why is willingness so important when it comes to solving conflicts?**

Activity. Holding up the blocks again, ask students to think about how their willingness blocks have gotten in the way when they've had conflicts. Have students pair up and discuss this together briefly.

Have students take out journals and do several minutes of automatic writing on the following topic: "A Time I Was Unwilling to Work Out a Conflict, and Why." Have students write for three to five minutes.

Afterward, ask for volunteers to share what they wrote. Ask each volunteer why he or she held onto the willingness block. What negative results came from holding onto it? Also ask the volunteers what they might have done differently if they were truly willing to work out the conflict.

Tell students they're going to be doing a visualization that will let them replay in their minds the conflict they just wrote about. Have students close their eyes, or cover them and look down, and picture the conflict they had. Say:

Take some slow, deep abdominal breaths. (Breathe with students.) **Feel yourself getting calmer and calmer. Picture yourself putting down your willingness block and leaving it on the floor.**

Picture yourself talking to the person you have your conflict with—the same person you just wrote about. Picture yourself getting ready to talk out the conflict using the Win/Win Guidelines. Say your calming statement in your head. Take another slow, deep breath. Think about the I-message you want to give. Now hear yourself say it to the other person. (Pause.)

Picture the person responding to you. See yourself listening to what the person has to say. (Pause.) **See yourself saying back the main idea of what you heard.** (Pause.) **Now see yourself and the other person talking over the problem and coming up with a fair solution.** (Pause.)

Picture yourself shaking hands and walking away satisfied. You've done it! You've resolved your conflict in a mature way, and you feel proud of yourself.

Have students open their eyes. Ask for one or two volunteers to share what they envisioned. Ask how the ending they envisioned differed from what happened in real life.

Wrap-Up. Affirm students for the important work they're doing to become truly willing to work out conflicts. Let students know that letting go of willingness blocks doesn't guarantee that the conflict will work out. But there's a greater chance that it will get resolved. Also, they'll feel better about how they handled themselves knowing they tried to be part of the solution rather than being part of the problem.

Extension. Encourage students to share their "What Are My Willingness Blocks?" handout with a trusted adult or friend. Have them talk with this person about what they're doing to try to let go of a willingness block.

Session 61: Let's Compromise
(10-Minute Time Cruncher)

conflict resolution • compromise • fairness • personal responsibility

Session 61 helps students open their minds to a variety of possible ways to compromise in a conflict situation.

Students will
- brainstorm ways to compromise in a conflict
- recognize that there are often many possible solutions

Materials
- chart paper and marker

Introduction. Write the word *compromise* on the board. Ask students what it means. Tie the idea of compromise to the concept of fairness.

Activity and Discussion. Ask students to think of conflicts that often come up in the classroom, on the playground, in the cafeteria, or somewhere else at school. Listen to their ideas and choose a conflict to focus on for this session—something all students will relate to.

Explain that you want the group to brainstorm all the ways someone could compromise to help work out this conflict. If you're comfortable, have students call out their ideas as they have them, allowing you time to list what they say on chart paper. Otherwise, pass a soft globe or ball to elicit ideas. Include your own ideas for compromising on the chart as well.

After several minutes, look at your list together. Ask: **Which of these ideas would be realistic for you to do in a conflict like this one?**

Wrap-Up. Tell students: **In nearly all conflicts, there's a way for both people to compromise, as long as they are willing to do so.**

Follow-Up. Encourage students to brainstorm in their journals or with a friend ways to compromise in a conflict they've had.

Extensions. Have students look up quotes about compromise on the Internet, copy down those they like best, and share them with friends. Students can also create a bulletin board or other class display with the quotes they found.

Session 62: Basement or Balcony? Part 1

conflict resolution • compromise • personal responsibility

Session 62 introduces the idea of "basement or balcony" as a metaphor for making negative versus positive choices in conflict.

Students will

- understand and develop their power to choose positive over negative responses to conflicts
- recognize that they feel better about themselves when they "go up to the balcony" and make positive choices in the face of conflict
- recognize that choosing the balcony is powerful and can lead to better outcomes for conflicts

Materials

- chart paper and marker
- handouts: "Basement or Balcony?" (page 149); "Basement or Balcony: Which Did You Choose?" (pages 150–151)

Note: Conduct this session and Session 63 in sequence.

Preparation. On chart paper, write the following: *"Be bigger than the problem."*

Introduction. Read aloud to students the following statement from a teacher:

"I realized that when I'm involved in a conflict and the other person is acting mean or nasty, if I do that, too, it's like I'm going down to the basement inside myself—to the lowest part of me. But if I choose to keep behaving with dignity and respect, then it's like I'm up in the balcony—the highest part of me. I feel better about myself when I choose the balcony."

Ask the class what these words mean to them. You might ask: **Where's the basement? Where's the balcony? What does this teacher mean by the "lowest part" of her? The "highest part"?** Reread the statement and invite any other student responses.

Discussion. Toward the top of the board make a large square, at least 2' x 3'. Above it write "Balcony." Toward the bottom of the board make another large square. Beneath it write "Basement." Ask students to think of negative ways they and others sometimes behave during conflicts—ways that put them in the basement. Write their ideas in the "Basement" box (yelling, blaming, being sarcastic, name-calling, not listening, rolling the eyes, making negative faces, threatening, hitting).

Now ask students: **What are some things people do to get to the balcony during a conflict?** Guide students to include many possible positive choices

(listening, compromising, taking responsibility, cooling off, keeping things in perspective, telling the truth, being respectful, refraining from name-calling, staying patient). List these in the "Balcony" box. Leave the boxes on the board for use in Session 63.

One by one, read the following quotes from real students, each time asking: **Did this person choose the basement or the balcony?**

- "I try not to say mean stuff."
- "When I'm in a conflict with people, I either call them names or get revenge."
- "I count backwards from 50 to let my anger out."
- "I do everything in my power not to hurt them or make a scene."
- "It's hard. If it's not my fault, I usually get mad and yell."
- "I try to calmly talk it out."
- "I usually say, 'You know what? I'm not going to argue.' Then I walk away."
- "I do my best to compromise."

Activity. Have students pair up and think of strategies and concepts they've used that have helped them stay in the balcony. After two or three minutes, reconvene in the circle and say: **No matter how much time we may have spent down in the basement, we have the power to go up to the balcony. It's always there for us, and when we choose to go there, we feel better about ourselves, and the conflict usually gets easier to deal with.**

Ask students to think of a time they went to the balcony instead of the basement. Ask how it felt to be up in the balcony, especially if they other person was down in the basement. Share your own example, too.

Distribute the "Basement or Balcony?" handout. Ask for volunteers to read each paragraph. After the second paragraph is read, refer to the sign you have made. Discuss the idea of being bigger than the problem. Then continue going over the handout.

Wrap-Up. Distribute the "Basement or Balcony: Which Did You Choose?" handout. Say: **Pay attention to what you do when you get into conflicts** this week. **Each time, ask yourself, "Did I go to the basement or balcony?" Don't judge yourself too hard if you found yourself in the basement. We've all gone there many times. Observing your own behavior is a powerful step in making new choices. If you're willing to take responsibility, getting to the balcony will be easier than you think.**

Tell students you'll be filling out the same handout, that learning how to stay in the balcony is something we all need to practice. Note that the handout will be used in Session 63 and is briefly discussed in Session 64.

Basement or Balcony?

Sometimes when people get us really mad, we automatically go down to the basement. We don't even think about it—we're just there. But the truth is, the balcony is available in every moment, and when we choose to go to the balcony, we feel better about ourselves, and the conflict usually works out a lot better.

Can you remember a conflict where you went up to the balcony instead of going down to the basement? How did it feel to be up in the balcony? For most people, going up to the balcony feels really good. Why? Because when we go to the highest part of ourselves, we feel proud and in control. We know we didn't let something or someone get the best of us. We discover that we can be bigger than the problem.

Now think of a time when you went down to the basement. What did you do? How did you end up feeling?

It's a big difference and an important choice: Basement or balcony? You have the power to choose the balcony each time you have a conflict. When you make this choice, you take a big step forward to becoming a conflict solver who knows how to get along with others. And when you do this, you start creating a pattern of success that can last the rest of your life.

Basement or Balcony: Which Did You Choose?

Observe yourself when you're involved in conflicts. Then fill out the sections below.

Conflict 1

Description of the conflict:

_____

_____

What I did in response to the conflict:

_____

_____

Where did I go—down to the basement or up to the balcony?

_____

_____

If I went down to the basement, what had me end up there?

_____

_____

If I went up to the balcony, how did I manage to stay there?

_____

_____

If the conflict ended in a negative way, what can I do differently next time?

_____

_____

If the conflict got resolved, what did I do that I can do in future conflicts?

_____

_____

Basement or Balcony: Which Did You Choose? (continued)

Conflict 2

Description of the conflict:

_____

_____

What I did in response to the conflict:

_____

_____

Where did I go—down to the basement or up to the balcony?

_____

_____

If I went down to the basement, what had me end up there?

_____

_____

If I went up to the balcony, how did I manage to stay there?

_____

_____

If the conflict ended in a negative way, what can I do differently next time?

_____

_____

If the conflict got resolved, what did I do that I can do in future conflicts?

_____

_____

Session 63: Basement or Balcony? Part 2

conflict resolution • compromise • personal responsibility

Session 63 guides students to reflect on their own choices in conflicts and take greater responsibility for their behavior. This session is a follow-up to Session 62.

Students will

- reflect on their "basement" or "balcony" reactions to conflict
- explore ideas for staying in the balcony during conflict
- understand that patience and practice can help them stay in the balcony more often

Materials

- completed handout: "Basement or Balcony: Which Did You Choose?" (pages 150–151)
- "Basement" and "Balcony" boxes (written on the board in Session 62—see page 147)
- "Ways to Chill" chart from Session 40 (see pages 100–101)
- student journals
- "Be bigger than the problem" sign from Session 62 (see page 147)

Introduction. Have students bring their completed "Basement or Balcony: Which Did You Choose?" handouts to the circle. Ask: **What did you notice when you observed yourself during conflicts? Did you spend more time down in the basement or up in the balcony? Why? What made it hard to go up to the balcony and stay there?**

Point out that going down to the basement is a conflict habit; we each have the power to change our conflict habits, even if it's hard at first. Give a personal example. Discuss.

Activity and Discussion. Ask: What "basement" kinds of things did you observe yourself doing? Discuss. Share your experiences, too. Then ask: **What "balcony" kinds of things did you do? What are some examples of how people were able to get themselves up to the balcony when there's been a conflict?** Affirm students for whatever they did to get to the balcony.

One at a time, share and discuss these examples of how two real students described how they get to the balcony:

- "I take time to cool off. Then I let the other person tell their side of the story."

- "I think about what happened and try to understand why the other person is reacting to it."

Ask students if they've tried doing these things. Continue the discussion, eliciting other things students do, or can do, to stay up in the balcony more often. Remind them to Stop, Breathe, Chill and to use calming statements, ideas from the "Ways to Chill" chart, or the temper tamers they listed in their journals (see page 112).

Ask students what they learned about themselves through this activity. Referring to the sign, ask if anyone did something that enabled him or her to experience being bigger than the problem. What was that like?

Wrap-Up. Remind students that we each have the power to go up to the balcony during conflict. It takes practice, patience, and willingness to try again when we fall short. Acknowledge students for the progress they are making. Be sure to acknowledge small steps, especially with students who've had difficulty getting to the balcony.

Session 64: Staying in the Balcony

conflict resolution • compromise • personal responsibility • fairness

Session 64 lets students explore a variety of positive ways to deal with conflict—to stay in the balcony. This is a follow-up to Session 62.

Students will

- explore a variety of ways to "stay up in the balcony" when faced with conflict
- role-play staying in the balcony by using a Peace Shield, calming statement, and I-messages

Materials

- "Be bigger than the problem" sign from Session 62 (see page 147)
- handout: "What Real Kids Have to Say About Staying in the Balcony" (page 154)

Note: The Peace Shield is introduced and explained in Session 47.

Introduction. Check in with students about how they're doing using Stop, Breathe, Chill and the Win/Win Guidelines in real conflicts to help them stay up in the balcony. Discuss progress and challenges. Share your own challenges and successes. The more authentic experiences you share, especially in terms of how you deal with challenges to peacefully working out conflicts, the more your kids are likely to buy in to doing so themselves.

Discussion. Refer to the "Be bigger than the problem" sign. Ask for examples of conflicts where students managed to stay in the balcony and be bigger than the problem when the other person was in the basement. Ask how they helped themselves stay up in the balcony.

Activity. Pass out copies of "What Real Kids Have to Say About Staying in the Balcony." Ask for volunteers to read aloud the quotes from real kids. After the quotes have been read, ask students to share what they found most helpful in hearing the experiences of other kids. Discuss.

Have students read the quotes again and circle one they find most useful, especially when dealing with someone who is down in the basement. Discuss.

Ask for volunteers to role-play the following scenario, shared by a fourth-grade girl (or use a scenario students suggest):

"This kid seems to have a problem with me. When I first moved here, I know I acted kind of annoying, but other kids get along with me, even

the kid's friends. But sometimes he acts like he hates me. I mean there are times he hits me, or he calls me terrible names. Other times we get along, and then I like him, but when he's mean I just want him to leave me alone."

Ask: **What can this girl do to solve the problem? Is there a way she can go up to the balcony as she stands up for herself?** Discuss, encouraging students to consider strategies they've learned that could be helpful (put on her Peace Shield, breathe deeply, use a calming statement). Remind students that they should never open themselves to abusive comments or physical harm from anyone. If that happens, they should walk away and seek the help of an adult.

Now ask for volunteers to role-play addressing the problem at a neutral time, like when the two students are getting along. Before the role play begins, coach the student who is being picked on to put on her Peace Shield, use a calming statement, and think about an I-message to deliver. When she feels fully prepared, have her approach the other role player and talk about the problem.

Wrap-Up. After the role play, ask for responses from the class, including other I-messages or approaches that could be helpful.

Extension. Have students work in pairs or small groups to come up with conflict scenarios and practice different ways to get to the balcony instead of the basement.

What Real Kids Have to Say About
Staying in the Balcony

In a national survey of more than 2,100 students in grades 3–6, kids wrote about positive choices they make in conflict situations. Here are some things they wrote:

"When I'm involved in a conflict, I tell the truth, try to calm down, and think about ways to handle it without hurting anyone. I try not to let my anger get to my head and cause me to say or do mean things."

"I try to figure out the problem and fix it in a fair and equal way."

"If I did something that bothered the other person, I say, 'Sorry I did that. I hope we can leave this behind and become friends again.' It works almost every time."

"I think about what happened and try to understand why the other person is reacting to it."

"I tell myself to back off and cool down."

"I try to calm the other person down, then tell myself not to get too involved. Later I write it out to vent my feelings."

"I walk away and try to clear my mind, and think about the good things in my life."

"When I'm in a conflict, one thing that really helps is I pretend my cat is next to me, and I feel better. Sometimes I talk to her in my imagination. It helps me come up with solutions."

"Sometimes I go in my room and find a little space where I just curl up in a ball. I'll read a book, and that really calms me down. Reading helps me think of solutions, too."

"I could have ended up in a fight with one of my friends when I tagged him during a game and he said, 'At least I'm not the one with bad eyes.' Instead of fighting, I decided to leave the park and ignore him. I decided to focus on how I feel about myself, which is good. I find if I take a break and talk to the person later, it works out. That's what I did with him."

Session 65: Introducing Assertiveness

conflict resolution • compromise • fairness • personal responsibility • assertiveness

Session 65 introduces the concept of assertiveness and helps students see the link between assertiveness and preventing and effectively solving conflicts.

Students will

- understand what it means to be assertive
- recognize the difference between being assertive and being aggressive
- role-play handling a conflict assertively

Materials

- chart paper and marker
- student journals
- handout: "Conflict Solver Interview" (page 156)

Preparation. On chart paper, write the following: *"Assertive—Strong and honest, yet respectful, saying what you need to say with confidence."*

Introduction. Say: **Today we're going to talk about being assertive. Does anyone know what** *assertive* **means?** Discuss briefly.

Say: **Here's an example of an assertive person I know: She gets along really well with others and always manages to say what's on her mind in a respectful way when she's in a conflict. Even when people try to argue or start a fight, she keeps a** *neutral* **facial expression and speaks in a firm but calm voice. She comes across as strong without being mean.**

Discussion and Activity. Ask students to describe what a neutral facial expression is. Discuss the importance of keeping a neutral facial expression and tone of voice, along with neutral body language that shows pride without being threatening. Ask for two volunteers to demonstrate neutral and non-neutral facial expressions, tone of voice, and body language.

Ask students: **What word describes people who can be strong and honest, stay respectful, and get their point across without bossing or threatening?**

Show the definition of *assertive*. Have students copy the definition into their journals. Lead a brief discussion of the difference between being assertive and being aggressive, making sure that students understand *assertive* means speaking our mind with

strength and respect, while *aggressive* means being ready to argue, threaten, or fight. Say: **Think of someone you know who is good at solving conflicts. Is the person assertive or aggressive?** Discuss.

Ask for two volunteers to role-play the following conflict, or another one students suggest, using the Win/Win Guidelines. Have both role players act assertively, not aggressively:

T.J. lent his friend Maya a book that needed to be returned to the library on Monday. Maya didn't return it on time and T.J. ended up having to pay a fine. T.J. is really annoyed.

Afterward, debrief with class. Were role players assertive, not aggressive? Did they resolve the conflict in a fair way? Did they both manage to stay up in the balcony? (See Session 62.) If so, how?

Wrap-Up. Pass out the "Conflict Solver Interview" handout and go over it with students. Make sure students know that adults as well as kids can be interviewed. Note that the completed handout will be used in Session 66.

Follow-Up. Check in with students to make sure they know who they can interview. As needed, help them figure out who this could be and how they can conduct their interview. (Some students may wish to record their interviews—this is fine as long as the interviewee agrees. They may also ask the person being interviewed to help complete the form as they talk.)

Conflict Solver Interview

Choose someone who you think is good at preventing or solving conflicts. This person should be someone you respect who gets along well with others, works out problems fairly, and speaks his or her mind assertively, without becoming aggressive.

Ask your conflict solver the following questions.
Write the answers below:

1. What do you do to keep your cool when someone gets you mad?

_____

_____

2. How do you stay calm during conflict?

_____

_____

3. What do you do to avoid using put-downs when you're in a conflict?

_____

_____

_____

4. Is there something you say to yourself that helps you keep your cool in conflict situations?

_____

_____

_____

5. What advice do you have for other people when it comes to handling conflict?

_____

_____

Session 66: Conflict Solver Interviews

conflict resolution • compromise • fairness • courage • personal responsibility

Session 66 asks students to share what they learned from conflict solvers they interviewed and reflect on how to apply any new understandings in their own lives. This session is a follow-up to Session 65.

Students will

- discuss ideas they have learned from interviewing effective conflict solvers
- recognize skills effective conflict solvers use to stay calm and handle conflicts assertively and fairly
- role-play assertive, respectful approaches to handling a typical classroom conflict

Materials

- completed handout: "Conflict Solver Interview" (page 156)
- sign with definition of *assertive* from Session 65 (see page 155)
- chart paper and marker
- student journals

Preparation. Prior to this session, pass out copies of the "Conflict Solver Interview" handout. Have students use it to interview someone they know who gets along well with others and is good at preventing and resolving conflicts. Post the sign that defines *assertive* to refer to as needed.

Introduction and Discussion. Have students bring their "Conflict Solver Interview" sheets to the circle. Put students in pairs. Give them five minutes to share the most important things they learned from the conflict solver they interviewed.

Afterward, ask students to share with the large group some of the most helpful things they learned from their conflict solvers. List key points on chart paper.

Go over the questions on the handout one by one, sharing and discussing interviewees' ideas and responses:

- What do you do to keep your cool when someone gets you mad?
- How do you stay calm during conflict?
- What do you do to avoid using put-downs when you're in a conflict?
- Is there something you say to yourself that helps you keep your cool in conflict situations?
- What advice do you have for other people when it comes to handling conflict?

Ask students if they have had the chance to apply anything they learned from the conflict solvers they interviewed. Discuss.

Activity. Ask for two volunteers to pretend they are the conflict solvers they interviewed. Have the students role-play a typical conflict that goes on in your room, but have them do so in a way their conflict solvers would likely resolve it. Guide role players to use the Win/Win Guidelines as they enact the scene.

Briefly discuss the role play; conduct additional role plays if time permits.

Wrap-Up. Remind students to keep applying what they're learning to real-life situations. Tell them you'll check in with them to hear how things are going.

Follow-Up. In their journals, have students reflect on what they learned from the conflict solver they interviewed. Have them include changes they want to make in the way they handle real-life conflicts, and how insights from these interviews can be applied.

Session 67: Staying Respectful with Someone You Don't Like

> **respect • tolerance • self-control • compassion • fairness • courage • personal responsibility**
>
> Session 67 guides students to choose to remain respectful even when dealing with people they don't especially like.
>
> **Students will**
> - understand why it's important to be respectful toward someone they don't wish to be friends with
> - recognize behaviors to avoid in order to remain respectful
> - learn and practice ways to stay respectful even when it's hard to do
>
> **Materials**
> - chart paper and marker

Preparation. On chart paper, write the following: *"We agreed we didn't need to be friends, we just needed to respect each other."*

Introduction. Say: **Sometimes it can be hard to be respectful to someone we don't like. Have you ever had that problem?** Briefly discuss. Say: **Here's something a real student wrote about handling the challenge of being around someone she didn't like:**

"I used to have a problem with this girl named Lanny. She wasn't a true friend. She would threaten that she wouldn't be my friend if I didn't do what she wanted to do. She would act mean to me. My mom said there will always be a Lanny in every grade you go into. She asked, 'What can you do to handle the one you're dealing with now?'

"I decided to talk to Lanny. We agreed we didn't need to be friends, we just needed to respect each other."

Ask: **What do you think is the most important lesson the girl who told this story learned from her experience?**

Discussion. Display the sign you prepared and have the class read it aloud together: "We agreed we didn't need to be friends, we just needed to respect each other." Ask: **Have you ever managed to treat someone you don't like with respect?** Discuss. Give a personal example.

Then ask: **What do you think people can do if they're in the same class, or on the same team, with someone they're no longer friends with? Or with someone they might not like? Think about how you would want to be treated by someone who may not like you.** Discuss and list students' ideas on chart paper.

Ask: **Even though you might not want to be friends with someone, what can you do to show basic respect? What things should you avoid doing?** Add responses to the list. Guide students to understand that there are minimum basic things we need to do to survive together in the same room or school, or on the same team, with someone we might not like. Add the following to the chart if they have not been mentioned:

- Avoid using negative face or body language.
- Refrain from whispering about the person when you see him or her.
- Resist talking behind the person's back.
- Refrain from texting or passing notes about the person.
- Be polite, and if you can, say hello (in a courteous, non-sarcastic way).

Activity. Say: **There are certain kinds of body language we need to avoid when we see someone we don't like.** One at a time, ask for several volunteers to model different kinds of negative body language. After each demonstration, say: **This is what we need to avoid doing. It's not respectful.**

Continue, asking for volunteers to model the following:

- giving a negative look or gesture
- leaning in toward each other and starting to whisper as a third role player walks by
- saying hello sarcastically

After each demonstration, repeat the line: **This is what we need to avoid doing. It's not respectful.**

Next, ask volunteers to model passing each other in the hall and being respectful even though they don't like each other. Invite at least three more sets of volunteers to model it as well.

Reiterate to students that, hard as it might be to do what was just modeled, it's critical that they do. Ask why this is so important. (It shows integrity, it helps us avoid starting conflicts, it's never cool to be cruel, it's a way to stay up in the balcony.)

Ask students: **What can you do if someone is going out of their way to be mean to you and you are doing all the things talked about today?**

Discuss, making sure to include these ideas as part of your conversation:

- Try talking to the person directly and privately to find out why she or he is acting that way. (Plan out what you're going to say first, and rehearse it.)

If you feel like you can't do this alone, ask your school counselor, teacher, or another trusted adult to help the two of you talk it out.

- If nothing you've tried works, seek the help of a trusted adult.

Wrap-Up. Ask if students have any questions. Reassure students that it isn't always easy to stay respectful, and it takes courage to commit to doing so. Emphasize that this is something they can get in the habit of doing through practice. Acknowledge students for the work they are doing to take responsibility for their behavior in challenging situations.

Follow-Up. To give students further help dealing respectfully with someone who isn't willing to cooperate or stay respectful, conduct Session 71 (pages 167–168).

Extension. Have students write skits or create additional role plays showing ways to handle being with someone they don't typically get along with at school, on the bus, at lunch, and in extra-curricular activities. Encourage students to demonstrate a variety of ways to stay respectful.

Session 68: The Dignity Stance

| courage • self-worth • calmness • assertiveness • self-control |

Session 68 introduces the Dignity Stance, an effective assertiveness tool students can use when they are involved in conflicts or mistreated by others.

Students will
- learn to use the Dignity Stance in conflict situations
- understand how to act assertively rather than aggressively or passively

Materials
- chart paper and marker
- handout: "The Dignity Stance" (page 162)

Preparation. On chart paper, write the steps for the Dignity Stance (see page 162).

Introduction. Tell students that today they're going to learn about an important way to stand up for themselves when they're involved in a conflict, or when they want to prevent a conflict or stop one from getting worse: the Dignity Stance.

Review with students what it means to be assertive (strong and honest, yet respectful, saying what you need to say with confidence).

Say: **You can show *assertiveness* in the way you hold your body and how you speak. The Dignity Stance is one way to do this.**

Activity. Tell students that starting with deep breaths and a calming statement will make it easier for them to use the Dignity Stance. Spend a few moments taking deep, abdominal breaths together; remind students to say a calming statement to themselves as they breathe.

Direct students' attention to the chart you have created. Go through each of the steps of the Dignity Stance with the group.

Stand tall with your head held high, feet apart, shoulders back. Demonstrate the Dignity Stance. Ask students to stand and also take the stance. Scan the class for kids who may need coaching. Some students might stiffen their bodies while others may take an aggressive stance, maybe even balling up their fists. Others will stand tall with head down shoulders hunched. Give coaching where needed.

Take slow, deep breaths to keep your cool.
Have students join in you in taking three slow, deep abdominal breaths. Remind them that they can do this "invisibly" (in a non-exaggerated way) and no one else will know they're doing it. Demonstrate how.

Keep your body language and facial expression neutral but strong. Emphasize that it's important to keep a *neutral* (nonemotional) expression that is strong but respectful. Demonstrate this for students. Then say: **Sometimes we have to act "as if." We need to act *as if* we are feeling brave, even if we're really scared. The more we act like we feel brave, the braver we will actually begin to feel. Our body language can help us look and *feel* brave and strong.**

Make direct eye contact. Demonstrate looking someone in the eye with confidence, not aggression.

Note: In some cultures, children are taught that looking someone in the eye is disrespectful. If you have students who have been raised to look downward or avert their eyes, let them know that, with many people, making direct eye contact is an important way to communicate respect and confidence. Help students identify when and how to do this comfortably.

Speak in a firm, steady tone of voice. Demonstrate with the following statement that can be used when facing an angry person: **"I know you're mad, but let's see if we can talk this out."** Have students turn to one another and make this statement standing tall, speaking in a steady, neutral tone of voice.

Select one student to join you before the group. Face your partner and say: **Now let's pretend you've just said something hurtful to me. First I'm going to take a deep breath and make my calming statement. Then I'm going to stand tall, look directly in your eyes, and in a firm, level voice I'm going to say how I feel.**

Still facing your partner, say: **"I find that insulting."** Now ask students to practice doing the same with the person next to them.

Walk away tall and strong. Demonstrate walking away tall and strong. Tell students that breathing deeply and repeating their calming statements will help them walk away with poise and dignity. Now have them practice walking away tall and proud. Give coaching where needed, and if you see any aggressive or passive postures or gestures help students modify them.

Remind your students of the way Martin Luther King Jr. carried himself during civil rights marches. Even when people were yelling racist words and threats, he would consistently stand tall, walk strong and proud, and maintain a neutral facial expression. This is the finest example of the Dignity Stance that exists for all of us.

Discussion. Have students sit back down in the circle. Ask for two volunteers to come to the center. Ask one student to imagine the other has just called him or her a name. Have the recipient of the put-down assume the Dignity Stance, give an assertive I-message, then walk away tall and strong.

Ask students to give feedback. Did the person stand and speak assertively, not aggressively? Did the person walk away tall and strong (not wimpy or aggressive)?

Ask students to come up with other assertive statements that can be used in similar situations. They might be I-messages or simple statements, but they should always be firm and respectful. Some examples are:

- "That wasn't funny."
- "Not cool."
- "I don't need to listen to this."
- "You're wasting your time."

Ask for more volunteers to come to the center of the circle, stand in the Dignity Stance, look the person in the eye, deliver a firm, steady response, and then walk away tall and strong.

Say: **If someone calls you a name or puts you down, the Dignity Stance is a way you can be strong and assertive without having to name-call back. You can walk away strong and brave, not scared and weak, just the way Martin Luther King Jr. did.**

Wrap-Up. Entertain questions and comments. Give students the "Dignity Stance" handout and suggest they tape it into their journal or onto the wall at home.

Extension. Suggest that students do the following visualization activity at home: **Tonight, while you're lying in bed before falling asleep, practice some deep breathing and picture yourself using the Dignity Stance. See yourself standing tall and brave, looking someone who has insulted you in the eye, and speaking assertively. See yourself walking away tall and strong.**

PART TWO

Preventing Conflict

The Dignity Stance

Stand tall with your head held high, feet apart, shoulders back.

Take slow, deep breaths to keep your cool.

Keep your body language and facial expression neutral but strong.

Make direct eye contact.

Speak in a firm, steady tone of voice.

Walk away tall and strong.

Session 69: Staying Out of Physical Fights

courage • self-control • respect

Session 69 introduces a practical, real-life approach students can use to stay out of physical fights. This session is a follow-up to Session 68.

Students will

- understand the importance of avoiding physical fights
- learn a realistic tool for staying out of fights
- come up with statements to use when faced with the possibility of a fight

Materials

- handout: "Staying Out of Fights" (page 164)
- "Dignity Stance" chart from Session 68 (see page 162)
- chart paper and marker

Introduction and Discussion. Say: Today we're going to talk about ways to stay out of physical fights. Here's some advice from a middle schooler who figured out a way to successfully do this. Distribute the handouts and invite a student or students to read the story from a real middle school student.

After the story has been read, ask: **Why does it take courage to walk away when someone's trying to pick a fight?** Discuss, and encourage students to be frank. For some kids, fighting is a way of life and a tool for proving one's worth.

Make it clear to students that avoiding physical fights doesn't mean letting people harm them. What it does mean is using every other option available. If students are in danger and need to defend themselves against oncoming violence, a physical response may be the only option, but that's the exception. Strongly emphasize the need to stay away from groups and places where fighting is likely. Say: **If you need to walk down another street on the way home from school to avoid a possible fight, do it. What else can you do?** Discuss.

Ask: **What happened to the boy in the story when he fought in sixth grade?** (He got suspended.) Ask students what the rules at school are regarding fighting. What are the consequences? Discuss. Also ask what would happen if they were adults and they got into a fight. Talk about adult consequences of fighting. Remind students that by learning how to resist fighting now, they're setting a pattern that can support them for the rest of their lives.

Ask students what technique the boy in the story came up with to keep himself from fighting when others were egging him on (Stop, Drop, Roll). Ask students: **What do you do to resist fighting? What else can you do?** Remind students of Stop, Breathe, Chill and the Dignity Stance.

Activity. Draw students' attention to the "Dignity Stance" sign, particularly "Speak in a firm, steady tone of voice." Put students in pairs and have them come up with statements that can be used if someone's trying to draw them into a fight. Give the following example that many kids use: "This isn't worth fighting over." After a few minutes, bring the class back together and ask for their ideas, listing them on chart paper.

Wrap-Up. Acknowledge students for their efforts to stay out of physical fights and get along better with others. Affirm them for honesty, respect, and respectful listening you've observed during the session.

Extensions. The middle school boy came up with his own unique strategy to stay out of fights: Stop, Drop, Roll. Students may want to come up with their own individual strategies to stay brave, respectful, and safe. Have students share their ideas through a classroom display.

If physical fighting is common in your school, introduce the following sometime after you've completed this session:

Tips for Staying Out of Physical Fights

- Don't provoke people.
- Resist hanging out with kids who get into physical fights.
- Find healthy ways to express anger; never go on the attack.
- Avoid places where fighting is likely to occur.
- Be willing to apologize if you've offended someone.
- Be guided by what you know is right, not your reactions.
- Remember the consequences of fighting and how that can affect your life.

Staying Out of Fights

A middle school boy discovered that he could keep himself out of fights by using the same saying that's used in fire prevention: "Stop, Drop, and Roll." This is what the boy recommends:

> Here's what I realized after I got suspended for fighting: If someone tries to tempt you to fight, don't do it. There's no realistic point to fighting. If somebody's picking on you, that person might have a troubled life. Their problems might lead them to act differently than they should. What I like to do when someone tries to get me to fight is stop, drop and roll.

> **STOP to think about it.**

> **DROP whatever you want to say or do that's not respectful.**

> **ROLL on over to what you're going to do next.**

> Instead of getting pulled into fights, focus on your schoolwork. That's what I do. Many a day, people try to get me involved in fights. If someone intentionally throws things at me, I don't let it get to me. People will egg me on and try to get me to hit the other person. I just try to let their words go and do what I know is right.

> I learned my lesson when I was in sixth grade. This kid was throwing things at me. We just came back from an assembly. So I pushed him and he pushed me back. We got sent to the office and we started kicking each other. It was a mistake. I could have just let it go, something stupid like that, but I didn't. We both ended up getting suspended. Now I know better.

Think About It

Is there a place in your life where you can Stop, Drop, and Roll to stay out of an argument or a fight?

_____

_____

_____

Responding to Conflict

The more your students are able and willing to work out conflicts, the less likely they will be to bully or stand by passively (or aggressively) and watch bullying happen. This section will help you teach kids how to resolve different kinds of common conflicts using the Win/Win Guidelines. The sessions will enable your students to role-play and resolve conflicts brought on by gossip, exclusion, hurt feelings, negative group dynamics, and other familiar conflict triggers. The activities in the Preventing Conflict sessions on pages 119–164 lay the groundwork for the Responding to Conflict activities in this section. Conduct at least some of those sessions before doing these.

Be sure to have these charts displayed: "Respectful Listening," "The Win/Win Guidelines for Working Out Conflicts," and "Stop, Breathe, Chill" (introduced in Sessions 2, 8, and 9), and "Ways to Chill" (see Session 40, pages 100–101).

70. Win/Win Guidelines for Working Out Conflicts (Review)
71. Working Out Conflicts with Someone Who Is Unwilling
72. Using I-Messages and Reflective Listening in Conflicts
73. Gossip and Conflict
74. Conflicts with Friends
75. Brainstorming Solutions (10-Minute Time Cruncher)
76. Group Conflicts: Talking Someone Down
77. Group Conflicts: Check In with Your Conscience
78. Confronting Someone Who Has Hurt You
79. Dealing with Exclusion and Rejection
80. The Problem with Fighting
81. Mediating a Friend's Conflict

Session 70: Win/Win Guidelines for Working Out Conflicts (Review)

respect • personal responsibility • conflict resolution

Session 70 offers a refresher on the Win/Win Guidelines and gives students the opportunity to practice using all the guidelines together through role play.

Students will

- review how they've been using the Win/Win Guidelines to resolve conflicts
- address challenges they've encountered using the Win/Win Guidelines
- role-play conflicts using the Win/Win Guidelines and evaluate how effectively the guidelines were applied

Materials

- chart paper and marker
- *optional handout:* "Win/Win Guidelines for Working Out Conflicts" (page 36)

Introduction and Discussion. Ask students how they've been using the Win/Win Guidelines to prevent or resolve conflicts. Refer to the "Win/Win Guidelines for Working Out Conflicts" chart and ask about different parts of the process: **What are you doing to cool off? Have you run into any challenges using I-messages? Which steps are most helpful? Most challenging?**

Refer to the Rules for Using the Win/Win Guidelines. Ask: **Are you remembering to use these rules? Are there any that are hard to stick to?** Discuss. Affirm students for progress they're making. Assure them that challenges are normal. With more practice and role-play, the guidelines will become easier and more natural to use.

Activity. Ask for two volunteers to role-play a conflict. You can have students choose a conflict that's fairly common and role-play that one, or use this idea: **Person A spread a mean rumor about Person B. Person B retaliated by gossiping about Person A.**

Have volunteers role-play the conflict, using the guidelines and rules. Allow the role players to work their way through without interruption, unless they get stuck and need help.

After they finish, ask the class if they noticed each guideline being used. Ask for specific examples. Ask if the role play went well. Why or why not? What improvements could have been made?

Give the role players a chance to replay the scene, incorporating ideas that came up in the discussion.

As time permits, invite other volunteers to role-play one or two more scenarios. Choose common conflicts that happen in your class, or ask students to suggest conflicts to enact. Each time, offer support only when role players seem stuck. After each role play, ask the class to evaluate how the Win/Win Guidelines helped students solve the conflict, suggesting ideas that might have made the process go smoother. Discuss.

Wrap-Up. End the session by affirming students for their continued efforts toward resolving conflicts peacefully and respectfully. You may want to distribute fresh copies of the handout for students to keep in their journals or tape inside their notebooks, desks, or lockers.

Follow-Up. Continue to check in with students on how they're doing as they use the Win/Win Guidelines. Provide refresher lessons on the guidelines, referring back to Sessions 9–14 as needed. You may want to provide fresh copies of the Win/Win Guidelines handout for students as well.

Extension. Have students develop conflict-solving skits to perform for younger students.

Session 71: Working Out Conflicts with Someone Who Is Unwilling

conflict resolution • compromise • fairness • respect

Session 71 explores how to talk out a conflict with a resistant person.

Students will

- recognize that it can be possible to resolve a conflict even when only one person is willing
- role-play resolving a conflict with an unwilling partner
- see the relationship between misunderstandings and willingness blocks

Materials

- chart paper and marker or "WILLINGNESS" skills sign from Session 58 (see page 141)
- large wooden block (to represent a "willingness block")

Note: If you have not conducted Sessions 58 and 59 (pages 141–144), read through them prior to conducting this one.

Preparation. If you have not done so before, create a sign that says the following:

"Working out conflicts requires WILLINGNESS to:
- *compromise*
- *hear out the other person*
- *be patient"*

Introduction. Display the sign and review or introduce the three willingness skills, making sure students understand that working on these will help them become better and better at working out conflicts with other people.

Discussion. If you've done Session 59, Willingness Blocks, ask students what willingness blocks are (things we think and feel that hold us back from working out problems). Otherwise give them the definition. Ask: **What are some examples of willingness blocks?** (Wanting to be right, not liking the other person, wanting to blame someone, not wanting to look like a wimp.)

Ask students: **Have you ever been willing to work out a conflict with someone, but the person seemed unwilling to work it out with you?** Discuss, sharing your own story as well.

Activity. Say, **Let's see if we can work out a real conflict where one person was really holding on to her willingness block.**

Read the following real conflict shared by a real student. The boy who wrote this story expressed deep frustration at the other person's unwillingness to work things out.*

"I was in a conflict where someone blamed me for something I didn't do. It started at recess when we were playing a game called four square. Someone threw a ball at my shoe. It flew up and hit a girl on the nose. The next day I tried to talk to her but she told me that she hates me because I hit her with the ball on purpose. Now you can see how much pressure I have! She doesn't want to be my friend anymore and she hates me for something I never actually did."

Ask for volunteers to role-play the conflict. Have one student be the boy who wrote the story. Have the other be the girl who's angry with him. Before attempting to resolve the conflict, have the boy rehearse in his mind what he's going to say, then steady his nerves by taking deep breaths and silently repeating his calming statement. Have him approach the girl at a neutral time, and then use the Win/Win Guidelines to try to talk out the conflict. Remind him to keep using deep breathing and his calming statement while he talks with the other student. Have the girl hold onto her willingness blocks (anger and blame). Ask her, at first, to actually hold a block in front of her to represent her unwillingness, then put it aside if and when her resistance starts to dissolve.

Note: If at any point during the role play either student gets overwhelmed, step in as mediator to help the two work out the conflict. Let your kids know

* Stories and quotes attributed to real students and teachers come from author interviews and from responses to the Survey About Conflicts conducted by the author and publisher. See pages 1 and 279–281 for further information.

that the option of asking a trusted adult to mediate is a good one if they need the help.

Afterward, debrief. Did the conflict get worked out? Did the girl let go of her willingness blocks? Why or why not? Is there something that could have been done differently?

Point out that this conflict was caused by a misunderstanding. Ask: **What was the misunderstanding?** Explain that the majority of all conflicts are caused by misunderstandings. Say: **Misunderstandings and willingness blocks go hand in hand.**

Ask students to think about a time they were involved in a conflict over a misunderstanding. Ask: **Did you hold onto a willingness block? Did the other person? What happened?**

Wrap-Up. End by reminding students that sometimes even if only one person is willing to talk things out, conflicts can be resolved. Ask students to notice times when they find themselves holding onto a willingness block. Have them ask themselves the following: "Why am I holding onto this willingness block? Could there be a misunderstanding here?"

Session 72: Using I-Messages and Reflective Listening in Conflicts

conflict resolution • fairness • compromise • respect • personal responsibility

Session 72 gives students practice using the Win/Win Guidelines for Working Out Conflicts with an emphasis on I-messages and reflective listening.

Students will

- review how to use I-messages and reflective listening

- observe and discuss a role play using the Win/Win Guidelines
- role-play using I-messages and reflective listening in conflict situations

Introduction and Discussion. Take three to five minutes to review I-messages and reflective listening. Ask students: **How do you feel when you're in a conflict and someone keeps saying "you" this and "you" that?** (Hearing things like "You started it" or "You're wrong" causes people to feel defensive, angry, blamed, or hurt.) **Why is it important to start from the word "I" when you're trying to work out a conflict?** (Doing so makes people feel less angry and defensive.) Point to Guideline 2: *Talk it over starting from "I," not "you."* Ask for a couple examples of I-messages. Remind students that using I-messages is not just about the words you speak, but also how your face and body look when you say them.

Next, ask students how they feel when someone truly listens to them. As they share, reflect back what was said. ("So you feel like someone really cares when that person truly listens to you?" Or, "I hear you saying that you feel respected when someone sincerely listens to what you have to say.") Emphasize

that when we have conflicts, truly listening to the other person can be really hard, but when we do so, we're much more likely to work things out. Ask why this is often the case. Briefly discuss.

Refer to the Win/Win Guidelines and tell students they are going to get extra practice with the guidelines today, with some special focus on I-messages and reflective listening (saying back what you heard).

Activity. Ask for a volunteer to come to the center of the circle and demonstrate the following conflict-solving scenario with you. The student will play Person A and you will play Person B. Spend five to ten minutes role-playing. As you do, point out to students each stage of the Win/Win Guidelines.

- Person A lent his kneepads to Person B, and Person B lost one of them. Now Person A is angry.

Have Person A take a few breaths to cool off, then give an I-message expressing his displeasure about what happened (Guidelines 1 and 2).

In your role as Person B, take some deep breaths as you hear his words, then paraphrase what he said (Guideline 3). Don't offer excuses or apologies at this time. Just listen and say back what was said. ("So you're really annoyed because you can't use your skateboard without your kneepads, and now one is gone. You were counting on me to take care of your things, and you feel let down.")

If Person A has more to say, continue to listen and say back.

Now deliver your I-message to Person A (Guideline 2). Example: "I feel really bad about losing the knee-pad. Sometimes I get really disorganized. I should have been more careful (Guideline 4), and I wish you wouldn't be angry with me."

Have Person A say back what you just said (Guideline 3).

Discuss possible solutions together and have the class help think of some, too (Guideline 5). Choose a solution with Person A.

Now go to Guideline 6: *Affirm, forgive, thank, or apologize.*

Next, have students get into pairs, choose a Person A and Person B, and role-play one of the following scenarios, or other scenarios students suggest, using the Win/Win Guidelines. Remind students to make sure to start from "I" and to say back what they hear the other person saying. Tell them to see if they can get to a resolution.

- Person A got a bad grade on a math quiz. Person B says sarcastically, "Way to go, genius."
- Person A gave Person B a look in the lunchroom, and Person B is offended.

Circulate as students role-play and offer guidance where needed.

Wrap-Up. Take a minute or two to debrief in the large circle. Ask students how it went in terms of taking deep breaths before speaking, using I-messages, and truly listening. Affirm students for whatever positives you observed.

Follow-Up. If time permits, invite some partners to reenact their role plays for the large group. Then discuss with the group how the role players used the skills and what other things they could have said or done.

Session 73: Gossip and Conflict

---

conflict resolution • personal responsibility • fairness • courage • compassion • respect

Session 73 guides students to consider the damage done by gossip and to see the link between gossip and conflict.

Students will

- role-play working out a conflict resulting from gossip
- understand the role gossip plays in creating and fueling conflicts
- recognize their responsibility for being part of the solution when it comes to gossip

Materials

- handout: "What Real Kids Have to Say About Gossip and Conflict" (page 171)
- chart paper and marker
- student journals
- *optional: Sixth Grade Secrets* by Louis Sachar

Introduction. Distribute handouts and read or have a student read the statistic at the top. Ask: **Does this sound right to you? Is gossip a big problem in our school? Do you think it leads to a lot of conflicts?**

Read or have a student read the quoted story from the handout. Invite responses from students. Ask: **Has anything like this ever happened to you? How does gossip affect the atmosphere in a class or school?**

Have students take a couple of minutes to complete the bottom of the handout. Invite a few volunteers to share their experiences with the class, either reading what they wrote or talking about it. Caution them not to use real names. Ask students: **Why do people gossip? Is it easy to do it without thinking? Is it hard not to gossip?** Discuss briefly.

Discussion. Write the word *conscience* on the board. Review its meaning—a feeling or knowledge of right and wrong that guides us to do what is right. Ask students: **When gossip is being spread, what does your conscience guide you to do?** Discuss, sharing these words from a fourth-grade student: **"If people are talking about someone, I walk away if I can. And I never say anything when kids ask, 'What do you think of So-and-So?' "**

Ask students to respond. Then ask: **What are some ways you can stop gossip in its tracks?** List students' ideas on chart paper under the heading "No More Gossip."

Activity. Using the Win/Win Guidelines, have a few students role-play the gossip scenario from the handout. Ask them to role-play it in two different ways: The first role play should show what happens when gossip is spread. The second should show what happens when someone takes a step to stop the spread of gossip.

Debrief with students after the role plays. Ask why it's so important to stop the spread of gossip.

Wrap-Up. Affirm students for the measure of personal responsibility they exhibited in coming up with solutions to gossip. Remind them that their task is to put these solutions into action in real life. Post the "No More Gossip" chart as a reminder of how to be part of the solution when it comes to the spread of gossip.

Follow-Up. Encourage students to write in their journals about how gossip has affected them, what they can do to avoid gossiping, or how they can help stop gossip when it's happening.

Extensions. Have students read *Sixth Grade Secrets* by Louis Sachar. Afterward, talk together about the negative results of secrets and gossip.

Discuss examples from books, movies, or TV shows that depict people gossiping. What often happens when gossip is spread? What could the characters have done to stop the spread of gossip and the conflicts that ensued as a result?

What Real Kids Have to Say About
Gossip and Conflict

In a national survey of more than 2,100 students in grades 3–6:

64% (1,394 students) said that rumors and gossip are a top cause of conflict in their lives.

Here's what one student wrote:

"Last year I got into a huge fight with four other girls. It all started with gossip. That is probably the #1 thing that starts fights in our school. One of the girls said something incredibly mean about another girl. The girl that she told it to, Corinna, was not very trustworthy, and she told the girl who the gossip was about! I was with Corinna so I got blamed, too, even though I never said anything. It was *not* fun.

"The girl who was gossiped about was so mad she told on both of us to the principal! I knew that I didn't do what she accused me of so I got extremely angry. Then I blurted out something that I was trying to hold in: 'If it wasn't for Corinna we wouldn't be in this mess!' I was ashamed of myself. Corinna started to cry. I apologized very sincerely but everyone was still mad. It was a mess.

"After a few days we ended up talking it over. Finally we all ended up forgiving each other."

What do YOU have to say about gossip and conflict?

Do you gossip? How do you feel when someone gossips about you? What can we do to stop gossip from happening?

_____

_____

_____

_____

_____

Session 74: Conflicts with Friends

personal responsibility • conflict resolution • compassion • respect • forgiveness

Session 74 helps students understand the value of taking responsibility, apologizing, forgiving, and working things out through compromise when conflicts come up between friends.

Students will
- reflect on what gets in the way of resolving conflicts with friends
- role-play working out conflicts with friends
- recognize that taking responsibility, compromising, and forgiving are essential for working out conflicts

Materials
- handout: "Being Willing to Stay Friends" (page 173)
- student journals

PART TWO
Responding to Conflict

Introduction. Distribute the handouts and read or have a student read the quote from a student who responded to the Survey About Conflicts. Invite comments from students about the quote. Ask if they ever find themselves waiting for an apology and then watching the conflict drag on and on. Discuss.

Ask: **In situations like this, what keeps you from being willing to apologize or talk things out? What willingness blocks get in your way?** (Wanting to be right, not wanting to take any responsibility, stubbornness, feeling too hurt to want to talk things out.) Discuss.

Activity and Discussion. Ask for two volunteers to role-play working out the following conflict, or another one students suggest, using the Win/Win Guidelines:

There's a boy in the class Mahli has a crush on. Mahli's friend Audra mentions it in passing to the boy's friend, and now the boy knows. When Mahli finds this out, she tells people in the class that she hates her friend Audra because she has a big mouth.

Afterward, debrief with the class. **Were Mahli and Audra willing to hear each other out? Did they try to understand each other's point of view? Were they willing to take responsibility, compromise, apologize, and forgive each other? Did the conflict get resolved? How? Did either girl do anything that worked against solving it? What helped them work things out? What else might have helped?** Discuss what students observed and other ideas they offer.

Have two different volunteers role-play working out the following conflict, or another one students suggest, using the Win/Win Guidelines:

Henry fumbled the ball during touch football, causing his team to lose the game. His friend screamed at him and called him a name for doing it. Henry got mad, pushed his friend down, and called him a name back. Now neither friend is talking to the other.

Again, debrief with the class. **Were Henry and his friend willing to hear each other out? Did they try to understand each other's point of view? Were they willing to take responsibility, compromise, apologize, and forgive each other? Did the conflict get resolved? How? Did either or them do anything that made it harder to resolve it? What helped them work things out? What else might have helped?** Discuss what students observed and other ideas they offer.

Wrap-Up. Tell students to silently ask themselves if they have any ongoing conflicts with friends where they need to compromise and work something out. Ask them to think about things they learned in this session that could help them do so. Remind students to keep applying what they are learning in real-life situations. Affirm them for acts of compassion, insights given, and helpful solutions.

Follow-Up. Have students write in their journals about any ongoing or repeated conflicts they have with friends. Is there something they need to take responsibility for? Is there a way they can see themselves compromising? Is there something they need to apologize for?

Being willing to Stay Friends
Advice from a Fifth Grader

In a national survey of more than 2,100 students in grades 3–6, kids wrote about conflicts they had with friends. Here's what one fifth-grader wrote:

> "The most important thing to remember when you get into a conflict with a good friend is this: If you're really good friends, there's nothing you *can't* work out. Sometimes you have to be willing to say 'I'm sorry' first. Some kids make the mistake of waiting for the other person to apologize first. That's the biggest mistake you could possibly make, because the conflict keeps going. Letting things go on too long can destroy the friendship."

Write about a conflict you had with a friend where **neither of you was willing** to say "I'm sorry." What happened?

_____

_____

_____

_____

_____

Write about a conflict you had with a friend where **one of you was willing** to say "I'm sorry." What happened?

_____

_____

_____

_____

_____

Session 75: Brainstorming Solutions
(10-Minute Time Cruncher)

conflict resolution • compromise • fairness • personal responsibility

Session 75 has students look at their own personal conflicts and brainstorm a variety of possible compromise solutions.

Students will

- brainstorm in journals possible solutions to an unresolved or ongoing conflict they have
- identify one or two solutions they can use to resolve their real-life conflict

Materials

- student journals

Introduction. Read aloud the following words from a fourth-grade student: **"Sometimes I write about conflicts in my journal. It really helps. I number the solutions I come up with. I memorize them and try to use them when the conflict happens again, or if it hasn't been solved."**

Ask students to each think of a conflict they've had that either isn't resolved or is likely to occur again. Give your own example. Ask for one or two examples from students.

Have students open their journals and briefly write a description of the conflict.

Activity. At the board demonstrate doing a quick brainstorming of solutions to the conflict you described in your example. Come up with five to ten solutions, and don't censor any of your ideas. Explain that brainstorming is a creative act. Something that might seem like a silly idea at first can actually hold the key to a solution.

In their journals, have students brainstorm a numbered list of possible solutions to the conflict they just wrote about. Tell them to let their ideas flow freely and without judgment. Encourage them to come up with five to ten solutions, and to write down all ideas that pop up.

Wrap-Up. When their brainstorming lists are completed, ask students to circle one or two solutions they like best. Tell them to try using one of the solutions to work out their conflict during the coming week. Let them know you'll check back in with them about how it went.

Follow-Up. Check in with students to hear if and how their solutions worked. Encourage them to continue looking for solutions to conflicts. If any students are having serious difficulty working out a conflict, remind them to talk to a trusted person to get some help with it.

Session 76: Group Conflicts: Talking Someone Down

conflict resolution • anger management • self-control • personal responsibility • integrity

Session 76 looks at a conflict on the verge of getting physical that was sparked by mean text messages. It helps students consider ways to be part of the solution, not part of the problem, when tempers flare.

Students will
- identify actions that cause a conflict to escalate
- consider the harmful and pernicious effects of nasty text messages
- come up with ideas to help de-escalate a conflict
- learn that "talking someone down" can help prevent some conflicts from getting physical

Materials
- chart paper and marker
- handout: "Tom's Story: Mean Texting Leads to a Fight" (page 177)
- *optional: Eagle Song* by Joseph Bruchac

Preparation. On chart paper, write: *"You can either be part of the problem or part of the solution."*

Introduction. Lead students in taking three slow, deep abdominal breaths. Remind them that deep breathing will help them calm down and stay in better control whenever there's a conflict.

Say: **Today we're going to look at a conflict that took place among a group of boys: Tom, Logan, and Jack. (These aren't their real names.) After the story, I'm going to ask you to think of ways Tom and Logan could have been part of the solution, rather than being part of the problem.**

Activity and Discussion. Distribute the handout. Ask for a volunteer to read Tom's story aloud to the class.

After the story has been read, ask students if mean texting is a problem in your school. Discuss briefly.

Ask students: **What started the conflict on the playground? What did Logan do to escalate the conflict—to make it grow? Remind students that in nearly all conflicts, both people are responsible in some way.**

Say: **What about Tom? He wrote that Jack threw the icicle at both Logan and him. What might Tom have done to provoke this?**

Ask: **Does it sound like Tom was part of the solution or part of the problem? Why? What might Tom have done to be part of the solution? Is there a way he could have helped prevent the conflict from getting out of hand?** Discuss.

At the top of a piece of chart paper, write "Talking Someone Down." Ask students: **What does it mean to talk someone down? Have you ever tried to talk down someone who was angry?** Ask for examples and give one yourself. Ask how the conflict that Tom wrote about could have been less serious if he or someone else had tried to talk Logan down. Or perhaps someone could have tried to talk Tom down when he started fueling the fire. Have students look back at the story and identify places where someone could have helped de-escalate things. Discuss.

Ask what tools students can use to calm themselves and the other person if a conflict is escalating. (Walk away together, take deep breaths, lower your voice if the other person's gets louder, use things on the "Ways to Chill" list, remind the other person that it's not worth getting into a physical fight.) Ask what else they might say to someone on the verge of losing his or her temper. List ideas on the "Talking Someone Down" chart.

Ask for two volunteers to play the roles of Tom and Logan. Have the student playing Tom role-play using some of the things that were just discussed to help Logan calm down. Invite other ideas from students.

Wrap-Up. Refer to the sign, "You can either be part of the problem or part of the solution." Invite someone to read it. Reiterate that in every conflict, each person has the choice of being part of the solution or part of the problem.

Reiterate that spreading rumors via texting or other means, threatening, or putting someone down is cruel and inevitably leads to conflict.

Follow-Up. Encourage students to keep making efforts to prevent and resolve conflicts in their lives at home and at school. Remind them to turn to a trusted adult if things get physical or they don't know what to do.

Extension. Have students read *Eagle Song* by Joseph Bruchac to find out how one boy turned an enemy into an ally.

PART TWO
Responding to Conflict

Tom's Story

Mean Texting Leads to a Fight

My best friend, who I'll call Logan, started getting all these bad texts from a kid I'll call Jack. When some of the texts came, Logan's cell phone was in his mom's pocket, so she saw them. She told Logan she was going to talk to Jack's mom about the texts after school the next day.

But during recess the next day, things got physical. Logan and I were with a couple other friends, and Jack was with a bunch of his. Jack said something mean to Logan, and Logan swore at Jack. People started saying things, then yelling. A kid from Jack's group got chased by someone in ours and ran away. Everybody was all riled up. I was about to charge in because of lies Jack told. A kid had to hold me back. Logan just kept yelling at Jack, and Jack ended up throwing a huge icicle at Logan's head and at mine. The bell rang and we had to go in, but we were all really mad!

Everyone at school was talking about what happened. The news got around and the principal heard about it. Eventually Jack got suspended and Logan was held in the principal's office till his mom came to school.

Think About It

When he got really mad Tom said he "was about to charge in." What would have happened if he had actually done that?

_____

_____

_____

When things started getting out of hand, how could Tom have talked himself down? How could he have talked Logan down and prevented the conflict from getting worse?

_____

_____

_____

Session 77: Group Conflicts: Check In with Your Conscience

conflict resolution • compassion • fairness • personal responsibility • respect • integrity • forgiveness

Session 77 has students evaluate an incident involving gossip and shunning through the lens of conscience.

Students will

- understand how gossip hurts friendship and leads to conflict
- reflect on the understanding that excluding others is cruel and unfair
- recognize the role each person can play in stopping the practice of shunning
- come up with solutions to a conflict involving gossip and shunning

Materials

- sign from Session 31: "Conscience—A feeling or knowledge of right and wrong that guides us to do what is right" (see page 76)
- handout: "Josie's Story: 'She Thinks She's So Great!'" (page 179)
- chart paper and marker
- paper and pencil for each group of four

Introduction. Say: Today we're going to look at a conflict that took place when a group of kids turned against another girl we'll call Josie. Distribute the handout. Ask for a volunteer to read the conflict aloud to the class.

Discussion. Ask students: **Have you ever had the experience of being shunned by a group—purposely left out and ignored? Do you know anyone this has happened to? How does it feel to be cast out in this way?**

Ask students if they've ever shunned someone else. Refer to the definition and say: **If you're shunning someone, check in with your conscience. Sometimes people excuse this kind of behavior by saying the other person deserves it. Is that true? Is it ever right to shun someone?** Discuss. Some students may have justified this kind of behavior to themselves. Guide them to think about how they would feel if they were the person who was cast aside. Point out that even if they're mad at someone, shunning is never okay.

Activity. Tell students they're going to work in groups to come up with solutions to the conflict in the story.

Put students into groups of four. Have each group choose a Leader, a Recorder, an Announcer, and an Encourager. Say: **Each group's goal is to come up with ways the kids in the story could have prevented this conflict from starting or escalating.**

What could Josie have done? What about Sasha and Kasi? Explain that the role of the Leader is to keep the group focused on the goal. The Encourager's job is to affirm people when they share ideas and to encourage those who are quiet to take part. Recorders should list ideas. Everyone in the group can contribute ideas. At the end of the discussion time, the Announcers will share their groups' ideas with the class.

Allow about five minutes for groups to discuss solutions. Then have students reconvene in the large circle. Ask the Announcer from each group to share ideas their group came up with. List the ideas on a chart labeled "Troubleshooting Group Conflicts."

Ask students if there are any group conflicts that exist now that could be put to an end with some of the solutions on the chart. Discuss without using real names.

Wrap-Up. Remind students that you'll be checking in with them to see how they're implementing the things they came up with.

Follow-Up. Continue to check in with students about ways they're preventing and resolving conflicts. Ask how they're doing in regard to excluding others. Checking in often is the key to holding students accountable. It also affords you opportunities to affirm progress and learn what help students might need with specific issues, skills, and questions.

PART TWO
Responding to Conflict

Josie's Story

"She Thinks She's So Great!"

A conflict happened when these rumors were being spread about me. People started saying that I thought I was really popular and I was too good for my friends. Even Sasha, my best friend in the world, was acting mad toward me. After a while none of my friends were talking to me anymore.

I tried to convince them that it wasn't true. Some people wouldn't even listen. Sasha said she didn't know who to believe and told me to leave her alone. I felt sick inside. I confronted Kasi, the girl who started the rumors, and we talked about it. She said that she wouldn't spread rumors about me anymore. I didn't really believe her, even though I wanted to.

Since then people have been a little nicer to me, but not like before. Sometimes I still cry because I wonder if I can ever really trust my friends anymore.

Think About It

Has something like this ever happened to you or someone you know? How did it make you feel? What could you have done to make things better?

_____

_____

_____

_____

_____

_____

_____

_____

_____

Session 78: Confronting Someone Who Has Hurt You

> **courage • conflict resolution • integrity • personal responsibility • respect • compassion • assertiveness**
>
> Session 78 gives students strategies for talking assertively and respectfully to another person when a conflict isn't sufficiently resolved. This session is a follow-up to Session 77.
>
> ### Students will
> - understand how to use a "think-aloud" to rehearse talking to someone you've been hurt by
> - role-play working out a conflict involving hurt feelings
> - gain a deeper sense of empathy regarding the impact of shunning and excluding
>
> ### Materials
> - computer or overhead projector
> - handout: "Josie's Story: 'She Thinks She's So Great!'" (page 179)
> - "Dignity Stance" chart from Session 68 (see page 162)
>
> **Note:** Before conducting this session, read or review Session 49 (Using Think-Alouds) and Session 68 (The Dignity Stance).

Preparation. Bring up the reproducible handout from the CD-ROM on a laptop, or make an overhead transparency so you can project the story for all students to read without having to use individual copies. You may wish to have students refer to their copies of the handout, which was used in Session 77, as well.

Introduction. Project the handout on your screen or wall and read or have a student read the story aloud. Tell students: **At our last session, we talked about ways this conflict could have been prevented or stopped. Today we're going to role-play ways Josie, the girl who was shunned, can stick up for herself and talk through the conflict with Kasi, the girl at the core of it.**

Ask a volunteer to play Josie. Say: **Although this conflict appears to be over, Josie still feels she can't trust her friends, particularly Kasi, who started the whole thing. Josie has decided that she needs to speak to Kasi.**

Activity. Have Josie start by doing a think-aloud, rehearsing what she's going to say. Refer to the "Dignity Stance" chart. Tell Josie to stand tall before a pretend mirror (or a pretend trusted person), take some deep breaths, and speak her words aloud, holding her head high, and making eye contact. Invite ideas from students about what Josie can say. Have them give help on body language and tone of voice if needed.

Ask a second volunteer to take the part of Kasi. After Josie is mentally prepared, have her role-play

approaching Kasi to talk things over using the Win/Win Guidelines. Have Josie start by taking some deep breaths, silently making her calming statement, and beginning with an I-message such as: "I have something on my mind that I'd like to talk with you about." As the students role-play, coach and invite input from the class as needed.

After the role play, debrief and have the class give feedback: **What worked? What didn't work? What else might Josie have said or done? Did Josie and Kasi come to an understanding? In real life, do you think you could stick up for yourself and talk things through like Josie did? Why or why not?**

If time permits, invite another set of role players to reenact Josie working out the conflict with Kasi.

Wrap-Up. Affirm the role players and the class for the work they're doing to solve conflicts peacefully, fairly, and respectfully. Ask if students would like to affirm someone in the class. Acknowledge that it takes courage to speak up for yourself, and doing it with dignity shows respect for both yourself and the other person.

Extensions. Tell students that Josie is still hurt because Sasha, her very best friend, let her down. Have students work in pairs to role-play Josie preparing to talk to Sasha, then using the Win/Win Guidelines to work out this conflict.

Have students think about characters from literature who were shunned by others. What helped them make things better?

Session 79: Dealing with Exclusion and Rejection

compassion • kindness • respect • conflict resolution • fairness

Session 79 builds empathy and fosters problem solving in conflicts that involve exclusion and rejection.

Students will
- see exclusion and rejection through the eyes of different people involved in a conflict sparked by being left out
- brainstorm and role-play solutions to a conflict where someone is excluded and rejected
- learn ways to be respectful, assertive, and realistic in working out conflicts

Materials
- handout: "Anna's Story: Feeling Rejected" (page 182)
- chart paper and marker
- student journals

Introduction. Say: Today we're going to look at a conflict that happened among three kids we'll call Anna, Sophia, and Carl. After we hear their story I'm going to ask you to think of ways each of them could have been part of the solution, rather than part of the problem.

Activity and Discussion. Distribute the handout. Ask for a volunteer to read Anna's story aloud to the class.

After the story has been read, ask students if they've ever been in a situation similar to Anna's. Ask: **Why might Sophia have left out Anna? What did Carl do that was hurtful? Why do you think he did that?** Discuss.

Have three volunteers role-play the conflict as described in the story. At the end of the role play refer to Win/Win Guideline 5: *Come up with a solution that's fair to each of you.*

Put students in pairs and have them brainstorm at least three more compromise solutions for the conflict. Have them list solutions on the handout or in their journals.

Have students share solutions they came up with. List these on chart paper under the title "Solutions to a Conflict Where Someone Is Left Out."

Now ask for three volunteers to replay the conflict using a new solution from the list.

Caution role players not to be "fake nice" but to act out the conflict taking into consideration real feelings that could contribute to a situation like this one. For example, Anna's cousin may have needed a break from playing with her and might have wanted time with her new friend; Carl may have feared that if he let Anna be included, *he* would be the one left out. Encourage role players to be real yet respectful, assertive yet kind. Guide them to come up with realistic solutions, not solutions that sound good but that they wouldn't actually use in real life.

Wrap-Up. When the role play is complete, remind students to use what they're learning when real-life conflicts come up. Tell students you'll be checking in with them about how they're applying what they've learned. Be sure to check in a few days from now.

Follow-Up. Have students write in their journals about a time they were excluded or a time they excluded someone else. Tell them to write about the feelings they experienced and the feelings the other person may have experienced. What can they do differently next time?

Extension. Discuss some of the reasons kids treat each other in mean ways. Review healthy strategies they can use to deal with strong feelings instead of hurting others or continuing to feel hurt and angry.

Anna's Story
Feeling Rejected

I got into a conflict when I was at my cousin Sophia's birthday party. Sophia was playing with this boy she never met named Carl. They were playing for about half of the party. I couldn't even find her, and when I did Sophia and Carl ran away from me.

I felt bad and asked my cousin, "Why aren't you playing with me?" That's when Carl said, "Sophia can do whatever she wants! You're not the boss of her!" I got mad and said some things back to Carl. Then he called me short and ugly. I started to cry.

Sophia *never* said a word to help. I couldn't believe my cousin was on Carl's side. I said to Sophia, "Why are you playing with him? He's calling me names!" My cousin said nothing. Then Carl said *they* were cousins! I knew it wasn't true, because if it was, he would be *my* cousin, too. I said to Sophia, "You should think about what you're doing. You don't even know this kid. I've known you ever since we were little babies!" She said nothing. Then I walked away heartbroken.

Think About It

What are some ways this conflict could have been prevented?
What can be done to resolve it?

_____

_____

_____

_____

_____

_____

_____

_____

Session 80: The Problem with Fighting

conflict resolution • fairness • courage • self-control • personal responsibility • integrity

Session 80 takes another look at a conflict that's in danger of becoming physical. It highlights the consequences of physical fighting.

Students will

- examine what to do when there's an escalating conflict that's about to get physical
- understand that intervening in a physical fight is not safe
- consider the long-term consequences of physical fighting

Materials

- handout: "Jason's Story: 'It's Worthless to Fight'" (page 185)
- *optional handout:* "Tips for Staying Out of Physical Fights" (page 186)

Note: Before conducting this activity, you may find it helpful to review Sessions 46 (Don't Get Physical) and 67 (Staying Out of Physical Fights).

Introduction. Lead students in taking three slow, deep abdominal breaths. Remind them that deep breathing will help them calm down, gain greater self-control, and think more clearly whenever they are faced with a conflict.

Discussion. Distribute the handout. Ask for a volunteer to read Jason's story aloud to the class. Then ask students for responses. Also ask: **What might have happened if the argument kept going?**

Avoiding Physical Fights: Students' Real Concerns

When you tell a student to get an adult when friends get in a physical fight, they may raise concerns such as:

"What if there's no adult around?" If a student asks this question, talk about realistic options such as running to get help, calling for help on a cell phone, taking themselves out of the fray so they don't get drawn into it, and imploring the kids to stop fighting as Jason did and, at the very least, not egging on people who are fighting or threatening to fight.

"I won't stand there and watch somebody beat up my friend." Reiterate to students that if they, or someone they know, are being physically attacked and there's *no one* around to help, this is the only time a physical response might be needed. Emphatically stress how critical it is to stay out of situations that can lead to a physical fight, and to avoid places where fights are likely to happen. Bring up the fact that physical fighting can lead to escalating forms of violence. Someone could have a weapon in a pocket or could decide to have several people help him or her retaliate after school or at another time. Tell students, "If you want to help your friend (or

yourself), sometimes running as fast as you both can is the best option."

"I don't want to look weak." Remind students that it takes more courage to resist fighting than to give in to it. As one middle school student said, "Sometimes the brave kids just walk away. Sometimes the unbrave kids fight and try to show off." Remind them of the example set by Martin Luther King Jr.

"My mom/dad told me to hit back." In response to this, say, "When you're here you need to obey the school rules. Physical fighting is against the rules of our school and our country." Remind students that adults who fight are often arrested and sent to jail, and kids who fight in school are suspended. Is it really worth it to fight?

"Going to an adult is snitching." Make it clear to kids snitching is telling on someone for the express purpose of getting the person in trouble. Seeking the help of an adult if someone's safety is in jeopardy is the responsible thing to do. Everyone has the right to be safe.

Then ask: **What if people had started punching and kicking? Would it have been safe for Jason to try to stop a physical fight? What could happen?** Make it clear to students that it is never safe to step in and try to stop a physical fight.

Ask students: **What should you do if friends get into a physical fight?** (Get an adult.)

Refer back to the story and ask students: **What if kids who were watching—bystanders—decided to get involved? What are some things they might have done that could have *escalated* the conflict?** (Take sides, get physical, egg people on, gossip about what happened after it ended.)

Write the word *neutral* on the board. Ask students if they know what it means. Define neutral as not taking sides. Ask: **Was Jason was neutral?** (He was: He addressed the problem, not taking sides.) **Why is it important to stay neutral when trying to help friends work out a conflict? What are some ways you can help yourself stay calm and neutral if you want to step in when friends are in a conflict?** (Use Stop, Breathe, Chill; calming statements; Peace Shield; Dignity Stance; Win/Win Guidelines.)

Activity. Have groups role-play the conflict in the story with the players trying not to let the argument grow. What can they do to prevent its escalation?

Ask students what the consequences of fighting are in your school. Discuss. Help students understand that if they get in the habit of yelling and fighting when they're in elementary or middle school, they'll have a hard habit to break when they get older.

Ask students to name some of the many consequences for adults who get into physical fights or shouting matches (physical harm to people, broken relationships, trouble with the law, bad reputation, low self-esteem, etc.). Discuss.

Reread Jason's statement. "It's worthless to fight." Ask students: **Is it worthless to fight? Why?** Help students recognize that fighting actually *is* worthless because it does not lead to a solution, it hurts people, and it escalates conflicts.

Wrap-Up. Acknowledge students for any acts of respect and good listening you have observed. See if any students want to acknowledge peers.

Extension. If fighting is a problem in your school, review and discuss the "Tips for Staying Out of Physical Fights" handout.

Jason's Story
"It's worthless to Fight"

A conflict I was involved in was when some of my friends got into a big argument. We were all in the middle of a ball game. I didn't know what to do. So, I went up to them and said, "What's wrong, guys?"

They just ignored me, so I asked again, and they ignored me some more. I tried to calm them down, but they didn't listen. So I said, "Stop!" in the firmest voice I could, and finally they backed up. But they just looked at me and said, "Bug off, buddy." Then I started reminding them about their friendship, and how we all have great times together. But, they were still really mad and kept arguing. They were shouting and calling each other names. One guy threatened another one. Nobody was hitting yet, but I was afraid they would start to. That's when I yelled, "STOP FIGHTING! IT'S WORTHLESS TO FIGHT!"

They all stopped and looked at me. And then they *did* stop. They must have realized it really *was* worthless to fight. After that, they were finally able to let go of what was bothering them and get back to playing the game.

Think About It

What helped stop this conflict from turning into a fight?
What could have made it worse?

_____

_____

_____

What can you do if your friends are about to fight?

_____

_____

_____

Tips for Staying Out of Physical Fights

- Don't provoke people.

- Resist hanging out with kids who get into physical fights.

- Find healthy ways to express anger. Never go on the attack.

- Avoid places where fighting is likely to occur.

- Be willing to apologize if you've offended someone.

- Be guided by what you know is right, not your reactions.

- Remember the consequences of fighting and how they can affect your life.

Session 81: Mediating a Friend's Conflict

conflict resolution • compassion • fairness • integrity • kindness • forgiveness

Session 81 addresses how and when to help friends resolve a conflict.

Students will

- recognize that there are times when they might be able to help friends resolve a conflict
- role-play a situation where an unbiased friend mediates a conflict for two friends using the Win/Win Guidelines
- understand the importance of remaining neutral and maintaining confidentiality when helping friends resolve a conflict

Materials

- chart paper and marker
- handout: "Bob's Story: Best Friends Since Kindergarten" (page 188)

Preparation. On chart paper, write:
"Mediate—To help settle a disagreement between two other people
Neutral—Not taking sides"

Introduction. Tell students that sometimes it's possible for friends to help other friends mediate a conflict, and that it's critical to remain neutral if they try this. Refer to the chart paper and clarify the definitions of the words *mediate* and *neutral* with students.

Say: **Today we're going to hear a real story of how a boy named Bob helped mediate a conflict that threatened to destroy the long-term friendship between Pennie and Maria. (These aren't their real names.)**

Activity and Discussion. Distribute the handout. Ask for volunteers to read each paragraph.

At the end ask: **How did Bob know Maria and Pennie had a conflict? What did he do to help?** (He suggested going to the Peace Place to work out the conflict, he reminded the girls of their friendship, he listened as both girls told their side of the story, he remained neutral, he didn't talk about who was wrong and who was right.)

Ask for three volunteers to role-play the scenario that took place in the Peace Place, following the Win/Win Guidelines.

Afterward, ask the class: **Did Bob stay neutral? Why is staying neutral important when you're helping friends work out a conflict?** Discuss.

Tell students: **When you're helping friends solve a conflict, the things they say to each other are personal. They need to trust that you won't tell anyone else what they said. Keeping a personal conversation confidential shows respect, integrity, and maturity.**

Discuss, making sure students understand how important it is to honor confidentiality between friends.

Note: An exception is if a student needs adult help. Occasionally in the process of mediating a conflict a student may hear something that makes him or her uncomfortable or seems dangerous. Make sure students understand that maintaining confidentiality among peers is not the same as keeping secret something that needs to be addressed with a trusted adult.

Ask: **Can you think of a conflict friends might have where it would be a good idea to try to mediate? Are there ever times it might *not* be wise to mediate friends' conflicts?** Discuss, making sure students understand that it's not appropriate to mediate when friends don't want the help. Make it clear that students should never try to mediate in the middle of physical fighting.

Wrap-Up. Draw students' attention to the Peace Table or Peace Corner in your room and remind them to use it when they need to work out a conflict or unhook from anger.

Follow-Up. Have students suggest some other scenarios where friends could help mediate a conflict. Have them role-play a few using the Win/Win Guidelines, in small groups or in front of the class.

Extension. Discuss how the conflict between Pennie and Maria could have been stopped earlier or avoided altogether. Have students role-play scenarios at the dance class and in the lunchroom in which Maria and Pennie find a way to resolve their conflict rather than say mean things about each other.

Bob's Story

Best Friends Since Kindergarten

Pennie and I were really good friends, and her closest friend in the world was Maria. They'd been best friends since kindergarten. But one day everything changed and I didn't know why.

They started saying bad things about each other. It really got to me when we were in the lunchroom. Pennie and I were at one table, and Maria was at the other. They were making fun of each other and trying to get the kids at their tables to join in. It made me sad to see them treating each other that way.

It bothered me so much I was ready to leave the table. But then I thought about the Peace Place, this corner in our room where you can go to work out conflicts. I decided to ask the teacher if we could all go there. I asked Pennie and Maria, and they agreed.

When we got there I said, "You guys are such good friends. Why are you fighting?" At first they just kept arguing. They kept blaming each other. So I decided to ask each of them to think of something good about each other. That kind of changed the mood between them.

Then the whole story came out. Maria said it all started in dance class the day before. Pennie was supposed to hold onto her hand while they were spinning around. But Pennie let go, and Maria ended up falling down and spraining her wrist. Maria thought Pennie did it on purpose, and she was really hurt and mad.

Pennie said the reason she let go of Maria's hand was because she got dizzy. In no way had she done it on purpose, and she was mad that Maria thought she would do something so mean. She actually felt bad Maria had gotten hurt.

Once Maria understood that it really was an accident, she let go of her anger. She and Penne both started talking about how bad they felt that it all had gotten so out of hand. They ended up hugging and apologizing.

I was so happy they made up! They'd been best friends for so long, and they almost lost their friendship over this conflict. By talking out the problem, they were able to work things out and stay best friends. They thanked me over and over again for helping them. I felt really good that I was able to help them work things out.

Addressing Name-Calling and Teasing

Name-calling, put-downs, and teasing can be precursors to bullying and, if the intent is to do deliberate harm, can qualify as actual bullying. This section of *No Kidding About Bullying* emphasizes the critical understanding that mean words, names, and gestures have no place in our schools or in our lives. The sessions give students strategies for responding to teasing, name-calling, put-downs, cruel words, and other forms of meanness. These strategies form a fundamental foundation for helping them deal with cruel behavior of any kind. (More on this is addressed in Dealing with Bullying, pages 217–260.)

In the Survey About Conflicts, girls and boys alike reported name-calling and teasing as two of the top three causes of conflicts. Sixty-eight percent of respondents (1,485 participants) reported that being teased or made fun of was a major source of conflict; sixty-four percent (1,389 participants) cited name-calling.

Many sessions from Fostering Kindness and Compassion (pages 51–81) introduce concepts revisited here, so it's suggested that you conduct some of those prior to introducing these. Also familiarize yourself with Sessions 38 (Calming Statements), 47 (Peace Shield), 65 (Introducing Assertiveness), and 68 (The Dignity Stance).

Be sure to have these charts displayed: "The Win/Win Guidelines for Working Out Conflicts" and "Stop, Breathe, Chill" (introduced in Sessions 8 and 9), "No More Hurtful Words" (Session 22), and "Dignity Stance" (Session 68).

82. Taking Responsibility for Mean Words
83. Effects of Name-Calling, Put-Downs, and Meanness
84. Dignity Stance Review (10-Minute Time Cruncher)
85. Assertive Responses to Mean Words, Part 1
86. Assertive Responses to Mean Words, Part 2
87. Mean Comments, Gestures, and Laughter
88. Unhooking from Mean Words and Actions
89. Tools for Unhooking
90. Learning to Detach
91. "I Was Just Kidding"
92. Don't Get Stung by Zingers
93. Becoming Zinger-Proof
94. Being an Upstander for Someone Who's Being Teased

Session 82: Taking Responsibility for Mean Words

personal responsibility • conscience • compassion • respect

Session 82 guides students to take responsibility for hurtful words they might have spoken to another person.

Students will

- understand how mean words hurt and lead to conflict
- reflect on how they want to be regarded by others
- take greater responsibility for their words and actions and refrain from treating others in mean ways

Materials

- chart paper and marker or sign from Session 16 (see page 52 and Preparation, below)
- handout: "Jenna's Story: 'I Said Something Really Mean'" (page 192)

Preparation. If you haven't done so before, on chart paper write: *"Our words and actions today create memories that will fill others' memory banks tomorrow."*

Introduction. Ask for a volunteer to read the sign. Ask students what these words mean to them. Briefly discuss, emphasizing that when we're hurtful to another person, we risk creating in him or her a negative memory of us that can last forever. Say: **Today you'll be hearing a real story from a girl named Jenna whose mean words deeply hurt a classmate named Renee. (These aren't the girls' real names.)**

Discussion and Activity. Distribute the handout. Ask for a volunteer to read Jenna's story aloud to the class.

Afterward, ask students if they've ever been in a situation similar to Jenna's. Discuss briefly.

Ask: **Have you ever said something mean that ended up hurting someone? Why did you say what you said?** Discuss briefly. **Can you remember ever having someone say mean things about you? How did it make you feel?** Briefly share responses.

Then ask: **What important insight did Jenna gain from this experience? What did she learn?**

Emphasize that Jenna ended up taking responsibility for what she did. Ask why this is so important.

Refer to Win/Win Guideline 4: *Take responsibility for your role in the conflict.* Say: **By taking responsibility, Jenna was able to make things better. If she had denied what she'd done, what might have happened? How might she have felt inside?**

Ask students to turn to a partner and share about a time they said or did something hurtful that they still

need to take responsibility for. Let students know this might relate to a conflict with a friend, a sibling, a family adult, or someone else.

After several minutes, ask students what they might say to the person they hurt if that person were here right now. Some examples are: "It was wrong of me to say what I did. I'm really sorry and I hope you'll forgive me." Or, "I feel really bad that I hurt your feelings before. I was having a stressful day, but it was still wrong for me to take it out on you." The latter is an excellent example of truly taking responsibility without trying to excuse one's bad behavior. (In contrast, the following attempt at self-justification cancels out any good done by the apology: "I feel really bad that I hurt your feelings before. I was having a stressful day, and you should have known better than to annoy me.")

Encourage students to seek out the person later and make amends. Have them practice doing this with their partners. Circulate and give help where needed.

Reconvene in the circle and say: **Jenna realized that she didn't want to say mean things about people behind their backs. How else could she have handled the resentment she felt toward Renee? What can she do differently if a situation like this comes up again?** Discuss. Remind students that I-messages are an ideal alternative to hurtful words. Say: **If you have an issue with someone, try speaking to the person directly, starting from "I,"** *instead* **of resorting to name-calling, sarcasm, put-downs, or talking behind the person's back.**

Ask students to think of an I-message Jenna could have used had she chosen to talk directly to Renee about how she felt.

Wrap-Up. Refer back to the sign: *"Our words and actions today create memories that will fill others' memory banks tomorrow."* Ask: **How do you want to be remembered by others? Discuss.**

Affirm students for their willingness to take responsibility, and for any acts or words of kindness, insight, and integrity during this session.

Follow-Up. Have students observe themselves as they go through their day, taking note of how they speak to others at school and at home. If someone gets on their nerves, do they react with a mean comment? If they do, are they willing to take responsibility afterward without making excuses for themselves?

Jenna's Story

"I Said Something Really Mean"

At the beginning of the year, I said something really mean about Stacy, this girl in my class who used to be my friend. I was mad at her because it seemed like she was the teacher's favorite kid. The mean thing I said got back to her during recess.

When we got inside I started crying because I knew I had done something really wrong. I found Stacy and told her I was sorry. I told her about 1 million times, but she was still mad. (I know I would be, too).

Later I started crying again and went to the girls' bathroom. There was Stacy. She was crying, too.

When she saw me crying, she realized how bad I really felt. She finally accepted my apology. Now she and I are good friends again.

The lesson I learned is that it's bad to talk about people behind their backs, because then you're just being like a bully. It is so true that no one is perfect. And it really hurts people when they find out you were talking about them. So why do it?

Think About It

How would you answer the question Jenna posed at the end of the story?

_____

_____

_____

If you have the urge to talk behind someone's back, what can you do instead?

_____

_____

_____

Session 83: Effects of Name-Calling, Put-Downs, and Meanness

compassion • kindness • respect • personal responsibility

Session 83 fosters empathy in students regarding the impact of name-calling, teasing, and mean words. It also clarifies the difference between teasing and bullying.

Students will

- understand that teasing is never okay to do if it makes the other person uncomfortable
- gain greater awareness of the hurt teasing and name-calling can cause
- gain empathy for people who are teased or put down
- resist engaging in hurtful teasing and name-calling

Materials

- handout: "Bullying vs. Teasing: What's the Difference?" (page 195)
- student journals
- chart paper and marker or "No More Hurtful Words" pledge from Session 22 (see page 62)

Preparation. If you have not conducted Session 22, write the pledge on chart paper as directed on page 62.

Introduction. Tell students that today they're going to be looking at how name-calling, put-downs, and mean words affect all of us. Say: **First let's take a few minutes to think about the difference between teasing and bullying. How are they different?** Invite a few responses. Then distribute the "Bullying vs. Teasing: What's the Difference?" handout and ask for volunteers to read it aloud. Discuss it briefly.

Tell students that hurtful teasing almost always involves name-calling, put-downs, and mean words. Cruel words of any kind create conflicts and hurt feelings, even if the other person seems to be going along with it. Discuss this briefly.

Discussion. Say: **Here's how some real kids feel about name-calling and put-downs.** Read the following student quotes* one at a time, inviting brief responses:

- "One time I decided to play basketball, but I took a shot and missed. Everyone started calling me names and scolding me. I hated it. One kid said, 'At least my only friend isn't my dad, unlike *you*.' It was very hurtful. I thought I would start to cry, so I left."

- "It makes me really mad when kids talk and look at me in mean ways, and say mean things about people I like, like my friends and family."

- "People say how ugly our clothes are and how cute theirs are. It really hurts. Not every kid can afford fancy clothes."

Ask students if name-calling, put-downs, and other forms of meanness have decreased since you've started doing the activities in *No Kidding About Bullying*. Say: **Since we've been working on creating a get-along classroom, are you getting better at treating people with kindness and respect, even when you're annoyed?** Encourage them to be honest. Discuss.

Ask if there are times or places where name-calling, put-downs, and meanness are still a big problem. Ask: **How do you feel when you see these things taking place?** Discuss.

Note: If you encounter any cavalier attitudes, like "I don't really care how other people feel. I like to make them feel bad," clearly voice how you feel when you see mean behavior.

Activity. Put students in pairs and have them briefly discuss how they are personally affected by name-calling, put-downs, and meanness, including as observers.

Now have students take out their journals to do automatic writing about the following question: **"How do name-calling, meanness, and put-downs affect you and the people you know?"** After about three minutes, ask if anyone would like to share what they wrote. (Be sure to write yourself, and consider sharing what you wrote, too.)

---

* Stories and quotes attributed to real students and teachers come from author interviews and from responses to the Survey About Conflicts conducted by the author and publisher. See pages 1 and 279–281 for further information.

Ask students to think of ways they might need to improve when it comes to using name-calling, put-downs, and other forms of meanness, including at home. Discuss.

Ask students if they need to get better at handling name-calling, put-downs, and other forms of meanness directed at them. Caution them not to use real names.

Ask: **What do you need help with when it comes to name-calling, put-downs, and other forms of meanness? Are there any important questions you need answered?** List what students say on chart paper, letting students know you will talk together about the questions in the near future.

Wrap-Up. Refer to the "No More Hurtful Words" pledge. End by saying the pledge together. Remind students to live the words of the pledge outside of school, too.

Follow-Up. Plan to follow up by addressing with the class concerns and questions listed on the chart. Engage students in brainstorming some answers to these questions. Help them become part of the solution.

Let students know they can also come to you privately to discuss their questions.

Bullying vs. Teasing: What's the Difference?

Bullying is when a person or group repeatedly picks on someone in order to purposely hurt and gain power over the person.

Teasing is a different story. Teasing can be annoying and upsetting, but it's generally not intended to gain power over another person or do serious harm. If teasing is done in an aggressive or unkind way, with the intent of gaining power over someone else, that's bullying. This includes when the teaser says she or he was "just kidding."

Sometimes teasing is meant to be light and playful without hurting the person's feelings. If it's fun for *both* people involved, and it truly *stays* playful for each of them, it can be okay to do. But if either person finds the teasing hurtful or uncomfortable, it's *not* okay to do.

Cruel teasing hurts many kids and creates lots of conflicts in their lives. In a national survey of more than 2,100 students in grades 3–6:

68% (1,485 students) said that **being teased or made fun of are top causes of conflicts** in their lives.

Think About It

Is there someone you like to tease? Is there someone who likes teasing you? Have you ever been in a situation where teasing hurt? Write about it.

_____

_____

_____

_____

_____

Session 84: Dignity Stance Review

(10-Minute Time Cruncher)

courage • personal responsibility • respect

Session 84 provides a review of the Dignity Stance, introduced in Session 68, which helps students deliver assertive responses.

Students will

- review and practice how to use the Dignity Stance in situations involving name-calling and meanness
- understand how to respond assertively and bravely without being aggressive

Materials

- "Dignity Stance" chart from Session 68 (see page 160)
- *optional handout:* "The Dignity Stance" (page 162)

Note: You may want to review Session 68 for background on helping students use the Dignity Stance.

Introduction. Post the chart and remind students that the Dignity Stance will help them stand up for themselves when they're involved in conflict or faced with name-calling or bullying. Say: **Today we're going to review how to use the Dignity Stance so you can respond to name-calling with both courage and respect.**

Activity. Have students take three slow, deep abdominal breaths to get to a calm place.

Ask students to stand. Take them through each step of the Dignity Stance, doing each step with them:

- Stand tall with your head held high, feet apart, shoulders back.
- Take slow, deep breaths to keep your cool.
- Keep your body language and facial expression neutral but strong.
- Make direct eye contact.
- Speak in a firm, steady tone of voice.
- Walk away tall and strong.

When you get to "Speak in a firm, steady tone of voice," have students imagine they are facing someone who just called them a name. Have them look at this imagined person and say, "I find that disrespectful," then turn and walk away.

Next, put students in pairs to practice the Dignity Stance with their partner. Have them say, "I find that disrespectful" (or something else you agree would work) and practice walking away with head held high.

Wrap-Up. Briefly review what it means to be assertive: strong and honest, yet respectful, saying what you need to say with confidence. Say: **Remember, the Dignity Stance will help you be strong and assertive without having to engage in name-calling or put-downs.**

If you wish, distribute copies of the "Dignity Stance" handout for students to keep.

Session 85: Assertive Responses to Mean Words, Part 1

respect • courage • personal responsibility • self-control

Session 85 helps students come up with assertive responses to teasing, put-downs, and insults.

Note: Conduct Session 68, The Dignity Stance, prior to this one. You will also find it helpful to read through Session 65.

Students will

- more fully understand the distinction between being assertive and being aggressive
- come up with assertive comebacks they can use in response to put-downs
- practice using assertive comebacks in conjunction with the Dignity Stance

Materials

- Sign with definition of *assertive* from Session 65 (see page 155)
- chart paper and marker
- "Dignity Stance" chart from Session 68 (see page 160)

Preparation. If you haven't done so before, write the following on chart paper: *"Assertive—Strong and honest, yet respectful, saying what you need to say with confidence."*

Introduction and Discussion. Start by leading students in taking three slow deep, abdominal breaths. Tell them that today's session will help them find the right words when someone picks on or teases them or someone they know.

Remind students that even though they may feel very angry or upset if they're picked on, or if they witness a friend being picked on, it's still important to be respectful (stay "up in the balcony"*) and respond assertively, not aggressively.

Display the definition of *assertive* and ask for a volunteer to read it aloud.

Ask students: **What's the difference between being *assertive* and being *aggressive*?** Make sure students understand that being *assertive* means speaking one's mind with directness and strength while remaining respectful. Being *aggressive* means responding by arguing, threatening, fighting, or hurting someone back with name-calling or put-downs.

Activity. Share with students this story from a third grader named Mia (not her real name):

"On my bus there are two boys who are really mean to me. They make fun of me and they say things like, 'You don't know anything 'cause you're just a girl. You'll never be as smart as we are!' Most

of the time I just ignore them, but that doesn't always work. Sometimes you have to speak up for yourself. One day I decided to outsmart them. I said, 'I bet you don't know how much 12 times 13 is.' They just looked the other way and got quiet, so I knew they didn't know the answer. I told them what the answer was and walked away, proud of myself. After that, they left me alone."

Ask students: **What did Mia do to respond to the kids who were teasing her?**

Ask students to think of some other assertive comebacks Mia could have given. Ask: **What I-messages could she have used?** Give the following examples: "I have no interest in listening to this." "I'm not interested in something this silly. Girls are smart, capable, and cool."

List students' responses on chart paper entitled "Assertive Comebacks."

Ask students to think of other common put-downs kids use. Now have them suggest assertive comebacks they can respond with. Add them to the chart.

Caution students against using sarcasm or veiled put-downs. Emphasize that how they deliver the comeback is just as important as the words they speak. Say: **Stopping and breathing first is critical. This will calm you down so you can think clearly and speak in a way you're proud of.**

Demonstrate delivering an assertive comeback. Stop and breathe first, assume the Dignity Stance, and use a firm, confident voice. Then walk away tall and strong. Remind students: **Do this even if the**

---

* This refers to the concept "Basement or Balcony?" addressed in Sessions 62 and 63. See pages 147–152.

other person tries to draw you back in. Repeat your calming statement in your head, ignore what they're saying, and remind yourself to be the bigger person.

Put students in pairs and have them practice some of the assertive comebacks they came up with, standing and delivering the comebacks using the Dignity Stance. Circulate to make sure students are on the right track.

After about five minutes, ask a few pairs to demonstrate in front of the group. Have the class take note of tone of voice, eye contact, body language, and posture. Point out or have students point out any hints of sarcasm or aggressiveness.

Wrap-Up. Acknowledge students for working on something that even adults find hard to do. Remind them that learning how to act assertively now will help them for the rest of their lives.

Follow-Up. Conduct Session 86, which gives students practice incorporating calming strategies into their assertive comebacks, or Sessions 88 and 89, Unhooking from Mean Words and Actions, and Tools for Unhooking.

PART TWO
Addressing Name-
Calling and Teasing

Session 86: Assertive Responses to Mean Words, Part 2

> **self-control • calming • personal responsibility • courage • anger management**
>
> Session 86 helps students integrate calming strategies and manage anger when delivering assertive comebacks. This session is a follow-up to Session 85.
>
> **Note:** Complete Sessions 38, Calming Statements, and 47, Peace Shield, prior to this one.
>
> **Students will**
> - review the difference between being assertive and being aggressive
> - practice delivering assertive comebacks
> - practice using calming statements, deep breathing, and the Peace Shield when someone treats them meanly
>
> **Materials**
> - "Assertiveness" sign and "Assertive Comebacks" chart from Session 85 (see page 197)
> - "Dignity Stance" chart from Session 68 (see page 160)
> - *optional:* student journals

Introduction. Review with students what it means to be assertive (strong and honest, yet respectful, saying what you need to say with confidence). Also review the distinction between being assertive and being aggressive (*aggressive* means being argumentative, demeaning, threatening, or hurtful).

Ask students what were the most important things they learned in the last session about body language, tone of voice, and facial expressions when delivering assertive comebacks.

Activity and Discussion. Say: Three things that will help you assertively deal with name-calling, put-downs, and teasing are your calming statement, deep breathing, and your Peace Shield. Think about your calming statement now. (Students wrote these in their journals during Session 38). Guide students in taking several slow, deep abdominal breaths and silently saying their calming statements. Have them visualize putting on their Peace Shield. Say: Picture yourself surrounded by your Peace Shield. See it protecting you from all mean words.

Now ask for volunteers to role-play the following scenarios, or others students suggest, using assertive comebacks.

- **You just got a haircut. The kid who sits next to you keeps making fun of it and tries to get others to join in.**

- **This kid in your class keeps putting down the shoes you're wearing today. Then she starts putting down your family, too.**

- **Your friend always does well on tests. Two kids in the class start calling him a nerd and try to get others to join in. You decide to say something to the kids who are teasing.**

Remind role players: **Before you speak, stop and breathe. Silently repeat your calming statement, put on your Peace Shield, and get into the Dignity Stance. Then, deliver your assertive comeback. When the words are out, turn and walk away with your head held high. Do this even if the other person keeps trying to draw you back in. If you feel angry as you walk away, continue breathing deeply, and silently repeat your calming statement to yourself.** Ask students: **What else can you remind yourself of as you walk away?** (For example, "I can be the bigger person.")

After each role play, ask the class to evaluate the comebacks that were used. Were they truly assertive? Were they delivered in an assertive way? Did the person use a firm, strong voice, without yelling? How was the person's body language? Was the student able to walk away tall and strong without getting drawn back in? As you discuss these things, add any new assertive comebacks to your chart.

Wrap-Up. Acknowledge students for their hard work in learning how to manage anger and be assertive. Remind them that knowing how to assertively handle disrespect and meanness will help them in situations they encounter for the rest of their lives.

Follow-Up. Tell students to rehearse using assertive comebacks at home (in the mirror or with a family member or trusted friend). Practice will build their confidence in real-life situations. Be sure to check in with students about how they're doing; address challenges they encounter.

PART TWO
Addressing Name-Calling and Teasing

Session 87: Mean Comments, Gestures, and Laughter

> **compassion • respect • kindness • personal responsibility • acceptance**
>
> Session 87 further sensitizes students to the impact of mean or critical comments and gestures and mocking laughter.
>
> **Note:** Conduct Session 22, "Words That Hurt," prior to this session.
>
> **Students will**
> - reflect on ways they can respond if they see someone being demeaned or ridiculed
> - role-play responding to situations where someone is being mocked
> - compose songs, raps, or poems that take a stand against cruelty toward others
>
> **Materials**
> - "No More Hurtful Words" pledge from Session 22 (see page 62)

Introduction. Ask a student to lead in the reading of the "No More Hurtful Words" pledge. Ask students how they're doing honoring the agreements on the pledge inside and outside of class. Discuss, affirming them for progress.

Discussion and Activity. Ask: **Aside from mean teasing and name-calling, how else do kids put each other down?** Guide students to think about mocking gestures, faces, negative body language, and laughter at someone else's expense. Discuss briefly. Share what you've observed.

Read aloud the following scenario:

Marina just moved here from another country. The lunch she brings to school today is totally different from what kids in her class are accustomed to. Some kids find it gross and make faces when they see it. Other kids start to join in, laughing and pointing at Marina's lunch.

Ask for a volunteer to play the role of Marina. Have several volunteers pretend to be kids sitting near Marina in the cafeteria responding in mean ways to the food she has (mocking faces, hostile laughter, pejorative remarks and gestures).

At the end of the role play, ask the student playing Marina how the comments and gestures made her feel. Ask students to think about how they would feel if they were in her shoes. Tell them how you would feel, and how you feel when you see such things happen. Ask students to specifically identify which gestures and actions were hurtful, negative, or demeaning.

Ask: **If you were watching something like this really happen, what could you do to help?**

Read aloud another scenario:

Lee often has trouble understanding things that are taught in class. Today he gives a wrong answer in front everyone. Kids start to laugh and do other hurtful things. Lee is clearly embarrassed.

Ask for a volunteer to play Lee and for other kids to play the part of students making fun of him. After the role play, ask the student playing Lee how the other students' behavior made him feel. Ask the class how they would feel in his place. As before, have students specifically identify the gestures and actions that were hurtful. Ask students how they felt observing this. Ask: **What could you do or say if you saw this happening in real life? If you want to help, what might stand in your way?** Reiterate that it takes courage to speak up on someone else's behalf.

Wrap-Up. Acknowledge students for the important work they're doing to create a kinder more compassionate climate in the classroom, school, and world.

Close by repeating the "No More Hurtful Words" pledge together.

Follow-Up. Put students in groups of three or four. Ask each group to compose a short poem, rap, or song taking a stand against cruelty in the classroom and school. Allow students time to complete and share their poems, raps, and songs with the class.

Extensions. Have students visit other classes to share what they wrote and to introduce the "No More Hurtful Words" pledge to the school at large.

Ask your principal if your students can share the poems, raps, and songs they created over your school's public address system or during an assembly.

Session 88: Unhooking from Mean Words and Actions

> **calming • courage • self-control • anger management • respect**
>
> Session 88 gives students a mindset for "unhooking" from mean words and actions and provides specific strategies to help them do this. This session is a follow-up to Session 85 and a lead-in to Session 89.
>
> **Note:** Complete Sessions 38, Calming Statements, and 47, Peace Shield, prior to this one. Also review Session 48, Using Think-Alouds.
>
> ### Students will
> - review assertive comebacks they can use when someone is mean to them
> - understand what it means to "unhook" from someone else's mean words or put-downs, and learn how to do it
> - role-play unhooking from mean comments and gestures
>
> ### Materials
> - "Assertive Comebacks" chart from Session 85 (see page 197)
> - "Dignity Stance" chart from Session 68 (see page 160)
> - handout: "Don't Get Hooked" (pages 203–204)
> - *optional:* student journals

Introduction and Discussion. Refer to the "Assertive Comebacks" chart. Ask students: **Have you had an opportunity to use assertive comebacks in real life yet? How did it go?** Discuss.

Remind students that even if the other person continues using put-downs or mean words after they've given their comeback, it's important to walk away and not get "hooked" back in. Say: **The other person may want to have the last word, and might continue saying mean things. If you react, you're just giving the person more power. By ignoring what's being said and walking away with your head held high (as opposed to weak and defeated), you keep your power where it belongs—*inside of yourself.* That's more important than having the last word.**

Stress that retaliating with more put-downs just adds fuel to the fire and leads to escalation. Ask if this has happened to any of them. Discuss.

Refer to the "Dignity Stance" chart. Tell students that even if they feel shaky inside, it's important to stand tall and speak assertively. Discuss.

Activity. Read aloud the following examples of unhooking, shared by real students:

- Ava's story: **"One time this girl in my class made up a story that I punched her on the bus. I knew she was lying and I didn't know what to do. After I thought about it, I realized that I really didn't care what she said. I decided to ignore her and I was happy I did. It made me feel good not to let her words get to me."**

- Kyle's story: **"There was this kid who was very mean to me. At first, he was my friend. Then he just turned on me. He called me names and put me down. He started making fun of other people I know, too. I told him to stop and he got mad at me. He started yelling more bad things at me and other people I know. It made some of us really upset. I decided to just try and stay away from him. He's still mean, but I've learned not to let it get to me. I don't need to act like him."**

Ask for students' responses to Ava's and Kyle's (not their real names) stories. Say: **When Ava and Kyle decided to ignore or stay away from the person who was being mean, they decided not to get "hooked." What can you do to keep from being hooked?**

Ask for volunteers to role-play the first scenario. Then have the student playing Ava face the class and do a think-aloud that expresses her decision to let things go and unhook from the lie that was being spread about her. If necessary, model doing the think-aloud first.

If time permits, have volunteers role-play Kyle's scenario, then have the student playing Kyle do a think-aloud in front of the class.

Wrap-Up. Many kids are afraid of looking weak if they don't respond with an aggressive comeback. Address this real concern. Remind students of Martin Luther King Jr. and others who rose above insults without stooping to the level of their aggressors. Say: **Real strength is being able to walk away as though the other person's words have no power over you.**

Follow-Up. Pass out the "Don't Get Hooked" handouts. Tell students to read the information, fill out "My Tools for Unhooking" on the back, and bring their sheets to the next session. Tell them to jot down any questions or comments they have in the margins or in their journals. Follow up by conducting Session 89.

Note: The handout includes a recommendation to write about angry feelings. Make sure students know that they should *never* write angry feelings on social networking sites or in texts or emails. Angry words written on the computer or cell phone can be transmitted to other people with a single click. Emphasize that the writing is intended for their eyes only.

Don't Get Hooked

Do you ever walk around with somebody's put-down taking up space in your brain? Do you ever spend time focusing on getting even?

Walking around with your head full of angry thoughts about getting even can drain your energy and make you feel worse. It's like walking around covered with a glob of slime. But you don't have to stay hooked that way. Here are four things to help you unhook and release the angry thoughts and feelings. They will enable you to leave that glob of slime on the ground where it belongs, and walk away with your own power in place:

1. Give yourself 30 minutes to stew. Take some time alone and be as mad as you want for those 30 minutes. On paper, write down what you're mad about. This is just for you, so don't show what you wrote to anyone else. When you're done, tear up the paper and throw it away. Once the feelings are out on paper, they won't clog up your brain as much.

2. Keep repeating your calming statement silently and do something that helps you chill out. If you're at school, wash your face and get a drink. If you're home, try exercising or listening to music. When angry thoughts pop back up, replace them with your calming statement so your mind doesn't get trapped in bad thoughts.

3. Talk to a trusted person. Make this confidential. Do this to get bad feelings out of your system—not to get even or get the person in trouble. It won't help to start gossiping about the person who made you mad—that will only make things worse. Come up with a plan of action. For example, you might plan to talk directly to the person who upset you, or to ignore the person. You might decide to ask for more help from a counselor, a teacher, or another adult for help.

4. Do something *constructive* (something useful and healthy). Help someone else, or get involved in a project. Helping others is one of the best ways to help yourself feel better. It turns the energy of anger and hurt feelings into something useful. This is a good step to take any time you feel sad, mad, or worried.

Make a conscious choice *not* to get hooked by someone else's negative words. Hold onto your power instead of giving it away. As one student said, "I refuse to let *their* words ruin *my* day."

Don't Get Hooked (continued)

My Tools for Unhooking

My calming statement is: _____

_____

My Peace Shield looks like this: (Draw and describe it here):

Three things on my list of ways to chill out are:

1._____

2._____

3._____

Two assertive comebacks I can use are:

1._____

2._____

A trusted person I can talk to is:

_____

If that person is not available, another trusted person is:

_____

Session 89: Tools for Unhooking

calming • courage • self-control • anger management • respect

Session 89 gives students more ways to "unhook" from mean words and actions and provides specific strategies to help them do so. This session is a follow-up to Session 88.

Note: Complete Sessions 38, Calming Statements, and 47, Peace Shield, prior to this one.

Students will

- understand how to "unhook" from someone else's mean words or put-downs
- learn how to use specific strategies for unhooking from mean actions
- raise real questions that come up for them about applying unhooking strategies in their lives

Materials

- "Assertive Comebacks" chart from Session 85 (see page 197)
- "Dignity Stance" chart from Session 68 (see page 160)
- completed handouts: "Don't Get Hooked" (page 203–204)

Preparation. Make sure students have read their handouts and completed "My Tools for Unhooking" on the back of the sheet. Do the same yourself. Have on hand some extra copies of the handout so students who forgot to bring theirs or have not yet completed it will have a personal copy.

Introduction. Have students take out their "Don't Get Hooked" handouts. Choose a few volunteers to share the most important insights they gained from reading the information and listing their tools for unhooking.

Activity and Discussion. Ask for seven volunteers to read aloud each of the seven paragraphs. Discuss.

Ask students to share questions and comments they've jotted down. Encourage them to be as honest as possible. Remind them that you don't want them to just say the "right thing" when they're in class and then do the "wrong thing" (act aggressively or passively) when they're confronted with real-life situations.

Ask: **How many of you would rather just get even if someone puts you down?** Guide them to understand that it's normal to feel that way sometimes, but taking revenge almost always makes things worse. It leads to escalating conflicts that inevitably end badly.

A student may say, "Sometimes you have to show you're stronger, so the other person doesn't keep trying to push you around." Respond by saying, "You can be strong without being mean. Saying something assertive, then walking away with courage and dignity, is what real strength is all about."

Remind students that the tools for unhooking will help them hold onto their strength and power and build it up. Put students in pairs and have them talk with partners about their tools for unhooking.

Afterward, ask a few students to share what they wrote. Share what you wrote, too.

Wrap-Up. Tell students to put their "My Tools for Unhooking" sheets in a place where they can refer to them often (such as taped to the front of their journal or hung on a wall at home). Say: **Remember to use everything we've talked about in real life.** Tell students you'll be checking in with them to hear how they're applying what they've learned.

Follow-Up. Continue to check back with students about the progress they're making in keeping from getting hooked by mean words and actions. Discuss difficulties that arise, and address students' questions and challenges. Affirm them for progress they make.

Session 90: Learning to Detach

self-control • self-respect • self-worth • anger management • courage

Session 90 teaches students how to create an attitude of detachment when they are teased or picked on.

Students will

- understand that they do not have to engage with people who are treating them unkindly
- learn about positive self-talk that can help them detach from people's mean words and actions
- reflect on other things they can do to help themselves unhook and detach

Materials

- handout: "What Real Kids Have to Say About Detaching from Name-Calling and Teasing" (page 207)
- a yellow marker or crayon for each student
- journals

Introduction. On the board, write the word *detach*. Ask if anyone knows what it means to *detach* from someone else's mean words. Guide students to understand that detaching from someone's mean words means unhooking and deciding not to let what was said get the best of you or make you feel bad about yourself. Say: **What we tell ourselves in the moment can really help us detach.** Give an example of something you tell yourself that helps you detach from rude comments, such as, **"**This isn't worth getting upset over.**"** Say: **Statements we tell ourselves that help us feel better are called** *positive self-talk.*

Ask students if they have any statements that help them detach from someone's mean words. Also ask what else they do to help themselves detach. Say: **Even though you may still feel the sting of someone's mean words, by using positive self-talk, deep breathing, and your calming statement you'll gain greater control over your reactions. Then you can either choose a response or walk away with your head held high.**

Ask students: **Can you think of a time you detached when someone called you a name or put you down? What helped you detach?** (Students might have said something to themselves, such as "I'm not going to take this personally," or they may have taken an action that helped.)

Activity and Discussion. Distribute the handout and say: **Here are some ideas from middle schoolers who've learned how to detach from mean words and put-downs. The first quote is from a girl who used to react all the time and ended up in lots of conflicts.** Ask a student to read the first quote from the handout.

Ask: **What did this student tell herself that helped her detach?** Discuss, emphasizing the idea of positive self-talk.

Now ask for volunteers, one at a time, to read aloud the rest of the quotes from real kids. Tell students to follow along and highlight in yellow the parts that can help them in their own lives.

Ask: **Why is it important to unhook, detach, and keep from investing your energy reacting to someone's rudeness?**

Refer to the bulleted "Positive 'Self-Talk'" quotes at the bottom of the handout. Ask students: **Which of these quotes would best help you detach next time someone says something mean to you?** Have them highlight the one they choose in yellow.

Review other things students can do to help themselves detach (deep breathing, calming statements, Peace Shield, one of their chill-out strategies).

Wrap-Up. Have students jot down in their journals the positive self-talk quote they chose. Ask them to jot down something else they can do to help themselves detach. Remind students that detaching will help them keep their power rather than give it away.

What Real Kids Have to Say About
Detaching from Name-Calling and Teasing

Tips from Middle Schoolers

Here's how some middle school students detach when someone teases them or calls them names (you can use these ideas, too):

"Here's how I look at it: If they're spending their time trying to get a reaction out of you, it's just not worth giving them the satisfaction. There's no point in talking back. It's better to just ignore what they're saying."

"It's not worth getting into a fight over this stuff. I know I'm a different kind of person than they are, and that's okay. It's good just to be your own self and let their words slide off your back."

"Sometimes classmates call people names just to be cool. They're trying to make you feel powerless and themselves powerful. Try to ignore it. Normally if I just walk away and ignore them they'll just forget about it. Sometimes I ask myself if I did something wrong. If I did I try to fix it. Other times I just realize that it's their loss. If it keeps on happening, I find an adult to talk to about it."

"If someone's name-calling I try to ignore them. If you're with people who are disrespectful, you need to hang around with the right people."

"My advice if they say things you don't like is to let it go. Don't even worry about it. They can talk all they want, but they can't hurt you if you don't let them. If it really bothers you, talk to the school counselor or someone who can keep it private."

Positive "Self-Talk" for Detaching from Mean Words

- "It's not worth getting into a fight over this stuff."
- "I know I'm a different kind of person than they are, and that's okay."
- "It's good just to be your own self and let their words slide off your back."
- "I just realize that it's their loss."
- "If people you're with are disrespectful, you need to hang around with different people."
- "They can talk all they want, but they can't hurt you if you don't let them."

Session 91: "I Was Just Kidding"

self-control • courage • compassion • respect • personal responsibility

Session 91 helps students respond assertively to mean joking or hostile comments masked in humor.

Students will

- understand that if something said in jest upsets another person, then it's not funny and not okay to say
- role-play and discuss assertive responses to sarcastic or hurtful joking
- strengthen their assertiveness skills

Materials

- "Dignity Stance" chart from Session 68
- "Assertive Comebacks" chart from Session 85
- handout: "That's Not Funny" (page 210, four copies)

Introduction and Discussion. Ask students if they've ever experienced someone saying something hurtful or aggressive, and then saying, "just kidding." Ask: **If something hurts or angers another person, does saying "just kidding" make it okay? Why or why not?** Discuss, emphasizing that it's never okay to cover up a mean remark by saying you were just kidding, nor is it okay to make a joke at someone else's expense.

Read aloud this statement made by a third-grade student:

"It makes me really mad when kids tease me and say they're just kidding, but they really weren't kidding at all."

Ask students to respond. Say: **How about if someone says something mean, sarcastic, or hurtful and then says, "I was only joking around"—is that ever okay to do?** Guide students to understand that it's never okay to mask hostility with humor. Say: **Remarks like this are called zingers. If someone says something that hurts your feelings, you don't have to smile and go along with it. If it hurts, it hurts. You have a right to feel how you feel.**

Activity. Tell students that today they're going to role-play using the assertiveness skills they've been learning to handle situations where someone tries to mask meanness and sarcasm with humor. Briefly review the skills you've worked on with students (Dignity Stance, I-messages, assertive comebacks, calming statements, deep breathing, positive self-talk).

Put students in pairs and have them come up with assertive comebacks or I-messages they can use if someone makes a mean comment and then says, "I was just kidding."

While pairs are working together, have three volunteers look over the dialogue on the "That's Not Funny" handout. Give them each a copy and keep one for yourself.

After a few minutes, have the class reconvene in a circle. Ask the three volunteers to act out the scenario from the handout in front of the class, reading aloud the dialogue. Have the student playing Amy assume the Dignity Stance when responding to Juan. Give her a quick prompt for each step (body tall, head high, feet apart, deep breaths).

After the role play, ask the class how they think it went. Ask "Amy" how she felt using assertiveness to respond to Juan. Ask "Juan" what effect Amy's assertive response had on him. Ask Ken the same question. Discuss. Ask the class: **Is there anything else Amy could have said or done to handle the situation more assertively? What could Ken have done differently so he could have been part of the solution rather than part of the problem?**

Remind students: **If the person giving the putdowns laughs or makes comments as you walk away, keep walking with your head held high. Having the last word isn't important. Removing yourself from the person who's trying to hook you in is. It takes the wind out of whatever he or she is trying to say. Acting as if you don't care what the person says gives the impression that you're not hooked in (even if you still are on the inside). This helps you detach and take back your power.**

Ask: **Do you think there's a way Amy could have responded with humor? What could she have said?** (For example, when Juan said, "Nice shirt. Where'd you get it? From your little sister?" Amy might have responded, "You like it? I'll ask my sister if she can give you one, too.") Tell students that responding with humor can often be effective if they're comfortable doing this. Sometimes a humorous comment can take away the impact of the put-down. Remind students to make sure their humorous comment isn't said with sarcasm or meanness.

Wrap-Up. Say: **Giving an assertive comeback and walking away with your head held high shows self-respect and confidence. Can you think of someone who's assertive, confident, and respected?** (Invite a few responses, and give an example of someone you know.) Say: **Next time someone tries to hook you in with mean words, ask yourself how that person might respond. Following that person's example can help strengthen your confidence.**

Follow-Up. Have students role-play other scenarios they suggest, focusing on how students targeted by mean joking can respond assertively.

"That's Not Funny"

This is a script to be enacted by three students playing the roles of Juan, Amy, and Ken.

Juan: *(laughing)* Nice shirt, Amy. Where'd you get it? From your little sister?

Amy: *(serious)* That's not funny, Juan. I like this shirt.

Juan: *(chuckling)* Hey, stop being so serious. I was just joking.

Amy: *(calm and direct)* I don't find your humor entertaining.

Juan: Oh, stop being so sensitive.

Amy: *(calm and direct)* Your joke just wasn't funny.

Juan: *(leaning in toward Ken and getting him to snicker)* Hey, Ken, have you noticed how Amy can't take a joke? She's soooo serious. *(makes a mocking face)*

Amy: *(in a grown-up voice)* That's not funny either. I'm finding your humor a little immature and I have other things I need to do right now. *(walks away confidently with head held high)*

Session 92: Don't Get Stung by Zingers

> **courage • self-control • self-respect • self-affirmation**

Session 92 helps students strengthen their internal resources and confidence to deflect "zingers"—sarcastic remarks and put-downs.

Students will
- recognize how zingers lead to a cycle of conflict
- learn ways to become zinger-proof
- begin to create a personal insurance policy against zingers

Materials
- chart paper and marker
- handouts: "Don't Get Stung by Zingers" and "Become Zinger-Proof" (pages 212–213, copied back-to-back); "Zinger Insurance Policy" (page 214)
- yellow marker or crayon for each student

Preparation. On chart paper, write: *"No one can make you feel inferior without your consent." —Eleanor Roosevelt*

Introduction. Display the quote and ask a student to read it aloud. Ask students what the quote means; make sure they understand the meaning of *inferior*. Ask students: **What does this quote mean to *you?***

Activity and Discussion. Pass out the "Don't Get Stung by Zingers" and "Become Zinger-Proof" handouts, copied back-to-back. Refer to the title "Don't Get Stung by Zingers" and go over what zingers are. Discuss briefly.

Tell students you'll be asking volunteers to read the handout aloud. Tell them that as the handout is being read, they should highlight anything that seems especially important or that they have questions about.

Choose three volunteers to read the first three paragraphs of "Don't Get Stung by Zingers." Ask students: **What do you think of Gus's ideas about zingers? Do you have the power to keep yourself out of a zinger match?** Discuss.

Choose other volunteers to read the last four paragraphs on the page. Pause for brief responses, then turn the handout over and have volunteers read the paragraphs in "Become Zinger-Proof." Remind students who are following along to underline anything they want to know more about.

Afterward, have students look at the passages they highlighted. Address their questions and comments. Encourage them to speak honestly.

Next, have students pair up and talk with partners about at least one thing they can put on each of the three lists:

- **List 1:** All the things they're good at, even little things
- **List 2:** All the people in their life who care about them, adults as well as kids
- **List 3:** Happy memories, from as far back as they can remember to the present

Wrap-Up. Bring the circle back together and distribute the "Zinger Insurance Policy" handout. Ask students to fill in the lists on the handout after class or later in the day. Let them know they can refer to their lists when they need a reminder of good things in their lives that help them feel strong on the inside. Have them bring completed handouts to the next session (Session 93).

Follow-Up. Conduct Session 93, "Becoming Zinger-Proof."

Don't Get Stung by Zingers

Zingers are sarcastic comments and put-downs. On TV and in videos, we hear zingers all the time—and people usually laugh at them. But when zingers are directed at us in real life, it can be a different story. If someone insults you with a zinger, you have the right to feel mad. You might feel as if you need to throw a zinger right back at the person. But that's not necessarily the case.

A boy we'll call Gus said this about zingers: "The kids in my class use zingers all the time. Every minute, someone's trying to outdo the next person with sarcastic remarks and put-downs. I refuse to get involved. I don't need to build my self-esteem by making someone else feel bad. I either walk away or think about something else."

Makes sense, doesn't it? Why let someone's put-downs ruin your day? And why be a part of ruining someone else's day? Sure, it can be hard to pull back from a zinger match, or to let harsh words bounce off you, but you have the *power* to do this.

If zingers are directed at you and you feel yourself reacting, remember to Stop, Breathe, Chill. Use your calming statement and some positive self-talk to activate the strength you have inside. Try telling yourself: "I don't need their approval," or "Their words are meaningless."

Some kids feel like they can't survive without returning zingers. It's normal to want to protect yourself. But sending zingers back usually makes things worse, and it won't make you feel better about yourself. The truth is, it's often better to let the zingers fly right past you. That's what Gus does. And since he doesn't take part, people are less likely to send zingers his way. He has plenty of things in his life that make him feel good about who he is, so he doesn't need to build himself up by throwing zingers at people.

If zingers are flying at you, and you don't want to just walk away, you can say something assertive like, "It's too bad you have to build yourself up by trying to put someone else down." Say this in a neutral, matter-of-fact way—not sarcastic or mean. Then, walk away with your head held high and focus on things that give you strength and confidence.

Remember the words of former First Lady Eleanor Roosevelt:

> *"No one can make you feel inferior without your consent."*

Become Zinger-Proof

Do you want to become zinger-proof? Make your own personal insurance policy against zingers. Start by writing these three lists:

List 1: All the things you're good at, even little things

List 2: All the people in your life who care about you, adults as well as kids

List 3: Happy memories, from as far back as you can remember to the present

These lists are your Zinger Insurance Policy. When someone says something that gets you down, don't let it take up space in your brain. Instead, think about all the things you're good at, or all the people who care about you, or a happy memory. Direct your focus to stuff that makes you feel better, not worse.

Whenever someone sends a zinger your way, remember this insurance policy. Then remember to breathe, stay calm, and stand tall. Say something assertive back if you want to, or ignore the person. Then walk away strong and tall. All these things will help you look confident and in control, even if you don't feel that way in the moment.

Over time, kids who want to throw zingers will see that they're not getting the result they're looking for. Remember this: The more you react, the more it encourages them. The less you react, the less likely they'll be to keep throwing zingers. You have the power to break this cycle!

Zinger Insurance Policy

For each list, write as many things as you can think of. You can add to these lists each day.

List 1: All the Things I'm Good At

List 2: All the People Who Care About Me

List 3: Happy Memories

On the back of this sheet, draw yourself wearing your Peace Shield as a protection against zingers.

Session 93: Becoming Zinger-Proof

courage • self-control • self-respect • self-affirmation • personal responsibility

Session 93 helps students strengthen their internal resources and confidence to deflect "zingers"—sarcastic remarks and put-downs. This session is a follow-up to Session 92.

Note: Complete Sessions 38, Calming Statements, and 47, Peace Shield, prior to this one.

Students will
- understand how zingers lead to conflict
- reflect on their personal insurance policies against zingers
- become more zinger-proof

Materials
- sign with Eleanor Roosevelt quote from Session 92 (see page 211)
- handouts: "Don't Get Stung by Zingers" and "Become Zinger-Proof" from Session 92 (pages 212–213, copied back-to-back)
- completed handout: "Zinger Insurance Policy" (page 214; see "Preparation," below)

Preparation. Have students complete the "Zinger Insurance Policy" handout prior to this session.

Introduction. Refer to the quote and ask students how Eleanor Roosevelt's words relate to their lives. Briefly discuss.

Discussion. Refer students to the "Don't Get Stung by Zingers" handout and ask the following questions:

- **Does anyone feel like Gus—not affected by zingers? What helps you feel that way?**

- **Does anyone like to throw zingers at others? Why? How do you suppose the person receiving zingers feels?**

- **What kinds of zingers do kids use on each other? How do you feel when zingers are flying toward you? Toward other kids?**

- **How do you respond to zingers that come your way? Is there a better way you could be responding?**

Activity. Have students take out their "Zinger Insurance Policies." Put students in pairs and have them share the lists they made.

After about five minutes, ask for a volunteer to act out the following (a student who is the target of zingers) as you read it aloud:

You are at home thinking about what will happen at school tomorrow. Two kids who sit next to you always toss zingers at you and everyone else. Tonight you decide to prepare yourself. Look over your "Zinger Insurance Policy" and zero in on some things that make you feel good about yourself. Put on your Peace Shield for protection. Take some deep breaths and practice your calming statement. Think about whether you want to just ignore the zingers or respond. In case you decide to respond, think of an assertive comeback you might use. Rehearse it in the mirror.

Ask for two volunteers to join the first one and role-play what happens at school the next day. Tell the central role player: **When the kids start throwing zingers, you feel ready and confident. When they try to draw you in, you know just what to do.**

Coach the central role player along, and invite feedback from the class.

Afterward, debrief. Ask the central role player how it felt to try to detach from the zingers. Ask the other players how it felt when someone didn't respond to sarcasm and put-downs. Ask the class to comment on what they observed.

Wrap-Up. Let students know that you'll be observing how they apply the strategies and understandings of zinger-proofing. Remind them that zingers have no place in a get-along classroom.

Follow-Up. Suggest that students team up with a friend to help stop zingers and put-downs. Say: **Talk together about ways you can help each other stay zinger-proof. Agree on a plan of action. You might use a signal like putting your hands in your pockets. Or maybe you can agree to say something like "This is probably making _____ uncomfortable." Or you can walk away together.**

Session 94: Being an Upstander for Someone Who's Being Teased

compassion • courage • respect • integrity • personal responsibility

Session 94 fosters in students the willingness to stand up for someone who's being teased or put down.

Students will

- understand the importance of being an upstander, even when it's hard to do
- visualize themselves speaking up for someone who's being put down
- create drawings of themselves as upstanders

Materials

- chart paper and marker
- student journals
- large sheets of drawing paper, markers, other art materials for creating posters
- *optional handout:* "8 Ways to Be an Upstander" (page 65)

Preparation. Make the following sign to post prominently in your room: *"If you have the opportunity to help someone and you don't do it, you're wasting your time here on earth." —baseball great Roberto Clemente*

Introduction. Say: **We all know how much it hurts to be picked on and put down. How do you feel when you see this happening to someone else?** Discuss. Tell students how you feel.

Continue: **We've talked about how hard it can be to stand up for someone, especially if you're the only one. Here's a story from a fourth-grade student who became an upstander:**

"I knew someone with special needs. She was being made fun of by one of my friends. It really bothered me. I tried to get him to stop, but he wouldn't listen to me. Finally I told the teacher what was going on. I ended up losing this friend, but helping someone who really needed it. I'm glad I did it."

Ask: **What do you think about what this student did? How hard do you think it was?** Discuss. Ask: **Was the friend in this story a true friend? Why or why not?** Discuss, emphasizing it's important *not* to follow the lead of someone who's doing the wrong thing for fear of losing that person's friendship. If you stand up for what's right and lose the friendship, the person wasn't a friend to begin with.

Display the Roberto Clemente quote and ask students to read it aloud in unison. Ask: **What does Roberto Clemente mean when he says "you're wasting your time here on earth" if you could help someone but don't?** Discuss, then ask students to write the quote in their journals.

Say: **The student who wrote the story we just heard is an upstander—someone who stands up for people who are mistreated. How about you?**

What might still hold you back from being an upstander for someone who's being picked on?

Activity. Explain that you're going to lead students in a short visualization that will help them find the courage to become upstanders. Take two or three minutes to have students close their eyes, breathe deeply, and look into the highest, bravest part of themselves. Have them picture themselves breathing deep, standing tall, and speaking out for someone who is being picked on. Have them picture the person thanking them. Have them picture themselves feeling full of strength, courage, and pride.

Wrap-Up. Have students open their eyes. Ask: **What strategies can help you find the courage to be an upstander for someone who needs your support?** Review willingness skills, Peace Shield, deep breathing, calming statements, Dignity Stance, I-messages, assertive comebacks, and rehearsing ahead of time.

Follow-Up. Give students drawing paper and have them create posters entitled "Be an Upstander." They can include Clemente's words along with pictures of themselves, or use other ideas about being an upstander that are meaningful to them. You may want to pass out copies of the "8 Ways to Be an Upstander" handout from Session 23 to prompt their thinking. When the posters are complete, have students display them throughout the school.

Extensions. Have students write a morning announcement for the school using Clemente's quote and encouraging others to be upstanders.

Create a bulletin board called "Quotations from Upstanders." Post the quote from Roberto Clemente and have students look for and post additional quotes that represent what it means to be an upstander.

Dealing with Bullying

What can you do when bullying takes place? This section gives you ways to help students recognize bullying and respond to it in healthy, assertive ways. It defines bullying as when a person or group purposely engages in actions, usually repeated over time, intended to harm someone else emotionally or physically and show power over the person. The sessions include a range of strategies to help kids who are bullied, a key strategy being to develop a culture of upstanders. This latter is especially critical given that 57 percent of the time, bullying stops in less than ten seconds when peers intervene on behalf of the child who is being bullied (Bullying.org, 2010).

Sessions in this section help students define and recognize bullying, respond to bullying if they are targeted, become upstanders if they witness bullying, and discuss and role-play real "bullying stories" from the perspective of all students involved. You will also find support for helping kids who are bullying stop doing so, and for fostering and reinforcing empathy and strong conscience in all students.

Note: Often the terms *bully* and *victim* are used to define the roles that occur in bullying situations. Because these terms label students, I prefer to use terms that emphasize the behavior that occurs: *the person who is bullying* and *the person who is being bullied.* While using this language can feel awkward, it makes the important point that people should not be defined by their behavior or role during a given moment in time.

Key tools for this group of sessions include the informational handouts introduced in Sessions 95, 96, 98, and 99. Many skills introduced in Managing Anger (pages 83–118) and Preventing Conflict (pages 119–164) will be helpful for students as they take part in these sessions, particularly those from Sessions 38 (Calming Statements), 65 (Introducing Assertiveness), 68 (The Dignity Stance), and 85 and 86 (Assertive Responses to Mean Words, Parts 1 and 2).

Your Role When Bullying Happens

If you are aware of someone in your class who's bullying a friend or classmate, speak first to the child who's being bullied. Students who have been bullied need to know that they have a right to be safe and that you want to help. If a friend has done the bullying, remind them that kids who hurt their friends are not true friends, and that the wise choice might be to hang out with someone else—someone who treats them with respect. Help a student in this situation make a new friend.

Then speak to the child who is bullying. Let this student know you're aware of what's been happening, and that no one ever has the right to harm other people, even if the student is hurt or angry. Give a consequence if there's been physical aggression in your classroom, and follow through with other school staff about consequences for bullying outside of your classroom. Offer to help the student stop bullying and find ways to get along better with other students. Alert other school personnel who are generally present during lunch, recess, or other out-of-class times at school.

Be sure to inform your principal or other designated school official about the situation so all students involved can get appropriate intervention and support. If you think the child who's bullying is experiencing physical aggression at home, follow your school's procedures for mandatory reporting and student support.

Session 95: What Is Bullying?

> **self-respect • courage • compassion • kindness • personal responsibility**
>
> Session 95 defines bullying and helps students understand that bullying is harmful to everyone involved, including those who witness it.
>
> **Students will**
> - learn the meaning of bullying
> - learn about the three roles in the bullying cycle
> - reflect on the harmful impact of bullying on all involved
>
> **Materials**
> - chart paper and marker
> - handout: "The Real Deal About Bullying" (pages 221–222)
> - blank sheet of paper for each student
> - small box (or other container) with a lid labeled "Question Box"

Preparation. On chart paper, write the title *"If You Are Bullied: Do's and Don'ts."* List these key points from the handout:

DO

- Get away if you don't feel safe.
- Tell an adult about it.
- Buddy up.
- Be an upstander for yourself.

DON'T

- Get physical.
- Threaten or call the person names.
- Cry in front of the person who is bullying you.
- Ignore bullying and hope it stops.

Introduction. Ask students if they think bullying happens much in their school or neighborhood.

Ask students how they've been personally affected by bullying. Discuss, but don't push students to reveal if they have been or are being bullied. Kids who are bullied sometimes feel ashamed about it, so ease into this slowly. Let them know that bullying is always harmful and is never okay to do.

Tell students they're going to be learning ways to handle bullying, but first you'll share some facts about it.

Activity and Discussion. Pass out the "Real Deal About Bullying" handouts. Explain that you will ask some questions and that they can find answers on the handout. Refer to your own copy of the handout as you ask and discuss the following:

What is bullying? Have someone share the definition from the handout. Briefly discuss examples of bullying.

Reiterate the difference between teasing and bullying. Teasing is usually not done to have power over another person. It can be annoying and upsetting, but can also be playful at times. Bullying is never playful and always does harm.

Ask: **What percentage of kids from the Survey About Conflicts say bullying goes on often, all the time, or every day? How often do you see bullying going on?**

What are the three roles in bullying? Ask students if they know what a bystander is (someone who stands by and watches bullying happen). Bystanders observe and don't try to help. Bystanders can actually make bullying worse just by providing an audience, even if it's just an audience of one.

Note: Sometimes students will rush to label less aggressive acts as bullying. Clarify that if someone leaves you out from time to time or calls you a name, that doesn't qualify as bullying. But if someone is truly cruel to you, and treats you this way often, that's bullying. If your students use labels like *bully* and *victim*, model the nonlabeling way *(person who bullies, person who's bullied)* and have them rephrase.

Who does bullying harm? The answer is everyone—the person who is bullied, the one who does the bullying, and the bystanders. Ask students why they think this is the case. You might ask: **How does bullying hurt those who are bullied? How does it hurt the people who watch it happening? How does it hurt those who do the bullying?** Help students understand that bullying creates an atmosphere of fear, danger, and "un-safety."

Ask students how they feel when they see someone bullied. Bring out the fact that bystanders often feel guilty and afraid.

What often happens to 25 percent of kids who bully? Explain that kids who develop a pattern of bullying can find it hard to break this pattern as they get older. The result can be law-breaking behaviors like harassment, assault, and vandalism.

Ask students what is the most important role they can play if they see bullying taking place (the role of an upstander). Also ask what an upstander can do for kids who are bullied (intervene to help stop the bullying). Let them know you'll be going over things to help them be upstanders in future sessions.

Ask students: **What do you think you can do to help end the cycle of bullying?** (Don't bully others, be an upstander for kids who are bullied, get help if you or others are being bullied.)

Briefly go over the chart: "If You Are Bullied: Do's and Don'ts," referring to the handout for elaboration and clarification. Let students know that in upcoming sessions they'll be learning more about how to be an upstander for themselves and others when bullying takes place. (Note that assertive comebacks are introduced in Session 85.)

Wrap-Up. Pass out paper and have students write "Question/Comments About Bullying" at the top of their sheet. Tell them to take their papers home and write down any questions or comments they have about bullying.

Show students the Question Box. Explain that they are to bring their questions and comments back to school and place them, folded, in the Question Box. Tell them you're going to read everything and emphasize that they don't have to put their name on their papers; however, if they want an individual answer from you, they should include their name.

Follow-Up. On an ongoing basis, read through the questions in the Question Box and select some that you can address with the class. Also follow up with students who want personal help. This session may bring out painful feelings for some of them. If this is the case, follow up confidentially. If you come across any questions or situations you need help addressing, discuss them with the school counselor, psychologist, social worker, principal, or students' parents. You are welcome to email me about any questions at help4kids@freespirit.com. Keep the Question Box available as you conduct other sessions and encourage students to add questions to the box whenever they have them.

The Real Deal About Bullying

In a national survey of more than 2,100 students in grades 3–6, **44% (963 students)** said that bullying happens often, every day, or all the time (in school or other places).

What Is Bullying?

Bullying: When a person or group purposely engages in actions intended to harm someone else emotionally or physically and show power over the person. Bullying often consists of a series of cruel acts repeated over time. It may include any of the following:

- hurting someone physically
- cruel teasing
- harmful threats
- spreading nasty rumors
- mean phone calls, texts, notes, and emails
- cruel name-calling, put-downs, and gestures
- excluding someone repeatedly and getting others to do it, too

Three Roles in Bullying

- the person who bullies
- the person who is bullied
- the bystander(s)—the person or people who watch acts of bullying

Bullying Harms Everyone

Bullying harms not only the person who's being bullied, but also those who watch it happen (bystanders) and even those who do the bullying. In fact, 25% of kids who bully over and over again eventually end up in trouble with the law.

The Real Deal About Bullying (continued)

If You Are Bullied: Do's and Don'ts

What If Someone Is Bullying You?

DO

- **Get away if you don't feel safe.** Walk (or run) away as fast as you can.

- **Tell an adult about it.** Telling isn't tattling—it helps you stay safe. Tell the adult where and when the bullying took place, what happened, and who did it.

- **Buddy up.** People who bully like to pick on kids who are alone, so stick with other kids.

- **Be an upstander for yourself.** If you feel safe, tell the person to stop bullying you. Use an I-message or another assertive comeback.

DON'T

- **Get physical.** Fighting might make the bullying worse. If someone physically threatens you, don't fight: Instead, get away as fast as you can. The *only* exception is if you are in immediate physical danger and have no other possible choice but to defend yourself.

- **Threaten or call the persons names.** This can cause the bullying to escalate—get worse.

- **Cry in front of the person who's bullying you.** Someone who is bullying might like to see you cry. Take deep breaths and try to stay calm. You can cry in private after you walk away and find someone to help.

- **Ignore bullying and hope it stops.** People who keep bullying aren't likely to stop or go away by simply being ignored. Decide whether to stand up for yourself or get help from a grown-up.

Session 96: Questions About Bullying

compassion • personal responsibility • integrity

Session 96 reviews the bullying information introduced in the previous session and addresses students' questions and comments on bullying. It also reinforces the concept that bullying harms everyone and that, by working together, we all have the power to stop it. This session is a follow-up to Session 95.

Students will

- discuss and respond to questions and comments about bullying from the Question Box
- reflect on the impact of bullying described in two stories from real kids
- understand the critical need to be an upstander rather than a bystander

Materials

- Question Box from Session 95 (see page 220) with students' questions
- handouts: "The Real Deal About Bullying" from Session 95 (pages 221–222) and "If You're Being Bullied" (page 225)

Preparation. Have students bring their "Real Deal About Bullying" handouts, distributed in Session 95. Have on hand some extra copies of the handout so students who forgot to bring theirs or were absent during Session 95 will have a personal copy.

Prior to this session go through the questions in the Question Box. Choose a few to discuss now.

Introduction. Have students put any remaining questions and comments in the box if they haven't already done so.

Gather in the circle and review information from "The Real Deal About Bullying" handouts, focusing on the definition of bullying, the bullying cycle, and the fact that bullying harms everyone involved.

Discussion and Activity. Choose a question you have preselected from the Question Box. Read it aloud and ask for student responses to it. Provide any information that's needed.

Discuss several more questions and comments.

Next, read aloud the following story, shared by a fourth-grade student:*

"My friends didn't like this one girl, so they made a club against her. They asked me to join. I didn't really know the girl, so I decided to go along with my friends. When the girl found out about the club, she was so upset she told the principal. We had to sit down with her and have a talk. The girl was so hurt by what we did she was crying. I never meant to hurt her and I didn't know what to say.

"After the talk, she ended up forgiving us. She and I ended up becoming good friends. Sometimes you might not know that what you're doing is bullying. I learned how important it is to be nice to everyone even if you don't know them, and to not always go along with your friends."

Ask students: **Why might the friends have started a club like this? Why do you think this student joined the club against the girl?** Review the student's statement: "Sometimes you might not know that what you're doing is bullying." Ask: **How was joining the club an act of bullying? What important lesson did this girl learn?** Discuss, emphasizing issues like peer pressure, thinking about how other people might feel, and checking in with one's conscience.

Read aloud another story, this one from a fifth-grade student:

"There is a boy at school who gets bullied all the time. It started last year and still goes on. Everyone I know, except me and my best friends, tease him. I feel so bad for him. I think he should learn better comebacks.

"Last year I was hoping they'd forget about him over the summer, but right after summer break was over, they kept bullying him. I wish it could stop, but it doesn't. I feel so bad for him."

Discuss, particularly the following, "They kept bullying him. I wish it could stop. But it doesn't. I feel so bad for him." Ask students: **Will bullying stop if no one says or does anything about it? What could this boy and his friends have done to be upstanders for this boy?**

Say: **The boy who told this story was being *passive*.** He cared, but was afraid to help, so he did nothing. Review what it means to respond assertively, as opposed to being aggressive or passive. Tell students that upstanders are always assertive, not mean. They respond to what's going on with directness and strength rather than getting down to the level of the person who's bullying.

Wrap-Up. Let students know that it's possible to put an end to bullying in a school. It can happen when *everyone* makes up their mind *not* to bully, and to be upstanders for kids who are being bullied, and for themselves, if they're bullied. Say: **This includes adults in the school, too. That's why it's important to let them know when bullying takes place. If they don't know about it, they can't help. We're doing** these sessions so we can have a school without bullying.

Pass out "If You're Being Bullied." Tell students to be sure to read it, highlight any parts they have questions about, and write comments in the margins. Let them know you'll discuss it with them during the next few days.

Follow-Up. Continue to discuss with students ways to recognize and stop bullying. Note that Session 97 addresses how students who are being bullied can respond to it.

Also continue to invite questions for the Question Box and to discuss these as a group or individually.

If You're Being Bullied

If you're being bullied, remember your own worth and value.

Kids who are bullied often think they're being picked on because there's something wrong with them. *This is absolutely not true.* If you're feeling that the bullying is your fault, let go of that idea. It's not your fault. No one deserves to be bullied. Period.

Too often kids who are bullied keep the problem inside because they feel embarrassed, ashamed, or scared. Doing this only makes it worse. Shame and silence can make you forget who you really are. Never forget the personal power you have inside yourself.

Some kids think everyone has to dress, talk, eat, think, act, and look alike. You don't have to be like everybody else to be worthy of respect. Your individuality is what makes you special. Don't let anyone else's words or actions make you feel "less" than anybody else. Always remember that you are a valuable person worthy of respect.

Session 97: What to Do If Someone Bullies You

courage • personal responsibility • self-respect • assertiveness

Session 97 provides skills and strategies students can use if they are being bullied. This session is a follow-up to Session 96.

Students will

- understand that the words of someone who bullies them should never be taken personally
- review what they can do if they are bullied
- understand that they don't have to shoulder bullying alone
- reflect on the fact that bystanders can become upstanders who help

Materials

- handouts: "If You're Being Bullied" from Session 96 (page 225) and "The Real Deal About Bullying" from Session 95 (pages 221–222)
- "If You Are Bullied: Do's and Don'ts" chart from Session 95 (see page 219)
- *optional:* student journals

Preparation. Have on hand some extra copies of the handouts so students who forgot to bring theirs or were absent during Session 95 or 96 will have personal copies.

Introduction and Discussion. Have students bring their "If You're Being Bullied" handouts to the circle. Ask: **What questions came up for you as you read through this?** Respond to questions and comments kids had about what they read.

Remind students that if they've ever been bullied, they're not alone. At least 50 percent of kids in all age groups are bullied.* Consider sharing your own story if you've ever been bullied, too. Doing so will help kids who've been bullied feel less alone and safer about opening up.

If anyone reveals having been bullied, allow time for discussion. Refer to both handouts and to the chart. Say: **If you're being bullied it's really important to remember that you have worth and value just as you are, no matter what the other person says or does.** Discuss.

Say: **Let's take another look at the story from a real student you heard in the last session. I'm going to be asking several of you to play the roles of the kids in this story. Then we're going to think about what the boy who was being bullied might have done to help himself.** Read the story aloud to your class:

"There is a boy at school who gets bullied all the time. It started last year and still goes on. Everyone I know, except me and my best friends, tease him. I feel so bad for him. I think he should learn better comebacks.

"Last year I was hoping they'd forget about him over the summer, but right after summer break was over, they kept bullying him. I wish it could stop, but it doesn't. I feel so bad for him."

Ask for a volunteer to play the role of the boy who was being bullied. Have two groups play the roles of the kids who bullied and the bystanders. Afterward, ask students: **What assertive comeback could this boy use to be an upstander for himself?** ("I don't deserve to be treated this way." "I'm not listening to you anymore.") Have the boy choose a comeback and speak up assertively. Then ask the class: **What other things could he do to deal with the bullying?** Discuss students' ideas, focusing on the "Do's and Don'ts."

Note: Sessions 107, Bullied on the Playground, and 109, Physically Bullied by a Group, address physical bullying in more depth and include a handout, "Keep Yourself Safe from Physical Harm." See page 250.

Ask the bystanders to face the class next, and ask: **What could these students have done to help instead of remaining silent?** Finally, ask the kids who bullied to face the class. Have the class suggest what these students should or could have done differently, especially those in the group who had guilty feelings about contributing to the bullying. Discuss, addressing students' fears about speaking out and their concerns about not going along with the crowd.

---

* New York University Child Study Center, January 2010.

226 No Kidding About Bullying

Wrap-up. Stress that in all three roles—the person who's bullied, the bystanders, or the student or students who are bullying—there are positive choices everyone can make. Reiterate that students who are being bullied do not ever deserve to be bullied.

Follow-up. Have students review with a trusted friend or family member things they can do to help themselves if they are ever bullied, and what might stand in the way of advocating for themselves. Suggest that they write about this in their journals, too.

"What If?" Questions About Getting Help from Adults

Students are likely to have concerns about telling an adult about bullying. Here are some questions they may ask and responses you can give:

"What if someone hurts me and they threaten to do it again if I tell?" Tell students: People threaten because they're afraid of getting in trouble. If someone threatens your physical or emotional safety in any way, don't remain silent. Talk to a trusted adult as quickly as you can.

"What if they tell me they're going to wait for me off the school grounds?" Tell students: This is all the more reason to talk to an adult, like the teacher or guidance counselor. The school has rules that are meant to protect you in school and on the way home. If you remain silent, you put yourself at greater risk.

"What if telling makes it worse?" Tell students: If this happens, it's time for a family grown-up (a parent or guardian) to meet with the principal. Adults at school and at home have an obligation to keep you safe. Don't let yourself be defeated by someone else's cruelty.

"What if it's someone from my group of friends who is threatening me? I feel like I need to be loyal." Tell students to think about this: If your best friend was being threatened, what advice would you give? Wouldn't you want to make sure your best friend was safe? So if the same thing is happening to you, you need to treat yourself like you would a good friend. Another thing to think about: If someone in your group is threatening or hurting you, do you really want to be loyal to this person?

"What if I'm too scared to tell anyone?" Tell students: By going to an adult, you can help yourself stop feeling scared. Plus, if you get help, you may help other kids find the courage to get help, too. One thing you might do is talk to an adult about how you can deal with the person who's picking on you. You can decide what to say and role-play it first for practice. If this assertive approach doesn't work, the adult can talk to the person who's bullying you.

Session 98: Help Yourself Deal with Bullying

personal responsibility • courage • compassion • assertiveness

Session 98 gives students strategies for dealing with people who bully them and for building confidence and assertiveness.

Note: Prior to conducting this session, it would be helpful to review Sessions 85 and 86, which focus on assertive comebacks students can use when dealing with mean words and put-downs.

Students will
- reflect on things they can do to prevent themselves from being bullied
- know what to do to deflect bullying if it should happen (or is happening) to them
- be empowered to be their own advocate if bullying takes place

Materials
- chart paper and marker
- handouts: "8 Keys to Making Yourself More Bully-Proof" (page 230)
- "Dignity Stance" chart from Session 68 (see page 162)
- student journals

Preparation. On chart paper, write the title *"8 Keys to Making Yourself More Bully-Proof."* List these key points from the handout:

1. *Don't believe a word they say.*

2. *Fake it till you make it.*

3. *Claim your dignity.*

4. *Use an assertive comeback.*

5. *Talk to a trusted adult.*

6. *Stick around other kids and adults.*

7. *Build yourself up from the inside out.*

8. *Reprogram your brain.*

Introduction. Pass out the "8 Keys to Making Yourself More Bully-Proof" handout. Let students know that these keys can do two important things: First, they can help students build the confidence and courage to handle bullying. Second, the 8 Keys can also help them send the message that they are not an easy target.

Activity and Discussion. Referring to the chart and the handout, go over the 8 Keys, discussing the following:

1. Don't believe a word they say. Ask a volunteer to read aloud this first key. Tell students that one of the biggest problems with bullying is when we believe the things the person says about us. Say: **Anyone who bullies is doing it to have power over another person. Even if the person has picked you to bully, they could just as easily bully someone else. If you're being bullied, it's** very important to remember that there's nothing wrong with you, no matter what the other person says. Discuss.

If you have conducted Session 47, Peace Shield (page 114), remind students about it and ask how their Peace Shield could help keep out the hurtful words.

2. Fake it till you make it. Ask someone to read this key aloud. Ask: **What does it mean to "fake it till you make it"? How can pretending to feel strong and brave help you?** Help students understand that even if they feel upset, it's critical to act as if they don't when in the presence of kids who are bullying. Make sure students know they can let the feelings out when they get home or privately at school with a trusted person.

3. Claim your dignity. Have a volunteer read this key aloud. Ask what students have learned that can help them do this. Briefly review the Dignity Stance, having everyone stand and go through each step.

4. Use an assertive comeback. Invite someone to read this key aloud, and briefly discuss assertive comebacks students might use if they are bullied.

5. Talk to a trusted adult. After having a student read this key aloud, ask: **Who are some adults that can help you?** (Examples include a teacher, guidance counselor, principal, parent or guardian, youth leader, and others.) Remind students that talking to a trusted person is critical; emphasize that they have the right to ask for help. The adult can either help solve the problem or find someone else who is better able to. Acknowledge that even if it's hard to get help, it's important not to stop trying.

If students say, "Asking an adult for help will make the bullying worse," tell them that if it does get worse, they need to go back for more help. Reiterate that bullying is against the law in many states, and against the rules of your school.

Note: Session 50, Getting Help with Anger, is a ten-minute time cruncher that focuses kids on figuring out adults they can go to for help.

6. **Stick around other kids and adults.** Have a student read this key aloud then ask: **How can this help you bully-proof yourself?** Briefly discuss situations where kids might be alone, and help them strategize ways they could buddy up or stay closer to other people. You might give this example: **Maybe you feel like hanging out by yourself during recess rather than play. Instead of sitting somewhere alone, see if you can get a friend to join you. If there's no one to do that, sit somewhere within the eyesight of a teacher or an aide.**

7. **Build yourself up from the inside out.** Have a student read this key aloud. Then ask: **What can you do to build your confidence? How can building yourself up inside help you become more bully-proof?** If you conducted Session 92, refer back to the "Zinger Insurance Policy" (page 214) and review it with students.

8. **Reprogram your brain.** Discuss how visualization—picturing yourself handling a situation in a strong, confident way—can help you become more strong and confident.

Note: Sessions 100 and 101 focus on keys 7 and 8 in more depth and detail.

Wrap-Up. Reiterate that bullying has no place in your school and that you are someone students can come to for help. If they do, let them know things will be handled with confidentiality and care.

Follow-Up. Conduct Session 100, Build Yourself Up from the Inside Out, and Session 101, Reprogram Your Brain.

8 Keys to Making Yourself More Bully-Proof

What does it mean to be bully-proof? It means you think and act in ways that show you won't let others have power over you. Here are 8 important steps you can take to help yourself become more bully-proof:

1. When people try to bully you with words, don't believe a word they say. It's more about them than you.

2. Don't let them see you sweat. "Fake it till you make it."

3. Claim your dignity. Stand tall and walk proud.

4. Use an assertive comeback like, "I don't have time for this stuff." Then walk away with your head held high.

5. Talk to a trusted adult. Report who bullied you, what happened, and where it happened. If it happened online, show the adult the email, text, or Web page.

6. Stick around other kids and adults. People who bully look for kids who are on their own.

7. Build yourself up from the inside out. Remind yourself of your own worth and value. Strengthen your natural skills and talents. This will give you back the energy that the person who bullies is trying to take away.

8. Reprogram your brain. Every night, picture yourself strong, confident, and standing up to the person who's bullying you. See yourself triumphing by being confident and assertive.

Session 99: If You've Bullied Others

self-control • personal responsibility • respect • compassion • fairness

Session 99 is a session to conduct with all students, focused on helping kids who have bullied or who are bullying recognize that they can change.

Students will
- review the three roles in the bullying cycle
- assess themselves to see if they've been bullying others
- learn ways to help themselves stop if they've been bullying someone

Materials
- chart paper and marker
- handouts: "Are You Bullying Anyone?" (page 233); "Help Yourself Stop Bullying: What to Do If You've Bullied Others" (pages 234–235)

Preparation. On chart paper, write:
"Three Roles in Bullying

- *the person who bullies*
- *the person who is bullied*
- *the bystanders"*

Introduction. Ask students: **What are the three *roles* in bullying?** Refer to the chart and go over each role. Ask students to define *bystander.* Emphasize that bystanders play an extremely important role. Bystanders can decide to help or to hurt. Often, bystanders remain silent, which doesn't help. If they start to laugh, do something to encourage the bullying, or join in themselves, they become part of the bullying. Say: **But bystanders can transform themselves into upstanders. How?**

Let students know that people may experience all three roles at some point in their lives. Briefly share your own examples of roles you've played. Be honest—this helps students be honest, too. Ask which roles students have experienced. Discuss briefly.

Note: Students may be reticent to disclose that they have bullied others. Don't push or put anyone on the spot.

Discussion. Refer again to the terms you wrote on chart paper and say: **Some people know they bully. Others bully without realizing it, or get drawn in without really meaning or wanting to.** Pass out the "Are You Bullying Anyone?" handout and say: **This is a quiz you can take home and fill out to figure out if you are bullying anyone.** Briefly review the items on the handout together; ask if students have any questions.

Tell students that if they have bullied someone else or are doing it now, today's session will help them stop.

Pass out "Help Yourself Stop Bullying: What to Do If You've Bullied Others" and ask for a volunteer to read the opening paragraph. Ask students how bullying hurts the person who is doing it. Discuss.

One by one, ask for volunteers to read the individual steps to stop bullying. Discuss each briefly, making sure students understand. Invite ideas for ways to own the problem, promise to stop, make amends, give yourself credit, and be part of a solution to the wider problem of bullying. Help kids identify appropriate adults to talk to also.

Activity. Ask for a volunteer to role-play the part of a student who has been bullying. Have another volunteer play the role of a trusted friend or adult. Have them play out the conversation that takes place when the child who bullies decides to do the things on the "What to Do If You've Bullied Others" handout.

Afterward, have the class give feedback. Ask: **How did it go? What else could the student have said or asked? Is this something you could do in real life?**

Note: Although recent research indicates that some kids bully strictly because of the desire for power, research also shows that kids sometimes bully because they're depressed or carrying around intense feelings of anger. They may be, or have been, the targets of bullying or abuse themselves. They may also be dealing with family issues like divorce, unemployment, mental health problems, serious illness, domestic violence, or substance abuse. Any time a child is at risk in these ways or seems motivated by cruelty, contempt, or anger, it's essential to take steps to help that child. Reach out to your school nurse, counselor, or psychologist for interventions and follow-up.

Wrap-Up. Reiterate to students that we all make mistakes, and that many people have bullied someone at one time or another. Every day is an opportunity to do better.

Let students know they can write you a note or come to you confidentially at any time to discuss these issues.

Acknowledge students for their honesty, respectful listening, and openness. See if students want to acknowledge others in the class.

Follow-Up. Be sure to check in with students in a day or two about what was discussed in this session. Follow up with any students who ask for help or appear to need it.

Extensions. Allow separate times for additional students to role-play ways to ask for help from an adult and to apologize and make amends.

Also allow a time for small-group discussions about ways to stop the problem of bullying in the school.

As a class, take the "No Bullying Pledge":

- I will not take part in any actions that purposely hurt another person.
- I will join with friends to stand up for kids who are being picked on.

Are you Bullying Anyone?

Some people know they bully—others bully without realizing it. To find out if you do things that could be considered bullying, take this quick self-test. Be honest and check off any statements that apply.

REGULARLY or OFTEN . . .

_____ I try to make someone else feel really bad or embarrassed.

_____ I make fun of someone in a mean or humiliating way.

_____ I take part in lots of mean name-calling.

_____ I leave people out on purpose and make them feel bad about it afterward.

_____ I purposely cause physical pain to another person.

_____ I threaten people.

_____ I try to make someone feel like she or he isn't as good as I am.

_____ I send mean emails, IMs and texts, or I post mean things on social networking sites about another person.

_____ I spread mean rumors about others.

_____ I try to get other people to do any of these things.

Need Help?

If you need help to stop bullying, talk to an adult you trust.

Think About It

What can you do to be part of the solution to bullying?

_____

_____

_____

Help Yourself Stop Bullying

What to Do If You've Bullied Others

When you bully, it hurts *you* as well as the person you're picking on. Kids who bully can form long-term negative habits: habits of meanness, trouble managing anger, difficulty getting along with others, broken relationships. But you don't have to go down that road. Here are six important things you can do to break the habit of bullying:

1. **Own the problem.** It takes a lot of courage to admit to yourself that you've done something wrong, but only by doing so can you change. If you've bullied and you're willing to be honest and face up to it, you're taking a BIG first step.

2. **Tell a trusted adult.** Telling an adult can help you feel better about yourself again. He or she can help you figure out how to stop bullying. You might say, "I've been really mean to someone. I feel bad about it and I want to stop, but I'm not sure how."

What adult can you talk to? It can be a parent, teacher, guidance counselor, nurse, social worker, principal, or a youth leader at an after-school program or at your place of worship. If you have big problems on your mind and feel bad inside, an adult can help you deal with these issues, too.

If you can't figure out who can help and need to talk to someone right now, call the Boys Town National Hotline: 1-800-448-3000. (Even though it says "Boys Town," the hotline is for everyone, girls and boys.) You can call anytime, day or night. A trained professional will be there to talk to you and your call will be confidential. Don't hang up if there's a little wait time. A real person who cares will be there.

Help Yourself Stop Bullying (continued)

3. **Make a promise to yourself to stop bullying now.** Write it down and put it in a safe place. You might want to share your promise with the adult you spoke to.

4. **Make amends.** This means apologizing to the person you've hurt, then doing something to make up for the pain you've caused. For example, you can start including the person in games, or telling your friends that you've gotten to know the person better and you're sorry you were mean. Or invite the person to your home or offer to help with a homework assignment or a sport.

5. **Give yourself credit for the steps you're taking to stop bullying.** It takes a lot of courage to own up to bullying and change. It's a big deal for the kid you've bullied and for yourself. You can use your journal to write down the steps you're taking and give yourself credit for taking them.

6. **Be an upstander to help stop bullying in your school.** Think of ways you can do this. Talk to your teacher and other kids about ending bullying in your school. Stick up for kids who are being picked on and get your friends to do it to. Be part of the solution.

Remember, bullying will only stop when enough kids make the decision to stop it. Congratulate yourself if you decide to become one of them.

Session 100: Strengthen Yourself from the Inside Out

self-respect • compassion • kindness • self-acceptance • personal responsibility

Session 100 helps kids build internal strength and courage in the face of bullying and supports healthy self-esteem for all students. This session is a follow-up to Session 98.

Students will

- create lists of their own talents and competencies
- write notes of affirmation to classmates
- reflect on other ways they can strengthen themselves from the inside out for the purpose of bully-proofing

Materials

- "8 Keys to Making Yourself More Bully-Proof" chart from Session 98 (see page 228)
- handout: "8 Keys to Making Yourself More Bully-Proof" (page 230)
- writing paper and pencils or pens for each student
- student journals

Introduction. Look together at the chart and the handout, briefly reviewing the first six keys.

Activity. Direct students' attention to the seventh key and have a student read aloud the text from the handout.

Have students pair up. Pass out paper and have them write the following heading: "Talents I Have and Things I'm Good At."

In pairs, have students discuss and list everything each of them is good at, including things such as helping, caring, being a true friend, being funny, and being kind. Encourage them to list at least ten things. Model ways kids can encourage each other to come up with more ideas. For example, a partner can ask, "What else are you good at?" or say, "I've noticed that you're good at _____." Allow five minutes or less for this activity; circulate and give coaching as needed.

When the lists are complete, have students exchange papers with their partners. On the back of their partner's sheet, have them each write a paragraph of affirmation about the partner, elaborating on all positive qualities they have noticed or discussed. You can model this ahead of time or read aloud the following example:

Dear Alex,

I think you're a really cool person. You're funny and nice. I would have been scared moving here and being the new kid in the class, but you handled it really well. I know you're good at math, building things, and running. It's cool the way you can explain a math problem

to people when they don't get it. It's been really nice getting to know you.

Mark

After students are done writing, have them exchange papers again, read the note from their partner, and then put their paper with the note into their journals. Then have them turn to a clean page and write the following heading: "I Did It." Tell them to take a minute or two to write at least three things they accomplished today. An accomplishment can be as simple as "I handed in my homework on time."

Discussion. Gather students back in a circle and ask: **How can the lists and paragraphs you wrote today help you strengthen yourself from the inside out?** Discuss. Make sure students understand that focusing on their strengths and accomplishments will help them gain confidence and remember their own worth and value. Ask: **How can this help you be more bully-proof? How can it help you find the courage to be an upstander or to stop bullying?**

Ask students what else makes them feel confident and happy. Discuss and have students write down other strengthening activities they can do. Say: **For example, if you like to draw, do it as often as you can.**

Wrap-Up. Tell students to add to their "Talents I Have and Things I'm Good At" and "I Did It" lists every single day, noting all their capabilities and accomplishments, large and small.

Let students know that these lists are an ongoing way to strengthen good feelings about themselves. Remind them to go back to their lists and the affirmation their partner wrote about them whenever they need to build their confidence or courage "muscles."

Session 101: Reprogram Your Brain

courage • self-respect • compassion

Session 101 has students engage in an envisioning exercise that builds confidence in the face of bullying and supports healthy self-esteem. This session is a follow-up to Session 98.

Students will
- reflect on the words of a real student who was bullied and still maintained a sense of confidence and pride
- further bully-proof themselves by envisioning their most "confident selves"
- understand that regularly envisioning their confident selves can strengthen them from the inside out

Materials
- "8 Keys to Making Yourself More Bully-Proof" chart from Session 98 (see page 228)
- handout: "8 Keys to Making Yourself More Bully-Proof" (page 230)

Introduction. Tell students that it's possible to be bullied and still manage to keep an attitude of confidence inside oneself. Read aloud the following story, reported by a fifth-grade girl, to illustrate this:

"I get bullied because of my lisp. This boy used to call me 'tongue-talker.' Every time I saw him, he made fun of me. It made me want to cry, but I didn't. Even though I felt mad, sad, and stressed, I figured out that when people bully you, you shouldn't listen to them or believe what they say. At all times, be yourself and believe in yourself."

Discussion. Ask: What did this student learn from the experience of being bullied? What were some of the feelings the student had at first? What does she know that helps her cope confidently? Discuss briefly.

Tell students that the dignity and confidence this girl expressed are possible for everyone, and the exercise you're going to take them through right now will help build it.

Activity. Look together at the chart and handout, briefly reviewing the first seven keys. Then direct students' attention to the eighth key and have a student read aloud the text from the handout.

Lead students in three rounds of slow, deep abdominal breathing. Ask why this kind of breathing is so important to do. (It calms the body and mind and helps us focus.)

Have students close their eyes. Read the following in a slow, calm, soothing voice:

Take another slow, deep breath, all the way down. Hold the breath inside yourself for a few seconds. (Pause.) Now let it out very slowly. Continue breathing slowly and deeply. Imagine that your mind is a blank movie screen. If any thoughts come up as I'm speaking, put them on a cloud, and let the cloud float the thoughts away. Then bring your mind back to the blank movie screen.

Project onto the screen of your mind an image of yourself. See yourself looking wonderful! You are happy, confident, strong, and proud. See yourself standing tall and smiling. You're filled with confidence and happiness. (Pause.)

Picture yourself feeling completely respected and cared for. Let those good feelings go directly into your heart and mind. Take another slow, deep breath as you bring feelings of self-care, confidence, and respect deeper inside yourself.

Now, if there's anyone who has ever hurt you, past or present, see yourself confidently walking over to that person. You are fully in charge. Tell that person whatever you need to say. Say it with strength, confidence, and respect. (Pause.)

Now see yourself walking away with your head held high. You are filled with pride and confidence. You will always have the power to be an upstander for yourself, because you know just what to do, and you deserve respect.

Pause a moment; then have students open their eyes. Ask how the envisioning was for them. Discuss. If any students had difficulty envisioning, or if negative thoughts intruded, remind them that the more they practice this the easier it becomes—the more they focus on the image of themselves that they envision today, the more calm and confident they will feel. It's like learning any other new skill.

Wrap-Up. End by telling students to practice this process every night before going to sleep. Doing so can reprogram their brains, helping them feel proud, confident, and empowered under any challenging circumstance. Remind students that this can help them deal with all aspects of bullying.

Follow-Up. Have students draw pictures of their most confident self, and write a statement of affirmation expressing their confidence and pride. Have them write in present tense. (For example: "I am happy and filled with confidence," or "I know exactly how to handle any challenge that comes my way.")

Session 102: Projects to Prevent Bullying

self-respect • courage • compassion • personal responsibility • cooperation

Session 102 provides students with sound advice from a teen who learned how to handle being bullied and to rise above it. They will also work on anti-bullying projects.

Students will
- be reminded of ways to hold onto their sense of self-worth if they are bullied
- learn some emotionally healthy ways to deal with the impact of being bullied
- begin projects that reinforce ways to "shake off" bullying

Materials
- handout: "'Shake It Off': Tips from Quinn About Being Bullied" (page 240)
- chart paper and marker
- paper, markers, crayons, chart paper, and pencils for each of six groups

Preparation. Write the following six ideas from the handout on six large strips of chart paper:

- *"Shake it off. Remember that nothing can diminish you."*
- *"No one can take away from you who you really are."*
- *"Talk to a trusted adult to let your feelings out and get help."*
- *"Let the bad stuff go. Don't keep replaying it in your mind."*

- *"Focus your mind on things you're good at and people who care about you."*
- *"Remember that at any given time there are probably more people who care about you than don't."*

Introduction and Discussion. Ask: How can bullying make people feel? Entertain responses. Remind students that everyone has worth and value, even if bullying causes them to temporarily forget that they do. Reassure them that the bad feelings will likely pass if they do the things they're learning to deal with bullying and bully-proof themselves.

If the bad feelings linger, it's critical to talk to a trusted adult.

Ask: **What are some things you've learned that can help you remember your worth and value?** Discuss ideas from handouts and activities you've covered in the "Dealing with Bullying" section, including students' "Talents I Have and Things I'm Good At" lists (Session 100), adults they've identified who can help them, and the "confident self" envisioning process (Session 101).

Pass out a handout to each student. Tell students they'll be reading ideas from Quinn today. Say: **Quinn is a teenager who was bullied in elementary and middle school. At first, he started feeling really lonely and wondered if there was something wrong with him. But then Quinn got help from an adult and started to remember his own worth and build his own confidence.** Ask for a volunteer to read aloud Quinn's words. Make sure students know what *diminish* means (to make someone feel less than they are). Ask students what the following words from Quinn mean to them personally: "Remember that nothing can diminish you. No one can take away from you who you really are." Say: **If you ever feel temporarily diminished by bullying, that's your signal to do the things you've learned to help yourself—including some of Quinn's idea.**

Discuss students' responses to this and to the rest of Quinn's advice. Then ask: **What did Quinn learn from his experience?** Discuss, making the point that after deciding to confide in a trusted adult, Quinn learned to strengthen himself from the inside out and started feeling better about himself.

Activity. Divide students into six groups. Pass one sentence strip to each group. Ask each group to discuss the words on their sentence strip, then choose one of the following activities to do together based on the words:

1. Make a group poster or collage using the words. Illustrate and decorate it.
2. Create a poem, rap, or song about the words on their sentence strip or the entire story.
3. Create a web with the words of their sentence strip in the middle, and four examples using pictures or words radiating out from the web's center.

Circulate as students work in groups making sure everyone understands the task. Compliment groups for positives you observe.

Wrap-Up. Acknowledge students for their hard work and for any positives you observed in the way they worked together and ask if they would like to acknowledge each other.

Follow-Up. Set aside time for students to complete projects and share them with the class. Have each group explain what they did and what they learned from working on this together. Display all projects in the room or hall.

Encourage students to complete the questions on the handout and keep it in their journals as another resource to help them when they need confidence and support.

"Shake It Off"

Tips from Quinn on Getting Past Being Bullied

Quinn is a teenager who was bullied in elementary and middle school. Based on what he learned through these experiences, Quinn has this to say to kids who are being bullied:

"Shake it off. Remember that nothing can diminish you. No one can take away from you who you really are. If a part of you feels sad, admit it to yourself and feel what you feel, *but don't try to do it alone.* Make sure you talk to a trusted adult so you can let the feelings out and get help. Then focus your mind on things you're good at and people who care about you. Do healthy things to help yourself shake off the bad stuff and see the good again. Don't keep replaying it in your mind. And remember that at any given time there are probably more people who care about you than don't."

Think About It

1. Do you have bad feelings you need to let go of relating to bullying or any other problem? Write about them on the back of this sheet or in your journal.

2. Who are two trusted adults you can talk to if you need help?

   _____   _____

3. If you can't see either adult in person, try using phone or email. Is there anyone else you can reach out to? If you can't figure out who can help and need to talk to someone right now, call the Boys Town National Hotline: 1-800-448-3000. (Even though it says "Boys Town," the hotline is for everyone, girls and boys.) You can call anytime, day or night. Don't hang up if there's a little wait time. A real person who cares will be there.

4. Quinn reminds kids who feel sad to focus on things they're good at and people who care about them. What are five things you're good at?

   _____

   _____

5. Name three people who care about you a lot.

   _____   _____   _____

6. What can you do to help yourself feel better when you're feeling down?

   _____

   _____

Session 103: Fostering Compassion—"I Know What It's Like"

compassion • kindness • courage • respect • personal responsibility

Session 103 fosters in students a deeper level of kindness and compassion and encourages them to be upstanders for those who are bullied and left out.

Students will

- reflect on a story from a real student who learned greater compassion from her experience of being bullied
- reflect on the importance of having compassion and acting in compassionate ways
- examine their level of willingness to be an upstander and reach out to kids who are bullied and excluded

Materials

- chart paper and marker
- handout: "Rena's Story: 'I Know What It's Like'" (page 242)

Preparation. On chart paper, write the following: *"Compassion: Understanding the feelings of others and feeling what they feel in your own heart."*

Introduction. Ask a student to read the definition of compassion. Make sure everyone understands the meaning. Ask: **How does being an upstander show compassion?** Tell students that expressing compassion through our actions is one of the highest forms of kindness.

Activity and Discussion. Pass out the handouts and introduce the story on the handout by saying: A girl named Rena was bullied throughout her years in elementary school. Now she's in high school. Rena understands what it's like to be bullied. Because of this, she has become a very compassionate person who likes to reach out to people. Rena is an example of someone who is a true upstander.

Have a student read aloud Rena's story from the handout. Then ask: **What did Rena learn from her experience of being bullied? Why is it important to have compassion for others? Why is it so important to act in compassionate ways?**

Discuss. Then ask: **What did Rena discover about people by reaching out?** (Everyone has something interesting about them. Everyone will respond to kindness.)

Ask students if they've ever reached out to someone who's been left out. Ask: **What did you gain from that experience?**

Ask if they've been an upstander in other ways for someone else. If so, have them describe what it was like.

Ask if anyone has had someone be an upstander for them. Discuss.

Ask why it's important to be an upstander, even if you feel nervous about doing it.

Wrap-Up. Ask your students to notice at lunchtime or on the playground if anyone is being teased or left out. Encourage them to be upstanders for that person. Encourage them to notice how willing they are to do this, and what might stand in their way.

Rena's Story

"I Know what It's Like"

I was bullied for a long time, so I know what it's like. That's why I always help kids who are left out.

There are some kids no one will sit with at lunch. I know how lonely it can be to sit by yourself and I know how it feels to be picked on, left out, and bullied. So I decided that I would be the one to sit with kids who are excluded. I've learned a lot from doing it, and it's actually become fun.

I've discovered that anyone will respond to kindness. Once you take the time to get to know someone, you see that everyone has something interesting. If you take an interest, it makes them happy and they open up more. Then they start to take an interest in you. I've become friendly with some of the kids I've sat with who were alone. Soon you end up with a whole table of friends you never knew before. Even if they're all people who don't necessarily fit in with the popular group, you fit in with each other. Sometimes kids who don't "fit in" are actually some of the nicest people.

Think About It

Is there anyone you know who is left out? Would you ever consider reaching out to that person with kindness the way Rena did? What might give you the courage to do it? What might stand in your way?

_____

_____

_____

_____

_____

_____

_____

Session 104: The Courage to Be an Upstander

courage • personal responsibility • compassion • kindness

Session 104 helps students build their courage and confidence so they can be upstanders for kids who are bullied.

Students will
- reflect on why it takes courage to be an upstander for someone who is bullied
- learn specific steps for building their courage and think of other ways to do this as well
- role-play being upstanders for someone who's being bullied

Materials
- chart paper and marker
- handout: "What Real Kids Have to Say About Being an Upstander When Someone Is Bullied" (page 245)

Preparation. On chart paper, copy the following, leaving blank spaces so students can suggest additional entries:

Build Your Courage to Be an Upstander Against Bullying

1. *Practice the Dignity Stance. It will help you stand tall to help others.*
2. *Use deep breathing to keep your cool.*
3. *Rehearse your words.*
4. *Picture yourself helping assertively.*
5. *Partner up. Have a friend join you to confront someone who's bullying.*
6.
7.
8.

Introduction. Tell students that today they'll be learning more ways to build their courage "muscles" so they can be upstanders for kids who are bullied. Ask: **What are you already doing to help when someone is being bullied?** Discuss.

Ask: **Why does it take courage to be an upstander? What stops you from helping someone who's being bullied?** Discuss, emphasizing that each time someone stands up against bullying, this helps put an end to it. Ask: **What are some things you've learned that can help you gain the courage to be an upstander for kids who are bullied?** Discuss and review strategies that have been introduced.

Discussion. Pass out copies of "What Real Kids Have to Say About Being an Upstander When Someone Is Bullied." Ask for five volunteers to read aloud

the quotes from kids who've been upstanders. Ask for students' responses.

Then direct their attention to "Build Your Courage to Be an Upstander Against Bullying" on the handout and chart. Go through steps 1–5 with students, discussing each one and answering questions. For the fifth step, help students recognize how partnering with another person can give them courage by not having to face the situation alone.

Then ask: **What else would give you the courage to be an upstander if you see someone who's being bullied?** Write suggestions on the board. Discuss, then ask students which two they find the most helpful. Add these to the chart. If there are more than two, include them as well.

Activity. Ask for four volunteers to role-play the following scenario, or another bullying scenario you think students will relate to:

Note: Confronting a bullying situation alone can be daunting. For this reason many experts believe that it's preferable for kids to be upstanders in partnership. However, if no one else is around to buddy up with, it's helpful for kids to know how to do it alone. For this reason, you will want to vary the role playing so students can practice being upstanders alone and with others.

Jeffrey sees Tommy being bullied by Stewart on the playground. He decides to be an upstander for Tommy. Jeffrey stands tall, breathes deep, thinks of words to say, and walks over. Then he speaks directly to Stewart about what he's doing. Finally, he asks Tommy to hang out with him on another part of the playground.

After the role play, ask the volunteer who played Jeffrey: **How did it feel to be an upstander for Tommy? Was it easy to do?**

Ask for one new volunteer to join the others and play the part of a student named Claire. Replay the scene, this time having Jeffrey ask Claire to partner up with him to be an upstander for Tommy. After the role play, ask the student who played Jeffery: **How did it feel this time to be an upstander? Was it easier to do with Claire helping?**

Also ask students: **What could have happened if no one had stepped in to help Tommy?** Discuss, making sure to address students' questions or concerns about being upstanders in bullying situations.

Wrap-Up. Remind students that each time they practice being an upstander for those who are bullied they will strengthen their courage muscle. Say: **The more upstanders we have, the closer we get to making ourselves and our school bully-proof.**

Follow-Up. Conduct Sessions 105, Stand Up to Bullying, and 106, More Practice for Being an Upstander, which provide more opportunities for students to role-play being an upstander.

What Real Kids Have to Say About
Being an Upstander when Someone IS Bullied

In a national survey of more than 2,100 students in grades 3–6, kids wrote about finding the courage to be an upstander for someone who is being bullied. Here are some things they wrote:

> "It's hard when you see someone being bullied for something they can't help. If you're scared to help them, do it anyway. You have the right to stand up."
>
> "I tell the person who is bullying to quit it. Then I take the person who was being bullied to another place, away from the bully."
>
> "I tell the person who is bullying that what they're doing isn't right and they should stop."
>
> "I tell the person bullying to stop, and try to comfort the person who was being bullied."
>
> "I help kids who are bullied by staying with them. I've learned that kids who bully don't go after people if they have at least one friend."

Build Your Courage to Be an Upstander Against Bullying

1. Practice the Dignity Stance. It will help you stand tall to help others.

2. Use deep breathing to keep your cool.

3. Rehearse your words.

4. Picture yourself helping someone by giving an assertive comeback or getting help.

5. Partner up. Have a friend join you to confront someone who's bullying.

6. _____

7. _____

8. _____

Session 105: Stand Up to Bullying

compassion • courage • personal responsibility • kindness • respect

Session 105 has students practice being upstanders by role-playing helping kids who are bullied. This session is a follow-up to Session 104.

Students will

- review the steps to being an upstander for someone who is bullied
- reflect on their willingness to be upstanders and anything that might stand in the way
- role-play situations where a student is being picked on and upstanders intervene
- envision a scenario where they serve as an upstander for someone in need of help

Materials

- "Build Your Courage to Be an Upstander Against Bullying" chart from Session 104 (see page 243)
- *optional handout:* "What Real Kids Have to Say About Being an Upstander When Someone Is Bullied" (students' copies from Session 104; see page 245)

Introduction and Discussion. Referring to the chart, review ideas about being an upstander when someone is bullied.

Ask students: **Since we last talked about this, has anyone helped someone who was being picked on or included someone who was left out? How did it feel to help?** Discuss. If no one helped out, ask what stopped them from doing so.

Activity. Ask for volunteers to role-play the following scenarios, or others students suggest. Suggest they use ideas from the class chart. After each role play, discuss briefly how it went, what worked, what was difficult, and why.

- Every day when Gabe, a second grader, is outside on the playground, one of the older kids pushes him down and takes his money. You decide to be an upstander.

- Audra is in a special class but comes to your class for social studies every day. That's when Ronnie and Ali pick on her and call her mean names. You decide to ask someone to help you be an upstander for her.

- On the bus, Nick and Marco always pull Zoey's hair and knock her down. You and your friends decide to be upstanders for her.

After all the role plays, ask the upstanders: **How did it feel to stand up for someone who was being bullied? What helped you do it?**

Ask all students: **What would make it easier to be an upstander?** Tell students that people who become upstanders often get the courage to do so by focusing on helping somebody rather than on the fear they might be feeling. They become stronger people with greater self-respect as a result. Discuss.

Wrap-Up. Close the session with a brief visualization exercise. Have students close their eyes and take three slow, deep abdominal breaths. Then read the following aloud to them:

Imagine yourself seeing someone who is being picked on. You feel really bad for that person. You decide you're going to tell the person who's picking on him to stop. See yourself as strong, brave, and confident. Think about what you want to say. (Pause.) Now picture yourself walking over to the person and saying your words. Picture the person hearing you and stopping. Picture the person you helped thanking you. Imagine yourself filled with a deep sense of pride and strength.

Now open your eyes and know that you have the power to do this in real life, either alone or with a friend.

Follow-Up. Encourage students to practice being an upstander this week. Remind them they don't have to do it alone.

Extension. Give students several days to write anonymous essays about their experiences with bullying—as someone who was bullied, as someone who bullied, or as a bystander. Share these essays with your principal. With students' permission, post the essays randomly in school to build awareness.

Session 106: More Practice for Being an Upstander

compassion • respect • courage • personal responsibility

Session 106 gives students practice being an upstander for kids who are bullied. This session is a follow-up to Session 104.

Students will

- review the steps to being an upstander for someone who is bullied
- discuss roadblocks to being an upstander and ways to overcome them
- role-play being upstanders for someone who's being bullied

Materials

- "Build Your Courage to Be an Upstander Against Bullying" chart from Session 104 (see page 243)
- *optional handout:* "What Real Kids Have to Say About Being an Upstander When Someone Is Bullied" (students' copies from Session 104; see page 245)

Introduction and Discussion. Start by leading students in a round of deep breathing. Tell them that during this session they will be practicing being upstanders. In real life, deep breathing will help them get mentally prepared to intervene.

Ask: **Why is it important to be an upstander? How does it help other people? How does it help you? How does it help our school?** Discuss. Emphasize that being an upstander not only helps the person being bullied. It also shows bystanders and the person who's bullying that someone cares enough—and is *brave* enough—to stand up and speak out.

Make sure students recognize that being an upstander for someone else will strengthen their courage muscle, give them more confidence, and make them feel proud of themselves.

Do a quick review of the chart and ask: **Since we last talked about this, has anyone been an upstander for someone who was bullied? How did it go?**

Ask if anyone observed bullying, but held back from helping. Discuss the reasons students hold back from being upstanders. Ask the class: **What can help you find the courage to be an upstander when it seems hard to do?** Let students know that the more they practice being an upstander, the easier it will get.

Activity. Have students role-play being upstanders in the following bullying situation:

Every day at recess, Rex calls Andy a loser and other mean things, and he makes mean remarks about Andy's family. Andy tries to ignore him, but Rex keeps doing this every day. Van and Jason always see this happening, and they feel really bad for Andy, but they're afraid that if they step in Rex will pick on them, too. One day, they decide Rex's abuse has to stop, and they are going to be upstanders for Andy.

Ask for volunteers to act out this story. Before the role play begins, talk the upstanders through the Dignity Stance and remind them to take deep breaths and think about the words they want to speak. Have them rehearse what they're going to say.

Afterward, debrief with the class about how it went, what worked, what didn't work, and what made it easy or hard to be an upstander.

If time permits, ask students for other situations that could be role-played (remind them not to use real names when bringing up incidents), or suggest some you think would be good ones for your group. Invite different volunteers to role-play each scenario. Briefly discuss each role play.

Wrap-Up. Ask: **Can you see yourself being an upstander like the ones we role-played today? Think about a situation where you could do this.**

Let students know you will continue to check in with them about how they're doing as upstanders in real life. Remind them they can talk with you about any questions or concerns they have in doing this.

Follow-Up. Encourage students to share with their families what they're learning about being upstanders for people who are bullied, and how they're preparing to do this in real life.

Extensions. Have students create upstander role plays to enact for a class of younger students, at a school assembly, or for a school podcast.

Invite students to write "I Was an Upstander" essays; collect the essays in a class book or display them for a parent conference or open house event.

Session 107: Bullied on the Playground

> **compassion • courage • respect • personal responsibility**
>
> Session 107 has students role-play being upstanders for someone who is being physically bullied; they will also reflect on things they could have done if they were the person who was bullied.
>
> ### Students will
> - consider what they can do if they're being physically bullied
> - learn how upstanders can help if they see someone being physically bullied
> - role-play a situation in which upstanders support a student who is being physically bullied
>
> ### Materials
> - handouts: "Jon's Story: 'No One Would Help Me'" (page 249); "Keep Yourself Safe from Physical Harm" (page 250)
> - charts: "Dignity Stance" from Session 68 (see page 162); "8 Keys to Making Yourself More Bully-Proof" from Session 98 (see page 230); "Build Your Courage to Be an Upstander Against Bullying" chart from Session 104 (see page 243)

Introduction. Say: Today we're going to look at a bullying situation that happened to a boy we'll call Jon. After you hear his story, you'll get a chance to role-play ways Jon's friends could have been upstanders for him.

Discussion. Distribute the handout and ask for a volunteer to read aloud Jon's story. Ask: **What did Jon do that finally ended the bullying?** (He talked to his dad and he talked to the parents of the kid who was bullying him.) Point out to students that Jon had to go for help to more than one grown-up. Emphasize the importance of continuing to look for adult help when it's needed.

Ask: **What might Jon have done before that to put a stop to the bullying?** (Go back to the teacher immediately after the kid beat him up, tell his dad sooner, go to the principal.)

Then ask: **What about Jon's friends? How could they have helped?** Have students pair up for a minute or two and talk about things the friends could have done to help him when they saw him being bullied on the playground. Address kids' real fears about being retaliated against if they intervene. Let them know that the more upstanders there are, the less likely retaliation will occur.

Afterward, discuss what students came up with. Refer to the "Steps You Can Take to Be an Upstander Against Bullying" and "Dignity Stance" charts.

Remind students that upstanders should never put themselves in physical danger. Tell students that if they see someone being physically harmed, they can do three things:

1. Shout out, "Leave him alone!" or "Leave her alone!" Sometimes that can be enough to get the person to stop.

2. Beckon for the student who's being harmed to come with them, then run fast together, preferably to a place where other people are. There's power in numbers.

3. *Always* let an adult know what happened as quickly as possible. Harming someone physically is against the school rules and against the law.

Activity. Ask for volunteers to play the roles of Jon, the kid who bullied him, and upstanders who decide to help him out.

After the role play, discuss how it went, what worked, what didn't work, and other options the friends or Jon might have used.

Have another set of students role-play the same scene, this time having a single student be the upstander on his or her own. Discuss. If time permits, do additional role plays using new ideas from the discussions.

Wrap-Up. Ask: **What have you learned from Jon's story and from our role play?** Remind students that they have the right to protect themselves against bullying. Emphasize that each time they serve as upstanders, they help put an end to bullying.

Distribute the "Keep Yourself Safe from Physical Harm" handout. Go over the information on the handout.

Follow-Up. Review the "Keep Yourself Safe from Physical Harm" handout with students. Cover in detail any questions they have.

Jon's Story
"No One would Help Me"

One day I was at recess just playing tag. It was a normal day until this kid pushed me over. Then I kept ending up on the ground because he kept tripping me. I didn't know how to stop him, so he kept doing it. Two of my friends were there, but they went over to the other side of the playground. I think they wanted to get away from him. He tripped me each time we played tag from May 3 to May 11. No one would help me. Finally I told the teacher.

The next week he beat me up at recess and told me not to ever tell on him again. I went home with a black eye and lied to my mom and told her I got hit by a football. The boy kept bullying me until July because we lived really close to each other. Finally I told my dad. He talked to this kid's parents, and the kid finally stopped bullying me.

Think About It

What could Jon have done to get more help sooner? What could his friends have done to help?

_____

_____

_____

_____

_____

_____

_____

_____

_____

Keep Yourself Safe from Physical Harm

If you're in danger of being physically harmed, you need to keep yourself safe. Here are ways to gain control and exit a dangerous situation:

• Stand up straight, look the person in the eye, and say in a firm, clear voice, "Leave me alone!" Then walk (or run) away quickly and calmly.

• Shout "Cut it out!" as loudly a you can, and get yourself away.

• Join a group of people nearby so you're not alone.

• If you're in real danger—for example, if you're facing a gang of kids who are about to harm you—run as fast as you can to a safe place, then seek the aid of an adult.

Session 108: Bullied by Friends

compassion • courage • respect • personal responsibility

Session 108 has students reflect on what can be done if they or someone they know is bullied by a friend.

Students will

- discuss in cooperative groups what kids can do if they're being bullied by a friend
- consider actions students can take when someone is bullying a friend
- understand that if someone is mistreating them, the person is not being a true friend

Materials

- chart paper and marker for each group of four students
- handout: "Bullied by Friends: Stories from Real Kids" (page 252)

Introduction. Distribute the handout and ask for volunteers to read aloud each of the stories. Invite brief responses.

Discussion. Ask students: **Why would a person bully a friend? Is someone who does this really a friend?**

Ask: **Have you ever been bullied by a friend, or known someone who was?** Discuss, reminding students not to mention real names.

Ask: **What if you have a friend who bullies someone and you want to help? What can you say to your friend? What if your friend bullies you? What can you do?** Discuss briefly. These ideas will continue to be in focus during the activity and final discussion.

Activity. Put students into groups of four. Have each group choose a Leader, a Recorder, an Announcer, and an Encourager. Say: **Each group's goal is to brainstorm four possible things people can do if they or someone they know is bullied by a friend.** Explain that the role of the Leader is to keep the group focused on the task. The Encourager's job is to affirm people for sharing ideas and to encourage everyone to take part. Recorders should write the ideas. Everyone in the group can contribute their ideas. At the end of the discussion time, the Announcers will share their groups' ideas with the class.

After five or ten minutes, have students reconvene in a large circle. Have Announcers share with the class what their group has come up with. Ask students to comment on each group's ideas. Discuss these and provide coaching and feedback as appropriate. Also ask about the role upstanders could play to help in such a situation. Be sure to share all of the following with students:

- If the person is bullying you, you can rehearse some assertive words you can say to that person. For example, "This bullying has to stop. I deserve to be treated with respect." Then use the Dignity Stance and speak to the person directly.
- If the person is bullying someone you know, be an upstander for the person being bullied. Do this on your own or with another friend.
- If the bullying doesn't stop, quit hanging out with the person. Find some new friends who treat you and others with respect.
- Talk to a trusted adult who can help get the bullying to stop. An adult can also help the person being bullied.
- If you are bullying a friend, get help from a trusted adult.

Wrap-Up. Remind students that they have the right to be safe. If they are ever in a situation where someone is harming them, it's important to go for help if nothing else has worked.

Note: Bullying between friends may occasionally be precipitated by a conflict. While mediation is rarely useful when dealing with bullying, you may want to try to mediate to get to the root of the conflict in cases where there was a real friendship that went sour. But it's extremely important to be mindful of any feelings of intimidation the child who was bullied might have. If you sense that the child is afraid to speak up in front of the friend who bullied him or her, do not try to mediate; instead, speak to each child separately. Remember that all acts of bullying need to have a consequence, regardless of whether you mediate.

Bullied by Friends
Stories from Real Kids

In a national survey of more than 2,100 students in grades 3–6, kids wrote about being bullied. Here are stories from a fourth-grade girl and boy:

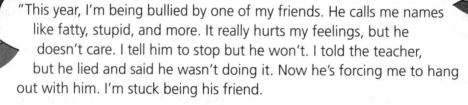

"At the beginning of the school year, when my friend got stressed she would hit me. She would hit me on the back, my arms, or my stomach. I told her to stop but she kept doing it. One day after class she picked up her textbook and whacked me across the back. She always says she's sorry, but she keeps on doing it. She calls me weak because I tell her it hurts. But, if I accidentally hit her with my pen, she calls me a name and starts crying.

"The problem still isn't solved, because she keeps doing it. My arms are sore from her hitting me. I can't tell her I don't want to be friends anymore. I'm afraid she'll hurt me more."

"This year, I'm being bullied by one of my friends. He calls me names like fatty, stupid, and more. It really hurts my feelings, but he doesn't care. I tell him to stop but he won't. I told the teacher, but he lied and said he wasn't doing it. Now he's forcing me to hang out with him. I'm stuck being his friend.

"I try to get other people to be my friend, but they're all *his* friends, so I'm stuck with him. He's still bullying me, and I don't know what to do."

Think About It

How can these kids get help? What would *you* do in their situation?

_____

_____

_____

Session 109: Listening to Your Gut

courage • compassion • kindness • respect • personal responsibility

Session 109 has students consider ways to stay safe and prevent situations where physical bullying by a group can occur.

Students will
- understand possible precursors of a physical attack
- reflect on ways to avert such an attack
- learn how to listen to their gut instincts when it comes to dangerous or threatening situations

Materials
- chart paper and marker

Introduction. Ask students if they've ever had a "gut feeling" about something. Share your own experience of having a negative gut feeling that guided you to take care of yourself. Say: **It's important to listen to our gut feelings. They can help us keep ourselves safe.**

Ask: **In terms of being bullied, what have you learned about keeping yourself safe?** (Stay around other people, seek help if you're being threatened.) **Also in terms of bullying, have you ever had a gut feeling that someone was planning to physically hurt you?**

Activity and Discussion. Write *"Listening to Your Gut"* at the top of the chart paper. Say: **There are often signals ahead of time that physical bullying might happen. What might those signals be?** Write students' ideas on the chart paper. Signals might include threats, aggressive put-downs, attempts at humiliation, and rumors that kids might be planning something. Discuss, guiding students also to understand that when there's impending danger, people often can sense that something's wrong on a gut level.

Ask: **If someone is getting threats or hearing lots of mean put-downs, and feels like a bullying situation is getting worse or is going to get worse, what can the person do?** (Let an adult know what's going on, make sure not to be alone.) **If you get a bad feeling in the pit of your stomach each time you see a kid or a group of kids, what should you do?** (Listen to your gut, don't ignore the bad feeling, stick with other people, talk to an adult, avoid secluded or unmonitored areas.)

Wrap-Up. Acknowledge students for the very important work they are doing in learning how to prevent and address bullying. Encourage them to continue to bring any questions to you.

Session 110: "Gay, Nerd, Freak"

> **compassion • acceptance • personal responsibility • kindness • respect**
>
> Session 110 impresses upon students painful consequences of name-calling and put-downs.

Students will

- understand that the term *gay* is not to be used as a put-down
- discuss other terms that are not to be used as put-downs
- recognize that cruel name-calling can lead to deep emotional pain
- role-play being upstanders for themselves and others in a bullying situation where a child has been the object of pejorative name-calling and put-downs

Materials

- handout: "'Everybody Decided I Was Gay': A Story from a Real Kid" (page 255)
- student journals

Introduction. Tell students that sometimes bullying can be so upsetting that some kids get extremely depressed as the result of it. Say: **This is what happened with the boy who wrote the story you are about to hear.** Pause to see if anyone wants to comment or respond.

Discussion. Distribute the handout and ask for a volunteer to read aloud the story.

Have students respond with three minutes of automatic writing. Give them the following prompt: **"What came into my mind as I listened to the story was . . . "**

After students have had time to write, ask how the boy in the story felt. Ask: **What names was he called? Why did that hurt so much?**

Ask what else the boy could have done to address the bullying. (Go back to the teacher; go to the principal, counselor, or nurse; tell his parents what was going on.)

Students sometimes also use words like *gay* in a way that's not meant to put down a particular person, as when they say "That's so gay." Stress that the word *gay* should never be used as a put-down or to mean *anything* negative. Ask why this is so. Make sure students understand that this is disrespectful to people who are gay as well as to those who aren't.

Ask: **What about calling someone a *nerd* because he or she is smart—isn't that disrespectful, too? What are some great things about being smart? Why would people put someone down for being smart?**

Ask: **What about *freak*? Why is that disrespectful?** As appropriate within your group, discuss other names or insults that are issues in your classroom or that students are concerned about, including racial or sexual slurs and cruel labels for those with disabilities.

Activity. Refer once again to the handout and ask: **What would it be like if no student ever had to be made to feel the way this boy did? How can you be a part of making this happen?** Put students in pairs and have them brainstorm ways they can be upstanders if they see anyone treated as the boy in the story was.

After a few minutes, have students do one or two role plays of standing up for someone in a similar situation.

Wrap-Up. Remind students that one of the most important things they can do if they or others are bullied is *not* to remain silent. Emphasize the need for all people to decide not to use cruel language and to speak out when they hear others using it.

Affirm students for their courage, kindness, and honesty during the session; encourage them to acknowledge each other, too.

Follow-Up. Check in with students to see if they have questions or want to talk about ideas that were discussed in the session.

"Everybody Decided I was Gay"

A Story from a Real Kid

In a national survey of more than 2,100 students in grades 3–6, kids wrote about being bullied. Here is a story from a fifth-grade boy:

"It started at lunch when everybody decided I was gay. So that's what they started calling me, and I'm not. They also called me freak because I don't buy lunch, and a nerd because I get straight A's. About a month ago this kid calls me a nerd and other names. So I go tell my mom. The next day his best friend hits me in the face because I told on his friend. Then I got mad and I wanted to hit him back, but I didn't. Now it's the end of the school year. It's like every day without crying is an accomplishment. Even some of my friends have turned on me."

Think About It

This boy is so sad, hurt, and lonely that he cries all the time. What got him this upset? Why do kids call people names like "gay" and "nerd"? What can be done to make kids stop this kind of name-calling? How can this boy get help?

_____

_____

_____

_____

_____

_____

_____

_____

_____

Session 111: Cyberbullying

Session 111 highlights the impact of cyberbullying and cautions students against using electronic media to harm another person in any way.

Students will

- learn what constitutes cyberbullying and reflect on its impact
- learn what to do if they are ever cyberbullied
- gain a deeper sense of responsibility regarding cyberbullying
- be encouraged to be upstanders if they know cyberbullying is taking place

Materials

- chart paper and marker
- handout: "Cell Phone Cyberbullying: Stories from Real Kids" (page 257)

Preparation. On chart paper, write the following: *Cyberbullying—Using a cell phone, computer, or any other form of electronic media to purposely harm another person. Cyberbullying happens in cyberspace: in email, instant messages, text messages, podcasts, blogs, chat rooms, Web pages, and on social networking sites.*

Introduction. Ask students: **Who has heard of cyberbullying? What is cyberbullying?** Show the definition and go over it with students, elaborating as needed. Ask if students know any examples of cyberbullying from the news, TV shows, videos, books, or stories they've heard. Discuss. Share an example that you're aware of.

Ask: **Why is cyberbullying bad?** Discuss.

Discussion and Activity. Pass out the handout. Have a student read the first story. Ask: **In what way was Amanda cyberbullied? What could she have done to help herself?** Discuss, guiding students to understand that it's important to do two things: save any available evidence and immediately get help from a trusted adult.

Ask: **Is it ever okay to bully? Is it ever okay to cyberbully? What if Amanda did something mean in the first place? Would it be okay for her friends to cyberbully her then?** Remind students that cyberbullying, like any other form of bullying, is never justified and is always wrong.

Read or have a student read Jay's story. Ask: **How was Jay cyberbullied? What could he have done to help himself?** Discuss, reiterating that it's very important to save available evidence and to show it to a trusted adult.

Let students know that even if the cyberbullying happened after school hours, if it affects kids when they're at school, it needs to be reported. Schools have rules against bullying, and those rules apply to cyberbullying as well.

Ask for volunteers to role-play one of the scenarios from the handout. Before beginning the role play, ask the class to coach the student who was bullied on how she or he could handle it. Ask: **What can _____ say to people who are involved? Who can she or he approach for help?** Have the volunteer playing the role of the student who was cyberbullied incorporate these suggestions into the role play.

Wrap Up. Ask students what they can do if someone they know is cyberbullying someone else. Remind them of the importance of being an upstander. Ask how else they can be upstanders when it comes to cyberbullying.

Follow-Up. Check in with students to make sure they remember the two things to do if they experience or know about cyberbullying.

Extension. Refer students to the Stop Bullying Now (www.stopbullyingnow.hrsa.gov). Have them click on "Cyberbullying" and find some new facts. They can also click on the kids' page and read up on bullying and what they can do about it.

Cell Phone Cyberbullying
Stories from Real Kids

Amanda's Story

"I had an argument with these girls who used to be my friends. That night they IM'd each other saying all these mean things about me. Someone downloaded one of the IM's, printed it, and brought it to school. She started passing it around to other people, making it sound like everything was my fault. I was so upset. But I didn't know what to do."

Jay's Story

"One day I woke up late and couldn't find any clean clothes. I threw on a dirty sweatshirt and some old jeans that were too short. There wasn't time to comb my hair, and I didn't realize there was jelly on my face from a donut I ate on the way to school. I looked like a mess. When I got to school some kids started laughing at me and saying mean things. I didn't know it right then, but one of them took a picture of me with his cell phone. Then he and his friends set up a Web page where they posted the picture. They called the Web page 'Jay's a Loser.' The next day all the kids were talking about it and laughing at me.It was horrible. I wanted to hide."

Think About It

Have you ever used the computer or cell phone to hurt someone or get even? If so, you're cyberbullying.

Why is it wrong to cyberbully?

_____

_____

What can you do if cyberbullying happens to you?

_____

_____

What can you do if someone you know is about to cyberbully someone else?

_____

_____

Session 112: Picture a School Without Bullying

personal responsibility • respect • collaboration • courage • compassion

Session 112 guides students to imagine and brainstorm ways your school can prevent, reduce, and eliminate bullying. If you wish, use it to lay the groundwork for Session 113.

Students will
- take part in an envisioning exercise that lets them imagine their school completely free of bullying
- brainstorm concrete actions your school can take

Materials
- chart paper and marker
- student journals
- *optional:* mural or poster paper, markers, and other art materials

Introduction. Say: Imagine putting an end to bullying in our school. Imagine all of us helping make this happen. Tell students that today they'll have a chance to think of what this might be like and ways they could help make that happen.

Activity and Discussion. Start by doing an envisioning activity to help students picture an end to bullying in the school. Say: **As we do this activity, I'm going to ask you to let go of the voice that says "It's not possible" and allow your mind to be completely open. Don't judge any ideas that come up, and let your mind be free to think of creative ideas to stop bullying.**

Have students sit comfortably in chairs or on the floor. Have them close their eyes or cover them and look down. Lead your kids in taking two or three slow, deep abdominal breaths. Then read aloud the following:

Take another slow, deep breath. Picture yourself capable of doing anything you set your mind to. Picture everyone in our class capable, kind, and working together on putting an end to bullying. (Pause.)

Imagine that you've all come up with an excellent plan to end bullying in our school. This is a plan that really works. Picture our principal thanking you. Picture the principal, teachers, students, and others putting the plan into action throughout our entire school. (Pause.)

Now picture our school becoming a place where all people are respected and accepted for exactly who they are. (Pause.) **Picture all kids treating each other with respect in the halls, in the lunchroom, on the bus, on the playground—everywhere. Picture all kinds of kids learning and playing together in peace. Everyone feels safe here, and no one, no matter how different they may seem, is left out or put down.** (Pause.)

What are *your* **ideas for ending bullying in our school? I'm going to give you a minute or two to let your ideas come into your mind. Don't stop or judge any ideas that come up. Just let your mind go free.**

After a minute or two have students open their eyes and write in their journals the ideas they came up with. Caution them not to judge their ideas. Next, have students get into pairs and share their ideas with their partners.

Wrap-Up. Bring students back to the circle and ask them to share a few ideas. Tell students that during the next session, they will share in more detail. Ask them to keep thinking of ideas and to note them in their journals.

Follow-Up. Be sure to follow up with Session 113, in which students can create a concrete list of ideas to present to the school administration.

Extension. Have students make posters or a mural depicting the school without bullying.

Session 113: Ways to End Bullying in Our School

personal responsibility • respect • collaboration • courage • compassion

Session 113 guides students to come up with concrete actions they and the school can take to reduce bullying in the school.

Students will

- come up with a cohesive list of actions your school can take to put an end to bullying
- prepare to present their ideas to the principal or other administrators

Materials

- chart paper and marker
- student journals

Preparation. On chart paper, write the "No Bullying Pledge":

- *I will not take part in any actions that purposely hurt another person.*
- *I will join with friends to stand up for kids who are being picked on.*

If you conducted Session 112, remind students to bring their journals with ideas they brainstormed about stopping bullying at school.

Introduction. Tell students that today they'll have a chance to think of things people in the school might do to reduce and prevent bullying, and to perhaps someday eliminate it completely. Ask: **What are some things you think would help us do this?**

Briefly discuss a few responses. If the idea surfaces that it's impossible to get rid of bullying, let students know that other schools have succeeded in drastically reducing bullying, and reducing bullying is the first step toward stopping it completely. Stress that every person can help make this happen.

Have students partner up and discuss ideas that could help eliminate bullying at school. (If you conducted Session 112, pair students up with partners from that activity.)

Discussion and Activity. After a couple of minutes, have students convene in the large circle. Ask them to share their ideas. Remind students not to judge each other's suggestions. List all the ideas on a chart entitled "Put a Stop to Bullying."

Next, go through the list with your students, and together choose five to ten ideas your class would like to present to the principal. Help your students

choose practical, doable activities that are low-cost and can be done schoolwide. Share the ideas from the list on page 260 to give them an idea of what other schools have done.

Wrap-Up. Display the "No Bullying Pledge." Recite it together, as a class.

(Alternatively, you and your students may instead want to create your own "No Bullying Pledge.")

Note: If any students hesitate or object to the pledge, see them after the session to hear what their considerations are. Encourage them to give the words of the pledge a chance, and let them know that they're an important part of helping reduce and prevent bullying.

Follow-Up. Invite the principal (or other appropriate administrator) into your room to hear your class's ideas for preventing and reducing bullying schoolwide. See which ideas she or he would like to see implemented. Follow through with the administrator and other school personnel to help bring students' ideas to fruition.

Choose a committee of students in your class to work on spreading the word schoolwide. Consider starting with a "Put a Stop to Bullying" poster contest. Your campaign might include a "No Bullying Pledge" and other ideas students come up with.

Extensions. Have your students work in small groups to start implementing ideas. Have them visit other classes to get more students involved.

Put a Stop to Bullying

This is a compilation of ideas from schools that have formed bully prevention and anti-bullying committees. Many of these committees are comprised of student and teacher representatives from each grade, the school counselor, and the principal:

- Quote of the Week read on intercom; responses from students to be posted on a "Respect Board" in the hallway
- "Stop Bullying" convocation at the start of the school year
- Each homeroom creates a poster and slogan to go along with a monthly character education/anti-bullying theme; these are posted throughout school
- "No Bullying" pledge posted in all classrooms
- Notes to parents about the school's bully prevention program
- Back-to-school night based on a motivational student-led activity with an anti-bullying message that focuses on respect
- Student-made respect posters and artwork in the showcase
- "Respect" message posted on a sign in front of the school
- Certificates for acts of respect, caring, and "upstander" behaviors
- Reward system for positive behavior
- Several assemblies throughout year on bullying prevention with students presenting skits and role plays

Accepting Differences

Much of the bullying that takes place among students is based on perceived differences. Research has shown that biases are a key source, be they ethnic, gender, religious, race-based, or related to sexual orientation. This section gets to the core of the issue, emphasizing that people are all the same inside even though different on the outside. Through the following sessions students can see that we are all a part of the same human family, one in which every person deserves to be treated with respect.

Many sessions from Fostering Kindness and Compassion (pages 51–81) and Addressing Name-Calling and Teasing (pages 189–216) introduce concepts that are relevant here, so it's suggested that you conduct some of those prior to introducing these. Also familiarize yourself with Session 68 (The Dignity Stance).

Be sure to have these charts displayed: "Respectful Listening" (introduced in Session 2), "The Win/Win Guidelines for Working Out Conflicts" and "Stop, Breathe, Chill" (Sessions 8 and 9), "No More Hurtful Words" (Session 22), and "Dignity Stance" (Session 68).

Session 114: Step into the Circle

acceptance • respect • compassion • kindness

Session 114 focuses students on their similarities and helps them see their connections to one another.

Students will
- discover ways they are like each other, even if they appear to be different
- gain in their understanding that all human beings have things in common
- consider what our world would be like if people were more accepting of differences

Materials
- chart paper and marker
- *optional:* student journals

Introduction and Activity. Tell students they're going to be playing a game called "Step into the Circle."*

Have them stand in a circle. Say: **Step into the circle if you have a heart that beats inside you.**

Of course, the whole class will step into the circle. Say: **Look around. Is this something we all have in common?**

Have students return to the exterior circle. Say: **Let's see what else people in our class have in common.** One at a time, read the statements below (or similar ones you come up with) and have students step into the circle every time one applies to them. After students step in, say: **Look around and see who you have this in common with.** Then have them step back to the exterior circle with the rest of the class.

Step into the circle if . . .

- your favorite color is red (blue, green, purple, etc.).
- your favorite subject is science (geography, English, Spanish, math, etc.).
- you like soccer (baseball, gymnastics, dancing, skateboarding, etc.).
- you like to draw.
- you hate homework.
- you enjoy reading.
- you enjoy playing video games.
- you care about your family.
- you like pizza.
- you like peppers.
- you like ice cream.
- you feel bad when someone calls you a name.
- you care about having a get-along classroom.
- you wish there was no bullying in our school.

Discussion. Afterward, ask students: **Were you surprised by any ways you're like some of your classmates? What surprised you? Were the same people always inside the circle, or were there different things that different people had in common?** Discuss responses briefly.

Then ask: **Did you notice you have things in common with people who look different from you on the outside?** (Examples: a boy and girl might both like soccer; a tall person and short person might both have red as their favorite color; a black person and white person might both feel bad when someone calls them a name; people of different nationalities might like video games or might dislike homework.)

Have students pair up. Give them two to three minutes to brainstorm at least five things all people have in common. Have them start by thinking about basic human needs.

Afterward, have students share what they came up with. Record their ideas on a chart entitled "Ways We Are All Alike."

Wrap-Up. End by asking students what our world would be like if people were more in touch with ways they are alike, rather than focusing on differences.

Hold up or point to the globe. Say: **We're all part of the human family. Each time we choose to accept the ways we're different and focus on ways we're alike, we help create a kinder, more peaceful world.**

Follow-Up. Encourage students to write in their journals about something they learned when they stepped into the circle. This might be a likeness they were surprised to share with someone, a difference that surprised them, or ideas that came to them about things students in the classroom or people in the world have in common.

* Many thanks to school counselor Paula Eisen for sharing the idea of "Come into the Circle."

Session 115: This Is Who I Am

respect • acceptance • compassion • kindness

Session 115 helps students see the commonalities they have with others.

Students will
- identify in writing things they feel and care about
- share what they've written with a partner and look for things they share in common
- practice good listening and respectful interactions with their partner

Materials
- handout: "This Is Who I Am" (page 264)

Introduction and Activity. Tell students that today they're going to take a few minutes to think about some things that are important to them. Distribute the handout and give students a few minutes to individually complete as much of it as possible.

Discussion. Have students bring their handouts to the circle. Tell them they will be pairing up to share their "This Is Who I Am" sheets with a partner. Ask: **As you share, how can you show your partner respect?** Be sure the discussion includes being good listeners, refraining from put-downs or negative body language, using reflective listening, and giving full attention.

Tell students that after one partner finishes sharing what he or she wrote on the handout, the other partner will then do two things:

1. Give a sincere compliment (for example, "You said drawing makes you happy. That drawing you did last week is really cool").

2. Tell the person things you realized you have in common as you listened (for example, "I'm scared of snakes, too. I didn't know you were").

Give students about ten minutes to share. Let them know that if they didn't finish filling out the handout, they can still talk about the ideas on it. Circulate as they do so, making sure everyone is on track.

After partners have shared, have the class reconvene in a large circle. Ask students what they learned about each other through this activity.

Wrap-Up. Affirm students on acceptance, respect, and good listening your observed.

Follow-Up. Allow time for students to finish filling in their handouts, including drawing pictures of themselves. Encourage them to write in their journals about what they learned about each other through this experience, what new insights or ideas occurred to them, and what they learned about themselves.

This is who I Am

_____ makes me happy.

_____ makes me sad.

_____ makes me laugh out loud.

_____ makes me mad.

_____ makes me feel frightened.

_____ makes me feel stressed.

Something I really need is: _____.

I really wish: _____.

What interests me most in life is: _____

These people are especially important to me: _____

_____

Something I care about more than anything else is: _____

_____

My greatest hope for the world is: _____

My name is: _____

On the back of this page or on a separate sheet of paper, draw a picture of yourself.

Session 116: Different and Alike Interviews

acceptance • compassion • kindness • respect

Session 116 helps students look at the likenesses and differences they share with classmates and see that some differences can be dynamic and interesting.

Students will
- interview each other to find out likenesses and differences
- see the positives in having certain differences
- be better able to accept and appreciate the differences in each other

Materials
- handout: "Different and Alike Interview Questions" (page 266)

Introduction. Pair students with partners who are different than they are in some way (sex, size, race, personality, interests, etc.). Have partners stand together in the large circle. Ask a few partners: **How are you different from each other?** Tell students that partners are now going to have a chance to learn more about ways they are different and alike.

Activity and Discussion. Pass out the "Different and Alike Interview Questions." Have students write their partner's name on their sheet. Then have them spend a few minutes interviewing each other, noting the answers to the questions on their sheets.

When students finish, have them reconvene in the circle. Ask students: **What did you learn about your partner? What are some ways you're alike? What do you have in common? What differences did you discover?**

After several students share ideas, ask: **Who learned something surprising or interesting about their partner? What did you learn? Why did that surprise or interest you?** Continue the discussion, emphasizing what's interesting and valuable about

differences among people as well as the many commonalities students share.

Ask the group: **Why is it important to be aware of the ways we are all alike?** (It helps us understand each other better and realize we're not alone; it helps us see that even if someone seems different on the outside, we still may have things in common.) **What if everyone were exactly like everyone else? What's good about the fact that we're all different in some ways, too? Why is it important to appreciate the ways we're different?** (We each have unique things to contribute to the class and the world; we learn from each other; without differences the world would be pretty boring.)

Wrap-Up. Remind students that all human beings have similarities, no matter how different they may appear to be. Encourage them to be open to getting along with and getting to know people who seem different than they are. Affirm students for things they did in today's session to accept and appreciate differences in each other.

Different and Alike Interview Questions

Talk About It

Find someone who is different from you in some way. Talk about the following questions together to discover what you do and don't have in common:

What do you care most about in the world? _____

Who do you care most about in the world? _____

What makes you happy? _____

What makes you angry? _____

What makes you sad? _____

What makes you most proud? _____

What is one special thing about you that many people don't know? _____
_____

If you could change the world in one way, how would you change it? _____
_____

If you could have three wishes granted, what would they be? _____
_____

Think About It

After you have both talked about all the questions, answer the following:

What are three things you both have in common? List them.

_____

_____

What's one way you and your partner are different from each other?
What's interesting about this difference?

_____

_____

Session 117: Differences Can Separate Us, Part 1

acceptance • respect • personal responsibility • compassion

Session 117 explores the ways differences can be a source of separation.

Students will

- reflect on ways all human beings are alike
- identify and reflect on the differences that separate us
- recall a time they were perceived as different and how they were affected by this

Materials

- handouts: "What Real Kids Have to Say About Differences" (page 268); "Many Kinds of Differences" (page 269)
- chart paper and marker
- student journals

Preparation. On chart paper, copy the web of differences depicted on the handout.

Introduction. Ask: **What are some of the ways all human beings are alike?** (We all need food, clothing, shelter, love; we all have a heart that beats and a brain that thinks; we all have feelings; we all need respect.)

Say: **Even though all human beings have so many things in common, what are some of the ways we might be different on the outside?** (Students might suggest size, gender, race, color, etc.) List a few on the board.

Discussion. Distribute the "Many Kinds of Differences" handout and direct students' attention to the chart you copied. Discuss the differences, and see if students suggest others to add.

Ask: **How can these differences separate us?** Discuss, bringing out the fact that people often judge each other negatively based on differences.

Distribute the "What Real Kids Have to Say About Differences" handout and ask for volunteers to read the statements from real kids. Then ask: **Do any of these sound familiar?** Say: **At one time or another just about all of us have had the experience of being seen as different in some way.** Ask students to think of a time they were treated negatively because they were seen as different. Ask for one or two volunteers to share. Share your own story.

After several responses, ask: **Why do people sometimes mistreat or make fun of people they see as different from themselves?** Discuss.

Activity. Have students take their journals to a place in the room where they feel comfortable writing, and have them do three to four minutes of automatic writing on the topic of what it's like to be treated negatively because of a perceived difference. Tell them to be sure to include what they learned from the experience.

Afterward, give students time to reread what they wrote. See if anyone would like to share.

Wrap-Up. Tell students: **Even though it can really hurt to be treated badly because you're seen as different in some way, sometimes the experience of being hurt can make us more compassionate (caring and understanding) toward other people.**

Follow-Up. Ask students to observe how they treat others throughout the rest of the day. Are they treating someone negatively because they see the person as different? Tell them to take home their "Many Kinds of Differences" handouts and their journals so they can write about this before the next session.

Plan to follow up with Session 118 as soon as you are able.

Extension. Read and discuss *In the Year of the Boar and Jackie Robinson* by Bette Bao Lord. In this book, ten-year-old Shirley Temple Wong arrives from China and struggles to be accepted until she discovers Jackie Robinson and is inspired by how he overcame tremendous odds.

What Real Kids Have to Say About
Differences

In a national survey of more than 2,100 students in grades 3–6, kids wrote about differences. Here are some things they said:

> "I get mad when people make fun of my culture and my name."
>
> "A bunch of kids pick on a guy on my bus because he's kind of overweight."
>
> "There's this kid with only one leg. Some kids are nice to her face, and then they make fun of her when she's not around. Why are people so mean?"
>
> "It makes me mad when people tease or insult kids about their race or religion."
>
> "I don't like it when someone gets teased because they're not American."
>
> "I get angry when I see people teasing others because they are different."
>
> "Why can't people just accept the fact that every living person on the face of the earth is different in their own way?"
>
> "I want people to learn that it's okay to be different."

What do YOU think about differences?

Why do people sometimes act mean or make fun of people who are different from them?

_____

_____

_____

_____

_____

_____

Many Kinds of Differences

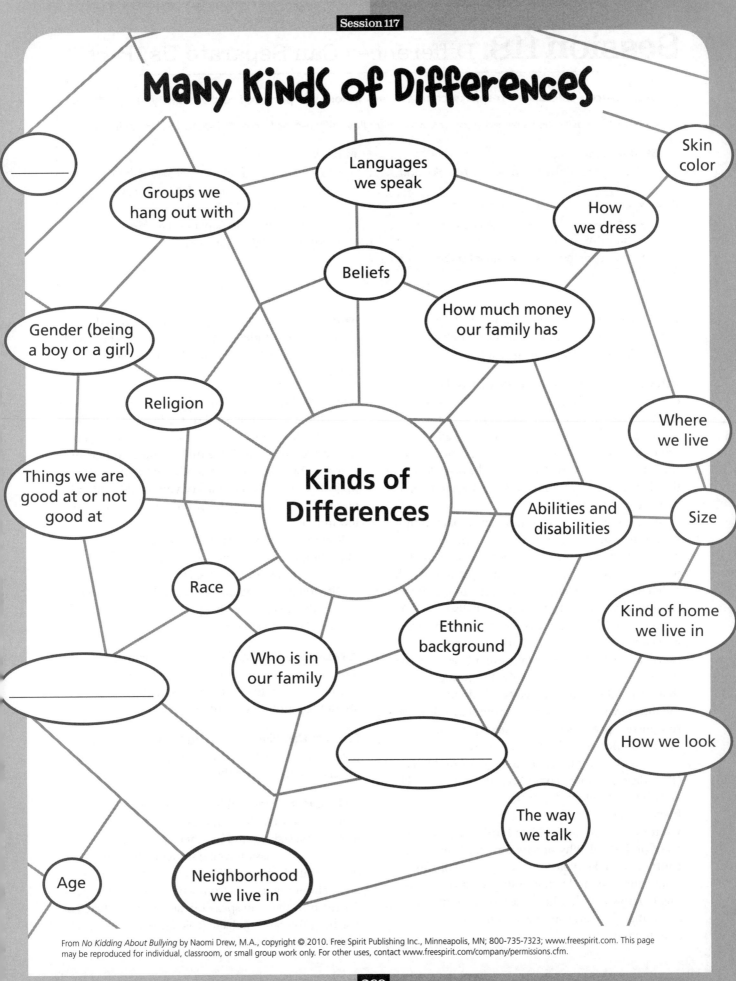

Skin color

Languages we speak

Groups we hang out with

How we dress

Beliefs

How much money our family has

Gender (being a boy or a girl)

Religion

Where we live

Kinds of Differences

Things we are good at or not good at

Abilities and disabilities

Size

Race

Kind of home we live in

Who is in our family

Ethnic background

How we look

The way we talk

Age

Neighborhood we live in

Session 118: Differences Can Separate Us, Part 2

acceptance • tolerance • respect • compassion • kindness • personal responsibility

Session 118 has students reflect upon the way they allow differences to create separations in their lives.

Students will

- understand the meaning of *prejudice* and *bias*
- examine their own prejudices
- understand that prejudice and bias are harmful
- reflect on how people can let go of prejudice

Materials

- chart with differences from Session 117
- handout: "Many Kinds of Differences" from Session 117 (page 269)
- poster or drawing paper and markers
- *optional:* student journals

Preparation. On chart paper, write: *"Prejudice: A strong feeling of unfair dislike toward a person or group because they seem different in some way."*

Introduction and Discussion. Display the differences chart from Session 117 and ask students what they've learned about themselves so far when it comes to differences. Do they tend to be accepting or not accepting? Do they feel like the different one sometimes? If so, how does that make them feel? Are they becoming more compassionate toward people they see as different? Discuss.

Bring out the fact that even the most open-minded people are not always open to every kind of difference. Display the definition of *prejudice* and go over it with students. Connect the idea of prejudice to the differences on the chart, such as race, color, gender, religion, size, and so forth. You might also add that another word for *prejudice* is *bias:* people can have a *prejudice* or *bias,* and they can feel or be *prejudiced* or *biased.* Say: **We all have certain prejudices, and that doesn't mean we're bad people. But it does mean that we need to open ourselves a little more to the difference we have a bias about. Each time we recognize a prejudice inside ourselves is an opportunity to open our minds some more.**

Ask: **Why is it important to let go of prejudices?** (Prejudices separate people; keep them from really knowing each other; stop them from becoming friends; lead to conflict, hatred, and war.) Also ask: **What leads to prejudice? Is it hard or easy to let go of prejudice? Why or why not? If it's hard, what could help make it easier?** (Recognizing prejudice inside ourselves and being willing to let go of it, getting to know people who we see as different, learning about their lives and cultures, opening our hearts and minds.)

Note: If someone brings up the issue of prejudice in the family, tell students that as we learn deeper levels of acceptance, we set an example for people in our families.

Activity. Remind students about the journaling you asked them to do after the last session. Ask: **Are there any attitudes about differences you have that you would like to change? Are there people and groups you are not as open and friendly to because of a prejudice? Is there a prejudice you would like to let go of?** Have students pair up and talk about this for a few minutes.

Reconvene in the circle and ask students why it's important to have an open heart and an open mind when it comes to differences. Discuss.

Distribute drawing materials and have students work individually or with a partner to create posters entitled: "Don't Let Differences Separate Us."

Wrap-Up. Affirm students for their willingness to look at their own prejudices and try to change them. Encourage them to continue writing in their journals about their attitudes about differences.

Follow-Up. Plan time for students to finish their posters. When they are completed, display them in the classroom or the halls.

Extensions. Have students be on the lookout for examples of prejudice and bias on the Internet, TV, movies, magazines, and in other aspects of public life. Have a discussion where students share examples they've found and consider ways they can learn more about themselves from what they observe. Also discuss how they can speak out against prejudice. The Teaching Tolerance website (tolerance.org) has excellent information on this.

Read and discuss *The Christmas Menorahs* by Janice Cohn, the true account of how the entire community of Billings, Montana, united to combat prejudice.

Session 119: Prejudice, Bias, and Stereotypes

acceptance • tolerance • respect • compassion • kindness • personal responsibility

Session 119 sensitizes students to the impact of prejudice, bias, and stereotyping.

Students will
- reflect on the meaning of *prejudice*, *bias*, and *stereotype*
- understand that any form of prejudice or stereotyping is wrong
- reflect on the impact of prejudice and stereotyping on two real kids

Materials
- chart paper and marker

Preparation. On a sheet of chart paper, write the following:

"Prejudice: A strong feeling of unfair dislike toward a person or group because they seem different in some way.

"Stereotype: An oversimplified and inaccurate judgment about a whole group of people based on prejudice."

Introduction. Invite one boy to come to the center of the circle. Ask him if he likes peanut butter. Depending on his answer, say: **Then I guess all the boys in the class must (like/not like) peanut butter because you're a boy and you like/don't like peanut butter. Aren't all boys the same?** Let the class respond to your comment. Discuss.

Invite one girl to come to the center of the circle. Ask if she is good at math. Depending on her answer, say: **Then I guess all girls (are/are not) good at math because you're a girl and all girls are the same, right?** Have students respond again.

Ask: **Is it a good idea to assume something about a whole group based on one person? Why or why not?** Display the definitions of *prejudice* and *stereotype* and go over these with students. Connect the idea of prejudice to things like gender, race, color, religion, size, and so forth. Help students understand that when we make blanket assumptions, we are stereotyping and showing prejudice or bias.

Activity and Discussion. Read aloud the following real-life story from a student named Khaled (not his real name):*

My family is from Iran so people call me a terrorist. The other day when we were playing baseball, a kid on the other team said, "Oh, you're probably happy about 9/11." I was crushed. How could he say that to me? How could he think something like that? I'm just as upset about 9/11 as everyone else in this country. I have an uncle who died in the World Trade Center. Why do people behave this way?

Ask: **How were people stereotyping Khaled? What bias were they showing toward him?**

Ask: **If you were Khaled, how would you feel about what people were saying about you?** Discuss. Ask if they have ever had a similar experience.

Then ask: **Why was it unfair for people to treat Khaled this way?** Discuss.

Share another story, this one from a fifth-grade girl called Jasmine (not her real name):

Once when I was just sitting around, this boy came up to me and said, "You look funny. What are you?" I replied to him that I was Dominican and Spanish. He told me, "You can't be Spanish, because you don't have long hair." I just walked away, because I knew he was being ignorant.

---

* Quotes and stories attributed to real students and teachers come from author interviews and from responses to the Survey About Conflicts conducted by the author and publisher. See pages 1 and 279–281 for further information.

The next day, he started talking about the color of my skin, saying I was dark chocolate. He said mean things about my family and made up a horrible song about us. Then he got all his friends to do these things every day. It got uncomfortable to be at school. When my friends stood up for me, this boy and his friends threw things at us.

I went to an adult even though it was hard. I needed someone. That person was my mom. I know I can count on my family to be there for me.

Ask students what they thought as they heard this story. Ask: **How were people stereotyping Jasmine? What bias were they showing toward her?**

Let students know that acts of prejudice can happen toward anyone, regardless of race or religion. They can be focused on many different groups of people. Ask the girls in the class if people ever assume particular things about them just because they're girls. Ask the boys the same question. Ask how it makes them feel when people assume things about them without knowing who they really are.

Tell students: **Any act of prejudice is unacceptable, even if someone says "I didn't mean it" or "It was only a joke."** Discuss.

Wrap-Up. Ask what Jasmine did to help herself. Emphasize that talking to a parent or another trusted adult is an important thing to do if they are ever treated the way Khaled or Jasmine were.

Hold or point to the globe and ask children to imagine what a world without prejudice might be like. Encourage them to talk about this with their families and friends and to write about it in their journals.

Follow-Up. Conduct Session 120, in which students come up with ways to respond to prejudice and stereotyping.

Extension. Read and discuss *The Watsons Go to Birmingham—1963* by Christopher Paul Curtis, which tells the story of an African-American family at the start of the civil rights movement from the perspective of a fourth-grade boy.

Session 120: Be Part of the Solution

acceptance • tolerance • compassion • respect • personal responsibility

Session 120 focuses on responding to prejudiced remarks and standing up against prejudice. This session is a follow-up to Session 119.

Students will

- learn ways to respond to words of prejudice
- role-play being an upstander in response to prejudice
- understand that each person needs to be part of the solution to prejudice

Materials

- chart paper and marker
- definitions of *prejudice* and *stereotype* from Session 119 (see page 271)
- *optional handout:* "You Belong" (see CD-ROM)

Introduction and Discussion. Say: Sometimes people who don't know better might speak words of prejudice. Sometimes they'll make jokes about another race, religion, or group of people. If that happens, what do you think you can do?

Discuss, noting students' ideas on chart paper. Be sure to include the following in your discussion:

- Don't join in if people are making jokes about or stereotyping people of a particular race, religion, gender, etc.

- Speak up. If you don't, people might think you agree.

After brief discussion, focus attention on the importance of speaking up respectfully. Relate this to the idea of being an upstander, rather than a bystander, in a bullying situation. People can be upstanders for themselves and others when it comes to prejudice and stereotyping, too.

At the top of a new sheet of chart paper, write "Responding to Prejudiced Remarks." Ask: **What are some things you could say if you hear a prejudiced remark, or if someone directs one at you?** Invite students' ideas about what to say, and note ideas for respectful responses on the chart. Include a range of suggestions. Here are a few to get you started:

- "I'm uncomfortable hearing that."
- "That's not funny."
- "Please don't make remarks like that."
- "People who are _____ (specific race, religion, nationality, etc.) are human beings and deserve respect."

- "All people deserve to be respected."
- "That comment wasn't right."
- "That's not cool."

Activity. Have students role-play using the previous comments and those they come up with themselves. Have them use the Dignity Stance and keep their body language neutral. Allow time for several students to practice different statements in pairs or with the larger group.

Wrap-Up. Remind students that each time they stand up against prejudice they are part of the solution to it. Point to the globe and tell students that standing up against prejudice makes the world better for all people.

Extensions. Have a brainstorming session to come up with ideas for making your school a place where all people feel safe, respected, and accepted. Follow up with something you can implement schoolwide, such as a poster, essay-writing, or video campaign.

Stress that we share this earth together, and we all belong to the human race. Give your students copies of the poem "You Belong" (from the CD-ROM). After reading it together, have them create their own poems based on the feelings the poem elicits for them. Students can share their poems with the class and school.

Session 121: Differences Writing Activities

personal responsibility • compassion • acceptance • kindness

Session 121 gives students writing projects to help reflect on their own personal responsibility, acceptance, and compassion toward others.

Students will

- write thoughtfully and critically about accepting differences or speaking up in response to prejudice
- work independently and in pairs
- recognize their role in building a classroom climate of acceptance

Materials

- differences chart from Session 117 (see page 267)
- definitions of *prejudice* and *stereotype* from Session 119 (see page 271)
- handout: "Writing About Accepting Differences" (page 275)
- *optional:* art, print, or technology resources for making a class book

Note: This session introduces one or more writing activities on topics related to accepting differences. Before conducting it, determine how you want to approach the assignment with students. Review the seven assignments on the handout and decide if you want to assign one topic only, assign several topics one at a time, or give students a choice of topics. Also consider whether you want students to write one- or two-page essays or if you want to offer the option of other genres (such poetry, short story, dialogue, or letter). Plan how much time students should have in and out of class to complete the assignment.

Preparation. If you want to distribute the handout to students, make photocopies. If you are assigning a single topic, write the topic on the board or chart paper.

Introduction and Discussion. Display the charts and review with students ideas you have discussed about commonalities, differences, and prejudice. Ask students: **What's prejudice? What's bias? What does it mean to stereotype? What have you learned about your own prejudices? About how it feels to be stereotyped?** Share something you have learned as well.

Activity. Explain the assignment and time frame and ask if students have any questions. Then have students partner up and talk briefly about the assignment—what they can write about, how they'll get started, who they might want to talk to for ideas, and so forth.

After just a few minutes, have students find places to write independently for the remainder of the session.

Wrap-Up. Reconvene in the circle and affirm students for the work they are doing to understand and accept differences among their classmates and others.

Follow-Up. Continue to allow time for students to finish their writing projects.

Extension. When the projects are completed, put together a class book or a Web page where students may share their writing if they wish.

writing About Accepting Differences

1. Write about a time you left someone out because you saw that person as different. How do you think he or she felt? What did you learn from this experience?

- -

2. Write about a character in a story, movie, or video who was left out because he or she was seen as different. What happened? How did the person feel? What lessons can be learned from this story or experience?

- -

3. Do you believe kids in our school accept people they consider different? Write about this. Give examples without using names.

- -

4. How can we help kids accept people they see as different? What are some possible solutions? Talk to friends and family members to get their thoughts.

- -

5. How would our world be different if people accepted each other they see as different? Write about this. What suggestions do you have for promoting acceptance? Talk to friends and family members to get their thoughts.

- -

6. What is prejudice? Look it up in the dictionary. Ask people you know what this word means to them. How does prejudice hurt all of us? What can you do to be part of the solution to prejudice?

- -

7. Who are some people who have fought prejudice? Write about one of them. What did this person do? What can you do to fight prejudice?

- -

Four Review Sessions You Can Use at Any Time

Here are four activities you can use to review content in this book. Insert them anywhere to help your students remember, digest, and reflect upon what they've been learning. Be sure to also question your students about how they are applying what they have learned in real-life situations.

Session 122: Ball-Throw Review

Purpose

To review key concepts and strategies

Materials

- soft ball suitable for being thrown in the classroom
- list of questions you have prepared based on what you've recently taught in *No Kidding About Bullying*

Procedure

Have students form a circle, standing or seated. Throw the ball to a student and ask one of the questions you have prepared. If the student answers correctly, he can throw the ball to another student who will get to answer the next question. If he answers incorrectly, he throws the ball back to you, and you choose the next student.

Encourage students to throw the ball to people who have not been chosen yet. After your questions have been answered, have students come up with their own questions and continue throwing the ball to each other to answer them.

Session 123: Brainstorming Web

Purpose

To have students create webs in which they brainstorm the key things they remember from content covered

Materials

- large piece of chart paper for each group of three
- marker for each student

Procedure

Place students in groups of three. Give each group a large sheet of chart paper and a marker. Instruct students to create a web on their chart paper including every key point they can remember from a given topic area you have covered. The center of the web should name whatever topic you want to review: "Getting Along," "Working Out Conflicts," "Being an Upstander," and so forth.

Give students about ten minutes to work on their webs. When they are finished, have each group share their web with the rest of the class, talking about concepts they have included. Every so often ask, "How are you applying this in real life?"

Session 124: Note Card Review/Reflect

Purpose
To help students recall the information they have learned and air questions and comments

Materials
- 3" x 5" note card and pencil for each student
- box, bowl, or bag to put the cards in

Procedure
Have students name strategies and concepts they have learned so far through sessions in this book. List these on the board.

Pass out note cards. Ask students to write down any questions or comments they have about anything they've learned thus far. Encourage them to ask the hard questions they're grappling with or to express comments they've been holding back, like, "Deep breathing is silly. I don't like to do it" or, "What if I

tell an adult and then the kid hurts me more?" Once the questions and comments have been written, have students put the note cards in the container.

Have a student come to the container, close her eyes, and randomly choose a question. Have another student read the question/comment aloud. Ask for responses from the class before you give yours. Sometimes kids will have already successfully dealt with challenges they are struggling with. If you get a question or comment you're not sure how to respond to, email me at Naomi@LearningPeace.com and I will do my best to answer it.

Encourage students to use their journals to list questions that come up as they're applying what they've learned. Every couple of weeks, gather together for five to ten minutes and go over these questions.

Session 125: TV Show Review

Purpose
To help students recall, in a fun and creative way, a wide range of ideas and strategies they have learned

Materials
- large piece of chart paper and marker for each group of four
- tape
- pretend microphone
- stickers or other small rewards

Procedure
Place students in groups of four. Have each group choose a recorder who is able to write quickly and an

announcer who will come to the "mic" to share the group's ideas with the class in an animated way.

Give each group chart paper and markers. Instruct students to brainstorm everything they remember learning thus far (or in the section you have just covered). Ask them to see how many ideas they can list in five minutes. Say, "1, 2, 3, GO!" and have groups begin brainstorming. After five minutes, ask each group to hang up their chart on the wall. The announcer holds the "microphone" and animatedly shares what the group has brainstormed. The group that has brainstormed the largest list of legitimate items gets a sticker or other fun, simple reward.

No Kidding About Bullying
Pre- and Post-Test

	Never	Sometimes	Usually	Always
Kids in my class are kind to each other even when no one's looking.	❏	❏	❏	❏
I am kind to other kids even when no one's looking.	❏	❏	❏	❏
Kids in my class get into lots of conflicts.	❏	❏	❏	❏
I get into lots of conflicts.	❏	❏	❏	❏
I know how to work out conflicts peacefully.	❏	❏	❏	❏
I wish I could handle conflicts better.	❏	❏	❏	❏
Kids in my class are mean to each other.	❏	❏	❏	❏
There are times I am mean to other kids.	❏	❏	❏	❏
Kids in my class know how to manage their anger.	❏	❏	❏	❏
I know how to manage my anger.	❏	❏	❏	❏
Kids in my class care about the feelings of others.	❏	❏	❏	❏
Kids in my class bully when no one's looking.	❏	❏	❏	❏
I get bullied.	❏	❏	❏	❏
I bully others.	❏	❏	❏	❏
I know what to do if someone bullies me.	❏	❏	❏	❏
I know how to help if someone bullies a friend.	❏	❏	❏	❏
Kids in my class get along with each other.	❏	❏	❏	❏
I feel emotionally and physically safe with my classmates, anywhere in and around school.	❏	❏	❏	❏

Survey About Conflicts

conflict: an argument, fight, or disagreement

About YOU

_____ I am a boy.   _____ I am a girl.   My age: _____   My grade: _____

About CONFLICTS

1. How often do you see conflicts happen in your school or other places? (check one)

____ never   ____ sometimes   ____ often   ____ every day   ____ all the time

2. How often do YOU get into conflicts? (check one)

____ never   ____ sometimes   ____ often   ____ every day   ____ all the time

3. Check whatever things below start conflicts for YOU _or_ OTHER KIDS. Use the lines to add things that aren't listed here.

____ being teased or made fun of   ____ rumors and gossip

____ being blamed for something   ____ threats

____ being picked on for being different ____ mean notes or text messages

____ being left out   ____ _____

____ someone being unfair   ____ _____

____ name-calling   ____ _____

____ cheating at games   ____ _____

Survey About Conflicts (continued)

4. What do you usually do to deal with conflicts you get into?

_____

_____

_____

5. How mean do you think kids are to each other on a scale of 1–10?
(circle a number)

1   2   3   4   5   6   7   8   9   10

not mean at all → → → → → → → → → → →   very mean

6. How do you keep yourself out of physical fights?

_____

_____

Would you like to learn more about how to do this?   ____ yes   ____ no

Why or why not? _____

7. How often does bullying happen in your school or other places?

____ never   ____ sometimes   ____ often   ____ every day   ____ all the time

8. Do you ever step in and help kids who are being bullied?

____ yes   ____ no

If so, how do you try to help? _____

_____

Survey About Conflicts (continued)

9. What do people do that makes you really mad? _____

_____

10. What do you do when someone gets you mad? _____

_____

11. What stresses you out? _____

_____

Very IMPORTANT Question

12. What would you most like to learn about conflict, anger, bullying, or getting

along with other kids? _____

_____

Optional: Tell YOUR Story

Tell about a conflict you were in. In at least 2–3 paragraphs, describe what happened. Did it get solved? If so, how? You can use the back of the paper if you need more room.

_____

_____

_____

_____

_____

Thank you for completing the Survey About Conflicts.

References and Resources

Books for Kids

Blubber by Judy Blume (Yearling, 1986). Fifth-grader Linda is teased and bullied by her peers for being overweight. Jill is drawn into the bullying because she wants to be accepted. This book is a powerful lens on the impact of bullying, the need to be an upstander, and the need for compassion and acceptance.

The Christmas Menorahs: How a Town Fought Hate by Janice Cohn (Albert Whitman, 2000). When a rock is thrown through the window of a house containing a menorah, the people of Billings, Montana, take a stand against bigotry and put menorahs in their windows. This story is a powerful example of what upstanders can do. It teaches personal responsibility, compassion, and acceptance.

Circle of Gold by Candy Dawson Boyd (Scholastic, 1996). After her father dies, Mattie Benson tries to bring her family back together with the help of a beautiful golden pin. Her story teaches integrity, conscience, problem solving, and conflict resolution. This book is a Coretta Scott King Award winner.

Crash by Jerry Spinelli (Laurel Leaf, 2004). Crash has bullied his neighbors and classmates his whole life. When his grandfather has a stroke, Crash finds that friends and family have a new meaning for him. This book highlights such issues as accepting differences, compassion, bullying, and the ability to change.

Dear Mom, You're Ruining My Life by Jean Van Leeuwen (Puffin, 1990). Sam is eleven and she's completely mortified by everything her mother does. Through Sam's story, readers learn to face issues of anger, problem solving, accepting differences, and dealing with peer pressure.

Eagle Song by Joseph Bruchac (Puffin, 1999). Danny Bigtree is teased and bullied when his family moves from a Mohawk reservation to Brooklyn. With the help of a legendary Iroquois peacemaker, Danny explores how he can transform anger, bullying, and adversity into friendship.

Ethan, Suspended by Pamela Ehrenberg (Eerdmans Books for Young Readers, 2009). As one of the only white kids in school, Ethan finds himself to be a racial minority in an almost entirely African-American and Latino junior high. Lessons about prejudice, acceptance, and understanding are explored.

Fourth Grade Weirdo by Martha Freeman (Yearling, 2001). Dexter is different, and through his humorous story, readers learn that, "Even if everybody thinks you're weird, you've gotta pay attention to the handsome guy inside." This book addresses put-downs, gossip, being different, and having feelings.

Gaffer Samson's Luck by Jill Paton Walsh (Farrar, Straus and Giroux, 1990). James has to move to a strange new place. He wants to be accepted by the kids there but ends up making friends with an old man next door. This book helps readers examine issues of exclusion, accepting differences, problem solving, anger, and avoiding physical fights.

In the Year of the Boar and Jackie Robinson by Bette Bao Lord (HarperCollins, 1986). Ten-year-old Shirley Temple Wong struggles to fit in when she moves to the United States from her home in China. She learns to overcome her own obstacles through her discovery of the courageous actions of Jackie Robinson, the first African-American Major League baseball player. This story addresses issues of exclusion, prejudice, and accepting differences.

The Janitor's Boy by Andrew Clements (Aladdin, 2001). Jake is embarrassed by his janitor father. His embarrassment causes him to lash out at his father until he learns some important lessons about acceptance and compassion.

Joshua T. Bates Takes Charge by Susan Shreve (Yearling, 1995). Joshua is supposed to be helping a new student who becomes the target of the fifth grade's biggest bully. This book helps address issues of conscience, peer pressure, personal responsibility, and avoiding physical fights.

Junebug by Alice Mead (Square Fish, 2009). When Junebug turns ten, he is confronted with the prospect of joining a gang. This book helps highlight such issues as keeping out of a fight, dealing with peer pressure, and making the right choice.

Just Kidding by Trudy Ludwig (Tricycle, 2006). D.J.'s friend Vince has a habit of teasing D.J. and then saying, "Just kidding," as if it will make everything okay. D.J. is afraid that if he protests, his friends will think he can't take a joke.

Losers, Inc. by Claudia Mills (Hyperion, 1998). Ethan can't compete with his older brother's perfect GPA, so he and his friend decide to start a Loser's Club. Ethan starts to reevaluate his quest for super-loser status when he meets a teacher he is determined to impress. This book helps kids look at bullying, compassion, and taking responsibility for one's actions.

The Misfits by James Howe (Atheneum, 2003). Overweight seventh grader Bobby Goodspeed and his five friends are all put down for being different. They form their own group and start a No Name-Calling Movement in their school. Teaches acceptance, compassion, kindness, and personal responsibility.

Mr. Peabody's Apples by Madonna (Callaway, 2003). Based on a 300-year-old tale, this picture book is a good teaching tool about the devastating impact of gossip. It fosters personal responsibility, compassion, kindness, and conscience.

My Secret Bully by Trudy Ludwig (Tricycle, 2005). When Monica's friend Katie begins to call her names and humiliate her in front of other kids at school, she feels betrayed and isolated. But with help from her mother, Monica gains the confidence to stand up to a bully disguised as a friend.

One City, Two Brothers by Chris Smith (Barefoot Books, 2007). Based on a folktale told by both Jewish and Arabic people, this picture book shows how the spirit of brotherhood can survive amid differences. It highlights compassion, kindness, acceptance, and altruism.

The Revealers by Doug Wilhelm (Farrar, Straus and Giroux, 2005). At Parkland Middle School, three seventh graders decide to share their personal bully stories via the Internet. Their forum, the "Revealer," allows other kids who are bullied to connect and share their stories. This book attests to the transformative power of speaking out.

Shiloh by Phyllis Reynolds Naylor (Aladdin, 2000). This Newbery Award–winning novel tells the story of eleven-year-old Marty who finds an abused dog and faces powerful ethical questions as a result. This is an excellent vehicle for examining issues of conscience, compassion, and personal responsibility.

Sixth Grade Secrets by Louis Sachar (Scholastic, 1994). This humorous book shows what happens when Laura and her friends start a secret club with secret messages and secret codes. This book helps readers look at gossiping, exclusion, fairness, conflict, and dealing with peer pressure.

Slump by Dave Jarzyna (Yearling, 2000). When longtime pal Annie orders him to shape up, Mitchie starts to think seriously about his bullying ways. This book fosters discussions about the impact of put-downs, taking responsibility for one's actions, and making positive and negative choices.

Sparks Fly Upward by Carol Matas (Clarion Books, 2002). Rebecca has to confront prejudices inside and outside her family when a fire forces her to live with a Ukrainian foster family. Rebecca eventually bonds with Sophie, the daughter in her foster family. Through her travels Rebecca learns courage, acceptance, and compassion.

Speak Up and Get Along! by Scott Cooper (Free Spirit Publishing, 2005). This book presents 21 assertiveness strategies kids can learn and use to express themselves, build relationships, end arguments and fights, halt bullying, and beat unhappy feelings. Includes examples and dialogue kids can practice and try.

Surviving Brick Johnson by Laurie Myers (Clarion Books, 2000). Alex is certain he will be bullied when Brick, the big new kid at school, sees Alex imitating him. But Alex has a lot more to learn about Brick than what he sees on the surface. Through the boys' relationship, readers examine issues of bullying, dealing with fear, accepting differences, and challenging one's perceptions.

There's a Boy in the Girls' Bathroom by Louis Sachar (Yearling, 1988). Bully Bradley Chalkers is the oldest boy in his fifth-grade class. He eventually learns to make some positive changes after he starts working with the new school counselor. Sheds light on bullying, acceptance, compassion, personal responsibility, anger, and how to stay out of fights.

Through My Eyes by Ruby Bridges (Scholastic, 1999). Bridges's moving memoir takes readers back to 1960 when she was escorted by federal marshals to be the first black child to attend an all-white school in New Orleans. This book speaks to the need for compassion, acceptance, and understanding.

Trouble Talk by Trudy Ludwig (Tricycle, 2008). Maya's new friend Bailey begins to talk too much, is hurting people's feelings, and is spreading harmful rumors. Maya realizes Bailey is not the friend she needs and discovers the harmful consequences of "trouble talk."

The Watsons Go to Birmingham—1963 by Christopher Paul Curtis (Laurel Leaf, 2000). This winner of the Newbery Honor and the Coretta Scott King Honor Awards tells the story of an African-American family at the start of the civil rights movement. Told by fourth grader Kenny, this book shows the results of prejudice and helps readers examine such issues as acceptance, compassion, and the need for kindness.

When Zachary Beaver Came to Town by Kimberly Willis Holt (Random House, 2001). Thirteen-year-old Toby Wilson learns some important life lessons when he befriends a newcomer known as "the fattest boy in the world." This book instructs readers on how to deal with difficult feelings, accept differences, and express the need for compassion.

The Wish by Gail Carson Levine (HarperTeen, 2005). When Wilma is granted the wish to become popular, she learns the true cost of popularity and begins to see the real meaning of her favorite quote, "To thine own self be true." Wilma's story addresses issues of integrity, peer pressure, accepting differences, and the true meaning of friendship.

Videos

Integrity Matters Character Videos for Kids. A collection of character education videos created for elementary school children. Integrity Matters teaches students how to become people of integrity through learning and practicing basic moral values including compassion, respect, self-control, acceptance, and kindness. For more information go to www.integrity-matters.com.

Let's Get Real. This thirty-five minute video features real kids and their own words about bullying and harassment. From the youth who are targeted, to the students who pick on them, to those who find the courage to intervene, *Let's Get Real* examines bullying from a full range of perspectives. Be advised that this video contains some harsh language. For more information go to groundspark.org/our-films-and-campaigns/lets-get-real.

Organizations, Programs, and Websites

Bullying UK
www.bullying.co.uk
This award-winning anti-bullying charity is full of valuable resources for parents, schools, and kids and teens.

Bully Police
www.bullypolice.org/grade.html
Learn how your state's bully law (or lack thereof) is graded and pick up best practices from other states and schools that make the grade.

The Cyberbullying Research Center
cyberbullying.us
This site includes research, stories, cases, fact sheets, tips and strategies, current news headlines on cyberbullying, plus downloadable materials for educators and parents to use and distribute.

i-SAFE
iSafe.org
i-SAFE is a nonprofit foundation sponsored by the U.S. Congress that provides a variety of educational opportunities, including classroom curriculum, a virtual training academy for adults, and the iMentors program for kids and teens.

KidsHealth
kidshealth.org
The award-winning KidsHealth website helps teachers, parents, and kids deal with bullying and other issues.

National Crime Prevention Programs
www.ncpc.org/programs
This site provides a quick set of facts on a variety of initiatives and campaigns dedicated to improving safety and reducing crime.

Olweus Bullying Prevention Program
www.olweus.org
This comprehensive program is designed to reduce and prevent bullying schoolwide. The program materials use thorough instructions to help teachers and school administrators mediate and control bullying in every school classroom and corner.

Responsive Classroom
www.responsiveclassroom.org
The Responsive Classroom approach follows seven guiding principles on how to incorporate social-emotional skills in schoolwide practice. Informed by independent research and teacher expertise, this site has much to offer toward the creation and maintenance a safe school. Sponsored by the Northeast Foundation for Children (NEFC).

The Second Step Program
www.cfchildren.org/programs/ssp
Organized by the Committee for Children, this classroom-based social skills program can be used in preschools through junior high schools. The program uses group discussion, modeling, coaching, and practice to teach empathy, impulse control, problem solving, and anger/emotion management.

Steps to Respect
www.cfchildren.org/programs/str/overview
Sponsored by the Committee for Children, this research-based anti-violence curriculum helps elementary students recognize, refuse, and report instances of bullying.

Stop Bullying Now
stopbullyingnow.hrsa.gov/kids
Sponsored by the U.S. Department of Health and Human Services, this kid-friendly website uses cartoon characters, games, and songs to get an anti-bullying message across while helping kids to reduce stress and have fun.

The Substance Abuse & Mental Health Services Administration's National Mental Health Information Center
mentalhealth.samhsa.gov/15plus/aboutbullying.asp
The Bullying section of SAMHSA's website includes downloadable public service announcements and resource-rich guides for students, educators, caregivers, mental health professionals, and community organization members.

Teaching Tolerance
tolerance.org
This anti-violence website includes teaching materials for every grade level on a large variety of issues related to promoting justice and equality. Type "bullying" into their search engine to find anti-bullying games, surveys, tips, and songs.

Hotlines

Boystown
1-800-448-3000
www.boystown.org
A 24-hour crisis hotline for any social-emotional troubles affecting kids and teens (both boys and girls) including anger, depression, and school issues. Available in Spanish.

Hopeline
1-800-784-2433
www.hopeline.com
A 24-hour national suicide hotline that is private and confidential. Available in Spanish.

Nineline
1-800-999-9999
nineline.org
A 24-hour toll-free hotline for crisis intervention, referral, and information for troubled youth and their families.

The Trevor Project
1-866-488-7386
www.thetrevorproject.org
A 24-hour crisis and suicide prevention helpline for lesbian, gay, bisexual, transgender, and questioning youth.

References and Resources

American Psychological Association. "The Mental Health Implications of Witness Status." *School Psychology Quarterly*, vol. 24, no. 4 (December 2009): 211–223.

Bluestein, Jane. *The Win-Win Classroom: A Fresh and Positive Look at Classroom Management.* Tyler, TX: Corwin, 2008.

Centers for Disease Control and Prevention and the National Center for Injury Prevention and Control. "Understanding Youth Violence: Fact Sheet 2008." Retrieved January 18, 2010, from www.cdc.gov/ncipc/pub-res/YVFactSheet.pdf.

Center for Social and Emotional Education. "Breaking the Bully-Victim-Witness Cycle." *School Climate Matters* 2, no. 2. (June 2008): 3.

Coloroso, Barbara. *The Bully, the Bullied, and the Bystander.* New York: HarperCollins, 2003.

Fredrickson, Barbara. *Positivity: Groundbreaking Research Reveals How to Embrace the Hidden Strength of Positive Emotions, Overcome Negativity, and Thrive.* New York: Crown Publishers, 2009.

Goleman, Daniel. *Social Intelligence: The New Science of Social Relationships.* New York: Bantam, 2006.

Goodman, Robin. "Aggression." New York University Child Study Center. Retrieved January 20, 2010, from www.education.com.

Health Resources and Services Administration Maternal and Child Health Bureau. "What We Know About Bullying." U.S. Department of Health and Human Services. Retrieved January 18, 2010, from njbullying.org/documents/whatweknowaboutB.pdf.

Kim, Bob, and Judy Logan. *Let's Get Real Curriculum Guide.* San Francisco: GroundSparks, 2004.

Olweus, Dan, Susan Limber, and Sharon Mihalic. *Blueprints for Violence Prevention, Book Nine: Bullying Prevention Program.* Boulder, CO: Center for the Study and Prevention of Violence, 1999.

Pepler, Debra, et al. "Developmental Trajectories of Bullying and Associated Factors." *Child Development* 79, no. 2 (March/April 2008): 325–338

Power, Samantha. *A Problem from Hell: America and the Age of Genocide.* New York: Harper Perennial, 2007.

Swearer, Susan M., Dorothy L. Espelage, and Scott A. Napolitano. *Bullying Prevention and Intervention: Realistic Strategies for Schools.* New York: Guilford, 2009.

Index

About the Author

Naomi Drew, M.A., is recognized around the world for her work in conflict resolution and bullying. A former teacher, she is the award-winning author of six widely used books. Her landmark book, *Learning the Skills of Peacemaking*, was one of the first to introduce peacemaking into public education. Her acclaimed book for middle school students, *The Kids' Guide to Working Out Conflicts*, has been lauded by educators and students as well as by *School Library Journal*, *Teaching K–8*, and *Voice of Youth Advocates*. Her work has been featured in magazines and newspapers across the United States, including *Time*, *Parents*, and *The New York Times*. She has been a guest on syndicated radio and national TV, and has served as a parenting expert for "Classroom Close-Ups," an Emmy-winning public television program.

Naomi is a dynamic speaker who has inspired audiences across the United States. She serves as a consultant to school districts, parent groups, and civic organizations and is a registered provider with the New Jersey State Department of Education Character Education Network. She would be happy to come to your area to do a workshop or keynote.

Naomi has two grown sons who were raised in accordance with the principles she writes about. With over twenty-five years of experience in the field, she has worked with thousands of people of every age. "Peaceful Parents," her online newsletter, has broad international readership, and her website, LearningPeace.com, is a valuable resource to educators and families worldwide.

For pricing information, to place an order, or to request a free catalog, contact:

Free Spirit Publishing Inc. • toll-free 800.735.7323 • help4kids@freespirit.com • www.freespirit.com